HANDBOOK OF INTERNATIONAL AND CROSS-CULTURAL LEADERSHIP RESEARCH PROCESSES

An invaluable contribution to the area of leadership studies, the *Handbook of International and Cross-Cultural Leadership Research Processes: Perspectives, Practice, Instruction* brings together renowned authors with diverse cultural, academic, and practitioner backgrounds to provide a comprehensive overview and analysis of all stages of the research process.

The handbook centers around authors' international research reflections and experiences, with chapters that reflect and analyze various research experiences in order to help readers learn about the integrity of each stage of the international leadership research process with examples and discussions. Part I introduces philosophical traditions of the leadership field and discusses how established leadership and followership theories and approaches sometimes fail to capture leadership realities of different cultures and societies. Part II focuses on methodological challenges and opportunities. Scholars share insights on their research practices in different stages of international and cross-cultural studies. Part III is forward-looking in preparing readers to respond to complex realities of the leadership field: teaching, learning, publishing, and applying international and cross-cultural leadership research standards with integrity. The unifying thread amongst all the chapters is a shared intent to build knowledge of diverse and evolving leadership practices and phenomena across cultures and societies.

The handbook is an excellent resource for a broad audience including scholars across disciplines and fields, such as psychology, management, history, cognitive science, economics, anthropology, sociology, and medicine, as well as educators, consultants, and graduate and doctoral students who are interested in understanding authentic leadership practices outside of the traditional Western paradigm.

Yulia Tolstikov-Mast, Ph.D., is a global leadership scholar, doctoral faculty, and authentic research advocate. Yulia is Professor of Ethical and Creative Leadership at the Interdisciplinary Ph.D. Program at Union Institute and University. She researches global leadership and followership, international professional communication, leadership education, and social change.

Franziska Bieri, Ph.D., teaches undergraduate social science classes at the University of Maryland Global Campus and doctoral global leadership and research methods courses at the Indiana Institute of Technology's Ph.D. Program in Global Leadership. Her areas of research include international nongovernmental organizations, global governance, and comparative labour markets.

Jennie L. Walker, Ph.D., is Lead Faculty and Associate Professor for Business Leadership at Forbes School of Business & Technology, University of Arizona Global Campus. She specializes in global leadership research and developing people and organizations for success in complex, diverse, and increasingly global environments.

Leadership: Research and Practice Series

Series Editor Ronald E. Riggio

Henry R. Kravis Professor of Leadership and Organizational Psychology and former Director of the Kravis Leadership Institute at Claremont McKenna College

In Memoriam
Georgia Sorenson (1947–2020)

Leadership and the Ethics of Influence
Terry L. Price

Becoming a Leader
Nine Elements of Leadership Mastery
Al Bolea and Leanne Atwater

Inclusive Leadership
Transforming Diverse Lives, Workplaces, and Societies
Edited by Bernardo M. Ferdman, Jeanine Prime, and Ronald E. Riggio

Leadership Across Boundaries
A Passage to Aporia
Nathan Harter

A Theory of Environmental Leadership
Leading for the Earth
Mark Manolopoulos

Handbook of International and Cross-Cultural Leadership Research Processes
Perspectives, Practice, Instruction
Yulia Tolstikov-Mast, Franziska Bieri, and Jennie L. Walker

Deepening the Leadership Journey
Nine Elements of Leadership Mastery
Al Bolea and Leanne Atwater

For more information about this series, please visit: www.routledge.com/Leadership-Research-and-Practice/book-series/leadership

Handbook of International and Cross-Cultural Leadership Research Processes

Perspectives, Practice, Instruction

Edited by Yulia Tolstikov-Mast, Franziska Bieri, and Jennie L. Walker

Routledge
Taylor & Francis Group

NEW YORK AND LONDON

Cover image: © Getty Images

First published 2022
by Routledge
605 Third Avenue, New York, NY 10158

and by Routledge
2 Park Square, Milton Park, Abingdon, Oxon, OX14 4RN

Routledge is an imprint of the Taylor & Francis Group, an informa business

© 2022 Taylor & Francis

The right of Yulia Tolstikov-Mast, Franziska Bieri, and Jennie L. Walker to be identified as the authors of the editorial material, and of the authors for their individual chapters, has been asserted in accordance with sections 77 and 78 of the Copyright, Designs and Patents Act 1988.

Library of Congress Cataloguing-in-Publication Data
Names: Tolstikov-Mast, Yulia, 1971- editor. | Bieri, Franziska, 1977-editor. | Walker, Jennie L, 1975- editor.
Title: Handbook of international and cross-cultural leadership research processes: perspectives, practice, instruction / edited by Yulia Tolstikov-Mast, Ph.D., Franziska Bieri, Ph.D., Jennie L Walker, Ph.D.
Description: New York, NY: Routledge, 2022. | Series: Leadership: research and practice | Includes bibliographical references and index.
Identifiers: LCCN 2021026404 (print) | LCCN 2021026405 (ebook) | ISBN 9780367436872 (hardback) | ISBN 9780367434335 (paperback) | ISBN 9781003003380 (ebook)
Subjects: LCSH: Leadership--Research. | Leadership--Cross-cultural studies.
Classification: LCC HM1261.H366 2022 (print) | LCC HM1261 (ebook) | DDC 303.3/4--dc23
LC record available at https://lccn.loc.gov/2021026404
LC ebook record available at https://lccn.loc.gov/2021026405

ISBN: 978-0-367-43687-2 (hbk)
ISBN: 978-0-367-43433-5 (pbk)
ISBN: 978-1-003-00338-0 (ebk)

DOI: 10.4324/9781003003380

Typeset in Bembo
by MPS Limited, Dehradun

Contents

Contents

Contents

Contributors

Yulia Tolstikov-Mast, Ph.D., is a Professor of Ethical and Creative Leadership at the Interdisciplinary Ph.D. Program at the Union Institute & University. Originally from Russia, Yulia experienced the Soviet system, perestroyka, and emerging market economy before relocating to the United States. Her scholarship appears in Advances in Global Leadership, Journal of Leadership Education, Women Courageous and The Study and Practice of Global Leadership books, among others. She published on the development of a global leadership discipline and articulated the concepts of global follower and global followership. She was the Country Co-Investigator in Russia for the GLOBE 2020 Project. Yulia is an advocate for culturally responsible and authentic research models. Her ongoing international project is a multi-stage exploratory study of Russian followership. Yulia is a Global Mindset Inventory Certified Facilitator with wide consulting experience. Yulia has a B.A. in Linguistics (Rostov State Pedagogical University, Russia), an M.A. in Professional Communication (Purdue University), and a Ph.D. in Communication (The University of Memphis).

Franziska Bieri, Ph.D., teaches undergraduate social science classes at the University of Maryland Global Campus and doctoral global leadership and research methods courses at the Indiana Institute of Technology's Ph.D. Program in Global Leadership. Her areas of research include international nongovernmental organizations, global governance, and comparative labour markets. She has written on the institutional contexts of public-private partnerships, the role of trust in civic engagement, and school-to-work transitions. She is the author of the book "From Blood Diamonds to the Kimberley Process: How NGOs Cleaned Up the Global Diamond Industry" (Routledge, 2010). Her research has also appeared in the International Journal of Sociology and Social Policy, Advances in Global Leadership, European Societies, and Sociological Forum.

Jennie L. Walker, Ph.D., is Lead Faculty and Associate Professor for Business Leadership at Forbes School of Business & Technology, University of Arizona Global Campus. She specializes in global leadership research and developing people and organizations for success in complex, diverse, and increasingly global environments. For the past 20 years, she has provided professional education and leadership development within Fortune 500 organizations, as a professor and executive in higher education and as a consulting partner to organizations globally. She is a multiple year award recipient of Faculty of the Year and is widely published across academic journals, books, magazines and digital media. Previous books include Developing Your Global Mindset: The Handbook for Successful Global Leaders and Teaching Methods in Business: Vol. 1. Experiential Exercises in the Classroom. Outside of her career, Dr. Walker is mother to four children, and enjoys travel, scuba diving, creative writing, films and pets.

Authors

David N. Avdul, Ph.D., is the Director of Compensation and HR Centralized Services and an Adjunct Professor at DePaul University in the College of Business. Avdul worked in the financial services and medical device industries for more than 20 years, and in higher education for over 5 years. He has been a guest lecturer at various colleges around Chicago and has taught various Human Resources Management courses, including a course in Manama, Bahrain. He was awarded a Dean's fellowship and scholarship to study Human Resources at Loyola University-Chicago, and has also earned industry awards for developing innovative corporate incentive plans and wellness programs. In business, Avdul has been in charge of many high profile projects in compensation, benefits, and HR information systems, both domestically and globally. He is passionate about implementing streamlined, best-practice solutions, leadership, global HR issues, and training and developing employees to perform at their highest levels.

Frank Banfill, Ph.D., is the Executive Vice President at KiDs Beach Club, a non-profit organization that provides character education for pre-teenagers. He is the executive producer of a weekly children's TV program and regularly consults on leadership and organizational development, especially for non-profit organizations. Dr. Banfill's 30+ year career has spanned the worlds of business, entertainment, religion, and education. He co-founded a global travel company, produced the movie *More Than Funny*, which debuted in 700+ theaters, trained leaders across six continents, and co-founded a college in Tanzania, Africa. Dr. Banfill has authored two books and has been a keynote speaker for numerous organizations and institutions including Liberty University and the U.S. Navy. He holds a PhD in Global Leadership-Organizational Management from Indiana Tech and a Senior Certified Professional certification in HR from SHRM. Dr. Banfill resides in the Dallas-Ft. Worth Metroplex with his wife of more than 30 years.

Jack Barentsen, Ph.D., professor of practical theology, Evangelische Theologische Faculteit, Leuven (Belgium). Jack Barentsen (PhD) studied physics, philosophy and theology in the US, and served in his home country the Netherlands first as pastor and church planter. In 2001, Barentsen started teaching at the Evangelische Theologische Faculteit in Leuven (Belgium), focusing on leadership development in early Christianity through the lens of modern leadership theory (*Emerging Leadership in the Pauline Mission*, W&S 2011). He currently serves as professor of Practical Theology at the ETF, researching contemporary forms of religious leadership in multiple countries with the Institute of Leadership and Social Ethics, and consulting with churches on leadership development. He also holds an appointment as Extraordinary Researcher in Practical Theology at the Faculty of Theology of North-West University in Potchefstroom, South Africa. He is married, has two daughters and an expanding family with two grandchildren.

Gabrielle Blackman, Ph.D., is a faculty member in the Graduate Psychology Department at Purdue University Global (PG). There, she advises graduate students who are working on their master's degree thesis projects. Dr. Blackman serves on various university committees and as the Faculty Advisor for PG's Psi Chi International Honor Society chapter. She currently chairs the Society for Industrial and Organizational Psychology's Committee for the Advancement of Professional Ethics. Her research focuses on positive leadership and organizational practices, processes, and outcomes, emphasizing ethics-based and humanistic approaches. She has presented her research findings at dozens of national and international conferences and within peer-reviewed journals and edited books. Previously, she was an Assistant Professor of Leadership Studies at Christopher Newport University and an Adjunct faculty member of George Mason University's (GMU) School of Management. She holds a Master of Arts and a Doctor of Philosophy in industrial and organizational psychology from GMU.

Ariel B. Blair, Ph.D., is an Assistant Professor (Lecturer) of Management at the University of Utah David Eccles School of Business, and a Visiting Professor at the Tuck School of Business at Dartmouth College. Her research interests include leadership and followership in diverse workforces focusing on cultural differences in innovation and employee voice. Ariel's publications include articles in the *Journal of Social Issues* and *OD Practitioner*, and book chapters in R. Koonce, M. Bligh, M. Carsten, and M. Hurwitz (Eds.), Followership in action: Cases and commentaries, and B. Jensen (Ed.), *What Is Your Life's Work?* She built a strong foundation for her research while working in corporate organizations. Ariel has worked in a wide range of industries while living in Japan, Spain, Thailand, and the United States.

Nina Collins, M.S., is the Scholarly Publishing Specialist at Purdue University Libraries and School of Information Studies, specializing in open access, scholarly publishing, scholarly communication, open scholarship, and publication ethics. Nina promotes open scholarship at Purdue, serving as primary contact for questions related to open access and transformative open access publishing agreements. She manages Purdue's institutional repository as well as the Purdue Libraries Open Access Publishing Support Fund. She frequently conducts workshops on deceptive or predatory publishing, open access, research metrics and publishing best practice. Nina holds Master's degrees in Library Science and Information Science from Indiana University, with a specialization in Digital Libraries.

Erika L. Dakin Kirby, Ph.D., is Professor of Communication Studies, the A.F. Jacobson Chair in Communication at Creighton University and a facilitator for the Anti-Defamation League and the Minnesota Humanities Center. An organizational communication scholar, she studies the everyday intersections of working and personal life, emphasizing how differing social identities (including race, class, gender, and ability) intersect with organizational structures. She teaches courses on race, gender, social justice, and communication, and engages in advocacy in her community. She co-edited two editions of *Gender Actualized: Cases in Communicatively Constructing Realities* with Dr. Chad McBride and has published over 45 manuscripts in numerous outlets in her discipline including the *Handbook of Organizational Communication*. She is past-president of the Organization for the Study of Communication, Language, and Gender and recipient of the Charles Woolbert Award of the National Communication Association for scholarly work that stands the test of time.

Julie A. de Jong, M.S., is a Survey Methodologist in the International Unit within the Survey Research Center, University of Michigan, and holds a Master's Degree in Survey Methodology from the University of Michigan. She collaborates in the design and direction of both mono-country and cross-national surveys, with a focus on promoting survey research best practices, specifically in countries with limited survey research capacity and infrastructure. She has authored and co-authored a number of book chapters, journal articles, reports, and quality assessments on the design and implementation of international, multinational, multiregional, and multicultural surveys. She has also co-authored several publications examining measurement error resulting from both interviewers and the interview setting in cross-national surveys.

Tonya Ensign, Ph.D., holds a Ph.D. in Global Leadership and Change, an M.A. in Organizational Management and undergraduate degrees in Finance and International Business. She has devoted 25 years to understanding the phenomenon of transformational change. Her career has focused on teaching, coaching, advising, and supporting leaders during this process. Dr. Ensign teaches in the PhD program in Global Leadership at Indiana Institute of Technology, leads their Independent Global Practicum program, and is considered an expert on Transformative Learning and Change.

Wendy Fox Kirk, Ph.D., is an Assistant Professor and Department Chair for Business Administration & Marketing in the Goddard School of Business & Economics. Her leadership research considers gender, power and identity aiming to address issues of disadvantage with a focus on women's careers and the gendered organization. She received the 2019 Outstanding Emerging Scholar Award by ILA's Women's Leadership Affinity Group. Publications include articles in *Gender in Management: An International Journal, Journal of Strategic Management Studies* and *Advances in Developing Human Resources,* and book chapters in Madsen, S. R. (Ed.). (2017). *Handbook of research on gender and leadership.* (Edward Elgar), and in Storberg Walker, J., & Haber Curran, P. (2017). *Theorizing women & leadership: New insights & contributions from multiple perspectives.* (IAP.) She is also a consulting editor for the *Journal of Education for Business.*

Kem Gambrell, Ph.D., is an Associate Professor & Chair of Doctoral Program in Leadership Studies at Gonzaga University. Originally from Boulder, Colorado, she has spent the last 30 years in the Midwest, previously teaching at the University of Nebraska and Viterbo University. Dr. Gambrell holds a bachelor's degree in Biology from Concordia College (Seward, Nebraska), a Masters degree in Leadership Studies, and a Ph.D. in Human Sciences (Leadership Studies) from the University of Nebraska. Dr. Gambrell's research has centered around exploring under-represented leadership paradigms, specifically focusing on Native American perspectives, as well as constructive development and the social construction of leadership. In addition, she has consulted for not-for-profit and medical organizations on a variety of leadership and organizational change over the past fourteen years.

Patricia Goerman, Ph.D., leads the Language and Cross-Cultural Research Group in the Center for Behavioral Science Methods at the U.S. Census Bureau. She has been a member of the Comparative Survey Design and Implementation (CSDI) executive committee since 2017 and has co-chaired the American Association for Public Opinion Research (AAPOR) Cross-Cultural and Multilingual Research Affinity Group since 2016. Dr. Goerman has 17 years of experience in the development and pretesting of multilingual survey instruments, with a focus on Spanish-language materials. Her research interests include questionnaire design and translation, cross-cultural issues in surveys, inclusion of respondent voices in questionnaire development through pretesting and interviewer doorstep messages. She has a Ph.D. in Sociology from the University of Virginia.

Elizabeth Hartney, BSc (Hons), MSc, MA, PhD, RPsych, has over 25 years of experience as a psychologist and clinician-researcher in the Canadian and UK health systems, and has held a variety of leadership roles, including Professor of Leadership Studies, Program Head of the MA Leadership (Health Specialization) program, and Director of the Centre for Health Leadership & Research at Royal Roads University, as well as guiding provincial policy as the in-house Licensed Psychologist at the British Columbia Ministry of Health. Her clinical experience includes providing front line care to First Nations Health Authority patients during the COVID-19 pandemic, as well as previously treating people with addictions and concurrent disorders in hospitals and clinics in British

Columbia and Alberta. She holds a PhD in Psychology and Master's degrees in Cognitive Science and Higher Education, and has published extensively in the fields of patient-centred care and leadership in health systems.

Kathy-Ann C. Hernandez, Ph.D., is a professor of leadership and research methods in the College of Business and Leadership and co-chair of the Ph.D. program in Organizational Leadership at Eastern University in Pennsylvania, USA. She is the co-author of *Collaborative Autoethnography* (2013, with Heewon Chang and Faith Wambura Ngunjiri) as well as the author/presenter on several other autoethnographic related scholarship projects. Her work has appeared in the *Handbook of Autoethnography*, T*he International Journal of Qualitative Studies in Education*, and *The Journal of Research Practice*. Her research is focused on the Black Diaspora and the salience of race/ethnicity, gender and social context in identity formation, leadership development, and social and academic outcomes for marginalized populations. She is also committed to interrogating and fostering more diverse and equitable organizational spaces, human flourishing, work-life integration, and the leadership development experiences of women and minorities in academic and public settings.

Marc Hurwitz, Ph.D., is Associate Director, Undergraduate and Non-degree Programs, Conrad School of Entrepreneurship and Business, University of Waterloo, Canada. He has written three books and numerous articles on followership, leadership, and collaboration. Marc also won the Sandford Fleming Teaching Award in 2019 for his work teaching leadership, consulting, and entrepreneurship at University of Waterloo. His career also includes 10 years working for large corporations including at an executive level, 15 years co-founding and running a leadership-followership consulting firm - FliPskills and FliPU - and nearly 20 years acting, directing, and writing. He holds a PhD in neuroscience, an MBA, and master's degrees in mathematics and physics.

Emerald Jay D. Ilac, CSIOP, RMP, Ph.D., is currently an Assistant Professor of the Ateneo de Manila Psychology Department, and Director for the Ateneo Center for Organization Research and Development. He worked in operations for over ten years in institutions such as KFC Philippines, Gloria Jeans Coffees and Seattle's Best Coffee, as marketing officer for Kenny Rogers Roasters, and as cluster manager for Netopia under ePLDT. His research on leadership, culture, and industrial-organizational psychology have been published in local and international journals and books. Moreover, he is a member and peer reviewer of the International Leadership Association and the Psychological Association of the Philippines where he was Chair of the Industrial-Organizational Psychology Division from 2018 to 2020. A licensed psychometrician under the Philippine Regulatory Commission and a Certified Specialist in Industrial-Organizational Psychology, he finished his undergraduate and doctorate degree in Leadership Studies from the Ateneo de Manila University.

Dara Kelly, Ph.D., is from the Leq'á:mel First Nation, part of the Stó:lō Coast Salish. She is an Assistant Professor of Indigenous Business at the Beedie School of Business, SFU. She teaches in the Executive MBA in Indigenous Business and Leadership program, and on Indigenous business environments within full-time and part-time MBA programs. Dr. Kelly is a recipient of the 2020 Early in Career Award for CUFA BC Distinguished Academic Awards. Her research helps fill in gaps in the literature on the economic concepts and practices of the Coast Salish and other Indigenous nations. In addition to her studies, Dara was a Researcher with the Mira Szászy Research Centre for Māori and Pacific Economic Development at The University of Auckland Business School. Dara also has professional experience in leadership development programming and seeks to maintain collaborative research ties with Aotearoa-New Zealand in the area of Indigenous economic development.

Kathleen Kephart, M.S., is a researcher specializing in questionnaire design and evaluation with the Center for Behavioral Science Methods at the U.S. Census Bureau. She has over 12 years of experience working in the field of survey research. She has worked on a variety of topics including address frame quality for address-based sampling, questionnaire design and evaluation, usability testing, and cross cultural survey research. In her current job duties she regularly works with other federal agencies to conduct pretesting of their surveys including NCES, BLS, USDA, and NCHS. Her current research interests include field training for cross cultural interviews, joint usability and cognitive testing, designing better cognitive interview probes, and household rostering techniques. She has a B.A. in Mathematics from St. Olaf College in Northfield, MN and a M.S. in Survey Research and Methodology from the University of Nebraska-Lincoln.

Wanda Krause, Ph.D., is Program Head of the MA in Global Leadership program and Associate Professor in the School of Leadership Studies at Royal Roads University. Her work focuses on Middle East politics, civil society, human rights issues, evaluation, women's participation, and global leadership. Her single author books include Spiritual Activism: Keys for Personal and Political Success. San Francisco CA; Turning Stone Press; *Civil Society and Women Activists in the Middle East: Islamic and Secular Organizations in Egypt.* London: IB Tauris (2012); and *Women in Civil Society: The State, Islamism, and Networks in the UAE.* New York: Palgrave-Macmillan (2008). Wanda has edited and contributed to further books, in addition to numerous book chapters and journal papers on related topics. She has led the founding or co-founded centers and programs in the Middle East and Canada.

Pamela A. Lemoine, Ed.D., is an Assistant Professor and Program Coordinator for the Global Leadership Ph.D in the Department of Leadership Development at Troy University. Dr. Lemoine previously held a faculty appointment at Columbus State University working with the masters, educational specialist, and doctoral programs. Dr. Lemoine completed a BA in English, an MA in Educational Technology, and an EdD in Educational Leadership at the University of Louisiana at Lafayette. Dr. Lemoine has over 30 years of experience in education serving as a school and district administrator. Dr. Lemoine's interests include leadership experiences with disruption in VUCA. She has authored or edited books, professional journals, numerous book chapters and presented at state, regional, national, and international professional organizations. Her current work includes examining challenges faced by immigrant and refugee children in the U.S. educational system as well as the impact of COVID-19 on P12 and higher education.

Anna Lilleboe, Ph.D., is a global leadership practitioner and scholar. She grew up in South East Asia and received her higher education in the United States. She completed her doctorate degree in Global Leadership at Indiana Institute of Technology in 2020. Her dissertation on global followership evaluated Japanese and American followers and their perspectives on ideal followership. Anna has more than twenty years of experience working with global companies to optimize their strategic initiatives. She is also an adjunct professor at Indiana Institute of Technology Graduate Business School, teaching global project leadership and human capital development. Anna calls Vancouver, WA home where she lives with her husband and family.

Petros G. Malakyan, Ph.D., MA, is Professor of Organizational Leadership and the Department Head of Communication and Organizational Leadership in the School of Informatics, Humanities and Social Sciences at Robert Morris University. Petros holds terminal degrees in Intercultural Studies with a Leadership concentration from the Graduate School of Intercultural Studies at Fuller Theological Seminary in Pasadena, California. Petros has created and taught more than two dozens of leadership courses in four continents of the world. Malakyan's expertise and research interests are in integrative and interdisciplinary studies of leadership; leadership and followership; leader-follower identities; curriculum design and development; and doctoral programs in leadership. He has published in the Journal of Leadership Studies, International Journal of Doctoral Studies, International Journal of Social Science Research, IntechOpen, and others. His recent research interests are in the areas of doctoral education, leadership in the digital age, cybersecurity leadership, and fluidity in leading and following.

Surbhi Malik, Ph.D., is Assistant Professor of English at Creighton University, where she teaches courses in multiethnic literature, transnational feminism, and global Bollywood. Her research examines the intersections of race, place, and gender in South Asian and Asian American diasporic literature and film. Her research has been published or is forthcoming in several peer-reviewed journals, including the *Journal of Creative Communications, Journal of Religion and Society, South Asian Review, Verge: Studies in Global Asias, South Asian Popular Culture,* and *ARIEL: A Review of International English Literature.*

Mikelyn Meyers, M.S., is a sociolinguist with more than ten years of experience researching the design of linguistically and culturally appropriate translated survey materials. She works in the Language and Cross-Cultural Research Group in the Center for Behavioral Science Methods at the U.S. Census Bureau. Her research interests include optimizing internet surveys for speakers of non-English languages, interviewer training on overcoming language barriers, and racial identity in immigrant families. She has a MS in Sociolinguistics from Georgetown University.

Arkadiusz Mironko, Ph.D., is an assistant professor of management at Indiana University East School of Business and Economics. Previously, he worked at the Rotterdam School of Management Erasmus University in the Netherlands, and the Anderson Graduate School of Management at the University of California, Riverside. Most recently, he is engaged in research on dynamics in global virtual teams and global leadership. His core research interests are in the area of global business strategy, global competition, and knowledge creation and transfer through R&D between multinational corporations entering developing economies and collaboration with indigenous firms. Mironko is the author of the book Determinants of FDI Flows within Emerging Economies: A Case Study of Poland, published by Palgrave Macmillan and several other publications. He teaches courses in global competition, business strategy, entrepreneurship, and leadership. He received his Ph.D. in International Business from Rutgers University.

Vera Mishina, Candidate of Sciences, is from Chelyabinsk, Russia. She graduated from Chelyabinsk State Academy of Culture and Arts where she studied philosophical anthropology and completed her postgraduate studies culminating with the Candidate of Science degree in 2009. In her candidate thesis, Vera investigated the relationship between innovation and self-realization of a personality, the peculiarities of creative and leadership behaviors within innovative processes. Later, Dr. Mishina continued her scientific and teaching activities in management at South Ural State University (SUSU, Chelyabinsk, Russia). Currently, she works at the Department of Modern Educational Technologies (SUSU). She is the author of more than 50 scientific publications, and her deep theoretical training and high creative and scientific potential make her a valuable contributor to international cooperation programs for university teachers. Vera is a Co-Investigator for GLOBE Project, Russia, a world-wide study on leadership effectiveness.

Zeina N. Mneimneh, Ph.D., is an Assistant Research Scientist in the Survey Methodology Program, and the Director of the International Unit within the Survey Research Center, University of Michigan. She is the director of the World Mental Health Data Collection Coordinating Center that supports the design and implementation of national mental health surveys in more than 35 countries. She is also the chair of the executive committee of the Comparative Survey Design and Implementation (CSDI) annual Workshop. Mneimneh has published more than 60 peer-reviewed publications and book chapters. Her research investigates factors affecting the reporting of sensitive information, including interviewer, respondent, and question characteristics, and contextual factors related to culture and the interview setting. Her recent work examines the use of social media data for social science research including consent to link survey data with social media data.

Henriette Müller, Ph.D., is Visiting Assistant Professor of Leadership Studies at NYUAD. Her research encompasses the comparative study of leadership both at the national and international level, as well as across diverse cultural regions. Her most recent book *Political Leadership and the European Commission Presidency* was published by *Oxford University Press* in 2020. She is the editor (together with Ingeborg Tömmel) of *Women and Leadership in the European Union* (*Oxford University Press*, forthcoming), as well as two special issues on *The Role of Leadership in EU Politics and Policy-Making* (*West European Politics*, 2020, 43/5) together with Femke van Esch, and *Women Opposition Leaders: Pathways, Patterns and Performance* (*Politics & Governance*, 2023, 11/1) together with Sarah C. Dingler and Ludger Helms. Her research has appeared among others in *Hawwa: Journal of Women of the Middle East and the Islamic World* and *Journal of European Integration*.

Rosemary Muriungi, Ph.D., has worked in Africa and the United States as an educator in institutions of higher learning and as a practitioner in global organizations advocating for children, human rights, and sustainable human development, including the United NationsHer recent roles involve Market Intelligence Research and Business Advising at the Washington Small Business Development Center (WSBDC) and teaching Strategic Leadership, Leadership and Human Potential, and Leadership in Global Business Environments at Gonzaga University. Her research interests focus on women, youth, organizational, and global leadership; small business development; higher education of under-served, vulnerable, and marginalized populations; humanitarianism; forced displacement and migration. Rosemary serves on Boards in Kenya and the United States. She is the current Board President to Partnering for Progress (P4P) in the United States. She is passionate about talent and leadership development of women and youth and has mentored and coached many over the years.

Jennifer Aden Murnane-Rainey, Ph.D., is a global leadership scholar and practitioner. She has held executive-level finance, sales, marketing, and operations positions for multinational organizations and played a key role in global strategic planning efforts for organizations in the financial services, business services, and education industries. Jennifer is an associate professor of management and finance at Midland University and runs her own strategy consulting company (JAM Group) where she has consulted on complex business issues to improve organizational performance in the corporate, government, and nonprofit sectors. She holds a Ph.D. from Iowa State University's Leadership Academy in Family & Consumer Sciences Education, as well as an MBA and a BSBA degree both from the University of Nebraska at Omaha.

Angie O'Brien, M.A., is a social scientist in the in Center for Behavioral Science Methods at the U.S. Census Bureau. She is a member of the Language and Cross-Cultural Research Group and has a master's in sociology and a bachelor's degree in Spanish language and cultural studies. Angie is currently a doctoral candidate at the Department of Sociology at University of Maryland, College Park. Her dissertation uses both quantitative and qualitative methods to explore how pregnancy behaviors and culture have changed over time. She is interested in survey methods, questionnaire design, gender, work, and family.

Dionne Rosser-Mims, Ph.D., is a Full Professor of adult education and former Dean of the College of Education at Troy University (TROY). Appointed Vice Chancellor of the Troy University Phenix City Campus in October 2020, Dr. Rosser-Mims completed Harvard's Women in Educational Leadership Institute and is a 2016 Chancellor's Fellow. Dr. Rosser-Mims has nearly 20 years of adult education experience. She has authored four books with the most recent 2020 co-edited publication titled *Pathways into the Political Arena: The Perspectives of Global Women Leaders.* Dr. Rosser-Mims is the co-founder of *Dialogues in Social Justice: An Adult Education Journal,* a peer-reviewed open-access journal. Dr. Rosser-Mims holds a doctorate in adult education and a master's in public administration from the University of Georgia. Her research interests include leadership development; international and comparative adult and continuing education; women and leadership; and leadership and intersectionality theory.

Lamia El Sadek, Ph.D., studied business management and information technology and has a Masters in Training and Development from North Carolina State University. She holds a PhD in Global Leadership from Indiana Tech. Lamia has extensive international business and finance experience in multinational corporations. Later in her career, she decided to pursue her true passion and work in the non-profit sector. Lamia has worked in international development and humanitarian relief throughout Africa, the Middle East, Australia, and Europe on issues ranging from economic development, forcibly displaced & refugee rights, to gender equity and youth empowerment. In 2010, Lamia was among an international humanitarian delegation to Gaza. In 2016 and 2017, she spoke at the United Nation's CSW on 'Economic Empowerment and Equity of Marginalized Groups' globally. Lamia is currently working on a book outlining the parallels between the recent global revolutions (Arab Spring) and the social movements within the U.S.

Anthony Scardino, Ph.D., has a BA in Political Science focused on International Relations, a Master of Public Policy in Economics, and a Ph.D. in Leadership and Organizational Change. His research is deeply embedded in Servant Leadership and Organizational Change focused on higher education, community engagement, and ethical business practices. Anthony is the author of a number of academic articles on leadership and economics. After many years in the traditional business world in various management positions and as a consultant, Anthony desired an opportunity to take his experience and share it within the classroom. Anthony's focus on quality leadership and change, he championed organizational change within the institution to create new pathways of success for the adult learner. Anthony is currently an Associate Professor and Vice President of the Faculty Senate at Felician University in NJ. He teaches Economics, International Business, Business Ethics and Leadership, and Entrepreneurship.

Sarah Singletary Walker, Ph.D., is currently the Interim Vice Provost for Institutional Diversity and Inclusion at Creighton University. She is also a Management Professor in the Heider College of Business at Creighton University where she teaches undergraduate, graduate, and doctoral-level students. Trained as an Industrial–Organizational Psychologist, she is an active researcher on topics related to diversity, equity, and inclusion for both Applied Psychology and Management journals. In addition, she has been awarded $1.1M in federal grant funds designed to increase the diversity of individuals pursuing Post- Baccalaureate degrees.

Carly Speranza, Ed.D., is the Director of Research and Assistant Professor of Management in the College of BILT at Marymount University, in the Washington D.C. metro area. She is also an Adjunct Faculty member at Creighton University and at Indiana Tech University. Previously she was the Associate Dean of the College of Strategic Intelligence and Associate Professor of National Security and Leadership Studies at National Intelligence University, an accredited federal university, in Washington

DC. She is a retired Lieutenant Colonel from the U.S. Air Force where she served on active-duty as an Intelligence Officer for over twenty years.

Elizabeth Stork, Ph.D., is Professor of Organizational Leadership. She earned her Ph.D. in Social Work – Social Administration from the University of Pittsburgh as well as her M.A. in Sociology in Gender, Race, and Class and M.S.W. Her B.A. in The Classics is from L.S.U. She has been teaching at RMU since 2005. Stork conducts research in a variety of subjects related to the social construction of leadership but her interests are strongly in patriarchal effects on women and men leaders and the persistence of gender stereotypes. Areas of research are in leadership entitlement, using film to study gender stereotyping, deconstructing leadership, and deconstructing diversity. Currently she is studying women activists in authoritarian, patriarchal countries such as Jordan, Armenia, and Ethiopia, interviewing women who accomplish things under oppressive social traditions. She teaches research methods, social movements, sex/gender and leadership, and leadership and democracy.

Amanda Wickramasinghe, Ed.D., Ph.D., is a scholar-practitioner in global competencies, global mindset, women's leadership, organizational development, and international studies. She is the Director of Education for ERA Brokers and an adjunct professor at Brandman University and National University. In addition to these and earlier leadership roles, she serves on multiple international outreach committees, creating global strategic partnerships. She has traveled extensively internationally, interviewing global leaders for her contributions to foreign policy. Amanda is a board member for the International Center for Global Leadership and an active member for the International Leadership Association, where she has chaired research panels and moderated keynote speaker events. She serves as an advocate for international affairs and is a founding member of the International Women's Innovative Network. She earned her EdD and PhD at Pepperdine University. She was appointed to the board of visitors and was recognized as an Inaugural 40 under 40 Honoree at Pepperdine University.

Brenda C. Williams, Ed.D., has had a two-decade long career in Higher Education in several areas: HR, Student Affairs, IT and Workforce Development and Continuing Education. Her research and scholarship are in: employment of people with disabilities and employment, at-risk populations, immigrant populations, global leadership, multiculturalism in qualitative research and community college leadership. Dr. Williams has taught as an adjunct for Indiana Tech University over 8 years as an adjunct in the PhD Leadership Program; Towson University, College of Education; an adjunct at Morgan State University, Community College Leadership Doctoral Program, an adjunct at UMUC, Human Resource Management, Business and Professional Programs; and as an adjunct at Capella University where she teaches Leadership and Systems Thinking. She holds B.S from New York University, MA Ed & HD from The George Washington University, and EdD in Higher Education Administration from The George Washington University.

Sarah Wipperman, LLM, is the Scholarly Communications Librarian at Villanova University, specializing in issues related to publishing, copyright, author rights, open access, and scholarly infrastructure. Sarah provides academic author consultations to help them understand and negotiate their publishing contracts. She also teaches frequent workshops on copyright, reuse, publishing criteria, sharing work outside of publication, and increasing research visibility. Prior to Villanova, Sarah held roles in scholarly communication, institutional repository management, and library publishing at the University of Pennsylvania Libraries. She holds a Master in Law from Penn Law, specializing in copyright and contracts.

Leon van den Broeke, Ph.D., studied economics, law and business studies, and theology. He is extraordinary professor Theology of Law and Church Polity, and Director of the Deddens Church Polity Centre at the Theological University Kampen; associate professor Religion, Law and Society, and chair of the Centre for Religion and Law at the Vrije Universiteit Amsterdam, the Netherlands. He also works as a consultant, trainer and mediator.

Maja Zelihic, Ph.D., is a Fulbright Specialist, Full Professor, and Department Chair of Advanced Management Studies at the Forbes School of Business and Technology, University of Arizona Global Campus. She is a Global Dialogue Partner at NAFSA, and serves on the Board of Advisors of the International Fellowship Program in Arbitration and Scientific Assessment, the comprehensive global academic review platform. She is an industry advisory member at the Amity University Novel Communication Lab (AUNCL). Dr. Zelihic is a Board member at the Center for Women's Leadership at the Forbes School of Business and Technology. She was listed as Top 200 Global Leaders to follow in 2021 by PeopleHum. She is published in over 20+ peer-reviewed journals, and her research ventures took her to Haiti, Cuba, Mexico, Panama, Jordan, Zambia, the Balkan region, among others. Her book on Perception, with Dr. Diane Hamilton, was released in December 2020 (https://drmajazelihic.com/)

Series Foreword

For most of the last century (hard to imagine that the 20th century is now far behind us), published leadership research was largely conducted by Western scholars, particularly scholars in North America and Western Europe. And, for the most part, the leaders (and followers) studied were primarily limited to those countries. This led to a very limited perspective on leaders and leadership. Thankfully, in the much more interconnected world of the 21st century we are seeing a sharp increase in the study of leadership from all corners of the globe. As you can imagine, this has greatly increased the complexity of both studying leadership internationally and cross-culturally, but also in expanding our understanding of leadership as it plays out in many diverse countries and cultures. Which brings us to this book.

When the editorial team, led by Yulia, first proposed this handbook, I had two main thoughts: First, I knew there was a need for a guidebook to assist the growing number of scholars who were studying leadership cross-culturally and internationally (and a need to inform more "provincial" scholars about this work that was being done). But, second, I was concerned that there might not be enough good scholarship to fill such an ambitious volume. On the second count, I was wrong. The editorial team of Yulia, Franziska, and Jennie have cast a broad net and sought diverse, expert authors who have knowledge of the theoretical, methodological, and practical issues that are required to study leadership in different countries, cultures, regions, and societies. The result is a true *handbook* that can be used by scholars, students, and practitioners, interested in leadership from an international and cross-cultural perspective. Not only will this volume increase current understanding of the many issues in international and cross-cultural research, but it will stimulate further thinking and advancement in this very important area of leadership studies.

When people ask me why I study leadership, I always say that I am fascinated by its complexity and awed by its importance to society and humankind. After diving into this handbook, I am even more convinced that leadership in all its forms in different countries and cultures is fantastically complex, and simply reading this book opens up new ways of thinking about, and planning to investigate, leadership in its many and diverse forms.

Ronald E. Riggio

Acknowledgements

Bringing a book of this magnitude to life requires a village, and we are grateful to the many partners and colleagues involved. First and foremost, we thank the authors herein who graciously shared life experiences and scholarly wisdom. Your contributions provide road signs to other scholars as they navigate the beautiful complexities of cross-cultural and international leadership research and build genuine partnerships with others in the process. They also provide compelling stories around the proverbial campfire, to support one another as we reflect on our journeys.

We hold our Series Editor, Dr. Ron Riggio, in great esteem for the ongoing forum for leadership scholarship that he created and continues to foster through the Leadership: Research and Practice series. His early and ongoing support of our ideas have made this project possible, and we extend our gratitude.

There are many in our village of supporters who have been generous with their feedback and suggestions to shape this work, such as our conference session participants at multiple academic conferences like the International Leadership Association Annual Meetings and the Bulgarian Comparative Education Society Conferences. Thank you! These panels and discussions were instrumental to further develop the vision of the Handbook.

To our families, we thank you for supporting us with the time and energy needed to produce the Handbook. We love you, and we do this work with you always with us in spirit. Perhaps one of the greatest privileges of scholarship is the ability to leave a humble but heartfelt mark on the world. Thank you for helping us do that.

Finally, we are grateful to you, our readers. We have relished the opportunity working with colleagues to bundle our combined scholarly wisdom into a vehicle that will serve you in doing the same for many years to come. To inspire your exploration of the Handbook, we invite you to begin by reflecting on the words of Dr. Wade Davis, whose quote captures our sentiments as we reflect on the journey that this book has taken us on, "The world can only appear monochromatic to those who persist in interpreting what they experience through the lens of a single cultural paradigm, their own. For those with the eyes to see and the heart to feel, it remains a rich and complex topography of the spirit." We wish you a rich journey.

Yulia, Franziska, Jennie

Introduction to the Handbook

Yulia Tolstikov-Mast, Franziska Bieri, and Jennie L. Walker

It is an exciting time to be in the flourishing field of leadership studies. It has been producing more scholarship than ever before, increasing its international reach, and examining new perspectives, such as exploring leadership as a multi-level phenomenon (e.g., individuals, teams, organizations, industries, nations), addressing followership, and analyzing the complexity of contextual influences (Dionne, 2017; Gardner et al., 2010; Marcy, 2020). Discussions about the evolution of leadership in the 21st century are of great interest to scholars and practitioners across sectors, due to the important role of leadership processes in the global economy, societies, organizations, international relations, and public health.

The diversity of interests in leadership and an application of the leadership phenomenon across disciplines makes leadership studies a truly multidisciplinary field. This is evidenced by a greater diversity of disciplines reported in analyses of Leadership Quarterly publications, including management, psychology, history, cognitive science, economics, anthropology, sociology, political science, medicine, engineering and other fields (Dionne, 2017; Gardner et al., 2010). Leadership studies have also expanded in recent years across cultures and societies (e.g., House et al., 2004; House et al., 2014; Jogulu, 2010; Leong & Fischer, 2011), with a noticeable increase in culture specific leadership theorizing within societies (Peus, Braun, & Knipfer, 2015; Pillai et al., 2011; Romero, 2004). For example, research looking at indigenous, Middle Eastern, Asian, Russian, and other racial, ethnic, and culturally-specific leadership practices are emerging across the globe (e.g., Eisenbeiß & Brodbeck, 2014; McDonald, 2011). Concepts and models from these studies are critically important to the field, as they have been developed based on the local values, beliefs, histories, traditions, and leadership practices, thus, viewing leadership through an authentically developed scholarly lens. Leadership scholars emphasize the importance of this cultural lens to capture complexity of context, especially in international or cross-cultural studies (Farid, 2011; Osland, Bird, & Oddou, 2012; Scandura & Dorfman, 2004; Shamir, 2012). Finally, growth in diverse leadership scholarship has inspired international research partnerships to collaborate, critically examine and question methodological approaches to leadership topics (Dorfman et al., 2012).

Although the increase in international, cross-cultural, and multicultural leadership research is evident, discussions about an appropriate research process, including nuances, challenges, or ways of conducting this type of research, are limited (Hanges & Shteynberg, 2004). Leadership researchers have no guide or frameworks to help them lead and collaborate effectively on international leadership research projects. However, the complexities within international studies (e.g., intersections of culture,

DOI: 10.4324/9781003003380-101

societal characteristics, histories) require non-linear and reflective research approaches not widely taught in traditional leadership curriculum. The need for alternative research frameworks has been acknowledged by a number of leadership scholars (Osland, Bird, & Oddou, 2012; Peterson & Hunt, 1997). A step-wise research process that is convenient for conventional leadership scholarship is not suited for studies with the goal to genuinely understand authentic local perspectives and practices.

Another challenge is a continued bias towards Western research methodology and use of a Western theoretical lens in observations of culturally unique phenomena (Karr, 2016; Kovach, 2009; Miller Cleary, 2013; Smith, 2003). This tendency is reported in many social science disciplines, including the field of leadership (e.g., Hage & Posner, 2015; Karr, 2016; Sidani, 2008). "One approach to knowledge developed by a small group of Europeans turned out to have such spectacular consequences for humanity," commented Godfrey-Smith (2003, p.5). Western universities mostly introduce social science subject knowledge shaped by Western thinkers (Karr, 2016). Other diverse and similarly valuable perspectives and methodologies remain overlooked or are treated as less important (Kovach, 2009). Ultimately, an application of Western epistemological and ontological views to understand non-Western leadership practices presents a risk for misrepresentation of leadership phenomena in other societies. The main goal of social science scientific observations is to reveal truths about human reality (Godfrey-Smith, 2003), and this cannot be reliably done by scholars who are not prepared for the complexities of international research.

Leadership studies should offer opportunities to learn how to engage in rigorous and authentic scholarship across cultures and societies, as well as to work productively in international research collaborations. To conduct leadership research in different societies and cultures does not mean only to travel abroad or work with internationally diverse samples. The handbook argues the importance of a unique intercultural and international research approach across the entire conceptual framework of a study, from a theoretical foundation to a research application.

Handbook Contribution

The *Handbook of International and Cross-Cultural Leadership Research Processes: Perspectives, Practice, Instruction* is a distinctive contribution to the area of leadership studies with attention to all stages of the research process. It provides an analysis of international and cross-cultural leadership scholarship, discusses international research collaborations, and makes recommendations for internalization of doctoral leadership research curriculum. A unique feature of this volume is that it curates personal reflections of leadership scholars from diverse cultural and international backgrounds about their research experiences to further illuminate the interactions among researcher, participants in research and the field of international leadership research. The reflections are intended to inspire readers, whether students, experienced researchers, or faculty who teach research, to consider their own preparation and approaches to research.

We have titled the handbook using the words 'international' and 'cross-cultural,' as these descriptors remain commonly utilized in the field. 'International' refers to research that crosses borders. 'Cross-cultural' research makes comparisons between different cultural groups. While most if not all international research is cross-cultural, not all cross-cultural research is international. International research is often unique in the research collaborations it requires (Committee on International Relations in Psychology, 2014). This made both terms important to capture the coverage herein. The considerations and framework discussed in this book have wide application in research with diverse societies across the globe. As research evolves in the future, we suspect that the considerations in this volume will not be relegated to "international" or "cross-cultural"; they will be integrated into research approaches across fields and disciplines in the recognition that regardless of where we stand in the world there remain bridges to be built across the diversity of human experiences.

Good intentions are not enough to uncover authentic cultural knowledge. Applying exclusively Western monocultural standards could lead to biased research, flawed study results, and non-replicable knowledge (Matsumoto & van de Vijver, 2011). This is why the Handbook includes several chapters discussing research integrity and standards for cross-cultural and international leadership research. "To cross cultural borders in research is a slippery and complicated endeavor, and good intentions, though essential, are not enough to help researchers make those crossings with respect those they research and with their own integrity intact" (Miller Cleary, 2013, p. 1). Miller Cleary (2013) summarizes what has been on the minds of international researchers who wrote chapters for the Handbook: how could we move our studies from a basic 'do no harm' imperative to "'ethic of care' and respect" (p. 11), "a humanitarian commitment" (p. 12) to represent those we research within their true leadership realities.

One of the main themes throughout chapters is the importance of different contextual considerations in leadership studies, both theoretically and methodologically, and how they necessarily influence the approach to research. The Handbook advocates that to conduct international research it's important to apply diverse epistemological and ontological perspectives, a "native" theoretical foundation, and relevant research methodology to capture local context in a truthful and unbiased way. Conceptually, we need to consider characteristics of study participants, their cultures, histories, perspectives, and current realities. In doing so we may find that there are no existing or relevant theoretical frameworks for a specific population or context. Methodologically, we need to include variables that can explain, partly or fully, observed cross-cultural differences to enhance study validity and address biases and inequivalence. This may require unique research designs, such as using multiple languages in interviews of bi-cultural leaders or having ongoing scholarly reflections throughout qualitative as well as quantitative studies (e.g., Matsumoto, & van de Vijver, 2011). To authentically explore diverse cultural contexts, researchers may find themselves at a cross-road between what they were 'taught' to do as researchers and what a study calls for.

While traditional leadership research publications are treated as guides with definitive answers, this Handbook does not take that approach. Instead, the authors often present questions to consider, such as: Which research questions should be asked to contribute to a body of knowledge? How do we address causes of the observed differences? (e.g., ecological fallacy; cultural attribution fallacy) (Matsumoto & Yoo, 2006). What can be learned from other disciplines about international and cross-cultural scholarship frameworks? (Berry at al., 2002; Matsumoto, & van de Vijver, 2011). How do we tell a more complete story without overly simplifying the intersection of many contexts? These are just a few of the questions that inspired this Handbook. Answers to these questions are not simple or straightforward. Thus, a multidisciplinary and multinational group of scholars and practitioners came together to explore them.

To study leadership within a local context and across cultural boundaries requires a particular set of research skills, multidisciplinary knowledge and knowledge of non-Western literature and perspectives. Thus, the Handbook argues that there is a need to enhance leadership research education in these areas. Moreover, engagement in leadership research across cultures needs researchers with a uniquely developed disposition, a cultivated international research integrity, ability to evoke diverse intellectual resources and integrate local context.

Handbook Vision

This publication has been a journey to learn from a diverse group of international researchers about their experiences, so we may offer the readers insights from real-world experience and a dynamic framework that will smooth out their own path. Like any journey, it had a starting point. Ideas for the Handbook began with the editors' shared passion for diversity and zest for international explorations, both in life and in research. We all had experience conducting research outside of our home countries and across cultures. However, our preparation for doing this research differed. Some of the differences were positive, in terms of approaches or methods, while others pointed to gaps in training that we had to learn through experience. Regardless of our individual journeys, we all agreed on the imperative for international research education for leadership scholars in our highly-globalized world. We share a glimpse into our individual journeys here.

Yulia's Story

In 2013, I traveled to my home country, Russia, to collect data for an exploratory study on Russian followership (see Chapter 4 for more details). This experience had many consequences. I realized the research process required additional steps that were different from qualitative studies I had performed in the U.S.A. This led me to search for scholarly literature that offered insights into studies outside of a Western leadership framework and context. At the same time, as Lead Faculty at a U.S. university, I was coordinating a redesign of core research courses for a doctoral program in global leadership. Since many doctoral students were interested in doing leadership studies in other countries or across cultures, I realized it was critical to introduce a new course in the curriculum that would provide foundational understanding of research contexts and approaches outside of familiar leadership epistemology.

The efforts to learn more about research in other countries and to design an international research course revealed a substantial and significant gap in literature. Discussions with like-minded researchers across disciplines and at the International Leadership Association inspired an idea for a detailed manual on international and cross-cultural leadership. However, when the publisher reviewed the book proposal, the decision was that the gap in literature called for a much larger undertaking – a handbook. Sharing the handbook vision with Jennie and Franziska was only natural, as they were experienced international leadership researchers, regularly trained doctoral students in international leadership (through the course I originally designed), and were advocates for the handbook goals.

Franziska's Story

As a native Swiss, naturalized American, and permanent resident of Bulgaria, international and cross-cultural realities are part of my personal fabric and daily routines. I grew up in a bilingual household, and we are raising our children with the three languages spoken in our family. In Sociology, I found a perfect match for my curiosity about society and interests in global and international issues.

I have conducted qualitative and quantitative studies focused on global, international, comparative cross-national, and local contexts. For my dissertation research I investigated how government, non-governmental, and industry leaders worked together to develop an international solution to end the trade in conflict diamonds. More recently, I have collaborated with colleagues in Switzerland and Bulgaria on a school leaver survey. I regularly teach graduate and undergraduate courses, including research methods classes with interdisciplinary and international foci.

Based on this background, Yulia's plans for a book featuring authors' visions for and insights from international research approaches immediately struck a chord with me. In fact, the editorial process of this Handbook itself crossed boundaries in terms of methodological and theoretical traditions, professional backgrounds, disciplines, and time zones.

Jennie's Story

Ever since I was in elementary school, I've been drawn to connect with people from other cultures. First, it was befriending foreign exchange students in my schools in the U.S.A, and then interacting with local peoples when I studied abroad several times in college – Spain, Argentina, Chile. I deeply enjoyed learning about other perspectives, traditions and histories. I also developed many great friendships that continue to this day.

My career continued to lead me across borders. As a corporate leadership development specialist, I taught cross-cultural leadership to managers and directors in several countries. My hobby-turned-side-job as a scuba instructor found me leading trips to Mexico. Most recently, I teach graduate courses in global leadership research and consult on cross-cultural leadership in organizations. For me, international and cross-cultural leadership have always been about building bridges between people. It's rich work, because the diversity of experiences and stories are without end as societies and cultures change over time.

When Yulia approached Franziska and I about the concept for this handbook, I was immediately interested, because of my experience as a scholar working across cultures and also as a professor training future scholars. Experience has taught me that working across cultures requires a different level of preparation that is not often covered in research courses or trainings. It tends to be lumped into contextual considerations related to sample or treated as a step in the research process, both of which over-simplify a necessarily complex undertaking. Furthermore, I see a compelling need across academic fields and disciplines to move away from compartmentalizing diversity in certain courses and programs to integrate it more fully into curriculum, such as processes for research itself.

Handbook Authors

The Handbook brings together authors with diverse cultural, academic and practitioner backgrounds. Our authors are from Armenia, Belgium, Bosnia, Bulgaria, Canada, Egypt, Germany, India, Kenya, Lebanon, Leq'á:mel First Nation (part of the Stó:lō Coast Salish), Poland, Philippines, Russia, Sri Lanka, Switzerland, Trinidad and Tobago, and the U.S.A. Their academic expertise and experiences come from the fields of anthropology, leadership, sociology, global leadership, marketing, management, political science, psychology, military leadership, practical theology, indigenous business studies, public policy, education, English, communication studies, and library sciences. Many of the authors are currently or have been professionals in a variety of industries including human resources, strategic planning, project management, non-profit socially-oriented organizations, education, consulting, and government organizations. The authors also vary in terms of their depth and breadth of international or cross-cultural research experiences. Some draw on insights from decades long research careers, while others reflect on their first systematic leadership study - their dissertation. The diversity of the authors creates a multidimensional and compelling exploration of perspectives, approaches and experiences when engaging in international and cross-cultural leadership research. The unifying thread among them is a shared intent to build knowledge of diverse and evolving leadership practices and phenomena across cultures and societies.

Handbook Structure

The Handbook of International and Cross-Cultural Leadership Research Processes has three parts. Part I introduces epistemological, ontological and conceptual traditions of the leadership field. The authors critically reflect on how established leadership and followership theories and approaches sometimes fail to capture local practices in different cultures and regions of the world. They underscore the importance of asking context-specific research questions, discuss the emergence of authentic culturally-immersive studies and theorizing, and offer unique frameworks to study leadership and followership in international and intercultural environments.

The chapters in Part II focus on methodological and design problems and opportunities when conducting research on global leadership topics. Scholars share insights on their research practices in different stages of international and cross-cultural studies. We have organized the chapters by these stages: planning and design issues (Part IIA); qualitative and quantitative data collection (Part IIB); and analysis and interpretation (Part IIC).

Part III is forward-looking. Authors consider how we prepare future researchers today and how research training must evolve to account for and respond to the complexities and realities of the field. There is a discussion on how we disseminate new knowledge gleaned from research, and consideration for how to be more inclusive in that process. Finally, the concluding chapters engage readers in a discussion of how we maintain integrity of research in the field and then provide them with a framework forged from the insights in this Handbook. The sections in Part III include, teaching and learning international and cross-cultural leadership research (Part IIIA); research publishing and application (Part IIIB), and leadership research standards (Part IIIC).

The Handbook includes examples of both theoretical and empirical works, from questioning the concept of "universal leadership theory" to discussing ethical research standards across cultures and setting standards for intercultural research approaches to rigor. Other topics are international sampling strategy, integrity and validity of international research, cultural assumptions and frames of reference and their influence on theory development, challenges with concept translation, international approaches to informed consent, and publication standards in international scholarly outlets. Additionally, the Handbook discusses challenges and rewards of conducting research across cultures and countries, the value and challenges of international research collaborations, as well as unique methodologies to understand leadership phenomena in different cultures. Many chapters offer practical recommendations and resource lists. Readers will find examples of leadership research within the indigenous context, as well as perspectives on how power and inequality shape research methods and epistemologies. Other chapters represent studies and research reflections across international (e.g., Russia, Japan) or cultural contexts (e.g., minority groups based on race, gender or sexual orientation, First Nation Peoples). What unites chapters is the focus on the research process, as authors reflect and offer insights based on their diverse research histories.

Handbook Audience

The Handbook is intended to be a resource for a broad audience that includes scholars across disciplines and fields, educators, consultants, and graduate and doctoral students who are interested in researching leadership practices outside of the traditional Western paradigm and across intercultural and international environments.

International and global leadership are relatively new and trending areas. Increasing number of universities are offering classes in these areas, and more graduate and doctoral students are engaging in international and global leadership research across research courses. In addition, many academic journals that publish leadership scholarship desire to feature studies with diverse samples and international and cross-cultural research approaches. Thus, this book is unique and timely to provide assistance with planning, conducting and publishing international leadership scholarship.

The *Handbook of International and Cross-Cultural Leadership Research Processes: Perspectives, Practice, Instruction* can be used for research courses in programs that focus on leadership. Relevant courses may include educational leadership, international management, organizational behavior, international business, leadership studies, and global leadership. The book can be a main text for a standalone cross-cultural, international or a global leadership research course, or it can supplement introduction to research or methodology specific courses (e.g., qualitative, quantitative, mixed methods).

Leadership research across cultures and societies is a global endeavor, and the book is intended for a global audience, featuring works of diverse scholars conducted in different regions of the world. Some readers may focus on specific stages in the research process, while others might select chapters that align most with the methodological design they are planning. Other readers may seek insights on research experiences in particular world regions or academic disciplines. The Handbook is structured so that it can be read in its entirety or explored selectively by chapter. No matter the approach, the overall goal of each chapter, section and the Handbook is to provide the reader with concrete ideas and practices to conceptualize, design, and conduct rigorous and authentic cross-cultural and international leadership studies.

References

Berry, J. W., Poortinga, Y. H., Segal, M. H., & Dasen, P. R. (2002). *Cross-cultural psychology: Research and applications*. Cambridge University Press.

Clifton, J., & Dai, W. (2020). A discursive analysis of the in situ construction of (Japanese) leadership and leader identity in a research interview. Implications for leadership research. *Leadership, 16*(2), 180–199. doi:10.11 77/1742715019856159

Committee on International Relations in Psychology. (2014). *Engaging in international collaborative research. Part of the series going international: A practical guide for psychologists*. Office of International Affairs. https://www.apa.org/international/resources/publications/research.pdf

Dionne, S. D. (2017). Leadership Quarterly Yearly Review: Multidisciplinary, multilevel, multisource, multi-skilled and multigenerational perspectives. *Leadership Quarterly, 28*(1), 22–23. http://doi:10.1016/j.leaqua.201 7.01.007

Dorfman, P. W., Javidan, M., Hanges, P., Dastmalchian, A., & House, R. (2012). GLOBE: A twenty-year journey into the intriguing world of culture and leadership. *Journal of World Business 47*(4), 504–518. doi:1 0.1016/j.jwb.2012.01.004.

Eisenbeiß, S., & Brodbeck, F. (2014). Ethical and unethical leadership: A cross-cultural and cross-sectoral analysis. *Journal of Business Ethics, 122*(2), 343–359. doi:10.1007/s10551-013-1740-0

Farid, M. (2011). Contextual leadership. *The Journal of Management Development, 30*(9), 865- 881.

Gardner, W. L., Lowe, K. B., Moss, T. W., & Mahoney, K. T. (2010). Scholarly leadership of the study of leadership: A review of The Leadership Quarterly's second decade, 2000–2009. *The Leadership Quarterly, 21*(6), 922–958. DOI:10.1016/j.leaqua.2010.10.003

Given, L. M. (Ed.). (2008). *The Sage encyclopedia of qualitative research methods. Cross-Cultural Research*, 180–181. doi:10.4135/9781412963909

Godfrey-Smith, P. (2003). *Theory and reality: An introduction to the philosophy of science*. University of Chicago Press.

Hage, J. & Posner, B. Z. (2015). Religion, religiosity, and leadership practices: An examination in the Lebanese workplace. *Leadership & Organization Development Journal, 36*(4), 396–412. doi:10.1108/LODJ-07-2013-0096

Hanges, P. J., & Shteynberg, G. (2004). Methodological challenges and solutions for leadership researchers. *Zeitschrift für Personalforschung, 18*(3), 346–358.

House, R. J., Dorfman, P. W., Javidan, M., Hanges, P. J., & DeLuque, M. S. (2014). *Strategic leadership: The GLOBE study of CEO leadership behavior and effectiveness across cultures*. Sage

House, R. J., Hanges, P. Javidan, M., Dorfman, P., & Gupta, V. (2004). *Culture, leadership, and organizations*. Sage

Jogulu, U. D. (2010). Culturally-linked leadership styles. *Leadership & Organization Development Journal, 31*(8), 705–719. doi:10.1108/01437731011094766

Karr, M. C. (2016, March 7). Dominance of Western perspectives troubles the social sciences. *Harvard Crimson*. https://www.thecrimson.com/article/2016/3/7/western-perspective-dominates-social-sciences/

Kovach, M. (2009). *Indigenous methodologies: Characteristics, conversations, and contexts*. Toronto, Ontario, Canada: University of Toronto Press.

Leong, L. Y. C., & Fischer, R. (2011). Is transformational leadership universal? A meta analytical investigation of multifactor leadership questionnaire means across cultures. *Journal of Leadership & Organizational Studies, 18*(2), 164–174.

Marcy, R. T. (2020). Leadership of socio-political vanguards: A review and future directions. *The Leadership Quarterly, 31*(1), Article 101372. https://doi.org/10.1016/j.leaqua.2019.101372

Matsumoto, D., & van de Vijver, F. J. R. (Eds.). (2011). *Culture and psychology. Cross-cultural research methods in psychology*. Cambridge University Press.

Matsumoto, D., & Yoo, S. H. (2006). Toward a new generation of cross-cultural research. *Perspectives on Psychological Science, 1*, 234–250.

McDonald, P. (2011). Maoism versus confucianism: Ideological influences on Chinese business leaders. *Journal of Management Development, 30*(7/8), 632–646. doi:10.1108/02621711111150164

Miller Cleary, M. (2013). *Cross-cultural research with integrity: Collected wisdom from researchers in social settings*. Palgrave Macmillan UK.

Oc, B., Bashshur, M. R., Daniels, M. A., Greguras, G. J., & Diefendorff, J. M. (2015). Leader humility in Singapore. *The Leadership Quarterly, 26*(1), 68–80.

Osland, J. S., Bird, A., & Oddou, G. (2012), The context of expert global leadership. In W. H. Mobley, Y. Wang, & M. Li (Eds.), *Advances in global leadership* (7th ed., pp. 107–124). Emerald.

Peterson, M. F., & Hunt, J. G. (1997). International perspectives on international leadership. *Leadership Quarterly, 8*(3), 203–231.

Peus, C., Braun, S., & Knipfer, K. (2015). On becoming a leader in Asia and America: Empirical evidence from women managers. *The Leadership Quarterly, 26*(1), 55–67. doi:10.1016/j.leaqua.2014.08.004

Pillai, R., Kohles, J. C., Bligh, M. C., Carsten, M. K., & Brodowsky, G. (2011). Leadership in "Confucian Asia": A three-country study of justice, trust, and transformational leadership. *Organization Management Journal, 8*(4), 242–259.

Prawat, R. (1989). Promoting access to knowledge, strategy, and disposition in students: A research synthesis. *Review of Educational Research, 59*(1), 1–41. doi:10.2307/1170445

Romero, E. J. (2004). Latin American leadership: El Patron and El Lider Moderno. *Cross-Cultural Management, 11*(3), 25–37. doi:10.1108/13527600410797828

Scandura, T., & Dorfman, P. (2004). Research in an international and cross-cultural context. *Leadership Quarterly, 15*(2), 277–307.

Shamir., B. (2012). Leadership in context and context in leadership studies. In M. G. Rumsey(Ed.), *The Oxford handbook of leadership*(pp. 343–358). Oxford University Press.

Sidani, Y. M. (2008). Ibn khaldun of north africa: An AD 1377 theory of leadership. *Journal of Management History, 14*(1), 73–86. doi:10.1108/17511340810845499

Smith, B. (2003). Worldview and culture: Leadership in Sub-Sahara Africa. *New England Journal of Public Policy, 19*(1), Article 15, 243–274. https://scholarworks.umb.edu/nejpp/vol19/iss1/15

Part I

Philosophical and Conceptual Traditions

Yulia Tolstikov-Mast

Part I introduces our readers to epistemological, ontological and conceptual traditions of the leadership field. Every academic field encompasses a range of epistemological and ontological traditions that serve as a foundation for creating knowledge (Guba & Lincoln, 1994). These traditions help understand the nature of reality, scholars' relationship to reality and the best ways to uncover knowledge. The leadership field, like all fields of study, evolves and changes as research unveils new insights, leading to shifts in the very foundations of knowledge (Bryman et al., 2011).

The three chapters in this section discuss earlier limitations of the field, where narrow philosophical assumptions, generalizations, limited populations, and interpretations of reality dominated. These limitations are not unusual for nascent fields (Taylor, 1987; Terman, 2011). The challenge is that some persist. Specifically, leadership theories and approaches historically have failed to capture how leadership is practiced in diverse cultures and regions of the world (Hunt & Fedynich, 2018). Because of that, leadership studies became a North American and Western European–centric field with fragmented knowledge about leadership practices outside of the traditional context (Avolio, Walumba, & Weber, 2009). Thus, valid knowledge outside of prescribed traditions remains hidden. These introductory chapters shine a spotlight on these issues and provide guidance to scholars searching for inclusive ways to conceptualize and study leadership.

In Chapter 1, Yulia Tolstikov-Mast and Jennifer Aden Murnane-Rainey address the cross-cultural and international reach of leadership scholarship. The chapter discusses epistemologies of traditional leadership research and acknowledges a bias towards Western cultures that has existed since the field's inception. While concerns remain about the dominance of the Western lens in research on non-Western societies, the authors discuss the noticeable scholarly shift to embrace the multiculturalism of leadership and culture-specific leadership theories. They also offer examples of progressive studies with authentic and emic or culture specific leadership paradigms. The chapter offers an outlook on new horizons in international leadership studies and concludes with examples of frameworks to study cross-cultural leadership.

In Chapter 2, Marc Hurwitz focuses on the other side of leadership, followership. An advocate of followership research, Hurwitz makes the case for the study of international followership being just as important as the study of leadership, since it is impossible to understand diverse perspectives of cross-cultural and international leadership without it. His deep dive into diverse followership research is thorough and detailed. Although there is a very limited number of cross-cultural and international followership studies and most of them adopt Western theories, tools and instruments,

Hurwitz shares examples of international followership research with unique approaches and conclusions grounded in local contexts.

Finally, Wanda Krause's Chapter 3 concludes the first part of this handbook. Krause asserts that the field of leadership studies, like many other social science fields, carries an inherent bias about human reality. Accustomed to familiar approaches, many leadership scholars fail to step outside of traditional paradigms and ask inclusive leadership questions. Thus, we are left wondering whose knowledge our leadership studies and theories represent. Krause shares her perspective-shaping experience with international research on civil organizations in the Middle East to illustrate how to ask better questions and be intentional in capturing diverse leadership realities.

Overall, Part I sets the tone for this handbook, demonstrating the need for epistemological, ontological and conceptual shifts in leadership research to embrace non-Western foundations of knowledge. The evolution is underway having the stream of studies with culturally unique models and methodologies, the inclusion of followership as a partnering process in cross-cultural leadership practices, and rethinking research questions to capture accurately local leadership experiences.

References

Avolio, B. J., Walumba, F. O., & Weber, T. J. (2009). Leadership: Current theories, research, and future directions. *Annual Review of Psychology, 60*, 421–449.

Bryman, A., Collinson, D., Grint, K., Jackson, B., & Uhl-Bien, M. (Eds.) (2011). *The SAGE handbook of leadership*. Sage.

Guba, E. G., & Lincoln, Y. S. (1994). Competing paradigms in qualitative research. In N. K. Denzin, & Y. S. Lincoln (Eds.), *Handbook of qualitative research* (pp. 105–117). Sage.

Hunt, T., & Fedynich, L. C. (2018). Leadership: Past, present, and future: An evolution of an idea. *Journal of Arts & Humanities, 8*(2), 20–26. 10.18533/journal.v8i2.1582

Taylor, C. (1987). Interpretive social science. In P. Robinson & W. Sullivan (Eds.), *Interpretive social sciences* (pp. 33–81). University of California Press

Terman, J. (2011). Comparative administration: Ontology and epistemology in cross-cultural research. *Administrative Theory & Praxis, 33*(2), 235–257. http://www.jstor.org/stable/29783184

1

Leadership Studies Across Cultures and Nations

Traditional Epistemology and New Horizons

Yulia Tolstikov-Mast and Jennifer Aden Murnane-Rainey

Introduction

Historically, the field of leadership studies has employed Western methodology and used English as the academic lingua franca to conduct and disseminate research (Bass & Bass, 2008; Chin, Trimble, & Garcia, 2017). The Western-centric and mono-linguistic practices have influenced the understanding of leadership. For example, the use of English in non-English-speaking cultures has led to questionable translations and an imposition of English meanings and concepts. The nuances of diverse leadership realities and leadership studies produced by scholars in non-English-speaking cultures have largely been overlooked (Bass & Bass, 2008; Schedlitzki et al., 2017; Stockemer & Wigginton, 2019). There has also been an implied expectation for publication and distribution in English language channels, as they are predominant in the field.

Over the past 30 years, leadership research has been evolving and becoming an increasingly inclusive scholarly area (Bass & Bass, 2008; Steinmann & Pugnetti, 2021). More international students study leadership and more non-Western scholars and practitioners question traditional leadership theories and applicability of leadership knowledge to their local contexts (e.g., Chin, Trimble, & Garcia 2017; Khan, 2020). This includes novel and authentic research designs and the emergence of non-Western leadership theorizing (e.g., Von Glinnow & Schneper, 2015; Zhang et al., 2012). As a result of the growth in international research and research collaborations, the meaning of leadership itself and what is considered leadership practice has come under greater scrutiny, due to differences across societies and cultures.

This chapter's goal is to offer a look at how cross-cultural and international leadership scholarship is currently positioned and approached within the broader field of leadership studies. In this chapter, we first offer a historical focus on leadership research across cultures, including when cross-cultural and international leadership research was recognized as a unique area of study. Then we discuss global leadership research and its views on leadership in multinational and complex settings. We further explore local, non-Western lenses to look at leadership practices. These approaches are increasing in number but not yet prominently represented within cross-cultural and international studies. Finally, this chapter concludes with how this handbook fits within these developments in the literature, featuring new research directions that account for cultural and societal nuances in leadership practices and diverse paradigms to study them.

DOI: 10.4324/9781003003380-1

Leadership Research Across Cultures and Societies: A Historical Focus

Traditional Epistemologies

Systematic leadership research began only in the 20th century (Bass, 1981). Early leadership conceptual and empirical developments emerged from management and psychology and, as a result, studies were initially quantitative, using survey instruments (Toor & Ofori, 2008a; 2008b). In the late 1990s, *leadership* started to gain prominence as a university program of study (Wheatley, 1994). Around this time, its application was expanded into many topical areas and professional contexts (i.e., healthcare, education, financial services) (Bass & Bass, 2008; Bryman et al., 2011). Leadership has always been an interdisciplinary area of study (Morris & Seeman, 1950). However, it has yet to achieve the cross-cultural and global objectives for reaching inclusiveness and comprehensiveness (Perkins, 2009).

Many scholars suggest that traditional leadership research has been biased toward North American contexts and cultures, since the field was originally grounded in Western scholarship and philosophy (Bass & Bass, 2008; Blair & Hunt, 1986; Bryman, 2004; Chin, Trimble, & Garcia, 2017; Den Hartog & Dickson, 2004; Yukl, 2010). More specifically, according to Peterson and Hunt (1997), leadership research has had a U.S. bias: the construct of *leadership* is an American notion with no universal meaning to fit a specific theory or group of scientific concepts (House, Wright, & Aditya, 1997). Snaebjornsson et al. (2015) state that "most of the leadership research in the past 50 years has come from the United States, Canada, and Western Europe and is strongly based on North American leadership paradigms" (p. 2). North American influence spread worldwide, and the bias transferred to other societies when English-speaking scholars with American leadership education conducted research, applying theories developed in the United States to other cultures and countries (House, Wright, & Aditya, 1997; Peterson & Hunt, 1997).

For example, the rapid increase in American multinational companies from the 1940s to 1980s had an influence on both cultural, commercial, and educational aspects of leadership in other societies and extended the Western view of leadership beyond the borders of the United States (Hunt & Fedynich, 2018; Middlehurst, 2008; Wee, 2010). Assessing the origins of leadership perceptions of Asian, Arab and African managers who had received a Westernized MBA education (in the United Kingdom), Mellahi (2000) found that Western leadership values were taught as the most important while local or culture-specific values of students' countries were neglected, thus, interpreted by international students as less important.

In the latter part of the 20th and earlier 21st centuries, leadership research started to evolve more internationally by including diverse country samples and research topics and conducting comparative studies (Dickson et al., 2003; Scandura & Dorfman, 2004; Steinmann & Pugnetti, 2021). International research collaborations, publishing in international outlets, and the use of qualitative and non-traditional designs also increased. The intersection of cross-cultural studies and leadership studies became a new field of study called *global leadership*. Global leadership shifted the leadership field from the mono-linguistic white male emphasis of earlier studies to a more holistic understanding of leadership across cultures and countries (Steinmann & Pugnetti, 2021). Early researchers in this field were international management scholars Perlmutter (1969) and Levitt (1983). When the field emerged, there were multiple classifications and categorizations of a new type of research, including multinational, multicultural, global leadership, international leadership, cross-cultural, cross-national, multicultural relations, and cross-border studies, without clearly established definitions, research scope and scale (Dickson et al., 2003; Mobley, Ming, & Wang, 2011; Peterson & Hunt, 1997; Scandura & Dorfman, 2004; Tsui et al., 2007). New journals and books specific to global leadership began to emerge and received multidisciplinary attention, such the journal *Advances in Global Leadership* and the book *Global leadership: Research, practice, and development* by Mendenhall and colleagues (2018).

Recognition of Cross-Cultural and International Leadership Area of Studies

First Scholarly Analyses

Several milestones helped position cross-cultural, international, and later, global leadership as unique and important areas of leadership studies. Important contributions include analytical summaries of scholarship by Peterson and Hunt (1997); House, Wright, and Aditya (1997); Smith (1997); Dorfman (1996) (updated Dorfman, 2003); and Dickson et al. (2003). Built on previous publications, Dickson et al. (2003) offers a 21st century perspective on leadership studies outside of the United States. The authors refer to the area as *"cross-cultural leadership."* Although the term is not clearly defined, the analysis of scholarship focuses on studies that cross cultural boundaries (including domestic, comparative, or multinational leadership research). Dickson and colleagues (2003) concluded that the level of emic (i.e., local) perspectives and approaches are becoming more refined and sophisticated (e.g., *The Leadership Quarterly*, *Advances in Global Leadership*), featuring more diverse groups of investigators and multinational studies than ever before (Dickson et al., 2003; Dorfman, 2003; House, Wright, & Aditya, 1997; Smith, 1997; Peterson & Hunt, 1997).

The GLOBE research project is an important example of research that began in the 1990's that has brought together hundreds of diverse researchers globally to collect data in nearly 200 societies over the last 25 years (Javidan et al., 2010). The study looks at the intersections of culture and leadership within societies. Earlier research on cultural dimensions informed global leadership research. Dickson et al. (2003) acknowledged Hofstede (1980) and Trompenaars and Hampden-Turner (1997) who have been important to the field of global leadership when exploring leadership approaches within and across societies. GLOBE research, for example, built on and expanded Hofstede's (1980) cultural dimensions, now including the following: uncertainty avoidance, power distance, societal collectivism, in-group collectivism, gender egalitarianism, assertiveness, future orientation, performance orientation, and humane orientation (House et al., 2002).

Global leadership and cultural dimension research have made important contributions to our understanding of how behaviors and expectations, especially as they relate to leadership, are influenced and shaped by culture. However, Dickson and colleagues' (2003) provide a counter-perspective that there is still work to do to build models of leadership from the unique vantage point of specific cultures. They reinforce that international journals continue to feature models from Western cultures that are typically comparative and quantitative in nature. To their point, cross-cultural leadership studies are largely characterized by quantitative perspectives to develop statistically supported typologies or culture clusters that measure dimensions of culture and allow for advanced data analysis techniques (Dickson et al., 2003; Dorfman, 2003; House, Wright, & Aditya, 1997; Peterson & Hunt, 1997; Smith, 1997). Dickson et al.'s (2003) work was important to present the value of non-Western leadership scholarship and research approaches to the academic community within leadership studies.

Inclusion of Cross-Cultural and International Leadership Perspectives in the Conventional Leadership Field

Another milestone was the appearance of sections on cross-cultural and international leadership research in prominent leadership handbooks. Avolio, Walumba, and Weber (2009) called for leadership studies to include cross-cultural, global, and comparative focus; where cross-cultural is understood as "across cultures" and global as "international experience". The authors restated the value of comparative studies for leadership effectiveness in different cultures or researching practices developed in one culture and applying them to other cultures.

The handbooks by Bass and Bass (2008), Nohria and Khurana (2010), and Bryman et al. (2011) are notable publications that provide updated overviews of the leadership field of studies. It is important to recognize that the latest editions of the mentioned publications include chapters dedicated to diverse and culture-specific issues in leadership research. We offer here a brief summary of the content of the chapters, as well as an analysis of how cross-cultural and international leadership scholarship are represented therein.

Bass and Bass's (2008) *Part VII Diversity and Cultural Effects* focuses on women and minorities as leaders and followers, and globalization and cross-national effects. The authors acknowledged that leadership research continued highlighting stereotypical views of women into the 21st century by applying "male" characteristics rather than focusing on understanding women leadership in context. Moreover, they stated "because changes are rapidly occurring for women in leadership roles, earlier research may need to be discounted. Progress toward seeing women as compatible with management continues, despite the handicaps of socialization, status conflicts, and stereotyping" (p. 942). They stressed that, "The same careful consideration is necessary to the development of a new appreciation of racial and ethnic differences in leadership" (p. 942). Studies should help understand views on leadership practices within specific groups across the spectrum of diversity (e.g., ethnic groups, genders, sub-cultures, ages, physical ability), as different factors may be important in each group.

In their extensive discussion of globalization and cross-national effects on leadership, Bass and Bass (2008) stressed the importance of further scholarly developments, including a more sophisti-cated understanding of cultural values and dimensions; a better understanding of characteristics that may be more universal in nature; offering a more detailed analysis of culture specific concepts of leadership within cultural clusters; and exploration of concepts that are authentic to specific groups (e.g., Ubuntu in Africa). For future studies, the authors recommended considering the origins of leaders, connections between cultures and institutions, differences in styles of leadership, or lea-dership in multinational firms.

For the research process, Bass and Bass (2008) offered a critique of current approaches, where most cross-cultural sampling is a matter of convenience and opportunity, within country samples are very small or unequal in size a representative sampling could be prone to underlying proprietary interests, organizational differences are not factored in, traditional designs might be culturally in-compatible, and overall, studies could be ethnocentrically biased (e.g., sources of concepts, theories, models) towards the USA or Europe. Overall, Bass and Bass (2008) encourage using authentic lenses in theorizing and performing empirical observations to study leadership across diverse gender, ethnic, and national groups, rather than applying traditional leadership frameworks that could help highlight stereotypes rather than demonstrate uniqueness.

Nohria and Khurana's (2010)*Handbook of Leadership Theory and Practice* is distinct from Bass and Bass (2008) in its discussion and representation of leadership studies within and between cultures and countries. It features a chapter on the Project GLOBE as a representation of leadership in the cultural context (Javidan et al., 2010), presenting details of its theoretical foundation and metho-dology. It also includes a chapter on women in leadership, offering conceptual discussions while also calling for emic models exploring cultural attitudes toward women (Ely & Rhode, 2010). Finally, Kanter's (2010) chapter on leadership in a globalizing world uses a sociological framework con-necting context and leadership characteristics mediated by the nature of a leaders' tasks. The chapter is based on Kanter's previous work and is a detailed analysis of macro trends that define globalization (uncertainty, complexity, and diversity), and places emphasis on leadership for social responsibility. Kanter advocates that companies have enormous potential to improve the state of the world; and leaders (whom she refers to as global leaders) need evidence-driven curriculum to develop relevant 21st-century skills.

Guthey and Jackson's (2011) chapter in the *Sage Handbook of Leadership* (Bryman et al., 2011) centers on the importance of the relationship between leadership and cultural context. The authors start with Hofstede's legacy and the application of Hofstede's culture typology in current studies. They also discuss cultural dimensions of the GLOBE Project. From an ontological perspective, the chapter stresses the importance of moving beyond quantitative comparative research and embracing the qualitative paradigm that could help understand how leaders "lived, enacted, and interacted with their cultures on a daily basis" (p. 173) and within a specific context. The chapter's conclusion introduces the concept of global leadership and highlights the importance of studying global leaders. It also emphasizes the relationship between a leader and diverse stakeholders to address world problems, similar to the conclusion in Nohria and Khurana's (2010) handbook.

Finally, the review of Northhouse's (2018) textbook *Leadership: Theory and Practice* is helpful to understand if cross-cultural and international research is taught or how. The text includes two relevant chapters: *Gender and Leadership* and *Culture and Leadership*. The first chapter's goal is to understand gender differences in leadership styles, the nature and consequences of prejudice, and gaps in current research. The chapter shows the importance of a greater emphasis on a cultural understanding of gender, and on an interaction among gender, values, and leadership processes. Finally, the chapter acknowledges that our knowledge about leadership and gender is very limited, is mostly about women in leadership roles, represents Western contexts, and thats a cannot be generalized across all genders or national cultures.

Northouse's *Culture and Leadership* chapter in the same textbook (Northouse, 2018) offers a traditional view on culture and its dimensions, and the connection between culture and leadership processes. Framed as a competency tool, culture is discussed in relation to working effectively worldwide. The GLOBE Project (House et al., 2004) is the main example in this publication to illustrate culture clusters and dimensions. One of the unique products of this research is the development of leadership "profiles" that suggest desired leadership behaviors for each country, based on the findings.

Overall existing analyses of cross-cultural and international leadership research is incomplete. The current works showcase large scale studies that treat culture as the only influencer, focus on cultural dimensions and their comparisons across societies, with leadership practices taking pace within an organizational context. Hofstede's (1980) cultural dimensions and the project GLOBE are referred to as the most influential cross-cultural leadership studies, foundational to the discovery of what we now know about leaders, their behavior and effectiveness across many countries. These studies determined differences and similarities between cultural communities and reasons behind them. At the same time, Hofstede's research and the GLOBE Project are bounded by their own foci, intents and samples. For example, these studies principally drew from samples of managers in organizations.

What is required is a greater appreciation of multiple models and views of leadership to form an inclusive perspective on cross-cultural and international leadership, especially within the contemporary global environment. Bass and Bass (2008) state, "As one crosses national and cultural boundaries, the differences in socialization in the various nations of the world give rise to different concepts of leadership" (p. 982). This conclusion is already well accepted by many leadership scholars. It is time to pass the acceptance stage and start analyzing diverse leadership frameworks that have already been proposed and even explained by scholars in and outside the United States. The next two sections discuss global leadership as an emergent field of studies and examples of locally derived leadership models and Indigenous studies.

Global Leadership Research: Leadership Realities Beyond Cultural Context

Global leadership emerged as a multidisciplinary field following new realities of international business, namely the globalization of operations (Mendenhall, 2018). Originally, the main scholarly contributions came from international business, cross-cultural and cognitive psychology, and intercultural communication. International affairs, anthropology, and sociology are some other fields that have natural intersections with global leadership research (Osland, 2018).

Scholars were concerned with challenges faced by global executives who operated in multi-national environments, relocated for international assignments and managed global teams and global operations (Mendenhall et al., 2018). Initial research revealed that an understanding of culture and knowledge of cultural dimensions were not the only determining factors for successful global leadership outcomes. To lead effectively in a global context requires a special intellectual capacity or global mindset and set of global skills (Osland et al., 2006). Debates about what constitutes global context, the scope of global leadership or the nature of the global leadership construct are ongoing (Mendenhall et al., 2012; Mendenhall & Reiche, 2018; Reiche et al., 2017). Empirical studies to understand global vs local leadership are still limited (Mendenhall et al., 2018).

Even though the global leadership field is still developing and more empirical evidence is needed, we can definitively conclude that global leadership scholars approach leadership practices differently than traditional leadership scholars. First, global leadership studies include a diverse group of multidisciplinary and international researchers (e.g., Mendenhall et al., 2018; Ngunjiri & Madsen, 2015; Zander, 2020). In addition to scholars from the United States and Western Europe, there are also academic scholars from Asia, the Middle East, Africa, and South America who are actively contributing to the field (e.g., Cremer, 2021; Jordans, Ng'weno, & Spencer-Oatey, 2020). Second, they focus on a multiplicity of contextual influences (rather than just culture), interdependence of many elements involved in global functioning (e.g., economies, technology, politics, health) and persistent ambiguity (e.g., multiple language, interpretations), rather than just cultural differences or categories (Mendenhall, 2018). To function within the complexity of global context, global leadership scholars are interested to know how leaders negotiate or reconcile cultures, span boundaries or deal with cognitive complexity, just to name a few research areas (Mendenhall, 2018).

Some current scholarly developments include the conceptualization of global followers and global followership as the partnering side of global leadership that focuses on relationship and mutual outcomes (Tolstikov-Mast, 2016), empirical advancements to understand typology of global leadership roles by studying task and relationship complexity (Reiche, Bird, Mendenhall, & Osland, 2017), examination of bi-cultural and multicultural leaders' behavior and identities (Shakir & Lee, 2017; Yoko Brannen & Thomas, 2010), complexities of global mindset (Hruby et al., 2018), and charting a responsible global leadership framework for the field (Mendenhall et al., 2018; Stahl et al., 2020). There is also rapidly growing research on women as global leaders that explores women's leadership in a global context with unique conceptualization, diverse methodologies, and international scholars (e.g., Breithaupt, 2015; Ngunjiri & Madsen, 2015).

Local and Indigenous Leadership Paradigms and Approaches

Two other research trends that require additional attention in summaries and analyses of cross-cultural and international leadership scholarship are local, culture-specific and Indigenous studies (Native American and First Nations) from different countries that use authentic (non-Western) frameworks. It is important to account for and promote this diverse leadership knowledge. Future publications can review, synthesize and categorize existing scholarship. The following are some examples to illustrate exciting research that helps open up a native perspective about leadership practices.

Local, Culture-Specific Leadership Studies

There is limited but compelling evidence about misalignment in application of some Western frameworks to leadership practices of different cultural groups. For example, a qualitative study of Japanese followers' leadership preferences evaluated the suitability of Bass and Avolio's (1997) full-range leadership model in Japan revealing misalignment with Japanese culture and preferences for culture specific leadership styles (Fukushige & Spicer, 2007). Blunt and Jones (1997) have argued that significant variations in leadership in East Asian and African societal cultures suggest the importance of diverse local leadership models. Most of this scholarship, however, is not published in mainstream academic journals or widely discussed in academia or college classrooms. For example, Andrews (2002) introduced a concept of parallel leadership (i.e., relationship between teacher leaders and principals based on mutual trust, shared directness, and individual expression), based on a five-year study in Australia. Analyzing appropriateness of the framework for research in China, Goh (2009) explains that *Lian,* one of the variations of the concept of *Face,* has a deep significance to Chinese people. It represents "confidence of society in the integrity of ego's moral character, the loss of which makes it impossible to function properly within a community" (Hu, 1944, p. 45). "When Lian is lost, it is irrecoverable and the individual's integrity of character is cast in doubt" (Goh, 2009, p. 337). This concept of *Face,* is unusual for the Western world, and is not captured in cultural dimensions, for example. The concept is equally inner- and outer-directed. Thus, "the ability to exercise caution to prevent hurting the face of others indicates good social skills and experience, as well as an individual's level of maturity" (Goh, 2009, p. 338). Using parallel leadership to investigate relationships with leaders in China would introduce a conflict as the perspective would be viewed "to be disrespectful or discourteous if teachers do not observe their status in the organization" (Goh, 2009, 338). Concluding the analysis, Goh (2009) references a list of scholars (e.g., Cheng & Wong, 1996; Dimmock & Walker, 2000) who have been asserting that intellectual traditions of other cultures should be used with extreme caution in different contexts. Instead, are often applied without questioning their inherent assumptions.

In recent years, there has been an increasing emergence of publications with authentic cultural leadership models. For example, Chin, Trimble, and Garcia (2017) present examples of culturally specific orientations to leadership with personal narratives, theoretical essays, case studies, by offering new paradigms and dimensions. The chapters introduce new theorizing from Africa (e.g., a view on trait theory from Liberia, Cameroon and South Africa; communal philosophies of Ubuntu) and Asia (e.g., Confucius thoughts in China). They offer perspectives on inclusive and multidimensional leadership from a non-Western lens (Indian, Indo-European or Muslim leadership), and an application of diverse views in contexts (e.g., service economy, social justice, higher education and military).

Looking at scholarship on women's leadership, Chao and Ha (Eds.) (2019) edited a groundbreaking publication offering an intersectional perspective on Asian women leaders, including interdisciplinary gender-centered cross-national and cross-sector comparison. Their book includes chapters written by international authors about various aspects of Asian women leaders in Asian and Western countries. Another recent publication, titled *Ready to Lead: Understanding Women's Leadership in the Middle East and North Africa,* features research that led to creation of the Middle East Women Leaders Index (MEWLI) (Khurma et al., 2020). The instrument was designed by a male and female team of scholars to quantify women's representation in leadership in the public sector in the MENA region. The study framework is based on the meaning of gender equality in public institutions and barriers for women to reach leadership positions, and the authority a women-leader can effectively wield once in power.

Indigenous Leadership Research Across Countries

Authentic studies have been emerging to tell a story of Indigenous leaders using not only critical theory perspective to discredit privileges of one voice over many others but also native frameworks (Calliou, 2006; Evans & Sinclair, 2016). These frameworks are grounded in the daily lives of Indigenous peoples and aim to improve lives of communities in meaningful ways (Julien, Wright, & Zinni, 2010; Kenny & Fraser, 2012). Although leadership literature on Australian, American, Canadian and New Zealand Native People is growing, this literature "is scattered throughout many academic journals and edited collections in a variety of disciplines, or is unpublished" (Calliou, 2006,

p. 2). Studies and theoretical discussions draw from native platforms of spirituality, consensus in decision-making, harmony, and respect among people. They focus on elements that native people encounter daily: an intersection of land, story, ancestors and elders (Kenny & Fraser, 2012).

Some notable publications offer comparative analysis of native vs traditional leadership theory perspectives (e.g., individual traits and actions; situational aspects, individual learning and a conceptual description of an ideal leader) (Julien, Wright, & Zinni, 2010; Kenny & Fraser, 2012) demonstrating unique philosophies and intellectual traditions embedded in the frameworks.

Examples of Indigenous methodology are rich and culturally unique. For example, Evans and Sinclair (2016) explore the leadership of Australian Indigenous artists with a framework of "territories" to capture influence of overlapping contexts in which Indigenous artistic leaders work. This approach demonstrates interconnection among individuals, leadership, and community. Thematic, narrative, and discursive analyses identify multiple practices of leadership that become a foundational model of the study. Other Indigenous studies employ local traditional designs including storytelling, use of personal narratives and case studies (Kenny & Fraser, 2012).

Some Indigenous leadership publications introduce the importance of blended Western and Indigenous approaches in Indigenous scholarship. There is a recurring theme that present-day Native people walk a thin line between several worlds: Indian country and mainstream societies; native, global, and virtual contexts (Evans & Sinclair, 2016; Kenny & Fraser, 2012). This situation requires consideration of both Western and Indigenous values, and even potential use of both Western and Indigenous frameworks. Another interesting theme is "offering" Indigenous lenses to Western leadership practices. For example, a framework of "territories" could have a broader applicability outside of Indigenous life and help reveal new insights about non-Indigenous leadership (Evans & Sinclair, 2016). Finally, Kenny and Fraser's (2012) edited book gives a voice to Native women who use their wisdom and daily practices to nurture and sustain their communities. The editors use a feminist philosophical view to look at realities of Native women, turning traditional feminism into Indigenous feminism. Although accepting feminism and searching for their feminist voices, Indigenous women want to do it their own way, prioritizing protection of their men and communities and finding strength in their own heritage.

Conclusion

The chapter offered a review of the historic and contemporary developments of the leadership field. We showed how the leadership field originally started from a Western focus and has given more space to multicultural perspectives in recent years. An analysis of the literature shows that cross-cultural and international leadership research have been recognized as unique areas of study, with global leadership research considering leadership in multinational and complex settings. We also explored emic, local, non-Western lenses to look at leadership practices. While these approaches are increasing in number, they are not yet sufficiently represented within cross-cultural and international studies of leadership.

Based on this backdrop, this handbook fills an important niche in the literature that has been acknowledged to be of great importance, but remains in limited supply: discussion of culturally unique research and research approaches. The chapters featured in this volume provide insights on diverse cultural and societal nuances in leadership practices along with discussion of the diverse paradigms used to study them. We recommend that readers explore the diverse perspectives on leadership and contextual considerations throughout this volume. Chapter 35 provides a useful framework and reflective questions to guide cross-cultural and international leadership research. The framework was developed from the insights gleaned from the chapters of this handbook. We hope that researchers reading the volume will continue deepening the body of knowledge in the field by creating novel scholarship, forming collaborative cross-cultural and international partnerships, and sharing their experiences, insights, and perspectives; for it is together that we advance the field.

References

Andrews, D. (2002) Parallel leadership: A clue to the contents of the "black box" of school reform. *International Journal of Educational Management 16*(4), 152–159. doi:10.1108/09513540210432128.

Arnulf, J. K., & Larsen, K. R. (2020). Culture blind leadership research: How semantically determined survey data may fail to detect cultural differences. *Frontiers in Psychology, 11*, 176. doi:10.3389/fpsyg.2020.00176

Avolio, B. J., Walumba, F. O., & Weber, T. J. (2009). Leadership: Current theories, research, and future directions. *Annual Review of Psychology, 60*, 421–449. doi:10.1146/annurev.psych.60.110707.163621.

Bass, B. M. (1981). *Stogdill's handbook of leadership: A survey of theory and research.* The Free Press.

Bass, B. M. & Bass, R. (Ed.) (2008). *The Bass handbook of leadership: Theory, research, and managerial application* (4th ed.). The Free Press.

Bass, B. M., & Avolio, B. J. (1997). *Full-range leadership development: Manual for the multifactor leadership questionnaire.* Mindgarden.

Batistič, S., Černe, M., & Vogel, B. (2017). Just how multi-level is leadership research? A document co-citation analysis 1980–2013 on leadership constructs and outcomes. *The Leadership Quarterly, 28*, 86–103.

Blair, J. D., & Hunt, J. G. (1986). Getting inside the head of the management researcher one more time: Context-free and context-specific orientations in research, *Journal of Management, 12*, 147–166. doi:10.11 77/014920638601200202.

Blunt, P., & Jones, M. L. (1997). Exploring the limits of Western leadership theory in East Asia and Africa. *Personnel Review, 26*(½), 6–23. doi:10.1108/00483489710157760.

Brannen, M. Y., & Thomas, D. C. (2010). Bicultural individuals in organizations: Implications and opportunity. *International Journal of Cross Cultural Management, 10*(1), 5–16. doi:10.1177/1470595809359580.

Breithaupt, J. R. (2015). Multiple intelligences of effective women global leaders: Emotional, social, and cultural competencies. In F. W. Ngunjiri & S. R. Madsen (Eds.), *Women and leadership: Research, theory, and practice. Women as global leaders* (pp. 73–93). IAP Information Age Publishing.

Bryman, A. (2004). Qualitative research on leadership: A critical but appreciative review. *The Leadership Quarterly,15*(6), 729–769. doi:10.1016/j.leaqua.2004.09.007h.

Bryman, A., Collinson, D., Grint, K., Jackson, B., & Uhl-Bien, M. (Eds.) (2011). *The SAGE handbook of leadership.* SAGE.

Butler, C. L., Sutton, C., Mockaitis, A. I., & Zander, L. (2020). The new Millennial global leaders: What a difference a generation makes! In L. Zander (Ed.), *Research handbook of global leadership: Making a difference* (pp. 141–163). Edward Elgar Publishing.

Calliou, B. (2006). *Research and dialogue: Leadership development for aboriginal nations.* Buffalo Mountain Drum.

Chao, C.-C., & Ha, L. (Eds.). (2019). *Asian women leadership: A cross-national and cross- sector comparison* (1st ed.). Routledge. doi:10.4324/9780429025815.

Chen, X-P., & Fahr, J. L. (2001). Transformational and transactional leader behaviors in Chinese organizations: Differential effects in the People's Republic of China and Taiwan. In W. H. Mobley & M. W. McCall, Jr. (Eds.), *Advances in global leadership* (Vol. 2, pp. 101–126). Emerald.

Cheng, K. M., & Wong, K. C. (1996) School effectiveness in East Asia: Concepts, origins and implications. *Journal of Educational Administration, 34*(5), 32–49.

Chin, J., Trimble, J., & Garcia, J. A. (2017). *Global and culturally diverse leaders and leadership: New dimensions and challenges for business, education and society.* Emerald.

Conger, J. A. (1998). Qualitative research as the cornerstone methodology for understanding leadership. *The Leadership Quarterly, 9*(1), 107–121. doi:10.1016/S1048-9843(98)90044-3

Covey, S. R. (2005). *The 8th habit: From effectiveness to greatness.* The Free Press.

Cremer, D. (2021). *On the emergence and understanding of Asian global leadership.* De Gruyter.

Den Hartog, D. N., & Dickson, M. W. (2004). Leadership and culture. In J. Antonakis, A. T., Cianciolo, & R. J. Sternberg (Eds.), *The nature of leadership* (pp. 249–278). Sage.

Den Hartog, D. N., House, R. J., Hanges, P. J., Ruiz-Quintanilla, S. A., & Dorfman, P. W. (1999). Culture specific and cross-culturally generalizable implicit leadership theories: Are attributes of charismatic/transformational leadership universally endorsed? *The Leadership Quarterly, 10*(2), 219–256. doi:10.1016/S1048-9843(99)00018-1.

Dickson, M. W., Den Hartog, D. N., & Mitchelson, J. K. (2003). Research on leadership in a cross-cultural context: Making progress, and raising new questions. *The Leadership Quarterly, 14*, 729–768. doi:10.1016/j.leaqua.2003.09.002.

Dimmock, C., & Walker, A. (2000) Globalisation and societal culture: Redefining schooling and school leadership in the twenty-first century. *Compare, 30*(3), 303–312.

Dorfman, P. W. (1996). International and cross-cultural leadership research. In B. J. Punnett & O. Shenkar (Eds.), *Handbook for international management research.* Blackwell (pp. 267–349).

Dorfman, P. W. (2003). International and cross-cultural leadership research. In B. J. Punnett & O. Shenkar (Eds.), *Handbook for international management research*(2nd ed.). University of Michigan.

Dorfman, P. W., & Howell, J. P. (1988). Dimensions of national culture and effective leadership patterns. *Advances in International Comparative Management, 3*, 127–150.

Ely, R. F., & Rhode, D. L. 2010). Women and leadership: Defining the challengesIn N. Nohria & R. Khurana (Eds.), *Handbook of leadership theory and practice* (pp. 377–410). Harvard Business Press.

Evans, M. M., & Sinclair, A. (2016). Navigating the territories of Indigenous leadership: Exploring the experiences and practices of Australian Indigenous arts leaders. *Leadership, 12*(4), 470–490. doi:10.1177/1742 715015574318.

Fraser, T. N. (2012). *Living Indigenous leadership: Native narratives on building strong communities.* UBC Press.

Fukushige, A., & Spicer, D. P. (2007). Leadership preferences in Japan: An exploratory study. *Leadership & Organization Development Journal, 28*(6), 508–530. doi:10.1108/01437730710780967.

Gannon, M. J., & Pillai, R. (Eds.). (2013). *Understanding global cultures: Metaphorical journeys through 31 nations, clusters of nations, continents, and diversity* (5th ed.). Sage.

Gardner, W. L., Lowe, K. B., Meuser, J. D., Noghani, F., Gullifor, D. P., & Cogliser, C. (2020). The leadership trilogy: A review of the third decade of *The Leadership Quarterly. The Leadership Quarterly, 31*(1), [101379]. doi:10.1016/j.leaqua.2019.101379.

Grint, K., Jackson, B. (2010). Toward "socially constructive" social constructions of leadership, *Management Communication Quarterly, 2*(2), 348–355. doi:10.1177/0893318909359086.

Guthey, E., & Jackson, B. (2011). Cross-cultural leadership revisited. In A. Bryman, D. L. Collinson, K. Grint, B. Jackson, & M. Uhl-Bien (Eds.), *The Sage handbook of leadership* (pp. 165–178). Sage.

Hanna, A. A., Smith, T. A., Kirkman, B. L., & Griffin, R. W. (2021). The emergence of emergent leadership: A comprehensive framework and directions for future research. *Journal of Management, 47*(1), 76–104. doi:10.1177/01492063209656831t.

Hofstede, G. (1980). *Culture's consequences: International differences in work-related values.* Sage.

Hofstede, G. (2001). *Culture's consequences: Comparing values, behaviors, institutions, and organizations across nations.* (2nd ed.), Sage.

Holmberg, I., & Åkerblom, S. (2006). Modelling leadership-implicit leadership theories in Sweden, *Scandinavian Journal of Management, 22*, 4, 307–329.

House, R. J., Hanges, P. J., Javidan, M., Dorfman, P. W., & Gupta, V. (2004). *Culture, leadership, and organizations: The GLOBE study of 62 societies.* Sage Publications.

House, R., Hanges, P. J., Ruiz-Quintanilla, S. A., Dorfman, P. W., Javidan, M., Dickson, M., Gupta, V., & GLOBE (1999). Cultural influences on leadership and organizations. *Advances in Global Leadership, 1*, 171–233.

House, R., Javidan, M., Hanges, P., & Dorfman, P. (2002). Understanding cultures and implicit leadership theories across the globe: An introduction to project GLOBE, *Journal of World Business, 37*(1), 3–10. doi:10.1016/S1090-9516(01)00069-4.

House, R. J., Wright, N. S., & Aditya, R. N. (1997). Cross-cultural research on organizational leadership: A critical analysis and a proposed theory. In P. C. Earley & M. Erez (Eds.), *New perspectives on international industrial/organizational psychology* (pp. 535–625). Jossey-Bass.

Hu, H. C. (1944). The Chinese concept of face. *American Anthropologist, 46*, 45–64.

Hunt, T., & Fedynich, L. C. (2018). Leadership: Past, present, and future: An evolution of an idea. *Journal of Arts & Humanities, 8*(2), 20–26. doi:10.18533/journal.v8i2.1582.

Hruby, J., de Melo, R. J., Samunderu, E, & Hartel, J. (2018). Unpacking the complexities of global mindset: A multi-lens analysis. In *Advances in global leadership* (Vol. 11, pp. 97–143). Emerald Publishing Limited. doi:10.1108/S1535-120320180000011004.

Goh, J. W. P. (2009). 'Parallel leadership in an "unparallel" world'– cultural constraints on the transferability of Western educational leadership theories across cultures. *International Journal of Leadership in Education, 12*(4), 319–345.

Insch, G. S., Moore, J. E., & Murphy, L. D. (1997). Content analysis in leadership research: Examples, procedures, and suggestions for future use. *The Leadership Quarterly, 8*(1), 1–25. doi:10.1016/S1048-9843(97)90028-X.

International Leadership Association. (2017). *Annual report 2017.* http://www.ila-net.org/about/annualreportsarchive/2017AnnualReport.pdf.

International Leadership Association (2021). *Leadership journals from ILA.* http://www.ila-net.org/Publications/Journals.htm.

Javidan, M., Dorfman, P., Howell, J. P., & Hanges, P. (2010). Leadership and cultural context: A theoretical and empirical examination based on project GLOBE. In N. Nohria & R. Khurana (Eds.), *Handbook of leadership theory and practice* (pp. 335–376). Harvard Business Press.

Jordans, E., Ng'weno, B., & Spencer-Oatey, H. (2020). *Developing global leaders: Insights from African case studies. Palgrave studies in African leadership.* Palgrave Macmillan.

Julien, M., Wright, B., & Zinni, D. M. (2010). Stories from the circle: Leadership lessons learned from aboriginal leaders. *Leadership Quarterly, 21,* 114–126.

Jung, D. I., Bass, B. M., & Sosik, J. J. (1995). Bridging leadership and culture: A theoretical consideration of transformational leadership and collectivistic cultures. *Journal of Leadership Studies, 2*(4), 3–18. doi:10.1177/107179199500200402.

Kanter, R. M. (2010). Leadership in a globalizing world. In N. Nohria & R. Khurana (Eds.), *Handbook of leadership theory and practice* (pp. 569–609). Harvard Business Press.

Klenke, K. (Ed.) (2008). *Qualitative research in the study of leadership.* Emerald.

Kozai Group (2020). *Research Blog.* https://www.kozaigroup.com/blog/.

Khurma, M. J., Pagan, C., Farley, A., & Horner, A. (2020). *Ready to lead: Understanding Women's public leadership in the Middle East and North Africa.* Wilson Center. https://www.wilsoncenter.org/sites/default/files/media/uploads/documents/MEP_2002_MENA%20report_v2_Corrected_0.pdf.

Lee, K., Scandura, T. A., & Sharif, M. M. (2014). Cultures have consequences: A configural approach to leadership across two cultures, *The Leadership Quarterly, 25*(4), 692–710. doi:10.1016/j.leaqua.2014.03.003

Levitt, T. (1983, May-June). The globalization of markets. *Harvard Business Review,* 92–102.

McLellan, K., & Uys, K. (2009). Using the career orientations inventory (COI) for measuring internal career orientations in the South African organisational context. *SA Journal of Industrial Psycholog, 35*(1), 21–30. doi:10.4102/sajip.v35i1.416.

Mellahi, K. (2000). The teaching of leadership on UK MBA programmes: A critical analysis from an international perspective. *Journal of Management Development, 19*(4), 297–308. doi:10.1108/02621710010322652

Mendenhall, M. E. (2018). Leadership and the birth of global leadership. In M. E. Mendenhall, J. S. Osland, A., Bird A., G. R. Oddou, M. L., Maznevski, M. J., Stevens, & G. K., Stahl (Eds.), *Global leadership: Research, practice, and development* (pp. 3–27). Routledge.

Mendenhall, M. E., Li, M., & Osland, J. 2016. Five years of global leadership research, 2010–2014: Patterns, themes, and future directions. In J. Osland, M. Li, & M. Mendenhall (Eds.), *Advances in global leadership* (Vol. 9). Emerald.

Mendenhall, M. E., Osland, J., Bird, A., Oddou, G. R., Stevens, M. J., Maznevski, M. L., & Stahl, G. K. (2018). *Global leadership: Research, practice, and development.* Routledge Taylor & Francis Group.

Mendenhall, M. E., & Reiche, S. B. (2018). Back to the future: Leveraging a typology of global leadership roles to guide global leadership research. In M. E. Mendenhall, J. S. Osland, A. Bird, A., G. R. Oddou, M. L., Maznevski, M. J., Stevens, & G. K., Stahl (Eds.), *Global leadership: Research, practice, and development* (pp. 391–406). Routledge.

Mendenhall, M. E., Reiche, B. S., Bird, A., & Osland, J. S. (2012). Defining the "global" in global leadership. *Journal of World Business, Elsevier, 47*(4), 493–503.

Middlehurst, R. (2008, October). Not enough science or not enough learning? Exploring the gaps between leadership theory and practice. *Higher Education Quarterly, 62*(4), 322–339.

Mobley, W. H., Ming, L., & Wang, Y. (2011). *Advances in global leadership* (Vol. 6). Emerald.

Morris, R. T., & Seeman, M. (1950). The problem of leadership: An interdisciplinary approach. *American Journal of Sociology, 56*(2), 149–155.

Morrison, H. (2008, January). Advisor reviews-standard review: Directory of open access journals (DOAJ). *The Charleston Advisor,* 19–26.

Manjunatha, G., Mamatha, V., & Kumara, B. (2019). An analysis of open access publication productivity of science and technology in DOAJ: An overview. *Online International Interdisciplinary Research Journal, 9,* 364–368.

Ngunjiri, F. W., & Madsen, S. R. (Eds.). (2015). *Women and leadership: Research, theory, and practice. Women as global leaders.* IAP Information Age Publishing.

Ngunjiri, F., & Nyathi, N. (Eds.). (n.a.). *Palgrave studies in African leadership.* Palgrave McMillan. https://www.palgrave.com/gp/series/14652.

Nohria, N., & Khurana, R. (Eds). (2010). *Handbook of leadership theory and practice.* Harvard Business Press.

Northouse, P. G. (2018). *Leadership: Theory and practice* (8th ed.). Sage Publishing.

Omeltchenka, A. E., & Armitage, A. (2006). Leadership prototypes: A Russian perspective. *Baltic Journal of Management, 1*(3), 315–338. doi:10.1108/17465260610690953.

Osland, J. S. (2018). The multidisciplinary roots of global leadership. In M. E. Mendenhall, J. S., Osland, A. Bird, G. R. Oddou, M. J. Stevens, M. L. Maznevski & G. K. Stahl (Eds.), *Global leadership: Research, practice, and development* (3rd ed., pp. 28–56). Routledge.

Osland, J. S., Bird, A., Mendenhall, M. E., & Osland, A. (2006). Developing global leadership capabilities and global mindset: A review. In G. K. Stahl & I. Bjokrmann (Eds.), *Handbook of research in international human resources management* (pp. 197–222). Edward Elgar Publishing.

Parry, K. W. (1998). Grounded theory and social process: A new direction for leadership research. *The Leadership Quarterly, 9*(1), 85–105.

Peachey, J. W., Zhou, Y., Damon, Z. J., & Burton, L. J. (2015). Forty years of leadership research in sport management: A review, synthesis, and conceptual framework. *Journal of Sport Management, 29*(5), 570–587. doi:10.1123/jsm.2014-0126.

Peng, T. K., Peterson, M. F., & Shyi, Y.-p. (1991). Quantitative methods in cross-national management research: Trends and equivalence issues. *Journal of Organizational Behavior, 12*(2), 87–107. doi:10.1002/job.4 030120203.

Perkins, A. W. (2009). Global leadership study. *Journal of Leadership Education, 8*, 72–87. doi: 10.12806/v8/i2/tf2.

Perlmutter, H. V. (1969). The tortuous evolution of the multinational corporation. *Columbia Journal of World Business, 1*, 9–18.

Peterson, M. F., & Hunt, J. G. (1997). International perspectives on international leadership. *Leadership Quarterly, 8*(3), 203–231. doi:10.1016/S1048-9843(97)90002-3.

Pettigrew, A. M. (1979). On studying organizational cultures. *Administrative Science Quarterly, 24*, 570–581.

Reiche, B. S., Bird, A., Mendenhall, M. E., & Osland, J. S. (2017). Contextualizing leadership: A typology of global leadership roles. *Journal of International Business Studies, 48*, 552– 572.

Reiche, B. S., Mendenhall, M. E., Szkudlarek, B., & Osland, J. S. (2019). Global leadership research: Where do we go from here? In J. S. Osland, B. S. Reiche, B. Szkudlarek, & M. E. Mendenhall (Eds.), *Advances in global leadership* (Vol. 12, pp. 213–234). Emerald. doi:10.1108/S1535-120320190000012013.

Riggio, R. (July 10, 2011). The top 10 books to REALLY learn about leadership. *Psychology Today.* https://www.psychologytoday.com/us/blog/cutting-edge-leadership/201107/the-top-10-books-really-learn-about-leadership.

Ritzer, G. (2012). Globalization. In *The Wiley-Blackwell encyclopedia of globalization.* Wiley.

Robertson, R. (2018). Glocalization. In *The international encyclopedia of anthropology.* Wiley.

Rudolph, C. W., Katz, I. M., Ruppel, R., & Zacher, H. (2021). A systematic and critical review of research on respect in leadership. *The Leadership Quarterly, 32*(10). doi:10.1016/j.leaqua.2020.101492.

Sadeghi, R. (2013). *Re: How to access and translate full-text foreign language articles?* https://www.researchgate.net/post/How_to_access_and_translate_full-text_foreign_language_articles/526691fcd11b8b633dd79453/citation/download.

Schedlitzki, D., Ahonen, P., Wankhade, P., Edwards, G., & Gaggiotti, H. (2017). Working with language: A refocused research agenda for cultural leadership studies. *International Journal of Management Reviews, 19*(2), 237–257. doi:10.1111/ijmr.12100.

Scandura, T., & Dorfman, P. (2004). Leadership research in an international and cross-cultural context, *The Leadership Quarterly, 15*(2), 277–307. doi:10.1016/j.leaqua.2004.02.00.

Sims, D., & Siew-Kim, J. L. (1993). Discovering an alternative view of managing: A study with Singaporean women managers. *Applied Psychology: An International Review, 42*(4), 365–377. doi:10.1111/j.1464-0597.1993.tb00751.x.

Smith, P. B. (1997). Cross-cultural leadership: A path to the goal? In P. C. Earley & M. Erez (Eds.), *New perspectives on international industrial/organizational psychology* (pp. 626–639). Jossey-Bass.

Shakir, F. Y. and Lee, Y.-T. (2017), Connecting across cultures: An empirical examination of multicultural individuals as global leaders. In *Advances in global leadership* (Vol. 10, pp. 89–116). Emerald Publishing Limited. doi:10.1108/S1535-120320170000010003.

Snaebjornsson, M., Edvardsson, I. R., Zydziunaite, V., & Vaiman, V. (2015, April). Cross-cultural leadership: Expectations on gendered leaders' behavior. *SAGE Open.* doi:10.1177/2158244015579727.

Steinmann, M., & Pugnetti, C. (2021). Leading in Switzerland and Poland: A case study of leadership practices in financial services. *International Journal of Financial Studies, 9*(1), 6. doi: 10.3390/ijfs9010006.

Stockemer, D., Wigginton, M. J. (2019). Publishing in English or another language: An inclusive study of scholar's language publication preferences in the natural, social and interdisciplinary sciences. *Scientometrics, 118*, 645–652. doi:10.1007/s11192-018-2987-0.

Stahl, G., Miska, C., Noval, L., & Patock, V. (2020). Responsible global leadership: A multi- level framework. In L. Zander (Ed.), *Research handbook of global leadership – making a difference* (pp. 178–201). Edward Elgar Publishing.

Thompson, W. & Hickey, J. (2005). *Society in focus*. Allyn and Bacon.

Tolstikov-Mast, Y. (2016). Global followership: The launch of the scholarly journey. In J. S. Osland, M. Li, & Y. Want (Eds.), *Advances in global leadership* (Vol. 9, pp. 109–150). Emerald.

Toor, S., & Ofori, G. (2008a). Grounded theory as an appropriate methodology for leadership research in construction. *Proceedings from the International Conference on Building and Education Research (BEAR)* (pp. 1816–1831). https://www.irbnet.de/daten/iconda/CIB11453.pdf.

Toor, S., & Ofori, G. (2008b). Leadership versus management: How are they different, and why. *Leadership and Management in Engineering*, *8*, 61–71. doi:10.1061/(ASCE)1532-6748(2008)8:2(61).

Trompenaars, F., & Hampden-Turner, C. (1997). *Riding the waves of culture: Understanding diversity in global business*. McGraw-Hill.

Tsang, D. (2007). Leadership, national culture, and performance management in the Chinese software industry. *International Journal of Productivity and Performance Management*, *56*(4), 270–284. doi:10.1108/17410400710745306.

Tsui, A. S., Nifadkar, S. S., & Yi, A. Y. (2007). Cross-national, cross-cultural organizational behavior research: Advances, gaps, and recommendations. *Journal of Management*, *33*(3), 426–478. doi:10.1177/0149206307300818.

Tung, R. L., & Verbeke, R. A. (2010). Beyond Hofstede and GLOBE: Improving the quality of cross-cultural research. *Journal of International Business Studies*, *41*(1), 1259- 1274. doi:10.1057/jibs2010.41.

Ulrich, D. (2010). *Leadership in Asia: Challenges, opportunities, and strategies from top global leaders*. McGraw Hill.

Van de Vijver, F. J. R., & Leung, K. (2000). Methodological issues in psychological research on culture. *Journal of Cross-Cultural Psychology*, *31*(1), 33–51. doi:10.1177/0022022100031001004.

Vijayakumar, P. B., Morley, M. J., Heraty, N. L., Mendenhall, M. E., & Osland, J. S. (2008). Leadership In the global context: Bibliometric and thematic patterns of an evolving field. In J. S. Osland, M. E. Mendenhall, & M. Li (Eds.), *Advances in global leadership* (pp. 31–72). Emerald Publishing Limited.

Vogel, B., Reichard, B., Batistič, S., & Cerne, M. (2021). A bibliometric review of the leadership development field: How we got here, where we are, and where we are headed. *The Leadership Quarterly*. doi:10.1016/j.leaqua.2020.101381.

Von Glinnow, M. A., & Schneper, W. D. (2015, November 30). Global and comparative leadership. *Oxford Bibliographies in Management*. doi:10.1093/obo/9780199846740-0051.

Vu, T-M. (2016). International leadership as a process: The case of China in Southeast Asia. *Revista Brasileira de Politica Internacional*, *60*(1). doi:10.1590/0034-7329201600109.

Wang, M., Zhou, L., & Liu, S. (2014). Multilevel issues in leadership research. The Oxford handbook of leadership and organizations. In D. Day (Ed.), *The Oxford handbook of leadership and organizations* doi:10.1093/oxfordhb/9780199755615.013.00.

Wee, C-H. (2010). Developing Asia's corporate leadership: Challenges and moving forward. In D. Ulrich (Ed.), *Leadership in Asia: Challenges, opportunities, and strategies from top global leaders* (pp. 44–52). McGraw Hill.

Wheatley, M. J. (1994). *Leadership and the new science: Learning about organization from an orderly universe*. Berrett-Koehler Publishers.

Wright, N. S., & Aditya, R. N. (1997). *Cross-cultural research on organizational leadership: A critical analysis and a proposed theory*. In P. C. Earley & M. Erez (Eds.), *The New Lexington Press management and organization sciences series and New Lexington Press social and behavioral sciences series. New perspectives on international industrial/organizational psychology* (pp. 535–625). The New Lexington Press/Jossey-Bass Publishers.

Yukl, G. A. (2010). *Leadership in organizations*. Prentice Hall.

Zander, L. (2020). *Research handbook of global leadership: Making a difference*. Edward Elgar Publishing.

Zefeiti, S. M. B. A., & Mohamad, N. A. (2015). Methodological considerations in studying transformational leadership and its outcomes. *International Journal of Engineering Business Management*. doi:10.5772/60429

Zhang, X., Fu, P., Xi, Y., Li, L., Xu, L., Cao, C., Li, G., Ma, L., & Ge, J. (2012). Understanding Indigenous leadership research: Explication and Chinese examples. *The Leadership Quarterly*, *23*, 1063–1079. doi:10.1016/j.leaqua.2012.10.009.

2

International Followership

A Research Review Including Issues, Challenges and Future Directions

Marc Hurwitz

Introduction

My biggest fear is that those of you who study leadership will skip past this chapter, thinking either that it lacks relevance to your research or that followership and the study of following is ancillary to your work. As Uhl-Bien and her colleagues (2014) note at the end of their review of followership research, "There is no leadership without followers, yet followers are very often left out of the leadership research equation" (p. 83). In this chapter, I hope to persuade you that international research is impoverished without including followership and, moreover, that there is a rich and growing body of work with the potential to inform and shape our understanding of leadership.

First, however, it is worth noting that the leadership industry, with estimated revenues over USD $370 billion in 2019 (trainingindustry.com, 2020) largely relies on U.S.-derived leadership models such as transformational leadership, situational leadership, Kouzes and Posner's framework from their book *The Leadership Challenge* (2002), or servant leadership. To what extent does this approach capture leadership models and modes of expression in other cultures? Does it preference white, male, cis-gendered Western practices? How can we claim theories have external validity outside the culture from which they are derived and within which the research is conducted? What other approaches might exist? And how might we extend current ideas to improve social or organizational outcomes? One remedy for this narrow focus of study – indeed, the theme of this compendium – is to refocus and redouble attention on research that originates beyond Western cultural and political borders, developing a greater awareness and sensitivity for how leadership is enacted in the rest of the world as well as within minority groups embedded in Western countries such as the Indigenous peoples of North America. This is important work.

At the same time, studying leadership as if it were the sole agentic role in team or organizational relationships is to promulgate an incomplete theory of human interactions. Followership is integral to leadership; there are no leaders without people willing and able to follow. Hollander (1992), for instance, suggests that leadership and followership are a social exchange where both roles exert influence, and "followers can affect and even constrain leaders' activity in more than passing ways" (p. 71). Omitting one of the partners and roles in any social exchange process marginalizes the missing role, and leads to theories that inevitably fail to capture important aspects of the relationship process. What is needed is for more international followership research including leadership research that includes and honors followership.

DOI: 10.4324/9781003003380-2

In my hopes to inform and persuade you of the importance of international followership research, I have divided the rest of the chapter into five sections. First, I suggest a number of reasons why we should care about studying international followership. The section addresses questions such as how followership is related to social justice, what goes wrong if we study leadership absenting the impact of followership and why followership matters to group outcomes. Section 3 considers why care must be taking using Western notions of followership to interpret experiences and processes in other cultures. Section 4 is a review of what are considered the main followership theories. The penultimate section reviews existing literature on international followership in peer-reviewed journals, books and PhD dissertations. And finally, in Section 6, I draw a few conclusions about leadership and followership, recommending directions for future research.

Why Study International Followership?

In this section, I propose three reasons for studying international followership: (1) it has the potential to transform ways of improving social justice through empowering people who see themselves as followers and therefore, in most leadership theories, are disempowered; (2) group outcomes are the result of complex social interactions and reducing these to a unidirectional leader-acts-on-followers model ignores powerful determinants and levers for success; and (3) followership is something different than leadership such that failing to distinguish what is unique about leadership (or followership) means we fail to understand it.

Followership Is Integral to Social Justice

From a social justice perspective, Ofumbi (2017) conducts a spirited defense of agentic followership by considering the negative impact that the leadership industry has had on the Acholi people of Uganda in their struggle to overcome authoritarian leaders. As Ofumbi writes, "Chinua Achebe (1984) observed that a crisis of poor leadership is the foremost challenge of Africa . . . however, according to the Acholi model (of leader-follower relations), Africa's foremost challenge is poor *leadership theory*, which cast a larger-than-life image of leaders in the mind of leaders and followers" (p. 329; italics added). Virtually all standard leadership theories are versions of the "Great Man" perspective, that leaders are the prime movers and determiners of social and organizational outcomes – what Meindl, Ehrlich, and Dukerich (1985) refer to as the "Romance of the Leader". Indeed, the more we double down on one role to the exclusion of both, the less useful such models become and there can even be unintended harmful consequences such as the empowerment of those with narcissistic tendencies (Steffens & Haslam, 2020) and the transposition of the idea that leaders should be good to the belief that goodness resides in leaders. For example, authentic leadership theory suggests that people should be their authentic selves as leaders. But what if the individual is a bully, or a narcissist, or suffers from other personality flaws that impair their ability to appropriately carry out their *role* as a leader (Alvesson & Einola, 2019)? For example, in the run-up to the 2016 U.S. elections it was suggested Trump would make a good leader because he showed his true self.

In a more positive light, for those who live in high power-distance cultures, giving weight and substance to followership can be a force for important social change. Schuder (2017) notes that in cultures such as Honduras, power inequality is seen as the bedrock of a stable and secure society. As a result, when a disempowered group wrestles control from those in authority, rather than change the structure of society the new regime often replaces one power structure with another and one set of inequalities with a new set, shuffling the deck rather than changing the game. Empowering people as followers using the lens of followership suggests new ways to tackle deeper, structural issues such countries have. In the case of Honduras, Schuder suggests five followership-based strategies for change including promoting common purpose and finding ways to "celebrate and express individualism to generate a sense that each person can contribute to the group's work" (2017, p. 60).

The Quality of Followership Is a Determinant of Group Outcomes

Imagine two teams, the first of which is composed entirely of "strong" followers. Most theories of followership claim that this includes behaviors such as initiative-taking, engagement in the team and leader goals, questioning directives to ensure understanding and challenging the leader (e.g., Chaleff, 1995; Hurwitz & Hurwitz, 2015; Kellerman, 2008; Kelley, 1992). Strong followers also possess traits such as honesty and integrity, dependability, and are supportive of the leader (e.g., Agho, 2009; Meilinger, 2001). The second team, by comparison, is composed of passive followers who need extensive direction, are unreliable, disengaged, or fail to support the mission of the team when the leader is absent. It is obvious that, *ceteris paribus*, the first team will be more effective than the second. Although many leader-centric theories propose followers as mediators of outcomes, few incorporate a model of strong followership that suggests specific dimensions of followership that mediate outcomes. In these models, followership characteristics are situational variables, not modifiable by followers themselves; it is assumed followers have neither agency nor choice and therefore do not change their behaviors to adapt to leadership. In other words, a complex human interaction – a systems perspective – is simplified to a one-way influence process. Is this simplification valid?

Good followership fosters better leadership; toxic followership can derail leadership. Andrea Manica and his colleagues conducted a series of experiments on how leadership and followership are enacted in fish, specifically the three-spined stickleback (*Gasterosteus aculeatus*; for a review of other articles on followership in fish, see Hurwitz, 2018). In one experiment (Harcourt et al., 2009), the researchers paired leader-type fish with follower-type fish to see how leader-follower interactions impact foraging behavior. Leader-type fish initiated far more trips when paired with follower-type fish than they did when acting alone. One possible reason is that when prey fish such as sticklebacks are put into groups, they do more than increase existing behaviors; they actually change behaviors to take on specific roles – some fish will forage while others stay vigilant for predators (e.g., Brandl & Bellwood, 2015). The overall impact is to increase foraging efficiency by foraging more often while occasionally exchanging foraging and vigilance roles. However, not every group of fish produce equivalent results. In a foraging experiment with guppies, Dyer and colleagues (2008) tested three types of shoal composition: (1) all leader-type fish, (2) all follower-type fish and (3) mixed groups equally split between leader and follower fish. The mixed group considerably outperformed the other two, more than doubling the success of the all leader groups, while both leader and follower fish in mixed groups foraged more effectively than in the homogeneous shoals. This result suggests that the effect is more than one type of fish taking on a single role but, rather, the fish improved coordination through role-switching within mixed groups; not only did strong leadership impact followers, strong followership impacted leaders. Put in human terms, when a team is responsive, creative and engaged, it allows the leader to do more, try more, step back from the leadership role when needed to take on other roles and be more responsive to the needs of the team. In addition, strong followers are able to reverse mentor leaders, helping them improve their leadership skills.

Leaders Can Create Better Followers, but Only If They Know What Constitutes Effective Followership

One role leaders engage in is that of mentor or coach, helping their team develop knowledge, skills, and abilities. To mentor effectively requires that leaders understand followership so that they can give precise, actionable advice. Another way leaders develop their team include performance appraisals, performance management, competency dictionaries and the like. For example, a large

Canadian financial institution defines the competency of creativity as follows: "Uses creativity to positively impact the business". This definition ignores the distinction in leader or follower roles in the creative process. Alternatively, this competency can be made role-specific, creating greater opportunities for assessment and development:

1. Leadership creativity: Manages the creative process productively; facilitates the use of creativity tools effectively; creates an environment that fosters the creative input of others.
2. Followership creativity: Introduces research, facts, ideas, and other support to the creative process; provides valued input that leads to novel solutions; respects and helps develop the ideas of others.

Being able to articulate clearly the differences in roles supports performance discussions, mentoring, and even the ability to help people develop their followership identity (Thompson, 2020).

Followership Is a Counterbalance to Poor or Toxic Leadership

While the previous discussion suggests how followers and leaders can support each other, a separate strand of followership theory proposes that followers can and should take an oppositional stance in situations where a leader lacks appropriate moral direction, exercises poor judgment, fails to provide vision or direction, damages team or individual morale, or is engaged in illegal activity (Chaleff, 1995; Kellerman, 2008). In other words, followership can remedy poor or toxic leadership. The extent to which such remedies are possible is limited by numerous cultural and organizational factors (Chordiya et al., 2020).

Toxic Followership Can Derail Leadership

Followership can also be a negative influence, what has sometimes been called toxic followership (Lipman-Blumen, 2005). Active forms of toxic followership include excessive flattery (Offerman, 2014), encouraging negative traits in their leader (Thomas et al., 2016), engaging in unethical practices that reflect poorly on the leader and not just the follower (Disque, 2018), and providing advice to a leader which sways a leader to pursue inappropriate goals or to take wrong actions (Chaleff, n.d.). Passive forms of toxic followership include resisting legitimate orders, purposefully misconstruing instructions or subverting the ability to achieve team goals for reasons such as careerism, doing less that what is asked, and disengaging from the team or task (Edmonds, 2021). Not only do such behaviors reduce follower output, they require additional leadership time, negatively impacting the followership of other team members.

Followership Is Not Leadership

There is confusion in the literature about what constitutes leadership due largely to the nomologically nebulous space it occupies. For example, the principal factor of a followership questionnaire developed by Ligon and colleagues (2019) accounts for 31% of the total variance and is comprised of nine items, listed here in the order each loads onto the primary dimension:

1. I evaluate activities that are necessary for organizational goal achievement.
2. I contribute my best at work.
3. I develop competencies in my work to increase my value to the organization.
4. I finish assignments that go beyond my job duties.
5. I generate and evaluate new ideas that contribute to organizational goals.

6. I spend time thinking about how my work contributes to my personal fulfillment.
7. The leader can give me an assignment without supervision, knowing that I will complete it.
8. Alignment between my personal and organizational goals helps me stay involved at work.
9. I think about how my work adds to society.

Other than item 7, the rest of the questions could as easily be about leadership as about followership; in other words, the face validity of this survey is debatable. Indeed, Agho (2009) conducted a survey of 300 senior U.S. executives using 20 items based on the instrument developed by Kouzes and Posner (2002) to measure perceptions of ideal leadership traits. While Agho found differences between the overall pattern of ideal leader versus ideal follower attributes, the top six traits were the same: honesty/integrity, competent, forward looking, inspiring, intelligent, and fair-minded. To what extent, then, does Agho's instrument measure followership? And to what extent does the Kouzes and Posner study measure leadership? Indeed, many of the GLOBE study leadership variables (House et al., 2004) could be interpreted as characteristics of either an outstanding leader or follower. I conducted an informal within-person test of this supposition with my colleagues in the leadership space by giving them a subset of GLOBE items, asking them to rate each for its relevance to outstanding leadership, and then rate it for its relevance to outstanding followership (or reversing the order). While there were differences in how some characteristics were valued, the majority of ratings were the same for both. Perhaps surveys such as GLOBE, which present leadership without followership, inadvertently tap into a "romance of the leader effect" (Meindl, Ehrlich, & Dukerich, 1985): if a trait is perceived as good, and leadership is positively framed or presented in isolation, then the trait is rated as important for leadership.

More qualitative study is needed of team behaviors in different cultural contexts, traditions, and situations to categorize behaviors as leadership or followership. And, once we do, what contextual clues lead to individuals switching between leadership and followership roles (Malakyan, 2014)? How does someone decide which role or behaviors they are engaging in and how are we, as researchers, going to evaluate that choice? How does this work in multicultural teams? And what other types of leader-follower systems exist outside of dyads, hierarchy, or leaderless teams?

Lord and Alliger (1985) propose that people form social perceptions based on frequency information on how often someone behaves in a certain way associated with a prototype such as leadership. In other words, speaking out in a Western context is seen as a sign of leadership. But is that equally true in other contexts? Are there cultural contexts where someone could be exhibiting excellent followership by speaking out, or poor leadership by speaking out? In developing lists of leadership and followership traits between countries, might it be the case that it is not leadership or followership that is being measured but, rather, matching preferences for certain skills, traits, and behaviors in co-workers to implicit prototypes for leadership or followership? Alternatively, when people hear the words *leader* or *follower*, they could be thinking "colleague" and would mostly answer the same regardless of the role-based context the experimenter uses. None of the studies have used manipulation checks to ensure that the construct being measured is followership rather than something else entirely.

1. A Western Perspective on Followership

Followership theories primarily originate in the USA, and research that has been done in other cultural contexts often uses this Westernized conception of followership to pose research questions and interpret outcomes. There is little research on how followership is enacted in other societies or how beliefs about it differ (later in this chapter, I review international followership research). There are two reasons this is uniquely problematic to international followership research, the first of which is that the language of followership is far from universal, and the second is that most people have poorly developed ideas about followership.

Followership Has No Universal Technical or Colloquial Definition

I teach a leadership/followership course three times a year to graduate students in engineering. About 80% of my students did their undergraduate studies in Southeast Asia, Eastern Asia and the Middle East with a smattering from Africa and South America. The rest (20%) were born in Canada, although that also includes first-generation Canadians. Some students hear the term *followership* on the first day of class and, as they attempt to wrestle with the idea, it is equally clear that there is a wide variety of implicit beliefs about the nature of followership (Hurwitz, 2017): who is a follower (is it everyone who is not the CEO, is it someone who is subservient or acts that way, etc.), what is good followership and does it even exist as a unique construct? This challenge is particularly acute in translation. For example, when Chaleff's book, *The Courageous Follower*, was published in Spanish, he worked with a translator, Dario Orlando Fernandez, to decide what Spanish word to use. Should it be *colaborador* or *seguidores* (Chaleff, private communication – he settled on *seguidores* but now wonders if *colaborador* might have been the better choice)? What do you do when the word "follower" has overtly religious or political connotations (Nurhadi, 2020)? And regardless of the word used in translation, what identities and schemas (Carsten et al., 2010) does it activate in the listener?

Furthermore, should the word *follower* be used to indicate an individual's status in a dyad based on power or hierarchy as is often done in leadership research? Is it a mental state, a role, or an identity? How does culture shape follower identity and what we think about followers (Steffens et al., 2018)? While these questions apply to all followership research, it is especially acute when confounded by culture, or when a model is exported to another country in a different language. Even the questions "Who is a leader?" and "Who is a follower?" add a layer of complexity outside the context of Western, for-profit organizations. For example, when a Canadian Indigenous elected chief meets with a hereditary tribal chief, can we automatically assume one has a "leadership" role? Is there the same automatic association between leadership and power or status with the Acholi of Uganda?

In my class, I teach a processual definition of leadership and followership: "Leadership is setting a framework that others adopt; followership is working within a framework created by another" (Hurwitz, 2018, p. 4; note the lack of influence in this definition). By the end of the semester, students mostly agree to it as usable and valuable, possibly because I am the instructor and wield expert power in the classroom quite expertly, but it is not universally accepted outside my class and I tell students as much. Unlike leadership, the word *followership* is not widely recognized and there is no direct equivalent in many languages. It is only recently that Google has stopped redirecting followership queries to "fellowship" and a whole slew of *Lord of the Rings* references. For these reasons, there is a need to research what the word means in translation and not assume that the same nomological network is being activated by it elsewhere, as might happen in a North American context. There is not a single study from the above literature review that tackles this important issue.

People Do Not Have a Well-Developed Sense of What Followership Is, or Is Not

When you ask someone about leadership, they most likely have had a lifetime of exposure to the concept; leadership is regularly discussed in media, commented on in books, required as an "enabling competency" by professional bodies such as CPA Ontario (The Chartered Professional Accountant Competency Map, 2012), and training provided at many post-secondary institutions and workplaces. In contrast, there are only four peer-reviewed journal articles on followership training (Jenkins & Spranger, 2020) and one book (Hurwitz & Thompson, 2020). While individuals might have constructed a (strong) leadership identity and tested it through active engagement with a variety of leadership constructs, few have a similarly well-developed followership identity, an observational perspective that is helpful in distinguishing different types of followership, or a nomological network that enables it to be disentangled from roles such as peer, teammate, employee or even leader.

For example, I recently conducted interviews with 40 chartered accountants in Ontario, Canada. A number of the interviewees mentioned that my initial e-mail to them was the first time they had heard the term *followership*. As interviewees attempted to answer my questions, many were thinking through what it means to be a follower and wrestling with identity work. Their responses at the beginning of the interview compared to the end suggested that even a half-hour conversation guided by specific questions about followership was enough for them to modify their formative notions. As well, interviewees could not accurately distinguish what was or was not an instance of followership, often describing something they did in a leadership position as if it was followership. More generally, then, even when survey participants list their implicit followership theories (IFTs) or implicit leadership theories (ILTs) or researchers develop their own lists, given the nascent understanding of followership, how should such lists be interpreted? What underlying constructs are actually being tapped into and how does the (cultural) context and language being used affect the results? As Offermann, Kennedy and Wirtz (1994) note: "Others then have used these lists (of traits developed through qualitative, interview-based research) with the tacit assumption that characteristics not generated spontaneously are not present in the person's implicit theory . . . certain characteristics of the implicit theory may still exist without spontaneously surfacing, due to poor memory search or lack of involvement in the procedures" (p. 46). In the case of followership, it is more than a memory retrieval issue. When researchers ask survey participants about followership, there is no shared understanding of the term. Do people think mostly about their personal experience of reporting in to someone, which is a hierarchical perspective? Do they assume it is trait-based and therefore does not apply to themselves? What other notions might they have? When we ask people in non-Western nations about followership, do we know how they interpret the word *followership*, or how it relates to leadership, or how it relates to Western notions?

In fact, even when we ask about leadership, it is possible that the responses are about followership. Mintzberg (1973), for example, reported that managers spent about 7% of their time communicating with superiors while Kurke and Aldrich (1983) found it was as high as 18% in their replication study, yet neither mentioned "follower" as a role managers possess. What other behaviors have been interpreted under the rubric of leadership that are followership or citizenship actions? It is important, for this reason, to use observational techniques and grounded research that pay special attention to unique acts of followership in other cultures. It may also be that what constitutes an act of followership and the construal of the same differs depending on cultural context. For example, in Chinese culture, respect for authority is an important value (Yang et al., 2020); however, Carsten et al. (2010) consider this passive followership while Sy (2010) identifies conformity as a negative followership trait. Although GLOBE (House et al., 2004) and other intercultural leadership research have promoted a healthy discussion about what it means to lead, the same is not yet true about following, and this is troublesome not only for followership studies but in understanding leadership as well.

2. Followership Theory Review

The next part of this chapter summarizes the main followership theories. As authors have previously noted (e.g., Baker, 2007; Brown & Thornborrow, 1996), followership theory originates from a Western perspective and my impression is that researchers from the USA, United Kingdom and Canada are the primary contributors to this endeavor. However, there has been a recent uptick in articles with an Asian perspective (see Table 2.1) and a growing but still small corpus of works from other countries and continents.

Robert Kelley (1988) is considered to have initiated modern followership studies, although Mary Parker Follett (1927) was the first management theorist to mention followership in print, introducing the idea of the two roles working together to produce outcomes ("power with"). Zaleznik (1965) posited the first typology of followers based on two dimensions: submissiveness vs.

Table 2.1 Country of Origin and/or Study

# Publications	Journal Articles	PhD Dissertations
1	Belgium, Botswana, Greece, Honduras, Iran, Ireland, Japan, Jordan, Lithuania, Portugal, Russia, Rwanda, Thailand, UAE	Americans embedded in a Korean-run company, Ethiopia, Ethiopian-Americans, Ghana, Korea, Libya, Uganda
2	India, Indonesia, Israel, Italy, Netherlands, Romania, Serbia and Macedonia, South Korea, Sweden	China
3–4	Australia (3), Germany (3), Nigeria (4), Pakistan (4)	Asian-Americans (3)
>4	China (11), Malaysia (6), cross-cultural (5)	Multi-cultural (8)

dominance, and passivity vs. activity. Kelley's (1992) model has a similar two axes: dependent vs. independent, and passive vs. active. Those in the active/independent quadrant are *Exemplary* followers, the passive/dependent followers are *Sheep*, and those in the middle are *Pragmatists* (the other two quadrants being *Alienated* and *Conformist*). His 1992 book, *The Power of Followership*, introduced a 20-item questionnaire (pp. 90–92) that has been widely used in quantitative studies. The next significant theoretical development was proposed by Ira Chaleff (1995) in which he outlined five practices of courageous followers, broadening the concept of courageous conscience introduced by Kelley (1992) to include assuming responsibility, serving the leader, challenging the leader, participating in transformation and taking moral action. Chaleff (2008) also contributed a typology of followers based on two dimensions: level of support for the leader, and the degree to which the follower challenges the leader. *Partners* are high in support and challenge, *Resources* are low in both, with the other two quadrants being occupied by *Implementer* (high support, low challenge) and *Individualist* (low support, high challenge).

A feature that distinguishes Chaleff's work is his belief that followers and leaders revolve around a common purpose (Bennis, 2007; Chaleff, 2008) rather than the leader's purpose. But he also takes the view that followers can remedy the toxic and dangerous tendencies of some leaders. This is a perspective shared by Kellerman (2008), who articulated a model of followership as a political and social force based on the single dimension of engagement. In particular, Kellerman argued that it is *Diehard* and *Activist* followers – the most engaged categories of followers – who can, should the necessity arise, overturn autocratic or fascist leaders and their regimes. In her conception, followership, leadership and situation form a three-legged stool that defines the leadership dynamic.

Identity studies represent a recent development that focuses on how individuals see themselves within a role and how they enact it as a result (Thompson, 2020). Collinson (2006) suggested three types of follower identities that people hold: conformist, resistant and dramaturgical (see also Epitropaki et al., 2017; Morris, 2014). By contrast, ILTs are the expectations people have about how others should behave in a particular role, and this may or may not be concordant with their identity perspective. Sy (2010) proposed that people also hold IFTs and presumed that it is distinct in both formation and use from an individual's ILT.

Many of these theories reverse the lens by focusing on followers and followership. A different approach suggests that followers actually create leaders and leadership (sometimes called a constructionist approach) based on the premise that people choose who and when to follow. One version of this (DeRue & Ashford, 2010) suggests that leadership and followership are claimed and granted in a mutual interaction that results in people taking on one role or the other. Note that this is different from a research paradigm that implicitly assumes leaders and followers can be identified hierarchically via organizational charts or titles. Another view is that leaders and followers work together to create outcomes and that both roles are equal and valuable (Follett, 1927; Fairhurst & Uhl-Bien, 2012; Shamir, 2007). A model of complementary leader-follower interactions was proposed by Hurwitz and Hurwitz (2015) in a system they call The Generative Partnership Model. The roles of leadership and followership in this model are defined by behaviors rather than positions (Hollander, 1974; Vanderslice, 1988) and, as such, are dynamic and non-exclusive. Hurwitz and Hurwitz do not propose a typology or a survey instrument, and there has been no independent research-backed assessment of their model.

A number of other authors have offered typologies, lists of best practices, behavioral characteristics, relational views (e.g., Hollander, 1992), evolutionary analyses (Balan & Vreja, 2019; Bastardoz & Van Vugt, 2019; Van Vugt, 2006), and constructionist perspectives (Uhl-Bien & Pillai, 2007; Shamir, 2012) with reviews that provide more detail (Baker, 2007; Crossman & Crossman, 2011; Hurwitz & Hurwitz, 2009; Uhl-Bien, Riggio, Lowe, & Carsten, 2014). However, all authors mentioned so far are from North America and the United Kingdom (except Crossman and Crossman from Australia), and express ideas that may or may not be applicable elsewhere, but are certainly influenced by Western perspectives on leadership and followership.

A final thread is a body of literature on non-human species. While leadership theory has been tested and explored within different species (e.g., Dyer et al., 2008; Fischhoff et al., 2007; Harcourt et al., 2009; Peterson et al., 2002), only a few papers explicitly investigate followership (Hurwitz, 2018; Nakayama et al., 2016; Stueckle & Zinner, 2008). The results, however, are intriguing because the dynamics these papers identify in non-humans could easily be applied to people. This line of research suggests that there are adaptive, ecological reasons for leader-follower dynamics, specifically, that leadership and followership is a universal phenomenon of social species. This perspective leads to interesting questions about existing theories; it would be odd, for example, to talk about "authentic leadership" in fish or wolves even though there is behavior we would call authentic were it done by people.

Another way to characterize followership research is by where the agency is assumed to reside, or by what role takes focus. Prior to the mid-1950s, most models assumed leadership was innate and success depended primarily on immutable traits (of the leader). While this approach is leader-centric, it also gives as little agency to the leader as it does to the follower. As trait approaches to leadership gave way to situational and other models, leaders were imputed to have agency to improve team outcomes. This perspective has largely dominated in the years since, even though Meindl and colleagues (1985) demonstrated through a series of studies that this was as much leadership romance as it was leadership reality. Indeed, there are no studies that I know of supporting the notion that leadership has a greater impact than the collective effect of agentic followers.

In their comprehensive literature review, Uhl-Bien and colleagues (2014) employed the concept of agency as a tool for classifying followership theories. They developed five categories of theory based on which role (leader or follower) is considered to be able to take independent action:

1. Leader-centric theories – leaders create outcomes. A leader acts through followers to produce outcomes (the follower is either a mediating or moderating variable). Interestingly, all the leadership theories in this category assume that only leaders have agency but Uhl-Bien and colleagues simply note that followers are moderators or mediators of leader influence on team outcomes and, as such, could have agency and influence on the outcomes if not on the leader (Oc & Bashshur, 2013). Theories in this category include most of the influential mid- to late-20th century (Western) leadership models such as trait, behavioral and contingency approaches.
2. Role-based theories or "reversing the lens" – followers create outcomes. Here, the focus is on how followers act (through leaders) to produce outcomes. Although power may still be exercised top-down, influence is exercised bottom-up. The theories in this category generally acknowledge the importance of leaders to outcomes, but the focus is on the impact followers

can have. For example, Kelley (1992) claims that followers are responsible for 80% of organizational outcomes and, regardless of the truth of this claim – it seems to be more a rhetorical device in his book although others have repeated it as if it were truth – it is representative of the belief that followers can and do make a significant impact (Hurwitz & Hurwitz, 2015).

The two most-cited theories in this category are Kelley's (1988) typology and Chaleff's (1995) courageous followership. Other influential ideas include Jean Lipman-Blumen's (2005) discussion of how followers can enable and sustain toxic leaders, and Sy's (2010) six-factor structure of implicit followership theories (IFTs) held by supervisors.

3. Relational views – followers and leaders act together on outcomes. In this category, leaders and followers engage mutually to create outcomes. The first modern theory of followership (Follett, 1927) of "power with" took this approach and, interestingly, transformational leadership as originally conceived by James MacGregor Burns (1978) did, too. As re-conceptualized by Bass (1985, 1988) and others, however, it became something leaders do to followers and, as such, transformed into another leader-centric theory (Uhl-Bien et al., 2014). Leader-Member Exchange (LMX) is a further instance of a relational theory (Graen & Uhl-Bien, 1995).

4. Follower-centric theories – followers act on leaders. Here, the theory is indifferent to outcomes – followers construct the social dynamic that allows for leadership. Leadership, in this view, is a social construct. People occupying the role of leader and their ability to be effective in it are often those considered prototypical of the role as is asserted by ILTs. No mention is made of outcomes or the impact of relationships to determining outcomes. Meindl's work on the romanticization of leadership and social identity theory are two examples in this category.

5. Constructionist followership – people co-create leadership systems. What unifies ideas in this category is the assumption that leader and follower roles are fluid and socially constructed; individuals can hold multiple identities or none, roles can switch, and the theoretical focus is on how systems are constructed rather than how goals are attained. For example, complexity theories do not require leaders or followers and the identification of a person with a role may be an artefact of the observational lens used to probe a particular relational system rather than an independent property of a complex system. Other theoretical perspectives include DeRue and Ashford's (2010) claiming and granting (Hogg, 2001) and Collinson's view on post-structuralist identities (2006).

While the review by Uhl-Bien and her colleagues covers many followership theories, there have been additional models put forward since 2014. As well, there are theories that do not fit a particular category well. Servant leadership, for example, is a leader-centric theory about how to behave as a follower; servant leadership theory suggests that the leader (by which is meant the hierarchical leader) "serves" their followers, but have they given up their leadership role in doing so? At what point is a servant leader able to object to what the follower does? At what point have they truly given up the privilege of leadership to serve instead? By contrast, the generative partnership model of Hurwitz and Hurwitz (2015) supposes that leadership and followership are fluid and complementary. For example, someone can take on the leadership role but only in the context of someone else taking on the follower role. Leaders and followers have a set of role-specific responsibilities that enable goal achievement and, as such, this model is a combination of categories 3–5 above.

An additional issue with the categories proposed by Uhl-Bien and her colleagues (2014) is that they are not based on a single definition of leadership:

Category 1: A leader is an individual who influences or acts on another.
Categories 2 & 3: Leaders are defined by hierarchy and power relationships.
Category 4: A leader is an individual given power by others.

Category 5: Leaders and followers are emergent properties of systems. In other words, it is the micro-interactions between individuals (or agents) and rules that govern such encounters – those moments of individual exchange – that are foundational and not the patterns that emerge which we observe and call leadership or followership. To take an example from statistical physics, temperature is a collective average of molecular energy, and heating and cooling are the results of energy transfer between molecules. Therefore, temperature is an emergent property of the system not the property of an individual molecule. This reinterpreting of temperature (and heat) in this way has fostered the invention of new solutions such as microwave ovens and induction stovetops that work without relying on "heat exchange".

While the categories above parse theories along a leader-follower relationship axis, they fail to account for purpose or context. In particular, the nationality or culture within which leadership-followership is embedded is crucial. Tolstikov-Mast (2016) notes, for example, that "global followers are distinct from traditional followers due to the nature and outcomes of the global context" (p. 126).

Normative Rather Than Descriptive Theories

Finally, very little of the peer-reviewed literature actually takes a grounded approach to developing leadership-followership theories. Given that many followership studies use surveys (see Section 4 of this chapter), it is normative theories that are being explored. Does this represent followership? As Chaleff (2020) notes, "each culture…has its own embedded language, narratives, symbols, and biases about leading and following that cannot be sidestepped" (p. 12). Is a Western-based instrument able to tap into non-Western followership schemas and constructs effectively? At what point does it become more relevant to look at what followership is in a particular culture or environment? And what happens when contexts collide, as often happens within global organizations (Hocagil, 2020; Tolstikov-Mast, 2016)?

3. International Followership Journal and Book Chapters Review

The book *Followership Education* (Hurwitz & Thompson, 2020) includes a chapter by Nurhadi (2020) detailing a challenge he had introducing followership training into Indonesia. Nurhadi is a marine engineer who, after attending a followership symposium as part of the International Leadership Association's annual conference in 2014, decided to devote himself to the study of followership because he felt it had "unique and practical importance" (2020, p. 87). After subsequently attending a Courageous Follower training session with Ira Chaleff in 2017, Nurhadi decided to bring followership to his home country of Indonesia. Like many in the followership space, Nurhadi believes that engaged and agentic followers can be a remedy for poor leadership (personal communication, see also Chaleff, 1995; Kellerman, 2008), and can bring positive value to the leadership process (e.g., Hollander, 1974).

The first surprise Nurhadi encountered was the difficulty getting attendees for his sessions in Indonesia (Nurhadi, 2020). He sent out a survey to find out why attendance was so poor. The survey contained questions such as "Are you interested in learning about followership?" to which 90.1% said yes. Fully 93% of respondents gave a definition of followership such as "followership is obedience to a leader", "followership is a member in a group" or "followership is the opposite of leadership". In Bahasa (the primary language of Indonesia), followership can hold negative connotations; there is even a pejorative for a type of follower, "Pembebek", which means blindly obeying orders and following directions. Nevertheless, 89.1% responded that followership had positive connotations for them. While many people expressed an interest in learning about followership few would even agree to attend an information session. The reason for this was nothing

Nurhadi had encountered or heard about from Western facilitators he had studied under including Ira Chaleff and Marc and Samantha Hurwitz.

Instead, what Nurhadi discovered through additional surveys and focus groups was that a particular translation of a well-known Hadith – a source of Islamic law comparable to the Quran – into Bahasa has created a cultural bias not found elsewhere. The hadith that is translated in many Islamic countries as "Every one of you is a **guardian** and every one of you is responsible (for his wards)" (Sayings and Teachings of Prophet Muhammad, n.d., see section 67/122) is translated into Bahasa as: "Every one of you is a **leader** and every one of you is responsible (for his wards)" (Nurhadi, 2020, pp. 93–94). As Nurhadi notes, "there is an embedded cultural value to leader and leadership based on the hadith that prioritizes it for most Indonesians over the concepts of follower and followership" (2020, p. 94). Followership, in Indonesia, is not just about organizational roles but is tied to deeply held religious beliefs. Rather than seeing the roles as complementary, they are exclusive and oppositional. By accepting training on followership, a workshop participant would be diminishing their chance of "becoming" a leader. In other words, leadership or followership once embraced cannot be replaced.

Nurhadi's experience is thought-provoking, and it further suggests the value of international followership not simply as an extension of Western ideas, but for the richness, depth and alternative perspectives it can add. In the next sections, the two main sources of research on international followership are reviewed. The first section covers journal articles and chapters while the second covers dissertations.

Peer-Reviewed Journal Articles and Book Chapters

Method

Articles and book chapters were identified through a search on the term "followership" in the title and keyword fields of two research databases: *Scopus* and *PsycInfo*. I also reviewed my personal collection of books and articles on the topic of followership. Note that this search fails to find articles which might have discussed followership from a leader-centric perspective (as noted earlier, this includes a huge number of studies with followers as the dependent variable or situational context). It also misses articles that use a substitute term for followership. I recognize this is a significant issue that limits the articles and books found, but is difficult to address. For example, some organizational citizenship behaviors have been equated with followership (Hurwitz & Hurwitz, 2015; Peterson, Peterson, & Rook, 2020), and LMX theory uses the word "member" to mean someone in a hierarchically determined followership role, but both were excluded from this survey.

It is also likely there are articles published in non-English language journals or books that discuss followership but are not indexed through *Scopus*, *PsycInfo* or my library's (University of Waterloo) search engine; I have no resources to find such articles. And, like the above, even when they are translated into English, it is quite possible that followership was not the term used by the translator given how uncommon and little known it is. Given that this chapter is about non-Western theories, these limitations may significantly underrepresent international studies on followership.

I then revised each of the items found using the above search and decided whether to include them based on a number of criteria:

1. Articles and chapters about followership in the USA, Canada or Great Britain and by authors from those countries were excluded unless they were about minority cultural experiences (none were).
2. In some cases, I was unable to obtain the text of the article or chapter and therefore it was not included (fewer than 10 articles or chapters fell into this category, mostly due to my library not having access online and the author not responding to a request for an English version).

3. If an article was unavailable in English it was excluded.
4. I found one incident of an article that was modified and republished in several low impact journals. In that case, I included the earliest version of the article only.
5. References cited in the article or chapter were investigated in case they had not otherwise been identified through the database search. The same criteria as above were then applied to these newly identified articles.

Each article was read and categorized according to the type of research conducted, primary region of focus (for studies this meant the culture of the target participants and for theory/perspective pieces it was the country of the authors), details of the method, and notes were made about the conclusions.

Results

A total of 68 articles and chapters were identified (see Table 2.1). The list includes five comparative studies across more than two countries, one of which was about followership at the United Nations. Most articles were published in low impact journals – only two articles each were in *The Leadership Quarterly* and *Journal of Leadership Studies*. Fifteen articles (excluding book chapters) were in leadership-focused journals. This may speak to the difficulty of getting followership work published even though some of the research featured high N, multi-instrument, multi-wave studies with relatively sophisticated models and methods.

Articles were of a variety of types: historical review, mixed methods, perspective-taking on followership, qualitative, quantitative, scale development and theory. The sole historical review was about the code of the warrior (Bushido) in feudal Japan (Pascoe, 2016).

The "perspective" category includes articles that discuss the importance of followership (e.g., Tolstikov-Mast, 2014b), or what followership means in a particular context. All four of the Nigerian articles fell into this category with a strong political theme to each. Indeed, my weekly Google Alert on the search term "followership" suggests that it is much discussed in the Nigerian press. This is possibly due to the influence of Ira Chaleff; in the early 2000s he conducted a government seminar on The Courageous Follower, gave away a number of books to the National Democratic Institute in Nigeria and President Obasanjo even mentioned that he had "made copies (of Chaleff's book) for my friends" (personal communication from I. Chaleff, August 2020).

Qualitative research on international followership is scarce. All the qualitative articles from a non-Western country (3) were conducted in Malaysia. Other than a brief period from 2013–2016, there has been no new qualitative research until this year (see Table 2.2). As a result, many of the quantitative articles are based on Western or Westernized theories and tools rather than emic-derived models. This is a significant gap in the literature.

Twelve quantitative studies used Kelley's five-category typology and his 20-item questionnaire as a survey instrument (Kelley, 1992). Note that others also used Kelley's typology (mixed methods – one, perspectives – two, qualitative – two, and scale development – one). Of the studies that used Kelley's model, six found that the most common type in the studied population was *Pragmatists*, while four noted that the largest number of respondents were *Exemplary* (two did not break out results by type); there were no obvious regional differences for which style was most prevalent. Only one quantitative study used Chaleff's model (Na-Nan et al., 2016) and it was unclear how the scale was developed as they appear not to use the Dixon and Westbrook (2003) instrument, which is the only validated one that I am aware of.

Few studies mentioned whether surveys were translated or how, since it is likely from the Methods sections that they were not presented to participants in English. Almost all the quantitative studies were survey-based. A number of the Chinese studies referred to ideas such as Confucianism, Daoist philosophy, benevolent leadership, yin-yang leadership, harmony, obedience, congruence,

Table 2.2 Publication Year and Study Methodology

Year	Total	Historical	Qual.	Quant.	Mixed Method	Scale Dev.	Theory	Perspective
1996	1		1					
2007	1						1	
2010	2						1	1
2011	1							1
2012	2			1				1
2013	8		2	4			2	
2014	7		1	1		1	3	1
2015	6		1	2	1		1	
2016	9	1	1	4		1	2	
2017	7			5			1	1
2018	7			5				2
2019	13			9	1	1	1	1
2020 (as of June)	5		1	2	1	1		

Guanxi and other "Chinese" perspectives on leadership and followership (Berman et al., 2013; Jia, Yan, Cai, & Liu, 2018; Lee & Reade, 2018; Wang, Li, Guo, & Liang, 2019; Wang & Peng, 2016), yet many of the questionnaires used were adaptations of Western instruments. Followership research is beginning to flourish in China as 8 out of 14 quantitative studies from 2018–2019 were done by Chinese researchers with Chinese participants, and all were large multi-scale surveys. Only one paper was about developing a new scale within a Chinese context and it is the most recent (Yang et al., 2020). In general, quantitative studies had N's from as low as 60 to the many thousands, with a median number of participants of 296.

Other findings from China include that leader-member exchange (LMX) improved when followers took responsibility for implementing effective work practices (Xu, Loi, Cai, & Liden, 2019), narcissistic leadership was negatively related to subordinates' followership but mediated by Guanxi (Wang et al., 2019) and that positive IFTs were associated with collegiality. In Thailand (Na-Nan et al., 2016), Chaleff's courage to perform was the highest-rated followership trait while courage to challenge was the lowest. And in a large multi-country (Asian) study, Berman and colleagues (2013) first equated followership with obedience because of its ties to Confucianism, and then found that managers in East Asia, Malaysia and India preferred greater levels of followership than in the USA.

In Pakistan (Ghias, Hassan, & Masood, 2018), courageous followers also tended to be exemplary leaders, but the most common type of follower was Kelley's *Pragmatist*, with *Exemplary* second (Urooj et al., 2020). Nonetheless, proactive followers generated greater trust by leaders (Shahzadi et al., 2017).

Theory articles advance specific ideas about the nature of followership and were largely based upon literature reviews and novel reflections. For example, Küpers (2007) suggests that leadership and followership are deeply interconnected with context in organizations that are typified by injustice and dominated by leaders. Another article (Van Gils, van Quaquebeke, & van Knippenberg 2010) suggests that disagreements about the quality of LMX cannot be explained by social exchange theory. Instead, it is the match of ILTs and IFTs to perceived behaviors (their own and their counterpart) that generate the quality of LMX perceived by each party.

Discussion

In Canada, where I live, Indigenous culture is appreciably distinct from that of the Europeans who came later, and from those who have immigrated to Canada more recently even after years of cultural assimilation and attempts to eliminate indigenous culture through government programs such as residential schools. In the indigenous context, band and tribal leadership is exercised through elected band councillors and chiefs, hereditary chiefs, and elders. A newsworthy event from 2019–2020 over the construction of the Coastal GasLink pipeline through Wet'suwet'en lands in the central interior of British Columbia (Kestler-D'Amours, 2020) illustrates how leadership (and followership) ideas can differ from Western notions. In this situation, the hereditary chiefs were opposed to the pipeline project, the elected band council chiefs were largely in favor of the project, and no mention was made of what elders said or did. Protests against the pipeline project rocked Canada for a number of weeks and included supporters inside the Wet'suwet'en community, other indigenous groups and a significant number of people from non-Indigenous communities. How, then, should we understand followership in a situation when the cultural patterns of influence and power are non-hierarchical and based on different traditions than those represented by our research literature? What additional forces are at play in a situation such as this? What biases are created by layering a Western framework over the actors and situation? How might that affect the theories they create about such events? And what tools should be used to investigate such phenomena? There is no research on followership in this community that I know of. My colleagues who study leadership in women, as well as leadership amongst African Americans, tell me it is lacking there, too.

As the article by the Nigerian authors Ogbonna, Ogundiwin and Uzuegbu-Wilson (2012) point out, leadership theory has quashed important discussions about what it means to follow, specifically in the Nigerian/African/Black context. They go on to assert that "leadership has perpetually failed Nigerians" (p. 68) and discussions are needed as to how followers can reshape leadership, constrain toxic leadership and enable greater democratic rule. Arowolo (2019) agrees, and further asserts that followers are "the foundation of democracy" (p. 108) but that strong followership includes such traits as humanity, loyalty, honesty, integrity, reliability, utility, synergy, intelligence, cooperativeness, diplomacy and sociability. How does this contrast with normative ideas of followership in China, defined by Li and colleagues (2019) as "the free will recognition of leadership in the commitment toward realization of the collectively adopted organization vision and culture" (p. 616), or of Berman et al. (2013) who equates followership with obedience? To what extent does this align with Sy's (2010) model of IFTs that contains two first order dimensions (and six second order ones): followership prototype (composed industry, enthusiasm, good citizen); and followership anti-prototype (conformity, insubordination, and incompetence)? Would conformity be considered an anti-prototype in other cultures? For example, Mohamad and Saad (2016) found that Malaysians were more dependent, subdued, high in obedience and conforming to directions while Idrus, Hashim and Raihanah (2015) relate that to the customary law of *adat* which still regulates people's lives and makes obedience a prototypical followership trait in Malaysia. Would Malaysian IFTs have a similar structure to that found by Sy? Is Sy's model, based as it is on normative beliefs and interpreted through a Western lens, a normative theory in other countries? Is it descriptive? And what do respondents have in mind when they hear the word followership, often for the first time?

One of the takeaways from this review, then, is that while there is an overall need for more international followership research, the lack of emic-centered research is particularly acute. This includes studies involving implicit beliefs about followership as well as those grounded in descriptive, qualitative research such as Mohamad and Saad (2016). The poverty of models about followership is also seen in the small number of theory papers.

As mentioned in the Methods section, little information was provided about how the surveys were translated (note that every quantitative study was survey-based). Followership is still an emerging concept in English – until recently, for example, a Google search on the word "followership" changed to "fellowship" which then turned up a list of *Lord of the Rings* references (Hurwitz & Hurwitz, 2020). I will return to this subject in the Conclusion section. In Russian, for example, there are five words for follower each of which represents very different perceptions of leader-follower relationships (Tolstikov-Mast, 2014a). Tolstikov-Mast also notes other issues for those doing followership research in a culture other than their own including designing questions in a foreign language, what it means to work with an international sample, ensuring the needed level of diversity or homogeneity in the sample, obtaining consent, transferring research questions and models in the context of the culture being studied, evolution of meaning over time, oral traditions and even assembling a research team.

PhD Theses

Method

I conducted a search on the term "followership" in three fields of the ProQuest database: Abstract, Title, and Keywords. It returned 329 hits (July 7, 2020). It is probable that some relevant theses were missed using these search criteria because, until recently, the term *followership* was uncommon (Riggio, 2020) – in fact, alternatives such as "partner", "member", "collaborator", "team" or "citizen" (such as in Leader-Member Exchange or Organizational Citizenship) have been used in the past. There may also be non-English language theses about followership which the search did not uncover. As with the journal articles, I used the Reference section of each thesis to look for additional theses (and articles) that had not been found through the database search.

Each thesis was reviewed for inclusion. The thesis had to be about followership or followers, not simply as a contextual element or passive agent, and also had to satisfy one or more of these conditions:

1. Published by a student at a university not located in Canada, USA, or UK;
2. About followership other than in Canada, USA, or UK; or
3. About followership of an immigrant community or bicultural group within Canada, USA, or UK;
4. About followership within a minority community.

The criteria narrowed the list to 20 dissertations. I was unable to obtain either the abstract or full text of one thesis, further reducing the number to 19 – all theses are cited in the "Dissertation" section of the Bibliography at the end of this chapter. Only three theses were completed prior to 2010 and the largest number (four) were written in 2019. There was a higher percentage of cross-cultural comparisons than for the journal articles – two theses involved multiple nationalities (seven and nine), one with three (Jamaica, USA and Thailand), and five comparing two cultures (for a total of 8 out of 19) – see Table 2.1. In addition, a number of theses studied cultural minorities (six in total compared to no journal articles on the topic): Mexican-Americans, Asian-Americans (two), Korean-Americans, a community within Uganda (the Acholi people), and an Ethiopian religious community (Kale Heywet church). In terms of who was studied, it included employees of for-profit organizations, students, nurses, church congregants and leaders (in three studies), authors, members of a political party and educators.

The earliest thesis was completed in 1983, five years before Kelley's seminal HBR article. The author (Castillo, 1983) applied Frew's Leadership and Followership Style Questionnaire (Frew, 1977; which used Fiedler's LPC theory as the theoretical basis for the survey) to 230 nursing students to compare and contrast leadership and followership beliefs held by those identified as Anglo-Americans versus Mexican-Americans. Interestingly, the author found that while student nurses held different beliefs about ideal followership, their beliefs about the traits of ideal leaders were indistinguishable (within the limitations of the power of the test). Castillo concludes with a call to teach both leadership and followership in the final two years of the four-year college nursing program at her college.

Despite the number of theses, the length of time since publication and that a number were from graduate schools recognized for excellence in leadership scholarship (tier one or two institutions), only Blair and Bligh (2016) has subsequently published Blair's work in a peer-reviewed journal.

The most recently published PhD thesis was on Asian-Americans (Kim, 2020) exploring why they are underrepresented in leadership roles. For example, even in the field of technology, where a disproportionate percentage of the workforce is Asian-American in the USA, there are 30% fewer Asian-American managers than would be expected based on their overall participation rate (Bureau of Labor Statistics, 2019). One surprise was the discovery that Asian-Americans were considered both better leaders and followers by Anglo-Americans. Kim conducted a second wave of studies, finding that Asian-Americans had formed stronger followership identities than Anglo-Americans which, alongside self-perceptions as more conforming and less intelligent, resulted in a lower desire to lead.

Fully 15 theses used a role-based approach (as per Uhl-Bien et al., 2014), one was leader-centric, one was constructionist and two were relational.

Discussion

As can be seen from Table 2.3, there has been a steady stream of dissertations over the last decade though in small numbers. Unlike journal articles, there is an even split between qualitative and quantitative studies and some of the qualitative studies deserve wider recognition. For example, Ofumbi's (2017) thesis on the Acholi of Uganda presents a narrative on followership and leadership that is quite different from Western models. Rather than supposing the leader-follower dynamic should be based on power and influence, he suggests that according to the Acholi worldview, "followership is the self-consciousness of and commitment to human dignity…Human dignity encompasses the agency to nurture and actualize human potential to thrive, reverence for the inherent worth of all humans, and unfettered access to equal opportunities" (pp. 139–140). Furthermore, he asserts that, "according to the Acholi model, Africa's foremost challenge is poor leadership theory, which cast a larger-than-life image of leaders in the mind of leaders and followers" (p. 329).

Antwi (2015) conducted a mixed methods study of followership in leader-follower dynamics of political parties in Ghana, uncovering an intimate relationship between corruption – politicians giving gifts to followers to curry favor and votes –ith expectations by those followers of the same.

Table 2.3 PhD Thesis Publication Year and Study Methodology

Year	Total	Historical	Qual.	Quant.	Mixed Method	Scale Dev.	Theory	Perspective
1983	1			1				
2011	1			1				
2012	1				1			
2013	2			1		1		
2014	2		2					
2015	2		1		1			
2016	2		1	1				
2017	2		1	1				
2018	1		1					
2019	3		1	2				
2020 (as of June)	2		1	1				

Hocagil (2020) conducted a study including seven countries of origin on following in a global context, uncovering four themes:

1. Following effectively. Sub-themes: being proactive, following and leading simultaneously, having the necessary skills, being in sync with the organizational culture, building trust and holding a team orientation;
2. Following globally (a unique category). Sub-themes: adjusting to the cultural norms of others in the team/organization, dealing with complexities, being flexible and maintaining an awareness of the environment;
3. Developing continuously. Sub-themes: being an autodidact through training opportunities, learning on the job and staying up to date.
4. Managing challenges. Sub-themes: being aware of and adapting to different ways of doing business, communicating effectively in a cross-cultural perspective, being trustworthy and having the courage to act.

A qualitative study with respondents from nine countries (Hong, 2014) found different themes between Western and non-Western participants. For example, while upwards communication was universally desired in ideal followers, Western followers wanted "to express their opinions freely, to ask questions, and to challenge leadership, while non-Western followers said that, even if they shared their opinions, they needed to be sensitive to timing" (p. 109). Similarly, Medcof (2012) noted in his study on Indians and Canadians that, "the majority (of Indian respondents) suggested that followers needed to keep a professional distance between their leaders and themselves in the workplace" (p. 143) while "developing a personal relationship with a leader might be unseemly…Canadians, on the other hand, had no such concerns" (p. 144). Indians used (upwards) communication for compliance and task-centered updates whereas Canadians emphasized relationship-building. The scale developed by Park (2013), based on Korean IFTs, had a four-factor structure different from the model of Sy (2010) based on American respondents: goal orientation (pursuing a common goal, goal alignment, embracing organizational goals), working towards goals (honest opinions, reaching agreement, high performance standards, upwards communication), enthusiasm (activeness, energy, engagement, relationship) and intellectuality (critical thinking, creativity, understanding job, self-development).

Only Chai's (2013) thesis made use of Kelley's 20-item questionnaire, in contradistinction to its frequency of use in journal articles. So, while surveys were still the dominant form of quantitative analysis in theses, their origin was from a wide variety of sources including Carsten and Uhl-Bien's (2012) proactive followership scale, Gallup's Q12 engagement survey, MLQ-5X, VanWhy's (2015) authentic followership scale, Sy's (2010) IFT scale, Epitropaki and Martin's (2004) ILT scale, as well as measures such as organizational commitment, culture and consideration.

Overall, the theses provide a rich source of new models and ways of thinking about followership, and hence leadership.

Conclusion

In this chapter, I have attempted to convince you that we need more research and study of international followership. To begin, I attacked the notion that leadership is enough to explain the social processes we observe. Hopefully, there are resources in the articles and theses that intrigue you to read more. For example, there were a number of excellent descriptive, qualitative studies in the list of theses such as Umer's (2019) five types of leadership-followership processes in the Ethiopian Kale Heywet church: individualism, authoritarianism, partnership, integration and *holoubuntu* (defined as the interconnected social process of a harmonious community through humanness, integrity and spirituality). Articles such as Idrus, Hashim, and Raihanah's (2015) look at Malaysian follo-wership in two popular television shows also present alternative perspectives on what "good" followership entails within a cultural context. But we need a richer, more diverse set of ideas about followership: how it is enacted; the impact it has on individuals, groups and societies; how it can be taught or developed; and how it intertwines with leadership.

Given some of the leadership and followership research in non-humans, I personally believe that there is an adaptive set of leadership and followership behaviors – what might be considered universal or optimal ways social animals engage. At the same time, there is clearly a diversity within that framework to be uncovered. While asking people what they think is the current dominant approach to exploring the phenomenon, it is not the only way and should be informed by different approaches.

These are some of the questions that keep me up at night and that make international followership an intriguing and needed area for leadership research in the future. Yes, we need more international leadership research focused only on leadership, but we also need much more international followership research, too. In 2019, six colleagues and I organized the first Global Followership Conference. The 130 attendees came from Southeast Asia, Africa, South America, Europe, Australia and, of course, North America. They included a number of the people whose work is referenced in this chapter. It was a start, at least, to exploring the phenomenon of followership globally. Going forward, I hope to see many more opportunities for international followership scholars to exchange ideas, and for international leadership and followership scholars to come together and explore this social behavior as the integrated, complementary *system* that it is. I hope to see many more cross-cultural studies looking at the leadership-followership dance: how we do it differently from each other and how it is similar across cultures. I hope to see more publication outlets available in high-quality journals. And I hope that one day there will something with a title like: "The Journal of *International Leadership with Followership Studies*" (to paraphrase the words of Mary Parker Follett in 1927).

References

Achebe, C. (1984). *The trouble with Nigeria.* Heinemann Educational Books.

Agho, A. O. (2009). Perspectives of senior-level executives on effective followership and leadership. *Journal of Leadership & Organizational Studies, 16*(2), 159–166. doi:10.1177/1548051809335360

Alvesson, M., & Einola, K. (2019). Warning for excessive positivity: Authentic leadership and other traps in leadership studies. *The Leadership Quarterly, 30*, 383–395. doi:10.1016/j.leaqua.2019.04.001

Arowolo, D. E. (2019). Leadership–followership disconnect and democratic decline in Nigeria. *Africa Review, 11*(2), 107–121. doi:10.1080/09744053.2019.1631078

Baker, S. D. (2007). Followership: The theoretical foundation of a contemporary construct. *Journal of Leadership & Organizational Studies, 14*(1), 50–60. doi:10.1177/0002831207304343

Balan, S., & Vreja, L. O. (2019). Leadership and followership. An evolutionary perspective. In Proceedings of the 13th *International Management Conference* (pp. 1185–1197).

Bass, B. M. (1985). *Leadership and performance beyond expectations.* Free Press.

Bass, B. M. (1988). The inspirational process of leadership. *Journal of Management Development, 7*, 21–31. doi:10.1108/eb051688

Bastardoz, N., & Van Vugt, M. (2019). The nature of followership: Evolutionary analysis and review. *The Leadership Quarterly, 30*(1), 81–95. doi:10.1016/j.leaqua.2018.09.004

Bennis, W. (2007). The challenges of leadership in the modern world: Introduction to the special issue. *The American Psychologist, 62*(1), 2–5. doi:10.1037/0003-066X.62.1.2

Berman, E., Sabharwal, M., Wang, C., West, J., Jing, Y., Jan, C., Liu, W., Brillantes, A., Chen, C., & Gomes, R. (2013). The impact of societal culture on the use of performance strategies in East Asia: Evidence from a comparative survey. *Public Management Review, 15*(8), 1065–1089. doi:10.1080/14719037.2013.816522

Blair, B. A., & Bligh, M. C. (2018). Looking for leadership in all the wrong places: The impact of culture on proactive followership and follower dissent. *Journal of Social Issues, 74*(1), 129–143. doi:10.1111/josi.12260

Brandl, S., & Bellwood, D. (2015). Coordinated vigilance provides evidence for direct reciprocity in coral reef fishes. *Science Reports, 5,* 14556. doi:10.1038/srep14556

Brown, A. D., & Thornborrow, W. T. (1996). Do organizations get the followers they deserve? *Leadership & Organization Development Journal, 17,* 5–11. doi:10.1108/01437739610105986

Bureau of Labor Statistics. (2019). *Labor force statistics from the current population survey: Employed persons by detailed occupation, sex, race, and Hispanic or Latino ethnicity.* Retrieved June 2, 2020, from https://www.bls.gov/cps/cpsaat11.htm

Burns, J. M. (1978). *Leadership.* Harper & Row.

Carsten, M. K., & Uhl-Bien, M. (2012). Follower beliefs in the co-production of leadership: Examining upward communication and the moderating role of context. *Zeitschrift Für Psychologie, 220,* 210–220. doi:10.1027/2151-2604/a000115

Carsten, M. K., Uhl-Bien, M., West, B. J., Patera, J. L., & McGregor, R. (2010). Exploring social constructions of followership: A qualitative study. *The Leadership Quarterly, 21*(3), 543–562. doi:10.1016/j.leaqua.2010.03.015

Chaleff, I. (n.d.) Toxic followers. *The followership exchange.* http://followership2.pbworks.com/w/page/12482156/TOXIC%20FOLLOWERS.

Chaleff, I. (1995). *The courageous follower: Standing up to and for our leaders.* Berrett-Koehler Publishers.

Chaleff, I. (2008). Creating new ways of following. In R. Riggio, I. Chaleff, & J. Lipman-Blumen (Eds.), *The art of followership: How great followers create great leaders and organizations* (pp. 67–87). Jossey-Bass.

Chaleff, I. (2020). Foreword. In M. Hurwitz & R. Thompson (Eds.), *New directions for student leadership: No. 167. Followership education* (pp. 11–13). Jossey-Bass.

Chordiya, R., Sabharwal, M., Relly, J. E., & Berman, E. M. (2020). Organizational protection for whistleblowers: A cross-national study. *Public Management Review, 22*(4), 527–552. doi:10.1080/14719037.2019.1599058

Collinson, D. (2006). Rethinking followership: A post-structuralist analysis of follower identities. *The Leadership Quarterly, 17,* 179–189. doi:10.1016/j.leaqua.2005.12.005

Crossman, B., & Crossman, J. (2011). Conceptualising followership – a review of the literature. *Leadership, 7*(4), 481–497. doi:10.1177/1742715011416891

DeRue, D. S., & Ashford, S. J. (2010). Who will lead and who will follow? A social process of leadership identity construction in organizations. *Academy of Management Review, 35,* 627–647.doi:10.5465/AMR.2010.53503267

Disque, B. M. (2018). Followership: Avoid being a toxic subordinate. *NCO Journal,* May 30, Article 11. https://www.armyupress.army.mil/Journals/NCO-Journal/Archives/2018/May/Followership/.

Dixon, G., & Westbrook, J. (2003). Followers revealed. *Engineering Management Journal, 15*(1), 19–25. doi:10.1080/10429247.2003.11415192

Dyer, J. R. G., Croft, D. P., Morrell, L. J., & Krause, J. (2008). Shoal composition determines foraging success in the guppy. *Behavioral Ecology, 20*(1), 165–171. doi:10.1093/beheco/arn129

Edmonds, W. M. (2021). *InTOXICating followership: In the Jonestown massacre.* Emerald Publishing Limited.

Epitropaki, O., Kark, R., Mainemelis, C., & Lord, R. G. (2017). Leadership and followership identity processes: A multilevel review. *The Leadership Quarterly, 28,* 104–129.doi:10.1016/j.leaqua.2016.10.003

Epitropaki, O., & Martin, R. (2004). Implicit leadership theories in applied settings: Factor structure, generalizability, and stability over time. *Journal of Applied Psychology, 89,* 293–310. doi:10.1037/0021-9010.89.2.293

Fairhurst, G. T., & Uhl-Bien, M. (2012). Organizational discourse analysis (ODA): Examining leadership as a relational process. *The Leadership Quarterly, 23*(6), 1043–1062. doi:10.1016/j.leaqua.2012.10.005

Fischhoff, I. R., Sundaresan, S. R., Cordingley, J., Larkin, H. M., Sellier, M., & Rubenstein, D. I. (2007). Social relationships and reproductive state influence leadership roles in movements of plains zebra, Equus burchellii. *Animal Behaviour, 73*(5), 825–831.doi:10.1016/j.anbehav.2006.10.012

Follett, M. P. (1927). Leader and expert. In H. C. Metcalf (Ed.), *The psychological foundations of management* (pp. 220–243). Shaw.

Frew, D. R. (1977). Leadership and followership. *Personnel Journal, 56*(2), 90–97.

Ghias, W., Hassan, S., & Masood, M. T. (2018). Does courageous followership contribute to exemplary leadership practices: Evidence from Pakistan? *NUML International Journal of Business & Management, 13*(1), 11–21.

Graen, G. B., & Uhl-Bien, M. (1995). The Relationship-based approach to leadership: Development of LMX theory of leadership over 25 years: Applying a multi-level, multi-domain perspective. *Leadership Quarterly 6*(2), 219–247. doi:10.1016/1048-9843(95)90036-5.

Harcourt, J. L., Ang, T. Z., Sweetman, G., Johnstone, R. A., & Manica, A. (2009). Social feedback and the emergence of leaders and followers. *Current Biology, 19,* 248–252. doi:10.1016/j.cub.2008.12.051

Hogg, M. A. (2001). A social identity theory of leadership. *Personality and Social Psychology Review, 5*(3), 184–200. doi:10.1207/S15327957PSPR0503_1

Hollander, E. P. (1974). Processes of leadership emergence. *Journal of Contemporary Business*, *3*, 19–33.

Hollander, E. (1992). The essential interdependence of leadership and followership. *Current Directions in Psychological Science*,*1*(2), 71–75. Retrieved April 20, 2021, from http://www.jstor.org/stable/20182133

House, R. J., Hanges, P. J., Javidan, M., Dorfman, P. W., & Gupta, V. (2004). *Culture, leadership, and organizations: The GLOBE study of 62 societies*. Sage Publications.

Hurwitz, M. (2017). Followership: A classroom exercise to introduce the concept. *Management Teaching Review*, *2*, 281–288. doi:10.1177/2379298117717468

Hurwitz, M. (2018). Exploring distributed leadership: A leader-follower collaborative lens. In N. Chatwani (Ed.), *Distributed leadership: Palgrave studies in leadership and followership* (pp. 1–25). Palgrave Macmillan. 10/1 007/978-3-319-5958108_1

Hurwitz, M., & Hurwitz, S. (2015). *Leadership is half the story: A fresh look at followership, leadership, and collaboration*. University of Toronto Press.

Hurwitz, M., & Hurwitz, S. (2009). The romance of the follower: Part 1. *Industrial and Commercial Training*, *41*(2), 80–86. doi:10.1108/00197850910939117

Hurwitz, M., & Hurwitz, S. (2020). Integrating followership into leadership programs. In M. Hurwitz & R. Thompson (Eds.), *New directions for student leadership: No. 167. Followership education* (pp. 23–36). Jossey-Bass.

Hurwitz, M., & Thompson, R. (2020). *New directions for student leadership: No. 167. followership education*. Jossey-Bass.

Idrus, M. M., Hashim, R. S., & Raihanah, M. M. (2015). Followership: Boosting power and position in popular TV fiction. *GEMA Online Journal of Language Studies*, *15*(1), 207–224. doi:10.17576/GEMA-2 015-1501-12

Jenkins, D., & Spranger, S. (2020). Followership education for postsecondary students. In M. Hurwitz & R. Thompson (Eds.), *New directions for student leadership: No. 167. Followership education* (pp. 47–63). Jossey-Bass.

Jia, J., Yan, J., Cai, Y., & Liu, Y. (2018). Paradoxical leadership incongruence and Chinese individuals' followership behaviors: Moderation effects of hierarchical culture and perceived strength of human resource management system. *Asian Business and Management*, *17*(5), 313–338. doi:10.1057/s41291-018-0043-9

Kellerman, B. (2008). *Followership: How followers are creating change and changing leaders*. Harvard Business School Press.

Kelley, R. E. (1988). In praise of followers. *Harvard Business Review*, *66*(6), 142–148. https://hbr.org/1988/11/ in-praise-of-followers

Kelley, R. E. (1992). *The power of followership: How to create leaders people want to follow and followers who lead themselves*. Currency/Doubleday.

Kestler-D'Amours, J. (2020). Understanding the Wet'suwet'en struggle in Canada. *Al-Jazeera* (March 1, 2020). from https://www.aljazeera.com/news/2020/03/understanding-wet-struggle-canada-200301200921070.html

Kouzes, J. M., & Posner, B. Z. (2002). *The leadership challenge* (3rd ed.). Jossey-Bass.

Küpers, W. (2007). Perspectives on integrating leadership and followership. *International Journal of Leadership Studies*, *2*(3), 194–221. http://www.regent.edu/acad/global/publications/ijls/new/vol2iss3/kupers/Kupers_Vol2Iss3.pdf

Kurke, L. B., & Aldrich, H. E. (1983). Note – Mintzberg was right!: A replication and extension of the nature of managerial work. *Management Science*, *29*(8), 975–984. doi:10.1287/mnsc.29.8.975

Lee, H., & Reade, C. (2018). The role of yin-yang leadership and cosmopolitan followership in fostering employee commitment in china: A paradox perspective. *Cross Cultural and Strategic Management*, *25*(2), 276–298. doi:10.1108/CCSM-12-2016-0216

Li, H., Zhao, Z., Müller, R., & Shao, J. (2019). Exploring the relationship between leadership and followership of Chinese project managers. *International Journal of Managing Projects in Business*, *13*(3), 616–647. doi:10.11 08/IJMPB-02-2019-0042

Ligon, K. V., Stoltz, K. B., Rowell, R. K., & Lewis, V. J. (2019). An empirical investigation of the Kelley followership questionnaire revised. *Journal of Leadership Education*, *18*(3). https://journalofleadershiped.org/ jole_articles/an-empirical-investigation-of-the-kelley-followership-questionnaire-revised/

Lipman-Blumen, J. (2005). *The allure of toxic leaders: Why we follow destructive bosses and corrupt politicians—and how we can survive them*. Oxford University Press.

Lord, R. G., & Alliger, G. M. (1985). A comparison of four information processing models of leadership and social perceptions. *Human Relations*, *38*, 47– 65. doi:10.1177/001872678503800103

Malakyan, P. G. (2014). Followership in leadership studies: A case of leader-follower trade approach. *Journal of Leadership Studies*, *7*(4), 6–22. doi:10.1002/jls.21306

Meilinger, P. S. (2001). The ten rules of good followership. In Richard C. Lester & A. Glenn Morton (Eds.), *AU-24 concepts for air force leadership* (pp. 99–101). Air University Press.

Meindl, J. R., Ehrlich, S. B., & Dukerich, J. M. (1985). The romance of leadership. *Administrative Science Quarterly*, *30*, 78–102. doi:10.2307/2392813

Mintzberg, H. (1973). *The nature of managerial work*. Harper and Row.

Mohamad, R., & Saad, N. M. (2016). Power distance culture and the construction of the followership identity. *Asia Pacific Journal of Advanced Business and Social Studies*, 2(1), 149–160. https://apiar.org.au/journal-paper/power-distance-culture-and-the-construction-of-the-followership-identity/

Morris, R. (2014). Constructions of following from a relational perspective: A follower focused study. *Journal of Leadership Education*, 13(4), 51–62. doi:10.12806/V13/I4/C7

Nakayama, S., Harcourt, J. L., Johnstone, R. A., & Manica, A. (2016). Who directs group movement? leader effort versus follower preference in stickleback fish of different personality. *Biology Letters*, 12(5). doi:10.1098/rsbl.2016.0207

Na-Nan, K., Thanitbenjasith, P., Ekkasitsanamthong, & Pukkeeree, P. (2016). The relationship between organizational cultures and courageous followership behaviors: What's the relationship and why does it matter? *International Business Management*, 10(18), 4384–4390.

Nurhadi, M. B. (2020). Development of a followership teaching strategy in Indonesia. In M. Hurwitz & R. Thompson (Eds.), *New directions for student leadership: No. 167. Followership education* (pp. 87–97). Jossey-Bass.

Oc, B., & Bashshur, M. R. (2013). Followership, leadership and social influence. *The Leadership Quarterly*, 24(6), 919–934. doi:10.1016/j.leaqua.2013.10.006

Offerman, L. R. (2014). When followers become toxic. *Harvard Business Review*, January 2004. https://hbr.org/2004/01/when-followers-become-toxic

Offermann, L. R., Kennedy, J. K., Jr., & Wirtz, P. W. (1994). Implicit leadership theories: Content, structure and generalizability. *The Leadership Quarterly*, 5, 43–58. doi:10.1016/1048-9843(94)90005-1

Ogbonna, E. C., Ogundiwin, A. O., Uzuegbu-Wilson, E. (2012). Followership imperative of good governance: Reflections on Nigeria's 'second chance' at democratization. *International Affairs and Global Strategy*, 4, 65–80. https://www.iiste.org/Journals/index.php/IAGS/article/view/2653

Pascoe, B. (2016). Followership and the samurai. *Journal of Leadership Studies*, 10(3), 54–57. doi:10.1002/jls.21494

Peterson, R. O., Jacobs, A. K., Drummer, T. D., Mech, L. D., & Smith, D. W. (2002). Leadership behavior in relation to dominance and reproductive status in gray wolves, Canis lupus. *Canadian Journal of Zoology*, 80(8), 1405–141. doi:10.1139/Z02-124

Peterson, T. O., Peterson, C. M. & Rook, B. W. (2020, pre-print). Exemplary followership. Part 2: Impact of organizational citizenship behavior. *Industrial and Commercial Training*. doi:10.1108/ICT-06-2020-0072. https://www.emerald.com/insight/content/doi/10.1108/ICT-06-2020-0072/full/html.

Riggio, R. E. (2020). Why followership?. In M. Hurwitz & R. Thompson (Eds.), *New directions for student leadership: No. 167. Followership education* (pp. 15–22). Jossey-Bass.

Sayings and teachings of Prophet Muhammad. (n.d.). Retrieved from https://sunnah.com/.

Schuder, K. L. (2017). Using followership to develop new leadership in cultures with greater power distance. *Journal of Leadership, 10 (Symposium)*, 3, 58–61. doi:10.1002.jls

Shamir, B. (2007). From passive recipients to active co-producer s: Followers' roles in the leadership process. In B. Shamir, R. Pillai, M. Bligh, & M. Uhl-Bien (Eds.), *Follower-centered perspectives on leadership: A tribute to the memory of James R. Meindl* (pp. ix–xxxix). Information Age Publishers.

Shamir, B. (2012). Leadership research or post-leadership research: Advancing leadership theory versus throwing out the baby with the bath water. In M. Uhl-Bien & S. Ospina (Eds.), *Advancing relational leadership research: A dialogue among perspectives* (pp. 477–500). Information Age Publishers.

Shahzadi, G., John, A., Qadeer, F., & Shamaila, M. (2017). Followership behavior and leaders' trust: Do political skills matter? *Pakistan Journal of Commerce and Social Science*, 11(2), 653–670. http://hdl.handle.net/10419/188310

Steffens, N. K., & Haslam, S. A. (2020). The narcissistic appeal of leadership theories. *American Psychologist*. doi:10.1037/amp0000738

Steffens, N. K., Haslam, S. A., Jetten, J., & Mols, F. (2018). Our followers are lions, theirs are sheep: How social identity shapes theories about followership and social influence. *Political Psychology*, 39(1), 23–42. doi:10.1111/pops.12387

Stueckle, S., & Zinner, D. (2008). To follow or not to follow: Decision making and leadership during the morning departure in chacma baboons. *Animal Behaviour*, 75(6), 1995–2004. doi:10.1016/j.anbehav.2007.12.012

Sy, T. (2010). What do you think of followers? Examining the content, structure, and consequences of implicit followership theories. *Organizational Behavior and Human Decision Processes*, 113(2), 73 - 84. doi:10.1016/j.obhdp.2010.06.001

The Chartered Professional Accountant Competency Map. (2012). Retrieved August 29, 2020, from https://media.cpaontario.ca/become-a-cpa/CompetencyMap.pdf

Thomas, T., Gentzler, K., & Salvatorelli, R. (2016). What is toxic followership?. *Journal of Leadership Studies, 10,* 62–65. doi:10.1002/jls.21496.

Thompson, R. (2020). Followership identity work. In M. Hurwitz & R. Thompson (Eds.), *New Directions for student leadership: No. 167. Followership education* (pp. 65–75). Jossey-Bass.

Tolstikov-Mast, Y. (2014a). *Relationship between science and wisdom.* Presentation at the 2014 fall immersion weekend of the global leadership program. https://www.youtube.com/watch?v=7H4Nf7D2_14.

Tolstikov-Mast, Y. (2014b). Followership in Russia: Understanding traditions and exploring meaning of current reality. *Journal of Leadership Education (Special 2014),* 100–110. doi:10.12806/V13/I4/C11

Tolstikov-Mast, Y. (2016). Global followership: The launch of the scholarly journey. *Advances in Global Leadership, 9,* 109–150. doi:10.1108/S1535-120320160000009013

Trainingindustry.com. *Size of the training industry.* https://trainingindustry.com/wiki/outsourcing/size-of-training-industry/

Uhl-Bien, M., & Pillai, R. (2007). The romance of leadership and the social construction of followership. In B. Shamir, R. Pillai, M. Bligh, & M. Uhl-Bien (Eds.), *Follower-centered perspectives on leadership: A tribute to the memory of James R. Meindl* (pp. 187–210). Information Age Publishers.

Uhl-Bien, M., Riggio, R. E., Lowe, K. B., & Carsten, M. K. (2014). Followership theory: A review and research agenda. *The Leadership Quarterly, 25,* 83–104. doi:10.1016/j.leaqua.2013.11.007

Urooj, U., Yasmeen, R., Khan, N.-U.-S., Qamar, K., Iqbal, R., & Khalil, H. (2020). "There's only one king and you are not him" Followership styles of medical residents in Pakistan. *Pakistan Armed Forces Medical Journal, 70*(2), 362–367. Retrieved from https://www.pafmj.org/index.php/PAFMJ/article/view/4190

Vanderslice, V. J. (1988). Separating leadership from leaders: An assessment of the effect of leader and follower roles in organizations. *Human Relations, 41,* 677–696. doi:10.1177/001872678804100903

Van Gils, S., van Quaquebeke, N., & van Knippenberg, D. (2010). The X-factor: On the relevance of implicit leadership and followership theories for leader-member exchange agreement. *European Journal of Work and Organizational Psychology, 19*(3), 333–363. doi:10.1080/13594320902978458

Van Vugt, M. (2006). Evolutionary origins of leadership and followership. *Personality and Social Psychology Review, 10*(4), 354–371. doi:10.1207/s15327957pspr1004_5

VanWhy, L. P. (2015). *Development of the authentic followership profile (AFP) test instrument* [Unpublished doctoral dissertation]. Regent University.

Wang, L., Li, X., Guo, Q., & Liang, H. (2019). The influence mechanism of narcissistic leader on subordinates' followership under the Chinese cultural background. *Ekoloji, 28*(107), 3661–3666.

Wang, X., & Peng, J. (2016). The effect of implicit-explicit followership congruence on benevolent leadership: Evidence from Chinese family firms. *Frontiers in Psychology, 7.* doi:10.3389/fpsyg.2016.00812

Xu, A. J., Loi, R., Cai, Z., & Liden, R. C. (2019). Reversing the lens: How followers influence leader–member exchange quality. *Journal of Occupational and Organizational Psychology, 92*(3), 475–497. doi:10.1111/joop.12268

Yang, Y., Shi, W., Zhang, B., Song, Y., & Xu, D. (2020). Implicit followership theories from the perspective of followers. *Leadership and Organization Development Journal, 41*(4), 581–596. doi:10.1108/LODJ-05-2019-0225

Zaleznik, A. (1965). The dynamics of subordinacy. *Harvard Business Review, 43*(3), 119–131.

Dissertations

Amgheib, A. I. A. (2016). *How leadership styles and follower characteristics predict follower work outcomes in Libyan organisations* [Unpublished doctoral dissertation]. Kingston University.

Antwi, E. O. (2015). *Party followership and political leadership: A study of governance in Ghana* [Unpublished doctoral dissertation]. Indiana Wesleyan University.

Blair, B. A. (2016). *Cultural influences on followers and follower dissent* [Unpublished doctoral dissertation]. Claremont Graduate University.

Castillo, M. H. M. (1983). *Perceptions of Mexican-American And Anglo-American nursing students toward an ideal leadership and followership style* [Unpublished doctoral dissertation]. New Mexico State University.

Chai, D. H. (2011). *Leading as followers: A followership study of the Korean congregational leadership of the Presbyterian church (U.S.A.)* [Unpublished doctoral dissertation]. Spalding University.

Chen, W. (2013). *The differences in leadership styles and followership styles between China and the U.S.: A cross cultural comparison* [Unpublished doctoral dissertation]. University of Phoenix.

Cheng Mung Lai, C. (2015). *A case study of successful teacher followership in a Hong Kong post-secondary school* [Unpublished doctoral dissertation]. University of Bristol.

Hallowell, E. G. (2015). *Courageous followership, exile and leadership in West African political fiction* [Unpublished doctoral dissertation]. Union Institute & University.

Hocagil, A. (2020). *Exploring global followership phenomenon in global organizational context: A study of global followers within global technology companies* [Unpublished doctoral dissertation]. Indiana Institute of Technology.

Hong, E. S. (2014). *A grounded theory of leadership and followership in multicultural teams in SIL* [Unpublished doctoral dissertation]. Biola University.

Imoukhuede, O. (2019). *The impact of entrepreneurial leadership on authentic followership in Nigeria and the United State*[Unpublished doctoral dissertation]. Regent University.

Kim, Y. (2020). *The Asian-White leadership gap: Interpersonal and extrapersonal explanations based on leader and follower stereotypes* [Unpublished doctoral dissertation]. University of Waterloo.

Lawrence III, T. O. (2017). *Followership in a global context: Examining the relationship between Chinese national culture and follower role orientation* [Unpublished doctoral dissertation]. Indiana Institute of Technology.

Medcof, T. (2012). *Followers and followership: An exploration of follower prototypes, national culture, and personality* [Unpublished doctoral dissertation]. York University.

Ofumbi, D. W. (2017). *Followership construction among the Acholi people in Uganda* [Unpublished doctoral dissertation]. Biola University.

Park, C. H. (2013). *Development and initial validation of an instrument to assess followership competency in a Korean manufacturing company* [Unpublished doctoral dissertation]. Pennsylvania State University.

Satrio, R. (2019). *American managers' lived experience in U.S. affiliates of Korean companies: A phenomenological study of cross-cultural followership* [Unpublished doctoral dissertation]. The George Washington University

Shin, L. J. (2019). *The link between culture and minority leadership: Implicit followership theory and the social identity model of organizational followership* [Unpublished doctoral dissertation]. University of California, Riverside.

Umer, H. K. (2019). *The relational theory of the leadership-followership process: Perceptions of leaders and followers in the Ethiopian Kale Heywet church* [Unpublished doctoral dissertation]. Biola University.

3

Whose Leadership Questions Do We Ask? Whose Leadership Knowledge Do We Capture?

Wanda Krause

Introduction

There are several leadership learnings I have had along the lifetime of my research, so far, that have guided me to ask better research questions. I have conducted research for well over 20 years in various intercultural and geographical settings. However, my MA degree offered me some of my larger learning opportunities that I focus on in this chapter in a discussion to elucidate bias in research. My MA comprised of opportunities for attuning to research questions and the research process in a culture, economic context and political context different to the one I was born into, and in a much more intensive and immersive way than I had previously experienced. My MA thesis was in the Political Science/International Relations Department at the University of Guelph, Canada, and the geographical location for my data location for my thesis was in Cairo, Egypt. My cultural preparation for the research journey was assisted through growing up in a multiracial household with Jamaican and German parents. Both were invested, to differing degrees, in my learning their cultural values and perspectives. The literature I was reading on the oppression of women in the Middle East assumed their passivity. Perhaps the research topics I have chosen were influenced by the awareness that despite the assumptions in much of the literature, my own great-great grandmother had fled her home in the Middle East to be with the man she loved. He was not from the Middle East and not of her religion, although he converted to her religion. Thus, she defied expectations of compliance, and put into question the dominant literature's view of women in the Middle East, for me.

Despite my inter-racial background and intercultural upbringing, and even despite the preparation with my MA supervisor, living and studying in this region presented culture shocks. I went to Egypt numerous times before embarking on my M.A. thesis research. Over those years, I studied the Arabic language and became fully immersed in everyday life by spending long stretches of time with families that did not speak any English. In that time, I researched and published on women's activism in Latin America and democracy and Islamism in Egypt. Most of my research had been indirect observations and ethnography, guided by discourse analysis, first-person research and a lot of informal inquiry. In essence, I was engaged in action-oriented research, which is an engagement method. During this research, I also was afforded many opportunities to get right in the lives of the women I was studying and participate on some projects, in turn, offering my insight while learning in iterative steps.

The following describes my journey through rethinking imported frameworks, identifying unconscious bias in worldviews and better understanding civil society as one conceptual framework.

DOI: 10.4324/9781003003380-3

The purpose of this chapter is to illustrate a journey to uncover bias in frameworks, the questions that can drive the inquiry, the specific questions we ask individuals and our own assumptions. I offer a greater perspective on how the knowledge researchers tend to capture can serve to exclude much of the richer and meaningful knowledges, ways of being and doing. I discuss what is problematic with both the research questions and questions embedded in the schedule of questions, with interviews, as examples. Throughout I illustrate the biases inherent in the civil society framework I have used, as an example for international researchers. At the end of the chapter, I offer new ways of knowing, being, and doing to help international researchers and students ask better research questions – to guide their research agenda, the research methods and their own thinking. My hope is to offer a deeper understanding of the risks and drawbacks of uninformed and biased questions and analysis in leadership-related research. This chapter includes my own journey as a way of instruction for navigating the quandaries of international research. Although I had a strong background that prepared me to embark on such research, the very lack of institutional learnings to prepare me is a large part of my motivation for this chapter. I hope, too, to offer insight and suggestions for peeling back bias, interrogating worldviews and finding means to be open to new ways of being, doing and seeing.

Rethinking Imported Frameworks

I chose my MA topic partly because I began to realize that the literature I was reading by mostly American, and also some European, authors on women in the Middle East told a story that did not align with my observations and experience visiting the Middle East. The literature held that women were so repressed they could not create better conditions for themselves (Hale, 1997; Paider, 1995; Mahmood, 2004; Singerman, 1995). Not in too few words, the literature argued that the West essentially had to save them. The West had to import democracy. For example, in the literature, women's forms of organization that are Islamic are pitted against what are categorized as the feminist ones viewed as more civilized forms. Al-Ali (2000) explains that from her fieldwork on Cairo women activists, "secular (feminism) has become highly misleading and homogenizing".

The frameworks I was using, to assist my inquiry, were not helpful because they excluded the issues and forms of mobilization that mattered to individuals I was studying and working with. Hence, they misconstrue, if not miss, examples of mobilization, struggle, leadership and activism that are often in response to and aligned to different contexts. I focus on two examples to illustrate how the frameworks used can be not only misaligned but when used without reflection on the inherent bias embedded in the concepts can further serve to marginalize and misconstrue those we are studying – feminism and civil society. For the first example, research on women tends to apply a feminist lens to understanding women's struggle and activism. In my work (2008, 2012, 2019), I learned that most of their activism is not motivated by a feminist agenda. If I were to insist on using a feminist framework to track and grasp change, I would miss "seeing" the bulk of struggle of these women. I would miss what matters and what does not matter for these women.

As Mahmood (2004) has argued in her analysis of women in religious lessons located in Cairo, feminist scholarship overemphasizes the politically subversive form of agency, while it has ignored other modalities of agency whose significance is missed within what she refers to as the "logic of subversions and resignification of hegemonic terms of discourse" (p. 155). Whereas secular feminists believe in grounding their discourse outside of religion so "religion is respected as a private matter for each individual" (Karam, 2000, p. 13), Muslim women activists do not see religion as a private matter (Krause, 2012). From my research, Islamists equate secularism with atheism (Krause, 2012). Al-Ali, thus, advocates using "women's activism" rather than "feminism", arguing that most Egyptian women activists reject that label.

With its plethora of organizations, illustrating potential for civil society, Egypt was a logical choice to study women's Islamic and secular organizations. Muslims comprise 90% of the Egyptian population (CIA World Factbook, 2020). There has long been interest in the literature on Muslim societies. Although, there may be much greater understanding of different Muslim communities in the West, today, my research area was in a new territory. It was exciting. However, to capture new insights and knowledge around the leadership capacities in the women I was researching required rethinking the frameworks and concepts I was applying, including feminism as a framework that is often viewed as highly positive.

Is There a Civil Society in the Middle East?

The dominant definition of civil society excluded those who were guided by religion because the concept of civil society became delinked from religion during the enlightenment period when religion was seen in Western traditions as incongruent with progress (Cohen & Arato, 1992). Hence, when I asked if there was a civil society in the Middle East, I was addressing the contention I had with this trajectory that not only viewed religion as antithetical to freedom, progress and civility, but Islam in particular. My further contention was with the marginalization of women as influencers of change in the Middle East. My research considered if women were expanding civil society in the Middle East. Decolonizing dominant frameworks and messaging must involve an approach that centers the voices of others.

I observed that women were mobilizing around creating pathways to achieving the things that mattered to them most, such as putting food on the table, creating an ethos of piety or charity for greater equality and access. They were not passive, as some of the literature frames them, at the least. Yet, most of the literature I was reading would frame women as so repressed and passive that they were incapable of pursuing what mattered to them (Singerman, 1995). Most of the literature claimed that there was no civil society in the Middle East to be found. However, if women were pursuing change and women were mobilizing around issues that mattered, the logic I used was that there were individual and collective acts of refusal of the status quo (see McGranahan, 2016).

In my research, the lenses that dominate, being from a Western trajectory and history, serve to prefer particular groups and marginalize others, and continue to do so. As with our biases, described previously, our lenses are often sourced from our culture, our past and current environment, our individual experiences and our upbringing. Antoun (2000) asserts that the gross oversight of what is constituted as civil society in contexts different to our own is due to the limitations of what is constituted as civil institutions. Antoun (2000) argues that the concept of civil society has "discounted important action arenas of civil society thus [having] obscured a significant process that has contributed to civil society in the Middle East for generations" (p. 441). The inclusion and exclusion of Islamic groups or associations as civil society institutions has also been a matter of considerable disagreement (Krause, 2012).

Thus, leadership begins with ourselves to critically interrogate the assumptions in the media and in the literature upon which we base our knowledge and approaches about an outside world. Ethical international leadership, thus, for me, entails critiquing what we have been taught. The tendency in current research on political Islam, for example, tends to focus on particular social movements over popular mobilization, as demonstrated by the women I study, around what matters to these groups. In so doing, such research focus obscures the many forms and nuances of movements and mobilization. Its narrow focus obscures the broader trajectories and developments that are emerging which are about so much more, including the pursuit of the good life and positive change. The pursuit of the good life may mean peace and prosperity but it is important to recognize that in order to have peace and prosperity the simple acts around putting food on the table or learning how to read and write are foundational – and often missed in literature on political change or leadership.

For example, several groups sought to teach women how to read the Qur'an as part and parcel of understanding and correctly practicing piety, according to how the group or organization understood piety. Such understanding may be in direct contradiction to other groups or organizations' perspectives on what piety looks like. As such groups may compete around what the good life looks like. Women were taught how to read the Qur'an in other cases to facilitate literacy. These different approaches to change and what change means obscures the political subjectivity development that is occurring. While political Islam may be viewed as incompatible with civil society development, such activism negates this dominant conceptualization of who should be at the margins of citizenship. Such mobilizes actors who are on the margins of that story around what comprises civil society although they may be exercising political Islam.

A further assumption that researchers may carry is the significance awarded to actions that are more easily observable, such as those that are addressed at the state. State-directed action or fighting patriarchy comprises only a few aspects of women's participation, in which women were involved. The literature on participation in the Middle East shows numerous misconceptions and biases that serve to delineate the kinds of questions we ask related to change here too. These approaches, and the resulting inquiries, function to exclude individuals whose activities are not directed at some "power-overing" force, such as the state. A significant bias in this respect is where politics is viewed as the sole domain of formal institutions. As Paider (1995) underscores: "One widespread assumption is the only political and economic domains worth studying in Muslim societies are the formal ones, and Muslim women are unimportant or at best marginal to these domains because they have few formal political and economic rights and make a limited contribution to formal domains" (p. 2).

Hence, civil society as a concept, I argue, is one that is universal, as it is predicated on the presence of civility and collaborations to create the good life. However, civil society activism takes on meaning based on its specific context. Activism in one place and time, thus, although based on universal principles of civility, may take different forms. In the Middle East, for example, Islam plays a key role, unlike in Western contexts, in shaping goals, desires and practices. Activism in situations of poverty may be that which are not routinely considered as necessarily important as in contexts of greater affluence. If the state is the locus for understanding positive change, then when actions are not directed at the state, civil society actions are viewed as non-existent, then leading to erroneous conclusions that civil society is absent. It should also be emphasized that collaborations in pursuit of the good life may be in the context of repression and authoritarian regimes. Hence, as a whole, the region may be considered to have a weak civil society but that does not mean civil society activism is absent. In fact, civil society activism may be rife because of such context. The challenge for the international researcher, in this example for a framework, would be to discern the forms of activism that take place under conditions different to one's own or the dominant literature and Western conception of civil society.

Unconscious Bias in Research Questions

For my MA thesis, I conducted 33 formal interviews in addition to continuing to engage in the methods of observation and engaging with the women on their projects and activism, as with those that follow. In my research I had to expand the narrow categories applied to international research, in particular, the framing of the concept of civil society itself. The leadership knowledge I was working from is a Western construct incapable of capturing the knowledge of the women whose actions are, in fact, expansive of civil society and empowering of women in many ways not fully understood from civil society framings and feminist conceptualizations. It is essential, therefore, to examine not only the frameworks applied and used to guide the inquiry but also the very questions we ask when engaging with the methods.

By applying both the frameworks and inquiry questions without questioning and revising them, I would have missed the numerous forms of activism and great work with which these women were engaged. These women's examples of activism included developing the self by teaching religious principles and accordingly what was deemed the right conduct. The activists found ways to cir-cumvent systems and structures of oppression that affected their communities by collaborating not just with women but with men. Everyday effort was put into doing good onto others, often through charity. In a few examples, groups opened daycares to help women be able to get out and earn income. They pooled money together to help each other advance financially through innovative lending schemes. There were several initiatives where literacy and other skills were taught. In one example, the women worked through religious scripts to prepare alternative views on freedoms that were curtailed by dominant interpretations of religion. There were initiatives to educate women about domestic abuse and support women out of those situations. In one example, democratic principles were taught. Orphanages and cheap, accessible healthcare was provided to poor com-munities. In many ways, these forms of activism are subtle and because not seen as fitting a feminist or civil society framing would be missed without endeavoring to ask with curiosity to truly learn new ways of being, doing and seeing.

I had key learning moments that pushed me to revise the understanding of context and appli-cation of dominant frameworks in different contexts different to the West or contexts of relative safety. I asked the director of one organization if I could interview her and two others who par-ticipated in the organization. The director introduced me to a participant she chose. She did not explain why we should remain in the room but she sat us in a room where we could all three get acquainted, before I would begin. It is customary to have tea and maybe sweets before going through any formal interview process. It was to some degree understandable that the director was nervous about what I might ask, given the government crackdown on any activity that is deemed remotely political. When I began to introduce my research and describe the interview process, I let the participant know that she could end the interview at any point and asked if I could record the interview. The director remained present and involved. I took out my sheet of questions, translated into Arabic by an Arabic speaker, although I verified them from my Arabic, and I proceeded to do my first interview, asking questions to get at demographic data. I asked about the participant's role and what she did in the organization.

Then I got to *the* question, where I asked the participant if she thought the work she was doing was political. I should have known better. The director ended the interview on the participant's behalf promptly and sent her away. Stunned, I remained seated as she walked back towards me sternly reprimanding me. She expressed that that question would send anyone in her organization flying out the windows. Their work was inherently political because their work was about changing the state by changing society, in particular through women, to deepen Islamic knowledge and better align themselves to what they deemed as Islamic piety and conduct. That said, *that* word (in Arabic, *siyasa*) could not be spoken, and for good reason, given the government crackdown. I was unable to continue the research in this organization. In the years to come, I would keep returning to do further research, during which time individuals in such organizations would become jailed on much larger scales than I imagined, at that time.

Although for my previous research, I had interviewed individuals who had been jailed for their activism, I would soon meet many more and learn of graver stories. On that evening, after the first formal interview in an Islamic women's organization, I went home and revised a few questions, stripping anything overtly related to the political. What I learned to do differently was to get to know the organizations and individuals before asking such direct questions. Once I got to know women to the degree that I would help them in their organizations, I could almost ask anything related to change. For this particular research, I sometimes did not even ask my questions until a third meeting. In subsequent research, I have even waited an entire year of meeting and gathering together for events of their interest before assessing I might be in a position to ask direct questions around politics. To assume I could ask about politics and they did not know me was naïve for a context where the state is highly nervous about its fragility.

While I have focused on this particular research for my master's thesis in this chapter to illustrate one of my greater learning pivots for further reflection, I ended up going back to some of these organizations and others subsequently for over a ten-year period, a few up to 13 years later. Reflecting and revising on the inquiry and the questions we ask is critical. A further critical lesson I could impart from this longitudinal engagement, however, is the deepening of relationship, trust, and understandings shared around worldviews and biases. Many researchers go into a community, collect data and then leave with actually minimal understanding of the context, challenges and dreams the researched share. The goal for me was to create change by creating space for the inclusion of voices, especially poor women, and engaging further in relationships. Understanding and peeling back misunderstanding must be pursued through inquiry occurring through revising the very questions we ask and, in particular, through time.

Unconscious Bias in Worldviews

Just as important is reflecting on our own personal bias and, thus, our own personal agendas and assumptions. Upon embarking on my thesis portion of my masters of arts abroad, my mother gave me her sage advice. As my mother and perhaps knowing fully well how the "other" is often framed, she advised, "You are there to collect data, not to tell anyone what is right or wrong. Whenever you have the urge during your interviews to say something to anything that doesn't sound right to you, bite your tongue". It went something like that. And bite my tongue I literally did a few times initially. There were numerous times when I heard things I judged as cringe worthy to my sensibilities that I wanted to say my thoughts out loud. Here it became important to know myself quickly as I was engaged in my research. My propensity, probably not disconnected from the cultures that have influenced me, was to speak my thoughts out loud directly and without mincing words. Curiosity, inquiry and humility as part of research would become my keys to research success. It is understandable that many researchers do not have opportunity to have been raised with these cultural influences or given such advice. As such, it is critical that researchers think about unconscious bias and consider learning who they are, how they think and how they interact with the rest of the world and are perceived by different others. This is learning self-awareness. My journey to get there is ongoing and has been through peeling back the unconscious bias that we all have and which shape our worldviews, the questions we ask and, therefore, what we see.

Our ability to be successful at international leadership research is directly related to our success at leading ourselves first. The ability to do good and ethical research internationally should begin with seeking to understand our own mindsets and human subjectivity. Subjectivity broadly refers to the ability of an individual or entity to act upon another entity with consciousness and agency (Allen, 2002). Kraus (2015) argued that one's subjectivity is in fact influenced by the world or environment in which one operates and the conditions of this reality. The assumptions we hold and so the kinds of research questions we ask in both the research design and the methods we use evolve from and are shaped by the cultures we are from. They are also shaped by the individual ways we have experienced and understand the world. This includes the way we have come to see the world and our place in relation to it.

Leadership, then, entails that we have to strive to be accountable to the values of ethical behavior, diversity, inclusion, transparency, humility, trust and honesty. We play a role in entrenching marginalization and exclusion through the choices we make for and in our research, which is also influenced by the way we see the world. Because we have the power to shape thoughts and actions of others, we ought to pay close attention to the ways in which we can empower or disempower through our research. Through the particular lenses we use and the frameworks we unwittingly apply, we can not only exclude important aspects or issues that matter to those who we are studying and working with, but misrepresent their truths. Thus, it is imperative for those engaged in international leadership research to seek the ways that make possible greater awareness in how we can also use our power to support ethical research. Such means being conscious of privilege we hold and can wield as researchers. It is, furthermore, essential to consider how to engage with those within different communities and cultures closer to home, too. Privilege refers to "an advantage a person holds due to their membership in a social group, in contexts where that membership shouldn't matter" (Lowe, 2020, p. 457). Privilege is, for example, "[the] white, thin, male, young, heterosexual, Christian, and financially secure" (Lorde, 2007, p. 116). Such includes gaining awareness of the bias we unconsciously thread into and shape our research.

If we are human, we are biased (Ross, 2020). Unconscious bias is the tendency to inadvertently avoid or dismiss unprejudiced consideration of a question. Unconscious bias happens when we make rapid judgments and assumptions of people and situations, without conscious awareness of the mental processes at play (Ross, 2020). Most people favor the group they are a part of, even though they may claim that they have no preference (Fiarman, 2016). Furthermore, people across groups show preferences for the "culturally valued group" (Fiarman, 2016, p. 11). Our own situation within the existing power structures has shaped our unconscious biases or inadvertent beliefs that a particular person or perspective is right. Citing a 2013 Gallup poll, whereby 45% of the American public stated that same-sex marriage should not be valid, Ross questions whether such bias can be seen as conscious (Ross, 2020, p. 3). In another example of unconscious bias, a Stanford study illustrates disproportionate punishment of black students compared with their white peers in a school setting. Teachers were shown student discipline records together with names assigned randomly. Half of the names, for example, Deshawn and Darnell, suggested that the students were black. Half of the names, for example, Greg and Jake, suggested that the students were white. The study found that teachers were more likely to assign a harsh punishment for repeated misbehavior to students they thought were black than to students they thought were white. In this study, teachers' perceptions of students' racial identity influenced their responses (Okonofua, Pauneskua, & Waltona, 2016).

Ross (2020) argues that our bias is shaped during and begins in childhood. The sources of our unconscious biases arise from the way we were raised, our education, our social, political or economic environments, past and present, individual experiences, our internal states and extent of exposure to different peoples, cultures and perspectives – in tandem with our openness to learning. Bias is also influenced by competencies, such as, trust, empathy, intercultural communication, curiosity, resilience and adaptability. These unconscious biases influence us even when they are in direct opposition to our espoused beliefs (Fiarman, 2016). "If we are human, we are biased" (Ross, 2020, p. 2).

Unconscious bias, thus, can serve to discriminate against people or groups on the basis of their characteristics, such as their gender, race, sexuality, disability and social class, and without re-cognizing we are discriminating. Unconscious bias occurs when we make judgments regarding who to include in research and who to exclude, based on identity or the frameworks we apply around who they are or represent. In my research, regarding Muslim women in the Middle East and, in particular, those who see their activism as guided by religion, are often excluded. Unconscious bias thereby might influence those of us leading international research – or research engaging other cultures closer to home – in how we determine which person to offer more time in interviews, decide on who is capable of supporting our thesis, as well as who does not have the competencies related to what we believe we are looking for.

Unconscious bias against a particular religion, especially one that is different to ours, can lead the researcher to make unconscious judgments about the religion of those studied. It can pose a barrier to digging deeper to understanding motivations of those who are choosing particular activism or pursuing particular goals. In most of my own research, becoming conscious of how large of a role religion plays in the communities and with the actors I am studying has been of significance to understanding motivations for and forms of activism leading to various forms of change, including positive change for civil society development. It is necessary to embed oneself in worldviews other than what we are raised with in order to provide ourselves the chance to appreciate how the self is shaped according to the numerous interconnecting influences and forces that shape one's conscience, disposition and even desires.

The Problem with the Questions We Ask

There are significant implications to using unexamined questions to guide the research agenda, ask many of the questions we do in the implementation of the research methods and when we fail to examine our own biases and worldviews. The societies I have researched are various, being mostly from the Middle East, but also Latin America, Europe and Indigenous communities in Northern Canada. What this journey has highlighted for me is that we are often asking questions that are embedded in our own worldviews that does not allow for or embrace other ways of being, knowing and doing. If one is studying Muslim societies, for example, how is it that we continue to apply the frameworks, such as, the dominant conception of civil society, that prefer and privilege non-religious expressions? Or how is it that we continue to work with concepts whose theorization has been driven by mostly men whose purview and interest have traditionally been state-centered and ignorant of the private sphere? If one is studying Indigenous communities whose practices have not informed the dominant understanding of governance, for example, how then can we apply a Western governance framework to these communities, and hope to add accurate and new perspectives? Asking questions embedded in a particular context and our own worldviews leads to exclusion. It leads to misrepresentation of others who do not conform to the worldview and interests of the privileged. It serves to uphold the status quo, entrenching dominant knowledge, ways of being and doing, that secure dominance over others.

The work of Islamic and Islamist individuals offers a case in point. The Islamic and Islamist women activists, whom I have studied throughout the years, cannot be placed effectively in such conceptual boxes. Their knowledge, their being, and what they are doing have implications for the public sphere and their societies. In fact, much of their work has transnational impact. Yet, many researchers serve to reduce their contributions. A little has been written on the Muslim Sisterhood, the women's arm of the Muslim Brotherhood, which is the mother organization to most Islamist organizations in the Middle East, established in 1928. It began activities during the rise of the organization through Hassan al-Banna to oppose British colonial control of Egypt. Yet, while I was in the field studying Islamic women's organizations in Egypt, only one other researcher to my knowledge, Shireen Hafez, was doing similar research, focused on redefining the concept of empowerment to illustrate how the work of Muslim women can contribute to their own empowerment and the empowerment of the marginalized through organizational participation.

Also, women in the Arab Gulf, have received even less attention and acknowledgment. In addition to the framings and focus mentioned, the focus in this region has largely been on oil money that is viewed to subdue popular participation in the region, the Arab Gulf, in particular. Due to the focus on oil politics and the assumptions that women are subdued and passive, very little research had been conducted on women's activism in the Arab Gulf, beyond Kuwait and Bahrain. In the UAE and Qatar, not only researchers but Emirati and Qatari women themselves, tend to be reductionist about women's contributions, seeing them in very limited ways. Islamic and Islamist women activists in the UAE and Qatar (as elsewhere) are in fact playing a critical role in political change, and in counter-acting, appropriating and even leveraging the more ambitious masculine expressions of political Islam. Such activists are engaged in the empowerment of others, seen as such from alternate points of view. The scale of their impact is unmatched because of the funding they receive from public and private donors. Through the avenues of networks and organizations, women enable women, men and young children to achieve basic rights to, for example, better living conditions, food and clothing, education and skills training (see Krause, 2008; Krause & Finn, 2018).

In such an example, the impact of women's critically significant work is lost in the prominent, politicized and epistemologically problematic focus on the state and the activism of Islamist men, wherewith women's activism becomes marginalized (see Krause, 2008; Krause & Finn, 2018). Far from being motivated by only piety or practical considerations related to the private realm, and far from being inconsequential to larger political processes and citizenship development, women's actions give momentum for positive developments that other activists have failed to accomplish (Krause, 2008, 2012). Women's pursuit of, and drive for, change in these Arab Gulf countries have been insufficiently theorized and, as such, the questions asked miss all the actions that contribute to change and the impact of women's activisms. The consequence of using concepts that lead researchers to ask the wrong questions marginalize key actions, actual grassroots transformations and the larger mobilizations remain in abeyance.

The issue is that Western, neo-liberal texts pit the West against other societies, in these examples, the Middle East, and Indigenous communities, as the higher in civility. Based on this judgment, most of the research is guided by questions that do not acknowledge the possibility that there are ways of knowing that are of equal value to the West's. In my examples, both the frameworks and the research questions guide answers to conclude that these societies are completely void of civil society or empowerment, as examples, and other processes. Recognizing the bias against the Middle East, Islam and/or women whose actions and goals were not rights-based, it is imperative to change the frameworks and the language of the questions we pose to be inclusive of thinking and action that fall outside the neo-liberal trajectory historically embedded in the histories of Europe. Re-evaluating the neo-liberal frameworks used to guide research inquiry and methods, we discover, in the examples above, that even tribal practices could be very collaborative, that Islam could be emancipatory, that poor women could be creative in their ways of attaining well-being and even more – we may be able to find better ways to address the large, global and planetary challenges of our times.

New Ways of Knowing, Being and Doing in Planning International Research

Inquiry must feature the voices of those studied, discussed and those impacted by the research itself. Those impacted include, first and foremost, those whose perspectives and stories are translated to others. For example, many of the women I studied in poor areas would not be able to tell their own stories outside their own contexts because they do not speak the language privileged in most places around the globe – English. Researchers, however, need to be sensitive to the protection of those who they are researching and impacting also during the process of research. In the example I provided earlier with the director, I could have mitigated the situation that engendered fear and anxiety by examining first my own privilege whereby discussing politics may not lead to my jailing for engaging on that topic as quickly and enduringly as it might for my research participant – although that can also be debatable in some contexts.

Researchers ought to think more systematically around how we can better support and include other perspectives for impact related to the promotion of human rights, empowerment of individuals and collectives, sustainability, and global health. Such is being integral. "Integral" means comprehensive, balanced and inclusive. For Wilber et al., a practice based on care is essential (Wilber, 1997; Wilber et al., 2008, p. 27). Care can be demonstrated in inquiry around what the needs, dreams, hopes, concerns and issues are for those you are studying. Care is illustrated when the researcher involves those most impacted in the design of the research. Care is shown in including the concerns of those impacted into the research and empowering them to offer their own recommendations to address issues with which they are concerned. I argue care ought to be an ethical imperative for international research. This approach would then help one "want to make a difference, to give more, to move past narrow and fragmented views and magnify the freedom, love, openness and depth in us, in others, and in the world" (Wilber et al., 2008, p. 4). This consciousness is a disposition of leading-the-self before leading others, one's community or initiatives (Esbjörn-Hargens, 2011) to include the marginalized and offer deeper knowledge.

If we can acknowledge that we are part of a larger interdependent system that we can influence, as Laszlo (1996) argues we will realize just how much impact we have as international researchers on research to be more inclusive and honoring of those we research. We might be able to lift our blinders enough to begin to recognize the concepts we are applying or roots of colonization, as practiced in historical and newer forms, the actions and approaches we are taking as research approaches, that serve to exclude or include, and, thus, the kinds of questions we are using to collect data. We can ask: what will be my change strategy for inclusive practice in my research agenda? How might I first gain understanding around the roots of colonization so that my research practice serves decolonization? How might I adapt my methods of inquiry to be more inclusive and curious of other ways of being, doing, and seeing? When people colonize they deny the very existence of a culture or merit among those they have colonized. Hence, decolonization entails rediscovery and recovery of the culture, language, identity and perspectives (Laenui Battiste 2003).

Through applying such an approach that can be open to new ways of being, doing and seeing, we have greater ability to become more conscious and capable of asking better questions, at least in recognizing the concepts and questions that serve to marginalize or include. We might consider how we are doing so on the individual level and collective. We can begin to ask better questions by asking: what is problematic with the framework that guides how we categorize individuals into those we deem to be politically relevant and those we believe are inconsequential to change? What concept of economic development have we been learning that focuses on what is wrong to the detriment of recognizing what is working? What values are our approaches based on? By shifting our thinking, being and doing in each, we might begin to see how our research can create shifts for better global and planetary leadership. We can then ask questions, such as, how can I lead myself in my international research to impact change on a global scale? How can I lead myself around local issues that are related to global issues to impact on a global scale? How do the concepts and models we have been using impact upon and influence economic, social, political and ecological change?

Conclusion

Inquiry must feature the voices of those studied, discussed and those impacted by the research itself. Inquiry, with the research questions and questions we use in our methods must identify in which ways terminologies, language, depictions, framing and criteria used for indicators privilege some and serve to further marginalize others. It is also imperative that we use self-reflective questions with ourselves. A key example of a concept, found throughout my research, is the term *civil society*. Impediments to the study of existing and substantive political processes persist even within frameworks that focus on change from the societal level. Large sectors of the population, such as women, people living in poverty or those who use Islamic frameworks within their strategies remain hardly represented and little understood from such frameworks as civil society (Krause, 2012, pp. 2–3). Inclusion of such other voices is significant because if, in this example, the state remains the focus, incomplete and grossly wrong conclusions about change will be drawn. If the activism of women's Islamic organizations, as one example, is discounted as ill-suited to change, here meaning positive change, perhaps one of the greatest resources for "civilizing" in the framing of civil society will be lost.

Women with whom I have conducted research in the Middle East, in addition to research in Latin America, Europe, Asia and North America, have had to find innovative and creative ways to secure a more peaceful and sustainable life and future, and are therefore wonderful examples of how to lead and navigate challenges and chart a future for global change on the macro level. These women create change within their own systems, and the global systems of oppression, individually and collectively. Hence, to see their contributions and appreciate their work, we ought to be guided by questions that allow us to view the limits of our concepts and recognize the ways in which we frame and approach others based on these narrow conceptions.

We have numerous biases to overcome and narrow conceptions of reality to expand. We need solutions to our current and overwhelming lack of international leadership research acumen, if we hope to contribute to change towards a more global and planetary consciousness in thinking, being and doing, one that is inclusive and respectful of knowledge that does not share Western roots. I argue that by overcoming these biases and approaches to inquiry, we might learn how to do better international research. Such has relevance to all leaders, especially those of us who are leading research internationally, and locally with communities and cultures that have been marginalized, as our research can have great implications to those we are researching, and the knowledge and practice that ensues from the frameworks we use and the questions we ask.

References

Al-Ali, N. (2000). *Secularism, gender and the state in the Middle East: The Egyptian women's movement.* Cambridge University Press.

Allen, A. (2002). Power, subjectivity, and agency: Between Arendt and Foucault. *International Journal of Philosophical Studies, 10*(2), 131–149. doi:10.1080/09672550210121432

Antoun, R. T. (2000). Civil society, tribal process, and change in Jordan: An anthropological view. *International Journal of Middle East Studies, 32*, 441–463.

CIA World Factbook. (2020). *Egypt people.* https://theodora.com/wfbcurrent/egypt/egypt_people.html#:~:text=Egyptian%2099.7%25%2C%20other%200.3%25%20(2006%20est.)&text=Religions%3A,10%25%20(2015%20est

Clark. J. (1994). *Islamic social-welfare organizations and the legitimacy of the state in Egypt: Democratization or Islamization from below?* [PhD dissertation]. University of Toronto.

Cohen, J. & Arato, A. (1992). *Civil society and political theory.* MIT Press.

Esbjörn-Hargens, S. (2011). *Integral theory in action: Applied, theoretical, and constructive perspectives on the AQAL model.* State University of New York Press.

Esbjörn-Hargens, S. (2009). Integral teacher, integral students, integral classroom: Applying integral theory to education. *Next Step Integral,* 1–42. http://nextstepintegral.org/wp-content/uploads/2011/04/Integral-Education-Esbjorn-Hargens.pdf

Fiarman, S. (2016). Unconscious bias. *Educational Leadership, 74*(3), 10–15.

Globe Framework. (n.d). *Principles of management.* https://opentextbc.ca/principlesofmanagementopenstax/chapter/the-globe-framework/#:~:text=However%2C%20basing%20their%20work%20on,term)%204)%20assertiveness%20orientation%20

Hale, S. (1997). *Gender politics in Sudan: Islamism, socialism, and the state.* Westview Press.

Karam, A. (2000). Feminisms and Islamisms in Egypt: Between globalization and postmodernism. In Marchand, H. & Runyan A.S. (Eds.), *Gender and global restructuring: Sightings, sites and resistances.* Routledge.

Kraus, B. (2015). The life we live and the life we experience: Introducing the epistemological difference between "lifeworld" (lebenswelt) and "life conditions" (lebenslage). *Social Work and Society. International Online Journal, 13*(2). http://www.socwork.net/sws/article/view/438

Krause, W., & Finn, M. (2018). Refusal and citizenship mobilization post-Arab revolts: An inquiry into Islamic women activists in Qatar. In P. Rivetti, & H. Kraetzschmar (Eds.), *Islamists and the politics of the Arab uprisings: Governance, pluralisation and contention.* Routledge.

Krause, W. (2012). *Civil society and women activists in the Middle East.* I.B. Tauris.

Krause, W. (2008). *Women in civil society: The state, Islamism, and networks in the UAE.* Palgrave-Macmillan.

Laenui, P. (Burgess, H.). (2000). Processes of decolonization. In Battiste, M. (Ed.)., *Reclaiming Indigenous voice and vision* (pp. 50–56). UBC Press.

Laszlo, E. (1996). *The systems view of the world: A holistic vision for our time.* Hampton Press.

Lorde, A. (2007). *Sister outsider: Essays and speeches.* The Crossing Press.

Lowe. D. (2020). Privilege: What is it, who has it, and what should we do about it? In B. Fischer (Ed.), *Ethics, left and right* (pp. 457–464). Oxford University Press.

Mahmood, S. (2004). *Politics of piety: The Islamic revival and the feminist subject.* Princeton University Press.

Markakis, D. (2016). *US democracy promotion in the Middle East: The pursuit of hegemony*. Routledge.

McGranahan, C. (2016). Theorizing Refusal: An Introduction. *Cultural Anthropology, 31*(3), 319–325. doi:1 0.14506/ca31.3.01

Molineaux, M. (1985), Mobilization without emancipation? Women's interests, the state, and revolution in Nicaragua. *Feminist Studies, 11*(2), 227–254.

Okonofua, J., Pauneskua, D., & Waltona, G. (2016). Brief intervention to encourage empathic discipline cuts suspension rates in half among adolescents. *Proceedings of the National Academy of Sciences, 113*(19), 5221–5226. doi:10.1073/pnas.1523698113

Paider, P. (1995). *Women and the political process in twentieth-century Iran*. Cambridge University Press.

Ross, H. (2020). *Everyday bias: Identifying and navigating unconscious prejudice in our daily lives* (2nd ed.). Rowman & Littlefield.

Singerman, D. (1995). *Avenues of participation: Family, politics, and the networks in urban quarters of Cairo*. Princeton University Press.

Wilber, K. (1997). *A theory of everything: An integral vision for business, politics, science, and spirituality* (2nd ed.). Shambhala.

Wilber, K., Patten, T., Leonard, A., & Morelli, M. (2008). *Integral life practice: A 21st century blueprint for physical healthy, emotional balance, mental clarity, and spiritual awakening*. Integral Books.

Part II

International Leadership Research Processes

Core Issues in Study Design, Data Collection and Analysis

Franziska Bieri

There as been a growth in cross-cultural and multinational research on leadership topics (Jogulu, 2010; House et al., 2013; Leong & Fischer, 2011; Peus, Braun, & Knipfer, 2015; Pillai et al., 2011; Osland, Bird, & Oddou, 2012, Mendenhall et al., 2018). Global leadership scholars have produced rich empirical data based on qualitative and quantitative data collected internationally. In an overview of the literature, Osland (2018) identified empirical research studies that have been published on global leadership. More than half of those empirical studies reviewed relied on qualitative interviews, about 30% on quantitative survey research, and the remaining studies included varied methods such as focus groups, archival data, or content analysis (pp. 68–73). What this illustrates is a broad foundation of methodologies applied in global leadership research. More surprising in that regard, is the relative lack of attention in the field on the hows and whys of design and method choices and implementation. Given the various intricacies that characterize cross-cultural or international research studies, discussion on the best practices of study designs and methodologies are particularly important to guide and advance global leadership scholars' inquiries. The chapters in Part II of the handbook "International Leadership Research Processes: Core Issues in Study Design, Data Collection, and Analysis" focus on methodological and design problems when conducting research on global leadership topics.

As highlighted in the introductory chapter to this volume, researchers need to consider context and cultural diversity throughout the research process. For this purpose, we feature here insights from scholars on practices in different stages of their international and cross-cultural studies: planning and design issues; qualitative and quantitative data collection; and insights on analysis and interpretation. The chapters are diverse in terms of disciplinary background, regions of the world where the research was conducted, different populations studied and qualitative or quantitative data collection.

Two contributions in this handbook section shed light on the intricacies and richness of the international research collaboration process. Tolstikov-Mast and Mishina describe the uniqueness of international research collaborations through their study on followership in Russia. Religious leadership is the subject of Barentsen and van den Broeke's chapter. The authors share insights on the experiences of a research group that focused on northwest Europe to investigate how faith communities are affected by cultural and social changes of recent times. The collaboration of an international research network was key and fostered an interdisciplinary dialogue, resulting in different perspectives for understanding and strengthening contemporary religious leadership.

Questions related to power, inequalities and minority populations are discussed in many chapters and the focus of several contributions in this handbook section. Authors reflect on unique local contexts in defining power differences and considerations when studying minority populations in terms of study design. Ilac explores research practices involved in conducting leadership research with the LGBTQ community. The author reflects on researcher bias, respondent's fear of self-expression due to oppression and suppression, the lack of cultural acceptance and how this shapes the research process with regard to participant selection, instrumentation and the protection of human subjects. Stork shares experiences from a phenomenological study and interviewing women activists in Armenia, Jordan and Ethiopia, shedding light on leadership in patriarchal, authoritarian contexts and offering reflections on oppression, subordination and violence. Bieri and Tolstikov-Mast explore how multiculturality, or the diverse cultural and social backgrounds of researchers and those researched, shape international leadership research. The authors consider multicultural contexts and identities as methodological issues in qualitative research. They highlight the imbalance of power and multiple dimensions of socio-cultural hierarchies that are at play in research interviews and share the best methodological practices from a variety of disciplines.

Considerations of power and inequalities is also a key feature of those authors who conduct and inform non-Western or Indigenous research methods and epistemologies. Gambrell explores the relationship between individuals and communities through a personal narrative based on her experiences with the Oglála Lakota, a Native American sovereign nation in the United States. Gambrell makes a case to conduct non-Western centered, culturally centered holistic research. In another contribution, Gambrell focuses on community impact based on her experiences with Sičáŋǧu Lakota in south-central South Dakota. Native and Indigenous people have been working to educate both themselves and settler colonialist/Western-trained scholars to decolonize research. Indigenous research methods and considering non-Western worldviews can have positive impacts on the knowledge creation on leadership as well as promote positive relationships and benefits for communities. Kelly explores oral history as a method for gathering data in leadership studies. The author reflects on the complexity of this method and lessons learned based on her experiences conducting oral history as an Indigenous researcher. Blair and Fox-Kirk discuss challenges to the cultural foundation of cross-cultural leadership theory and research based on observations from cross-cultural collaboration research in Jamaica, Thailand and the United States. They point to the importance for cross-cultural researchers to understand the context of the epistemological approaches as embedded within particular cultural foundations as a way to escape epistemic colonialism. Hartney and Krause show how to give voice to marginalized perspectives. By developing greater awareness and intercultural competence, researchers are contributing to multiple ways of knowing, and more nuanced and informed methods to address pressing issues of our times.

Ethical considerations are particularly relevant in international research that involve diverse participants, different norms and values as well as differences in legal regulations guiding data collection. Ethical issues involved in global leadership research are detailed in Blackman's chapter. The author provides an overview on ethics in the research preparation stages, including IRB questions, informed consent, as well as ethical issues regarding data-sharing and dissemination in the context of international research.

Political leadership and structures are the focus of two chapters. Müller explores how to study political leadership comparing the relationship between leaders and their institutional-structural environments in democracies and various types of authoritarian regimes, offering a model on how researchers can go about comparing leaders of varying political systems. Speranza reflects on the complexity of government bureaucracy but also the opportunities to do research on public servants at all levels of government based on her own research experience.

Best practices in international quantitative survey research is the focus of three chapters. Goerman, Meyers, Kephart and O'Brien synthesize the vast literature on survey translation and pretesting. The chapter presents methodological tools including how to involve respondent voices in the survey development process through pretesting of translated surveys. Mneimneh and de Jong outline the growth in international and comparative population-level surveys and the development of multinational, multiregional and multicultural (3MC) survey methods. The authors provide an overview of common challenges in collecting population-based survey data in international and 3MC settings and highlight some solutions that would benefit the field of global leadership studies. Lilleboe reflects on the role of bias in cross-national survey research. She considers important considerations that need to be made regarding quantitative research in non-Western contexts from her own experience in leadership research in Japan.

The chapters feature diverse methodologies. For example, social media research is the focus of Gabrielle Blackman's contribution, showing how global leadership research can apply online communication technologies in research. Crowdsourcing platforms can be helpful when working with hard to reach populations, facilitating the recruitment of participants from multiple cultures or across borders, and when studying online leader behaviors. Blackman outlines both the strengths and limitations of those methodologies and reviews the best practices in this field. Ensign shares reflections on a qualitative content analysis of archived research in the area of adult learning. The author shares what she learned through her study on disorienting experiences and transformative learning and reflects on the challenges of multicultural analysis when conducting archival research.

Diversity is also evident in terms of the locations where the empirical studies presented in the chapters were conducted. Walker discusses international leadership research in the context of lesser-understood societies, which necessitates foundational cultural research and a creative research approach. The author provides insights on two cultural studies performed between 2013−2015 in Suriname and Haiti. The multi-faceted research approach is detailed along with discussions on research scope, assessing researcher fit and the preparation needed for successful field interviews. Zelihic explores the multifaceted leadership realities through several comprehensive research studies conducted in Haiti, Zambia, Cuba and Mexico between 2017 and 2020. The chapter's author shares her unique perspective exploring differences and similarities within leadership realities of each region while focusing on the most impactful variables related to leadership effectiveness and sustainability. Furthermore, the chapter provides the unique perspective and experiences of international research ventures through a researcher's lens facing and overcoming challenges while gaining an insightful knowledge of different cultures, leadership styles and business operations.

Part II is structured in three sections following the chronological order of the research process, from planning and design considerations (Part A), the actual implementation and collection of qualitative and quantitative data (Part B) followed by chapters that address questions on data interpretations (Part C). We hope that the readers find value in those chapters as they prepare or embark on their own international and cross-cultural research and that these works spark further deliberate discussion on methodological questions in the global leadership field as it relates to how we consider unique context and international complexities in each stage of the research process.

References

House, R. J., Dorfman, P. W., Javidan, M., Hanges, P. J., & de Luque, M. F. S. (2013). *Strategic leadership across cultures: GLOBE study of CEO leadership behavior and effectiveness in 24 countries.* Sage Publications.

Jogulu, U. D. (2010). Culturally-linked leadership styles. *Leadership & Organization Development Journal, 31*(8), 705−719.

Leong, L. Y. C., & Fischer, R. (2011). Is transformational leadership universal? A meta-analytical investigation of multifactor leadership questionnaire means across cultures. *Journal of Leadership & Organizational Studies*, *18*(2), 164–174.

Mendenhall, M. E., Osland, J. S., Bird., A., Oddou, G. R., Stevens, M. J., Maznevski, M. L., & Stahl, G. K. (Eds.). (2018). *Global leadership: Research, practice and development* (3rd ed.). Routledge.

Osland, J. S. (2018). An overview of the global leadership literature. In M. E. Mendenhall, J. S. Osland, A. Bird, G. R. Oddou, M. J. Stevens, M. L. Maznevski, & G. K. Stahl (Eds.), *Global leadership: Research, practice, and development* (3rd ed., pp. 57–116). Routledge.

Osland, J.S., Bird, A., Oddou, G. (2012). The context of expert global leadership. In W. H. Mobley, Y. Wang, & M. Li (Eds.), *Advances in global leadership* (7th ed., pp. 107–124). Emerald.

Peus, C., Braun, S., & Knipfer, K. (2015). On becoming a leader in Asia and America: Empirical evidence from women managers. *The Leadership Quarterly*, *26*(1), 55–67.

Pillai, R., Kohles, J. C., Bligh, M. C., Carsten, M. K., & Brodowsky, G. (2011). Leadership in "Confucian Asia": A three-country study of justice, trust, and transformational leadership. *Organization Management Journal*, *8*(4), 242–259.

Part A

Planning and Designing Leadership Research in International Contexts

4

Early Stages of an International Research Collaboration: A Followership Study in Russia

Yulia Tolstikov-Mast and Vera Mishina

Introduction

This chapter is a result of the research collaboration between two Russian scholars employed by different international universities, residing in Russia and the United States, with research training in their respective countries. This chapter stresses the importance of the research planning stage to avoid frustrations and misunderstandings during an actual international research work. More specifically, the authors advocate for appreciation and respect of partners' research traditions to be more open and collaborative in international scholarship. With significant education reforms in the country, Russian researchers are compelled to engage in international collaborations. This chapter helps international leadership scholars learn about the current state of Russian research, influences of research traditions, current research internalization strategies, existing academic programs in leadership studies. This chapter includes the authors' reflections on what it meant to plan followership research in Russia and anticipate working with a Russian-trained or an American-trained scholar. The authors argue that one of the first steps in international research collaborations should be reviewing similarities and differences between collaborators' research foundations and experiences to become familiar with each other's research language and to conduct a study blending the approaches to produce a truly international leadership research.

The number of international research collaborations has been increasing exponentially around the world (e.g., Castillo & Powell, 2020; Gui et al., 2019; Lebeau & Papatsiba, 2016; Owens, 2018; Sadeghi-Bazargani et al., 2019). The American Psychological Association (APA) defines *international research collaborations* as "research projects that involve active participation of investigators whose primary institutional affiliations are in different countries" (Committee on International Relations in Psychology, 2014, p. 4). Although a study topic, its scope, or number of collaborators may change, the approach to a joint nature of an international research process remains the same. It is when "cross-national teams jointly initiate, perform, and report empirical research in an area of common interest" (Committee on International Relations in Psychology, 2014, p. 4). This chapter adopts the APA view of an international research collaboration.

Globalization influences science like any other aspect of our existence (Gui et al., 2019). World complexities and interrelated concerns demand diverse resources, broad thinking, and expertise to produce new knowledge and solutions. If effective, international collaborations create unique "ways of addressing research questions, extending existing research to other populations, constructing

DOI: 10.4324/9781003003380-4

meaning and drawing implications that would not have been otherwise possible" (Committee on International Relations in Psychology, 2014, p. 5). However, working in or managing collaborations is not easy and never smooth: situational, institutional or national challenges are interconnected; and researchers often need to deal with many influencing socio-cultural factors at once (Gui et al., 2019; Kwiek, 2020; Porter & Birdi, 2018). Some are minor and easy to adjust while others can create significant barriers for research. Factors could range from a macro-level (e.g., history, economy, geographical distance, cultural values, relationship between countries), organizational (e.g., institutional reputation) and project management (e.g., funds, coordination) to individual influences (e.g., individual productivity, professional research training, level of expertise) (Hoekman et al., 2010; Katz & Martin, 1997; Kwiek, 2020; Luukkonen et al., 1992).

Although international researchers do consider many macro- and micro-level influences, they are often prone to overlooking potential differences in research traditions and assuming a universal approach to research. On the one hand, a view on research is similar across disciplines and societies: it is a process of a new knowledge creation to understand a phenomenon, its role in the overall environment and applications to life (Traore, 2004). On the other hand, concept definitions as well as research standards could vary, especially in studies about humans (their behavior, perceptions, feelings, etc.) where research methodology, design assumptions, language connotations, data collection protocols, ethical standards and even a meaning of research could differ depending on local research traditions and local approaches to knowledge creation (Cheng, 1994; Gagnon et al., 2004; Msoroka & Amundsen, 2018). Literature on research collaborations stresses the importance of socio-cultural contexts that influence how research is understood and conducted (Papoutsaki, 2006). However, recommendations often do not go beyond socio-cultural contexts, thus scholars who plan to engage in international research partnerships might not even think about them as potential influencers in the joint research work.

Planning Followership Research in Russia: Collaborators' Reflections

The researchers' reflections start the chapter and introduce ideas behind the Russian followership study, an apparent need for an international collaboration, collaborators' challenges and "aha" moments. Two Russian international researchers, Yulia Tolstikov-Mast and Vera Mishina, open up about their unique research motivations and assumptions and discuss the importance of learning about the current world of research in Russia and training and expectations of Russian researchers during the research planning stage.

A Russian Heritage and Western Research Training: How I Unexpectedly Stumbled

I am Yulia Tolstikov-Mast, a Russian born and raised. In 1993, I graduated with a degree in Russian as a Second Language (RSL), Literature, and English Language from Rostov State Pedagogical University in Russia. Later, I taught RSL and English at several Russian universities, had administrative responsibilities in international student' affairs, worked in international business, tutored English and briefly entered a post-graduate program in linguistics. In 1998, I moved to the United States and earned an MA in professional communication at Purdue University (in Fort Wayne).

Learning about the communication discipline, exploring many intersections of Russian culture, business and communication and enjoying science, inspired me to continue my research education in the Ph.D. program in Communication at the University of Memphis. After graduation, my research training continued with numerous conference presentations, publications, positions at U.S. universities and finally, a leadership role at a doctoral program, that required teaching research subjects and supervising dissertation work. By the time I went to Russia to conduct research, I was an experienced researcher-generalist who felt comfortable across methodologies and designs. At the same time, my research training was exclusively in English and at the U.S. social science programs.

The story of the Russian followership research started in the summer of 2013 when I traveled to Moscow on a Lilly Grant to collect data for a qualitative study on Russian followership. The main purpose of the grant was to explore the followership roles of Russian people and the relationship between Russian leaders and followers. Those topics were untapped, and I chose an exploratory research method with a range of open-ended questions. Maxwell's (2005) approach to qualitative inquiry was my guide in planning a study. Based on my understanding of Russian epistemology, I was cautious in my application of Western leadership frameworks in a Russian socio-cultural context (Littrell et al., 2014; Tolstikov-Mast, 2014). At the same time, scholarly discussions on followership in Russia did not really exist, and anything I was able to find, in Russian or English, was from historical, religious and pop-culture perspectives. Thus, I relied on a very limited theoretical foundation to frame the study.

With a literature review draft, research design, IRB approval and interview questions written in English, I embarked on my research journey. And I stumbled at the first step: translation of an interview protocol. I was aware of the translation requirements (e.g., Fryer, 2019; Harkness, 2004) to align American English and Russian meanings in the interview protocol. I also relied on my knowledge of comparative English-Russian linguistics. With that, I took the first stab at the translation of the interview protocol into Russian. Although I expected to have challenges translating "follower" and "followership", I overlooked that Russian language actually has a range of words that represent the study concepts, all with subtle historical, political, or social connotations (Littrell et al., 2014; Tolstokov-Mast, 2014a; Tolstokov-Mast, 2014b).

The main stumble was the realization of "losing" some of my Russian language fluency. After the translation, I asked my cousin, who met characteristics of a potential study participant, to review my translation for clarity. His response was: "We don't really say it like that in Russian". Although my Russian grammar was correct, the sentence structure had mistakes, and some nuances of Russian language were missing. Reflecting on this experience, I saw that some phrases were constructed as an English-Russian exact translation and not an adaptation of English terminology to Russian language. The second realization was my lack of knowledge of how to formulate interview questions for Russian study participants since my research training was exclusively in English and in the U.S. social science programs. Finally, my affiliation with a U.S. university was not well-accepted by some Russians based on a historical suspicion about intentions of American scientists (Cohen, 2001), constraining a sample recruitment.

Initial roadblocks led me to rethink my study: to focus, first, on understanding which "followership" and "follower" terms are most commonly used in Russian language in the context of my study and on piloting the interview protocol; and second, on locating a research partner in Russia. The second task actually became the priority in order to create an appropriate approach to data collection. I reached out to several of my Russian colleagues, but quickly learned that, although they had degrees in social science fields, they never received training in data collection with human subjects similar to my training in the United States.

The second surprise was a number of researchers who were reluctant to engage in a collaboration with an American researcher, even one who was a native Russian. Dr. Natalya Sarahanova from St. Petersburg State University of Economics was the first researcher who met my proposal with enthusiasm. I would like to acknowledge her significant role in the study development: from numerous discussions of a back-and-forth translation, making a connection to a Russian linguist to help us understand a range of Russian equivalents for "follower" and "followership", to discussions about scientific approaches in Russia. We co-presented at conferences, and Natalya collected the first data with a refined study protocol (Littrell et al., 2014; Tolstikova-Mast, & Sarakhanova, 2013).

An informed consent design for Russian study participants was a lengthy process as it was not a common practice in Russia in 2013. In fact, it remains an uncommon practice at the time of this publication in 2021. The majority of my discussions with Natalya centered on reconciling Russian and American views on science and research, on understanding qualitative vs. quantitative inquiry and on philosophical assumptions associated with research methods and designs. Since I learned terminology and empirical traditions in the United States, Natalya and I had to use a dictionary to look up Russian equivalents and descriptions of research terminology. While we were both well-trained researchers, we realized that our Russian and Western research training differed.

The data collection process was intense. My pilot project took a month, resulting in 8 interviews, and Natalya's 10 interviews were a two-month process. Influenced by the Soviet system, Russians still refused to participate in studies, especially qualitative ones and coordinated by a Western researcher. Later, I encountered articles that address similar data collection challenges in Russia around the time of my research endeavors (Flick, 2014; Goode, 2009; Resch & Enzenhofer, 2018; Voldnes et al., 2014). For example, Goode (2009) reported that the main challenge in doing research in Russia is to access study participants and ensure the credibility of observations. Qualitative studies still could be viewed with suspicion – as an intrusion or potentially unsafe activity, both politically and socially.

Drained from the process, I suspended the data collection and focused on the data analysis. However, with limited interviews, I felt it was important to have additional data for a more complete portrait of a Russian follower, the socially constructed reality of followership and relationship between Russian leaders and followers.

Four years later, in 2018, I was introduced to another researcher, Dr. Vera Mishina. Employed at a newly formed research university, Vera was trained in conducting interviews in the field of marketing and also was aware of the U.S. social science research expectations. At the same time, we still had to reconcile the meanings of follower and followership, research in Russian and American social sciences, or an appropriate structure for a theoretical foundation and the overall study. Vera is the co-author of this manuscript. Below she shares her reflection on what it meant for her to start a study with a Western research partner who had a similar Russian heritage but was, otherwise, pretty Western in her research planning.

Engaging in the International Research Collaboration: A Russian Scientist with the Russian Research Training

I work at the South Ural State University (SUSU). The motivating factor for me to collaborate with Yulia was SUSU's newly acquired status (in 2010) of a "national research university". It meant expectations from faculty to effectively engage in teaching and scholarly activities at the international level. In 2015, the university entered the 5-100 strategic plan – a government program to strengthen leading Russian universities (Project 5-100, n.a.). Simultaneously, SUSU engaged in active recruitment of international students, and I was able to contribute to the university mission by teaching international students due to my high command of English. To prepare for class discussions, I reviewed many high-quality articles published in international academic outlets.

Inclusion of Russian universities into the world rankings is a very important achievement. In 2017, SUSU received a higher university rating in the Webometrics Ranking of World Universities and was included into the Round University Ranking. In 2018, the university appeared on the list of best world universities in QS World University Rankings. And in early 2020, the university competitiveness in international education was emphasized in Times Higher Education. Currently, the main goal of SUSU is transformation into SMART-university, which will become the main basis for sustainable development of the region, and make a significant contribution in global education and science (Project 5-100, n.a.).

For the SUSU faculty, the university participation in the 5-100 Project and a status of national research university means increased demand for higher-level publications (Tier 1 academic journals).

Study results should be published in scientific journals indexed in SCOPUS and Web of Science (Q-1, Q-2). We are strongly encouraged to participate in international research collaborations and projects, and I am personally very interested in these initiatives. At the same time, the university supports faculty with many resources including English writing assistance in academic publications, and integration of faculty into scientific societies.

In 2018, I took professional development classes to prepare for the IELTS – the International English Language Test. It is designed to help applicants work, study or migrate to a country where English is the native language. On the one hand, the classes helped me increase my knowledge of the scientific language of research and presentation of scientific data. On the other hand, a successfully passed exam would allow me to participate in scientific international internships and even enter a doctoral program in another country. Currently, the university is actively implementing the EMI (English Medium Instruction) Program. It is a method of using English for teaching academic disciplines because of an increase in the number of international students. The program allows faculty to master scientific English language needed to understand international scientific texts, articles and books. In this program, we are also considering cultural nuances of researchers from different cultures. The spread of international contacts leads to acute demand in scientific communication. In general, the university is open to international collaborations in the spheres of science and education.

Finding myself with new expectations at work, conditions where I was expected to publish in Tier 1 journals, I studied many journals in my academic area and related fields, considered a structure of articles and even attempted (together with a SUSU colleague) to submit an article to a relevant Western journal. However, publishing in international journals appeared harder than we originally expected. With our own efforts, we were able to get to Tier 3 and 4 journals and conference proceedings. Almost immediately, broker firms emerged in Russia that offered their services to "place" an article in high-quality journals, including improving quality and offering translations. Service fees ranged between $1,000–$2,000, and a payment did not guarantee publication in a promised journal. Thus, it became evident that communication, scientific exchanges and collaborations would be important to understand the process of structuring, writing and formatting an article based on the results of scientific observations.

In this uneasy situation I began my collaboration with Yulia. Naturally, I had doubts and concerns about my abilities, professionalism, and peculiarities of a Western scientific research process. A very important argument for my engagement with Yulia was a personal connection. Our mutual colleague, who already had experience in international collaborations, introduced me to Yulia. It meant I was able to trust and was assured that the work would be productive.

One of my first questions was: if necessary, would I be able to deviate from the traditional research plan I have been accustomed to in Russia (frameworks, formulation of hypotheses, results and discussions)? The challenge is, there is no determined structure of a scientific article in Russia, with exception of general comments, relevance, feasibility and conclusion sections. Within an article, we can have many variations: discussions of terminology, analysis of different points of view regarding a scientific problem, comments on tables and graphs, analysis of graphs, etc. Everything depends on the area of investigation, journal mission and subjects and page limitation. For example, it is popular to divide the dissertation into sections and submit them as journal articles. That is why a researcher could accumulate a range of different articles: theoretical, applications, analytical. Not to fall into my established scientific habits, I decided to follow Yulia's plan and take part in writing distinctive parts based on the best practices of Western research journals.

I was hesitant about the comparability of our research knowledge and training. The experience from several years ago left an unsettling feeling. In 2008, I presented at the *XX World Philosophical Congress* in Seoul, South Korea. After my presentation, in the division of philosophical anthropology, the audience was silent. After a few minutes of silence, the first questions came from a student who was pursuing a master's degree in the USA: "I don't quite understand what research method you use? Was it an abductive approach"? I was surprised and only nodded in reply. When I got home, I started digging into this question. It appeared that in the courses on "History and Methodology of Science" we learned only about induction and deduction. In reality, we have been using adjudication in most of our studies without applying a correct terminology – it is when we transfer main concepts and approaches from one discipline to another. To this day, I am very thankful that this master's student asked me the questions at the conference. Now, my research colleagues use the term "abduction" as the main methodological method base for a study. There is also transduction; however, it hasn't been discussed in any of our research philosophy courses.

My next scholarly concern was the ability to offer practical applications for research. I can share my own example of conducting, writing and defending my candidacy thesis in the philosophy of anthropology. I was actually lucky: my committee chair worked with modern topics and creative approaches; and his doctoral students were allowed to articulate a practical side of a study, to some degree. However, when it was time for my defense, negative comments emerged from other dissertation reviewers. They noted that doctoral students should focus on a topic of special novelty or mention opportunities for practical application of results. I was told "an aspirant's dissertation is a learning experience. It requires a deep theoretical and historical analysis of literature. That is pretty much it! More complex topics with practical application should be left for the doctoral type of a dissertation".

The third important question for me was what types of literature (types of sources) would my scientific collaborator prefer? What major studies would she use as the base for her research? What method and what databases would my international partner use to collect data? In Russia, literature review falls into a data collection category. Russia has wide opportunities to access scientific literature. There are very large libraries in cities with a significant populations exceeding a million people as well as equivalents of these libraries on the internet (e.g., the famous "Lenin" library in Moscow (The Russian State Library, n.a.) and databases of scholarly articles (Scientific Electronic Library, n.a.). Most of the large Russian universities now have subscriptions to complete international databases. However, Russian scientists often choose two directions to gather literature: physically go to the library (as a habit) or completely trust search results on the Internet (without checking scholarly databases). The first and second options would create gaps in knowledge since some sources would be omitted. To avoid gaps, I was proactive in discussing with Yulia databases, types of sources and main seminal authors to choose for the study theoretical foundation.

The fourth question was on how we could stay connected and have timely discussions in the planning stage of the study. Traditionally, in Russia, work and private emails are not viewed right away, at least not on the same day. It also happens that emails go to spam (especially university accounts). At the same time, the planning stage requires efficiency. That is why we discussed communication right away and tried to use different communication channels including Skype, Zoom, or WhatsApp. Those channels often saved us some trouble, and their importance increased during the COVID-19 pandemic. Overall, any type of instant communication is useful to allow immediate updates about upcoming meetings, to interact without interruptions, as well as to receive voice and text information and exchange files promptly.

The fifth question was about my university's technology capabilities (e.g., SPSS). Up until recently, not every Russian university had or used university-wide data analysis software. After 2016, universities started purchasing licenses that largely increased university expenses. At times, not every university employee has access to every database or software. For example, specialized software could be purchased exclusively for a college or a department, and installed only on one or two computers. Thus, a university-employed researcher might not know about available data analysis software, does not have skills to work with it, and certainly cannot access the program from a home computer.

And finally, the last and most pressing question I am currently facing is am I ready to sacrifice my personal time for research if my place of employment increases the workload? Everyone is experiencing uncertain times. Who would have thought a year ago that COVID-19 pandemic would force us to restructure our work routines, and do online conferences and webinars in teaching and research. People across spheres see increased workloads because of the online transactions. However, time for research is not scheduled or financially rewarded by universities. That is why the question of time for research is rather difficult. Often it is a choice between private life and research, sleep and research, family time and research.

Overall, an international research collaboration is like a long adventure that is influenced by a large number of factors: from language barriers and socio-cultural differences to technological resources of each member of a group. What's greatly important is the quality of your partner's research preparation: the better the foundational knowledge and training, the higher the results. If research collaborators actively participate in international conferences, we can also hope they have high capabilities for collaborations and tolerance for cultural nuances of collaborators.

Conclusion

The reflections offer an overview of the local Russian research context that is relevant to know about in order to successfully work with Russian scholars. Both Yulia and Vera often pondered what international researchers would need to understand to engage successfully in scholarly activities with Russians. What knowledge of Russia, beyond socio-cultural and language variations, could be beneficial for international research collaborators? In their reflections, the Russian researchers agree that in understanding of the Russian science system, including its traditions and current evolution, terminology and understanding of disciplines, meaning of research, approaches to research training and a world perception of Russian research quality and trust in research evidence are important for productive research collaborations. It's also critical to understand the experiences of Russian scientists: the increased university demands for publications, a realization of limitations in their knowledge of Western research standards or recognition of deeply philosophical traditions of Russian science, among others.

Yulia and Vera's collaboration is ongoing. We are finishing the data collection stage, and are excited to publish in both Russian and Western outlets and present at Russian and Western conferences. The process of reconciling Russian and U.S. research traditions is also ongoing. Vera took a lead in data collection making this process comfortable for study participants who prefer to work with a Russian researcher. Data analysis will be led by Yulia who is more experienced at it. The literature review section will be written by both scholars and will be a blend of Russian and U.S. standards of writing and literature analysis. Finally, data interpretation and recommendations will be highly collaborative and contextual, taking into consideration potential readers, language of presentations and publications and other culturally specific aspects.

The next section of this chapter is the result of discussions between Yulia and Vera about specific information that Western scholars would need to know about Russian approaches to research to have effective research collaborations in the area of leadership studies. There is not much written about Russian research and research education (Chigisheva et al., 2017). Thus, facts and details in this section are critical for English-speaking professionals with Western research training and interest in research projects in Russia.

The World of Russian Science

Russian Science and a Push for Global Competitiveness

Russians have been dominating the fields of hard and applied sciences for centuries and their discoveries continue to shape many disciplines (Chalyan, 2018; Famous Russian Scientists and their Discoveries, n.a.). Simultaneously, of the Soviet regime were unkind to social sciences as public opinion was manipulated or disregarded. Moreover, social science research was not encouraged or popularized. The collapse of the Soviet Union brought chaos and stagnation to every field of the Russian sciences. Decades of underfunding, bureaucracy, opposition to reforms, and inadequate salaries led to a science brain-drain forcing thousands of Russian scientists to leave research or move abroad (Chigisheva et al., 2017; Gaponenko, 1995; Schiermeier, 2013). Researchers who stayed were obligated to have their work vetted before they can submit it to foreign journals or were cut from "undesirable" foreign grants (e.g., Dynasty Foundation, Open Society Foundations; Schiermeier, 2013).

In the past 10 years, Russian President Putin's administration started paying more attention to science, including tangible steps to make science and innovation the top national priorities (e.g., significant increase in investments, public science spending; Schiermeier, 2013; Vorotnikov, 2018). These developments are aimed to change the culture of Russian higher education and research and to align the entire approach to scientific discoveries with Western standards (Bothwell, 2019). At the same time, some Russian scholars voice skepticism about fund allocations, where money could go to universities that have a strong lobby influence within the government but are not necessarily the best institutions (Vorotnikov, 2018).

5-100 Russian Academic Excellence Project

The first incentive to reform a Russian approach to science was the adoption of the Bologna Process by the Russian Federation to increase "unification of educational standards with ones of the EU" being "the main trend in the development of Russian education" (Vorontsov & Vorontsova, 2015, p. 1163). Thus, in 2013, Russia initiated Project 5-100, a state program to support leading Russian universities (5-100 Project, n.a.). Its goal is to increase competitiveness of Russian education in the global educational and scientific realms and to maximize the competitive position of the group of leading Russian universities. As a consequence, these universities could join prestigious educational rankings, such as Quacquarelli Symonds, Times Higher Education and Academic Ranking of World Universities.

To start, 54 Russian universities competitively entered into the 5-100 Project; and 21 were the finalists selected by the International Council and the Ministry of Education and Science of the Russian Federation (5-100 Project, n.a.). Later, a Key Performance Indicators (KPI) model was introduced in Russia as a measurable value to demonstrate how effectively a person is achieving the most important goals of contributing to organizational competitiveness (Marr, 2020). KPI consists of many factors, but mainly requires university faculty to publish in high rating international subject journals. National research universities and global universities included in the Project 5-100 are the most active in producing scholarship in Russia with the highest expectations for KPI.

On March 4, 2020, a global analytical agency QS Quacquarelli Symonds released results of the academic subject ratings of the best universities (QS World University Rankings by Faculty; and QS World University Rankings by Subject). The Russian academy was represented by 22 universities (13 were Project 5-100 members) with three universities (members of the Project 5-100) included into 100 best world universities (QS World University Rankings, n. a.). This increase in rating is a significant milestone for Russia as it elevates Russian universities' standings in global education competitiveness.

Russian analysts assert that changing the Russian research system requires efforts beyond an increase in funding, policy ambitions, improved efficiency and performance of universities but new methods as well as interdisciplinary and international collaborations (Karaulova et al., 2016; Marshakova-Shaikevich, 2010). And the Russian government has been pushing to expand network boundaries, attract foreign scientists to national universities and encourage international alliances (Konovalov, 2019; Vorotnikov, 2015). The Russian International Affairs Council (RIAC), a non-profit academic think tank, pledged to facilitate Russia's integration into the global community by facilitating cooperations between Russian scientific institutions and foreign analytical centers and scholars (Konovalov, June 24, 2019). Thus, Russian researchers now have a more compelling reason to engage in international collaborations.

However, analysis of collaborative publications in Russia demonstrates dominance of the old approaches to the research system: prevalence of partnership within one discipline and domestic alliances over international partnership (Marshakova-Shaikevich, 2010). At the same time, the visibility of Russian publications is higher when co-authored with international partners. Research publications with only Russian authors are cited on average 2.5 times when the average number of internationally cited publications is 4.33 times (170% increase) (Marshakova-Shaikevich, 2010; Karaulova et al., 2016). Overall, research collaborations in Russia mostly follow old research networks through familiar and already established interactions (Karaulova et al., 2016). Analysts report that some international research meetings are censored, and some Russian scientists have to inform the ministry in advance about meeting plans and follow-up about the content of the conversations. Moreover, a scientist's private meetings with foreign colleagues outside of working hours could require permissions from a research center's management (Bershidsky, 2019).

All the examples in the section on the Russian current research reforms show new vs. old research traditions, including a research production conflict, regulatory contradictions and continued political constraints. At the same time, the increase in international collaborative publications is an optimistic sign.

Social Science Disciplines and Leadership Studies in Russia

Emergence of social science disciplines is a natural progression of knowledge development to understand the social world. Each discipline, however, has a unique story, its own set of assumptions about the nature of state and society, and ideological undertones (Manicas, 1990, 1991). The United States has a wide range of social science disciplines developed based on British or American models (Manicas, 1990). Russian science, influenced by the Soviet regime, offers a restricted number of disciples at universities. Analysts blame it on suppression of social science research that began during Stalin's era and lasted for over 70 years (Graham, 1972; Hesli & Kessel, 2001; Gaponenko, 1995). Some disciplines, like communication, did not exist until recently due to an association with freedom of speech (Tolstikov-Mast & Keyton, 2002); and some fields of studies, like leadership, still do not have an adequate disciplinary representation.

Our extensive search revealed the only clearly identifiable program in leadership – the Graduate School of Leadership (GSL). The program does not associate itself with any type of sciences or a discipline. It is a part of Saint Petersburg Christian University (SPbCU) that was established in 2010 for the purpose of cultivating effective and ethical leadership in Russia and beyond (School of Leadership, n.a.). SPCU is an international affiliate member of the Council of Christian Colleges and Universities (CCCU) of higher theological training institutions from around the world. The School of Leadership mission is listed as "*Promotion* of biblical principles and effective approaches in leadership; *Advancement* of knowledge and research in Leadership Studies; *Development* of effective organizations and healthy communities; *Honoring* God through the practice and promotion of effective and ethical leadership in all areas of life; and *Service* to leaders in Russia and beyond, by equipping them to lead well in churches, businesses, educational and non-profit organizations" (School of Leadership, n.a.).

The multidisciplinary program embraces many contexts (from churches, businesses, educational and non-profit institutions) and claims to critically examine leadership traditions, theories and practices and the way towards highly effective leadership and followership based on a Christian perspective. The school also offers leadership consulting, coaching and training to various organizations. According to the school website, faculty and students conduct research and publish on leadership with attention to the historical and cultural uniquenesses of the Russian and Eurasian context. However, the search for publications or consulting areas did not yield any leadership-specific topics (List of Faculty Publications, n.a.).

Another example of an emerging academic and practitioner interest in the subject of leadership is the Centre for Education Leadership. Publicly available information about the center is limited. It appears to have a across-disciplinary focus and a narrow approach to leadership within a field of education (Center for Education Leadership, n.a.). The final evidence is the availability of leadership training for emerging Russian researchers. On October 23, 2020, the College of Europe e-welcomed a group of young researchers from all over Russia (Online visit to the College of Europe organized for Russian researchers; 10/23/2020). It seems the focus of the training is practical: on raising research initiative and empowering emerging Russian researchers to work in or lead international research projects.

Conclusion

Putin's administration made science and innovation top national priorities and introduced changes to transform the approach to science and increase Russian universities competitiveness. If you plan to initiate a joint leadership or followership study with Russian colleagues, they will be eager to engage. At the same time, research support is still connected to political influences and lobbying; thus, not every university has adequate resources or research training.

Enthusiasm for research is also counteracted by increased pressure on university faculty. It seems that Russia's scientific system adopted the "publish or perish" slogan so familiar to scholars in American U.S. and European countries. Old-style bureaucracy and hierarchy among scientists are still prevailing. However, there is also evidence that many Russian scientists look for innovative interdisciplinary and international collaborations.

Although it is important to understand the Russian scientific system in order to have an effective research collaboration, Western scholars could encounter more serious challenges with misalignment of Western vs Russian disciplinary knowledge, meaning of research and research training. Russian views on the nature of research, education and methodologies have similarities as well as differences with Western social science approaches. The section below explains nuances of the Russian perspective on research.

The Meaning of Research in Russian Social Science Areas

Russians are introduced to the word "research" at school, in the first grade (Deubel, 2017; Batina, 2015; Kuznetsova, 2011). Kindergarten graduates are told that they are going to school to study and learn about the world around them. In Russia, nobody really explains the term at school but schoolchildren are asked to present results of some sort of investigative projects throughout their school years. Later on, children learn different approaches and research methods in chemistry, biology or physics without clearly understanding their involvements in research. Further on, even in college, pursuing bachelor's degrees, Russian students are not truly asked to do research. In 1–2 years, they are required to take a sociology course that is feared by every student. The course introduces the basics of statistical analysis. In Russian instructors' opinions, this first encounter with a research process is overwhelming. Students do not have a clear understanding of the needs for research or knowledge derived from empirical evidence. Nevertheless, undergraduates further take research courses in philosophy of science, modern natural sciences or history as well as relevant research methods courses in graduate and post-graduate degrees.

Research Training: Aspirantura and Doktorantura

In Russia, after receiving bachelor and master degrees, students could continue their research and pedagogical activities in Aspirantura and Doktorantura. Those are the highest research degrees offered by the largest Russian universities with a special status. For admission to Aspirantura, students have to take exams in their subject area, in philosophy and a foreign language. For admission to Doktorantura, the requirement is to be a Candidate of Science (a result of defended dissertation in Aspirantura), a significant list of publications and have developed materials for a doctoral dissertation.

Both Aspirantura and Doktorantura culminate with a dissertation. In Russia, a dissertation is a product of a scientific inquiry where an investigator establishes a research problem, defines an object of investigation, research purpose, solves problems and comes to definitive results (Polozheniye o Vysshey attestatsionnoy komissii, n.a.; Stepin, 2003).). The Russian Higher Attestation Commission (HAC) defines dissertation as a scientific qualifying work where an investigator has to solve scientific problems of a certain level with the use of a chosen methodology. HAC reviews a dissertation cases; and the dissertation council makes a decision about awarding the degree of candidate or doctor of sciences.

A dissertation defense is a scientific discussion. It takes place at a meeting of an academic council in front of about 20 of its members. Prior to the defense in Aspirantura, a Candidate of Science is expected to produce about 20 publications. While in Doktorantura, a Doctor of Science is required to have about 50 publications of different types, including international and peer-reviewed articles as well as research books (Karpov, 2014; Polozheniye o Vysshey attestatsionnoy komissii, n.a.).

Currently, the Russian Federation has about 700 federally accredited institutions. The final count is challenging because of seminaries and theological universities where this count does not take place. Moscow State University and Saint Petersburg State University are above the classification as two elite institutions that have the highest education status in Russia (Martynenko, 2019). They are followed by federal universities. Special status goes to national research universities with a focus on one area of study (e.g., pedagogical university, physics and math university).

The Bologna Process and Putin's science reforms influenced postgraduate research training to comply with the new national policy. As a basis for research training, post-graduate education is expected to equip students with necessary competencies to conduct research (Chigisheva, Soltovets, & Bondarenko, 2017). However, this type of education was the last one to undergo reforms since university changes were introduced from the bachelor's level first, with the master's education to follow (Chigisheva, Soltovets, & Bondarenko, 2017).

According to Chigisheva, Soltovets, and Bondarenko (2017) and Morgan (May 31, 2018), the process of reforming Russian research training is far from being successfully completed. One of the fundamental Soviet-era higher education divides was between receiving subject education in universities and actually engaging in research in the Russian Academy of Sciences. This tendency is still alive in some Russian universities. A new idea is to create a new science research approach to drive the integration of research and teaching forward conceptually. This is where professionals could work both for the Russian Academy of Sciences and universities, and where teaching faculty could also conduct research. 5-100 Russian Academic Excellence Project intends to do just that (Morgan, May 31, 2018).

Even in Aspirantura, research training is limited and mainly takes place with a dissertation committee chair (Volkov, 2009; Karpov, 2014; Maksimov, 2013; Nevolina, 2001). Although there is *How to write and defend a dissertation* (2016) and other books on dissertation writing (250,000 based on the search in Russian State Library database; The Russian State Library, n.a.), these sources are mostly introductory. University researchers or students planning to do advanced research designs or data analysis look for answers to their research questions in their scholarly networks, at scientific associations, and conferences.

Issues of Methodology

Methodology is studied only in Aspirantura where aspirants learn that scientific research includes a process of investigation that follows a specific scientific method. There are four main methodological levels used in research: a philosophical methodology (meta-methodology), general scientific methodology, industry methodology and methodology of a specific discipline. The latest is what American scholars call a research method. It is used to expand theoretical or empirical knowledge, a complex of ideas about the specifics of an object and subject of cognition, and a set of techniques and research procedures (Fedorova, 2016; Fillips, 1999; Potapov, 2013; Shakhovskaya, 2017).

Knowledge of general philosophical principles and philosophy of science are paramount for creation of new scientific knowledge in Russia. They are integral forms of scientific knowledge, including knowledge about society, cultures, history and human existence. For example, Russian Hermeneutics is widely used in studies due to their connection to cognition and reflexivity (Moore, 2009). A dialectical method is also popular and includes a philosophical investigation where phenomenon is considered flexibly, critically, consistently, taking into account its internal contradictions, changes, developments, causes and effects, and unity and struggle of opposites (Maksimov, 2013; Nevolina, 2001). Overall, the Russian philosophical view of methodology is very similar to scientific approaches in other countries (Maksimov, 2013; Nevolina, 2001). However, if in the United States, a philosophy of science is foundational but peripheral, giving priority to an application of research methods via designs; in Russia, philosophical depth is important for every step in research.

Russian studies accept empirical and theoretical levels of investigation. Empirical is consistent with Western quantitative traditions and is based on observations and experiments that lead to supporting or rejecting a hypothesis. A method of scientific investigation is applied to both theoretical or methodological parts (e.g., methodological foundation for investigation, theoretical-methodological foundation). Theoretical studies are theoretical concepts, principles or ideas. Methodology in theoretical studies is used to organize theoretical arguments. Theoretical investigations have a very broad set of methods: idealization, formalization, analysis and synthesis, ascent from abstract to concrete, and induction and deduction (Chigisheva, Soltovets, & Bondarenko, 2017; Fedorova, 2001; Fillips, 1999).

In Russian social and humanitarian disciplines, the research process includes the following (Chigisheva, Soltovets, & Bondarenko, 2017; Fedorova, 2001; Fillips, 1999):

- A general structure: a statement of a problem, research goals and objectives, explanation of a methodology, description of data collection and data analysis and conclusions.
- A theoretical study also includes: a conceptual model of investigation, description of concepts, categories and connections among them;
- Analytical part: characteristics of different approaches found during theoretical analysis and selection of one of the approaches for the practical part of a study.
- Practical/applied part: justification for future studies and data application in practice.

Traditionally, research rarely focuses on practical applications. The practical or applied part is an elective. It is standard for some dissertation committee chairs to limit their research candidates explaining that the practical part could only be in the highest-quality studies (meaning doctoral dissertations). At the same time, in doctoral dissertations, the theoretical part followed by analysis and conclusion of the entire document significantly outweigh other parts of a study. Simultaneously, modern research could differ in its intent and even have an initial goal to find practical application for practical problems.

Theoretical studies are prevalent in Russian social and humanitarian sciences. A methodology of a specific discipline (in the United States this approach is called "research methods") is less popular. Qualitative and quantitative research methods are taught in the discipline of sociology, considered pretty difficult and require calculations and availability of data analysis software that is not widely accessible to every researcher. For example, software could be available on only a few computers in one department.

To help international readers visualize the structure of research articles in Russia, there are two examples. Chigisheva, Soltovets, and Bondarenko's (2017) research represents the most common study where literature (policies in this study) is reviewed analytically (applying specific philosophical methodology) to formulate conclusions. On the other hand, Karaulova, Gök, Shackleton, and Shapira's (2016) research is an example of methodology more familiar to American social science researchers. The study is based on a mixed-method design. With a quantitative part focusing on a bibliometric analysis of scientific publications by Russian authors; and a qualitative part is a series of semi-structured interviews.

Overall, there is not much published on current social science research training and curriculum in Russia. Searches in both Russian and English revealed just a few programs that have research courses similar to what you could see at U.S. universities. There is a semester-long research methods course at a higher school of economics offered at a bachelor's program of foreign languages and inter-cultural communication (Research Methods, 2019/2020). The course is taught in English (requires at least an intermediate level), and introduces the basics of social science research skills, including philosophical assumptions, conceptual framework, research methods (qualitative and quantitative), data analysis, data collection techniques, sampling and measurement, research limitations, research writing and others. The course also includes analytical frameworks and methods of research in contemporary linguistics. Interestingly, the course has a module on the difference between Russian and Western traditions in research.

Conclusion

Russian research in social and humanitarian sciences has unique philosophical traditions and a re-search training process. The majority of studies are conducted by aspirants and doctorants. The post-graduate stage is also when students learn about research methods and designs. Undergraduate students, however, have a scarce and mostly philosophical and theoretical research education. This is different from, for example, American research training, where many undergraduate programs al-ready offer independent or collaborative research opportunities in classes or in grant-sponsored projects with their faculty (Kinzie, Husic, & Elrod, 2010).

Reforms of Russian research training are underway but are far from being completed. Teaching and research are still performed by different professionals employed by more teaching-oriented institutions or research academies. Another unique characteristic of Russian sciences is the appli-cation of scientific methodology to theoretical and empirical research with the majority of new scientific knowledge generated from theoretical studies; although modern research is emerging with observations and practice-focused research goals.

Overall, American and Russian scholars have university pressures to publish to maintain or increase university ratings and recognition. Thus, both sides could use it as a motivation to engage in studies of Russian leadership and followership – areas with very limited empirical knowledge. Additionally, both sides could enrich their epistemological and ontological understanding from learning and applying elements of each other's research processes. Collaborative work could also lead to diverse conference presentations and publications to reflect on international studies with Russian counterparts.

Trust in Russian Science

In addition to unique methodological standards and meaning of research, Western scholars en-counter another challenge in scientific collaborations with Russians – a perception of corruption in research. Bothwell (March 7, 2019) comments that "The Soviet legacy of mistrust, excessive oversight and data fabrication prevails across many institutions. Besides, the current political environment provides no good support to building trustworthy and sustainable partnerships with centers of excellence in the West, on which some successful projects of Russian universities depended during the previous two decades".

Only recently the Russian government started seriously auditing scientific publications (Antiplagiat, n.a; Dissernet, n.a.; Konovalov, 2019; Singh Chawla, 2020). For example, the Russian Science Foundation started taking more serious precautions to prevent duplicate funding by cross-checking and screening applications with other research funders (RFBR, Ministry of Science and Higher Education). It also calls for funding agencies in Russia and abroad to take further steps to isolate and confront duplicate awards (Konovalov, 2019).

It is reported that academic journals in Russia have retracted 800 papers following a probe into unethical publication practices by a commission appointed by the Russian Academy of Sciences (RAS). It showed a long history of unethical practices in Russian scientific literature, including plagiarism, self-plagiarism, and gift authorship (addition of co-author who did not contribute any work). In March 2018, Dissernet, an independent network of experts, researchers and reporters dedicated to uncovering scientific plagiarism and falsification, identified more than 4,000 cases of plagiarism and questionable authorship among 150,000 papers in about 1,500 journals (Dissernet, n.a.). In September 2019, Antiplagiat, the first top-quality Russian software to detect plagiarism (Antiplagiat, n.a.), reviewed 4.3 million Russian-language studies and found that more than 70,000 were published at least twice and a few were published as many as 17 times, demonstrating widespread self-plagiarism. It is reported that "brokers" are selling slots on manuscripts written by others that were already accepted by journals (Singh Chawla, 2020), and in 2019, the commission asked 541 journals to retract a total of 2,528 papers.

Unethical research conduct is a global problem. In Russia, like in other parts of the world, it is the result of pressure to publish and obtain research funds. Thus, the issue is in need of worldwide solutions.

Conclusion

Vera and Yulia developed a successful research collaboration. Success is attributed not only to their common heritage but mostly to understanding the mutual value of the collaboration and determination to make it work. Their reflections are a testament of international researchers' vulnerabilities and a need to accept and incorporate diverse epistemologies and ontologies. Open-mindedness to understand and reconcile Russian and Western approaches to research is not about choosing one over the other but embracing multi-philosophy and multi-methodology in research.

This chapter is one of a few publications that opens a world of Russian science to Western scholars and explicates knowledge about Russian science system, meaning of research and methodologies and unethical publication practices needed for successful collaborations with Russian scholars. Additionally, the chapter introduces the emergence of leadership studies in the country with highly centralized power, restricted human rights and very limited space left for civic activism (Russia Events of 2021, n.a.). The situation calls for more international research collaborations to empower and support Russian scholars in their research and application of studies for public and organizational good. Joint efforts could help address complex research questions, extend research, develop new meanings and draw implications that would not have been otherwise possible.

To conclude, we are offering suggestions to create an effective collaboration with Russian social and humanitarian sciences scholars in leadership studies.

1. Learn about social-cultural and epistemological approaches to research in general and in leadership/followership studies, in particular.

2. Read about current developments in the Russian sciences (considering ongoing reforms).
3. Consider a partner university with available research resources and research training.
4. For leadership and followership research, very likely you will not be able to locate an exact expert. Thus, look beyond leadership studies and focus on forming an interdisciplinary international research team.
5. The most qualified Russian research partner would be the one with a Candidate of Science (completed Aspirantura) or professor degree (completed Doktorantura).
6. Expect Russian scientists to have strong philosophical and theoretical research education and have less experience in empirical studies. Research method and design; research assumptions, limitations and delimitations, as well as research applications are the most challenging sections in research reports.
7. When Russian research partners are identified and research commitments are obtained, invest time in pre-research discussions about each other's research expectations, meanings of research, research experiences, understanding of ethical research conduct and desired research outcomes.
8. Truly international studies are inclusive with epistemologies and ontologies; make sure Russian as well as your own research views are considered and incorporated.
9. Getting to know and developing relationships with international colleagues as well as conducting a research SWOT analysis are critical steps (Committee on International Relations in Psychology, 2014; Stead & Harrington, 2000). SWOT helps assess skills and resources needed to accomplish research goals and find complimentary collaborators (Stead & Harrington, 2000).
10. Considering current political tensions between Russian and European and U.S. governments, it's important to check current regulations and policies on publishing with Russian scholars. As we were finishing this chapter, in February of 2021, Yulia emailed an editorial assistant at the publishing house with a few manuscript-related questions. The editorial assistant responded requesting to pre-screen the Russian research co-author as part of an International Trade Sanctions Policy for residents of a number of countries (including Russia) (U.S. Sanctions on Russia: An Overview, March 23, 2020). She asked for the Russian research partner's name and address to compare to a database of sanctions. The verification process took three days. A sanctions compliance team response was positive, and the publisher gave permission to include the chapter in the handbook (See International Trade Sanctions Policy and references for details; Frequently Asked Questions About Copyright, n.a.).

References

5-100 Project Official Web-Site 5-100 Project Official Web-Site. (n.a.). https://5top100.ru/en/.

Antiplagiat. (n.a.). https://www.antiplagiat.ru/en/.

Batina, L. V. (2015). Vozmozhnosti proyektirovaniya i issledovaniya v nachal'noy shkole/L. V. Batina// Problemy i perspektivy razvitiya obrazovaniya: materialy VII Mezhdunar. nauch. konf. Krasnodar, Novatsiya (pp. 59–63). https://moluch.ru/conf/ped/archive/203/8646/.

Bershidsky, L. (2019, August 16). Russia tells its scientists to steer clear of foreigners. *Bloomberg Opinion*. https://www.bloomberg.com/opinion/articles/2019-08-16/putin-tells-russian-scientists-to-steer-clear-of-foreigners.

Bothwell, E. (2019, March 7). Questions on Russia's research reforms. *Inside Higher Ed*. https://www.insidehighered.com/news/2019/03/07/experts-have-doubts-russias-plans-reform-research-efforts.

Castillo, J. A., & Powell, M. A. (2020). Research productivity and international collaboration: A study of Ecuadorian science. *Journal of Hispanic Higher Education*, *19*(4), 369–387. 10.1177/1538192718792151.

Center for Education Leadership. (n.a.). Institute of Education. https://ioe.hse.ru/en/.

Chalyan, D. (2018, February 7). 5 times Russia absolutely owned science. *Science & Tech*. https://www.rbth.com/science-and-tech/327520-russia-scientific-discoveries-mars.

Cheng, J. L. C. (1994). On the concept of universal knowledge in organizational science: Implications for cross-national research. *Management Science*, *40*(1), 162–168. http://www.jstor.org/stable/2632851.

Chigisheva, O., Soltovets E., & Bondarenko, A. (2017). Internationalization impact on PhD training policy in Russia: Insights from the comparative document analysis. *Journal of Social Studies Education Research, 8*(2), 178–190. https://pdfs.semanticscholar.org/3d53/5daa88d095dbcf756c2c136e8647e740efe5.pdf?_ga=2.675101 61.1038264939.1605112410-1727776997.1605112410.

Committee on International Relations in Psychology. (2014). Engaging in international collaborative research. *Part of the Series Going International: A Practical Guide for Psychologists.* Office of International Affairs. https://www.apa.org/international/resources/publications/research.

Cohen, S. F. (2001). *Failed crusade: America and the tragedy of post-Communist Russia.* W.W. Norton.

Deubel, P. (2017, July 26). Conducting research-based projects in elementary grades with safety in mind. *The Journal.* https://thejournal.com/articles/2017/07/26/conducting-research-based-projects-in-elementary-grades-with-safety-in-mind.aspx.

Dissernet. (n.a.). https://www.dissernet.org/about/

Faculty of Social Sciences. (n.a.). *HSE.* https://social.hse.ru/en/.

Famous Russian Scientists and their Discoveries. (n.a.). *Study in Russia.* https://studyinrussia.ru/en/why-russia/traditions-of-education/scientists-and-discoveries/.

Fedorova, Ye. P. (2001). Kak uspeshno napisat', oformit' i zashchitit' magisterskuyu dissertatsiyu [Tekst]: metodicheskiye rekomendatsii dlya magistrantov, obuchayushchikhsya po napravleniyu podgotovki 38.04.01 – Ekonomika/Ye. P. Fodorova, A. P. Meshkova, Ye. O. Vostrikova; M-vo obrazovaniya i nauki RF, Astrakhanskiy gos. un-t. – Astrakhan': Astrakhanskiy un-t, 2016. – 26.

Fillips, E. M. (1999). Kak napisat' i zashchitit' dissertatsiyu: Prakticheskoye rukovodstvo/Estell M. Fillips, D. S. P'yu; [Per. s angl. V. Bochkareva i dr.]. – Chelyabinsk: Ural, 1999. – 285.

Flick, U. (Ed.). (2014). Challenges for qualitative inquiry as a global endeavor [Special issue]. *Qualitative Inquiry, 20,* 1059–1127.

Frequently Asked Questions About Copyright. (n.a.). CENDI. https://cendi.gov/publications/04-8copyright.html.

Fryer, C. E. (2019). An approach to conducting cross-language qualitative research with people from multiple language groups. In P. Liamputtong (Ed.), *Handbook of research methods in health social sciences.* Springer. doi:1 0.1007/978-981-10-5251-4_38.

Gagnon, A. J., Ruppenthal, L., Merry, L., Small, R., Ogilvie, L., Liegl, B., Schindlauer, D., Frideres, J., Akbari, A. H., Reichhold, S., & Märtenson, H. (2004). Conceptual clarity in international collaborations: A point of departure for policy-relevant research on discrimination. *Journal of International Migration & Integration, 5*(4), 477–494. doi:10.1007/s12134-004-1024-8.

Gaponenko, N. (1995). Transformation of the research system in a transitional society: The case of Russia. *Social Studies of Science, 25*(4), 685–703. doi:10.1177/030631295025004005.

Graham, L. R. (1972). *Science and philosophy in the Soviet Union.* New York.

Goode, P. (2009). Redefining Russia: Fieldwork, qualitative methods, and Russian politics. *APSA 2009 Toronto Meeting Paper.* https://ssrn.com/abstract=1451654.

Gui, Q., Liu, C., & Du, D. (2019). Globalization of science and international scientific collaboration: A network perspective. *Geoforum, 105,* 1–12. doi:10.1016/j.geoforum.2019.06.017.

Harkness, J., Pennell, B.-E., & Schoua-Glusberg, A. (2004) Survey questionnaire translation and assessment. In S. Presser, J. M. Rothgeb, M. P. Couper, J. T., Lessler, E., Martin, J. Martin, & E. Singer (Eds.), *Methods for testing and evaluating survey questionnaires* (pp. 453–473). Wiley.

Hesli V. L. & Kessel B. L. (2001). The state and social science research in Russia. In P. Ratcliffe (Ed.), *The politics of social science research. Migration, minorities and citizenship* (pp. 202–238). Palgrave Macmillan. doi:10.1 057/9780230504950_10.

Higher School of Modern Social Sciences. (n. a.). Lomonosov Moscow State University. https://www.msu.ru/en/admissions/general-programs/higher-school-of-modern-social-sciences.ph.

Hoekman, J., Frenken, K., & Tijssen, R. J. W. (2010). Research collaboration at a distance: Changing spatial patterns of scientific collaboration within Europe. *Research Policy, 39,* 662–673.

House, R. J., Dorfman, P. W., Javidan, M., Hanges, P. J., & Sully de Luque, M. F. (2013). *Strategic leadership across cultures: GLOBE study of CEO leadership behavior and effectiveness in 24 countries.* SAGE.

Javidan, M., Dorfman, P., De Luque, M., & House, R. (2006). In the eye of the beholder: Cross cultural lessons in leadership from Project GLOBE. *Academy of Management Perspectives, 20*(1), pp.67–90.

Kak napisat' magisterskuyu dissertatsiyu [Tekst]: uchebno-metodicheskoye posobiye. 2-ye izdaniye, stereotipnoye. – Moskva: Izdatel'stvo «FLINTA», 2016. – 174.

Kanke, V.A. Metodologiya nauchnogo poznaniya [Tekst]: uchebnik dlya magistrov/V. A. Kanke. – Moskva: Omega-L, 2013. – 255.

Karaulova, M., Gök, A., Shackleton, O., & Shapira, P. (2016). Science system path-dependencies and their influences: Nanotechnology research in Russia. *Scientometrics, 107,* 645–670. doi:10.1007/s11192-016-1916-3.

Karpov, A.S. Prakticheskoye posobiye dlya aspirantov i soiskateley [Tekst]: (kak postupit' v aspiranturu, kak napisat' dissertatsiyu, avtoreferat, nauchnuyu stat'yu, kak podgotovit' k zashchite i zashchitit' dissertatsiyu)/ A. S. Karpov, V. A. Karpov. - 2-ye izd., pererab. – Moskva: Nauch. tekhnologii, 2014. – 265.

Katz, J. S., & Martin, B. R. (1997). What is research collaboration? *Research Policy, 26*, 1–18.

Kinzie, J., Husic, D., & Elrod, S. (2010). Research and discovery across the curriculum. *Peer Review, 12*(2). https://www.aacu.org/publications-research/periodicals/research-and-discovery-across-curriculum.

Konovalov, S. (2019, June 24). Research ethics in Russia: Challenges for the Russian Science Foundation. *The Russian International Affairs Council (RIAC)*. https://russiancouncil.ru/en/blogs/konovalov/research-ethics-in-russia-challenges-for-the-russian-science/.

Kuznetsova, T. V. Soderzhaniye i etapy obucheniya proyektno-issledovatel'skoy deyatel'nosti v nachal'noy shkole: dissertatsiya... kandidata pedagogicheskikh nauk: 13.00.01/Kuznetsova Tat'yana Vladimirovna; [Mesto zashchity: Tom. gos. ped. un-t]. – Tomsk, 2011. – 191 p.

Kwiek, M. (2020). Internationalists and locals: International research collaboration in a resource-poor system. *Scientometrics, 124*, 57–105. doi:10.1007/s11192-020-03460-2

Lebeau, Y., & Papatsiba, V. (2016). Conceptions and expectations of research collaboration in the European social sciences: Research policies, institutional contexts and the autonomy of the scientific field. *European Education Research Journal, 15*(4), 377–394. https://journals.sagepub.com/doi/full/10.1177/1474904111 6642777.

Lebedev, S.A. Metodologiya nauchnogo poznaniya [Tekst]/S.A. Lebedev. – Moskva: Prospekt, 2015. – 257.

List of Faculty Publications. (n.a.). St. Petersburg Christian University. http://spbcu.ru/en/academics/list-of-faculty-publications/.

Littrell, R. F., Puffer, S. M., McCarthy, D. J., Dorfman, P., Tolstikov-Mast, Y., & Sarahanova, N. (2014, October). Russian leadership: Is it evolving toward more international styles? *Academy of Management Annual Meeting Proceedings, 1*, 13201. doi:doi:10.5465/AMBPP.2014.13201symposium.

Luukkonen, T., Persson, O., & Sivertsen, G. (1992). Understanding patterns of international scientific collaboration. *Science, Technology, & Human Values,17*(1), 101–126.

Maksimov, S.N. Metodologiya i metodika nauchnogo tvorchestva (kak napisat' i zashchitit' dissertatsiyu) [Tekst]: uchebnoye posobiye/S. N. Maksimov; M-vo obrazovaniya i nauki Rossiyskoy Federatsii, Federal'noye gos. byudzhetnoye obrazovatel'noye uchrezhdeniye vyssh. prof. obrazovaniya "Sankt-Peterburgskiy gos. ekonomicheskiy un-t". – Sankt-Peterburg: Izd-vo SPbGEU, 2013. – 202.

Manicas P.T. (1990) The Social science disciplines: The American model. In P. Wagner, B. Wittrock, & R. Whitley (Eds.), *Discourses on society. Sociology of the sciences yearbook* (Vol. 15). Springer. doi:10.1007/978-0-5 85-29174-1_3.

Manicas, P. T. (1991). *History and philosophy of social science*. Wiley-Blackwell.

Marr, B. (2020) *What is a KPI?* https://www.bernardmarr.com/default.asp?contentID=762.

Marshakova-Shaikevich, I.V. (2010). Scientific collaboration between Russia and the EU countries: A bibliometric analysis. *Herald of the Russian Academy of Sciences, 80*, 57–62. doi:10.1134/S1019331610010077

Martynenko, A. (2019, January 21). *Vuzy Rossii, kakogo statusa oni byvayut*. https://univer.expert/vuzy-rossii-kakogo-statusa-oni-byvayut.

Maxwell, J. A. (2005). *Qualitative research design: An interactive approach*. SAGE.

Moore, C. (2009). Tracing the Russian hermeneutic: Reflections on Tarkovsky's cinematic poetics and global politics. *Alternatives: Global, Local, Political, 34*(1), 59–82. http://www.jstor.org/stable/40645258.

Morgan. J. (May 31, 2018). New Russian push on science. *Inside Higher Ed*. https://www.insidehighered.com/news/2018/05/31/russia-makes-new-push-research.

Msoroka, M. S., & Amundsen, D. (2018). One size fits not quite all: Universal research ethics with diversity. *Research Ethics, 14*(3), 1–17. doi:10.1177/1747016117739939.

Nauka: vozmozhnosti i granitsy [Tekst]/V.S. Stepin i dr; Rossiyskaya akad. nauk, In-t filosofii. – Moskva: Nauka, 2003. – 292.

Nevolina, E.M. Kak napisat' i zashchitit' dissertatsiyu: Kratkiy kurs dlya nachinayushchikh issledovateley/Ye. M. Nevolina. – Chelyabinsk: Ural L.T.D., 2001. – 190.

Polozheniye o Vysshey attestatsionnoy komissii pri Ministerstve nauki i vysshego obrazovaniya RF. https://vak.minobrnauki.gov.ru/about#tab=_tab:polojenie~.

Potapov, V.I. Kak vypolnit' nauchnoye issledovaniye, napisat', oformit' i zashchitit' magisterskuyu dissertatsiyu [Tekst]: uchebnoye posobiye/V. I. Potapov, D. V. Postnikov; Minobrnauki Rossii, Federal'noye gos. byudzhetnoye obrazovatel'noye uchrezhdeniye vyssh. prof. obrazovaniya "Omskiy gos. tekhnicheskiy un-t". – Omsk: Izd-vo OmGTU, 2013. – 117.

Online visit to the College of Europe organized for Russian researchers. (10/23/2020). College of Europe. https://www.coleurope.eu/events/online-visit-college-europe-organized-russian-researchers.

Owens, B. (2018, November 7). The benefits and challenges of international research collaboration. *University Affairs (UA)*. https://www.universityaffairs.ca/features/feature-article/the-benefits-and-challenges-of-international-research-collaboration/.

Papoutsaki, E. (29 November–1st December 2006). De-westernising research methodologies: Alternative approaches to research for higher education curricula in developing countries. Presented at the Second International Colloquium on Research and Higher Education Policy. UNESCO Headquarters, Paris Project 5-100. South Ural State University. https://www.susu.ru/en/project-5-100.

QS Rankings by Faculty and Subject Place Project 5-100 Institutions Among World's Best https://5top100.ru/en/news/118938/.

QS Top Universities. (n. a.). *SUSU*. https://www.topuniversities.com/universities/south-ural-state-university-national-research-university#372363.

QS World University Rankings. (n. a.). *Top Universities*. https://www.topuniversities.com/university-rankings/world-university-rankings/2020.

Research Methods. (2019/2020). Bachelor's programme 'foreign languages and intercultural communication. https://www.hse.ru/en/ba/lang/courses/292674983.html.

Resch, K., & Enzenhofer, E. (2018). Collecting data in other languages – strategies for cross-language research in multilingual societies. In *The sage handbook of qualitative data collection* (pp. 131–146). SAGE. doi:10.4135/9781526416070.

Russia Events of 2021. (n.a.). *Human Rights Watch*. https://www.hrw.org/world-report/2021/country-chapters/russia.

Russian Social Science Review. (n. a.). *Taylor & Francis*. https://www.tandfonline.com/toc/mrss20/current

Sadeghi-Bazargani, H., Bakhtiary, F., Golestani, M., Sadeghi-Bazargani, Y., Jalilzadeh, N., & Saadati, M. (2019). The research performance of Iranian medical academics: A National Analyses. *BMC Medical Education*, *19*, 449. doi:10.1186/s12909-019-1892-4.

Schiermeier, Q (2013). Russian science chases escape from mediocrity. *Nature*. https://www.nature.com/articles/d41586-018-02872-8.

School of Leadership. (n.a.). St. Petersburg Christian University. http://spbcu.ru/en/course/school-of-leadership/.

Scientific Electronic Library. (n.a.). https://www.elibrary.ru/defaultx.asp

Shakhovskaya, L.S. Kak podgotovit' i napisat' kachestvennuyu magisterskuyu dissertatsiyu [Tekst]: uchebnoye posobiye/L. S. Shakhovskaya, YA. S. Matkovskaya; Ministerstvo obrazovaniya i nauki Rossiyskoy Federatsii, Volgogradskiy gosudarstvennyy tekhnicheskiy universitet. – Volgograd: VolgGTU, 2017. – 73P.

Singh Chawla, D. (2020, January 8). Russian journals retract more than 800 papers after 'bombshell' investigation. *Science*. https://www.sciencemag.org/news/2020/01/russian-journals-retract-more-800-papers-after-bombshell-investigation.

Social Sciences. (n.a.). *East View Press*. https://www.eastviewpress.com/resources/journals/social-sciences/

Stead, G.B., & Harrington, T.F. (2000). A process perspective of international research collaboration. *The Career Development Quarterly*, *48*, 323–331.

SUSU Re-enters the World Ranking of THE University Impact Rankings 2020. (2020, April 13). https://www.susu.ru/en/news/2020/04/23/re-enters-world-ranking-university-impact-rankings-20.

Vorotnikov. E. (November 25, 2015). Russia creates plan to recruit foreign researchers. *The Chronicle of Higher Education*. https://www.chronicle.com/article/russia-creates-plan-to-recruit-foreign-researchers/?cid2=gen_login_refresh&cid=gen_sign_in.

The Russian State Library. (n.a.). https://www.rsl.ru/en.

Tolstokov-Mast, Y. (2014a). Followership in Russia: Understanding traditions and exploring meanings of current reality. *Journal of Leadership Education*, *13*(4), 100–110. doi:10.12806/v13I14/C11.

Tolstikov-Mast, Y. (2014b). *Relationship between science and wisdom*. Presentation at the 2014 Fall Immersion Weekend of the Global Leadership program. https://www.youtube.com/watch?v=7H4Nf7D2_14.

Tolstikov-Mast, Y., & Keyton, J. (2002). Communicating about communication: Fostering the development of the communication discipline in Russia. In I. N. Rozina (Ed.), *Theory of communication and applied communication. Bulletin of Russian Communication Association*(Issue 1, pp. 119–134). Institute of Management, Business, and Law. (Reprinted in ERIC database ED 461905).

Tolstikova-Mast, Y., & Sarakhanova. N. (October, 2013). *Social construction of followership in Russia: Exploratory research*. Paper competitively selected by the Leadership in Russia & Global Context Conference, Higher School of Economics (Moscow, Russia) and by the Centre for Cross Cultural Comparisons & Auckland University of Technology (New Zealand).

Traore, A.S. (2004). Liens Entre les Programmes de Reserche et les Politiques Bilateralles et Multilaterales de Developpement en Afrique Subsaharienne. Paper presented at the 5th Annual Global Development Conference, January 28, New Dehli, India.

U.S. Sanctions on Russia: An Overview. (March 23, 2020). *Congregational research service: In focus*. https://fas.org/sgp/crs/row/IF10779.pdf.

Voldnes, G., Grønhaug, K., & Sogn-Grundvåg, G. (2014). Conducting qualitative research in Russia: challenges and advice. *Journal of East-West Business*, *20*(3), 141–161. doi:10.1080/10669868.2014.935548.

Volkov, Y. G. Kak pisat' i zashishyat' dissertatsiju [Tekst]: uchebnoye posobiye/YU. G. Volkov. - 2-ye izd., pererab. i dop. – Moskva; Rostov-na-Donu: MarT, 2009. – 133.

Vorontsov, A, & Vorontsova, E. (2015). Innovative education in Russia: The basic tendencies analysis. *Procedia - Social and Behavioral Sciences*, *214*, 1147–1155. doi:10.1016/j.sbspro.2015.11.731.

Vorotnikov, E. (2018, April 14). Putin to boost science research funding by 150%. *University World News: Russia*. https://www.universityworldnews.com/post.php?story=20180413111636641.

5

Leaders Around the World

New Avenues for the Comparative Study of Political Leadership

Henriette Müller

Introduction

Comparative research on political leadership – the performance, effectiveness and impact of political leaders – has so far largely been confined to the study of leadership in either democracies or autocracies,[1] hardly engaging in direct comparisons across these two major types of political systems (Guriev & Treisman, 2020; Maerz, 2019; Elgie, 2018; Helms, 2016; Huskey, 2016; Ezrow & Frantz, 2011; Elgie, 1995; Helms, 2005). Moreover, studies that do engage in comparative analyses of political leadership, such as the recent one by Teorell and Lindberg, focus on accession to and dismissal from power across political systems, yet without studying leaders' performances *during* their incumbencies (2019, p. 67). This is true of other recent analyses as well, including a comparison of leadership succession across the democratic/autocratic divide by Helms (2020) and a study on personal characteristics of leaders around the world by Gerring et al. (2019). Comparative studies of democrats and various types of autocrats do exist in the subfield of political psychology; however, they mainly focus on personality traits or beliefs, and do not thoroughly incorporate the institutional, structural and political contexts of democracies and autocracies (Krasno & LaPides, 2015; Hermann, 2005).

In sum, we can observe that, unlike in other disciplines such as management, business and organizational studies, where a variety of cross-regional and -cultural comparisons on leadership exists (Gupta & Van Mart, 2016; Muna, 2011; Jogulu, 2010), cross-regime comparative research of political leadership is scarce in the discipline of political science. This has been largely due to the gross institutional differences political leaders face when acting in democracies versus autocracies. Although the difference is the very foundation of comparison, in this particular case, the inarguably important differences have inhibited cross-regime analysis. The effect on scholarship of this institutional divide is often reinforced by a lack of systematic data availability and access to comparable research material across regime types. The pursuit of expert interviews in autocracies, for example, on questions related to political leadership likely entails additional, deterrent risks for researchers (Grimm et al., 2020). Furthermore, in non-democratic settings the access to and availability of political speeches or public approval polls of political leaders may be limited, and international surveys that facilitate comparisons between countries may have difficulties operating in unfree societies (Guriev & Treisman, 2020, p. 2). Notwithstanding these practical constraints on thorough cross-regime studies of political leadership, since "political leadership belongs to those fundamental features of political regimes that are shared by

DOI: 10.4324/9781003003380-5

democratic and non-democratic regimes […], careful cross-regime analysis of political leadership has [not only] gained importance" and academic salience, but is essential to the understanding of political performances in different political systems (Helms, 2012, p. 12).

In this regard, cross-regime economic studies have provided initial findings that heads of government and state have a measurable impact on the economic development of their countries (Jones & Olken, 2005; Jones, 2009). Since it is difficult to model agency effects, however, the researchers drew their conclusion from correlating a leader's death in office (either natural or accidental) with national economic growth rates in the immediately following years (Jones & Olken, 2005, p. 836). Their findings suggest that there is a divide in terms of leaders' effects on economic growth between heads of government and state in democracies and those in non-democracies, with a leader's impact strongest in autocratic settings. While this conclusion could be applied to the disastrous economic policies of Robert Mugabe in Zimbabwe or the successful ones of Lee-Kwan Yew in Singapore, the correlation of a leader's death with economic growth rates again does not inform us about that leader's political performance, strategies and policy choices – in short, the provision of political leadership – *during* his or her tenure.

Additionally, the researchers potentially underestimate the capacity of national executives in democracies to substantially influence the economic fate of the societies they govern. While leaders in democratic settings are generally able to influence only the broad framework in which economic development takes place, they may at times and especially during severe economic crises exert substantial agency. The New Deal policies of U.S. President Franklin D. Roosevelt and German Chancellor Gerhard Schröder's Hartz IV reforms cannot comfortably be subsumed under "degrees of agency" (Jones, 2009, p. 4; see also Skocpol & Finegold, 1982, pp. 255, 278; Helms, 2001, pp. 163ff.). Most importantly, the occasion of death is an awkward basis for the study of the relationship between leaders' performances and the development of national economies, since it tells us nothing about their agendas, rhetoric or behavior. In light of advancing international leadership research, new conceptual approaches are thus necessary to systematically compare the exercise of political leadership by national executives *during* their incumbency *and* across different political systems, especially democracies and autocracies.

To help close this research lacuna, this chapter studies the role political leadership may play in different political systems by specifically focusing on the relationship between political leadership and economic development across regime types. It reflects as well on research implications for cross-regime comparisons of political leadership and suggests how the lack of systematic data availability across regime types might be bridged. Taking the institutional differences as a starting point, this chapter shows that all regime types are in need of political leaders and hence benefit from the exercise of political leadership. All leaders, whether democrats or autocrats, are in need of legitimacy, and, hence, engage in different yet complex processes of legitimation (Tannenberg et al., 2020; Weber, [1922] 1978). Moreover, this chapter shows that the distinct leader-environment relations within regime types have become more complex and ambiguous in both types of political systems in recent times. Taking the relationship between political leadership and economic policy as a conceptual basis, it underscores why and how the development of the national economy can provide particularly fertile ground for the pursuit of cross-regime comparative research of political leadership in the future.

Political Leadership: Structure and Agency across Regime Types

Politics is a critical context in the study of leadership. International leadership research could thus not be advanced without a closer look at what defines political leadership and how it is embedded in and across different political systems and contexts around the world. International leadership research needs to engage more, both theoretically and methodically, in the comparative analysis of political leadership that involves different political systems. This section will thus first explore what political leadership is. Second, it will compare the foundations of and recent trends in the occurrence and exercise of political leadership across regime types. Third, it will evaluate the research implications resulting from consideration of the different political systems for the comparative study of political leadership.

Conceptualizing Political Leadership

As a special part of social leadership, political leadership is a sociopolitical phenomenon apparent in all political systems, whether democratic or non-democratic (Helms, 2012, p. 12; Masciulli et al., 2016b, p. 6). "Leadership is an essential feature of all government and governance: weak leadership contributes to government failures, and strong leadership is indispensable if the government is to succeed" (Masciulli et al., 2016b, p. 3).

Applied to political systems – i.e., the organization and processes of government and governance – leadership "is the process by which one individual [or set of individuals] consistently exerts more impact than others on the nature and direction of group activity", doing so not "by position, or *headship*, [but] by the relationship between leader and followers, or *leadership*" (Kellerman, 1984, p. 70, emphasis in original). Through such relationships, leaders obtain greater attention and influence, but not without regard to the power recipients' interests and values, implying that followers do have a choice to follow or not (at least initially) (Brown, 2014, p. 21).

Political leadership, in other words, derives from a reciprocal process between leaders and followers in the realm of politics, in which individual leaders exert influence rather than coercion. Power and authority play important roles in the exercise of political leadership, but they should not be confused with it (Müller, 2020, p. 17). Whereas power and authority imply a unidirectional hierarchy of political decision making, political leadership derives from the reciprocal process between leaders and followers, in which individual leaders exert influence – both positive and negative (Collinson, 2017). In this sense, leadership is a value-neutral phenomenon; any given leader's "impact can be constructive and empowering and/or destructive and oppressive" (Collinson, 2017, p. 274). Considered as this sort of reciprocal-dynamic interaction, political leadership in executive offices, whether in democracies or non-democracies, does not depend solely on the institutional *structure* of the office – i.e., the political system. It equally involves the incumbent's *agency* to lead – i.e., his or her exercise of leadership – thereby avoiding "a simple dichotomy between social structures and political agency" (Masciulli et al., 2016b, p. 8).

What do these manifold links between power, authority and followers in the context of political leadership indicate for its comparative analysis across different political systems? Taking, for example, the potential followers' ability to choose and follow voluntarily, political leadership seems not to apply in the institutional contexts of authoritarian regimes. At the same time, political leadership is a contested concept in democratic politics. Here, leadership is sometimes seen as undemocratic, since it indicates a tension between "the need for a leader to provide stability and direction, and on the other, the principle that the people should rule" (Elgie, 2015, p. 25). Moreover, coercion and manipulation are often present in democracies; they occur regularly in democratic parliaments, for example, when votes need to be whipped and party discipline is enforced (Elgie, 2015, p. 28). Does this mean that "true" leadership may not even be possible in democracies?

Turning to autocracies, the lack of functioning institutional checks and balances substantially constrains the opportunity for followers to follow voluntarily. The lack of separation of powers allows for the unlimited use of coercion against citizens. However, while the unfettered use of power is not in fact considered a form of political leadership, overreliance on it has been shown to be highly dysfunctional in non-democratic settings. In this regard, Tucker (1995) points out that "authoritarian regimes characteristically strive to mobilize popular support for their policies by persuasion before resorting to the coercive methods that they hold in reserve for use when persuasion fails" (p. 61). In other words, even in non-democratic contexts there may be people who follow authoritarian leaders voluntarily (Elgie, 2015, p. 28).

Political Leadership in Different Political Systems

Representative democracies feature electoral regimes that practice universal suffrage. This encourages political competition among different political parties that offer distinct policies. In this context, leaders' legitimacy derives from the political agendas they propose, on which grounds they get elected and which they are expected to pursue during their time in office. This dynamic between political legitimacy and competition can be considered the very essence of democracy for political leaders: Democratic presidents and prime ministers are vested with procedural and institutional legitimacy, but they face uncomfortable incumbencies as they are exposed to public accountability for their performance and policy choices (Kane & Patapan, 2012, chap. 5, p. 1). For their non-democratic counterparts, this relationship is generally reversed. Autocrats usually lack independent authority and institutional legitimacy but are safe in office and better shielded from public challenge, at least in the short term (Frantz & Stein, 2012, p. 295; Lake & Baum, 2001, p. 618). This does not mean that they do not need to attain political legitimacy at all; rather they must acquire it through non-electoral means (Gerschewski, 2013).

Power-wielding alone does not ensure consistent support among citizens. Non-democratic rulers also need to engage in political tasks in which the exercise of leadership may be essential. These include "the selection of personnel, the adoption of public choices, the cultivation of a compelling personal image, and the construction and manipulation of national symbols, rituals, and narratives" (Huskey, 2016, p. 70). In other words, although authoritarian regimes have the potential to use unmitigated power, its practice is demonstrably a strategy with poor odds of return in the long run (Kane & Patapan, 2012, chap. 1, p. 7; Gerschewski, 2018).

In the context of democratic government, presidents and prime ministers are the most obvious (positional) leaders of the core executive, and trends of personalization in both offices have been observed in recent decades to varying degrees and intensities (Renwick & Pilet, 2016, chap. 11, p. 3; Peters & Helms, 2012, pp. 31–32; Karvonen, 2010, p. 106; Poguntke & Webb, 2005, pp. 4, 11). Due in part to profound structural changes in the social composition of many democracies, the decrease of party cohesiveness and constituencies' attachments to party-ideological programs, and the development of electronic mass media systems, individual political actors have gained relatively more prominence in the executive and electoral arenas than collective actors (e.g., parties or cabinets), especially during times of economic crisis (Peters & Helms, 2012, p. 29; Lobo & Ferreira da Silva, 2018, pp. 1162–63).

This trend, in which individuals instead of issues become pivotal in some contemporary democracies, indicates that democracies are at increased risk of being undermined by both individual leaders as well as more structural shifts. Where relative expansion of the executive's political power occurs, it often coincides with and is reinforced by several other features of contemporary democratic politics, among them a decline of (party) political competition accompanied by high electoral volatility, a decline in party memberships, and a tendency toward low electoral turnouts, lower rates of government alternation and the increasing professionalization of politicians (Mair, 2013, pp. 42–44; Mair, 2008, p. 220; Helms, 2016, p. 462; Ieraci, 2012, p. 546; Mattila & Raunio, 2004, p. 282). The personalization of politics has manifested with widely varying scope and intensity – short-lived and superficial in some countries, more permanent in others (Karvonen, 2010, pp. 102, 105). In any event, it makes the contingent and relatively unpredictable factor of a leader's personality more potentially influential in democratic decision making, especially in the realm of party-political direction-setting and political communication (Higley & Pakulski, 2012, pp. 336, 345; Körösényi, 2005, pp. 367–68, 370).

By contrast, in many autocracies, governmental authority is invested in a ruling coalition of individuals, elites, families or party officials who together hold enough power to ensure the survival of the government. The institutional and structural variations between autocrats and groups of elites suggest the existence of four major regime subtypes (and several sub- and hybrid systems) of autocracy: single/dominant-party, monarchic, military and personalist rule (Geddes, 1999, pp. 121ff.; Geddes et al., 2014, pp. 317–18).[2] Interrelations and status of political institutions in autocracies do not mirror the separation of power and political legitimacy of democratic institutions. Still, the relationship between the leader and the ruling elites suggests that power sharing and even separation, albeit imperfectly, take place in autocracies too, and are in some cases able to offer (at least) a limited counterbalance to autocratic power (Gandhi, 2008, pp. 187–88). Moreover, recent trends suggest that non-democratic rulers not only aim to establish and maintain legitimacy within the national context, but in many cases also seek international approbation, thereby engaging in political tasks in which the exercise of leadership is essential (Gerschewski, 2013, pp. 18ff.; Maerz, 2019, pp. 8–9).

Single/dominant-party and dynastic monarchic regimes are structurally and institutionally better equipped to counterbalance their leaders than are, for example, personalist or military dictatorships, and generally provide more stability and continuity over time (Frantz & Stein, 2012, p. 298; Geddes et al., 2014, pp. 317–18; Stockemer & Kailitz, 2020, p. 721). Ideal-typical depictions of single/dominant-party autocracies often provide the broadest base of support within the realm of autocratic regimes. Although the trappings of democratic competition in single/dominant-party states are superficial, the "party organization exercises some power over the leader at least part of the time" (Geddes, 1999, p. 124). In dynastic monarchies, the political legitimacy of the leader and regime stability derive from family lineage, thereby often incorporating the entire family into ruling the state (Ezrow & Frantz, 2011, p. 242; Herb, 1999, pp. 2–3). The royal families function as political institutions that control leadership selection and "exercise complete political power", often relying on consultative councils for advice and governance (Frantz & Stein, 2012, p. 297). As such, the institutions of strong party dominance and dynastic monarchy embed their leaders in a relatively broad network of institutions and groups of elites, often constraining the autocrat from exercising unmitigated power (Svolik, 2012, p. 115; Geddes et al., 2014, p. 321; Frantz & Stein, 2012, 301).

In conclusion, a direct comparison indicates that both regime types need leaders and that leaders need legitimacy, though they have to gain and maintain it through different means and strategies (Tannenberg et al., 2020, p. 6). The distinction between leaders of democracies and rulers of autocracies is essential both in normative and actual terms, as the former compete for office and are exposed to public contests and accountability. There is no evidence that leaders of democratic and autocratic systems converge in their patterns of performance (Gerschewski, 2018, p. 661). Still, while Lake and Baum (2001) have argued that "[p]oliticians differ not in their goals but in the institutional contexts in which they seek to satisfy their desires" (p. 618), this section has shown that these different institutional contexts are more complex in their leader-environment relations than their ideal-typical depictions often suggest. Additionally, given autocrats' different exposure to structural constraints, a cross-regime analysis by Lührmann et al. (2018) indicates that once clear-cut regime distinctions have become more ambiguous in recent times (p. 66).

Regarding the relationship between structure and agency in democratic politics, the latest developments suggest a shift toward more leader-centered politics. While specific manifestations of this shift may often be temporary in nature and certainly affect different democracies to varying degrees, they potentially provide leaders with "wide room for political manoeuvre even against the instruction of the citizen" (Helms, 2016, p. 470). In contrast, the subtypes of authoritarian rule discussed above "shape leader-elite relations and define the nature of competition" and political leadership in non-democratic settings (Frantz & Stein, 2012, p. 299). The institutions of strong party dominance and dynastic monarchy – through their often more collective forms of rule – not only facilitate the more stable exercise of power, mitigation of conflict, and power transition, as a consequence of which they are generally more balanced and durable than military or personalist rule; they also embed their leaders in a broader network of institutions and groups of elites, and are overall better equipped to constrain the autocrat from exercising unmitigated power. These regime-type differentiations suggest that the level of a leader's structural embeddedness is in the end an empirical question that needs to be studied on a comparative, case-by-case basis rather than solely through the lens of ideal-typical depictions.

Comparative Political Leadership: Implications for International Research

As the study of political leadership in both democracies and autocracies has shown, international research on political leadership and related themes (e.g., followership and elites) that directly compares both democracies and non-democracies across a variety of world regions has been scarce due to the distinct institutional and structural differences of political systems within which the respective leaders are embedded and act. While the distinction between leaders of democracies and rulers of autocracies is essential in both normative and actual terms, Masciulli et al. (2016b) point out that "if we decided to limit the studied universe of leaders by weeding out all tyrants, egoistic 'power-wielders' and morally deficient individuals, the remaining number of cases might be too few from which to draw any meaningful conclusions" (p. 10).

In this regard, these different institutional contexts are more complex, dynamic and often non-linear in their leader-environment relations than their ideal-typical depictions suggest, as touched on above. A direct comparison indicates that both regime types need leaders and that leaders need legitimacy, though they have to gain and maintain it through different means and strategies. In non-democratic settings, leaders have the power to co-opt followers and lead (if necessary) by acclamation, while leaders of democratic settings have to interactively engage with followers. In either case, their actual performance needs to be studied in-depth rather than evaluated through ideal types of regimes.

Thus, rather than focusing on the institutional designs as such, as is often done in political science, a closer study of the specific structural dynamics that leaders face may contribute to a reciprocal conversation between leadership scholars of both democracies and autocracies, allowing for the meaningful study of the different patterns of performance that both democratic and non-democratic leaders employ in their respective contexts. Even the most wide-ranging edited volumes on political leadership, *The Oxford Handbook of Political Leadership* (Rhodes & 't Hart, 2014), *Comparative Political Leadership* (Helms, 2012), *Personality, Political Leadership, and Decision Making: A Global Perspective* (Krasno & LaPides, 2015), and *The Ashgate Research Companion to Political Leadership* (Masciulli et al., 2016a), do not engage in direct comparative analyses, but rather feature individual chapters in which scholars focus either on democratic or non-democratic leaders and Western or non-Western regions separately. As previously discussed, this often stems from flawed presumptions about leadership based on the irrefutable institutional differences between the different political systems, often reinforced by a lack of availability of similar research materials. In addressing both these gaps, national economic development and, in particular, economic policy may provide fertile angles from which to engage in such comparative leadership research.

Economic Policy and Political Leadership: Moving International Research Forward

In the burgeoning scholarly literature on political leadership, the role of the national economy as a decisive institutional and situational arena for the exercise of leadership by national executives has gained relatively little attention. This is equally true in reverse. Economists in their study of economic growth have only rarely incorporated the perspective of individual actors into their analysis.

Although the literature on economic growth focuses on the organizational framework and "how the 'rules of the game' vary across countries, and [how] differences can be powerful sources in explaining different development paths," few theories of economic growth acknowledge and specifically focus on the impact of leadership (Jones, 2009, p. 2). While it has been acknowledged that the fact that "market mechanisms do not always work efficiently" does drive "the need for leadership in the [economic] context" (Zehnder et al., 2017, p. 68), a stronger research angle on agency and leadership is overdue in the disciplines of both economics and political science.

National executives across all states need to engage and deal with economic policy (Mulligan et al., 2004, pp. 71–72; Stockemer & Kailitz, 2020). "Governments are generally expected to promote prosperity, and many authoritarian leaders actively advertise their economic achievements" (Guriev & Treisman, 2020, p. 6). In this regard, economic performance is often used as a proxy to evaluate government performance as well as citizens' national approval and perceptions in international comparative analyses. In the words of Guriev and Treisman (2020), "In all types of regimes, citizens approve of their government more when they see the economy booming" (p. 18). This also means that the potential lack of data availability to study political leadership across regime types can at least partly be overcome, since many economic indices, from the World Bank indicators to the World Economic Forum's Global Competitiveness Index to surveys and approval polls, such as Gallup's, do have a global comparative reach. "Moreover, economic perceptions [among citizens], even though not perfectly accurate, do track objective indicators," thus enabling thorough comparative cross-regime analysis in the realm of political leadership (Guriev & Treisman, 2020, p. 31).

Political leaders of both democracies and non-democracies are highly affected by the condition and development of their respective national economies and their economies' international interdependence through the global capitalist system. This renders the national economic context central to any national leader's structural environment and for any leader's performance and agency. Whereas a consensus might be easily reached on the objective of fighting extreme poverty by raising per capita income, the variety of objectives and means regarding economic development increases greatly with more improved and diversified living conditions. "Political leaders then face the choice between seeking consensus or imposing their own judgment; and their leadership may be more readily contested" (Arndt, 1984, p. 58). The supposedly easy target of higher economic growth entails major challenges for anyone holding executive office since there are many different potential avenues on how to pursue it (e.g., more production, higher productivity, greater investment, technological innovations etc.), and it is rarely clear which of various political strategies will be most effective in achieving them (Arndt, 1984, p. 58).

Understanding political institutions as the formal and informal rules of political and economic markets, "they structure the [policy] environment, providing agents different incentives to supply factors of production, to specialize, and to innovate" (Pinto & Timmons, 2005, p. 27). In particular, political institutions that are based on the rule of law and non-arbitrary legitimacy are better equipped to provide political certainty and constancy, crucial ingredients for economic development (Faust 2007a, p. 308, n. 2). In the long term, democracies have a positive effect on economic development due especially to their institutional stability, competitive inclusiveness and regulation of political succession (Acemoglu et al., 2019; Papaioannou & Siourounis, 2008; Magee & Doces, 2015, p. 223). Since economic growth is largely a step-by-step process, the positive correlation between democracy and economic development mainly derives from a country's regime record and long-term perspective with little or no "statistically significant effect on economic growth […] in a given year" (Gerring et al., 2005, p. 349).

At the same time, autocracies also vary in terms of structural leader-and-elite constellations; for instance, "broader ruling coalition[s] have incentives to mimic[] certain features of democra[tic]" institutions (Faust, 2007a, p. 312). Non-democratic leaders have substantial room for political maneuver not only concerning basic economic conditions but the direction and speed of economic development, especially when their economies are based on extracting mineral resources. The relatively stable power coalitions of some autocracies – e.g., single/dominant-party states and dynastic monarchies – have "an interest in overall economic growth because growth will [both] maximize the overall resources, from which [they] can extract [their] economic privileges", and help them to better maintain power and political as well as economic stability (Faust, 2007a, p. 312; Kailitz, 2012, pp. 515–16; Stockemer & Kailitz, 2020, pp. 723–724). Moreover, "it is easier to manipulate diffuse feelings of safety than to fool people about the prices they see in stores and the numbers on their paychecks" with "citizens' direct experience of changing wages, prices, and employment levels limit[ing] the power of censorship and propaganda" in autocracies (Guriev & Treisman, 2020, pp. 32, 34). Furthermore, economically wealthy non-Western countries such as Singapore or Qatar have subscribed to the Western capitalist system and are highly dependent on international market mechanisms (Kailitz & Stockemer, 2017, p. 339). Altogether, this variety of factors, including power coalitions, citizens' perceptions and international interdependence, indicate that autocratic leaders might be overall relatively more constrained in the context of economic policy and development than in other domains of society.

Conclusively, political leaders of both democracies and non-democracies are highly affected by the condition and development of their respective national economies and international interdependence, rendering the domain of economic policy central for cross-regime analysis of leaders. Not only is more economic data available across regime types, but authoritarian manipulation of followers' perceptions might be less pronounced in the economic than in other domains of society, allowing for stronger cross-regime comparative study of followership as well. In the words of Treisman (2014), "faster growth […] entrenches incumbent leaders, whether dictators or democrats" (p. 928).

Times of economic crisis highlight the significance of such contexts and reciprocal relations. Due to the pivotal effect of successful economies on leaders' legitimacy, both types of leaders face serious threats during times of economic crises, since both experience "conditions of uncertainty and ambiguity" with regard to their institutional and structural environments (De Clercy & Ferguson, 2016, p. 105). It is thus surprising that studies focusing on political leadership in precarious contexts have done so, yet again, mainly from the perspective of democratic settings (see, for example, De Clercy & Ferguson, 2016; Boin et al., 2005). Both democratic and "autocratic leaders seek to avert unrest, reiterate their authority, and deflect blame", as they endeavor to look competent in economic matters vis-à-vis followers and the national constituency as a whole (Windsor et al., 2014, p. 451). Studying in depth the different means and strategies that democratic and non-democratic leaders have at their disposal and employ during times of crisis is thus a fertile prospect for international leadership research.

On the one hand, the capacity of democracies to provide participation, deliberation and negotiation in policy-making processes as well as the rule of law is often more constrained and distorted during times of economic and financial market turmoil (Enderlein, 2013, p. 715): "the crisis becomes the excuse for any and all political agendas that can plausibly (or even implausibly) be linked to the crisis" (Zywicki, 2012, p. 202). Patterns of policymaking in democracies demonstrate that political executives tend to shift the *modus operandi* in less democratic directions during economic and financial crises (Enderlein, 2013, p. 715). Non-democratic rulers, by contrast, are more likely to mimic liberal-democratic institutions and/or make political and economic concessions when put under pressure and threatened with the loss of legitimacy (Windsor et al., 2014, p. 451). Economic upheavals are particularly likely to incentivize such shifts (Ezrow & Frantz, 2011, p. 102). In sum, economic crises that create substantial uncertainty regarding redistribution effects and long-term economic outcomes generate pressure to act on political leaders of any regime type (Morlino & Quaranta, 2016, p. 621). Whether and to what extent these likely shifts in the performance of political leaders indicate, for example, a trend toward an erosion of democracy in democratic settings, a trend toward democratization in non-democratic settings, or are of temporary nature without any long-term political or institutional repercussions will be a central question of future comparative leadership research.

In conclusion, despite "large-*n* statistical studies find[ing] it hard to capture the significance of the quality and style of particular political leaderships" (Brown, 2016, p. 6), the preceding points indicate that while the individual agency of heads of government and state needs to become a central feature in the analysis of regime types and economic development, the domain of economic policy provides a particularly bountiful field for the study of political leadership across regime types, specifically for tracing the various strategies and patterns of performance that both democrats and autocrats employ. In light of the substantial differences between democracies and autocracies that embed their political leaders in different institutional-structural environments, which has inhibited international comparative research of political leadership thus far, the focus on economic policy could substantially contribute in bridging that research gap.

Treating economic policy as a field in which to exercise political leadership as well as to legitimize one's leadership is a central strategy of political leaders across both democracies and non-democracies, albeit apparent through different modes and patterns of performance. How do heads of government and state address economic challenges? What economic policies and politico-economic strategies do they propose? How do their speeches and rhetoric differ in regard to the respective national or international economy? Through the variety of international economic indices, researchers can pinpoint the performance of political leaders with more objective data both in regard to national economic performance as well as governmental approval rates among citizens, which tend to be less biased with regard to the economic domain than other sectors (Guriev & Treisman, 2020).

While, for example, healthcare policy can differ significantly from country to country in terms of governmental prioritization, heavily depending on the extent of a country's investments in social welfare measures, economic policy, the condition and development of the national economy and its international interdependence are always central for political leaders of both democracies and autocracies. Considering diverse political systems, economic policy is thus both an essential tool to legitimize one's leadership in either a democracy or an autocracy, and a sectorial research angle that allows scholars to bridge the long-term research gap in the systematic study of political leadership across different political contexts, moving beyond the democratic/autocratic divide. Focusing on economic development would allow international leadership scholars to trace the various strategies and patterns of performance of both democrats and autocrats during their incumbencies, evaluating directly performance, impact and outcome – in short, the study of comparative political leadership.

Conclusion

While the comparative study of political leadership has so far largely been confined to analyses of either democracies or autocracies, this chapter has provided some considerations of the relationship between political leadership, regime type and economic policy that can contribute to the conceptualization of careful cross-regime studies of political leadership in the future, engaging scholars across the disciplines of political science and economics in interdisciplinary and international leadership research.

In doing so, this chapter has shown that both democracies and non-democracies need leaders and that leaders need legitimacy, though they have to gain and maintain it through different means and strategies. The trends of presidentialization/prime-ministerialization and personalization in democracies and single/dominant-party regimes and dynastic monarchies' growing desire for international legitimacy indicate that leader-environment relations across both regime types will become increasingly complex. The chapter has also pointed out that economic policy and inter alia national economic development are crucial fields where leadership through various means and strategies is exercised across regime types, opening a particularly fertile domain for careful cross-regime analysis of leadership performances. While scholars of international leadership research often encounter lack of systematic data availability across diverse political systems, the study of economic development across countries and regions is overall better equipped, providing central research resources for leadership scholars to pinpoint their analyses. The central relationship between political leadership and economic development, while often underestimated in both political science and economics, thus offers a tremendous research reservoir for future interdisciplinary scholarship of leadership. The time is ripe to move beyond the analysis of leaders' deaths as the signature impacting factor of national executives on economic growth, and investigate the complex relationship between agency, economy and regime type on a broader conceptual, international and interdisciplinary research basis.

Notes

1 The terms "autocracies" and "non-democracies" are used interchangeably in this chapter for variation in wording.
2 For the purpose of this chapter, the typology established by Geddes (1999) and updated by Geddes Wright and Frantz (2014) serves as the methodological point of reference, since their distinction of regime types focuses on "the rules that identify the group from which leaders can come and determine who influences leadership choice and policy" (i.e., distinction of 'leadership groups' within autocracies, p. 314). For other classifications of autocratic regime types, for example, see Kailitz (2013), who adds to the four-fold typology two further types of autocratic regime, namely ideocracy (a regime having a strong ideology) and electoral autocracy (where several parties compete with each other, though there are low levels of electoral integrity). See also Stockemer & Kailitz, 2020, pp. 714, 715, on this point. Lührmann Tannenberg and Lindberg (2018) distinguish between closed autocracies (no elections for the chief executive or the legislature) and electoral autocracies (de jure multiparty elections for the chief executive and the legislature) (pp. 62–63).

References

Acemoglu, D., Naidu, S., Restrepo, P., & Robinson, J. A. (2019). Democracy does cause growth. *Journal of Political Economy*, *127*(1), 47–100.

Arndt, H. W. (1984). The role of political leadership in economic development. *Canadian Journal of Development Studies*, *5*(1), 51–63.

Bennister, M., & 't Hart, P. (Eds.). (2017). *The leadership capital index: A new perspective on political leadership*. Oxford University Press.

Boin, A., 't Hart, P., Stern, E., & Sundelius, B. (2005). *The Politics of Crisis Management: Public leadership under pressure*. Cambridge University Press.

Brown, A. (2014). *The Myth of the Strong Leader: Political leadership in the Modern Age*. The Bodley Head.

Brown, A. (2016). Against the Führerprinzip: For collective leadership. *Dædalus*, *145*(3), 109–123.

Collinson, D. (2017). Critical leadership studies: A response to Learmonth and Morrell. *Leadership*, *13*(3), 272–284.

De Clercy, C., & Ferguson, P. A. (2016). Leadership in precarious contexts: Studying political leaders after the global financial crisis. *Politics and Governance*, *4*(2), 104–114.

Elgie, R. (1995). *Political leadership in liberal democracies*. Palgrave Macmillan.

Elgie, R. (2015). *Studying political leadership: Foundations and contending accounts*. Palgrave Macmillan.

Elgie, R. (2018). *Political leadership. A pragmatic institutional approach*. Palgrave Macmillan.

Enderlein, H. (2013). Das erste Opfer der Krise ist die Demokratie: Wirtschaftspolitik und ihre Legitimation in der Finanzmarktkrise 2008–2013. *Politische Vierteljahresschrift*, *54*(4), 714–739.

Ezrow, N., & Frantz, E. (2011). *Dictators and dictatorships: Understanding authoritarian regimes and their leaders*. Continuum.

Faust, J. (2007a). Autocracies and economic development: Theory and evidence from 20th-century Mexico. *Historical Social Research*, *32*(4), 305–329.

Faust, J. (2007b). Democracy's dividend: Political order and economic productivity. *World Political Science Review*, *3*(2), 1–26.

Frantz, E., & Stein, E. A. (2012). Comparative leadership in non-democracies. In L. Helms (Ed.), *Comparative political leadership* (pp. 292–314). Palgrave Macmillan.

Gandhi, J. (2008). *Political Institutions under dictatorship*. Cambridge University Press.

Gandhi, J., & Przeworski, A. (2007). Authoritarian institutions and the survival of autocrats. *Comparative Political Studies, 40*(11), 1279–1301.

Geddes, B. (1999). What do we know about democratization after twenty years? *Annual Review of Political Science, 2*, 115–144.

Geddes, B., Wright, J., & Frantz, E. (2014). Autocratic breakdown and regime transitions: A new data set. *Perspectives on Politics, 12*(2), 313–331.

Gerring, J., Bond, P., Barndt, W. T., & Moreno, C. (2005). Democracy and economic growth: A historical perspective. *World Politics, 57*(3), 323–364.

Gerring, J., Oncel, E., Morrison, K., & Pemstein, D. (2019). Who rules the world? A portrait of the global leadership class. *Perspectives on Politics, 17*(4), 1079–1097.

Gerschewski, J. (2013). The three pillars of stability: Legitimation, repression, and co-optation in autocratic regimes. *Democratization, 20*(1), 13–38.

Gerschewski, J. (2018). Legitimacy in autocracies: Oxymoron or essential feature? *Perspectives on Politics, 16*(3), 652–665.

Grimm, J, Koehler, K., Lust, E. M., Saliba, I., & Schierenbeck, I. (2020). *Safer field research in the social sciences.* SAGE Publications.

Gupta, V., & Van Mart, M. (2016). *Leadership across the globe.* Routledge.

Guriev, S., & Treisman, D. (2020). The popularity of authoritarian leaders: A cross-national investigation. *World Politics*, 1–38.

Helms, L. (2001). the changing chancellorship: Resources and constraints revisited. *German Politics, 10*(2), 155–168.

Helms, L. (2005). *Presidents, prime ministers, and chancellors: Executive leadership in western democracies.* Palgrave Macmillan.

Helms, L. (Ed.) (2012). *Comparative political leadership.* Palgrave Macmillan.

Helms, L. (2016). Democracy and innovation: From institutions to agency and leadership. *Democratization, 23*(3), 459–477.

Helms, L. (2019). When less is more: 'Negative resources' and the performance of presidents and prime ministers. *Politics, 39*(3), 269–283.

Herb, M. (1999). *All in the family: Absolutism, revolution, and democracy in the middle eastern monarchies.* State University of New York Press.

Hermann, M. (2005). Assessing leadership style: Trait analysis. In J. Post (Ed.), *The Psychological Assessment of Political Leaders* (pp. 171–212). University of Michigan Press.

Higley, J., & Pakulski, J. (2012). Elite and leadership change in liberal democracies. *Historical Social Research, 37*(1), 333–350.

Huskey, E. (2016). Authoritarian leadership in the post-communist world. *Dædalus, 145*(3), 69–82.

Ieraci, G. (2012). Government alternation and patterns of competition in europe: Comparative data in search of explanations. *West European Politics, 35*(3), 530–550.

Jogulu, U. D. (2010). Culturally-linked leadership styles. *Leadership & Organization Development Journal, 31*(8), 705–719.

Jones, B. F. (2009). National leadership and economic growth. In Palgrave Macmillan (Eds.), *The New Palgrave Dictionary of Economics.* Palgrave Macmillan. doi:10.1057/978-1-349-95121-5_2969-1.

Jones, B. F., & Olken, B. A. (2005). Do leaders matter? National leadership and growth since World War II. *Quarterly Journal of Economics, 120*(3), 835–864.

Kailitz, S. (2012). Macht der Autokratietyp einen Unterschied für das Wirtschaftswachstum? *Politische Vierteljahresschrift, Sonderheft, 47*, 500–527.

Kailitz, S. (2013). Classifying political regimes revisited: Legitimation and durability. *Democratization, 20*(1), 38–60.

Kailitz, S., & Stockemer, D. (2017). Regime legitimation, elite cohesion and the durability of autocratic regime types. *International Political Science Review, 38*(3), 332–348.

Kane, J., & Patapan, H. (2012). *The democratic leader: How democracy defines, empowers and limits its leaders.* Oxford University Press/Oxford Scholarship Online.

Karvonen, L. (2010). *The personalisation of politics: A study of parliamentary democracies.* ECPR Press.

Kellerman, B. (1984). Leadership as a political act. In B. Kellerman (Ed.), *Leadership: Multidisciplinary perspectives* (pp. 63–89). Prentice-Hall.

Körösényi, A. (2005). Political representation in leader democracy. *Government and Opposition, 40*(3), 358–378.

Krasno, J., & LaPides, S. (Eds.) (2015). *Personality, political leadership, and decision making.* Praeger.

Lake, D. A., & Baum, M. A. (2001). The invisible hand of democracy: Political control and the provision of public services. *Comparative Political Studies, 34*(6), 587–621.

Lobo, M. C., & Ferreira da Silva, F. (2018). Prime ministers in the age of austerity: An increase in the personalisation of voting behaviour. *West European Politics, 41*(5), 1146–1165.

Lührmann, A., Tannenberg, M., & Lindberg, S. I. (2018). Regimes of the world (RoW): Opening new avenues for the comparative study of political regimes. *Politics and Governance, 6*(1), 60–77.

Maerz, S. F. (2019). Simulating pluralism: The language of democracy in hegemonic authoritarianism. *Political Research Exchange, 1*(1), 1–23.

Magee, C. S. P., & Doces, J. A. (2015). Reconsidering regime type and growth: Lies, dictatorships, and statistics. *International Studies Quarterly, 59*(2), 223–237.

Mair, P. (2008). The challenge to party government. *West European Politics, 31*(1/2), 211–234.

Mair, P. (2013). *Ruling the void: The hollowing of western democracy.* Verso.

Masciulli, J., Molchanov, M. A., & Knight, W. A. (Eds.). (2016a). *The Ashgate research companion to political leadership.* Routledge.

Masciulli, J., Molchanov, M. A., & Knight, W. A. (2016b). Political leadership in context. In J. Masciulli, M. A. Molchanov, & W. A. Knight (Eds.), *The Ashgate research companion to political leadership* (pp. 3–30). Routledge.

Mattila, M., & Raunio, T. (2004). Does winning pay? Electoral success and government formation in 15 West European countries. *European Journal of Political Research, 43*(1), 263–285.

Morlino, L., & Quaranta, M. (2016). What is the impact of the economic crisis on democracy? Evidence from Europe. *International Political Science Review, 37*(5), 618–633.

Müller, H. (2020). *Political leadership and the European commission presidency.* Oxford University Press.

Mulligan, C. B., Gil, R., & Sala-i-Martin, X. (2004). Do democracies have different public policies than nondemocracies? *Journal of Economic Perspectives, 18*(1), 51–74.

Muna, F. A. (2011). Contextual leadership. A study of Lebanese executives working in Lebanon, the GCC countries, and the United States. *Journal of Management Development, 30*(9), 865–881.

Papaioannou, E., & Siourounis, G. (2008). Democratisation and growth. *Economic Journal, 118*(3), 1520–1551.

Peters, B. G., & Helms, L. (2012). Executive leadership in comparative perspective: Politicians, bureaucrats and public governance. In L. Helms (Ed.), *Comparative political leadership* (pp. 25–55). Palgrave Macmillan.

Pinto, P. M., & Timmons, J. F. (2005). The political determinants of economic performance: Political competition and the sources of growth. *Comparative Political Studies, 38*(1), 26–50.

Poguntke, T., & Webb, P. (2005). The presidentialization of politics in democratic societies: A framework for analysis. In T. Poguntke & P. Webb (Eds.), *The presidentialization of politics: A comparative study of modern democracies* (pp. 1–25). Oxford University Press.

Renwick, A., & Pilet, J.-B. (2016). *Faces on the ballot: The personalization of electoral systems in Europe.* Oxford University Press.

Rhodes, R. A. W., & 't Hart, P. (Eds.) (2014). *The Oxford handbook of political leadership.* Oxford University Press.

Skocpol, T., & Finegold, K. (1982). State capacity and economic intervention in the early new deal. *Political Science Quarterly, 97*(2), 255–278.

Stockemer, D., & Kailitz, S. (2020). Economic development: How does it influence the survival of different types of autocracy? *International Political Science Review, 41*(5), 711–727.

Svolik, M. W. (2009). Power sharing and leadership dynamics in authoritarian regimes. *American Journal of Political Science, 53*(2), 477–494.

Svolik, M. W. (2012). *The politics of authoritarian rule.* Cambridge University Press.

Tannenberg, M., Bernhard, M., Gerschewski, J., Lührmann, A., & von Soest, Christian. (2020). Claiming the right to rule: Regime legitimation strategies from 1900 to 2019. *European Political Science Review,* 1–18. doi:1 0.1017/S1755773920000363.

Treisman, D. (2014). Income, democracy, and leader turnover. *American Journal of Political Science, 59*(4), 927–942.

Tucker, R. C. (1995). *Politics as leadership.* University of Missouri Press.

Weber, M. ([1922] 1978). *Economy and society: An outline of interpretive sociology* (Vol. 1). University of California Press.

Windsor, L. C., Dowell, N., & Graesser, A. (2014). The language of autocrats: Leaders' language in natural disaster crises. *Risk, Hazards & Crisis in Public Policy, 5*(4), 446–467.

Zehnder, C., Herz, H., & Bonardi, J.-P. (2017). A productive clash of cultures: Injecting economics into leadership research. *Leadership Quarterly, 28*(2), 65–85.

Zywicki, T. (2012). Economic uncertainty, the courts, and the rule of law. *Harvard Journal of Law and Public Policy, 35*(1), 195–212.

6

Planning to Address Ethical Challenges of International Leadership Research

Gabrielle Blackman

Introduction

International leadership research contributes unique insights into our understanding of leadership attributes, behaviors and competencies across cultures (Brodbeck et al., 2007). It addresses questions such as how do leadership practices differ across cultures (House, 2004)? How well does transformational leadership style predict employee performance across countries (Crede, Jong, & Harms 2019)? What competencies must a leader possess to be effective in international settings (Caligiuri & Tarique, 2016)? Beyond comparative research, scholars examine global leadership within diverse, multi-cultural organizations (Osland, 2018), which often involves engaging with diverse organizational and operating practices, stakeholders and governments (Mendenhall, 2018). The global context increases the complex nature of leadership roles, particularly during a crisis, such as a worldwide pandemic (e.g., coronavirus (COVID-19)). Thus, an ongoing inquiry into leadership practices from the international perspective will ensure researchers maintain an accurate understanding of the factors involved, and practitioners have access to evidence-based recommendations.

Data collection and research collaborations across countries enable us to identify, develop, and analyze theories and frameworks that guide practice. Increased interests of researchers to work across borders (Cleary, 2013) also introduces opportunities to learn about cross-cultural and international leadership. However, international research brings challenges (Illinois State University, n.d.-a). Laws, policies, institutional regulations, and professional practice often differ across countries. Differences in social, economic, justice, cultural, religious and political factors also increase the complexity of international research (Anderson, 2011). For example, in many Muslim communities, a research participant's family members play a larger role in decision making than in other communities. The norm of family involvement in decision making requires a distinct approach to the research process, including allowing space for the participant's relative(s) to engage in the informed consent process (Packer, 2011). These factors make international leadership research both scientifically enriching and challenging to navigate. How do researchers plan and design studies to meet the ethical challenges involved?

Those planning and designing international leadership research must prepare at the profession field level (e.g., examining professional regulations and ethical standards in the country of interest), country-level (e.g., investigating laws, regulations and policies associated with research) and local-social level (e.g., exploring cultural, religious and social norms). Obtaining knowledge about ethical

DOI: 10.4324/9781003003380-6

issues and standards will contribute to effective planning and research design. Researchers can then develop ethical proposals and protocols that address their research population's socio-cultural needs and interests. Simultaneously, they can contribute to research and practice in significant ways. On a broader level, ethical research practices help ensure that international research continues, as local collaborators will be more likely to partner with researchers who maintain ethical standards (Steneck, 2011).

This chapter explores ethical factors researchers should consider when conducting international leadership research. International leadership research examines topics, concepts, and models in the leader/leadership and follower/followership domains studied from the international lens, including global leadership (Osland, 2018). It includes studies on participants residing in a country that differs from the researcher's country and studies involving cross-cultural comparisons. The information presented in this chapter will apply most directly to studies involving (a) social scientific frameworks, (b) empirical methods, (c) data collection from human participants and (d) direct collaborations among researchers from two or more countries. The information will be particularly useful to doctoral students, researchers who are inexperienced with international research or who want to add an international dimension to their studies, as well as experienced international researchers who want to examine the ethical dimensions of their research.

Many ethical issues, standards and principles apply to international leadership research. This chapter focuses on a select set of factors, chosen due to their relevance at the planning and design stages of international research, including institutional review boards (IRBs), informed consent, professional competencies, travel for research purposes and data-sharing in the context of international leadership research. This chapter provides examples and short cases to illustrate ethical issues. Researchers should consider these issues when planning and designing their studies, using them as starting points for anticipating other problems that may arise in their research. The short cases are based on or adapted from real events. To protect the privacy of individual researchers, the author uses pseudonyms.

Learning About Research Ethics

Research ethics are critical to ensuring responsible science and the protection of participants. Reviewing guiding documents and ethical principles and standards prescribed by one's profession prepares researchers to remain sensitive to emerging issues and situations that could pose ethical problems. Ethical sensitivity enables researchers to plan their research activities and design studies more effectively.

Table A6.1 provides a list of guiding documents and resources that will help researchers to understand ethical principles related to research (see Appendix). It includes guiding documents, such as the Belmont Report (National Commission for the Protection of Human Subjects of Biomedical and Behavioral Research, 1979), Declaration of Helsinki (World Medical Association, n.d.) and Nuremberg Code (National Institutes of Health, n.d.). It also includes resource portals and select country-specific ethical guidance pertaining to research with human subjects. Notable resources include "Ethics around Europe", an online portal to ethics-related resources for those in psychology residing or conducting research in European Union (EU) countries, with links to the ethics committee webpages for EU professional associations. Another resource, "The International Compilation of Human Research Standards", provides information about and links to research ethics agencies, laws, regulations and guidelines for over 100 countries. Also included is the "UNESCO Code of Conduct Social Science Research", which provides ethical standards for international research. The RESPECT Project provides ethical guidance for researchers in the EU exploring socio-economic issues. The country-specific resources in Table A6.1 include ethical guidance from a sample of countries, including Australia, Canada, Finland, Malaysia, Norway, Russia, South Africa, Sweden, Thailand and the United

States (US) (see Appendix). Starting with the guiding documents, researchers can use these resources as a starting point for learning about research ethics.

Guiding Documents

The history of research ethics is extensive. Some of the more influential moments in this history include the publication of the Nuremberg Code, Declaration of Helsinki and Belmont Report. Researchers should review these guiding documents to understand the general principles that underlie research ethics. Notably, within the Nuremberg Code, the Declaration of Helsinki and many professional ethics codes and standards related to research, we find an emphasis on research benefiting the research population.

Nuremberg Code

During World War II, Nazi scientists conducted studies that constituted war crimes, causing death and significant harm to those subjected to the research. These crimes contributed to an international focus on research ethics, culminating in the Nuremberg Code of 1949 (Annas, 2018). The Nuremberg Code comprises 10 principles to which researchers should adhere to protect research participants. The principles focus heavily on the protection of human participants. For example, the Code establishes guidelines for modern informed consent, posits that participants may leave a research study after it starts and explains that the benefits of participating in a study must outweigh the risks (National Institutes of Health, n.d.). While the authors developed the Nuremberg Code to address medical-related research, it has influenced ethical research in various disciplines, including the social sciences.

Declaration of Helsinki

The World Health Association (WMA) published the Declaration of Helsinki in 1964, last updating it in 2013. Like the Nuremberg Code, the WMA developed the Declaration for the context of medical research; however, it has influenced research in a wide range of fields. While it aligns with the Nuremberg Code, the Declaration is much more extensive. It includes a Preamble, 13 General Principles and principles regarding risks, burdens and benefits; vulnerable groups and individuals; scientific requirements and research protocols; research ethics committees; privacy and confidentiality; informed consent; and other aspects of research (WMA, 2013).

Belmont Report

The U.S. National Commission for the Protection of Human Subjects of Biomedical and Behavioral Research published "The Belmont Report" in 1979. The Belmont Report presents three ethical principles that should underlie research: respect for persons, beneficence and justice. Respect for persons refers to the importance of preserving the dignity of individuals in research settings. Beneficence refers to the principle of helping, as opposed to harming, those affected by the research. Justice refers to the principle of fairness, including fairness in deciding who may participate in a research study. In addition to these principles, the Report outlines specific applications. It provides standards for informed consent, including criteria for information, comprehension and voluntariness. It has strategies for assessing the risks and benefits of research. Finally, it guides the fair selection of participants. The Commission provides specific methods for applying informed consent, limiting risks and maximizing benefits and obtaining research participants in ways consistent with the principles of respect for persons, beneficence and justice (Office of Human Research Protections, 2019).

Professional Codes of Ethics

Researchers should also examine their discipline's professional ethics code for additional guidance regarding researching in international settings. International partners may have different ethical standards, leading to differences in expectations, decision making and actions. Thus, an international researcher must also be aware of the ethical standards for research of their international research partners. If a researcher is conducting an empirical study with human participants in a country outside of their own, they must also examine research and professional ethics and legal considerations in the other country. Leadership scholars and researchers will find relevant codes within psychology and management, among other disciplines. Professional societies and government agencies or boards are often the sources of ethics codes (see Table A6.1 for examples).

For example, researchers with a psychology background will often find professional codes of ethics through their country's professional societies and government. There are commonalities across countries when comparing the ethics codes within this profession. For example, the Canadian Code of Ethics for Psychologists (Canadian Psychological Association, 2017), European Federation of Psychologists' Association's Meta-Code of Ethics (European Federation of Psychologists' Association, 2005), APA's (2012) Ethical Principles of Psychologists and Code of Conduct, South Africa's (2002) Ethical Code of Professional Conduct and the Code of Ethics of the Russian Psychological Society (2012) provide similar guidance on ethical standards for informed consent, conducting assessments, dealing with conflicts of interest, confidentiality and other aspects that would be relevant to researchers studying international leadership (see Table A6.1 in the Appendix for resources).

However, countries may differ in terms of the emphasis and level of detail they provide on certain standards of these codes. Differences may reflect each country's particular ethical concerns and values. Thus, while it may be challenging due to leadership's multidisciplinary nature, it is important to consult the most relevant codes of ethics based on one's profession and country.

Formal Training in Research Ethics

Researchers should consider formal ethics courses before planning an international research project. Research-focused universities often provide professional development workshops on research ethics. There are also well-established online providers of research ethics courses. Collaborative Institutional Training Initiative (CITI Program) (www.citiprogram.org) provides formal, online research ethics training to researchers. Researchers can choose from basic and advanced ethics courses, including some coursework related to international research. Completing a formal course on research ethics will prepare researchers to develop ethical sensitivity and competencies to formulate research plans and designs that ensure compliance.

Cross-cultural research partners may find it valuable to participate in a CITI Program together to establish shared expectations. Using CITI Program courses as a guide, researchers can adopt the same processes and principles related to important topics such as conflicts of interest, information security, working with human participants and research conduct. Large scale, international research programs with many researchers working together would benefit from experiencing the same formal training in these areas.

The CITI Program may provide a good starting point for researchers; however, it has limitations. CITI offers various webinars and courses on broad topics such as conflicts of interest, data management and privacy and confidentiality (CITI Program, n.d.-a). However, CITI does not currently offer a course that focuses exclusively on international research collaborations. They do offer a module (one lesson within a larger course) on international research, within their social-behavioral-educational (SBE) human subjects course. The module addresses international research collaborations, how to work within the local research context, as well as IRB and informed consent in international research

(CITI Program, n.d.-b). However, the training is limited in its breadth and depth of coverage. Another limitation is that, while available to international participants, CITI Program courses appear to be based on Western contexts, particularly the United States. For example, many courses focus specifically on U.S. laws and regulations. Researchers from the United States may find it helpful to complete courses on the Health Information Portability and Accountability Act (U.S. Department of Health and Human Services, n.d.) or the Revised Common Rule (Office of Human Research Protections, 2019). Researchers outside of the United States may find such modules do not apply to their research settings. Thus, researchers should use additional resources, such as those in Table A6.1, to learn more about international research ethics (see Appendix).

Planning for Institutional Review Boards

IRBs were first established in 1966 (National Institutes for Health, 2017), in response to guidelines in the Surgeon General's Directive on Human Experimentation (1966). Those conducting federally funded research in the United States must adhere to specific policies concerning the IRB process, and the U.S. federal policy currently influences the guidelines for the Protection of Human Subjects (i.e., "Common Rule"). Universities and institutions throughout the world now have IRBs in place. A typical IRB consists of five or more professionals from within and outside of the institution. The IRB reviews research proposals to assess the study's risks and benefits, providing feedback and, ultimately, an outcome to the researchers (Buelow, 2011). A result of "approval" is typically required for researchers to conduct their studies. IRBs ensure researchers protect participants and evaluate risks; however, some have criticized the IRB system (Buelow, 2011). For example, some suggest that reviewers on IRBs often lack cross-cultural competencies to assess international research (Nichols, 2016). Other issues arise when managing IRB processes across multiple international sites. On the contrary, others have found it challenging to work with participants in developing countries when there is no local IRB (Lescano et al., 2008).

Local IRBs

Typically, researchers conducting studies in a different country must seek local IRB approval, in addition to the approval of their home IRB. The University of Pittsburgh's Human Research Protection Office (n.d.) recommends that researchers work with a local collaborator to identify a local IRB. They suggest that researchers consult the Office of Human Research Protections (OHRP) Database for Registered IRB Organizations, IRBs, Federalwide Assurance and Documents (https://ohrp.cit.nih.gov/search/irbsearch.aspx?styp=bsc). Researchers can find details for IRBs throughout the world using the database. The university also recommends that researchers use the local Department of Ministries or government agencies when there is no local ethics review committee available.

Many universities guide researchers on how to proceed when a local IRB is unavailable. For example, Northwestern University recommends that researchers work with local experts or leaders within the community to obtain support for the research project in the absence of a local IRB. Researchers must document the steps they take to secure approvals from a local IRB or obtain support from experts or leaders in the community (Office of Research, n.d.). The University of Southern California provides similar guidance, suggesting that researchers obtain approval from an expert who is familiar with the local area's culture. In cases where there is minimal risk, the university may even accept a letter of approval from the research site (e.g., an agency or organization with which the researcher has partnered to collect data (Office of the Protection of Research Subjects, n.d.). Thus, researchers interested in conducting studies in an area that lacks a local IRB should explore other options, consulting their IRB to see what would be acceptable.

Bhat and Hedge (2006), of the United States, collected data from participants of "an isolated village" in India (p. 535). Before conducting the study, the researchers submitted their proposal to Princeton University's IRB. They also attempted to locate a local IRB but could not find one. The authors did not disclose the village name and, by now, there may be a local IRB available to support research in that village. The researchers adapted their approach to ensure that their plans represented their participants' needs.

They recommend three principles upon which other researchers could establish strategies in the absence of a local IRB. Firstly, they suggest that researchers submit their proposals to at least one IRB and provide information about the participants' culture and context to the IRB. For example, a researcher planning an international study could request that an academic expert on the culture and context provide background information about the population to the IRB. Secondly, Bhat and Hedge (2006) suggest that an advocate for the local population provide subject-matter-expertise to the researchers *during* the planning stages. The advocate should provide information to the researchers regarding how procedures and methodological decisions may affect participants. Thirdly, the participants should have the opportunity to review the research proposal. Participants should provide insights into how the procedures would affect them. The authors note that this is also an opportunity for researchers to gain insight into how the study could benefit participants (Bhat & Hedge, 2006).

Notably, the authors emphasized that they anticipated not having a local IRB and planned to address this. They had previously examined the local environment during the planning stages. Thus, they could develop a plan to ensure they could conduct the study following ethical standards of the local area (Bhat & Hedge, 2006).

IRBs for Multiple Sites Research

Working on research involving multiple sites can slow the review process. One place may require evidence of IRB approval from another site before reviewing an IRB proposal. These requirements may cause delays simply because the proposal must be approved by one before submitting it to another. For example, researchers from Johns Hopkins Medicine would need to submit evidence of local IRB approval before applying for IRB approval through John Hopkins instead of simultaneously undergoing review at both institutions. Similarly, researchers at Illinois State University (ISU) collaborating within international organizations, such as the Peace Corps, would need approval from the Peace Corps before submitting their proposal to ISU (Illinois State University, n.d.-b). Sometimes the IRBs across research sites view the same research proposal differently; one place may approve the proposal, while another may require significant changes or reject the proposal outright (Musoba et al., 2014). Suppose the researcher obtains approval for their research protocol from the local IRB. The local IRB process takes four weeks. Once approved, they submit the research protocol to their university's IRB. However, their university IRB requests changes to the research procedures to minimize a potential threat to participants' anonymity. The researcher may then need to take the revised protocol back to the local IRB for a subsequent review. Even small issues that arise may add a significant amount of time to the IRB review process when multiple IRBs are involved.

Recently, in the United States, revisions to the Common Rule have helped mitigate these issues for those working on certain federally funded research. The regulations allow eligible researchers from multiple sites to submit their proposals to only one accepted IRB (Office of Human Research Protections, 2019). This change may serve as a model for IRBs in general and across countries in the future.

To avoid unexpected delays, collaborators should attempt to anticipate any aspects of their research proposals that may cause concern for their IRB; if possible, all research collaborators should consult with members of their IRBs about potential issues before finalizing their proposals. They should inquire about policies related to research in collaboration with others or on multiple sites.

Through careful planning and communicating with collaborators and IRBs, researchers can reduce the likelihood of unexpected obstacles with the IRB.

Planning for Ethical Informed Consent

Informed consent is one of the most emphasized practices of ethical research. Established in the Nuremberg Code in modern history, and elaborated upon since that time, this standard ensures that human participation in research is voluntary and with knowledge of the potential benefits and risks involved (NIH, n.d.). While the practice appears simple, the international context brings many obstacles to informed consent, such as language differences, literacy differences, the cross-cultural validity of consent and distribution methods. For example, those conducting qualitative studies may need to be particularly mindful of whether interview questions may elicit responses that could harm participants, considering cultural and political factors. Researchers should inquire with local collaborators and others with expertise on the culture regarding factors that may put participants at risk.

Informed Consent and Language Differences

Researchers planning to conduct international research should consider the language(s) spoken by their intended samples (Jack et al., 2014). With the support of local partners, they should carefully assess their research population's language characteristics to determine the most appropriate language and manner of communicating information throughout the consent process. This is particularly important in countries where participants may speak multiple languages, with varying fluency levels across them. For example, India recognizes 22 languages in the constitution, with 122 languages spoken by significant numbers of people (10,000 or more) (Office of the Registrar General, 2011). Generally, researchers should anticipate the language characteristics of their study population and obtain translated versions of the informed consent instead of having someone orally translate the form for each participant during data collection (University of California San Francisco, 2016).

Researchers who pursue translation of research materials should take precautions to ensure validity and accuracy. When planning a research study with a population that speaks a different language, researchers should work with a local collaborator or expert to review the translations to ensure the concepts espoused in the informed consent material translate accurately. For example, the researcher may obtain translations and back-translations of the informed consent form from another investigator in the host country. Researchers employed with universities may also obtain access to translation services at their universities. For example, the University of Arizona's National Center for Interpretation offers fee-based translation services to employees at the university (University of Arizona, n.d.). There are also reputable companies that provide translation services. For example, the University of California San Francisco (UCSF) offers a list of companies, such as The Language Bank (www.language-bank.com), for researchers who must translate study materials. The University also recommends including a notarized statement from the translator, in which the translator confirms that they are fluent in both languages (University of California San Francisco, 2017). Researchers planning to translate study materials should also check Table A6.2 for an additional resource: the GLOBE Project Translation Protocol. In their handbook, the GLOBE Foundation presents a systematic guide for establishing valid translations of study materials (see Appendix).

Guidance and best practices on survey translation is an evolving area. Interested researchers should consult de Jong and Mneimneh's (2021) chapter on survey design and implementation, as well as the Goerman et al. (2021) chapter on survey translation and data quality within this handbook. Researchers can use these resources, and those presented in this section to take steps towards ensuring accurate and appropriate survey translations.

Informed Consent and Literacy Differences

Another issue that relates to language and informed consent is the diversity of literacy rates across countries. In some countries, literacy rates are exceptionally low. Some participants cannot read an informed consent form with fluency (Sil & Das, 2017), and they may hesitate to self-identify as a person with reading challenges. They may agree to participate, but they have not based their decision on having read and understood the informed consent form. Researchers often communicate study information through a detailed, written document. Using a written method to communicate study information when participants lack literacy skills jeopardizes the validity of the informed consent process (Sil & Das, 2017). Researchers who are engaging in international leadership research should explore the literacy rates of the research population. Alternative methods for sharing the information in the consent form should be available for those with low literacy skills. For example, it may be appropriate for a representative of the participant to read the informed consent form to the participant (Sil & Das, 2017).

Informed Consent and Indigenous Communities

According to cross-cultural research expert Cleary (2013), research involving indigenous populations must begin with the community's agreement. Ideally, researchers and community leaders cultivate a relationship and then the agreement. Based on interviews with international researchers, Cleary highlights that researchers should establish research plans with their host communities. The community must be aware of research plans and agree to them. Gaining approval at the community level may be a lengthy process, as there may be multiple layers of people the researcher should consult (Cleary, 2013). For example, Abdel-Messih (2010) describes how in Egypt, the consent process would involve several layers. First, the researcher should consult with the community or religious leader (e.g., the Imam). If the leader approves, the researcher would consult with the heads of families for the potential participants. Finally, researchers would present the research opportunity to the potential participants. Researchers would be most successful in obtaining these consents if they involve the community in the research planning and protocol development process. The reason is that cultural characteristics can be challenging to consider when planning and designing the research without the support of the community (Abdel-Messih, 2010).

Table A6.2 provides examples of resources researchers can consult when planning studies that involve Indigenous peoples (see Appendix). Across the resources, a major theme emerges regarding the need to respect the indigenous community's culture when conducting research. The Australian Institute of Aboriginal and Torres Strait Islander Studies (AIATSIS) outlines 14 ethical principles, emphasizing the interactions between these communities and researchers. For example, Principle 4 involves the "Rights in the traditional knowledge and traditional cultural expressions of Indigenous peoples must be respected, protected and maintained." Similarly, the National Health Council of Brazil's guidelines involving Indigenous people states that researchers must demonstrate respect for the worldviews, beliefs and language of Indigenous communities involved in research (National Health Council of Brazil, 2000). The University of Alaska Fairbanks (UAF) emphasizes the need for researchers working with Indigenous Alaskan communities to demonstrate respect for the cultural traditions of the community (University of Alaska Fairbanks, n.d.). Another common theme that emerges is that conducting research with Indigenous populations often involves non-traditional consent procedures.

Table A6.3 includes a resource from the World Health Organization (WHO) that shows an example of a community consent form. Researchers could consult this example when developing consent procedures for an Indigenous community. It also includes an example agreement resource from WHO, which researchers could consult when planning research with an Indigenous community (see Appendix).

Cross-Cultural Validity of Informed Consent

Some authors argue that the standards for informed consent common in Western countries are inappropriate for other settings. Krogstad et al. (2010) argues that informed consent criteria do not align with the decision-making approaches, norms and characteristics of some in developing countries. For example, informed consent is directed at the individual participant, while many cultures would make decisions regarding participation at the community level (e.g., with elders or community leaders making decisions on behalf of community members).

In some cultures, signing one's name has a distinct meaning and is reserved for specific functions; thus, signing one's name to an informed consent form may seem inappropriate to some participants (Krogstad et al., 2010). For example, Abdel-Messih (2010) explains that researchers may find it difficult to elicit signatures on consent forms in Egypt. Signatures are reserved for a select few documents (e.g., birth certificates). Despite agreeing to participate, participants may not be willing to sign their names to informed consent forms. One way to overcome this challenge is to request that participants orally express their agreement to participate, with the researcher recording the oral agreement to document consent (Abdell-Messih, 2011). Some university IRBs and government agencies provide guidance on how to verify informed consent when working with populations unable to sign a consent form. For example, the National Institute for Research in Reproductive Health (2017) of India provides standard operating procedures for recording the informed consent process to document consent. They provide guidance, such as to include the witness in the video frame throughout the full informed consent process when video recording a participant's oral consent to research.

Informed Consent and Employees

Those researching leadership often work within organizations to collect data. Often, this involves collecting data from employees. Researchers conducting international studies within organizations should consider the potential risks regarding coercion, privacy, confidentiality, undue rewards and misconceptions regarding voluntary versus mandatory participation (University of Pittsburgh Human Resource Protection Office, n.d.).

A research scientist was visiting an employment site on an arranged data collection visit in the United States. She put informed consent forms on the conference room tables. As the employees arrived, they began to review the documents. Then, the research scientist reviewed the informed consent forms verbally with the employees. Some employees started laughing when she explained that their participation was voluntary. When she inquired about their response, one employee explained that their supervisor told them they had to participate in the research. Consistent with her informed consent form, the researcher spent several minutes reassuring the employees that the study was voluntary. She would not disclose the names of employees who chose not to participate. One employee left the room, and the research scientist wondered whether others secretly wanted to do the same. On her next data collection trip, she discussed these issues with the host prior to data collection to ensure they were on the same page regarding voluntary participation.

According to the U.S. Department of Health and Human Services (n.d.), researchers must avoid coercing or unduly influencing people to participate. Coercion and undue influence involve presenting rewards or threats that would affect the employee's decision to participate in the research in a way that undermines the notion of volunteerism and autonomy. For example, it would be unethical for a manager to threaten employees with poor working conditions should they decline to participate. Researchers conducting studies in international settings must be aware of power dynamics that could give the impression of an undue reward or punishment. Researchers must also examine relevant laws and policies for the country within which they will collect data (see Table A6.1 in the Appendix). What regulations are in place, if any, to protect employees? Do you anticipate contradictions between what you state in the informed consent form and how an employer presents the research opportunity to their employees?

Planning for Professional Competency Requirements

Professional competencies and regulations are also relevant for those planning to conduct international leadership research. Countries vary in their policies and laws governing professional practice (e.g., Bourgeault & Grignon, 2013). Some research activities may fall under restrictions. For example, national and local governing bodies often regulate professional competencies involved in psychological testing and assessment.

Dr. Atalay has a background in organizational psychology and resides in Turkey. Through a mutual connection, Dr. Atalay meets Dr. Taylor, a registered psychologist who lives in Australia. Dr. Taylor requests Dr. Atalay's assistance with a leadership project. Initially, Dr. Atalay did not contribute to data collection. However, as new phases of the research began, he was invited to facilitate a series of focus groups and administer psychological tests to a sample of managers in Australia. Dr. Taylor assured Dr. Atalay that she would handle the IRB process and that Dr. Atalay should focus on travel arrangements.

However, Dr. Atalay later learned through a colleague that the host country, Australia, regulates who can administer and use psychological tests. Dr. Atalay examined these requirements further and sought advice from a reputable authority. He determined he should refrain from collecting data because he was not a registered psychologist in Australia. While he decided this before the data collection events, Dr. Atalay had already made travel arrangements. Dr. Taylor suggested that Dr. Atalay was overreacting and complained about the inconvenience the situation was causing. The events affected the trust and team dynamics within the research team.

Researchers can often avoid ethical issues by assessing the potential ethical risks involved before committing to a project or research plan. In this case, Dr. Taylor should have been aware that it would be unethical for Dr. Atalay to collect data and refrained from inviting him to do so. Still, Dr. Atalay should have evaluated the opportunity further, considering professional and ethical responsibilities, before committing to it. While the regulations were unexpected, Dr. Atalay likely could have discovered them sooner. If he had taken time to consider whether there may be ethical and legal issues associated with the plan, he likely would have found this information sooner and refrained from committing to data collection.

Planning for Ethical Travel When Conducting International Research

When developing international research plans, researchers should examine the travel policies and laws of any countries they plan to visit when conducting their studies. They should learn about each country's entry and visa requirements. Some countries have more rigid entry requirements compared to others, and countries may have different entry requirements depending on the visitor's country. For example, South Africa, like other countries, allows residents of many countries to visit visa-free, but for different durations of time (Department: Home Affairs Republic of South Africa, 2020). Some countries also have arrangements with others that allow residents of either country to travel more freely between the two (e.g., Australia and New Zealand; New Zealand Government, 2020). Many countries require researchers to enter on a particular visa category other than a tourist visa, which may involve greater scrutiny and longer wait periods. For example, India (Government of India, n.d.), Spain (Consulate of Spain, n.d.) and Thailand (Royal Thai Embassy, n.d.) require research visas. These requirements may vary depending on the type of research and the length of stay. For example, a researcher visiting France partnering with an institution may be eligible for a "Passeport Talent" visa, allowing them to stay for up to four years. A visiting doctoral candidate may enter on a long-stay visa. In some cases, depending on their sponsorship, a doctoral candidate may enter on a student visa and engage in paid research (Campus France, 2017). Some countries closely monitor international research initiatives, and researchers should prepare for obstacles, should their research plans come under scrutiny. It would be unethical to enter a country on a visa that does not allow research if one plans to conduct research there.

Researchers should also be aware that visa and travel restrictions may arise during crises, such as the global COVID-19 pandemic. For example, during the COVID-19 pandemic, countries worldwide restricted travel (U.S. Department of State, 2020). These restrictions may make it difficult or impossible for researchers to travel to other countries to conduct research.

Case of the Wrong Visa

Alder is a doctoral student who planned to travel to India for one month to collect data for his dissertation study. Before his trip, Alder was quite busy working on his dissertation and juggling work and family responsibilities. A few weeks before his departure, he realized that he never applied for a visa to travel. His host had provided him with an invitation letter and other documents he would need to lodge his application several months ago. However, Adler did not realize how long the process would take and put it aside for a later date. Adler felt he had an obligation to travel as planned because his host had arranged for his arrival. He decided to travel on an eTourist visa and entered the country without any problems. However, his host later became aware of the visa situation. The situation created distrust in the working relationship, and the researcher put the sponsor at risk for allowing someone to conduct research without the appropriate permissions to do so.

Due to a lack of planning, Adler put himself into a position where he felt pressured to look for unethical alternatives. He made an unethical choice to address the situation. Through careful and early planning, Adler could have applied for the appropriate visa and not risked his reputation or jeopardized his host. Likewise, if he had been honest with his host after realizing the time constraints would not allow him to apply for a proper visa, he could have rescheduled the trip. This would have allowed Adler to secure an appropriate visa, uphold ethical standards, protect his host and maintain the relationship with his collaborators.

Political Climate and Research Travel

Ramzi, a citizen of Morocco residing in the United States, was completing his doctoral studies when changes to U.S. policies caused him to change his international research plans. He originally planned to collect data in Canada. At the time, U.S. President Trump issued Executive Order 13769 that prohibited people from several African and Middle Eastern countries (i.e., Chad, Iraq, Iran, Libya, Sudan, Somalia, Syria and Yemen) countries from entering the United States (White House, 2017a). Despite legally residing in the United States, Ramzi was concerned that he might be unable to re-enter if he traveled to Canada to collect data. Thus, he decided to collect data online, using the Zoom (www.zoom.com) video-based communication platform. This example illustrates how the political climate can bring challenges to international leadership researchers. A related example is President Trump's Proclamation on the Suspension of Entry that specifically prevents some graduate students and researchers of China from entering the United States (White House, 2020b). The political climate may affect whether it is possible and safe to travel to collect data or to meet with research collaborators.

Planning for Ethical Data Sharing

Researchers engaged in international research commonly collaborate with partners, such as researchers at other institutions, organizations or companies. Collaborations may require researchers to share information, including participant data. For example, researchers collaborating with the GLOBE Foundation enter a data-sharing arrangement with the foundation (GLOBE Foundation, n.d.). Some leadership journals, such as The Leadership Quarterly, encourage researchers to share their data publicly (e.g., through direct links between the research article and data repositories) (Elseveir, 2020). Data sharing has become an increasingly common practice, with some institutes adopting ethical standards concerning the value of sharing data for the progress of science (NIH, 2020).

Data sharing requires careful planning. Participant data may be private, sensitive, classified or otherwise confidential. Researchers have an ethical responsibility to share data in secure ways and establish safeguards over the use and future use of data (American Psychological Association, 2012). Collaborations involving researchers and partners from multiple countries require additional sensitivity to data sharing matters as the norms, expectations and regulations surrounding data sharing may differ between collaborators. Thus, researchers planning to conduct international leadership research should establish protocols and plans for sharing information to prevent the misuse of data and protect participants. The first step in this process involves developing a data-sharing agreement.

Data-Sharing Agreements

Data-sharing agreements involve formal, often signed documents that detail how researchers and other collaborators will transfer data. These agreements have become increasingly common in the age of big data and open science. Researchers in medical fields and natural sciences commonly use data-sharing agreements amongst researchers, government bodies, companies and other entities. Social scientists are also turning to data-sharing agreements to facilitate responsible sharing.

A recent study by Polanin and Terzian (2019) examined researchers' perceptions of data sharing when data-sharing agreements are available. Their sample consisted of 247 researchers in the social sciences. They did not provide demographic information for the participants, which would have been helpful for determining whether there were international or cultural differences in the findings. Polanin and Terzian's study employed an experimental design in which they presented participants with the scenario that another researcher asked the participant to provide research data for a meta-analysis. In one condition, the participants received a data-sharing agreement, and in the other condition, participants received a standard data request. They provided participants in the data-sharing agreement condition with information about the primary investigator of the hypothetical meta-analysis study, rights and responsibilities of the parties involved, how the information would be stored and other details. The researchers were significantly more likely to share data when the requestor provided a data-sharing agreement (Polanin & Terzian, 2019).

International researchers may find this helpful when requesting access to data from international collaborators. Initiating a data-sharing agreement may increase the likelihood that international collaborators would share data, while facilitating the ethical transfer of data. An example of a research group that provides transparent information about data-sharing is the GLOBE Foundation. The GLOBE Foundation collaborates with hundreds of leadership researchers around the world. They clearly explain that when they partner with researchers, the GLOBE Foundation maintains ownership of the data associated with each researcher's country. They also explain that they will share the data that researchers from each country collect with the respective researcher (e.g., a researcher collecting data for the project in Kenya would receive the data set of leader responses drawn from Kenya) (GLOBE Foundation, n.d.). Having data-sharing information up front, potential collaborators can make informed decisions about whether to partner with the GLOBE Foundation.

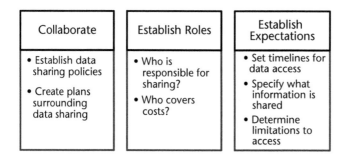

Figure 6.1 A Summary of APA's (2015) Best Practices for Data Sharing

Data-Sharing: Ethical Practices

In 2015, the American Psychological Association (APA) assembled experts to establish best practices for data sharing (see Figure 6.1). Acknowledging the benefits of data sharing to science, the APA provided specific strategies researchers should use to share data in a secure, responsible manner. Firstly, they note that researchers should work with collaborators to establish policies and plans surrounding data sharing. Researchers should clearly define the conditions and expectations surrounding their plans and agreements. Examples of details to include are timelines for data access, the specific information to be shared, limitations to access and conditions surrounding access. Researchers should consider who will take responsibility for sharing the data through a proper repository and who should cover the costs involved with data sharing (American Psychological Association, 2015).

To prepare for data sharing, researchers should consider what they tell participants during the informed consent process. If a collaborator or other researchers may request access to the data, the researcher should consider this when planning the informed consent procedures. Researchers should avoid suggesting that they will only use the data in the present study (NIH, 2020). Researchers may opt to use language in the informed consent form that ensures participants are aware that other researchers may view data. Disclosing the potential for data sharing will ensure the consent process does not pose obstacles should the researcher decide to share the data with collaborators.

Ethical Issues in Sharing Qualitative Data

Some leadership scholars use a mix of quantitative and qualitative data collection methods. Quantitative data involves information with numeric values, such as numeric responses to a survey. In contrast, qualitative data include information that is non-numeric, such as written information, speeches, recordings and similar sources of data (Bordens & Abbott, 2017). When sharing data, researchers must consider the nature of qualitative data, such as video recordings, which may significantly threaten participant anonymity (American Psychological Association, 2015). In some cases, participants may already feel reluctant to share information in qualitative studies. For example, Voldnes et al. (2014) describe the challenges researchers face when conducting qualitative studies in Russia. Leaders are often reluctant to participate in interviews due to distrust in the research process and researchers' motives (Voldnes et al., 2014). Researchers must be mindful of their participants' privacy, particularly if data sharing is likely and the political climate or other contextual factors require heightened sensitivity to safeguard participants.

Experts note that "for international research, policies and procedures for sharing data should be sensitive to the regulations, norms, and other socio-cultural characteristics of the setting in which the data are collected" (American Psychological Association, 2015, p. 2). Researchers should be particularly mindful of qualitative data that may disclose information that could harm participants in international settings. For example, suppose the research topic relates to behaviors that may be illegal or socially taboo in the research country or cultural environment. In that case, researchers should consider whether sharing data could bring harm to participants (DuBois et al., 2018).

Researchers who are planning international research should consider these issues before committing to a data-sharing plan or agreement. For example, a researcher interviewing leaders about their responses to the COVID-19 pandemic might consider whether information shared could have legal ramifications if made public. Considering the worst-case scenario, would a potential breach of data security lead to harm to participants? Suppose a research collaboration is contingent upon sharing data. In those cases, researchers should carefully investigate the nature of the data, the degree to which the researcher can maintain the anonymity of participant data, the credentials of collaborators, the credibility of collaborators, and whether collaborators would uphold commitments to maintain this anonymity and confidentiality after you share the data.

DuBois et al. (2018) recommend that researchers take the following precautions when sharing qualitative data in data storage centers. Firstly, researchers should ensure there is no identifying information included with the data. This recommendation goes beyond reviewing a dataset for unintentional inclusion of characteristics that could lead someone to guess the identity of the participant(s). Researchers must thoughtfully consider whether the nature of the data (i.e., audio recordings) and the information participants provide could jeopardize participant anonymity. Secondly, the authors recommended that the information be maintained securely through encryption methods. Researchers should also attempt to collect informed consent from participants, particularly when it is not possible to maintain confidentiality (DuBois et al., 2018). Researchers can use these steps to help ensure that data sharing is a secure, ethical process.

Conclusion

Researchers must adhere to a complex web of legal and ethical standards in any research setting, and this complexity increases within the international research context. The dilemmas common in this domain can be novel, complex and multi-faceted. Failing to adhere to legal and ethical expectations could lead to various consequences such as distrust, loss of credibility, legal liability, professional or licensure consequences, fines and unintended harm to participants or collaborators. Ethics resources and guiding documents help well-intentioned leadership scholars understand important requirements, such as informed consent, to ensure ethical and legal compliance. These resources also prepare researchers to be ethically sensitive to new or unexpected ethical issues that may emerge, allowing them to design studies that align with ethical standards. By adhering to ethical and legal frameworks, researchers can secure trusting relationships with stakeholders, maintain credibility and research partnerships (Steneck, 2011), demonstrate respect for participants and their communities, ensure data collection and interpretation accuracy and ensure that all stakeholders benefit from the research.

This chapter highlights ethical issues for researchers planning and designing international leadership research. Researchers can use the information provided to gain insight into the types of ethics-related problems that may emerge. One cannot underestimate the importance of planning for ethical research. Taking time to plan, thoughtfully assessing the research context and anticipating risks and ethical issues enables researchers to address ethical considerations proactively much of the time. By understanding the importance of ethics in research and establishing a firm commitment to uphold ethical standards, researchers will be ready to make ethical decisions when faced with unexpected issues.

References

Abdel-Messih, I. A. (2010). In M. S. Anderson & N. H. Steneck (Eds.), *International research collaborations: Much to be gained, many ways to get in trouble* (pp. 251–260). Routledge.

American Psychological Association. (2012). *Ethical principles of psychologists and code of conduct*. https://www.apa.org/ethics/code/.

American Psychological Association. (2015). *Data sharing: Principles and considerations for policy development*. https://www.apa.org/science/leadership/bsa/data-sharing-report.pdf.

Anderson, M. S. (2011). What can be gained and what can go wrong in the context of different national research environments. In M. S. Anderson & N. H. Steneck (Eds.), *International research collaborations: Much to be gained, many ways to get in trouble*(pp. 3– 8). Routledge.

Annas, G. J. (2018). Beyond Nazi war crimes experiments: The voluntary consent requirement of the Nuremberg Code at 70. *American Journal of Public Health*, *108*(1), 42–46. doi:10.2105/AJPH.2017.304103

Bhat, S. B., & Hedge, T. T. (2006). Ethical international research on human subjects research in the absence of local institutional review boards. *Journal of Medical Ethics*, *9*, 535–536.

Bordens, K. & Abbott, B. (2017). *Research design and methods: A process approach*. McGraw-Hill Education.

Bourgeault, I. L., & Grignon, M. (2013). A comparison of the regulation of health professional boundaries across OECD countries. *European Journal of Comparative Economics*, *10*(2), 199–223.

Brodbeck, F. C., Chhokar, J. S., House, R. (2007). Culture and leadership in 25 societies: Integration, conclusions, and future directions. In R. House, J. Brodbeck, F. C. Chkokar, & J. Singh (Eds.), *Culture and leadership across the world: The GLOBE book of in-depth studies of 25 societies* (pp. 1023–1099). Psychology Press.

Buelow, P. A. (2011). The institutional review board: A brief history of attempts to protect human subjects in research. *Clinical Nurse Specialist: The Journal for Advanced Nursing Practice*, *25*(6), 277–280.

Caligiuri, P., & Tarique, I. (2016). Cultural agility and international assignees' effectiveness in cross-cultural interactions. *International Journal of Training & Development*, *20*(4), 280–289. doi:10.1111/ijtd.12085.

Campus France. (2017). *Research in France: Come to France*. https://ressources.campusfrance.org/pratique/guides/en/choisir_recherche_en.pdf.

Canadian Psychological Association. (2017). *Canadian code of ethics for psychologists* (4th ed.). https://cpa.ca/docs/File/Ethics/CPA_Code_2017_4thEd.pdf.

CITI Program. (n.d.a). *Explore our courses*. https://about.citiprogram.org/en/courses/.

CITI Program. (n.d.b). *Social-behavioral-educational (SBE) basic*. https://about.citiprogram.org/en/course/human-subjects-research-2/.

Cleary, L. M. (2013). *Cross-cultural research with integrity: Collected wisdom from researchers in social settings*. Palgrave Macmillan. doi:10.1057/9781137263605.

Crede, M., Jong, J., & Harms, P. (2019). The generalizability of transformational leadership across cultures: A meta-analysis. *Journal of Managerial Psychology*, *34*(3), 139–155. doi:10.1108/JMP-11-2018-0506.

Consulate of Spain in Washington. (n.d.). *Visa information and requirements*. http://www.exteriores.gob.es/Consulados/WASHINGTON/en/Consulado/Pages/Visas.aspx.

de Jong, J. A., & Mneimneh, Z. N. (2022). Survey design and implementation considerations in international and cross-national research. In Y. Tolstikov-Mast, F. Bieri, & J. Walker (Eds.), *Handbook of International and Cross-Cultural Leadership Research Processes*. Routledge/Taylor and Francis.

Department: Home Affairs Republic of South Africa. (2020). *Countries exempt from South African visas*. http://www.dha.gov.za/index.php/immigration-services/exempt-countries.

DuBois, J. M., Strait, M., & Walsh, H. (2018). Is it time to share qualitative research data? *Qualitative Psychology*, *5*(3), 380–393. doi:10.1037/qup0000076.

Elseveir. (2020). *The leadership quarterly: An international journal of political, social and behavioral science*. https://www.elsevier.com/journals/the-leadership-quarterly/1048-9843?generatepdf=true.

European Federation of Psychologists' Association. (2005). *Meta-code of ethics*. http://ethics.efpa.eu/metaand-model-code/meta-code/.

GLOBE Foundation. (n.d.). *GLOBE 2020: Country co-investigator handbook*. https://globeproject.com/about?page_id=cci#globe2020_cci.

Goerman, P., Meyers, M., Kephart, K., & O'Brien, A. (2022). The relevance of survey translation and data quality in leadership studies: How to Include Diverse voices in survey design. In Y. Tolstikov-Mast, F. Bieri & J. Walker (Eds.), *Handbook of International and Cross-Cultural Leadership Research Processes*. Routledge/Taylor and Francis.

Government of India. (n.d.). *Visa categories*. https://indianvisaonline.gov.in/visa/visa-category.html.

House, R. (2004). Illustrative examples of GLOBE findings. In R. J. House, P. J. Hanges, M. Javidan, P. Dorfman, & V. Gupta (Eds.), *Culture, leadership, and organizations: The GLOBE study of 62 societies* (pp. 3–9). SAGE.

Illinois State University. (n.d.a). *IRB international research requirements*. https://research.illinoisstate.edu/ethics/human-subjects/international/.

Illinois State University. (n.d.b). *Local research and ethics review*. https://research.illinoisstate.edu/ethics/human-subjects/international/local/.

Institute for Employment Studies. (n.d.). *The RESPECT Project*. http://www.respectproject.org/main/index.php.

Jack, C., Singh, Y., & Mars, M. (2014). Language, cultural brokerage and informed consent – will technological terms impede telemedicine use? *South African Journal of Bioethics & Law*, 7(1), 14.

Krogstad, D. J., Diop, S., Diallo, A., Mzayek, F., Keating, J., Koita, O. A., & Touré, Y. T. (2010). Informed consent in international research: The rationale for different approaches. *The American Journal of Tropical Medicine and Hygiene*, 83(4), 743–747. doi:10.4269/ajtmh.2010.10-0014.

Lescano, A. R., Blazes, D. L., Montano, S. M., Kochel, T., Moran, Z., Lescano, A. G., & Martin, G. J. (2008). Supporting the creation of new institutional review boards in developing countries: The U.S. Naval Medical Research Center Detachment experience. *Military Medicine*, 173(10), 975–977.

Mendenhall, M. E. (2018). Leadership and the birth of global leadership. In M. E. Mendenhall, J. Osland, A. Bird, & G. Oddou (Eds.), *Global leadership: Research, practice, and development* (3rd ed.). Routledge, Taylor & Francis Group.

Musoba, G. D., Jacob, S. A., & Robinson, L. J. (2014). The Institutional Review Board (IRB) and faculty: Does the IRB challenge faculty professionalism in the social sciences? *Qualitative Report*, 19(51), 1–14.

National Commission for the Protection of Human Subjects of Biomedical and Behavioral Research. (1979). *The Belmont Report: Ethical principles and guidelines for the protection of human subjects of research*. https://www.hhs.gov/ohrp/sites/default/files/the-belmont-report-508c_FINAL.pdf.

National Health Council of Brazil. (2000). *Resolution N#304*. http://conselho.saude.gov.br/resolucoes/2000/Res304_en.pdf.

National Institutes for Health. (2020). *Data sharing*. https://grants.nih.gov/faqs#/data-sharing.htm?anchor=question50619

National Institutes of Health. (n.d.). *The nuremberg code*. https://history.nih.gov/research/downloads/nuremberg.pdf.

National Institutes for Health. (2017). *Timeline of laws related to the protection of human subjects*. https://history.nih.gov/about/timelines_laws_human.html.

National Institute for Research in Reproductive Health. (2017). *Audio visual (AV) recording of informed consent process*. http://www.nirrh.res.in/wp-content/uploads/2018/08/10-Audio-Video-Consent.pdf.

New Zealand Government. (2020). *Passport and visa when you go to Australia*. https://www.govt.nz/browse/leaving-nz/travel-or-move-to-australia/passports-and-visas-when-you-go-to-australia/.

Nichols, A. S. (2016). Research Ethics Committees (Recs)/Institutional Review Boards (Irbs) and the globalization of clinical research: Can ethical oversight of human subjects research be standardized? *Washington University Global Studies Law Review*, 15(2), 351.

Office of Human Research Protections. (2019). *The revised common rule's cooperative research provisions*. https://www.hhs.gov/ohrp/regulations-and-policy/single-irb-requirement/index.html.

Office of the Protection of Research Subjects. (n.d.). *International research*. https://oprs.usc.edu/irb-review/international-research/.

Office of the Registrar General, India. (2011). *Census of India: Language, India states, union, and territories*. https://www.censusindia.gov.in/2011Census/C-16_25062018_NEW.pdf.

Office of Research: Institutional Review Board Office. (n.d.). *IRB review of international research*. https://www.irb.northwestern.edu/irb-review-of-international-research-2/.

Osland, J. S. (2018). An overview of the global leadership literature. In M. E. Mendenhall, J. Osland, A. Bird, & G. Oddou (Eds.), *Global leadership: Research, practice, and development* (3rd ed.). Routledge, Taylor & Francis Group.

Packer, S. (2011). Informed consent with a focus on Islamic views. *Journal of the Islamic Medical Association of North America*, 43(3), 215–218.

Polanin, J. R., & Terzian, M. (2019). A data-sharing agreement helps to increase researchers' willingness to share primary data: Results from a randomized controlled trial. *Journal of Clinical Epidemiology*, 106, 60–69. doi:10.1016/j.jclinepi.2018.10.006.

Psychological Society of South Africa. (2007). *South African professional conduct guidelines in psychology 2007*. https://www.psyssa.com/wp-content/uploads/2016/12/SOUTH-AFRICAN-PROFESSIONAL-CONDUCT-GUIDELINES-IN-PSYCHOLOGY-2007-PsySSA_updated_01-12-2016pdf.pdf.

Royal Thai Embassy. (n.d.). *Visa: 11. Non immigrant visa – research and science "RS."* http://www.thaiembassy.org/dakar/en/services/4463/52524-11.-NON-IMMIGRANT-VISA---RESEARCH-AND-SCIENCE-&quo.html.

Russian Psychological Society. (2012). *Code of ethics of the Russian Psychological Society*. http://www.psyrus.ru/en/documents/code_ethics.php.

Sil, A., & Das, N. K. (2017). Informed consent process: Foundation of the researcher--participant bond. *Indian Journal of Dermatology, 62*(4), 380–386. doi:10.4103/ijd.IJD_272_17.

Steneck, N. H. (2011). Research integrity in the context of global cooperation. In M. S. Anderson & N. H. Steneck (Eds.), *International research collaborations: Much to be gained, many ways to get in trouble*(pp. 9–20). Routledge.

Surgeon General. (1966). *Surgeon General's directives on human experimentation.* https://history.nih.gov/research/downloads/Surgeongeneraldirective1966.pdf.

United States Department of Health and Human Services. (n.d.). *Informed consent FAQs.* https://www.hhs.gov/ohrp/regulations-and-policy/guidance/faq/informed-consent/index.html.

United States Department of Health and Human Services. (n.d.). *Summary of HIPAA security rule.* https://www.hhs.gov/hipaa/for-professionals/security/laws-regulations/index.html.

United States Office of Human Research Protections. (2019). *International compilation of human research standards.* https://www.hhs.gov/ohrp/sites/default/files/2019-International-Compilation-of-Human-Research-Standards.pdf.

United States Department of State. (2020). *COVID-19 country specific information.* https://travel.state.gov/content/travel/en/traveladvisories/COVID-19-Country-Specific-Information.html.

University of Alaska Fairbanks. (n.d.). *Research with indigenous peoples.* https://www.uaf.edu/irb/indigenous/

University of Arizona. (n. d.). *Translation services.* https://nci.arizona.edu/translation-request.

University of California San Francisco. (2017). *Consenting non-English speakers.* https://irb.ucsf.edu/consenting-non-english-speakers#translating.

University of California San Francisco. (2016). *Quick guide: Consenting non-English speaking subjects.* https://irb.ucsf.edu/consenting-non-english-speakers#translating.

University of Pittsburgh Human Resource Protection Office. (n. d.). *Research involving employees as research participants.* https://www.irb.pitt.edu/content/research-involving-employees-research-participants.

Voldnes, G., Grønhaug, K., & Sogn-Grundvåg, G. (2014). Conducting qualitative research in Russia: Challenges and advice. *Journal of East-West Business, 20*(3), 141–161.

White House. (2017a). *Executive order protecting the nation from foreign terrorist entry into the United States.* https://www.whitehouse.gov/presidential-actions/executive-order-protecting-nation-foreign-terrorist-entry-united-states-2/.

White House. (2017b). *Proclamation on the suspension of entry as nonimmigrants of certain students and researchers from the People's Republic of China.* https://www.whitehouse.gov/presidential-actions/proclamation-suspension-entry-nonimmigrants-certain-students-researchers-peoples-republic-china/.

World Medical Association. (n.d.). *WMA declaration of Helsinki: Ethical principles for medical research involving human subjects.* https://www.wma.net/policies-post/wma-declaration-of-helsinki-ethical-principles-for-medical-research-involving-human-subjects/.

Appendix

Table A6.1 A Sample of Resources for Learning about Research Ethical Standards

Resource
American Psychological Association Ethics Code.https://www.apa.org/ethics/code/
Australia's National Statement on Ethical Conduct in Human Research.https://www.nhmrc.gov.au/about-us/ publications/national-statement-ethical-conduct-human-research-2007-updated-2018#toc__1491
The Belmont Report: Ethical Principles and Guidelines for the Protection of Human Subjects of Research.https://www.hhs.gov/ohrp/sites/default/files/the-belmont-report-508c_FINAL.pdf
Canadian Code of Ethics for Psychologists.https://cpa.ca/aboutcpa/committees/ethics/codeofethics/
Collaborative Institutional Training Initiativehttps://about.citiprogram.org/en/homepage/Declaration of Helsinki: Ethical principles for medical research involving human subjects.https://www.wma.net/policies-post/wma-declaration-of-helsinki-ethical-principles-for-medical-research-involving-human-subjects/
Ethics around Europe.http://ethics.efpa.eu/ethics-around-europe/
European Meta-Code of Ethics (Psychology).http://ethics.efpa.eu/metaand-model-code/meta-code/
Finnish National Board of Research Integrity.https://tenk.fi/sites/tenk.fi/files/Ihmistieteiden_eettisen_ ennakkoarvioinnin_ohje_2019.pdf
Forum for Ethical Review Committees in Thailandhttp://www.fercit.org/file/Guideline_English_version.pdf
Government of Canada Ethics Resource.https://www.canada.ca/en/health-canada/services/science-research/ science-advice-decision-making/research-ethics-board/ethics-resources.html
International Compilation of Human Research Standards (Worldwide).https://www.hhs.gov/ohrp/ international/compilation-human-research-standards/index.html
The Malaysian Code of Responsible Conduct in Researchhttps://uitmethics.uitm.edu.my/v1/images/stories/ guidelines/my_code.pdf
*The Nuremberg Code*https://history.nih.gov/research/downloads/nuremberg.pdf
The Norwegian National Research Ethics Committees.https://www.forskningsetikk.no/en/guidelines/social-sciences-humanities-law-and-theology/
RESPECT Project (EU Countries) – Institute for Employment Studies.http://www.respectproject.org/main/ index.php
Russian Psychological Society Code of Ethics.http://www.psyrus.ru/en/documents/code_ethics.php
South Africa Ethical Code of Professional Conduct.https://www.psyssa.com/wp-content/uploads/2016/12/ SOUTH-AFRICAN-PROFESSIONAL-CONDUCT-GUIDELINES-IN-PSYCHOLOGY-2007-PsySSA_updated_ 01-12-2016pdf.pdf
Swedish Ethics Review Authorityhttps://etikprovningsmyndigheten.se/for-forskare/vad-sager-lagen/
UK RIO Good Practice in Research: Internet Mediated Researchhttp://ukrio.org/wp-content/uploads/UKRIO-Guidance-Note-Internet-Mediated-Research-v1.0.pdf
UNESCO Code of Conduct Social Science Research.http://www.unesco.org/new/fileadmin/MULTIMEDIA/ HQ/SHS/pdf/Soc_Sci_Code.pdf

Table A6.2 Resources for Researchers Conducting Studies with Indigenous Populations

Resource	Description
AIATIS. https://aiatsis.gov.au/research/ethical-research	Ethical guidance for conducting research with Australian Indigenous people
National Health Council. http://conselho.saude.gov.br/resolucoes/2000/Res304_en.pdf	Ethical guidance for conducting research involving indigenous people (Brazil)
Indigenous People and Participatory Health Research. https://www.who.int/ethics/indigenous_peoples/en/index9.html	The World Health Organization provides ethical standards for conducting research with indigenous populations.
Research with Indigenous Peoples. https://www.uaf.edu/irb/indigenous/	The University of Alaska Fairbanks provides guidance on ethical issues involved in conducting research with indigenous people.
Protocols and Principles for Conducting Research in an Indigenous Context. https://www.uvic.ca/hsd/research/igovprotocol.pdf	The University of Victoria provides guidance on ethical issues involved in conducting research with indigenous people. They emphasize partnership, participation, and protection in these research relationships.

Table A6.3 Examples of Research Ethics-Related Forms and Procedures

Resource	Description
Agreement between Researchers and Indigenous Community. https://www.who.int/ethics/indigenous_peoples/en/index14.html	The WHO provides an example of an agreement between a research group and Indigenous community.
Consent for Data Sharing Forms. https://ukdataservice.ac.uk/manage-data/legal-ethical/consent-data-sharing/consent-forms	Examples of information sheets and informed consent forms for research involving data sharing, such as in cases in which researchers collaborate across a consortium
Ethics Review Form that Includes Questions to Assess the Researcher's Cultural Competencehttps://research.usp.ac.fj/wp-content/uploads/2013/11/human_ethics_handbook.pdf	The University of the South Pacific's Ethics Review form includes a section for researchers to demonstrate cultural competence in relation to their research population.
GLOBE Project – Translation/Back-Translation.https://globeproject.com/about?page_id=cci#globe2020_cci	The GLOBE Project presents the steps involved in their translation/back-translation process.
Informed Consent – Indigenous People – Collective Consent.https://www.who.int/ethics/indigenous_peoples/en/index16.html	The WHO provides an example of a "collective consent" from an Indigenous Organization form.
Quick Guide: Consenting Non-English Speaking. Subjects.https://irb.ucsf.edu/consenting-non-english-speakers#translating	UCSF provides guidance on informed consent with non-English speaking participants.

7

Conducting International Leadership Research within the Government Sector

Context from an Interpretative Phenomenological Analysis (IPA) Study

Carly Speranza

Introduction

Beginning in 2013, as an active-duty military officer in the U.S. Air Force completing my doctorate, I began to search for a research topic to focus my doctoral dissertation and complete my doctoral studies in interdisciplinary leadership. After some time, I finally asked myself, "What do I already know? Where has my experience taken me, and what am I passionate about?" After a period of critical self-reflection, I realized that I had traveled to over 40 countries, was passionate about global issues, and had served as a female expatriate leader in eight nations across the globe. As a result, I formulated a plan and began a study to answer the following research question: "How do females in the U.S. government experience their leadership in overseas multinational organizations?" In the end, I was able to research the "lived experience" of expatriate leadership without leaving Washington, D.C., and at minimal cost. I was able to accomplish this without travel because I interviewed each female participant after they had completed their expatriate tour(s) overseas and returned home to the United States.

The government sector can be a complex sector filled with bureaucracy, gate keepers, and a culture that outsiders may find difficult to access and navigate (Jiwani & Krawchenko, 2014). However, the government sector provides an extraordinary opportunity to research international leadership through public servants and their important local-, state- and national-level work. In fact, while limited research has been done in this area (Trottier et al., 2008), the government sector remains open to research and provides researchers a challenging, yet virtually untapped arena to conduct important research on international leadership.

This chapter will describe how through my study I learned not only the experiences of women leadership overseas, but also the nuances of conducting international leadership research with U.S. government employees, and within U.S. government facilities. While I was a U.S. government employee at the time of my IPA study, I have also worked overseas and served with multiple non-U.S. governments in non-U.S. government facilities overseas and was able to incorporate this information and experience into this chapter. As a result, this chapter will explore both my research

DOI: 10.4324/9781003003380-7

and professional overseas' experience in order to help future researchers navigate this ever-important sector full of research possibilities.

Why Conduct a Leadership Study Using a Government Entity and/or Its Employees

In the field of leadership, especially international leadership, public servants, to include political and military leaders, provide an exemplary subject to showcase how leadership happens on the national and international stage. In fact, often a leadership biography or autobiography on a national leader will find itself on a bestselling book list because people want to know intimate details about public figures, what they eat, how much they sleep, their educational background, but more importantly how they made it to the national stage and how they maintain their success or why they failed. Subsequently, many of these details are built around an individual's character traits and effectiveness as a leader.

Second, studying leadership within the government provides an excellent opportunity to study how leaders and followers interact within an inherently bureaucratic entity, something that may be difficult to find in a non-government environment in some cultures (Trottier et al., 2008). How is transactional versus transformational leadership employed within a hierarchy? How important is ethical leadership in the government? How do leadership dynamics change during an election process or when a newly elected official takes office? How can servant leadership theories be applied in a hierarchical environment?

Third, local and federal government employees provide critical leadership and services to their constituents. Because many of their decisions are a matter of public record and may have an extraordinary influence on people and society (Hassan et al., 2014), one can research decision making and impact to the public sector on a number of areas to include economic and fiscal policy over various periods of time, advancement and availability of healthcare, education reform, international treaties, environmental laws and impact and energy policy. While corporate and other industry leaders also make tough decisions, they are often influenced by their boards and other stakeholders and do not sit in elected or politically appointed positions.

Fourth, one can use the government sector to compare leadership styles and elements against non-profit or for-profit organizations, especially in the areas of strategic planning and implementation. According to Bryson (2018), prior to the early 1980s, strategic planning within the government sector applied mostly to statecraft at the national level, or military strategy. However, today, strategic planning is conducted across local, regional and national levels around the globe. Subsequently, strategic planning may vary amongst non-profit, government, or for-profit organizations due to identification of stakeholders and differences in fiscal expectations, especially in those organizations that deliver public services (Bryson, 2018).

Fifth, the government sector is an excellent place to study crisis leadership. From natural disasters, to pandemics and terror attacks, local, state and national governments are often at the forefront of crisis management. In fact, the leadership environment can often be influenced by crises and how political leaders engage during them (De Clercy & Ferguson, 2016). Subsequently, this sector can offer excellent opportunities to explore international leadership before, during and after crises.

An Overview of a Study on How Females in the U.S. Government Experienced Leadership in Overseas Multicultural Organizations

As mentioned earlier, I conducted a study to answer the research question: "How do females in the U.S. government experience their leadership in overseas multinational organizations?" While I had served overseas on multiple occasions, I wanted to understand how other females experienced leadership where there are fewer women than men, and where women often experience limited opportunities for leadership advancement (Eagly & Carli, 2007). Part of this exploration was to seek out how each woman experienced her environment and how she professionally and personally adjusted to "being" female in the overseas male-dominated environment. Analysis was also conducted on how female leaders experienced cross-cultural environments, cultural adjustment and leadership in cross-cultural, international environments.

Ultimately, the U.S. government was selected for study because it is an arena that has frequently employed women as expatriates over the last 20-plus years; yet, limited if any research had been published on women expatriates in this sector. The U.S. State Department has sent women overseas for decades to operate in hundreds of embassies, consulates, diplomatic missions and to assist with ongoing efforts to increase women's participation in peace and security initiatives (State.gov, n.d.). Since 9/11, the U.S. military has consistently sent female military members overseas for multiple purposes, to include combat roles, cultural engagement and support to humanitarian operations (Katzenberg, 2019). These government assignments can last anywhere from three months to three or four years. As a result, the U.S. government offered an excellent pool of experienced female expatriate leaders to draw lessons from to inform multiple industries (Speranza, 2017). While several of these female expatriates were found through personal relationships and my previous position in the government, a researcher outside the government could find possible participants through organizational websites or social media platforms.

As a research method, I selected interpretative phenomenological analysis (IPA), a qualitative method because it provided an opportunity to conduct in-depth interviews and apply interpretation and analysis, defined as the double hermeneutic, based on verbal and non-verbal cues (Smith et al., 2009). Having served as a female expatriate myself, I was eager to examine other females employed by the U.S. government in effort to categorize both common and uncommon experiences as they were "lived" as leaders in multinational organizations outside of the United States (Speranza, 2017).

Ultimately, the following criteria were used to select female participants for the study: (a) served in the U.S. government, to include any organization within the Department of Defense or the U.S. military (b) served overseas in a multinational organization (e.g., NATO, the UN); and (c) served in a mid-to-senior level leadership position, which was defined by 15 years or more in the U.S. government.

I began finding qualified participants by reaching out to a few women that I personally knew had led overseas and met the research criteria. However, after that initial few, the remaining participants were recommended by others and a result of snowball sampling. Each potential subject was extended an official letter inviting her to participate in the study. This letter informed potential subjects that pseudonyms would be used in the study to protect personal details, interviews would be audio recorded, and that all participants could withdraw at any point from the research study. Ultimately, I contacted 15 potential participants, and 9 were willing and able to participate in the study.

The female participants had a wide variety of experience as depicted by Figure 7.1. Of the nine participants, five had previous or current military experience. As for length of time in the U.S. government, the participants' service spanned from 15 to 36 years, with an average of 28 years in the government. With regard to overseas experience, the participants had an impressive array of travel and work that spanned the globe. Two women spent over half of their careers overseas and every woman worked in more than one overseas location and often on two or more continents.

With regard to education, all study participants possessed at least a master's-level degree, and three had completed a law degree. Seven of the nine women, at the time of the interview, filled senior or executive-level positions within the U.S. government. In fact, three of the women interviewed were the first women in their professional field to reach their leadership rank and position. Consequently, this pool of participants was a rare find, especially amongst female expatriates.

Because few females at the time had reached these leadership levels, I took great care to use pseudonyms and to not personally identify the female participants. As such, each subject was informed that they would remain anonymous and that sensitive data would be masked to provide

Participants' Pseudonym	Military or Government Rank	Real-world Experience
Janet	Lieutenant Colonel	15+ years in the U.S. Air Force; Grew up overseas: Served in UN Mission in Democratic Republic of Congo
Diane	(2-Star) Major General	33+ years in the U.S. Air Force; Grew up overseas; Served in Afghanistan
Crystal	Minister Counselor	34+ years in the State Department; Served 16 years overseas: South Africa, Brazil, Mexico, Saudi Arabia, Somalia & Kenya
Helena	Director	23+ years experience; Government Contractor, USAID, Council of Foreign Relations; Served in Angola and Afghanistan
Laura	Deputy Undersecretary of Defense	36+ years in the U.S. military and as a civilian in Department of Defense; Served in Germany, Switzerland, South Korea, and extensively with NATO
Cathy	Ambassador	25+ years in the U.S. Government; Member of the National Security Council & Ambassador; Served extensively in Africa
Irene	FS-01 / GS-15	25+ years in the State Department; Served 12 years overseas: Russia, Croatia, Nicaragua, and Mexico
Felicia	(3-Star) Lieutenant General	28+ years in U.S. Army; Served in Germany and Iraq
Vivian	(2-Star) Major General	33+ years in the U.S. Air Force; Served overseas: Korea, Germany, Latin America, and Afghanistan

Figure 7.1 Female Study Participants

Note. From "Expatriate Leadership: A Phenomenology Study on How Females in the U.S. Government Experienced Leadership in Overseas Multinational Organizations by C. Speranza, 2015 [Doctoral dissertation, Creighton University]. http://hdl.handle.net/10504/74382

confidentiality to them and their information. This was especially critical as these women served at various levels in the U.S. government and may have inadvertently exposed sensitive relationships or data during the interview process.

Limitations of the Study

Later in the chapter, I will discuss possible limitations of conducting research in the government sector. These are a few of the limitations that I experienced in this particular study.

The first limitation of this study was that because many of these women were high-level government employees, I could not access them easily or expect multiple interviews based on their daily job requirements. As a result, data collection was limited to a single session focused on the participants' personal reflections about their leadership experience overseas. Creswell (2013) mentioned that phenomenological data collection typically involves multiple interviews while Moustakas (1994) stated that a subsequent interview might be required. Additionally, Smith et al. (2009) discussed that many IPA studies utilize "straightforward designs" that employ one-time data collection. Subsequently, while this was a limitation, the selected research method provided the ability to determine the number of interviews with each participant based on unique circumstances.

A second limitation was that while my participants led across the globe, from Angola, to Afghanistan and Brazil, they were all Americans and likely led from a Western Leadership perspective. As a result, my study findings may not extend to women of all nationalities and cultures.

A third limitation was my potential bias and possible misinterpretation of the data provided by the subjects in my study. As the researcher, I had personally experienced this particular phenomenon on multiple occasions. While it is acceptable to insert personal experience into an IPA study and, in fact, Moustakas (1994) states that "personal history brings the core of the problem into focus" (p. 104), in this study I decided to bracket my own experience so that I did not taint that of the subjects'. As such, I attempted to interpret my subjects' verbal and nonverbal responses as best as I could as a researcher and not as an experienced female expatriate.

Qualitative Interviews

IPA data collection is typically elicited through semi-structured, one-on-one interviews (Smith et al., 2009). While nine questions were prepared prior to the interview, questions were slightly modified throughout each interview based on the subjects' responses. To meet the intent of IPA, interview questions were open-ended to encourage the participants to speak about their experience (s) at length without interruption from the researcher (Smith et al., 2009). As an example, here are three of the nine questions that I asked my study participants during their interview:

- Please describe your experience of adjusting to the expatriate work environment and the local culture.
- How did you experience leadership in the multicultural environment?
- What, if any, modifications did you make to your own leadership style to ensure effectiveness in the cross-cultural environment?

Each interview varied in time and depended on how the participants responded to the questions. Overall, the majority of the interviews went approximately 45 minutes, with the shortest interview around 30 minutes, and the longest interview approximately one hour. Since a verbatim transcript of each interview was required for in-depth post interview analysis, I electronically recorded every interview, and used a third party outside of the United States to provide transcripts.

In effort to ensure that each study participant felt comfortable and so that I could record the interview free from outside interruptions, the location of each interview was jointly decided by the subject and myself. While two interviews took place in subjects' homes, the remaining seven interviews were conducted in the subjects' workplace and within government buildings. On one occasion, I was unable to bring a recording device into the government facility; however, the organization provided me an approved device and provided me a recording via compact disc

Table 7.1 Female Expatriate Leadership Overseas Study Themes

Theme	Description
Expatriate experience is professionally and personally rewarding	Through the positive nature of the expatriate experience, each woman discovered professional or personal attributes about themselves that strengthened their ability to lead and pursue goals in the future.
Being a female expatriate can be isolating, but not lonely	While these women felt isolated at times due to their sex, they often maintained contact with friends and family back home in an effort to stay connected.
Expect others to go through an adjustment period when first working with a female expatriate leader	Most subjects were surprised at how others reacted to their gender overseas. Several women encountered men during their overseas experiences that did not know how to act because they were unaccustomed to working with females, especially as peers or in leadership positions.
Specific leadership traits and behaviors can reduce cultural and gender barriers	The women often had to diagnose the environment, which was slightly different for each woman. Then, they needed to decide how to modify their leadership style to be more effective in the expatriate environment. A few of these include competence, display of respect and listening.
Cultural adjustment is challenging; immerse in the culture early	In an effort to understand the culture, most of the women, especially those with extensive overseas experience, began studying the culture of the country and oftenfamiliarized themselves with the language, well before they embarked on their expatriate assignment.
Relationships are critical to expatriate success	Within the expatriate environment, often due to cultural barriers, relationships can take even longer to build. However, once relationships were established, each participant found them critical to networking, stakeholder engagement and overall support in a professional, and sometimes personal sense.
Senior-level females are often tested or ignored after they first arrive	Several participants found that nations unfamiliar with women in senior leadership positions expressed initial doubt or refusal to acknowledge their presence.
Serving as a female expatriate can make a way forward for other women	While overseas these women were also able to have a strong, positive effect at the local level where they served as expatriates.

afterwards. With the exception of one interview where I drove several hours to meet the participant, each interview was within 45 minutes of my workplace and residence. This was one of the benefits as a researcher living in Washington, D.C., at the time of my study.

Analysis

IPA analysis requires full-text transcripts to complete the analysis of the data (Smith et al., 2009). During the analytical phase I attempted to comprehend the subject's account while also using "interpretative resources" (e.g., non-verbal cues during the interview) to analyze the data presented (Brocki & Wearden, 2006). As such, I took extensive notes during each interview to assist in the later interpretation of the transcripts.

Review and analysis of the data provided involved looking holistically at the data gathered, breaking down the data into individual parts and interviews, providing interpretation analysis and then looking holistically again at the data to ensure the analysis and interpretation truthfully represents the data gathered. In this process, I applied Ricoeur's theory of interpretation in effort to restore the transcript "to a living communication" (Tan et al., 2009).

Study Results

Overall, analysis of the interview data resulted in the following eight themes (see Table 7.1).

My hope is that this description of an international leadership study conducted in the government sector provided you with additional ideas and inspiration to conduct your own. The next section continues with additional recommendations drawn from my overseas experience and scholarly literature to further inform you of the challenges and opportunities that the government sector provides to international leadership researchers.

Reflection and Recommendations

As stated earlier, the government sector is a complex environment where each agency and level of government has its own nuanced and contextual culture. Additionally, as Jiwani and Krawchenko (2014) found in studying the Canadian federal service and communication within it, it can be difficult to access government personnel and conduct research within a culture that often practices information control. As a result, researchers may find it difficult to find government research participants and ultimately get their research questions answered. The following are several recommendations based on my experience in the government sector and also bolstered by others who have published government studies and are framed as likely chronological pre-, during and post-study recommendations and considerations when conducting international leadership research.

Pre-Study Considerations

Access to Government Personnel

As with any research study that requires participants, once you map out the study design and complete the Institutional Review Board (IRB) process (if required, or an equivalent), you must set out to find participants. In my case, I sought out individuals to interview; however, whether quantitative or qualitative, you must recruit individuals to participate in your study within the government. This can be quite challenging, especially if you are not a government employee or have government connections. Even more so, this can appear almost impossible for foreign researchers as some governments may be hesitant to talk to foreigners due to security concerns (Scoggins, 2014). My own IRB process went through my university and was quite seamless; however, some government entities, especially if you are going through an agency for a study and have no university affiliation, may have their own IRB process that may prove a bit more cumbersome. That being said, your participants may also need to seek approval from their government organizations to participate in your study. Subsequently, it is important to understand the full IRB and subsequent government approval process prior to embarking on government research to ensure that you and your participants do not inadvertently go against regulations or policy.

First, expect that it will take longer to recruit government personnel than civilian personnel to participate in your study. One reason for this is that government personnel often have strict guidelines, and their position may require them to get approval from their government institution, specifically through legal counsel, prior to participating in a study (Jiwani & Krawchenko, 2014). Subsequently, they may require a legal or ethics review of the provided research participation letter, or other details of your study, to ensure that the institution and employee(s) are not at risk by participating.

Second, some government institutions have an Office of Research (or an equivalent) where all research requests must filter through for approval before participants can be approached. For instance, if you want to conduct funded human research in the U.S. Department of Defense, you must seek approval from the U.S. Army Medical Research and Material Command Office of Research Protections, Human Research Protection Office, before you can launch a research study (Department of Defense, 2019). Consequently, if you must submit your request through a third party it may be months before you receive approval (if at all) to begin your research project.

The majority of research interview requests for government employees originate through professional networks (Jiwani & Krawchenko, 2014). As mentioned earlier in the chapter, I found my first participants through personal relationships. However, I managed to find a few participants over the Internet and "cold-called" them. To enlist participants, I first sent an email with several details about the study. Then, I followed up with a phone call to make the invitation a bit more personal. The first person that I spoke with on the phone did not meet the participant criteria; however, they recommended two colleagues to contact and provided me their email information. In the end, I ended up interviewing both of the recommended women for my study. Thankfully, I had a quick 30-second pitch (i.e., an elevator speech) that I could provide quickly over the phone to solicit volunteers for my study. While a quick pitch of your research is always recommended, it is even more crucial when you are an outsider trying to conduct research in an organization that you do not belong to.

Third, government employees, especially those that are more senior, may have limited time to engage in research activities (Peabody et al., 1990). As I discovered in my study, I needed to complete my data collection in one sitting because many of my participants had schedules that would not allow for multiple sessions. Additionally, with a few participants, I had to wait several weeks to find space on their calendar to conduct an interview, and even then, I was only granted up to an hour at most. Also, most mid to high-level employees do not control their own calendar and often have secretaries, aides or executive officers, otherwise known as "gatekeepers," who you must go through to get an appointment. It is important that you understand who your subject's gatekeeper is to ensure you contact and work with the appropriate person to ensure your meeting is successful (King & Horrocks, 2010; Peabody et al., 1990).

Fourth, you must be aware of safety and security concerns to yourself and participants when engaging with foreign governments. If you choose to travel to a foreign country, be certain to check the news and embassy websites to ensure the area is safe to travel to. Also, there are governments that, depending on your citizenship, you may not be provided access to. For instance, if you are a U.S. citizen, it is unlikely that you will be granted access to several governments (e.g., North Korea, Iran, Venezuela) based on current political challenges. The same goes for South Koreans that seek to enter North Korea because South Koreans are forbidden by their government to communicate directly with North Korea (Deutsche Welle, n.d.). However, according to Armstrong (2011), other nations have been able to conduct research with North Korea through North Korean embassies in other nations, or through other international collaboration opportunities.

While your personal safety should be a primary concern, you must also consider safety to your participants that may not be prevalent in your home country. For instance, if you choose to look at LGBT policies within governments you should be aware that roughly 72 nations criminalize same-sex sexual activity and 15 nations criminalize the gender identity and/or expression of transgender people (Human Dignity Trust, 2020). As such, you need to protect your subjects and potentially their identities so that they remain unharmed now and in the future. To do this, I recommend you become familiar with laws and customs that may relate to your research topic and consider how they could adversely affect any study participants. To prepare further, I highly recommend Felbab-Brown's working paper for Brooking Institute entitled "Security Considerations for Conducting Fieldwork in Highly Dangerous Places or on Highly Dangerous Subjects" (2014).

Access to Government Facilities

In some cases, you may not be required to enter a government facility to gather or receive data for your study; however, there is a strong likelihood that you will need to get access to a government building, especially for interviews or focus groups. If this is the case, you will probably need someone to sponsor and escort you into the facility (Richardson, 2014). This may be your study participant(s), or someone identified by them to escort you in for an appointment. It is advisable that you have a firm appointment and arrive to the building roughly 15–20 minutes prior to the appointment to allow time for possible security procedures. I have visited government buildings in roughly 15 countries, and in almost every case I have needed extra time to get through security and escorted to the relevant office.

When planning your trip to the government building, ensure that you consider public transportation or parking facilities as many government facilities will not let visitors park near their buildings due to security concerns. If this is the case, ask your contact at the organization to possibly get you a parking pass or advanced access. If you are visiting an embassy or a government building within a city center, definitely consider using public transportation and plan your route out ahead of time because minimal parking, if any, will be available to visitors.

Prior to your appointment, you may have to share personal information (e.g., birthdate, address, email) with your contact to get cleared for entrance. It is not unusual prior to, or upon arrival, to show two forms of identification (passport if outside your home country) to security to gain access to the building. Additionally, you may be required to wear a badge that allows you escorted or un-escorted access in the building. Also, be prepared for x-ray screening when you enter the facility, and bag checks when you enter and depart the facility. Depending on the particular nation and government facility, security may check your person at any point during your visit.

Access to Government Reports and Data

In cases where a study does not require participants and instead seeks information and data, the researcher will need to find the appropriate government office to request the information through. Expect the release of data to take some time, a minimum of several months and do not expect the office to collate or organize the information for you. Additionally, do not expect to receive the whole of your request as the information may be deemed sensitive or classified and unable to be released or at a minimum redacted throughout (Walby & Larsen, 2012).

Many governments have avenues for citizens and others to request information. For instance, if you are seeking information from the U.S. government, your first avenue should be to submit a Freedom of Information Act (FOIA) request. You can submit this through the U.S. government's FOIA website: www.foia.gov. As another example, if you would like to get information from Canada's government, most Canadian government organizations have a freedom of information coordinator that you can locate online (Ministry of Government and Consumer Services, 2020). Subsequently, with today's technology and a little bit of digging, you may be able to find the organization or person to request government data and information from through the Internet.

Conducting the Study

Tape-Recording Interviews or Events

Every government facility has different rules on electronic and video recordings within their facility. This is especially important to understand if you enter classified areas to conduct research, so be certain to ask for permission to record prior to your appointment. During my research, I recorded the interviews and brought in two recording devices to every interview in case one failed to work. In fact, I did have a recording device at one point not work properly, so I recommend to always have a back-up. Also, one facility I entered would not allow me to use my phone to record, and another facility allowed me to use my phone only once I verified that cellular service was disabled and placed on airplane mode. As such, be prepared to adapt to government facility restrictions, and consider possibly meeting and conducting interviews outside of the facility if you cannot bring in recording devices. I recommend contacting your participant beforehand and asking if you are allowed to electronically or video record inside the government facility prior to your appointment to avoid last minute issues.

Building Trust with Government Personnel

As a researcher, especially if conducting qualitative research, it is important to quickly build a sense of rapport with your study participants. As explained by King and Horrocks (2010), "rapport is essentially about trust – enabling the participant to feel comfortable opening up to you" (p. 48). This can be more difficult if you are not a government employee, are a foreigner, or do not have a previous connection, personally or professionally, with your subject; moreover, government employees are often even more constrained with their information (Jiwani & Krawchenko, 2014) and time than participants in other fields. However, here are a few suggestions to break the ice when you arrive to interview a government employee.

First, I discovered during my study that it is best, when able, to be introduced by someone who knows you and your subject, prior to the interview. For instance, prior to interviewing five of my subjects, friends or colleagues sent an email to the subject endorsing my study and myself as a reputable individual. Also, there were several third-party individuals that helped me to get interviews with a few of my higher-ranking study subjects because I could not contact them directly due to protocol issues and my military rank at the time.

Second, prior to the interview you should review the subject's biography and position to understand a little bit about them so that you can plan at least one or two comments or questions to break the ice when you arrive. During my study there were moments when I showed up for the interview and was escorted to someone's office that I had never met before to begin an interview. Especially in qualitative studies, you want the subject to be comfortable answering personal questions. Thus, preparing a few comments to break the ice before the interview begins can be critical in getting your subject comfortable to answer your questions. In fact, if you have a few moments before the interview, take time to look around the office and prepare to comment on one or two artifacts you see to get the participant to talk a bit about themselves and begin to build a rapport (Peabody et al., 1990).

Third, while we have talked about conducting interviews within government facilities, it is important that you ask your study participants where they would like the interview to occur. This is especially important because government personnel may not feel comfortable meeting in their offices, or they may feel more comfortable meeting in their offices where they can control the environment. Also, you may want to interview public servants who are retired or currently working outside of the government; thus, it is important that you are flexible to meeting them at a location of their choosing to ensure a comfortable environment and interview (Babbie, 2014; King & Horrocks, 2010). I interviewed several participants inside of their government agency, and a few in their homes. I found that both worked well and let each participant know that I would meet them wherever they were most comfortable to conduct a recorded interview. However, as discussed earlier, for safety and security purposes, you may or may not have access, especially if you are not a citizen, to other governments' facilities. Also, if you are in a country that you are unfamiliar with and meeting outside of a government facility, you may want to consider bringing along a second person to an interview for safety reasons.

Fourth, how you present yourself to your subjects will also determine how comfortable they are with you as a researcher (King & Horrocks, 2010). To prepare for your "self-presentation", I recommend you consider (1) your words and (2) your appearance. You should prepare a short 3–5-minute explanation of your study and how you intend to conduct the interview. While you likely have already sent out information on the study through email or a phone call, your government participant is busy and has possibly forgotten why you are there. Thus, it is your responsibility to remind them and prepare them for the next hour together. Additionally, especially if you are visiting a government facility, you should plan to dress business-like and on the conservative side to convey that this interview is a professional meeting, in a professional environment. For example, men might want to consider wearing a sport coat and slacks, while women should consider wearing a nice top and slacks or a skirt, or a dress. Remember, you set the tone for the interview and your appearance is the first thing your participant(s) will notice.

Interviewing Political Elites

As a researcher, you may choose to interview high-ranking political party members or government officials, also known as "elite interviewing," because their insights may be extremely valuable to your field (Richardson, 2014). While all of the considerations that we have discussed up to this point remain true, there are a few additional items to consider when interviewing a political elite (Lilleker, 2003). First, you should understand that "gaining access to elites can prove to be one of the most challenging aspects of the research process" (Richardson, 2014, p. 182). Case in point, as cited by Richardson (2014) found that to garner an interview with an elite took an average of 15–20 calls to the elite's place of work. Additionally, Richardson (2014) found that elites often respond more frequently to phone calls than to emails due to the personal nature of a phone call.

Second, once you secure an interview you may have to trim the number of questions you ask based on the time you are allowed. For instance, if your participant has a national-level position you may only be allowed 10 minutes with them. Therefore, you must be prepared beforehand to ensure you get your most important questions asked first (Lilleker, 2003). Subsequently, do not ask the participant questions that you can find the answers to through another source (e.g., The Internet) unless a first-hand source is preferred, as these will only take up valuable time (Peabody et al., 1990).

While you want to prepare questions for a shorter interview based on time allowed, be prepared to expand the interview as necessary. Often, gatekeepers may provide you only 10–15 minutes, especially if they don't know you; however, once you are in the interview the subject may move their schedule around to allow more time if they find your research important and are enjoying the interview. During my research, I interviewed several participants that were considered politically elite and on every occasion my participant expanded their schedule to allow for additional time.

I highly recommend that you conduct a few pilot interviews before you interview political elites if possible (Peabody et al., 1990). This will allow you time to test your recording equipment, test your interview guide, and get an idea of on average how long it will take to answer your proposed questions. Also, you can test out different probes and prompts, and get more comfortable with your sequencing (King & Horrocks, 2010). For this reason, if you have several participants to interview for your study, I recommend that you save your high-ranking individuals for later to ensure you have plenty of practice and have honed your interview guide for this particular study. Additionally, political elites are more likely to request a full transcription of the interview due to political sensitivities so be prepared in case they make that request (Lilleker, 2003).

Post-Study and Publication

Using Pseudonyms or Real Names

One area that researchers always need to consider for ethical and identification purposes is whether or not to use pseudonyms or real names for their participants when presenting their research findings. Pseudonyms can be used for many reasons to include maintaining confidentiality and putting the subject at ease with the enhancement of anonymity (Yu, 2008). Because public sector personnel hold a unique position, and in many cases can be tied to a political party and politically sensitive policies and projects, you may want to consider the use of pseudonyms. Moreover, to further ensure anonymity you may choose to mask your participants' job title, government organization or other key characteristics that could identify your participants (Wiles et al., 2008).

In my research study, because I interviewed higher-ranking government officials about their leadership experiences, to include important decisions made during their work, I selected to use pseudonyms. However, to improve the readability and personal nature of their stories, I opted to use names versus letters, numbers or other codes. Additionally, when publishing quotes or information about my participants, I also made sure to remove dates and locations as necessary to ensure their identity was protected as best as possible (Wiles et al., 2008).

Clearance for Publication

It is important to note that I did not have my study participants review their transcripts post-interview. First, this was not a requirement of the selected IPA method (King & Horrocks, 2010). Additionally, because IPA also has an interpretation component integrated within analysis and can expand beyond the written transcripts, I purposely engaged in "thick description" of the phenomena (King & Horrocks, 2010) and provided some context outside of the written transcripts that rendered review of the transcripts by the participants in possible opposition of my interpretation as a researcher. Because of this, each of my participants signed a consent form that did not provide them an opportunity to review transcripts prior to publication. Furthermore, none of my study participants withdrew from the study or requested to review their transcripts post-interview.

While my participants did not review their transcripts, because I was a government employee at the time, I was required by the Defense Intelligence Agency to submit my study report and publication to both their security and public relations office to ensure that my information did not harm the U.S. government. Within the U.S. government this process is officially referred to as "Pre-publication Review" and is in place to ensure that no classified or sensitive information is accidentally released to the public (ODNI, n.d.). This process can take anywhere from 2–3 months and involves a handful of forms that the researcher must complete when they send in their draft publication (NDU, n.d.). My draft was returned within 45 days and no edits were required on my part prior to publication; however, the government may require you to redact or edit certain material if they deem it harmful to the government. As such, ensure that you take the pre-publication timeline and possible edits into consideration when you are working with government entities.

Government Universities: An Untapped Resource

While there are public and private universities, there are also a handful of universities across the globe that are fully funded and governed by federal governments. For instance, in the United States, the U.S. government fully funds several universities in an effort to provide specialized higher education and research. A few of these universities include, National Defense University, each of the U.S. Military Academies, the Uniformed University of Health Services and the university that I worked at during my IPA research. While I was active duty in the military at the time when I conducted my IPA study (I have since retired), I was assigned to National Intelligence University in Washington, D.C., an accredited federal university that grants bachelor's and master's degrees in the field of Intelligence.

While civilians outside of the government may not be able attend these federally-universities (depends on the government), they can be an important avenue for civilian researchers to obtain data or engage in research partnerships. For instance, in Sweden, the Swedish government runs the Swedish Defense University (SDU). While this university provides multiple degrees, they also operate federally funded research centers. In fact, one of the research centers at this university is the Centre of Natural Hazards and Disaster Science that is funded by the Swedish government but brings together SDU and two Swedish civilian universities to conduct research in this specific area (Swedish Defense University, n.d.).

Within this chapter it is impossible to name every government-funded university across the globe; however, I mention these few examples because government universities are a great avenue to possibly seek information on a government, without having to go directly to government agencies. Additionally, research centers at government universities may be a great gateway to establish research partnerships and possibly funding; therefore, keep government universities in mind when you decide to begin your next study within the government sector.

While this section has provided several sage recommendations, realize that conducting international leadership research within the government can prove easier or more difficult depending the context of the research itself (e.g., location, method, relationships). However, the most important thing to consider throughout the research process should be personal safety to yourself and your participants. Subsequently, when possible do not go it alone and if this is your first time conducting research in the government sector remember to seek advice from other scholars who have conducted research in this sector to ensure you are well prepared.

Conclusion

My hope is that this chapter has provided useful and accessible information that will assist readers to conduct successful international leadership research within the government sector. Remember, the government sector is individualized to each country, and possibly each region, and will likely be difficult to navigate, especially for the novice researcher. As such, prepare for a few roadblocks, quite a bit of extra time to gather data and a challenging, yet extremely fruitful and often untapped resource. If you are up for an adventure that may take you to some far-off lands, or behind doors that you never imagined existed, then I highly advise you take the leap and research the government sector.

References

Armstrong, C. K. (2011). Trends in the study of North Korea. *The Journal of Asian Studies*, 70(2), 357–371. doi:10.1017/S0021911811000027

Babbie, E. (2014). *The basics of social science research* (6th ed.). Wadsworth.

Brocki, J. M. & Wearden, A. J. (2006). A critical evaluation of the use of interpretative phenomenological analysis (IPA) in health psychology. *Psychology and Health*, 21(1), 87–108. doi:10.1080/14768320500230185

Bryson, J. M. (2018). *Strategic planning for public and non-profit organizations* (5th ed.). Wiley.

Creswell, J. W. (2013). *Qualitative inquiry & research design: Choosing among five approaches*. Sage Publications.

De Clercy, C. & Ferguson, P. A. (2016). Leadership in precarious contexts: Studying political leaders after the global financial crisis. *Politics and Governance, 4*(2), 104–114. doi:10.17645/pag.v4i2.582

Department of Defense. (2019). *A primer for conducting Department of Defense (DoD) funded human research with military populations – June 2019.* https://cdmrp.army.mil/pubs/pdf/Conducting%20Research%20Military%20Pop%20DoD_funded_20%20May%202019.pdf

Deutsche Welle. (n.d.). How to do scientific research in – and with – North Korea. *Deutsche Welle.* https://www.dw.com/en/how-to-do-scientific-research-in-and-with-north-korea/a-47678500

Eagly, A. H. & Carli, L. L. (2007). *Through the labyrinth: The truth about how women become leaders.* Harvard Business School Publishing Corporation.

Felbab-Brown, V. (2014). *Security considerations for conducting fieldwork in highly dangerous places or on highly dangerous subjects.* The Brookings Institution. https://www.brookings.edu/wpcontent/uploads/2016/06/06_security_considerations_fieldwork_felbab_brown_report.pdf

Hassan, S., Bradley W. E., & Yukl, G. (2014). Does ethical leadership matter in government? *Public Administration Review, 74*(3), 333–343.

Hofstede, G. (1991). *Cultures and organizations: Software of the mind.* McGraw-Hill Book Company.

Human Dignity Trust. (2020). *Map of countries that criminalise LGBT people.* Human Dignity Trust. https://www.humandignitytrust.org/lgbt-the-law/map-of-criminalisation/

Jiwani, F. N. & Krawchenko, T. (2014). Public policy, access to government, and qualitative research practices: Conducting research within a culture of control. *Canadian Policy Policy, 40*(1), 57–66. doi:10.3138/cpp.2012-051

Katzenberg, L. (2019, March 8). 40 stories from women about life in the military. *The New York Times Magazine.* https://www.nytimes.com/2019/03/08/magazine/women-military-stories.html

King, N. & Horrocks, C. (2010). *Interviews in qualitative research.* SAGE Publications.

Lilleker, D. G. (2003). Interviewing the political elite: Navigating a potential minefield. *Politics, 23*(3), 207–214.

Ministry of Government and Consumer Services. (2020). *How to make a freedom of information request.* Ministry of Government and Consumer Services. https://www.ontario.ca/page/how-make-freedom-information-request

Moustakas, C. (1994). *Phenomenological research methods.* SAGE Publications.

National Defense University. (n.d.). *Prepublication review.* https://www.ndu.edu/prepub-review/

Office of the Director of National Intelligence. (n.d.). *Pre-publication review.* https://www.dni.gov/files/documents/Pre%20Pub%20FAQs.pdf

Peabody, R. L., Hammond, S. W., Torcom, J., Brown, L. P., Thompson, C. & Kolodny, R. (1990). Interviewing political elites. *PS: Political Science and Politics, 23*(3), 451–455.

Richardson, P. B. (2014). Engaging the Russian elite: Approaches, methods and ethics. *Politics, 34*(2), 180–190. doi:10.1111/1467-9256.12036

Scoggins, S. E. (2014). Navigating fieldwork as an outsider: Observations from interviewing police officers in China. *PS: Political Science and Politics, 47*(2), 394–397.

Smith, J. A., Flowers, P. & Larkin, M. (2009). *Interpretative phenomenological analysis: Theory, method and research.* SAGE Publications.

Speranza, C. (2017). Women expatriate leaders: How leadership behavior can reduce gender barriers. *Creighton Journal of Interdisciplinary Leadership, 3*(1), 20–32.

Swedish Defense University. (n.d.). The Centre of Natural Hazards and Disaster Science (CNDS). https://www.fhs.se/en/centre-for-societal-security/research/the-centre-of-natural-hazards-and-disaster-science-cnds.html

Tan, H., Wilson, A. & Olver, I. (2009). Ricoeur's theory of interpretation: An instrument for data interpretation in hermeneutic phenomenology. *International Journal of Qualitative Methods, 8*(4), 1–15.

Trottier, T., Van Wart, M. & Wang, X. (2008). Examining the nature and significance of leadership in government organizations. *Public Administration Review, 68*(2), 319–333.

U.S. Department of State. (n.d.). *About us.* https://www.state.gov/about-us-office-of-global-womens-issues/.

Walby, K. & Larsen, M. (2012). Access to information and freedom of information requests: Neglected means of data production in the social sciences. *Qualitative Inquiry, 18*(1), 31–42. doi:10.1177%2F1077800411427844

Wiles, R., Crow, G., Heath, S. & Charles, V. (2008). The management of confidentiality and anonymity in social research. *International Journal of Social Research Methodology, 11*(5), 417–428.

Yu, K. (2008). Confidentiality revisited. *Journal of Academic Ethics, 6,* 161–172.

8

Courage Required

LGBTQ Leadership Research in Multifaceted Realities

Emerald Jay D. Ilac

Introduction

Ulrich (2010) posits that, given the differences in cultural heritage, political systems, demographics and social structures, it is difficult to understand leadership without acknowledging the diversity in leadership phenomena in international contexts. Studying leadership, therefore, must respect certain specificities nuanced and imperative in understanding these milieus: the historical (development history or maturing process of leaders in their specific context), societal (social structure or networks of a specific context) and cultural (values, ideational systems, and behavioral models) facets influencing leadership outcomes (Zhang et al., 2012). Cultural values for instance influence leadership practices (Alves et al., 2005), making leadership phenomena in one culture not easily applicable to other cultures (Steers et al., 2012).

Scholarly work on leadership has yet to consider the characteristics and perspectives that sexual minorities may bring to the process of leadership (Fassinger et al., 2010). This chapter focuses on forwarding the dynamism of leadership research highlighting gender diversity, specifically for the LGBTQ community. Gender diversity and sexual expression continually become part of the future direction of leadership research (e.g., Morton, 2017; Fine, 2017; Muhr & Sullivan, 2013; Renn, 2007; Linstead & Pullen, 2006; Fuss, 2001) since the volatile, uncertain, complex and ambiguous [VUCA] world embrace the variedness in gender occupying leadership roles across multiple contexts (i.e., political, academic, corporate). Gender diversity in leadership may come in the form of women and members of the lesbian, gay, bisexual, transgender and queer (LGBTQ) community occupying leadership roles when the traditionally accepted view is that these posts should be awarded to heterosexual males. As leadership phenomena operate in unique circumstances and dynamic contexts that consistently alter common notions and tried-and-tested leadership models, advances in technology use brought by the Fourth Industrial Revolution for instance can be used to allow a more global and wide-reaching approach in data gathering, without jeopardizing ethical standards.

In this light, I hope to contribute to understanding processes and critical facets within leadership research focusing on gender diversity, specifically highlighting LGBTQ leadership research. In writing this chapter, I discuss as well the challenges, expectations, needs, dangers and the uniqueness of conducting LGBTQ leadership research on an international level, by highlighting empirical work done on this topic by various scholars and researchers expert on this agenda. In doing so I aim to not just only bring to awareness the research protocols involved in conducting LGBTQ leadership

DOI: 10.4324/9781003003380-8

research, but also to help researchers on what to look out for in conducting these kinds of research to successfully execute them. I then end the chapter with recommendations in addressing these to forward LGBTQ leadership research.

LGBTQ Leaders on the Rise

Sitting at the core of leadership research is how people behave and the rationale behind these behaviors. To understand leadership, therefore, means to fathom the complex interplay of factors affecting individuals as they behave within their respective diverse contexts. This echoes what Kurt Lewin, the father of modern social psychology, postulated when he declared that to understand any situation it was necessary that "one should view the present situation – the status quo – as being maintained by certain conditions or forces" (Lewin, 1943, p. 172) operating within any affecting context. This is exemplified in his formula $B = f(p, E)$ where B is behavior is a function of the interaction between p, the person, and E, the environment. It stipulates any observable behavior is a by-product of the interaction of the person operating within a specified environment or "field." Thus, part and parcel of this interplay is the intrinsic personality of the leader persona that influences the way they behave and impacts their followers within their social contexts. In understanding and researching leadership, therefore, following Lewin's Force Field Theory, one has to look at both the individual and the situation where that individual operates. This is mirrored by Dunham and Pierce in 1989 in their Leadership Continuum model, which looks at the interaction of leaders and followers operating in an environment resulting in an expected outcome.

Looking at the LGBTQ community members, it is clear they are moving upward occupying leadership roles in politics and in business without creating public stir nor highlighting their individual gender identities. Echoing Lewin's Force Field Theory, these LGBTQ leaders have learned to read the context they are operating to successfully lead. If leaders cannot decipher their environment, it may result in failure of leadership. For instance, in the political arena, there are famous LGBTQ leaders in world history who have effectively read, deciphered and navigated their contexts to attain their success. Included in this list, to name a few, are the Macedonian King Alexander the Great, transgender Roman Emperor Elagabalus, King William II of England, Queen Kristina of Sweden, Confucian ruler of the Qing dynasty Qianlong, American President James Buchanan, Iceland's first lesbian Prime Minister Jóhanna Sigurðardóttir, Xavier Bettel who was prime minister of Luxembourg, and Ana Brnabić who became prime minister of Serbia (Ogles, 2017). The same skills in discerning contexts and understanding the environment were also utilized by LGBTQ business leaders who were able to maneuver across roadblocks and eventually succeed. Some of these leaders would be CEO of Apple Inc. Tim Cook, Qantas Airlines' CEO and Companion of the Order of Australia Alan Joyce, co-founder of PayPal Peter Thiel, Martine Rothblatt who is CEO of United Therapeutics, Lloyd's of London's CEO Inga Beale, co-founder of Prezi Peter Arvai, Joel Simkhai of Grindr, Chris Hughes of Facebook, Claudia Brind-Woody of IBM and David Geffen the founder of DreamWorks (Kerrigan, 2018).

Now, certain contexts and societies have acknowledged LGBTQ members and might be more comfortable recognizing their diverse gender identities. With the help of public recognition, they continue to populate hierarchical positions, influencing the very context they are operating in and molding societal paradigms in general. If leadership is construed broadly as an influence process in which an individual moves other people in a particular direction (attitudinally, cognitively, or behaviorally), then our list of successful LGBTQ leaders proves they have enacted these behaviors crucial to leadership (Fassinger et al., 2010). Our list of LGBTQ political and business leaders above, as they ascended to leadership posts by successfully navigating their domains, have used different leadership skills necessary to rise and achieve success. They understood how people and organizations behave, how to create and strengthen relationships, how to handle conflict, build commitment, establish group identity and adapt behavior to increase effectiveness (Bennis & Nanus, 1985; Burns, 1978; Kets de Vries, 2001; Pfeffer, 1988; Stogdill & Bass, 1990). For instance, Xavier Bettel is the first openly gay prime minister to be re-elected a second term (Anderson, 2018), while Tim Cook doubled Apple's revenue, profit, and market value in 2020 despite the Coronavirus pandemic (Mickle, 2020).

Confounding Issues in LGBTQ Leadership Research

However, despite the increasing number of LGBTQ leaders in the public arena, few leadership scholars are researching their stories and experiences. To analyze why there is not much extensive scholarly research on theorizing LGBTQ leadership – and synchronous to the Lewinian principles on conditions and forces affecting human behavior – it is only fitting to dissect the situation through its three fundamental elements: the researchers themselves and their biases, the members of the LGBTQ community as participants and samples of leadership research and the social strata and culture where these two groups are functioning in.

Issue: Researcher Bias

Breslin and colleagues (2017) notes leadership literature has thus far only considered male-female dichotomies and failed to examine the sexual orientation dimension beyond this dichotomy (for an exception see Lee et al., 2008 which courageously looked at public administration leadership acknowledging the multiplicity of genders). Extending this dichotomy, a quick review of research shows three topics on gender and leadership: the difference in the leadership styles of men and women, gender and leadership effectiveness (e.g., are men more efficient leaders than women or vice versa); and the glass ceiling or cliff phenomenon or the obstacles that prevent women from reaching top management positions in organizations (i.e., Northouse, 2007; Sabharwal, 2013; Bertrand et al., 2018; Chisholm-Burns et al., 2017; Faniko et al., 2017; Lathabhavan & Balasubramanian, 2017; Lewellyn & Muller-Kahle, 2020; Bear et al., 2017; Shen & Joseph, 2020; Larsson & Alvinius, 2019). Prior research highlight more the male-female gender dichotomy rather than exploring and acknowledging the pluralities of gender and how these multifaceted lenses impact leadership behavior of the individual, followership and the socio-cultural consciousness.

In 1997, Clark and Serovich found through a meta-analysis of 13,217 articles across 17 family-therapy journals three primary reasons that contribute to the dearth of LGBTQ research: (1) authors chose to publish in LGBTQ-specific journals only thus constraining studies of the phenomenon from reaching a wider readership and thereby creating limited researcher interest, (2) existing heterosexist bias in theory and research design and (3) a pervasive heteronormative assumption that whatever is applicable in heterosexual research can be directly applied to LGBTQ research. In their analysis, Clark and Serovich (1997) state that since authors select only LGBTQ-specific journals, information that would be valuable for other researchers would be "marginalized in specialized publications" (p. 247). Clark and Serovich (1997) also claim that the heterosexist bias appears because scholars are hesitant of conducting LGBTQ research out of fear that other people will question their own orientation or reasons for initiating research on LGBTQ. Lastly, Clark and Serovich (1997) take the stand that a direct application of heteronormative processes in conducting non-heteronormative research will eventually lead to failure as the nuances and contexts of LGBTQ members are unique and at times exclusive to their own experiences. For instance, scholars agreed that theory use in research conceptualization, results interpretation, and methodological rigor would lead to enhanced knowledge that would advance different fields of study (Bengtson et al., 2005; Demo & Allen, 1996; Lavee & Dollahite, 1991 as cited in van Eeden-Moorefield et al., 2018). Yet this is of particular concern on research on LGBTQ individuals with their own families since past research in family studies uses theories developed based on heterosexual, cisgender individuals and their families which will lead to faulty interpretation of the LGBTQ nuances, context and experience. This scarcity of sexuality-sensitive research suggested a need for further scrutiny, especially in light of research postulating that LGBTQ leadership is affected by sexual identity and heteronormative contexts (e.g., Morton, 2017; Fine, 2017; Muhr & Sullivan, 2013; Renn, 2007).

There exists also a particular fear for the researchers to be labeled as "queer scholars" if ever they decide to get their feet wet with LGBTQ research. Heterosexual researchers, heterosexual men in particular, may avoid LGBTQ research topics for fear of being typecast or presumed gay when they engage in these (Harding, 2007; Nayak & Kehily, 1996).

Researchers brave enough to explore beyond the duality of gender and reconnoiter this uncharted territory of leadership research need to vanquish their own biases (as stated by Clark and Serovich in 1997) and view LGBTQ leadership research through an objective lens unaffected by their reflexivities. This consideration of their own heterosexist bias is relevant not only for those conducting LGBTQ leadership research but even for researchers with no specific interest in LGBTQ issues but will encounter LGBTQ individuals as they conduct their research in whatever field (Blair, 2016).

Heterosexist bias must be acknowledged, cogitated and evaluated at every stage of the research process, from the theory that generates the research question up to the presentation and dissemination of results. If the theory used in the research design a study is based on heterosexist and heteronormative beliefs, or does not fit with the LBGTQ perspective, then the entire research agenda will demonstrate bias (Blair, 2016), producing findings most possibly non-reflective of LGBTQ paradigms. For instance, leadership theory may naturally focus on the abstractions of the constructs within leadership (i.e., conceptualization of leadership definition, listing prescriptive agentic roles for leaders, or describing leadership processes) (see Bass, 2008 for a thorough listing of these theories and frameworks). On the other hand, LGBTQ leadership would work with these same theories to create social change, promote advocacies, improve social justice and increase awareness of contextual paradigms that might be hindering LGBTQ inclusion. This is the rationale why queer theory was eventually conceptualized: it began as a critique of heteronormativity, the framework of normative social structures that insist on demarcating between essentially male and female sexual identities and on rendering abject anyone unable to coherently align their sex, gender expression and sexual desires to this heterosexual matrix (Butler, 1990, 1993). Thus, selecting the right theory will help the LGBTQ community achieve its goal of being heard through participating in leadership research.

Aside from theory selection, Blair (2016) also highlights that research bias happens when a researcher fails to ask about sexual or gender identities as a variable in demographic profiling, or conducts research that automatically excludes sexual and gender minorities. Researchers should acknowledge the gender identities of their participants since failure to acknowledge this perpetuates experiences of marginalization of the LGBTQ.

In particular, one major bias researchers may carry is the rationale behind doing LGBTQ research (Blair, 2016). Researchers need to make manifest their personal beliefs, partialities and even motivations for pursuing LGBTQ research. Individuals conducting research on LGBTQ – whether heterosexual or non-heteronormative – must demonstrate personal clarity by discerning why are they conducting LGBTQ-themed research. Are they conducting studies because they are allies invested in promoting and upholding LGBTQ community advocacies to address the social issues and injustices associated with and experienced by the LGBTQ community? Or is it because they themselves are members of the LGBTQ community and therefore find research as an avenue for forwarding their suffered social inequities to public awareness? Knowing this intent will bring to awareness the parameters of conducting the research, that it is aimed to counter heteronormative norms in support of the LGBTQ cause, and is conducted in a non-biased, non-heterosexist manner.

On the opposite end of the spectrum of a strongly heteronormative bias in conducting LGBTQ leadership research is being too absorbed with the LGBTQ advocacies that it becomes impossible for the researcher to dissociate one's own strong personal predispositions, which may tarnish the entire research agenda, methodologies and result interpretations. For example, a researcher on LGBTQ leadership behaviors should not select data or findings that would exclusively support their hypotheses and reject all other information contrary to their intention. By being more open to possibilities of results, LGBTQ leadership researchers can provide an unbiased reporting of actual human behavior and practice. Thus, it is imperative researchers must acknowledge their assumptions, biases, prerogatives, and values that might influence the entire research agenda. As Blair (2016) notes, it is expected that LGBTQ researchers should be open to any possible findings that may come out as a result of the research, and interpret them objectively, even if it may go against their expectations. Also, ethical researchers of LGBTQ leadership must explore studies that do not just emphasize the negativities experienced by the LGBTQ leaders but must as well showcase the positive experiences (i.e., tenacity or resilience) reported by LGBTQ leaders (Blair, 2016). Presenting both strengths and areas of development of LGTBQ leaders will demonstrate the researcher's objectivity and neutrality, and show confidence in the collected data that will lead to unprejudiced interpretations. This kind of perspective in conducting research is found more evident in psychological and socio-anthropological research, as there is more thrust to acknowledge what Willig (2001) and Mills and colleagues (2006) calls researcher reflexivities, or sensitivity to reflexivity that allows acknowledgment of personal lenses brought by researchers into the study.

Issue: Experiences of Suppression of the Research Participants

LGBTQ individuals, in general, are afraid to come out into the open to have their leadership experiences scrutinized. This mode of self-suppression becomes a dilemma when conducting research. Research on LGBTQ leadership shows it is closely connected to and affected by non-heterosexual leaders' LGBTQ identities and their heteronormative contexts. Issues of trust and openness necessary in the research process are placed in question because LGBTQ members are afraid of the shame and malignancy they will face if they come out in the open. This issue limits securing LGBTQ people willing and trusting to reveal their leadership experiences to researchers, which makes LGBTQ leadership research prohibitive in terms of sampling feasibility.

With sexual orientation generally understood as a concealable identity unlike gender and race which are highly visible (Ng & Rumens, 2017), experiences of LGBTQ leadership, therefore, are marked by fears of rejection from heterosexist colleagues once their identity comes out together with having concomitant self-monitoring behaviors (Courtney 2011). Self-identified LGBTQ leaders working along with heterosexuals with substantive interests in these populations may still encounter conflicts, heterocentrism, heterosexism, homophobia and hostility from other people both within and outside of certain social circles especially when their identities are revealed (LaSala et al., 2008). Being subordinated to a heteronormative context may push LGBTQ leaders to push back and view leadership as a commitment to disrupt prejudicial behaviors and promote queer acceptance in their settings (Courtney, 2014), but this may not always spell success. Renn and Bilodeau (2005) extend this by saying LGBTQ leadership experiences supported leader identity development. Prior literature emphasizes the overlaps between leadership development and LGBTQ identity development as these individuals navigate within their social contexts. A number of these studies describe how leaders make meaning of leadership, how it affects their sexual orientation, and their resulting political activism (Miller & Vaccaro, 2016).

One method LGBTQ leaders in general use in handling the fear of rejection resulting from the stigma associated with non-heteronormative self-identities – especially those performing within the public sphere – is to conceal their sexual identity in the closet (Fidas & Cooper, 2014; Hewlett & Sumberg, 2011). This is true in locations where LGBTQ individuals face prejudice and discrimination in the workplace around the globe based on sexual orientation and gender (Köllen, 2016; Ragins, 2004). LGBTQ individuals who do not wish to disclose their sexual orientation can adopt identity management strategies to conceal their sexual identity in the workplace (Ragins et al., 2007). In particular, LGBTQ identity management would involve evaluating the repercussions of disclosing their own identity with members of their heteronormative social circles (e.g., Button, 2004; Chrobot-Mason et al., 2001) and analyzing how this would impact them. LGBTQ people may attempt as one practice to "pass," presenting themselves as heterosexual or choosing not to correct the assumption that they are heterosexual (Barreto et al., 2006; Berger, 1990) by intentionally hiding undisclosed information or unintentionally passing where they assume an acceptable social identity (DeJordy, 2008; Goffman, 2009). Passing can be further divided into "counterfeiting" a false heterosexual identity (i.e., introducing dates of the opposite gender) or "avoiding" the issue of sexuality altogether (Button, 2004; Chrobot-Mason et al., 2001). Yet through fabricating or shunning off the topic, LGBTQ leaders protect themselves from the consequences of social stigma and oppression (Kanuha, 1999); particularly in certain settings where intolerance exists, staying in the closet or remaining their real identity secret to heteronormative colleagues and superiors may be the better alternative than acquiescing to stigma and fear.

Due to the fear of discrimination and silencing, LGBTQ leaders often choose not to disclose their sexual identity or may even "re-closet" themselves to avoid biases through concealing their sexual orientation and restricting statements and actions perceived to be typical of LGBTQ persons (Madera, 2010). The LGBT Foundation (n.d.) therefore reiterates participants must be able to trust researchers will not share any of the information given to them to anybody and keep their identities secret. To do this, it is suggested to use participant codes instead of actual names, and to ensure there would be no identifying information anywhere on the data. Details such as locations, appearance, or other distinctive information about a participant should be avoided altogether, as these can enable identification even if the sample is big (LGBT Foundation, n.d.).

It is not expected that LGBTQ members with leadership roles should first come out of the closet and willingly reveal their current gender identities at the time of the research; that decision is a personal choice inherent to the individual and should not be affected or coerced by anyone's research agenda. As Blair (2016) points out, the researcher should ask this but the decision to respond will come from the willingness of the respondent. However, what is imperative is that the research agenda should consider the ethical implications of conducting leadership research with members of the LGBTQ community, regardless whether they are leaders or not. There should be a balance between protecting the safety, dignity, anonymity and confidentiality of LGBTQ participants to ensure their trust and confidence in research, while still guaranteeing equal access to research participation and that their lives and experiences are not excluded from bodies of research under the guise of paternalistic protection (Blair, 2016; LGBT Foundation, n.d.; Roffee & Waling, 2017). Procedures should protect the dignity of LGBTQ research participants to ensure confidence and trust in the researcher and the entire research process, and the ethical way to do this is to evaluate whether we as researchers have taken the necessary steps to ensure the safety of our participants coming from this vulnerable population. This is our paramount burden being leadership scholars as LGBTQ leaders unravel their experiences in forwarding leadership theory.

Issue: Social (Non-)Acceptance of the LGBTQ Community

Probably acting simultaneously as both the biggest aid and hindrance, society and culture plays an indelible crucial factor in LGBTQ leadership research as this is the stage where both scholars and the LGBTQ community interact. For participant LGBTQ leaders in LGBTQ leadership research, cultural context determines acceptability of their sexual orientation, gender identity and gender expression, and therefore, they will most likely alter the intersection of their identity accordingly dependent on how strong the cultural context is (Paisley & Tayar, 2016), giving sexual orientation greater potential for rearrangement and ambiguity than other axes of identity (Sedgwick, 1990). Members of the LGBTQ community may see leadership either as another space wherein they must comply with heterosexist norms or, conversely, as an opportunity to promote queer acceptance (Courtney, 2014) through advancing their advocacies. Heterosexist norms refer to societal-level ideologies and patterns of institutional oppression directed to non-heterosexuals (Herek, 2000), while a society that promotes prejudicial affective or behavioral response, passive avoidance and active aggression directed toward an individual because he or she is perceived to be homosexual (Cerny & Polyson, 1984; Roderick et al., 1998; Bernat et al., 2001, as cited in Lottes & Grollman, 2010) is considered homonegative.

In many cultures, homosexuality is not acceptable and even deemed illegal especially those with strong homonegative standards; disclosing oneself as a member of the LGBTQ community in these societies is ill-advised and may lead to social ostracization and even incarceration. In their study done about LGBT expatriates who move and relocate between different countries and cultures because of the demand of work, Paisley and Tayar (2016) state there is a range of cultural facets to be considered that influence LGBTQ acceptance at differing social levels, from national to organizational to sub-cultures within organizations. Each of these levels operates simultaneously but will influence the LGBTQ individual in different degrees depending on how closely the individual identifies themselves within each level. These levels can be described in terms of tight cultures (or those that may exhibit social and legal discrimination of LGBT individuals because of the rigid social norms) versus loose cultural contexts (or those that are accepting of gender differences and have less rigid social norms), as stated by Triandis and Gelfand in 1998.

In tight cultures, such as in Japan, China, Malaysia, Russia and countries in the Middle East, there is agreement on cultural norms and acceptable correct behavior as individuals operate in society, including expected gender and social norms which must be adhered to be accepted (Paisley & Tayar, 2016). In Russia, for instance, the government is heterosexist and strongly heteronormative with homophobic laws in effect − such as the recent constitutional change that ended the hope of the possibility of gay marriage (NBCnews.com, 2020) − and with reports of groups openly torturing gay men in Chechnya (Human Rights Watch, 2019). China still considers homosexuality an illness despite it being removed from psychiatric texts in China in 2001, adopting the rhetoric of "tongxinglianbing" or "homosexuality illness" where same-sex sexual attraction is considered abnormal and a mental disorder that required a cure (Blain, 2019). Muslim-majority countries are least accepting of non-heteronormativity, with Islamic societies from Africa to Southeast Asia demonstrating strong denouncement and incrimination of any homosexual displays (Pew Research Center, 2013). However, the same Pew Center report notes as well that "countries where religion is less central in people's lives" tend to be "among the richest countries in the world," indicative of the possibility that wealth and better education rather than religiosity determine social acceptance of non-heteronormativity (Pew Research Center, 2013).

Meanwhile, countries with populations of diverse backgrounds are laxer and loose as they accept more of the diversity and are more tolerant with individual differences (Paisley & Tayar, 2016) such as in Canada, the United States of America, Latin America, Australia and even South Korea. In these countries, differences in gender expressions are likely acceptable, making LGBTQ leadership research more feasible and tolerated. In other countries with loose cultural contexts such as Argentina, Uruguay and Brazil report more advanced status in terms of upholding LGBTQ rights as compared to other nations in the world and subsequently have produced LGBTQ political literature on forwarding LGBTQ rights (for recent examples see Encarnacion, 2020; Salinas et al., 2020; Schulenberg, 2019; Strickler, 2017). They allow same-sex marriages and civil unions, and have strong anti-discrimination laws with the courts and social movements defending LGBTQ rights (Corrales, 2015a).

Though this may be the case for those with laxer contexts, researchers should still not rest on their laurels. Despite the openness of some cultures, it is still best to side with caution and exercise prudence when conducting research within these contexts to demonstrate care and protection when working with the LGBTQ community. For instance, dissimilarity in LGBTQ protection and expression is salient sometimes even in the same country such as in Brazil which simultaneously safeguards LGBTQ rights but is one of the world's murder capitals for LGBTQ individuals (Corrales, 2015a). The rationale for this disparity would include the increasing number of people with higher educational levels and rising income levels which equate to economic prosperity and is associated with stronger tolerance to political rights, greater chances of democratization and a better chance of social acceptance (Corrales, 2015b).

In a study done in 2013, it notes the interesting position of the Philippines in LGBTQ research as having the same situation of simultaneous acceptance and persecution. It is a devoutly Catholic country – the strongest Catholic faith in Southeast Asia – and still has a representative Muslim minority (Pew Research Center, 2013). LGBTQ individuals are situated in a unique "contradictory reality" (Cardozo, 2014, p. 6) in the country where they experience a paradoxical context of simultaneous tolerance and hostility.

In terms of tolerance, the Philippines has been labeled as one of the most LGBTQ-friendly countries in Southeast Asia (Manalastas et al., 2017) where LGBTQ individuals are free to publicly express their gender identities without persecution as compared to its other SE Asian countries. Despite centuries of colonial rule, same-sex sexual behavior has never been criminalized, unlike in neighboring Malaysia and Singapore. Homosexuality is rooted in Philippine indigenous constructions of gender diversity that blend same-sex sexuality and transgenderism (Garcia, 2013), with languages that may refer to either same-sex attracted men, especially feminine gay men, or to male-to-female transgender individuals (Nadal & Corpus, 2013).

However, in relation to hostility, there are accounts of "nuances of oppression" that permeate the experiences of LGBTQ Filipinos (Garcia, 2008, p. 402). One factor that influences this is the Catholic church's 400-year stronghold on the country: its subtly homonegative teachings have resulted in the sedimentation of strongly unfavorable opinions towards the LGBT community and the eventual escalation of these sentiments into oppressive acts (Pew Research Center, 2013; Slootmaeckers & Lievens, 2014). In addition to this, no law protects LGBTQ individuals against transgressions of their rights. Thus, in this dual contradictory context, LGBTQ leaders try to operate and reveal themselves to a select few and back up advocacies to promote their welfare.

Forwarding LGBTQ Leadership Research

Conducting leadership research becomes more difficult if the besmirchment is compounded by additional factors such as race, ethnicity, economic status, education levels, disability and other demographic aspects. The openness to research by the participants themselves, the biases and motivation of those conducting the research, and the culture where both researcher and participant are embedded – all these influence the available types and dearth of LGBTQ research. In a study by van Eeden-Moorefield and colleagues in 2018 for instance, content analysis of LGBTQ research finds that in counseling journals from 1978 to 1989 only 0.65% focused on LGBTQ highlighting on university-based lesbian and gay samples with 73.7% using surveys and lacking on information about race or ethnicity (Buhrke et al., 1992 as cited in van Eeden-Moorefield et al, 2018). Recently, Hartwell and colleagues (2012) report an increase in LGBTQ content in family therapy journals since the 1970s, jumping from 77 to 173 articles: most were clinical articles (43.9%), followed by quantitative studies (39.3%), qualitative studies (13.3%) and mixed methods (2.9%). Blumer, Green, Knowles, and Williams's (2012) content analysis of 17 clinical journals highlight the dearth of transgender research between 1997–2009, publishing only 9 papers out of 10,739. Ng and Rumens (2017) echo this by stating although the number of LGBTQ individuals may be numerically small, it is apparent that the amount of research attention assigned to LGBTQ workplace issues would appear to be disproportionately low compared to other marginalized groups such as women, those with physical disabilities and racial minorities.

As for LGBTQ leadership research, a quick desktop review for instance of the journal *The Leadership Quarterly* for articles published between 1990 to 2020 shows three journal articles searched with the keyword "LGBT", 10 with the keyword "homosexual", two using the word "queer", and two for "LGBTQ". Running the same process for the journal *Leadership* since its inception in 2005, the keyword "LGBT" produced six journal articles, 12 for "homosexual," 11 for the keyword "queer", and one for "LGBTQ". This shows there are studies conducted on LGBTQ leadership, but still not yet that many in comparison to the volume of research these two major journals have produced on leadership. Under Google Scholar, running the words "LGBT leadership" produce 18,700 hits for the year range 2010 to 2020. Research using these keywords vary from advancing LGBT rights in society or in work (i.e., Ng & Rumens, 2017; Paisley & Tayar, 2016; Cook & Glass, 2016; Lewis & Pitts, 2017; Steiger et al., 2020; Hollis & McCalla, 2013), forwarding LGBT advocacy such as gender and legal qualities (i.e., Lucio & Riforgiate, 2019; Nogueira, 2017; Byers et al., 2019, Corrales, 2015a, 2015b; DeFilippis, 2016), looking at status of LGBTQ experiences across countries (i.e., Adihartono & Jocson, 2020; Ngwa Nfobin, 2014; Manalastas et al., 2017), LGBTQ practices in different contexts (i.e., Renn, 2010; Nicol, 2011) or protecting LGBTQ members through reiterating ethical practices (i.e., Adams et al., 2017; Blair, 2016; LGBT Foundation, n.d.; Roffee & Waling, 2017; Sell & Holliday, 2014; Cisneros & Bracho, 2019).

Under LGBTQ leadership research, there are journal articles that tackle LGBTQ experiences on leadership effectiveness (i.e., Morton, 2017; Bullard, 2015), leadership styles and strategies (i.e., Fine, 2017; Harding et al., 2011) and leadership development (i.e., Renn & Bilodeau, 2005; Ryan, 2016; Lee, 2020; Olive, 2015). Though this list is not exhaustive, there are more studies about LGBTQ experiences in general rather than those that focus on LGBTQ leadership itself.

This opens the possibilities for the changing direction and future of LGBTQ leadership research. For instance, LGBTQ leadership research can bring its focus on the intersection of topics that take LGBTQ leadership differently. Researchers can look at the LGBTQ leadership experience of those in public offices such as in politics (local and/or national level), military and even the judiciary. To look at a different corporate angle, LGBTQ leadership experiences can be explored within social enterprises, grassroots communities, non-government and non-profit organizations and small-and-medium family businesses. LGBTQ leadership can be explored within ethnocultural and indigenous contexts, alongside the creation of communities of LGBTQ leaders, and even LGBTQ leadership across generational differences. Given the movements in the current VUCA (volatile, uncertain, complex, and ambiguous) world as a result of technology and health pandemics, it would be essential to see how LGBTQ leaders adjust and adapt to change, and how they lead their followers through the influx of global changes. Would they have a different set of skills or competencies unique as leaders as they navigate in their specific contexts? Are LGBTQ leaders more task or relationship-oriented as they execute their programs? How do they behave in decision making, or even in the practice of creativity, or in the formation of a learning organization? The research possibilities are myriad.

Methods in LGBTQ Leadership Research

It is important to ask now: how should research in LGBTQ leadership research be designed and forwarded? To answer this, it is important to turn to the methods that can be used in conducting LGBTQ leadership research.

Samples

Searching and selecting LGBTQ participants will entail tapping into various networks discreetly and relying on directions from other LGBTQ members who are brave enough to come forward publicly. A purposive sampling method in participant gathering might prove essential given the level of anonymity and confidentiality leadership research will entail. Using this technique in participant gathering may help future leadership scholars go beyond students and utilize a wider spectrum of possible participants across various industries and leadership backgrounds. Purposive sampling delimits a sample in such a way as to control for many extraneous influences, ensuring the sample includes those who most closely represent the population of interest while reducing some biases and enhancing validity (van Eeden-Moorefield et al., 2018). Participants gathered must be representative and inclusive of the diversity of the LGBTQ population. Most LGBTQ research continues to include mainly samples of the middle class, White, educated groups, and lack intersectional analyses (Bowleg, 2013; Tasker & Patterson, 2007) concerning race, ethnicity and socio-economic status which can be included to ensure better demographic representation. By expanding this demographic profile, leadership research can truly be representative of the LGBTQ community and not just address the concerns or issues of a limited few. The challenge to LGBTQ leadership researchers is to enlarge the possible sources of data to ensure that the complexity of LGBTQ is acknowledged, studied and covered to really bring about a more thorough and in-depth analysis of the LGBTQ experiences to fully contribute to leadership theory.

The research must also ensure sample sizes are adequate to ensure the representativeness of the population. The number of participant respondents must be sufficiently large to capture meaningful samples of the community. Sample sizes are further reduced when exploring the intersection of race, ethnicity, nativity and disability (Waite & Denier, 2019).

Instruments

Materials used in conducting LGBTQ leadership research must remove heterosexist biases scholars may unknowingly include. The way recruitment materials are stated should be free from this bias (i.e., using "women leaders" but excluding transsexual women from participating). Measures utilized in LGBTQ research must use language acknowledging the diversity of participants, is understood by all regardless of gender and is respectful of the diverse sexual orientations and expressions. One classic example is the dichotomy of gender options ("male" or "female") which fails to consider diverse gender identities: this construes research as prohibitive in gender identification beyond these two preferences and is indicative that the research agenda is not interested nor respectful in the participation and life stories of the LGBTQ community. Research that fails to ask about sexual or gender identities, or research that automatically excludes sexual and gender minorities, further perpetuates marginalization and stigmatization (Blair, 2016). To aid and show sensitivity to LGBTQ leaders in tight cultures (Triandis & Gelfand, 1998), Paisley and Tayar (2016) recommends providing "choices about the expression of their identities... to fit with cultural context" (p. 775) by such as the different typologies of sexual identity rather than choosing among categories such as the strict male-female dichotomy.

The American Psychological Association Publication Manual in its most current edition is also straightforward in using non-sexist and non-derogatory languages in tool construction, regardless of whether it is for quantitative or qualitative research designs, across culture and across countries. In fact, there is now an entire section on "Bias-Free Language Guidelines" which stipulates to "use the singular 'they' to avoid making assumptions about an individual's gender" (see Section 5.5). Avoiding cis- and heteronormative implications is also imperative and recommends "assigned sex at birth" over "birth sex" because of the implication the latter is binary. It also states to avoid "preferred pronouns" and instead use "'identified pronouns,' 'self-identified pronouns,' or 'pronouns'" as these avoid the implication of choice in using someone's correct pronoun. As one of the more commonly used writing guides for researchers in the social sciences regardless of country, culture and ethnicity, the APA Manual emphasizes that researchers should "respect the language people use to describe themselves; that is, call people what they call themselves... [and that researchers should] ask participants which designations they use and/or consult self-advocacy groups that represent these communities" (p. 218), demonstrating sensitivity to context. Thus, it notes "LGBT" alone as a terminology is considered outdated but there is no consensus on which permutation of abbreviations beyond "LGBTQ" is ideal. Moreover, identity-first language is recommended to avoid collapsing sexual identity diversity and expressions under the label "homosexual". For identities outside the LGBTQ+ umbrella, the manual writers offer a soft recommendation of "straight" over "hetero-sexual" to veer away from the frequently used homosexual/heterosexual dichotomy.

Research Methods

A critique of leadership scholarship is its fixation on gendered leadership styles. Berg, Barry and Chandler (2011) stresses it is more relevant to dissect how male and female leaders differentially embody gendered leadership vis-à-vis masculinist leadership discourses since this accomplishes the more imperative task of revealing how leaders collectively reproduce or transform inequitable gender structures. These arguments point to a need to emphasize the "various layers of embeddedness [unto] power structures, dynamics, and relationships...central to interpretation" (Duerst-Lahti, 2007, p. 10). To address this, LGBTQ leadership research must use postmodern interpretive approaches that analyze the everyday embodiment of leadership performance and yield holistic insights on how context, in-dividual hermeneutics, and societal discourses influence it (Van Wart, 2013).

Qualitative methods would be more advantageous in advancing LGBTQ leadership research. Barker (2001) suggests "a new framework for leadership studies [must] be built upon a direct, phenomenological experience of leadership" (p. 483). He argues quantitative research predicts behavior through dissecting between subjects and objects (Barker, 2001), whereby the leadership phenomenon has a predicted beginning and end, and a hypothesized cause and effect. Qualitative methods, on the other hand, allow researchers to view leadership as a complex social process, where the interaction of culture and context shape its fundamental understanding. Therefore, to understand leadership exercise as embedded within the social process of specific social strata, qualitative research will provide vividness and a large density of essential information regarding the concept (Avolio et al., 2002) given this field is rarely probed. This was echoed by Tasker and Patterson (2007) who stressed qualitative research highlighted important insights regarding the context of LGBTQ communities. This does not mean quantitative methodologies are less powerful, but given the dearth of LGBTQ studies, an exploratory lens is more beneficial.

Renn (2010) expands the discussion on LGBTQ research methodologies by stating that re-gardless of theoretical approach or research paradigm (qualitative, quantitative, mixed methods), existing studies of LGBTQ issues too frequently rely on convenience samples, limited data, and unsophisticated data analysis and/or interpretation. Collecting random samples of LGBTQ people for quantitative studies and purposeful, criterion-based samples for qualitative studies can be difficult, and scholars have to acknowledge these difficulties in whatever methodological paradigm they are operating in. Qualitative leadership research therefore must provide meaningful interpretations of the LGBTQ leadership experience, and uses the correct epistemological theoretical lens is fitting the research agenda.

Research Ethics

Procedurally, LGBTQ leadership research needs to be comprehensively adequate in complying with ethical requirements of confidentiality, anonymity, privacy and protection from harm (LGBT Foundation, n.d.). It should be practiced that data should not have any identifying information that might allow witch-hunting of participants which may lead to detrimental effects especially for leaders in the upper echelons of an organization or those working in the public sphere such as in government. Even in a paper I co-authored with my students on LGBTQ public leadership, the journal we submitted to had to clarify if the names written in the paper were in fact pseudonyms to ensure the protection and safety of our respondents (Gamboa et al., 2020).

The LGBT Foundation emphasizes participants must be made aware of how their data will be handled so they can make a properly informed decision whether to participate or not: who will have access to the data, where will it be kept, how long will it be kept, and how secure the data storage will be. "Digital documents and recordings can be stored in password-protected folders, while physical documents can be placed in a locked cabinet" (LGBT Foundation, n.d.). Researchers should destroy the data (i.e., deleting digital files and folders or shredding actual surveys) after an agreed period of time (i.e., 1 year), so that the information given by the participants does not remain long after the project is complete or the paper is published.

Critical as well in conducting qualitative LGBTQ research done face-to-face is the guardianship of the participant's psychological and physical well-being. Though published leadership research usually does not provide in-depth details on how the psychological and physical well-being of their LGBTQ respondents was guaranteed, undergoing through the Ethics Review Board is fundamental to ensure that the research agenda is done correctly (American Psychological Association, 2017). Researchers must observe sensitivity when asking questions, know what the right questions are, detect when LGBTQ respondents prefer to not answer questions and learn how to treat discomfort during the data-gathering process (British Psychological Society, 2014). In the event LGBTQ participants feel threatened or distressed as a result of the data-gathering process, they should be informed of offices and centers that can offer resources and LGBTQ-affirming and supportive professionals to address any psychological repercussion. As Blair (2016) notes, if there are few LGBTQ resources available, the onus is on the researcher to provide enough resources before commencing the study. The last thing we need is to destroy the trust and rapport we have built with our LGBTQ participants just because we are insensitive to their context and situation. When this occurs, there is a higher probability the participant will not join future research, inhibiting theory-building capability and knowledge generation apart from destroying the interpersonal connection.

Final Words

Leadership research for the LGBTQ community is never easy. In the times I have personally endeavored to work with this community to look at the plight of leaders and their experiences, I have always walked on eggshells as it requires a heightened level of sensitivity and discernment. True enough, LGBTQ leadership research is not for the fainthearted, it is for those who are courageous to brave the field with an understanding of their context. Researching sans acknowledgment of the situation and the LGBTQ individual will lead to failure and more damage than expected positive returns.

Just like any kind of research, working with LGBTQ leaders as a data source requires a test of feasibility and inspection of researcher motivation. However, unlike any other kind of empirical research, working with the LGBTQ community requires comprehension of their struggles, fears and determination to bring to greater consciousness their experiences, successes and hardships. It requires a determined purpose as to why this research is significant and valid and should showcase explicitly how it can help forward literature, theory and the advocacies this community values. LGBTQ leadership research will test the capacity of the researcher to work with a marginalized social group, and having worked on various research with them, I can say that it is both challenging yet rewarding at the same time.

I began this chapter by saying at the core of leadership research are people and comprehending individual human behavior. In this vein, LGBTQ leadership research is not simply just about theoretical implications and factors in leadership, but is more importantly about the voice of a community ostracized, bashed and left at the margins of society. They have a vital role in contributing to understanding leadership phenomena and its agency. All that is needed is the courage to bring this voice forward.

References

Adams, N., Pearce, R., Veale, J., Radix, A., Castro, D., Sarkar, A., & Thom, K. C. (2017). Guidance and ethical considerations for undertaking transgender health research and institutional review boards adjudicating this research. *Transgender Health*, *2*(1), 165–175.

Adihartono, W., & Jocson, E. U. (2020). A comparative analysis of the status of homosexual men in Indonesia and the Philippines. *Journal of Southeast Asian Human Rights*, *4*(1), 271–305.

Alves, J., Manz, C., & Butterfield, D. (2005). Developing leadership theory in Asia: The role of Chinese philosophy. *International Journal of Leadership Studies*, *1*, 3–27.

American Psychological Association. (2017). *Ethical principles of psychologists and code of conduct*. https://www.apa.org/ethics/code/ethics-code-2017.pdf

Anderson, E. (2018, October 16). *Xavier Bettel asked to form next Luxembourg government*. https://www.politico.eu/article/xavier-bettel-asked-to-form-next-luxembourg-government/

Avolio, B., Sosik, J., Jung, D., & Berson, Y. (2002). Leadership models, methods and application. In W. Borman, D. Ilgen, & R. Klimoski (Eds.), *Handbook of psychology* (Vol. 12, pp. 277–307). Wiley and Sons.

Barker, R. (2001). The nature of leadership. *Human Relations*, *54*, 469–494.

Barreto, M., Ellemers, N., & Banal, S. (2006). Working undercover: Performance-related self-confidence among members of contextually devalued groups who try to pass. *Journal of Social Psychology*, *36*(3), 337–352.

Bass, B. (2008). *The Bass handbook of leadership: Theory, research, and managerial applications* (4th ed.). Free Press.

Bear, J., Cushenbery, L., & London, M., & Sherman, G. (2017). Performance feedback, power retention, and the gender gap in leadership. *The Leadership Quarterly*, *28*(6), 721–740.

Berg, E., Barry, J., & Chandler, J. (2011). Changing leadership and gender in public sector organizations. *British Journal of Management*, *43*, 1492–1509.

Berger, R. (1990). Passing: Impact on the quality of same-sex couple relationships. *Social Work*, *35*(4), 328–332.

Bennis, W., & Nanus, B. (1985). *Leaders*. Harper and Row.

Bengtson, V. L., Acock, A. C., Allen, K. R., Dilworth-Anderson, P., & Klein, D. M. (2005). Theory and theorizing in family research: Puzzle building and puzzle solving. In V. L. Bengtson, A. C. Acock, K. R. Allen, P. Dilworth-Anderson, & D. M. Klein (Eds.), *Sourcebook of family theory & research* (pp. 3–33). Sage Publications, Inc.

Bertrand, M., Black, S., Jensen, S., & Lleras-Muney, A. (2018). Breaking the glass ceiling? The effect of board quotas on female labour market outcomes in Norway. *The Review of Economic Studies*, *86*(1), 191–239.

Bernat, J. A., Calhoun, K. S., Adams, H. E., & Zeichner, A. (2001). Homophobia and physical aggression toward homosexual and heterosexual individuals. *Journal of Abnormal Psychology*, *110*(1), 179–187.

Blain, H. (2019, July 13). *A history of homosexuality in China*. The Culture Trip. https://theculturetrip.com/asia/china/articles/a-history-of-homosexuality-in-china/

Blair, K. (2016). Ethical research with sexual and gender minorities. In A. Goldberg (Ed.), *The SAGE encyclopedia of LGBTQ studies* (pp. 375–380). SAGE Publications Inc.

Blumer, M., Green, M., Knowles, S., & Williams, A. (2012). Shedding light on thirteen years of darkness: Content analysis of articles pertaining to transgender issues in marriage/couple and family therapy journals. *Journal of Marital and Family Therapy*, *38*, 244–256.

Bowleg, L. (2013). "Once you've blended the cake, you can't take the parts back to the main ingredients": Black gay and bisexual men's descriptions and experiences of intersectionality. *Sex Roles*, *68*, 754–767.

Breslin, R., Pandey, S., & Riccucci, N. (2017). Intersectionality in public leadership research: A review and future research agenda. *Review of Public Personnel Administration*, *37*(2), 160–182.

British Psychological Society. (2014). *Code of human research ethics*. https://www.bps.org.uk/sites/bps.org.uk/files/Policy/Policy%20-%20Files/BPS%20Code%20of%20Human%20Research%20Ethics.pdf

Buhrke, R., Ben-Ezra, L., Hurley, M., & Ruprecht, L. (1992). Content analysis and methodological critique of articles concerning lesbian and gay male issues in counseling journals. *Journal of Counseling Psychology*, *39*, 91–99.

Bullard, E. (2015). Queer leadership in higher education. *International Journal of Organizational Diversity*, *15*(3), 1–11.

Button, S. (2004). Identity management strategies utilized by lesbian and gay employees a quantitative investigation. *Group & Organization Management, 29,* 470–494.

Burns, J. (1978). *Leadership.* Harper and Row.

Butler, J. (1990). *Gender trouble.* Routledge, Chapman & Hall.

Butler, J. (1993). *Bodies that matter.* Routledge.

Byers, D., Vider, S., & Smith, A. (2019). Clinical activism in community-based practice: The case of LGBT affirmative care at the Eromin Center, Philadelphia, 1973–1984. *American Psychologist, 74*(8), 868–881.

Cardozo, B. (2014). *A 'coming out' party in Congress?: LGBT advocacy and party-list politics in the Philippines* [MA Thesis], UCLA eScholarship, Los Angeles, CA.

Cerny, J. A., & Polyson, J. (1984). Changing homonegative attitudes. *Journal of Social and Clinical Psychology, 2*(4), 366–371.

Chisholm-Burns, M., Spivey, C., Hagemann, T., & Josephson, M. (2017). Women in leadership and the bewildering glass ceiling, *American Journal of Health-System Pharmacy, 74*(5), 312–324.

Chrobot-Mason, D., Button, S., & DiClementi, J. (2001). Sexual identity management strategies: An exploration of antecedents and consequences. *Sex Roles, 45,* 321–336.

Cisneros, J., & Bracho, C. (2019). Coming out of the shadows and the closet: Visibility schemas among undocuqueer immigrants. *Journal of Homosexuality, 66,* 715–734.

Clark, W., & Serovich, J. (1997). Twenty years and still in the dark? Content analysis of articles pertaining to gay, lesbian, and bisexual issues in marriage and family therapy. *Journal of Marital and Family Therapy, 23,* 239–253.

Cook, A., & Glass, C. (2016). Do women advance equity? The effect of gender leadership composition on LGBT-friendly policies in American firms. *Human Relations, 69*(7), 1431–1456.

Corrales, J. (2015a). The politics of LGBT rights in Latin America and the Caribbean: Research agendas. *European Review of Latin American and Caribbean Studies, 100,* 53–62.

Corrales, J. (2015b). *LGBT rights and representation in Latin America and the Caribbean: The influence of structure, movements, institutions, and culture.* The LGBT Representation and Rights Institute. University of North Carolina.

Courtney, S. (2011). Lesbian, gay, and bisexual (lgb) identity and school leadership: lgb english school leaders' perspectives [MA Thesis], The University of Manchester, Manchester, UK.

Courtney, S. (2014). Inadvertently queer school leadership amongst lesbian, gay and bisexual (LGB) school leaders. *Organization, 21*(3), 383–399.

DeFilippis, J. (2016). "What about the rest of us?" An overview of LGBT poverty issues and a call to action. *Journal of Progressive Human Services, 27*(3), 143–174.

DeJordy, R. (2008). Just passing through stigma, passing, and identity decoupling in the workplace. *Group & Organization Management, 33,* 504–531.

Demo, D. H., & Allen, K. R. (1996). Diversity within lesbian and gay families: Challenges and implications for family theory and research. Journal of Social and Personal Relationships, 13, 415–434.

Duerst-Lahti, G. (2007). Reflections on studying public leadership so as to take gender and race seriously: Person, position, political location and perception in the gendered and raced leadership of Wisconsin's major agencies. In *Leading the future of the public sector: The third transatlantic dialogue* (pp. 1–37). The University of Delaware.

Dunham, R. B., & Pierce, J. L. (1989). *Managing.* Scott Foresman.

Encarnacion, O. G. (2020). The gay rights backlash: Contrasting views from the United States and Latin America. *The British Journal of Politics and International Relations.* doi:10.1177/1369148120946671

Faniko, K., Ellemers, N., Derks, B., & Lorenzi-Cioldi, F. (2017). Nothing changes, really: Why women who break through the glass ceiling end up reinforcing it. *Personality and Social Psychology Bulletin, 43*(5), 638–651.

Fassinger, R., Shullman, S., & Stevenson, M. (2010). Toward an affirmative lesbian, gay, bisexual, and transgender leadership paradigm. *American Psychologist, 65*(3), 201–215.

Fidas, D., & Cooper, L. (2014, June 4). *The cost of the closet and the rewards of inclusion: Why the workplace environment for LGBT people matters to employees.* https://issuu.com/humanrightscampaign/docs/cost_of_the_closet_may2014

Fine, L. (2017). Gender and sexual minorities' practice and embodiment of authentic leadership: Challenges and opportunities. *Advances in Developing Human Resources, 19*(4), 1–15.

Fuss, D. (2001). Theorizing hetero- and homosexuality. In S. Seidman & J. C. Alexander (Eds.), *The new social theory reader: Contemporary debates* (pp. 347–352). Routledge.

Gamboa, L. L., Ilac, E. D., Carangan, A. M., & Agida, J. S. (2020). Queering public leadership: The case of lesbian, gay, bisexual and transgender leaders in the Philippines. *Leadership.* doi:10.1177/1742715020953273

Garcia, J. (2008). *Philippine gay culture: Binabae to bakla, silahis to MSM.* University of the Philippines Press.

Garcia, J. (2013). Nativism or universalism: Situating LGBT discourse in the Philippines. *Kritika Kultura*, *20*, 48–68.

Goffman, E. (2009). *Stigma: Notes on the management of spoiled identity*. Simon and Schuster.

Harding, N., Lee, H., Ford, J., & Learmonth, M. (2011). Leadership and charisma: A desire that cannot speak its name? *Human Relations*, *64*(7), 927–949.

Harding, T. (2007). The construction of men who are nurses as gay. *Journal of Advanced Nursing*, *60*(6), 636–644.

Hartwell, E., Serovich, J., Grafsky, E., & Kerr, Z. (2012). Coming out of the dark: Content analysis of articles pertaining to gay, lesbian, and bisexual issues in couple and family therapy journals. *Journal of Marital and Family Therapy*, *38*, 227–243.

Herek, G. M. (2000). The psychology of sexual prejudice. *Current Directions in Psychological Science*, *9*(1),19–22.

Hewlett, S., & Sumberg, K. (2011). For LGBT workers, being "out" brings advantages. *Harvard Business Review*, *89*(7/8), 28–30.

Hollis, L. P., & McCalla, S. A. (2013). Bullied back in the closet: Disengagement of LGBT employees facing workplace bullying. *Journal of Psychological Issues In Organizational Culture*, *4*(2), 6–16.

Human Rights Watch. (2019, May 8). *Russia: New anti-gay crackdown in Chechnya*. https://www.hrw.org/news/2019/05/08/russia-new-anti-gay-crackdown-chechnya

Kanuha, V. (1999). The social process of "passing" to manage stigma: Acts of internalized oppression or acts of resistance? *Journal of Sociology and Social Welfare*, *26*(4), 27–46.

Kerrigan, S. (2018, July 5). *27 Most successful LGBT+ entrepreneurs, executives and opinion leaders*. https://interestingengineering.com/27-most-successful-lgbt-entrepreneurs-executives-and-opinion-leaders

Kets de Vries, M. (2001). *The leadership mystique: A user's manual for the human enterprise*. Financial Times Prentice Hall.

Köllen, T. (2016). *Sexual orientation and transgender issues in organizations: Global perspectives on LGBT workforce diversity*. Springer

Larsson, G., & Alvinius, A. (2019). Comparison within gender and between female and male leaders in female-dominated, male-dominated and mixed-gender work environments. *Journal of Gender Studies*. doi:10.1080/09589236.2019.1638233

LaSala, M., Jenkins, D., Wheeler, D., & Fredriksen-Goldsen, K. (2008). LGBT faculty, research, and researchers: Risks and rewards. *Journal of Gay & Lesbian Social Services*, *20*(3), 253–267.

Lathabhavan, R., & Balasubramanian, S. A. (2017). Glass ceiling and women employees in Asian organizations: A tri-decadal review. *Asia-Pacific Journal of Business Administration*, *9*(3), 232–246.

Lavee, Y., & Dollahite, D. (1991). The linkage between theory and research in family science. Journal of Marriage and the Family, 53, 361–373.

Lee, C. (2020). Courageous leaders: Supporting and celebrating LGBT school leaders. *Impact: Journal of the Chartered College of Teaching*, *1*(9), 53–55.

Lee, H., Learmonth, M., & Harding, N. (2008). Queer(y)ing public administration. *Public Administration*, *86*(1), 149–167.

Lewellyn, K. B., Muller-Kahle, M. I. (2020). The corporate board glass ceiling: The role of empowerment and culture in shaping board gender diversity. *Journal of Business Ethics*, *165*, 329–346.

Lewin, K. (1943). Psychological ecology. In D. Cartwright (Ed.), *Field theory in social science*. Social Science Paperbacks.

Lewis, G. B., & Pitts, D. W. (2017). LGBT–Heterosexual differences in perceptions of fair treatment in the federal service. *American Review of Public Administration*, *47*(5), 574–587.

LGBT Foundation. (n.d.). *Ethical research: Good practice guide to researching LGBT communities and issues*. https://s3-eu-west-1.amazonaws.com/lgbt-website-media/Files/1a884870-453a-429d-a213-399a9502472c/Ethics%2520Guide.pdf

Linstead, S., & Pullen, A. (2006). Gender as multiplicity: Desire, displacement, difference and dispersion. *Human Relations*, *59*(9), 1287–1310.

Lodola, G., & Corral, M. (2010). Support for same-sex marriage in Latin America. *Americas Barometer Insights*, *44*. http://www.vanderbilt.edu/lapop/insights/I0844.enrevised.pdf.

Lottes, I., & Grollman, E. (2010). Conceptualization and assessment of homonegativity. *International Journal of Sexual Health*, *22*, 219–233.

Lucio, W., & Riforgiate, S. (2019). Collective communication within LGBT leadership: Sharing the vision. *Ohio Communication Journal*, *51*, 115–131.

Madera, J. (2010). The cognitive effects of hiding one's homosexuality in the workplace. *Industrial and Organizational Psychology*, *3*, 86–89.

Manalastas, E., Torre, B., Ojanen, T., Ratanashevorn, R., Hong, B., Kumaresan, V., & Veeramuthu, V. (2017). Homonegativity in southeast Asia: Attitudes toward lesbians and gay men in Indonesia, Malaysia, the Philippines, Singapore, Thailand, and Vietnam. *Asia-Pacific Social Science Review, 17*(1), 25–33.

Mickle, T. (2020, August 7). How Tim cook made apple his own. *The Wall Street Journal.* https://www.wsj.com/articles/tim-cook-apple-steve-jobs-trump-china-iphone-ipad-apps-smartphone-11596833902

Miller, R., & Vaccaro, A. (2016). Queer student leaders of color: Leadership as authentic, collaborative, culturally competent. *Journal of Student Affairs Research and Practice, 53*(1), 39–50.

Mills, J., Bonner, A., & Francis, K. (2006). The development of constructivist grounded theory. *International Journal of Qualitative Methods, 5,* 25–35.

Morton, J. W. (2017). Think leader, think heterosexual male? The perceived leadership effectiveness of gay male leaders. *Canadian Journal of Administrative Sciences, 34,* 159–169.

Muhr, S., & Sullivan, K. (2013). "None so queer as folk": Gendered expectations and transgressive bodies in leadership. *Leadership, 9*(3), 416–435.

Nadal, K. L. & Corpus, M. J. H. (2013). 'Tomboys' and 'baklas': Experiences of lesbian and gay Filipino Americans. *Asian American Journal of Psychology, 4*(3), 166–175.

Nayak, A., & Kehily, M. (1996). Playing it straight: Masculinities, homophobias and schooling. *Journal of Gender Studies, 5*(2), 211–230.

NBCnews.com. (2020). *Russian constitution change ends hopes for gay marriage.* https://www.nbcnews.com/feature/nbc-out/russian-constitution-change-ends-hopes-gay-marriage-n1233639

Ng, E., & Rumens, N. (2017). Diversity and inclusion for LGBT workers: Current issues and new horizons for research. *Canadian Journal of Administrative Sciences, 34,* 109–120.

Ngwa Nfobin, E. (2014). Homosexuality in Cameroon. *International Journal on Minority & Group Rights, 21*(1), 72–130.

Nicol, H. (2011). College student leadership within the LGBT community. *International Journal of Arts & Sciences, 4*(25), 15–25.

Nogueira, M. B. (2017). The promotion of LGBT rights as international human rights norms: Explaining Brazil's diplomatic leadership. *Global Governance: A Review of Multilateralism and International Organizations, 23*(4), 545–563.

Northouse, P. G. (2007). *Leadership. Theory and practice* (4th ed.). Sage Publications.

Ogles, J. (2017, September 29). *31 LGBT leaders from world history.* https://www.advocate.com/people/2017/9/29/31-lgbt-leaders-world-history#slide-0

Olive, J. (2015). The impact of friendship on the leadership identity development of lesbian, gay, bisexual, and queer students. *Journal of Leadership Education, 14*(1), 142–159.

Paisley, V., & Tayar, M. (2016) Lesbian, gay, bisexual and transgender (LGBT) expatriates: An intersectionality perspective. *The International Journal of Human Resource Management, 27*(7), 766–780.

Pew Research Center. (2013). *The global divide on homosexuality: Greater acceptance in more secular and affluent countries.* Pew Research Center. https://www.pewresearch.org/global/2013/06/04/the-global-divide-on-homosexuality/

Pfeffer, J. (1988). *The human equation: Building profits by putting people first.* Harvard Business School Press.

Ragins, B. R. (2004). Sexual orientation in the workplace: The unique work and career experiences of gay, lesbian and bisexual workers. In *Research in personnel and human resources management*(pp. 35–120). Emerald Group Publishing Limited.

Ragins, B., Singh, R., & Cornwell, J. (2007). Making the invisible visible: Fear and disclosure of sexual orientation at work. *Journal of Applied Psychology, 92*(4), 1103–1118.

Renn, K. (2007). LGBT student leaders and queer activists: Identities of lesbian, gay, bisexual, transgender, and queer-identified college student leaders and activists. *Journal of College Student Development, 48*(3), 314–328.

Renn, K. (2010). LGBT and queer research in higher education: The state and status of the field. *Educational Researcher, 39*(2), 132–141.

Renn, K., & Bilodeau, B. (2005). Queer student leaders: An exploratory case study of identity development and LGBT student involvement at a midwestern research university. *Journal of Gay & Lesbian Issues in Education, 2*(4), 49–71.

Roderick, T., McCammon, S. L., Long, T. E., & Allred, L. J. (1998). Behavioral aspects of homonegativity. Journal of Homosexuality, 36(1), 79–88.

Roffee, J. A., & Waling, A. (2017). Resolving ethical challenges when researching with minority and vulnerable populations: LGBTIQ victims of violence, harassment and bullying. *Research Ethics, 13*(1), 4–22.

Ryan, T. (2016). The deepening of identity: How leadership affects lesbian, gay, and bisexual student sexual identity development. *New York Journal of Student Affairs, 16*(1), 36–48.

Sabharwal, M. (2013). From glass ceiling to glass cliff: Women in senior executive service. *Journal of Public Administration Research and Theory*, 25(2), 399–426.

Salinas, G. C., Martinez, J., & Vidal-Ortiz, S. (2020). LGBT studies without LGBT studies: Mapping alternative pathways in Perú and Colombia. *Journal of Homosexuality*, 67(3), 417–434.

Schein, E. (1983). The role of the founder in creating organizational culture. *Organizational Dynamics*, Summer, 13–28.

Schein, E. (1985). *Organizational Culture and Leadership*. Jossey-Bass.

Schulenberg, S. (2019). LGBT rights in Chile: On the verge of a gay-rights revolution? *Sexuality, Gender & Policy*, 2(2), 97–119.

Sedgwick, E. (1990). *Epistemology of the closet*. University of California Press.

Sell, R., & Holliday, M. (2014). Sexual orientation data collection policy in the United States: Public health malpractice. *American Journal of Public Health*, 4(6), 967–969.

Shen, W., & Joseph, D. (2020). Gender and leadership: A criterion-focused review and research agenda. *Human Resource Management Review*. doi:10.1016/j.hrmr.2020.100765

Slootmaeckers, K., & Lievens, J. (2014). Cultural capital and attitudes toward homosexuals: Exploring the relation between lifestyles and homonegativity. *Journal of Homosexuality*, 61(1), 962–979.

Steers, R., Sanchez-Runde, C., & Nardon, L. (2012). Leadership in a global context: New directions in research and theory development. *Journal of World Business*, 47, 479–482.

Stogdill, R., & Bass, B. (1990). *Stogdill's handbook of leadership: A survey of theory and research*. The Free Press.

Streiger, R., & Henry, P. J. (2020). LGBT workplace protections as an extension of the protected class framework. *Law and Human Behavior*, 44(4), 251–265.

Strickler, J. A. (2017). *Variation in Latin American LGBT rights* [Unpublished master's thesis]. University of Miami.

Tasker, F., & Patterson, C. (2007). Research on gay and lesbian parenting: Retrospect and prospect. *Journal of Gay, Lesbian, Bisexual and Transgender Family Issues*, 3, 9–34.

Triandis, H., & Gelfand, M. (1998). Converging measurement of horizontal and vertical individualism and collectivism. *Journal of Personality and Social Psychology*, 74, 118–128.

Ulrich, D. (2010). Leadership in Asia. In D. Ulrich (Ed.), *Leadership in Asia: Challenges and opportunities* (pp. 1–21). McGraw Hill.

van Eeden-Moorefield, B., Few-Demo, A., Benson, K., Bible, J., & Lummer, S. (2018). A content analysis of LGBT research in top family journals 2000-2015. *Journal of Family Issues*, 39(5), 1374–1395.

Van Wart, M. (2013). Administrative leadership theory: A reassessment after 10 years. *Public Administration*, 91(3), 521–543.

Waite, S., & Denier, N. (2019). A research note on Canada's LGBT data landscape: Where we are and what the future holds. *Canadian Review of Sociology*, 56(1), 93–117.

Willig, C. (2001). *Introducing qualitative research in psychology*. Open University Press

Zhang, Z., Waldman, D. A., & Wang, Z. (2012). A multilevel investigation of leader-member exchange, informal leader emergence, and individual and team performance. Personnel Psychology, 65, 49–78.

9

Research with Native American Communities—Experiences with the Lakota[1]

Kem Gambrell

At its core, Native and Indigenous leadership is relational (Kenny, 2012). Kenny (2012) notes that "in healthy tribal societies, individuals acted on behalf of others in the community" (p. 7). It was this focus on relationships that kept the nation together, and promoted collectivism and community thriving (Kenny, 2012). Perhaps it is this community and relational focus that has enthralled white[2] people with Native and Indigenous peoples.[3] Over 150 years ago, author D. H. Lawrence focused on the issue of the North American identity "suggesting that American consciousness was essentially 'unfinished' and incomplete" (Lawrence, 1990, as cited in Deloria, 1998 p. 3) and as such dominant culture in the United States has continually searched for self-insights by exploring Native peoples. Zheng (2016) supports this by speculating that privileged people gain knowledge and self-insight at the expense of marginalized peoples' well-being. As Deloria (1998) notes, "Indians represented instinct and freedom" for Americans, who wanted both to "savor civilized order and savage freedom at the same time" (p. 3). Thus, "there has been all the time, in the white American soul, a dual feeling about the Indian…the desire to extirpate [him]. And the contradictory desire to glorify him" (Deloria, 1998, p. 4).

As a result of this incomplete identity and subsequent fascination, non-Native people have been doing research with sovereign[4] Native American tribes and Indigenous people for generations. Often these projects have generally been implemented by researchers with little reflection as to the communities need for the research, or the often-traumatizing impact that might occur due to what Hodge (2012) calls "scientific racism". Consequently, these settler colonial and racist practices have been damaging in educational, health and research policies and practices to Native and Indigenous participants and community/tribes for decades.

To counter these harms, as well as to center culturally appropriate, sensitive and ethical research, the purpose of this chapter is to explore dynamics including; how to de-center a settler colonialist paradigm, considerations to being culturally intentional and sensitive in research and provide examples through a specific research setting. For the intent of this paper, reflections from leadership research done with the Sičáŋǧu Lakota[5] in south-central South Dakota will be used as an example for this discussion. Furthermore, ways of being that I believe are essential to conducting research with Native and Indigenous peoples will be examined. These aspects rise from insights from research processes that include:

- Positionality
- Intention and Awareness

DOI: 10.4324/9781003003380-9

- Cultural Liaisons and Translators
- Being in Relationship
- Land is Central
- Hold the Space
- Indigenous Worldviews
- Research is Transformative

Background

Traditionally, Western views of leadership tend to focus on the leader (Archuleta, 2012) and "reflect the bureaucratic, hierarchical organizational paradigms of industrial structures" (Archuleta, 2012, p. 163). This incomplete mindset has placed tremendous inadequacies on leadership scholarship and understanding. As Yukl (1999) reflects, "The leadership actions of one individual are much less important than the collective leadership provided by members of an organization" (p. 93).

However, regardless of these insights, "there has been a pattern of non-Indigenous leadership practices being forced upon Indigenous communities" (Voyageur et al., 2015, p. 3) that includes not just governmental systems, but also the projection of a Western, colonialist paradigm in *how* Native and Indigenous leadership is understood. As such, research that stems from authentic and sincere relationships within communities, needs that rise from these relationships and ethically and cultural-relative studies in partnership with these communities is essential.

While several Western leadership scholars have suggested other models forwarding progress in these endeavors (e.g., see Uhl-Bien, Marion & McKelvey, 2007), to date there are limited scholarly publications that center leadership from a non-Western paradigm. Having access to more recently established research-oriented books written by Indigenous, First Nation, Indian and Aboriginal peoples (e.g., see Chilisa, 2012/2019; Kovach, 2010; Lambert, 2014; Smith, 1999/2012; Wilson, 2008) may be the evolution that leadership scholarship needs. This is important because these scholars de-center a Western paradigm creating an important and much needed space for other ways of thought that include Indigenous ontology,[6] epistemology[7] and axiology.[8] De-centering the dominant narrative and model, especially in the field of leadership, might just be one way to counter the enduring harm that often follows with this incomplete way of thinking. As Veracini (2017) reflects, if "my humanity is to come; it will follow genuine decolonialization" (p. 2).

While there are several ways to de-center the dominant paradigm, to do so requires a focused and intentional process for those of us who were "trained" and/or raised in this worldview. Furthermore, this also requires an understanding of *how* colonialization continues to perpetuate marginalization, oppression, ethnocentrism, and other systemic tribulations. It also necessitates having the desire to create a more holistic, equitable, and inclusive way of being in the world (Blaut, 1993). Thus, as a settler colonialist and researcher there are several things I can do to counter these harms when I conduct research with Native communities. For example, intentionally and consistently unpacking my identity and privilege, perception checking the cultural assumptions I unintentionally and unknowingly place on others, and having others assist me to "see" where I am projecting my worldview onto others is imperative to culturally competent research. As Vercini (2017) writes, "I am a settler, but indigenous resurgence is my interest. It will make me a better human being and a worse settler" (p. 2).

To begin this process, in this chapter I will attempt to de-center my settler colonial-ness by respecting Native and Indigenous wisdom and methodology and provide the reader with examples and rational as to why this is imperative to conducting research with the Sičáŋǧu Lakota, one of the 574 U.S. federally recognized Native Nations (National Conference of State Legislatures, n.d.). Furthermore, these ponderings may also be considered for other Native/Indigenous groups as a place of consideration.

Tipi as cultural way of reporting findings/process

- **Intention and Awareness** (direction the tipi opening is placed
- **Cultural Liaisons and Cultural Translators** (shape, size, & materials)
- **Be in Relationship** (where placed in conjunction with others)
- **The Land is Central** (where one is Indigenous to)
- **Hold the Space** (inside the tipi)
- **Indigenous Worldviews** (entire process of setting up the dwelling)
- **Research is Transformative** (reflection)
- **Positionality** (who am I as a researcher)

Figure 9.1 Setting up a Tipi: Findings and Process.

The Tipi

The tipi is the dominant structure or dwelling of plains tribes such as the Lakota and great intention went into the placement, materials, contents and location of the tipi in conjunction with others in the community. Like the bottom or circular shape of the tipi, these reflections are written in a linear form, they are not actions to be taken in a specific order. Instead, they are fluid, circular, ebbing and flowing with the coalition and context (Figure 9.1).

To begin to do some of this de-centering, the use of a Lakota cultural reference, in this case a *tipi*,[9] will be used to demonstrate a non-Western way of reporting research insights with the culture in which they originate and reside in. A cultural reference "refers to the extent to which the research emanates from the culture in which it is conducted" and "its customs, norms or behaviors not found in the West" (Adair et al, 1993 as cited in Chilisa, 2012, p. 102). By doing this, I also attempt to call out the "power of the storyteller, while drawing attention to the relationship between the colonizer and the colonized" (Q'um Q'um Xiiem, et al., 2019, p. 5). To do this, I start with positionality.

Positionality

To start, one must consider who they are in relationship to others. However, as a white, Western settler colonialist, to also understand that "my role is not to draw conclusions for another or to make an argument" (Wilson, 2008, p. 133) is counter to what the academy teaches. However, as Posthumus (2019) writes "I firmly believe in the importance of describing to the best of our abilities the worldviews of people different from ourselves and seriously engaging with other belief systems" (p. 4). This is the paradox.

Chilisa (2012) uses the term "academic imperialism" to describe the academy's tendency to exclude and dismiss as "irrelevant knowledge embedded in the cultural experiences of the people and the tendency to appropriate indigenous knowledge systems" (p. 55). Omi and Winant (1994) discuss that white people use racial ideologies and associated discourses to produce racial privileges while justifying continued discrimination, impeding anti-white criticism and limiting potential avenues for racial justice. Decentering whiteness and/or a Western paradigm is the act of removing this dominant perspective from its position of power and integrating it as one of multiple perspectives (Cotter, 2016; Pedro, 2017; Regan, 2017). Therefore, decentering a settler colonialist and/or white Western paradigm challenges us to more deeply explore and understand the values, beliefs and practices associated with those that are largely based on the principles of conquest and exploitation (Hitchcock & Flint, 2015). Arvin (2014) notes one way that:

> settler colonialism and white supremacy buttress each other, but are not exactly the same, is that "racial mixture" is encouraged under settler colonialism, in order to make Indigenous peoples, and their particular claims to land, less distinct from settlers. Any kind of "mixture" allows Indigenous peoples to be seen as less "authentic," as "dying out." However, the goal of settler colonialism is to mix the population in such a way that it is closer in proximity to whiteness. (para. 7)

Therefore, a central part of our work as Western-trained researchers is to explore our projection and practice of this settler colonialist and academic imperialism that many have been schooled into. To do so requires the consistent practice of discernment and perception checking with cultural liaisons as researchers and scholars. These are the challenges that I try and invite myself into contemplating when I engage with others in research.

Intention and Awareness

Another consideration of working with the Sičáŋǧu Lakota and Native peoples, specifically in the United States, in addition to my white-Western-trained paradigm, is that Tribal Nations are sovereign entities "with the inherent right to self-government, including the authority to create their own laws and protect the health and welfare of their citizens" (Hershey, 2019, p. 55). Of the hundreds of federally recognized tribes in the United States, many have distinct languages, customs and worldviews. To generalize all Native peoples and customs into one "racial" group severely negates the historical, cultural, physical, spiritual and other differences these people have. In addition, many of these nations have practices and policies regarding working with non-Native and Indigenous people conducting research that also must be considered. For example, some tribes have their own IRB, or require tribal government permission to gather data. Kanehe (2007) also notes that "individual members of the tribe or other Indigenous group cannot consent for the entire population" (p. 117).

As well as the ethnic differences between Native and Indigenous peoples, non-Natives, land and relationship to the Earth is central to the knowledge and pedagogy of place (Wilson, 2008). As Westerners, it is easy to forget that the land on which we reside is the homeland and ancestral lands of people that have been residing in for thousands if not tens of thousands of years. Origin stories of Native and Indigenous people clearly articulate a long historical connection to place (Treuer, 2012). Discussion of geographical events such as glacial events, massive floods and other incidents modern science can easily mark as having occurred thousands of years before the invasion of Europeans or Spanish conquistadors (Mann, 2005).

Yet, even with this historical evidence, dominant culture often overlooks or negates the long history of Native and Indigenous peoples (Deloria, 1997), and the trauma that many of these groups have faced because of war, genocide, reservation assignment, boarding schools and allotment policies by the government (see Child, 2000; Heinrichs, 2013; Deloria, 1997: Yuan et al., 2014). Scholars are often no different. To recognize the land and the peoples that inhabited it thousands of years before settler colonialism began enables the start of a different relationship with Native people. To understand how nearly all Indigenous peoples in the United States have been forcefully moved and their traditional homelands unceded, stolen and besmirched, and how they have suffered as a result of governmental and settler-colonial policies begins a long acknowledgment of the harms that Native people have suffered. As Tuck and Yang (2012) comment, "until stolen land is relinquished, critical consciousness does not translate into action" (p. 19). Tuck and Yang (2012) reflect settler nativism "is an attempt to deflect a settler identity, while continuing to enjoy settler privilege and occupying stolen land" (p. 11). Thus, non-Native researchers must begin the very process of relationship with Native peoples starting with themselves and the land on which they inhabit. To decenter this settler nativism, we can ask questions such as:

- On what Indigenous homelands do I reside or occupy?
- How were these lands acquired by dominant culture?
- What is/are the treaty(ies) that were signed with the regional Indigenous groups, and what is the history of these agreements?
- Where are the Indigenous people of this land today?
- If the Indigenous people of the land still exist, how is their language, cultural practices and tribal well-being surviving and thriving today?

These questions and others begin to demonstrate how the historical context is crucial to grounding the intent of the research and their relationship with the community. To sit clearly in relationship means not just where a community is going, but also its history, context and strengths.

Direction of the Tipi: Intention

To begin a research project, setting the intention, or reason and energy desired as a researcher and community member/guest is important. To set up camp, understanding the land and the elements such as wind, sunrise, time of year, etc. is pivotal to how the tipi is assembled. This focus and intention set the stage for the work, and how the relationships and, as a reflection, the research, is conducted. Like a purpose statement at the beginning of a project, intention is the corner and touch stone that grounds the research and individuals in times of challenge and unclarity.

The Lakota often talk about coming in a "good way" or being intentional in their relationships. As Mirsky (1937) suggested, an individual's social standing was determined by how well he or she "interfaced with the group in terms of kinship, observing the proper degree of duties, avoidances, respect, and joking in the correct contexts" (p. 402). This "Lakota way of life" necessitates embracing not only the cultural aspects of being Lakota, but also all the values, virtues and traditions of putting others' needs first (Marshall, 2001). Lakota spirituality is viewed as more than a religious practice; it is described as a way of being (Deloria, 1944/1998; Marshall, 2001; Petrillo, 2007). Thus, setting a clear intention of relationship and research in partnership with tribal community is foundational to ethical research with Native Americans.

Cultural Liaisons and Translators

Another factor for those wishing to do research with Native people is having cultural liaison and translators (CLT) as part of the research project. First, to be a cultural liaison and translator means to be *from* that community, respected by, and seen as a representative of the community *by* the community. As Bends et al. (2013) comment, the skills CLTs bring to this position are "learned through their experience living and working on their reservations, being taught by family and other tribal members about the unique histories and philosophies of their tribes, proper protocol, and how to navigate in the local arenas" (p. 354). Previous researchers such as Edmonds et al. (1996), Reiber et al. (1992) and Watson et al. (2001) discuss the use of community members as peer educators, but this is generally done as part of a government or grant research project after needs have been "imposed" and the implementation of findings are being done. While this is also an important role, even more essential is developing relationships and setting the research stage with CLTs long before the project begins. Thus, as researchers we must consider *who* as a researcher one is aligning with, *how* these relationships are developed, the length of time these relationships have been in place and whether CLTs are respected within the community. To do this requires relationships within the community as researchers, and continued perception checking and feedback from community members. In addition, having several CLTs as part of the research project who are not only accountable to their community, but also responsible to community organizations is helpful.

Indigenous leadership is founded on the "interconnection of all things, the power of influence, the burden of leadership, and the role of persuasion" (Kenny, 2012, pp. 11–12). Consequently, conducting research having cultural liaisons and translators within the community are those that: (a) understand and are from the culture; (b) speak the language fluently and understand local slang and jargon; (c) are respected within the community and can speak to the needs and desires of the community accurately. Often these individuals are highly active in the community, have been chosen as informal leaders (i.e., they are elders and work in community-based organizations) or have held elected positions. These relations not only substantiate the project on many levels, but also honor the true nature of relationship for Sičáŋǧu Lakota and other Native people, who are much more relational and collectivist in nature (Gambrell, 2017).

Tipi Materials: Cultural Liaison and Translators

Tipi size, shape and the kind of materials are also important to setting up a successful camp. This is also true with cultural liaisons and translators. While there are different kinds of tipis made today, there is also the understanding that different sizes, shapes and materials are place-based, and withstand the elements differently given the climate and surroundings. People are much the same way in that not all ways of being work in every context. To assume that because someone is Native, or from the community, that they can navigate the political and tribal ways of the area is naïve and can be disastrous for relationships. As history has shown, many times the U.S. government and its imperialist systems have enforced laws and treaty "negotiations" under the premise that it "was supposed to be good for the Indians" (Echo-Hawk, 2010, p. 19). These acts often included enforcing a white patriarchal paradigm onto Natives forcing individuals to "speak" for their people to the point that not only were these "appointed people" not recognized by the tribes but were often also bribed by the government to do so (Hodge, 2012).

Different Native/Indigenous communities have different expectations, cultures and ontologies and, like the tipi materials, cultural liaisons are the bridge and translator, contextually appropriate for non-Natives to better understand and incorporate cultural/environmental nuances. Thus, having the best tipi-cultural liaison-for the environment is pivotal to not just surviving, but thriving.

Being in Relationship

For leadership researchers, being in relationship seems obvious, specifically when considering that leadership at its essence is all about connections. However, one thing that has become apparent is the need for authentic and sustained connections with the community. According to Smith (2012) the idea of community is "defined or imagined in multiple ways: as physical, political, social, psychological, historical, linguistic, economic, cultural, and spiritual spaces" (p. 128). Some authors refer to these examples and multiple layers of belonging as "nested identities" in the sense that many Native and Indigenous people have a multi-layered identity which can incorporate each one of the communities that he or she has inherited as well as the broader Native identity (Smith, 2012,

153

p. 129). As Mora and Diaz (2004) note, "The entire research endeavor must be participatory in nature in order to produce qualitatively different research that is based on community-identified problems and needs" (p. 24). Too often Native communities, including the Lakota, have shared stories of white researchers coming into their community with the desire to do research, and then abruptly leaving afterwards (Lambert, 2014; Smith, 2007). As Hodge (2012) reflects, research with Native and Indigenous populations has generally been implemented by governmental researchers with the aid of a "trusted member of the community" who acted as a translator, even when the community scarcely recognized these individuals.

Sadly, there are numerous examples of settler colonialists causing extensive harm within Native and Indigenous communities, and who were obviously not engaged in relationships with these groups. Instances such as the French and Indian War of 1756 to 1763 when small-pox-infected blankets were distributed to the Native American communities and thousands succumbed to the disease (Hodge, 2012; Kiger, 2019), to researchers drawing more than 200 blood samples for diabetes research from Havasupai tribal members (Hodge, 2012). Incidents such as these not only caused death and suffering among Native peoples, but in the case of the blood samples, these items were not only removed from the study site without the tribe's knowledge, but they were also used for other studies that contradicted the very core of the Havasupai's traditional beliefs negating their origin stories (Hodge, 2012). Hodge (2012) observes that, "American Indians/Alaska Natives have a troubling history of scientific racism that has led to multiple research abuses; violations of basic human rights; and, in some cases, genocidal tactics against American Indians" (p. 431). Subsequently, being in close relationship can help mitigate the potential for some of these types of future harms.

It is more difficult to use these scientific racist and ethnocentric tactics if one is truly in relationship with the people and community of which one is closely collaborating with. Chilisa (2012) frames this as relational axiology, describing it as being "built on the concept of relational accountability" (p. 22). This responsibility includes accountability, respectful representation, reciprocal appreciation and rights and regulations during the research process (Chilisa, 2012, p. 22). Even becoming an informal member of a Sičáŋǧu Lakota community means being a family or "relative" (tiošpaye[10]), which takes time and sustained effort. Thus, the level of care, relationship and responsibility naturally increases. The other aspect of this is that by being in relationship the researcher's "desires" are secondary, and the community needs rise as the priority (Chilisa, 2012, p. 294).

Being in Relationship: Tipi Location to Others

Relationship is key to research and to leadership. Connection to others, alignment with individuals and how the greater community aligns and configures is also key to the health, social dynamics and politics within a community. Thus, asking ourselves as researchers where our relationships lay, how healthy and genuine these relationships are and who we align ourselves with is central to the cultural quality, ethics and in turn, community benefit from the research. As such, *where* we set up camp in conjunction with others shows not just where our relationships are, but also how we understand the community, and what our role and responsibilities are within the community. As Posthumus (2019) notes, for the Lakota, an individual could not survive without a group of relatives to cooperate with. Smith (2007) writes, "the new relationship has to respect all of the other relationships around it" (p. 79).

Author's Application

As a Western-educated social scientist, understanding the cultural importance of an authentic relationship was difficult at first. I had been trained to ask the questions and drive the conversation/study towards the purpose I had designed. However, one of the best lessons I learned was to be quiet and *notice* what was going on around me. Observing who was talking to who, and which individuals (genders, etc.) were not present and why. As a Lakota *tuŋwiŋ*[11] gently scolded me, "Stop asking questions and watch. Your answers will come if you are open to them". Therefore, being willing to set aside my Western training, and to intentionally notice was (and still is) one of the more difficult lessons working the with the Lakota has taught. This noticing has served me well in ceremony, in relationship and in working with community. It helps me to start de-centering my settler-colonial worldviews and assumptions when working with others.

Prior to my initial research with the Lakota, I had been going to the reservation for over eight years. At first, I was invited by a Lakota woman I had been in the same friendship circle with. Eventually, I was able to develop long-term relationships with community members, and I continue to go to South Dakota at least annually. Since the original trip, I have attended weddings, graduations and funerals, as well as ceremonies to honor these relationships.

Land Is Central

As Wilson and Laing (2019) write, "As Indigenous people, our cultures are shaped by knowledge and ways of knowing that are connected to the land" (p. 136). The authors reflect that the most critical aspects of Native culture are those that are not seen, value systems, deep philosophies, cosmology and how all of that connects to how Native people go about being in the world. "Everything in the universe is speaking to us" and, as such, Indigenous literacy is based on the cosmos (Styres, 2019, p. 26). By inhabiting spaces – by being present in those spaces, to occupy these spaces and to story those spaces, to (re)member and (re)cognize those spaces – they become place*ful* (Styres, 2019). Casey (1996) writes that we are never without "emplaced experiences…we are not only in places, but of them" (p. 19).

For Native people, the land expresses a duality that refers not only to the "place as a physical geographical space, but also to the underlying conceptual principles, philosophies and ontologies of that space" (Styres, 2019, p. 27). Even in an urban context, the relationship to place and space stems from a different relationship than many settler-colonialists can epitomize or comprehend. As Orange (2018) writes, "everything here is formed in relation to every other living and non-living thing from the earth. All our relations" (p. 11). Many Native people's relationship to the land and animals creates the fabric of their society and a culture deep-rooted in relationship with the space.

However, the U.S. government, along with other imperialistic entities have, through their settler colonial practices, invariably destroyed the habitat that supports the tribal way of life (Echo-Hawk, 2010). As one example, Echo-Hawk (2010) discusses how "the plains habitat of the Pawnee Nation was virtually destroyed as countless millions of buffalo and wolves were slaughtered and steel plows were pulled through Native plant communities" (p. 361). Echo-Hawk (2010) suggests that the deforestation and destruction of the natural environment and the related wild animals and plants that had sustained the Native Indian tribes has led directly to their collapse. So much so that many went extinct following "the conquest of nature in North and South American since 1492" (Echo-Hawk, 2010, p. 361).

To be in relationship with Native and Indigenous people, and in turn to understand the needs and worldviews of that community, requires a strong sense of land and the people and history directly associated with it. As Smith, Tuck and Yang (2019) state, "*to say water is life, land is our teacher,* and to ignore Indigenous presence and relationship with those lands and waters, is to miss the point entirely" (p. 1, italics in original). Simpson (2016) aptly reminds: "[T]here is no decolonization without Indigenous present on Indigenous land and waters" (p. 20).

Land Is Central: Geographic Location of Tipi

Styres (2019) reflects, "[L]and expresses a duality that refers to not only to place as a physical geographic space but also to the underlying conceptual principles, philosophies, and ontologies of that space" (p. 27). Fundamentally, understanding that *where* camp is established is a direct connection to the earth and relationship of the people who are *of* that place. "Land as an Indigenous philosophical construct is both space (abstract) and place/land (concrete); it is also conceptual, experimental, relational, and embodied" (Styres, 2019, p. 27). As settler-colonial individuals, often white researchers believe we can "set up camp" anywhere. This assumption creates not just a scientific racist paradigm, but also negates how community is formed, especially as Native people.

Author's Application

As a researcher, unpacking the historical trauma and continued harm that policies by the U.S. Government continue to induce is part of the deconstruction of the leadership narratives the Lakota tell. Awareness of how these policies and related practices have potentially embedded themselves in the very stories and understanding the Lakota have is paramount to exploring leadership as a Native phenomenon, rather than a Western and colonial imposition.

To engage with the Lakota, first, an invitation to join gatherings and events needs to be made by community members. After years of accepting these invitations, ultimately an invitation to other events in the same community allowed for deeper acceptance and relationship to space, and the extended family/community (*tiošpaye*[12]). Needless to say, I made a number of mistakes and violated "where I could set up camp." And like many relationships, sometimes I was just not welcome. After a while, I learned to pay closer attention to the environment around me. This allowed for fewer mistakes, a greater awareness and, graciously, more invitations to be part of the community and relationship. This, in turn, allowed for collaborative research.

Styres (2019) emphasizes this by writing "Land is an articulation of ancient knowledges grounded in the experiences of self-in-relationship to place" (p. 24). If, as in the case of the Lakota, the land has been stolen and one's ancestors have been forcefully placed on a reservation, then one's worldview and its related narratives has been impacted by colonialization and often its related historical trauma.

Hold the Space

In research, especially when using Indigenous methods, qualitative, or action/participatory research, holding the space for participants to feel comfortable, safe and authentic is key to gaining meaningful insights into the phenomena and meaning making from the participants. It is part of the higher quality relationship, and the often rather therapeutic nature of listening. As Wilson (2008) comments:

> In our cultures an integral part of any ceremony is setting the stage properly. When ceremonies take place, everyone who is participating needs to be ready to step beyond the everyday and to accept a raised state of consciousness. You could say that the specific rituals make up the ceremony are designed to get the participants into a state of mind that will allow for the extraordinary to take place. (p. 69)

While holding the space is closely related to the concept of intent, this concept moves past just setting the intention, to one of deliberately holding a state of increased mindfulness throughout the research and being in relationship (Wilson, 2008). As such, holding the space is a litmus test and cornerstone to how we as researchers engage with those we are doing research with, and *how* we want to be and stay in those relationships. To consider "how the researcher listens, pays attention, acknowledges, and creates space for the voices and the knowledge systems of the Others" is all part of holding space (Chilisa, 2012, p. 22). How this is manifested and demonstrated can shift and evolve with time and the deepening of connection; it cannot, however, be undersold or devalued in the importance of it. Furthermore, one cannot take it lightly or impose a Western relational under-standing regarding intent, either through informality, a colonial understanding or a transactional interpretation.

Hold the Space: Inside the Tipi

Kapferer (2008) noted that Lakota spirituality and ritual clearly function to maintain a sense of indigeneity and the distinctiveness for Lakota identity and tradition. This decolonizing strategy works in "opposition and resistance to non-Lakota belief and practice, neocolonialism, and the homogenizing effects of globalization and multiculturalism" (Posthumus, 2019, p. 6). While in Lakota tradition there are several community members that can create and hold the space, in ceremony these individuals are often spiritual, "medicine people" or elders, and as a patriarchal tribe, often men (Gambrell, 2009, p. 90).

Creating and holding a specific intention and purpose for ceremony is a humbling and am-biguous responsibility. As Fools Crow reflected, having a high moral compass, clear purpose and a humble heart are needed when individuals engage in ceremony (Mails, 1979, pp. 49–54). Therefore, carrying the intention of relationship and working in and with community as one moves forward with research is not a light endeavor. Like the inside of one's dwelling, this is a space held where family and friends come and stay, and where safe, healthy and productive connections can reside.

Smith (1999) proposes that researchers must go beyond simply recognizing one's personal beliefs, assumptions and effects they have on others. In addition, continued perception-checking and ac-countability play into holding the space. This kind of discernment includes asking questions such as:

- Who defined the research question?
- For whom is this study worthy and relevant? Says who?
- What knowledge will the community gain from this study?
- What are some likely possible positive and negative outcomes from this research?
- To whom is the researcher accountable? (Smith, 1999, p. 173)

Author's Application

To hold the space and set an intention for research, having many community conversations is required to identify the need for the study. To do this, I have discussions with individuals at length before the formal research begins and ask permission in a traditional manner, to speak formally to each of my participants. Often this involves a tobacco offering, or *opaǧi* asking for guidance, or permission (White Hat, 2012) and sets the stage for respect, reciprocity and ac-countability (Wilson, 2008, p. 99). In addition, unlike many qualitative or quantitative methods, multiple "interviews" and observations are held. This method allows for a more sustained re-lationship, deeper understanding and the ability to explore their perspective through story and narrative. Furthermore, it allows me to listen deeply, and be present, instead of focusing pre-dominantly on the interview questions. Last, and more importantly, this manner of conversation also sets the stage for understanding, as a researcher, what information and stories are shared as friends, and are not for wider disbursement. Came (2013) reflects on this in her discussion of the *Te Ara Tika* Māori framework, which incorporates the elements of relationships, justice and equity, research design and cultural and social responsibility. As other authors note, bringing reverence to the study through my interactions with the participants works to ensure that I respected their requests and that I honored their stories and their trust (e.g., see Chilisa, 2012, 2019; Smith, 1999/2012; Yuan et al., 2014).

Indigenous Worldviews

Thankfully, more and more Indigenous and Native scholars and researchers are sharing their wisdom with the wider community. Examples include Lakota author Joseph Marshall III (e.g., 2001, 2004, 2014, 2016) who has written many books on Lakota worldviews. In addition, Vine Deloria (e.g., 1997, 2003) challenged the academy in several of his books. In addition, Linda Tuhiwai Smith (1999/2012) set the stage for decolonizing research in her groundbreaking book and, since, many others have followed. "Unfortunately, we mostly hear that version from a dominant perspective that has assumed the right to tell the stories of the colonized and the oppressed that they have re-interpreted, re-presented, and re-told through their own lens" (Smith, Tuck, & Yang, 2019, p. xi).

> It galls us that Western researchers and intellectuals can assume to know all that it is possible to know of us that the West can desire, extract and claim ownership of our ways of knowing, our imagery, the things we create and produce, and the simultaneously reject the people who created and developed those ideas and seek to deny them further opportunities to be creators of their own cultures and own nations. (Smith, 2012, p. 2)

However, while white, non-Native people cannot be "Indigenous researchers", because only Native peoples carry Indigenous worldviews, we can intentionally use Indigenous research methods to better engage with communities. For instance, Wilson (2008) discusses this when he writes about the four dominant research paradigms that Western researchers often ground their work in: positivism, post-positivism, critical theory and constructivism (p. 35–37). As Wilson notes:

> There is a common thread of thinking that runs through them. The commonality is that knowledge is seen as being individual in nature. This is vastly different from the Indigenous paradigm, where knowledge is seen as belonging to the cosmos of which we are a part and where researchers are only the interpreters of this knowledge. (p. 38)

This key distinction between Indigenous and dominant/non-Indigenous and the "ownership" of knowledge is one major difference in worldviews.

Ways to Engage in Indigenous Research Methods

As non-Native individuals, to begin using Indigenous research methods there are things that ought to be considered:

1. Consider the epistemology being used – Wilson (2008) comments that using an Indigenous perspective is not enough, but rather Indigenous research must leave behind dominant paradigms. As Smith (1999) contends, research, especially with Indigenous people, needs to de-center a colonized mindset. While this is not the ultimate end-goal, decolonialization[13] is a step towards centering the voices of the Native/Indigenous people, and de-centering the dominant voices, including those of the researcher(s) (Figure 9.2).
2. Writing and reporting – Smith (1999) states that for Indigenous people–"Every aspect of the act of producing knowledge has influenced the ways in which indigenous ways of knowing have been represented" because the writings; (a) do not reinforce Native/Indigenous values, actions, customs, etc., (b) often express information in ways that imply Native/Indigenous do not exist,

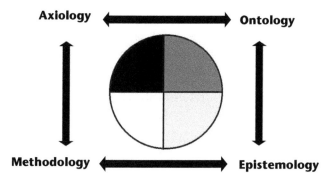

Figure 9.2 Indigenous Research Paradigm.
Source: See Wilson (2008, p. 70).

(c) may be writing about Native/Indigenous but are writing things that are untrue, and (d) are writing about Native/Indigenous but are writing things that are culturally insensitive" (p. 19). Thus, the researcher(s) should consider *how* reporting the information will impact the community from which the information came.

3. Responsibilities to community-Numerous ethics protocols guide research with Native/Indigenous communities. As such, "resisting the colonizer/colonized relationships that embrace deficit theorizing and damage-focused research about the Other", as well as "embracing ethical protocols that draw from cultural practices informed by connectedness" can guide the researcher(s) (Chilisa, 2012, p. 295).

Using these guidelines as a foundation to research will not only begin to de-center a Western paradigm, but they can also interrupt, at least to some degree, what Chilisa (2012) called "deficit theorizing, damaged-focused assumptions, prejudices, and stereotypes" (p. 57) that Western-trained scholars have often used in research methodology, analysis, and interpretation in a study.

Research Is Transformative

As Shawn Wilson (2008) so beautifully articulates, if we are doing our research in a good way, it transforms us. Working with communities and commemorating their resiliency, strengths, assets and needs cannot but intensify the depth of relationship, insights and profound honor that working with Native/Indigenous people can bring. Having the reverence to gain deeper insights, understanding and to ultimately, if we are fortunate, help the community is a humbling and amazing experience. Furthermore, the opportunity to de-center ourselves as researchers and work together with others is not only extremely rewarding, but it also provides an opportunity to transform ourselves as settler colonialists. As Wilson (2008) proposes, "if research doesn't change you as a person, you didn't do it right" (p. 135).

Transformational Experience and Reflection

Wilson (2008) reminds his readers that research is ceremony. Honoring the process as such enables researchers to learn from others, and get a glimpse into deeper understanding, awareness and an opportunity to explore our own understanding of the world around us in a more insightful and transformative way. And while the research itself is often enlightening, more so are the relationships and various perspectives that engaging in research can bring.

In my relationship with the Sičáŋǧu Lakota, I have truly been transformed by their profound and amazing generosity, resiliency and humanity. The Lakota are a proud, resourceful and strong people.

They, like many people and tribes, have shown great forte and resolve. Like other Native and Indigenous groups, the Lakota and their associated reservations and communities are also challenged by many things, most of which have stemmed from the imperialistic and colonialization of the United States and the related practices of the U.S. government.

These relationships have changed me for the better, and, I believe, helped me become a better researcher and teacher. Most importantly however, I believe they have helped me become a better relative.

Concepts and the Tipi

As discussed previously, the concepts used here emerged from many years of relationship, engagement and work with the Sičáŋǧu Lakota. The connections made here reflect my personal reflection and understanding of these notions, but also the understanding that nothing is permanent, and application of these ideas historically, or even today might not be how others understand or would explain them. This, too, is a Lakota way of understanding, as I can only speak from my personal perspective, and not for others (Marshall, 2001). In addition, while these things are written in a linear form, they are not steps to be taken in a specific order. They are fluid, circular, ebbing and flowing with the relationship and context.

Final Thoughts

There have been many lessons I have learned from my Lakota teachers, more than can candidly be discussed here. I have tried to share some of them, however, there is no real way to depict the depth and breadth of being in relationship from a Lakota sense, while still wearing Western, settler colonialist lenses. However, one last thought emerges as I conclude this chapter. And that is that there are just some stories that are not meant to be shared. Having had others sit with me as a compassionate friend, as someone who just needed to get the words out to look at and consider for myself, then having a friend and confidant who will just listen, knowing the story was not theirs to share, to fix or to navigate was profound and exceptionally helpful. While there are these personal stories, there are also community and cultural stories that are just that, so sacred that they are not for common knowledge or dispersion, especially from a Westerner.

As a qualitative researcher there have also been times where I have had participants share something that was personal, sacrosanct even. And it is in that moment, and again when reviewing the transcripts, that as a researcher and as a relative, having the opportunity to discern how deeply I am connected to the person/people in front of me, and if that particular story is meant for a broader community, or instead, is like dandelion seed fluff in the wind...here one moment, and off the next. This is the power of relationship, that not only are we blessed as researchers with these moments that deeply connect us to one another, but this also allows us to truly consider if the information and story was for our ears only, or meant for the wider society to learn and grow from. This challenges the very fundamental question and belief as a settler colonialist and Western-trained scientist. Thus, asking myself the questions such as "Do I have the *right* to this knowledge and truth" and even if this information or knowledge has been shared with me, is it "'mine' to share with others, are important to begin unsettling my dominant training and paradigm. Additionally, I should not assume that I have been trained well enough, or have listened, observed or understood sufficiently to have "discovered" any new truth or knowledge, or even that I have drawn accurate conclusions as I conduct research. However, being in a continued place of acknowledgment, intention, awareness, cultural liaisons and translators, relationships, setting and holding the space, recognizing my positionality and potential transformation helps navigate some of these dilemmas.

Last, this depth of relationship from the Lakota understanding or other Native/Indigenous worldviews are not taught as part of the dominant, Western and settler-colonist paradigm from my experience. And as such, to truly walk in relationship with the land, and the Lakota who have a profound, cultural and ancestral connection to it, we as guests must tread gently, working to respect and honor the gifts we are given. Archuleta (2012) comments that "leadership is in the midst of change" (p. 163), and I agree. Using non-Western ways of research and being in relationship can be at the leading edge of this change.

Note About Lakota Language

Lakota is an oral language, and while it has been transformed to written, there are several ways readers may see spellings (and definitions) of words. For this chapter, two sources were consulted: White Hat (1999) Reading and Writing the Lakota Language. The University of Utah Press; and Buechel and Manhart (2002). Lakota Dictionary. University of Nebraska Press.

Notes

1 I choose to capitalize the term Indigenous here to de-center the dominant narrative and honor Indigenous authors and researchers.
2 In this piece, to begin the process of de-centering a dominant paradigm, I choose to not capitalize the term "white."
3 Indigenous, First Nation, Aboriginal, Indian and Native American are all terms used, albeit in different areas of the globe, for peoples indigenous to the specific geographical place since time immemorial. For the sake of this piece, I will generally use the terms Native, Native American and Indigenous. I choose to capitalize the term Indigenous here, as Native and Indigenous authors do.
4 Sovereign nation: The power to do everything necessary to govern itself. Native American tribes are sovereign nations that retain many of their pre-colonial rights. Sovereign immunity is one of those rights.
5 Sičáŋǧu Oyáte (the Upper Brule Sioux Nation) – are also known as Sičáŋǧu Lakota, and the Rosebud Sioux Tribe, a branch of the Lakota people and one of the seven council fires (tribes) of the Lakota. Rosebud Reservation is in south-central South Dakota.
6 Ontology is the theory of the nature of existence, or the nature of reality. Ontology asks, what is real?
7 Epistemology is the study of the nature of thinking or knowing. It involves the theory of how we come to have knowledge. As such, it asks, how do I know what is real?
8 Axiology is the ethics that guide the search for knowledge and determines which information of worthy searching for. Thus, it asks the question, what is ethical to do in order to gain this knowledge, and what will it be used for?
9 A tipi is a plains Indians traditional dwelling.
10 The Lakota term for extended family unit.
11 Lakota for aunt.
12 Extended family or band.
13 Decolonialization has been described as a process which engages with imperialism and colonialism at multiple levels, working to decenter these systems. For researchers, this means having a deep understanding of the underlying assumptions, motivations and values which inform research practices.

References

Archuleta, M. (2012). Approaching leadership through culture, story, and relationships. In C. Kenny & T. Ngaroimata (Eds.), *Living Indigenous leadership: Native narratives on building strong communities* (pp. 162–175). UBC Press.

Arvin, M. (2014, June 2). Possessions of whiteness: Settler colonialism and anti-blackness in the Pacific. *Decolonization-Indigeneity, Education & Society*. https://decolonization.wordpress.com/2014/06/02/possessions-of-whiteness-settler-colonialism-and-anti-blackness-in-the-pacific/

Bends, A., Burns, C., Yellowman-Caye, P., Rider, T., Salois, E. M., Sutherland, A., Todd, M., LaVeaux, D., & Christopher, S. (2013). Community-university research liaisons: Translating the languages of research and culture. *Pimatisiwin: A Journal of Aboriginal and Indigenous Community Health, 11*(3), 345–357.

Blaut, J. M. (1993). *The colonizer's model of the world. Geographical diffusionism and eurocentric history.* The Guilford Press. ISBN 0-89862-348-0

Came, H. A. (2013). Doing research in Aotearoa: A Pākehā exemplar of applying Te Ara Tika ethical framework. *Kotuitui: New Zealand Journal of Social Sciences.* doi:10.1080/1177083X.2013.841265

Casey, E. S. (1996). How to get from space to place in a fairly short stretch of time: Phenomenological prolegomena. In S. Feld & K. Basso (Eds.), *Senses of place* (pp. 13–52). School of American Research Press.

Child, B. J. (2000). *Boarding school seasons: American Indian Families, 1900–1940.* University of Nebraska Press.

Chilisa, B. (2012). *Indigenous research methodologies.* SAGE.

Chilisa, B. (2019). *Indigenous research methodologies* (2nd ed). SAGE.

Cotter, H. (2016, September 15). An artist redefines power. With sanitation equipment. *New York Times.* https://www.nytimes.com/2016/09/16/arts/design/an-artist-redefines-power-with-sanitation-equipment.html.

Deloria, P. J. (1998). *Playing Indian.* Yale University Press.

Deloria, E. C. (1944/1998). *Speaking of Indians.* University of Nebraska Press.

Deloria, V. (1997). *Red earth, white lies. Native Americans and the myth of scientific fact.* Fulcrum Publishing.

Deloria, V. (2003). *God is red: A native view of religion.* Fulcrum Publishing.

Echo-Hawk, W. R. (2010). *In the courts of the conqueror: The 10 worst Indian law cases ever decided.* Fulcrum Publishing.

Edmonds, M.E., Van Acker, K., Foster, A. V. M. (1996). Education and the diabetic foot. *Diabetic Medicine, 13,* S61–S64.

Gambrell, K. (2009). *Healers and helpers, unifying the people: A qualitative study of Lakota leadership* [Unpublished doctoral dissertation]. University of Nebraska-Lincoln.

Gambrell, K. (2017). The case for an Indigenous collectivist mindset. In J. L. Chin, J. E. Trimble & Garcia, J. E. (Eds.), *Global and culturally diverse leaders and leadership (Building leadership bridges)* (pp. 21–39). Emerald Publishing Limited. doi:10.1108/S2058-880120170000003001.

Heinrichs, S. (2013). *Buffalo shout, salmon cry: Conversations on creation, land justice, and life together.* Herald Press.

Hershey, T. B. (2019). Collaborating with sovereign tribal nations to legally prepare for public health emergencies. *The Journal of Law, Medicine & Ethics, 47*(2), 55–58.

Hitchcock, J., & Flint, C. (2015). *Decentering whiteness.* Center for the Study of White American Culture.

Hodge, F. S. (2012). No meaningful apology for American Indian unethical research abuses. *Ethics and Behavior, 22*(6), 431–444.

Kanehe, L. M. (2007). From Kumulipo: I know where i come from-an Indigenous Pacific critique of the genographic project. In P. Mead & S. Ratuva (Eds.), *Pacific genes & life patents. Pacific Indigenous experiences & analysis of the commodification & ownership of life*(pp. 114–129). Call of the Earth Llamado de la Tierra and The United nations University Institute of Advanced Studies.

Kapferer, B. (2008). Beyond symbolic representation: Victor Turner and variations on the themes of ritual process and liminality. *Suomen Antropologi: The Journal of the Finnish Anthropological Society, 33*(4), 5–25.

Kenny, C. (2012). Liberating leadership theory. In C. Kenny, & T. N. Fraser (Eds.), *Living indigenous leadership: Native narratives on building strong communities* (pp. 1–14). UBC Press.

Kiger, P. J. (2019, November 25). Did colonists give infected blankets to native Americans as biological warfare? *History Stories.* https://www.history.com/news/colonists-native-americans-smallpox-blankets.

Kovach, M. (2010). *Indigenous methodologies: Characteristics, conversations and contexts.* University of Toronto Press.

Lambert, L. (2014). *Research for Indigenous survival: Indigenous research methodologies in the behavioral sciences.* Salish Kootenai College Press.

Mails, T. E. (1979). *Fools crow.* University of Nebraska Press.

Mann, C. C. (2005). *1491: New revelations of the Americas before Columbus.* First Vintage Books.

Marshall III, J. M. (2001). *The Lakota way: Stories and lessons for living.* Penguin Compass.

Marshall III, J. M. (2004). *The journey of Crazy Horse.* Penguin Books.

Marshall III, J. M. (2014). *Returning to the Lakota way: Old values to save a modern world.* Hay House, Inc.

Marshall III, J. M. (2016). *The Lakota way of strength and courage: Lessons in resilience from the bow and arrow.* Sounds true.

Mirsky, J. (1937). The Dakota. In M. Mead (Ed.), *Cooperation and competition among primitive peoples* (pp. 382–427).

Mora, J. & Diaz, D. (Eds.) (2004). *Latino social policy: A participatory research model.* Haworth Press.

National Conference of State Legislatures. (n.d.). *Federal and state recognized tribes.* Retrieved on October 18, 2020, from https://www.ncsl.org/research/state-tribal-institute/list-of-federal-and-state-recognized-tribes.aspx

Omi, M., & Winant, H. (1994). *Racial formation in the United States: From the 1960s to the 1990s*. Routledge.

Orange, T. (2018). *There, there*. Penguin Random House.

Petrillo, L. (2007). *Being Lakota: Identity and tradition on the pine ridge reservation*. University of Nebraska Press.

Pedro, L. (2017, November 7). Rashaad Newsome recenters blackness in art history. In sculpture and collage, Newsome explores agency, feminism, and what we think we're looking at. *Hyperallergic*. https://hyperallergic.com/410233/rashaad-newsome-recenters-blackness-in-art-history/.

Posthumus, D. C. (2019). The ritual thiyóšpaye and the social organization of contemporary lakota ceremonial life. *Journal for the Anthropology of North America, 22*(1), pp. 4–21. doi:10.1002/nad.12091.

Q'um Q'um Xiiem, J. A., Lee-Morgan, J. B. & De Santolo, J. (2019). Decolonizing research: Indigenous storywork as methodology. In J. A. Q'um Q'um Xiiem, J. B. Lee-Morgan, & J. De Santolo (Eds.), *Decolonizing research: Indigenous storywork as methodology*. (pp. 1–16). Zed Books.

Regan, S. (2017). Redefining art through an intersectional lens. *Hyperallergic*. https://hyperallergic.com/399492/redefining-american-art-through-an-intersectional-lens/.

Reiber, G. E., Pecoraro, R. E., & Koepsell, T. D. (1992). Risk factors for amputation in patients with diabetes mellitus, a case control study. *Annals of Internal Medicine, 117*, 97–105.

Simpson, L. (2016). Indigenous resurgence and co-existence. *Journal of the Critical Ethnic Studies Association, 2*(2), 19–34.

Smith, L. T. (1999). *Decolonizing methodologies: Research and Indigenous peoples*. Zed Books.

Smith, L. T. (2007). Getting the story right-telling the story well. Indigenous activism-indigenous research. In P. Mead & S. Ratuva (Eds.), *Pacific genes & life patents. pacific indigenous experiences & analysis of the commodification & ownership of life*(pp. 74–81). Call of the Earth Llamado de la Tierra and The United nations University Institute of Advanced Studies.

Smith, L. T. (2012). *Decolonizing methodologies: Research and indigenous peoples* (2nd ed.) Zed Books.

Smith, L. T., Tuck, E., and Yang, K. W. (2019). *Indigenous and decolonizing studies in education: Mapping the long view*. Routledge.

Styres, S. (2019). Literacies of the land: Decolonizing narratives, storying and literature. In L. T. Smith, E. Tuck, & K. W. Yang, (Eds.). *Indigenous and decolonizing studies in education: Mapping the long view*. Routledge.

Treuer, A. (2012). *Everything you wanted to know about Indians but were afraid to ask*. Borealis Books.

Tuck, E., & Yang, K. W. (2012). Decolonization is not a metaphor. *Decolonization: Indigeneity, Education & Society 1*(1), 1–40. http://decolonization.org/index.php/des/article/view/18630/15554.

Uhl-Bien, M., Marion, R. & McKelvey, B. (2007). Complexity leadership theory" shifting leadership from the industrial age to the knowledge era. *Leadership Quarterly, 18*(4), 398-318.

Veracini, L. (2017). Decolonizing settler colonialism: Kill the settler in him and save the man. *American Indian Culture and Research Journal, 41*(1), 1–18.

Voyageur, C., Brearley, L, & Calliou, B. (Eds.). (2015). *Restorying Indigenous leadership: Wise Practices in community development*. Banff Centre Press.

Watson, J., Obersteller, E. A., Rennie, L., & Whitbread, C. (2001). Diabetic foot care: Developing culturally appropriate educational tools for Aboriginal and Torres Strait Islander peoples in the Northern Territory, Australia. *The Australian Journal of Rural Health, 9*(3). 121–127.

White Hat, A. (2012). *Life's Journey-Zuya.: Oral teachings from Rosebud*. (J. Cunningham, Ed.). University of Utah Press.

Wilson, S. (2008). *Research is ceremony: Indigenous research methods*. Fernwood Publishing.

Wilson, A. & Laing, M. (2019). Queering Indigenous education. In L. T. Smith, E. Tuck, & K. W. Yang (Eds.), *Indigenous and decolonizing studies in education* (pp. 131–155). Routledge.

Yuan, N. P., Bartgis, J., & Demers, J. (2014). Promoting ethical research with American Indian and Alaska Native people living in urban areas. *Framing Health Matters, 104*(11), 2085–2091.

Yukl, G. (1999). An evaluation of conceptual weaknesses in transformational and charismatic leadership theories. *Leadership Quarterly 10*(2), 285–305.

Zheng, L. (2016, May 15). Why your brave space sucks. *The Stanford Daily*. https://www.stanforddaily.com/2016/05/15/why-your-brave-space-sucks/.

10

Researching Religious Leadership in a Postmodern, Northwest European Context

Jack Barentsen and Leon van den Broeke

Introduction

Religion and religious leadership play hugely different roles across the world. In many countries, religion is a matter of birth and culture and is often intimately connected with structures of governance. Yet, many Western societies have experienced strong secularizing tendencies that have relegated religion to personal choice and the private sphere. This has resulted in major declines in church membership, and the closure of hundreds of church buildings. Consequently, religious leadership – at least in northwest Europe – no longer occupies a significant public place in politics, business, education or health but appears to be an internal matter for religious communities (Taylor, 2007; Paul, 2017; Root, 2019). Recent developments, however, also demonstrate contrary trends, since the influence of religious leadership is widely felt in Western societies (Cartledge et al., 2019; Barentsen, 2020). Many religious leaders have received positive press for their public involvement in peace-making, issues of race, anti-poverty or sustainability, while other religious leaders attract a substantial following with mindfulness, meditation, yoga, reading cards and dozens of other spiritual practices (Carrette & King, 2005; Christerson & Flory, 2017; Stanton, 2019). On the other hand, some religious leaders drew negative media attention, for instance, because of sexual abuse, misuse of funds or religiously motivated violence. Clearly, the public presence of religion and the societal impact of its leaders is undeniable in Western societies in spite of decades of secularization (Zonderop, 2018).

These cultural evolutions have created a turbulent context for the practice and the interpretation of religious leadership during the last 50 years. One of the main challenges of religious leaders is to navigate their religious communities through the rough waters of a secularizing society on the one hand, and of the increasing religious diversification on the other, while maintaining relevant connections with their own religious traditions (Barentsen & Foppen, 2020b). Considering the impact of religious leadership in Western societies, it is vital that these dynamics are investigated, both by scholars who count themselves religious and by other scholars of organizational and public leadership (Barentsen, 2016b).

This chapter narrates the research process of a Dutch/Belgian ecumenical research group that has collaborated in researching religious leadership for nearly a decade, in which the current authors participated. The first phase of this Dutch-speaking research group focused on the Dutch/Belgian context, had an ecumenical, that is, a multi-Christian membership and focus, and was recently completed. This phase focused on pastoral leadership in Christian traditions represented in northwest Europe. This is hardly representative of religious leadership in various religions and across the world,

DOI: 10.4324/9781003003380-10

but already this limited scope demanded a variety of expertise, knowledge, and traditions to accomplish the limited objective. New phases of research may be initiated by widening the research scope to include the entire European context or even various global contexts. Another extension of research may involve religious leadership in other world religions. In this chapter, we point to lessons learned to enable this further and broader research into this significant field.

The research from the ecumenical group is framed with a broader review of the vast literature on religious leadership, specifically within Christian faith communities. We can only do so in exemplary fashion, selecting complementary sources to offer a comprehensive survey of the terrain. We conclude with lessons learned and an agenda for the future of research on religious leadership. Finally, we offer this review in the hope that in general it will encourage scholarship and leadership research across many domains and especially in the areas of religious studies and religious leadership. We narrated explicitly about the internal deliberations in our research group in order to provide insights for education in leadership research.

The Formation of a Dutch/Belgian Ecumenical Research Group (DBERG)

The Netherlands and Belgium have a rich Christian history, with Reformed traditions represented mostly in the northern provinces of the Netherlands, and Roman Catholicism mostly in the southern provinces and in Belgium. Secularization tendencies led to major losses in church membership since the 1960s while simultaneously the population grew more open towards a great diversity of religious and spiritual influences (Bernts & Berghuijs, 2016). In these cultural dynamics, the function of religious leadership was under stress, and research was urgently needed.

In 2009, the Centre for Religion and Law, a joint venture of the Faculties of Theology and of Law at the Vrije Universiteit Amsterdam, organized a symposium on pastoral and denominational leadership of faith communities at the supralocal level. The Centre invited experts in religion, law, governance, canon law and religious leadership from several universities, to discuss church governance and translocal supervision. Several participants (had) served as pastor or bishop (previously). The symposium focused on questions like: Who is in charge? What is the religious or theological legitimation for their authority? To what extent do structures of leadership function as identity markers and represent deeply treasured values for faith communities, both local and translocal?[1]

Answers to these questions varied greatly by tradition. Evangelical and Pentecostal faith communities are primarily locally organized and locally oriented. They are autonomous and independent, without formal connections to other local churches; yet they cooperate on various matters more informally. These are labeled "congregational churches." Faith communities like the Roman Catholic Church are primarily nationally and internationally organized. These so-called "episcopal churches" are organized in a centralized, hierarchical fashion with a top figure, like the Pope. In between these congregational and episcopal churches are the so-called "synodical-presbyterial" churches that emphasize both local governance and translocal connections and supervision. Although these three types of churches are theoretically distinct, in practice they function like a typology with great variety and some overlap.

The 2009 symposium investigated this situation from an ecumenical (i.e., multi-Christian) perspective. Biblical and historical scholars offered perspectives on translocal leadership in the Early Church (the first centuries AD) and throughout the Middle Ages. Systematic theologians and canon law scholars discussed the episcopal perspective of the Roman Catholic Church, the (im)possibility of a translocal supervisor in Protestant denominations and the congregational perspective on the bishop as from below instead of being hierarchically appointed from above (Houtepen et al., 2011).

This symposium and its proceedings led in January of 2010 to the formation of a long-term Dutch-Belgian Ecumenical Research Group (DBERG) on local and translocal religious leadership under the auspices of the Netherlands School for Advanced Studies in Theology and Religion (NOSTER).[2]

Theologians from various Christian traditions and with expertise in biblical studies, systematic or practical theology, leadership and church polity, gathered several times each year until 2019. The group started with 7 scholars in 2010, invited external specialists to present their research at their meetings, and thus grew to a peak of 15 scholars in 2014.[3] It focused mainly on religious leadership of churches in the Netherlands and Belgium, with the aim of broadening the group to study religious leadership in the European post-Christendom context. The group's diversity of expertise and Christian traditions presented a unique opportunity to study religious leadership from a multidisciplinary and ecumenical perspective, different from the typical internal discussions in each Christian tradition among its own specialists.

During its early years, the group identified three dimensions of religious leadership that needed further investigation: the individual, institutional and educational dimensions of religious leadership (details follow). These dimensions became the framework for the next phase of qualitative research.

In 2015, four focus group sessions were conducted with Dutch and Belgian church leaders (in Dutch). In countries where only 25% of the population claimed any form of church membership in 2015 (Bernts & Berghuijs, 2016), down from 75% in 1980,[4] religious leaders from 15 major denominations were selected as a representative sample. These denominations sent 27 representatives (both pastors and denominational leaders), divided over the first two focus groups. Next, educational leaders from schools of theological education from these same denominations were invited, and 15 delegates responded, which again were divided into two focus groups.

For each focus group session, many members of the DBERG were present. The invited participants shared and discussed their prepared answers to three questions. These questions focused on (1) how they evaluated the changing cultural climate and its effects on religious leaders, (2) which aspects of the Bible and their church tradition they felt were absolutely necessary for future church leaders and (3) what consequences this should have for theological education, its curriculum and its effect on personal formation. Subsequently, the DBERG discussed and analyzed the results, which become the foundational chapters of *Religieus leiderschap in post-christelijk Nederland* (ET: *Religious Leadership in the Post-Christian Netherlands*) (van den Broeke & van der Borght, 2020). Other chapters offered interpretations of these results following each DBERG scholar's expertise.

In summary, the formation and activities of the Dutch Belgian Ecumenical Research Group represented a timely response from relevant faculties of theology to current cultural and societal pressures on faith communities and religious institutions. Given the task of these faculties in educating new generations of religious leadership, they needed to investigate the dynamics of religious leadership within their constituencies. The resulting data showed much shared concern over cultural developments and leadership challenges, even if research participants represented a significant diversity of leadership structures, leadership principles and community functions.

Developing a Common Language and Research Framework

During the early years, the DBERG devoted much time to developing a common language and research framework. The diverse specialties on the research team led to some polarization between the concepts of religious leadership as *office* and as *leadership*. Those favoring the terminology of *office* and *ministry* defined the leadership role in biblical, theological and institutional terms, where concepts like calling, representation and ordination play a large role. Others favored the language of *leadership* to highlight the human and social nature of the leadership function within the group or community, with concepts like management, power, collaboration and identity. Slowly, mutual understanding developed over the course of a number of meetings, which was reflected in a few publications (van den Broeke & van der Borght, 2012; and also much later Barentsen, 2018).

This discussion reflects a number of different research traditions. The first research tradition comes from biblical studies since religious leadership is almost always rooted in particular interpretations of sacred texts. Since the 1970s, social scientific models have been used in the study of biblical texts about leadership. Holmberg used Weber's theory of authority to interpret leadership developments in the missionary work of the apostle Paul (Holmberg, 1978). Clarke used cultural-anthropological research on status and patronage to interpret leadership roles in the early Corinthian church (Clarke, 1993). Marchal used the lenses of feminist theory and power constructs to study a small New Testament letter, *Philippians*, while Ehrensperger extended the use of theories of power and identity in understanding Pauline leadership (Ehrensperger, 2007). Barentsen combined theories of leadership and power with social identity theory to reconstruct leadership development in the Pauline mission (Barentsen, 2011). Stewart-Sykes offered the latest reconstruction of church leadership in the first two centuries AD (Stewart-Sykes, 2014), combining various lines of historical, cultural and social scientific analysis of biblical texts.

A second research tradition focused on historical studies of the development of church leadership in more recent centuries. For instance, Heitink traced the development of the pastoral office in the Netherlands from the 16th through the 20th century (Heitink, 2001). In the process, he developed the model of *person/office/profession* to understand the dynamics and tensions of pastoral leadership, which a number of DBERG scholars used with appreciation. Similar historical research has been done in the USA (Holifield, 2007), in the United Kingdom (Billings, 2010) and in Germany (Klessmann, 2001). Such historical developments describe the structures and functions of religious organizations and leadership in their historical and cultural contexts.

A third research tradition focused on a theological understanding of religious leadership, often drawing on ecumenical debates such as in the World Council of Churches. This resulted in systematic theological and historical theological studies about church office, which employed careful analysis of concepts like ordination, calling, apostolic succession, Christ representation and sacrament (Graafland, 1999; van der Borght, 2007). Another study proposed adding the office of bishop to existing Protestant ministry structures (Kronenburg, 2003). These studies typically compare normative historical documents, interpretations of biblical texts, and practices from various traditions to legitimate and refine existing structures of leadership, occasionally to create new structures to unify distinct traditions. This research focuses mainly on negotiating normative theological principles.

A fourth research tradition represents empirical theological research on the current practice of religious leadership, often with the help of current leadership theory. Brouwer investigated the professionalization of pastoral leadership in the Netherlands (Brouwer, 1995), while Volland employed models of entrepreneurial leadership in qualitative research on innovative church leadership (Volland, 2013). This type of research has also been conducted by members of the Academy of Religious Leadership (mostly in the USA, see their *Journal of Religious Leadership*), in which Barentsen published a study on adaptive church leadership and identity construction (Barentsen, 2015). This research attempts to bridge the languages of traditional theological analysis and the social sciences.

The debate between the languages of *office* and *leadership* in the DBERG thus has deep roots in a number of research traditions, that were all represented in the DBERG. Each research tradition is to some extent interdisciplinary in approach; joining these four in one research group presented additional interdisciplinary challenges, sometimes simply of understanding one another. It presented the unexpected need for developing a common language and research paradigm. One of the fruits of this period was a small postdoc seed grant in 2014 for one of the current authors, with Peter-Ben Smit, professor of Old Catholic Church Structures at Utrecht University (member of DBERG) and Paul 't Hart, specialist in public leadership at the School of Governance of Utrecht University (not a DBERG member), to map the previous two decades of empirical research on religious leadership. Although two publications resulted (Barentsen, 2016b, 2016c), advocating a practical-theological approach to church leadership by correlating theological and organizational literature, unfortunately, no further funding or projects resulted from this.

The DBERG never quite succeeded in shaping one common language, although progress was sufficient to move forward as a research group. Even in its final publication, the various contributions sometimes still breathe different atmospheres and speak different languages (van den Broeke & van der Borght, 2020). Although it is tempting to discern clusters of scholars within the DBERG that favored one or another approach, this is nearly impossible because various scholars were themselves quite interdisciplinary in approach, but of course not as comprehensive as the group together. This continued "common language" challenge is not very surprising if one takes into account that different languages and perspectives are not only academically rooted but also deeply embedded in personal spiritualities.

As the DBERG moved through its phase of empirical research in 2015, it turned out to be very difficult to do the analysis of the focus groups and write the agreed-upon interpretive articles. At times, the project seemed to have come to a halt. This was, in part, due to the interdisciplinary nature of the study of religious leadership. It is of such importance to the functioning and identity of Christian faith communities, that all theological disciplines investigate it intently. This was, of course, reflected in the interdisciplinary nature of the research group. Yet, this also prevents the study of religious leadership from becoming a distinct, institutionally embedded subdiscipline in theology. Without such institutional embedding, no one group or department seemed to fully "own" the project and its agenda. It was easy for the usual academic pressures, such as the demands of teaching and curriculum development, departmental research programs and new job roles, to take priority.

Finally, scholars of the DBERG, with their different approaches and perspectives, probably operated from different epistemologies, in which theological traditions played different normative roles. Some of the researchers focused on textual interpretation (close textual reading) and on literature research, while others engaged in quantitative and qualitative research. The different epistemologies involved were never intentionally addressed in the group's meetings. However, if this project is to become more global, including leadership in other religions, the task of aligning epistemologies becomes more important.

In the end, the DBERG can be evaluated as successful in negotiating a common language and research paradigm, which enabled scholars from different (interdisciplinary) research traditions to participate, while valuing the different contributions based on diverse scholarly backgrounds, epistemologies and personal spiritualities. Even though all DBERG members count themselves Christians by personal conviction, as well as theologians by academic profile, this success is not so self-evident as the group might at first have expected.

Individual Dimensions of Religious Leadership: Methodological Diversity in Conducting and Interpreting Focus Group Responses

One of the three dimensions of religious leadership, that the DBERG identified early in its meetings is the individual dimension. This reflects 20th-century tendencies in leadership practice and research with a strong focus on the leader: traits, skills, character and style (Northouse, 2015). Such a leader-centric focus is contested today within leadership studies generally, often criticized as the "romance of leadership" (Meindl, Ehrlich & Dukerich, 1985; Uhl-Bien & Pillai, 2007). Most scholars in the DBERG were not aware of this trend in general leadership studies. Instead, they found this individual dimension relevant for their context, since it was theologically and ideologically legitimated in most Christian traditions represented in the group.

Their sense of the relevance of the individual dimension was confirmed in the focus group interaction, especially when church representatives participated (see previous description). Responses indicated that most religious leaders view their role as focused on proclamation based on sacred texts and on pastoral care. They valued tasks in leadership and governance much lower. Yet, their responses also signaled a desire to learn about communicative skills, group dynamics, and identity formation. These responses are tangible evidence of the tension that these respondents felt between their own, mostly theological, understanding of their own role, and the reality that required them to engage in leadership. In other words, they signaled a tension between their sense of calling and their actual job demands (see further analysis in Barentsen & Foppen, 2020a). This finding led to a renewed discussion in the DBERG about how to understand and define leadership, which revealed that the same tension still existed within the research group.

In subsequent research, the DBERG devoted a considerable amount of time and energy to this individual dimension, using a variety of methods. One DERG member conducted quantitative surveys with another scholar who had presented her work in the DBERG meetings. Together, they investigated the well-being of pastors in the Netherlands. These surveys focused on work satisfaction ($N = 110$), and burnout and work-related passion ($N = 643$). Overall, these scholars reported that pastors generally do not self-identify as leaders and that they manifest a clear internal focus for their work (Stoppels & Bisschops, 2020). This research built on earlier research among Dutch Reformed pastors in the Netherlands (Evers & Tomic, 2003), and parallels research carried out independently in Germany (Stahl et al., 2019) and the USA (Chandler, 2010).

The DBERG took note of existing qualitative research on the professionalization of religious leaders in the Netherlands. Roman Catholic priests were found to have a low appreciation for their professional functioning since their theological language with its well-worn metaphors ("shepherd", "soul care") seemed far removed experientially from the norm of professional functioning (Schilderman, 1998). Reformed pastors reported feelings of inadequacy and identity crisis when facing the professional demands of their work (Brouwer, 1995). Similar studies were conducted independently, again in Germany (Karle, 2001) and the USA (883 telephone surveys with pastors, in addition to many more Congregational Life Surveys, Carroll, 2006). In different ways, these research projects pointed to the tension between a theological self-understanding of pastors and their calling, as compared with a leadership-oriented self-understanding. Extending these findings, two DBERG members reflected on the understanding of "office" in late modern society in a philosophical and theological contribution, noting that the emphasis is shifting again, now from professionalization to personalization (Paas & Saane, 2020).

Additional interaction with the personal dimension of religious leadership came from other DBERG members. The tension between the theological and the professional legitimization of religious leadership highlighted questions of authority. To what extent could religious authority be founded on theological concepts and spiritual sources, and to what extent on professional competence? Two scholars investigated the authority of religious leadership through sociological and theological literature research (Paas & Saane, 2020). These scholars also inquired as to whether entrepreneurial religious leaders in Europe demonstrated a different personality profile from established religious leaders (Foppen et al., 2017).

Another scholar conducted interview research to document shifting authority structures and the tasks of religious identity construction (Barentsen, 2016, 2016a), while additional literature research with a separate research group resulted in a theological and social psychological study on the nature of authority (Barentsen, 2017).

A number of DBERG scholars engaged in theological literature research to investigate the individual dimension of religious leadership. By analyzing and comparing various theological proposals, Koffeman – a systematic theologian – concluded that ordination to the office of religious leadership is founded in liturgy and worship. Ordination distinguishes a pastor from other functional ministries or church offices and identifies the leader with the sacramental ordained ministry. This type of leadership comes "from outside" or "from above", and not "from inside" or "from below" (Koffeman, 2014). Similar theological research had been conducted earlier by van der Borght (a DBERG member) in an examination of ecumenical documents related to church leadership (van der Borght, 2007). Interestingly, such research had also been done in a qualitative fashion by van Holten (not a DBERG member) who investigated the relationship between calling, role, and task in a series of depth interviews with three categories of respondents: advanced students, beginning pastors and experienced pastors (van Holten, 2009). As the work of the DBERG neared completion, several interpretive chapters connected these findings about the individual dimensions of religious leadership through literature research with how the concept of "office" functioned in a particular tradition, and how it was affected by secularization in postmodern society (Evers, Koffeman & van der Schee, 2020; van der Schee & Witte, 2020).

In summary, the individual dimensions of religious leadership have been investigated by a variety of methodologies. It was first investigated through specific questions in the four focus groups and then analyzed further by the DBERG scholars. They used quantitative (survey) and qualitative (interview) methods, and then employed theological, philosophical, sociological, and psychological literature study to interpret the empirical results and situate them in broader societal and religious trends. Various spin-off publications resulted that were noted in the DBERG meetings, but conducted and published in other academic settings and research groups. During these proceedings, various understandings of leadership manifested themselves both in the focus group responses and in the ongoing work of the DBERG. Two chapters in the final publication sought to resolve this tension (Paas & van Saane, 2020; Abrahamse et al, 2020).

Institutional Dimensions of Religious Leadership: Focus Groups and Spin-Off Research

As the discussion of the work of DBERG progresses from the personal to the institutional dimensions of religious leadership, it should be noted that the early distinction between these two dimensions did not always work well in practice. Often the personal and institutional dimensions overlap: are well-being, burnout and professionalization personal or institutional phenomena? Should ordination and calling be understood as personal or institutional dimensions of leadership? As research progressed, it was evident that these were closely connected, even though the distinction presented a helpful way to initially frame the focus group sessions. Hence, the final publication of the DBERG did not subdivide the publication into these three dimensions of leadership, but into two major sections: I. Explorations and II. Interpretations. The first section features five chapters with the sociological context of religion in the Netherlands and Belgium, and with empirical research from surveys, focus group sessions and interviews. The second section then interpreted these findings in six chapters through the lens of various disciplines in theology, sociology and leadership studies without any further empirical research.

As narrated above, the DBERG originated in a conference that investigated translocal religious leadership, referring to the leadership of a number of churches or a denomination (regional, national or international). Thus, the institutional dimension of religious leadership was at the forefront of the group from the beginning. This conforms to wider trends in organizational and leadership research, that point out the importance of the follower, the group and the social context in understanding leadership (e.g., Haslam et al, 2020; Uhl-Bien & Ospina, 2012). The first years of the DBERG thus devoted much time to exploring existing research on this institutional dimension. In their meetings, experts presented research on the functional well-being of ministers, and on the perception of their leadership within faith communities (2013); on how Christian denominations responded theologically and structurally to changing leadership roles in a secular society (2014); and on mapping how faculties of theology and seminaries adapted their program and curricula in response to fewer candidates for ministry with changing candidate profiles (2015).

Next, focus groups were organized in 2015. The participating religious leaders (pastors, denominational leaders, educational leaders) responded to three questions (see section 2 previously) about the future of the church in the current postmodern climate (as reported in Schaeffer & Witte, 2020). All participants were acutely aware of the changing culture and its effects on their faith communities, although they evaluated it differently. Some pointed out the importance of social-communicative and organizational skills, some highlighted the urgency of spiritual and theological formation, and others aimed to increase hermeneutical awareness of the surrounding culture for faith communities and their pastors.

Church responses also differed, depending on their size and context. Small churches, often without a full-time pastor, struggled to survive. Some churches transitioned to become more missional, i.e., more outwardly focused. Migrant churches aimed to position themselves in what was for them a new ecclesial, societal, and political context. Larger churches often needed to reorganize while they wrestled with questions about their public relevance. Participants also wrestled with two dilemmas: (1) balance between openness and identity maintenance and (2) orientation towards *Christendom* (institutional religion as part of culture) versus *post-Christendom* (deinstitutionalized religion in the margins of society).

There was broad recognition within the focus groups that religious leadership was in crisis: the traditional practice of religious leadership no longer seemed to fit their post-Christian context. Consequently, theological education was also under significant stress to adapt to this new situation (as reported in Schaeffer, 2020). This new post-Christian situation often implies that the role of the priest or preacher as a "Man/Woman of God", central to the functions and purposes of the faith community, is gradually overtaken by various forms of collaborative leadership (Barentsen & Foppen, 2020a).

Earlier indications of this trend towards collaborative leadership come from outside and inside the DBERG. In the mid-1990s, Vermeulen conducted practical-theological, ethnographic research (combining participant observation, structured interviews, and document analysis) to investigate the role of volunteers in pastoral leadership in four Roman-Catholic parishes in Rotterdam (Vermeulen, 1998). He found that pastoral leadership had become a collaborative effort of professionals and volunteers, similar to the much later responses in the DBERG focus groups. One of the DBERG members had investigated collaboration in denominational leadership before the group started. Van den Broeke investigated the precarious relationship between local, regional and national leaders in the merger of three Dutch Protestant regional church councils (*classes*) by means of historical research in church archives and more extensive literature research in church polity (van den Broeke, 2005). Later, he extended this research by conducting focus group sessions with six regional church councils, which found that collaboration between professionals and volunteers is key to vital regional governance and supervision (van den Broeke, 2009) and also that the societal and political context of such classes plays an important role (van den Broeke, 2020b). This collaborative approach was also examined by experts in church polity and canon law, to gauge its effect on the legal status of professional and lay leaders that collaborated in a particular network (Post et al., 2008).

During the focus group sessions, some initiatives in revitalizing existing churches or the start-up of new ones were noted. For many focus group participants, all well-established within their own traditions and fields, this appeared as a marginal development, sometimes challenging existing religious traditions. However, it was significant enough for the DBERG to take notice: several members collaborated in depth-interviews with six Dutch pioneer leaders, who were engaged in starting up new Christian communities. The interviews inquired into personal motivation, competencies, institutional embedding and the target group. The results were analyzed using a familiar model with four components (person, tasks, acts, practices) (Abrahamse et al., 2020). This complements research into innovative religious communities that is widely undertaken in various countries (USA: Branson & Warnes, 2014; UK: Goodhew et al., 2012; Germany: Pompe et al., 2016).

Two other DBERG members extended research on entrepreneurial religious contexts in other academic settings. Barentsen conducted survey research to inquire into the self-understanding of entrepreneurial religious leaders (Barentsen, 2019a), supplemented by literature research on the social impact of such leadership (Barentsen, 2019b). Van den Broeke investigated the legal dimension of religious freedom for faith communities and religious leaders, which is relevant for entrepreneurial leaders and their new communities (van den Broeke et al., 2019a) in order to have a better understanding of civil law – more research is urgently needed in this field. Moreover, van den Broeke wrote about the missional leadership of the classes in the Protestant denominations with view to church planting, as the church is missional in nature, something which is sometimes neglected or misunderstood in the ecclesial context (van den Broeke, 2019b, pp. 91–103).

DBERG research into the institutional dimension of religious leadership is only a small segment of significant research in Europe and worldwide. One could note the rapid rise of networks of independent, often charismatic, leaders and their churches, often through digital media (Christerson & Flory, 2017). The social or civic impact of religious leaders is receiving significant research attention (Smidt, 2016; Cartledge et al., 2019). The structures of religious leadership are changing, so that new research focuses on "interim pastor" as more than simply a temporary stop-gap measure (Jordan, 2008), or on the reli-entrepreneur, who enters the religious marketplace by offering spiritual services to people of a variety of faiths or no faith at all (Hero, 2016). These phenomena of religious leadership are relatively new, and it attracted some attention during various DBERG meetings. Yet, research on these phenomena is only beginning.

Amidst these international trends, the DBERG represents a small regional research group with (at its peak) 15 participating scholars to investigate ongoing developments in the structures and styles of religious leadership in northwest Europe, mostly focused on the Netherlands and Belgium. This research built on previous research by most participating scholars, and produced numerous spin-offs that members contributed in other academic conferences and publications. However, since changes in the nature and structure of religious leadership run largely parallel in various European countries, the DBERG intends to develop a European research project together with other viable European partners to work together in multidisciplinary collaboration. This network should include a greater diversity of denominations and educational institutes, both in the research group and in the respondents approached in empirical research. We hope that the lessons learned by DBERG members will be helpful for this future venture, as documented in this chapter, and in its final publication *Religieus leiderschap in post-christelijk Nederland* ET: *Religious Leadership in Post-Christian Netherlands*; van den Broeke & van der Borght, 2020).

Educational Concerns for the Future of Religious Leadership: International Perspectives

One of the surprises in reflecting on the DBERG research and its publications is that relatively little has been made of the educational dimension of religious leadership. One of its early proposals was to include an educational dimension, i.e., to inquire into the methods and curricula for training religious leaders. This framed the focus group sessions, both in the selection of respondents for sessions 3 and 4 (educational leaders) and in the questions to which all respondents were asked to respond. The results in terms of educational concerns were summarized in one chapter (Schaeffer, 2020). In hindsight, this concern deserved more attention.

Yet, as the DBERG prepared for the focus groups, they developed important questions about theological education and curriculum development. What changes in the profile of future pastoral leaders can be expected? Which aspects of church tradition are carefully maintained and which might be open to change? How do these expectations affect theological curriculum development? How can institutions adequately prepare young (and often older) students for their future leadership roles?

These questions are indeed important and urgent. The reported stresses and changes in religious leadership raises concerns about new curriculum needs for skill and knowledge development and for spiritual formation. The growing diversity in religious and cultural backgrounds in student bodies generates uncertainty about religious identities and traditions; how can training institutions educate students with a clear sense of religious (confessional) identity, while also enabling them to function in a pluralistic and diverse environment where boundaries and beliefs are more fluid? The decreasing number of theological students force institutions to a greater "market-orientation" to attract students with relevant theological education. And changes in society are reflected in accreditation frameworks that demand an explicit accounting of curriculum content in relation to societal needs. The educational leaders who participated in the focus groups not only signaled these questions and needs, but also indicated that their curricula were gradually being adapted (Schaeffer, 2020).

DBERG scholars had input into two further research projects in this field. First, Doornenbal conducted an extensive review of the literature on entrepreneurial church leaders and enriched his findings with a number of in-depth interviews with theological educators from three major training institutions that were represented in the DBERG. Although the literature indicated the need for training in missional or entrepreneurial leadership, the interviews showed that the then current state of theological education did not meet this need (Doornenbal, 2012). Second, Erwich reflected on autobiographical material collected from theology students in the Netherlands to unravel patterns and characteristics of student spiritual development, which he then interpreted through Marcia's framework of identity statuses. The author proposed that student spirituality and personal formation should take a more significant place in theological education than thus far (Erwich, 2018). In the years after the focus group research, several Dutch schools initiated specialized programs for such needs, but this came too late to figure significantly in the DBERG research report.

Still, the paucity of notice of this educational dimension in the further work of the DBERG does not mirror the significant research time and funding that is devoted to this topic internationally. For instance, the Learning Pastoral Imagination Project in the USA collected and analyzed stories of seminarians in their last year of study, then again two years later, and compared them with interviews with pastors in ministry (5–35 years). In several publications, the project examined how students moved from the intellectually and cognitively demanding seminary classroom setting to the more embodied and relational practice of ministry with its intense emotions and overwhelming complexity, culminating in a 5-year report (Scharen & Campbell-Reed, 2016). In South Africa, a very different and culturally complex corner of the world, theologians equally wrestle with the shape of theological education. Ministerial formation practices are vital, not only to educate people from various cultural and educational backgrounds, but also to foster personal spirituality and integrity, to develop discernment in working with various people, and to train in contextual skills for social and theological analyses in a country of great differences (Naidoo, 2012). Many more projects could be mentioned, in Canada (Wong et al., 2019), Australia (Ball, 2013) and the Majority World (Shaw & Dharamraj, 2018), to name but a few.

Clearly, the educational dimension of religious leadership is a field that deserves much further exploration than the DBERG was able to accomplish thus far. Yet, it is clear that traditional pedagogies and curricula, focusing on cognitive knowledge and development, with the aim of enabling students to locate themselves firmly in a particular tradition, are under stress. Boundaries have liquified, traditions appear to lose relevance easily and personal development has become everyone's major life task. This situation calls for greater attention to personal and spiritual formation, for being able to root oneself firmly in a particular religious identity while yet being able to operate in very diverse environments. It also requires leadership skills that serve changing religious communities and institutions that wrestle intently with their socio-religious identity. As the DBERG seeks to expand its scope and research, perhaps it can focus increasingly on promoting healthy development of future religious leaders.

Researching Religious Leadership: An Agenda

This section concludes our review of research conducted by the Dutch/Belgian Ecumenical Research Group, which we labeled DBERG for ease of reference. The group consisted of theologians and experts on religious leadership that are located in the Netherlands and Belgium. This review locates the DBERG research in an international, mostly Western context, where the Christian tradition has been pushed out of the public square in a movement that has been interpreted sociologically as secularization. At the same time, a multitude of religious forms and expressions has arisen in Western societies, that compete in the broad religious marketplace for adherents and for public influence.

The DBERG story began by bringing together an interdisciplinary team – albeit only Christian theologians – with prior research experience in religious leadership, that highlighted the need for further research in *supralocal* religious leadership. The group began by widely exploring research on religious leadership to frame further research, and (by hindsight) also to build a common language and research framework. This unexpected task of developing a common language highlights the need at the beginning of any research journey, especially if it is to be interdisciplinary like much of leadership research, to acknowledge and reconcile different registers of academic discourse.

Four focus groups were initiated on the basis of an early analysis of the state of the question, which identified the individual, institutional and educational dimensions of leadership as needing further investigating. Working with professional educators and leaders in the religious sphere brought new challenges of attunement, now to reconcile academic and professional practitioner perspectives in a manageable research framework.

Subsequently, there was a great methodological diversity in understanding and interpreting these focus group results, with each expert contributing from his or her own discipline and specialty. This is where the diversity in the research group paid good dividends in enabling the methodological diversity within one project. It also involved each researcher discovering and defining their own identity as academic researcher in the context of a larger interdisciplinary group of scholars.

The previous review also demonstrated that DBERG research was extended by group members outside of the group. In other words, DBERG research produced numerous spin-offs by its members in other research groups and conferences. This was documented primarily from the work of the current authors since these spin-offs were produced individually, outside of the purview of the group as a whole.

The group's research brought together a variety of denominational perspectives from two countries, which provided a helpful setting for learning across traditional boundaries. Yet, the main focus was not on analyzing the role of various Christian traditions as variable in different leadership structures, nor on comparing the two countries for cultural differences. Each country and each Christian tradition has its own unique characteristics, which are vitally significant (and sensitive!) for insiders. Perhaps that is a reason why the group did not produce general advice or recommendations for improving theological education in such diverse traditions. However, from a broader perspective, these traditions and countries have much in common, primarily because the group focused on the northwest European contexts, which share a common narrative of secularization, globalization, digitalization, individualism, etc. Evidently, a broader orientation, for instance towards the Global South, towards ethnicity and gender and other concerns, remains an important part of the future research agenda.

The picture that emerges from this review is of a kaleidoscope of forms, roles and activities of religious leadership, and of a broad toolbox of research methodologies to investigate this leadership. Clearly, research on religious leadership is multifaceted in its methodology. A large segment of this research employs theological, historical and philosophical methods that are text-based. The language of "sacrament", "call" and "ordination" figures largely in these forms of research. Another large segment of research correlates these findings with literature research in sociology, (social) psychology, pedagogy, organizational studies and leadership studies. Increasingly, however, qualitative and quantitative empirical research methods are used, sometimes in mix-method research design, and recently also in ethnographic research. Quantitative surveys have often been conducted from a sociology of religion perspective. Within a more psychologically oriented research framework, interviews are frequently used in phenomenological research. In addition, focus groups and participant observation play an important role in the research we reviewed. Remarkably, the use of (auto)biographical narrative is also gaining currency, often in ethnographic approaches.

In terms of leadership content and context, religious leadership is observed to participate in broad societal tendencies that affect all manner of leaders and institutions. In a society where institutions decrease in value, where boundaries become fluid, and where charismatic leaders gain credibility, religious communities and their leaders inevitably participate in these changes. Hence, research on religious leadership is an ongoing need for societies where religion might be devalued in terms of institutional presence, but where religious experience represents a significant motivation for large numbers of people, with major impact on public debate, education and politics. Further research on the religious identity of adherents and its social impact, and again on the impact of religious leadership in the public domain, is vital for the future of our societies.

A glaring lack in this review is, of course, its focus on only one religion, namely Christianity. It is abundantly clear by now that "Christianity" is not monolithic, but contains within itself many different kinds of religious experiences, communities, practices and leadership, although they all ultimately focus on Jesus Christ and the Bible. Similar research needs to be and is being done within other religions. Here too, most world religions are not monolithic but contain a great variety of traditions and communities within themselves. One review could not possibly do justice to them all; this one cannot even do justice to the entirety of Christianity. However, what is presented is sufficiently representative of Western Christian traditions to be helpful in evaluating the potential that religious leaders have to lead not only their own communities, but also to impact the public square in which they participate. Certainly, the research group demonstrated in its workings and results that research into religious leadership is vital to interpret and influence societal developments in which religious motivations and movements continue to play an important though changing role – in addition to the many other new developments in leadership research and leadership education generally.

Hence, we end this review by emphasizing the need for establishing more international research networks to understand, interpret and shape religious leadership, and to pay closer attention to the educational dimension of theological institutes for new generations of religious leaders. This presents a great opportunity for junior researchers, beginning their research journey, to develop particular approaches that will enrich new leadership research and, in turn, leadership education. There is a need for broader models of religious leadership that are not only theologically or religiously, but also sociologically and psychologically rooted (see such noteworthy efforts as Brouwer, 2019; Percy et al., 2019). And perhaps, an international database on religious leadership (like Callahan, 2013) might be helpful to facilitate the study of religious leadership across contexts and cultures.

Notes

1 For conference information and proceedings, see https://centre-religion-law.org/nl/symposia-en-lezingen, accessed October 6, 2020.
2 A cooperative platform for 12 faculties of theology or religious studies in the Netherlands and Belgium. See https://noster.org/, accessed October 6, 2020.
3 The authors of this review are both members of the DBERG, and from a Protestant-Evangelical tradition. Other DBERG experts are from Roman Catholic, Old Catholic and Orthodox traditions.
4 https://opendata.cbs.nl/statline/#/CBS/nl/dataset/37944/table?fromstatweb, accessed October 6, 2020. Figures for the Netherlands, but comparable to those in Belgium.

References

Abrahamse, J. M., Broeke, L. van den, Leer, T. van der, & Witte, H. P. J. (2020). Pionierend leiderschap: Een verkenning. In E. A. J. G. van der Borght & L. van den Broeke (Eds.), *Religieus leiderschap in post-christelijk Nederland* (pp. 105–131). KokBoekencentrum.

Abrahamse, J. M., Bakker, H., Koffeman, L. J., & Smit, P.-B. (2020). Geordineerd ambt en leiderschap. In E. A. J. G. van der Borght & L. van den Broeke (Eds.), *Religieus leiderschap in post-christelijk Nederland* (pp. 257–293). KokBoekencentrum.

Ball, L. (2013). *Transforming theology: Student experience and transformative learning in undergraduate theological education*. Wipf & Stock.

Barentsen, J. (2011). *Emerging leadership in the Pauline Mission: A social identity perspective on local leadership development in Corinth and Ephesus* (Princeton Theological Monograph Series, Vol. 168). Wipf & Stock.

Barentsen, J. (2015). Church leadership as adaptive identity construction in a changing social context. *Journal of Religious Leadership, 15*(2), 49–80.

Barentsen, J. (2016a). Changements dans les structures d'autorité de l'Église – comment les interpréter? In A. Join-Lambert, A. Liégeois, & C. Chevalier (Eds.), *Autorité et pouvoir dans l'agir pastoral* (pp. 267–278). Lumen Vitae.

Barentsen, J. (2016b). Practising religious leadership. In J. Storey, J. Hartley, J.-L. Denis, P. 't Hart, & D. Ulrich (Eds.), *Routledge companion to leadership* (pp. 260–277). Routledge.

Barentsen, J. (2016c). Van ambtstheologie naar leiderschapsdiscours: Zoektocht naar een nieuwe visie op religieus leiderschap. *Nederlands Theologisch Tijdschrift, 71*(4), 305–320. doi:10.5117/NTT2016.70.305.BARE

Barentsen, J. (2017). The end of authority – and its legitimate future: A theological assessment. In J. Barentsen, S. van den Heuvel, & P. Lin (Eds.), *The end of leadership* (Vol. 4, pp. 13–29). Peeters.

Barentsen, J. (2018). Ambt en leiderschap in praktisch-theologisch en oecumenisch perspectief. *Handelingen: Tijdschrift Voor Praktische Theologie En Religiewetenschap, 2018*(1), 65–75. https://ixtheo.de/Record/1642430536

Barentsen, J. (2019a). The pastor as entrepreneur? An investigation of the use and value of "entrepreneur" as metaphor for pastoral leadership. In S. Jung, V. Kessler, L. Kretzschmar, & E. Meier (Eds.), *Metaphors for leading—leading by metaphors* (Vol. 6, pp. 75–88). Vandenhoeck & Ruprecht.

Barentsen, J. (2019b). The religious leader as social entrepreneur? In S. C. van den Heuvel & L. Bouckaert (Eds.), *Servant leadership, social entrepreneurship and the will to serve: Spiritual foundations and business applications* (pp. 235–253). Palgrave Macmillan.

Barentsen, J. (2020). Leading oneself in a VUCA world: Lessons from the field of religious leadership. In E. van Zyl, A. H. Campbell, & L. Lues (Eds.), *Chaos is a gift: Leading oneself in uncertain and complex environments* (pp. 211–224). KR Publishing.

Barentsen, J., & Foppen, A. (2020a). Leiderschap, hermeneutiek en groepsidentiteit in een maatschappij zonder grenzen. In A. J. G. van der Borght & L. van den Broeke (Eds.), *Religieus leiderschap in post-christelijk Nederland* (pp. 167–198). KokBoekencentrum.

Barentsen, J., & Foppen, A. (2020b). Post-christendom context in Nederland en België. In A. J. G. van der Borght & L. van den Broeke (Eds.), *Religieus leiderschap in post-christelijk Nederland* (pp. 17–36). KokBoekencentrum.

Bernts, T., & Berghuijs, J. (2016). *God in Nederland 1966-2015*. Ten Have.

Billings, A. (2010). *Making God Possible: The task of ordained ministry present and future*. SPCK.

Branson, M. L., & Warnes, N. (2014). *Starting missional churches: Life with God in the neighborhood*. InterVarsity Press.

Brouwer, R. (1995). *Pastor tussen macht en onmacht. Een studie naar de professionalisering van het hervormde predikantschap*. Boekencentrum.

Brouwer, R. (Ed.). (2019). *The future of lived religious leadership* (Vol. 7). VU.

Callahan, S. H. (2013). *Religious leadership: A reference handbook* (2 vols). Sage.

Carrette, J. R., & King, R. (2005). *Selling spirituality: The silent takeover of religion*. Routledge.

Carroll, J. W. (2006). *God's potters: Pastoral leadership and the shaping of congregations*. Eerdmans.

Cartledge, M. J., Dunlop, S., Buckingham, H., & Bremner, S. (2019). *Megachurches and social engagement: Public theology in practice*. Brill. doi:10.1163/9789004402652.

Chandler, D. J. (2010). The impact of pastors' spiritual practices on burnout. *Journal of Pastoral Care & Counseling, 64*(2), 1–9. doi:10.1177/154230501006400206.

Christerson, B., & Flory, R. (2017). *The rise of network christianity: How independent leaders are changing the religious landscape*. Oxford University Press.

Clarke, A. D. (1993). *Secular and Christian leadership in Corinth: A socio-historical and exegetical study of 1 Corinthians 1-6*. Brill.

Doornenbal, R. J. A. (2012). *Crossroads: An exploration of the emerging-missional conversation with a special focus on "missional leadership" and its challenges for theological education*. Eburon.

Ehrensperger, K. (2007). *Paul and the dynamics of power: Communication and interaction in the early Christ-movement*. T&T Clark.

Erwich, R. (2018). Studying theology: Between exploration and commitment – researching spiritual development of higher education students of theology. *International Journal of Christianity & Education, 22*(3), 214–232. doi:10.1177/2056997118782517

Evers, H., Koffeman, L. J., & van der Schee, W. (2020). De boel bij elkaar houden: Leiderschap in een presbyteriaal-synodale kerkorganisatie. In L. van den Broeke & E. A. J. G. van der Borght (Eds.), *Religieus leiderschap in post-christelijk Nederland* (pp. 199–220). KokBoekencentrum.

Evers, W., & Tomic, W. (2003). Burnout among Dutch Reformed pastors. *Journal of Psychology & Theology, 31*(4), 329–338. doi:10.1177/009164710303100403

Foppen, A., Paas, S., & van Saane, J. (2017). Personality traits of church planters in Europe. *Journal of Empirical Theology, 30*(1), 25–40. doi:10.1163/15709256-12341349

Goodhew, D., Roberts, A., & Volland, M. (2012). *Fresh! An introduction to fresh expressions of church and pioneer ministry*. SCM Press.

Graafland, C. (1999). *Gedachten over het ambt*. Meinema.

Haslam, S. A., Reicher, S., & Platow, M. J. (2020). *The new psychology of leadership: Identity, influence and power* (2nd ed.). Routledge.

Heitink, G. (2001). *Biografie van de dominee*. Ten Have.

Hero, M. (2016). The marketing of spiritual services and the role of the religious entrepreneur. In J.-C. Usunier & J. Stolz (Eds.), *Religions as brands: New perspectives on the marketization of religion and spirituality* (pp. 75–87). Routledge.

Holifield, E. B. (2007). *God's ambassadors: A history of the christian clergy in America*. Eerdmans.

Holmberg, B. (1978). *Paul and power: The structure of authority in the primitive church as reflected in the Pauline Epistles*. CWK Gleerup.

Houtepen, A. W. J., Schoon, D., Kronenburg, J., Bakker, H., Roukema, R., Eijk, T. van, & Broeke, L. van den. (2011). Speciaal nummer, "De Bisschop." *Nederlands tijdschrift voor kerk en recht, 5*, 14–162.

Jordan, E. (2008). The place of ordained local ministry in the church of England. *Practical Theology, 1*(2), 219–232. doi:10.1558/prth.v1i2.219

Karle, I. (2001). *Der Pfarrberuf als Profession: Eine Berufstheorie im Kontext der modernen Gesellschaft* (Praktische Theologie und Kultur, Vol. 3). Chr. Kaiser Verlagshaus.

Klessmann, M. (2001). *Pfarrbilder im Wandel: Ein Beruf im Umbruch*. Neukirchener.

Koffeman, L. J. (2014). *In order to serve: An ecumenical introduction to church polity*. LIT Verlag.

Kronenburg, J. (2003). *Episcopus Oecumenicus: Bouwstenen voor een theologie van het bisschopsambt in een verenigde reformatorische kerk* (IIMO research publication, Vol. 62). Meinema.

Meindl, J. R., Ehrlich, S. B., & Dukerich, J. M. (1985). The romance of leadership. *Administrative Science Quarterly, 30*(1), 78–102. doi:10.2307/2392813

Naidoo, M. (Ed.). (2012). *Between the real and the ideal: Ministerial formation in South African churches*. Unisa Press.

Northouse, P. G. (2015). *Leadership: Theory and practice* (7th ed.). Sage.

Paas, S., & Saane, J. W. van. (2020). Leiderschap en ambt in de laatmoderne samenleving. In A. J. G. van der Borght & L. van den Broeke (Eds.), *Religieus leiderschap in post-christelijk Nederland* (pp. 151–166). KokBoekencentrum.

Paul, H. *De slag om het hart: Over secularisatie van verlangen*. Boekencentrum, 2017.

Percy, M., Markham, I., Percy, E., & Po, F. (Eds.). (2019). *The study of ministry: A comprehensive survey of theory and best practice*. SPCK.

Pompe, H.-H., Todjeras, P., & Witt, C. J. (2016). *Fresh X – Frisch. Neu. Innovativ: Und es ist Kirche*. Neukirchener Aussaat.

Post, H. A., Beek, A. van de, Ploeg, T. J. van der, Eijk, A. H. C. van, & Meijers, A. P. H. (2008). Speciaal nummer, "Kerkelijk werkers en pastoraal werkers." *Nederlands tijdschrift voor kerk en recht, 2*, 1–77.

Root, A. (2019). *The pastor in a secular age: Ministry to people who no longer need a god*. Baker Academic.

Schaeffer, J. H. F. (2020). Theologische opleidingen in relatie tot de toekomst van religieus leiderschap. In E. A. J. G. van der Borght & L. van den Broeke (Eds.), *Religieus leiderschap in post-christelijk Nederland* (pp. 77–104). KokBoekencentrum.

Schaeffer, J. H. F., & Witte, H. P. J. (2020). Kerkleiders over de toekomst van kerkelijk leiderschap. In E. A. J. G. van der Borght & L. van den Broeke (Eds.), *Religieus leiderschap in post-christelijk Nederland* (pp. 55–67). KokBoekencentrum.

Scharen, C., & Campbell-Reed, E. R. (2016). Learning pastoral imagination: A five-year report on how new ministers learn in practice. *Auburn Studies, 21*, 1–62.

Schilderman, H. (1998). *Pastorale professionalisering: Een empirisch-theologisch onderzoek onder rooms-katholieke pastores naar de betekenis van de ambtstheologie voor de professionalisering van pastorale arbeid* (Theologie & Empirie, Vol. 29). Kok.

Shaw, P., & Dharamraj, H. (Eds.). (2018). *Challenging tradition: Innovation in advanced theological education*. Langham Global Library.

Smidt, C. E. (2016). *Pastors and public life: The changing face of american protestant clergy*. Oxford University Press.

Stahl, B., Hanser, A., & Herbst, M. (Eds.). (2019). *Stadt, land, frust?: Eine Greifswalder Studie zur arbeitsbezogenen Gesundheit im Stadt- und Landpfarramt* (Kirche im Aufbruch, Vol. 26). Evangelische Verlagsanstalt.

Stanton, G. D. (2019). A theology of complexity for Christian leadership in an uncertain future. *Practical Theology*, *12*(2), 147–157. doi:10.1080/1756073X.2019.1595318

Stewart-Sykes, A. (2014). *The original bishops: Office and order in the first Christian communities*. Baker.

Stoppels, S., & Bisschops, A. M. H. (2020). Pastores en hun leiderschap: Uitdagingen en welbevinden. In L. van den Broeke & E. A. J. G. van der Borght (Eds.), *Religieus leiderschap in post-christelijk Nederland* (pp. 37–54). KokBoekencentrum.

Taylor, C. (2007). *A secular age*. Belknap Press of Harvard University Press.

Uhl-Bien, M., & Ospina, S. (Eds.). (2012). *Advancing relational leadership research: A dialogue among perspectives*. Information Age Pub.

Uhl-Bien, M., & Pillai, R. (2007). The romance of leadership and the social construction of followership. In B. Shamir, R. Pillai, M. C. Bligh, & M. Uhl-Bien (Eds.), *Follower-centered perspectives on leadership: A tribute to the memory of james R. Meindl* (pp. 187–210). Information Age Publishing.

van den Broeke, L. (2005). *Een geschiedenis van de classis: Classicale typen tussen idee en werkelijkheid (1571-2004)* [Ph.D. Dissertation]. Vrije Universiteit.

van den Broeke, L. (2009). *Classis in crisis: Om de classicale toekomst*. Boekencentrum.

van den Broeke, L., & van der Borght, E. A. J. G. (2012). De toekomst van religieus leiderschap. *In de Waagschaal: Tijdschrift voor theologie, cultuur en politiek*, *11*, 4–7.

van den Broeke, L., Overbeeke, A. J., van der Ploeg, T. J., & van der Schyff, G. (Eds.). (2019a). *Perspectieven op de godsdienstvrijheid en de verhouding tussen staat en religie: Bundel ter gelegenheid van het tienjarig bestaan van het NTKR. Tijdschrift voor recht en religie*. Paris Uitgeverij.

van den Broeke, L. (2019b). The missional bishop: Classical assembly, church planting, church renewal. In B. Ensign-George, & H. Evers (Eds.). *Church polity, mission and unity: Their impact in church life. Proceedings of the international conference, Princeton, New Jersey, USA, 18–20 April, 2016* (pp. 91–103). Church Polity and Ecumenism: Global Perspectives 5. LIT Verlag.

van den Broeke, L., & van der Borght, E. A. J. G. (Eds.). (2020a). *Religieus leiderschap in post-christelijk Nederland*. KokBoekencentrum.

van den Broeke, L. (2020b). The challenge of the classis: A buffer between ecclesial individualism and regional catholicity. In L. van den Broeke, & A.J. Janssen (Eds.). *A collegial bishop revisited: Classis and presbytery at issue* (pp. 37–53). Deddens Kerkrecht Serie 4. Summum Academic Publications.

van der Borght, E. A. J. G. (2007). *Theology of ministry: A reformed contribution to an ecumenical dialogue*. Brill.

van der Schee, W., & Witte, H. P. J. (2020). Secularisatie van het ambt? Verkenningen. In A. J. G. van der Borght & L. van den Broeke (Eds.), *Religieus leiderschap in post-christelijk Nederland* (pp. 221–234). KokBoekencentrum.

van Holten, J. (2009). *Rol & Roeping. Een praktisch-theologisch onderzoek naar de rolopvatting van aanstaande, beginnende en oudere predikanten gerelateerd aan hun roepingbegrip*. Boekencentrum.

Vermeulen, F. (1998). *Patronen van pastoraal leiderschap*(Vol. 7). Gooi en Sticht.

Volland, M. (2013). An entrepreneurial approach to priestly ministry in the parish: Insights from a research study in the diocese of Durham [Ph.D. Dissertation]. Durham University, Cranmer Hall.

Wong, A. C. K., Bill McAlpine, Thiessen, J., & Walker, K. (2019). Are you listening? The relevance of what pastoral/denominational leaders and theological educators are saying about preparing leaders for ministry. *Practical Theology*, *12*(4), 415–432. doi:10.1080/1756073X.2019.1609255

Zonderop, Y. (2018). *Ongelofelijk: Over de verrassende comeback van religie*. Prometheus.

11

Women Leaders and Activists in Authoritarian, Patriarchal and Religiously Traditional Societies

Elizabeth Stork

Introduction

I have been interested in how everyday people live in different countries since I was quite young. I have traveled extensively and lived in Japan as a child and in Germany as a young spouse and mother. I also have had an interest in how religion shapes societies, especially those with state-sponsored religion, such as Islam in Jordan and Apostolic Christianity in Armenia. Since religion imposes and reinforces traditions, especially patriarchy (Al-Hassan & Takash, 2011; Devnew et al., 2017; Johnson, 2014; Moghadam, 2004), many societies are more conservative, authoritarian and patriarchal than non-religion affiliated societies (Fox, Alzwawi, & Refki, 2016; Hofstede, 2001; Johnson, 2014; Kassa & Sarikaksis, 2019; Walters 2017). Countries in which religion is state-sponsored or embodied in laws and practices around family and institutions rely on designated scriptural works and traditions to organize society. Adherence is not usually optional, particularly in public. All of the major Abrahamic religions (Islam, Judaism and Christianity) and most of their denominations are patriarchal and reify the role of women as subordinate to men; this in and of itself is a conservative and authoritarian stance. I have been curious how people negotiate the terms of a modernizing society and globally influenced, rapidly changing norms within such traditionalism (Haghighat, 2014; Hofstede, Hofstede & Minkov, 2010; Rayyan, 2016).

I am a feminist researcher, trained in Western research traditions, who is highly curious about the lives of women in social systems that seem desperate to maintain "traditional" ways, ways in which women's agency and self-determination are unimportant if noticed at all, in the face of the spread of norms from secular and nominally more equal systems. How do women, especially when knowing they are subordinated and "less than", assert themselves to have better and different lives? Do they wish for change? In this chapter, I explain my experiences undertaking research in three countries to learn how women who are expected to conform to traditional gender roles find ways to assert themselves to bring about social change in their societies. This two-fold narrative is about navigation when doing international leadership research: navigating contexts – worlds new to me to learn about how women live daily, and navigating process – to locate extraordinary ordinary women to speak with. This chapter describes one way to make a contribution to the field of international leadership research.

DOI: 10.4324/9781003003380-11

Envisioning and Preparing

My Context as Researcher

As a woman who came of age in the 1970s in a politically liberal, military family practicing Catholicism, I struggled with conforming to the pressure of religion and our inevitable patriarchal social structure that privileged men's entitlement over women's autonomy. I also came of age as feminism and other civil rights arguments were front page news. The process was slow for me, but organic, starting with noticing how my accomplished and income-producing mother could not get a credit card in her own name, to recognizing the subliminal gender stereotypes to which I was expected to conform. As a curious and justice-minded young woman, this led to reading and eventually formally studying how religion influences sexism (Lerner, 1986; Stone, 1976), to analyzing the institution of marriage and the roles of wives and mothers, politics and policies (Armstrong, 1986; Blank, 2007; Coontz, 2005), as well as the portrayal of sexism in film and television (Alcolea-Banegas, 2009; Stead & Elliott, 2009). I advocate for women's and girls' right to be autonomous and to recognize that their fears of intimidation and subordination are true and at the same time unjust, especially because I raised four daughters through the 1990s and 2000s. I wanted to acquire some understanding of how some women think and take action in the developing world where but for the luck of my birth could have been my home and my context.

Patriarchy persists (England, 2010; Gilligan & Snider, 2018; Johnson, 2014; Seguino, 2011; Sen, 2007), authoritarianism is on the rise (Diamond, Plattner, & Walker, 2016; Economist Intelligence Unit EIU, 2016, 2018) and religion enforces and reinforces traditional values and patriarchy itself, and is invariably authoritarian (Adely, 2012; Johnson, 2014; Kassa & Sarikakis, 2019; Seguino, 2011). In many developing countries, the lack of vocal and visible aspirations to become other than (or in addition to) a wife, mother and care-taking daughter or daughter-in-law is the norm (Adely, 2012; Genovese, 2013; Joseph, 1999; Kassa & Sarikaksis, 2019). However, I didn't believe some women didn't want more than what was dictated for them and their daughters by their societal values. Knowing how hard it is to turn off automatic biases (Loeske, 2017), I tried not to assume that women in traditional societies, that is, where gender roles are narrowly prescribed and men have a public life and women generally do not, who comply with traditional roles and norms, were not happy or fulfilled. But I knew that real social problems with unfortunate consequences such as child marriage and frequent as well as dangerous childbirth, the inability to divorce without lifelong sanctions, the high prevalence of abuse and violence against women and children were mainstays of those societies (Armenia, 2019; Ethiopia, 2019; Jordan, 2019). Rules, rewards and punishments meted out by male religious leaders and the family's men abound in strict, conservative, religious societies (Adely, 2012; Kassa & Sarikakis, 2019). I wanted to know who the women are who step out of bounds, how they are able to do it and for what reasons. Thus, I developed a research plan that would couple my love for travel and other cultures with my keen interest in the lives of women in gender-normed, gender-role-circumscribed societies. The main focus was on how and why some women become leaders and activists to bring unjust, social conditions to light in their societies. My research approach was to analyze a social perspective by getting as close to it as I could through biographical narratives. Being present would mean taking part in what is observed, taking a role in how participants tell their stories and reflecting on them, which then would lead me and might lead them to new insights and taking some part in changing the world (Flick, 2007). The method was biographical, listening to women tell their stories and how their life experiences brought them to activism and how their environment influences how they act for a belief or cause.

My goal was to interview women leaders and activists who are attempting to improve some condition or create social change in their societies where the needs and interests of women as equal citizens with men are not. The three countries have clear and strong track records of governing without the protections and privileges of civil rights for women, minorities and marginalized people. In short, they are authoritarian countries with patriarchal systems entrenched by tradition and religion to maintain the status quo of women in subordination to men. I was also very interested in the upbringing these women had, assuming that parents', primarily fathers', attitudes toward women in general or their daughters specifically, played an important role in their pursuit of education, work outside of the home and social activism responsibility. I wanted to learn and understand to inform my students and others about how similar and different some cultures are with regard to women and possibly to dispel assumptions that are commonly held by Westerners about the generalized notion of the oppression of "women in traditional, religious cultures" in developing countries. When I teach about women leaders, I want to bring to life women leaders outside our usual and known domains who take action and influence others, primarily in difficult conditions. When I teach about social movements or diversity, I want to be able to share that our fears about others are because of what we do not know, not because others are people to be feared.

Naturally I had many informed assumptions, both personal and educated, about how women are treated in deeply religious societies from my upbringing by a profoundly religious mother and my 10-year first marriage to an evangelical Christian. Later, my understanding came from observations of and conversations with acquaintances who are fundamentalists in the West and traditionalists in the Middle East and North Africa. Yet these experiences and lives are not only those of women in developing countries, they are widespread in the United States, too (Bartkowski & Read, 2003; Johnson, 2014; Seguino, 2011), and I lived it myself for several years while trying to maintain a relationship with an unmovable, religiously fearful father to my children. I also believed that if women wanted their lives to be different, it could be at great risk to them to articulate or act on such an idea. Women maintain homes and families, the foundational structure of patriarchal societies (England, 2010; Johnson, 2014; Seguino, 2011; Sen, 2007), and to upset that or deviate would come at a cost; violence, imprisonment and shunning notwithstanding (Abeya, Afework & Yalew, 2012; Johnson, 2014; Lenze & Klasen, 2017; Mengistu, 2019; Zamfir, 2018).

I assumed that women in cultures with strict beliefs about women would require a man's imprimatur or permission to step outside of normative bounds to be in public, advocating for some kind of change in her society. And I assumed that some women would find it risky to talk to a Western woman about her family life and her advocacy work so precautions would have to be taken about how to initiate such a meeting and where and when to meet.

I assumed that I could move relatively freely in countries where women are seen but not heard because of my white Western privilege which was true. I do note: traveling while female is not particularly different from being female at home in the United States.

I assumed that I would be able to find the kinds of women I was seeking and they would talk with me. I also believed that the women I sought and who would speak would be few and far between, which was not the case; there were many, it just took effort and persistence to find them because they rarely make for good news coverage and easy public identification.

Methodology for a Traveler-Researcher

I began thinking about doing something really different, and that I thought mattered, when I applied for a sabbatical for 2018. I wanted to do a project that enabled me to conduct research and to travel to far-off lands. I learned of summer research funding offered by my university, so I crafted a proposal for both the funding that summer and the subsequent sabbatical for the spring of 2018. Writing a proposal for funding, even for small sums at the university level, was a crucial start to articulating a rationale for why I could and should do such research. In the end, I received the summer funding and the sabbatical.

There are, of course, common and standard procedures for carrying out qualitative research that I planned to follow, but language, far-flung travel and complexities with making initial contact with strangers required being flexible with my approach (Flick, 2007). My research design was loose, meaning that my concepts were not strictly defined and my procedures were not firmly fixed (Miles & Huberman, 1994); my framework was feminist theory, the perspective that structural sex and gender inequality exist and that the male viewpoint is not the human viewpoint (Adely, 2012; England, 2010; Kassa & Sarikaksis, 2019; Seguino, 2011). My method was partially guided by grounded theory because I aimed to gather a diversity of experiences and purposes of the women I interviewed through theoretical sampling and analytical induction, and data were biographical stories.

Context Is Everything: Selecting International Locations

The selection of countries to visit was methodical and pragmatic. Authoritarianism was my first criterion because the governmental control and influence over activism may make it dangerous to engage in (Abdel-Samad, 2017). I discovered the Economist's Intelligence Unit (EIU) annual *Democracy Index 2016*. It relies on a rigorous methodology and explains changes around the world over the past year while listing countries in order of their democratic functioning.

The EIU developed 60 indicators in five scored categories to evaluate a country's political environment: electoral process and pluralism, civil liberties, the functioning of government, political participation, and political culture (Economist Intelligence Unit, 2017, 2018, 2019). Total scores between 8 to 10 identifies a Full Democracy, 6 to 7.9 indicates a Flawed Democracy, 4 to 5.9 a Hybrid Regime, and below 3.9 Authoritarian. The 2016 report categorized 167 nations of which 51 were authoritarian regimes. By 2019, authoritarian regimes increased by three (Economist Intelligence Unit, 2019). Civil liberties such as free speech, assembly and association encompass the territory in which promoting social change occur, and political culture and participation enable or restrict the advancement by popular demand of those social changes. Media freedom enables the dissemination of ideas. As these decline around the world, I felt that my research into the voices and actions of dissenters of the status quo was even more relevant than when it started.

I narrowed down the 51 authoritarian regimes on the 2016 list by eliminating countries ranked at the bottom (e.g., Chad, Syria, North Korea), places in which wars, kidnapping and violent conflict were ongoing or could erupt and where anti-American sentiments and State Department warnings are high. The annual *Democracy Index* as well as the U.S. Department of State are quite specific and prescriptive about this and I accepted their warnings. I focused on the countries that were religious more than secular, authoritarian more than democratic, and patriarchal more than equal. Other countries with highest scores in authoritarianism had drawbacks as simple as my not knowing anyone living in them, not being able to find the "right" interview candidates and newly enacted curtailment of liberties for travelers from the United States (e.g., U.S. Dept. of State Travel Advisories).

Armenia and Jordan, and later Ethiopia, were selected on these bases in addition to the democracy-to-authoritarian scores: differences in political systems (an autocratic monarchy, a post-Soviet, unstable and transitioning republic, and an uneasy one-party republic), different state-sponsored or affiliated religions (one a Muslim nation; one a Christian nation; and one mixed Muslim, Christian and not state-sponsored

Table 11.1 Scores from the EIU's Annual Democracy Index, 2016–2019, for Countries in the Sample

Country	Regime	2016	2017	2018	2019[*]
Armenia	Authoritarian > Hybrid	3.88	4.11	4.79	5.54
Ethiopia	Authoritarian	3.60	3.42	3.35	3.44
Jordan	Authoritarian	3.96	3.87	3.93	3.93

Note

[*] For context, Norway was ranked first with an overall score of 9.87 and North Korea last with an overall score of 1.08; the United States ranks 25th, with a total score of 7.96 (2019).

but strongly religious) and all with entrenched patriarchal social systems and traditional expectations for gender roles and conformity (Bureau of Democracy, Human Rights, and Labor, 2017, 2018a-d, 2019a-f, 2020a-f). They are also suffering poverty rates of nearly one-third their populations, and they are located in regions of instability; all have had recent conflicts (Table 11.1).

Sampling: Contacts and Participants

Sampling strategies and site selection were deliberate to collect a body of empirical examples to explore the varieties of the phenomenon (Flick, 2007) of women activists under culturally restrictive norms. My criteria for selecting participants was theoretical (Charmaz, 2006; Glaser & Strauss, 1967; Miles & Huberman, 1994), ostensibly resulting in the same knowledge of when to stop interviewing as does data saturation (Charmaz, 2006): women who were challenging the status quo in some public way, and women who were brought up in the country they lived in and therefore had lived experience with some forms of restrictions on women and their activities. I expected some interviews would be less targeted and useful than others, but something could be learned no matter what. My conversations with participants were planned to be systematic semi-structured life-world interviews, in-depth, focused and with purpose, and clearly cross-cultural (Kvale, 2007).

For several reasons I could not get serious about using social media, particularly Facebook. I was not interested in the minutiae often posted, and didn't trust the cloaked manipulation I carefully studied (Vaidhyanathan, 2018). I was encouraged to use it, however, to locate people who were activists or knew activists, but I wasn't very savvy about doing so.

It is not difficult to find the names of organizations, and often individuals, in news stories from other countries that can be reliably translated to English, plus authors of books and research or news articles could be easily contacted through the medium. I also tracked down information about organizations and individuals by searching the internet using targeted key words. I expected I would be able to create a list of potential interviewees from news stories and online queries, and hoped to identify more participants once I made contact with the first set because of their ability to help.

I was not initially interested in speaking to government officials because I was repeatedly told that in authoritarian countries access to ministers by an outsider with nothing valuable (money, influence, introductions) to offer in exchange is difficult. Also, "reality" may be understood differently by political ministers than by women seeking law and policy changes. This is common when interviewing "elites" because access, asymmetry of power, and my own knowledge differential would be additional concerns over the already cross-cultural context (Kvale, 2007). There was also the risk of only hearing the "party-line" either because of belief in it or fear to speak otherwise and be recorded (Abdel-Samad, 2017; P. Malakyan, personal communication, May 9, 2018).

I hoped and believed that academics and leadership practitioners in social science arenas would know about grassroots and NGO activities, as so many do in my local work, and send me in the right direction to find those who could speak to the matters I was bringing forth. I expected that if I found names of people or organizations, and asked those I was in contact with, that I could gain access to them or to people like them. Thus, I depended mostly on searching the internet and local university websites for information about events, organizations and people who were convening, researching, teaching and publishing in areas aligned with activism, leadership, women and the topics of religion, politics and human rights. I also read the U.S. Department of State's and the United Nations' websites to search for the work they are funding or doing in these areas. I made lists of people and searched online for contact information and affiliations so I could email them. My lack of trust in social media may or may not have hampered getting access to the women I wanted to reach, but I felt at least as well informed and prepared without it. At later times, when given a Facebook page that women used to promote their activities, they were, naturally, almost all in the local language and therefore unavailable to me anyway unless I called on people I know who could translate. Because making those requests, maybe repeatedly, seemed onerous I did not ask. However, I was directed to specific pages which could be and were translated into English in which notices of upcoming events and videos of other events were covered. I relied on snowball sampling and was rewarded with great interest from my initial contacts who introduced me to other women willing to talk.

Interviewing Considerations

I received IRB approval from my institution; informed consent would be obtained by way of agreement to be interviewed following an explicit request for that approval at the start of the interview. My interviewing plan was quite simple once I had meetings scheduled with participants. I had a short list of questions, a few about their interests, experiences, purposes and goals for activism and others about how they got to the place where they became activists. The specific locations, timing and sequence depended on the country because of whether I was managing the process myself, as in Jordan and Ethiopia, or had help, as I did in Armenia.

I planned to ask: What have you been working on [as an advocate, activist or normal citizen]? Why? How did you decide to do [activity]? How do your family and friends think about you and [your activity]? I would follow up with questions about the woman's education and family life, listening for how the men in her family thought about her activities and whether she felt supported or thwarted. Based on my research, I had expectations that for a woman in the strongly traditional and patriarchal countries I was working in to find her voice and use it she would need the support or at least the allowance from the men in her family. Even if she was well-educated and working outside the home, it would be because of male approval. I wanted to know if the women I interviewed who were activists of some kind had that experience.

I knew language barriers would likely exist given that I did not speak Arabic, Armenian or Amharic, but I would also have to bridge the myriad other cultural differences between me and my participants that were likely to be quite stark. For instance, I am a white, middle-aged, blond, single, female academic, traveling alone to countries I was unfamiliar with. I would be asking women to talk to me about their work, their activism, their families and background so I could learn from them, but the only thing I was ostensibly offering was an opportunity to tell their story to an American academic woman who planned to write about them. I felt it was important to show them my interest for the sake of one woman listening to another about how she creates a life with meaning, respecting her choices and experiences as things I would never really understand the same way she did. I believed, too, that there might be a benefit to be able to speak aloud about her beliefs and activities. My best effort, then, would be to learn as much as I could about the history and current events of her country so I could place her story in some context that would be built on as I listened to other women's stories.

While I was no expert on the social, political and economic issues women face in Armenia, Jordan and Ethiopia, I could demonstrate that I took the time and effort to learn the names and positions of leaders, recent events and acquired a general sense of recent history, as well as efforts of activists to ask about. The women I was interested in interviewing would know the issues, be critical and insightful, had hope and maybe a plan, and were expressive of the nationality they lived in. I found, for the most part that my homework was appreciated; in a few cases I was corrected about the meaning of events and predictions for the future, and was given so much more detail and interpretations to understand. To be a full participant myself in this undertaking, I had responsibilities, too, to the people who were making time for me to really listen and ask clearly what I wanted to know. I asked about how they felt about the politics of their countries, the development and changes occurring and about specific events. My participants were all working to change a condition or raise awareness and they offered their perspective on the importance of their goals even within the political structures surrounding them, but I also wanted to know about their backgrounds, how and why they were doing what they were doing. I was not always able to learn as much as I wanted about every participant's personal life because I wanted to respect their privacy. When any one woman offered personal information, I would ask more thinking a door was opening, all the while gauging her receptiveness to answering those questions. When the answers were short or clipped, or they changed the subject, I did not press. More than once I was told that they feared being identified so they would rather not say too much and asked me not to use their names or any identifying information about them.

I did fret about how to handle the likely need for translations. Some researchers claim that translators cannot do justice to a conversation because they may intentionally or inadvertently embed their own agendas or biases (Kvale, 2007). On the other hand, international research should not hinge on only following through with the absolute best practices, but should try to explore for an understanding of how people make sense of their lived experiences while striving for rigor. Something gained, even if not under the best conditions, is something gained, and with care and insight, new understanding as incomplete as it will inevitably be without being in the individual's shoes is worth the effort and result. Learning another language with such fluency to comprehend what an interviewee is saying is an example of best getting in the way of good. I knew I was at a disadvantage not knowing the languages, never mind extra-linguistic communication, but one can't wait to be fully prepared for everything or one would never undertake anything. My many previous experiences in foreign countries where I was unable to speak the language did not diminish the gains I did receive by working a little harder and taking it a little slower to understand what I could. Reading literature on communication practices in those places informed me about differences I might experience (e.g., *Culture Shock* series, travel guides, phrase books).

I bought myself some phrase books, but because all three countries use a different alphabet, not only was reading the transliteration one thing, seeing the words was completely another. I took advantage of the likelihood that many people around the world speak English, and if I was disabused of that notion in my travels, I could look up translation providers and hire one. I made the decision to just go and find out what language barriers I might encounter and figure out how to deal with them then. I was confident from early contacts that enough people I would meet with could speak English; my contacts in all three countries wrote emails or texts to me in English. It turned out that I did not need an official translator in any of the countries because through the snowball recruitment technique, an original contact or interviewee translated or provided a translator.

Financing Travel

Clearly, conducting research abroad is an expensive effort. For my first excursion to Armenia and Jordan, I used the $3,500 in funding I received from a summer fellowship. The next academic year, 2018–2019, I had my own travel fund with a small sum from the sale of a house. I had applied for two small travel grants from private foundations with tangential funding priorities, but did not receive them. There is no doubt that without my own investment in this research project, I would not have been able to go to these places a second time or to Ethiopia the first time. The timing was right for me to travel and grant possibilities were restrictive, constraining and funding if awarded was too far off in the future. I wanted to do this research, so I spent my own money. It is difficult to separate the costs associated with my research travels because I bracket research work with excursions in the countries and travel to other places on the way or in proximity to where I need to be. I estimate it cost about $6,000 for two visits to Armenia and Jordan and one to Ethiopia, of which I contributed $2,500. Airfares were half that total cost. I stayed in apartments I found using Airbnb, bought some groceries and cooked and had some meals in cafes. I rented a car for part of one trip only, in Jordan, because I wanted to travel afterwards, and used it to get to my interviews.

Accommodations were not expensive, however fueling up a car was more so than iin demonstran the U.S.

Being There, Doing Research

Armenia

Armenia is a new republic (since 1991) with an elected head of state, but only is recently emerging as a hybrid authoritarian-democratic nation. At the time of my travels, politicians and rich business men owned the news media and could and did prevent negative coverage; journalists feared reprisals (Bureau of Democracy, Human Rights, and Labor, 2017, 2018a, 2019a). A bloodless revolution (The Velvet Revolution) occurred in the spring of 2018 with the long-ruling president ousted and a new, presumably democratic reformer president in his place. Voter turnout and participation in demonstrations has increased, as has confidence in the government, although that is tenuous. Political activity without government interference occurs and accountability and transparency are improved, but not the prevalence of corruption (Bureau of Democracy, Human Rights, and Labor, 2020a). On the two long north to south borders of this small and landlocked country are political and ethnic enemies; borders are closed and patrolled. Armenia's scores on the Democracy Indices have increased slightly over the past three years (see Table 11.2).

I discussed my interest in women in authoritarian and patriarchal countries with my academic department head and that I was thinking about traveling and interviewing women. He suggested I visit Armenia, his home country, where he had started a non-profit and still had many contacts and friends. He talked for hours with me about his experiences growing up in Soviet Armenia and working in the Soviet Union, and he told me a great deal about the political uncertainties there. I also read several books about the post-Soviet transition in Armenia, its history with its neighbors, the horrific genocide a hundred years ago, and Armenia's food, culture and religion.

I made three trips to Armenia. My first "gatekeeper" was a woman, N, who was asked by my department head, her former supervisor and current patron, to assist me which she did amiably and knowledgably in all three visits. I told her by email that I was looking for women who were doing work that seemed designed to change some condition, such as concerning property or divorce rights, low participation of women in high paying jobs or government, and working for domestic violence awareness. From perusing Armenian English newspapers online for stories about activism and women, I gave her some names. I went to Armenia for the first time in July 2017, prepared to interview at least a dozen women over a 10-day period that N set up for me. After reading about concerns Armenians might have about voice recordings, given their caution about "the authorities," I chose not to record the interviews but, it turned out I probably could have because when I asked my colleague "gatekeeper" after a few interviews, she suggested I could have asked each participant and maybe received permission.

Table 11.2 Selected Countries' 2016 and 2019 Scores on Democracy Index Categories (EIU)

	Electoral Process & Pluralism	Functioning of Government	Political Participation	Political Culture	Civil Liberties
Armenia	4.33/7.50	2.86/5.36	4.44/6.11	1.88/3.13	5.88/5.59
Ethiopia	0.00/0.42	3.57/3.57	5.56/5.56	5.63/5.00	3.24/2.65
Jordan	4.00/3.58	4.29/4.29	3.89/3.89	4.38/4.38	3.24/3.53

A few of the women I talked with could understand English but not speak it quickly or with as much detail as their own languages, so translations provided by N were done so I could understand the interviewee rather than the other way around or in both directions. After introducing myself, I asked the first question, whether the woman I was talking with considered herself an activist in any way. She would invariably understand my question, or ask for a definition of activist (which I gave as some variation of: "someone who cares about something strongly enough that she takes public actions to do something about it"), apparently understanding my speech, then answer in rapid-fire Armenian. N would listen and translate, and I would write furiously and make notes about the environment, her manner and appearance and other observations. N found for me the retiring government Minister of Education who, among many other things, brought about the first policy of inclusive education of any post-Soviet country; a journalist and Radio Free talk show host who had been beaten and arrested a few times by angry oligarchs she reported on; a social work professor who could not tell me her last name or what she did outside of work because she feared reprisals from the university; an epidemiologist who has provided scientific reports to the government about the high risk of endocrine cancers in women because of the Soviet-age toxic waste dumps in the country and who eventually forced the government to begin clean-up efforts; and a disability rights activist who by 2019 became a government minister of health and disability rights. I located two university professors on my own, one who co-founded the first women's shelter and runs a center for education and activism around domestic violence, and one studying women and politics and arranged my interviews to take place in their offices on campus.

N was very helpful and I would have struggled to accomplish as much as I did without her, but I learned on my last visit that she did not really approve of what I was doing because she is herself a conservative, traditional, religious woman and thinks her country works best when women do what women are supposed to do, and more people can be happier if they conform. She opposes many liberal causes and rights as potentially destructive to the fine balance the country is trying to achieve between bringing down the old Soviet oligarchs and bringing back the underground religion and family traditions of Armenian. She also believes that a man has the right to discipline his wife and children as he sees fit because Christianity says so. She only provided full translations for two women whose stories did not quite fit my research, and because she was very professional and also complying with a request from her beloved mentor to assist me, I did not question her trustworthiness with regard to the content of the translations she did provide.

Jordan

Jordan is an authoritarian monarchy. The king controls the political arena and most everything in the lives of the people. There are no real, oppositional political parties because of the control of the country by the monarch, and it has a weak and restricted civil society and widespread poverty (Abdel-Samad, 2017). Speech against the king, foreign countries and Islam, among other things, are criminal offenses (Bureau of Democracy, Human Rights, and Labor, 2018c, 2019e, 2020e). The press is not free, and is subjected to gag orders from time to time. Impunity for corruption is pervasive, and there is no real transparency in much of what the government does. However, some democratic activities such as elections for lower house representatives occur, mostly for the appearance of democracy to other nations. In addition to its economic issues, Jordan has accepted more than 650,000 Syrian refugees (Bureau of Democracy, Human Rights, and Labor, 2020e). There are sporadic protests against austerity measures; the latest one resulted in the stepping down of the prime minister (Economist Intelligence Unit, 2018). Except for economic growth and recognition by richer governments, social change is not sought by and large. Dealing with water shortages, a growing refugee population, and its physical location among wars and enemy countries are more important government priorities. Jordan's score on the Democracy indices has remained low and steady (see Table 11.2).

I had been to Jordan once before in 2009 where I had a guide who met me at the Israeli-Jordan border, took me through passport control and showed me over five days most of the inhabited parts of the country; he told me a lot about everyday lives of people. I read about Jordan's formation, its Bedouin and Palestinian people, its neighbors and culture. I also have kept up with a former doctoral student, S, from Jordan who had been inviting me to visit him and his family after they relocated from the United States back to Jordan after his degree was completed. I made three visits to Jordan for this research.

S invited me to stay with his family of seven in his three-bedroom apartment and offered to take me to interviews in Amman when I arrived for my first visit for my research in 2017. I explained to S prior to arriving what I was planning to do and the kinds of women I wanted to interview, but he was not particularly helpful with contacts. He was my first gatekeeper in Jordan. I now know my interests were in conflict with his notions about women, what is possible in his country and what is generally important. I met his office mates and did talk with one female faculty member for a few minutes who vehemently stated she was not an activist or working on "women's issues, although they are certainly important". I conducted two interviews, and spent time with a female colleague who now resides in the United States that S introduced me to visiting historical sites. She was a good source of information about women in Jordan in general, but not about activists. It was a special opportunity to live with S's family for a week (which I did three times all together) and participate in or observe the dynamics of this religious family in Jordan. S's wife dresses and acts as traditional Muslim wives do, but she speaks some English and over my visits has taught me much about her life and family life like hers. One of my visits with his family was near an election. S and his relatives and friends went to hear the men speak who were running for office, but ignored the women. S told me that only women care about what women candidates say; the men would never show up to hear them and would never vote for them.

When I planned my second research trip in 2019, I was not going to rely on S for assistance because of his disinterest and reticence although I was welcome to stay with his family. I noticed an increasing religiosity at home, a loss of interest in returning to the United States (which had been a hope after S gained experience in Jordan) and a near reversal in their teenage daughter's desire to be Western when she decided she would follow her mother in her practice of Islamic traditions for women. Instead, I scoured English-language Jordanian newspapers for stories about women in the news to find my own participants to interview. I found out about a woman, a well-known but controversial journalist, who wrote a book on the practice of honor killings (Husseini, 2009). I emailed her; she replied, willing to do an interview. I also emailed a woman employed in the Jordan office of the United Nations, and she, too, agreed to meet with me to help with possible participants. She gave me the name of Dr. Salma Nims, the Secretary of the Jordanian Commission on Women, whom I emailed. Dr. Nims offered to meet with me as well as introduce me to women activists. I was grateful for this introduction in spite of the fact that I wanted to avoid officials. I had no luck identifying individual women doing activism in Jordan in the news as I was able to do in Armenia because news stories are not written about them, so I started where I could.

On my 2019 trip to Jordan, I drove myself to my interviews with the help of my phone GPS. The buildings did not look like what I imagined government offices would look like; they were old-looking, not polished, with few signs indicating what the building housed, but with guards and barriers to access the parking areas. Inside, additional guards asked whom I wanted to see and arranged for someone to accompany me to Dr. Nims' office.

The Secretary of the Commission on Women was a beautiful woman dressed in Western clothing, very stately and professional. She welcomed me, served tea and was open, friendly and very helpful. She gave me an interview about how she came into the semi-governmental agency position she was in (from a western-educated, well-known and respected Christian family – Christians make up about 3% of the population (Bureau of Democracy, Human Rights and Labor, 2018c, d; 2019e, f), and she appeared to sincerely want to improve the conditions for women. Nims served in this position at the pleasure of the king who appointed her, and she had a simple office with many people working on women's issues. Her job, she said, was to promote advocacy organizations' goals where policy change is necessary. Several issues were in the forefront, for example, to change laws that prevent children born to non-Jordanian women married to Jordanian men from having citizenship and basic rights – those children cannot go to free government schools, have passports or obtain healthcare; to get the government out of deciding which occupations and what hours women can work since only 14% of women in Jordan are in the paid workforce and women's occupational opportunities are tightly controlled; and to stop discrimination in women teachers' pay in privately-owned schools, which is often considerably less than minimum wage ($200 per month compared to $80 per month for women). To complain is to assure job termination.

Nims was proud of a recent victory for women which was the abolishment of the "rape marriage". This law stated that any man who engages in sex with a women under 18 has committed rape, but it allowed men to escape criminal punishment if they married their victims and stayed with them for three years (Tahhan, 2017). Victims had been "encouraged", or forced by their families to marry their rapists to protect her father's family's honor. Far too often, the young wife was treated as a servant for the man's family and abused, then promptly divorced. Divorced women too often end up in "shelters" because the men in their families will not accept them back into the family. Thousands of women are in these places which are like jails. They are not free to leave unless a man has them released into his custody (S. Nims, personal communication, Oct. 12, 2019).

Women had been working on this issue for years and Nims readily got behind it when she took the commissioner role. Their goals were to end the practice of forced "rape" marriage all together and to enable the prosecution of the rapist by the courts. She told of an organized protest the women's group planned, and with support from her office it was able to take place. She showed me photos and videos of hundreds of women with signs protesting loudly in front of the Parliament building; the protestors were rallied by what she called an electronic storm, a large social media blitz. Parliament's Legal Committee, which included women, was against abolishing the law. But because of the intense pressure and attention from the media, the Royal Committee and the king pressured Parliament (and Parliament only does what the king wants) to abolish the law, so the drive was successful. However, it only applies to women under 18, so there is still work to be done according to Dr. Nims.

At my last visit, Dr. Nims invited two activist leaders of the teachers' pay movement to explain to me their efforts to date. The two women did not speak English but they were eager to share their efforts and frustrations about the conditions for women teachers. An assistant to Dr. Nims who was involved in the project served as an excellent translator and explained the context. Women are only allowed to teach young children and girls. They are challenged from every direction, but their fight is to be paid fairly and to have the right to remain employed even if they speak up against a practice.

I would not have learned about these activist women if I had not interviewed at the government level. In spite of the anger and frustration of women over certain conditions and practices, locating women who are calling for change is difficult. Language is a barrier as is my being an outsider. There are real risks to criticizing the government, to the point that my host, S, became concerned about my using his name in any publication. It is also illegal to say anything negative about the king or his family. It takes courage and family support to speak up about changes to the status quo.

Ethiopia

Ethiopia is a federal republic, ruled by one party which holds all parliament seats (Bureau of Democracy, Human Rights, and Labor, 2019c, 2020c). The government uses informants, surveillance and searches, and it controls the media and the internet. People loyal to the party receive preferences for jobs, housing and freedom from some interference (Ethiopia, 2019c, 2020c). Here, too, a new government is anticipated to bring about democratic reforms such as those that demonstrate respect for human rights and the rule of law (Bureau of Democracy, Human Rights, and Labor, 2020c). The population is optimistic. Recently, the newly appointed prime minister, who won the Nobel Peace Prize in 2019 for ending a long-running war with Eritrea to its north, added women to his cabinet and appointed a woman to be a figurehead president which is constantly touted as enlightened (Ahmed & Freytas-Tamura, 2018). People now have access to websites that were banned (Bureau of Democracy, Human Rights, and Labor, 2020c). With about 82 ethnic groups and nearly as many languages, conflicts have been common and the new prime minister has been popular in all the regions and among a wide range of tribes. But the use of lethal force to put down protests has blemished his record. And there is still only one real political party even though several are organized (Economist Intelligence Unit, 2018). Since my travel there, the prime minister has engaged in war and violence to bring down opposition, seemingly a return to the way things have been since the dictatorship of Mengistu. Ethiopia's score on the Democracy Index has worsened (see Table 11.2).

I have made just one visit to Ethiopia, therefore my experiences in country and with Ethiopians are fewer. I knew no one in Ethiopia or anyone who had ever been to Ethiopia. With all the courage I could muster, I decided to give it a try because of its interesting and unique history and current situation. I read about Ethiopia's recent leaders, its desire and increasing opportunities to be important to Africa, its struggle to keep the country unified and its relationship with others now and through its history. I posted a request for assistance on the International Leadership Association's (ILA) website and received replies from two members. They made introductions to women they thought might be of assistance through email and I corresponded with them to learn of study participants who would fit with my project, although neither resided in the country. I found some names in English-language news; however email addresses and phone numbers were not easy to find, and I added those names to my list to work on when I got to the country. I had the names of three potential study participants, two university professors and a lawyer. I called them and left messages about who I was, why I was calling and I left my contact information. One professor called back saying she could not meet but gave me the names of two people who might; I did not hear from anyone else even after a couple of follow-up phone calls.

I left for Ethiopia without any commitments for participants, but was advised by my contacts that I should use WhatsApp to call people once I was in the country. I booked a private tour online a couple of months prior to my trip to see the country for 10 days before returning to Addis Ababa for my interviews. I flew to five different northern regions inside the country and traveled around the south to small villages where people still practice the same traditions they have for centuries. It was a quick view of a large and diverse country, but it was important to me not to just drop into the capital city and think I knew anything about the country.

I interviewed a young woman at the university who had lived in the United States for a few years and spoke excellent English. She and I discussed experiences she and her friends had that were dismissive and discriminating because of their sex, and also about the lack of jobs for educated women. Her interests were in colorism and she was heading to the United States for graduate school. A student group of mixed sexes was preparing an alternative Valentine's Day message for university students by preparing roses to give out with the message of obtaining consent for sexual activity and invited me to observe, but I did not get to speak to any of them because of their schedules and deadlines. The most informative interviews I conducted were with several members of an activist and advocacy organization.

I met with the staff of an organization called Setaweet, a word which means to "start the conversation" in Amharic about sexual violence. They produced a gallery showing of "What She Wore" that the Washington Post (Schemm, 2018) covered in which the actual clothing that girls from ages 7 to 17 were wearing when they were raped was hung up for viewing. As expected, none of it was revealing or otherwise "asking for it", the purpose of the showing. It was with these women that I heard one say, "We want better days, when it is not a challenge every day to be a woman". They told that rape and sexual abuse is all too common. She quickly revised her statement to say that her first remark was meant to be about women being in public, but being at home was even more dangerous because of the entitlement fathers, uncles, brothers and cousins feel they have about women. I also heard and read about the abuse of women and girls by men who use battery acid to disfigure and maim them because they think the women deserve punishment. One goal of Setaweet is to reduce the cheap and easy procurement of battery acid in hope of reducing this particular form of violence which was becoming more widespread. The cost of the acid was the equivalent of $3 for a gallon and widely available. But the organization's main activity is teaching high school students to think about sex the same way one thinks about having tea with a friend – one doesn't just take a cup from another, or just helps himself, one asks for a cup. Sexual activity is often coercive; the goal of the training is to teach respect for women as human beings with rights to their own bodies. The program, which was voluntary and attended on Saturdays by the students is now a privately funded program in schools because of the success of the efforts of these young people. Funding for such activities must be obtained within the country since new laws forbid more than 10% of any funding for any program from coming from outside. This policy was instituted to prevent more "liberal" activities from outside the country from being funded.

I know where to pick up again when I return to Ethiopia. That first trip felt a little less successful than my second and third trips to Armenia and Jordan, but I need to remember that my first trips were not as satisfactory as my subsequent ones were, either. My plan is to return to all three countries to re-interview the women I met to learn more about how their activism has shifted, whether anything important has resulted and what they thought or what changed in themselves since we last spoke. Much has changed in this short time, however. The COVID-19 pandemic has curtailed travel and wars have occurred in Armenia (which they lost politically and at much larger cost, mentally) and still are occurring in Ethiopia. Economic conditions are worse in all three countries, which is a known factor for social retrenching not social change (Diamond et al., 2016). World powers are in some flux. Authoritarianism continues to rise.

Reflections and Lessons Learned

It was impossible to quiet my mind as I reflected on not only what women told me, but how much anger, frustration and the sadness they carried. At the same time, they projected courage, hope and an assurance that they were right to uncover the hidden, bring wrongs into the light, and discredit practices that allowed and enabled men and the systems they built and supported to subordinate and harm women. System change was a distant goal, but attitude and belief changes were an immediate need and a glimmering possibility. And they emphasized what many activists know: one person conversing with another person can bring about awareness and support for change. The tentative expression of emotions, mixed as they were from anger to hope to fear of upending the known, and the unambiguous righteousness expressed could be exhausting, and it often was for me. Making the time for paying attention to something else was crucial to be able to start again the next day listening, especially when conducting three, four or five interviews in a single day. Distractions could help relax the mind whether a walk, a meal, a streaming film to watch or some other activity was necessary to settle the brainwaves for sleeping and refreshing.

As my interviews proceeded, I began to search, through listening and reading my notes, for concerns and issues I had not already identified, and seeking the names and stories of women I had no information about yet who had those stories to tell. My concern was that I would draw conclusions prematurely based on patterns found early in the process, taking strongly stated ideas or overt claims as representative of the phenomenon (Charmaz, 2006).

Handwriting notes during the interview then typing them up within a couple of weeks of returning home brought all the swirling thoughts and emotions back to the surface, but this time it was with an organized and analytical mind. Filling in small details was easy when done early, not so much when done weeks later.

It may be difficult to identify and locate the people of interest for a study, especially if they are minorities and women in countries where neither are respected figures. However, because many people do step up and speak out, people with interests in the issues will know who those people are. Newspaper stories and social media are ways to find them or find contacts who can provide relevant information. Then the snowball method of recruiting study participants is most rewarding. Using the name of the person who identified a potential participant is helpful, but even more so is having that person make the first contact with a simple request.

Making a donation to an organization or effort is a good way to thank someone for an interview. I did that in Armenia for all the work N provided; $100 goes a long way to help with procurement of supplies like paper and other tools used daily. Asking if there is a contribution you can make to a cause is very much appreciated.

Having their stories told to the Western world is a significant reason some women spoke with me, which they made a point to say. Their deep knowledge of the complicated issues and solutions is seldom shared with anyone but their close allies. They may not be able to speak completely honestly or tell all sides of an issue for concern that their opinions may not be kept private. Establishing a comfortable environment and trust takes time, authentic interest and openness that has to be evident in one's own conversational style – body language, facial expressions and a listening posture are important to be aware of. Having said that, unlocking the passion someone has for the work they do seemed to come easily for them once I told them who I was and that I wanted to learn from them, and as we found other common grounds like talking about our children, having traveled around their city or country, eating their food or having a passion for the same issues. I have never been so aware of what active listening was until doing this research.

I found that few if any of the women I spoke with considered themselves "feminists". The word is fraught with tension and is less meaningful or significant than it sometimes feels in the United States too, especially among younger women who feel far removed from the initial anger about sexism that fueled the original Western movement. None of the women I spoke to seemed to hope for equality or an end to sexism; they were more focused on specific harms they felt and solutions to those problems. The opportunity to work in safety, earn an income, not to be seen as superfluous to society except for the "rewards" of marriage, not to be bodies created for men's use, and the primary members of society to carry so many physical and emotional burdens were day-to-day hardships they knew kept them pushed down. They were fighting to end the violence within and without the home that so many of them experienced. They were fighting to be heard about laws and the law enforcement needed to protect them. I stopped asking the question about whether they saw themselves as feminists. My participants sounded almost afraid of the term or being described by it. They repeated the refrain I have often heard among American women that "feminism" has a bad connotation, because it suggests that the world would be better off with women in charge, without men at all and other extreme ideas. Female equality was premature to even imagine in societies where women must obtain permission to leave their homes, are the vessels for their family's honor and live in nearly constant fear of being harmed by the very men that are supposed to protect them. They wanted to participate in public life in safety, and to be heard and understood. In subsequent interviews, I asked women just to explain what they were doing and why. What were their immediate goals and where did they hope those achievements would lead? I also stopped asking if they thought of themselves as activists and let them use the term if they chose to. *Activism* is what I thought they were doing, but they just felt it was work for raising awareness and changing policies. A conclusion for me was not to use terms that researchers use to describe actions and belief systems but to infer what I could from how they recounted their experiences and said what they were drawn to do.

I know traveling alone to a foreign country where one does not speak the language, know anyone or has never been, to collect data by interviewing and observing people is not for the faint of heart. It is easy to get frustrated by the myriad things that do not work the way we anticipate or expect, from lack of electricity to government-controlled internet to finding an address when house or building numbers are not used. The constant awareness of difference can be exhausting. International researchers should expect and plan for that.

Having a slightly guarded sense of trust about the general and innate goodness of people goes a long way. In my considerable experience, people who approach you when you are obviously a tourist or outsider often really do desire to help you understand how to buy train tickets, find a street or meal, or tell you about an event you are witnessing. Sometimes, traveling while female, it is hard to dismiss a man who was being initially helpful, but everyone understands the word and body language of No. Sometimes you will spend more money than you should have (and likely will not even realize it) because you do not understand enough about the culture or you are taken for a wealthy person because you have traveled so far. Sometimes people will take advantage of you. It will always take longer than you expect to get where you are going. There will be days when being constantly aware of your surroundings is tiresome. But the wonderful insights gained, the connections to your fellow human beings made, the possible friends and colleagues you will be introduced to and the rich experiences you bring back to your friends, colleagues and students are so worth the effort.

The women I met risked health, safety, happiness and security to bring about awareness of issues, speak truth to power, provide services and education and forums. They make inroads in policy and laws, they protest, they expose corruption and gross inequalities and they lead other activities where they are heard and seen in societies and countries where women can suffer for not keeping their heads down and their voices silent. Conducting research in international settings, as rich and rewarding as it is and as exhausting and intimidating as it also is, without a doubt provides an important way to learn about how people in so many ways unlike us deal with the world they live in and seek to change it, as do so many people just like us. To glean insights into how people lead, how they influence their constituents and followers, how they use the tools and resources they find, and how they sometimes risk their safety, jobs, reputations and futures for the change they believe must come is valuable to our audiences. Your experiences will be different from mine because nothing is static and all the factors vary all the time. The more we venture out, the more questions we ask, the more people we make connections with and the more we discuss our findings and insights with others, the more sense we can make of the world we inhabit.

References

Abdel-Samad, M. (2017). Legislative advocacy under competitive authoritarian regimes: The case of civil society in Jordan. *Voluntas 28*, 1035–1053.

Abeya, S. G., Afework, M. F., & Yalew, A. W. (2012). Intimate partner violence against women in west Ethiopia: A qualitative study on attitudes, woman's response, and suggested measures as perceived by community members. *Reproductive Health, 9*(14), 3–11.

Adely, F. J. (2012). *Gendered paradoxes: Educating Jordanian women in nation, faith, and progress.* University of Chicago Press.

Ahmed, H., & de Freytas-Tamura, K. (2018, Oct 25).Ethiopia appoints its first female president. New York Times.

Al-Hassan, S., & Takash, H. (2011). Attributions and attitudes of mothers and fathers in Jordan. *Parenting: Science and Practice, 11*, 142–151 doi:10.1080/15295192.2011.585559.

Alcolea-Banegas, J. (2009). Visual arguments in film. *Argumentation 23*(2), 259–275.

Armstrong, K. (1986). *The gospel according to woman.* Doubleday.

Bartkowski, J. P., & Read, J. G. (2003). Veiled submission: Gender, power, and identity among evangelical and Muslim women in the United States. *Qualitative Sociology, 26*(1), 71–92.

Blank, H. (2007). *Virgin: The untouched history.* Bloomsbury.

Bureau of Democracy, Human Rights and Labor. (2017). Armenia. *2016 Country reports on human rights practices.* United States Department of State. https://www.state.gov/reports/2016-country-reports-on-human-rights-practices/armenia/.

Bureau of Democracy, Human Rights and Labor. (2018a). Armenia. *2017 Country reports on human rights practices.* United States Department of State. https://www.state.gov/reports/2017-country-reports-on-human-rights-practices/armenia/.

Bureau of Democracy, Human Rights, and Labor. (2018b). Armenia. *2017 Report on international religious freedom.* United States Department of State. https://www.state.gov/reports/2017-report-on-international-religious-freedom/armenia/.

Bureau of Democracy, Human Rights, and Labor. (2018c). Jordan. 2017 *Report on international religious freedom.* United States Department of State. https://www.state.gov/reports/2017-report-on-international-religious-freedom/jordan/.

Bureau of Democracy, Human Rights and Labor. (2018d). Jordan. *2017 Country reports on human rights practices.* United States Department of State. https://www.state.gov/reports/2017-country-reports-on-human-rights-practices/jordan/.

Bureau of Democracy, Human Rights and Labor. (2019a). Armenia. *2018 Country reports on human rights practices.* United States Department of State. https://www.state.gov/reports/2018-country-reports-on-human-rights-practices/armenia/.

Bureau of Democracy, Human Rights, and Labor. (2019b). Armenia. *2018 Report on international religious freedom.* United States Department of State. https://www.state.gov/reports/2018-report-on-international-religious-freedom/armenia/.

Bureau of Democracy, Human Rights, and Labor. (2019c). Ethiopia. *2018 Country reports on human rights practices.* United States Department of State. https://www.state.gov/country-reports-on-human-rights-practices/ethiopia/.

Bureau of Democracy, Human Rights, and Labor. (2019d). Ethiopia.*2018 Report on international religious freedom.* United States Department of State. https://www.state.gov/reports/2018-report-on-international-religious-freedom/ethiopia/.

Bureau of Democracy, Human Rights and Labor. (2019e). Jordan. *2018 Country reports on human rights practices.* United States Department of State.

Bureau of Democracy, Human Rights, and Labor. (2019f). Jordan. 2018 *Report on international religious freedom.* United States Department of State. https://www.state.gov/reports/2019-report-on-international-religious-freedom/jordan/.

Bureau of Democracy, Human Rights and Labor. (2020a). Armenia. *2019 Country reports on human rights practices.* United States Department of State. https://www.state.gov/reports/2019-country-reports-on-human-rights-practices/armenia/.

Bureau of Democracy, Human Rights, and Labor. (2020b). Armenia. *2019 Report on international religious freedom.* United States Department of State. https://www.state.gov/reports/2019-report-on-international-religious-freedom/armenia/.

Bureau of Democracy, Human Rights and Labor. (2020c). Ethiopia. *2019 Country reports on human rights practices.* United States Department of State. https://www.state.gov/reports/2019-country-reports-on-human-rights-practices/ethiopia/.

Bureau of Democracy, Human Rights, and Labor. (2020d). Ethiopia. *2019 Report on international religious freedom.* United States Department of State. https://www.state.gov/reports/2019-report-on-international-religious-freedom/ethiopia/.

Bureau of Democracy, Human Rights and Labor. (2020e). Jordan. *2019 Country reports on human rights practices.* United States Department of State. https://www.state.gov/reports/2019-country-reports-on-human-rights-practices/jordan/.

Bureau of Democracy, Human Rights and Labor. (2020f). Jordan. *2019 Report on international religious freedom.* United States Department of State. https://www.state.gov/reports/2019-report-on-international-religious-freedom/jordan/.

Charmaz, K. (2006). *Constructing grounded theory: A practical guide through qualitative analysis.* Sage.

Coontz, S. (2005). *Marriage, a history.* Penguin.

Devnew, L. E., Austin, A. M. B., Le Ber, M. J., & Shapiro, M. (2017). Women's leadership aspirations. In S. R. Madsen (Ed.), *Handbook of research on gender and leadership* (pp. 165–179). Edward Elgar.

Diamond, L., Plattner, M. F., & Walker, C. (2016). *Authoritarianism goes global.* Johns Hopkins University Press.

Economist Intelligence Unit (EIU). (2016). *Democracy index 2016: Revenge of the "deplorables."* http://www.eiu.com.

Economist Intelligence Unit. (2017). *Democracy index 2017: Free speech under attack.* http://www.eiu.com

Economist Intelligence Unit. (2018). *Democracy index 2018: Me, too: Political participation, protest and democracy.* http://www.eiu.com.

Economist Intelligence Unit. (2019). *Democracy index 2019: A year of democratic setbacks and popular protest.* http://www.eiu.com.

England, P. (2010). The gender revolution: Uneven and stalled. *Gender & Society, 24*(2), 149–166.

Flick, U. (2007). *Managing quality in qualitative research.* Sage.

Fox, A. M., Alzwawi, S. A., & Refki, D. (2016). Islamism, secularism and the woman question in the aftermath of the Arab Spring; Evidence for the Arab Barometer. *Politics and Governance, 4*(4), 40–57. doi:10.17645/pag.v4i4.767.

Gilligan, C., & Snider, N. (2018). Why does patriarchy persist? *Polity.*

Glaser, B. G., & Strauss, A. L. (1967). *The discovery of grounded theory: Strategies for qualitative research.* Aldine.

Husseini, R. (2009). *Murder in the name of honor.* OneWorld Publ.

Hofstede, G. (2001). *Culture's consequences: Comparing values, behaviors, institutions, and organizations across nations.* Sage.

Hofstede, G., Hofstede, G. J., & Minkov, M. (2010). *Cultures and organizations: Software of the mind* (3rd ed.). McGraw Hill.

International Leadership Association. (2020). ila-net.org

Johnson, A. (2014.) *The gender knot: Unraveling our patriarchal legacy.* Temple University Press.

Joseph, S. (Ed.) (1999). *Intimate selving in Arab families: Gender, self, and identity.* Syracuse University Press.

Kassa, B. E., & Sarikaksis, K. (2019). Social media trivialization of the increasing participation of women in politics in Ethiopia. *Journal of African Media Studies, 11*(1), 21–33. doi:10.1386/jams.11.1.21_1

Kvale, S. (2007). *Doing interviews.* Sage.

Lenze, J., & Klasen, S. (2017). Des women's labor force participation reduce domestic violence? Evidence from Jordan. *Feminist Economics, 23*(1), 1–29. doi:10.1080/13545701.2016.1211305

Lerner, G. (1986). *The creation of patriarchy.* Oxford University Press.

Loeske, D. R. (2017). *Methodological thinking* (2nd ed.). Sage.

Mengistu, A. A. (2019). Socioeconomic and demographic factors influencing women's attitude toward wife beating in Ethiopia. *Journal of Interpersonal Violence, 34*(15), 3290–3316. doi:10.1177/0886260519842179

Miles, M. B. & Huberman, A. M. (1994). *Qualitative data analysis: A sourcebook for new methods* (2nd ed.). Sage.

Moghadam, V. M. (2004). Patriarchy in transition: Women and the changing family in the Middle East. *Journal of Comparative Family Studies, 35*(2), 137–162.

Rayyan, M. (2016). Jordanian women's leadership styles in the lens of their masculinity- femininity value orientation. *Journal of Transnational Management, 21*(3), 142–161. doi:10.1080/15475778.2016.1192916

Schemm, P. (Dec 10, 2018). Will Ethiopia's reforms include its women? *The Washington Post.* Retrieved from https://www.washingtonpost.com/world/africa/will-ethiopias-reforms-include-its-women/2018/12/09/934a1d14-edb4-11e8-8b47-bd0975fd6199_story.html?utm_term=.f327d584a4f3

Seguino, S. (2011). Help or hindrance? Religion's impact on gender inequality in attitudes and outcomes. *World Development, 39*(8), 1308–1321.

Sen, G. (2007). Informal institutions and gender equality. In J. Jutting, D. Drechsler, S. Bartsch, & I. de Soysa (Eds.), *Informal institutions: How social norms help or hinder development* (pp. 49–72). OECD.

Stead, V., & Elliott, C. (2009). *Women's leadership.* Palgrave Macmillan.

Stone, M. (1976). *When god was a woman.* Harcourt, Brace, Jovanovich.

Tahhan, Z. (Aug 1, 2017). "Historic day" as Jordanian parliament repeals rape law. *Al Jazeera English*. https://www.aljazeera.com/indepth/features/2017/08/day-jordanian-parliament-repeals-rape-law-170801103929836.html

Vaidhyanathan, S. (2018). *Anti-social media*. Oxford University Press.

Walters, B. R., & Perez, S. (2016). Cultural commitments and gender parity: Human rights and implicit religion. *Implicit Religion, 19*(4), 481–505. doi:10.1558/imre.28273

Zamfir, K. (2018). Returning women to their place? Religious fundamentalism, gender bias and violence against women. *Journal for the Study of Religions and Ideologies, 17*(51), 3–20.

Part IIB

Quantitative, Qualitative and Unique Design Considerations

12

The Relevance of Survey Translation and Data Quality in Leadership Studies

How to Include Diverse Voices in Survey Design

Patricia Goerman, Mikelyn Meyers, Kathleen Kephart, and Angie O'Brien

Introduction

Survey data are of critical importance in enabling leaders to make sound policy decisions. Leaders at all levels, including national and local government, Non-Governmental Organization (NGOs), businesses and non-profit organizations use survey data in their decision making. Whether such data are gathered through large nationally representative surveys, small panel surveys or via qualitative methods such as focus groups, one critical component is always present: for data to be relevant and comparable across all members of a society, respondents from as many social, cultural and linguistic groups as possible need to be included. For this reason, sound survey translation methods are of critical importance. Survey designers, analysts and end data users should all have a basic awareness of sound practices in this area. Furthermore, leaders who make data-driven decisions should ask questions about how survey instruments were developed and how the data were gathered.

For leadership researchers who would like to collaborate across countries, focusing on best practices for survey translation can help with setting up sound research projects as well. There can be many challenges with translating concepts unique to a particular culture or group. This chapter focuses on best practices for survey translation, particularly on how to bring the voices and perspectives of people from diverse backgrounds into the process via pretesting and qualitative research. Moreover, many of the concepts and recommendations in this chapter are applicable to other aspects of international leadership research.

Survey translation is a complex task that has the end goal of creating functionally equivalent materials in order to include the perspectives of more members of a population than a monolingual instrument could do. This chapter presents insights into the complexity of high quality multilingual survey design and discusses implications for the leadership studies field.

In this chapter, we discuss the collection and interpretation of data across languages and cultures in the context of U.S. government household surveys that have the goal of producing nationally representative data. The chapter covers three main topics. First, we discuss the complexity of multilingual survey design. Second, we give a brief overview of best practices for survey translation. Third, we discuss the inclusion of respondent voices and perspectives in the process through pretesting. The

DOI: 10.4324/9781003003380-12

chapter then concludes by tying multilingual questionnaire development best practices to the field of leadership studies. It is only through inclusion of diverse respondent voices and perspectives in research that leaders can effectively make policy and practice decisions that affect all the members of a society or organization.

Review of the Literature

As countries grow more internally diverse and the public and private sectors become increasingly international, the need for multilingual and cross-cultural research grows (Elo et al., 2016; Lane et al., 2014; Peterson & Hunt, 1997). Yet, the utility of the policies and practices developed based on the leadership studies literature is highly dependent upon the quality of data produced in any given study (Brackstone, 1999; Schintler & Kulkarni, 2014). Although the leadership studies literature provides a number of theoretical perspectives on cross-cultural research, its cross-cultural methodological literature is less developed (see handbook introduction).

In order to effectively lead, governments need to be able to collect and interpret meaningful data about their populations (Elo et al., 2016; Lane et al., 2014). As such, it is essential that surveys include and are representative of all members of diverse populations to the extent possible (De Heer, 1999). In a country as large and heterogeneous as the United States, the government needs to be able to effectively conduct surveys across languages and cultures (Barreto et al., 2018). Specialized research groups in U.S. government agencies have increasingly begun to focus on these issues over the years (Leeman, 2016; Pan et al., 2014). For example, the U.S. Census Bureau has a Language and Cross-Cultural Research group that focuses on questionnaire design and pretesting of translated survey instruments.

The Complexity of Multilingual Survey Development

The main goal in developing multilingual surveys is to design an instrument that asks the same questions across diverse survey respondents, both within and across language groups. Survey designers strive for comparable understanding of the questions by respondents, given that the ultimate goal is collection of parallel data across groups. These goals are neither straightforward nor easy to achieve since not every language and culture share the same concepts, interpretations of terms or even institutions.

Numerous studies document that not all words and concepts can easily be conveyed in other languages or cultures (Fukuhara et al., 1998; Leeman, 2018; Pan et al., 2014; Samady et al., 2008). Sometimes these incongruences arise predominantly from linguistic issues. For instance, Fukuhara et al. (1998) encountered difficulties when translating a quality of life survey from English into Japanese. Factor analysis of the questionnaire revealed that "physical" quality of life was difficult to differentiate from "mental" quality of life in the Japanese translation. Furthermore, focus groups demonstrated that the phrase "limited" [by health or mental capacity] in English was interpreted as "limited by a doctor" in the Japanese version. Thus, the researchers determined that additional translation was necessary to acquire reliable data for policymakers and leaders in the healthcare industry (Fukuhara et al., 1998).

Differences in culture and societal institutions can cause translation issues as well. For example, Balbinotti et al. (2007) found that business terms can be difficult to translate when two countries have significantly different financial markets and systems. For example, they found that many Brazilian CFOs were unfamiliar with financial tools and concepts that are uncommon in emerging markets, such as "credit ratings" or "earnings per share dilution". Consequently, the researchers had to conduct multiple rounds of translation, revision and validation to ensure more parallel data collection across languages. Similarly, in his study of business texts, Becher (2011) found that

German-English and English-German translations of business texts often had issues with "explicitation" and "implicitation". In other words, the German and English languages differ in whether meaning is more often stated explicitly or whether it is implied, which can have implications for translation.

The U.S. Census Bureau's American Community Survey (ACS) question series on education level provides a good illustration of the complexity of multilingual survey design and translation (Goerman, Fernandez & Quiroz, 2018a). The ACS is a monthly survey that samples 3.5 million addresses a year. It is a multi-mode survey with instruments that are administered through the Internet, paper questionnaires, by phone and in-person with interviewers. At the time of the study, the survey had two Spanish versions with minimal differences between them, one used in the continental United States and one used in Puerto Rico. One challenge with measuring education level in the United States is the country's diverse population made up of many immigrants who have completed schooling in different countries at various times. U.S. education levels such as "high school" do not have an exact counterpart in many immigrants' countries of origin.

In the years leading up to and immediately after 2010, the U.S. Census Bureau completed several cognitive testing studies of the Spanish language version of the ACS. A Spanish translation of the survey had been in use but it had not been tested with respondents previously. This effort was an early project undertaken by a recently established language research team housed in the questionnaire design and pretesting area of the agency. The Spanish language questions were cognitively tested in the interviewer administered mode with 46 Spanish speakers and 10 English speakers, divided across two rounds of testing (Goerman et al., 2018c). Testing of the English version of the survey was included in the project in order to determine whether any issues identified were translation issues or crosscutting issues that affected both languages. Cognitive interviewing is a survey pretesting method whereby a draft version of a survey under development is administered to respondents with various characteristics to gauge their interpretation of the questions. Typically, the survey is administered to the respondent and then the researcher administers probing questions to learn about the person's interpretation of key terms and questions. The goal is to determine whether respondents are interpreting and answering questions as intended by the survey designers. When problems are identified through the testing, survey designers make changes to the questions and often retest in an iterative manner. Cognitive interviewing is a qualitative research method and is not typically conducted with representative samples (Willis, 2005). However, researchers typically strive for as much diversity as possible in respondent characteristics and living situations. For more on the method, see Schoua-Glusberg and Villar (2014) and Willis (2005).

The ACS includes a series of questions about education level. One particular question that illustrates the difficulty with multilingual surveys quite well is as follows in English and Spanish:

> "The next questions are about schooling and education. At any time <u>in the last 3 months</u>, have you attended school or college? Include only nursery or preschool, kindergarten, elementary school, home school, and schooling that leads to a high school diploma or a college degree".
> "Las siguientes preguntas son sobre instrucción y educación. En cualquier momento <u>durante los últimos 3 meses</u>, ¿asistió usted a una escuela o universidad? Incluya solo guardería infantil o preescolar, kindergarten, escuela elemental, enseñanza en el hogar y escuela que conduce a un diploma de escuela secundaria o un título universitario".

This example wording showcases three different potential respondent difficulties with translation: (1) confusing terms, (2) complex question structure and (3) conceptual mismatch across cultures. In terms of confusing terms: Spanish speakers had trouble with the term used for "attended" (asistió). The respondents explained that "asistió" could be interpreted as "attended" – as in English – but could also be interpreted as "went to", such as to drop off a child, meet with a teacher, etc. This was particularly problematic because of the examples of nursery school, preschool and kindergarten included in the question. Many parents did "go to" school frequently in order to drop off their children.

Additionally, the testing showed that complex question structure was an issue in both languages in the above example. People had trouble with the length and number of clauses in the question, as evidenced by the fact that many people asked for the question to be repeated. This issue was particularly pronounced in Spanish, where many respondents asked the researcher to re-read the question before they could provide an answer.

Finally, researchers noticed issues of conceptual mismatch with terms such as "home school". Home schooling is an official program in the United States, whereby parents follow a curriculum and educate their children at home rather than sending them to a public or private school. Cognitive testing showed that Spanish-speaking immigrants interpreted the translation used for home school, "enseñanza en el hogar" or literally "teaching in the home" as a variety of things, such as Bible lessons, teaching children about manners or about moral principles, etc. The danger with this interpretation was that people might mistakenly respond "yes" to the question when thinking about these rather common activities even though they had not been enrolled in formal schooling. This response error could result in an overestimation of the number of homeschooling families in the United States. Other researchers have identified issues with translation of educational levels in surveys as well (Schneider, 2009; Schneider et al., 2016, Schoua-Glusberg et al., 2008).

U.S. Census Bureau researchers attempted a variety of approaches to resolve the above education question issues between the rounds of cognitive testing. The easiest type of problem to address was revision of confusing terms, such as the translation for "attended" school. Rather than "asistió", the researchers tested the term "estudió" or "studied" and discovered that this term worked better. In terms of complex question wording, researchers recommended dividing the question into shorter sentences with fewer clauses. However, this was not an option for the survey sponsor in this case given that the question had appeared in many iterations of the survey and the sponsor wanted data across years to remain comparable. To address the issue of conceptual mismatch, one strategy that was tested was to add an English term in parenthesis to the Spanish translation. In this case, the translation for "home school" in Spanish became "enseñanza en el hogar (home school)" for Round 2 testing. This revision was found to be helpful in Puerto Rico, where many Spanish speakers were familiar with both the home school program and English terminology, but it did not resolve all issues for stateside Spanish speakers. Another strategy that was attempted to address the conceptual mismatch was the addition of a "read as necessary" definition for the term "home school". This addition was helpful in our second round of testing.

The previous example illustrates the complexity involved in the translation of just one survey question. The survey methodology field has increasingly focused on language and cross-cultural issues related to survey design. The next section discusses survey translation and some current best practices.

Best Practices for Survey Translation

There have been quite a number of publications related to survey translation over the years (Behr & Shishido, 2016; Harkness, 2003; Pan et al., 2020). Traditional guidelines about translation state that a translation should (1) use the same register or degree of formality as the source; (2) include the same material as the original version without clarifying or adding content; and (3) include equivalent qualifiers and modifiers, such as adjectives and adverbs, though word order should be modified to be appropriate for a given language (Harkness et al., 2010).

Harkness et al. (2010) pointed out a number of issues with these assumptions. First, they asked whether it is possible and desirable to match register, or level or degree of formality, across languages.

Different populations have different average educational and literacy levels. This is particularly the case when you are surveying immigrant populations within a host country. When the goal is to collect parallel data across groups, it may not be desirable to use the same degree of formality or complexity in all languages. Second, it may be necessary to omit content or add explanations in pursuit of equivalent meaning across languages in a survey. The home school example that we discussed earlier is a good example. This program does not exist in some countries and it may require explanation for some groups but not others. The third assumption is based on the theory that equivalent qualifiers and modifiers exist across languages, which is not always the case. A particularly challenging type of survey "jargon" to translate are response scales, where respondents are asked to rank their answers with qualifiers such as "strongly agree", "somewhat agree" and so on. Whether there is an exact translation and whether people interpret the gradations in answer scales in the same way across languages is an open question (Harkness et al., 2010).

Translation of Answer Scales

The literature on translation of answer scales shows evidence that language, culture and meaningfulness all influence response style (Renteria et al., 2008; Si & Cullen, 1998). In order for results to be valid, answer scales must function comparatively in all languages and cultures (Berkanovic, 1980; Hulin & Mayer, 1986; Villar, 2009). There are many challenges to achieving this goal. In his 2009 study, Collazo (2005) details issues in translating a nine-point hedonic scale from English into Spanish. This study tested three different versions of a translation: (1) a literal translation (word-for-word); (2) a liberal translation (a translation that focused more on conveying similar meaning and register across languages rather than being word-for-word); and (3) a liberal translation written at a child's reading leveling (lower register translation). Overall, the liberal version at a child's reading level worked best, although 30% of the respondents ranked the translated responses differently than in the English version.

The literature also documents many challenges in the translation of intensity modifiers, or words that qualify the meanings of other words, such as adjectives or adverbs. Intensity modifiers can both drastically increase or decrease the reliability of a translation (Villar, 2009). For example, the probability of selecting an extreme response varies across languages and cultures. In their study of gender role attitude scales, Gibbons et al. (1999) found that (English/Spanish) bilingual respondents were more likely to select extreme responses in Spanish on one survey. Additionally, on another survey, the researchers found that respondents were more likely to select more extreme responses when answering in their native language than in their second language, yet differences in their real-life situation could not account for all the differences in response style that a person showed across languages (Gibbons et al., 1999). There is some research finding that intensity modifiers can actually render scale points less functional in cross-national surveys. In her study examining the International Social Survey Programme, Villar (2009) found that adding intensity modifiers, such as "strongly" agree, "somewhat" agree, "neither agree nor disagree" and so on, to an eight-point scale made it more difficult to measure respondents' underlying attitudes than the same scale without the intensity modifiers. One suggested solution was not to label all points on the scale to minimize differences in interpretation.

Translation Methods

There are a number of common survey translation methods. In the more recent survey translation literature, translation via the team or committee approach is considered to be a best practice, as opposed to older methods such as back translation, which was en vogue years ago (Mohler et al., 2016). Back translation is a method whereby a translator converts the source language to a target language. A second translator then translates the material from the target language back to the source language so that monolingual survey sponsors can compare the two source language versions to try to spot any differences, which might indicate translation errors. This method can be problematic for several reasons. The biggest issue is that researchers are not actually evaluating the target translation but rather they are evaluating a translation of a translation (Behr, 2017). This can lead to several problems: (1) when comparing the source material to a back translation it is very easy to miss mistakes in the target translation, and (2) since words and concepts often cannot be translated one-to-one across languages, let alone cultures, often some degree of cultural adaptation is necessary. If the source material and back translation look similar, this does not mean the translation is of high quality and it is no guarantee that it is functionally equivalent to the source. It also may appear that a back translation into the source language looks like a "poor translation" because the text is very different, when in reality the translation includes appropriate adaptations to make the two versions functionally equivalent.

Committee translation is typically completed using a team of translators and researchers with expertise in language, survey methodology, cross-cultural issues and subject-matter expertise. In this process, team members individually translate the entire survey or segments of the survey. Team members then review all the translations produced during individual translation. Individual translation is followed by a reconciliation or adjudication meeting where the team members agree on final wording. An adjudicator makes final decisions when team members cannot reach consensus on a particular issue (Pan 2005). The final steps of the translation involve review, respondent pretesting and documentation of the process, as illustrated in the TRAPD (Translation, Review, Adjudication, Pretesting and Documentation) model laid out in the Cross Cultural Survey Guidelines (Mohler et al., 2016). It is often the case that different team members bring different expertise to a translation committee, for example subject-matter experts are sometimes not fluent in the target language/s but they often provide critical information about the intent of survey questions. Different agencies and different projects will likely have different resources available to form teams for a given project. It is sometimes the case that a committee approach can be applied during the review stage in the event that an organization was not able to conduct the translation itself this way (see Goerman et al., 2018c for more detail on this type of approach to translation review).

Innovative Translation Methods

Some agencies, such as the European Social Survey, have adopted innovative methods such as advance translation (Dorer, 2015). This method involves systematically checking the source questionnaire before it is finalized for translation. In this method, both experienced survey translators and survey researchers are asked to translate a pre-final version of the source questionnaire in advance of the source version being finalized and to make written comments. They are asked to do a "problem oriented translation" in order to point out problems, which are then addressed in the source version prior to completing a final translation. The goal is to improve the source questionnaire before official translation is done. The initial translation of the survey is only the first step in the search for parallel instruments for use across languages.

Expert Review of Survey Translations

Expert review is a tool that can improve the quality of survey translations. This procedure can be completed prior to respondent pretesting, or when time or funding does not allow for respondent pretesting, it can also provide a basic evaluation of a survey translation (Goerman et al., 2018c). Typically, expert review involves three or more independent reviewers who are fluent in the target language with different types of expertise, such as (1) subject-matter expertise, (2) being a certified translator and/or having language and cultural expertise, (3) methodological expertise (such as being a survey methodologist). Each individual reviewer may not have all three types of expertise.

The steps involve each reviewer researching and commenting on an initial survey translation independently. A team lead typically compiles all the reviewer comments. Team members then attend consensus meetings to discuss their recommendations. Similar to the steps of a committee translation, if consensus cannot be reached, an adjudicator (typically the team lead) makes a decision. Finally, the recommendations are documented. An advantage of expert review is that this method is often lower cost and faster than respondent pretesting. However, expert review should supplement rather than replace respondent pretesting when possible. As we will discuss in the next section, respondents may react quite differently than experts do to a particular translation.

Pretesting of Multilingual, Multicultural Survey Instruments: Including Respondent Voices in the Survey Development Process

While committee translation and expert review can go a long way towards increasing the comparability of different language versions of a survey instrument, the inclusion of respondent voices is a critical component in survey development. It can be very difficult for expert survey designers to be aware of all possible backgrounds and life circumstances that might influence respondents' interpretations of survey questions. The best way to factor in this information is through pretesting survey questions with people with a variety of backgrounds and demographic characteristics relevant to the target population/s of a given survey. By observing respondents' reactions to survey instruments, their interpretation of questions and how they formulate their responses, researchers can make great strides towards improving the quality of survey data that can be collected with the final instruments (Miller et al., 2014; Willis, 2005).

The U.S. Census Bureau and other federal agencies have data quality standards to ensure high-quality data products (U.S. Census Bureau, 2016). These standards include guidance on data collection instrument development and pretesting (U.S. Census Bureau, 2015). Common survey methodology pretesting methods can be divided into two categories: pre-field and field methods. Pre-field methods include expert review, cognitive testing and usability testing. Common field methods of pretesting include behavior coding, split panel field testing, field observation and online non-probability panels. For an inventory of common pretesting methods see the U.S. Office of Management and Budget (2016b) working paper.

This chapter focuses on including the voices and perspectives of respondents in translated survey instruments, and cognitive and usability testing are key methods for doing this. These methods are common pre-field survey development methods used to ensure that survey translations are as parallel as possible to the source. As discussed previously, cognitive interviewing involves testing with respondents via one-on-one interviews to evaluate whether respondents interpret, comprehend and respond to survey questions as intended.

Usability testing involves measuring efficiency, effectiveness and satisfaction while a respondent completes tasks on a website or in an application. For usability testing of surveys, we focus on evaluating the user experience while respondents complete a survey, specifically looking for places where the respondent does not answer questions accurately or easily. Typical goals are determining whether the respondent can access the survey and finish it in a reasonable amount of time.

Typical cognitive and usability interview methods involve asking the respondent "probing" questions, such as "what does the term 'foster child' mean to you in this question?" (Willis, 2005; Geisen & Romano Bergstrom, 2017; Goerman & Caspar, 2010b). Probing can either be concurrent, where the interviewer breaks in during the survey taking event to ask questions, or retrospective, where questions are asked only after the respondent has finished answering the survey questions. Sometimes a combination of the two methods is used. In deciding when to administer probes, the researcher must balance two competing concerns. First, if respondents are probed too long after they answer the survey question, they may forget what they were thinking or why they chose a particular answer. Second, if they are probed during or immediately after answering a survey question, it may disrupt their thought processes or change their responses to later questions. When we conduct usability testing of web surveys at the U.S. Census Bureau, we often limit probing to be retrospective in order to avoid interfering with the respondent's natural path through the web survey.

There are a number of typical types of cognitive interview probes, including think aloud, meaning oriented, process oriented, paraphrasing and recall probes. A think-aloud procedure is when respondents are asked to talk out loud while they fill out a form or decide how to answer a question. Many researchers use meaning-oriented probes to understand respondent interpretation of concepts, such as, "What does the term 'home schooling' mean to you in this question?" Process-oriented probes are questions such as, "How did you arrive at or choose that answer?" Interviewers often ask paraphrasing probes, such as, "Can you tell me in your own words what that question is asking?" to gauge which concepts are salient to a respondent in a survey question. Finally, recall probes ask questions such as, "How do you remember that you (saw a dentist 3 times) in the last year?" (Goerman & Caspar, 2010b; Willis, 2005).

Survey pretesting is often done with surveys that are only administered in one language. However, when surveys are done in the 3MC (Multinational, Multicultural and Multiregional, context), there are many considerations that need to be taken into account (Cross Cultural Survey Guidelines, 2016). In practice, there is often a lack of complete pretesting of multilingual instruments. This limitation is typically related to cost or a lack of knowledge as to how to best carry out such testing.

In current practice there are two main contexts for cognitive testing in 3MC projects. First, cognitive testing is often part of the development of cross-cultural/cross-national instruments (e.g., European Social Survey, 2014). The goal is to develop and pretest an instrument that works across multiple countries. A second context is the testing of pre-existing or newly developed translations, which is more common in the United States in agencies such as the U.S. Census Bureau. The main goals of this type of work are to identify terms, concepts or questions that function differently across cultures and subsequently make edits and retest to verify that changes have created more parallel questions across languages.

There is one important caveat about multilingual pretesting. Some researchers have identified cultural differences among cognitive interview respondents and have found that the method may not work as smoothly in some groups as in others. Many researchers have noted that the cognitive testing method was designed with Western respondents in mind (Willis, 2015). Willis (2015) provides a history of the introduction of the cognitive interviewing method in the survey methodology field in the 1980s through the interdisciplinary Cognitive Aspects of Survey Methodology (CASM) framework. This movement was the result of collaboration between researchers in the fields of cognitive psychology and survey methodology. Initial research in this area was based in the United States and Western Europe and the focus was not on survey translation. So called 3MC research in the survey field became more common with the founding of organizations such as the Comparative Survey Design and Implementation (CSDI) group in 2002.

Research done in this vein has uncovered evidence that some language/cultural groups have difficulty with typical cognitive interview techniques and probe wording (Mneimneh et al., 2018; Goerman, 2006; Pan et al., 2010). For example, Goerman (2006) has found that without upfront explanation, Spanish-speaking respondents in the United States sometimes interpreted cognitive interview probes to be a sort of "test" of their knowledge and Pan et al. (2010) found that Chinese speakers sometimes expressed reluctance to respond to cognitive interview probes due to interpreting them as a request to speak for others. Some possible reasons for respondent difficulty are differing communication styles across languages and cultures, different levels of topic sensitivity across cultures, lower education levels of some monolingual immigrant populations with whom testing is often done, and lack of familiarity with surveys in some populations. The literature also includes ways to adapt the cognitive interviewing technique to different groups, but more research is needed on this topic.

Additionally, there is ongoing research on target populations for testing web surveys in non-English languages in the United States. Researchers have asked questions such as how fluent in English, how internet proficient, and how literate respondents should be (Goerman et al., 2018c; Garcia Trejo 2017Garcia Trejo & Schoua-Glusberg, 2017). In our questionnaire development research at the U.S. Census Bureau, we typically assume that the users for our translations will be monolingual speakers of the target languages. If they were very proficient in English, we might expect them to use the English version of our websites or questionnaires. However, in some of our cognitive and usability pretesting in Spanish, we have found that the more monolingual respondents, even those who were literate in the target language and had experience using smartphones or computers, lacked a specific kind of Internet proficiency and form literacy that was needed to complete web surveys (Garcia Trejo & Schoua-Glusberg, 2017). Surveys are often conducted in multiple modes and when they participate, respondents with lower literacy will more often fall into interviewer administered modes (i.e., telephone or in person) as opposed to self-administered modes (i.e., paper questionnaires or Internet). Because of this tendency, cognitive and usability testing are often conducted with these different types of modes in mind (Pan et al., 2020). More research is needed regarding the best types of respondents to test different instruments in different modes, though some research has begun into that topic (Goerman et al., 2018b).

Practical Guidance for Multilingual Cognitive Testing

There are a number of decisions that need to be made when managing a 3MC survey pretesting project (Goerman & Caspar, 2010b). They include composition of the research team, development of study materials, cognitive interviewer training, selection of study participants and analysis and reporting of results.

Particular skills are needed for the composition of a survey translation pretesting team. Those include fluency in the languages of interest, cultural knowledge and survey methodology background. There are a number of roles to fill on a translation pretesting project as well. At the U.S. Census Bureau, translation pretesting teams typically include survey methodologists, recruiters, interviewers, analysts, cultural experts and subject-matter experts. In some cases, the same person can fill multiple roles. However, it is more common that each team member does not have all of the necessary skills. For example, some survey methodologists and subject-matter experts may not speak all of the target languages needed in a study. The team for each project needs to be put together based on the staff skills and resources available, which may vary quite a bit depending on where and when a study takes place.

Cognitive interview protocol development is another area in which researchers have to make some decisions at the outset of a project. Interview protocols are like interview guides that contain the list of survey questions to be tested along with research goals and probes to be asked of each respondent. When designing an interview protocol, researchers need to decide whether to use scripted or emergent probes. Scripted probes are planned in advance; emergent probes are based on issues that come up through the course of the interview. Ideally, researchers use both types of probes. However, less experienced interviewers often need to rely more heavily on scripted probes. For work in less commonly spoken languages, it is often difficult to find experienced survey methodologists who are fluent in the language and also experienced cognitive interviewers.

Cognitive interviewer training is another area that needs to be considered. The typical components of the training are: (1) general training on how to conduct a cognitive interview; (2) project-specific training that addresses the goals and potential issues with the questions in the survey; and (3) linguistic and cultural sensitivity issues related to the target population. It is highly recommended that interviewers be given some time to do some practice interviews in the target language as part of their training. Paired practice with one person pretending to be a respondent is a common method.

Another decision point is which language to use in interviewer training. It is ideal to train in the language in which the interviews will be administered whenever possible. Often it is the case that all parties involved in the study will not speak all target languages. At a minimum, there should be some in-language practice interviews conducted as well as some brainstorming by those with cultural knowledge about any issues they think may arise. If translators without experience in survey translation are employed, training for the nuances of survey translation would also be ideal (Pan et al., 2020).

Choosing the number and types of cognitive interview respondents is also an important topic (Blair & Conrad, 2011; Goerman, 2010). Researchers in the United States have looked at the issue of how many English language participants are ideal (Blair & Conrad, 2011). While there is no consensus on this issue, Blair and Conrad (2011) did empirical research on the number of interviews that continue to uncover major issues with a questionnaire. They recommended far more interviews than are often done, up to 50. This work did not take into account multi-language projects, which may have even more potential issues with the survey instrument and translations. Practically speaking, the number of respondents included in a project is tightly tied to project timeline and budget. Our research center typically includes between 10–20 respondents per round of testing. We try to have two to three rounds of testing where revisions to question wording can be tested based on findings from earlier rounds of testing.

In addition to typical variation in demographic characteristics that we look for in monolingual projects (e.g., age, education level, gender, region of the country where respondents live), it is important to consider respondents' country of origin, as well as characteristics of interest related to questions being tested. For example, for Internet access questions, people who live in rural areas where different types of service are available or not available would be of interest. For questions about race, one might want to include people likely to pick more than one category and some people who might pick each of the different categories.

Spanish speakers in the United States are from many different national origins and there may be important linguistic and cultural differences among them. Goerman (2010) looked at the issue of variation in terminology used by Spanish speakers from different national origins living in the United States. In that study, Goerman found less variation when the terminology was related to basic demographic topics, but more variation in terminology related to more specialized topics like appliances and activities. More research is needed on this topic. The ideal number and types of respondents needed can vary by topic and how many different questions are being tested, as well as by the demographic characteristics of the respondent population.

Finally, for a 3M cognitive testing project, it is important to plan for reporting of results. One needs to decide whether to create transcripts or summaries of each case. Transcripts can be useful if researchers would like to analyze exact wording used by respondents and when resources are available. Summaries are often less time consuming to create and can focus on exactly the issues the researcher is examining. For summaries, the researcher must first choose the language in which to write the summaries. If summaries are written in the target language/s, they may need to be translated into the source language or common project language, in case some team members are monolingual. If this is the case, key terms and concepts still need to be included in the target language, since testing typically uncovers alternative wording to be further tested or implemented.

When it is time for analysis, researchers must decide how issues will be coded across cases. This decision allows researchers to see how frequently a problem is occurring and whether the frequency varies across language groups, which might indicate translation problems. When reports are written in the source language, it is important to include key concepts in the target language, along with an explanation of what was problematic and meanings of newly recommended terms. In summary, there are many complex decision points that need to be tailored to each project.

Including Both Source and Target Languages in 3MC Pretesting Projects

One lesson that we have learned to be true through many U.S. Census Bureau translation pretesting studies is that it is important to test the source and translated versions of a questionnaire together. Testing of translated questions can uncover problems in the original English wording, especially with long and complex questions or concepts. In early translation pretesting studies, it was sometimes assumed that any misunderstandings respondents had were because the translation was "wrong or unclear". However, sometimes these misunderstandings result from unclear source material. In one study where we tested just the Spanish wording of an instrument in the first round, and the Spanish and English versions together in a second round, we found that there were a number of different types of problems that were only uncovered when testing both languages together (Goerman & Caspar, 2010a). We found what we called: (1) problematic translations, (2) cross-cutting issues, (3) source language findings and (4) combination findings.

An example of a problematic translation identified in a questionnaire pretesting study is the term "single family house" (Goerman et al., 2014). The original Spanish translation for this concept was "casa para una sola familia". This wording caused large numbers of Spanish speaking respondents to think of a "small home" or literally a "house for just one family", a place where only one family happens to be living as opposed to a housing type. This misinterpretation could cause response error as respondents focused on who lives there as opposed to the type of place.

An example of a cross-cutting finding is the term "enumerator", which appears in some U.S. Census materials as referring to the field interviewers for the Decennial census population count (Goerman & Caspar, 2010a). Testing showed that the term was not well understood by people in either language group, though actually it was better understood in Spanish as "someone who counts something".

A source language finding is a term that was only problematic in the original English version of the survey (Goerman & Caspar, 2010a). An example is the term "parent-in-law", which was translated as "suegro(a)" (meaning "father-in-law or mother-in-law"). Spanish speakers had a much easier time locating the term "suegra" on the questionnaire when they were looking for the concept of "mother-in-law" than did English speakers, who struggled to find the less common term "parent-in-law".

Finally, combination findings are those in which both the source and translation exhibit problems, but they are different in nature. An example of this type of situation is the household member relationship category "roomer or boarder", translated in Spanish as "inquilino o pupilo". Spanish speakers understood "inquilino o pupilo" to be referring to a "renter or student" (when they knew the term "pupilo" at all), but upon closer examination it was apparent that many English speakers did not understand the phrase "roomer or boarder" well either.

Translation and Adaptation: How to Handle Differences Across Languages and Cultures

In a large agency, such as the U.S. Census Bureau, there are logistical difficulties in terms of multilingual survey development. We often work with longitudinal surveys and surveys that have been administered over decades. It is important to be able to examine trends over time and question wording cannot be changed lightly. Sometimes data quality issues in problematic question wording have to be weighed against the repercussions of interrupting time series data. As a result, non-English pretesting findings can sometimes uncover issues that are then shelved.

This is particularly the case when testing uncovers situations where adaptations may be needed. An adaptation can be defined as a deviation in translated wording, where the translation does not match the original source wording exactly. Adaptations are done in order to improve parallel understanding across language versions when there is a cultural or linguistic difference that cannot easily be bridged.

For example, testing of the U.S. Census Bureau's Hispanic origin question has shown that the different word order in the Spanish and English versions sometimes cause confusion for Spanish speakers (Childs et al., 2007; Goerman et al., 2014). The question reads:

> "Are you of Hispanic, Latino, or _Spanish_ origin?"
> "Es usted de origen hispano, latino o _español_?"

We have underlined and italicized the term "Spanish" in both languages for emphasis. The Spanish language version of the question ends with the word "Spanish" and testing has shown that respondents can sometimes interpret the question as asking which of the three terms best describes them. Sometimes Spanish-speaking respondents have even answered "no" to the question altogether, after appearing to hear it as a question about whether they are "español" (Spanish), which is sometimes interpreted as asking if they are literally from Spain. One possible explanation for this type of respondent behavior is that for people who are answering the survey in Spanish, this question violates conversational norms governing the communication of relevant information (Grice, 1975). Many respondents would assume the interviewer knows they must be "of Hispanic, Latino, or Spanish origin" if they are completing the survey in Spanish. Therefore, they often decide the question must be asking which of the three ethnicities they identify with, rather than being a simple yes/no question.

The question on Hispanic ethnicity is a long-standing item included on the U.S. decennial census form and many other surveys. Consequently, changing the word order in one language would not be a small decision. Regardless of whether changes are possible at the time of pretesting, having information about how respondents are interpreting a question can be extremely helpful in interpreting results and understanding the data that policy makers and other leaders use to make decisions.

In some cases, adaptations are implemented as a result of testing. The end goal is to have parallel questions and comparable data across language groups. A great illustration of this is testing of an ACS question about plumbing (Goerman et al., 2014). The question was originally worded:

> "Do you have COMPLETE plumbing facilities in this house or apartment; that is, (1) hot and cold piped water, (2) a flush toilet and (3) a bathtub or shower?"

The question was divided and reworded in part to read:

> "Does this unit have hot and cold running water?"

When the edit occurred, the data being gathered through the question revealed some serious concerns in Puerto Rico. Around 8% of respondents typically answered "no" to the original, longer question wording. When the question was broken into three items, "no" answers to just the hot and cold running water item suddenly jumped to almost 25%.

Researchers had been in the process of conducting cognitive testing of the Spanish wording when this issue arose. We had completed one round of Spanish testing, which included some Puerto Rican Spanish speakers living in Chicago. We did not observe any obvious problems in their responses. We speculated that this might be a double-barreled question, where respondents were being asked two different things: whether they had running water and whether they had "hot and cold" water. We also noticed that the phrase "hot and cold" was the last thing respondents heard in

Spanish (italicized below for emphasis), whereas "running water" was the last thing English speakers heard. We wondered whether the word order might be making one part of the double-barreled question stand out more in Spanish than in English.

"Does this unit have *hot and cold* running water?"
"¿Tiene esta vivienda agua por tubería *caliente y fría*?"

Based on these observations, the Spanish word order was revised to read:

¿Tiene esta vivienda agua caliente y fría por tubería?

We tested the new word order again with Puerto Rican origin respondents living in Chicago and we did not find issues. The change was made in the instrument but upon the next round of data collection, the issues with the Puerto Rican data remained. There were still increased "no" answers over the original compound question. During subsequent cognitive testing and research completed in Puerto Rico, researchers found that people in Puerto Rico do not have "hot and cold running water". Many of those who have running water have water that arrives at the house at only one temperature. People then have hot water heaters attached to specific sinks but do not necessarily have hot and cold water at every sink. While they may not have hot and cold water throughout the whole house or at all, many people did have running water.

An adaptation was introduced to address this issue with the addition of a new question in Puerto Rico in 2013. The new question series reads:

1. Does <building type> have running water?
2. Does <building type> have a water heater?

An important takeaway from this study was that cognitive testing of the Puerto Rican survey instrument should really be done in Puerto Rico. When we interviewed Puerto Rican respondents in Chicago (in an attempt to save money), they did not have this issue while living in Chicago, so it was not uncovered.

Multilingual Pretesting: Areas for Future Research

There are a number of areas in which future research is needed on pretesting. First, more research is needed to develop best practices for 3MC cognitive and usability testing. Empirical research is also needed on other pretesting methods for use in the 3MC context such as expert review, usability testing and field tests.

An exciting area of innovation in multilingual survey research involves pretesting using online non-probability panels such as offered by Qualtrics or Mturk (Hadler & Parent-Thirion, 2019). These panels are not representative of the U.S. population, and typically provide respondents with a small incentive to complete surveys. U.S. Census Bureau researchers have begun testing survey materials in non-English languages in non-probability panels by administering survey questions that are followed by probes. While some probes are closed-ended (i.e., respondents must choose between a discrete list of response options), these probes can also appear with open-text fields where respondents can type out longer answers to the probes. Forthcoming research by our team highlights the need to include open-ended probes as an important component for assessing data quality. In particular, the responses to open-ended probes help us identify respondents who are doing the bare minimum to complete the survey (what we think of as "satisficing") or who are not paying attention to the task (García Trejo et al., under review).

One important consideration when designing multilingual testing projects using non-probability panels is ensuring that the members of these panels are similar to the target audience for the translations being tested. When comparing the target audience of the translation to the members of the online non-probability panel, researchers should take into account how bilingual the respective respondents are, whether they reside in the country where the survey will ultimately be administered, as well as their education level and other demographic characteristics that might influence respondent interpretation of survey questions.

There are advantages to multilingual non-probability panel pretesting, including quick turnaround times with larger sample sizes and lower costs when compared to in-person testing. However, there are also important limitations to this pretesting mode. The data from these testing projects is not as rich when compared to in-person testing. It is also labor intensive to code the responses to open-ended probing questions.

Finally, our forthcoming research indicates that data quality concerns may be more pronounced in non-probability panel testing with speakers of languages other than English. For example, we have observed more respondents typing in random combinations of letters and numbers, or off-topic nonsense in Spanish than in English. Some extreme examples include respondents in our Spanish speaking pretesting panels that have typed in a note saying that they do not actually speak Spanish. We are currently researching the impact that different security and data quality measures have on monolingual and bilingual Spanish-speaking pretesting respondents, including measures to identify fraudulent respondents who are posing as speakers of the target language in order to collect an incentive.

Summary: The Importance of Survey Design, Translation and Pretesting in Leadership Studies

This chapter has discussed the complexity of translating data collection instruments into multiple languages. We have outlined best practices for completing survey translations and summarized the importance of pretesting translated materials with respondents to collect feedback from the intended users of a survey instrument.

Survey translation is a complex task because there is not necessarily a one-to-one correlation between the words or concepts in one language and the words or concepts in another language. Common pitfalls include confusing terminology in the source language, complex source language question structure, and conceptual mismatches across cultures. In addition, there are nuances to capturing subtle gradations in answer scales. Sometimes modifications to the source language wording are needed to improve translatability. In other cases, revisions to the source language would be ideal, but it can be difficult to make changes to source language text when a particular question has been asked for many iterations of a survey.

Translation via the team or committee approach is now considered the gold standard of survey translation methods, although advance translation is a newer method that is currently being researched. Once a translation has been completed, back translation is no longer considered a best practice for evaluating the translation quality. Researchers now recommend completing an expert review as a minimal level of review of translated survey materials. Inclusion of respondent voices and perspective in the survey development process through respondent pretesting using a method like cognitive or usability testing is the ideal way to evaluate and improve the quality of a translation.

A newer line of research in the field of multilingual survey design is the usage of online non-probability panels in order to complete respondent pretesting virtually. While this type of online pretesting may be faster and more cost effective, the data is not as rich as data collected via in-person testing, and it may be harder to guarantee that respondents reflect the demographic characteristics of the target population.

While the availability of accurate survey data that reflects diverse populations is important to help leaders in government and industry make decisions, it is also important that leaders be able to assess the methodology used to collect data in order to know if they are sound and reliable. Similarly, leadership researchers who are collaborating in a transnational context also need a firm understanding of best practices for translation and survey data collection in a multilingual research environment.

As this chapter makes clear, there are many challenges to producing high quality translations of survey instruments and other research materials. It is important for both leaders and leadership scholars to understand the complexity of the process and the care that is needed to ensure high quality data. It is also important to ask questions about how data were created and to recognize data sources that do not contain representative or high-quality data about diverse populations. High-quality translations can help to ensure that underrepresented populations are included in policy discussions and decisions.

Disclaimer

This chapter was written to inform interested parties of research and to encourage discussion. The views expressed are those of the authors and not those of the U.S. Census Bureau.

References

Balbinotti, M. A. A., Benetti, C., & Terra, P. R. S. (2007). Translation and validation of the Graham-Harvey survey for the Brazilian context. *International Journal of Managerial Finance, 3*, 26–48.

Barreto, M. A., Frasure-Yokley, L., Vargas, E. D., & Wong, J. (2018). Best practices in collecting online data with Asian, Black, Latino, and White respondents: evidence from the 2016 Collaborative Multiracial Post-election Survey. *Politics, Groups, and Identities, 6*(1), 171–180.

Becher, V. (2011). *Explicitation and implicitation in translation. A corpus-based study of English-German and German-English translations of business texts* [Dissertation].

Berkanovic, E. (1980). The effect of inadequate language translation on Hispanics' responses to health surveys. *American Journal of Public Health, 70*(12), 1273–1276.

Behr, D. (2017). Assessing the use of back translation: The shortcomings of back translation as a quality testing method. *International Journal of Social Research Methodology, 20*(6), 573–584. doi:10.1080/13645579.2016.1252188

Behr, D., & Shishido, K. (2016). The translation of measurement instruments for cross-cultural surveys. In C. Wolf, D. Joye, T. W. Smith, & Y. Fu (Eds.), *The SAGE handbook of survey methodology* (pp. 193–209). SAGE Publications.

Blair, J. & Conrad, F. G. (2011). Sample size for cognitive interview pretesting. *Public Opinion Quarterly, 75*(4), 636–658.

Brackstone, G. (1999). Managing data quality in a statistical agency. *Survey Methodology, 25*(2), 139–150.

Childs, J. H., Landreth, A., Goerman, P., Norris, D., & Dajani. A. (2007). *Behavior coding analysis report: Evaluating the English and the Spanish version of the Non-Response Follow-Up (NRFU)*. Statistical Research Division Study Series Report: Survey Methodology #2007-16. Retrieved on May 15, 2020 from https://www.census.gov/srd/papers/pdf/ssm2007-16.pdf.

Collazo, A. A. (2005). Translation of the Marlowe-Crowne social desirability scale into an equivalent Spanish version. *Educational and Psychological Measurement, 65*(5), 780–806.

Cross Cultural Survey Guidelines. (2016). *Guidelines for best practice in cross-cultural surveys* (4th ed.). Retrieved on September 3, 2020 from https://ccsg.isr.umich.edu/.

De Heer, W. (1999). International response trends: Results of an international survey. *Journal of Official Statistics, 15*(2), 129.

Dorer, B. (2015). Carrying out advance translations to detect comprehensibility problems in a Source questionnaire of a cross-national. *Translation and Comprehensibility, 72*, 77.

Dorfman, P. W., Howell, J. P., Hibino, S., Lee, J. K., Tate, U., & Bautista, A. (1997). Leadership in Western and Asian countries: Commonalities and differences in effective leadership processes. *Leadership Quarterly, 8*(3), 233–274.

Elo, I., Hummer, R., Rogers, R., Van Hook, J., & Drew, J. R. (2016). *Recommendations regarding the proposed 2018 redesign of the NHIS Population Association of America June 30, 2016.*

Emmerling, R., Boyatzis, R. E., Gutierrez, B., Spencer, S. M., & Zhu, G. (2012). Thinking globally, leading locally: Chinese, Indian, and Western leadership. *Cross Cultural Management: An International Journal, 19,* 1

European Social Survey. (2014). *ESS round 7 translation guidelines.* ESS ERIC Headquarters, Centre for Comparative Social Surveys, City University London.

Fukuhara, S., Bito, S., Green, J., Hsiao, A., & Kurokawa, K. (1998). Translation, adaptation, and validation of the SF-36 Health Survey for use in Japan. *Journal of Clinical Epidemiology, 51*(11), 1037–1044.

García Trejo, Y., Meyers, M., Martinez, M., Goerman, P., O'Brien, A., Otero Class, B. (under review) "Identifying data quality challenges in online non-probability opt-in panels using cognitive interviews in English and Spanish". Journal of Official Statistics.

Garcia Trejo, Y. A., & Schoua-Glusberg, A. (2017). Device and internet use among spanish-dominant hispanics: implications for web survey design and testing. *Survey Practice, 10*(3), 2779.

Geisen, E., & Romano Bergstrom, J. (2017). *Usability testing for survey research.* Elsevier.

Gibbons, J. L., Zellner, J. A., & Rudek, D. J. (1999). Effects of language and meaningfulness on the use of extreme response style by Spanish-English bilinguals. *Cross-Cultural Research, 33*(4), 369–381.

Goerman, P. L. (2006). An examination of pretesting methods for multicultural, multilingual surveys: the use of cognitive interviews to test Spanish instruments Conducting Cross-National and Cross-Cultural Surveys. *ZUMA Nachrichten Spezial Band, 12,* 67–79.

Goerman, P. L. (2010). Number and nationality of spanish-speaking immigrant respondents for U.S. cognitive testing studies. Paper presented at the 65th Annual Conference of the American Association for Public Opinion Research (AAPOR), Chicago, Illinois May 13–16, 2010. JSM Proceedings, American Statistical Association, Alexandria, VA. pp. 5924–5937. Retrieved May 3, 2020 from www.asasrms.org/Proceedings/y2010/Files/400114.pdf.

Goerman, P., & Caspar, R. (2010a). Managing the cognitive pretesting of multilingual survey instruments: A case study of pretesting the U.S. Census Bureau Bilingual Spanish/English Questionnaire. In J. Harkness, M. Braun, B. Edwards, T. P. Johnson, L. E. Lyberg, P. Mohler, B. Pennell, & T. W. Smith (Eds.), *Survey methods in multicultural, multinational, and multiregional contexts.* Wiley Press.

Goerman, P., & Caspar, R. (2010b). A preferred approach for the cognitive testing of translated materials: testing the source version as a basis for comparison. *International Journal of Social Research Methodology, 13*(4), 303 - 316, First published on: 16 November 2009 (iFirst).

Goerman, P., Clifton, M., Quiroz, R., McAvinchey, G., Reed, L., & Rodriguez, S. (2014). *Census American Community Survey Spanish CAPI/CATI Cognitive Testing Phase II Final Report.* Center for Survey Measurement Study Series. Survey Methodology #2014-08. Retrieved on 5/15/20 from https://www.census.gov/srd/papers/pdf/ssm2014-08.pdf.

Goerman, P., Fernandez, L., & Quiroz, R. (2018a). Translation of country-specific programs and survey error: Measuring the education level of immigrants. *Translation & Interpreting, 10*(2), 21–33.

Goerman, P. L., Meyers, M., Sha, M., Park, H., & Schoua-Glusberg, A. (2018b). Working toward comparable meaning of different language versions of survey instruments: Do monolingual and bilingual cognitive testing respondents help to uncover the same issues. *Advances in comparative survey methods: Multinational, multiregional, and multicultural contexts (3MC)* (pp. 251–269). doi:10.1002/9781118884997.ch12.

Goerman, P., Meyers, M., &García Trejo, Y. (2018c). *The place of expert review in translation and questionnaire evaluation for hard-to-count populations in national surveys.* In GESIS symposium on surveying the migrant population: Consideration of linguistic and cultural aspects (Vol. 19, pp. 29–41). DEU.

Goerman, P., Quiroz, R., McAvinchey, G., Reed, L. and Rodriguez, S. (2014). *Census American Community Survey Spanish CAPI/CATI Instrument Testing Phase 1, Round 2—Final Report.* U.S. Census Bureau, Study Series, Survey Methodology #2014-06. Retrieved May 15, 2020 from https://www.census.gov/srd/papers/pdf/ssm2014-06.pdf.

Grice, P. (1975). Logic and conversation. In P. Cole & J. Morgan (Eds.), *Syntax and semantics. 3: Speech acts* (pp. 41–58). Academic Press.

Hadler, P., & Parent-Thirion, A. (2019) Combining cognitive interviews and web probing for cross-cultural cognitive pretesting: the case of the european working conditions survey. *Harmonization, 5*(2).

Harkness, J. A. (2003). Questionnaire translation. In J. A. Harkness, F. J. R. Van de Vijer, & P. Mohler (Eds.), *Cross cultural survey methods* (pp. 35–36). John Wiley & Sons, Inc.

Hulin, C. L., & Mayer, L. J. (1986). Psychometric equivalence of a translation of the job descriptive index into Hebrew. *Journal of Applied Psychology, 71*(1), 83.

Harkness, J. A., Villar, A., & Edwards, B. (2010). Translation, adaptation and design. In J. A. Harkness, M. Braun, B. Edwards, T. P. Johnson, L. Lyberg, P. Mohler, & T. W. Smith (Eds.), *Survey methods in multinational, multiregional and multicultural contexts* (pp. 117–140). John Wiley & Sons, Inc.

Harkness, J. A., Braun, M., Edwards, B., Johnson, T. P., Lyberg, L., Mohler, P., & Smith, T. W. (Eds.), (2010). *Survey methods in multinational, multiregional and multicultural contexts* (pp. 117–140). John Wiley & Sons, Inc.

Johnson, T. P., O'Rourke, D., Burris, J., & Owens, L. (2002). Culture and survey nonresponse. In D. A. Dillman, J. L. Eltinge, R. M. Groves, & R. J. A. Little (Eds.), *Survey nonresponse* (pp. 55–69). John Wiley & Sons.

Lane, J., Stodden, V., Bender, S., & Nissenbaum, H. (Eds.). (2014). *Privacy, big data, and the public good: Frameworks for engagement.* Cambridge University Press.

Leeman J. (2016) Censuses and large-scale surveys in language research. In K. King, Y. J. Lai, & S. May (Eds.), *Research methods in language and education. Encyclopedia of language and education* (3rd ed.). Springer. doi:10.1007/978-3-319-02329-8_8-1.

Leeman, J. (2018). It's all about English: the interplay of monolingual ideologies, language policies and the US Census Bureau's statistics on multilingualism. *International Journal of the Sociology of Language, 252,* 21–43.

Miller, K., Willson, S., Chepp, V., & Padilla, J. L. (2014). *Cognitive interviewing methodology.* John Wiley & Sons.

Mneimneh, Z., Cibelli Hibben, K., Bilal, L., Hyder, S., Shahab, M., Binmuammar, A., & Alwaijri, Y. (2018). Probing for sensitivity in translated survey questions: Differences in respondent feedback across cognitive probe types. *Translation & Interpreting, 10*(2).

Mohler, P., Dorer, B., de Jong, J., & Hu, M. (2016). *Translation overview. Guidelines for best practices in cross-cultural surveys.* Survey Research Center, Institute for Social Research, University of Michigan. Retrieved May, 2, 2020 from http://www.ccsg.isr.umich.edu/index.php/chapters/translation-chapter.

Pan, Y., & de la Puente, M. (2005). *Census Bureau Guideline for the translation of data collection instruments and supporting materials: documentation on how the guideline was developed.* https://www.census.gov/srd/papers/pdf/rsm2005-06.pdf.

Pan, Y. Landreth, A., Park, H., Hinsdale-Shouse, M., & Schoua-Glusberg, A. (2010). Cognitive interviewing in non-English languages: A cross-cultural perspective. In Harkness, J., Braun, M., Edwards, B., Johnson, T. P., Lyberg, L. E., Mohler, P., Pennell, B., & Smith, T. W. (Eds.), *Survey methods in multicultural, multinational, and multiregional contexts.* Wiley Press.

Pan, Y., Leeman, J., Fond, M., & Goerman, P. (2014). Multilingual survey design and fielding: Research perspectives from the US Census Bureau. *Survey Methodology, 1.*

Pan, Y., Sha, M., & Park, H. (2020) *The sociolinguistics of survey translation.* Routledge.

Peterson, M. F., & Hunt, J. G. J. (1997). International perspectives on international leadership. *The Leadership Quarterly, 8*(3), 203–231.

Renteria, L., Li, S. T., & Pliskin, N. H. (2008). Reliability and validity of the Spanish language Wechsler Adult Intelligence Scale in a sample of American, urban, Spanish-speaking Hispanics. *The Clinical Neuropsychologist, 22*(3), 455–470.

Samady, W., Sadler, G. R., Nakaji, M., & Malcarne, V. L. (2008). Translation of the multidimensional health locus of control scales for users of American sign language. *Public Health Nursing, 25*(5), 480–489.

Schintler, L. A., & Kulkarni, R. (2014). Big data for policy analysis: The good, the bad, and the ugly. *Review of Policy Research, 31*(4), 343–348.

Schneider, S. L. (2009). *Confusing credentials: the cross-nationally comparable measurement of educational attainment: DPhil thesis* [Doctoral dissertation]. University of Oxford, UK. Retrieved from http://ora.ouls.ox.ac.uk/objects/uuid%3A15c39d54-f896-425b-aaa8-93ba5bf03529

Schneider, S. L., Joye, D., & Wolf, C. (2016). When translation is not enough: Background variables in comparative surveys. In C. Wolf, D. Joye, T. W. Smith, & Y. Fu (Eds.), *The SAGE handbook of survey methodology* (pp. 288–307). SAGE Publications.

Schoua-Glusberg, A., & Villar, A. (2014). Assessing translated questions via cognitive testing. In K. Miller, S. Willson, V. Chepp, & J. L. Padilla (Eds.), *Cognitive interviewing methodology.* (pp. 51–67). John Wiley & Sons.

Schoua-Glusberg, A., W. Carter, & E. Martinez-Picazo. (2008). *Measuring education among Latin American immigrants in the U.S.: A Qualitative examination of question formulation and error.* Paper presented at the 3MC Conference, June 25–29. Berlin, Germany.

Si, S. X., & Cullen, J. B. (1998). Response categories and potential cultural bias: Effects of an explicit middle point in cross-cultural surveys. *The International Journal of Organizational Analysis, 6,* 218–230.

Trottier, T., Van Wart, M., & Wang, X. H. (2008). Examining the nature and significance of leadership in government organizations. *Public Administration Review, 68*(2), 319–333.

Trottier, T., Van Wart, M., & Wang, X. (2008). Reinforcing the need for more sophistication in leadership studies in the government sector. *Public Administration Review, 68*(6), 1172–1174.

U.S. Census Bureau. (2015). *Appendix A2: Questionnaire testing and evaluation methods for censuses and surveys.* Retrieved on September 3, 2020 from https://www.census.gov/about/policies/quality/standards/appendixa2.html.

U.S. Census Bureau. (2016). *Statistical quality standards.* Retrieved on September 3, 2020 from https://www.census.gov/about/policies/quality/standards.html.

U.S. Office of Management and Budget. (2016a). *OMB statistical policy directive No. 2 addendum: Standards and guidelines for cognitive interviews.* Retrieved from https://obamawhitehouse.archives.gov/sites/default/files/omb/inforeg/directive2/final_addendum_to_stat_policy_dir_2.pdf.

U.S. Office of Management and Budget. (2016b). *OMB statistical policy working paper 47: Evaluating survey questions: An inventory of methods.* Statistical and Science Policy Office, Office of Information and Regulatory Affairs, Office of Management and Budget. Retrieved from https://s3.amazonaws.com/sitesusa/wp-content/uploads/sites/242/2014/04/spwp47.pdf.

Whitehead, G. E., & Brown, M. (2011). Authenticity in Chinese leadership: A quantitative study comparing western notions of authentic constructs with Chinese responses to an authenticity instrument. *International Journal of Leadership Studies, 6*(2), 162–188.

Willis, G. B. (2015). The practice of cross-cultural cognitive interviewing. *Public Opinion Quarterly, 79*(Special Issue), 359–395.

Willis, G. B. (2005). *Cognitive interviewing: A tool for improving questionnaire design.* Sage Publications, Inc.

Villar, A. (2009). *Agreement answer scale design for multilingual surveys: Effects of translation-related changes in verbal labels on response styles and response distributions.* University of Nebraska.

Yousef, D. A. (2000). Organizational commitment: a mediator of the relationships of leadership behavior with job satisfaction and performance in a non-western country. *Journal of Managerial Psychology, 15*, 6–24.

13

Multicultural Research Contexts

Franziska Bieri and Yulia Tolstikov-Mast

Introduction

There has been significant growth in cross-cultural and multinational research on leadership topics (Jogulu, 2010; House et al., 2004; Leong & Fischer, 2011). Similarly, we can observe an increase in culture-specific leadership theorizing and leadership studies that use non-Western perspectives (Peus, Braun, & Knipfer, 2015; Pillai et al., 2011; Romero, 2004; Farid, 2011; Osland, Bird, & Oddou, 2012; Shamir, 2012; Scandura & Dorfman, 2004). These trends are mirrored also in the expansion of international collaborations, including large-scale projects, such as GLOBE, which connect leadership scholars from around the world (Dorfman et al., 2012). Similarly, leadership scholars have extensively examined multicultural competencies in leaders and followers (for an overview, see Bird, 2018, Bird & Stevens, 2018). Still, scholars in the field have remained relatively silent on how we go about engaging in global leadership research and what the best methodological practices are to more effectively collect data across national and cultural borders. There is a need for critical examinations of how diverse socio-cultural characteristics of the researcher and the re-searched impact the research design and data collection and the implications this has for global leadership methodologies. Specifically, there are limited methodological reflections in the leadership field on the intricacies of international qualitative interviewing and how social, economic and cultural diversity shape the research process. In this chapter, we examine how multiculturality shapes the interview research process from study design, to data collection and then during the analysis and dissemination stages.

International or cross-cultural research is a process of data collection in a foreign country, a different culture, or across two or more countries or cultures with the purpose of capturing responses of an international or culturally diverse sample in a rigorous way (see Chapter 1 in this volume). Rigor of international and cross-cultural studies requires extra steps since such research faces an additional set of challenges. Those challenges might include triangulation of translation, working with interpreters, cultural or research training misalignment with international collaborators or gatekeepers and others. One of the unique issues in international and cross-cultural research is multiculturality – the multiple socio-cultural backgrounds that characterize both researcher and study participants. Researchers as well as study participants in leadership studies embody diverse cultural and social backgrounds, or multiculturality. Zhang and Guttormsen (2016) describe multiculturality as the variety of individual characteristics including nationality, gender, race, ethnicity or language. Nguyen and Benet-Martínez (2010) define multicultural

DOI: 10.4324/9781003003380-13

characteristics as follows: "individuals and societies who position themselves between two (or more) cultures and incorporate this experience (i.e., values, knowledge, and feelings associated to each of these identities and their intersection) into their sense of self" (p. 106). For international leadership research, these forms of diversity and their implications appear particularly salient. According to Mendenhall et al. (2018), "Global leadership is the processes and actions through which an individual influences a range of internal and external constituents from multiple national cultures and jurisdictions in a context characterized by significant levels of task and relationship complexities" (p. 23). We could easily replace here "global leadership" with "global research" as global researchers – not unlike global leaders – are tasked to navigate and manage complex situations, achieve results in cross-cultural settings, and engage in sense making in and of culturally unique and diverse experiences of others. How researchers can better navigate and manage the complexity of international research is important to consider.

Popularity of the Quantitative Research Method in Building the Leadership Field

Historically, quantitative methods have dominated the leadership field, specifically the use of self-administered questionnaires. "The dominance of…quantitative instruments reflects the wider epistemological orientation of many leadership researchers in that it exemplifies the commitment to a natural science model of the research process and to positivism in particular" (Bryman, 2011, p. 15). A pioneer in the field of cross-cultural management studies, Geert Hofstede proposed a model to look at culture as "the collective programming of the mind which distinguishes the members of one group or category of people from another" (Hofstede, 1991, p. 5). The core cultural dimensions identified by Hofstede are individualism/collectivism, hierarchy, status and power distance, uncertainty avoidance, masculinity/femininity and long- versus short-term orientation. Although widely used, this model faced criticism that the categorizations stereotype, ignored the complexity and diversity within nations and lost sight of the why and how those differences shape meanings and interactions. As Osland (2018) put it, "if we want to become more competent international cultural leaders, we need to move beyond such sophisticated stereotyping by using sense making to purposefully seek out evidence that challenges our cultural stereotypes and broadens our understanding of specific intercultural interactions" (p. 169).

Other international leadership surveys have considered a more multidimensional and multilevel approach to measuring contexts and cultures. For example, GLOBE focuses on nine attributes or dimensions of culture assessing those at both societal and organizational levels, and what the current perceived state is and what the desired situation would be by respondents (House et al., 2004). In 2003, Dickson, Hartog and Mitchelson concluded that with the help of quantitative inquiry, cross-cultural leadership studies have reached a level of sophistication with more refined measurements of culture and its dimensions. While the majority of cross-cultural leadership research is still quantitative, there is a growing number of culture specific and indigenous studies that use qualitative methodologies. Osland's (2018) comprehensive review of 32 empirical global leadership revealed that 17 are based on interviews, 9 feature survey data and the rest of the studies include focus groups, meta-analysis, archival data analysis and content analysis. Thus, qualitative interviewing arguably is an often-used form of data collection within a qualitative research method (Osland, 2018).

Qualitative Interviewing

Research Interview Methods

Let us briefly introduce the different types of research interviews commonly used (Weiss, 1995; Bryman, 2011; Kvale & Brinkmann, 2009). Qualitative forms include focus group interviews, informal interviews and semi- or unstructured in-depth interviews. Surveys or standardized interviews are quantitative in nature and mainly contain closed-ended question items with some open-ended questions, which are coded quantitatively during or after the interview. While the respondents complete survey questionnaires on their own, in a survey interview the questions and answers are read to them by the interviewer. Thus, quantitative interviews also may involve an interaction between the respondents and the interviewers, as do qualitative interviews. Survey or standardized interviews follow a rigid interview schedule with the goals to minimize interviewer effects and to conduct all interviews using the same protocol. Qualitative interviews, on the other hand, follow an interview guide. Some interviews are based on formal interview guides with specific questions to be asked. Other interviews are guided by a more flexible guide, which may list topics rather than specific questions. In any in-depth interview it is important to allow for flexibility and to follow cues and information provided by respondents. In this process, active listening is required and follow up questions are important. Similarly, good rapport is crucial in the interview process. Such rapport also requires respect toward respondents and a non-judgmental attitude of the interviewer. The goal is to actively listen and gather information as it is conveyed by the respondents.

In this chapter, we focus on qualitative in-depth interviews, which contain particular features:

> A researcher who uses in-depth interviewing commonly seeks "deep" information and knowledge – usually deeper information and knowledge than is sought in surveys, informal interviewing, or focus groups, for example. This information usually concerns very personal matters, such as an individual's self, lived experience, values and decisions, occupational ideology, cultural knowledge, or perspective. (Johnson & Rowlands, 2012, p. 100)

As such, in-depth interviews require knowledge of the cultural characteristics of research participants. Similarly, acknowledging one's own biases is necessary to effectively identify and actively listen to different worldviews.

Research in the international or cross-cultural setting is shaped by power dynamics as Zhang and Guttormsen (2016) describe:

> There is a power relationship between the interviewer and the interviewee in every interview situation, as there are different hierarchies of power associated with the different sub-elements of multiculturality. For example, a power imbalance occurs when the interviewer and interviewee belong to different ethnic groups or speak different languages with accents. This imbalance transpires when a sub-element, or a combination of different sub-elements, influences the process of securing and conducting interviews. (p. 233)

Inherent in the interview process is the power difference of the interview situation: the interviewer is in charge of the conversation and determines the agenda and takes the lead in the conversation (Holstein & Gubrium, 2003). There is also an inherent power difference in terms of who reveals information: interviewers generally do not share personal information, although different interview techniques suggest doing just that (Holstein & Gubrium, 2003), while it is expected that the respondents disclose their personal views and experiences. Similarly, where the interview takes place also is shaped by and in-turn shapes power dynamics. For example, Carly Speranza's chapter in this handbook offers a detailed discussion on the importance of selecting the location for in-depth interviews (Chapter 7).

The interviewer–interviewee relationship and resulting power inbalances is further complicated in the international area. "The pertinence of power imbalance relates to the fact that every cross-national interview is also an 'intercultural encounter' between the interviewer and the interviewee, and within a specific context" (Zhang & Guttormsen, 2016, p. 235). Social categorizations and language shape these power imbalances. This matters when securing and conducting interviews. It is not just language but also accents that matter; accents may be an indicator of ethnicity or social class. Transcriptions can often make accents invisible even though they may be key to describe the content and context of the interview. These linguistic nuances and methodological approaches to handle them will be discussed further below. Next, we explore the role of the researcher in qualitative interviews.

The Researcher in Qualitative Interviews

"[R]esearchers themselves are products of specific cultural contexts. The kinds of questions they tend to ask, and the ways they go about answering them, are influenced by their immediate cultural milieu" (Guthey & Jackson, 2011, p. 171). A qualitative researcher is a primary data collection and analysis tool (Denzin & Lincoln, 2017). This role is never neutral but challenging as qualitative researchers navigate in a complex and contradictory environment where they need to account for many things to record accurately their own observations while unwrapping meanings of their subjects' experiences (Denzin & Lincoln, 2017). Denzin and Lincoln (2017) explain that a researcher enters a study with his or her history and research traditions, views of self and others, and confronts the ethics and politics of research. This "biography" shapes all stages of the research process, from a theoretical perspective to data interpretation and evaluation (Denzin & Lincoln, 2017, p.12). The "biography" encompasses a researcher's membership or belonging to a similar or different group from a population of a study (Adler & Adler, 1987, 1994; Asselin, 2003; Dwyer & Buckle, 2009; Chaudhry, 1997; Denzin & Lincoln, 2017). A researcher always needs to connect to study participants by developing rapport around issues important for study participants. Those issues could include identity, language, age, gender or common experiences outside the scope of a study. Honesty, trust and openness can also be developed by admitting that a researcher did not have similar experiences and cannot claim to understand them but hopes to learn to share correct perspectives with others (Adler & Adler, 1987; Asselin, 2003; Dwyer & Buckle, 2009; Kanuha, 2000). Flexibility is required to develop rapport and negotiate complex power dynamics (Merriam et al., 2001).

Insider-Outsider Status

An insider status refers to researchers belonging to the group that they study, while an outsider does not belong the group studied. The group could be defined by nationality, race, gender, by cultural or ethnic heritage, membership in an organization or a certain social class, etc.

> [B]eing an insider or outsider may affect the way in which the researcher enters the field, the obligations that the researcher has to research participants, the ongoing nature of contact with research participants, and the level of trust demonstrated by research participants. (Given, 2008, p. 433)

Reflecting on their studies and work with research participants, qualitative scholars describe different experiences about their belonging or not belonging to a group in the eyes of the participants and the researcher's ability to present a trusted picture of experiences or of being accused of overly adjusting and pretending to understand all the experiences (Dwyer & Buckle, 2009; Chaudhry, 1997). However, the relationship between a researcher and researched as only an insider or outsider is overly simplistic (Schmalenbach & Kiegelmann, 2018; Chaudhry, 1997). Adler and Adler (1987) point out that an insider versus outsider status is not equal to either/or, one or the other, you are in or you are out. Rather, there is a complexity in similarities and differences, and in the same study, a researcher can be treated as an insider or outsider by different study participants or use different frames of references to make connections with people with similar characteristics. "In a dialectical approach, differences are not conceived as absolute, and consequently the relation between them is not one of utter antagonism" (Fay, 1996, p. 224). To complicate the dynamic, a study sample is never homogeneous, and differences in people's reactions toward a researcher are to be expected.

A good example of this more nuanced approach to the insider-outsider status is provided in Chapter 4 of this handbook, where one of the authors and co-author of the present chapter (Yulia Tolstikov-Mast) describes how she was perceived as both Russian but also a U.S.-affiliated researcher and expat when conducting research in Russia. A similar experience is described and interpreted by Zhang and Guttormsen (2016) where the first author of this article describes being

> socially categorised as an external "Westernised" outsider working for a foreign institute, as opposed to a fellow countrywoman, even though sharing the same characteristics ethnically and linguistically. Thus, in this particular context, her role as an "outsider", that is, not from inside the company, and the attributed meaning of "whiteness" (being grouped into the "white" expatriate group), were more dominant than the more salient characteristics of the shared skin colour and native language proficiency and accent. This demonstrates that social categorisation cannot always be placed on a continuum; the perceptions being played out and held by the interviewees do not correlate to which socio-biological traits are more salient than others and are thus context dependent. The activation of the "right" ethnicity is also subject to context and relationality. For example, having the same dark skin colour as the locals could result in the authors being treated as both "insiders" and "outsiders" in different field research projects, depending on the context. (Zhang & Guttormsen, 2016, p. 243)

As illustrated in the previous quote, a researcher's professional and personal identity can play a role in data collection. Access to information strongly depends on the identity or roles members of a community assign to a researcher (Chaudhry, 1997). Thus, researchers have to think to introduce themselves as an expert or novice, based on the marital status, ethnic background, religious affiliation or other aspects of his or her personal identity relevant to gaining access and obtaining trust of gatekeepers as well as study participants. "By strategically managing identities and roles together with skillfully executing assigned roles, a researcher may strongly enhance the success of a study. Failure to do this may jeopardize the whole enterprise" (Chirkov, 2016, p. 264).

Global leadership research studies include diverse samples in terms of nationality, socio-economic status, culture, level of trainings, international experiences and race/ethnicity. To conduct effective studies to reflect these diverse realities, this type of research should be highly contextual. Context is represented by study participant's and study environment characteristics, and multiculturality of a research sample should be treated as a valuable part of a study.

Multiculturality and Research Methodologies

While multiculturalism is generally used as a macro concept describing diversity in society, multiculturality refers to individual level characteristics rooted in macro structures. Multiculturality is an individual's diverse background that includes but is not limited to "nationality, ethnicity, gender, language and skin colour, and also how these elements interplay and perform as integral social phenomena" (Zhang & Guttormsen, 2016, p. 232). Those elements influence interactions between a researcher and their study participants as well as perceptions of reality of all actors in a given situation. Observations are situated in social worlds of an observer and the observed where "any gaze is always filtered through the lenses of language, gender, social class, race, and ethnicity" (Denzin & Lincoln, 2017, p. 12). In *Cross-cultural research with integrity: Collective wisdom from researchers in social settings* book, Cleary (2013) also discusses differences in life experiences and backgrounds between the researcher and the researched as a potential source of challenges: "Though the traditional research publication bio most often acknowledges only simplistic and academic parts of one's identity, in the research itself there is a danger in similarly simplistic takes on identity" (Cleary, 2013, p. 85). Thus, the researcher must consider the complexity of their own identity and its effect on their relationship with study participants, data collection and analysis.

Especially in international and cross-cultural contexts, those characteristics are not fixed traits but dynamic. "Different aspects, or boundary markers, of multiculturality are activated depending upon the particular situation as well as the physical location" (Zhang & Guttormsen, 2016, p. 234–235). People label each other and perceive one another in different ways depending on context. As such our identities and perceptions of the others are socially constructed – they are not inherent but bound by context and mutual understanding of individuals in a given situation. What is important to remember is that diversity characteristics of both the interviewee and the interviewer are relevant, as well as the unique combination(s) that is created in the encounter.

There is a danger in overlooking participants' multicultural identities. Cleary (2013) introduces "hybridity" as a term that captures a more complicated view of identity in research – e.g., bi-ratiality or multi-racial hybridity. "The hybrid border crossers, be it with gender hybridity or racial hybridity, or even for economic class cross-overs, develop double consciousness and often double existence due to experience in both cultures" (Cleary, 2013, p. 86). This hybridity complicates a study of "colonized" or under-privileged populations "as having [feeling] power in their dislocated lives" (p. 87) and is critical to prevent oppressor-oppressed relationships. Researchers interviewed by Cleary (2013) for her book suggest having participants investigate their own identities through participant narratives that they can find power in words and potentially redefine themselves and to find power in their complicated identities. The hybridity concept introduced by Cleary (2013) is also relevant with regard to cultural and linguistic backgrounds. We will explore this in the following section.

Bilinguals and Biculturals

Multilinguals or "[b]ilinguals are individuals who actively use more than one language" (Kroll, Dussias, Bice, & Perrotti, 2015, p. 377). Bilinguals are diverse. Some are exposed to two languages from birth and use them continuously in their daily activities through adulthood, or have one dominant language and occasionally (but regularly) use the second language. The other type of bilinguals acquire a second language later in life (Kroll et al., 2015). Similarly, for many this description is valid for more than two languages as multilingualism is widespread in many cultures and societies (Kroll et al., 2015; Mathews, 2019). We refer here to bilinguals (and biculturals) with the understanding that many may be multilingual (multicultural).

Biculturals are people who identify with more than one culture and have internalized several sets of cultural profiles (Brannen & Thomas, 2010; Fiske & Taylor, 1984). Those profiles or schemas are socially constructed and represent knowledge about the values, attitudes, beliefs and behavior of a culture (Fiske & Taylor, 1984). Biculturals could be migrants, children of migrants, children and grandchildren of multicultural households or members of indigenous groups. Bicultural individuals have several uniquely represented cultural identities (Hong et al., 2000). Research confirms that biculturals share the ability to shift between cultural identities depending on situations (Hong et al., 2000). They can access diverse cultural knowledge learned as a result of significant exposure to multiple cultures (Hong et al., 2000). They develop increased cognitive complexity and higher-order cognitive processes required to manage this complexity (Tadmor et al., 2012). Thus, they tend to be flexible (Hong et al., 2000), tend to have well-developed analytical skills to weigh between perspectives and alternatives, integrate diverse ideas and come up with unique and novel ideas

(Leung et al., 2008). They have greater tolerance for ambiguity, lesser information overload (Tadmor et al., 2012) and possess greater empathy (Brannen & Thomas, 2010). However, it does not mean all biculturals are the same, as there are multiple variations in the ways they experience their identities or perform frame switching. Still, studies on biculturals repeatedly indicate that these individuals have strong abilities to work successfully across cultures and considered as a potential global leadership talent in their organizations (Brannen & Thomas, 2010). Thus, the likelihood of their participation in global leadership studies is high. Since global leadership practices require professionals with world-wide experiences who can relate effectively to individuals similar as well as dissimilar from them, it is reasonable to assume that study participants in global leadership studies often speak more than one language, have resided in different countries, and have experience with or even acquired multiple cultures. Similarly, researchers in the field of global leadership may also be multilingual and/or bicultural. With that, it is important to understand how to collect data effectively in multicultural settings and develop relevant methodological approaches that are culturally responsive.

Strategies to Be More Culturally Responsive

Effective scholars and global leaders continually record and reflect on their experiences and critically examine their own personal biases and cultural background and how this shapes unconsciously made assumptions that can influence the course of a study (Zhang & Guttormsen, 2016). The self-reflexive approach in international research is important to examine whether a researcher's personal biases and cultural background led to unconsciously made assumptions that can influence the course of a study (e.g., data collection, coding of interview data, emerged interview themes). In qualitative international or cross-cultural studies, what is of particular importance is how the researcher's own multifaceted background has influenced a study.

Pranee Liamputtong's (2010) "Performing qualitative cross-cultural research" book is an insightful publication that addresses largely neglected issues of *culturally sensitive methodology* rather than an application of Western methodology to international contexts, specific to qualitative research. The book is dedicated to answering a fundamental question for any intercultural research: how do we acquire culturally appropriate knowledge we can trust? She talks in depth about the "human side" of a study – when people research people: about participants' vulnerability (e.g., suspicion, fear), importance to collaborate with locals (reciprocity of relationship) or researchers' well-being (as international research can take a physical and emotional toll). Perhaps one of the most significant parts of the book for cross-cultural and international leadership scholars is the chapter titled *Cross-cultural communication and language issues*. The chapter discusses language issues, the importance of training for bicultural researchers, limitations of working with interpreters, transcription challenges and data translation strategies some of which we will review in more detail below.

Zhang and Guttormsen (2016) identify five strategies to manage multitculturality in in-depth interviews. Those are:

1. activating the "favored" ethnicity – multicultural researchers may stress the ethnic background that is most valued by the respondent;
2. putting the "desired" passport forward – the multinational researcher can opt to use the nationality that provides the greatest access (for example, in national trade associations or expat networks);
3. reassuring of belonging to the "right" social category – researchers should carefully evaluate tension in the interview as signs of being placed in the "opposite" group and use small talk to reassure shared belonging and to be re-accepted to the relevant social group;

4. bonding in the mother tongue of the respondent – researchers can strategically use language for small talk to establish shared backgrounds;

5. adopting a multilingual approach with code switching – multilingual interviewers can strategically switch languages during the interview to (re)establish rapport, gain power or level the power field.

Those recommendations are indeed very useful for leadership research that is qualitative in nature and crosses borders or cultures and we will refer back to those guiding strategies in the next section.

Research indicates that journaling is a successful form of the action-reflection as it encourages individuals to reflect about new ideas or experiences they encounter in their lives (Zhang & Guttormsen, 2016). To illustrate this process, we share a pedagogical example from a global research practicum of a Global Leadership doctoral program. The following are questions from a doctoral global research practicum assignment *My Experience as an International Researcher* developed by one of the authors of this chapter, Yulia Tolstikov-Mast. Students completed this assignment as part of field research and interviews during their global practicum. Reflection questions right after interviews aim to capture the researcher's and study participant's multiculturality and the resulting social interaction and meaning emerging from this. The goal of the assignment and the global practicum is for students to move from knowledge to practice to transformation. Especially for the last process of transformation as an international scholar, pause and reflection is key in order to process experiences and learn from them, but also to develop an action plan to modify future behavior. The following questions are adapted from Zhang and Guttormsen's (2016) suggested questions and can serve as a guide for anyone seeking to adopt a semi-structured self-reflection guide.

During and after interviews, please reflect on the following questions:

1. *Activating preferred ethnicity or culture: when you contemplated the study and engaged in interviewing your study participants, did you try to emphasize or downplay your cultural background or ethnicity (to appear similar to your study participants or separate yourself from them)?*

2. *Relating via gender differences/similarities: have you tried to relate to your study participants because of your gender similarities, or have you tried to separate yourself, or appear neutral?*

3. *Belonging to the "right" category: during your interviews, have you experienced situations when you felt belonging to a different category – maybe due to differences in social status or interviewer-interviewee different categories? How did you overcome this misalignment?*

4. *Language strategy: when you conducted interviews, did you try to appear similar or different to your study participants in accent or non-verbal language?*

5. *Code-switching: have you experienced situations when you feel that you needed to switch among different categories (e.g., researcher, woman, Pakistani, American research)? Explain your thoughts and reasons.*

6. *International research project: comment on your experience planning and designing an international study; what have you learned about engaging in international studies?*

7. *Reflection as an international researcher: how do you see yourself as a global leader-researcher? How have you changed as a result of engaging in an international pilot study? Explain what you have learned about yourself and how you plan to put this knowledge into practice.*

Roulston (2010) describes the benefits of self-reflexive practices vis-à-vis "objective", non-contextualized approaches:

> reflexivity opens up possibilities to provide more complicated representations of research data and multi-layered accounts incorporating the researcher's voice as an alternative to un-situated accounts from 'neutral' researchers who absent themselves from their texts through the use of third person and passive voicing. (p. 118)

At the same time, there are also criticisms about reflexivity especially with regards to paying lip service to inequalities and "masking of inherent power relationships in research". (Roulston, 2010, p. 118)

As researchers, there may be little we can change about the immediate fundamental social assumptions made with regard to characteristics which may award or withhold power. However, we must be keenly aware of the privileges or forms of oppression that are "attached" to those identities we and the people we study hold and how those experiences of oppression or privilege shape our and others' views of the world and social reality.

Bilingual Interviews and Translation Issues

In the past 25 years, research investigating the consequences of bilingualism for language processing, cognition and brain functioning increased significantly (Marian & Spivey, 2003; Dijkstra, 2005; Kroll et al., 2006; Kroll et al., 2015). The findings are remarkable, demonstrating that the two languages are part of one language system stretched in different directions. It means both languages are always active when bilinguals listen, read or speak in either of the languages; and both languages impact each other's lexicon (e.g., Jared & Kroll, 2001), the grammar (e.g., Dussias, 2003) and the phonology (e.g., Sundara, Polka, & Baum, 2006). This parallel and bidirectional influence can be conscious or unconscious, and the degree of the influence can vary. At the same time, the first language is forever modified due to the interaction with the second language; and the second language is continuously shaped by the first language. We introduce a few authors below which have conducted research involving bicultural populations and who have shared valuable insights in how they managed the intricacies of such linguistic complexity in the data collection and analysis process.

Based on a signal case life history study of a young female science teacher in Pakistan, Halai (2007) analyzed her challenges of working with bilingual interview data in Urdu (the national language of Pakistan) and English. The article is unique, since it focuses on methodological issues that have not received sufficient attention, and research lessons can be applied to any bilingual data in any two languages. Halai is from the same culture as her research participants and is fluent in both Urdu and English. The interviews were conducted in Urdu, since Pakistani teachers in her sample preferred to speak Urdu rather than English. However, both researcher and researched were fairly fluent in English and switched from Urdu to English and back to account for language nuances and precision in conveying meanings. "…interviews are not just words spoken at a certain time in response to a social situation, they are embedded in the culture of the place…", commented Halai (2007, p. 345). The researcher identified at least three reasons for this code-switching: (1) "Special Science Vocabulary" (many science concepts are English words); (2) "English Words Used as Urdu Words" ("school," "teacher," "desk," and "pencil" have been integrated into Urdu; and (3) Minglish (common use of English mixed with other local languages in Pakistan).

Collecting and making sense of bilingual data was very time consuming (Halai, 2007). Since, literature on how to deal with bilingual data is generally sparse, Halai had to improvise and develop procedures and rules. Since most of the interview data was in Urdu but the research report had to be written in English, the next step of research involved translation. She went from translating some sections of the interviews to translating the first six full interviews and continued using the bilingual transcripts for the analysis of the remaining seven interviews. An additional challenge was reading data in two languages, where English is written from left to right and Urdu from right to left. Halai made a decision to move from "exact equivalence" (which became impossible) to "inexact equivalence", that helped convey the essentials. Halai concludes:

Language is context based; some words carry a world of meaning within them and cannot be easily conveyed in another language and to another culture. Sometimes the cultural barrier seemed so huge as to be almost insurmountable. I wondered to myself in my reflective journal, 'How much can I explain, elaborate, footnote, and interpret for my readers?' The final translated materials I have called transmuted texts as they have been converted from one language to another, and though the essence might be the same, they have changed in the process. (pp. 351–352)

Inhetveen (2012), a sociologist; Filep (2009), a social geographer; Holmes et al. (2013), applied linguists; and Rosenberg (July 26, 2019), a researcher-practitioner, add to the conversation based on their research experiences. They all agree that few practical methodological tools exist that guide researchers with issues of working with bilingual populations. We will briefly review those studies in the order listed above.

Inhetveen (2012) discusses her work with a culturally diverse and vulnerable sample (refugees) who did not share a common language with the researcher. She used a combination of oral and written translation stressing that oral translation (when working with an interpreter or local research assistant) and written translation (post-interview) should always be compared. These comparisons revealed complex statements and decisions about choice of a meaning. It also helped explain the role of an interpreter (e.g., which interview sentences or parts were translated right away and which parts were additional explanations; decisions made during oral translation), as well as create follow-up questions for future studies.

Filep's (2009) research took place in the Carpathian Basin. The area encompasses parts of Hungary, Slovakia, Ukraine, Romania, Serbia, Croatia, Slovenia and Austria. Although the area was dominated by Hungarians for centuries, it became more diverse following Turkish and Habsburg rule, and currently includes Hungarians, Slovaks, Ukrainians, Ruthenians, Romanians, Serbs, Croats, Germans, Roma, Jews and many more groups with distinct traditions and languages. Filep (2009) treats language not as a neutral medium but as an important element of identity where gender, ethnicity, religion, residency and other characteristics are mirrored in languages. The researcher advocates conducting problem-centered interviews in multilingual qualitative studies to watch for specific words that alter the course of an interview. Those words can be associated with local meanings (that are dominant in specific cultural groups), thus, making interviews with multilinguals a sensitive "detective" work. Filep engaged in a detailed literature review to find answers to common dilemmas and issues in multilingual research and the following strategies emerge: (1) find an alternative common language with the interviewee (preferably foreign for both parties); (2) "mix" languages (speaking several languages during interviews) to explain certain experiences better; (3) actively search for solutions and apply various communication and translation strategies; and (4) research and use accurate historical, cultural and societal knowledge about the context.

Holmes, Fay, Andrews and Attia's (2013) "Researching Multilingually" project aimed to explore theoretical and methodological frameworks for researching multilingually. Data included more than 25 narrative profiles of researchers working multilingually and 35 audio-recorded Powerpoint presentations. Study participants were asked to write narratives reflecting on the experience of researching multilingually and on their growing awareness of a multilingual research process. A key conclusion was the need to stay flexible and work in research collaborations. Multilingual researchers also felt conducting interviews or writing research reports in several languages was very natural and a norm. Finally, data revealed that multilingual researchers produced reflections of differing types depending on the language they used thus bringing richness to a study. Some participants commented that if they had to work monolingually, the data would only tell a "half-truth". The findings also raised the following important questions in multilingual studies: who is involved in a study, what are researcher-researched relationships, how are relationships negotiated and managed;

and which languages are used in researcher-researched relationships? This study challenges views on traditionally reported limitations in studies with multicultural and multilingual researchers and study participants where interviews are typically conducted and findings presented in one language.

The final example comes from practitioner's literature. Paula Rosenberg (July 26, 2019) is a researcher-practitioner with 10 years of experience conducting multi-country international qualitative studies. She shares that too many times her clients talk about international qualitative research like it is just an extension of the U.S. research standards. Rosenberg immediately contests this idea. In her experience, qualitative data collection has a mix of the U.S. traditional and local elements. For example, Rosenberg's bilingual (Hindi and English) speaking focus group participants started in English. However, as the conversation grew animated, they proceeded in "Hinglish" (alternation of English and Hindi, sometimes even in the same sentence). As a researcher, Rosenberg was unprepared for this dynamic but later developed a solution by having a translator with her at all times. Rosenberg shares some "lessons learned" to help international researchers across industries to learn international research nuances.

First, she suggests staying flexible during data collection and being ready to adjust methodology (e.g., time difference, data collection protocols, translation over a telephone can present challenges). Second, a cross-cultural meaning of "time" is similar for all activities. Expectations for research or business meetings fall into the same category of "time" management. For example, Rosenberg stayed flexible with the start and end times for focus groups in Latin American countries (start late-end late); but she was punctual in Germany or Japan (everything is on time). Third, the length of the interview often gets overlooked. A 60-minute interview in the United States in English is different from an interview with an interpreter in a different country, the nature of languages and associated cultural communication standards (e.g., longer greetings, extra time for building rapport, thoughtful pauses, different expressions or ways to explain experiences). Fourth, data collection day and time can be different per country (e.g., more flexible to miss some work for an interview, not willing to miss work and are only available on evenings or over the weekend). The previous examples also show the intricate links between language and culture.

Lessons and Further Questions

Globally, scholars are facing an increasing diversity of languages and cultures when collecting data. Bilingualism or multilingualism are important characteristics of multicultural people that influence their experiences and interactions.

> Those interactions, and the constant activation of the two languages, create demands on cognitive systems and the neural mechanisms that control them so that the bilingual is able to function fluently in each language and, at the same time, mix languages when switching is desirable or necessary. (Kroll et al., 2015, p. 392)

Thus, international researchers should consider relations between language use and cognition when designing and conducting their studies.

We need to have cross-disciplinary collaborations to look into how to capture the correct meanings of interviews when working with international samples. Should we allow study participants to express ideas in both languages and how? Do we acknowledge language-related limitations in research? How do we comment on a monocultural researcher-multicultural study participants or multicultural research and study participants? Should we have a standard protocol with required reflective criteria to capture bilingual or multilingual experiences? (e.g., context in which the two languages are used during data collection; proficiency in both languages). What protocols can we use or develop for working with multilingual data? What if the use of specific terms or phrases differs from one language or cultural context to another? How do we determine if we need to do literal or non-literal translation; or deal with a word or phrase that does not have an exact equivalent in a language of an interview? Answering those types of questions will require active methodological conversations between leadership scholars and across disciplines.

Future Directions: Building Multicultural Research Competencies

Based on the information provided in the chapter, it becomes evident that multicultural researchers working with multicultural samples need to consider these complexities in the various stages of the research process. With increasing globalization, multilingual and multicultural samples are ever more common, especially in the type of research inquiries global leadership focuses on. Thus, adopting and further building intercultural research standards is key and developing global research competencies becomes ever more important.

Niemczyk (2018) formulates an emerging definition on the competencies of international scholars:

> [a] globally competent researcher possesses knowledge, skills, values, and attitudes necessary to conduct respectful and rigorous research in diverse contexts. Globally competent researchers are aware of a wider world, critical global issues and their impact on education in different contexts. They are committed to collaborate within multicultural and multidisciplinary settings. Globally competent researchers value diversity, social justice, and manifest intercultural sensitivity conducting and reporting research. (p. 176)

This definition was developed based on an open-ended survey to both novice and expert scholars in the field of education. The cornerstones of these competencies match closely the arguments presented in this chapter regarding challenges and considerations for cross-cultural and international in-depth interviews. To promote those competencies, leadership researchers, their professional associations, and graduate programs should initiate methodological investigations and engage researchers and aspiring researchers in the field to learn more about such multicultural characteristics.

Global leadership literature has developed a rich knowledge base on features and practices of global leaders and followers operating effectively across cultures and in diverse settings (Mendenhall et al., 2018). Those insights can serve as a lens to adopt similar competencies and effective methodological practices that guide the study design of global leadership researchers with respect to language and culture. Also, global leadership qualities and competencies have received much attention in the field of global leadership. Bird (2018) points to the range of competencies including personal characteristics such as inquisitiveness and conscientiousness, attitudinal predispositions like appreciation for cultural diversity, results orientation, cognitive features like intellectual intelligence, motivation to learn, global knowledge or behavior skills like cross-cultural communication (p. 122). Many of those qualifications of global leaders bear close resemblance to the qualities that researchers involved in cross-cultural research should bring to the table, as we discussed in the preceding pages. Translating the global leadership competency insights into research competencies would be an obvious first step. Given the interdisciplinary nature of the global leadership field, drawing on methodological best practices from other fields is important. As we have identified in this chapter, multiculturality is a useful framework that can guide qualitative global leadership researchers and help advance qualitative methodology. Looking forward, we hope for a more systematic methodological debate and knowledge base in the field of global leadership, to develop a comprehensive understanding of the core skills sets required which can then inform education, training and the evaluation of research.

References

Abeyewardene, A., Abu-Lughod, L., Abu-Lughod, L., Ahmed, Q., Asad, T.,...Zaslavsky, C. (2003). Cross-cultural interviewing. In Holstein, J. A., & Gubrium, J. F. (Eds.), *Inside interviewing* (pp. 429–448). Sage

Adler, P., & Adler, P. (1987). *Membership roles in field research.* Sage

Adler, P. A., & Adler, P. (1994). Observational techniques. In N. K. Denzin & Y. S. Lincoln (Eds.), *Handbook of qualitative research* (pp. 377–392). Sage.

Asselin, M. E. (2003). Insider research: Issues to consider when doing qualitative research in your own setting. *Journal for Nurses in Staff Development, 19*(2), 99–103.

Bird, A., & Stevens, M. J. (2018). Assessing global leadership competencies. In M. E. Mendenhall, J. Osland, A. Bird, G. R. Oddou, M. J. Stevens, M. Maznevski, & G. K. Stahl (Eds.), *Global leadership: Research, practice, and development.* Routledge.

Bird, A. (2018). Mapping the content domain of global leadership competencies. In M. E. Mendenhall, J. Osland, A. Bird, G. R. Oddou, M. J. Stevens, M. Maznevski, & G. K. Stahl (Eds.), *Global leadership: Research, practice, and development.* Routledge.

Brannen, M. Y., & Thomas, D. C. (2010). Bicultural individuals in organizations: Implications and opportunity. *International Journal of Cross Cultural Management, 10*(1), 5–16

Bryman, A. (2011). Research methods in the study of leadership. In *The SAGE handbook of leadership* (pp. 15–28). Sage.

Chaudhry, L. N. (1997). Researching "my people," researching myself: Fragments of a reflexive tale. *Qualitative Studies in Education, 10*(4), 441–453.

Chirkov, V. (2016). *Fundamentals of research on culture and psychology: Theory and methods.* Routledge.

Cleary, L. M. (2013). *Cross-cultural research with integrity: Collective wisdom from researchers in social settings.* Palgrave Macmillan

Denzin, N. K., & Lincoln, Y. S. (Eds.). (2017). *Handbook of qualitative research* (5th ed.). Sage.

Dickson, M. W., Den Hartog, D. N., & Mitchelson, J. K. (2003). Research on leadership in a cross-cultural context: Making progress, and raising new questions. *The Leadership Quarterly, 14*(6), 729–768.

Dijkstra, T. (2005). Bilingual visual word recognition and lexical access. In J. F. Kroll & A. M. B. de Groot (Eds.), *Handbook of bilingualism: Psycholinguistic approaches* (pp. 179–201). Oxford University Press.

Dorfman, P. W., Javidan, M., Hanges., P., Dastmalchian, A., & House, R. (2012). GLOBE: A twenty year journey into the intriguing world of culture and leadership. *Journal of World Business, 47*(4), 504–518.

Dussias, P. (2003). Syntactic ambiguity resolution in L2 learners: Some effects of bilinguality on L1 and L2 processing strategies. *Studies in Second Language Acquisition, 25*(4), 529–557.

Dwyer, S. C., & Buckle, J. L. (2009). The space between: On being an insider-outsider in qualitative research. *International journal of qualitative methods, 8*(1), 54–63.

Farid, M. (2011). Contextual leadership. *The Journal of Management Development, 30*(9), 865–881.

Fay, B. (1996). *Contemporary philosophy of social science: A multicultural approach.* Wiley-Blackwell.

Fiske, S. T., & Taylor, S. E. (1984). *Social cognition.* Addison-Wesley Pub.

Fiske, S. T., & Taylor, S. E. (2013). *Social cognition: From brains to culture.* Sage.

Filep. B. (2009). Interview and translation strategies: Coping with multilingual settings and data. *Social Geography, 4*, 59–70.

Given, L. M. (2008). *The Sage encyclopedia of qualitative research methods.* Sage.

Guthey, E. & B. Jackson. (2011). *Cross-cultural leadership revisited. The Sage handbook of leadership* (pp. 165–178). Sage.

Halai, N. (2007). Making use of bilingual interview data: Some experiences from the field. *The Qualitative Report, 12*(3), 344–355.

Hofstede, G. (1991). *Cultures and organizations: Software of the mind.* McGraw-Hill.

Holmes, P., Fay, R., Andrews, J., & Attia. M. (2013). Researching multilingually: New theoretical and methodological directions. *International Journal of Applied Linguistics, 23*(3), 285–299.

Holstein, J., & Gubrium, J. F. (2003). *Inside interviewing: New lenses, new concerns.* Sage.

Hong, Y. Y., Morris, M. W., Chiu, C. Y., & Benet-Martinez, V. (2000). Multicultural minds: A dynamic constructivist approach to culture and cognition. *American Psychologist, 55*(7), 709.

House, R. J., Hanges, P. J., Javidan, M., Dorfman, P. W., & Gupta, V. (2004). *Culture, leadership, and organizations: The GLOBE study of 62 societies.* Sage Publications.

Inhetveen, K. (2012). Translation challenges: Qualitative interviewing in a multi-lingual field. *Qualitative Sociology Review, 8*(2), 28–45.

Jared, D., & Kroll, J. F. (2001). Do bilinguals activate phonological representations in one or both of their languages when naming words? *Journal of Memory and Language, 44*(1), 2–31.

Jogulu, U. D. (2010). Culturally-linked leadership styles. *Leadership & Organization Development Journal, 31*(8), 705–719.

Johnson, J. & Rowlands, T. (2012). The interpersonal dynamics of in-depth interviewing. In *The SAGE handbook of interview research: The complexity of the craft* (pp. 99–114). Sage.

Kanuha, V. K. (2000). "Being" native versus "going native": Conducting social work research as an insider. *Social Work, 45*(5), 439–447.

Kroll, J. F., Dussias, P. E., Bice, K., & Perrotti, L. (2015). Bilingualism, mind, and brain. *Annual Review of Linguistics, 1*, 377–394.

Kroll, J. F., Bobb, S. C., & Wodniecka, Z. (2006). Language selectivity is the exception, not the rule: Arguments against a fixed locus of language selection in bilingual speech. *Bilingualism, 9*(2), 119.

Kvale, S., & Brinkmann, S. (2009). *Interviews: Learning the craft of qualitative research interviewing.* Sage.

Leong, L. Y. C., & Fischer, R. (2011). Is transformational leadership universal? A meta- analytical investigation of multifactor leadership questionnaire means across cultures. *Journal of Leadership & Organizational Studies, 18*(2), 164–174.

Leung, A. K. Y., Maddux, W. W., Galinsky, A. D., & Chiu, C. Y. (2008). Multicultural experience enhances creativity: The when and how. *American Psychologist, 63*(3), 169.

Liamputtong, P. (2010). *Performing qualitative cross-cultural research.* Cambridge University Press.

Marian, V., & Spivey, M. (2003). Competing activation in bilingual language processing: Within-and between-language competition. *Bilingualism, 6*(2), 97.

Mathews, J. (April 25, 2019). Half of the world is bilingual. What's our problem? *Washington Post.* https://www.washingtonpost.com/local/education/half-the-world-is-bilingual-whats-our-problem/2019/04/24/1c2b0cc2-6625-11e9-a1b6-b29b90efa879_story.html.

Mendenhall, M. E., Osland, J., Bird, A., Oddou, G. R., Stevens, M. J., Maznevski, M., & Stahl, G. K. (Eds.). (2018). *Global leadership: Research, practice, and development.* Routledge.

Merriam, S. B., Johnson-Bailey, J., Lee, M. Y., Kee, Y., Ntseane, G., & Muhamad, M. (2001). Power and positionality: Negotiating insider/outsider status within and across cultures. *International Journal of Lifelong Education, 20*(5), 405–416.

Nguyen, A. D. & Benet-Martínez, V. (2010). Multicultural identity: What it is and why it matters. In Richard J. Crisp (Ed.), *The psychology of social and cultural diversity* (pp.87–114). Wiley-Blackwell.

Niemczyk, E. K. (2018). Developing globally competent researchers: An international perspective. *South African Journal of Higher Education, 32*(4), 171–185.

Osland, J. S., Bird, A., Oddou, G. (2012). The context of expert global leadership. In W. H. Mobley, Y. Wang, & M. Li (Eds.), *Advances in global leadership* (7th ed., pp. 107–124). Emerald.

Osland, J. S. (2018). An overview of the global leadership literature InM. E. Mendenhall, J. Osland, A. Bird, G. R. Oddou, M. J. Stevens, M. Maznevski, & G. K. Stahl (Eds.), *Global leadership: Research, practice, and development.* Routledge.

Peus, C., Braun, S., & Knipfer, K. (2015). On becoming a leader in Asia and America: Empirical evidence from women managers. *The Leadership Quarterly, 26*(1), 55–67.

Pillai, R., Kohles, J. C., Bligh, M. C., Carsten, M. K., & Brodowsky, G. (2011). Leadership in "Confucian Asia": A three-country study of justice, trust, and transformational leadership. *Organization Management Journal, 8*(4), 242–259.

Romero, E. J. (2004). Latin American leadership: El Patron and El Lider Moderno. *Cross Cultural Management, 11*(3), 25–37.

Rosenberg, P. (July 26, 2019). Lessons learned traveling the world to conduct qualitative research. *Escalent.* https://escalent.co/blog/lessons-learned-traveling-the-world-to-conduct-qualitative-research/.

Roulston, K. (2010). Theorizing the researcher: The reflective interviewer. In *Reflective interviewing: A guide to theory and practice* (pp. 115–129). Sage.

Scandura, T., & Dorfman, P. (2004). Research in an international and cross-cultural context. *Leadership Quarterly, 15*(2), 277–307.

Schmalenbach, C., & Kiegelmann, M. (2018). Juggling and joining perspectives and relationships – Multicultural researchers in multilocal frames of reference. *Forum: Qualitative Social Research, 19*(2).

Shamir, B. (2012). Leadership in context and context in leadership studies. In M. G. Rumsey (Ed.), *The Oxford handbook of leadership* (pp. 343–358). Oxford University Press.

Sundara, M., Polka, L., & Baum, S. (2006). Production of coronal stops by simultaneous bilingual adults. *Bilingualism, 9*(1), 97.

Tadmor, C. T., Hong, Y. Y., Chao, M. M., Wiruchnipawan, F., & Wang, W. (2012). Multicultural experiences reduce intergroup bias through epistemic unfreezing. *Journal of Personality and Social Psychology*, *103*(5), 750.

Weiss, R. S. (1995) *Learning from strangers: The art and method of qualitative interview studies*. The Free Press.

Zhang, L. E., &. Guttormsen, D. S. A. (2016). "Multiculturality" as a key methodological challenge during in-depth interviewing in international business research. *Cross Cultural & Strategic Management*, *23*(2), 232–256.

14

Indigenous Oral History Methods in Leadership Research

Dara Kelly

Introduction

For budding and seasoned researchers alike, knowing when Indigenous principles and practices of oral history differ from, or are the same as oral history methods is an ongoing challenge. This chapter discusses an underexplored approach to conducting leadership research that encompasses Indigenous principles of oral history and outlines its similarities and distinctions from oral history as a methodology in management and organizational research more broadly. This chapter first defines Indigenous oral history in relation to the broader context of collective knowledge systems. Secondly, it explores oral history as a method for gathering data in leadership studies, highlighting some key distinctions between the two. Based on qualitative interviews that capture oral history with Māori leaders conducted in my master's thesis, this chapter presents considerations to navigate in data collection across both understandings. I provide examples from my experience conducting oral history as an Indigenous researcher navigating leadership research within an Indigenous environment different from my own cultural background and share lessons learned about engaging across these distinct worldviews.

Within the context of Indigenous knowledge systems, oral history represents the collective body of knowledge that is passed down through generations of Indigenous peoples within kinship structures (Archibald, 2008; Henry & Pene, 2001; Mahuika, 2012; Weir & Wuttunee, 2004). In Indigenous communities, to mention oral history is to conjure an understanding about the nature of knowledge as the embodiment of collective identity, senses of place, belonging in community, and relational responsibility with the human, and non-human world (Cajete, 2000). Indigenous oral historical knowledge usually has long legacies that tie human existence to ancient and ancestral origins, often referring to cosmological roots, the beginning of the world or spiritual emergence within the universe (Marsden, 2003). It also connotes ways of knowing that are passed down through oral traditions, or the social structures and protocols that stipulate how oral history is passed from one generation to another.

Oral history is also used in management and organization studies research as a way to gather data, typically drawing upon the oral testimony of individuals to shed light on their experience and interpretation of significant organizational events. Leadership studies that draw upon leaders' biographies or life stories emphasize the experiences of individual leaders and their influence among followers (Bryman, 2004; Portelli, 1997). In traditional leadership research, oral history draws on thick

DOI: 10.4324/9781003003380-14

descriptions from qualitative interviews and emphasizes individual memory to shed light on historical events or pivotal moments of social change. The goal is to gain experiential, and context-specific insight from leaders, stakeholders, and other actors about organizational dynamics that may extend leadership theory, or its application in organizational settings (Hoffman & Hoffman, 1994; Shamir, Dayan-Horesh & Adler, 2005). When conventional organizational research oral history methods intersect or overlap with Indigenous oral history contexts, competing assumptions about their purpose and the processes of data collection present potential complications to research outcomes.

Applied to appropriate design methods for conducting research that explores Indigenous leadership, what is important to bear in mind regarding Indigenous epistemologies is that leadership is not separate from a broader context of collective intergenerational teachings (Royal, 2009). Indigenous leaders today are contemporary reflections of those before them, and I argue that accounting for Indigenous underpinnings of oral history within research design processes allows us to see leadership as part of an extended kinship principle. Using research methods that reflect Indigenous knowledge systems facilitate processes that "encourage us as Indigenous researchers to connect research to our own worldviews and to theorize based on our own cultural notions in order to engage in more meaningful and useful research for our people" (Archibald, Lee-Morgan, & De Santolo, 2019, p. 6). Indigenous research methodology works within community frameworks of everyday reality such that what happens at an individual level is inextricably linked to unfolding macro-level collective realities (Sandoval, Lagunas, Montelongo & Diaz, 2016). This integration of knowledge is reflected in approaches to research design starting first and foremost with understanding Indigenous worldview in order to ensure that researchers engage in relational and respectful processes to align how and why research is done. Kovach illustrates this alignment as:

> ...the interplay (the relationship) between the method and paradigm and the extent to which the method, itself, is congruent with an Indigenous worldview. From this perspective, one could argue that the focal discussion of Indigenous methodologies ought to be a deep concentration of worldview or paradigm. (2010, p. 40)

Indigenous oral history overlaps with processes of research design, storytelling and its affiliated social structures and asks researchers to hone not only listening skills, but engage with cultural practices that are typically learned in ceremonial contexts such as witnessing, embodied presence and spiritual attentiveness (Archibald, 2008; Kovach, 2009, 2010; Mahuika, 2012; Miller, 2011; Sandoval et al., 2016).

Training Across Indigenous Oral History Methods

In my life as a budding academic, I was trained in research at The University of Auckland Business School in Aotearoa-New Zealand and completed both my master of commerce and doctorate of philosophy there. Having spent nine years in Aotearoa-New Zealand, I became familiar and comfortable with understanding the Māori Indigenous experience of oral history and found many similarities to what I know from my Indigenous heritage, the Stó:lō Coast Salish traditions situated outside what is now the City of Vancouver in Canada.

Māori are descendants within the broader group of Polynesian language-speaking people throughout the Asia-Pacific region. Māori have been in Aotearoa-New Zealand for approximately 1,000 years and carry ancient traditions of ocean navigation from their cosmological roots having arrived at the islands on seven original canoes (Salmond, 1983). During my time as a student, I had the privilege to bear witness to the oratory of testimony given by Māori elders and intellectuals as part of a national treaty claims process between Māori and the government of New Zealand in 2010 (Hēnare & Hannah, 2010). I regularly attended Māori gatherings where te reo Māori, the Māori language was spoken exclusively. In retrospect, I realized that my Māori research mentor and supervisor exposed me to Māori oral history as a deliberate epistemological intervention to accompany the formal methodological training I received in university courses. I was encouraged to balance both perspectives with equal consideration and explore knowledge contributions about leadership across this divide.

Balancing Many Oral History Traditions

From my experience of conducting qualitative interviews in alignment with two different Indigenous cultural contexts, my own, and Māori, it became apparent that what shaped valuable insights to Indigenous participants emerged from their ability to capture and convey ancestral knowledge. The way they did that best was to share from oral history learned in their family and community settings. Instead of speaking from the perspective of a first-person singular experience, by and large, the point of reference was in the plural, expressed with language around "us", "we", and "our". This collective perspective caused me to reflect deeply in terms of assumptions we may carry as researchers about temporality, audience, accountability, and how to measure validity in oral history. It also highlighted the importance of a shifting context in which the conventions of oral history in management research terms were at times less relevant in Indigenous settings. Likewise, in academic conference and methodology settings, the nuanced conventions of Indigenous oral history were not as salient without the broader community context to give it meaning.

I have identified five main differences between Indigenous oral history and oral history as research methods in the Academy in Figure 14.1. These concern: (1) public/private sharing of knowledge; (2) temporal aspects of knowledge that represents collective, intergenerational wisdom as compared to knowledge at a fixed moment in time; (3) purpose for sharing knowledge from the participants' perspectives; (4) to whom one is accountable when sharing knowledge; and (5) temporally bound processes to validate and verify oral historical knowledge. These distinctions impacted how as a researcher-in-training, I intuitively balanced what I knew about oral history from an Indigenous perspective with what I learned about in university as a means to methodologically capture research data.

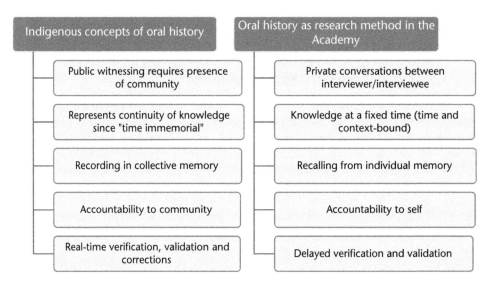

Figure 14.1 Summary Table of Indigenous Concepts of Oral History and Oral History as Research Method

Understanding these distinctions brings to light aspects of oral history that can have significant impacts on findings, but may go unnoticed when it comes time to interpret and analyze qualitative interviews. For example, on the first set of distinctions in Figure 14.1, I found that sometimes Indigenous elders carry the assumption that when asked to participate as an interviewee, they view it as an opportunity to exercise their responsibility to share knowledge as they would with Indigenous public audiences; however, they might agree to a private interview because that is the only option provided by the researcher. This culturally specific assumption can translate within the interview itself through layers of discourse. In a face-to-face interview between two people with appropriate consent and ethics compliance, the narrative may be coded with cultural subtext because it carries the potential to reach audiences beyond the research itself by virtue of the written nature of academic knowledge capture. This point highlights assumptions two, three, and four in Figure 14.1– that the interview may be seen as an opportunity to record and pass on knowledge within collective memory to be accessed by future generations. At the same time, because it is for future generations, the knowledge shared must also be informed by ancestral knowledge (from time immemorial) and therefore adhere to conventions of community accountability embedded in Indigenous oral history. The fifth distinction in Figure 14.1 is probably the most challenging to resolve in research between the two systems of oral history. What is shared in a one-to-one interview will never replicate or mirror oral history as a real-time community dialogue that gives the opportunity for an immediate response, debate, and ongoing discussion. In this instance, my advice is simply to understand the key differences, and know that one is not a substitute for the other. Nonetheless, Figure 14.1 shows how many Indigenous principles and practices of oral history apply not only within community settings but also apply within research contexts (Absolon, 2011; Archibald, 2008).

Understanding Indigenous Oral History

Indigenous oral history serves as a network of collective memory (Carlson, 2010; Kovach, 2009, 2010). Oral history functions as a symbolic and literal mechanism to bring genealogy to life because it "anchors the present in the past" (Cruickshank, 1994, p. 407), and is a crucial "linkage between past and present social organization" (1994, p. 412). The medium for that linkage is through shared knowledge, collective memory and ancestral relationships. These are distinguishing factors that differentiate knowledge transmission using oral traditions from a historical approach that captures and re-tells events of the past. By keeping these connections alive, Indigenous oral historians maintain their ancestral ties by contributing to collective knowledge.

There are long legacies of ethnographic research that capture Indigenous oral histories at a time when the romanticized notion of Indigenous peoples as a dying race prevailed (Bauer, 2017). Luckily, there has been a groundswell of Indigenous researchers over the past 25 years who have shaped a more balanced approach to research that honors Indigenous ontology and epistemology (Sumida Huaman & Mataira, 2019). Indigenous ontologies vary widely all over the world, but maintain similarities in key components of being such as an integrated sense of human belonging with, and among non-human relations (Archibald, 2008; Cajete, 2000; Marsden, 2003). Indigenous worldviews include all aspects of physical and spiritual life grounded in Indigenous philosophy from ancient and cosmological origins (Cajete, 2000). Indigenous epistemologies are similarly relational in their focus (Kovach, 2009; Wilson, 2008) but reflect the specific ways that Indigenous knowledge is collectively created, maintained, disseminated and shared. Indigenous epistemologies are guided by principles of engagement that speak predominantly to the spirit of intent, or the alignment of one's body, mind and spirit to receive knowledge as a sacred gift. Because Indigenous knowledge represents the "voices of the ancestors" (Kelly, 2017; Nicholson, 2019), Indigenous epistemologies refer to ways of accessing or gathering knowledge that can include dreaming, storytelling, conversational methods, family histories and interaction with the natural world.

In Miller's book, *Oral History on Trial* (2011), detailed discussion about Coast Salish Indigenous oral history sheds light on a common practice called oral footnoting (see pp. 146–147). This is a process that links narrators of a story to their oratory forebears from whom they learned the story and protocols around it. Oral footnoting reveals lineages of knowledge that can be verified and corroborated through processes of triangulation with other oral historians. What is most important within the process of oral footnoting is careful attention by the speaker to situate themselves within a larger unbroken line of storytellers to whom they are accountable and against which their story is measured as valid. It is this same network of storytellers who have cultural training and therefore expertise to assess the validity of Indigenous oral history. For example, a common practice that occurred in the interviews I conducted involved interviewees referencing who their mentors were before answering a research question. This allowed them to distinguish for me when they were expressing an opinion as compared to sharing from collective Indigenous knowledge.

Archibald (2008), a renowned Coast Salish scholar in Indigenous education theorizes on the concept of "storywork" that she coined while researching Indigenous oral traditions. Storywork refers to the interconnected processes of meaning-making, cultural protocols and synergies that arise between storyteller and listener. Each voice in oral history research (including the researcher's) is valued for individual insights, but together, individual voices contribute to an interconnected collective story of survival and existence guided by the wisdom of elders past, present and future. Indigenous oral history is cumulative in nature, temporally cyclical and intergenerational, collectively held and collectively remembered and contains both the ordinary and most sacred of human experiences. Together, it is the collective work of storytelling that ensures Indigenous knowledge is passed down from generation to generation, and this is a sacred responsibility to carry forward. Archibald explains below:

> Patience and trust are essential for preparing to listen to stories. Listening involves more than just using auditory sense. We must visualize the characters and their actions. We must let our emotions surface. As the Elders say, it is important to listen with "three ears: two on the sides of our head and the one that is in our heart". (2008, p. 8)

A particularly common characteristic across Indigenous oral history is the element of active participation in the story exchange. Articulating elements of Māori oral history in Aotearoa-New Zealand, Mahuika explains how principles of genealogy are applied through processes of reading oral history, and the living generations who access them:

> They are viewed as living documents, not just because they are oral, but because their outward expression represents an active connection that acknowledges a cultural and spiritual inheritance essential to who we are. (2012, p. 5)

The process of reading oral history keeps the stories alive, activating oral history as a methodology to inform contemporary thinking about ancient knowledge.

Using Oral History Interviews in Leadership Research

Shifting focus to uses and application of oral history in mainstream leadership research, characteristics of oral history methods include exploring insights into leadership from the perspective of those who experienced it (both leaders and followers) while accounting for depths and layers of context that also contribute to that experience (Batty, 2009; Cassell, 2009). The primary source of knowledge in leadership interviews is the individual person and their reflections and sense-making; by and large, the unit of analysis is at the individual level (Hoffman & Hoffman, 1994; Klenke, 2016; Neuenschwander, 1978;

Portelli, 1997; Yow, 1995). In addition, oral history methods may be used to record gaps in history that complement media records, and official documentation relating to historical events so that fuller versions of history are accessible to future generations. As Shamir, Dayan-Horesh and Adler explain, "the story itself represents an interpretation of the narrators' experiences, and in the sense that the researcher uncovers and articulates the meaning system embedded in the story" (2005, p. 19).

What makes oral history an appealing methodology for leadership research is the affective dimension of connecting with first-hand human experiences. Yet, a cursory search in *The Leadership Quarterly* shows that since 2008, only four articles specifically mention "qualitative interviews" and zero results for "oral history". The human experience of interpersonal connection that comes with oral history in leadership research is relatively lacking. Since 2005, only four articles specifically mention "oral history" from a search in the journal, *Leadership* that is known to be more oriented toward qualitative research. The four articles in *Leadership* include: (1) highlighting the leadership role of a professor who helped mitigate race tensions in the U.S. south in the 1960s and 1970s (Lowe, 2008); (2) a focus on the leadership of Dutch politician, Dirk Stikker who was Secretary General of NATO from 1961–1964 (Hoogenboezem, 2009); (3) a look at the merits of improvization in jazz music as providing insight into the performative mindset needed in leadership development (Harrison, 2017); and (4) an article that mentions the need for researchers to conduct qualitative interviews following historical analysis of female political leaders in Scotland during the 1990s (Robinson & Kerr, 2018).

A search for "case study" in *Leadership* produces 119 articles that may or may not include qualitative interviews as part of the case method and a separate search for "qualitative interview" produced three articles. Without drawing conclusions that are too definitive from these broad search terms, this is only to introduce the point that these low numbers may signal to a factor of oral history research that is well known and accepted in Indigenous research – that qualitative interviews take time. In Indigenous research, the most time-consuming aspect of qualitative interviews is gaining access by establishing meaningful relationships and trust to get high-quality interview data. It may simply mean researchers tend to choose other methods that produce larger sample sizes, data that is more readily available such as secondary sources and more efficient results over oral history methods and qualitative interviewing specifically. Nonetheless, interviews are not the only way to gather organizational stories. Gabriel (2018) discusses stories in organizations in terms of texts and narratives that often have work to do; in other words, stories contain detailed information about organizational cultures, identities and knowledge which makes them rich sources of research data. Together, like pieces of a mosaic, oral histories illustrate the untold individual story with the rawness of emotion layered with processed and unprocessed sense-making.

Although there are not a lot of examples to draw from to illuminate oral history methods in leadership studies, emphasis on the role and impact of stories in the study of leadership are prevalent with a search of "story" producing 276 articles in the journal *Leadership* since 2005. I now turn to issues that arise concerning validity of Indigenous oral history data and specifically address the representation of knowledge from individual versus collective perspectives.

Understanding Validity in Indigenous Oral History

One methodological concern with researchers looking to use oral history to design qualitative research is the issue of how to evaluate the validity of human memory over time. Accounting for human error, forgetting, memory gaps and shifting meaning with shifting experience is a challenge (Hoffman & Hoffman, 1994). Inconsistencies in memory become especially complex when more sources of data (such as written sources) add to, contradict or bring into question aspects of oral testimony. Hoffman and Hoffman (1994) utilize methods for corroborating components of oral history through triangulation with archival and historical evidence to reveal a "truth" that may be reasonably agreed upon within the scholarly community.

Triangulation in organization studies utilizes complementary qualitative and quantitative methods to verify consistency of findings (Bryman, 2004). Methods of triangulation are used in Indigenous oral history as well, but for different reasons. Instead of bringing together a range of analytical approaches to understand an issue or event of concern in collective memory, triangulation is used in Indigenous oral history to gather a mosaic of individual memories that together, give a broader sense of what occurred, regardless of how it was interpreted by the listener. A multiplicity of interpretations are important because when triangulation occurs, the process of remembering and recalling from memory in discussion revives the oral history anew, thus perpetuating its impact in each generation as a living history. There are additional layers of culturally mediated shared values that influence how collective memory is evaluated in processes of triangulation, including issues such as age, reputation, status and wisdom, generally attributed to respected elders whose lifetime of experience is honored and valued. Cultural nuance makes processes of triangulation for the purposes of finding "truth" inappropriate and offensive if applied within Indigenous oral history settings. The role of a researcher involved in Indigenous oral history is to listen and witness the process of storytelling rather than act as a conduit to a series of facts and historical evidence for the researcher to evaluate, code, analyze and extract meaning from.

The spiritual and metaphysical dimension of oral history sets out a complex system of reference within Indigenous knowledges. In the circumstance of one-on-one interviewing, adherence to Indigenous protocols of oral history is important because the knowledge represents the culmination of people and processes who have passed it on for many generations. In the precedent-setting court case *Delgamuukw v. British Columbia* (Delgamuukw v. British Columbia, 1997; Hurley, 1998), for the first time, oral history was accepted as evidence in court. This shift in the legal environment created new challenges for legal experts because it raised questions around how oral evidence should (and whether it could) be properly evaluated by a judge. In a research setting that involves Indigenous oral history, similar questions arise as to whether researchers are equipped to adequately understand the richness and depth of knowledge contained within Indigenous oral history. It is not about the inherent value of knowledge itself that matters; rather it is what the knowledge can do (Cajete, 1994, 2000; Miller, 2011).

To provide a concrete example, I share a story from my Indigenous background, the Stó:lō Coast Salish. In our culture, oral history was the only method to record significant events since time immemorial – the time before memory (Carlson, 2010). The oral history record contains transactions and collective histories as far back as we can trace our genealogy within the territories that we continue to occupy today. In one Stó:lō elder's story told in 1950, Mrs. Robert Joe traced her lineage back to the time when the most sacred ceremonial mask was brought to the Stó:lō people from the bottom of a lake (Blomfield et al., 2001). Anthropologists calculated that temporally, she traced her lineage back to approximately 1780, before contact with European settlers (Blomfield et al., 2001). As an oral historical account, no other sources of archival data existed to corroborate her story, but in many ways, to do so would diminish her testament to the continuity of Stó:lō oral history as an ancient practice. In this specific case, oral history offers a powerful statement of authority and belonging within place that may apply in Indigenous governance and leadership contexts, but there are ongoing debates about the uses of Indigenous knowledge alongside other forms of material, archaeological and scientific facts as evidence (Berkes, 2009; Todd, 2014; Whiteman, 2004). The caution here concerns hierarchies of knowledge, and the historical tendency to undervalue Indigenous knowledge when compared to Anglo-Western "facts". Valuing and centering processes of Indigenous oral history in research design may encourage insights that are more relevant to Indigenous people and communities.

In research processes there is a layer of delayed verification in transcript review that creates a differential between the protocols and traditions of Indigenous oral history and oral history as a data collection method in organizational research. In Indigenous cultural settings where oral history is traditionally shared in public, having the opportunity to validate knowledge in real time creates a form of public debate. It enables a more extensive process for addressing differences of memory, and disagreements such that cultural protocol enables dialogue and back-and-forth exchanges based on ancient principles of respectful discourse and oratory as an art form that takes generations to master. When you have an interview captured on video/audio recording that is transcribed and sent back to only the interviewee, there are no opportunities for community members, and particularly those with respect in the community to verify and validate collectively held knowledge against a "long-standing" record. This is an important process of collective co-creation, collaborative dissemination and course correction that occurs in public fora such as ceremonial settings. Research interviews create new issues that hinder or eliminate collective accountability immensely within Indigenous knowledge communities. In my experience, although interviews can facilitate elements of sacred exchanges, sacred interactions between two people differ significantly from sacred interactions conducted in public.

Issues of validity are complex in Indigenous oral history as researchers need to carefully consider assumptions from non-Indigenous research paradigms that ask for checks that may contradict Indigenous processes of validation. They may simply be inappropriate for the context. Additionally, Indigenous validity checks are not always feasible within the confines of qualitative interviews that uphold tertiary institutional standards of privacy, confidentiality and anonymity. It may not be possible to ensure validity is upheld with vastly different measures, and Gabriel reminds us that "there is no foolproof way of validating narrative research" (2018, p. 74). Instead, Gabriel suggests that this is why reflexivity is a process for researchers to engage in critical discussion about methodology as an ongoing and emergent scholarly discourse.

Navigating Oral History "On the Ground"

As an Indigenous researcher having conducted oral history to collect data in both my master's and doctoral research, some of the most perplexing and enlightening research moments involved navigating between worlds of training within formal tertiary institutions and training to understand Indigenous epistemology. Although use of oral history is common in Indigenous research across many disciplines in health sciences, social work, arts and humanities and law, oral history is not a common research method used at the University of Auckland Business School. It was an approach that I formally learned about during undergraduate study in an Indigenous Studies program within a faculty of arts degree. I implicity grew to recognize and appreciate oral history through exposure to Māori Indigenous community and political events that I attended over a six-month "shadowing" period with a Māori research supervisor.

When it came time to embark on my own research planning and design, it was hard to imagine conducting research that would not involve qualitative interviews given the richness of oratory I had seen at community events up until that point. I was developing an acute awareness to approaching qualitative research across many sets of knowledge systems. In my master's degree, I was operating within three sets of knowledge: (1) Coast Salish Indigenous knowledge from my own cultural heritage and upbringing; (2) Māori Indigenous knowledge held by Māori interviewees; and (3) institutional knowledge through university training. Operating across ways of knowing led to critical research design decisions that depend on appropriate alignment between epistemology and ontology. I provide concrete examples below.

Where Indigenous oral histories are captured in written form, there are additional layers of interpretation to consider for validity purposes including: how was oral history captured, who captured the original narrative, did it involve a mediator such as a translator, what was the medium used to capture the narrative and under what circumstances did the original narrative unfold? Coast Salish oral historian, Sonny McHalsie, gives advice on how to interpret written oral histories in archival and historical records, and says,

> When I read Duff or Hill-Tout, I'm not reading what he wrote, but what the person who told him said. I'm not in Duff's mind, but that of the person who told him. I look at [and account for] the filters imposed by academics. (McHalsie cited in Miller, 2011, p. 97)

McHalsie highlights that even if sources are written by Indigenous individuals, there are additional layers of translation to consider such as whether or not an informant was literate, or writing under duress or surveillance – conditions common at the time of colonization. A primary concern with shifting from one mode of transmission to another is when knowledge is decontextualized. This is a primary reason why Indigenous scholars center understanding Indigenous ontology and epistemology prior to embarking on research design and data collection. Print sources that contain Coast Salish philosophy provide insights from the voices of our ancestors that continue to speak to their descendants, as they do in oral history passed down orally.

Conducting Oral History Interviews on Ancestral Leadership

When I set out to interview on the topic of ancestral leadership (Kelly & Nicholson, 2021; Kelly, 2012; Kelly, Jackson & Hēnare, 2014), I drew from existing business networks within a research center at the University of Auckland Business School to access interviewees. Because that network is regional, it was easy to find interviewees with shared tribal affiliations. For approximately half of the interviews, a unifying factor was a shared identity to a particular Māori tribe called Ngāti Hine. How that unfolded in the interviews were specific conversations about the ancestress of Ngāti Hine, named Hine-ā-maru. She was alive approximately 500 years ago. In the interviews, I learned how her legacy of leadership continues to live through her descendants. I explored with them how their everyday lives are shaped by the collective memory of Hine-ā-maru, known for her tenacity, staunch disposition and endurance through hardship. She is attributed with a stringent, resilient character that has enabled Ngāti Hine people to endure and persist despite their challenges (Hēnare & Hannah, 2010).

In the process of conducting the interviews, there were two interviews that occurred separately, but back-to-back on location at one of the sacred houses within Ngāti Hine territory. Inside the sacred house, the interviews were conducted next to a carved representation of Hine-ā-maru whose presence came to life as an active participant. Although she could not physically speak, when I asked questions about her leadership and the legacy that is carried on through the work of her descendants, the interviewees spoke to her directly, gestured to her carving and responded as though they were conveying leadership wisdom on her behalf. In this instance, because I am not a member of the tribe, it was clear that I am not someone who needed to know about the legacy of Hine-ā-maru in order to pass down the knowledge to next generations. However, through these interviews inside the sacred house, a dialogue formed that involved interviewing Hine-ā-maru through her descendants. I acted as a conduit to an intimate conversation across generations that gave insight into an under-explored aspect of ancestral leadership as a contribution to the larger body of global theories on leadership.

In other interviews involving Māori business leaders with different tribal affiliations in the same region, interviewees shared aspects of broad Māori mythology and cosmology. They also shared private, sacred knowledge held within their families but chose not to disclose everything with the video camera on. In two cases, private knowledge was explicitly not shared. One participant made it clear that the context of the interview itself was not appropriate because she could not be certain about who might read the findings in the future. She was comfortable sharing with me informally and off-camera specific ways that she understood leadership as a spiritual relationship and how that was manifest in her life experience. The other participant also did not want to share on camera for a similar reason – because her spirituality is private, although she explained that it informs her leadership practice. For that portion of the interview, the camera was shut off. We made a verbal agreement that what was said would not be formally reported in the research findings.

In order to conduct interviews with Māori business leaders, I selected video recording as the medium for data collection over audio recording or note-taking because I wanted to analyze the data in terms of tacit observations with the ability to listen and replay notable facial expressions, body language, and remarkable silences. My choice to use video recording was not meant to replace or replicate intimacies of Indigenous oral historical traditions exactly; however, as a means for gathering data, video recording fostered elements of the relationship between storyteller and listener that bring Indigenous oral traditions to life such as synchronous animation of body, voice and a transfer of energy within detailed narratives given by the interviewees. There were no objections to my use of the video camera. There is a depth to video that further enabled me to represent the interviewees in the thesis in a way that reflected their individual identities, their active participation in selecting interview locations, and acknowledged the impact and influence of facial expressions and clothing within the larger narrative of Indigenous leadership.

It is not simply the content of what the interviewees said that shaped new insights into leadership, but how they communicated an embodied ancestral knowledge, interacted with me, and reacted to the interview questions that enhanced the quality of interviews (Makokis, 2001). With video as a medium to watch the interviews again and again during phases of data analysis, I was able to cross-reference more than the words they said. I revisited their interview narratives on the videos and transcripts paying attention to emotion, intergenerational wisdom and contextual political-historical impacts in real time.

Discussion

For Indigenous researchers aspiring to use oral history methods to explore leadership topics, my experience demonstrates that there were aspects of being an outsider (by not being Māori) that served me well as a researcher. My perspective brought a different Indigenous lens to expand on what might have been taken for granted as typical or even uninteresting within the day-to-day leadership experiences of Māori people. For example, similar to those articulated by the Māori participants, I feel an embodiment of leadership principles in my life that I attribute to my ancestors through specific and often risky decisions and actions they took. I feel that I understand their leadership decisions from their lasting legacies captured in family oral history. Yet, I had not had the opportunity to explore this as a theoretical lens to view leadership more generally. I called on personal intuition to drive my intellectual curiosity, but through the practice of applying Indigenous research methods, found a way to expand oral history beyond my cultural understanding.

A consideration in the process of conducting oral history research is preparation by the researcher beforehand to understand what it is that Indigenous interviewees are agreeing to share with a wide audience (Bull et al., 2019). Researchers should also consider why Indigenous interviewees are agreeing to share with a researcher (as opposed to members of the family or extended kinship and community groups) (Ellis & Earley, 2006). A further question to ponder might ask what (if any) the scholarly medium offers toward achieving Indigenous oral history objectives (Sandoval et al., 2016). For someone like me, who did not get to meet my grandparents, the interviews I conducted offered an opportunity for me to establish my own genealogical connection to an ancestral past that was challenging to access in other ways.

For non-Indigenous researchers who have had little exposure to Indigenous ways of being and knowing, there are aspects of Indigenous knowledge that depart significantly from Anglo-Western approaches to the study of leadership demonstrated in the comparison table in Figure 14.1. Resolving these conflicts entail criticality that challenges over-emphasis on the role of the individual-as-leader and emphasizes leadership as an intergenerational process that accounts for cultural identity, belonging and spirituality. I found that Indigenous interviewees responding to questions that are overly individualistic in nature actively resituate themselves within collectively held belief systems so that their perspectives are either reflecting one of many points of view, or representative of a collective voice. Depending on the leadership context, research questions that ask about someone's opinion or personal feelings may be less important to Indigenous interviewees than the processes of collective decision making or shared experience.

These pivots that occur while conducting oral history research are subtle and serve as a reminder that despite the appearance of all-encompassing and normative research methodologies within the academy, localized Indigenous knowledge tells a different story about the purpose of stories. The way that Indigenous storywork unfolds in research contexts means sometimes the work of the researcher is to pay attention to when these epistemes depart and when they come together. Renowned Indigenous scholar, Kovach warns that the dangers of not knowing these differences come at the cost of both the integrity of the research and the safety of Indigenous communities:

> What is contested, however, is that story is an apolitical, acultural method that can be applied without consideration of the knowledge system that sustains it. From that perspective, engaging with tribal stories means understanding their form, purpose, and substance from a tribal perspective. To attempt to understand tribal stories from a Western perspective (or any other cultural perspective) is likely to miss the point, possibly causing harm. This has been a significant finding since the dark years of anthropological research on Indigenous culture. (2009, p. 97)

Understanding how the validity of Indigenous oral history can or should be assessed in research contexts raises important questions about the task of the university-trained researcher who is also collecting oral history but doing so under very different assumptions. It raises issues regarding time, space and scientific versus cultural methods of recording and passing on knowledge.

Conclusion

Having used oral history to conduct research in the "training" stages of my academic career, I have gained insights into key distinctions between ways that oral history is understood within Indigenous knowledge contexts, and ways that oral history is taught as a method for data collection in research. In research methods literature and training within universities, the validity of oral history is measured by the extent to which narratives may or may not align with other documented records such as historical and archival secondary data. Within Indigenous oral history, validity involves a public process of community dialogue in real time. From the very foundations of epistemological and ontological assumptions, Indigenous oral history calls forth significantly different expectations about the purpose and intention behind sharing knowledge.

From a methodological standpoint making those assumptions visible requires an understanding of time beyond linear thinking so that kinship relations inform past, present and future generations of leadership. Navigating different epistemological assumptions is not always a clear process, as oral history is both a rich and nuanced method for data collection. Oral history is also a method with high potential for misunderstanding, missing layers of what is "really" being said, for whom and misapplication of the culturally specific context that can drastically impact research findings. While conducting oral history research, the researcher is influential in shaping the quality of relationships between themselves and the interviewee. Additionally, they might consider how they are in relationship with the leadership findings that unfold as the research advances.

I offer some final thoughts on oral history as a method for data collection in leadership research. As an Indigenous researcher, I found that for reasons not related to my academic identity but related instead to my Indigenous identity, I played a role in sharing Indigenous knowledge as a sacred gift bestowed by the interviewees. I felt that I joined an extended lineage of leadership knowledge keepers and it was and continues to be my responsibility to care for that knowledge. While validity in oral history research is not the same as validity in Indigenous oral history, neither are they in contradiction to one another; instead, oral history operates in ways that serve the epistemological purpose of each respective worldview.

Understanding these fundamental differences when conducting research with Indigenous communities can help to clarify how one receives knowledge as an interviewer, and how one interprets processes of oral history temporally. Measuring validity to meet both standards within the academy and within Indigenous epistemology requires a comprehensive grasp of how knowledge operates and for whom knowledge is intended to benefit. The findings from the study on Māori ancestral leadership taught me that engaging wholly in Indigenous oral history unearthed legacies of ancient knowledge that inform contemporary Indigenous leadership practice. The work of Indigenous leadership is contained within the sacred histories and identities embedded within oral history and these oral histories are embedded in cultural processes of change while remaining true to deep ancestries.

References

Absolon, K. E. (2011). *Kaandossiwin: How we come to know*. Fernwood Publishing.

Archibald, J. (2008). *Indigenous storywork: Education the heart, mind, body and spirit*. UBC Press.

Archibald, J., Lee-Morgan, J., & De Santolo, J. (2019). Introduction. In *Decolonizing research: Indigenous storywork as methodology*. Zed Books Ltd.

Batty, E. (2009). Reflections on the use of oral history techniques in social research. *People, Place & Policy Online, 3*(2), 109–121. doi:10.3351/ppp.0003.0002.0004

Bauer, Jr., W. (2017). Oral history. In C. Andersen & J. OBrien (Eds.), *Sources and methods in Indigenous studies* (pp. 160–168). Routledge, Taylor & Francis Group.

Berkes, F. (2009). Indigenous ways of knowing and the study of environmental change. *Journal of the Royal Society of New Zealand, 39*(4), 151–156.

Blomfield, K., Boxberger, D. L., Carlson, K. T., Duffield, C., Hancock, R. L., Lutz, J., McHalsie, S., Ormerod, P., Peters, T., Rafter, T., Robur'n, A., Schaepe, D. M., Smith, D., & Woods, J. R. (2001). In K. T. Carlson, C. Duffield, S. McHalsie, L. L. Rhodes, D. M. Schaepe, & D. A. Smith (Eds.), *A Stó:lō-Coast Salish historical atlas*. Douglas & McIntyre.

Bryman, A. (2004). Qualitative research on leadership: A critical but appreciative review. *The Leadership Quarterly, 15*(6), 729–769. doi:10.1016/j.leaqua.2004.09.007

Bull, J., Beazley, K., Shea, J., MacQuarrie, C., Hudson, A., Shaw, K., Brunger, F., Kavanagh, C., & Gagne, B. (2019). Shifting practise: Recognizing Indigenous rights holders in research ethics review. *Qualitative Research in Organizations and Management: An International Journal, 15*(1), 21–35. doi:10.1108/QROM-04-2019-1748

Cajete, G. (2000). *Native science: Natural laws of interdependence*. Clear Light Publishers.

Carlson, K. T. (2010). *The power of place, the problem of time: Aboriginal identity and historical consciousness in the cauldron of colonialism*. University of Toronto Press.

Cassell, C. (2009). Chapter 29: Interviews in organizational research. In D. Buchanan & A. Bryman (Eds.), *The Sage handbook of organizational research methods* (pp. 500–515). SAGE Publications Ltd.

Cruickshank, J. (1994). Oral tradition and oral history: Reviewing some issues. *Canadian Historical Review, LXXV*(3), 403–421.

Delgamuukw v. British Columbia. (1997). Supreme Court of Canada. No. 23799.

Ellis, J. B., & Earley, M. A. (2006). Reciprocity and constructions of informed consent: Researching with Indigenous populations. *International Journal of Qualitative Methods, 5*(4), 1–13. doi:10.1177/160940690600500401

Gabriel, Y. (2018). Stories and narratives. In C. Cassell, A. Cunliffe, & G. Grandy (Eds.), *The SAGE handbook of qualitative business and management research methods: Methods and challenges* (pp. 63–81). SAGE Publications Ltd. doi:10.4135/9781526430236

Harrison, R. T. (2017). Leadership, leadership development and all that jazz. *Leadership, 13*(1), 81–99. doi:10.1177/1742715016681120

Hēnare, M., & Hannah, K. (2010). *Summary northern tribal landscape overview for Te Paparahi o Te Raki inquiry* (p. 34). University of Auckland Business School.

Henry, E., & Pene, H. (2001). Kaupapa Māori: Locating Indigenous ontology, epistemology and methodology in the Academy. *Organization, 8*(2), 234–242. doi:10.1177/1350508401082009

Hoffman, A., & Hoffman, H. (1994). Reliability and validity in oral history: The case for memory. In J. Jeffrey & G. Edwall (Eds.), *Memory and history. Essays on recalling and interpreting experience* (pp. 107–130). University Press of America.

Hoogenboezem, J. A. (2009). Hidden success: A case study of Secretary-General Dirk Stikker's leadership at NATO. *Leadership, 5*(4), 403–421. doi:10.1177/1742715009343035

Hurley, M. (1998). *Aboriginal title: The Supreme Court of Canada decision in Delgamuukw v. British Columbia* (BP-459E).

Kelly, D. (2012). *Ngā Kete e Toru o te Wānanga: Exploring feminine ancestral leadership with Māori business leaders.* The University of Auckland.

Kelly, D. (2017). *'Feed the people and you will never go hungry': Illuminating Coast Salish economy of affection.* The University of Auckland.

Klenke, K. (2016). *Qualitative research in the study of leadership* (2nd ed.). Emerald Group Publishing Limited.

Kovach, M. (2009). *Indigenous methodologies: Characteristics, conversations, and contexts.* University of Toronto Press.

Kelly, D., Jackson, B., & Hēnare, M. (2014). 'He Apiti Hono, He Tātai Hono': Ancestral leadership, cyclical learning and the eternal continuity of leadership. In Robert Westwood, Gavin Jack, Farzad Rafi Khan, & Michal Frenkel (Eds.), *Core-periphery relations and Organisation Studies* (pp. 164–184). Palgrave Macmillan.

Kelly, D., & Nicholson, A. (2021). Ancestral leadership: Place-based intergenerational leadership. *Leadership.* doi:10.1177/17427150211024038

Kovach, M. (2010). Conversational method in Indigenous research. *First Peoples Child & Family Review: An Interdisciplinary Journal Honoring the Voices, Perspectives and Knowledges of First Peoples through Research, Critical Analyses, Stories, Standpoints and Media Reviews, 5*(1), 40–48.

Lowe, M. (2008). An unseen hand: The role of Sociology Professor Ernst Borinski in Mississippi's struggle for racial integration in the 1950s and 1960s. *Leadership, 4*(1), 27–47. doi:10.1177/1742715007085768

Mahuika, N. (2012). *'Kōrero Tuku Iho': Reconfiguring oral history and oral tradition.* The University of Waikato.

Makokis, L. (2001). *Teachings from Cree elders: A grounded theory study of Indigenous leadership* [PhD]. University of San Diego.

Marsden, M. (2003). The woven universe: Selected writings of Rev. Māori Marsden (Charles Royal, Ed.). Te Wānanga-o-Raukawa.

Miller, B. (2011). *Oral history on trial.* UBC Press.

Nicholson, A. (2019). Hau: Giving voices to the ancestors. *Journal of the Polynesian Society, 128*(2), 137–162. doi:10.15286/jps.128.2.137-162

Neuenschwander, J. A. (1978). Remembrance of things past: Oral historians and long-term memory. *The Oral History Review, 6*, 45–53.

Portelli, A. (1997). Tryin' to gather a little knowledge: Some thoughts on the ethics of oral history. In A. Portelli (Ed.), *The battle of Valle Giulia: Oral history and the art of dialogue* (pp. 55–71). The University of Wisconsin Press.

Robinson, S., & Kerr, R. (2018). Women leaders in the political field in Scotland: A socio-historical approach to the emergence of leaders. *Leadership, 14*(6), 662–686. doi:10.1177/1742715017710592

Royal, C. (2009, September 16). *Te Kaimānga: Towards a new vision for Mātauranga Māori.* Macmillan Brown Lecture Series, Christchurch.

Salmond, A. (1983). The study of traditional Māori society: The state of the art. *Journal of the Polynesian Society, 92*(3), 309–332.

Sandoval, C. D. M., Lagunas, R. M., Montelongo, L. T., & Diaz, M. J. (2016). Ancestral knowledge systems: A conceptual framework for decolonizing research in social science. *AlterNative: An International Journal of Indigenous Peoples, 12*(1), 18–31.

Shamir, B., Dayan-Horesh, H., & Adler, D. (2005). Leading by biography: Towards a life-story approach to the study of leadership. *Leadership, 1*(1), 13–29. doi:10.1177/1742715005049348

Sumida Huaman, E., & Mataira, P. (2019). Beyond community engagement: Centering research through Indigenous epistemologies and peoplehood. *AlterNative: An International Journal of Indigenous Peoples, 15*(3), 281–286. doi:10.1177/1177180119871705

Todd, Z. (2014). Fish pluralities: Human-animal relations and sites of engagement in Paulatuuq, Arctic Canada. *Études/Inuit/Studies, 38*(1–2), 217–238.

Weir, W., & Wuttunee, W. (2004). Respectful research in Aboriginal communities and institutions in Canada. In B. Fairburn & N. Russell (Eds.), *Co-operative membership and globalization* (pp. 207–236). Centre for the Study of Co-operatives.

Whiteman, G. (2004). Why are we talking inside?: Reflecting on traditional ecological knowledge (TEK) and management research. *Journal of Management Inquiry, 13*(3), 261–277.

Wilson, S. (2008). *Research is ceremony: Indigenous research methods.* Fernwood Publishing.

Yow, V. (1995). Ethics and interpersonal relationships in oral history research. *The Oral History Review, 22*(1), 51–66.

15

Survey Design and Implementation Considerations in International and Cross-National Research

Julie A. de Jong and Zeina N. Mneimneh

Introduction

Survey research is an important tool used to collect data from individuals to inform policy-making, allocation of resources, and other decision-making efforts. It is a quantitative approach used to systematically gather information from a sample of entities, such as individuals, households or organizations living in a certain geographic boundary during a specific period of time and to generate quantitative estimates of certain attributes or associations within the larger population. The attributes studied vary and include measures of health and well-being, educational attainment, employment, labor, economic behavior, political and social attitudes, community engagement and a host of other metrics important for assessing current needs and barriers to fill the needs of a population (Groves et al., 2009; Wolf et al., 2016). Surveys can be conducted locally in the researcher's country of residence, *internationally* (outside of the researcher's country of residence) or *cross-nationally* in more than one country, with the objective of comparing country estimates. Irrespective of the type of the survey, the goal is to collect high-quality data that accurately represent the population under investigation so that local and global decisions, such as program prioritization and resource allocation, are based on valid and reliable estimates.

While the field of quantitative survey research has deep roots in the social sciences, the use of surveys has also been adopted by many researchers in the nascent field of global leadership research alongside qualitative approaches as a complementary method to understand how global leaders manage and navigate global change (Mendenhall et al., 2017; Reiche et al., 2019). The implementation of quantitative methods in global leadership research is not without challenges, however. Global leaders, whether in governmental, philanthropic, or private organizations and businesses, are often a heterogenous population, spanning multiple cultural and socio-political contexts. While the diversity of the cultural background, and all of its richness, adds a great value to understanding potential cultural effects in global leadership research, challenges in isolating true cultural differences from those differences caused by variations in study design and implementation across different cultural groups can jeopardize the comparability of the results. In the last two decades, there has been a growing awareness of the challenges inherent in such comparative research that is deliberately designed to collect and compare findings from two or more populations. This increased awareness has led to the recognition of comparative surveys as a distinct category of research with some unique features and a commonly used name: Multicultural, Multiregional and

DOI: 10.4324/9781003003380-15

Multinational (3MC) surveys (Johnson et al., 2019; Survey Research Center, 2016; Harkness et al., 2010; Lyberg et al., 2021). Additionally, as survey research has proliferated in international settings, novel solutions to specific contextual challenges have been fueled as well (Survey Research Center, 2016). It is our hope that some of these culturally relevant methods will reach the field of global leadership studies, leading to cross-fertilization and blending of different research approaches, both qualitative and quantitative.

In this chapter, we take a first step towards bridging the disciplines of survey methodology and global leadership studies by illustrating challenges and sharing lessons learned from international and 3MC quantitative survey research. We do this by first presenting several examples of research programs in order to illustrate the varied utility and complexity of the international and 3MC survey landscape. We then discuss specific aspects of the survey lifecycle in international settings where common challenges often occur, affecting the quality of the data collected. We end with a discussion of the future of survey data and how advances in the field may impact global leadership research, focusing on several strategies for improving data quality. Throughout the chapter, we use the term *international* to refer to studies conducted outside the researcher's country of residence and the term *cross-national* to studies designed with the objective of collecting comparable data from two or more countries (cross-cultural studies are one type of 3MC studies) (Harkness et al., 2010; Johnson et al., 2019; Survey Research Center, 2016).

3MC and International Survey Research

Before delving into the challenges and strategies for improving data quality in quantitative international and cross-national survey research, we describe some of the long-standing surveys that have been providing international or regional data offering insights into the voices, needs and living circumstance of the people and driving important policy decisions that affect the well-being of nations.

Cross-National Health-Related Survey Data

The Demographic and Health Surveys (DHS) Program includes more than 400 surveys on a myriad of health topics in over 90 countries (DHS, 2020). These data have been used by the U.S. Agency for International Development (USAID) to monitor trends across health program areas and set priorities for funding, interventions, and policy development (USAID, 2020). Similarly, the Multiple Indicator Cluster Surveys (MICS), conducted in over 100 countries, are an important driver of UNICEF resource prioritization and allocation. DHS and MICS, along with many other valuable surveys (see, for example, Greenleaf et al., 2019), produce a vital source of health data, particularly on women and children. Reviews focused specifically on these programs substantiate their critical importance, noting the paucity of good quality survey data necessary to understand disparities more generally in Low and Middle Income Countries (LMIC), and especially on re-productive, maternal, newborn and child health topics (Hancioglu & Arnold, 2013; World Health Organization, 2011, 2017). The critical need for such data has driven many global organizations such as the United Kingdom Research and Innovation (UKRI) and the Bill and Melinda Gates Foundation to open funding programs and allocate resources for both primary data collection on metrics of health and health disparities (Greenleaf et al., 2019) as well as secondary data analyses of DHS, MICS and other survey data (Ewerling et al., 2018; Hancioglu & Arnold, 2013; Miedema et al., 2018). Global policy interventions related to infectious disease outcomes such as malaria have also been informed by comparative survey data collected in malaria-endemic countries within sub-Saharan Africa. These data have been used to assess the coverage of preventive treatment, resource use and antenatal care, and to identify individual and country-level factors that affect such coverage (Galactionova et al., 2015; Van Eijk et al., 2013).

Cross-National Education Survey Data

The Programme for International Student Assessment (PISA), funded by the Organisation for Economic Co-operation and Development (OECD) and conducted every three years, measures reading, mathematics and science knowledge and skills of children aged 15 years in about 80 countries. Data from PISA have been used by researchers in the field of education and instructional development to produce recommendations for curriculum (Yore et al., 2007) and equity policies within education systems (Gillis et al., 2016; Ho, 2010; Knipprath, 2010; see also Yore et al., 2010 for a complete review). OECD also funds a similar survey among the adult population in over 40 countries, the Programme for the International Assessment of Adult Competencies (PIAAC), to assess cognitive skills, including literacy, numeracy and problem solving. Globally, there has been an increased interest in such data to inform investments in life-long learning opportunities (i.e., adult education) (Tsatsaroni & Evans, 2014) and identify adult participation inequalities, calling on government leaders and global leaders in supranational institutions to adequately fund relevant organizations focused on adult education programs (Desjardins, 2014).

Cross-National Social Survey Data

The European Social Survey (ESS) is an ongoing cross-national survey conducted every two years across most countries in Europe to measure the attitudes and behaviors of adult populations on a number of social issues. A recently conducted impact study of the ESS documented many instances where these data have informed policy decisions and public and political debates. Highlighted topics include how data was used to influence alcohol-related policy in Belgium and to provide evidence for legislative proposals on the extension of a basic income scheme in Austria, on protections of the rights of sexual minorities in Estonia and on reforms to family policy in Slovenia, among others (Kolarz et al., 2017).

The European Quality of Life Survey (EQLS) is also a cross-sectional survey that is conducted every three to four years measuring topics related to the well-being and quality of life of adult populations in over 30 countries. These data have been used to call for policies related to recreational and green areas in many European countries to reduce socioeconomic inequality in mental well-being (Mitchell et al., 2015) and to urge leaders to rethink the design of policies aimed at achieving quality for EU citizens, given the documented gender gap in subjective well-being (Arechavala & Espina, 2019).

These findings, along with those from numerous other surveys, speak to the critical role that robust international survey research plays. Yet, methodological research conducted as part of these and other cross-national surveys provides ample evidence that collecting reliable, valid and comparable data has many design and implementation challenges. In the following section, we review the stages of the survey life cycle focusing on contextual conditions in international and cross-national studies that could threaten the quality of the data collected. As the global leadership field expands to blend data methods and conduct more quantitative comparative global surveys, such challenges will be at the forefront and will require innovative solutions.

Survey Design and Implementation Challenges in International Settings

Achieving high-quality survey data requires understanding and minimizing the potential sources of error that could occur at the different stages of the survey life cycle (Figure 15.1). One of the guiding frameworks that organizes the different sources of survey error is the Total Survey Error (TSE) framework (Groves et al., 2009). The TSE framework takes into consideration both how well survey questions *measure* the key constructs, as well as the extent to which the adjusted sample of

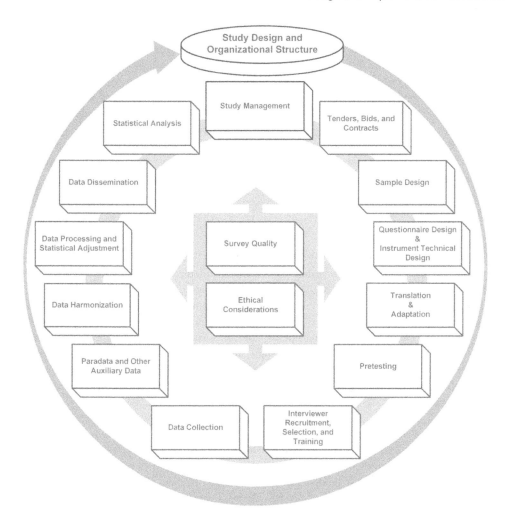

Figure 15.1 The Survey Life Cycle

respondents *represent* the population of interest (Groves et al., 2009) given a specific budget. Sources of measurement error include interviewers, respondents, mode of data collection, aspects of the questionnaire and its translations, the survey setting and data processing (Groves & Lyberg, 2010). In contrast, representation error – the extent to which one can generalize to the population of interest using sample survey data – is rooted primarily in inefficiencies of the sampling frame vis-à-vis the target population and in nonresponse among sampled respondents. In comparative, cross-national surveys, the TSE framework has been expanded to also include the concept of "comparison error" (Pennell et al., 2017; Smith, 2019). Potential sources of error often differ across study countries and present challenges to achieving a standard design and implementation protocol, thereby potentially increasing comparison error. While operationalization of such errors will look different depending on whether data is collected in a large-scale population-level survey or among a smaller target population of global leaders, the general nature of such errors will be similar.

While the TSE framework and its different sources apply to all types of surveys, factors that can contribute to these sources can differ across settings. For example, in LMIC settings, limitations in infrastructure (e.g., Internet access and coverage), the absence of comprehensive sampling frames, the geographical environment (e.g., access to certain areas due to infrastructure or armed conflict), the survey environment (e.g., norms against recording interviews for quality control), specific cultural dimensions (e.g., collectivism, masculinity, etc.) and limited survey expertise and capacity could magnify the magnitude of certain error sources. Furthermore, in cross-national studies, variations in these factors across countries can lead to differences in the magnitude of survey errors and subsequently the comparability of survey estimates. Hancioglu and Arnold (2013) discuss examples of such design and implementation challenges in DHS, MICS and older cross-national survey programs that have jeopardized data comparability. In the sections below we discuss four stages from the survey life cycle where challenges are commonly encountered in international and cross-national studies and which are highly relevant when implementing quantitative approaches in global leadership research.

Study Design

Survey Mode

Determining the study design and associated organizational structure occurs early in the survey life cycle. During this phase, the choice of the data collection mode(s) (face-to-face, telephone, web, etc.) shapes many other design considerations. Mode decisions are generally based on available sampling frames,[1] the literacy and cultural norms of the target population, the budget and available infrastructure. For example, limited postal infrastructure in many LMIC countries can render impossible a mail survey or postal invitation to an online survey. Even in countries with high levels of internet coverage, low functional literacy can also preclude web surveys. While telephone surveys could address the issue of illiteracy and internet and mail coverage, establishing telephone frames that include both landline and cell phone numbers (if needed) can be a challenge in certain countries. And even if telephone frames exist, ensuring non-differential telephone coverage with respect to key constructs or their correlates is needed. For example, in a number of countries in Africa (e.g., Mozambique, Niger and Malawi) cell phone ownership in the adult population is less than 60% and there is a large gender gap in ownership, with males owning the majority of cell phones (Lau et al., 2019; L'Engle et al., 2018). This renders face-to-face to be, to date, the most commonly used method in international and cross-national surveys, albeit the most costly. Still, armed conflicts, civil disturbances or the presence of a significant contagion like the coronavirus that caused the COVID-19 pandemic of 2020 forces many researchers to explore alternatives to face-to-face surveys or utilize mixed modes of data collection.

In certain cross-national surveys, variations in mode coverage have necessitated the implementation of different modes in different countries. For example, the Gallup World Poll relies on a telephone mode in countries where at least 80% of the target population has access to telephone and face-to-face in countries with lower telephone coverage (Gallup, Inc., 2015). When the International Social Survey Programme (ISSP) began, while the required mode was self-administration, low literacy levels in some countries required the use of interviewers (de Leeuw & Berzelak, 2016). Such design differences between countries can confound substantive between-country differences. While the introduction of alternate modes may present less of a challenge in surveys of global leaders, there still may be differences in access across some settings, particularly among the lower echelons of leadership. Thus, attempts to isolate and measure the magnitude of such confounding differences by conducting pilot-mode experiments are recommended.

Organizational Structure

The need for a strong organizational structure to coordinate all aspects of the design and implementation is particularly important in a cross-national survey where there are multiple countries, languages and populations. Ideally, such a central team is complemented by experts and country representatives to ensure that design decisions account for contextual variations including language, dialects, political and economic conditions and physical terrain and access restrictions (Pennell & Cibelli Hibben, 2016). Organizational structures can take many forms and vary on a continuum of tight central coordination to very loose or no central coordination (Cibelli Hibben et al., 2016). When a tight central coordination is coupled with a common funding source for all countries, the coordinating center can be empowered to require adherence to study protocols and may have significant central oversight. However, models with decentralized structures where multiple hub institutions lead surveys across a set of countries or where individual countries attempt to coordinate together allow more freedom in modifying survey protocols to the specific country context. When certain essential survey features are modified, comparability of data is jeopardized. For example, relying on probability samples (where every unit has a known non-zero chance of being selected) for certain populations but on non-probability samples in others (such as a snowball approach or convenience sample) will cause differential sampling error and affect the comparability of the results. As cross-national projects develop, leaders must consider what structure best fits the project, recognizing that no two structures may be exactly alike given the differences across projects. However, the development of a strong structure to address ongoing challenges in research and respond effectively and efficiently is critical to producing high-quality data (Lyberg et al., 2021).

Stakeholders

Data collected in international settings may have multiple stakeholders who are actively involved, have a vested interest in the project or are affected by it. Stakeholders may include the funding agency, the researchers, the in-country data collection agency, government officials, political groups, media outlets and the respondents themselves. In such circumstances, stakeholders will have varying degrees of understanding of the most critical elements of the survey methodology and the need for accurate data. Depending on the differential power, the actions of some stakeholders may result in a specific type of survey error such as when certain types of respondents are unable or unwilling to participate in a study (potentially resulting in nonresponse error), while others may halt the study altogether such as when political leaders block certain types of surveys from being conducted (Mneimneh et al., 2014). Thus, a central role of the project management team is to balance the aspirations, needs and political interests of the different stakeholders and the constraints of project scope, cost and timeline in such a way to allow for the best data quality even if on a limited set of measures and survey populations. In a cross-national survey, there is also an added complexity of comparability and the need for balancing both standardization and localization as well as contractual obligations and local expertise. Stakeholders are not always aware of the time and effort required to design and implement a quality cross-national survey across many countries (see for example, de Jong & Cibelli Hibben, 2018; European Social Survey, 2018). In such studies, a strong central coordinating center is an imperative stakeholder for developing and disseminating standard processes and communicating with each study site about acceptable adaptations for the local context. Infrastructure funding for such a strong central coordinating center becomes essential (Lyberg et al., 2021; Scott et al., 2019).

Tenders, Bids and Contracts

In international surveys, researchers may independently recruit and manage the field staff in the study setting or may collect data remotely (e.g., using a telephone call center located outside the study country). More commonly, however, fieldwork is coordinated with a local entity such as a governmental statistical bureau, a for-profit market research company or a non-profit organization

(Orlowski et al., 2016). In such an organizational setup, the researcher is an additional step removed from the fieldwork, which can lead to challenges in certain aspects of project management and concerns about the data quality and data security. When subcontracting field work to a local entity, the tendering (request for proposal) or contractual stage allows the researchers to define and detail project responsibilities, study specifications, quality frameworks and a data security plan, all of which are expected to be followed and fulfilled. The International Organization for Standardization (ISO) recommends that submitted proposals reference ethical codes in social, market, and public opinion research, providing the principle investigator with leverage if quality issues arise in later stages of the survey process (International Organization for Standardization, 2012; see also Orlowski et al., 2016). For example, the EQLS sponsor released a quality management framework alongside the tender requiring bidders to submit an accompanying quality proposal (de Jong & Cibelli Hibben, 2018). While it may be undesirable for the local contracted entity to disclose obstacles to adhering to the specifications, researchers should acknowledge potential cultural and contextual challenges and encourage bidders to be honest about realistic challenges in implementing the study specifications. For example, while the tender may specify the use of a probability sample, countries without existing sampling frames may deviate from the requirement and implement an alternate design instead, such as the random walk approach discussed in the following section on Sample Design. Thus, bidders are encouraged to be specific in the processes that they are able to and commit to follow, even if they deviate from the protocol encouraged in the tender. Moreover, before contracting the work to any local organizations, researchers need to spend time collecting information and understanding the cultural setting. It can be particularly useful to ask local or regional contacts to provide information about the bidders and to understand any existing local practices that deviate from the specified protocol and the likelihood of acknowledging such deviations.

Human Subjects Protection

A core step in the design process is the development of human subjects protection. Researchers have the ethical responsibility to protect the rights of respondents, interviewers and other research personnel employed in the data collection process (Groves et al., 2009; Joe et al., 2016; Singer, 2008). This is especially true in certain international and cross-national surveys, where the research includes populations with a limited survey research tradition and where sociopolitical factors engender vulnerable populations in need of rigorous ethical protections (Tourangeau et al., 2014). First, local ethical review committees might not be easily identifiable or even available. Allocating time to identify or put together a local ethical committee in each research setting (e.g., each study country) to review the survey protocol is essential. Second, in cross-national studies, researchers may confront situations that necessitate careful consideration and possible design trade-offs in order to comply with ethical principles and minimize sources of survey error while maintaining comparability (de Jong, 2019). For example, maintaining sensitivity to cultural differences by having other family members present during an interview may conflict with ethical obligations to protect confidentiality and to minimize error in respondent reporting (Mneimneh et al., 2020). Recognizing this type of conflict at the design stage allows for identifying features such as alternate modes for sensitive items, offering both respondent privacy and cultural sensitivity. Additionally, and particularly relevant in global leadership research, it is critical to implement processes to protect respondent confidentiality if there is the possibility that the respondent is completing the survey at his/her place of employment. Third, equitable and noncoercive inclusion is also an inherent challenge in some settings, especially those occurring at least partially in disaster or conflict regions. For example, even in studies of global leaders, where the average respondent is not likely to be as vulnerable as a respondent in a general population survey, the specific cultural context may produce a coercive situation where the respondent feels that participation in the survey is compulsory (e.g., due to institutional hierarchy). In such cases, it is crucial to protect both respondents and interviewers from psychological and physical harm, to recognize the potential for increased respondent and interviewer burden, and to clarify any benefits, or lack thereof, to respondents (Pennell et al., 2014; de Jong et al., 2016).

Sample Design

Probability sampling, wherein every element in the target population has a known non-zero probability of being selected, is recommended in any population-level survey. The target population could be the entire adult population of a country (e.g., study countries in the European Social Survey and World Mental Health surveys), a more specific subset such as married women of child-bearing age (e.g., study countries in the standard Demographic and Health Surveys) or, in the case of global leadership research, the CIOs of companies in a specific industry across several countries. However, in international settings, the ability to design and implement a strict probability sample can be jeopardized by a number of factors. For example, the terminology and definitions used across countries have the potential to jeopardize the soundness of the sample design (Lepkowski, 2005; Mneimneh et al., 2014, 2016; Pennell & Cibelli Hibben, 2016). In comparative cross-national studies, variations in these contextual factors can lead to sample design differences across sites, potentially introducing comparison error in the sample design process and affecting data comparability.

Sample design starts with the specification of the target population, ensuring that all elements have a known non-zero probability of inclusion in the sample. Determining whether exclusion of one or more specific sub-group within the target population occurred is essential for any type of inference or decision made from the survey estimates. Exclusions of specific concern include remote populations, which are costly to contact, areas of armed conflict which may be impossible to access, and displaced populations which may be difficult to identify. In population-level research, these sub-groups might be the most vulnerable members of a society and precisely those in need of priority attention from leaders seeking to make informed policy decisions. Exclusions may also be applied in settings with significant heterogeneity in spoken language, where cost constraints limit the number of translations of the survey instrument and the recruitment and training of interviewers with adequate language skills (Lepkowski, 2005).

In studies of global leadership, particularly in the comparative context, challenges at the sampling design phase may arise from unintentional differences in specification of the target population and subsequent production of the sampling frame. For example, the GLOBE CEO Project of 2014 included as its target population the direct reports of CEOs, whose names were to be provided by each CEO's administrative assistant, with potential for variation in interpretation and implementation of these instructions (House et al., 2013). In other studies, the target population may be even more nebulous (e.g., managers specializing in international relations). Any between-country variation in the definition of the target population, i.e., who is considered a CEO or what defines a manager specializing in international relations would lead to unintended cross-country variations that could impact the generalizability and comparability of the findings.

Once a target population is agreed upon, identifying or creating a sampling frame that includes all members of the target population is the next step. While government registries or other residential lists (e.g., utility customers, voter registries, etc.) are available in some countries, such lists are generally rare, especially in LMIC settings (Maineri et al., 2017; Minnesota Population Center, 2015). When a potential sample frame is identified, understanding its coverage properties is essential and can be very challenging in many international settings. Coverage properties are affected by both undercoverage (e.g., exclusion of certain members such as recent migrants, homeless population, new construction, refugees) and overcoverage (e.g., multiple residences among the middle- and upper-class in countries where seasonal residences are common). For example, in the GLOBE Project, any potential in how the CEO administrative assistants were identified, the definition of "administrative assistant", or the process of generating the names across countries could potentially lead to coverage differences (House et al., 2013).

In the absence of recent sampling frames, many international face-to-face surveys rely on constructing or updating existing frames through the use of multistage area probability sampling methods. Such a design typically begins with identifying available population size estimates (e.g., census data or large household surveys) to select and allocate the sample into primary stage units or enumeration areas followed by a subsequent selection stages of smaller geographic areas, households, and then individuals (Kish, 1965; Ustun et al., 2005). Typical challenges in this design begin with obtaining accurate population size estimates of the primary stage unit. In many LMIC countries, disruptions in the collection of census and other statistical data due to political sensitivities, political turmoil and conflict, lead to outdated population estimates. For example, Sudan conducted its most recent census in 2008, Cameroon in 2005 and Lebanon as distantly as 1932 (Salibi, 1988). Meanwhile, internal and external migration can significantly change the geographical population distribution in such countries in a short period of time. In other countries, economically motivated rural-to-urban internal migration can also lead to informal residential areas (e.g., slums, areas of land encroachment, etc.), where population estimates are dubious. Adjusting population size estimates in such circumstances is needed.

Another challenging aspect of multistage area probability sampling is the household selection process. After selecting the set of geographic clusters (enumeration areas, neighborhoods, sections of a village, blocks, etc.) a list of housing units that are located in each of these clusters is needed. When an updated list is not available, enumerators or interviewers are instructed to list all units in each geographic cluster. Once a list is constructed, a prespecified number of units is selected. This approach reduces the chance that interviewers would substitute selected households "on-the-fly" and also provides a way to control the size of selected households from each cluster and manage it more efficiently. However, due to existing survey traditions, cost, and safety concerns, full enumeration may not be implemented; rather, a *random walk* approach is often used. Random walk relies on interviewers locating the geographic cluster, identifying a random start and attempting to select and interview every nth household thereafter (Noelle, 1963). Unfortunately, evidence from household surveys suggests that the more freedom interviewers have in selection of households, the greater the risk of bias, possibly due to substitution (Eckman & Koch, 2019; Kohler, 2007; Menold, 2014). Recent research suggests that an alternative form of this approach may reduce bias if the random walk approach is retained (Bauer, 2016).

Recently, advances in geographic information systems (GIS), graphical positioning systems (GPS) and satellite images, have led to the use of grid sampling techniques in places where good quality sampling frames are lacking. In grid sampling, population density estimates at the 1 km grid level (or lower) are calculated utilizing multiple sources of information (census data, satellite imagery, nighttime lights, land use data, the presence of roads and city and village locations) and state-of-the-art population mapping models. Grid-based sampling lends itself well to cluster sampling, often being used as the final areal unit in a multistage sample. For example, the Eurobarometer uses 1 km grids developed by Geostat as secondary sampling units in a multistage design. A recent study (Cajka et al., 2018) surveying countries in South and Central America, Asia and Africa also used 1 km grids from Landscan as secondary sampling units before going on to select subgrids of variable size in the final areal stage. Grids could also have applications in other types of sampling such as developing an adaptive sampling frame for relatively rare and clustered populations (Peyrard et al., 2013).

The final step in the sampling process in most population-level surveys is the selection of a respondent within the household. This requires listing all or a sub-group of household family members and requisite eligibility. Before implementing this stage, it is essential to develop a definition for what is considered a household or a family as these can vary greatly across countries (Lepkowski, 2005). For example, it is not uncommon in some settings for multiple family units to share one household unit, along with potentially the same household entrance. There can also be confusion about whether to include other residents such as live-in servants or drivers, potentially resulting in coverage error. This could happen if such members are considered part of the target population and have no other residence in which to be counted. Once a household list is established, a random method to select the respondent is implemented through either automation (if a computer interviewing method is used) or using a Kish grid (if the instrument is on paper) (Kish, 1965; see also Appendix C in de Jong, 2016). Still, in many international surveys, establishing a full list of household members may be considered burdensome, time-consuming or intrusive (Gaziano, 2005; Rizzo et al., 2004). In these situations, a next birthday or the last birthday method is often used, though evidence suggests that this approach introduces bias (Koch, 2019). Le, Brick, Diop, and Alemadi (2013) suggest an alternate probability method that is less intrusive and that can be particularly suitable for larger households often prevalent in international settings.

Questionnaire Design

When designing a survey questionnaire, researchers may elect one or a combination of several strategies: (1) reuse questions, (2) adapt existing questions and (3) write new questions (van de Vijver et al., 2003). Before using any of these strategies and especially in international settings, the research team needs to identify any contextual or cultural factors that might dictate whether a question could be asked in the first place and how the questions will be perceived by all types of respondents needs to be implemented. In some settings, the questionnaire might have to be reviewed by national government entities, local authority or community leaders before approval to go into the field. Such reviews may result in deletion of certain questionnaire items (Kuechler, 1998). For example, in a cross-national survey in a number of countries in the Middle East, the government of Saudi Arabia did not permit inclusion of attitudinal questions about democracy on the questionnaire (de Jong & Young-De Marco, 2017). Survey questions that may be considered innocuous in one culture may be threatening or taboo in other cultures and while not necessarily prohibited from inclusion, may lead to nonresponse and even security concerns for the interviewer. Andreenkova and Javeline (2019) discuss how understanding the reasons for sensitivity and determining the extent to which they differ across countries can help in the evaluation of potential effects on data comparability and offer strategies for detecting and addressing such differences in a comparative context. In the questionnaire design phase, identification and evaluation approaches include soliciting expert opinion from specialists in cultural issues and from social scientists or experimenting with different approaches to elicit truthful responses and evaluating these approaches (Langhaug et al., 2010; Lara et al., 2004; Phillips et al., 2010). One strategy for improving the reporting of sensitive information that is perceived as socially desirable/undesirable or private is the use of self-administered mode. For example, an interviewer may administer the majority of the interview to the respondent in the traditional face-to-face mode, but then give the interviewing device (e.g., tablet, laptop, etc.) to the respondent for independent completion. In such cases, audio computer-assisted self-interviewing (A-CASI) is often used and can be particularly helpful in low-literacy settings. In A-CASI, respondents listen to an audio track recording of each survey question using a headset to complete the. If illiterate, survey respondents can be instructed to push color-coded buttons on a touchscreen or keyboard or have graphical representations of answer categories to indicate their response to each question (Hansen et al., 2016). While self-administered mode is challenging to implement in low literacy settings, there have been some successful attempts through the use of innovative solutions. For example, a study measuring sensitive attitudes about caste in rural India implemented an inexpensive, low-tech solution, wherein respondents listened to a prerecorded instrument on a basic MP3 player and entered responses on an answer sheet using simple shapes (Chauchard, 2013). Similar approaches using color-coded keyboards for primarily dichotomous questions have been used elsewhere (Hewett et al., 2004; Mensch et al., 2003). From a questionnaire design perspective, development of an instrument for administration to a target population of global leaders can incorporate similar strategies, considering the extent to which topics may be sensitive given the specific cultural context(s) and, accordingly, the application of alternate data collection modes.

There is also accumulating evidence on how *cultural frames, scripts, or language* can affect respondents' cognitive processes (Peytcheva, 2020; Schwarz et al., 2010; Tourangeau et al., 2000; Uskul et al., 2010; Uskul & Oyserman, 2006).[2] Oyserman (2017) explains that while general themes or ways of being (e.g., individualism) are present in each culture and arise from universal human evolutionally needs (survival, cooperation, conflict limitation), societies or cultures differ in the propensity in which specific themes guide everyday life. These themes in turn affect how information is processed and preserved in the memory and on what information it is acceptable to report. Cultural themes that receive the most attention in the literature are collectivism, individualism and honor (Hofstede, 2001; Hofstede et al., 2010; Oyserman, 2017; Schwarz et al., 2010). For example, interdependent cultures value indirect communication, requiring more sensitivity to conversational contexts to determine what is said "between the lines". When first asked how satisfied they are with their marriage and then with their life-as-a-whole, conversational norms of nonredundancy in interdependent cultures encourage respondents not to consider their marriage when they answer the life-as-a-whole question, much as if it were worded "Aside from your marriage…" (Schwarz et al., 1991). However, in independent cultures, respondents only observe the nonredundancy norm when the introduction renders it salient. As a result, answers to specific-general question sequences (which pose a nonredundancy problem) differ between cultures because of cognition variations causing differences in the means as well as the correlation between questions and changing substantive interpretations (Haberstroh et al., 2002; Schwarz et al., 2010). Hofstede Insights provide a tool for researchers and practitioners to learn about the prevalence of certain cultural themes in specific countries.[3]

Cultural differences also influence what people attend to and how they organize information. Collectivist cultures put a premium on "fitting" in and they tend to monitor their own behavior as well as the behavior of others to avoid standing out. Attending to certain events more closely affects how information is represented in memory and how it is recalled. Ji and colleagues (Ji et al., 2000) demonstrate how Chinese vs. American students differ in their recall strategies for survey items when asked about observable vs. unobservable behaviors. In terms of reporting information, social desirability bias where respondents intentionally (impression management) or unintentionally (self-enhancement) alter their answers to survey questions to fit social norms has been also found to be positively associated with collectivism (Bernardi, 2006; Bond & Smith, 1996; Lalwani et al., 2006; Triandis, 1995). Other studies have examined the impact of cultural frames on acquiescence (the tendency to choose "agree" or "yes" responses), extreme and middle category response styles on survey responses (see Yang et al. (2010) for a detailed review and discussion).

Such cultural differences in cognitive processes and associated impact on survey responses may compromise comparisons among cultural and country populations if observed differences in responses at the individual or group level do not reflect true differences on a particular construct. Accounting for these cultural effects in the questionnaire design process is particularly challenging because it is often difficult to generalize findings from one specific culture to another, evidence is still accumulating, and such effects are often topic dependent (DeCastellarnau, 2018).[4] However, there are pretesting methods that can be employed during the design process and that can help identify differences in cognitive processes.[5] In the international and particularly cross-national survey context, the pretesting method of cognitive interviewing (CI) is effective in uncovering problems with translated and adapted survey items that were originally designed in a different language or for a different a culture (for a review, see Willis, 2005; see also Schoua-Glusberg & Villar, 2014). CI typically consists of in-depth interviews with a small, purposive sample of respondents. Respondents first answer a survey question and describe how and why they answered the way they did, with follow-up probes by the interviewer relevant to the question or answer given. Questions found to have problems can then be modified to reduce errors in the cognitive process (Miller et al., 2014; Willis, 2005). If used to investigate the constructs captured by the questions, CI can help identify questionnaire issues that could affect the validity and cross-cultural comparability, which is particularly essential for studies seeking to make comparative estimates (Miller, 2019). However, research has also shown that different cultural and linguistic groups may respond differently to particular CI methods (Kelley et al., 2015; Pan et al., 2010), and Park and Goerman (2019) provide specific recommendations when conducting CIs among Chinese-, Korean- and Spanish-speaking respondents. While there is limited evidence in the literature to indicate that global leadership researchers have widely incorporated CI approaches in survey questionnaire design, integration of CI can be a valuable tool in understanding how cultural frameworks differentially affect the response process and can contribute to measurement error, particularly in comparative research.

Finally, when translating a questionnaire to a different language, additional recent approaches have been recommended to detect cultural and linguistic issues, determine the feasibility of translation, and identify potential translation challenges early in the questionnaire design process. These approaches include translatability assessment (TA), wherein the source (original) questionnaire is assessed during the initial instrument development stage to identify potential problems in translation and adaptation (Conway et al., 2014; Sperber et al., 2014), as well as advance translation (AT), in which an informal translation of the source questionnaire is produced to find problems in the source text that are apparent only when translation is attempted (Dorer, 2011). Evidence is still accumulating about their effectiveness, but recent publications point to the benefit of both approaches at enhancing the translatability and the cultural adaptability of questionnaires, and arguably of subsequent data quality (Acquadro et al., 2018; Dorer, Forthcoming). Other strategies for improving quality of the questionnaire ahead of translation and relevant in many international settings include software tools and approaches to identify potential problems in the wording or structure of the questions that may lead to difficulties in question administration, miscommunication or other failings, including the Question Understanding Aid (Graesser et al., 2006), the Survey Quality Predictor (Saris et al., 2011), and the Question Appraisal System (Willis & Lessler, 1999) and its adaptation for comparative research (Dean et al., 2007).

For a discussion of best practices for translating and adaptation survey instruments in international and cross-cultural settings, readers are encouraged to refer to the Cross-cultural Survey Guidelines (Survey Research Center, 2016).[6] A further discussion about translation in global leadership research is provided in Chapter 12 of this volume.

Data Collection

Data collection implementation encompasses a wide range of activities relating to interviewers, systems development and implementation and quality control, all presenting numerous logistical challenges in an international setting and threats to comparability in cross-national settings. Integral to the face-to-face data collection process are interviewers, who implement the survey design and are the primary link to respondents. Varying research traditions and, at times, limited exposure to state-of-the-art survey methodology current best practices can affect interviewer recruitment, training, assignment, remuneration and quality control practices, all with a direct effect on data quality.

Interviewer Recruitment, Training and Remuneration

In international contexts, where there is an increased likelihood of contact with more insular communities, recruiting and selecting interviewers who share characteristics with the local context can improve both cooperation and quality of data collected (Alcser et al., 2016). In settings with multiple questionnaire translations, an adequate number of interviewers with appropriate language skills will be required, alongside a staffing plan to match interviewers and respondents on language. Interviewer language abilities also need careful assessment due to the risk of interviewers overstating conversational, reading, and writing fluency in his or her non-native language(s). It also may be necessary to gender match interviewers to respondents in certain regions or countries or when investigating specific topics such as reproductive health. For example, in a national study conducted in the Kingdom in Saudi Arabia, all face-to-face interviews with household members were gender matched. This required, at times, sending both a male and female interviewer together to the same household so that a male interviewer could interview the male respondent and a female interviewer the female respondent (Al-Subaie et al., 2020).

Whether new or experienced interviewers are being recruited, conducting a comprehensive training is essential. The training needs to include components of standardized interviewing techniques, respondent cooperation, tailoring interviewer behavior to gain cooperation, sample management system use, completing contact attempt details and specific training on the study-specific questionnaire (Alcser et al., 2016).

Interviewer remuneration plays an important role in the quality of the collected data. In many countries, the research tradition is to pay interviewers by the completed interview rather than hours worked. While this practice may work well if all sampled members require the same level of effort to complete an interview, in reality individuals vary in their living conditions, demands on time, attitudes toward interviewing and family environment. Such variations make certain members easier to interview than others. If the level of effort needed to complete an interview is not factored into the interviewer remuneration protocol, interviewers may be tempted to deviate from the data collection protocol, recruiting "easier" members or fabricating interview data to shorten the interview (Mneimneh et al., 2019).[7]

Computerized Systems and Tools

The specific instrumentation used by the interviewer is also an important determinant of data quality. In settings where industry best practices are not widely diffused or where infrastructure is limited, adapting the latest technologies for computer-assisted interviewing (CAPI) might not be feasible, necessitating the use of traditional paper and pencil administration (PAPI) (Groves et al., 2009). Moreover, even in settings where CAPI is institutionalized, numerous data collection software platforms are currently in use and availability of features relating to sample management and quality control vary significantly. The use of a sample management system that facilitates releasing assigned sample lines to specific interviewers and requires interviewers to record contact attempt history (such as time and day of the attempt, mode of contact its outcome) is essential for understanding nonresponse rates and how they vary across countries and regions within a country. Furthermore, when such systems are integrated with the questionnaire system and have the capability to connect to the internet, near-real time (or even daily) exploration of the data routinely will allow for assessing interviewers' compliance reducing sources of error (Kreuter, 2013). Thus, differences in data collection mode (CAPI vs. PAPI), software and related institutional capacities and local resources and infrastructure (e.g., widespread Internet coverage) directly affect the type of quality control processes implemented and threaten the validity of the survey estimates and their comparability in cross-national settings (Pennell et al., 2017; Smith, 2019a; Smith, 2011).

Paradata

Paradata is defined as the data captured during the process of producing a survey statistic (e.g., time stamps, keystroke data), as well as observational data (e.g., observed neighborhood conditions)

(Kreuter, 2013). Paradata such as contact history details are essential for optimizing contact and cooperation and monitoring nonresponse bias (Groves, 2006). Nonresponse bias is a product of the nonresponse rate and the difference between respondents and nonrespondents. The nonresponse rate refers to the proportion of eligible sample units who fail to complete an interview, while the latter refers to the differences between respondents and nonrespondents on the measures of interest. If there is no such difference between respondents and nonrespondents, then there is no non-response bias, regardless of the magnitude of the response rate. However, if nonrespondents differ from respondents, the lower the response rate, the higher the bias is likely to be (Groves, 2006; Groves & Peytcheva, 2008). Survey nonresponse has been increasing, leading to concerns about nonresponse bias (Beullens et al., 2018; Brick & Williams, 2013; de Leeuw et al., 2019; Groves, 2011; Kreuter, 2013; Peytchev, 2013; Sastry et al., 2020; Wagner & Stoop, 2019). This is parti-cularly true when the topic of interest is stigmatizing (Gaia, 2015) or raises security concerns among respondents (Benstead & Malouche, 2015; Tannenberg, 2017), and when select elements of the target population are difficult to access (Tourangeau et al., 2014). Unfortunately, it is difficult to assess nonresponse bias because little data is typically available about nonrespondents. In the absence of more general guidelines about minimum response rates, researchers and organizations typically strive to achieve the highest response rate possible given budgetary constraints. Moreover, paradata is increasingly being used to drive responsive designs. The objective of such a design is to reduce nonresponse rate and ideally nonresponse bias through monitoring real-time selected paradata as indicators of quality, monitoring sample balances and altering design features during the course of data collection that could reduce nonresponse error (Groves & Heeringa, 2006).

However, adaptation of integrated systems allowing for such paradata analyses for quality control and responsive design in LMIC (and even in higher-income settings) remains relatively rare (Mneimneh et al., 2019). Successful adaptation of integrated systems requires a capacity-building endeavor and adequate budget, additional interviewer training, and expertise for software and server setup, and data analysis and processing. Still, integrated systems have been successfully implemented in several studies in international settings. Mneimneh et al. (2019) present a series of case studies on data-driven approaches to monitoring interviewer behavior in several international and cross-national surveys, offering real-world examples of how interviewer-level data collected in real-time can be used to detect potential interviewer deviations from study protocols via a range of quality indicators (e.g., interview length, nonresponse rate, etc.). Mneimneh et al. (2019) also discuss the additional financial and human resources needed to implement data-driven interviewer monitoring as well as the additional training, usability testing and efficient coordination needed to complement more traditional quality control procedures.

Interview Privacy in the Study Context

As discussed in the questionnaire design section, the respondent's propensity to report socially desirable responses can lead to over-reports of attitudes and behaviors perceived to be desirable as well as under-reporting of undesirable outcomes. Given the sensitive nature of some survey topics, it is important to understand how this bias might also be manifested differentially across contexts and how it interacts with the setting of the interview. For example, in face-to-face interviews, having a third person present (other than the respondent and the interviewer) varies greatly across countries, with estimates ranging between 17% and 82% of interviews, jeopardizing the privacy of the in-terview setting (Casterline & Chidambaram, 1984; Mneimneh et al., 2018; Mneimneh, 2012), and potentially affecting the reporting of sensitive information depending on the relationships between the respondent and the third party present (Aquilino, 1993; Aquilino et al., 2000; Moskowitz, 2004, Mneimneh et. al, 2018). The presence of a third party during the interview has been found to be associated with a number of respondent-level characteristics such as gender, education, income, as well as household level characteristics such as household size (Mneimneh et. al, 2018). Interviewers also vary in rates of private interviews obtained and recent literature has found some interviewer-level characteristics to be associated with the presence of a third party (Mneimneh et al., 2020) Researchers are thus encouraged to implement procedures to enhance interview privacy and account for it during analysis (Mneimneh et al., 2015, 2018). Less is known about the association between interview privacy and reporting in the field of global leadership research, but researchers need to consider the topic of the study and whether the privacy setting of the interview, the potential presence of others in the organization and their relationship to the respondent could affect the reporting of certain type of questions. The presence of a third party in an interview focusing on global leadership issues has the potential to disrupt candid reporting, particularly in the third party differs from the respondent in the organizational hierarchy and where the survey protocol requires a private setting.

The Future of International and Cross-National Research

The complexity of conducting research in an international setting, and particularly across multiple settings, presents significant challenges to data quality. However, there are important steps that researchers can take, both at the individual as well as the organizational level, to increase data quality as well as meet the fiduciary and ethical obligations inherent in survey data collection.

While it can be challenging to monitor quality in international and comparative studies, several cross-national surveys, including ESS, PIAAC, and EQLS have performed both internal quality audits and have commissioned external quality assessments (de Jong & Cibelli Hibben, 2018; Gallup Europe, 2010; Malter et al., 2018; Petrakos et al., 2010; Vila et al., 2013; Wuyts & Loosveldt, 2019). Quality reviews and evaluation studies are less common in most other comparative and single-country settings, but can result in important recommendations to improve data in future surveys. Researchers who are conducting quantitative surveys in the global sphere and who have not yet been exposed to the recent advances in the field of cross-cultural survey methodology are encouraged to consider external quality reviews as they are a relatively inexpensive tool to identify areas of improvement in the implemented design and offer valid recommendation that could improve the quality of the collected data.

Another important direction towards improving data quality in international settings, regardless of the topic of interest, is capacity-building – that is, developing the ability for local actors to conduct and analyze high-quality research independently. A capacity building approach is different than other approaches, sometimes referred to as "parachute consultations", where researchers become involved in conducting research and collecting data in an international setting without significant engagement by local scientists and practitioners (Finau et al., 2000; Panapasa et al., 2012). Capacity-building efforts, while essential, can be more costly and more time-consuming than "parachute" consultations and could be met with local resistance common to any change. Such resistance is usually caused by lack of trust in the benefit of the change, perceptions of the difficulty of proposed changes, or fear of the unknown (Finau et al., 2000; Panapasa et al., 2012). Identifying local long-term collaborators, establishing trust between the collaborators and their institutions, and adhering to transparency principles are essential for a capacity building effort to be fruitful. The achieved progress from such capacity building efforts can be incremental and it may be that each project in the region/country introduces a new skill set to the researchers, survey operations and/or other trainees which can be integrated into future studies and the accumulation of which produces the full set of expertise to conduct and collect high-quality data independently.

Although this chapter has been focused primarily on population-based face-to-face data collection methods and related challenges, it has been written during the time of the COVID-19 2020 pandemic where there has been a need to consider alternate modes of data collection, primarily telephone.[8] In many LMIC countries, telephone surveys face particular challenges in sampling design, where landline and mobile telephone penetration vary widely by country. Landline penetration lags well behind mobile penetration in much of the world, and while mobile coverage is greater, general population mobile surveys tend to over-represent young, male, urban and educated residents (Lau et al., 2019; L'Engle et al., 2018; see also Gibson et al., 2017 and Greenleaf et al., 2017 for reviews of recent literature). Related to the relative paucity of telephone surveys in LMIC settings is the limited research on nonresponse and measurement issues associated with this mode, particularly vis-à-vis cultural and contextual differences in a comparative context. These challenges are present for researchers across disciplines and present an opportunity to pilot alternate modes in these settings, where circumstances such as unanticipated political instability, natural disasters and other events may necessitate rapid mode transition in the future, even after the anticipated end of the pandemic.

Notes

1 A sampling frame is a list or group of materials used to identify all elements (e.g., persons, households, establishments) of a survey population from which the sample will be selected.
2 See also Pennell et al. (2017) and Harkness et al. (2014) for further discussions.
3 See https://www.hofstede-insights.com/product/compare-countries/.
4 For additional discussion on the effect of response styles, see also Lee et al., 2019; Liu et al., 2019; Yan & Hu, 2019.
5 See Caspar et al. (2016) for an overview of pretesting methods.
6 The Cross-cultural Survey Guidelines are available at http://ccsg.isr.umich.edu.
7 There is a significant literature on quality control strategies, including detection of fabricated data. See Kuriakose & Robbins (2016) and Robbins (2019) in addition to those noted in the section below on Paradata.
8 The current shift in population studies has occurred from face-to-face to telephone because while it is challenging, it is more feasible in many settings to collect data using a probability sample of telephone numbers, even in many LMIC countries. However, even in non-LMIC settings, conducting a web survey using a probability sample is very challenging. A sampling frame of email addresses from which to draw a probability sample is rare, and nearly impossible in LMIC settings.

References

Acquadro, C., Patrick, D. L., Eremenco, S., Martin, M. L., Kuliś, D., Correia, H., Conway, K., & Research, I. S. (2018). Emerging good practices for translatability assessment (TA) of patient-reported outcome (PRO) measures. *Journal of Patient-Reported Outcomes, 2*(1), 8.

Alcser, K., Clemens, J., Holland, L., Guyer, H., & Hu, M. (2016). *Interviewer recruitment, selection, and training* [*Guidelines for best practice in cross-cultural surveys*]. Survey Research Center, Institute for Social Research, University of Michigan. http://www.ccsg.isr.umich.edu/

Al-Subaie, A. S., Al-Habeeb, A., & Altwaijri, Y. A. (2020). Overview of the Saudi National Mental Health Survey. *International Journal of Methods in Psychiatric Research, 29*(3), e1835.

Andreenkova, A., & Javeline, D. (2019). Sensitive questions in comparative surveys. In T. P. Johnson, B.-E. Pennell, I. Stoop, & B. Dorer (Eds.), *Advances in comparative survey methods: Multinational, multiregional and multicultural contexts (3MC)* (pp. 139–160). John Wiley & Sons, Inc.

Aquilino, W. S. (1993). Effects of spouse presence during the interview on survey responses concerning marriage. *Public Opinion Quarterly, 57*(3), 358–376.

Aquilino, W. S., Wright, D. L., & Supple, A. J. (2000). Response effects due to bystander presence in CASI and paper-and-pencil surveys of drug use and alcohol use. *Substance Use & Misuse, 35*(6–8), 845–867.

Arechavala, N. S., & Espina, P. Z. (2019). Quality of life in the European Union: An econometric analysis from a gender perspective. *Social Indicators Research, 142*(1), 179–200.

Bauer, J. (2016). *Errors in random route samples.* 1st SERISS Survey Experts Forum Workshop, Munich, Germany.

Benstead, L. J., & Malouche, D. (2015). Interviewer religiosity and polling in transitional Tunisia. *Midwest Political Science Association Annual Meeting*, April, 16–19.

Bernardi, R. A. (2006). Associations between Hofstede's cultural constructs and social desirability response bias. *Journal of Business Ethics, 65*(1), 43–53.

Beullens, K., Loosveldt, G., Vandenplas, C., & Stoop, I. (2018). Response rates in the European social survey: Increasing, decreasing, or a matter of fieldwork efforts? In *Survey methods: Insights from the field (SMIF)*. doi:1 0.13094/SMIF-2018-00003.

Bond, R., & Smith, P. B. (1996). Culture and conformity: A meta-analysis of studies using Asch's (1952b, 1956) line judgment task. *Psychological Bulletin, 119*(1), 111.

Brick, J. M., & Williams, D. (2013). Explaining rising nonresponse rates in cross-sectional surveys. *The ANNALS of the American Academy of Political and Social Science, 645*(1), 36–59.

Cajka, J., Amer, S., Ridenhour, J., & Allpress, J. (2018). Geo-sampling in developing nations. *International Journal of Social Research Methodology, 21*(6), 729–746.

Caspar, R., Peytcheva, E., Yan, T., Lee, S., Liu, M., & Hu, M. (2016). Pretesting. *Cross-Cultural Survey Guidelines*. August.

Casterline, J., & Chidambaram, V. C. (1984). The presence of others during the interview and the reporting of contraceptive knowledge and use. In *Survey analysis for the guidance of family planning programs* (pp. 267–298). Ordina Editions.

Chauchard, S. (2013). Using MP3 players in surveys: The impact of a low-tech self-administration mode on reporting of sensitive attitudes. *Public Opinion Quarterly, 77*, 220–231.

Cibelli Hibben, K. L., de Jong, J., Hu, M., Durow, J., & Guyer, H. (2016). *Study design and organizational structure* [Guidelines for best practice in cross-cultural surveys]. Survey Research Center, Institute for Social Research, University of Michigan. http://www.ccsg.isr.umich.edu/

Conway, K., Acquadro, C., & Patrick, D. L. (2014). Usefulness of translatability assessment: Results from a retrospective study. *Quality of Life Research: An International Journal of Quality of Life Aspects of Treatment, Care and Rehabilitation, 23*(4), 1199–1210.

de Jong, J. A. (2016). Data collection. In *Cross-cultural survey guidelines*. http://ccsg.isr.umich.edu/datacoll.cfm

de Jong, J. A., Cibelli Hibben, K., & Pennell, S. (2016). *Ethical considerations* [Guidelines for best practice in cross-cultural surveys]. Survey Research Center, Institute for Social Research, University of Michigan. http://www.ccsg.isr.umich.edu/

de Jong, J. A., & Young-DeMarco. (2017). Best practices: Lessons from a Middle East survey research program. In *The Arab spring and changes in values and political actions in the Middle East: Explorations of visions and perspectives*. Oxford University Press.

de Jong, J. A. (2019). Ethical considerations in the total survey error context. In T. P. Johnson, B.-E. Pennell, I. Stoop, & B. Dorer (Eds.), *Advances in comparative survey methods: Multinational, multiregional and multicultural contexts (3MC)* (pp. 665–682). John Wiley & Sons, Inc.

de Jong, J. A., & Cibelli Hibben, K. (2018). *European quality of life survey 2016: Quality assessment*. Eurofound.

de Leeuw, E. D., & Berzelak, N. (2016). Survey mode or survey modes? In C. Wolf, D. Joye, T. W. Smith, & Y. Fu (Eds.), *Sage handbook of survey methodology* (pp. 142–156). Sage Publications, Inc.

de Leeuw, E. D., Suzer-Gurtekin, T. Z., & Hox, J. J. (2019). The design and implementation of mixed-mode surveys. In *Advances in comparative survey methods: Multinational, multiregional and multicultural contexts (3MC)* (pp. 387–408). Wiley & Sons.

Dean, E., Caspar, R., McAvinchey, G., Reed, L., & Quiroz, R. (2007). Developing a low-cost technique for parallel cross-cultural instrument development: The question appraisal system (QAS-04). *International Journal of Social Research Methodology, 10*(3), 227–241.

DeCastellarnau, A. (2018). A classification of response scale characteristics that affect data quality: A literature review. *Quality & Quantity, 52*(4), 1523–1559.

Desjardins, R. (2014). *Participation in adult education opportunities: Evidence from PIAAC and policy trends in selected countries*. https://escholarship.org/uc/item/1k1203tn

DHS. (2020). *Demographic and health surveys*. https://dhsprogram.com/

Dorer, B. (2011). Advance translation in the 5th round of the European Social Survey (ESS). *FORS Working Paper Series*, paper 2011-4. FORS.

Dorer, B. (Forthcoming). *Advance translation as a means of improving source questionnaire translatability? Findings from a think-aloud study for French and German*. Frank & Timme.

Eckman, S., & Koch, A. (2019). Interviewer involvement in sample selection shapes the relationship between response rates and data quality. *Public Opinion Quarterly, 83*(2), 313–337.

Ewerling, F., Victora, C. G., Raj, A., Coll, C. V., Hellwig, F., & Barros, A. J. (2018). Demand for family planning satisfied with modern methods among sexually active women in low-and middle-income countries: Who is lagging behind? *Reproductive Health, 15*(1), 42.

Finau, S. A., Finau, E., & Ofanoa, M. (2000). Research imperialism in Pacific health: The case of Tonga (1966-1997). *Pacific Health Dialog*, 7(2), 109–114.

Gaia, A. (2015). *Social desirability in reporting paying for sex and risky behaviours: Comparing two techniques for handling missing data* (Dissertation). University of Milan, Bicocca.

Galactionova, K., Tediosi, F., De Savigny, D., Smith, T., & Tanner, M. (2015). Effective coverage and systems effectiveness for malaria case management in sub-Saharan African countries. *PloS ONE*, 10(5).

Gallup Europe. (2010). *Quality assessment of the 5th European working conditions survey*. Eurofound.

Gallup, Inc. (2015). *How does the gallup world poll work?* http://www.gallup.com/178667/gallup-world-poll-work.aspx

Gaziano, C. (2005). Comparative analysis of within-household respondent selection techniques. *Public Opinion Quarterly*, 69(1), 124–157.

Gibson, D. G., Pereira, A., Farrenkopf, B. A., Labrique, A. B., Pariyo, G. W., & Hyder, A. A. (2017). Mobile phone surveys for collecting population-level estimates in low- and middle-income countries: A literature review. *Journal of Medical Internet Research*, 19(5), e139.

Gillis, S., Polesel, J., & Wu, M. (2016). PISA data: Raising concerns with its use in policy settings. *The Australian Educational Researcher*, 43(1), 131–146.

Graesser, A. C., Cai, Z., Louwerse, M. M., & Daniel, F. (2006). Question understanding aid (QUAID) a web facility that tests question comprehensibility. *Public Opinion Quarterly*, 70(1), 3–22. 10.1093/poq/nfj012

Greenleaf, A., Aliou, G., Turke, S., Battle, N., Saifuddin, A., Moreau, C., Guiella, G., & Choi, Y. (2019). *Performance monitoring and accountability 2020 technical report – comparison of remote data collection modes to monitor family planning progress in Burkina Faso: Representativeness, data quality, and cost*. Bill & Melinda Gates Institute for Population and Reproductive Health, Johns Hopkins Bloomberg School of Public Health.

Greenleaf, A. R., Gibson, D. G., Khattar, C., Labrique, A. B., & Pariyo, G. W. (2017). Building the evidence base for remote data collection in low- and middle-income countries: Comparing reliability and accuracy across survey modalities. *Journal of Medical Internet Research*, 19(5), e140. 10.2196/jmir.7331

Groves, R. M., Fowler, F. J., Couper, M. P., Lepkowski, J. M., Singer, E., & Tourangeau, R. (2009). *Survey methodology*. John Wiley & Sons Inc.

Groves, R. M., & Heeringa, S. G. (2006). Responsive design for household surveys: Tools for actively controlling survey errors and costs. *Journal of the Royal Statistical Society: Series A (Statistics in Society)*, 169(3), 439–457.

Groves, R. M. (2006). Nonresponse rates and nonresponse bias in household surveys. *Public Opinion Quarterly*, 70(5), 646–675.

Groves, R. M. (2011). Three eras of survey research. *Public Opinion Quarterly*, 75(5), 861–871.

Groves, R. M., & Lyberg, L. (2010). Total survey error: Past, present, and future. *Public Opinion Quarterly*, 74(5), 849–879.

Groves, R. M., & Peytcheva, E. (2008). The impact of nonresponse rates on nonresponse bias: a meta-analysis. *Public Opinion Quarterly*, 72(2), 167–189.

Haberstroh, S., Oyserman, D., Schwarz, N., Kühnen, U., & Ji, L.-J. (2002). Is the interdependent self more sensitive to question context than the independent self? Self-construal and the observation of conversational norms. *Journal of Experimental Social Psychology*, 38(3), 323–329.

Hancioglu, A., & Arnold, F. (2013). Measuring coverage in MNCH: Tracking progress in health for women and children using DHS and MICS household surveys. *PLoS Medicine*, 10(5).

Hansen, S. E., Lee, H. J., Lin, Y. C., & McMillan, A. (2016). *Instrument technical design*. [*Guidelines for best practice in cross-cultural surveys*]. Survey Research Center, Institute for Social Research, University of Michigan. http://www.ccsg.isr.umich.edu/

Harkness, J. A., Braun, M., Edwards, B., Johnson, T. P., & Lyberg, L. E. (2010). *Survey methods in multicultural, multinational, and multiregional contexts*. John Wiley & Sons.

Harkness, J. A., Stange, M., Cibelli, K. L., Mohler, P. Ph., & Pennell, B.-E. (2014). Surveying cultural and linguistic minorities. In R. Tourangeau, B. Edwards, T. P. Johnson, K. Wolter, & N. Bates (Eds.), *Hard-to-survey populations*. Cambridge University Press.

Hewett, P. C., Mensch, B. S., & Erulkar, A. S. (2004). Consistency in the reporting of sexual behaviour by adolescent girls in Kenya: A comparison of interviewing methods. *Sexually Transmitted Infections*, 80, 43–48.

Ho, E. S.-C. (2010). Assessing the quality and equality of Hong Kong basic education results from PISA 2000+ to PISA 2006. *Frontiers of Education in China*, 5(2), 238–257.

Hofstede, G. (2001). *Culture's consequences: Comparing values, behaviors, institutions and organizations across nations*. SAGE Publications.

Hofstede, G. H., Hofstede, G. J., & Minkov, M. (2010). *Cultures and organizations: Software of the mind* (3rd ed.). Mcgraw-hill New York.

House, R. J., Dorfman, P. W., Javidan, M., Hanges, P. J., & Luque, M. F. S. de. (2013). *Strategic leadership across cultures: GLOBE study of CEO leadership behavior and effectiveness in 24 countries*. SAGE Publications.

International Organization for Standardization (ISO). (2012). *Market, opinion and social research – Vocabulary and service requirements (ISO 20252)*.

ISO. (2015). *ISO 17100:2015 translation services*. ISO.

Ji, L.-J., Peng, K., & Nisbett, R. E. (2000). Culture, control, and perception of relationships in the environment. *Journal of Personality and Social Psychology*, 78(5), 943.

Joe, K., Raben, F., & Phillips, A. (2016). The ethical issues of survey and market research. In C. Wolf, D. Joye, T. W. Smith, & Y. Fu (Eds.), *The SAGE handbook of survey methodology* (pp. 77–86). Sage.

Johnson, T. P., Pennell, B.-E., Stoop, I., & Dorer, B. (Eds.). (2019). *Advances in comparative survey methods: Multinational, multiregional and multicultural contexts (3MC)*. John Wiley & Sons, Inc.

Kelley, J., Cibelli Hibben, K. L., Pennell, B.-E., & Yan, T. (2015, May). Analyzing cognitive interviews for cross-national studies. Proceedings of the *American Association for Public Opinion Research Annual Conference*.

Kish, L. (1965). *Survey sampling*. John Wiley & Sons.

Knipprath, H. (2010). What PISA tells us about the quality and inequality of Japanese education in mathematics and science. *International Journal of Science and Mathematics Education*, 8(3), 389–408.

Koch, A. (2019). With-in household selection of respondents. In T. P. Johnson, B.-E. Pennell, I. Stoop, & B. Dorer (Eds.), *Advances in comparative survey methodology* (pp. 93–109). John Wiley & Sons, Inc.

Kohler, U. (2007). Surveys from inside: An assessment of unit nonresponse bias with internal criteria. *Survey Research Methods*, 1, 55–67.

Kolarz, P., Angelis, J., Krcál, A., Simmonds, P., Traag, V., & Wain, M. (2017). *Comparative impact study of the European Social Survey (ESS) ERIC*. Technopolis Group.

Kreuter, F. (Ed.). (2013). *Improving surveys with paradata: Analytical uses of process information*. John Wiley & Sons, Inc.

Kuechler, M. (1998). The survey method: An indispensable tool for social science research everywhere? *American Behavioral Scientist*, 42(2), 178–200.

Kuriakose, N., & Robbins, M. (2016). Don't get duped: Fraud through duplication in public opinion surveys. *Statistical Journal of the IAOS*, 32(3), 283–291.

Lalwani, A. K., Shavitt, S., & Johnson, T. (2006). What is the relation between cultural orientation and socially desirable responding? *Journal of Personality and Social Psychology*, 90(1), 165–178.

Langhaug, L. F., Sherr, L., & Cowman, F. M. (2010). How to improve the validity of sexual behaviour reporting: Systematic review of questionnaire delivery modes in developing countries. *Tropical Medicine & International Health*, 362–381. doi:10.1111/j.1365-3156.2009.02464.x

Lara, D., Strickler, J., Olavarrieta, C. D., & Ellertson, C. (2004). Measuring induced abortion in Mexico A comparison of four methodologies. *Sociological Methods & Research*, 32, 529–558.

Lau, C. Q., Cronberg, A., Marks, L., & Amaya, A. (2019). In search of the optimal mode for mobile phone surveys in developing countries. A comparison of IVR, SMS, and CATI in Nigeria. *Survey Research Methods*, 13(3), 305–318.

Le, K. T., Brick, J. M., Diop, A., & Alemadi, D. (2013). Within-household sampling conditioning on household size. *International Journal of Public Opinion Research*, 25(1), 108–118.

Lee, S., Keusch, F., Schwarz, N., Liu, M., & Suzer-Gurtekin, T. Z. (2019). Cross-cultural comparability of response patterns of subjective probability questions. In T. P. Johnson, B.-E. Pennell, I. Stoop, & B. Dorer (Eds.), *Advances in comparative survey methods: Multinational, multiregional, and multicultural contexts (3MC)* (pp. 457–475). John Wiley & Sons, Inc.

L'Engle, K., Sefa, E., Adimazoya, E. A., Yartey, E., Lenzi, R., Tarpo, C., Heward-Mills, N. L., Lew, K., & Ampeh, Y. (2018). Survey research with a random digit dial national mobile phone sample in Ghana: Methods and sample quality. *PloS ONE*, 13(1), e0190902.

Lepkowski, J. (2005). Non-observation error in household surveys in developing countries. In *Household sample surveys in developing and transition countries: United Nations* (pp. 149–170).

Liu, M., Suzer-Gurtekin, T. Z., Keusch, F., & Lee, S. (2019). Response styles in cross-cultural surveys. In T. P. Johnson, B.-E. Pennell, I. Stoop, & B. Dorer (Eds.), *Advances in comparative survey methods: Multinational, Multiregional, and Multicultural Contexts (3MC)* (pp. 477–499). John Wiley & Sons, Inc.

Lyberg, L. E., Pennell, B. E., Cibelli Hibben, K. L., & de Jong, J. A. (2021). *Task force report on quality in comparative 3MC survey research*. American Association for Public Opinion Research/World Association for Public Opinion Research.

Maineri, A., Scherpenzeel, A., Bristle, J., Pflüger, S.-M., Mindarova, I., Butt, S., Zins, S., Emery, T., & Luijkx, R. (2017). *Report on the use of sampling frames in European studies*.

Malter, F., Schuller, K., & Borsch-Supan, A. (2018). *SHARE compliance profiles—Wave 7*. MEA, Max Planck Institute for Social Law and Social Policy.

Mendenhall, M. E., Osland, J., Bird, A., Oddou, G. R., Stevens, M. J., Maznevski, M., & Stahl, G. K. (2017). *Global leadership: Research, practice, and development*. Routledge.

Menold, N. (2014). The influence of sampling method and interviewers on sample realization in the European Social Survey. *Survey Methodology, 40*(1), 105–123.

Mensch, B. S., Hewett, P. C., & Erulkar, A. S. (2003). The reporting of sensitive behavior by adolescents: A methodological experiment in Kenya. *Demography, 40*, 247–268.

Miedema, S. S., Haardörfer, R., Girard, A. W., & Yount, K. M. (2018). Women's empowerment in East Africa: Development of a cross-country comparable measure. *World Development, 110*, 453–464.

Miller, K. (2019). Conducting cognitive interviewing studies to examine survey question comparability. In T. P. Johnson, B.-E. Pennell, I. Stoop, & B. Dorer (Eds.), *Advances in comparative survey methods: Multinational, multiregional and multicultural contexts (3MC)* (pp. 203–225). John Wiley & Sons, Inc.

Miller, K., Willson, S., Chepp, V., & Padilla, J. L. (Eds.). (2014). *Cognitive interviewing methodology*. Wiley.

Minnesota Population Center. (2015). *Integrated public use microdata series, international: Version 6.4 [Machine-readable database]*. University of Minnesota.

Mitchell, R. J., Richardson, E. A., Shortt, N. K., & Pearce, J. R. (2015). Neighborhood environments and socioeconomic inequalities in mental well-being. *American Journal of Preventive Medicine, 49*(1), 80–84.

Mneimneh, Z., Axinn, W. G., Ghimire, D., Cibelli, K. L., & Alkaisy, M. S. (2014). Conducting surveys in areas of armed conflict. In Roger Tourangeau, B. Edwards, T. P. Johnson, K. M. Wolter, & N. Bates (Eds.), *Hard-to-survey populations* (pp. 134–156). Cambridge University Press.

Mneimneh, Z., Lyberg, L. E., Sharma, S., Vyas, M., Sathe, D. B., Malter, F., & Altwaijri, Y. (2019). Case studies on monitoring interviewer behavior in international and multinational surveys. In T. P. Johnson, B.-E. Pennell, I. Stoop, & B. Dorer (Eds.), *Advances in comparative survey methods: Multinational, multiregional and multicultural contexts (3MC)* (pp. 731–770). John Wiley & Sons, Inc.

Mneimneh, Z., Pennell, B.-E., Kelley, J., & Cibelli Hibben, K. L. (2016). Surveys in societies in turmoil. In *Handbook of Survey Methodology* (pp. 178–190). Sage Publications, Inc.

Mneimneh, Z., Tourangeau, R., Pennell, B.-E., Heeringa, S. G., & Elliott, M. R. (2015). Cultural variations in the effect of interview privacy and the need for social conformity on reporting sensitive information. *Journal of Official Statistics, 31*(4), 673–697.

Mneimneh, Zeina N., de Jong, J., & Altwaijri, Y. (2020). Why Do Interviewers Vary on Interview Privacy and Does Privacy Matter? In K. Olson, J. D. Smyth, J. Dykema, A. L. Holbrook, F. Kreuter, & B. T. West (Eds.), *Interviewer effects from a total survey error perspective*. CRC Press.

Mneimneh, Zeina N., Elliott, M. R., Tourangeau, R., & Heeringa, S. G. (2018). Cultural and interviewer effects on interview privacy: Individualism and national wealth. *Cross-Cultural Research, 52*(5), 496–523.

Mneimneh, Z. N. (2012). *Interview privacy and social conformity effects on socially desirable reporting behavior: Importance of cultural, individual, question, design and implementation factors* (Doctoral Dissertation). The University of Michigan.

Moskowitz, J. M. (2004). Assessment of cigarette smoking and smoking susceptibility among youthtelephone computer-assisted self-interviews versus computer-assisted telephone interviews. *Public Opinion Quarterly, 68*(4), 565–587. doi:10.1093/poq/nfh040

Noelle, E. (1963). *Umfragen in der Massengesellschaft: Einführung in die Methoden der Demoskopie*. Verlag für Demoskopie.

Orlowski, R. A., Antoun, C., Carlson, R., & Hu, M. (2016). Tenders, bids, and contracts. In *Guidelines for best practices in cross-cultural surveys*. Survey Research Center, Institute for Social Research, University of Michigan. http://ccsg.isr.umich.edu/index.php/chapters/tenders-bids-contracts-chapter

Oyserman, D. (2017). Culture three ways: Culture and subcultures within countries. *Annual Review of Psychology, 68*, 435–463.

Pan, Y., Landreth, A., Park, H., Hinsdale-Shouse, M., & Schoua-Glusberg, A. (2010). Cognitive interviewing in non-English languages: A cross-cultural perspective. In *Survey methods in multinational, multiregional, and multicultural contexts*. John Wiley & Sons.

Panapasa, J. J., Jackson, J., Caldwell, C., Heeringa, S., McNally, J., Williams, D., Coral, D., Taumoepeau, L., Young, L., Young, S., & Fa'Asisila, S. (2012). Community-based participatory research approach to evidence-based research: Lessons from the Pacific Islander American Health Study. *Progress in Community Health Partnerships: Research, Education, and Action, 6*(1), 53.

Park, H., & Goerman, P. L. (2019). Setting up the cognitive interview task for non-English speaking participants in the U.S. In T. P. Johnson, B.-E. Pennell, I. Stoop, & B. Dorer (Eds.), *Advances in comparative survey methods: Multinational, multiregional and multicultural contexts (3MC)* (pp. 227–249). John Wiley & Sons, Inc.

Pennell, B.-E., & Cibelli Hibben, K. L. (2016). Surveying in multicultural and multinational contexts. In C. Wolf, D. Joye, T. W. Smith, & Y. Fu (Eds.), *Sage handbook of survey methodology* (pp. 157–177). Sage Publications, Inc.

Pennell, B.-E., Cibelli Hibben, K. L., Lyberg, L., Mohler, P. Ph., & Worku, G. (2017). A total survey error perspective on surveys in multinational, multiregional, and multicultural contexts. In P. Biemer, E. De Leeuw, S. Eckman, B. Edwards, F. Kreuter, L. Lyberg, C. Tucker, & B. T. West (Eds.), *Total survey error in practice*. John Wiley & Sons Inc.

Pennell, B.-E., Deshmukh, Y., Kelley, J., Maher, P., & Tomlin, D. (2014). Disaster research: Surveying displaced populations. In R. Tourangeau, B. Edwards, T. Johnson, K. Wolter, & N. Bates (Eds.), *Hard-to-survey populations*. Cambridge University Press.

Petrakos, M., Kleideri, M., & Ieromnimon, A. (2010). *Quality assessment of the 2nd european quality of life survey*. Eurofound.

Peyrard, N., Sabbadin, R., Spring, D., Brook, B., & Mac Nally, R. (2013). Model-based adaptive spatial sampling for occurrence map construction. *Statistics and Computing, 23*(1), 29–42.

Peytchev, A. (2013). Consequences of survey nonresponse. *The ANNALS of the American Academy of Political and Social Science, 645*(1), 88–111.

Peytcheva, E. (2020). The effect of language of survey administration on the response formation processes. In M. Sha & T. Gabel (Eds.), *The essential role of language in survey research* (pp. 3–22). RTI Press.

Phillips, A. E., Gomez, G. B., Boily, M. C., & Garnett, G. P. (2010). A systematic review and meta-analysis of quantitative interviewing tools to investigate self-reported HIV and STI associated behaviours in low-and middle-income countries. *International Journal of Epidemiology, 39*, 1541–1555.

Reiche, B. S., Mendenhall, M. E., Szkudlarek, B., & Osland, J. S. (2019). Global leadership research: Where do we go from here? In *Advances in global leadership* (Vol. 12, pp. 211–234). Emerald Publishing Limited.

Rizzo, L., Brick, J. M., & Park, I. (2004). A minimally intrusive method for sampling persons in random digit dial surveys. *The Public Opinion Quarterly, 68*(2), 267–274.

Robbins, M. (2019). New frontiers in detecting data fabrication. In T. P. Johnson, B.-E. Pennell, I. Stoop, & B. Dorer (Eds.), *Advances in comparative survey methods: Multinational, multiregional and multicultural contexts (3MC)* (pp. 771–805). John Wiley & Sons, Inc.

Salibi, K. (1988). *A house of many mansions, the history of Lebanon reconsidered*. IB Tauris.

Saris, W., Oberski, D., Revilla, M., Zavala-Rojas, D., Lilleoja, L., Gallhofer, I., & Gruner, T. (2011). *The development of the program SQP 2.0 for the prediction of the quality of survey questions* (RECSM Working Paper 24).

Sastry, N., Ananthpur, K., Axinn, W. G., de Jong, J. A., Bhat, S., & Sridharan, G. (2020). *Challenges and solutions to nonresponse for household surveys in India: An illustration from the Tamil Nadu Household Panel Survey* [Working Paper]. Survey Research Center, Institute for Social Research, University of Michigan.

Schoua-Glusberg, A., & Villar, A. (2014). Assessing translated questions via cognitive interviewing. In K. Miller, S. Willson, V. Chepp, & J. L. Padilla (Eds.), *Cognitive interviewing methodology* (pp. 51–67). Wiley.

Schwarz, N., Oyserman, D., & Peytcheva, E. (2010). Cognition, communication, and culture: Implications for the survey response process. In J. A. Harkness, M. Braun, B. Edwards, T. P. Johnson, L. Lyberg, P. Ph. Mohler, B.-E. Pennell, & T. W. Smith (Eds.), *Survey methods in multinational, multiregional, and multicultural contexts* (pp. 177–190). John Wiley & Sons, Inc.

Schwarz, Norbert, Strack, F., & Mai, H.-P. (1991). Assimilation and contrast effects in part-whole question sequences: A conversational logic analysis. *The Public Opinion Quarterly, 55*(1), 3–23. JSTOR.

Scott, L., Mohler, P. Ph., & Cibelli Hibben, K. L. (2019). Organizing and managing comparative surveys. In T. P. Johnson, B.-E. Pennell, I. Stoop, & B. Dorer (Eds.), *Advances in comparative survey methods: Multinational, multiregional and multicultural contexts (3MC)* (pp. 707–729). John Wiley & Sons, Inc.

Singer, E. (2008). Ethical issues in surveys. In *International handbook of survey methodology* (pp. 78–96). Lawrence Erlbaum Associates.

Smith, Tom W. (2019). Improving multinational, multiregional, and multicultural (3MC) comparability using the total survey error (TSE) paradigm. In T. P. Johnson, B.-E. Pennell, I. Stoop, & B. Dorer (Eds.), *Advances in comparative survey methods: Multinational, multiregional and multicultural contexts (3MC)* (pp. 13–44). John Wiley & Sons, Inc.

Smith, T. W. (2011). Refining the total survey error perspective. *International Journal of Public Opinion Research, 23*, 464–484.

Sperber, A. D., Gwee, K. A., Hungin, A. P., Corazziari, E., Fukudo, S., Gerson, C., & Whitehead, W. E. (2014). Conducting multinational, cross-cultural research in the functional gastrointestinal disorders: Issues and recommendations. A Rome Foundation working team report. *Alimentary Pharmacology & Therapeutics, 40*(9), 1094–1102.

Survey Research Center. (2016). *Guidelines for best practice in cross-cultural surveys.* Survey Research Center, Institute for Social Research, University of Michigan. http://www.ccsg.isr.umich.edu/

Tannenberg, M. (2017). The autocratic trust bias: Politically sensitive survey items and self-censorship. *AfroBarometer Working Paper No. 176.* https://media.africaportal.org/documents/afropaperno176_autocratic_trust_bias.pdf

Tourangeau, R., Rips, L. J., & Rasinski, K. A. (2000). *The psychology of survey response.* Cambridge University Press.

Tourangeau, Roger, Edwards, B., Johnson, T. P., Bates, N., & Wolter, K. M. (Eds.). (2014). *Hard-to-survey populations.* Cambridge University Press.

Triandis, H. C. (1995). *Individualism and collectivism.* Westview Press.

Tsatsaroni, A., & Evans, J. (2014). Adult numeracy and the totally pedagogised society: PIAAC and other international surveys in the context of global educational policy on lifelong learning. *Educational Studies in Mathematics, 87*(2), 167–186.

USAID. (2020). *The demographic and health surveys program.* https://www.usaid.gov/what-we-do/global-health/cross-cutting-areas/demographic-and-health-surveys-program

Uskul, A. K., & Oyserman, D. (2006). Question comprehension and response: Implications of individualism and collectivism. In Y.-R. Chen (Ed.), *National culture and groups* (Vol. 9, pp. 173–201). Emerald Group Publishing Limited.

Uskul, A. K., Oyserman, D., & Schwarz, N. (2010). *Cultural emphasis on honor, modesty, or self-enhancement: Implications for the survey response process.* doi:10.1002/9780470609927.ch11.

Ustun, T. B., Chatterji, S., Mechbal, A., & Murray, C. J. L. (2005). Quality assurance in surveys: Standards, guidelines, and procedures. In United Nations Statistical Division & United Nations Department of Economic and Social Affairs (Eds.), *Household surveys in developing and transition countries* (pp. 199–230). United Nations.

van de Vijver, F. J. R., Harkness, J. A., Mohler, P.Ph., van de Vijver, F. J. R., & Crosscultural Psychology. (2003). Bias and equivalence: Cross-cultural perspectives. In *Cross-cultural survey methods* (pp. 143–155). Wiley.

Van Eijk, A. M., Hill, J., Larsen, D. A., Webster, J., Steketee, R. W., Eisele, T. P., & ter Kuile, F. O. (2013). Coverage of intermittent preventive treatment and insecticide-treated nets for the control of malaria during pregnancy in sub-Saharan Africa: A synthesis and meta-analysis of national survey data, 2009–11. *The Lancet Infectious Diseases, 13*(12), 1029–1042.

Vila, J., Cervera, J., & Carausu, F. (2013). *Quality assessment of the third European Quality of Life Survey.* Eurofound.

Wagner, J., & Stoop, I. A. L. (2019). Comparing nonresponse and nonresponse biases in multinational, multiregional, and multicultural contexts. In T. P. Johnson, B.-E. Pennell, I. A. L. Stoop, & B. Dorer (Eds.), *Advances in comparative survey methods: Multinational, multiregional, and multicultural contexts (3MC)* (pp. 807–833). John Wiley & Sons, Inc.

Willis, Gordon B., & Lessler, J. T. (1999). *Question appraisal system BRFSS-QAS: A guide for systematically evaluating survey question wording.* Research Triangle Institute: CDC/NCCDPHP/Division of Adult and Community Health Behavioral Surveillance Branch.

Willis, G. B. (2005). *Cognitive interviewing: A tool for improving questionnaire design.* Sage Publications, Inc.

Wolf, C., Joye, D., Smith, T. W., & Fu, Y. (2016). *The SAGE handbook of survey methodology.* SAGE.

World Health Organization. (2011). *Monitoring maternal, newborn and child health: Understanding key progress indicators.* WHO.

World Health Organization. (2017). *Commission on information and accountability for women's and children's health: Keeping promises, measuring results.* WHO.

Wuyts, C., & Loosveldt, G. (2019). *Quality matrix for the European Social Survey, Round 8.* European Social Survey.

Yan, T., & Hu, M. (2019). Examining translation and respondents' use of response scales in 3MC surveys. In *Advances in comparative survey methods: Multinational, multiregional and multicultural contexts (3MC)* (pp. 501–518). Wiley & Sons.

Yang, Y., Harkness, J. A., Chin, T., & Villar, A. (2010). Response styles and culture. In *Survey methods in multinational, multiregional, and multicultural contexts* (pp. 203–223). John Wiley & Sons.

Yore, L. D., Anderson, J. O., & Chiu, M.-H. (2010). Moving PISA results into the policy arena: Perspectives on knowledge transfer for future considerations and preparations. *International Journal of Science and Mathematics Education, 8*(3), 593–609.

Yore, L. D., Pimm, D., & Tuan, H.-L. (2007). The literacy component of mathematical and scientific literacy. *International Journal of Science and Mathematics Education, 5*(4), 559–589.

16

Research in Unchartered Territories

Lessons from Suriname and Haiti

Jennie L. Walker

Introduction

International leadership research necessarily involves understanding the social culture in which the respective organization operates, including the many factors that have shaped it. History, politics, diversity of people in the region, social life and the economic and business climates all contribute to manifestation of culture and the mental models people use within a culture (Lindsay, 2000). Existing literature can provide a foundational understanding for many cultures, but not all. Geert Hofstede's initial work in the 1970s illuminated cultural dimensions in 50 countries (Hofstede, Hofstede, & Minkov, 2010). The GLOBE (Global Leadership and Organizational Behavior Effectiveness) Project, built on and extended cultural research with an initial publication that looked at 62 societies in 2004 (House, Hanges, Javidan, Dorfman & Gupta, 2004). Aperian Global's GlobeSmart tool also provides insights on cultural dimensions for 100 countries (Aperian Global, 2021). Research coverage has grown steadily since the turn of the century. As of 2021, GLOBE research has now expanded to 167 countries (GLOBE Project, 2021). These large-scale research projects provide useful insights into cultural norms, values and behaviors that help cross-cultural researchers prepare for immersion in these societies. There are, of course, also many independent research projects that have focused on single cultures.

As of 2021, there are 195 sovereign nations in the world (Nations Online, 2021) with many diverse groups within. This means that there are cultures that remain unexplored. There are also disputes about additional nations to be recognized and ongoing struggles for independence in foreign controlled regions of the world (Hardingham-Gill, 2020). Even among those that have been researched, smaller nations have not always received the attention that more populous and economically powerful countries have. Within the field of cultural research, there is refinement being made with respect to how social culture is measured. The study of culture has often been looked at in the context of national culture, such as with Hofstede's studies. However, GLOBE research frames cultural study a bit differently, by looking at societies. This acknowledges the reality that national culture is not always representative of diverse subgroups within those nations.

When preparing to perform research in a cultural environment with which one is unfamiliar or has not traveled to in some time, research materials on the culture are critical. In their absence, a unique research approach is needed. This chapter provides insights on two cultural studies I performed between 2013–2015 in Suriname and Haiti. The projects were associated with employee

DOI: 10.4324/9781003003380-16

engagement focused consulting engagements. The multinational clients in each case aimed to have a better understanding of the local cultures they were working in; cultures that were quite different than their own. Their initial attempts to engage employees were not successful, as evidenced by their employee engagement metrics. Employee engagement metrics were both philosophically and practically important for leaders in the companies, as they knew that their productivity and working climate were compromised due to the cross-cultural disconnect. Their objective in seeking outside assistance was to better understand the local social and leadership practices and to modify their employee engagement strategies for cultural relevance. This was wise, as research on intercultural and global leadership competencies shows that understanding culture helps us empathize and relate to others through shared meanings and experiences (Bird & Stevens, 2013). It can help us modify our behaviors to be more culturally appropriate, increasing our success in forming relationships, as well (Alon & Higgins, 2005). In business, the ability to form positive, long-term relationships is key to successful leadership and management (Uhl-Bien, 2011).

While I was highly experienced in cross-cultural leadership development and employee engagement, I personally had not been to these two societies. As a researcher and a consultant, I knew that the first step to properly analyse the organizational case for each operation was to have a firm understanding of the social cultures. I began by looking to well-known research sources, only to find that their publications were either non-existent or limited. An in-depth literature search revealed that publications were generally sparse, in the case of Suriname, and outside the context of research, in the case of Haiti. Publications on Haiti are plentiful when it comes to humanitarian aid work, but little is written about leadership in an organizational or business context.

I chose to discuss both cases in this chapter, as they share similarities from a research perspective, in terms of the lack of relevant literature about them, their development challenges as nations and their unique cultural features. Leadership and business practices are rarely addressed in research on these societies. This means that international leadership scholars and business practitioners have little available information to work with. From a development perspective, Suriname and Haiti are both small, underdeveloped societies. This makes them of limited interest to foreign national companies. This means they receive less research attention by both scholars and consultants, as well. Anecdotally speaking, I had placed personal calls to a few research institutes that specialize in cultural and country reports to inquire about any information they had on these countries. The responses all centered on a lack of demand. Existing publications written by travel guides, sociologists or anthropologists tend to focus on social characteristics, values and behaviors.

While these small nations are not high-profile locations for business ventures, there are multi-national businesses and organizations operating in both that need to properly understand these cultures to work with them in respectful and culturally relevant ways. The companies I had been contracted by specifically chose these locations due to their strategic importance in access to Caribbean shipping lanes. They did not have previous experience working in these countries to inform their current operations. Since politics, both governmental and social, in these societies are complex, it underscores the importance of having a firm foundational understanding of the culture to be able to navigate daily life and business. This certainly applies to understanding language use, since each of these societies shares diversity of languages that are linked to social strata and ethnic groups. In fact, language choice became pivotal issues in both employee engagement studies.

Multifaceted Research Strategy and Process

At the outset of each project, I knew that one of the final deliverables would be a report on business and society that could be used for leadership development purposes. I also was keenly aware of my personal need to be well informed prior to in-country field research. Therefore, I began each cultural study by creating a framework of critical topics that would need to be addressed. In an effort to be comprehensive,

I studied existing country and cultural reports on other nations to see what categories of information were addressed. There was no common framework; so, I added categories as I found them. I created special sections to address unique considerations or pressing issues in each culture, as well.

Researching a social culture involves a great deal of networking, time and creativity. While all comprehensive research involves generating ample and diverse search terms, in the case of novel socio-cultural research it also involves searching in other languages and pursuing different avenues for finding information. I began with scholarly research via library database searches, Google Scholar and researcher forums, such as relevant professional associations (AOM, ILA, AIB) and networks (Research Gate, Academia). My search terms were broad, including the country names and various culturally oriented search terms (e.g., culture, society, life, customs, business, leadership). Findings were sparse, leading me to look at a wide range of publications online, including books, magazine articles, news stories and blogs. I had greater success through the non-scholarly literature in gathering a number of resources. However, gaps remained.

As I identified gaps in information and unique topics for further exploration, I began to look outside of my search terms. This involved pulling in creative works (e.g., photography, fiction), histories and publications in other languages. In the case of Suriname, photography and works in other languages led to much useful and interesting information. I found much more written on Suriname in Dutch than I did in English, for example. These did require special purchases and an inter-library loan. For Haiti, it was works of fiction and feature articles on daily life that helped me formulate novel questions for further investigation. Local authors provided a glimpse of social dynamics, thoughts and feelings that are rarely expressed so poignantly in scholarly research. In each case, the initial research took several months. Had the intent of the research been to write an in-depth manuscript (i.e., a book) on the culture, it very well would have taken a year or more. However, the learning was deeply satisfying, often punctuated with engaging insights and new perspectives to explore.

Cultural Interviews

Interviewing people at the operations within the countries was an integral part of the research plan at the start of the project. However, I hadn't planned to do interviews outside of the organizations, especially during the foundational research stage of each project. It was the limitations of available information and the many questions raised in the initial research that led me to conclude that additional interviews were needed. I decided to incorporate a series of interviews with both local natives and foreigners who had spent extensive time in each respective country. The latter was important to understand an outside perspective on unique attributes of society and leadership.

Pre-trip interviews were another enjoyable aspect of the research, as the insights from those who were either from the culture or had spent much time there were invaluable to paint a picture of daily lives and the rich stories woven through them. Since the projects both involved field research in the organizations for whom I was consulting, I started with virtual interviews of stakeholders and leaders at headquarters and in the field operations. As with any relationship, building trust takes time and trust is imperative for authentic sharing of information (Wang, Yen & Tseng, 2015). So, I found that multiple conversations were helpful to further open conversation over time.

Outside of the company, I sought out expatriates and other business people with experience in-country. I began with my own personal network, searching LinkedIn for any first- or second-degree contacts with ties to these countries. Given the strong representation of the Haitian diaspora in North America, I found many interviewees originally from Haiti living in other parts of the world. I also interviewed expatriates from diverse fields such as business operations, medical missions and religious organizations. Suriname was more difficult. Ultimately, I found two strategies helpful – a general web search and a Facebook search. The general web search led me to Surinamese membership groups (i.e., clubs); Facebook led me to interesting contacts outside of my personal network

– including a professional travel photographer and a film producer who had served in the Peace Corps. The pre-trip interviews often confirmed information I had found in my literature search, which gave me confidence in the thoroughness of my research. However, there were also new insights that I gained that became incredibly helpful. For example, a topic that I had deemed tangential to the research became central, namely religion.

In my initial draft of the cultural reports before the field visits, religion was lightly mentioned. From an employee engagement and leadership perspective, I had noted that the diverse ethnic groups had different religious traditions that may require some workplace accommodations. However, I didn't consider the importance of this topic in manager-employee relations. While I cannot divulge the details of the incidents themselves, religion ended up being a pivotal issue in employee engagement in both studies. My literature search didn't alert me to the importance of religion in daily social life, which inevitably intersected with working life through social biases and discriminatory behaviors. The interviews, both pre-departure and then on-site, illuminated the issues. Religious discrimination and oppression is one example of an issue that can be commonly known in a society, but rarely discussed openly. This is where interviews can be very helpful to surface cultural undercurrents.

Cultural Dimensions and Assessments

It is helpful to look at an existing and well-utilized tool like Hofstede Insight's country comparison tool (Hofstede Insights, 2021) to understand its utility and its limitations when analyzing less understood cultures. The tool allows users to select one or more countries for comparison based on cultural dimensions. For example, it illustrates the distinct differences in cultural dimensions between Netherlands and Suriname. I've chosen these two societies as an illustration to show that despite 300 years of colonial history being ruled by Netherlands, Surinamese culture has evolved quite distinctly. Hofstede's cultural dimensions are helpful to illustrate distinct cultural differences between the two societies. Power distance is significantly higher in Suriname at 85/100 versus 38/100 in Netherlands, for example. This aligns with the findings of the field research that managers and senior leaders tend to operate with a distinct sense of hierarchy. Individualism in Netherlands is quite high at 80/100 versus 47/100 in Suriname. The preference for collectivism is quite evident in my experience of the employee interviews, especially within certain ethic groups in Suriname. Since ethic identity is of great importance in Suriname, cultural traditions are largely preserved within groups. The heritage of several ethnic groups in Suriname come from collectivist traditions and values. Uncertainty avoidance is incredibly high in Suriname at 92/100 versus 53/100 in Netherlands. The various instabilities of development, resources and politics in Suriname likely contribute to this extreme score. The comparison tool and cultural dimensions provide a quick, informative snapshot of potential differences to inform further exploration. The picture is incomplete, however.

Fang (2005) argues that Hofstede's cultural dimensions themselves do not represent the dynamic complexity of culture. "National cultures are living organisms, not time free fossils" (Fang, 2005, p. 81). He suggests a paradigm shift from looking at culture like an onion with layers to peel back to looking at culture like an ocean with shifting currents (Fang, 2005). This is arguably the case with the Surinamese sample. First of all, the sample for Suriname is drawn from a small group of IBM employees in Suriname in the 1970s (Minkov & Kaasa, 2020). Social cultures are dynamic and do show some change over time (Fang, 2005), so there is a need for more current data. Perhaps more significant is the nature of the sample itself. The advanced technical nature of work at IBM at that time in Suriname could have led to a sample that was not necessarily representative of broader social culture.

It is unlikely that any one model or tool will capture the complexities of culture. In fact, there have been strong criticisms of the oversimplification of cultures through models like Hofstede and GLOBE (Venaik & Brewer, 2016). In practice, as both a researcher and as a leadership development professional, I personally have found the models useful as a starting point, and for this reason I argue that researchers must look across many different resources to analyze the current reality and context they are researching. It is important to note that Haiti is not discussed in this section, because it is an example of a country for which one will not find data in Hofstede Insights, GlobeSmart or GLOBE. Until GLOBE's 2020 research data is published, half of the world's national cultures remain unrepresented by models or databases.

Culture Report Design

Because the culture reports were being produced for leadership development purposes, I felt it was important to begin with an initial discussion of the concept of culture, its practical importance and guidance on how to use cultural knowledge wisely. Readers were encouraged to maintain an open mind to develop new insights that may not be captured in this research, and to look forward to new experiences and new colleagues they would meet along their own journeys.

Each report then included a multifaceted introduction to the society followed by sections on history, the people, social life, the economic environment and the business environment. Many topics were addressed in the introduction to the cultural analysis, including politics, population, geography, climate, languages, travel considerations and unique attributes of the culture. Because history has an enduring influence on culture, each report discussed pre-colonization, colonization and the present-day societies. In the case of Suriname and Haiti, this included the road from colony to independence.

The section on the people presented a discussion of diversity that addressed cultural groups and what is known about dynamics between them. Social life included a discussion of foods, clothing, housing, transportation, music and dance, religions, holidays and celebrations, family life, educational access, work, health and healthcare, communication and media and recreation. There were also some special sections on issues that were particularly pertinent to respective societies, such as the evolution of women's legal rights and roles in Suriname.

The discussion of the economic environment included an overview of the economic climate, including the standard of living. Principle economic activities were profiled along with their relative importance to global business. Given the challenges of both societies with respect to economic and human development, each report discussed the specific challenges including unemployment.

The section on business environment presented information on business customs, such as approach to time and working hours, as well as communication norms. The discussion of management and leadership was the most challenging to complete in both cases, due to limited published information. Much of the information was supplemented through interviews with local natives and also expatriate managers. It included discussions of hierarchy of management, decision-making processes, employment laws, hiring and working with employees, group dynamics and motivating employees. The last topic in this section was on working with the local and national government agencies.

When designing leadership development resources, there is always a balancing act between breadth and depth of information. Coverage must be broad enough to address the scope of exploration, while providing a manageable and relevant depth of information. This is why each report was only about 50 pages in length. It was understood that leaders would be provided more in-depth information in local human resources laws, for example, and that they may choose to do further study on their own. Each report ended with a list of resources for continued exploration. To further engage leaders in using the information, each report was also presented in a video format, allowing leaders to watch an hour-long discussion highlighting and explaining key cultural considerations.

Preparing for Field Research

While I was researching the cultures, I concurrently planned for the future site visits. This included travel arrangements and coordination with the local operations. During field research, time is precious. In both Suriname and Haiti, I only had a week to work with. This was largely due to travel expenses, but also the time the organizations were willing to take employees away from their jobs. Since there were nearly 100 employees in Suriname and more than 200 in Haiti, this required advanced planning, scheduling and communication and coordination with supervisors. The goal for both projects was to interview as many employees as possible. We were successful in speaking to more than 90% of employees through focus groups or individual interviews because of advanced planning and communication, but also flexibility to accommodate employee needs. This last point became quite important as additional insights were gained about the culture in the field.

Field research among cultures began with anthropological studies in the early 1900s that were focused on observation through a colonial lens (Givens, 2008). Early studies have been criticized for the objectification of other cultural traditions. However, field research has evolved philosophically and ethically over time to place emphasis on the protection of and advocacy for research participants. It now crosses disciplines and includes a wide range of methods, largely tied to ethnography (Givens, 2008). I begin with this explanation, because it sets the stage for the design of the field research components of the projects.

I approached field research with some key learnings from cultural scholarship over my career in mind:

- Not all cultural insights apply to all people (Tung, 2008).
- A person's cultural identity depends on his/her individual life experiences (Moore & Barker, 2012).
- Some aspects of identity will be more salient (e.g., more obvious or emphasized) than others, depending upon what is important to an individual (Ting-Toomey, Yee-Jung, Shapiro, Garcia, Wright, & Oetzel, 2000).
- Cultural insights are only a starting point for understanding others (Trompenaars & Hampden-Turner, 2011).

I knew that my initial exploration of these cultures would provide information that confirmed my initial research, as well as information that contradicted it. Each person and situation encountered would be different, and it was important to anticipate that. I was clear that my intention was to be intentional in not promoting stereotypes. Rather, I aimed to provide organizational leaders with an idea of what they might experience or encounter in these particular cultural environments.

Assessing Researcher Fit

An important consideration in any field research is who conducts it. Naturally, as the person who was tapped to do the research, I was interested in being in the field myself. In the case of Suriname I was, which I will discuss later in the chapter. However, I made the difficult but ultimately best decision for research on the ground in Haiti to be conducted by native Haitians.

There were several reasons for selecting native Haitian researchers, including language, trust and safety. The field operation was quite large with several layers of leadership and employees. However, the majority being interviewed were production employees. Preliminary interviews with operation leaders revealed that most of the population spoke limited French, using Haitian Kreyol as their primary language. This would have necessitated a translator, which I was prepared to contract. However, further research indicated that there was often a distrust of foreigners. My interviews with the non-Haitian stakeholders of the research confirmed this. I knew that trust would be key to opening conversation with participants. Negative bias going in would make participants uncomfortable, require additional time, and therefore expense, and could ultimately jeopardize the research. Furthermore, reported kidnappings of foreigners were on the rise, namely for ransom.

Given the importance of trust, language and the safety of everyone involved in the study, I decided to partner with experienced consultants who were originally from Haiti. My preliminary research proved valuable in this regard, by helping me locate qualified individuals via my professional connections on Linkedin. I would remain the project lead, coordinating the overall design and implementation of the study in partnership with my new colleagues.

Research in Suriname

Once the cultural reports were complete, I moved to field research. However, I press pause here in the chapter to introduce readers to a brief overview of the country and people of Suriname. Because a foundational cultural understanding is important prior to engaging in field research, this section will introduce readers to the cultural context for the research. The information in this section is drawn from Business and Society in Suriname (Walker, 2014).

Introduction to Surinamese Culture

Republiek Suriname (Republic of Suriname) is a very small country on the northern coast of South America. The population is 541,638 (2012 census), with about half living in the capital Paramaribo. It has been an independent nation since 1975. Previously it was Dutch Guiana, a colony of The Netherlands. To understand current society in Suriname requires an understanding of the history. Even though colonization began almost 400 years ago, by the Spanish, English and then the Dutch, its effects remain hard to ignore. Years of colonization shaped the economy and society and its ongoing trajectory.

Modern society in Suriname was principally influenced by Dutch occupation that lasted from 1667 until 1975. They wanted Suriname for its high agricultural productivity and wealth. Intensive labor was needed to run these plantations, however, and the population of the country was quite small. The Dutch first captured and transported African slaves as their principle labor force, followed by contracted Asian laborers from China, India and Indonesia. Because these labor forces were so large relative to the population in the country, distinct enclaves developed in society. Surinamese society is extremely diverse, due to these hundreds of years of importation of slave and indentured labor by the Dutch.

The population is small due to a slow growth rate (less than 2%) and a mass exodus from the country during transfer of power from the Netherlands to an independent Surinamese republic in 1975. All citizens were given the choice to remain Dutch or become Surinamese nationals. Many of the people who were well educated and had resources, largely of European and Creole descent, emigrated to the Netherlands, literally abandoning houses and businesses. There are now almost as many Surinamese living in the Netherlands than in all of Suriname. While the transition to independence was peaceful, Suriname has experienced political and economic turmoil ever since.

While the government is a constitutional democracy, Suriname is plagued by corruption in government and the judiciary. The U.S. Bureau of Economic and Business Affairs reported in 2012 that the areas of government most affected by corruption are in procurement, land policy, taxation and license issuance. Suriname was ranked 88 out of 176 countries surveyed in Transparency International's 2012 Corruptions Perception Index. The judiciary suffers from corruption through political influence. Organized crime, mostly in drug and human trafficking, and police brutality are also concerns. An example of corruption concerns that made international news was a law that passed in 2012 that gave amnesty to the then current president and his former military colleagues accused of torturing and murdering 15 political opponents in public in 1982. The Netherlands responded by withdrawing aid funds for a short time. In 2020, when the president was ousted in the election, he did end up being criminally charged and sentenced to a lengthy prison term.

Language is perhaps one of the most complex aspects of the Surinamese social mosaic. Suriname is the only Dutch speaking country in South America. Dutch is the official language, and it has a slightly unique dialect in Suriname compared to the Netherlands. However, the local language, Sranan Tongo, is most commonly spoken. Sranan Tongo is a blend of African languages, English, Portuguese, and Dutch. Each ethnic group tends to use its own language within the group, but Sranan Tongo is a unifying language used by many ethnic groups to communicate with one another. There are three Asian languages spoken – Sarnami Hindi, Surinamese Javanese and Hakka Chinese; two Maroon languages – Auka and Saramaka; and several Ameridian languages including Arawak, Akurio, Carib, Trio, Warao and Wayana. There is some degree of English spoken and understood, since English is widespread in popular media and is a required language class in secondary school. An influx of Brazilian immigrants has increased the prevalence of Portuguese, as well. There are media outlets in Dutch, English and Sranan Tongo, and sign postings can be seen in all these languages as well as in Hindi and Portuguese. Code switching between groups about which language to use happens through high-context social cues.

Even though Sranan Tongo is most commonly used in daily life and there is a developing body of literature and music in it, efforts to make it the national language have failed to gain widespread support. This is because Surinamese take pride in their linguistic diversity and strong ties remain to countries of origin and ethnic groups. Social tensions have arisen over the question of language for both political and practical reasons. The continued use of Dutch, for example, is problematic, due to its link to colonial history and the fact that it continues to be the language of educational instruction among populations that do not commonly speak it in their communities. Dutch is particularly problematic for populations in lower socio-economic strata, where the inability to speak or read Dutch precludes them from formal education or basic services, such as the ability to apply for a driver's license.

Despite the problematic state of government and organized crime in Suriname, it is important to note that daily life, especially in the main towns, is relatively peaceful and people are quite friendly overall. The diverse mix of people creates a unique atmosphere ripe with opportunities to meet interesting people and experience a wealth of cultural treasures in music, food and artesian crafts. Citizens take great pride in their nation's cultural diversity and tolerance. Tolerance is an important word to describe the social culture, because while there is little open conflict, society is really a juxtaposition of many small groups that tend to socialize among themselves. Most citizens are proud to be Surinamese in nationality as well as actively preserving and practicing their specific ethnic cultures. As a result, there is less emphasis on Creolization – the blending of cultural groups – in Suriname compared to other countries in the Caribbean region. One explanation for the low degree of ethnic conflict is that there is no one majority, creating a society with less polarization. Hindustani and Maroon populations are relatively equal in size, for example. While Creole and Javanese populations are comparatively smaller in size, they do have active participation in politics, government and social life.

Instead of focusing on a unifying nationalism, Suriname has embraced a dominant plural ideology. Attempts by the Dutch to assimilate all ethnic groups through Dutch language, laws and customs proved difficult, especially with Javanese and Hindustanis. Around 1930, the Dutch began recognizing Asian cultural traditions, such as marriage practices. After independence, Suriname leaders once again began promoting an integrated Surinamese identity, but it lost support when the military regime associated with it began committing human rights abuses to disempower rival political groups. Today, all ethnic groups have representative leaders in government, including the indigenous groups. Personal identity and social life is closely tied with ethnicity in Suriname.

The ethnic groups are not just distinct, they remain culturally intact through ongoing use of their languages and customs. They also organize as such, in distinct communities, social and political groups. This organization may be helpful for the purposes of within group protection and representation of the groups' interests in society. For example, my research and interviews revealed that loyalty to one's ethnic group often trumped organizational hierarchy. That is, if a person was in a leadership role, their loyalty and protection of their employees within their ethnic group might be stronger than for other groups. Within group protection did not dissipate through organizational status. There is some evidence that this organization by ethnic group was shifting somewhat in younger generations, as my interviews revealed greater social mixing between young people.

Few foreigners do business in Suriname, so those visiting the country for the first time should anticipate that locals may show curiosity, asking many questions, or be particularly guarded until they known more about them. Businesses entering the market for the first time may want to consider hiring a reputable, well-connected agent or distributor to help them navigate local laws and cultural practices. The business community in Suriname is small and close-knit, so a local will have an easier time helping a business integrate successfully. Also, logistics may be difficult due to limited infrastructure and extreme weather patterns. A local professional will know how to navigate these issues or at least help prepare their business partners for what to expect.

Field Research in Suriname

After months of research and interviews, I believed that I was well prepared for the in-country research. However, my arrival in Suriname taught me an important lesson in staying up-to-the-moment on current events. I had been so focused on "wrapping up" my research pre-travel, that I hadn't been looking for daily news coming out of the country.

When I arrived in Suriname the first time, I was the first off the airplane, but the last to leave the airport. The security team made a point of searching all my belongings, asking many questions and detaining me for a long period for no apparent reason. While I cannot be sure of the motives, one of my local contacts shared with me later that there was some resentment toward the U.S.A. by Surinamese nationals in support of then President Bouterse. His son had recently been arrested by the U.S. Drug Enforcement Agency and then sentenced to 16 years in prison for criminal activities, including drug and weapons charges. It seems that I had found myself in some mild political crossfire. Being aware of this situation would have been helpful to have better understood in real time what may have been happening, especially if the treatment had been more than just a delay and discomfort. This learning became instrumental to better inform my daily research and research design for the Haiti project a year later. When researching a social culture and doing field research or consulting, a daily check of news is important to stay well informed. Since Suriname does not often make international headlines, one must actively seek information through local and regional news sources and targeted searches. After the airport, I'm glad to say that I did not have any other incidents like this.

The scope of research in Suriname was a week-long visit to the operation. It included 4 days of in-depth interviews through a variety of modalities with organizational leaders and employees at all levels. The first day was reserved for a site tour, initial introductions throughout the organization and private interviews with senior leaders. On day two, three large group sessions were held with different shifts to discuss the purpose of the visit, review the employee engagement survey results, and provide an open forum for discussion. Since the employee engagement survey indicated low ratings for the company on communication with employees, the large group sessions were important to organizational leaders to make sure everyone felt included and welcome to discuss questions and concerns openly. However, I knew that the low scores on trust and communication would necessitate more private forums. This is why during the large group sessions, employees were invited to participate in a variety of ways through the week: focus groups, small group discussions, individual meetings in a private office, written feedback or anonymous communication via written feedback or by phone. I provided my business cards to them. Because various languages were involved, I also introduced my translator who would be accompanying me throughout the week. She would translate Dutch, English and Sranan Tongo. Regardless of modality, employees were encouraged to communicate in their language of choice. Between the multi-modal approach and coverage of multiple languages, I felt relatively confident that the research would be successful in engaging employees. However, it became apparent that translation and modality were not the only considerations for participation.

My initial research on Surinamese ethnic groups pointed to unique characteristics of each, namely customs and cultural expressions. But it did not prepare me for cultural preferences when it came to sharing personal and sensitive information. Some people did share information in the large group sessions and focus groups, but I noticed that not everyone came and there were also a number of people who didn't participate. In fact, some of them didn't seem to be mentally present or engaged in the session. There were also few people who signed up for private interview times. After the first day of focus groups, my intuition and experience led me to conclude that my research strategy would need to change if I were going to connect with all employees. I discussed my concerns with organizational leaders and asked that they announce a series of open drop in times in a more secluded area of the operation. The floodgates of feedback opened, as a result, and I came to understand why the group sessions were not entirely fruitful.

Employees had been hesitant, fearful or simply unable to share feedback in the planned sessions. They also did not trust me sufficiently, as an unknown person who was clearly being hosted by the organization, to make individual appointments at first. Hesitance to share was related to social and organizational power dynamics. I had experienced this in other focus group sessions in previous research endeavors, so I understood this. What I didn't fully appreciate is the extraordinarily high risks associated with this in a small, interconnected society like Suriname. Employees shared how saying the wrong thing wouldn't just lead to marginalization or even a lost job, it could impact their families in other areas of their lives. Their fear was, therefore, understandable.

Inability to share was something I had not prepared for at all. During individual interviews, I came to understand why some employees seemed not to be mentally present or engaged. They didn't speak any of the languages being translated. This took some of the research stakeholders by surprise, as well. There had been an assumption that between Dutch and Sranan Tongo that everyone would be included. However, many of the Javanese employees in particular spoke neither. It was a Javanese employee that shared this with me. In fact, he had been sent as an appointed representative of a larger group of Javanese employees to speak on their behalf. At the end of our conversation, he invited me to meet with the larger group. I could tell that he had been sent to make me aware of the language issue, but also to evaluate whether the group would be comfortable sharing information with me.

When we met the next day as a group, I thought that many people would share. However, the same person sat in the middle of the group and communicated a series of points, occasionally looking at different members of the group as if to verify that he had communicated their concerns. At the end of the session, a few individuals communicated a few additional points to their spokesperson, which he translated for me. This particular interview was pivotal in unearthing specific employee engagement issues that were not being communicated and could be addressed. It also led me to ask more questions about communication preferences among different ethnic groups. When asked about Javanese preferences, for example, many people shared the importance of a designated spokesperson. This had not surfaced in my research or pre-interviews. Again, this was a socio-cultural norm that was known but unspoken. I found that there were distinct preferences for some groups based on social culture. Other preferences were influenced by social culture, but were tied more directly to socio-economic status.

Written feedback was option available to all employees. What I did not anticipate, however, is lack of literacy. While my initial cultural research discussed illiteracy as a problem especially outside of the capital city, I did not anticipate that this would be the case among employees at this operation, because my interviews with stakeholders and organizational leaders did not surface the issue. Writing and use of computers was not often required among production employees, so it may not have been a known issue. It was brought to my attention through an individual interview with an employee that I wouldn't likely get much written feedback due to literacy issues. The comment was that this was a shame, because these same people would be unlikely to sign up for an interview time as well. This made the drop-in sessions ultimately quite important. In fact, I converted focus group times to drop-in sessions and employees started coming in waves.

Thanks to the initiative of a few employees from different cultural groups to educate me on their needs, I was able to shift my research strategy and meet them where they needed to be. I was able to interview and collect feedback from nearly all employees, resulting in 44 pages of comments over 12 hours of interviews. The interviews and focus group sessions were very powerful, characterized by strong emotions and detailed stories of their experiences.

I do believe that my express emphasis on protection of their anonymity and evidence of this through the variety of research modalities set an important foundation to establish trust. Ultimately, trust explained much of why the employee engagement surveys were not accurate to begin with. After realizing how prevalent language, literacy and trust issues were, I realized that the employee engagement survey that all employees were required to sit and take couldn't be accurate. The original survey had been in Dutch. The administrator of the survey had flagged the results as having an abnormal skew to "neutral" as a response. The explanation for this was now clear. In the absence of understanding Dutch, employees chose the neutral response clear down the survey. Combine this with the general fear of giving negative feedback in society, and the neutral responses down the survey were likely a protective strategy.

Learnings About Leadership in Suriname

Because there is a heavy undercurrent of politics and corruption in society and businesses in Suriname, it is important to anticipate that Surinamese will be cautious with new people. The largely autocratic leadership style in Suriname leads employees to be risk averse in communications and interactions with others. Managers tend to be overtly direct in their communications with employees, with little explanation or interactive discussion. However, relationship status may soften communication between friends, even if there is power distance by position.

Surinamese leadership tends to be autocratic and patriarchal. So, hierarchy tends to be both respected and leveraged. Centralization is often preferred to maintain the center of power, oversight and control in organizations. An ideal boss in Suriname is a "benevolent autocrat". It is to be expected that he or she is direct and commanding in interactions, but should also show kindness and care to employee needs to some degree.

Because of the autocratic leadership environment, workplace politics tend to foster divide and conquer behaviors for those who want to rise up the ranks or protect their status. Ambitious employees may align themselves with leaders to garner favor or behave in unfair or unjust ways to gain advantage over their peers. There are usually few female executives, administrators or decision-makers in positions of power, making Surinamese business environments largely patriarchal.

Society in Suriname has fostered an environment where people tend to take care of their social groups. For those in power, this may translate into hiring or promoting people within one's social or ethnic group. For the average worker, this usually means sticking together on issues of importance to the group. However, loyalty among friends or allies is paramount and may override most other social rules, like taking care of one's group.

In terms of decision making in business, position matters. Decisions tend to be made from the top down and take time. Workplace politics are active, with people aligning themselves by friendship for protection or by position to receive favor. Since corruption is a long-standing concern in Suriname, leaders are often assumed to be bending rules or giving exceptions to those whom they favor.

Management in Suriname centers on being able to effectively manage groups. Since groups tend to form by ethnicity, it is important for a manager to understand the cultural norms and dynamics among diverse groups. Conflicts are generally resolved by compromise and negotiation within or between groups in the workplace. When dealing with conflicts, it may be helpful for managers to identify formal or informal group leaders to discuss issues privately before opening the discussion to the whole group.

Many Surinamese are used to working with diversity in the workplace. However, social patterns tend to replicate themselves in the workplace, where people socialize mostly with their own groups. Conflict between groups may be subtle, but is still present in the form of stereotypes, prejudices and discriminatory acts in hiring, preferential treatment and discipline. Because Surinamese pride themselves on cultural unity, the word discrimination may be seen as offensive. Subtle acts of discrimination may not be viewed as problematic and, therefore, may require education especially among management. Social class differences, especially in education, are pronounced. For example, while there is a large Hindustani population in Suriname, the traditional Indian caste system is not very active. The more divisive status in this population is socio-economic class, which may determine acceptable people with whom a person socializes, does business and even marries.

In Suriname, work is mostly seen as a means of making a living, not the focus of life. The focus is on personal and family well-being. People value equality, solidarity and fair treatment in their working lives. Incentives such as free time and flexibility are favored. Transparency and fair treatment are imperative to maintain trust. Interviews with Surinamese workers revealed several points to motivate employees:

- Fair and equal treatment
- Transparency and honesty
- Honoring work-life balance
- Social events and celebrations
- Paying well
- Financial incentives
- Professional development opportunities

Working with Surinamese employees requires strong knowledge of and responsiveness to the myriad of local cultural preferences and needs.

- Be sensitive to treating people fairly, equally and with respect always.
- Plan for introductory and ongoing training that may include some basic education.
- Structure staffing with the Surinamese desire for work-life balance in mind.
- Be sensitive when mixing diverse groups of people to proactively manage any tensions or conflicts.
- Be creative in recruitment strategies and benefits, as filling labor-based jobs may be challenging due to a generally negative view of manual labor and the active informal economy making formal work unappealing for some people.
- Plan for multi-lingual communications to engage all groups as needed.
- Offer development opportunities as incentives and for succession planning.
- Honor local events and holidays, and sponsor workplace celebrations and events.

The point of sharing this field research was to highlight reflections and learning I had in the process of performing research in a novel cultural environment, especially one in which little previous study has been done. However, I think it is important to also share the high-level results of this study as well, because leadership research is ultimately done to inform practice.

Translating Research to Practice in Suriname

The findings from the site visit informed a series of recommendations on improving the organizational effectiveness and overall climate at the operation. The foreign national country management team worked with on-site Surinamese leaders to implement several of the recommendations during the remainder of the year, prior to the next employee engagement survey. Within 6 months of the site visit, the employee engagement survey showed a 25.4% improvement in the overall labor environment, with specific improvement in 18 of the 25 survey sub-categories. The overall improvement achieved 93.9% of the organizations' set goal. This was the greatest one-year improvement any of their operations had realized in employee engagement. I attribute this to the importance of cross-cultural understanding. I completed a follow-up site visit the next year, and found that the improvement in work environment and morale among employees was evident.

Research in Haiti

While the focus of the study in Haiti was similar – to research employee engagement – the research design and practice were quite different than in Suriname. The next section will introduce readers to the cultural context for research in Haiti. The information in this section is drawn from Business and Society in Haiti (Walker, 2015).

Introduction to Haitian Culture

The Republic of Haiti is a small nation that is home to more than 10.9 million people. It is located in the Caribbean, sharing the island of Hispaniola with the Dominican Republic. Haiti is the most populous full member-state of the Caribbean Community (CARICOM). It is consistently ranked as the poorest country in the Americas, and has the lowest Human Development Index. While economically poor, the legacy of Haiti as a nation is rich.

Haiti declared its independence from France on January 1, 1804, making it the first post-colonial, independent black-led nation in the world. At this time, it was also the only nation that was independent in Latin America and the Caribbean. It is the only country in the western hemisphere to have defeated three European superpowers: Spain, Britain and France. It is also the only nation in the world that gained its independence through a slave revolt. As a result, Haitians take great pride in their independence as a nation and in their personal freedom. Stories of past Haitian heroes are passed down in local culture and education.

Most Haitians (90%) are descendants, in full or in part, of African slaves who were brought to the island beginning in the 16th century and continuing through the 18th century. This is largely because Haitian blacks and mulattos expelled the French and other Europeans from the country at the time of independence. Only about 5–10% of Haiti's people are of purely European or Middle Eastern descent, and many of these people are descendants of immigrants who came to Haiti during World War I in the early 1900s or when the Arab-Palestinian conflict erupted in the 1940s.

While the overall birth rate in Haiti is high, the growth rate is low at 1% per year. This is due to emigration to other countries, high infant mortality and poor health. Many Haitians live in the United States (e.g., Florida, New York), Canada (e.g., Montreal) and Cuba. For example, Haitian Kreyol is the second most common language spoken in Cuba, due to the more than 300,000 Haitian immigrants who live there. Of course, there are many Haitians living and working in the neighboring Dominican Republic, as well. Since so many Haitians live outside of Haiti, the Haitian diaspora is referred to as the tenth department of Haiti – a reference to the other official departments within the country.

The government is an elected democracy divided into 10 departments, all with local representation. However, ongoing political instability makes it difficult for citizens to trust government or to rely on public services. There have been at least 32 government coups in the 200 years Haiti has been a nation. Voter turnout is generally low overall, but the reasons differ between urban and rural areas. Urban citizens may not vote due to distrust of the political system, while rural citizens may not be accustomed to or informed about voting.

The government is often heavy-handed, and the police force and judiciary suffer from corruption and ineffectiveness. Corruption is common in the public sector and in urban areas, but not as common in the private sector or in rural Haiti. Haitians do not always enjoy free speech, press or assembly, but this has improved since the Duvalier dictatorship that ended in the 1970s. Public protests and riots are common. United Nations Peace Keepers have been present in Haiti since 2004 to facilitate fair elections and to control violent and ongoing clashes between government and opposition groups. Their presence is controversial, however, and sometimes characterized as occupation.

There is a long-standing love-hate relationship between Haiti and the U.S.A., as well, due to a history of occupation. U.S. troops invaded and occupied Haiti between 1915–1934 under the U.S. Monroe Doctrine. There were concerns by President Woodrow Wilson that Haitian alliances with Germany, combined with ongoing political coups and murders in Haiti, threatened U.S. business interests- namely the Haitian American Sugar Corporation. During the 19-year occupation, the United States disbanded the Haitian military, controlled the country with Haitian figure heads, changed the law to allow non-Haitian land ownership, and made significant improvements to infrastructure. There were two citizen rebellions against the United States at this time that both resulted in the deaths of many Haitians by U.S. Marines. As the great depression set in in the United States, resources were precious and the government pulled out its troops in 1934. While it has been nearly a century since occupation ended, the relationship remains tenuous at times. For example, post–natural disaster humanitarian aid has been another source of conflict.

The massive earthquake that devastated the island in 2010 brought in an outpouring of international aid and aid workers. In the decade after the quake, however, many people still live in tent cities, causing concerns about proper allocation of donations. This has added to the distrust of both local and foreign officials. Estimates vary widely, but somewhere between 1 to 3 million people were affected by the 7.0 magnitude earthquake, and more than 100,000 (some estimates say up to 300,000) people were killed. International aid organizations have had an ongoing presence in Haiti to provide basic services. Additionally, many orphanages and adoption agencies have been established to care for children who were left without families or whose families could no longer take care of them.

Because the income gap in Haiti is extreme, social life, work and worldview are strongly influenced by social class. Social class refers to a person's wealth and status in society, which impacts access to resources, such as education, work, and basic needs. Like many modern societies, there are class divides between rural and urban residents and working class and professional Haitians. However, these divides can be more extreme in Haiti, where access to basic resources like clean water, housing, and trash collection are luxuries that the majority of residents (as many as 80%) do not have. There are often physical distinctions among the upper and lower classes as well, where light skin and straight hair are associated with a higher class status. Language is also a marker for social class.

The official languages of Haiti are Haitian Creole (Kreyol) and French. While most citizens use Haitian Kreyol in daily conversation, French is often used in government and business. This is because French remained the language of government and of power generally throughout society, even after independence. However, language is a complex and sensitive issue in Haiti, because it is tied to both education and social class. French is typically only used by those with education beyond primary school (i.e., elites and middle class) and many Haitians do not have access to higher education. Because French appears to have more prestige than Kreyol, especially in the workplace, many Haitians identify themselves as French speakers when they are not truly fluent in the language. At the same time, those who are not fluent in French may be offended if a conversation begins in Haitian Kreyol, believing that others perceive them as lacking education or social refinement. Offering communications in both languages is important to reach everyone and ensure understanding.

Haitians are the largest creole language speaking community in the world. Kreyol is a blend of French, Taino, English, Spanish and various African languages. It is traditionally an oral language, but does have a written form that has gained popularity since the 1940s when literacy programs were introduced in Haiti. While it has similarity to creole languages spoken on Guadeloupe and Martinique, Haitian Kreyol has a distinct variation. Spanish may be prevalent along the border with Dominican Republic. English is a common second language with varying degrees of fluency.

In Haitian culture, oral forms of communication are still preferred over written. For example, radio broadcasts in Haitian Kreyol are the most important media in the country. There are several hundred stations. Word of mouth remains important in spreading news and information throughout communities. Even in private communications, sending audiotapes rather than letters may be favored. Written communication itself is challenge for many due to illiteracy. Some argue that there is also a remaining fear in society about writing information that may be used against the writer or the community, due to former dictatorships and a long history of government oppression and brutality. Oral communication is also quite important for the Haitian diaspora throughout the world, where Haitian radio stations within cities like New York, Boston and Miami relay information coming out of Haiti for those living abroad. Television is a luxury in Haiti, but there are some local channels.

Haitian people are known to be warm and personable in their interactions, and tend to be family-oriented. Hospitality and generosity are important and common features of Haitian society, especially within social groups but also in lending a hand to others in the community. Haitians value self- and artistic-expression. People find it important to express their opinions and feelings, and this is visually evident in the widespread artistic expression through music, painting, dance and crafts. It shows up in even mundane daily necessities, like transportation where buses and taxis are colorfully decorated.

Diversity issues among Haitians center on social class and "colorism". "Colorism" refers to the distinction between lighter and darker skin colors, where lighter skin and straighter hair is often given preferential treatment in society and business. There is a strong historical link between skin color and social class that still exists today, making it an important diversity issue to be aware of. Social class in Haiti is determined by many interrelated factors, such as:

- *Income*
- *Social connections*
- *Educational access/achievement*
- *Skin color/tone*
- *Land/property ownership*
- *Place of residence (urban vs. rural)*

There are four notable class divides that have variations within them as well. They are the rural working class, urban working class, urban middle class and elites.

Opportunities for work are largely tied to geography and social class in Haiti. This is rooted in history. Prior to the Haitian Revolution, plantations were the principle source of wealth for the elite. After the revolution, common people were parceled out land and the elites focused on government and administrative work. Today, about 1/3 of Haitians still work in small subsistence farms throughout rural Haiti. Some of these farmers do sell their products in local markets, most popularly through traveling saleswomen called Madam Sara.

The business culture in Haiti tends to follow a relaxed, Caribbean style where schedules and time frames tend to be loose. There is often a preference to establish personal relationship before discussing business. Personal connections are particularly influential in getting things done. Doing business in Haiti is best done with the help of reputable, well-connected agents which are sometimes called "fixers". This is because much of the economy is informal, requiring local knowledge of laws, business practices, services and infrastructure. Political instability, corruption and social unrest also require special understanding of how to reduce potential problems.

Field Research in Haiti

The scope of research in Haiti was also a one week-long visit to the operation. The first day included a site tour, initial introductions throughout the organization, and private interviews with senior leaders. The operation was twice the size of the one in Suriname, so the research design was centered on focus groups to allow the researchers to involve everyone. We were hopeful that that the combination of shared culture and languages between the researchers and the participants and the researchers' status as external consultants (i.e., not directly in the organizational hierarchy) would help participants feel comfortable sharing. Ultimately, it did, with more than 90% participation in 15 focus groups.

The number of focus groups required a great deal of advanced coordination with the human resources department and managers to account for everyone in the scheduling, especially because the formation of focus groups required attention to position and shared socio-cultural characteristics, such as language and social class. Both were exceptionally sensitive issues that were known to be divisive in society and the workplace itself. So, it was of critical importance that the focus groups be carefully constructed.

Focus groups were formed based on similar positions. My co-researchers and I knew that mixing hierarchies of power would jeopardize authentic sharing of information in a group setting, even if the groups were small. Based on the researchers' intimate knowledge of the culture and our research within the organization itself, there was reasonable certainty that employees in similar positions would have similar socio-economic status, education level and language needs. This ended up being the case for most employees. There were a few cases where employees did switch to another group. Some of this was based on personal preference and/or social dynamics within groups. Simply said, some people prefer to share information among friends. Employees also were provided with options for personal interviews and anonymous written feedback, although few chose these options.

There was a marked difference in the reception to focus groups in Haiti compared to Suriname. Our analysis was that the shared culture and language of the researchers was helpful in gaining trust more quickly. There were fewer cultural obstacles to navigate, since no translation was needed and high context social cues were immediately understood. However, the Haitian socio-cultural context also made the focus groups more effective. There was a commonly shared ethnic culture within focus groups in Haiti. Divisions and dissention between social classes was pronounced, as our research said it would be. The markers for social class that were identified in research also held true – language use, education and employment (i.e., job level and salary). However, the shared ethnic culture with fewer representative languages was easier to navigate in the research process. The careful design of the focus group compositions was ultimately instrumental in ensuring open and authentic communication.

The findings from the site visit informed a series of recommendations on improving the organizational effectiveness and overall climate at the operation. The foreign national country management team worked with on-site Haitian leaders to implement several of the recommendations and were successful in making improvements to work environment and employee morale.

Learnings About Leadership in Haiti

Haiti's political and economic history have created a business environment where management and leadership are not well defined. Revered leaders from the past are largely revolutionaries who rallied people against a common enemy. In modern times, with more than 32 coups in 200 years and several oppressive dictatorships, it is difficult for Haitians to agree on what effective leadership looks like *within* the Haitian community. What is abundantly clear in interviews and research, is that there is a strong desire for mutual respect, collaboration and inclusion between managers and employees. In the absence of accepted cultural norms for leadership and professional development in this area, organizational cultures are largely influenced by the individual personalities and preferences of local owners and managers. It is strongly advised that organizations implement inclusive and culturally sensitive management and leadership training to create a positive organizational culture rather than allowing individuals or the business environment determine that culture.

Structurally, it is common for organizations to have a simple hierarchy of a director or owner who has assistants or supervisors working directly for him/her and with a layer of workers below. Since corruption is widespread, Haitians will be cautious in trusting managers or leaders at any level until they have a personal relationship and history established with that person. It is important to establish personal and genuine relationships with people to gain their trust and engagement in the workplace.

Group work in Haiti is important but sometimes contradictory in nature. On one hand, group work is necessary and mutually beneficial to accomplish goals. For example, on one day a whole community may help a single farmer harvest his crops. The next day, the same group may help a different farmer build a new farmhouse. Communal sharing of work is known as "konbit". When a task is defined as one that is shared by all, it is much easier to find people who are willing to work. However, group work is also perceived as problematic at times. There is a Haitian saying "Ayisyen se krab", which translates to "Haitians are crabs". This refers to what happens when crabs are in a bucket – when tries to escape, the others pull it back down. The idea that people will pull each other down can make Haitians very sensitive to who is contributing their fair share of work and also to who may be holding them back from career growth and success. There can be resentments in groups where one person or a few receive recognition, additional privileges or advancement. This is because limited resources and opportunities in Haiti can create a sense of competition.

It is important that recognitions, privileges and advancement be transparent and possible to attain for others. Each member of the group should clearly understand what is required to excel and behaviors/deliverables should be rewarded fairly and consistently. Workloads should also be carefully managed to ensure that workers feel each person is contributing their "fair share". Favoritism, whether real or perceived, is very destructive to teamwork in Haiti.

Discussing or pointing out issues of diversity in terms of disability or sexuality may cause great discomfort in groups. It is rare for people in Haiti to discuss disabilities, whether acquired or lifelong. Disabilities may be viewed as mysterious and even dangerous, brought as a punishment to a person from the supernatural world rather than being a medical issue. This belief is especially common among the working class. There may be aversion to working with someone with a visible disability, as there may be fear of contracting not just the disability but also the "curse" itself. People with disabilities in Haiti are largely isolated from society and work. On the topic of sexuality, while there are some organizations in Haiti that advocate for equal treatment of gays and lesbians, people who do not identify as heterosexual continue to be marginalized and even actively discriminated against.

In Haiti, work is mostly seen as a means of making a living, not the focus of life. The focus is on personal and family well-being. People value equality, solidarity and fair treatment in their working lives. They feel valued when they are included in decision making. While transparency and fair treatment are imperative to maintain trust. Incentives such as free time, flexibility and career development are favored. Interviews with Haitian workers revealed several points to motivate employees:

- Empathetic and respectful managers
- Inclusion in decision process
- Being informed
- Transparency and honesty
- Honoring work-life balance
- Social events and celebrations
- Paying well and on time
- Fair and equal treatment, including workload
- Recognition, such as awards, financial incentives or paid vacation
- Professional development opportunities

Working with Haitian employees requires strong knowledge of and responsiveness to local culture. Effective leadership behaviors and actions include:

- Treat people fairly, equally, and with respect always.
- Keep employees informed and be transparent.
- Communicate in both Haitian Kreyol and French to engage all.
- Involve employees in decision making as possible.
- Form genuine and trusting relationships with employees.
- Provide ongoing training, including some basic education.
- Structure staffing with desire for work-life balance in mind.
- Offer development opportunities as incentives and for succession planning.
- Honor local events and holidays, and sponsor workplace celebrations and events.

Lessons Learned Across Studies

Throughout this chapter, I have shared the learnings I had along the way in researching "uncharted territories" in terms of culture and leadership studies. In the process of completing these studies, I learned valuable lessons about the wide scope of research needed for lesser explored cultural environments, including the importance of pre-trip interviews, assessing researcher fit and the preparation needed for successful field interviews. As I said early in this chapter, history has a long memory. I find it to be instrumental to understanding modern day societies. To those embarking on research of a lesser understood social culture, I recommend a scope that includes a long view of history and current events, along with government, politics, economy and popular culture. Narratives, such as those found in fiction, poetry and music, can be quite informative to understand the daily joys and challenges of life within the culture. It is also helpful to gather both "insider" and "outsider" perspectives through interviews. People within a culture are often too close to it to see its unique characteristics, or they may not have experience in other cultures to note the differences.

A researcher must also understand how their own national culture is perceived in the society where they will perform research. Communication and trust-building are important in any cross-cultural interactions, but when there is a pre-existing negative perception these take on heightened importance. Collaboration with native researchers and local experts is helpful, regardless. It may sometimes be necessary, however, for research to proceed smoothly.

When gathering data among diverse sub-groups within societies, a multifaceted data collection approach is helpful. Alternative options for commentary and interview location are important for wide participation. The researcher must also be on the lookout for what is not being communicated, as that may become just as important (or more so!) than what is being shared. Staying curious, open-minded and flexible to modify approaches for the needs of the sample is imperative to build trust and gather data.

When embarking on international leadership research in these studies, perhaps my most striking realization was that there is much about cultures and leadership in the world that we do not yet know. Even when written information exists, there are many known but unspoken and unpublished characteristics of culture that we must learn about. Furthermore, the slow but evolving nature of societies necessitates that we periodically reexamine culture and leadership, especially when there are dramatic socio-cultural shifts. The field of international leadership research remains rich with opportunity for researchers.

References

Alon, I., & Higgins, J. M. (2005). Global leadership success through emotional and cultural intelligences. *Business Horizons, 48*(6), 501–512.

Aperian Global. (2021). GlobeSmart Work Style Profile. https://www.globesmart.com/features/work-style-profile/

Bird, A., & Stevens, M. J. (2013). Assessing global leadership competencies. *Global Leadership: Research, Practice, and Development, 2*, 113–139.

Fang, T. (2005). From "onion" to "ocean": Paradox and change in national cultures. *International Studies of Management & Organization, 35*(4), 71–90.

Given, L. M. (Ed.). (2008). *The Sage encyclopedia of qualitative research methods.* Sage publications.

GLOBE Project. (2021). GLOBE 2020. https://globeproject.com/

Hardingham-Gill, T. (July 2020). *What it's like to visit a country that doesn't officially exist.* CNN. https://www.cnn.com/travel/article/visit-country-that-doesnt-exist/index.html

Hofstede Insights. (2021). *Compare countries.* https://www.hofstede-insights.com/product/compare-countries/

Hofstede, G., Hofstede, G. J., & Minkov, M. (2010). *Cultures and organizations: Software of the mind* (Vol. 3). McGraw-Hill.

House, R. J., Hanges, P. J., Javidan, M., Dorfman, P. W., & Gupta, V. (Eds.). (2004). *Culture, leadership, and organizations: The GLOBE study of 62 societies.* Sage publications.

Lindsay, S. (2000). Culture, mental models, and national prosperity. *Culture matters: How values shape human progress* (pp. 282–295). Basic Books.

Minkov, M., & Kaasa, A. (2020). A test of 'Hofstede's model of culture following his own approach. *Cross Cultural & Strategic Management.* doi:10.1177/10693971211014468

Moore, A. M., & Barker, G. G. (2012). Confused or multicultural: Third culture individuals' cultural identity. *International Journal of Intercultural Relations, 36*(4), 553–562.

Nations Online (2021). *Countries and regions of the world from A to Z.* https://www.nationsonline.org/oneworld/countries_of_the_world.htm

Ting-Toomey, S., Yee-Jung, K. K., Shapiro, R. B., Garcia, W., Wright, T. J., & Oetzel, J. G. (2000). Ethnic/cultural identity salience and conflict styles in four US ethnic groups. *International Journal of Intercultural Relations, 24*(1), 47–81.

Trompenaars, F., & Hampden-Turner, C. (2011). *Riding the waves of culture: Understanding diversity in global business.* Nicholas Brealey International.

Tung, R. L. (2008). The cross-cultural research imperative: The need to balance cross-national and intra-national diversity. *Journal of International Business Studies, 39*(1), 41–46.

Uhl-Bien, M. (2011). Relational leadership theory: Exploring the social processes of leadership and organizing. In *Leadership, gender, and organization* (pp. 75–108). Springer.

Venaik, S., & Brewer, P. (2016). National culture dimensions: The perpetuation of cultural ignorance. *Management Learning, 47*(5), 563–589.

Walker, J. L. (2014). *Society and business environment in suriname.* Najafi Global Mindset Institute.

Walker, J. L. (2015). *Society and business environment in Haiti.* Najafi Global Mindset Institute.

Wang, H. K., Yen, Y. F., & Tseng, J. F. (2015). Knowledge sharing in knowledge workers: The roles of social exchange theory and the theory of planned behavior. *Innovation, 17*(4), 450–465.

17

The Colonization of Cross-Cultural Leadership and Followership Research

Ariel B. Blair and Wendy Fox-Kirk

Introduction

In many ways, cross-cultural research parallels the wonder and challenge of traveling to different cultures. Both can be characterized by an interest in discovery and challenge. When physically traveling to different cultures, understanding the milieu of the culture provides context for the traveler that helps her engage with people in the culture rather than simply observing it through her own cultural lens. Similarly, as cross-cultural researchers, we must understand the context of our epistemological approaches and how those approaches to understanding culture form a lens embedded within particular cultural foundations. In contrast to the emic and etic debate, which asks which cultural values and norms are appropriate for evaluating phenomena, we discuss challenges to the cultural foundation of cross-cultural leadership theory and research. We argue that this context limits how research is conducted in ways that reflect patterns of epistemic colonialism, defined later.

This chapter grew out of a cross-cultural collaboration analyzing the experience of one of the authors in conducting empirical dissertation research in Jamaica, Thailand and the United States (U.S.), and subsequent research in France and Japan. That research examined whether the followership construct varied across cultures using a survey design that, measured dependent variables minority dissent and employee voice (Blair, 2017). The research highlighted challenges in translation and administering a survey in many countries. We will discuss these challenges and the concomitant lessons learned later in the chapter. Ultimately, the study found that the factor structure of followership varied across countries suggesting that testing hypotheses within countries might be appropriate, but comparing those hypotheses across cultures was not (Blair, 2017).

The Challenge

On their own, each of the lessons learned from the research appears a problem to be solved. Questions around translation of the word followership into different languages, or around collecting data in different cultures, may test a researcher's ingenuity. Those lessons learned, when told individually, could serve as a "how-to" guide to help others planning empirical research across national boundaries. The problem we kept encountering was that many of the recommendations which resulted challenge accepted approaches to empirical research. That led us to step back and ask why it seemed so difficult to do cross-cultural research in a way that felt, well, cross-cultural. Our

DOI: 10.4324/9781003003380-17

backgrounds provided a key to what we propose. We hail from different national cultures, one from a nation that colonized (Great Britain) and one with roots in two that were colonized (Jamaica and the United States). In addition, each author reflects different theoretical disciplines, cross-cultural leadership and critical management approaches to leadership.

We acknowledge that our approach occupies new ground and, as a result, includes assertions not answered in the current literature, and we encourage others to join us in exploring how established academic approaches can limit diverse cultural lenses, thus resulting in what we will describe as the colonization of cross-cultural research.

We use the research process to structure the chapter. The first section outlines the theoretical frame. Next, five sections address challenges in research design, translation, data collection, data interpretation and knowledge dissemination. Finally, we recommend new individual-level and discipline-level directions to help develop more inclusive approaches to cross-cultural leadership research.

Theoretical Framework

Epistemic Dominance

This chapter explores the epistemology of cross-cultural research. Epistemology is best understood as "the rules by which practitioners know what they know" (Cech et al., 2017, p. 744). It refers to the study or science of knowledge. Epistemology includes the examination of the nature of human knowing, claims to knowing, and interrogates the methods or tools related to how we make claims to knowledge.

Before we define the colonization of cross-cultural research, we need to clarify some key terms. Epistemic cultures refer to "those amalgams of arrangements and mechanisms – bonded through affinity, necessity and historical coincidence – which, in a given field, make up *how we know what we know*. Epistemic cultures are cultures that create and warrant knowledge" (Knorr-Cetina, 2009, p. 1).

Epistemic dominance results when one way of knowing is presented as better than other ways of knowing. Prior to the Renaissance, for instance, religious ways of knowing comprised the dominant epistemic culture. Today, scientific objectivism dominates the social sciences, including the management and leadership literature (Collinson, 2014). Next, we discuss the concentration of leadership theory development in certain cultural regions which may lead to epistemic cultural dominance.

Cultural Concentration of Theory Making

Historically, the largest concentration of organizational theory originates in two of the nine world regions defined by values rather than by geographic location, "English speaking" and "Protestant Europe" (ESPE). The dimensions that drive the regional grouping are traditional versus secular-rational values on one axis, and survival versus self-expression values on the other axis (Inglehart & Welzel, 2010). The culture-based view of the world proposed by Inglehart and Welzel allows us to recognize the concentration of similar cultural-values-based perspectives to organizational theory. Using this view, we see that the norms by which we operate come from cultures high in secular rational and self-expression values.

This handbook confirms that interest is growing for researchers exploring cultural differences in leadership and followership. Although a relatively small number of researchers from regions outside of ESPE are developing leadership and followership theories, most empirical research in this field applies theories that originate in a narrow range of cultures that utilize scientific objectivism as the dominant approach to research (Fairhurst & Grant, 2010; Collinson, 2014; Gantman et al., 2015).

Objectivist Approaches

The idea of taking an objective stance in research rather than a subjective one seems to make sense. If research is to make claims of epistemic authority, then it follows that all subjectivity (for example, personal biases) should be removed. However, this view has long been criticized along several lines (Cunningham, 1973). One major concern is whether humans can ever truly be objective (Rorty, 1998).

A recognition that humans are subjective is why common scientific methods aim to insert objectivity through processes like double-blind designs, control of potentially confounding variables and replication of studies. Many thus maintain that scientific objectivity can be achieved with the appropriate use of rigorous tools. This process will then lead to the uncovering of general underlying laws; this is known as universality. Yet this idea is based on the foundational assumption that a neutral world exists out there, whether humans are there or not. This view makes sense when we consider the law of gravity, for example. Gravity was there before it was discovered; put another way, Isaac Newton did not create it! However, when we look at social phenomena, the scientific approach to objectivity breaks down. Think about marriage. It is socially constructed and differs in meaning across historical time, and cultures. In this case, the search for universal, underlying laws is not sufficient if we want to understand more about marriage.

Building a body of robust knowledge must include gathering data on local practices while ensuring that the sensemaking of those practices comes from local knowledge. Based on these limitations of an objectivist approach, we question to what extent mainstream leadership and followership theories are valid across all cultures, given that they originate from limited cultural perspectives. We argue that a social-constructionist approach to leadership and followership, although not perfect, allows inclusion of differing cultural lenses. The social-constructionist approach views these concepts not as objective and undisputed, but as socially constructed. This view does not consider that either leadership or followership can be fixed, universal phenomena (Grint, 2005; Uhl-Bien & Pillai, 2007). In addition, taking a step beyond theoretical approaches, we suggest that assumptions and practices in conducting research and interpreting the results privilege certain cultures over others; in other words, they provide evidence of the colonization of cross-cultural research. As stated earlier, however, scientific objectivism is often a poor methodological fit for studying social constructs because researchers often treat the phenomena under scrutiny as though they are free from the influences of power, politics and other subjectivities (Alvesson & Sveningsson, 2012).

Cultural Colonization

Using these concepts, and building on Kerr (2014), we define the colonization of cross-cultural research as the process of epistemic cultural dominance, whereby the scientific hierarchy created by colonialism presents objectivist methodologies as the "ideal". Turning from the general to the specific, the way knowledge is created in the leadership field privileges methodologies that come out of a limited cultural framework over methodologies that arise from other cultural frameworks. As stated earlier, scholars developing leadership theory and research methods overwhelmingly come from, or are educated in, cultures that prioritize secular rational and self-expression values. As a result, those values have become the "ideal" against which cross-cultural research is measured.

In order to understand the colonization of cross-cultural research, it is necessary to return to basic concepts. For example, the phenomenon one researches is linked to how one researches it. If one seeks to measure productivity in a manufacturing plant, then an objectivist approach will lead to quantifying the level of productivity in different units – this becomes a "how much" question. However, if productivity is particularly low in one of the units, research may focus on a "why" question; now one is not measuring a known variable but trying to create an explanation for the phenomenon. For the latter case, a qualitative approach is more appropriate. This basic principle is sometimes forgotten or ignored (Johnson & Duberley, 2000). It is important to clarify the distinction between method and methodology. Methods are the tools used to conduct data gathering, whereas methodology is the research strategy. Objectivist methodologies can use both quantitative and qualitative methods (Silverman, 2016). When we talk about a qualitative approach or methodology, we are talking about a strategy that focuses on understanding why a phenomenon is the way it is within a particular context. The dominant approach to research can become the only way to research. This is problematic because using an ill-fitting approach can lead to poor explanations and incorrect or partial theory (Johnson & Duberley, 2000). At worst, it can reproduce existing power inequalities (Cech et al., 2017).

Examples of two different ways of researching will help elucidate these concepts. In the first case, imagine that you would like to research the incidence and spread of a disease across different countries. The dominant objectivist approach will likely garner useful data and lead to powerful explanations and theory. This approach works here because the phenomenon, the disease, is identifiable and measurable. A test for a disease works in the same way in all countries. As a researcher, you can be certain that the disease is present if the test is positive, which makes the comparison of incidence and spread meaningful. The aim of the research is to identify differences between countries, and the differences identified can help with disease management. For example, water conditions might be a key variable linked to increased spread in some countries. Knowing this, we can reduce disease incidence by improving water conditions. Central concepts of objectivist research such as validity, control and generalizability are important in this example, and essential for providing valuable knowledge.

In the second case, imagine researching a social or cultural phenomenon such as leadership. Not only is there no universally agreed test for leadership, but also the way the construct is understood and expressed is embedded within culture and language. As Warren Bennis suggests, "It is safe to assume that leadership and followership, like cuisine, have distinctive flavors from one culture to another" (Bennis, 2007, p. 5). The danger of using an objectivist approach in this case is that, by trying to develop a valid, controllable and generalizable measure of leadership, the researcher overlays their world view. Most published researchers are from cultures that are high in secular rational and self-expression values, which Inglehart and Welzel (2010) call ESPE backgrounds; thus it is likely that the ESPE worldview that prioritizes secular rational and self-expression values dominates. In other words, the claims of objectivity result in a hidden subjectivity (Silverman, 2016). The knowledge produced by this type of research is likely to stifle local differing, cultural ways of knowing leadership. What will occur is a benchmarking of leadership in other cultures against that expressed in the researcher's culture.

The above is an example of epistemic dominance (Knorr-Cetina, 2013; Kerr, 2014). The way we think about things in ESPE cultures becomes the "only" or "best" way to think. Bourdieu (2001) refers to this as false naturalization, or the process through which dominant discourses are unconsciously accepted and internalized. These discourses are considered "natural" or "inevitable" when in fact they are ideologically or socially constructed. In our example, the ESPE way of defining leadership becomes "culture-free", the "natural" way to think about leadership. This hegemonic discourse leaves no recourse to the fact that U.S.-dominated leadership research is shaped by U.S. cultural values. This U.S. subjective view becomes an internalized schema for "ideal leadership" and is presented by U.S.-trained scholars as if it were the only "truth".

Implicit Leadership Theory

Contrast the knowledge produced from this research to the disease research. How useful is it to know that leadership in other countries is not "ideal leadership"? The worry is that other ways of doing leadership and followership are likely to be positioned as not optimal, or ineffective. This imposition of "ideal leadership" is a form of leader and follower prototyping, also known as implicit leadership theory (Lord et al., 1999; Lord et al., 2001; Lord & Hall, 2005) and implicit followership theories (Carsten et al., 2010). Lord and his colleagues, working from an information processing stance, assert that each of us has within our long-term memory store a complex and enduring set of beliefs of expected leadership related characteristics and behaviors. These beliefs constitute what they refer to as the "implicit leadership theory" or "leader prototype" (Lord et al., 1984; Van Knippenberg, 2011).

We develop schema from early childhood that represents an internalization of the dominant societal and cultural views in which the individual is raised (Epitropaki & Martin, 2004). The leader and follower prototypes then act as the guiding schema through which individuals engage with the world; it is through this perceptual filter that we make judgments about leader and follower identities and leader effectiveness. Perceptual filters are utilized to create a match between observed behaviors of individuals and the internal prototype. If there is a mismatch, the individual is less likely to be identified as a "leader" or at least as an effective one. A failure to question the impact of leader and follower prototyping results in academic colonialism, not a genuine search for new knowledge. As Osland and Bird (2000) discuss, the common cultural dimensions of Hofstede (1980) and Hall (1989) are themselves based in a particular cultural schema. Those dimensions originate from comparisons to "western" norms that emerge from western dualism and can result in sophisticated stereotyping (Osland & Bird, 2000). As researchers, our cultural schema informs our work. Thus, cross-cultural research of social phenomena requires different approaches to objectivism.

Why is this important for cross-cultural researchers? These examples demonstrate that, if we are not mindful, we generate impaired knowledge. Put most simply, objectivist approaches may distort our view. Attempts to control potentially confounding variables in empirical research strips away meaning, especially local cultural meanings. Objectivist approaches view language as unproblematic; a word has a clear association with an external object or phenomenon in the real world. There is no room for differing interpretations of words, as highlighted by Wittgenstein (Stern, 1996). For example, the word "wicked" can take on different meanings in different contexts. It often means bad or evil, while in other cultural settings it may mean "good" or "excellent". This is particularly problematic for the phenomena that cross-cultural researchers examine as they are shaped and imbued with linguistic interpretations. Rather than recognizing that lenses exist through which to view the world, there is a tendency for objectivist approaches to dominate the world of management research (Alcadipani & Rosa, 2011).

We argue that social constructionist epistemologies are more appropriate for most cross-cultural research. These approaches rest upon the assumption that all knowledge, including research, is embedded in historical and political social practices. This suitably places knowledge practices within a power relations framework (Foucault, 1982) and combats the epistemic dominance of existing research.

According to Cech et al. (2017), the epistemic dominance of objectivist views has created a monopoly on "truth" claims. Other epistemologies are disadvantaged or delegitimized. In cross-cultural research, this epistemic dominance can result in the marginalization and silencing of voices expressing local ways of knowing (Terman, 2011). More specifically, listening to local interpretations of a phenomenon may be constrained by a need to impose the ESPE worldview. Researchers may try to corral local sensemaking into dominant knowledge frameworks. At another level, the dominance of objectivist approaches can create barriers to publishing for researchers with divergent voices, especially those that emanate from local experiences.

Resource Limitations

To demonstrate how colonialism permeates cross-cultural research, we share examples from research conducted across five countries. Based on propositions suggesting relationships between cultural values and norms, proactive followership and minority dissent (Blair & Bligh, 2018), the empirical research tested whether followership was the same in France, Jamaica, Japan, Thailand and the United States. Those studies highlight challenges with the research process. The researcher was a PhD student who managed the process with a minimal budget of approximately U.S. $5,000. The implications of that budget were that much of the work was done by colleagues who volunteered their help. In several cases, those colleagues managed the translations and back translations done by their graduate students. In the first study, in Jamaica, Thailand and the United States, samples were sourced through academic networks (Blair, 2017). In the second study, panels were purchased from a survey company. The limited budget precluded following the highly structured "best practices" outlined in the Cross Cultural Survey Guidelines (Mohler et al., 2016) used by large international research teams. As an example, the guide recommends two parallel translations that can be compared by a team. This approach is cost prohibitive for many researchers. Large and well-funded teams are yet another example of how epistemic dominance is maintained.

As the sections that follow show, even though research was conducted in different countries, the norms and rules of academia forced assimilation of researchers from different cultural backgrounds, potentially stifling their unique perspectives. Questions arose where there was the "accepted" way (e.g., the objectivist approach) versus what seemed best based on advice from local experts, cultural informants. These cultural informants were all academics, and the majority were educated in the United States or Western Europe. Yet, there were times when their advice on how to approach their home culture was different than the dominant epistemic culture or generally accepted approach of the academy. Translation and back translation is one example of a widely accepted methodological approach that presented issues related to translating gender in Japan and Thailand. We will discuss examples of this cultural colonialism in the following section.

Research Design Challenges

If we look at the research design decisions that face cross-cultural researchers, we gain a better understanding of how the dominant objectivist way of knowing prevails over local ways of knowing. From an academic practice perspective, the issue is one of consistency. Researchers often find it difficult to apply fully consistent methods to control for confounds. Yet cultures are unique and so may require different culturally sensitive approaches. The dilemma then becomes, do we follow objectivist norms of controlling for consistency and ignore cultural differences? Or, as we discuss later in the section on data collection, do we risk creating confounds by honoring the guidance of local partners and being sensitive to cultural norms? In other words, researchers face the predicament of managing ethnocentric research methods versus respecting cultural norms. Below, we discuss specific examples of dilemmas from one research design, recognizing that this is a small sample of a much larger set of possibilities. We use the research process as an organizing framework.

Cultural Limitations of Existing Research

Most research begins with an examination of the current state of knowledge in the field. Often researchers start with the question, "What do we currently know about the issue?" The first point of reference is the current literature in the relevant field. In our field of leadership and followership, the conversation in the literature depends on studies from only a few regions. Schemas from limited cultural perspectives dominate the field. As a result, we tend to measure the same variables based on available scales, even though they are not appropriate to that culture, as was found in the dissent scale (De Dreu & West, 2001). Next, in empirical research, we endeavor to define and operationalize the main concepts of interest. In the case of this research, the main concept was "followership". The question to ask now is, "Does the main concept in my research have a robust agreed definition?" In cross-cultural research it is essential to add a supporting question, "Does this construct differ across cultures?" Objectivist approaches assume that models and constructs are consistent across cultures.

There are questions about the efficacy of widely used cultural values frameworks to predict behavior (Minkov & Blagoev, 2012). Such frameworks include Hofstede (1980) and GLOBE (2004). Instead, there is broad evidence, supported in the two unpublished studies that are the foundation for this chapter, that when measured with these widely accepted values frameworks, within country differences are greater than between country differences (Leung & Morris, (2015) – a finding that again raises the specter of whether these values are simply sophisticated stereotypes (Osland & Bird, 2000). Adding variables beyond cultural values offered a potential improvement over research based solely on values. Accordingly, the study included tightness-looseness norms (Triandis, 1989). Though theoretically grounded, the tightness-looseness scale (Gelfand et al., 2011) did not demonstrate acceptable reliability outside of the United States, resulting in a missed opportunity to evaluate the efficacy of combining norms and values. An equally important design question arose in studying followership.

Followership – An Emerging Construct

Among leadership scholars, the construct of followership is still nascent. From its historical roots as the study of leadership from a follower's perspective, the construct has broadened to include the concept of examining how followers view their role in co-constructing leadership (Uhl-Bien et al., 2013). The leadership relationship is a one-way street where the leaders set the direction and followers do what leaders set forth. This role-based view of leadership puts the follower into a passive role (Uhl-Bien et al., 2013). It is a leader-centric model that continues to dominate much leadership research (Hoption et al., 2015; Fox-Kirk, 2017; Thoroughgood et al., 2018). According to Uhl-Bien and Pillai (2007), "this view romanticizes leadership and subordinates followership" (Uhl-Bien et al., 2013, p. 89). With role-based views, followership is seen as something only followers do. Those in leadership positions do not ever do followership. Research shows that this is incorrect, leaders do often engage in following behaviors (Fairhurst & Hamlett, 2003; Larsson & Lundholm, 2013). Further, role-based views set leadership and followership within a power-based hierarchical structure. This approach reifies norms; behaviors exhibited by those in the formal leader roles are leadership behaviors, while those exhibited by people in the formal follower role, i.e., subordinates, are followers.

Followership – A Social Construct

The construct of followership has expanded to include more proactive views of followers, views where followers envision their role to range from being passive to being active in co-creating leadership. The followership construct that we adopted for the research – a constructionist approach – places followers on a spectrum from passive to being actively involved in co-creating leadership (Uhl-Bien et al., 2013).

Let us ask the question of whether followership differs across cultures. Based on Carsten and Uhl-Bien's (2012) constructionist approach to followership, it was possible that the theory would vary based on cultural values, and might lead to a construct that works across cultural boundaries. In fact, Carsten et al. (2010) acknowledge that their sample is limited to the United States and Canada. They explicitly suggest that followership will vary based on cultural differences such as individualism and collectivism, and power distance. In addition to viewing followers with a broader lens, this construction views followers on a spectrum. That spectrum provides a construct more likely to encompass a range of cultural interpretations of the follower role. For this reason, we chose to use Carsten and Uhl-Bien's (2012) definition of follower co-production beliefs: "the extent to which individuals believe the follower role involves partnering with leaders to advance the mission and achieve optimal levels of productivity" (p. 211). This definition includes a subjective view of the follower role. Due to its constructionist nature, we assume that this construction of followership includes a range of possible schemas around that role. In order to understand how to approach the followership construct, it is necessary to turn to research partners, cultural informants or translators.

Translation

Our local partners, cultural informants or translators know the best way to express the concepts that are being translated into their language and cultural context. We have local partners or cultural informants for a good reason. At times, there is a dilemma, a decision that is not clear because it pits "good research practice" against cultural or language norms. For this research, dilemmas arose in several facets of the research design: how to translate followership, whether or not to use gendered language for the cultural values scale and whether to collect data online or on paper.

As discussed in the section on resource limitations, the most current "best practices" of having teams compare parallel translations (Mohler et al., 2016) is likely not an options for studies with limited resources. As a result, the researcher chose to use translation and back translation (Brislin, 1970), a widely accepted process of translation for this type of research. The idea, straightforward enough at first glance, is to translate the text into the target language and then have a different person translate the first translation back into the original text. The wrinkles that one might not expect include the need to repeat this process several times to ensure that the translation accurately reflects the same ideas in both languages. Local partners who can assist with the process of refining the final text help immeasurably. The translation process is costly and time consuming, privileging researchers who have greater access to resources.

In addition to translation, control of language is one of the pillars in the colonization of research. Those who create new theory also define the language used to describe that theory. As a result, the language of the theory creator becomes the language of the theory. The central role of English can create challenges that arise from word choice issues. As an example, languages define the word "followership" differently which presents a layer of complexity. In some languages, finding a word for followership proved difficult. For example, Japanese does not have a word for followership. So this led to the question of whether to use a phonetic spelling of the word using characters that are used to write foreign words (Katakana) or if there was a Japanese word (Kanji). Another example of the challenge of translating the construct of followership was in French. Multiple French words that could be used were close but imperfect, e.g., "dirigés" and "suiveur". Each word suggested one of the different followership roles that we were measuring. In other words, one French word suggested a more passive role than another. The senior leadership scholars in France had energetic but differing arguments about which word was best.

The Power of Dominant Instruments

Another difficult translation decision pertained to measuring cultural values using Schwartz's refined values theory (Schwartz et al., 2012). The theoretically based scale was a central part of the research. Some of the 19 sub-scales were a good match for the research focus, supporting or challenging the status quo. As a widely used and accepted scale in cross-cultural research, the scale seemed a safe choice. The scale, which has been used countless times, calls for separate female and male versions. However, local partners in Japan and Thailand advised against specifying gender in the scale translations. Using gendered pronouns was technically correct, but sounded awkward. Their advice directly contradicted the directions for the cultural values scale that specify gendered translation (Schwartz et al., 2012). This situation thus forced the researcher to make a difficult choice between following the dominant approach, which dictates using the form widely accepted in the literature, or the constructionist approach, which honors the wisdom of local partners. This complication not only concerned language; the need for male and female versions caused additional complexity in collecting samples. The accepted method demonstrates how epistemic dominance (Cech et al., 2017) of an objectivist approach can impair the pursuit of knowledge.

Next, we will discuss how culturally appropriate methods challenge the epistemologically dominant approach to the next stage of the research process, data collection.

Collecting Data

Once the research design is complete, and data collection tools are ready, the research can move to the next phase. Project management presents a major challenge for an individual researcher running a study across multiple countries. Several necessary decisions at this stage have implications for the research. Local partners can offer advice. The process of managing the details of multiple data collection efforts is often stressful, again, privileging large and well-funded research teams as was the case with translations.

When collecting data, unanticipated issues often arise that force a change in plans. Such challenges can be more taxing when they occur in different countries, cultures or languages. Differences in technology infrastructure and technology acceptance raised challenges. In our work, for example, an unexpected technology glitch occurred when a professor at Chulalongkorn University in Bangkok, Thailand, asked her students to participate during a class. The students pulled out their phones to take the survey. Though we had tested the survey, the system configurations were different from those we had used in our tests. Sometimes, the survey worked on participants' phones, but many participants were dropped part way through. Finding participants was difficult, and we could not afford to lose many of them to unstable technology.

Given that participants in Jamaica were taking the survey on paper, we decided to shift to paper in Thailand, as well. This created added costs of formatting the survey on paper, printing, distributing and collecting the surveys and finally entering the data. All of those added steps extended the time and budget needed to collect data. The fact that cross-cultural research requires more time and funding than single-nation research privileges researchers with greater access to resources. In general, researchers from universities in ESPE nations have more resources, so the dominance of their views is perpetuated without challenge.

Selecting Participants

Another source of cultural difference in data collection surrounds finding study participants. This speaks to a need to vary the research process across countries. In high-context cultures, we usually need to build relationships to find participants (Hall, 1989; Hall & Hall, 2001). At the University of the West Indies at Mona in Kingston, Jamaica, courses have administrators who manage class operations and determine if, how, and when research can take place. As a result, the course administrators are gatekeepers who hold access to student participants. For a researcher from a different academic system, discovering the existence of the administrators presents the first hurdle. Then come the time-consuming steps of contacting administrators and enlisting them to help with the project. When the research planning takes place in a low-context cultural environment, it is easy to forget how much time and energy are needed for relationship building. Once all of their questions were answered, and a greater level of trust was built, the course administrators proved a valuable resource. But an objectivist perspective assumes that adapting the research process and method to the specific culture reduces control and objectivity. Thus, using these administrators would be considered "bad" research, or at least a device likely to skew research. That highly structured view privileges the cultures in which it was developed and discounts research done in nations with less individualistic and higher context cultures.

Interpreting Data

Interpreting analysis of samples from different nations based on culturally bounded tools poses multiple challenges. Our original research question asked if followership is viewed the same way in different countries. Using the dominant objectivist epistemological approach here required a number of assumptions. First, we assumed study participants interpreted translated terms such as followership the way that was intended. Second, we assumed that samples collected via diverse methods provided sound data. Finally, we assumed that we could employ statistical tools in hopes of gaining insight into the constructs.

The initial assumption posed challenges during data analysis. There were significant problems with scale reliability in critical variables. In some countries, reliability was unacceptably low (i.e., 0.44 for tightness in Thailand and 0.53 for minority dissent in Jamaica), suggesting that random error could account for most of the score variance (Kline, 2011). Was lack of appropriate cultural context possibly a source of error? Was the translation the problem? Or was the construct inappropriate?

Based on the final assumption that statistical tools will facilitate insight, a multigroup, confirmatory factor analysis suggested that the data fit the statistical model differently across countries. The results of this factor analysis, the use of dominant objectivist epistemologies raised the question of whether the regression analyses proposed for hypothesis testing can be justified. Acceptance of the confirmatory factor analysis suggests that testing the hypotheses is meaningless. The finding potentially takes us back to the larger question of whether using theories developed in a narrow cultural context are appropriate for use across a wide range of cultures – or if, instead, their use constitutes epistemic dominance.

The second assumption that data can be collected with different practices leads to the question: how should we manage dilemmas when cultural norms conflict with research methods? A challenge arose for us when cultural informants suggested differing ways of collecting data. In Jamaica and Thailand, paper surveys, distributed through relationships, were most effective. In contrast, data from France and Japan was purchased from panels. Should only well-funded researchers be able to do international studies? Can we determine the extent to which study results have been influenced by using culturally appropriate methods? An objectivist approach questions these culturally responsive methods and possibly delegitimizes their perspectives (Cech et al., 2017).

Disseminating Knowledge

We conclude our tour through the research process by examining how scholars disseminate their work. Significant barriers prevent divergent perspectives from entering the conversation, such as language barriers and competition to gain access to journal space. As a result, divergent voices have been largely absent from the followership conversation.

In terms of dissemination, colonization operates at two levels. First, as stated previously, objectivist epistemologies dominate academia (Zaidi et al., 2016; Cech et al., 2017). It is harder to publish works underpinned by non-dominant epistemologies, especially indigenous epistemologies, which are often seen as inferior. Second, the English language prevails in academic publishing. Going back to the contrast between natural science and social science, the overreliance on objectivist concepts such as universalism and control can suppress local ways of knowing (Matthews, 2012). What results is a privilege for research that supports dominant epistemologies, thereby propping up the status quo. Other ways of knowing can result in questioning existing knowledge bases, and shaking the foundations of the empire is always going to be unpopular. The status quo narrows the channels for researchers with new ways of knowing, especially local and indigenous ones, and even more so for those who have findings that question the current state of the art. Hence, colonialism perpetuates through the whole research process, even at the point of dissemination.

In the end, we offer a cautionary tale, but not an unduly pessimistic one. We like to think these examples will help fuel meaningful discussion around approaches to international leadership research.

Individual-Level Future Research

We offer the following recommendations for leadership researchers, aware that they propose individual-level actions and thus do not address the system-level problems of epistemic dominance. However, there is value in making change at all levels in the field.

1. Take the time to uncover your own biases and place your research in the appropriate onto-logical and epistemological frame. For example, you could use Burrell and Morgan's (1979) paradigmatic model, which uses two dimensions (objectivity or subjectivity, and regulation or radical change) to identify where your personal approach fits. You can use this as a check to ensure that your research question, design, methods and analyses align with that paradigm.
2. Look at literature outside that of leadership and management. Anthropology and sociology offer valuable tools when considering multiple worldviews. Other fields may also have some highly relevant research on your topic.
3. When collecting data, research how to enhance cultural engagement with your chosen research tools, and be prepared to adjust.
4. When making decisions about your main concepts and interpreting the results, involve cultural informants, translators and participants. Expect that there will be more of these conversations than you can remember, and, as a result, keep a reflective account to remind you of your thought process and provide transparency concerning your decisions. Sharing your difficulties will help other researchers to avoid the same issues.
5. If you have difficulty getting published, try journals outside your field, or write a book chapter. You can also consider the careful use of social media, blogs and developing your own website to raise interest in your work. This route can also delegitimize your work, but some researchers have used it to good effect; see the work of Sara Ahmed as an example. Her website, "Feminist Killjoys", publishes material widely cited in academic journals (https://feministkilljoys.com/).
6. Pursuing research that does not fit objectivist methodologies can lead to constant questioning. Make the best decision possible with the available information – and then move on. Record important concerns in your research notebook so that you can remember them over time.

Field-Level Future Research

The colonization we discuss is institutionalized in the field. As a result, meaningful change must take place at the system level. Therefore, to address the colonization of cross-cultural research, we suggest that those leading the field need to develop policy and practice in the following areas.

1. People in the cross-cultural leadership field must reflect on the power dynamics within the field and decide whether the current structure that privileges certain cultures is acceptable.
2. If the practice of privileging a few cultures is not acceptable, then the field must address the question of how to reduce the structural bias in the current approaches. We must look for ways to remove epistemic dominance of certain cultures.
3. We need research methods that allow all researchers – regardless of resources – to participate fully in the conversation.

4. There is a need to develop theories and related measures that are truly cross-cultural. Developing this body of work will require cross-cultural research teams that collaborate to build constructs that embrace varied epistemological approaches, broader ways of knowing. Further, the resulting measures must allow for language differences rather than requiring exact translation.

5. Opportunities for publication need to be inclusive. In much the same way that corporate boards do not reflect the diversity of a society, editorial boards do not reflect the range of cultural perspectives. A systematic change to create culturally diverse editorial boards will lead to strategic changes in the way manuscripts are solicited. Casting a wider net will broaden the cultural range of voices that are published and heard.

Conclusion

Undertaking cross-cultural research is a mammoth task. It requires researchers to consider many more potential obstacles than within-culture research. Learning from those who have gone before you will help relieve some of the burdens of traveling on this journey. Obviously, knowing the details related to research design, methods of sampling, data collection and analysis are of great importance, especially when senior researchers can highlight effective and robust remedies to common problems. In this chapter, we have not only the story of one researcher's experience of doing complex, cross-cultural research but have also shared a deeper learning that emerged through later reflection. We were interested to explore the roots of the tensions between the dominant practices in leadership/followership research and cross-cultural research.

What emerged was a tale of power. First, there is the power to set the agenda of what counts as authoritative knowledge in research. Second, there is the power to steer novice researchers toward common practices and methods without considering that these practices are imbued with a particular worldview – a view from the old empires imposing their values and ways of knowing on others with different values and ways of knowing. What we observed, in short, was the subtle process of epistemic dominance. The outcomes of this dominance are many, including the continued use of research tools that are a poor fit when applied to different cultural contexts. As we have illustrated, these culturally bound tools and processes can exclude valuable and highly relevant knowledge. The result is the playing down of the embedded nature of language "as" culture, the viewing of it as simply a barrier to access culture. What occurs is the stripping away of culture and context, not a deeper understanding of how different cultures create meanings of phenomena of interest.

We cannot learn more about culture by removing it from the phenomenon we are studying. This results in reinforcing the Empire's way of knowing as the "best" or "only" way of knowing. In technical terms, the dominant epistemology is considered the "truth". Other epistemologies, such as indigenous ways of knowing, become "other" or "less than" – merely exotic or peripheral ways of knowing. This is how research is colonized. Cross-cultural research, in contrast, can be thought of as the search to understand others so we can better understand ourselves and our relationships with others. If we truly wish to develop meaningful knowledge frameworks, then change at the individual level is not sufficient. We need change at the discipline level. We hope, with this chapter, we have been able to shine a light on some key areas to expand that change.

References

Alcadipani, R., & Rosa, A. R. (2011). From grobal management to glocal management: Latin American perspectives as a counter-dominant management epistemology. *Canadian Journal of Administrative Sciences/ Revue Canadienne des Sciences de l'Administration*, 28(4), 453–466.

Alvesson, M., & Sveningsson, S. (2012). Un- and repacking leadership: Context, relations, constructions and politics. In S. Ospina & M. Uhl-Bien (Eds.), *Advancing relational leadership theory: A conversation among perspectives.* (pp. 203–206). Information Age Publishing.

Bennis, W. (2007). The challenges of leadership in the modern world: Introduction to the special issue. *American Psychologist, 62*(1), 2.

Blair, B. A. (2017). Cultural influences on followers and follower dissent [ProQuest Information & Learning]. In *Dissertation abstracts international section A: Humanities and social sciences* (Vol. 77, Issue 12–A (E)).

Blair, B. A., & Bligh, M. C., (2018). Looking for leadership in all the wrong places: The impact of culture on proactive followership and follower dissent. *Journal of Social Issues, 74*(1), 129–143.

Bourdieu, P. (2001). *Masculine domination.* Stanford University Press.

Brislin, R. (1970). Back-translation for cross-cultural research. *Journal of Cross-Cultural Psychology, 1,* 185–216.

Burrell, G. and Morgan, G. (1979). *Sociological paradigms and organisational analysis: Elements of the sociology of corporate life.* Heinemann Educational Press

Carsten, M. K., & Uhl-Bien, M. (2012). Follower beliefs in the co-production of leadership: Examining upward communication and the moderating role of context. *Zeitschrift Für Psychologie, 220,* 210–220. doi:10.1027/2151-2604/a000115

Carsten, M. K., Uhl-Bien, M., West, B. J., Patera, J. L., & McGregor, R. (2010). Exploring social constructions of followership: A qualitative study. *The Leadership Quarterly, 21,* 543–562. doi:10.1016/j.leaqua.2010.03.015

Cech, E. A., Metz, A., Smith, J. L. and deVries, K., (2017). Epistemological dominance and social inequality: Experiences of Native American science, engineering, and health students. *Science, Technology, & Human Values, 42*(5), pp. 743–774.

Collinson, D. (2014). Dichotomies, dialectics and dilemmas: New directions for critical leadership studies? *Leadership, 10*(1), 36–55.

Cunningham, F. (1973). *Objectivity in social science.* University of Toronto Press.

De Dreu, C. W., & West, M. A. (2001). Minority dissent and team innovation: The importance of participation in decision making. *Journal of Applied Psychology, 86,* 1191–1201. doi:10.1037/0021-9010.86.6.1191

Epitropaki, O., & Martin, R. (2004). Implicit leadership theories in applied settings: Factor structure, generalizability, and stability over time. *Journal of Applied Psychology, 89*(2), 293.

Fairhurst, G. T., & Hamlett, S. R. (2003). The narrative basis of leader-member exchange. In G. Graen (Ed.), *Dealing with diversity* (pp. 117–144). Information Age.

Fairhurst, G. T., & Grant, D. (2010). The social construction of leadership: A sailing guide. *Management Communications Quarterly 24*(2): 171–210.

Foucault, M. (1982). The subject and power. *Critical Inquiry, 8*(4), 777–795.

Fox-Kirk, W. (2017). Viewing authentic leadership through a Bourdieusian lens: Understanding gender and leadership as social action. *Advances in Developing Human Resources, 19*(4), 439–453.

Gantman, E. R., Yousfi, H., & Alcadipani, R. (2015). Challenging anglo-saxon dominance in management and organizational knowledge. *Revista de Administração de Empresas. Revista de Administração de Empresas.Hoption, 55*(2), 126–129 doi:10.1590/S0034-759020150202

Gelfand, M., Raver, J. L., Nishii, L., Leslie, L. M., Lun, J., Lim, B.,…Yamaguchi, S. (2011). Differences between tight and loose cultures: A 33-nation study. *Science, 332,* 1100–1104. doi:10.1126/science.1197754

Grint, K. (2005). Problems, problems, problems: The social construction of 'leadership'. *Human Relations, 58*(11), 1467–1494.

Hall, E. T. (1989). *Beyond culture.* Anchor.

Hall, E. T., & Hall, M. R. (2001). Key concepts: Underlying structures of culture. In *International HRM: Managing diversity in the workplace* (pp. 24–40). Blackwell.

Hofstede, G. (1980). *'Culture's consequences, international differences in work-related values.* Sage publications.

Hoption, C., Christie, A., & Barling, J. (2015). Submitting to the follower label. *Zeitschrift für Psychologie, 220,* 221–230.

Inglehart, R., & Welzel, C. (2010). Changing mass priorities: The link between modernization and democracy. *Perspectives on Politics, 8,* 551–567. doi:10.1017/S1537592710001258

Johnson, P. and Duberley, J., (2000). *Understanding management research: An introduction to epistemology.* Sage.

Kerr, J. (2014). Western epistemic dominance and colonial structures: Considerations for thought and practice in programs of teacher education. *Decolonization: Indigeneity, Education & Society, 3*(2), 83–104.

Kline, R. B. (2011). *Principles and practice of structural equation modeling* (3rd ed.). Guilford Press.

Knorr-Cetina, K. (2009). *Epistemic cultures: How the sciences make knowledge.* Harvard University Press.

Knorr-Cetina, K. D. (2013). *The manufacture of knowledge: An essay on the constructivist and contextual nature of science.* Elsevier.

Larsson, M., & Lundholm, S. E. (2013). Talking work in a bank: A study of organizing properties of leadership in work interactions. *Human Relations, 66*(8), 1101–1129.

Leung, K., & Morris, M. W. (2015). Values, schemas, and norms in the culture-behavior nexus: A situated dynamics framework. *Journal of International Business Studies, 46*(9), 1028–1050. doi:10/1057/jibs.2014.66

Lord, R. G., Foti, R. J., & De Vader, C. L. (1984). A test of leadership categorization theory: Internal structure, information processing, and leadership perceptions. *Organizational Behavior and Human Performance, 34*(3), 343–378.

Lord, R. G., Brown, D. J., & Freiberg, S. J. (1999). Understanding the dynamics of leadership: The role of follower self-concepts in the leader/follower relationship. *Organizational Behavior and Human Decision Processes, 78*(3), 167–203.

Lord, R. G., Brown, D. J., Harvey, J. L., & Hall, R. J. (2001). Contextual constraints on prototype generation and their multilevel consequences for leadership perceptions. *The Leadership Quarterly, 12*(3), 311–338.

Lord, R. G., & Hall, R. J. (2005). Identity, deep structure and the development of leadership skill. *The Leadership Quarterly, 16*(4), 591–615.

Matthews, G. (2012). Contesting Anglo-American anthropological hegemony in publication. *Journal of Workplace Rights, 16*(3-4), 405.

Minkov, M., & Blagoev, V. (2012). What do Project 'GLOBE's cultural dimensions reflect? An empirical perspective. *Asia Pacific Business Review, 18*(1), 27–43.

Mohler, P., Dorer, J., & Hu, M. (2016). Translation. *Guidelines for best practice in cross-cultural surveys.* Survey Research Center, Institute for Social Research, University of Michigan. Retrieved September 28, 2020 from https://ccsg.isr.umich.edu/

Osland, J. S., & Bird, A. (2000). Beyond sophisticated stereotyping: Cultural sensemaking in context. *Academy of Management Perspectives, 14*(1), 65–77.

Rorty, R. (1998). *Truth and progress: Philosophical papers* (Vol. 3). Cambridge University Press.

Schwartz, S. H., Vecchione, M., Fischer, R., Ramos, A., Demirutku, K., Dirilen-Gumus, O.,…Konty, M. (2012). Refining the theory of basic individual values. *Journal of Personality and Social Psychology, 103*, 663–688. doi:10.1037/a0029393

Silverman, D. (Ed.). (2016). *Qualitative research.* Sage.

Thoroughgood, C. N., Sawyer, K. B., Padilla, A., & Lunsford, L. (2018). Destructive leadership: A critique of leader-centric perspectives and toward a more holistic definition. *Journal of Business Ethics, 151*(3), 627–649.

Stern, D. G. (1996). *Wittgenstein on mind and language.* Oxford University Press on Demand.

Terman, J. (2011). Comparative administration: Ontology and epistemology in cross-cultural research. *Administrative Theory & Praxis, 33*(2), 235–257.

Triandis, H. (1989). The self and social behavior in differing cultural contexts. *Psychological Review, 96*, 506–520.

Uhl-Bien, M., & Pillai, R. (2007). The romance of leadership and the social construction of followership. In *Follower centered perspectives on leadership: A tribute to the memory of James R. Meindl* (pp. 187–209). Inormation Age Publishing.

Uhl-Bien, M., Riggio, R. E., Lowe, K. B., & Carsten, M. K. (2013). Followership theory: A review and research agenda. *The Leadership Quarterly*, doi:10.1016/j.leaqua.2013.11.007

Van Knippenberg, D. (2011). Embodying who we are: Leader group prototypicality and leadership effectiveness. *The Leadership Quarterly, 22*(6), 1078–1091.

Waller, V., Farquharson, K., & Dempsey, D. (2015). *Qualitative social research: Contemporary methods for the digital age.* Sage

Zaidi, Z., Verstegen, D., Naqvi, R., Morahan, P., & Dornan, T. (2016). Gender, religion, and sociopolitical issues in cross-cultural online education. *Advances in Health Sciences Education, 21*(2), 287–301.

18

Social Media and Crowdsourcing for International Leadership Research

Untapped Potential

Gabrielle Blackman

Recently, some leadership researchers have been using social media (e.g., He et al., 2019) and crowdsourcing (e.g., Gerpott et al., 2019) platforms to conduct empirical studies. Social media includes digital platforms that enable people to share information, generate content, interact and work together (McFarland & Ployhart, 2015). In addition to social media, people often organize through crowdsourcing platforms to share ideas and complete tasks online. Crowdsourcing occurs when organizations (or researchers in this case) "outsource" functions to people (crowds) outside of the organization and is often associated with companies soliciting innovative ideas from non-employees (Ghezzi et al., 2018). It may involve recruiting "crowds" to participate in studies using online crowdsourcing platforms (Mason & Suri, 2012). Social media and crowdsourcing platforms connect people virtually, making them valuable research tools. However, few international leadership (IL) researchers have taken advantage of the opportunities they present. One reason may be the lack of discipline-based guidance and best practices for using these platforms in international research contexts.

Scholars in the behavioral sciences (e.g., Hunt & Scheetz, 2019), behavioral accounting (Buchheit et al., 2018), management (Ghezzi et al., 2018), medical sciences (Franz et al., 2019), organizational psychology (Cheung et al., 2017) and social sciences (Kosinski et al., 2015) highlight the strengths, limitations and best practices for applying these platforms to conduct research. However, no discipline-specific guidance exists for IL researchers. This chapter aims to help fill this gap in the literature. It encourages IL researchers to consider using social media or crowdsourcing more often, when appropriate, particularly in the following contexts: research involving crises, hard-to-reach populations, culturally diverse communities, multinational populations and leader online behavior. To illustrate research applications, it includes examples from leadership and IL research, as well as from training and education, psychology, medical and health research contexts. This chapter also encourages IL researchers to empirically examine these platforms' strengths and limitations and establish best practices for applying them in valid, reliable ways to advance the IL field.

Examples of Social Media and Crowdsourcing Platforms

Table A18.1 includes examples of social media platforms. It includes Facebook, LinkedIn, Twitter, Vkontakte, WeChat and WhatsApp. Researchers can create free accounts to join each of these platforms. These platforms provide similar functions. Each includes publicly available content from users, including content from political and business leaders, activists, influencers, experts and others

DOI: 10.4324/9781003003380-18

in leadership, follower and constituent roles. Most have options to post advertisements to promote research opportunities and recruit participants. WeChat and WhatsApp currently do not offer paid advertising options useful for advertising research. However, Facebook provides targeted advertisement options based on demographic characteristics, interests, location, behavior (i.e., device usage) and connections (Facebook, n.d.) (see Appendix).

LinkedIn also offers targeted advertising options. Researchers can direct advertisements to members based on job experience, education, and other characteristics. An IL researcher could advertise to a targeted audience of senior leadership members, in specific industries, of companies of a particular size, and with specific demographic characteristics, using LinkedIn's advertising options (LinkedIn, n.d.) (see Appendix).

Table A18.1 includes examples of crowdsourcing platforms, including Amazon's Mechanical Turk (MTurk), Dynata, Opinion Access, SurveyCircle, SurveyMonkey's Audience and Qualtrics. Each enables researchers to access registered users available to participate in research. Except for SurveyCircle, these platforms involve compensating participants to complete research studies. MTurk allows researchers to set the compensation amount, and "workers" in the system can choose to participate in the study. Whereas SurveyMonkey's Audience platform sets the costs, and the amount the researcher pays depends on factors, such as limitations to participant characteristics. Similarly, Qualtrics offers access to participant panels, which academic researchers can recruit to participate in studies. Like Audience, Qualtrics sets the costs for participant panels. With SurveyCircle, researchers earn points by completing other studies on the platform and use those points to collect data for their research. Participants do not earn money for completing surveys and studies on SurveyCircle (see Appendix). The sections that follow provide further analysis of the strengths, limitations and opportunities of social media and crowdsourcing platforms for IL research contexts.

Current Use of Social Media and Crowdsourcing in IL Research

Some leadership scholars have recently used social media and crowdsourcing for empirical research studies. A recent EBSCO library database search for peer-reviewed journal articles containing "leader" in the title and "Amazon Mechanical Turk" in the article resulted in nine peer-reviewed articles published from 2017–2020. Their topics included leader sleep devaluation (Barnes et al., 2020), leader-safety motivation (Sawhney & Cigularov, 2019), leader arrogance (Borden et al., 2018), implicit leadership theory (Tavares et al., 2018), empowering leadership (Kim & Beehr, 2017), gender and leadership (Baldner & Pierro, 2019) and political leadership (Renshon et al., 2018; Wagoner & Barreto, 2019). Each involved quantitative data collection (i.e., surveys, including scenario-based experimental designs). In the IL literature, social media and crowdsourcing technologies are less common. An EBSCO library database search for peer-reviewed journal articles published from 2017–2020 with "leader" and international, global, cross-cultural, cross-country, multinational or multicultural in the title produced 1981 search results. There were four empirical studies involving social media or crowdsourcing for data collection or analysis when adding a set of search terms representing social media or crowdsourcing platforms. Of the four studies, three were qualitative studies (i.e., analyzing Twitter, Instagram) (e.g., Peres et al., 2020), and one was a quantitative study (Akdevelioglu & Kara, 2020). While not based on an exhaustive literature search, these results suggest that IL researchers miss opportunities to expand their research using these technologies.

Untapped Opportunities to Apply Social Media and Crowdsourcing in IL Research

The sections that follow discuss five contexts in which these technologies present opportunities for IL research. The first three contexts comprise *research during a crisis*, research with *hard-to-reach populations* and research on *culturally diverse communities*. The sections that follow present opportunities, risks and best practices for recruiting participants using social media for those three research contexts. The fourth context involves researching *international samples*, focusing on applying crowdsourcing technologies to recruit participants. The fifth context involves *analyzing user-generated content* (e.g., a top manager's Twitter feed), focusing on using social media for content analysis research. The five contexts are examples, not the only, contexts that may benefit from these technologies.

Social Media for IL Research in Crisis

Social media presents some IL researchers opportunities to recruit participants online using social media, mainly when mobility is limited. For example, during the COVID-19 pandemic, many countries limited in-person interactions in workplaces, universities and public places (Buchholz, 2020). Conducting face-to-face research was impossible at times. In the examples below (Mishra et al., 2020; Yang & Ren, 2020), the researchers continued to conduct studies during the crisis. The examples show how social media facilitated timely data collection. Some IL researchers who typically travel to collect data or meet with participants may find these examples illustrate alternative opportunities.

Mishra et al. (2020) investigated the effects of the Indian government-administered lockdown during the initial stages of the COVID-19 crisis on trainees participating in ophthalmic training programs. The researchers advertised their study using three social media platforms, posting to groups affiliated with the training program on Facebook, WhatsApp and Telegram. Participants completed surveys administered through Google Forms. The survey was active for 72 hours during the lockdown, and the researchers obtained 716 responses. They learned valuable insights into how they could support trainees.

Yang and Ren (2020) examined the effects of public leadership and moral obligation on collective action to prevent and control pandemics during the COVID-19 crisis. Due to its high rate of COVID-19 cases, the researchers chose the Henan province in China. They used WeChat to recruit participants, applying WeChat filters to limit recruitment to people in Henan. It is unclear how they initially contacted the participants in this region or if they purchased advertisements. Over 11 days, a sample of 533 participants completed their survey using WeChat. The authors noted that 70% of people residing in China use the social media app and that WeChat's region-filtering feature was useful; they did not identify further strengths or limitations to using social media. They acknowledged that people in the region tend to adhere to moral principles (Yang & Ren, 2020). Perhaps these cultural characteristics contributed to participants' willingness to participate and to the validity of their responses. Based on their findings, the researchers provided recommendations for how government and public leaders could mitigate the spread of COVID-19.

Social media may facilitate quick data collection. Mishra et al. (2020) collected 712 responses in three days; Yang and Ren (2020) collected 533 responses in 11 days. Cultural and other factors may influence this speed. For example, both of these studies took place in Asian countries. India and China share a high power distance orientation, demonstrating respect for people in authority positions (Hofstede Insights, n.d.). Cultural characteristics may have contributed to their willingness to respond to the requests for participation in the studies, which both came from researchers whom participants may have viewed as authority figures.

Data collection speed has implications for theory development, allowing science to progress faster because of the opportunities to test theories quickly (Buchheit et al., 2018). Additionally, if they waited until after the pandemic, participants would have based their responses on memory. Over time, answers may be less accurate due to flawed memories, decreasing the validity of the findings (Bordens & Abbott, 2017). IL researchers may find it useful to use social media to recruit participants during crises because of its timeliness and accessibility.

The speed and viability of collecting data using social media or crowdsourcing depend on the population's access to the Internet. According to the International Telecommunication Union (International Telecommunication Union, 2019), only a little over half (54%) of the world's people are Internet users. Cross-country comparisons show that these numbers vary greatly (e.g., 28% of people in Africa versus 87% in Europe use the Internet). Gender differences in Internet use are also present (48% of women versus 58% of men use the Internet). Costs, literacy rates and relevant computer skills appear to account for Internet use (International Telecommunication Union, 2019).

Similarly, while many platforms are available throughout the world, users differ in their preferences for venues, and the popularity of a forum may change over time. For example, a 2017 survey of Brazilians showed that 91% use WhatsApp daily (Statista, 2017). In the same year, only 73% of those in Saudi Arabia, 49% in South Africa and 40% in Indonesia actively used WhatsApp (Statista, 2018). Various agencies track social media usage across countries. Researchers could consult the World Economic Forum's web resources on social media (World Economic Forum, n.d.) and Statista's social media reports (Statista, 2020) to find current international trends of social media use. IL researchers should be aware that, in some cases, a lack of Internet access, access to social media or social media preferences might prohibit timely research using these platforms during a crisis.

Some governments also restrict social media access, preventing IL researchers interested in specific populations from using these platforms. For example, China banned Facebook, Instagram and Twitter (Hutt, 2017). Russia banned LinkedIn (Samuelson, 2016). India banned 59 mobile apps, including WeChat (Press Information Bureau Government of India, 2020). Similarly, President Donald Trump of the United States (U.S.) signed an executive order in 2020, banning WeChat, as well as TikTok (The White House, 2020). However, the status of TikTok may change amid ongoing discussions of its partnership with a U.S.-based company (Fung & Wang, 2020). IL researchers should consider that social media platforms' availability varies across countries due to the political climate, with access to them subject to change. Considering these factors, some IL researchers may be interested in populations that may be difficult to reach using these platforms.

When researching during a crisis, researchers should also remember that Internet access may change, and Internet Service Providers may have difficulty providing services. Thus, even in places that have widespread Internet access, crises may lead to changes in access. For example, a natural disaster may interrupt electricity and Internet services. Depending on the context, researchers may find current Internet access statistics as a crisis unfolds by referring to online resources. For example, in April 2020, the Pew Research Forum surveyed 34 countries regarding Internet use during the coronavirus pandemic. The majority of people surveyed in 32 countries (e.g., Australia, Japan, Philippines, Russia, South Korea, Tunisia and the United States) reported using the Internet.

In contrast, less than half of the people in Kenya and India reported using the Internet at that time (Schumacher & Kent, 2020). In the United States, as of June 2020, data usage increased by 47% during the COVID-19 pandemic, with social media use also increasing (e.g., Facebook 27% increase and LinkedIn 26%) during nationwide lockdowns (Cohen, 2020). In some events, such as when people must stay home but maintain Internet access, they may be affected by these technologies' overuse, influencing research participation. For example, some people report experiencing "zoom fatigue" when engaging in video-based social interactions through platforms such as Zoom, Facetime and Facebook Messenger. The fatigue is, in part, due to the increased strain people experience when they must attend to verbal communication without many non-verbal cues that are present in face-to-face interactions (Sklar, 2020). Thus, a crisis may affect the research population, participation rates, and participant responses when using these technologies to conduct studies during crises. However, in appropriate research contexts, these platforms open opportunities for IL researchers to collect data at critical times, allowing them to identify issues and solutions in times of need.

Social Media for IL Research with Hard-to-Reach Populations

IL researchers seeking participants from "hard-to-reach" populations, such as a small, geographically dispersed population or those with sensitive characteristics or interests (e.g., individuals with anti-government views) should explore the opportunities of social media recruitment while assessing its risks and limitations. In a recent example from psychology, Garcia (2020) recruited participants using social media to examine how losing a sibling affected twins versus non-twins. Garcia describes why she chose to use Facebook to collect data:

> Using Facebook as a recruitment tool for my master's thesis was my first choice to be able to reach as many participants as possible. Considering I had to target a very precise population, finding participants was as simple as looking for groups that catered to sibling loss. Although I could not directly access the groups, reaching out to the group's administrator and having them disseminate my survey link proved an effective method that provided me with an ample population sample. (K. Garcia, personal communication, July 29, 2020)

Twins make up only 3% of births in the United States (Martin & Osterman, 2019), her country of residence, and she was interested in those within this population who had lost a twin sibling. The size of her geographically dispersed population made it hard to reach. She recruited 113 non-twin participants and 43 twin participants using unpaid advertisements on Facebook. She posted the research announcement in the news feeds of groups such as "Twinless Twins Support Group International" and "Sibling Loss Awareness groups". For 11 weeks, she reposted the information to ensure it was present in the group members' news feed. She did not limit participants to her country of residence, nor did she report their countries of residence. Thus, it is not possible to assess whether cultural factors contributed to her participant response rate.

Many social media platforms include groups or other gatherings of users based on shared interests, experiences, or needs. IL researchers interested in hard-to-reach populations may find social media special interest groups (e.g., Garcia's sibling bereavement groups) provide a method for reaching members of that population. However, those interested in populations with sensitive interests who could face stigmatization or harm if exposed should be mindful of the social media context. In some countries (e.g., Cuba), authority figures closely monitor the Internet and violate users' privacy (Freedom House, n.d.), likely increasing the risk of harm and decreasing participant volunteering through social media. IL researchers should also assess factors such as restrictions, such as state-led surveillance, affecting their population's ability to safely participate in research. For example, researchers could use Freedom House (freedomhouse.org) as a starting point to assess the risk levels. Freedom House ranks countries based on the degree of government surveillance and the likelihood of experiencing negative repercussions when expressing oneself online (Freedom House, n.d.). When social media or Internet-based research poses risks to participants, IL researchers should explore alternative data recruitment and collections methods.

At times, researchers may offer greater protection over participant anonymity when collecting data online than in a face-to-face research environment (Chandler & Shapiro, 2016). For example, a researcher interested in unsafe work conditions may find that participants feel more comfortable responding to an anonymous, online survey than in a face-to-face interview. However, participants are arguably less accountable for what they say in an anonymous setting than in a face-to-face interview, potentially affecting the research's validity.

Chandler and Shapiro (2016) note that participants involved in online research studies may also be more likely to withdraw from a study than in face-to-face settings. Online participants can simply "close out" if they no longer wish to participate (Chandler & Shapiro, 2016). Knowing they can quickly stop participating, participants may be more likely to volunteer. IL researchers may leverage social media opportunities to overcome some of the challenges of studying sensitive topics, enabling them to contribute important insights to the academic literature.

Social Media for IL Research with Culturally Diverse Communities

IL researchers conducting studies involving people from multiple cultures may find that promoting a study using targeted social media advertising helps them reach their target populations. For example, Tsai et al. (2019) used Facebook advertisements to recruit participants from within the United States who had specific racial and ethnic backgrounds. They sought Chinese, Korean or Latin American cancer survivors to complete a quantitative survey. They translated advertisements into Chinese (simplified and traditional), Korean and Spanish. The researchers did not explain how they ensured that people from these populations would see the advertisement. Information regarding these steps would have helped other researchers in future studies.

Initially, 115 people registered to complete the study, of which they obtained a sample of 26 participants who completed the full study. While the sample size was small for a quantitative study, the research was a "feasibility" study to determine whether Facebook would effectively reach these populations in future research studies. They concluded that advertisements on Facebook, translated into their target populations' languages, would be an appropriate and useful method for future participant recruitment. The cost of advertising the study for 48 days was approximately USD $1,200. They also compensated participants with USD $10 gift cards (USD $260 total). Some international researchers may be able to apply similar strategies in their research. For example, a researcher interested in how constituents with different cultural backgrounds perceive political candidates could recruit a diverse participant pool using social media ads translated into the target populations' languages.

In another example, health researchers Pechmann et al. (2020) aimed to recruit participants for a longitudinal health study that involved a smoking cessation intervention administered on Twitter. They used Facebook to recruit 908 participants with four advertisement campaigns for over 61 weeks. One campaign targeted residents throughout the United States. Two targeted residents living in ZIP codes with high populations of Black or African American and Hispanic or Latino people and a high rate of cigarette purchases. The other targeted U.S. residents who speak Spanish and wanted to quit smoking. They used Facebook's advertising options to promote the study to people who searched using keywords such as "quitting smoking". Facebook did not allow them to choose race or ethnicity characteristics to direct advertisements (members do not need to report their race or ethnicity to join Facebook). The researchers identified ZIP codes in which relatively high numbers of people with these racial and ethnic backgrounds resided (Pechmann et al., 2020). Similarly, IL researchers who aim to recruit participants across different racial, ethnic or cultural backgrounds may find strategies to ensure that research announcements reach their target population using social media. To increase the likelihood of obtaining racially and ethnically diverse samples, researchers could consider targeted advertisements to various geographic locations, even within the same countries.

IL researchers must evaluate the research expenses these approaches would incur to determine whether they are cost-effective. Budget cuts and reductions to funding occurring in higher education may increase the importance of cost reductions (Friga, 2020), making paid advertisements less feasible for some researchers. Reagan et al. (2019) reviewed various research studies using Facebook paid ads to recruit participants. Comparing across 10 studies, they found a broad range of costs from roughly USD $378 to USD $11,103 for advertisements. The six studies reporting cost details showed that the "per participant" costs ranged from USD $0.13 to USD $68.64. In a review of Facebook as a social science research tool, Kosinski et al. (2015) similarly noted the wide range of costs involved in using social media for research purposes. They suggested that researchers become aware of the factors affecting prices to reduce advertising costs. For example, advertisement costs vary depending on the countries the researcher targets. Overall, they suggested, "with proper training, traditional social science studies can be conducted online at a lower cost and larger scale than ever before" (Kosinski et al., 2015, p. 554). Some IL researchers may find the costs are worthwhile, particularly if they have difficulty obtaining representative samples using traditional methods (e.g., flyers).

Crowdsourcing for IL Research with International Samples

IL researchers interested in cross-country comparisons may find opportunities to obtain representative samples using crowdsourcing platforms. Gerpott et al. (2019) conducted two studies using crowdsourcing platforms to assess the relationship between perceptions of ethical leadership and follower organizational citizenship behaviors (OCBs), as well as the mediating role of follower moral identity. They also examined whether participants' perceptions of the leader being "prototypical" of the group moderated the relationship between ethical leadership and follower OCBs. Study 1 was an experiment with a sample of 138 participants who were 43% female, with an average age of 36.5 years, and resided in the United States. Their most common employment industries included information technology, healthcare and public sector jobs. They recruited participants using MTurk, compensating participants USD $1. Using MTurk, they randomly assigned participants to one of four conditions. Participants wrote a short essay about how they envisioned it would be to work with the leader depicted in the vignette and completed an OCB questionnaire. Overall, the results supported their hypothesis, showing that participants' perceptions of the leader in the scenario affected their likelihood of engaging in OCBs in that setting. When participants viewed the leader as typical of the group, the relationship between their perceptions and OCBs increased (Gerpott et al., 2019).

In Study Two, the authors sought to replicate their initial findings using a field sample. They recruited a sample of 225 participants using CrowdFlower, a platform that drew from other labor pools to enlist participants for research studies. CrowdFlower is no longer in business. Participants included a slight female majority (54%), with an average age of 38. Most (84%) worked in service and related industries (e.g., technology and healthcare), with others (14%) in goods-producing and associated industries. The researchers compensated participants USD $0.70. This time, they limited participation to employees across various industries in Western countries (i.e., Canada, [unnamed] European countries, and the United States). The authors found support for their hypotheses, replicating the Study 1 results in a field sample (Gerpott et al., 2019).

Gerpott et al. (2019) illustrate how IL researchers could use crowdsourcing platforms to conduct multiple phases of research (e.g., scenario-based experiments, followed by field studies). By setting limits to who could participate, the researchers created a structure for assessing "employees" without collaborating with specific organizations. They obtained a sample of employees from multiple industries and countries, which would be advantageous to some IL researchers. Some IL researchers may find this opportunity aligns with their research needs, mainly when collecting quantitative data, such as to assess follower perceptions of leadership practices, behaviors and attributes.

Past research has established that participants recruited from crowdsourcing platforms, such as MTurk, share characteristics with general populations; however, research in this area is limited to certain countries (i.e., the United States). For example, Goodman et al. (2013) compared samples drawn from MTurk (107 participants) and people recruited from a middle-class community in the United States (60 participants). They found no substantial differences in gender, age, cognitive ability or the ability to pass instruction checks. However, they did find some differences in values. For example, they found differences in the degree to which MTurk and community participants valued time and money, with MTurk participants prioritizing money over time and vice versa for the community participants. They also found some personality differences, such as higher introversion levels in MTurk participants, compared to community participants. Finally, they found evidence that MTurk participants were more likely to "cheat" when asked knowledge-related questions, seeming to research answers online. Cheating behaviors included using the Internet to search for answers to questions rather than responding based on their existing knowledge. When researchers compensated participants for correct answers, participants were more likely to use the Internet to look for correct answers to questions (Goodman et al., 2013). Research regarding cross-cultural differences in honesty is still evolving. Preliminary research suggests that some online research participants engage in cheating and dishonest behaviors across countries; however, the frequency at which this occurs differs across cultures and countries (Hugh-Jones, 2016). IL researchers should consult with local partners and experts of the culture to assess the likelihood of dishonesty affecting the validity of results when using a crowdsourcing platform.

Researchers in the social sciences, business, management and related fields often conduct studies using university students as participants (e.g., university students complete research studies and receive course credit). Compared to student samples, there are strengths and limitations to using MTurk participants. Goodman et al. (2013) found that MTurk participants (average of 31 years) were older than students (average of 19 years), which may appeal to IL researchers interested in employed populations or leadership experience. However, they also found that MTurk participants (207 participants) were less likely than students (131 participants) to respond correctly to instruction manipulation checks (IMCs). That is, when asked to complete a reading comprehension task to test whether participants were paying attention, students were more likely than MTurk participants to demonstrate that they were paying attention (Goodman et al., 2013).

IL researchers should evaluate these factors when determining whether crowdsourcing platforms would be appropriate for their research studies. For example, if a researcher will administer assessments of knowledge, they should consider the possibility of participants "cheating" and potential threats to their study's validity. Goodman et al. (2013) suggested that instructing participants not to use the Internet to look up answers correlates with a decrease in cheating behaviors. Based on their research findings, giving these instructions should reduce this threat to validity.

IL researchers should keep in mind that recruiting participants using a crowdsourcing platform may also decrease external reliability (i.e., the generalizability of results) compared to other sampling methods (e.g., random sampling). A sample derived from MTurk, for example, may not be representative of the researcher's population of interest and would not be equated to drawing a random sample from the general public (Mason & Suri, 2012). Researchers should consider using country-specific crowdsourcing platforms to increase the chances of obtaining a representative sample. For example, Majima et al. (2017) note that MTurk would not provide a representative sample of the Japanese population. Thus, they encourage researchers interested in the Japanese population to use a local crowdsourcing platform in Japan. They also encourage international researchers to collaborate with local researchers who can help support the use of local crowdsourcing platforms.

IL researchers must weigh the benefits of timeliness with the dangers of inaccurate data that could lead to invalid theory. They should take steps to minimize threats to the reliability and validity of research derived from crowdsourcing. The GLOBE Foundation recommends that its Country Co-Investigators take steps to reduce the risks that data derived from crowdsourcing are inaccurate. Specifically, they recommend the following:

- Use screening questions (e.g., to inquire about residency and management role).
- Use an instruction check to screen for participants paying attention.
- Collect more data than needed in anticipation of the need to remove cases (e.g., due to respondents who do not pass instruction checks).

- Within the instructions, include the statement, "The quality of the answers that you provide will be checked during this survey as well as after the survey responses are completed".
- Remove participants with duplicate IP addresses.
- When using MTurk, hire only participants with a high rating (90%+) (GLOBE Foundation, 2020). Requesters, those hiring and paying MTurk workers, contribute to these ratings. The ratings represent the percentage of tasks the MTurk worker has completed to a satisfactory level, "approved of" by the task requestors (Amazon MTurk, 2019).
- Remove participants who complete the survey too quickly (i.e., <.33 of the median time).
- Calibrate participant compensation to avoid over-motivating participation (GLOBE Foundation, 2020).

Several of the GLOBE Foundation's recommendations are common practices when using crowdsourcing platforms in research. For example, researchers often use screening questions to determine whether a participant is part of the population of interest. Find an example of a screening questionnaire for an MTurk study in Hunt and Scheetz's (2019) analysis of the platform. Those researching an international setting should review potential screening questions with a local partner, particularly if there are language and cultural differences. Consulting with a local partner helps ensure researchers ask critical screening questions, using the most appropriate language while considering cultural norms.

Wessling et al. (2017) suggest that researchers using MTurk take steps to reduce participants' likelihood of engaging in character misrepresentation. Character misrepresentation reflects a tendency for some participants to respond to questions inaccurately to qualify for paid studies (Wessling et al., 2017). For example, suppose an IL researcher was interested in surveying people whose companies furloughed them during the COVID-19 crisis. The researcher includes a screening questionnaire to determine whether respondents meet the criteria and qualify for the paid study. Based on the screening questions, some respondents guess the population of interest and respond accordingly, even though their employers did not furlough them. These respondents then complete the paid portion of the study, further responding inaccurately. Such character misrepresentation threatens research validity (Wessling et al., 2017).

Wessling et al. (2017) suggest that respondents will typically misrepresent themselves only when there is a reason to do so. They recommend that researchers take all respondents who meet minimum criteria (i.e., approval rating thresholds on MTurk), allowing them to complete the study and receive compensation. Then, the researcher can organize the data as appropriate after collecting responses. For example, researchers may remove cases in which participants would not have met screening criteria, use all of the data and examine the effects of individual differences, or combine studies and direct participants to different questionnaires, depending on their screening responses. Again, the purpose of this approach is to remove the monetary source of some participants' motivation to misrepresent themselves (Wessling et al., 2017).

IL researchers should also be aware that cultural characteristics and language differences may lead participants to demonstrate character misrepresentation. According to Bernardi (2006), some people respond to surveys inaccurately because they aim to appear as a person who behaves in culturally accepted (socially desirable) ways. Therefore, respondents may deny bad behaviors (e.g., stealing) and affirm good behaviors (e.g., helping others) inaccurately. Populations with high collectivist (e.g., valuing the group over the individual), as opposed to individualistic, values are more likely to respond to surveys in these socially desirable ways (Bernardi, 2006). IL researchers in collectivist settings should consider whether participants might respond agreeably to screening questions due to social desirability bias. To reduce this bias, researchers should explain the importance of responding honestly, and the risks to the research should participants respond inaccurately. Language barriers could also lead to a participant describing their thoughts, viewpoints and experiences inaccurately.

Again, IL researchers would benefit from discussing these details with a local partner to assess whether they can overcome any potential obstacles that may lead to character misrepresentation.

As the GLOBE Foundation (n.d.) recommends, researchers should also consider using IMCs. When Gerpott et al. (2019) used a sample derived from MTurk to examine ethical leadership, they used IMCs. They identified 10 out of 170 participants who did not follow the given instructions. They used three items, for which they asked participants to mark a particular response option (i.e., mark the letter "a"). If participants are not paying attention enough to follow simple instructions, it is unlikely that their survey responses would be valid or reliable. Furthermore, Franz et al. (2019) established a time minimum for survey completion for quality control, similar to what the GLOBE Foundation recommends. In their study, they excluded data from participants who completed the survey in less than five minutes. IL researchers can use strategies such as these, as well, to improve the validity of crowdsourcing research.

Social Media for Researching Leader Online Behavior

Another research context in which IL researchers may find opportunities involves studying leader online behavior, such as social media activities during a crisis (Xiaocong, 2017). User-generated content such as videos, blogs, comments, other written content and photos is a central feature of social media. Users also make decisions and take actions, such as "voting" for and "liking" content (Obar & Wilderman, 2015). Given the amount of content present on social media platforms, some leadership researchers have recently analyzed user-generated data to draw conclusions about leadership phenomena.

For example, Men et al. (2018) conducted a content analysis study of "dialogical communication", examining how CEOs interact with the public on Facebook. They collected data from social media posts that are publicly available on the companies' Facebook pages. Men et al. (2018) selected leaders from Hootsuite and Xinfu's list of the "Top 100 CEOs on Social Media". The researchers identified 24 leaders who fit additional research criteria and randomly selected 30 posts from each leader's Facebook page. In total, the researchers analyzed 658 posts from the CEOs, along with 502 comments from members of the public. They assessed public engagement using existing Facebook data, such as the number of "likes", the number of times shared and emoticon reactions to posts. They assessed various other factors, such as the number of replies CEOs made to comments on their posts or times they "liked" a commenter's response, CEO personalization of reactions to members of the public (i.e., using the person's name) and use of inclusive language. The researchers identified the strategies that top social media CEOs employed on Facebook. They assessed the effectiveness of these messages by the degree of public engagement in response to CEO messages (e.g., number of likes or shares of the CEO's posts). Social media provided a platform to study leaders from various industries and countries. For example, included in their sample were Alan Sugar of the United Kingdom's Amshold Group, Jean-Pascal Tricoire of France's Schneider Electric, and the United States' Arne Sorenson of Marriot International (Men et al., 2018). There is no way of knowing whether the leaders in this study authored their own social media posts and comments (e.g., an assistant or public relations staff could have composed some).

Considering the number of posts and comments they were able to obtain, a large amount of data was available. Still, they noted that relying only on the posts and comments was a limitation in this study. Incorporating additional data collection methods, such as interviews, would have strengthened the study. Additional data from other social media sources, such as Twitter, would have also supported the existing content that they analyzed. Furthermore, they acknowledged that it is impossible to gauge the public's full response to the leader's social media activities based only on the comments obtained (Men et al., 2018).

Men et al. (2018) did not include information regarding obtaining informed consent from their research subjects. Buchanan (2017) notes that researchers and ethicists continue to analyze the ethical issues involved with collecting data from social media users, such as "tweets" and social connections on Twitter, without users' permission. Data mining and big data approaches shift the dynamics between researchers and participants, with participants becoming more like research "subjects" (Buchanan, 2017). A central tenant of research ethics is that researchers should obtain informed consent from research participants (e.g., American Psychological Association, 2010). Research involving social media data (e.g., user-generated content, such as posts on Facebook) may be considered "exempt" from this requirement by many institutional review boards (IRBs); however, some question the appropriateness of this exemption (Buchanan, 2017). Samuel et al. (2019) note that subjects may perceive such research of their user-generated content as a privacy violation. As Buchanan notes, research communities do not yet have a solid stance on the ethical implications of using publicly available social media records. The scientific community grapples with these issues, and researchers should be aware of this lack of concrete standards when conducting research. IL researchers should consult with colleagues, mentors, IRBs and resources in the next section to identify ethical issues related to their studies and ways to limit harm to participants.

When considering research that involves extracting data from social media accounts, researchers should be clear about what information they will obtain from participants' accounts. Below is an example excerpt from an informed consent form involving a social media study that explains what data the researchers would collect:

> Specifically, public profile, friend list, email address, custom friends lists, messages, News Feed, relationships, birthday, work history, status updates, education history, groups, hometown, current city, photos, religious and political views, videos, personal description, likes and your friends' relationships, birthdays, birthdays, work histories, status updates, education histories, groups, hometowns, current cities, photos, religious and political views, videos, personal descriptions and likes were listed. (Wee & Lee, 2017, p. 14)

IL researchers conducting studies involving collecting social media data that is not publically available should consider including similar information as applicable.

According to Kosinski et al. (2015), the profile information, status posts and interactions a person engages in on social media differ substantially from responses on a self-report measure completed in a laboratory setting. When people create content or express themselves on social media, they are typically unaware that a researcher will later analyze this content. A participant in a laboratory completing a self-report measure is aware of the research context, potentially affecting how the participant responds to the measure (Kosinski et al., 2015). Biases associated with self-report data (e.g., social desirability bias) are unlikely present in the same ways in data collected from user-generated social media content (Kosinski et al., 2015). For example, suppose Ali participates in a study on his college campus, and the researcher asks Ali to complete a leadership inventory. When completing the questionnaire, Ali responds in a way that would lead to high scores on valued attributes in his culture. If the researchers instead collected Ali's Facebook content from the previous two years and drew conclusions by analyzing this content, the research context would not have the same effect on Ali's leadership scores. However, other biases may be present in Ali's user-generated content available on social media (e.g., Facebook posts).

Public social media posts may be inaccurate (Franz et al., 2019). Posts, comments and other content may represent how the user wants to appear to the public. According to Yang et al. (2017), social media users tend to develop "e-personalities". When managing their reputations, some social media users present false information about themselves. The interactions people have and the content they produce online may reflect their "ideal" selves, as opposed to their true selves, the authors warn. E-personalities may include more positive or more negative dispositions than the person's offline character (Yang et al., 2017).

Furthermore, Men et al. (2018) note that research that relies on social media metrics (i.e., the number of likes on a post), as opposed to interviews or surveys, are limited in depth. Convenient, accessible data such as emoticon reactions to posts neglect the context surrounding these responses to user-generated content. When reading a CEO's tweet, two people could "like" it, but for different reasons; furthermore, they could like it to varying degrees. To gain a more accurate understanding of participants or subjects, researchers should consider collecting data from multiple social media accounts and other data sources (Men et al., 2018). For example, rather than relying only on a leader's blog posts published on LinkedIn, the researcher could collect content and data from the same leader's Twitter feed.

IL researchers should also consider establishing profiles for leaders they study, considering their cultural and other characteristics for further analysis. In a recent IL study of the communication patterns of 61 political leaders (e.g., King Salman bin Abdulaziz Al Saud) across 48 countries, Peres et al. (2020) assessed user-generated content from Twitter (300,000 total messages) to identify similarities and differences in the leaders' rhetoric. They created profiles for each leader to account for multicultural and international factors. The profiles included information about the country's gross domestic product (GDP), cultural standing on Hofstede's cultural dimensions, democratic state status and other variables. Surprisingly, they did not find significant effects for cultural factors on the leaders' messaging overall; instead, they found that most of the leaders addressed similar topic (e.g., economic issues) with a similar sentiment (i.e., positive tone), typically mirroring information portrayed in the news media (Peres et al., 2020). While they did not find significant differences across cultures, they would have been unable to draw these conclusions without creating country-specific profiles for the leaders. IL leaders considering research on user-generated content may want to account for similar cultural factors in their studies to establish a method for assessing cross-cultural factors concerning their research questions.

Resources for Using Social Media and Crowdsourcing for Research

Resources regarding these platforms for research purposes are limited. Table A18.2 includes resources for researchers applying social media and crowdsourcing platforms. Sloan and Quan-Haase's (2017) comprehensive handbook covers social media study design, qualitative and quantitative research, research and analytical tools and social media platforms. Franz et al. (2019) provide a primer for using Facebook to conduct qualitative research. Kosinski et al. (2015) analyze the strengths and limitations of using Facebook in research and give advice for using it effectively. Reagan et al. (2019) provide guidance for recruiting participants using Facebook. Buchheit et al. (2018) and Cheung et al. (2017) present methodological issues, strengths, and limitations of research with the MTurk platform. Kees et al. (2017) compare data quality across samples drawn from MTurk, student and professional panels. They also provide guidance for maximizing validity when using MTurk (see Appendix). The author could not find definitive resources describing best practices for using social media or crowdsourcing in research through national government websites, such as the U.S. Department of Health's Office of Human Research Protections.

Table A18.3 also includes several websites with guidance on using these platforms for research. Lehigh University discusses ethical issues, informed consent and best practices for using crowdsourcing to conduct research. The National University of Singapore presents ways of connecting with the public for research and problem-solving purposes using crowdsourcing platforms. The University of Waterloo explains how to use crowdsourcing to collect data and compensate participants. Stanford University, the University of Massachusetts and the University of California (Berkeley) provide ethical guidance on using MTurk for research purposes. Emory University,

Indiana University, Lindenwood University, Singapore Psychological Society and the Synergies for Europe's Research Infrastructure in the Social Sciences (SERIESS) provide further ethical guidance for collecting data using social media. The World Economic Forum presents social media usage statistics across countries. IL researchers should also consult their IRBs regarding ethical considerations relevant to their research (see Appendix).

Discussion

This chapter aims to help fill a gap in the IL research literature by analyzing opportunities for using social media and crowdsourcing technologies. These platforms provide opportunities and alternatives to traditional research approaches that may support IL researchers' aims. IL researchers should apply social media and crowdsourcing platforms when appropriate, such as in research involving crisis, hard-to-reach populations, culturally diverse communities, international populations, and leader online behavior. Examples of ways IL researchers could apply the platforms include recruiting participants through social media and crowdsourcing platforms, as well as analyzing user-generated content from social media. As shown in the research examples, researchers prepared to conduct studies using virtual modalities may adapt quickly when crises arise, enabling them to create and share knowledge at critical times.

Furthermore, almost all *Fortune* 500 companies actively engage in social media (99% on LinkedIn, 96% on Twitter, and 95% on Facebook) (Center for Marketing Research, 2020). Many political leaders actively engage with constituents using social media. For example, as of October 2020, U.S. President Donald Trump has 87 million followers (Trump, n.d.), Indian Prime Minister Narendra Modi (Modi, n.d.) has 62 million followers and Jordan Queen Rania Al Abdullah (Abdullah, n.d.) has 10.4 million followers on Twitter. IL researchers must study these communication modes and their outcomes, considering that many leaders and followers engage through social media. IL researchers can use their research findings derived from these technologies to contribute novel insights, guidance and solutions for contemporary local and global issues.

However, as discussed in this chapter, there are limitations associated with these platforms. IL researchers must weigh these and consider their research participants, topics, countries, cultures of interest and other factors to determine whether these platforms are appropriate. Furthermore, the field lacks empirical evidence demonstrating the reliability and validity of these participant recruitment and data collection methods in the IL field.

By cautiously applying these methods in international contexts and sharing their findings, IL scholars will better understand when and how to use these technologies to maximize their benefits and reduce risks. For example, IL researchers could examine the reliability associated with these platforms when collecting quantitative data. Reliability reflects the degree to which a measurement approach operates similarly across participants each time a researcher uses it (Miller & Lovler, 2019). IL researchers could incorporate these platforms into their existing studies, collecting data to assess reliability. For example, an IL researcher's primary interest may be to examine the role of gender in social judgment skills in global leadership settings. The researcher collaborates with a multinational company to collect data from employees at different sites, administering a survey to them on their company computers during the workday. Simultaneously, she uses an online crowdsourcing platform to administer the same survey to employed people of the same industry in the same countries. The researcher analyzes the data and summarizes the findings concerning her primary research questions. As a secondary focus, she compares the reliability statistics (e.g., internal consistency coefficients) associated with the company's survey results and those from crowdsourcing, sharing her findings in a journal article. This is just one example of how IL researchers could build a discipline-specific understanding of these platforms.

IL researchers can also contribute to the field's understanding of these platforms by transparently describing their research methods, costs and activities they use when conducting such studies. Reagan et al. (2019) called for researchers to provide more information regarding their recruitment strategies, demographic characteristics and recruitment expenditures when using social media to recruit participants. Many questions exist regarding social media use as a recruitment tool because researchers often do not include enough details in their research reports (Reagan et al., 2019). Similarly, a recent review showed that few researchers provide details regarding why they reject respondents when using MTurk (crowdsourcing) or their full criteria for selecting respondents, with some failing to report basic sample characteristics (Porter et al., 2020). Thus, the field would benefit if researchers provided detailed descriptions of the recruitment strategies, outcomes of those strategies, sample demographic characteristics and the costs involved.

Additionally, academic journals, such as management and leadership journals, and editorial boards, should open opportunities for researchers to publish international research, particularly studies that use these technologies. Increasing the number of internationally focused empirical studies in academic journals will ensure that international perspectives and knowledge is available. It will also help ensure that the IL field can establish best practices for applying these technologies in international research. With these initiatives, the IL field would establish a discipline-based understanding of the strengths, limitations and best practices for using these platforms to advance IL research.

References

Abdullah, R. A. (n.d.). *Rania Al Abdullah*. https://twitter.com/QueenRania.

American Psychological Association (APA). (2010). *Ethical principles of psychologists and code of conduct*. https://www.apa.org/ethics/code/.

Akdevelioglu, D., & Kara, S. (2020). An international investigation of opinion leadership and social media. *Journal of Research in Interactive Marketing, 14*(1), 71–92.

Baldner, C., & Pierro, A. (2019). The trials of women leaders in the workforce: How a need for cognitive closure can influence acceptance of harmful gender stereotypes. *Sex Roles: A Journal of Research, 80*, 565–577. doi: 10.1007/s11199-018-0953-1.

Barnes, C. M., Awtrey, E., Lucianetti, L., & Spreitzer, G. (2020). Leader sleep devaluation, employee sleep, and unethical behavior. *Sleep Health: Journal of the National Sleep Foundation, 6*(3), 411–417. doi: 10.1016/j.sleh.2019.12.001.

Bernardi, R. (2006). Associations between Hofstede's cultural constructs and social desirability response bias. *Journal of Business Ethics, 65*(1), 43–53. doi: 10.1007/s10551-005-5353-0.

Bordens, K., & Abbott, B. B. (2017). *Research design and methods: A process approach* (10th ed.). McGraw Hill.

Borden, L., Levy, P. E., & Silverman, S. B. (2018). Leader arrogance and subordinate outcomes: The role of feedback processes. *Journal of Business & Psychology, 33*(3), 345–364. doi: 10.1007/s10869-017-9501-1.

Bosch, T. (2019). Social media and protest movements in South Africa. In M. Dwyer & T. Molony (Eds.), *Social media and politics in Africa: Democracy, censorship and security*. Zed Books.

Buchanan, E. (2017). Considering the ethics of big data research: A case of Twitter and ISIS/ISIL. *PLoS ONE, 12*(12), 1–6. doi: 10.1371/journal.pone.0187155.

Buchheit, S., Doxey, M. M., Pollard, T., & Stinson, S. R. (2018). A technical guide to using Amazon's Mechanical Turk in behavioral accounting research. *Behavioral Research in Accounting, 30*(1), 111–122. doi: 10.2308/bria-51977.

Buchholz, K. (April, 2020). *What share of the world population is already on COVID-19 lockdown?* https://www.statista.com/chart/21240/enforced-covid-19-lockdowns-by-people-affected-per-country/

Center for Marketing Research, University of Massachusetts, Dartmouth (January, 2020). *Oversaturation and disengagement: The 2019 Fortune 500 social media dance*. https://www.umassd.edu/cmr/research/2019-fortune-500.html.

Chandler, J., & Shapiro, D. (2016). Conducting clinical research using crowdsourced convenience samples. *Annual Review of Clinical Psychology, 12*, 53–81. doi: 10.1146/annurev-clinpsy-021815-093623.

Cheung, J., Burns, D., Sinclair, R., & Sliter, M. (2017). Amazon Mechanical Turk in organizational psychology: An evaluation and practical recommendations. *Journal of Business & Psychology*, *32*(4), 347–361. doi:10.1007/s10869-016-9458-5.

Cohen, J. (2020). *Data usage has increased 47 percent during COVID-19 quarantine.* https://www.pcmag.com/news/data-usage-has-increased-47-percent-during-covid-19-quarantine.

Facebook. (n.d.). *Ad targeting: Help your ads find the people who will love your business.* www.facebook.com/business/ads/ad-targeting.

Franz, D., Marsh, H. E., Chen, J. I., & Teo, A. R. (2019). Using Facebook for qualitative research: A brief primer. *Journal of Medical Internet Research*, *21*(8), e13544. doi:10.2196/13544.

Freedom House. (n.d.). *About freedom on the net.* https://freedomhouse.org/report/freedom-net.

Friga, P. N. (April, 2020). Under Covid-19, university budgets like we've never seen before. *The Chronicle of Higher Education, Commentary.* www.chronicle.com/article/under-covid-19-university-budgets-like-weve-never-seen-before/.

Fung, B. & Wang, S. (2020). *TikTok will partner with Oracle in the United States after Microsoft loses bid.* https://www.msn.com/en-us/money/news/oracle-will-partner-with-tiktok-in-the-united-states-after-microsoft-loses-bid/ar-BB18ZEL8.

Garcia, K. J. (2020). *Twin versus non-twin siblings: Differences in depression and grieving after loss of a sibling* [Unpublished master's thesis]. Purdue University Global.

Gerpott, F. H., Van Quaquebeke, N., Schlamp, S., & Voelpel, S. C. (2019). An identity perspective on ethical leadership to explain organizational citizenship behavior: The interplay of follower moral identity and leader group prototypicality. *Journal of Business Ethics*, *156*(4), 1063–1078. doi:10.1007/s10551-017-3625-0.

Ghezzi, A., Gabelloni, D., Martini, A., & Natalicchio, A. (2018). Crowdsourcing: A review and suggestions for future research. *International Journal of Management Reviews*, *2*, 343. doi:10.1111/ijmr.12135.

GLOBE Foundation. (n.d.). *GLOBE 2020: Country co-investigator handbook.* https://globeproject.com/about?page_id=cci#globe2020_cci.

Goodman, J. K., Cryder, C. E., & Cheema, A. (2013). Data collection in a flat world: The strengths and weaknesses of Mechanical Turk samples. *Journal of Behavioral Decision Making*, *26*(3), 213–224. doi:10.1002/bdm.1753.

He, G., An, R., & Hewlin, P. F. (2019). Paternalistic leadership and employee well-being: A moderated mediation model. *Chinese Management Studies*, *13*(3), 645–663. doi:10.1108/CMS-10-2018-0724.

Hofstede Insights. (n.d.). *Country comparisons.* https://www.hofstede-insights.com/country-comparison/china,india/.

Hughes-Jones, D. (2016). Honesty and beliefs about honesty in 15 countries. *Journal of Economic Behavior & Organization*, *127*, 99–114.

Hutt, R. (2017). *The world's most popular social media mapped.* https://www.weforum.org/agenda/2017/03/most-popular-social-networks-mapped.

Hunt, N. C., & Scheetz, A. M. (2019). Using MTurk to distribute a survey or experiment: Methodological considerations. *Journal of Information Systems*, *33*(1), 43–65. doi:10.2308/isys-52021.

International Telecommunication Union. (2019). *New ITU data reveal growing Internet uptake but a widening digital gender divide.* https://www.itu.int/en/mediacentre/Pages/2019-PR19.aspx.

Kees, J., Berry, C., Burton, S., & Sheehan, K. (2017). An analysis of data quality: Professional panels, student subject pools, and Amazon's Mechanical Turk. *Journal of Advertising*, *46*(1), 141–155. doi:10.1080/00913367.2016.1269304.

Kim, M., & Beehr, T. A. (2017). Directing our own careers, but getting help from empowering leaders. *Career Development International*, *22*(3), 300–317. doi:10.1108/CDI-11-2016-0202.

Kosinski, M., Matz, S. C., Gosling, S. D., Popov, V., & Stillwell, D. (2015). Facebook as a research tool for the social sciences: Opportunities, challenges, ethical considerations, and practical guidelines. *American Psychologist*, *70*(6), 543–556. doi:10.1037/a0039210.

LinkedIn. (n.d.). *Reaching your audience: Targeting on LinkedIn.* https://business.linkedin.com/content/dam/me/business/en-us/marketing-solutions/resources/pdfs/linkedin-targeting-playbook-v4.pdf.

Majima, Y., Nishiyama, K., Nishihara, A., & Hata, R. (2017). Conducting online behavioral research using crowdsourcing services in Japan. *Frontiers in Psychology*, *8*, 378. doi:10.3389/fpsyg.2017.00378.

Martin, J. A., & Osterman, M. J. K. (2019). *Is twin childbearing on the decline? Twin births in the United States, 2014–2018.* https://www.cdc.gov/nchs/products/databriefs/db351.htm.

Mason, W., & Suri, S. (2012). Conducting behavioral research on Amazon's Mechanical Turk. *Behavior Research Methods*, *44*(1), 1–23.

McFarland, L. A., & Ployhart, R. E. (2015). Social media: A contextual framework to guide research and practice. *Journal of Applied Psychology*, *100*(6), 1653–1677. doi:10.1037/a0039244.

Men, L. R., Tsai, W.-H. S., Chen, Z. F., & Ji, Y. G. (2018). Social presence and digital dialogic communication: Engagement lessons from top social CEOs. *Journal of Public Relations Research, 30*(3), 83–99. doi:1 0.1080/1062726X.2018.1498341.

Miller, L. A., & Lovler, R. L. (2019). *Foundations of psychological testing: A practical approach* (6th ed.). SAGE.

Mishra, D., Nair, A., Gandhi, R., Gogate, P., Mathur, S., Bhushan, P., Srivastav, T., Singh, H., Sinha, B., Singh, M., Nair, A. G., Gandhi, R. A., Gogate, P. J., Sinha, B. P. & Singh, M. K. (2020). The impact of COVID-19 related lockdown on ophthalmology training programs in India – Outcomes of a survey. *Indian Journal of Ophthalmology, 68*(6), 999–1004. doi:10.4103/ijo.IJO_1067_20.

Modi, N. (n.d.). *Narendra Modi*. https://twitter.com/narendramodi.

Obar, J. A., & Wilderman, S. (2015). Social media definition and governance challenge: An introduction to the special issue. *Telecommunications Policy, 39*(9), 745–750.

Pechmann, C., Phillips, C., Calder, D., & Prochaska, J. J. (2020). Facebook recruitment using zip codes to improve diversity in health research: Longitudinal observational study. *Journal of Medical Internet Research, 22*(6), e17554. doi:10.2196/17554.

Peres, R., Talwar, S., Alter, L., Elhanan, M., & Friedmann, Y. (2020). Narrowband influencers and global icons: Universality and media compatibility in the communication patterns of political leaders worldwide. *Journal of International Marketing, 28*(1), 48–65. doi:10.1177/1069031X19897893.

Porter, N. D., Verdery, A. M., & Gaddis, S. M. (2020). Enhancing big data in the social sciences with crowdsourcing: Data augmentation practices, techniques, and opportunities. *PLoS ONE, 15*(6), 1–21. doi:1 0.1371/journal.pone.0233154.

Press Information Bureau, Government of India. (June, 2020). *Government bans 59 mobile apps which are prejudicial to sovereignty and integrity of India, defence of India, security of state and public order*. https://pib.gov.in/PressReleseDetailm.aspx?PRID=1635206.

Reagan, L., Nowlin, S. Y., Birdsall, S. B., Gabbay, J., Vorderstrasse, A., Johnson, C., & D'Eramo Melkus, G. (2019). Integrative review of recruitment of research participants through Facebook. *Nursing Research, 68*(6), 423–432. doi:10.1097/NNR.0000000000000385.

Renshon, J., Dafoe, A., & Huth, P. (2018). Leader influence and reputation formation in world politics. *American Journal of Political Science, 2*, 325–339. doi:10.1111/ajps.12335.

Samuel, G., Derrick, G. E., & van Leeuwen, T. (2019). The ethics ecosystem: Personal ethics, network governance and regulating actors governing the use of social media research data. *Minerva: A Review of Science, Learning & Policy, 57*(3), 317–343. doi:10.1007/s11024-019-09368-3.

Samuelson, K. (2016). *Russia to ban access to LinkedIn due to personal data concerns*. https://time.com/4568102/russia-ban-linkedin/.

Sawhney, G., & Cigularov, K. P. (2019). Examining attitudes, norms, and control toward safety behaviors as mediators in the leadership-safety motivation relationship. *Journal of Business & Psychology, 34*(2), 237–256. doi:10.1007/s10869-018-9538-9.

Schumacher, S. & Kent, N. (2020). *8 charts on internet use around the world as countries grapple with COVID-19*. https://www.pewresearch.org/fact-tank/2020/04/02/8-charts-on-internet-use-around-the-world-as-countries-grapple-with-covid-19/.

Sklar, J. (2020). *'Zoom fatigue' is taxing the brain. Here's why that happens*. [National Geographic] https://www.nationalgeographic.com/science/2020/04/coronavirus-zoom-fatigue-is-taxing-the-brain-here-is-why-that-happens/.

Sloan, L. & Quan-Haase, A. (2017). *The SAGE handbook of social media research methods*. SAGE.

Statista. (2017). *Most used social network apps in Brazil as of June 2017*. https://www.statista.com/statistics/746969/most-popular-social-network-apps-brazil/.

Statista. (2020). *Number of global social network users 2017–2025*. www.statista.com/statistics/278414/number-of-worldwide-social-network-users/.

Statista. (2018). *Share of population in selected countries who are active WhatsApp users as of 3rdquarter 2017*. https://www.statista.com/statistics/291540/mobile-internet-user-whatsapp/.

Tavares, G. M., Sobral, F., Goldszmidt, R., & Araújo, F. (2018). Opening the implicit leadership theories' black box: An experimental approach with conjoint Analysis. *Frontiers in Psychology, 9*(100), 1–11.

The White House. (August, 2020). https://www.whitehouse.gov/presidential-actions/executive-order-addressing-threat-posed-wechat/.

Trump, D. J. (n.d.). *Donald J. Trump*. https://twitter.com/realdonaldtrump.

Tsai, W., Zavala, D., & Gomez, S. (2019). Using the Facebook advertisement platform to recruit Chinese, Korean, and Latinx cancer survivors for psychosocial research: Web-based survey study. *Journal of Medical Internet Research, 21*(1), e11571. doi:10.2196/11571.

Wagoner, J. A., & Barreto, N. (2019). Out-group leadership and subgroup schisms: An examination of the 2016 U.S. presidential election. *Group Dynamics, 23*(1), 22–43. doi:10.1037/gdn0000095.

Wee, J., & Lee, J. (2017). With whom do you feel most intimate?: Exploring the quality of Facebook friendships in relation to similarities and interaction behaviors. *PLoS ONE, 12*(4), 1–16. doi:10.1371/journal.pone.0176319.

Wessling, K. S., Huber, J., & Netzer, O. (2017). MTurk character misrepresentation: Assessment and solutions. *Journal of Consumer Research, 44*(1), 211–230. doi:10.1093/jcr/ucx053.

World Economic Forum. (n.d.). *Social media.* www.weforum.org/agenda/archive/social-media.

Xiaocong Tian. (2017). A text analytic approach to study host country nationalist sentiments and MNE responses during national conflicts. *AIB Insights, 17*(3), 18.

Yang, L., & Ren, Y. (2020). Moral obligation, public leadership, and collective action for epidemic prevention and control: Evidence from the corona virus disease 2019 (COVID-19) emergency. *International Journal of Environmental Research and Public Health, 17*(8). doi:10.3390/ijerph17082731.

Yang, S., Quan-Haase, A., Nevin, A. D., & Chen, Y. (2017). The role of online reputation management, trolling, and personality traits in the crafting of the virtual self on social media. In L. Sloan & A. Quan-Haase (Eds.), *The SAGE handbook of social media research methods* (pp. 72–100). SAGE.

Appendix

Table A18.1 Examples of Social Media and Crowdsourcing Platforms for Conducting Research

Platform	Examples of Research Functions	Learn More
Amazon Mechanical Turk (MTurk) (crowdsourcing)	Participant Recruitment: • retains registered users available to participate in paid research	Amazon Mechanical Turk www.mturk.com/ CloudResearch www.cloudresearch.com/
Dynata (crowdsourcing)	Participant Recruitment: • retains registered users available to participate in paid research – Note: the platform is for businesses collecting consumer dataData Collection • Archival data • Content analysis	Dynata – Online, Qualitative Research www.dynata.com/services/online-qualitative/ Dynata – Samplify www.dynata.com/dynata-insights-platform/
Facebook (social media)	Participant Recruitment (paid/unpaid advertisement) Data Collection • Archival data • Content analysis • Facebook Data for Good partners with -non-profits and researchers. • Existing datasets available Research Management • Collaborate with researchers • Share information with researchers • Communicate with participants	Facebook www.facebook.com Facebook for Good dataforgood.fb.com/ Facebook Resources for Educators https://about.fb.com/company-info/
LinkedIn (social media)	Participant Recruitment (paid/unpaid advertisement) Data Collection • Archival data • Content analysis	Advertise on LinkedIn: https://business.linkedin.com/marketing- solutions/ads
Opinion Access (crowdsourcing)	Participant Recruitment • retains registered users available to participate in paid research Data Collection • Survey research • Scenario-based experiments	Opinion Access www.opinionaccess.com/
Qualtrics (crowdsourcing)	Participant Recruitment • retains registered users available to participate in paid research Data Collection • Survey research • Scenario-based experiments	Qualtrics https://www.qualtrics.com/ Qualtrics Panels https://www.qualtrics.com/research-services/
SurveyCircle (crowdsourcing)	Participant Recruitment • the platform retains registered users available to participate in research for "points;" researchers must "pay" for participants in "points"	SurveyCircle www.surveycircle.com/en/welcome-survey-manager/

(Continued)

Table A18.1 (Continued)

Platform	Examples of Research Functions	Learn More
	earned through participation in other research Data Collection • Survey research • Scenario-based experiments	
SurveyMonkey Audience (crowdsourcing)	Participant Recruitment • retains registered users available to participate in paid research Data Collection • Survey research • Scenario-based experiments	SurveyMonkey Audience www.surveymonkey.com/market-research/solutions/audience-panel/
Twitter (social media)	Participant Recruitment (paid/unpaid advertisement) Data Collection • Archival data • Content analysis	Twitter www.twitter.com Twitter Advertisements https://ads.twitter.com/login
Vkontakte (social media)	Participant Recruitment (paid/unpaid advertisement) Data Collection • Archival data • Content analysis	Vkontakte https://vk.com/ Guide to Vkontakte Advertising https://www.konstantinkanin.com/en/guide-vkontakte-advertising/
WeChat (social media)	Participant Recruitment (unpaid advertisement) Data collection (administer surveys) Research Management (Communicate with participants)	Wechat.com/en walkthechat.com/get-started-wechat/
WhatsApp (social media)	Research Management • Communicate with participants and researchers • Share information	WhatsApp www.whatsapp.com/about/

Gabrielle Blackman

Table A18.2 Resources for Researchers Using Crowdsourcing and Social Media

Resource	Description
Buchheit et al. (2018)	• Presents limitations of MTurk • Provides guidance for maximizing validity when using MTurk
Cheung et al. (2017)	• Presents methodological issues with the MTurk platform • Analyzes strengths and limitations of using MTurk • Provides guidance for maximizing validity when using MTurk
Franz et al. (2019)	• Provides a primer for using Facebook to conduct qualitative research
Kees et al. (2017)	• Compares data quality across samples drawn from MTurk, student samples, and professional panels • Provides guidance for maximizing validity when using MTurk
Kosinski et al. (2015)	• Analyzes strengths and limitations of using Facebook in research • Provides guidance on using Facebook effectively in research
Reagan et al. (2019)	• Provides guidance for recruiting participants using Facebook
Sloan and Quan-Haase (2017)	• A comprehensive handbook on social media and research; includes 39 chapters, covering social media study design, qualitative and quantitative research, research and analytical tools, and social media platforms
Lehigh University, *"Introduction to Crowdsourcing"*, research.cc.lehigh.edu/crowdsourcing	• Discusses ethical issues, informed consent, and best practices for using crowdsourcing to conduct research
National University of Singapore, *"Unleash the Power of Crowdsourcing in the Policy Cycle"*, https://lkyspp.nus.edu.sg/gia/article/unleash-the-power-of-crowdsourcing-in-the-policy-cycle	• Summarizes innovative ways of connecting with the public for research and problem-solving purposes
University of Waterloo: Research Ethics, *"Use of Crowdsourcing Services"*, uwaterloo.ca/research/office-research-ethics/research-human-participants/pre-submission-and-training/use-crowdsourcing-services	• Explains how to use crowdsourcing to collect data and compensate participants

Table A18.3 Resources List: Ethical Guidance for Using Crowdsourcing and Social Media

Resources	Location
Emory University *"Guidelines for Using Social Media to Recruit Research Participants"*	www.irb.emory.edu/documents/Guidance-Using_Social_Media_Recruit_participants.pdf
Indiana University *"Research Using Online Tools and Mobile Devices"*	https://research.iu.edu/compliance/human-subjects/guidance/mobile.html
Lindenwood University *"Guidance for Use of the Internet and Social Media Research"*	www.lindenwood.edu/files/resources/20180129-use-of-the-internet-and-social-media-in-r.pdf
National Ethical Guidelines for Biomedical and Health Research Involving Human Participants	https://www.iitm.ac.in/downloads/ICMR_Ethical_Guidelines_2017.pdf
Singapore Psychological Society Section "1.4 Social Media and Technology"	https://singaporepsychologicalsociety.org/wp-content/uploads/2019/07/SPS-Code-of-Ethics-1st-Edition.pdf
Stanford University *"Amazon Mechanical Turk: IRB Considerations"*	https://www.uwsp.edu/acadaff/orsp/Documents/Bailey_SBER-mTurk-slides-Stanford-University.pdf
Synergies for Europe's Research Infrastructures in the Social Sciences (SERISS), European Union *"Guidelines on the Use of Social Media Data in Survey Research"*	https://seriss.eu/wp-content/uploads/2019/08/SERISS-D6.2.-Guidelines-social-media-data-.pdf
University of Massachusetts *"MTurk Guidance"*	https://www.umass.edu/research/guidance/mturk-guidancea
University of California, Berkeley *"Mechanical Turk (MTurk) for Online Research"*	https://cphs.berkeley.edu/mechanicalturk.pdf
University of Rochester Medical Center *"Guidelines for Research Using Social Media"*	www.rochester.edu/ohsp/documents/ohsp/pdf/policiesAndGuidance/Guideline_for_Research_Using_Social_Media.pdf

19

Planning a Quantitative Study on Leadership in Japan

Anna Lilleboe

Introduction

Globalization has created a new working environment that is becoming more and more culturally diverse; and more companies are recognizing the need to have employees with global leadership competencies. Geographical borders are disappearing as more companies conduct business across continents (Perez, 2017). Consumers and the workforce are becoming more culturally diverse (Cui, Jo, Na, & Velasquez, 2015; Oyakanmi, 2009; Trask & Anguiano, 2012). Cultural differences and similarities influence employees' expectations for their leaders and what leaders need to do to be effective (Aritz & Walker, 2014). The World Economic Forum (WEF) reported that the shortage of global leaders is one of the top critical issues in today's organizations (Maznevski, Stahl, & Mendenhall, 2013). Global leadership also impacts local and domestic companies as globalization increases local workforce diversity and competition from foreign businesses (Arita, Hermachandra, & Leung, 2014; Oyakanmi, 2009). As a result, more organizations need employees with global leadership competencies to successfully operate in a global environment, even if those employees operate solely within their country of origin (Cumberland, Herd, Alagaraja, & Kerrick, 2016; Mendenhall, Reiche, Bird, & Osland, 2012).

The Role of Culture in Leadership

Despite the widespread recognition of how culture is an integral part of leadership, most leadership theories originated in Western countries and are based on Western views (AlSarhi, Salleh, Za, Mohamad, & Amini, 2014; Ly, 2020; Rowley, Oh, & Jang, 2019). Leadership literature disproportionately reflects Western perspectives which further reinforces Western notion on leadership (Wang, James, Denyer, & Bailey, 2014). Many current leadership theories lack consideration of non-Western cultural values (AlSarhi et al., 2014). Chen and Miller (2011) highlighted that when it comes to global leadership, there was still a notion of the West leading the East. Adler and Gundersen (2008) also argued that most organizational theories reflect the cultural context of the West, especially the cultural context of the United States as one of the most dominant Western countries. Uncritical application of Western-based theories in non-Western context creates an "emic-as-etic" condition, which is the belief that what works in the West applies globally (Li, 2012).

DOI: 10.4324/9781003003380-19

This creates a challenge for Western-based researchers specifically, as they can be biased by their Western cultural influence when conducting global leadership research.

Western-based views may also create a challenge for non-Western researchers who receive their research training or education in Western countries. In the United States alone, the number of international students in universities almost doubled from 2006 to 2018 (Mostafa & Lim, 2020) with the largest population of those coming from Eastern countries (Heng, 2018). Zhou (2015) found that interest in research was one of the major motivations for international students to pursue their doctoral degrees in the United States. The education and training the students receive are more likely to normalize Western biases (Pritlove, Juando-Prats, Ala-leppilampi, & Parsons, 2019) which, in turn, may create a Western bias as they conduct research in their native countries (Singh & Meng, 2013).

The call for examination of the applicability of Western-based leadership research in non-Western context is not new. For example, in 1939, a recommendation was made to Dr. Kanoe Sakumo at Kyushu University in Japan to assess the generalizability of recent U.S.-based leadership research in Japan (Lewin, Lippitt, & White, 1939). The recommendation led to a 30-year research on Japanese leadership which contributed to the development of Misumi's PM (performance-maintenance) theory of leadership (Misumi & Peterson, 1985). The theory focuses on the leadership interaction with the performance function vs the maintenance function of the groups. Misumi and Peterson (1985) found that Japanese leadership at the lower and middle management levels contributed more towards group performance compared to their American counterparts. Pressentin (2015) raised specific questions regarding the relevancy of Western-based leadership models and concepts in Asia. Examination of and testing the generalizability of leadership research findings from Western population to non-Western context allow for researchers to achieve parsimony and contribute to global leadership scholarship by addressing research limitations introduced by Western context, bridging the gap between Western and non-Western perspectives, as well as expanding the research lens to represent a global context.

As global leadership knowledge continues to expand, there has been an increasing number of leadership research representing non-Western perspectives. Multiple researchers have argued against the applicability of some leadership theories outside of Western context. For example, Chen and Mason (2018) argued that Western's concept of leadership differs from that of East Asia's due to differing cultural values. Kim and McLean (2015) proposed an integrative framework for global leadership competency that is adaptable to different cultures and countries. Santoso (2019) specifically compared and highlighted the differences in Asian versus Western leadership theory development. Alves (2004) discussed the incorporation of Chinese philosophy in Asian leadership theory development. Lang, Irby, and Brown (2012) proposed a new leadership model based on Confucian principles and East Asian cultural values.

When we consider non-Western perspectives, East Asia represents one of the regions where a good contrast with the West can be seen. Hofstede's classification of cultural dimensions introduced in 1980 revealed that Asian countries tend to have higher power distance and higher collectivism (Hofstede, 1980; Liden, 2012) compared to Western countries. Many researchers have highlighted other differences between East and West. For example, Yiend et al. (2019) found there was a significant difference in the level of cognitive biases between participants in the United Kingdom versus those in Hong Kong. Boyle et al. (2020) discovered significant group differences in personality, motivation and cognition levels between Thai and Australian university students.

Overall, global leadership research should represent a global view, which includes nuances across the globe and cross-cultural aspects. It is easier to see and recognize cultural differences, but it is more challenging to understand how to take such differences into consideration when it comes to conducting a global research. The purpose of this chapter is to provide some examples and recommendations that can help guide researchers who consider conducting their global leadership research in Japan or those who consider involving Japanese participants in their studies, as well as researchers who wish to develop theoretical foundations based on the Japanese-derived notion of leadership.

Japanese Leadership: Cultural Values, Research and Business Practices

Japan is one of the oldest countries in East Asia and has risen into one of the most prominent countries in the world. After the second World War, Japan has grown into an industrialized and modern society, characterized by high economic performance and advanced technological infrastructure (Chung, 2007). Despite being considered a modern society, Japanese rich cultural heritage and deep-rooted traditions continue to govern and be reflected in the Japanese way of life. For example, many Japanese still practice the unique cultural traditions such as sumi-ye or the art of the ink, ikebana or the art of flower arrangement, origami, or the art of paper folding, and Chado, or the way of tea (Caldarola, Shimpo, & Ujimoto, 2011).

Japanese Cultural Values

Researchers who consider conducting their research in Japan or research involving Japanese participants in their global research should pay attention to Japanese cultural characteristics and their contrast with Western cultural values. Using Hofstede's (1980) cultural dimension classifications, the majority of Western societies are classified as low power distance while Japan is classified as a high-power distance society (Harada, 2017; Qie et al., 2019). Consistent with characteristics of a high-power distance society, Japan is governed by a strong hierarchical structure.

Hofstede (1980) also classified Japan as a collectivist society in contrast to many Western countries which are more individualistic. Collectivist societies place heavy emphasis on group harmony, conformity, and the collective interest of the group. This influences the way Japanese make decisions as consensus become more critical in collectivist societies compared to individualistic ones (Truong, Hallinger, & Sanga, 2017). People in collectivist societies tend to be more cautious with how they express or offer opinions (Campion & Wang, 2019). If the opinion is not in line with that of the group, the person can be seen as disruptive or causing disharmony.

Japanese Leadership Research

Despite Japan's prominence in the global business context, research on Japanese leadership is still limited (Fukushige & Spicer, 2007). However, existing studies provide important insights into how Japanese cultural values influence the way Japanese view leadership comparing to traditional leadership knowledge of Western-based leadership theories and models. For example, servant leadership is viewed as a positive leadership model in the United States, yet it was not endorsed as an effective model in high-power distance societies such as Japan (Mittal & Dorfman, 2012). Mittal and Dorfman (2012) went as far as arguing that servant leadership will be counterproductive in the business setting in these societies. The idea of the leader serving his or her subordinates conflicts with the hierarchical nature of high-power distance societies. House's path-goal theory is another leadership theory that some researchers found to be inapplicable in Japan (Rodrigues, 1990; Kreitner, 1995) because it is not aligned with Japanese preferences to hold oneself accountable. The path-goal theory specifies that employees' performance depends on their leader's ability to provide clear paths to the goals, which aligns with the principles of servant leadership.

Findings from other studies lend support to some leadership differences between Japan and Western countries. For example, Mujtaba and Isomura (2012) found Japanese leaders to be more relationship-oriented than task-oriented compared to some Western countries such as the United States. Fukushige and Spicer (2011) research involving multiple instruments (that were developed with Western samples) with British and Japanese participants found significant differences in leadership preferences between Japanese and British employees. More specifically, the Multifactor Leadership Questionnaire (MLQ) showed low reliability for the Japanese participants, which raised concerns over the scale's universality. While multiple researchers have utilized MLQ in different non-Western countries including Malaysia (Jogulu & Ferkins, 2012), Hong Kong (Lui & Johnston, 2019), and Papua New Guinea (Muddle, 2020), some of the research results revealed the criticality of ensuring instrument's validity in cross-cultural context. For example, Lui and Johnston (2019) found that their confirmatory factor analysis (CFA) for the MLQ scale did not produce satisfactory results for their sample with participants from Hong Kong.

Regarding theoretical frameworks, scholars found support for some Western-based leadership theories' applicability in Japan. For example, transformational and transactional leadership theories can be adapted to various cultural contexts which makes them more universal across global environments (Pauliene, 2012). In Japan, transformational leadership style was found to be positively associated with leadership success (Perrin et al., 2012). Additionally, Jogulu (2010) discovered that Japanese cultural values allow Japanese leaders to adopt transformational leadership style more easily than transaction leadership style as Japanese values are more aligned with transformational leadership characteristics.

Japanese Business Practices

In examining leadership practices in Japan, one should recognize Japanese business practices that also offer a significant contrast to business practices in the United States. For example, employee loyalty towards one's leader or organization is expected (Moran, Abramson, & Moran, 2014; Morishima, 1996; Rousseau, 1990). There is still a strong negative connotation associated with employees who are deemed as disloyal, who abandon their employer and disobey their leaders (Guerra, Giner-Sorolla, & Vasiljevic, 2012; Nitobe, 2009). Japanese employees tend to prefer a long tenure in one company (Mujtaba & Isomura, 2011). Discussions to reach a decision are often informal and implicit (Porter, Takeuchi, & Sakakibara, 2000; Haghirian, 2010). Once the leader decides, the subordinates are expected to obey without question (Nitobe, 2009; Qie et al., 2019). These behaviors are consistent with multiple research findings that found high power distance societies to be positively associated with higher obedience level (Gu et al., 2017; Mone, Benga, & Opre, 2016).

The hierarchical nature of Japanese society creates certain rules within Japanese business practices. For example, the highest-level person in the hierarchy should be introduced first, seated first, etc. (Coulter et al., 2011). The Japanese language also reflects such hierarchical nature with honorific words as required grammar to address other people in higher hierarchy such as teacher, supervisor, etc. (Qie et al., 2019).

Japan also exhibits some differences in practical leadership behaviors compared to other countries. Through surveys and interviews involving 2,000 of the Forbes' largest corporations in the world, Karaszewski (2010) found multiple unique leadership practices in Japan compared to other countries' organizations. For example, while motivating and inspiring team members was viewed as incredibly important by the majority of organizations across the globe, Japanese leaders deemed this activity to be of very little importance. Rather than inspiring their team members with a vision as most leaders from other countries reported, Japanese leaders indicated higher frequency of having their subordinates create their own vision. Compared to leaders from other countries in the study, Japanese leaders also reported lower levels of agreement regarding the need to engage in activities to encourage subordinates to undertake certain tasks, which could be explained by the higher likelihood of Japanese subordinates to obey orders without needing to be encouraged. Equality in the workplace or equal treatment among employees was significantly more important for American employees compared to their Japanese counterparts (Uy et al., 2008). This could be because Japanese also demonstrated lower levels of individuality or the concept of "self" compared to Americans (Shuzo, Bagozzi, & Sadarangani, 2008).

Quantitative Research Considerations for Japan

Researchers who intend to conduct their research in Japan and/or involving Japanese participants within Japanese societal context have several factors to consider. From a theoretical foundation, conceptual framework, to data gathering and an analysis approach, the unique Japanese culture as well as practices may influence and distort the research results due to misinterpretation caused by Western-based lens. For example, the word "Hai" in Japanese, is usually translated as "Yes" by Westerners (Ciubancan, 2015). However, in Japanese context, the response is merely an expression of acknowledgement rather than a sign of agreement that it is often mistaken for.

Many researchers found that cultural diversity has a positive relationship with organizational performance (Choi, 2007; Talke, Salomo, & Rost, 2010; Pieterse, Van Knippernberg, & Van Dierendonck, 2013; Van Knippenberg, De Dreu, & Homan, 2004). However, Japan became one of the industrial leaders in the global world even though the Japanese population is highly homogenous with low cultural diversity (Yi, 2017), suggesting that there are other contributing factors than diversity within the Japanese population that influence performance and its success. Thus, international research should consider cultural values, business practices, personal practices and customs of the different societies in their studies (Rodd, 2013).

Theoretical Foundation and Conceptual Framework

Some Western-based leadership theories may not be applicable to Japanese context as they may not reflect Japanese realities. For example, Mittal and Dorfman (2012) as well as Hale and Fields (2007) argued that the servant leadership theory proposed by Robert Greenleaf may not be applicable in high power distance culture such as Japan. Servant leadership involves leaders putting their followers' needs above them which may conflict with the expected inequality in high power distance societies. House's path-goal theory is another leadership theory that may be suspect in Japanese context because it implies that employee's performance is depended on the leader, which is not aligned with Japanese preferences to hold oneself accountable (Rodrigues, 1990; Kreitner, 1995).

Construct equivalence is critical and a necessary condition in cross-cultural research. Without construct equivalence, the results may be misinterpreted as there might be other sources of variance beyond cross-cultural differences (McArthur, 2007). Researchers should consider potential construct differences across different cultures. For example, there are differences with regards to how Western and Asian societies view certain leadership concepts. Witt and Stahl (2016) found significant differences in how executives in Japan view responsible leadership versus executives in the United States. Takuma and Mizuki (2018) also highlighted different ways in how Japanese define ethical leadership in comparison to other countries such as the United States and Germany.

Data Gathering, Instruments and Analysis Approach

Although the number of Japanese who are fluent in English is increasing, it is still a recommended practice to have research communication and data-gathering instruments to be in a local language, Japanese. The country has long accepted that English proficiency is essential to operate successfully in the global world (Sakamoto, 2012). Japan's Ministry of Education, Culture, Sports, Science, and Technology (MEXT) made English a mandatory subject in all levels of schooling and has been actively promoting its use (MEXT, 2002, 2011). However, the English language continues to be deemed as foreign (Lieb, 2019). Furthermore, the actual level of English proficiency in Japan remains low even when compared with other countries in Asia (Reisel, 2018). Karaszewski (2010) found that although he sent out his research survey to Japanese participants in two different languages, English and Japanese, all responses he received were in Japanese, demonstrating Japanese participants' preference towards their native language. In addition to challenges associated with English proficiency, a survey in English may also cause response bias from Japanese participants as Japanese participants are more likely to choose a neutral response in English Likert-scale surveys (Harzing, 2006; Hayashi, 1996). The propensity towards a neutral response is consistent with preference towards harmony and conformity associated with collectivist societies.

Presenting research questions in English to Japanese participants also increases the risk associated with cultural acculturation. Cultural acculturation presents a risk to the validity of studies involving comparison of cultures as participants' indigenous cultural values might be influenced by the foreign cultural values resulting in cross-cultural bias (Hemert, Baerveldt, & Vermande, 2001). English language development may cause cultural acculturation where one becomes cognitively influenced by the cultural aspects of the language during the learning process (Richard & Toffoli, 2009). Cultural acculturation represents the incorporation or adoption of a different culture into one's own (Newman, Hartman, & Taber, 2012). For example, the Japanese, being a society with high context communication style, tend to be more indirect in their communication, yet they may be compelled to be more direct when communicating in English (Kanduboda, 2016). Measurement of participants' levels of acculturation can improve the validity of cross-cultural research (Hermet, Baerveldt, & Vermande, 2001).

Many researchers preferred to utilize an existing instrument as it is faster and often easier than developing a new instrument (Ali, 2016). However, similar to how the majority of leadership research is Western based, the majority of leadership research instruments and scales are also originated in English. An important consideration for effective translation of the research information as well as the research instruments is to ensure the translated version has an equal concept with the original version as the translation quality may affect the research validity (Ali, 2016). It will be extremely rare to be able to have one-to-one word match in the translation. In addition, often times equivalent meanings in two different languages require different words or phrases versus having a literal word translation. Beaton et al. (2000) proposed a guideline that has been adopted by multiple researchers when it comes to cultural instrument translation or adaptation. The guideline includes multiple steps involving forward translation (original language to target language) and backward translation (target language back to the original language). These steps may need to be repeated multiple times until both the original version and the translated version have equivalent meanings.

With regards to quantitative research specifically, simple comparative scores between Japanese and non-Japanese participants may yield to a misleading conclusion. For example, Lincoln and Kalleberg (1990) found that while Japanese employees demonstrate higher organizational commitment than their American counterparts, they would report lower scores in surveys because the standards by which they assess their level of commitment are higher than American employees. Researchers should consider whether the survey instruments they wish to utilize may involve unequal baselines for assessments. For example, terms such as "often", "regular", "frequent", "seldom", etc. tend to be more subjective as what one considers to be "often" may be different from someone else's interpretation. Such misalignment in interpretation may yield to unreliable comparative scores. Thus, researchers may be able to obtain more accurate results by including specific scale-statements in capturing frequency information, such as "less than once per day", "more than twice a week", etc.

Gender gap in the workforce continues to be a prominent issue in Japan. According to the Ministry of Internal Affairs and Communications (2007), the number of full-time female employees in Japan only counted for about half of full-time male employees. For managerial positions, the gap was even wider, especially when compared to Western countries. For example, as recently as 2016, female representation in managerial positions was only 13% compared to approximately 43% in

United States and 39.2% in Sweden (Binder et al., 2019). Female representation in executive po-sitions was even lower, with only approximately 3.4% in Japan compared to 17% in the United States and 30% in France. Researchers should consider this gender imbalance as they plan to conduct global leadership research in Japan, especially as the gender gap might be wider in some industries than others. For example, Schutte (2019) reported that a low number of female Japanese participants was a significant limitation in his research regarding comparative leadership styles in the wine in-dustries. Researchers may need to increase their sample size if they wish to obtain a certain number of female representations in their study.

Hamada (2018) proposed some contributing factors to Japanese gender gap in the workforce that might be helpful to understand as part of a research consideration. For example, many Japanese women did not seem to consider a leadership career to be appealing and voluntarily excluded themselves from promotional opportunities. This suggestion was consistent with the findings from the Japanese Productivity Center survey in 2015, which showed that about 70% of companies surveyed reported their female employees did not consider career advancement to be attractive. Many female employees cited significant personal hurdles against their careers such as increased working hours and lack of alternative childcare options (Zhou, 2015).

Survey instruments that have not been validated for Japanese participants may present a threat to validity and reliability. Researchers first must take careful measures to ensure the survey instruments are translated effectively into the Japanese language, with attention to the common language translation challenges such as specific terms and nuances that may yield to different meanings. Researchers also should consider additional steps to minimize threats to the instrument's validity and reliability. Validity and reliability are critical components of any research instruments. Validity can be defined as the degree of which the instrument measures what it is intended to measure while reliability represents the degree of consistency or reproducibility of the results (Zamanzadeh et al., 2015). Brown (2000) highlighted specific threats to validity for research in Japan were often due to insufficient number of questions, unclear description, absence of pilot testing, inadequate item analysis procedures, insufficient reliability studies and not enough validity analysis. Instrument va-lidity analysis may include examining results from content analysis, factor analysis, multi-trait/multi-method studies, etc. (Brown, 2000). Higher number of questions in the survey designed to measure a construct can help determine the internal reliability commonly measured by Cronbach's α (Rickards, Magee, & Artino Jr., 2012).

Researchers can adopt, adapt or create instruments for their international or cross-cultural study (He & Vijver, 2012). Adoption involves a close translation of the instrument to a target language. Adaption usually involves additional changes compared to adoption as a close translation associated with adoption might be inadequate for construct equivalence. Finally, researchers have the option to create a new instrument.

Additionally, researchers should consider whether the survey instruments they are planning to utilize are valid and reliable for Japanese participants. This can be a challenging effort as there is not a single way to confirm validity, and thus the validity of the research instrument should be shown through a collection of evidence. Sometimes the study results revealed that the instrument may not be valid when applied in a different culture or country. Such study still has value as it provides empirical evidence of the inapplicability of the instrument and provides support towards the need for either adaptation or complete exclusion of such instrument for that particular population.

Testing the instrument with a pilot group prior to utilizing it in the broader study can help in improving the validity of the instrument. Meng, Elliott and Hall (2010) argued that piloting the instrument in cross-cultural studies is essential to determine if the relevant construct in one culture is applicable to another before cross-cultural comparison can be analyzed. Results from the pilot can be useful in the evaluation of variance, calculation of reliability scores and determining composite score correlations (Rickards, Magee, & Artino Jr., 2012). Such results can provide important insights into the reliability of the instrument.

Focus groups discussion following the pilot are also useful in the adaption process of an instrument for utilization in a different culture or language (Fuller et al., 1993). The focus groups comprised of participants of the pilot who can offer important insights into potential adjustments that need to be made to the instrument to increase its validity. Input and feedback from the focus group can have insights into whether the instrument is effective in measuring what it is intended to measure in a different culture or country (Rickards, Magee, & Artino Jr., 2012). Multiple researchers have utilized focus groups in adapting their instrument for use in another country. For example, Bostjancic, Johnson and Belak (2018) used two focus groups in their effort to adapt the Cultural Intelligence Scale (CQS) for Slovenian populations. Jayawickreme et al. (2012) had six focus groups in adapting several scales intended to measure well-being and mental health for Sri Lankan participants. Chiba, Miyamoto and Kawakami (2010) utilized a focus group to adapt the Recovery Assessment Scale (RAS) for Japanese participants.

Survey instruments involving a Likert scale may also presents a challenge, as Japanese participants tend to favor a neutral response or the middle option that reflects their collectivist cultural value and preference towards group harmony as well as conformity (Hayashi, 1996). In general, middle or neutral responses may present a challenge in cross-cultural comparisons as differences or similarities may be more difficult to identify. As such, Likert-scale survey instruments may be more effective when the neutral or middle option is not offered.

Conducting a pilot study is an important part of research, particularly for international research. A pilot involves employing the research protocols, data collection approach and instruments, sampling strategies, as well other research techniques in the study to a much smaller group than the total planned sample size (Hassan, Schattner, & Mazza, 2006; Henson & Jeffrey, 2016). There are several critical benefits of a pilot study. Malmqvist et al. (2019), who conducted their study in Sweden based an adaptation of an Irish project, argued that a pilot study can better prepare researchers for the challenges associated with the overall study and can increase the confidence in the data collection instruments. Seidman (1998) recommended a pilot study for researchers to test their research approach and assess the effectiveness of such approach. Through the pilot, researchers can gain insights into potential problems with the research such as potential shortcomings in the research protocols, incompatible instruments, etc. that may present significant threats to the research validity and reliability. For example, the researchers can calculate preliminary Cronbach's alpha from the pilot results to provide an initial insight into the scale's reliability. Researchers can then adjust or make the necessary modifications to their research approach to ensure they obtain the intended results.

Reflections from Personal Research Experience

I conducted my research on courageous followership involving a comparison between Japanese and American followers. I did not grow up in Japan, but I grew up nearby in Southeast Asia and feel a strong cultural connection with Japanese values. I learned Japanese for several years through college and am inspired by Japanese discipline and approach to innovation. At the time I conducted my study, I was also working for a Japanese-owned financial services company where I had to interact frequently with colleagues and team members from Japan. I was intrigued to conduct my research involving a comparison of Japanese and American followers because of the cultural contrast that I experienced between the two cultures as well as my interest to expand the knowledge of followership.

My study revolved around the courageous followership concept and the main purpose was to assess whether the concept of courageous followership as a representation of ideal followership applies outside of the United States, specifically, in Japan. The contrasting cultures presented an important opportunity to explore the role that culture might have on ideal followership perception and demonstrated behaviors. My study tested the following hypotheses:

H10: There is no significant difference in the belief that courageous followership is a cultural ideal between American and Japanese participants.

H1A: American participants (i.e., personal cultural orientations are high in individualism and low on power distance) will report that courageous followership is a cultural ideal more so than Japanese participants (i.e., those with opposite scores in those personal cultural orientations).

H20: There is no significant difference in a level of actual courageous followership behaviors between American and Japanese participants.

H2A: American participants will report engaging in higher levels of courageous followership than will Japanese participants.

H30: There is no significant difference in the differential score of actual vs idealized courageous followership behaviors between American and Japanese participants.

H3A: The difference between American participants' actual behaviors vs. idealized courageous followership behaviors will be smaller than the difference between Japanese participants' difference in actual versus ideal behaviors.

I utilized two instruments: The Followership Profile (TFP) to measure the courageous followership behaviors (Dixon & Westbrook, 2003), and the Personal Culture Orientation (PCO) to assess the cultural dimensions (Sharma, 2010). The study included responses from 160 participants, which comprised of 80 U.S. employees and 80 Japanese employees. Through a quasi-experimental mixed factor repeated measure design, analysis of variance with covariates revealed how followers from each country perceive courageous followership behaviors as ideal and how often these followers practice such behaviors.

I utilized Qualtrics, a panel aggregator, to recruit my study participants and provided my sample characteristics which Qualtrics utilized to screen and ensure only eligible participants were included. My sample criteria included the specifications that participants must either be Japanese or American nationals (who live and work in their respective countries) and were in middle management or above. An automated routing feature from Qualtrics allowed for Japanese participants to be presented with the study information and survey in Japanese, while American participants were presented with equivalent information in English.

My research was not limited to specific industries, though my sample was limited to full-time employees in middle level management or above. I was able to obtain fairly equal representation of gender in my sample (71 males and 87 females). Table 19.1 outlines the final respondents' demographics by nationality and gender. Note that I provided an option of "Other" for gender to make sure respondents who may not identify themselves as "male" or "female" did not feel forced to specify themselves as one or the other.

I learned several valuable lessons as I conducted my research and after I completed my study. Indeed, there is no such thing as a perfect research. There are always limitations that either fall outside the researcher's control or that a single research cannot address. For example, researchers usually only have access to a limited representation of the study population which may not provide true representation of the overall population (Theofanidis & Fountouki, 2018). There are also limitations associated with studies involving self-reported data that are common in social science research, as such data will be exceedingly difficult to be independently verified (Price & Murnan, 2004). However, I hope the lessons I have learned throughout my research journey can help improve future research, including my own.

Table 19.1 Respondents Demographic by Nationality and Gender

Demographic	N	Percentage
American		
Male	28	35
Female	52	65
Japanese		
Male	43	53.8
Female	35	43.7
Other	2	2.5

Because my research involved comparison between American and Japanese employees, I understand the importance of offering the survey in the participant's native language, either Japanese or English. I did encounter a challenge here as the translation process took longer than I anticipated. It took approximately one month for the translation process to be completed. I followed the guidelines established by Beaton et al. (2000) which involved multiple steps of forward and backward translations. I obtained the translation services available through the company I was working for at the time. Because I worked for a U.S. division of a Japanese company, I had access to resources for the translation services I needed.

The first translation forward step involved having the original material in English translated into Japanese by native Japanese speakers with English fluency. Afterwards, native English speakers with Japanese fluency translated the Japanese version back into English as part of the second step of backward translations. I continued through this cycle of forward and backward translations until the original version and the backward translated version achieved conceptual equivalence. It included two cycles of forward and backward translations. The process involved two independent Japanese translators and two independent English translators.

Conceptual equivalence as the standard for the translation quality has been regarded as a critical foundation for international research since the 1950s (Zhou & Hua, 2021). Identifying conceptual equivalence was also a challenge for me as it was virtually impossible to obtain a word-for-word match. I consulted with a few professors and solicited input from several peers to help me determine that conceptual equivalence had been established between the original survey and the translated version.

I was fortunate to be able to identify native Japanese individuals with English fluency and vice versa. Some researchers may find it more challenging to do so and as such, may need to consider additional time as well as methods for identifying the needed translators. Utilizing multiple independent translators and review groups can be immensely helpful in the translation process, and something I highly recommend to any researchers needing to translate their survey instruments to another language. There are professional institutions available who specialize in providing translation services for a variety of languages. University resources may also have referrals for translation services.

In addition to translating the survey into Japanese, I also modified my survey response options. With the understanding that Japanese participants may favor the neutral or middle option in responding to a Likert-scale survey, I eliminated the neutral or middle option. This helped me in capturing the potential contrast I wanted to measure between American and Japanese responses. I further examined my survey questions to ensure there were no subjective terms that can yield to unequal baseline for assessments such as "often", "seldom", etc.

I utilized a pilot by starting the survey with a smaller group, approximately 10% of the size of my target population. It was extremely helpful in validating the instruments and provided confidence in releasing the survey to the wider targeted population. The pilot was released and temporarily closed after I received 15 responses (which was about 10% of my total sample size). I had some time to analyze the results from the pilot and had the opportunity to make any adjustments if needed including but not limited to changing the survey structure or even changing the instruments altogether. Results from the pilot enabled me to calculate and validate average completion time. I was also able to calculate the preliminary reliability score (Cronbach's alpha) that provided confirmation regarding the effectiveness of the instrument for my study. The pilot did not raise any alarms or red flags such as a large number of incomplete responses, and had a much faster completion time than anticipated, etc. From the pilot, I obtained sufficient reliability scores, which helped me confirm that both the instrument and the translation of such an instrument were effective. Following satisfactory results from the pilot, I released the survey again to the rest of the target population until I received the needed number of responses. Although I did not make any changes or modifications to my instruments following the pilot, following best practice, I did not include results from the pilot into the final analysis.

Despite these considerations, there were still some limitations in my study. For example, for the total sample, one of the measures in my surveys had a slightly less than the standard acceptable level for Cronbach's Alpha associated with the Japanese participants ($\alpha = .69$). I moved forward with the results after consultation with a few other professors who oversaw my study. However, future studies involving these measures in Japan may benefit from additional validations. I do not know whether another pilot or a larger pilot size would have identified this risk though I suspect it would have helped. If I had the opportunity to re-do my study, I would most likely increase my pilot size. I also might increase my overall sample size. It will be interesting to repeat the study and observe if the results are consistent or if additional validations can be obtained.

One of my survey instruments, the Followership Profile (TFP), to my knowledge at that time, has not been applied outside of the United States. It creates a threat to the instrument's validity and reliability. I had my reasons for moving forward with the instrument, including that it served a preliminary attempt to also test the instrument's applicability outside of the United States, or in Japan specifically. If the instrument was found not to be valid within a Japanese context, I wanted to at least be able to show that as there were no previous studies to determine the instrument's applicability in Japan. However, researchers can reduce threats to their research' reliability and validity by utilizing instruments that have been verified in the global context.

As I reflected on my experience, below are the recommended steps for any researchers who are planning to conduct their studies in Japan and/or who are planning to include Japanese participants in their studies:

1. Conduct comprehensive literature review to assess the applicability or potential limitation of the theoretical foundation or conceptual framework of the study. Determine whether the limitation might introduce risk to the research validity and/or reliability. If so, determine how such risk can be reduced or addressed.
2. Assess the construct equivalence associated with the study. Assess the applicability of a measure or instrument involved in the study. If the instrument has not been validated for utilization in Japan or for utilization with a Japanese population, determine how to address the threat to the research validity and reliability.
3. Translate the consent form, information about the study, and the instrument into Japanese. Ensure the translated version has conceptual equivalence with the original version. Follow the translation process recommended by Beaton et al. (2000) which included forward and backward translation process along with committee review to ensure conceptual equivalence has been achieved.
4. Pay special attention to words that may have unequal baselines for assessment such as "often", "frequent", etc. as what one considers to be "often" may be different from someone else's interpretation. Utilization of such words should be minimized or eliminated.

5. If the survey involves a Likert scale, consider adapting the scale by removing the middle or neutral option as Japanese participants are more inclined to select the middle or neutral option.

6. Due to their high power distance culture, consider where and how the invitation to participate in the study will come from. If the invitation comes from authority figures, respondents may feel more pressured to participate.

7. Conduct a pilot study or pre-test with a smaller sample group. The results from the pilot may provide insights into the feasibility of the study protocols, potential flaws in the survey that may need to be adjusted, reliability of the instrument, etc. A pilot study can also provide support for the reliability and the validity of the instrument.

8. Consider conducting a focus group discussion with members of the pilot study to determine if the instrument should be modified further for better adaptation for Japanese context to increase its validity and reliability.

Some of the examples and recommendations I have presented in this chapter may be specific to a Japanese context, however, they may also be applicable to other cultures. I hope the information helps guide researchers as they consider their global studies and help improve the advancement of global leadership. Only through continuous improvement and an extension of existing studies can we grow our knowledge and advance our understanding of global leadership.

References

Adler, N. J. & Gundersen, A. (2008). *International dimensions of organizational behavior* (5th ed.). Thomson Higher Education.

Ali, M. M. (2016). Are we asking the same questions in different contexts: Translation techniques in cross-culture studies in science education. *Journal of Turkish Science Education, 13*(1), 31–44.

AlSarhi, N. Z., Salleh, L. M., Mohamad, Z. A., & Amini, A. A. (2014). The West and Islam perspective of leadership. *International Affairs and Global Strategy, 18*(2014). 42–56.

Alves, J. C. (2004). Developing leadership theory in Asia: The role of Chinese philosophy. *International Journal of Leadership Studies, 1*(1), 3–25.

Arita, S., Hermachandra, D., & Leung, P. (2014). Can local farms survive globalization? *Agricultural and Resource Economics Review, 43*(2), 227–248.

Aritz, J., & Walker, R. C. (2014). Leadership styles in multicultural groups: American and East Asians working together. *International Journal of Business Communication, 51*(1), 72–92.

Beaton, D. E., Bonbardier, C., Guillemin, F., & Farraz, M. B. (2000). Guidelines for the process of cross-cultural adaptation of self-report measures. *SPINE, 25*(24), 3186–3191.

Binder, B., Dworkin, T. M., Nae, N., Schipani, C. A., & Averianova, I. (2019). The plight of women in positions of corporate leadership in the United States, the European Union, and Japan: Differing laws and cultures, similar issues. *Michigan Journal of Gender & Law, 26*(2), 279–340.

Bostjancic, E., Johnson, R. B., & Belak, U. (2018). Cross-cultural adaption of research tools: A study on the cultural intelligence scale adaptation in Slovenian. *Europe's Journal of Psychology, 14*(2), 386–403.

Boyle, G. J., Wongsri, N., Bahr, M., Macayan, J. V., & Bentler, P. M. (2020). Cross-cultural differences in personality, motivation, and cognition in Asian vs Western societies. *Personality and Individual Differences, 159*(1). doi:10.1016/j.paid.2020.109834

Brown, J. D. (2000). What is construct validity? *JAT Testing & Evaluation SIG, 4*(2), 8–12.

Canals, J. (2014). Global leadership development, strategic alignment and CEOs commitment. *Journal of Management Development, 33*(5), 487–502.

Caldarola, C., Shimpo, M., & Ujimoto, K. V. (2011). Sakura in the land of the maple leaf: Japanese cultural traditions in Canada. *Canadian Ethnic Studies Journal, 43*(1), 303–305.

Campion, L. L., & Wang, C. X. (2019). Collectivism and individualism: The differentiation of leadership. *TechTrends, 63*(3), 353–356.

Chen, C. & Mason, D. S. (2018). Postcolonial reading of representations of non-Western leadership in sport management studies. *Journal of Sport Management, 32*(2), 150–169.

Chen, M. J., & Miller, D. (2011). West meets East: Toward an ambicultural approach to management. *Academy of Management Executive, 24*(4), 17–24.

Chiba, R., Miyamoto, Y., & Kawakami, N. (2010). Reliability and validity of the Japanese version of the Recovery Assessment Scale (RAS) for people with chronic mental illness: Scale development. *International Journal of Nursing Studies, 47*(3), 314–322.

Choi, J. N. (2007). Group composition and employee creative behavior in a Korean electronics company: Distinct effects of relational demography and group diversity. *Journal of Occupational and Organizational Psychology, 80*(2), 213–234.

Chung, W. K. (2007). Westernization of business organizations in Japan and China: Continuity and change. In R. Raud (Ed.), *Japan and Asian modernity* (pp. 239–260). Routledge.

Ciubancan, M. (2015). Principles of communication in Japanese indirectness and hedging. *Romanian Economic Business Review, 10*(4), 246–253.

Coulter, S., Lee, J., Sheldon, A., & Meraz, J. (2011). Doing business in Japan. *Conflict Resolution & Negotiation Journal, 2*(1), 96–103.

Cui, J., Jo, H., Na, H., & Velasquez, M. G. (2015). Workforce diversity and religiosity. *Journal of Business Ethics, 128*(4), 743–767.

Cumberland, D. M., Herd, A., Alagaraja, M., & Kerrick, S. A. (2016). Assessment and development of global leadership competencies in the workplace: A review of literature. *Advances in Developing Human Resources, 18*(3), 301–317.

Dixon, G., & Westbrook, J. (2003). Followers revealed. *Engineering Management Journal, 15*(1), 19–25.

Dorfman, P. W., & House, R. J. (2004). Cultural influences on organizational leadership. In R. J. House, P. J. Hanges, M. Javidan, P. W. Dorfman, & V. Gupta (Eds.), *Culture, leadership, and organizations: The GLOBE study of 62 societies.* Sage Publications.

Fukushige, A., & Spicer, D. P. (2007). Leadership preferences in Japan: An exploratory study. *Leadership & Organization Development Journal, 28*(6), 508–530.

Fukushige, A., & Spicer, D. P. (2011). Leadership and followers' work goals: A comparison between Japan and the UK. *The International Journal of Human Resource Management, 22*(1), 2110–2134.

Fuller, T., Edwards, J., Vorakitphokatorn, S., & Sermsri, S. (1993). Using focus groups to adapt survey instruments to new populations: Experience from a developing country. In Morgan, D. L. (Ed.), *Successful focus groups: Advancing the state of the art* (pp. 89–104). SAGE Publications, Inc.

Grossman, I., Karasawa, M., Izumi, S., Na, J., Varnum, M. E. W., Kitayama, S., & Nisbett, R. E. (2012). Aging and wisdom: Culture matters. *Psychological Science, 23*(10), 1059–1066.

Gu, J., Cavanagh, K., Baer, R. A., & Strauss, C. (2017). An empirical examination of the factor structure of compassion. *PLoS ONE, 12*(2), 1–17.

Guerra, V. M., Giner-Sorolla, R., & Vasiljevic, M. (2012). The importance of honor concerns across eight countries. *Group Process and Intergroup Relations, 16*(3), 298–318.

Haghirian, P. (2010). *Innovation and change in Japanese management.* Palgrave MacMillan.

Hale, J. R., & Fields, D. L. (2007). Exploring servant leadership across cultures: A study of followers in Ghana and the USA. *Leadership, 3*(4), 397–417.

Hamada, T. (2018). Japanese company's cultural shift for gender equality at work. *Global Economic Review, 47*(1), 63–87.

Harada, Y. (2017). A cultural comparison of business practices in Thailand and Japan with implications for Malaysia. *Journal of Cogent Social Sciences, 3*(1), 1–9.

Harzing, A. W. (2006). Response styles in cross-national survey research: A 26-country study. *International Journal of Cross-cultural Management, 6*(2), 243–266.

Hassan, Z. A., Schattner, P., & Mazza, D. (2006). Doing a pilot study: Why is it essential? *Malays Farm Physician, 1*(2–3), 70–73.

Hayashi, C. (1996). *Structure of Japanese mind: Assessing culture and mind.* Toyokeizai-shinpo-sha.

He, J., & Vijver, F. (2012). Bias and equivalence in cross-cultural research. *Psychology and Culture, 2*(2), 251–277.

Heng, T. T. (2018). Different is not deficient: Contradicting stereotypes of Chinese international students in US higher education. *Studies in Higher Education, 43*(1), 22–36.

Henson, A., & Jeffrey, C. (2016). Turning a clinical question into nursing research: The benefits of a pilot study. *Renal Society of Australasia Journal, 12*(3), 99–105.

Hemert, D. A., Baerveldt, C., & Vermande, M. (2001). Assessing cross-cultural item bias in questionnaires: Acculturation and the measurement of social support and family cohesion for adolescents. *Journal of Cross-cultural Psychology, 32*(4), 381–396.

Hofstede, G. (1980). *Culture's consequences: International differences in work-related values.* Sage.

Hofstede, G., Hofstede, G. J., & Minkov, M. (2010). *Cultures and organizations: Software of the mind* (3rd ed.). McGraw Hill.

Jayawickreme, N., Jayawickreme, E., Pavel, A., Goonasekera, M. A., & Foa, E. B. (2012). Are culturally specific measures of trauma-related anxiety and depression needed? The case of Sri Lanka. *Psychological Assessment, 24*(4), 791–800.

Jogulu, U. D. (2010). Culturally-linked leadership style. *Leadership & Organization Development Journal, 31*(8), 705–719.

Jogulu, U. D., & Ferkins, L. (2012). Leadership and culture in Asia: The case of Malaysia. *Asia Pacific Business Review, 18*(4), 531–549.

Kanduboda, P. B. (2016). Communication strategies among trilingual speakers: Switching and borrowing among Sinhala, English & Japanese languages. *Theory and Practice in Language Studies, 6*(9), 1732–1739.

Karaszewski, R. (2010). Leadership in global business environment through a vision creation process. *The TQM Journal, 22*(4), 399–409.

Kim, J., & McLean, G. N. (2015). An integrative framework for global leadership competency: Levels and dimensions. *Human Resources Development International, 18*(3), 235–258.

Kreitner, R. (1995). *Management* (6th ed.). Houghton Mifflin.

Lang, L. Irby, B., & Brown, G. (2012). An emergent leadership model based on Confucian virtues and East Asian leadership practices. *International Journal of Educational Leadership Preparation, 7*(2), 1–14.

Lewin, K., Lippitt, R., & White, R. K. (1939). Patterns of aggressive behavior in experimentally created "social climates." *The Journal of Social Psychology, 10*, 271–299.

Liden, R. C. (2012). Leadership research in Asia: A brief assessment and suggestions for the future. *Asia Pacific Journal of Management, 29*(2), 205–212.

Lieb, M. M. (2019). Investigating the relationship between cultural dimensions of learning and English language proficiency. *The Electronic Journal for English as a Second Language, 24*(2), 1–22.

Li, P. P. (2012). Toward an integrative framework of indigenous research: The geocentric implications of Yin-Yang Balance. *Asia Pacific Journal of Management, 29*(4), 849–872.

Lincoln, J. R., & Kalleberg, A. L. (1990). Commitment, quits, and work organization in Japanese and U.S. Plants. *ILS Review, 50*(1), 39–59.

Lui, J., & Johnston, J. M. (2019). Validation of the nurse leadership and organizational culture (N-LOC) questionnaire. *BMH Heal Services Research, 19*(1), 469–478.

Ly, N. (2020). Cultural influences on leadership: Western-dominated leadership and non-Western conceptualizations of leadership. *Sociology and Anthropology, 8*(1), 1–12.

Malmqvist, J., Hellberg, K., Mollas, G., Rose, R., & Shevlin, M. (2019). Conducting the pilot study: A neglected part of the research process? Methodological findings supporting the importance of piloting in qualitative research studies. *International Journal of Qualitative Methods, 18*(2019), 1–11.

Maznevski, M., Stahl, G. K., & Mendenhall, M. (2013). Towards an integration of global leadership practice and scholarship: Repairing disconnects and heightening mutual understanding. *European Journal of International Management, 7*(5), 493–500.

McArthur, D. N. (2007). Construct equivalence in international business research: The first and the last of it. *Journal of Business Inquiry: Research, Education & Application, 6*(1), 28–38.

McDonald, P. (2012). Confucian foundation to leadership: A study of Chinese business leaders across Greater China and South-East Asia. *Asia Pacific Business Review, 18*(4), 465–487.

Mendenhall, M., Reiche, B., Bird, A., & Osland, J. (2012). Defining the "global" in global leadership. *Journal of World Business, 47*(4), 493–503.

Meng, J., Elliott, K., & Hall, M. (2010). Technology Readiness Index (TRI): Assessing cross-cultural validity. *Journal of International Consumer Marketing, 221*(1), 19–31.

Minkov, M., & Hofstede, G. (2011). The evolution of Hofstede's doctrine. *Cross Cultural Management, 18*(1), 10–20.

Ministry of Internal Affairs and Communications. (2007). Basic survey on employment structure. http://www.stat.go.jp/data/shugyou/2007/gaiyou.htm. Retrieved on 8 March 2020.

Mittal, R., & Dorfman, P. W. (2012). Servant leadership across cultures. *Journal of World Business, 47*(2012), 555–570.

MEXT. (2002). *Developing a strategic plan to cultivate "Japanese with English abilities."* Retrieved from http://unpan1.un.org/intradoc/groups/public/documents/APCITY/UNPAN008142.htm

MEXT. (2011). *Five proposals and specific measures for developing proficiency in English for international communication.* Retrieved from http://www.mext.go.jp/component/english/__icsFiles/afieldfile/2012/07/09/1319707_1.pdf

Misumi, J., & Peterson, M. F. (1985). The performance-maintenance (PM) theory of leadership: Review of a Japanese research program. *Administrative Science Quarterly, 30*(2), 198–223.

Mone, I. S., Benga, O., & Opre, A. (2016). Cross-cultural differences in socialization goals as a function of power distance, individualism-collectivism and education. *Romanian Journal of Experimental Applied Psychology*, 7(1), 330–334.

Moran, R. T., Abramson, N. R., & Moran, S. V. (2014). *Managing cultural differences*. Routledge.

Morishima, M. (1996). Renegotiating psychological contracts: Japanese style. In C. L. Cooper & D. M. Rousseau (eds). *Trends in organizational behavior* (pp. 139–158). John Wiley.

Mostafa, H., & Lim, Y. (2020). Examining the relationship between motivations and resilience in different international student groups attending US universities. *Journal of International Students*, 10(2), 306–319.

Muddle, G. R.(2020). The relationship between leadership style and hospital employee engagement in Papua New Guinea. *Asia Pacific Journal of Health Management*, 15(4), 42–55.

Mujtaba, B. G. & Isomura, K. (2012). Examining the Japanese leadership orientations and their changes. *Leadership & Organization Development Journal*, 33(4), 4010–4420.

Newman, B. J., Hartman, T. K., & Taber, C. S. (2012). Foreign language exposure, cultural threat, and opposition to immigration. *Political Psychology*, 3(3), 635–657.

Nitobe, I. (2009). *Bushido, the Soul of Japan*. GP Putnam's Sons.

Oyakanmi, A. O. (2009). Globalization: Its implications and consequences for developing countries. *African Journal of International Affairs and Development*, 14(1–2), 69–90

Pauliene, R. (2012). Transforming leadership styles and knowledge sharing in a multi-cultural context. *Business, Management, and Education Journal*, 10(1), 91–109.

Perez, J. R. (2017). Global leadership and the impact of globalization. *Journal of Leadership, Accountability and Ethics*, 14(3), 48–52.

Perrin, C., Perrin, P. B., Blauth, C., Apthorp, A., Duffy, R. D., Bonterre, M., & Daniels, S. (2012). Factor analysis of global trends in twenty-first century leadership. *Leadership & Organization Development Journal*, 33(2), 175–199.

Pieterse, A. N., Van Knippernberg, D., & Van Dierendonck, D. (2013). Cultural diversity and team performance: The role of team member goal orientation. *Academy of Management Journal*, 50(3), 782–804.

Porter, M., Takeuchi, M., & Sakakibara, M. (2000). *Can Japan compete?* MacMillan Publishing.

Pressentin, M. (2015). Universal leadership approaches & cultural dimensions: The expression of Asian leadership traits. *Amity Global Business Review*, 10(2015), 19–38.

Price, J. H., & Murnan, J. (2004). Research limitations and the necessity of reporting them. *American Journal of Health Education*, 35(2), 66–67.

Pritlove, C., Juando-Prats, C., Ala-Leppilampi, K., & Parsons, J. A. (2019). The good, the bad, and the ugly of implicit bias. *Lancet*, 393(10171), 502–504.

Qie, N., Rau, P. P., Wang, L., & Ma, L. (2019). Is the Senpai-Kouhai relationship common across China, Korea, and Japan? *Social Behavior & Personality: An international Journal*, 47(1), 1–12.

Reisel, M. (2018). From "Galapagos Syndrome" to globalization: Japanese businesses between tradition and virtual reality. *International Journal of Business Anthropology*, 7(2), 1–21.

Richard, M. O., & Toffoli, R. (2009). Language influence in responses to questionnaires by bilingual respondents: A test of the Whorfian hypothesis. *Journal of Business Research*, 62(10), 987–994.

Rickards, G., Magee, C., & Artino Jr., A. R. (2012). You can't fix by analysis what you've spoiled by design: Developing survey instruments and collecting validity evidence. *Journal of Graduate Medical Education*, 4(4), 407–410.

Rodd, J. (2013). Reflecting on the pressures, pitfalls, and possibilities for examining leadership. In E. Hujala, M. Waniganayake & J. Rodd (Eds.), *Researching leadership in early childhood education* (pp. 31–46). Tampere University Press.

Rodrigues, C. A. (1990). The situation and national culture as contingencies for leadership behavior: Two conceptual models. In S. B. Prasad (Ed.), *Advances in International Comparative Management* (pp. 51–68). JAI Press Inc.

Rowley, C., Oh, I., & Jang, W. (2019). New perspectives on East Asian leadership in the age of globalization: Local grounding and historical comparisons in the Asia Pacific region. *Asia Pacific Business Review*, 25(2), 307–315.

Rousseau, D. M. (1990). New hire perceptions of their own and their employer's obligations: A study of psychological contracts. *Journal of Organizational Behavior*, 11(5), 389–400.

Sakamoto, M. (2012). Moving towards effective English language teaching in Japan: Issues and challenges. *Journal of Multilingual and Multicultural Development*, 33(4), 409–420.

Santoso, C. B. (2019). Exploration of Asia leadership theory: Looking for an Asian role in the field of leadership theory. *Journal of Leadership in Organizations*, 1(1). doi:10.22146/jlo.44599

Schutte, N. (2019). East meets West: A comparative analysis of leadership styles in Canadian and Japanese wine industries. *International Journal of Economics and Finance Studies*, *11*(2), 1–19.

Seidman, I. (1998) *Interviewing as qualitative research: A guide for researchers in education and the social sciences* (2nd ed). Teachers College, Columbia University.

Sharma, P. (2010). Measuring personal cultural orientations: Scale development and validation. *Journal of the Academy of Marketing Science*, *38*(6), 787–806.

Shuzo, A., Bagozzi, R. P., & Sadarangani, P. (2008). An investigation of construct validity and generalizability of the self-concept: Self-consciousness in Japan and the United States. *Journal of International Consumer Marketing*, *8*(3–4), 97–123.

Singh, M., & Meng, H. (2013). Democratizing western research using non-western theories. Ranciere and mute Chinese theoretical tools. *Studies in Higher Education*, *38*(6), 907–920.

Takuma, K., & Mizuki, N. (2018). Ethical leadership and its cultural and institutional context: An empirical study in Japan. *Journal of Business Ethics*, *151*(3), 707–724.

Talke, K., Salomo, S., & Rost, K. (2010). How top management team diversity affects innovativeness and performance via the strategic choice to focus on innovation fields. *Research Policy*, *39*(7), 907–918.

Theofanidis, D., & Fountouki, A. (2018). Limitations and delimitations in the research process. *Perioperative Nursing*, *7*(3), 155–162.

Trask, B. S., & Anguiano, R. V. (2012). The critical importance of understanding cultural diversity from a global perspective for family and consumer sciences research and practice. *Family and Consumer Sciences*, *41*(2), 115–117.

Truong, T. D., Hallinger, P., & Sanga, K. (2017). Confucian values and school leadership in Vietnam: Exploring the influence of culture on principal decision making. *Educational Management Administration & Leadership*, *45*(1), 77–100.

Uy, A. O., Murphy Jr., E. F., Greenwood, R. A., Ruiz-Gutierrez, J. A., Manyak, T. G., & Mujtaba, B. (2008). A preliminary exploration of generational similarities and differences in values between the United States, United Kingdom, Iceland, Japan, Korea, Colombia, and the Philippines. *DLSU Business & Economic Review*, *18*(1), 29–46.

Van Knippenberg, D., De Dreu, C. K. W., & Homan, A. C. (2004). Work group diversity and group performance: An integrative model and research agenda. *Journal of Applied Psychology*, *89*(6), 1008–1022.

Wang, L., James, K. T., Denyer, D., & Bailey, C. (2014). Western views and Chinese whispers: Re-thinking global leadership competency in multi-national corporations. *Leadership*, *10*(4), 471–495.

Witt, M. A., & Stahl, G. K. (2016). Foundations of responsible leadership: Asian versus Western responsibility orientations toward key stakeholders. *Journal of Business Ethics*, *136*(3), 623–638.

Yi, Y. (2017). The status quo of racial discrimination in Japan and the Republic of Korea and the need to provide for anti-discrimination laws. *Columbia Journal of Race & Law*, *7*(2), 410–467.

Yiend, J., Andre, J., Smith, L., Chen, L. H., Toulopoulou, T., Chen, E., Sham, P., & Parkinson, B. (2019). Biased cognition in East Asian and Western cultures. *PLOS ONE*, *14*(10). doi:10.1371/journal.pone.0223358

Zamanzadeh, V., Ghahramanian, A., Rassouli, M., Abbaszadeh, A., Alavi-Majd, H., & Nikanfar, A. (2015). Design and implementation content validity study: Development of an instrument for measuring patient-centered communication. *Journal of Caring Sciences*, *4*(2), 165–178.

Zhou, J. (2015). International students' motivation to pursue and complete a Ph.D. in the US. *Higher Education*, *69*(5), 719–733.

Zhou, Y. (2015). Career interruption of Japanese women: Why is it so hard to balance work and childcare. *Japan Labor Review*, *12*(2), 106–123.

Zhou, X., & Hua, Y. (2021). Culture-loaded words and translation equivalence. *Theory and Practice in Language Studies*, *11*(2), 210–215.

20

When Archived Research Is the Data Set

Reflections on a Qualitative Content Analysis Study

Tonya Ensign

Introduction

Nearly a century ago, John Dewey (1933) reshaped the way researchers and educators view the role of scholarly reflection by suggesting it is the process of revisiting a subject or experience over and over in one's mind, resulting in the potential to act in new and deliberate ways. Since then, reflection has played an important role in advancing academic scholarship. In this chapter, I share reflections on my desire to understand the cultural nuances of a data set consisting of existing, published studies that examined international populations and were authored by scholars around the world (hereinafter referred to as *archived research*).

When archived research is the data set, content analysis is an appropriate method for exploring and understanding the meaning of the qualitative data in the documents (Lindgren et al., 2014; Schreier, 2012). As a case in point for this reflection, I present a qualitative content analysis study that drew on archived research as the data set and is titled *The Seed of Transformation: A Disorientation Index* (Ensign, 2019a). The data set consisted of peer-reviewed, empirical studies published by more than 100 scholars from around the world. Although the research questions for the study were not specifically concerned with country culture, I noticed interesting country culture nuances during the analysis phase. This spawned more questions and, after publishing my research, drew me back to the data set with a new lens that sought to explore country culture across studies. The experience shined a spotlight on the importance of being deliberate and intentional about the cultural information we choose to include and omit when writing and publishing studies. It caused reflection about how we, as scholars, publish peer-reviewed studies that become the archived research and foundation upon which others build. As Dewey (1933) timelessly suggested, I am hopeful that this chapter may inspire scholars to act in new and deliberate ways as we contribute to the body of knowledge that we call the academic literature.

I have structured the chapter based on a well-known theoretical model for scholarly reflection posited by Gibbs (1988) known as the Gibbs' Reflective Cycle: description of the experience, thoughts and feelings about the experience, evaluation of the experience, analysis to make sense of the situation, conclusions about what I learned and recommendations for the future. Following Gibbs' model, these phases of reflection are organized into three sections.

DOI: 10.4324/9781003003380-20

In Section 1, I describe the experience. First, I provide an overview of the study as a case in point and backdrop for my reflection. I summarize the purpose of the study, the research design, data set, analysis method, and a key finding of the study. I also explain qualitative content analysis as a research method to provide additional information for the reflection. I conclude this section by describing the specific experience during the analysis phase that triggered deep reflection for me. In Section 2, I discuss my thoughts and feelings about the experience and provide an evaluation of the experience leading to how I have made sense of it, as well as offer rhetorical questions for scholars to consider. In Section 3, I provide concluding thoughts about writing and publishing studies.

Section 1: Description of the Experience

This chapter reflects on aspects of my experience conducting a study titled, *The Seed of Transformation: A Disorientation Index* (Ensign, 2019a), hereinafter referred to as the *Disorientation Index study*. This qualitative, content analysis study was situated in the domain of adult learning and contributed to the evolution of transformative learning theory (Mezirow, 1978a, 1991). Additionally, the study contributed to the field of global leadership development (which is the intersection of global leadership and adult learning) and to the field of international education, specifically with respect to study abroad as a pedagogical primer for transformative learning (see Ensign, 2019b for further significance of the study). These are fields of study often explored by international leadership researchers.

Background of the Disorientation Index Study

Nearly half a century ago, Jack Mezirow's (1978a, 1978b) seminal research first introduced transformative learning theory as a unique way that adults learn. Since then, transformative learning theory has been called the new andragogy, the central theory of adult learning and the most researched theory in adult learning (Howie & Bagnall, 2013; Taylor, 2007; Taylor & Cranton, 2012). Transformative learning is a unique type of adult learning. It is different from learning a new skill or learning information from a book; when we experience transformative learning, our perspectives – or mental models – are transformed in significant, lasting and irreversible ways (Hoggan, 2016b; Mezirow, 1978a, 1978b, 1991). The iterative transformative learning process begins with a disorienting experience and includes self-examination, reflection, exploration, planning, learning, trying on and building competence in new roles and integrating a new perspective into one's life (Mezirow, 1978a, 1991).

As a seasoned change management practitioner and global executive coach, I have worked with hundreds of individuals and organizations who were disoriented by changes in their personal and/ or organizational situations. For example, a senior executive client of mine who moved his family overseas for an expatriate assignment experienced disorientation during his role change and was primed for transformative learning. Organizationally, change initiatives I have been involved with, such as mergers and acquisitions or turnover in top leadership, often left employees disoriented (also with the potential for transformative learning). Oftentimes, in my experience with situations such as these, disorientation is misunderstood, handled poorly, unsupported and, as a result, viewed negatively versus being viewed as an opportunity to transform. My work is global, and I also noticed that this phenomenon is international in nature – it spans countries and cultures across my global clientele. For these reasons, I wanted to gain a deeper understanding of the disorientation phase as an initiating circumstance for transformative learning. I also set out to contribute to the evolution of transformative learning theory as well as uncover ways to better serve my clients. Thus, as a Ph.D. in Global Leadership and Change student, this topic became the focus of my dissertation research.

Problem, Purpose and Research Question

The concept of a disorienting experience triggering transformation is shared across disciplines such as education, the management sciences, leadership studies, psychology and others (Adler, 1975; Dohrenwend & Dohrenwend, 1974; Erikson, 1977, 1994; Erikson & Erikson, 1998; Festinger, 1962; Furham & Bochner, 1986; Kim, 1988; Kim & Ruben, 1988; Kozai Group, 2008; Louis, 1980; Louis & Sutton, 1991; Mendenhall et al., 2018; Schank, 1982, 1999; Weick, 1995). It also spans country borders (Kozai Group, 2008; Mendenhall et al., 2018; Taylor, 1993). However, despite more than 40 years of research on transformative learning, including hundreds of published studies, more than 150 doctoral dissertations, an academic journal, international conferences and more than a dozen books (Kitchenham, 2008), the first phase and catalyst of this process remained under-researched (Taylor, 1997, 1998, 2000, 2005, 2007; Taylor & Cranton, 2012). Instead, most of the research in this area consisted of understanding phases of the transformative learning process *other than the disorienting dilemma phase*, for example, the reflection phase (Mälkki, 2010, 2012); critiques of transformative learning theory, for example, suggestions that the theory was too cognitive in nature or lacked attention to context (Clark & Wilson, 1991; Collard & Law, 1989); and empirical studies using transformative learning theory as the theoretical framework for the studies, for example, determining if a group of students that participated in a service learning study abroad trip experienced transformative outcomes (Kiely, 2005). There are hundreds of studies that have used transformative learning theory as a theoretical framework and the contexts of these studies have varied considerably: ranging from being disoriented as a result of diagnosis of an illness to disorientation traveling in a foreign land to disorientation caused by surviving a natural disaster (see Ensign, 2019a for a full review of contexts studied). While most of these studies mentioned the disorienting dilemma as the trigger for transformative learning, there was not an examination of the disorienting experience phenomenon *across* studies. The specific gap in the literature was that the *anatomy of the disorienting dilemma experience* was under-researched and not fully understood; there was no language to articulate nuances, dimensions or aspects of this phenomenon across contexts (Taylor 2007, Taylor & Snyder, 2012). Thus, the purpose of my Disorientation Index study was to move toward a better understanding of the anatomy of the disorienting dilemma phenomenon and provide evidence-based language to articulate the nuances of this important experience that has the potential to trigger transformative learning. To do this, I explored how scholars have conceptualized the disorienting dilemma in archived research and the overarching research question that guided the Disorientation Index study was: How do scholars conceptualize the disorienting dilemma in the transformative learning literature?

Research Methodology and Design

Selecting a research approach includes making several important decisions. One of the first decisions is deciding whether to conduct a qualitative, quantitative, or mixed-methods study. Qualitative research is an approach that seeks to explore and understand the meaning of a social or human problem (Creswell, 2014; Denzin & Lincoln, 2018). Since the overarching research question for the Disorientation Index study was open-ended and exploratory, I selected a qualitative research approach. There are three primary ways to collect qualitative data for analysis: via interviews, observations and/or documents (Patton, 2002). In the Disorientation Index study, peer-reviewed studies (documents) published in academic journals widely acknowledged as top journals in the field of adult education provided the qualitative data.

Data Collection and Data Corpus

To answer my overarching research question, I curated an initial data set of 256 peer reviewed, published articles on transformative learning from three highly respected, global academic journals where much of Mezirow's transformative learning research stream resides: *Adult Education Quarterly, Adult Learning,* and *The Journal of Transformative Education.* I then filtered the articles to 53 empirical studies where the scholarly researchers (hereinafter referred to as the *scholars*) used transformative learning theory as the theoretical framework for their studies and they claimed the participants they studied (hereinafter referred to as the *samples*) experienced transformative outcomes. These 53 studies yielded 82 disorienting dilemmas that I examined to understand how these scholars conceptualized the disorienting dilemmas experienced by samples they studied.

The articles that constituted my data set were written by 114 scholars from around the world. Specifically, the following regions were represented: Africa, Asia, Australia, New Zealand, Europe, North America and South America. Thus, the 53 studies, yielding 82 disorienting dilemmas and comprising more than 1,000 pages of textual data, provided a desirable, global representation of scholars' conceptualization of the disorienting dilemma and became the data corpus.

Qualitative Content Analysis

Qualitative content analysis was first recognized as an analysis method in 1941 and has had a long history in the field of nursing and also in non-English-speaking countries (Mayring, 2014). It is also recognized as an important research method in the Anglo-American literature (Elo & Kyngäs, 2008; Hsieh & Shannon, 2005). The use of qualitative content analysis has recently exploded in communications, business, psychology, journalism, sociology and other disciplines partly because of the sheer amount of textual data generated by the Web 2.0 (Neuendorf, 2017). This is the analysis method I used in the Disorientation Index study.

Holsti (1969) described qualitative content analysis as "a research method for investigating problems by systematically and objectively identifying characteristics of the message for the purpose of making inferences" (p. 14). Forty years later, Hsieh and Shannon (2005) upheld this basic definition, explaining qualitative content analysis as "a research method for the subjective interpretation of the content of text data through the systematic classification process of coding and identifying themes or patterns" (p. 1278). More recently, Krippendorf (2012) similarly described it as a systematic process that involves reading and re-reading a body of texts, images and/or symbolic matter to identify patterns in such data, typically in an inductive (i.e., theory-building) manner, with an aim to reduce its complexity. The goal of content analysis is to further the knowledge and understanding of one or more phenomena under study (Downe-Wamboldt, 1992). As these methodologists have agreed, this analysis method is appealing for large amounts of data because it provides a method for extracting the meaning of the data in a systematic way that, in turn, allows researchers to report findings (Schreier, 2012). Qualitative content analysis is also characterized by multiple realities and multifaceted perceptions of phenomena (Lincoln & Guba, 1985), which fit well with the constructivist worldview of the Disorientation Index study.

Latent Meaning and Manifest Meaning in Qualitative Content Analysis

A distinct feature of qualitative content analysis is that it analyzes both *latent* meaning and *manifest* meaning (Graneheim & Lundman, 2004; Schreier, 2012). Latent meaning is meaning that is not immediately obvious and requires taking context into account as the researcher interprets the textual data within their own mind. It is the *red thread* between the lines in the text (Graneheim & Lundman, 2004). Dooley (2016) explained:

> In latent content analysis, a human researcher reads the relevant text(s) and then responds to the research question at hand with a textual response—the interpretation and encoding of the text being analyzed takes place within the mind of the researcher. (p. 1)

Berg (1995) described the latent content analysis process as an examination of the texts' "deep structural meaning" (p. 176). In contrast, manifest meaning is factual or literal meaning in the text such as the frequency of certain words, or descriptive data such as the publication name, publication year, author name, number of authors, and authors' affiliations (Schreier, 2012).

In the Disorientation Index study, I analyzed both latent and manifest data. In order to answer my overarching research question and capture how the scholars conceptualized the disorienting dilemma in their studies, I read and re-read each study multiple times to explore, understand, and interpret their descriptions. Using NVivo software, qualitative content analysis (Schreier, 2012), and a constant comparative process (Corbin & Strauss, 2007), aspects of the disorienting dilemma began to emerge. Each time a study revealed a new dimension of the disorienting dilemma, I went back through every study, compared each study and coded each study to the new dimension. When eight dimensions, grounded in the data, were revealed, saturation was reached. This part of the analysis was the latent data analysis, specifically utilizing an inductive approach, also called data-driven approach (Schreier, 2012) or text-driven approach (Krippendorf, 2012). The text of the published studies was analogous to interview transcripts or textual survey responses.

I also analyzed manifest data such as the year of publication for each of the archived research studies, the scholars' institutional affiliations and the scholars' institutional locations around the world. In some cases, manifest data assisted in providing context for latent data analysis. Manifest data was analogous to the demographic attributes of interviewees or survey respondents. In analysis methods such as qualitative content analysis, sometimes results can be further stratified based on manifest data. For example, Witkamp et al. (2016) interviewed relatives of patients who died while in hospitals to better understand how to interact with these relatives. She used latent content analysis to learn about several needs expressed by the relatives of the deceased. Witkamp et al. (2016) further segmented the results based on manifest data that reported the type of relative: spouse, parent, caregiver, etc.

Latent Data Analysis Findings

Latent analysis revealed several findings. The key finding is presented here: a new Disorientation Index. Please reference the full study for other findings and a more thorough discussion of the findings (Ensign, 2019a).

The key finding in the Disorientation Index study was a new eight-dimension Disorientation Index that is grounded in the data and provides contemporary scholars with language for and understanding of the nuances of disorientation as a catalyst for transformative learning (Ensign, 2019a). It also provides a new tool for practitioners in global leadership development and international education (Ensign, 2019b). The Disorientation Index offers a framework for understanding dimensions of the disorienting experience, which can be acute (sudden) or epochal (bounded with a beginning or end), or not acute or epochal (ongoing with no clear beginning and/or ending); it can be experienced alone or with others; it might be an externally generated experience that others can see, or an internal disorientation in our own minds or hearts that is not visible to others unless we reveal it; we may have encountered this type of disorientation before, or it may be new to us; we may consider it a negative experience; however, in many instances the experience was not characterized as negative; it might take place in an educational setting, but most of the time disorienting experiences occur in familiar places such as our homes and where we work; sometimes a new geographical location causes disorientation, however, in the data set, many disorienting experiences did not take place in a new geographical location; and finally, the data set revealed that about half of the time, disorienting experiences were thrust upon the samples studied, but about half of the time they voluntarily chose the experience.

> The most common type of disorienting experience was an acute or epochal, externally generated, negative experience, that was experienced alone but in a familiar place, by someone who had no prior experience with this type of dilemma. In just over half of the studies, the person or population chose this general experience, and in just under half of the studies, the experience was thrust upon them. The data also revealed that most disorienting experiences in this data set did not take place in educational settings. (Ensign, 2019a, p. 124)

One of the most notable findings was that the disorienting dilemma (as it has been referred to for decades) does not have to be a negative experience. In fact, in 28% of studies, disorientation was not negative and in 55% of studies the participants chose or volunteered for the disorienting experience. We see this when we choose to travel or study abroad, choose a new career path, or choose to become parents; these are typically events that are disorienting but not necessarily negative. Thus, I suggest the first phase of transformative learning theory be renamed the *disorienting experience* instead of the *disorienting dilemma*.

Manifest Data Analysis Findings

Three key manifest variables were analyzed in the Disorientation Index study: the names of the journals in which the archived research was published, the years of publication for each of the archived research studies and the geographical locations of the scholars' affiliations.

First, the three source journals, *Adult Education Quarterly, Adult Learning* and *Journal of Transformative Education,* served as sampling filters. These journals are dedicated to adult education and much of the global transformative learning literature has been published here. In a 2016 study, Chad Hoggan curated a similar data set utilizing these journals, and his findings revealed a typology of six transformative learning outcomes. In the Disorientation Index study, I built on Hoggan's (2016a, 2016b) study and data set; I sought to bookend Hoggan's transformative learning outcomes study by exploring the initiating circumstance or disorienting experience. Second, the years of the publications also served as sampling filters to ensure all archived research in the data corpus was published between 2003 and 2017. Figure 20.1 displays the frequency of articles in the data corpus by publication year.

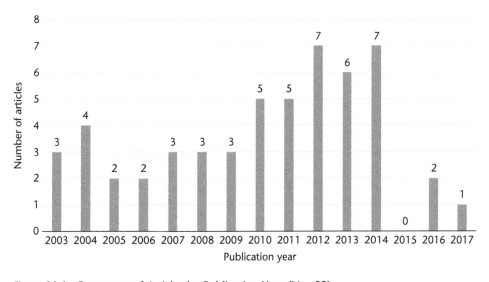

Figure 20.1 Frequency of Articles by Publication Year (N = 53)

Table 20.1 Authors' Global Affiliations

Number of Authors	Global Region	Country	Province, State or City
3	Africa	Botswana	unknown
		South Africa	unknown
6	Asia	Malaysia	Perak
		Taiwan	Changhua
			Taichung
			Taipei
6	Australia & New Zealand	Australia	Queensland
			Sydney
		New Zealand	Dunedin
7	Europe	Finland	Helsinki
		United Kingdom	Huddersfield
			Newcastle
			Nottingham
			Tyne
			West Yorkshire
91	North America	Canada	Alberta
			British Columbia
			Nova Scotia
			Winnipeg
		United States	27 states
1	South America	Ecuador	Guayaquil
114	Total Authors		

Note. For each global region, the number of authors affiliated with the region as well as the country, province, state or city is listed. The table is in alphabetical order by global region.

Last, the manifest data analysis also revealed that the authors of the studies were affiliated with institutions around the world, with 33% being outside the United States. The country of scholars' affiliations served as an indicator of a global sample of archived research. Table 20.1 provides the number of authors from each global region, and indicates countries, provinces, states and cities within each region that was represented.

Conclusion of the Study

The research approach, data set and rigorous analysis process were effective for answering the Disorientation Study's research question: How do scholars conceptualize the disorienting dilemma in the transformative learning literature? The study provided several key findings, including a new Disorientation Index and a deeper understanding of the varied contexts in which disorientation can catalyze the transformative learning process.

There are also several implications and opportunities for future research to build on this study. For example, the new Disorientation Index provided language for both scholars and practitioners in global leadership and international education who are utilizing disorientation as a pedagogical primer for learning and development (Ensign, 2019b). Furthermore, future research may seek to understand correlation (if any) or causation (if any) of the eight dimensions of the disorienting experience to Hoggan's six transformative outcomes. Future research may also seek to understand cultural nuances of the disorientation experience.

Of course, there are challenges in conducting research, and specific challenges with qualitative research of this nature. Denzin and Lincoln (2018) stated, "Everything cannot be done; choices must be made: How are they to be made, and how are they to be justified?" (p. 781). I evaluated the entire study in a special Epilogue section in the published study and point readers to the Epilogue for additional reflection (Ensign, 2019a). The following section focuses on specific aspects of the archived research that caused deep reflection after the Disorientation Index study was completed.

Specific Experience That Caused Deep Reflection

While conducting the Disorientation Index study, I read all, or large portions of, 256 articles in order to curate the 53-article data corpus of archived research. I then read, re-read and analyzed the 82 disorienting instances described in the studies. During the analysis process, I noticed that, in some of the studies, country culture played a role in how the scholars conceptualized the disorienting experience. That is, in the data analysis, clear statements about the location and sample of studies indicated cultural diversity.

For example, one study was conducted in an area of Africa that had been ravaged by war and poverty (Cox & John, 2016). In this study, youth were living in a constant state of disorientation. The study revealed that an *orienting* program – that is, a program that provided safety and structure for youth – acted as the initiating circumstance to trigger transformative learning. Cox and John (2016) suggested that by phrasing the initiating circumstance for transformative learning as a *disorienting* dilemma, we were viewing it through a Western lens. In their study, disorientation was the norm and the disruption experienced by the youth was a shift to being oriented (Cox & John, 2016).

In another study, Coryell (2013) sought to transcend Western cultural influences by investigating personal perceptions of students in a Master of Arts in Adult Learning and Teaching program. She exposed students to international educational settings and used narrative analysis to understand the students' educational narrative. Coryell (2013) claimed, "Knowledge is transformed through global intersections of society, the workplace, politics, economics, and lifelong learning" (p. 300), and her findings, which indicated an initial Western educational metanarrative, reiterated a need to broaden adult educators' perspectives beyond the majority demographics and cultures and to value these voices when facilitating transformative learning outcomes (Brookfield, 2003; Brown et al., 2000; Coryell, 2013).

Another qualitative, phenomenological study examined how international graduate students studying in the United States experienced transformative outcomes (Erichsen, 2011). In this study, the sample consisted of German, South Korean, Kenyan, Lao, Turkmen and Chinese students. Erichsen (2011) found that the international students she studied were continually transforming their understanding of the world and also transforming their identities; however, her findings did not reveal the highly individualistic, rational process of transformative learning as described in the Western literature. Erichsen (2011) summarized that Mezirow's (1978a) description of transformative learning was helpful but presented a process that was more cognitive and rational than the process she encountered with international graduate students which shifted conceptions of their self-identities including adaptation and reinvention of self within a new context.

As a scholar of global leadership, these studies cause me to ponder how cultural differences might play a role in the phenomenon of the disorienting experience. For example, how might people of Eastern cultures and Western cultures experience disorientation as a catalyst for transformative learning similarly and how might they experience it differently? Furthermore, might the scholars' cultures have impacted the lenses through which they conceptualized and described the disorienting experiences in their studies? Might scholars in the East conceptualize the disorienting experience differently than those in the West? What about studies authored by multiple scholars of diverse cultures?

After publishing the findings of the Disorientation Index study, I returned to my data set. I poured through the 82 disorienting instances again, this time looking for specific country culture attributes.

However, despite the data set providing culturally rich studies from far reaching places such as Ecuador, South Africa and Taiwan, without specific manifest data in the form of definitive cultural attributes of the scholars or the samples they studied, I found it was simply not possible to draw cultural or cross-cultural conclusions. Approximately a quarter of the disorienting instances (23%) in the data set were clearly international with statements of cultural diversity, however, the manifest data that were provided for these studies (as well as the other three quarters of disorienting incidences) were not specific enough to code in a way that allowed valid and reliable cultural or cross-cultural analysis. For example, even though the scholars' affiliations were provided and ensured international representation at a high level, for analysis purposes, I could not assume that their affiliations were also their countries of origin. A scholar from the United States might be teaching at a New Zealand university at the time of the study, hence, reported a New Zealand institutional affiliation in the manifest data, but the scholar might have brought a U.S. cultural bias to the study. Or, in many cases, there was more than one culture represented by multiple authors of a single study.

In addition to lack of cultural manifest data about the scholars, information about the countries from which the samples were curated were often vague or not even mentioned. Samples were commonly described as *a group of graduate students* or *a sample of women from a support group* without mentioning their country of origin or other demographic information. In some cases, the region of the world where the study was conducted was provided, but the specific country was not named.

As this experience unfolded, I became more aware of challenges we face as we strive to conduct international research when building on each other's research. While the academic journals from which I drew the sample of studies were international, and while they did provide the scholars' current global affiliation, they did not provide the variables necessary to analyze or draw country culture-related conclusions about the scholars or about the samples in their studies.

Section 2: Thoughts, Feelings and Sense Making

When I realized I would not be able to further understand cultural or cross-cultural aspects of the disorienting experience, my initial thoughts and feelings were mostly surprise and disappointment. I had spent nearly a year curating the data set and living in the data. I had published the Disorienting Index study and wanted to go back into the data to understand cultural implications. I was disappointed that such a rich data set of global disorienting experiences curated via high quality, peer-reviewed journals did not provide the manifest data needed for further country culture analysis. However, as a newly minted Ph.D., these feelings quickly turned to determination and a desire to understand the academic research and publishing process more deeply in order to make sense of and objectively evaluate the experience. I became curious about how we, as academic researchers and publishers, have developed the current protocols, processes, and technological systems for creating and disseminating knowledge.

Two key areas of my reflection were a lack of cultural manifest data about the scholars themselves and a lack of cultural manifest data about the samples they studied. Eventually, several possible – and somewhat discrete – explanations emerged that helped make sense of our current environment. Each of these areas is summarized below and rhetorical questions are posed as an invitation for further research and innovation.

The Absence of Information Is Information

My personal reflective process included telling and retelling my experience to colleagues. One colleague and experienced researcher pointed out that the mere fact that we do not know much about the scholars who conducted these studies is very telling. Is this intentional? Is it forced as a result of restrictive publication fields? Does this help or hinder our understanding of the studies?

Might we become biased readers if we did know this information? Tillman (2002) highlighted the importance of understanding "whether or not the researcher has the cultural knowledge to accurately interpret and validate the experiences" (p. 4) of the samples being studied. Without published manifest data about the researcher, it is not possible for readers to make this assessment.

Multiculturality Is Complex

Multiculturality is complex with limiting paradigmatic and institutional systems (Westwood & Jack, 2007). For example, postcolonial research and Western epistemology has dominated management knowledge (Jaya, 2001; Prasad, 2003; Wong-MingJi & Mir, 1997) and continues today as, "There is no one point at which colonialism formally ceased" (Westwood & Jack, 2007, p. 246). Scholars focusing on international management research methodology have demonstrated that methods employed to study the non-West are often *universalizing* and *nonreflexive* (Jack & Westwood, 2006; Westwood, 2004; Westwood & Jack, 2007). Critical race theorists assert that ethnicity and race should be explicit in all research, as they are endemic and engrained (Milner, 2007). In an article summarizing key theoretical concepts from postcolonial scholars and thought leaders in the field, Özkazanç-Pan (2008) exemplified the complexity of multiculturality by articulating her own position as a "third world woman scholar writing in English within a first-world business school location" (p. 966). She continued, "based on this, for whom do I speak and for whom can I speak?" (Özkazanç-Pan, 2008, p. 966).

Multiculturality also comes in at multiple levels. Invisible and implied manifest data exist in peer-reviewed, published studies. For example, some nonpredatory journals charge high submission fees and some journals are published only in English. These are barriers to entry for some scholars. These data are one level below published manifest data because we do not know which studies were eliminated from ever becoming published.

Interdisciplinary Research Has Reached a Tipping Point

When scholars publish a study in one academic discipline, for example education, they are not necessarily thinking about how researchers in other disciplines, for example international leadership studies, might use or build on their research in an interdisciplinary manner. However, interdisciplinary research is increasing rapidly; it has crossed the tipping point as an emerging paradigm for contribution of new knowledge and can no longer be denied (Repko & Szostak, 2021). Klein (2010) argued, "Interdisciplinarity is associated with bold advances in knowledge, solutions to urgent societal problems, an edge in technological innovation, and a more integrative educational experience" (p. 2). When we publish studies with information only pertinent to the academic discipline in which the study is situated, we may fuel a silo mentality between academic disciplines and inhibit interdisciplinarity. For example, in the Disorientation Index study, the three journals housing much of Mezirow's stream of transformative learning research are dedicated to the field of adult learning. Despite being a global area of study, these and other journals do not put emphasis on the multicultural aspects of the field and, instead, project a more ethnocentric and *ethno-disciplinary* stance. How might academic research – particularly education, social sciences, management sciences, and humanities research – benefit from and advance if scholars routinely embraced a more interdisciplinary and global mindset? Are we providing the data needed by our fellow scholars in other disciplines to explore multicultural research questions?

Researcher Reflexivity Is Important

As researchers, we approach our work with assumptions and beliefs about the topics we study. This can lead to both conscious and unconscious biases in our research. Creswell (2013) explained, "How we write is a reflection of our own interpretation based on the cultural, social, gender, class, and personal politics that we bring to research. All writing is 'positioned' within a stance" (p. 215). There is a widely held assumption in research that unconscious bias is undesirable, and we have a responsibility to examine and acknowledge our research positionality. Assessments such as the Implicit Association Test allow people to discover potential prejudices (Greenwald et al., 2015), however, these assessments are not part of the typical research process. Instead, researchers are encouraged to examine their bias more informally through reflexivity, or continuous reflection of the researcher on the research process. In some structured research formats, such as the United States doctoral dissertation, an explanation of the researcher's positionality is a required component of the study, however, even here researchers do not always report their ethnicity or race. Milner (2007) argued the importance of researchers understanding deep racial and cultural knowledge about themselves and the communities they are studying. He introduced "a framework to guide researchers in this process of racial and cultural awareness, consciousness, and positionality as they conduct education research" (Milner, 2007, p. 388). Milner's (2007) helpful framework offers a process for researchers to examine themselves, themselves in relation to others, reflective practices regarding their representation and methods for shifting from a focus on the self to the system. Milner (2007) argued that researchers must pay attention to their own racialized and cultural systems because these systems have molded their very ways of knowing. These embedded systems can bring accompanying dangers that are seen, unseen and unforeseen. For example, higher education is an environment ripe for bias in research. Frequently, higher education faculty (who often conduct research) have similar biases as graduate students (who are often the subjects being studied) in that they may both highly value learning and education. Additionally, in education and other disciplines, color- and culture-blind ideologies and research approaches can lead to seen, unseen and/or unforeseen exploitation and misrepresentation of individuals and communities of color (Banks, 2001; Lewis, 2001). Deeply reflecting on the unexpected country culture limits I encountered when I returned to my international data set postgraduation, has reinforced the importance of researcher-reflexivity for me as a scholar (see Epilogue in Ensign, 2019a for more about this).

Stereotyping Occurs in Research

In some cases, when publishing their findings, scholars may feel that revealing their own ethnicity or race might lead to stereotyping by their publishers or their readers. For example, if cultural attributes of the scholars are revealed during the journal submission process, the prevailing global political or economic climate may consciously or unconsciously play a role in which studies are approved for publication and how readers interpret the studies. Prevention of such prejudices in publishing is a driving force behind the blind peer-review process. However, after a publication has been approved and published, readers may bring their own bias to interpretation of a study based on the scholars' ethnicity or race, if their ethnicity or race are identified. Similarly, readers may bring their own bias to interpretation of a study based on the demographics of participants being studied. How can the academic community become aware of stereotyping and move toward a more nonprejudicial environment? What lessons might we borrow from human rights activists, social justice scholars and critical race theorists?

Academic Database Fields Have Not Kept Pace with the Globalization of Research

Designated data fields specifically identifying countries or cultures being studied are not available in most digital library user interfaces or library search engines. Margaret Hedstrom (1997), an associate professor teaching in the areas of archives, electronic records management and digital preservation posited that this is largely driven by a focus on the inputs available from suppliers (publishers) versus the outputs serving customers (researchers and students). Because our digital library systems are not designed to be searched by country, this information is often buried in the text of the articles or omitted all together. As international leadership researchers, we must rely on a time-consuming process of searching for keywords and stringing together Boolean phrases in a trial-and-error method that may or may not return desired results. So, the problem of getting at the multiculturality of authors of studies and samples being studied is also systemic. The technology exists to make this information available via search engines with discrete search fields such as these, however, user interfaces have not been designed this way nor have they been updated to reflect the globalization of research. How might our research strategies and outcomes benefit from searchable fields for ethnicity, race and country culture in our library user interface systems? Are there also downsides or might there be unintended consequences to making this information more easily searchable?

Section 3: Concluding Thoughts

Throughout the process of conducting the Disorientation Index study and subsequently reflecting on the research experience it afforded, I not only learned more about the disorienting experience and transformative learning, but also about the academic research and publishing process. In particular, I became more aware of challenges and limitations with respect to multicultural analysis when archived research is the data set. There is no easy way to address these deeply rooted institutional, societal and systemic challenges. However, I will offer the following concluding thoughts for scholars.

I urge researchers to consider the full life cycle of their work. Oftentimes we view the research process as linear. In its most simplistic form, a linear research process is depicted in Figure 20.2.

However, academic research is actually an organic, ever-evolving body of knowledge, thus, it has a complete life cycle. Figure 20.3 shows how the outcomes of our research become the inputs of future research as we continually build upon existing archived research. Perhaps this is most obvious

Figure 20.2 **Research as a Linear Process**

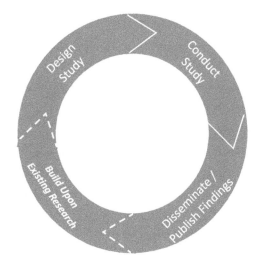

Figure 20.3 **Research as an Evolving Body of Knowledge**

in the stage of research where we conduct a literature review to understand what is known and what is still unclear or unknown about the topic at hand, but it is also foundational to qualitative content analysis studies, meta-analysis studies and any other research methodology where archived research is the data set.

If we embrace the idea that the research process is cyclical instead of linear, then we should not limit our research approaches to an end goal of revealing the outcomes of our own studies. Instead, in our research designs, we should consider how our studies might be of use by readers and also of use to other researchers who will likely build upon our work. Practically speaking, to do this we must adopt a mindset that includes intentionality in the type of information we publish. In addition to publishing the parochial findings of our own studies, we must think beyond our own findings to the greater research community, to global and interdisciplinary prospects and to how our research becomes archived knowledge contributing to future studies. As colleagues in the academy, we must acknowledge that an underlying tenet of our collective work is to build upon each other's research.

References

Adler, P. S. (1975). The transitional experience: An alternative view of culture shock. *Journal of Humanistic Psychology, 15*(4), 13–23. doi:101177/002216787501500403.

Banks, J. A. (2001). Citizenship education and diversity: Implications for teacher education. *Journal of Teacher Education, 52*(1), 5–16.

Berg, B. L. (1995). *Qualitative research methods for the social sciences* (2nd ed.). Allyn and Bacon.

Brookfield, S. D. (2003). Putting the critical back into critical pedagogy. *Journal of Transformative Education, 1*, 111–119. doi:101177/1541344603001002007.

Brown, A. H., Cervero, R. M., & Johnson-Bailey, J. (2000). Making the invisible visible: Race, gender, and teaching in adult education. *Adult Education Quarterly, 50*, 273–288. doi:101177/074171360005000402.

Clapp-Smith, R., & Wernsing, T. (2014). The transformational triggers of international experiences. *Journal of Management Development, 33*(7), 662–679. doi:101108/JMD-05-2012-0063.

Clark, M. C., & Wilson, A. L. (1991). Context and rationality in Mezirow's theory of transformational learning. *Adult Education Quarterly, 41*(2), 75–91. doi:101177/0001848191041002002.

Collard, S., & Law, M. (1989). The limits of perspective transformation: A critique of Mezirow's theory. *Adult Education Quarterly, 39*(2), 99–107. doi:101177/0001848189039002004.

Cook, G. (2012, February 12). Why scientists are boycotting a publisher. *The Boston Globe*. http://www.bostonglobe.com/opinion/2012/02/12/why-scientists-are-boycotting-publisher/9sCpDEP7BkkX1INfakn3NL/story.html.

Corbin, J., & Strauss, A. (2007). *Basics of qualitative research: Techniques and procedures for developing grounded theory* (3rd ed.). Sage.

Coryell, J. (2013). Collaborative, comparative inquiry, and transformative cross-cultural adult learning and teaching: A Western educator metanarrative and inspiring global vision. *Adult Education Quarterly, 63*(4), 299–320. doi:101177/074171361247420.

Cox, A. J., & John, V. M. (2016). Transformative learning in postapartheid South Africa: Disruption, dilemma, and direction. *Adult Education Quarterly, 66*(4), 303–318. doi:101177/0741713616648376.

Creswell, J. W. (2013). *Qualitative inquiry and research design*. SAGE publications.

Creswell, J. W. (2014). *Research design*. SAGE publications.

Denzin, N. K., & Lincoln, Y. S. (2018). *The Sage handbook of qualitative research*. Sage Publications.

Dewey, J. (1933). *How we think: A restatement of the relation of reflective thinking to the educative process*. Henry Regnery Co.

Dohrenwend, B. S., & Dohrenwend, B. P. (1974). A brief historical introduction to research on stressful life events. In B. S. Dohrenwend & B. P. Dohrenwend (Eds.), *Stressful life events: Their nature and effects* (pp. 1–6). John Wiley & Sons.

Dooley, K. J. (2016). Using manifest content analysis in purchasing and supply management research. *Journal of Purchasing and Supply Management, 22*(4), 244–246. doi:101016/j.pursup.2016.08.004i.

Downe-Wamboldt, B. (1992). Content analysis: Method, applications, and issues. *Health Care for Women International, 13*(3), 313–321. doi:101080/07399339209516006.

Elo, S., & Kyngäs, H. (2008). The qualitative content analysis process. *Journal of Advanced Nursing*, *62*(1), 107–115. doi:101111/j.1365-2648.2007.04569.x.

Ensign, T. (2019a). *The seed of transformation: A disorientation index* [Doctoral dissertation]. Pepperdine University. https://lib.pepperdine.edu/login?url¼https://search-proquest-com. lib.pepperdine.edu/docview/2240030131?accountid¼13159.

Ensign, T. (2019b). Triggers of transformative learning in global leadership development: The disorientation index. In J. Osland, B. Sebastian Reiche, B. Szkudlarek, & M. E. Mendenhall (Eds.), *Advances in global leadership* (Vol. 12). Emerald Publishing Limited.

Erichsen, E. A. (2011). Learning for change: Transforming international experience as identity work. *Journal of Transformative Education*, *9*(2), 109–133. doi:10.1177/1541344611428227.

Erikson, E. H. (1977). *Life history and the historical moment: Diverse presentations*. Norton.

Erikson, E. H. (1994). *Identity and the life cycle*. Norton.

Erikson, E. H., & Erikson, J. M. (1998). *The life cycle completed* (extended version). Norton.

Festinger, L. (1962). *A theory of cognitive dissonance* (Vol. 2). Stanford University Press.

Furham, A., & Bochner, S. (1986). *Culture shock*. Methuen.

Gibbs, G. (1988). Learning by doing: A guide to teaching and learning methods. *Further Education Unit*. https://www.brookes.ac.uk/ocsld/.

Graneheim, U. H., & Lundman, B. (2004). Qualitative content analysis in nursing research: Concepts, procedures and measures to achieve trustworthiness. *Nurse Education Today*, *24*(2), 105–112. doi:101016/j.nedt.2003.10.001..

Greenwald, A. G., Banaji, M. R., & Nosek, B. A. (2015). Statistically small effects of the Implicit Association Test can have societally large effects. *Journal of Personality and Social Psychology*, *108*, 553–561.

Hedstrom, M. (1997). Digital preservation: A time bomb for digital libraries. *Computers and the Humanities*, *31*(3), 189–202.

Hinds, J., & Joinson, A. N. (2018). What demographic attributes do our digital footprints reveal? A systematic review. *PLoS ONE*, *13*(11), 1–40. doi:101371/journal.pone.0207112.

Hoggan, C. (2016a). A typology of transformation: Reviewing the transformative learning literature. *Studies in the Education of Adults*, *48*(1), 65–82. doi:10108002660830.2016.1155849.

Hoggan, C. (2016b). Transformative learning as a metatheory: Definition, criteria, and typology. *Adult Education Quarterly*, *66*(1), 57–75. doi:101177/0741713615611216.

Holsti, O. R. (1969). *Content analysis for the social sciences and humanities*. Addison-Wesley.

Howard J. (2010, June 8). *University of California tries just saying no to rising journal costs*. The Chronicle of Higher Education. http://chronicle.com/article/U-of-California-Tries-Just/65823/.

Howie, P., & Bagnall, R. (2013). A beautiful metaphor: Transformative learning theory. *International Journal of Lifelong Education*, *32*, 816–836. doi:101080/02601370.2013.817486.

Hsieh, H. F., & Shannon, S. E. (2005). Three approaches in qualitative analysis. *Qualitative Health Research*, *15*, 1277–1288. doi:10.1177/1049732305276687.

Internet World Stats. (n.d.). *Internet world stats usage population statistics*. https://www.internetworldstats.com/stats.htm.

Jack, G., & Westwood, R. (2006). Postcolonialism and the politics of qualitative research in international business. *Management International Review*, *46*, 481–501.

Jaya, P. S. (2001). Do we really 'know' and 'profess'? Decolonizing management knowledge. *Organization*, *8*, 227–233. doi:101177/1350508401082008.

Jha, A. (2012, April 9). Academic spring: How an angry maths blog sparked a scientific revolution. *The Guardian*. http://www.theguardian.com/science/2012/apr/09/frustrated-blogpost-boycott-scientific-journals.

Kiely, R. (2005). A transformative learning model for service-learning: A longitudinal case study. *Michigan Journal of Community Service Learning*, *12*, 5–22. https://files.eric.ed.gov/fulltext/EJ848477.pdf.

Kim, Y. Y. (1988). *Communication and cross-cultural adaptation: An integrative theory*. Multilingual Matters.

Kim, Y. Y., & Ruben, B. D. (1988). Intercultural transformation. In Y. Y. Kim & W. B. Gudykunst (Eds.), *Theories in intercultural communication* (pp. 299–321). Sage.

Kitchenham, A. (2008). The evolution of John Mezirow's transformative learning theory. *Journal of Transformative Education*, *6*(104), 104–123. doi:101177/1541344608322678.

Klein, J. T. (2010). *Creating interdisciplinary campus cultures: A model for strength and sustainability*. John Wiley & Sons.

Kozai Group. (2008). *The global competencies inventory qualified administrator training resources*. The Kozai Group.

Krippendorf, K. (2012). *Content analysis: An introduction to its methodology* (3rd ed.). Sage.

Larivière, V., Haustein, S., & Mongeon, P. (2015). The oligopoly of academic publishers in the digital era. *PloS ONE*, *10*(6), e0127502. doi:101371/journal.pone.0127502.

Lewis, A. E. (2001). There is no "race" in the schoolyard: Color-blind ideology in an (almost) all-White school. *American Educational Research Journal, 38*(4), 781–811.

Lincoln, Y. S., & Guba, E. (1985). *Naturalistic inquiry*. Sage.

Lindgren, B. M., Sundbaum, J., Eriksson, M., & Graneheim, U. H. (2014). Looking at the world through a frosted window – Experiences of loneliness among persons with mental ill-health. *Journal of Psychiatry Mental Health Nursing, 21*(2), 114–120. doi:101111/jpm.12053.

Louis, M. R. (1980). Surprise and sensemaking: What newcomers experience in entering unfamiliar organizational settings. *Administrative Science Quarterly, 25*(2), 226–251. doi:102307/2392453.

Louis, M. R., & Sutton, R. I. (1991). Switching cognitive gears: From habits of mind to active thinking. *Human Relations, 44*(1), 55–76. doi:101177/001872679104400104.

Mälkki, K. (2010). Building on Mezirow's theory of transformative learning: Theorizing the challenges to reflection. *Journal of Transformative Education, 8*(1), 42–62. doi:101177/1541344611403315.

Mälkki, K. (2012). Rethinking disorienting dilemmas within real-life crises: The role of reflection in negotiating emotionally chaotic experiences. *Adult Education Quarterly, 62*(3), 207–229. doi:101177/0741713611402047.

Mayring, P. (2014). Qualitative content analysis: Theoretical foundation, basic procedures and software solution. Free download pdf version; copyright Philipp Mayring. Klagenfurt, Austria, 2014. https://www.beltz.de/.

McGuigan G. S., & Russell R. D. (2008). The business of academic publishing: A strategic analysis of the academic journal publishing industry and its impact on the future of scholarly publishing. *Electronic Journal of Academic and Special Librarianship, 9*(3). http://southernlibrarianship.icaap.org/content/v09n03/mcguigan_g01.html.

Mendenhall, M. E., Osland, J., Bird, A., Oddou, G. R., Stevens, M. J., Maznevski, M., & Stahl, G. K. (Eds.). (2018). *Global leadership: Research, practice, and development* (3rd ed.) Routledge.

Mezirow, J. (1978a). *Education for perspective transformation: Women's re-entry programs in community colleges.* Centre for Adult Education, Teachers College, Columbia University.

Mezirow, J. (1978b). Perspective transformation. *Adult Education, 28*(2), 100–110. doi:101177/074171367802800202

Mezirow, J. (1991). *Transformative dimensions of adult learning*. Jossey-Bass.

Milner, H. R., IV. (2007). Race, culture, and researcher positionality: Working through dangers seen, unseen, and unforeseen. *Educational Researcher, 36*(7), 388–400. doi:103102/0013189X07309471.

Neuendorf, K. A. (2017). *The content analysis guidebook* (2nd ed.). Cleveland State University.

Nordrum A. (2016). Popular Internet of things forecast of 50 billion devices by 2020 is outdated. *IEEE Spectrum.* https://spectrum.ieee.org/tech-talk/telecom/internet/popular-internet-of-things-forecast-of-50-billion-devices-by-2020-is-outdated.

Nguyen, A. (2017). Intercultural competence in short-term study abroad. *Frontiers: The Interdisciplinary Journal of Study Abroad, 29*(2), 109–127.

Osland, J. S. (2001). The quest for transformation: The process of global leadership development. In M. E. Mendenhall, T. M. Kühlmann, & G. K. Stahl (Eds.), *Developing global business leaders: Policies, processes, and innovations* (pp. 137–156). Quorum Books.

Osland, J., Bird, A., & Gunderson, A. (2007). *Trigger events in intercultural sensemaking* [Unpublished manuscript].

Özkazanç-Pan, B. (2008). International management research meets "the rest of the world." *Academy of Management Review, 33*(4), 964–974. doi:105465/amr.2008.34422014.

Patton, M. (2002). *Qualitative research and evaluation methods* (3rd ed.). Sage.

Prasad, A. 2003. The gaze of the other: Postcolonial theory and organizational analysis. In A. Prasad (Ed.), *Postcolonial theory and organizational analysis* (pp. 3–43). Palgrave Macmillan.

Repko, A. F., & Szostak, R. (2021). *Interdisciplinary research: Process and theory*. Sage publications.

Savicki, V., Adams, I., Wilde, A., & Binder, F. (2008). Intercultural development: Topics and sequences. *Frontiers: The Interdisciplinary Journal of Study Abroad, 15*, 111–126.

Schreier, M. (2012). *Qualitative content analysis in practice*. Sage publications.

Schank, R. C. (1982). *Dynamic memory: A theory of reminding and learning in computers and people* (Vol. 240). Cambridge University Press.

Schank, R. C. (1999). *Dynamic memory revisited*. Cambridge University Press, 1999.

Tarrant, M., Rubin, D., & Stoner, L. (2014). The added value of study abroad: Fostering a global citizenry. *Journal of Studies in International Education, 18*(2), 141–161. doi:101177/1028315313497589.

Taylor, E. W. (1993). *A learning model of becoming interculturally competent: A transformative process* [Doctoral dissertation]. Pepperdine University. Retrieved from https://lib.pepperdine.edu/login?url¼https://search-proquest-com.lib.pepperdine.edu/docview/304046909?accountid¼13159.

Taylor, E. W. (1997). Building upon the theoretical debate: A critical review of the empirical studies of Mezirow's transformative learning theory. *Adult Education Quarterly, 48*(1), 34–59. doi:101177/074171369704800104.

Taylor, E. W. (1998). *The theory and practice of transformative learning: A critical review.* Office of Educational Research and Improvement.

Taylor, E. W. (2000). Analyzing research on transformative learning theory. In J. Mezirow(Ed.), *Learning as transformation: Critical perspectives on a theory in progress* (pp. 285–328). Jossey-Bass.

Taylor, E. W. (2005). Making meaning of the varied and contested perspectives of transformative learning theory. *The Proceedings of The Sixth International Conference on Transformative Learning.* 459–464.

Taylor, E. (2007). An update of transformative learning theory: A critical review of the empirical research (1999–2005). *International Journal of Lifelong Education, 26*(2), 173–191. doi:101080/02601370701219475

Taylor, E., & Cranton, P. (2012). *The handbook of transformative learning: Theory, research, and practice.* Jossey-Bass.

Taylor, E. W., & Snyder, M. J. (2012). A critical review of research on transformative learning theory, 2006–2010. In E. W. Taylor & P. Cranton (Eds.), *The Handbook of Transformative Learning: Theory, Research, and Practice* (pp. 37–55). Jossey-Bass.

Tillman, L. C. (2002). Culturally sensitive research approaches: An African-American perspective. *Educational Researcher, 31*(9), 3–12. doi:103102/0013189X031009003.

Weick, K. E. (1995). *Sensemaking in organizations* (Vol. 3). Sage.

Westwood, R. (2001). Appropriating the other in the discourses of comparative management. In R. Westwood & S. Lin-stead (Eds.), *The language of organization* (pp. 241–282). Sage.

Westwood, R. (2004). Towards a postcolonial research paradigm in international business and comparative management. In R. Marschan-Piekkari & C. Welch (Eds.), *Handbook of qualitative research methods for international business* (pp. 56–83). Edward Elgar.

Westwood, R. I., & Jack, G. (2007). Manifesto for a post-colonial international business and management studies. *Critical Perspectives on International Business, 3*(3), 246–265. doi:101108/17422040710775021.

Witkamp, E., Droger, M., Janssens, R., van Zuylen, L., & van der Heide, A. (2016). How to deal with relatives of patients dying in the hospital? Qualitative content analysis of relatives' experiences. *Journal of Pain and Symptom Management, 52*(2), 235–242. doi:101016/j.jpainsymman.2016.02.009.

Wong-MingJi, D., & Mir, A. H. (1997). How international is inter-national management? Provincialism, parochialism, and the problematic of global diversity. In P. Prasad, A. J. Mills, M. Elmes, & A. Prasad (Eds.), *Managing the organizational melting pot: Dilemmas of workplace diversity* (pp. 340–364). Sage.

Part II C
Data Interpretation and Conclusions

21

Global Civil Society and Planetary Health

Overcoming the Myth of Objectivity

Elizabeth Hartney and Wanda Krause

Introduction

Colonialism and capitalism have had profound and lasting impacts on humanity throughout the world, and our connection to the earth. If we hope to support decolonization, peace and a trajectory to a healthy planet, we need to consider the notion of objectivity in progress, development and change implicit within these concepts. Otherwise, the environmental and spiritual cost will be destruction of civilization, cultural values and the planet (Whitmee et al., 2015). Socio-political and economic developments have created power dynamics which interact at a systemic level to shape our organizations, collective institutions, and experiences, on an individual and community level (Krause, 2019). Hartney brings insights and experience into this chapter, having worked with the Nuu-chul-nuth, Stó:lô, and Haida peoples in British Columbia, Canada. Krause having worked with Indigenous communities in Yukon, Canada, and researched, worked and consulted in the Middle East, Asia and Latin America, similarly expands on the concepts introduced through her own insights and experience. The authors demonstrate how international researchers can include the voices and perspectives outside the status quo, reducing inequities between the privileged and the marginalized. Such an endeavour includes understanding how researchers continue to dominate in the literature and present their subjective viewpoints as objective truth.

The concept of "public health" has been expanded into the concept of "global health" (Jamison et al., 2013), established through social, economic and political determinants (Holst, 2020). "Planetary health" is a broader and more comprehensive concept still. Emerging in the 1970s, it connects the individual to the planet (Prescott & Logan, 2019). Planetary health is an approach to life which attempts to address inequities, with the objective that all people on the globe have the ability to enjoy health and well-being (Gostin et al., 2018), in order to leave no one behind (Holst, 2020; UN Committee for Development, 2018). Global and cross-cultural researchers have a leadership role in acknowledging and influencing the power relationships that are established through these determinants through shifting the discourse to one that promotes the empowerment of marginalized voices and advances practices that are intersectional and decolonizing, ultimately promote planetary health.

Planetary health recognizes human impacts on the environment, and specifically, those that the exploitative practices initiated by colonialism and maintained by capitalism have on the natural systems of the planet, ultimately threatening human health. As planetary health researchers, we

DOI: 10.4324/9781003003380-21

recognize the interconnections between political, social, environmental and psychological discourses in shaping human behavior and creating systems which are damaging on every level. We also recognize the potential power of research to re-define societal values to promote justice, and through changing discourses and collective value systems, to promote human and planetary health.

In this chapter, the authors rely on the more comprehensive concept of planetary health, and further define and explain key concepts for global and cross-cultural leadership researchers, illustrating their role in the framing research to maximise the empowerment of under-represented peoples, and to create space for the process of decolonization of academic, government, and institutional research, policy and practice. Central to our discussion is the argument that the role of beliefs, expectations, and agency is essential to linking narrative and planetary health (Prescott & Logan, 2019, p. 1). As researchers, our ability to better understand whose interests are privileged, and, therefore, how to better approach our research, will guide our decisions and choices and to ultimately, promote a more equitable, peaceful and healthy world. This chapter begins with further key concepts pertinent for global and cross-cultural leadership researchers, explains the myth of objectivity, how to define the research question, power dynamics and unconscious bias to be considered, the utility of reflexivity and, finally, the initiative of ownership, control, access and possession (OCAP®) (First Nations Information Governance Centre, 2014).

Key Concepts for Global and Cross-Cultural Leadership Researchers

Ethnocentrism

Ethnocentrism is a well-established concept which refers to the tendency to use one's own group's standards as paramount when viewing other groups, thereby placing one's own group at the top of a hierarchy (Sumner, 1906). Researchers in the Northern Hemisphere are typically deeply entrenched in Eurocentric literature, that assumes the superiority of Western academic and societal standards, which are likely to form the basis of evaluations of the validity of the perspectives of others. We might, for example, consider the contributions of developed countries to human accomplishment, without considering their human and planetary costs. While science has made positive contributions, such as greater longevity the eradication of many diseases, from a broader view of the impact of human development on the world, it is clear that the prioritization of industrial development has resulted in subjugation of far more people than it has empowered. Even in the developed world, there is widespread psychological suffering and lack of autonomy at all levels of society, as we are all forced to conform to upholding the priorities of power structures that were built on and are maintained by oppression of the masses (Kessler & Bromet, 2013).

By the same token, we implicitly and explicitly cast judgment on individuals, communities and cultures that are disadvantaged by Western ethnocentric dominance. For example, academics privilege the English language as the most acceptable form of communication, both verbally and in writing (Altbach, 2007). It is unusual for an English-speaking academic to be required to speak or write in a second language; yet, it is essential for academics whose first language is not English. They are thereby immediately disadvantaged, even if fluent in English, by being required to express ideas through the limitations of English, and through being required to continually translate their ideas. This extends to the verbal expression of research participants; everything must be translated and back-translated, at best – simply translated to English without back translation at worse. The idea that the English language can capture, reflect or communicate ideas which may not even exist in English speaking mental models and world views is ethnocentric, and stifles the voices of those it seeks to represent. It is essential, therefore, that English-speaking researchers begin by giving voice to participants and interviewers in the language of the culture they seek to represent, for example, by hiring privileged access interviewers from within the culture (Johnson & Richert, 2016).

This step is particularly important when research is intended to represent the views and experiences of Indigenous peoples and communities (Whorf, 1956). Hartney has a deep recognition of this importance, having worked with the Nuu-chul-nuth and Haida peoples in British Columbia, Canada, as does Krause, who has worked with Indigenous communities in Yukon, Canada, and researched, worked and consulted in the Middle East, Asia and Latin America. Many Indigenous peoples in Canada were forced to speak English during the era of the residential schools, so speaking Indigenous languages is empowering and healing, and keeping the language alive is of central importance in these communities. Sensitivity is required in recognizing that the effects of colonialism have resulted in many Indigenous people not being able to speak their traditional languages. Privileging both the language itself and the ideas it conveys are important aspects of grounding the research in Indigenous and non-Western knowledges.

The process of research is itself an ethnocentric construct (Berry et al., 2002). By recognizing this, researchers can reduce ethnocentricity in the knowledge creation to which we contribute, by suspending our value judgements and considering perspectives which, although ethnocentric in themselves, may hold insights into how we might redress injustices and promote planetary health and healing. This may involve decentralizing Western human civilization as the focus of research while centering relations with others and nature as a key locus, and recognizing when the dominant Eurocentric culture suppresses and marginalizes other voices. Krause, being raised by her Jamaican mother and German father in Canada, learned early on how the perspectives and views of different cultures become marginalized. However, her research endeavour to de-center dominant voices and create space began when she started researching women in the Middle East borne out of an acute awareness that women in the region exercised power to advance their goals, despite the literature overwhelmingly indicating Middle Eastern women needed to be saved (Krause, 2008, 2013, 2019). Her own great, great grandmother fled the Middle East to marry the man she loved and make a life on her own terms. Hartney and Krause have endeavoured to change ethnocentric views, by scrutinizing the certainty of truth of a dominant Western, liberal trajectory, assumed objectivity, their own personal bias, bias in the literature, power dynamics and structures that serve more systemically to marginalize some and privilege others politically and economically, and through a conscious and reflective process to change the framing of phenomena through inquiry.

The Myth of Objectivity

Closely related to, and supportive of Western ethnocentric viewpoints, is the myth of objectivity. The success of colonialist viewpoints was highly dependent on the concept of objectivity, which is the idea that one point of view (typically the most widely accepted), is devoid of bias and reflects a more universal truth than other, subjective, positions, which are explicitly embedded in the perspective of the viewer. The claim that some viewpoints are more objective and, therefore, more truthful and worthy of privilege than others, is central to maintaining existing power structures, and perpetuating the social inequalities on which they depend (Berry et al., 2002). As philosophers such as Mannan (2016) have articulated, while scientists might strive for their knowledge to reflect an objective, factual description of the real structure of the world, strictly based on observations, experiments, and logical analyses of concepts, in fact, as scientists are social beings, we are inevitably impacted by our own psychology, ideology and sociology. We contend that this is a fundamental flaw in Western thought. The myth of objectivity also occurs with the presumption that criteria themselves are objective or that what is an indicator for something in one place is an indicator of the same in another place. Recognizing this myth is crucial for global and cross-cultural researchers to shift the dominant discourses to those that represent a broader range of perspectives.

Dismantling the myth of objectivity begins with oneself. Hartney and Krause, for example, became acutely aware of what had influenced their worldviews as they began their research, but they continue to peel back layers of understanding the self reflexively, the self in relation to others, and the self in the larger systems, recognizing the risk of becoming complacent with the passing seasons. They respectfully hold each other accountable through a discursive process of dialogue and debate. As discussed above, Krause situates herself by her intersectionality and therefore how she tends to view the world. However, an added layer is how she is viewed by others that defines how she relates to the world in different contexts. Thus, her identity is not the same, and how she influences the research context also differs. This has impacted her level of acceptance in some communities which in turn has impacted how much is shared in the research. Being a woman has enabled her to have access to women's only spaces in the Middle East, which has helped her to redress biases and assumptions in some of the literature written by men on the Middle East. Krause, however, has learned that being female does not mean that other women share the same experience or may even feel comfortable or confident sharing experiences that she may be perceived not to have had, given that she was, as one example, raised in the West with relative financial and political safety. Early on in her research career, during her undergraduate years, she immersed herself in a poor area of Egypt for several months to begin the journey of learning. This entailed culture shock before she could research with a better understanding of the barriers for different women, power dynamics that exist with not just men but other women, community and state, or of the different motivations women have to create change or even seek to control and quash change. Self-awareness and understanding the self in systems and, in particular, a self that is connected to the creation of stronger civil societies and planetary health is critical, and takes time.

For Krause's early journey, she is able only later to look back at the early years where she had limited understanding of the motivations mothers have to pursue the kinds of things they might, based on the experience and responsibility of being a mother. In Egypt, she collected data on women forming groups to care for their children to allow themselves freedom to pursue what they wanted but she minimized the key role this form of mobilization had on impacting their freedoms and capacities until she had her own children – soon enough beginning during her undergraduate years – to really grasp the significance of the women making this step happen. The many activities women were involved in were in fact motivated by sense of responsibility to serve their children, including pursuing income generating activities, learning how to read and write and various forms of activism.

> How patriarchy is subverted does not begin within an organization that aims its activities at the state; it begins within the home, within the village and among women whose concerns, dreams, and ingenious ways to achieve these practical things in life do matter. When these women together formed a daycare out of one of their homes to host their several children and take turns caring for the children in that home so that they could all together improve their economic circumstances, they contributed to their empowerment. They are perhaps not subverting government policies that marginalize women more generally and nor are they necessarily strategizing that such is their goal. They are, however, subverting economic constraints that oppress not only them but also all members of their immediate society. (Krause, 2012, p. 6)

To understand global civil society in context, Krause conducted research on women's activism of protesting in the streets against the mass disappearance of mostly male activists in Chile and Argentina. She recognized they were mostly the sons and husbands that were disappeared, motivating women to risk their lives pursuing justice for and knowledge about their missing family members. By opening up to the possibility that motherhood could be a key motivator for courageousness and acts of defiance for change, her work boldly argued for the centrality of motherhood in understanding change and the pursuit of democracy (Krause, 2004). Change and the creation of stronger civil societies globally is contextualized by experience and one's lived reality. For Krause, her own personal journey into motherhood was revelatory, leading to a journey of incredible learning, and believes it is important to be aware of how our identities, life experiences, states we are in, or propensities we have influence the lenses through which we not only see the world, but interpret the data, or even choose what data to include or exclude.

The myth of objectivity can be further understood in the use of objective criteria. Krause's research exposes how criteria used for evaluating the impact of women on civil society become erroneous. Centred on understanding to what degree women's organizations in the Middle East serve to expand civil society or hamper its expansion, Krause has also examined if there is any difference in the political impact of the different types of women's organizations on civil society. Firstly, much of the literature succeeds in establishing within the minds of many enquirers into state-society relations the view that if women are not seen in government, it is a reflection on their level of participation in what matters. Hence, objectively, on the basis that women are not found in government, for example, in Egypt, one might quickly conclude that women are not able to make any changes (Krause, 2012).

Krause (2008, 2012, 2013) argued that if a woman disrupts the patriarchal, patrimonial or even economic frameworks that govern her everyday life, that creates a ripple effect on the world outside the home. It follows then that participation within the most everyday ways or within the organizational types that support her to pursue her context specific needs, and secure sometimes the most basic rights, must be included in any serious study of civil society or planetary health. Krause recognized the criteria for evaluating their impacts excluded these everyday experiences which, in many of the countries in the Middle East, are shaped by poverty (2008, 2013). Yet, the focus on rights-based activism – which cannot happen easily within high levels of repression – reveals very little as to what women are pursuing and how they are pursuing their goals and more immediate needs. The myth of objectivity can be found in some feminist perspectives, as well – where all women, at all times, everywhere must be seen to want the same things.

Researchers must be fully immersed in the culture and aware of the political, social and economic dynamics that determine, in our case, what empowerment, change, peace and health mean to those studied. In contrast, Hartney, a woman of third generation Irish and Canadian immigrant descent growing up in England, and living for the past two decades in Canada, recognizes herself as an outsider, both of Indigenous communities, and of mainstream Canadian culture. She experiences being perceived as not belonging on a daily basis, yet she recognizes how her white privilege and fluent English first language grants her access to academia and other institutions, from which many other immigrants and marginalized people may be excluded. Her outsider perspective enables her to question dominant Canadian discourses, due to having been schooled in a more critical and historically informed educational system in the United Kingdom, one in which anti-racist discourse has been voiced since the 1990s, juxtaposed with and in stark contrast to the unconscious racism and stifling class system that still underlies and dominates British culture.

Yet the racism still experienced by Indigenous peoples in Canada remains appalling to Hartney, a part of her culture shock that remains unsettling after 20 years. Perhaps this is because very little obvious Indigeneity remains within mainstream British culture, with the occasional exception of Welsh, Scottish and Irish minority voices, who, despite being oppressed by English rule, experience marginalization quite differently from that of Indigenous peoples of Canada. Hartney is acutely aware that her outsider perspective may result in noticing the explicit yet unconscious racism towards Indigenous peoples inherent in Canadian culture, but is under no illusions that this reflects objectivity, grounded as it is in her early life imprinting by the world dominant, ethnocentric British worldview. Expressing this with humility has allowed Hartney to develop trust with Indigenous peoples, who recognize the authenticity of her outrage at their treatment, without her claiming to understand or empathize in any genuine way with their oppression, given the comparative limitations of her lived experience of exclusion as a bearer of white privilege. By respectfully engaging and privileging Indigenous voices and protocols, and positioning herself as a learner by listening and reflecting on the perspectives of Indigenous peoples, she models attempts to support and influence anti-racism discourse within the Canadian health system to emerging health leaders and allies. She communicates her intent to take action alongside those she conducts research with, rather than stay silent and complicit with the continued oppression of Indigenous peoples within Canadian society. Anti-racist discourse is validated and considered credible to policy-makers in healthcare when viewed as shedding light on objective statistics which reflect marginalization, such as the enormous health disparities (Adelson, 2005) and high suicide rates (Pollock et al., 2018) among Indigenous peoples in Canada and globally.

Power Dynamics

Power dynamics concern the influence and control that privileged groups and individuals in society have over others, to the point of the oppression and silencing of entire communities and sub-populations for the benefit of others (Allard-Tremblay, 2019). As researchers, we do not function outside of the power structures that have defined and enabled privilege; indeed, we hold a power position that has the potential to enable or suppress the influence of different perspectives, and to determine and refine whose voices are relevant to the solving of problems inherent in addressing planetary health. Our approach and choice of research participants is central to allowing different perspectives to be brought to light and considered, and our role as thought leaders allows us to determine the steps that must be taken for such perspectives to be acted upon by institutions that have the power to create systemic and societal change.

As discussed previously, the privileging of secular women whose activism is state-centric over poor women whose activism is around more immediate and practical goals (Molineaux, 1985) is perpetuated through applying "objective" frameworks which ignore the realities on the ground, such as Western feminist frameworks in countries where women do not identify their struggles with feminist ideals. Hence, it is essential to be critical of the concepts and frameworks we use by applying an inclusive and health-focused lens. The power dynamics that Hartney and Krause have sought to dismantle and disrupt includes the privileging of the settler communities over Indigenous communities, the privileging of the masculine and hierarchical over the feminine and practical goals and activism, the privileging of state-focused activism over acts of refusal and the generative forms of activism that actually serve to create a distribution of power and an enabling of empowerment within society, or the public-private divide.

The private sphere is typically defined as comprising the family, neighborhood or community and interpersonal relations between friends and acquaintances (Bystydzienski, 1992). The women in Krause's studies illustrate numerous examples of how change is created within the private sphere, and so thought to be apolitical, and consequently eliminated from study or concern. In their work, they show the fallacy of a divide defining what is civil and deemed uncivil where those deemed uncivil are silenced. They illustrate how researchers have the power to shift the discourse and including those marginalized. They further argue that it is a moral imperative for researchers to lead such change by reframing, dismantling those frameworks that marginalize, including marginalized voices and concerns and, in fact, opening space for those voices to speak.

Unconscious Bias

Unconscious bias is the tendency to discriminate against people or groups on the basis of characteristics such as gender, race, sexuality, disability and social class without recognizing this discrimination. This is particularly pervasive in those whose espoused values of equality are inconsistent with their attitudes and behaviors (Perry et al., 2015). Unconscious bias happens when we make rapid judgments and assumptions of people and situations, without conscious awareness of the mental processes at play. Obvious examples include assumptions that someone of Chinese descent is great at math or that an elderly female, disabled Arab should not be given a mortgage. More pervasive unconscious bias occurs when we make judgments regarding promotions between people in the workplace, based on their identity or judgments we make about who they are or represent. Unconscious bias thereby might influence leaders regarding who receives more training, who has the competencies to lead a project etc. Due to our cultural or educational influences, we can unconsciously prefer particular traits or competencies and thereby marginalize those individuals who we perceive to not have them.

Researchers have a responsibility to recognize the fundamental role we have in shaping the thoughts and actions of those in power. We might inadvertently disempower those who most need our advocacy, or reinforce existing and pervasive power structures by supporting belief systems that are rooted in discrimination, autocracy, bigotry and other forms of unconscious bias. Furthermore, our own situation within the existing power structures has shaped our unconscious biases or inadvertent beliefs that a particular person or perspective is right. The sources of our unconscious biases arise from the way we were raised, our education, our social, political or economic environments, past and present, individual experiences, our internal states and extent of exposure to different peoples, cultures and perspectives. Bias is also influenced by competencies, such as, trust, empathy, intercultural communication, curiosity, resilience and adaptability. If we are human, we are biased.

We can also make judgments with awareness that we are giving preference or even privilege to a particular person or group and even awareness that we are cutting the opportunities and access of a person or group, based on prejudiced judgments of them. This includes judging they are less deserving or capable, based on, for example, their being of a particular gender, race, age or an understanding we hold of intelligence. When Krause began her research on women in the Middle East, most of the literature she could get a hold of was disparaging of women's capacities to change their own conditions for the better due to the bias of the literature against women's capacities due to, for example, education, patriarchy, culture, religion, understanding of human rights or level of income. Krause studied Western, neo-liberal texts that pitted the West against the Middle East as the higher in civility and based on this judgment most of the research she had at her disposal concluded that the Middle East was completely void of civil society. While this is an example where researchers may be conscious of creating dominance, it is worthy with this example to show that those with good intentions may also inadvertently sustain the *status quo* of domination.

Hartney's work with Indigenous communities was precipitated by her work as a mental health expert in government. She noticed the disproportionate rates of morbidity and mortality among Indigenous peoples in routine statistical reports, yet found she was quickly shut down and repeatedly silenced when she raised questions concerning the need to address these issues in health policy. Only by entering academia was she able to address the need for Indigenous-led healthcare through research, but in doing so finds herself deeply constrained through the structures both that define and evaluate the quality of research, and the role of principal investigator in Western research systems. Ironically, this chapter is an example of how Hartney addresses issues related to the need for privileging Indigenous voices in health research, through her "expert" status as a doctoral level researcher. Yet this insight has been informed by listening to Indigenous Elders who have been disadvantaged in every way, and most notably through their educational disadvantage, being forced to "learn" through the abusive residential school system which was created to destroy their Indigenous knowledges.

Reflexivity

As researchers, we can develop appropriate goals to mitigate discrimination through raising our own awareness of the issues that we have the expertise and ability to influence, coupled with the process of reflexivity. Reflexivity is the process of critical self-awareness, by which we acknowledge the importance of power at the micro level of ourselves, and our relationships with others, as well as at the macro levels of society (Hankivsky, 2014). Reflexive practice therefore allows us to recognize the value of perspectives typically excluded from existing knowledge bases. While unconscious bias has been found to be an automatic cognitive process which is the result of deeply engrained societal prejudices, it is not completely beyond our control. Experimental research has demonstrated the ability of those with egalitarian goals to exhibit stereotype inhibition (Mosiowitz & Peizhong, 2011).

By raising our own consciousness through listening to and privileging marginalized voices, we can provide leadership for change in the system to challenge oppressive systems. By approaching inquiry with people of the culture researched with curiosity, which open our consciousness to different ways of knowing and being, we can become more attuned to planetary health and, consequently, promote human health and well-being on a global scale. To enable listening to other perspectives, Krause's research has argued for acknowledging that others had much to say to their own environments and ideas for their own well-being. She argued, firstly, that well-being is part and parcel of rights, and that well-being and individual or collective health is (or at least should be) the purpose and spirit of laws, policies and good governance. Secondly, she argued that the West does not have a monopoly on determining truth on what constitutes well-being and individual or collective health. However, in order to enable alternative or marginalized viewpoints, Krause has had to enable a more inclusive framework of what civility, and what democratic principles, and practice entail, and what "well-being" and "health" mean. By expanding the rigid boundaries around what civil society is, by listening to and privileging the marginalized voices of often poor, Muslim, women, in research on the Middle East, and elsewhere, Krause has led to change in the capacity to view and understand those who lead their own transformation without necessarily any help from the West.

Hartney also focuses predominantly on listening to the voices of those she hopes to support through her research. She is aware that her ability to paraphrase these voices into phrases and questions that sound and read as acceptable to Western academics inevitably loses some of the essence of the speaker, while appearing more closely aligned with language that is acceptable to those she seeks to influence. Continually checking with those she seeks to give voice to, reflecting on her own bias towards changing the system, she seeks critique from those around her in an ongoing attempt to mitigate her unconscious bias, as a non-Indigenous researcher raised in the culture of the oppressor.

Colonialism refers to the process by which one society overpowers and controls another, and in this context, refers to the overpowering of many parts of the world, in particular, the Americas, Africa and most of Asia in the period of the 15th to 19th centuries. This included the use of brutality and force to exploit and use people and natural resources for capitalist gain. A key practice was the transatlantic slave trade, primarily based in Africa, whereby human beings were forcibly taken from their land under threat of death, and transported to foreign countries to be sold as commodities to carry out the work of those in power positions. In the Americas, land was stolen from Indigenous peoples, who were controlled to the point of complete marginalization and oppression through the Indian Act and the reserve system. These abuses have created racialized peoples throughout the world, who represent the vast majority of the world's population, and are still experiencing oppression and disadvantage on a massive scale at all levels of society. The immorality of these colonial practices seems obvious today, yet the social inequalities that were created through these events are maintained through colonial knowledge systems which contain inherent biases that are based in privileging dominant, white, male, oppressor and exploiter perspectives, which prioritize the production of goods and services for profit, over human and planetary health and well-being.

Solutions

How to Define a Research Question

A research question is a starting point for any research endeavour. Without a question, we make the assumption that our current understanding is adequate. By framing our research with a strong research question, we identify the parameters of the knowledge we are seeking. The question should therefore cover the full scope of our research project, while attempting to confine the answers to the subject under scrutiny.

Defining research questions in this way is inherently flawed in that it narrows our focus, and attempts to negate or ignore the bigger picture, and the interconnections between the topic of our research and all other related topics. Yet it is a necessary starting point for beginning the dialogue between ourselves as essentially ignorant, and our research participants, who hold the knowledge which can broaden our perspectives. We can somewhat address the inherent flaw of confining our research to a specific question by recognizing and acknowledging other related topics for future study, without getting sidetracked from our original research question.

When we are working with marginalized communities, a useful place to begin defining research questions is by seeking the input of the people most affected by the research. One way researchers can do this is by developing relationships with the people they wish to better understand, to enable participants to become the co-researchers, in an engaged process of learning, giving and receiving. This goes against some of the traditional tenets of colonial research practice, whereby we specifically avoid the development of relationships with research subjects, in order to maintain an objective viewpoint, thereby objectifying those we intent to represent. Yet the idea of an objective researcher is a myth which is impossible to achieve. Researchers always bring their subjective opinions to their research, and by failing to acknowledge this, they run a greater risk of inadvertently reinforcing unconscious biases which have been created by oppressive power structures.

Although researchers are embedded within the colonial academic and government systems, they can sometimes access resources which allow greater involvement of marginalized voices in defining research questions. For example, Hartney's (2019) work with Indigenous communities in British Columbia allowed her to facilitate dialogue between First Nations people and health system partners, to define priorities for research based on the self-identified needs of the communities. While the topic of focus was mental health and substance use, openness to the viewpoints expressed by Indigenous voices included a wider scope of potential research questions and ideas, including not only physical health, but broader issues such as the role of traditional healers and mentors within the community, the function of ceremony, and connection to the land in healing through traditional food preparation. The privileging of oppressed voices began the process of building trust for future collaboration on research. Similarly, Hartney's work with people who use(d) substances and physicians developed alliances that had previously been absent, as the voices and leadership of patients was privileged and expert, while physicians discarded the mantle of superiority and listened to viewpoints which were crucial to the effectiveness of their work with these populations (Hartney, Barnard, & Richman, in press).

How to Develop Survey and Interview Questions

Surveys have their utility and have served to help us understand phenomena, such as through uncovering the stratification of systems or patterns. However, surveys by their very nature assume that the researcher already knows what is important and the role of the participant is to simply indicate the degree to which they agree with these pre-defined concepts. For this reason, surveys are often not helpful for representing different viewpoints from the established positions from those in authority (with notable exceptions, such as the Luxenborg Income Study, which exposed macro level issues on marginalization and poverty (Mahler & Jesuit, 2006).

Interview schedules which are structured, or even semi-structured, have the same inherent flaw. They define the scope of what the participant can discuss in a way that is biased towards validating and reinforcing the researcher's existing viewpoint. This can be avoided through the methods which allow the participant to define what is important, such as unstructured or narrative interviews, talking circles or journaling. Researchers often avoid these approaches because of the inconvenience of transcribing and analyzing large amounts of data which they consider irrelevant to their topic. This attitude is grounded in the counter-productive notion that the researcher understands the problem better than the participant does, and that the participant is essentially a commodity to be exploited to further the aims of the researcher.

Transformative Methods

Action research, community-based research, advocacy research and social justice research can be described as transformative methods, as they go beyond describing and understanding social phenomena, to engage those affected and produce emancipatory social change within the research context itself. This surpasses processes such as member checking, whereby validation is sought by data or results being presented back to participants to check for accuracy and resonance with their experiences (Birt et al., 2016), to actively involve participants or community representatives as co-researchers.

Hartney and the DESTINED project team (2020) took an open-ended approach to talking circles and interviews with Indigenous Elders, in an attempt to improve trauma-informed care in hospital emergency departments. Two important methodological decisions were made which allowed Indigenous voices to be privileged in this research: firstly, the leading of the data collection by Indigenous team members, and secondly, the use of just one open-ended question to begin the dialogue. The facilitator or interviewer could, of course, ask additional questions to clarify and expand the ideas being shared, however, by following the lead of participants, the research team avoided defining the responses according to existing perspectives.

In her research on the Middle East, Krause employed a variety of approaches in her endeavor to improve understanding of those marginalized and, in fact, give voice to those who are marginalized. Krause began visiting the Middle East in 1992 sometimes yearly and at times more often during a given year. As mentioned, her interest in the Middle East began during her undergraduate years while taking courses in the Orientalistik department, as it was called then, in Germany – the name used to lump a broad region into one that seemed fascinating to early European explorers. Krause then went on to do her MA on women's Islamic organizations and women's secular organizations in Cairo and then her PhD on a variety of women's organizations in the UAE, from which she then developed her research in the region. She has interviewed literally hundreds of men and women in the region and in other parts of the world. However, her work has included other methods for data collection beyond survey and interview methods to involve observation, reflection and action research to inform the kinds of questions that need to be asked. As Bradbury (2015) argues:

> Action researchers represent the possibility of re-enchanting knowledge creation for a flourishing world. We are called to engage with rather than merely understand, the unprecedented and compounding challenges that surround us, such as poverty, inequality, climate change, globalization, the ethical use of technology, the information technology revolution, and fundamentalism of all types … Action researchers are concerned with the conduct and application of research but, unlike applied researchers, we engage stakeholders in defining problems, planning and doing research, interpreting results, designing actions, and evaluating outcomes. We step beyond applied research into the democratization of research processes…. (p. 3)

Through involving herself in research, Krause could not help getting involved in the activism of many of the women she was researching. The approach to action research, whereby she participated in the activities, enabled the ability to not only understand but to a greater extent be with the women in pursuit of change, pursuing oftentimes shared goals and dreams for a better life, locally and collectively, for larger systems, planetary transformation and health. Krause evolved in all such contexts of togetherness, a reshaping of the questions that need to be asked. That process is a lived process, meaning that each researcher is invited to better inform their understanding, approaches and questions by recognizing that objectivity is a myth, and while participation might very well change what is being researched, the truth is that we are all shaping and influencing what we believe we are merely observing anyway. Participating allows for a better capacity to see from the inside out and position the questions to better reflect multiple worldviews and in particular those from which the experience is occurring.

Ownership, Control, Access and Possession (OCAP®)

As transformative researchers, Hartney and Krause recognize the importance of those studied maintaining "ownership" of the data they share, and input into its interpretation and dissemination. This is particularly important in anti-oppressive, anti-racist work with Indigenous peoples, who have developed Ownership, Control, Access and Possession (OCAP®) principles to guide research involving Indigenous peoples. OCAP® is a registered trademark of the First Nations Information Governance Centre (First Nations Information Governance Centre, 2014). Readers are directed to the FNIGC's website (www.FNIGC.ca/OCAP), so they can read and understand the full definition of OCAP®.

OCAP® is a set of principles about working with Indigenous peoples that takes important steps towards decolonizing research. Central to OCAP® is the recognition of community harm that has been inflicted on Indigenous peoples by researchers. Several types of harm are identified in OCAP®, including physician harm, psychological harm, social harm, economic harm and relational harm. There is a recognition that non-Indigenous researchers can benefit from Indigenous research, through academic prestige and advancement. The OCAP® principles aim to ensure that engaging in research with Indigenous peoples does not cause harm to the people it sets out to help.

This includes protocols which aim to ensure that abusive research is not conducted with Indigenous communities. For example, there have been cases of non-Indigenous researchers obtaining consent forms which identify the scope of research as smaller than how the data was actually used. In order to avoid this from occurring, Indigenous communities should be involved in determining the collection, use and dissemination of the research. By asserting ownership, researchers are accountable to the community for the use of the data. By asserting control, Indigenous communities are able to determine how data are managed, shared and destroyed. By asserting access, data and research findings cannot be kept from the Indigenous community from which they were extracted without the knowledge of that community. And by possessing and therefore governing the use of the data, Indigenous communities are able to hold data within their jurisdiction, allowing them to steward the data appropriately. This is lost when data are given over to academic institutions and governments to determine how data are used. By owning, controlling, having access and possession of research data, Indigenous peoples are able to determine the benefits and harms of the use of their own information. OCAP® therefore benefits not only Indigenous people, through creating processes for re-building trust with researchers, but also researchers, as it enhances the integrity of their research, and the ethical status of the research process itself.

Unfortunately, OCAP® is currently a voluntary process for researchers, even those engaged in direct research with First Nations peoples. Consequently, even when researchers commit to following OCAP® principles, they are often judged by peers who hold colonial worldviews which put them at a disadvantage when adhering to OCAP®. This can ultimately lead to researchers being judged as less productive in comparison to peers who do not follow such respectful guidelines, and can create barriers to advancement for non-Indigenous researchers. Adoption of OCAP® for all researchers would help to rectify this fundamental injustice within the academic system, would enable more researchers to work with Indigenous communities, and would allow Indigenous peoples to benefit from the insights that research can provide.

Conclusions

In supporting global civil society and planetary health, there are many ways international leadership researchers must work to address marginalization. International leadership researchers are urged to reconsider their biases, and to think about how to include people whose voices have been suppressed and silenced in research and in many other ways. In particular, they should reflect on the safety and privilege they enjoy, as constructed by the dominant society and, consequently, the inherent ethnocentrism of the research. Despite their expertise, such researchers should avoid the assumption that their perspective is objective, and instead recognize it is inherently subjective and defined through the lens of their privileged life experience and education. They should take a stance of listening, and immersing themselves in understanding the meaning, if not the language, of the people they intend to represent. As the authors have argued, objectivity is a myth.

Further, researchers should recognize their inherent power over their participants, reflected in their reporting. Reflexivity and awareness of the likelihood of unconscious bias can help to mitigate the potential harm to participants through misrepresenting their views. Member checking, translation and back-translation and extensive community engagement can further help to mitigate the potential for harm. OCAP® (First Nations Information Governance Centre, 2014) provides a set of principles to guide researchers to conduct research in a way that redresses the balance of power, and researchers are urged to follow OCAP® principles and engage in OCAP® training prior to working with Indigenous peoples. Academic and government organizations are urged to make OCAP® training a routine aspect of professional preparation for researchers, in a similar vein to the TriCouncil Policy Statement: Ethical Conduct for Research Involving Humans (TCPS 2).

Finally, international leadership researchers are urged to recognize the inherent ethnocentricity of the research paradigm itself, no matter how shrouded in community consultation, engagement and Indigenization. We caution readers, particularly, against taking a checklist approach to research validation, which primarily provides reassurance to the researcher, not necessarily to those who stand to gain or lose in the present, and into the future, as a consequence of data being interpreted and reinterpreted by those whose goals are not aligned with planetary health. Global and planetary health can become explicit through identification of multiple benefits of taking a larger perspective of the myth of objectivity around what is to be considered development and health in way of creating civilization and human health.

References

Adelson, N. (2005). The embodiment of inequity: Health disparities in Aboriginal Canada. *Canadian Journal of Public Health, 96*, S45–S61. doi:10.1007/BF03403702

Allard-Tremblay, Y. (2019). Rationalism and the silencing and distorting of Indigenous voices. *Critical Review of International Social and Political Philosophy*. doi:10.1080/13698230.2019.1644581

Altbach, P. (2007). The imperial tongue: English as the dominating academic language. *Economic and Political Weekly, 42*(36), 3608–3611. www.jstor.org/stable/40276356.

Berry, J. W., Poortinga, Y. H., Segall, M. H., & Daren, P. R. (2002). *Cross-cultural psychology: Research and applications*. Cambridge University Press.

Birt, L., Scott, S., Cavers, D., Campbell, C., & Walter, F. (2016). Member checking: A tool to enhance trustworthiness or merely a nod to validation? *Qualitative Health Research, 26*(13), 1802–1811. doi:10.1177/1 049732316654870

Bradbury, H. (2015). *The Sage handbook of action research* (3rd ed.). Sage.

Bystydzienski, J. M. (1992). *Women transforming politics: Worldwide strategies for empowerment*. Indiana University Press.

First Nations Information Governance Centre. (2014). *Ownership, control, access and possession (OCAP^{TM}): The path to first nations information governance*. https://fnigc.inlibro.net/cgi-bin/koha/opac-retrieve-file.pl?id=5 776c4ee9387f966e6771aa93a04f389

Gostin L., Meier B., Thomas R., Magar V., & Ghebreyesus T. (2018). 70 years of human rights in global health: Drawing on a contentious past to secure a hopeful future. *Lancet, 392*(10165), 2731–2735. doi:10.1016/ S0140-6736(18)32997-0

Hankivsky, O. (2014). *Intersectionality 101*. Institute for Intersectionality Research and Policy, Simon Fraser University. http://vawforum-cwr.ca/sites/default/files/attachments/intersectionallity_101.pdf.

Hartney, E., Barnard, D. K., & Richman, J. (2020). Development of best practice guidelines for primary care to support patients who use substances. *Journal of Primary Care & Community Health, 11*. doi:10.1177/2150132 720963656

Hartney, E. (2019). *Indigenous mental health & substance use leadership research planning initiative: Final report*. Centre for Health Leadership and Research, Royal Roads University. doi:10.25316/IR-4419

Hartney, E. and the DESTINED Project Team. (2020). *Developing Elders Support for Trauma Informed Emergency Departments (DESTINED): Final report*. Centre for Health Leadership and Research, Royal Roads University. doi:10.25316/IR-14929

Holst J. (2020). Global Health – Emergence, hegemonic trends and biomedical reductionism. *Globalization and health, 16*(1), 42. doi:10.1186/s12992-020-00573-4

Jamison D., Breman J., Measham A., Alleyne G., Claeson M., Evans D., et al. (2013). Global health 2035: A world converging within a generation. *Lancet, 382*(9908):1898–1955. doi:10.1016/S0140-6736(13)62105-4

Johnson, B. & Richert, T. (2016). A comparison of privileged access interviewing and traditional interviewing methods when studying drug users in treatment, *Addiction Research & Theory, 24*(5), 406–415. doi:10.3109/1 6066359.2016.1149570

Kessler, R. C. & Bromet, E. J. (2013). The epidemiology of depression across cultures. *Annual Review of Public Health, 34*, 119–138.

Krause, W. (2004). The role and example of Chilean and Argentinean mothers in democratisation, *Development in Practice Journal, 14*(3), 366–380.

Krause, W. (2008). *Women in civil society: The state, Islamism, and networks in the UAE*. Palgrave-Macmillan.

Krause, W. (2012). *Civil society and women activists in the Middle East*. I.B. Tauris

Krause, W. (2013). Deep democratization in Egypt: How women are driving the changes," *Informed Comment*, July, 2013.

Krause, W. (2019). Leading in times of cultural diversity: Achieving wellbeing, inclusivity and organizational performance. In J. Marques (Ed.), *The Routledge companion to management and workplace spirituality*. Routledge.

Lancet editorial. (2019, January). The bigger picture of planetary health. *The Lancet Planetary Health, 3*(1-E1). doi:10.1016/S2542-5196(19)30001-4

Mahler, V. A., & Jesuit, D. K. (2006). Fiscal redistribution in the developed countries: New insights from the Luxembourg Income Study. *Socio-Economic Review, 4*(3), 483–511. doi:10.1093/ser/mwl003

Mannan, A. (2016). Science and subjectivity: Understanding objectivity of scientific knowledge. *Philosophy & Progress, LIX-LX*, 44–71.

Molineaux, M. (1985). Mobilization without emancipation? Women's interests, the state, and Revolution in Nicaragua. *Feminist Studies, 11*(2), 227–254.

Mosiowitz, G. B. & Peizhong, L. (2011). Egalitarian goals trigger stereotype inhibition: A proactive form of stereotype control. *Journal of Experimental Social Psychology, 47*(1), 103–116. doi:10.1016/j.jesp.2010.08.014

Perry, S. P., Murphy, M. C., Dovidio, J. F. (2015). Modern prejudice: Subtle, but unconscious? The role of bias awareness in Whites' perceptions of personal and others' biases. *Journal of Experimental Social Psychology, 61*, 64–78. doi:10.1016/j.jesp.2015.06.007

Pollock, N. J., Naicker, K., Loro, A. et al. (2018). Global incidence of suicide among Indigenous peoples: A systematic review. *BMC Medicine, 16*, 145. doi:10.1186/s12916-018-1115-6

Prescott, S. & Logan, A. (2019). Narrative medicine meets planetary health: Mindsets matter in the Anthropocene. *Challenges 2019, 10*(17), 1–26. doi:10.3390/challe10010017

Sumner, W. G. (1906). *Folkways*. Ginn & Co. Cited. In Berry, J. W., Pootinga, Y. H., Segall, M. H., & Dansen, P. R. *Cross-cultural psychology: Research and Applications* (2nd ed.). Cambridge University Press.

Whitmee, S., Haines, A., Beyrer, C., Boltz, F., Capon, A. G., & Dias, B. (2015, July). Safeguarding human health in the Anthropocene epoch: Report. Lancet commission. *The Rockefeller Foundation-Lancet Commission on Planetary Health, 386*(10007-P19732028). doi:10.1016/S0140-6736(15)60901-1

Whorf, B. L. (1956). *Language, thought and reality*. (J. Carroll, Ed.). MIT Press.

UN Committee for Development. (2018). *Policy, report on the twentieth plenary session. Supplement No. 13 (E/2018/33)*. United Nations. https://sustainabledevelopment.un.org/content/documents/2754713_July_PM_2_Leaving_no_one_behind_Summary_from_UN_Committee_for_Development_Policy.pdf

22

Canteyuke

Exploring the Lakota Virtue of Generosity in Relationships and Research

Kem Gambrell

Out of the seven major values of the Lakota,[1] perhaps the most difficult to grasp from a Western paradigm is that of generosity or *canteyuke*,[2] which Gambrell and Fritz (2012) found to be central to Lakota leadership. Contrary to those raised in a capitalistic society, giving away many of one's belongings and personal treasures in honor of birthdays, graduations, and the death of a loved one is not a typical Western practice. For those raised and/or taught in a Western worldview, watching a *wóplia*[3] or potlatch ceremony can be extremely juxtaposed to the more materialistic attitude often displayed in dominant society. These ceremonies, honoring both those individuals who have had great accomplishments or those who have passed on, are ways that the Lakota and other Native Americans show a deeply embedded cultural practice of generosity.

The axiology and practice of generosity is grounded deeply in tradition and has served Native communities, and more specifically the Lakota, for many generations. Moreover, generosity, and its close companion gratitude, has allowed extended families, *tióśpeye*, and tribes to survive in times of great struggle. Generosity, in all its complex and nuanced manners, has been modeled for centuries and is a major aspect of understanding and conducting research with the Lakota and other Native and Indigenous[4] communities.

Chilisa (2012) describes Indigenous research as having four components: (1) it focuses on a local phenomenon; (2) it is context-sensitive, creating locally relevant constructs, methods, and theories; (3) it can integrate both Indigenous and Western theories; and (4) its assumptions are informed by an Indigenous research paradigm (p. 13). Furthermore, Kovach (2010) reflects that "giving back" is a central and a foundational characteristic of Indigenous research methods. Embracing and weaving in generosity as a core tenant throughout one's research is paramount to understanding operating and "walking in a good way" with Native communities. For the Lakota, this loosely means being a good relative-thinking of others first, being in relationship, and centering the needs of community before oneself (Gambrell & Fritz, 2012; White Hat, 2012). Walking in a good way also applies directly to conducting research with Native and Indigenous communities. Central to this, the concept of generosity, is more than just giving a "gift," it is deeply embedded in culture and a philosophical way of engaging with the world around us. Rather, the virtue of generosity sits firmly within the core of Lakota relationships, rooted solidly in gratitude of the earth, and all her inhabitants (Marshall, 2001).

To explore the Lakota virtues of generosity and gratitude, this chapter will integrate a personal narrative as well as context this within a relationship-research setting. "Narrative is a theme throughout Indigenous scholarship. All cultures are sustained through stories that integrate past,

DOI: 10.4324/9781003003380-22

present, and future" (Kenny, 2012, p. 7). The intent of this is to invite non-Native/Indigenous researchers to: (1) consider their positionality as outsiders, (2) to encourage research practices that are culturally centered and appropriate, and (3) to reduce the trauma and harms that Native and indigenous people have encountered from researchers. Smith (2012) writes, "the ways in which scientific research is implicated in the worst excesses of colonialism remains a powerful re-membered history for many of the world's colonized peoples. It is a history that still offends the deepest sense of our humanity" (p. 1). To encourage a de-colonial perspective, I use the term *relationship-research* intentionally, due to the influence of Indigenous research scholars such as Linda Tuhiwai Smith (1999, 2007), Shawn Wilson (2008) and others. These individuals adeptly write that "the problem with 'outsiders' researching Indigenous peoples is that there is always a comparison made between the culture of the 'studied' and the 'studier'…with the inevitable consequence of rating one over the other" (Wilson, 2008, p. 17). Smith (2012) goes on to explain this by writing, "the West can desire, extract and claim ownership of our ways of knowing … then simultaneously reject the people who created and developed those ideas and seek to deny them further opportunities … it angers us" (p. 1). As both authors discuss, the tendency of Western researchers is to compare ways of being, which has often placed peoples such as Native and Indigenous ways as less than (Chin & Trimble, 2012).

For leadership scholars, this notion of comparison has been solidly grounded in Western research methods. Considerable numbers of studies on leadership compares leaders, with the goal of finding the more successful trait, characteristic or leader behavior (Kenny, 2012). This way of thinking and researching leadership tends to minimize the complexity of the relationships and situation and centers the "leader." While the field has begun in ways to unpack this assumptive and narrow focus (i.e. see complexity leadership), it still perpetuates a dominant culture paradigm, limiting both understanding and other ways of being. As Wilson (2008) notes, the problem with this is "that we can never really remove the tools from their underlying beliefs" (p. 13).

While I will address my personal positionality shortly, part of the goal here is not to "compare" but rather, to unearth some of the assumptions my Western scientific training imbedded in my earlier meaning-making, and how some of the experiences I will share have exposed the limitations and hegemony of these methods. Lorde (2015) notes that "For the master's tools will never dis-mantle the master's house. They may allow us to temporarily beat him at his own game, but they will never enable us to bring about genuine change" (p. 98). Given the cultural differences that scholars must navigate when conducting research with cultures different than our own, having insights into gratitude and generosity, specifically from a non-dominant lens, will only increase the chances of success in developing and maintaining relationships. While some qualitative research methods such as Narrative Inquiry and Portraiture discuss the importance of trust and relationship (Clandinin, 2013; Clandinin & Connelly, 2000), generally these are still framed from a Western mindset. Here, when I discuss the practice of *relationship-research*, I define this as showing the "appropriate levels of respect, reciprocity, and responsibility" (Wilson, 2008, p. 99) to both the individual relationships *and* the community in which the research is being done. This framework creates not just an opportunity for research, but more importantly, it creates long-term connections and accountability to which both the researcher and the community are responsible. As the Lakota would say, we become *relatives* (White Hat, 2012).

In addition, unlike more traditional Western research processes, this chapter will incorporate a storied approach, with the hope that the reader will garner the lessons and insights they need, rather than providing a prescriptive or linear approach. Not only does a narrative approach parallel more of an Indigenous research method, but it is also my attempt to de-center methods that tend to minimize oral tradition and history (Yuan et al., 2014). To provide a one-approach-fits-all approach negates the vast cultural and philosophical differences and understandings of Native and Indigenous peoples. Yuan et al. (2014) note, we seek to promote ethical research and enhance the research capacity of urban AI/AN communities, and that scholars note that Native and Indigenous peoples have had a "long history of eradication and termination" (p. 2085). However, the authors go on to comment that "strong collaborations are needed for future development of research policies and implementation strategies at local and national levels that will have lasting benefits

for Native and Indigenous communities and peoples (Yuan et al., 2014, p. 2085).

With this understanding, the intent of this chapter is to show the complexity and nuances of working with individuals and communities different from the researcher. As scholars, it is imperative to carefully consider, respect, and be in relationship with those we are fortunate enough to collaborate with in research using the philosophy of gratitude and generosity (Chilisa, 2012; Kovach, 2010; Smith, 1999, 2012; Wilson, 2008). However, as part of this aim, I must position myself as a non-Native individual, and have the reader be aware that the following stories, observations, and reflections are mine alone. As such, they are only offered as a place of contemplation and discernment for others, and not as either a Native perspective or the "right" way for others. All mistakes and misconceptions are my own.

An Early Encounter

To begin- It was a beautiful June day, and I was traveling with two friends to a little community outside of Porcupine on the Pine Ridge Reservation of the Oglala Lakota. We were jovial as we drove through the beautiful sandhills of Nebraska on our way to South central South Dakota, and the current homelands of the Oglala Lakota. The long strands of greening prairie grass and wildflowers danced magically in the rolling hills, swirling in the soft breeze, seemingly waving to the world and all those passing by. As we traveled through the vast landscape of the central plains, the hills rose and fell, scattering pockets of marshland and small ponds here and there. Navigating the long narrow ribbon of the two-lane highway, it was not hard to picture large herds of buffalo that once roamed the area in herds of thousands, and the people whose existence was in direct relationship with the *tatáŋka*.[5]

A proud and resilient people, the Oglala are most known for their famous relative, Crazy Horse (Marshall, 2004). *Tašuŋke Witkó*, or Crazy Horse (Marshall, 2004, p. xiv) as he is known in English, is so legendary that in 1948 Korczak Ziolkowski began carving a monument to him in the Black Hills, an area revered to the Lakota and other plains tribes. Today thousands of tourists visit the Crazy Horse Monument, which sits ironically about 30 minutes from Mount Rushmore. Paying tribute to the "founding fathers," Mount Rushmore honors four individuals who, among other things, helped perpetuate colonization of the United States, and by extension the Lakota and other Native people. Paradoxically, both monuments are carved from the granite of the Black Hills, lands from which the Sioux[6] continue to perceive as sacred territory.

All these thoughts flowed through my mind as we weaved along the lush green hills winding our way along the two-lane highway that took us towards Pine Ridge. The sky was a deep blue, and it was a wonderfully warm summer day after a long winter. None of us had been to the reservation with the objective of this trip, although all of us had been participating in *inípi*[7] ceremonies for several years after being invited by a friend. My first time on Pine Ridge, nearly four years prior, I was curious and naive, not knowing what to expect. This time, while I was early in my journey of awareness, I had a little more insight into the culture and ceremonial ways of the Lakota. Even with these experiences, and perhaps even more pronounced in retrospect, my white[8] friends and I were culturally incompetent in the ways of the Lakota and blind to our privilege.

This entire trip was predicated on one of the earliest and more profound experiences I had with the Lakota. After a couple of years participating in *inípi* ceremonies in my hometown, I had met and gotten to know a medicine man that worked with my *inípi* community. "Mato," as I will call him, traveled occasionally from Pine Ridge Reservation to the city where I lived. Mato was a good friend of Bob, the individual that introduced me to the *inípi ceremony* (Treuer, 2012, p. 65). Mato and Bob had participated together in various Lakota ceremonies for years on the reservation, and Bob was instrumental in creating a space for incarcerated Native Americans to attend sweat lodge and practice their traditional way of prayer. Mato would travel from the reservation to support Bob and the Native inmates that were released for a few hours every week to pray.

The *inípi* ceremony, or sweat lodge as it is more commonly known, is a beautiful way to connect with one's self, the earth, and focus completely on community and prayer. White Hat (2012) explains that *inípi* means "they are bringing new life, physically and spiritually. *I* refers to the energy or resource, *ni* means 'to be alive', and *pi* is the plural form" (p. 172). Generally conducted in a round, dome-like structure made of willow branches and tarps, rocks are heated on a large fire, and placed in the center inside the structure. Water is then poured on the rocks, while traditional songs and prayers are performed. Many Native people use sweat lodges to pray, and today it is one of the most well-known and widely used Native ceremonies. Treuer (2012) notes however, that there is a wide variation in practices and structures for this ceremony across Native cultures (p. 65). In these ceremonies, as I understand the teachings from the Lakota, prayers are always for others, never oneself. This external focus allows people to contribute to the community as one of the many ways that generosity is grounded in Lakota ontology.

After spending several years in *inípi* community and developing a personal relationship with Bob and Mato, I was invited to Mato's Sundance, where I was able to observe him on the reservation in a larger community and as a Sundance intercessor, or leader. The Sundance is one of the most important ceremonies for the Lakota, where people come together for four intense days of prayer (Mails, 1978, 1998). It was after the ceremony that I *opaġi*[9] and asked Mato, requesting spiritual guidance and teaching from him. Fast forward several years to the trip my friends and I were taking to South Dakota to visit Mato and his family in a small community outside of Pine Ridge where he lived.

As a spiritual teacher and medicine man, Mato holds the traditional understanding of his role in community. By that I mean Mato does not "work" in the conventional sense of the word, but rather, had a "call" through his dreams to serve community in this capacity. Due to this role, anything he does–prayers for people, healing ceremonies, mentoring, guidance, community support and so many other things – Mato does for the well-being of the people, and not for a salary. To serve the community, traditional Lakota have an understanding that for those who are summoned by the spirits to serve others, it is then the community's responsibility to make sure these individuals and their families have what they need (for example see Mails, 1991). Thus, to receive the assistance of a medicine person, one should offer some sort of a *wohoyake* or offering to ask for help. As White Hat (2012) explains, a *wohoyake* is:

> The offering of compensation given to a medicine man. What-ever is given, the value de-monstrates how much the ceremony is appreciated. It's a way of saying thank you. A medicine man will accept gifts but will never charge for a ceremony; it's up to the one being helped to determine the compensation. (p. 176)

While many tribal communities in North America use tobacco as an offering and the customs around its use vary, "most Indians believe that any spiritual request made of the Creator of one's fellow human beings must be 'paid for'. Tobacco is viewed as an item of not just economic but primarily spiritual value. It is a reciprocal offering" (Treuer, 2012, p. 51).

Initial Lessons

From these first encounters, I gained several insights that later served me in the research I colla-borated on with the Lakota. First, and most importantly, relationship is central. Before any research was conducted, authentic and sustained relationships had been developed. These relationships were years in the making to develop trust and connection, but to also cultivate insights into the needs of the community. Second, as a leadership scholar, being in relationship allowed me to observe and engage with Lakota peoples as leaders, community members, and relatives. These observations also developed opportunities for greater cultural competence. All of this formed a basis for deconstructing my initial narrative around leadership, but also Western research that tends to negate the oral tradition and historical trauma that many Native and Indigenous peoples have experienced.

Offerings

After I asked Mato for spiritual instruction, I began preparing for the ceremony with help and guidance from Lakota mentors. Whether it is *wiwaŋg wácípi* (Sundance), *inípi* (sweat lodge), or *haŋbléceya*[10] (vision quest), these preparations often take months, if not years for the participants. In addition, obligations for ceremony for both the Sundance and the vision quest are at least a four-year commitment for both the spiritual teacher as well as the mentee. Not only are there the long-term obligations for the participant, but there is also an emotional and physical aspect, setting a clear intent, and preparing one's body for the long arduous ceremonies. Additionally, there are also many mental and ritualistic preparations as well. Because of this longstanding commitment by both the individual who made the request (the one who *opaġi*) and the receiver (a Native medicine person or Native elder), a clear intention and deep dedication is needed. This alone begins to set the stage for a deep and long-term relationship that is not to be taken lightly.

When we arrived at Mato's home, we found one of his younger daughters and many grandchildren. Unpacking the many sacks of groceries, house supplies, clothing, and other *wohoyake* items we had brought to Mato and his family allotted us access to his simple and modest mobile home. As we entered, the living room was barren except for a few camping chairs and a sagging couch that had piles of blankets, sleeping bags, and pillows next to it- clear evidence that many people slept in the living room on the floor. We would learn that many people on the reservation "couch-surfed" to be around Mato for days or weeks to receive spiritual guidance.

While we carried the items into the house, Mato's daughter Angel started unpacking them. It was amazing to watch…we had brought enough food for a family to eat for several weeks, and yet Angel divided all the groceries and other items into multiple piles. Soon, others began arriving, and I realized that she was immediately sharing the *wohoyake* with community members in need. As folks arrived, they shook our hands, joking and chatting with one another as they picked up the share allotted to them. The younger children ran around, each with a Kellogg's pop tart from the box that had inadvertently been carried inside. Now, as I reflect on the food we had meant to keep for ourselves had managed to end up in the piles now being distributed to others, I realize this was yet another lesson- that I would not go hungry while being on the reservation and to remove attachment to material things. While Mato and his family were obviously limited in their resources, they were not restricted in their ability to share generously with others. It was, and continues to be, a humbling moment. From the first moment we walked in the door, we were fed, constantly offered coffee (a reservation staple) and the use of their home for basic needs while we camped on their lands. For the Lakota:

> Nothing is too good to give away. We give away most everything, we give some relatives a place to stay, and we give away blankets, food, clothes, and shoes. It's helped me really live with the philosophy that nothing's permanent, it's just here to enjoy. (Gambrell & Fritz, 2012, p. 319)

Perhaps this inherent generosity starts with the Lakota understanding of *mitakuye oyas'iŋ*, which means "all my relatives" (Marshall, 2001, p. 211; White Hat, 2012, p. 173), and is grounded in the philosophy and intentional focus on relationships. Marshall (2001) comments that the phrase *mi-takuye oyas'in,* is "essential to and used in all of our ceremonies...its definition reminds us of that connection. And served to remind us of our place in the great scheme of life" (p. 211).

Intentional Student

After the initial insights, these continued experiences further shaped my understanding of generosity and gratitude that became foundational in my relationships with my Lakota friends and mentors, as well as my research. One such lesson includes the discernment around the term *mitakuye oyas'in.* From my Western training as a social scientist, I was encouraged to remain distant and objective (Creswell & Creswell, 2018). However, from a Native and Indigenous perspective, by the mere nature of "being a relative" and "related to all," which is what the more nuanced understanding of *mitakuye oyas'in,* means, I have noticed that becomes more and more difficult to be objective when I have shared meals with someone and observed their struggles and triumphs. Mitchell (2020) articulates this well by writing, "Indigenous kinship systems provide models for reciprocal care" (p. 24).

The other lesson I learned from the reflection above is the profound care the Lakota show to others. This care manifests in so many ways, including generosity of their material things, but also their deep desire and beliefs around connection to all things that include human "relatives," but also the animals, plants, and the world around them. And this connection starts with an ingrained and natural bond and gratitude for the people and their environment. Thus, when we can "extend our view of kinship beyond our anthropocentric view, a whole new world of knowledge becomes available to us" (Mitchell, 2020, p. 24).

Where Am I?

Central to a Native and Indigenous paradigm and to Indigenous Research Methods is relationship to the land. Wilson (2008) reflects this when he writes "Knowledge itself is held in the relationships and connections formed with the environment that surrounds us" (p. 87). He goes on to comment that the "environment is the knowledge or the pedagogy of place" and that "knowledge, theories and ideas are not only knots in the strands of relationality that are not physically visible but are nonetheless real" (p. 87). Robin Wall Kimmerer (2013) reflects:

> After all of these generations since Columbus, some of the wisest of Native elders still puzzle over the people who came to our shores. They look at the toll on the land and say "The problem with these new people is that they don't have both feet on the shore. One is still in the boat. They don't seem to know whether they're staying or not." (p. 207)

Linda Tuhiwai Smith, Eve Tuck, and K. Wayne Yang (2019) further this notion by writing that "to say water is life, land is our first teacher, and to ignore Indigenous presence and relationship with those lands and waters is to miss the point entirely" (p. 1). While I continue to reflect on my own transient nature in my life this perspective seems more veritable. The recognition that my relationship with the land and my neighbors differs when I think about being a part of the place, versus the place being a resource for my convenience and use. As Villanueva (2018) reflects, "What makes a people indigenous? Indigenous people believe they belong to the land, and non-indigenous people believe the land belongs to them" (p. 22). One way to address this as Kimmerer (2013) reflects, is to become "indigenous to place" (p. 207).

To become indigenous to place, as I have come to understand it as a non-Native, means becoming present to where I am. This means taking the opportunity to be deliberately attentive to relationships; the land, area, people, and the history of the place and space in which I am. It means settling in, for at least a full cycle of seasons, and watching the change and impermanence that is imbedded in the natural world. It also means seeing myself and acting as if I am a steward to the land- seeing it not as a resource, but rather as something to be grateful for and in relationship with.

These lessons have served me as a leadership researcher. If leadership is about relationship (Kenny, 2012) influence (Yukl & Falbe, 1990), and complexity (Uhl-Bien & Marion, 2008), then how better to become a better observer of the leadership phenomena then by being present and grounded in the place and space around me? From this positionality, needs of the community rise naturally, and my relationships and connections allow for ease of engagement, research, and action that can create lasting benefits. This sense of connection, and the resulting desire for respect, reciprocity, and responsibility lends itself to a stewardship perspective to both relationship to the people and the land.

Picking Sage

Perhaps one way to explain this stewardship as a lesson I learned from Mato's older sister. During one of the days of ceremony on Pine Ridge, *tuŋwiŋ*,[11] pulled several of the women aside, and talked about how to collect sage for the ceremony. *Peji hota*, is translated to mean "gray grass," and is used in various ceremonies to "clarify the mind...the smoke purifies the space and clears the area of any negative energy" (White Hat, 2012, p. 173). Both the individuals participating in, and the ceremony itself requires sage to cleanse and purify.

As *tuŋwiŋ* spoke, it seemed clear that she was frustrated with several of the women and used this time to talk about a deeper way of being with the land. She spoke of the medicine that sage brings, and how when we collect it we should gather it from our homelands, not from the ceremonial grounds. This, she would go on to explain, was for several reasons. First, if we are present to the land in which we live, we could be present to all the cycles and seasons. As such, we would better understand where the larger patches of sage are, not taking the first sage seen, rather, being able to monitor it to avoid over-harvesting. Additionally, we can better conceive of ways that we only take what we need, spreading the gathering over both time and place. In addition, *tuŋwiŋ* talked about being a part of giving-back to the land, creating a sustainable relationship with both the plant, and the area it grows. As Kimmerer (2013) notes, "If we use a plant respectfully it will stay with us and flourish. If we ignore it, it will go away. If you don't give it respect, it will leave us" (p. 157). Native and Indigenous peoples have been reiterating this for decades. Oglala Lakota Chief John Hollow Horn commented years ago

> Some day the earth will weep, she will beg for her life, she will cry with tears of blood. You will make a choice, if you will help her or let her die, and when she dies, you too will die (Mitchell, 2020, p. 27).

This was important information. It has not been uncommon for me to observe individuals picking sage, usually those holding a Western mindset, gathering it in massive amounts, stripping the area of both the plant as well as the opportunity for future patches. In these cases, there would not be a tobacco offering to ask permission of the plant, or the use of scissors or a small knife to cut each stem carefully leaving enough of the plant stem so it would continue to grow. Instead weed whackers and hedge trimmers are used, causing decimation and irreparable harm. I have also seen sage pulled up by the roots, leaving nothing but small holes in the ground like pock marks where huge patches of the gray grass once flourished. It turns out that the land can never really be healed once completely disrupted, and that many plant species are lost in these approaches. Kimmerer (2013) notes similar practices: "when the forests around here grow back after agricultural clearing, the trees come back readily, but the understory plants do not" ... "Even after a century of regrowth, the post farming forests are impoverished, while the untilled forests just across the wall are an explosion or blossoms. The medicines are missing, for reasons ecologists do not yet understand" (p. 200).

As *tuŋwìŋ* understood, to be in relationship with the land was not that we can't consume or collect the food and other resources that we need, rather it means that we honorably take what is given. Being honorable means, as Kimmerer (2013) describes, that human beings should not forget that these are all *gifts*, which is why we need to take care of, and to be stewards of the earth. Thus, we give back, in reciprocity and in gratitude for what has been given. Since the teachings of *tuŋwìŋ*, finding wild patches of sage has become harder and harder. The lesson was clear. As Kimmerer (2013) notes, "we need acts of restoration, not only for polluted waters and degraded lands, but also for our relationship to the world" (p. 195).

In these teachings, it was apparent that *tuŋwìŋ's* frustrations came not so much from the small group of white women around her, but rather due to the deep desire to restore an honor to the way we live, and "receive the respectful acknowledgement of the rest of the earth's beings" (Kimmerer, 2013, p. 195). Kimmerer (2013) calls this the "honorable harvest" and like *tuŋwìŋ*, is trying to encourage people to "remember what is good for the land is also good for the people" (p. 195). "Human beings have fallen out of alignment with life…people have forgotten how to live in relationship with the rest of creation" (Mitchell, 2020, p. 20).

By these simple lessons: (1) be present and in relationship with the land; (2) be grateful-make an offering; (3) collect only what is needed; (4) be intentional in collecting; (5) wander, taking only small amounts here and there to harvest honorably; (6) when possible, leave the seeds or other means for the plants to return; and, (7) thank the plant each time it is used- *tuŋwìŋ* was asking us to care for and respect all of our relations. These are also good research practices as well.

Stewardship of Knowledge

This philosophy of stewardship can also come in the form of what researchers can and should do with the gifts of insight they have obtained. From my Western scientific methods training, knowledge was something I had "a right" to, and little thought was given to how it was obtained, and how sacred the information truly was. One such disturbing example is the "2004 lawsuit won by the Havasupai Tribe against the Arizona Board of Regents and Arizona State University researchers for their misuse of DNA samples" (Yuan et al., 2014, p. 2086). Yuan and colleagues explained that while the "blood samples were collected for a diabetes study" which the tribe had supported, they were "later analyzed for unrelated investigations on schizophrenia, migration, and inbreeding that were not approved by the tribe" (p. 2086). This example parallels to some degree what I was taught in my Western education. If my white teachers signed off on it, IRB approved it, and I collected it, then the data was "mine" to do with as I wanted. However, I have now come to realize the self-oriented and colonized mindset this perpetuates. Wilson (2008) counters this narrative by writing:

> Accountability is built into the relationships that are formed in storytelling within an oral tradition. As a storyteller, I am responsible for who I share information with, as well as ensuring that it is shared in an appropriate way, at the right place and time. (p. 126)

Unfortunately, it seems as humans, and even more so as those trained in Western research methods, we forget the inherent respect and responsibility in our research-relationship with others. As Smith (2012) purports, "It appalls us that the West can desire, extract and claim ownership of our ways of knowing, or imagery, the things we create and produce, and then simultaneously reject the people who created and developed those ideas" (Smith, 2012, p. 1).

Another challenge observed from centering a Western paradigm and research method is how knowledge and understanding is created. Kimmerer (2013) talks about how "names are the way we humans build relationships, not only with each other, but with the living world" (p. 208). However, she also discusses that "once some folks attach a scientific label to a being, they stop exploring who it is" (p. 208). However, my sense is that if leadership and other social science researchers can be *present to* and *grateful for* the ever-changing impermanent world around us, then we will be more able to think more holistically about the complexity we encounter. I believe that the precursor to this is a mindset of gratitude. This is particularly true when doing research with others we are in relationship with. To hold central to everything we do tenant of being present to where we are allows researchers to ground ourselves not in the Western orientation of self, but rather the understanding and commitment to a sustainable and "honorable harvest" both with the land, as well as those we do research with. "There is no separation between ceremony and our daily walk in the world. Everything is interrelated and recognized for its sacred place" (Mitchell, 2020, p. 20), and in this mindset, gratitude is understood at being at the center.

Taking Off Your Boots

Not only have many of my experiences with the Lakota helped me understand relationships more deeply with people and the land, but they have also helped me show up better as a relative. By being a better relative, I have been able to reflect upon how I engage in these relationships and interact with others more holistically. Taking time to pause, especially when confronted with situations that are not comfortable, or when it seems I or others are at odds with each other, has been a valuable lesson. And like many other teachings, I believe being able to take time and pause, to intentionally respond is a personal and researcher virtue strongly grounded in gratitude and generosity.

Several years ago, while at Sundance, I was able to observe one of the leaders gracefully navigate a situation with implications that could have been ultimately very destructive to the larger community. While on the surface it might have seemed like a small incident, on the larger scale, especially in a community that is very political in nature, a long-term impact, should this situation have gone south, was in the making.

To explain- one central aspect of the Sundance is the continuous smudging, or "cleansing" the area with smoke using plant material. While sage leaves are an important piece, another plant relative, cedar needles, or *ḣaŋté,* is used as a primary way that cleansing is done with the dancers and all those who work to support them (Treuer, 2012, p. 62). This aspect of the ceremony is the first thing that happens in the early dawn hours and is one of the last things that is done to close the day. Depending on the size of the Sundance, "smudging" requires a small group of people to complete.

Like any invitational gathering that brings hundreds of people together, the Sundance, while a prayer ceremony, also has its fair share of human drama. People come from all around the world, and all walks of life. This is a beautiful aspect of ceremony, where people assemble for the specific purpose of intentional prayer and purposeful community. However, with all this amazing and rich opportunity for connection, learning, and relationship, also comes individuals with a sense of knowing the "right-way." While these folks are not bound by race, gender, nation, or tribal community, in the case of dominant society members, being ensconced in white privilege and white fragility often creates a particular dynamic in these situations. Smith (1999) discusses some of this mindset when she unpacks the concepts and impact of imperialism and colonialism, stating that "Imperialism still hurts, still destroys and is still reforming itself constantly" (p. 20). This understanding frames the following example of white assumption and interventionism.

One early morning, I was asked by Ted, one of the Lakota leaders, to take the 12-year-old daughter of one of the locals to the East gate, to teach her how to smudge the Sundancers entering into the circle for the ceremony. When Jade and I arrived at the East gate, however, there was another white woman, new to this Sundance standing at the East gate with a smudge can. When I greeted her, she promptly gave me a handout with the "rules" from another Sundance and commented that she had been at ceremony for years and had decided it was "her turn" to smudge in the dancers that morning. When I asked if Ted had spoken to her about this, she said that he had not, but that she "knew what she was doing," and that she "was there first." Quickly I understood that this was not my place or time to challenge (and in reality, on the reservation as a white woman, it is not ever my place to "correct" others), and as such we waited for Ted, who was always one of the East gate morning smudgers as a leader.

Within ten or so minutes, Ted arrived. Seeing that the white woman, and Jade and I were at the gate, he paused, looking at me questioningly. He asked me what was going on, and I quietly said that the other woman had resolved to smudge at the East gate herself. Instead of approaching and confronting her, Ted calmly sat down. Leisurely, Ted began to unlace his tall ash-covered leather work boots. Two minutes became five as he slowly and methodically removed his shoes and his socks in such a manner that he could easily don them again later. Then Ted stood, calmly walking over to the woman in his bare feet. Quietly, although I could still hear the conversation, Ted asked the white women to do him a favor, sending her on her way to complete a "very important task" that he entrusted only her to do. I stood there watching the scene unfold, as Ted gently, without anger or animosity, spoke to and persuaded the woman to change her objective.

I believe that generosity and gratitude is rooted in this scenario in many ways. First, I have come to believe that Ted was practicing generosity by not shaming or treating the other woman in a patriarchal manner. He had, by taking the time to be intentional and creatively thoughtful, found a task that was needed. This allowed the woman to step away from her current course of action (seemingly embedded in white entitlement), to save face and feel essential. In addition, by finding a solution, Ted was centering another Native, Jade, encouraging her to start becoming part of the ceremony, of which she is an active member to this day. In addition, through his actions, he was intentional, modeling a kind of grace and composure that seems scarce in today's world. As Diewert (2013) comments "our greatest challenge is to recognize, resist, and dismantle the structures of oppressive power, not just to reform their most harmful policies" (p. 136). From my perspective, this is exactly what Ted was able to do, not just for the other woman, but for Jade and me as well, by modeling of intentionality and generosity.

This lesson has served me well as a researcher. It reminds me that while there are important things, they need not be rushed. To stop, consider, reflect, and then act with generosity has not only allowed me to de-center some of my white privilege and entitlement, but has also created a space within me that encourages curiosity, considerations of others' perspectives and needs, and open to other cultural ways of being in relationship. These insights have also helped me as researcher honor the knowledge of others in a new way.

Haŋbleĉeya at Mato's

After a restful night under the stars at Mato's place, my friends and I gathered to start making final preparations for my *haŋbleĉeya,* or "going on the hill." The original reason for my desire for spiritual guidance from Mato, I had been preparing for months, setting my prayers in the pinches of tobacco placed in little brightly colored pieces of cloth. Mato spoke to us about the ceremony, and things that might happen "on the hill" during the ceremony. He talked of the Lakota values of gratitude, and how everything around us is a relative, and that we are connected and dependent beings. Mato went on to explain that the core tenants of Lakota spirituality are grounded in the premise of gratitude and that to start, be thankful for what we are given. And as he spoke, Mato reminded me to always pray for others, and to center the needs of the community, while also focusing on my reason and intent for going on the hill. He also reiterated that everything that happens on the hill is a gift, to take the lesson or message and to thank the creator for it…Even if I did not ever understand its full meaning. As Mitchell (2020) reflects,

> The entire span of human life exists within each one of us, going all the way back to the hands of the Creator. In our bodies, we carry the blood of our ancestors and the seeds of the future generations. We are the living conduit to all life. (p. 21)

At the time I was extremely focused and unable to understand many of the lessons he was trying to share. Today I appreciate the level of commitment that Mato and those who supported me during this time devoted. Food was cooked, the fire was kept the entire time, support *inipi* (sweat lodges) and prayers were offered, and a number of people worked to assist me in so many ways. I used to think that the person or people "in ceremony" were the important ones. Now I understand that without a strong and supportive community, none of these ceremonies would occur. They literally cannot be done in isolation. To center another's prayers and help provide support to the space needed for these is perhaps one of the greatest examples of generosity shown.

This too is a lesson about research. From my Western training, research is often focused on the desires and needs of the academic. Centered is ownership of knowledge, and sharing of the insights gained from others, often not for their benefit, but rather for the advancement of the scholar. Smith (2007) reflects this by saying that "the institution of research by its nature alienates" (p. 75). However, when Mato finally came and got me from my little spot on the hillside, I returned to his house to find a large feast had been cooked. Soups, fry bread and chokecherry *wojapi,* and many other dishes had been prepared to feed the dozens of community members involved. While it had seemed that I was all alone during the days of *haŋblećeya,* it soon became evident that there were many people supporting Mato and I, and the prayer community that had been formed unbeknownst to me.

This perhaps is another critical lesson when doing research with others- that it is never done in isolation or for the sole purpose or interests of the researcher. Instead, research is done in relationship, with the desires and inquiry rising from the needs of the community, of which the researcher is a member (Wenger et al., 2002, pp. 36–37). Wenger et al. (2002) comment:

> Members of a healthy community of practice have the sense that making the community more valuable is to the benefit of everyone. They know that their own contribution will come back to them…This kind of reciprocity is neither selfless nor simple tit for tat, but a deeper understanding of mutual value that extends over time. (p. 37)

Conceivably this is one of the most striking contradictions from Western research training, and a challenge to the messages of individualism and competition that I received from the academy (Smith, 2007, p. 76). However, this perspective of relationship-research is central to community development and change (Smith, 2007, p. 76). I believe it is also a much more socially just way of conducting research. As Kelley et al. (2013) reflect "Conducting research in an ethical manner within indigenous communities necessitates an active awareness of the extent to which federal government agencies and affiliated institutions have oppressed, discriminated against, and engaged in culturally biased practices with these communities" (p. 12).

Final Researcher Ponderings

As a non-Native individual, I have often read, reflected on, and had multiple conversations regarding how to de-center a Western scientific paradigm in my research and in my understanding. I believe as a leadership scholar and student this deconstruction of a Western mindset helps stop perpetuating colonization and harm, but it also creates a more holistic and deeper understanding of the phenomena of leadership. It is not easy, and I am often not confident that I have been successful in this endeavor.

> Researchers enter communities armed with goodwill in their front pockets and patents in their back pockets, they bring medicine into the villages and extract blood for genetic analysis. No matter how appalling their behaviors, how insensitive and offensive their personal actions may be, their acts and intentions are always being justified as being for the "good of mankind. (Smith, 2012, p. 25)

While I have little doubt that I have been offensive and even harmful to those I have studied and done research with, albeit unintentionally, my hope in sharing some of these stories is to confer the need for gratitude and generosity as a core component of doing research with any group, including Native and Indigenous peoples. More importantly, my desire as a researcher *and* relative is to center other ways of being as I work with people and communities where I am not indigenous to. Similar to Kelley et al. (2013) and associates reflection on Western oriented researchers, "Some have viewed research involving AIAN groups as an extension of colonization, given the ethnocentric foundation of Western scientific principles and their application within indigenous contexts" (p. 13). This ethnocentrism has not only harmed our Native and Indigenous relatives, it also drastically minimizes our own understanding and knowledge, limiting our ability to connect with ourselves and others. This only perpetuates a limited paradigm, propelling all phenomena through this one worldview. Unfortunately, this only perpetuates racism and trauma within Native peoples and communities. Kelley et al. (2013) observe that:

> The impact of these practices extends to the present-day health of indigenous people, who experience health disparities that stem from racism, loss of native language, loss of land, and complex socioeconomic factors. Prior to their contact with European settlers, North American indigenous people had socioeconomic, spiritual, and linguistic structures that supported an indigenous worldview, that is, a perceptual understanding of the world based on holistic, cyclical, sacred, and spiritual connections. However, European contact influenced indigenous people's worldviews, and Western European perspectives on science and reason have since ruled supreme. (p. 12)

To re-center a Native or Indigenous perspective to change some of the structures and heal the related trauma by, "focus on decolonizing knowledge in the disciplines is a method for emancipating colonized peoples" (Nakata et al., 2012, p. 120) is one way to begin the healing process, as well as expanding our understanding of relational phenomena such as leadership.

Action Steps

To counter these harms, there are several things that both the academy and researchers can do. First, as many authors propose, the academy can begin by truly honoring diverse cultural values and worldviews (Chin & Trimble, 2012; Smith, 1999, 2012; Wilson, 2008). I would suggest that this includes not just exploring other cultures in education but working to imbed a variety of philosophies and worldviews throughout curriculum that de-centers a dominant and colonizer narrative. Second, for those researchers trained in or are from a dominant culture, consideration of how colonial and racist practices have influenced both oneself and the institutions one is a part is critical. Reflecting upon, exploring and unsettling these narratives as "natural," "default" and "assumed" is central to conducting ethical cross-cultural research. Chin and Trimble (2015) note that "too many leadership scholars and researchers carry out their affairs as though a universal approach remains appropriate (p. 9). A central part of this practice is doing identity work. Like Helms (2020) eloquently notes, "Whites seem to be the only racial group that spends more time and effort wondering about the implications of race for other groups than it does for itself" (xiii). Last, Western trained scholars can consider using alternative research practices such as Indigenous research methods (e.g., see Archibald et al., 2019; Chilisa, 2012; Kovach, 2009; Smith, 1999; Wilson, 2008). Mitchell (2020) notes that "the overall lack of diversity within the patriarchal colonial paradigm has had a suffocating impact on creative intelligence and a divisive impact on society" (p. 23). The use of research methods that are based on healthy relationships between researchers, communities, and participants that include the key facets of respect, reciprocity, and accountability with which the research is partnering is not just socially just, it is ethically and culturally grounded. While these tenants Wilson (2008) and others believe are core, they manifest differently in different cultural and ethnic people. To begin this process however, researchers can start with the concepts of gratitude and generosity in themselves and their relationships, identifying *where* and *how* these beliefs are practiced within the communities and individuals their research resides.

In essence, there is no one-way to engage in gratitude and generosity. These concepts are understood and practiced differently between individuals and communities, tribes, and cultures. As I have come to understand it, to engage in generosity, I must genuinely *feel* gratitude and appreciation for what has been given. To feel gratitude and appreciation, mindfulness and relationship must be present and embodied. Simpson (2013) notes to be mindful, present and show gratitude and appreciation, we not only need to "unsettle the settler within," dismantling a colonial paradigm, but that we also need "many more unsettled settlers" (p. 53).

> "I suspect all of our security concerns will be addressed if we enact spiritual ways of living that promote systems of life-enhancement, not just the enhancement of our human lives, but life-enhancement in a world full of relatives" (Wildcat, 2013, p. 309). As researchers, we have the responsibility to engage in the difficult processes of truth-telling and sustained practices of decolonization alongside our Indigenous brothers and sisters. "Decolonization for white settlers will inevitably require a deepening understanding of past and present colonial violence, and a relentless refusal to reproduce that violence through consistent practices of solidarity" (Diewert, 2013, p. 137). This is the characterization of Native leadership, ad of gratitude and generosity, "an aesthetic engagement-one that brings us to the beauty of our lives-on the land, with each other, and in relationship to all living things" (Kenny, 2012, p. 7).

Mitakuye oyas'iŋ.

Note about Lakota language

Lakota is an oral language, and while it has been transformed to written, there are several ways readers may see spellings (and definitions) of words. For this chapter, two sources were consulted: *White Hat (1999) Reading and Writing the Lakota Language*. The University of Utah Press; and Buechel and Manhart (2002). Lakota Dictionary. University of Nebraska Press.

Notes

1 The Lakota are a plains tribe that include seven council fires. Often known as part of the great Sioux nation (which also includes the Dakota and Nakota tribes) they are one of the largest Native American nations today. The Lakota once roamed the central and Northern Central US. Today the Lakota are centralized in North and South Dakota on reservations.
2 Defined as to give, to share, to have a heart.
3 Generally translated as "to give thanks, rejoice or be glad." This is also used as a common Lakota term for a give-a-way or thanksgiving ceremony.
4 Native is a term, for the purpose of this paper, refer to Native Americans, or people whose homelands are in the U.S. The term Indigenous is used for those people around the world. I choose to capitalize the term

Indigenous here, as many Native and Indigenous authors do. The term Indigenous means as been described as meaning "born of the land" or "springs from the land."

5 Lakota term for Bison.

6 Sioux is a generic term for the Lakota, Dakota and Nakota Nations.

7 Inipi ceremony is often called "sweat lodge" in English. It is a prayer ceremony that includes sweating in an enclosure, with rocks that have been heated over a large fire.

8 To decenter a dominant culture positionality, I intentionally chose to not capitalize "white.".

9 *Opaği* is a Native American pipe that is loaded with tobacco and ready to be offered. It can also be a tobacco offering to individuals, asking for guidance, healing, or permission.

10 Vision quest, or *haŋbléčeya* is four-day ceremony where the individual is placed in a small obscure place to focus on their prayers and ask for a vision or purpose from the spirits.

11 Lakota term for aunt. Using it is a sign of respect for an elder or respected woman in the community.

References

Archibald, E., Xiiem, Q. Q., Lee-Morgan, J. B., & De Santolo, J. (Eds.). (2019). *Decolonizing research: Indigenous Storywork as methodology*. ZedBooks.

Buechel, E., & Manhart, P. (2002). *Lakota dictionary*. University of Nebraska Press.

Chilisa, B. (2012). *Indigenous research methodologies*. SAGE.

Chin, J. L., & Trimble, J. E. (2012). *Diversity and leadership*. SAGE.

Clandinin, D. J. (2013). *Engaging in narrative inquiry*. Left Coast Press, Inc.

Clandinin, D. J. & Connelly, F. M. (2000) *Narrative inquiry: Experience and story in qualitative research*. Jossey-Bass.

Creswell, J., & Creswell, D. (2018). *Research design: Qualitative, quantitative, and mixed methods approaches* (5th ed.). SAGE Publishing.

Diewert, D. (2013). White Christina settlers, the Bible, and (de)colonialization. In S. Heinrichs (Ed.), *Buffalo shout, salmon cry. Conversation on creation, land justice, and life together* (pp. 127–137). Herald Press.

Gambrell, K. M., & Fritz, S. M. (2012). Healers and helpers, unifying the people: A qualitative study of Lakota leadership. *Journal of Leadership & Organizational Studies, 19*(3), 315–325. doi:10.1177/1548051812442749

Kimmerer, R. W. (2013). *Braiding Sweetgrass. Indigenous wisdom, scientific knowledge, and the teachings of plants*. Milkweed editions.

Kelley, A., Belcourt-Dittoff, A., Belcourt, C., & Belcourt, G. (2013). Research ethics and indigenous communities. *American Journal of Public Health, 103*(12), 2146–2151.

Kenny, C. (2012). Liberating leadership theory. In C. Kenny & T. N. Fraser (Eds.), *Living indigenous leadership: Native narratives on building strong communities* (pp. 1–14). UBC Press.

Kovach, M. (2010). *Indigenous methodologies: Characteristics, conversations, and contexts*. University of Toronto Press.

Lorde, A. (2015). The master's tools will never dismantle the master's house. In C. Moraga & G. Anzaldua (Eds.), *This bridge called my back* (4th ed., pp. 98–101). State University of New York Press.

Mails, T. E. (1978, 1998). *Sundancing: The Great Sioux piercing ritual*. Council Oaks Books LLC.

Mails, T. E. (1991). *Fools crow: Wisdom and power*. Council Oaks Books LLC.

Marshall III, J. M. (2001). *The Lakota way: Stories and lessons for living*. Penguin Compass.

Marshall III, J. M. (2004). *The journey of crazy horse*. Penguin Books.

Mitchell, S. (2020). Indigenous prophecy and Mother Earth. In A. E. Johnson & K. K. Wilkinson (Eds.), *In all we can save. Truth, courage, and solutions for the climate crisis.* (pp. 16–28). One World.

Nakata, N. M., Nakata, V., Keech, S., & Bolt, R. (2012). Decolonial goals and pedagogies for indigenous studies. *Decolonization: Indigeneity, Education & Society, 1*(1), 120–140.

Simpson, L. (2013). Liberated peoples, liberated lands. In S. Heinrich (Ed.), *Buffalo shout, salmon cry* (pp. 50–60). Herald Press.

Smith, L. T. (1999). *Decolonizing methodologies: Research and indigenous peoples*. Zed Books LTD.

Smith, L. T. (2007). Getting the story right-telling the story well. Indigenous activism-indigenous research. In P. Mead & S. Ratuva (Eds.), *Pacific genes & life patents. Pacific indigenous experiences & analysis of the commodification & ownership of life* (pp. 74–81). Call of the Earth Llamado de la Tierra and The United nations University Institute of Advanced Studies.

Smith, L. T. (2012). *Decolonizing methodologies: Research and indigenous peoples* (2nd ed.) Zed Books.

Smith, L. T., Tuck, E., & Yang, K. W. (Eds.). (2019). *Indigenous and decolonizing studies in education. Mapping the long view*. Routledge.

Treuer, A. (2012). *Everything you wanted to know about Indians but were afraid to ask*. Borealis Books.

Trimble, J. L., & Trimble, J. E. (2015). *Diversity and leadership*. SAGE.

Uhl-Bien, M., & Marion, R. (Eds.). (2008). *Complexity leadership: Part 1: Conceptual foundations*. Information Age Publishing, Inc.

Villanueva, E. (2018). *Decolonizing wealth: Indigenous wisdom to heal divides and restore balance*. Berrett Koehler.

Wenger, E., McDermott, R., & Snyder, W. M. (2002). *Cultivating communities of practice*. Harvard Business School Press.

White Hat, A. (2012). *Life's Journey-Zuya.: Oral teachings from Rosebud*. (J. Cunningham, Ed.). University of Utah Press.

Wildcat, D. (2013). Enhancing life in a world of relatives. In S. Heinrich (Ed.), *Buffalo shout, salmon cry* (pp. 295–314). Herald Press.

Wilson, S. (2008). *Research is ceremony. Indigenous research methods*. Fernword Publishing.

Yuan, N. P., Bartgis, J., & Demers, J. (2014). Promoting ethical research with American Indian and Alaska native people living in urban areas. *Framing Health Matters, 104*(11), 2085–2091.

Yukl, G. & Falbe, C. (1990). Influence tactics and objectives in upward, downward, and lateral influence attempts. *Journal of Applied Psychology, 75*, 132–140.

23

Exploring and Understanding Multifaceted International Leadership Realities

Maja Zelihic

Introduction

Historically, the study of managerial and leadership effectiveness has employed traditional Western-style corporate attributes and behaviors as its success indicators (Gavin & Westwood, 2009). The behaviors of leaders in those corporations have seemingly become the benchmark for leadership, to be applied in any enterprise, market, country, or culture (Gavin & Westwood, 2009). The original and quite outdated assumption was that leadership and operational practices within a company, such as Ford in the United States, should be applicable to companies in other countries, such as Sony in Japan or Ikea in Sweden. While operational effectiveness and leadership principles may show some similarities across the world, as key indicators are observed, important differences emerge. In studies looking at the intersection between culture and leadership, roughly half of the variation in national cultural orientations is unique to each country (Beugelsdijk & Welzel, 2018). Therefore, as we study different cultural contexts, such as major corporations in France, emerging enterprise in Bali, or a small coffee shop in Havana, we must be mindful of the unique expressions of leadership within each culture.

It is becoming increasingly evident that the "one size fits all" approach to the examination of leadership effectiveness fails to capture cultural nuances. The GLOBE project research attempted to develop a theory of observing, describing, understanding and predicting the impact cultural variables have on leadership, focusing on behavioral patterns, attitudes, cultural norms, societal atmosphere and obstacles (House, Javidan, Hanges, & Dorfman, 2002). Cultural dimensions studied by GLOBE researchers included uncertainty avoidance, power distance, collectivism, gender egalitarianism, assertiveness, and future, organizational, and humane orientation (House, Javidan, Hanges, & Dorfman, 2002). While the research ventures described in this chapter are not focusing on the GLOBE's cultural dimensions at their core, the clear majority of the above-mentioned cultural dimension variables are touched upon.

The purpose of this chapter is to discuss the multifaceted leadership realities faced in the course of several international research studies I completed. These studies in Haiti, Cuba, Zambia and Mexico illustrate distinct variables influencing the expression of leadership and its perceived effectiveness in the context of national culture, local business practices and organizational culture. These nations, along with many other regions of the developing world, are undergoing some form of transformation, each having its own unique layers of difficulties impacted by their different realities. The chapter will provide explicit discussion of my experiences and perspectives as an international

DOI: 10.4324/9781003003380-23

researcher. By exploring these perspectives, the reader will develop an appreciation for the diverse expressions of leadership in different cultures and better understand the complexities of leadership research in different regions of the world.

Haitian Leadership Study

From 2017 to 2018, I had the opportunity to engage in a joint research venture in Haiti. While I had extensive experience with international research and research funding through a fellowship grant at my university, I had not had the opportunity to research in Haiti previously. This made my co-researcher's cultural guidance particularly important for this study. He is Haitian-American, and had both personal and business experience in Haiti. The first-hand cultural insights would be important to aid in narrowing our focus to businesses within regions he was most familiar with, Cap-Haitien in the North Province and Port-au-Prince in the West Province, as well as access to our desired sample population. These regions represent two out of five main Haitian business markets.

Study Overview

The purpose of our study, *A Study of Motivation and Personal Characteristics Among Haitian Entrepreneurs Facing "Obstacle" Variables in Small Business Arena,* was to explore entrepreneurial motivations and leadership effectiveness, identifying challenges small business leaders must contend with to succeed. The study was concentrated on motivations influencing Haitian entrepreneurs to start new businesses, persevere though a multitude of obstacles, and, ultimately, create a sustainable business. Motivational factors were examined using a modified Scheinberg and MacMillan motivational model (Scheinberg & MacMillan, 1988), which is a cross-cultural cognitive model of new venture creation. Scheinberg and MacMillan (1988) identified six motivational factors entrepreneurs across cultures in eleven countries shared, including need for approval, perceived instrumentality of wealth, communitarianism, need for personal development, need for independence, and need for escape. This study specifically examined problems faced by the entrepreneurs, both during the start-up stage and in their current operations, and attempted to develop a reflecting the relationship between motivation, personal characteristics of Haitian entrepreneurs, and success.

Intersection of Leadership and Culture in Haiti

One of the aims of research was to better understand Haitian leadership norms and behaviors in practice. Haitian leaders across economic sectors and industries are faced with persistent economic, social, political and environmental challenges that shape their leadership. Haiti suffers from record unemployment rates, with 70% of the able-bodied workforce without a steady job (Thorpe, 2017). Forty-five percent of Haitians are illiterate and living in poverty, with a quarter of them living in extreme poverty (Gordon, Plumblee, Higdon, Davis, & Vaughn, 2017).

The island Haiti shares with the Dominican Republic, Hispaniola, is prone to earthquakes and hurricanes. While these natural disasters impact both countries, Haiti tends to suffer more intense damage and longer-term recovery due to "a killer combination of geography, poverty, social problems, slipshod building standards and bad luck" (Borenstein, 2019). This has made particularly violent natural disasters, such as the 2010 earthquake and 2016 hurricane, devastating to the already fragile infrastructure and social services available (Park, 2016). Basic services, such as weekly garbage collection, are not provided.

Frequent changes within the government and political unrest further complicate the situation. While one can attempt to lead his/her business in the best way possible, businesses do not exist in a vacuum and are prone to a multitude of problems from the external environment. Political protests in the capital and other major cities often turn into riot situations, which halts already fragile economic development (Whitney, 2019). Corruption is widespread in government and business sectors, with bribery as a standard business practice (Klitgaard, 2010).

The intensity of social and environmental challenges facing Haitian business leaders have limited growth in the business sector. GDP annual growth averaged only 1.3% over the past two decades (World Bank, 2020). While there have been growth periods (Mesidor, 2014), ongoing natural disasters and political instability backtrack progress. Additionally, Haiti has received "billions in foreign aid, yet persists as one of the poorest and worst governed countries" (Buss & Gardner, 2005). Still, the entrepreneurial sector has leaders who are successfully overcoming a shortage of adequate equipment funding, supplies, trained workforce, and proper infrastructure (Peart & Knowles, 2018). This makes leadership research particularly important in Haiti to identify success factors that may aid aspiring entrepreneurs. Successful entrepreneurship is of crucial importance in the developing world, where traditional employment opportunities are limited (Margolis, 2014).

Research Challenges in Haiti

Prior to traveling to Haiti, we took a traditional approach of exploring literature using online peer-reviewed databases. Once we were in country, however, the majority of research had to be done in person and manually. For example, additional literature review had to be done by physically going to a library. We also had a lengthy in-person meeting with the Ministry of Commerce to better understand how entrepreneurship functions within Haiti. The Ministry helped us with identification of enterprises of interest, as well.

Our time in the capital, Port au Prince, was marked by protest. This caused us to be trapped in one section of the city for 12 hours to escape demonstrators. After a somewhat frightening encounter with the protesters, we were able to leave the capital for the quiet villages of Grand Goave province. Traveling from Port Au Prince, it takes approximately two hours to get to the province of Grand Goave (Grangwav in Creole) in the southwest of Haiti, even though the actual distance is only 64 km. This is because the roads are very rough and damaged, which cause create hazards for cars. Due to insufficient funding, many roads are unmarked, and traffic lights only exist in major urban areas. The tropical climate does not help matters. Both cars and roads are often damaged, due to seasonal torrential rains (Haiti Infrastructure, Power, & Communication, 2017).

The area was completely devastated during the 2010 earthquake, with 90% of its infrastructure being destroyed (DesRoches, Comerio, Eberhard, Mooney, & Rix, 2011). For example, the dam on the Grand Goave river has been in danger of breaking ever since the earthquake, despite relief efforts by the USA army in the immediate aftermath of the disaster. Almost every governmental building, school, church, and residential home suffered damage or was destroyed. Industrial development ceased throughout the region. Despite the obstacles, in this quiet province with peaceful fishing villages reminiscence of some more prosperous periods, two small enterprises are thriving and employing local workers.

The primary data for the Haitian study was collected through in-person structured interviews, surveys, and in-depth case studies conducted at two different businesses that included a livestock operation and an automotive distributor. To avoid heavy traffic and several hours driving, we stayed in the local village, which was close to the establishments we chose for our study. While conveniently located near our research subjects, the village had no running water or electricity. The electric power we used sporadically to save gas was supplied using generators. Water was poured from the top of the roof every few days to give us enough for showers and cooking. Power outages and infrequent water supply were problems both businesses we observed dealt with on a daily basis.

Staying in the village enabled us to immerse into the local culture, interact with locals, observe and participate in local customs, and experience delicious Haitian food. From a research perspective, living daily life alongside the community gave us a real-life appreciation for some of the obstacles each business faced daily.

Findings

The unreliable and limited basic resources created ongoing challenges for the businesses, while also strengthening the agility of these entrepreneurs to exercise agility in adapting to fluctuating conditions. Leadership agility was a key theme in our findings. It extended beyond resource constraints and living conditions to navigation of the complex and often corrupt political environment. Local business owners routinely were required to negotiate with politicians, landlords, and government officials, resorting to bribery and sometimes the need to restart the business again from scratch. The entrepreneurs regarded these unfortunate setbacks as the price of managing a business enterprise in the culture. As a result, ingenuity, tenacity, and patience were viewed as requirements for sustainable business leadership. So it was not surprising that the final data analysis found a positive correlation between motivations, personality characteristics, and success. A compelling research question for the future is whether the intensity of the challenges was, in fact, instrumental in the development of the leadership competencies and behaviors needed to thrive in this environment.

In the following section, we go to a different corner of the world, exploring leadership in the Southern African country of Zambia.

Zambian Leadership Study

I served as a Fulbright Specialist when I studied leadership in Zambia with a team of researchers. The researchers included the Executive Dean of the Forbes School of Business and Technology, who was leading the first Fulbright project, and I was in charge of the second project. The team who collaborated on the research article are from Mulungushi University and Uganda Management Institute. Our research initiative, Empowering Global Leaders Through Workplace Sustainability (Daugherty, Zelihic, Deresa, Nga'mbi, & Ssekamatte, 2021), consisted of two separate projects in Zambia over ten months in 2018 and 2019.

The first Fulbright project aimed to explore the evolving nature of Zambian leadership skills the 21st-century workplace demands, while understanding multifaceted complexities, challenges, and opportunities in the southern African region. Fulbright Specialists did not set out to share Western best practices with the audience. Instead, through sharing survey findings, they attempted to identify an effective path for leaders within Zambian societal and cultural frameworks while reflecting on some comparable Western leadership experiences. The second Fulbright project aimed to conduct a comprehensive assessment of current state of Zambian leadership, with its full range of challenges and opportunities through research data gathered from the leaders of Zambia across 18 different industries.

Study Overview

The Fulbright project involved surveying Zambian leaders across different industries to understand the framework for leadership in rapidly developing African economies, like Zambia. The study looked at adaptability for change, implementation strategies, and complacency avoidance. A descriptive survey design was adopted for the study. Data was collected using a survey questionnaire triangulated with focus group data from 246 Zambian leaders across 18 different industries. Quantitative data was analyzed using descriptive statistics, while qualitative data was analyzed using thematic analysis.

Intersection of Leadership and Culture in Zambia

The landscape of African leadership is changing. It is being molded by changing demographics, new technologies, and the influences of emerging markets and the global political environment. The African continent was experiencing significant economic development prior to the 2020 pandemic (African Development Bank Group, 2017; World Bank, 2020). In 2017, the African Development Bank Group reported that Africa had the second fastest growing economy in the world. Zambia, for example, experienced economic growth in 2017 due to crop harvest and better electricity supply (World Bank in Africa, 2018). The growth continued in 2018 with accommodative monetary conditions helping the financial sector (World Bank in Africa, 2018). If the skill of African labor supply matches its pure demographic growth, then some regional economies could expand by 22 percent by 2030, reducing poverty for 51 million people (World Bank, 2014). However, as is the case in many parts of the African continent, the region faces a myriad of challenges typically associated with underdeveloped countries, centered explicitly around its infrastructure. According to Umez (2000), African problems can be categorized into the following categories: colonial legacy, corruption at different layers of the society, and prolonged absence of democracy in some areas.

Strong leadership is needed to support progress. However, the crisis of leadership appears as the most pertinent problem confronting the African continent today (Olalere, 2015). "Although the negative legacy of colonial dominance has contributed to a culture of corruption, poverty, tribalism and violence, charismatic leaders frequently invoke indigenous cultural values and means to overcome these problems" in Sub-Saharan African cultures, such as Zambia (Wanasika, Howell, Littrell & Dorfman, 2011). This unique cultural approach to leadership was the focus of our research study.

Some of the complexity of Zambian leadership style is rooted in a desire for openness, tempered by caution rooted in historical abuses by colonizers. For example, Zambian leaders in our study stated that they realized that isolation was not a winning strategy in the long run. However, they remained cautious about being too open to global opportunities, lest Zambia be taken advantage of, as it had been in the past. China has been characterized as the new colonizer of Zambia (Negi, 2008). The economy has largely been dependent on copper mining and an increased monopoly of Chinese-based businesses and their investments (Gadzala, 2010). While Zambian consumers may benefit from newly opened businesses and their products, the Chinese companies have been accused of only providing low quality jobs to Zambians (Kamwanga & Koyi, 2009), rather than improving the overall employment climate and upskilling for the local population. However, there are notable contributions to infrastructure development, such as the Zambian railway (Van Bracht, 2012) and refurbishment of copper mines, which led to increased export rates (World Bank in Africa, 2018). The relationship between China and Zambia, ultimately, is complex and sometimes punctuated with public dissent and protest (Van Bracht, 2012).

Research Challenges in Zambia

Zambian infrastructure, while not ideal, allowed us to travel to both Kabwe and Livingstone, where Mulungushi Universities have campuses. The main campus in Kabwe is located a few hours from its capital Lusaka, depending on traffic. Thanks to both the host university and our Fulbright stipend, our accommodations were quite comfortable, and we were able to appreciate the richness of Zambian cuisine both at the hotel and visiting our Zambian colleagues. One of the complexities of this research is that we had to conduct surveying prior to arriving in Zambia via online surveys, while focus groups were conducted at the seminars. Ideally, it would be terrific to get both surveys and focus group data from the same group of participants, but that was not a possibility. While we had some overlaps between the survey participants and focuss group participants, a perfect match was not feasible.

This study is limited to the data pool of Zambian leaders. To ensure significant findings in the entire southern African region, similar studies need to be conducted in the neighboring countries. The clear majority of participants were in the middle- to high-level leadership positions. Leaders in lower-ranking leadership positions might have different perspectives. The male and young leaders were overrepresented in the data pool, but this reflects the current demographics of Zambian leadership.

The survey and focus group participants expressed optimism for Zambian leaders being able to pursue their unique path of leadership, creating political, economic and social structures that will take local natural and human resources to enhance Zambian development and growth. Researchers used a qualitative approach focusing on the determinants of leadership for understanding gaps in Africa at large, with a focus on Zambia in particular. The research used descriptive surveying and focus groups as data-gathering instruments 246 Zambian leaders participated in the survey across 18 different industries, including 25.71% from the government, 11.45% from the business sector, 9.39% from the agriculture sector and 4.90% from the mining industry (Daugherty, Zelihic, Deresa, Nga'mbi, & Ssekamatte, 2021). In addition, at each seminar we conducted two focus groups. Focus group participants were asked to share their views and participants regarding what needs to be performed to promote trans-formative leadership and workplace sustainability. Many of them recommended a review of the education system, improvement of communication and working environment, as well as promotion of local solutions and innovation (Daugherty, Zelihic, Deresa, Nga'mbi, & Ssekamatte, 2021).

Findings

It emerged that Zambian leaders face challenges of lack of proper talent management and infra-structure, effective mentoring, and human resource gaps. Findings indicate that offsetting leadership gaps will require a focus on education, talent management, empowerment of women leaders and finding a unique African leadership path. Zambian leaders' reality is at times forcing them to re-plicate Western-style leadership or pursue a path that is forced on them by the foreign firms which are currently monopolizing the Zambian market.

This unique combination of leadership styles drawing from their rich uniquely African heritage with some global, predominately Western elements has allowed the region to maximize its strong history and traditions of its leadership practices, all the while; it has begun its transformation to establish consistency with the rest of the world. As countries around the globe undergo some form of change given the issues of technology and global competition. Cuban leadership reality, in-troduced in the next section is vastly different from its Zambian counterparts.

The survey and focus group participants expressed optimism when it comes to Zambian leaders being able to pursue their unique path of leadership creating political, economic and social structures, which will take advantage of Zambian natural and human resources in order to enhance Zambian development and growth. Furthermore, the project incorporated discussion on the empowerment of female leaders, innovative approaches in addressing the gender gap, and cultural sensitivities in ad-dressing the workplace gender issue within the developing world. The gender focus was important to highlight the significant role men play in enhancing female progress in the work environment.

Furthermore, the researchers and audience members analyzed multigenerational workforce challenges with a focus on unconscious bias at a 21st-century Zambian workplace. The participants agreed that as digital natives collide with digital immigrants at any workplace, it becomes imperative for business leaders to maintain the delicate balance of talent and technology capitalization while ensuring the ideal of a harmonious relationship between employees. The project also included discussion of offsetting the leadership gap in the developing world through education, talent management, emerging technology utilization (cloud-based technology), and adaptability to rapid change environment; and analysis of a unique African path to global leadership with a focus on its rich pre-colonial tradition. The seminar participants agreed that African leaders should not mimic their Western counterparts but instead develop their unique styles positioned adequately within their respective societies.

Cuban Leadership Study

Our Cuban research took place in the summer of 2019. The research was funded by the fellowship grant at the chapter author's university. There were only two researchers in our team, including myself, due to the constraints and complexities of traveling to Cuba. Cuba as a research interest, was selected during the time when the United States eased its restrictions, but unfortunately, the actual trip took place as restrictions were being placed back on.

Study Overview

The research venture titled *Transformation of the State-operated Enterprises into a Free Market Business Entities in Cuba,* primarily focused on leaders within three small, non-government owned enterprises. The research purpose was to identify variables that are the most beneficial in creating sustainable businesses operations navigating a complex business arena in the current Cuban transition environment. If those "transitional success variables" are identified, the path towards more sustainable business transformational model which is fitting the current period within the Cuban society.

Cuban enterprises must face societal, cultural, and business transformation from an outdated restrictive communist model to a capitalistic, free-market model. While on the surface, communism appears to be flourishing in Cuba, the free market is "burrowing irresistibly from within" (Mandell, 2014, para. 8). Capitalism is slowly evolving on the island without being openly discussed (Mandell, 2014). We aimed to identify variables that are the most beneficial within the business arena in the current Cuban transition environment. If those "transitional success variables" are identified, the leaders' path towards more sustainable transformational fitting the current period within the Cuban society will be much easier. While many small business owners perceivably embrace the changes, many companies struggle to create a sustainable business model in order to operate within a free market arena effectively (Jorge, 2003).

As we studied Cuban leaders, the focus was on three variables: risk-taking, acceptance of change, and experience with the emerging free market. The research aimed to correlate the mentioned variables with the Cuban bureaucratic regulatory system, acceptance and adaptability within market adjustment, and creation of a sustainable model. Studying variables impacting Cuban leadership we focused on the following hypotheses:

- The higher the risk-taking index of Cuban small-business leaders the higher the enterprises' adaptability factor in embracing market changes.
- There is a positive relationship between the leader's willingness to accept constant change working within and their ability to navigate the bureaucracy of Cuban business regulations.

Intersection of Leadership and Culture in Cuba

The U.S. boycott of trade further depleted the Cuban economy, which did "an excellent" job deteriorating on its own over the last few decades of failed ideology and inept leadership (Mandell, 2014). At this juncture, the Cubans economy is in even worse shape due to coronavirus, which impacted its currency and Trump's administration attempts to "strengthen the decades-old trade embargo" (Augustin & Robles, 2020, para. 4).

The cost of U.S. sanctions was enormous for both sides. The economic embargo in place since the 1960s cost the U.S. economy 1.2 billion per year without even an accurate calculation of how much it cost Cuba (Feffer, 2016). While Cuba-US relationship started improving during Obama administration, in the last year or so, much of the improvement has been reversed, and new sanctions were imposed (*US-Cuba Relations,* 2020).

Immediately after the U.S. imposed embargo, Cuba was forced to depend on a "single benefactor and a single commodity," Soviet Union and sugar subsidies (Mandell, 2014, para.4). This hindered the Cuban ability to develop other sectors, experiencing a severe crisis after the Soviet Union collapsed in the 1980s (Feffer, 2016).

One should go no further than to observe once breathtaking housing in old Havana, built before the 1960s, deteriorating at a stunning rate of three collapsed houses per day, due to the lack of maintenance and capital needed for refurbishment (Mandell, 2014). Whether Cuba has the strength to weather the transitional storm while avoiding turbulence of experience of transitioning from the state to a market-based economy, similar to what China and Russia experienced a few decades prior, remain open (Mandell, 2014).

Within this grim reality, new enterprises are opening, in the last decade, and old enterprises are transitioning into a new system. One can only hope that once the proper set of variables are identified in correlation to the effectiveness of a transformational enterprise, that same knowledge can be applied to other countries going through a similar change. Some experts feel that Cuba is already successfully on its way to a market-based economy, while the official government stance is that communism is there to stay (Miroff, 2012). However, Cuba is known to be one of the countries often exposed to major setbacks. While during the Obama administration, relaxing some embargo parameters proved to help the Cuban economy, in the last few years, some reinstated and some newly imposed sanctions prevented petroleum delivery to Cuba and significantly reduced commercial flights from the US impacting Augustin & Robles, 2020, para. 4).

As Cuba emerges from the years of government-regulated business model ridden with multitude of issues, including huge bureaucracy, poor infrastructure, the clear majority of workers still employed by the state, and the perceived irrevocability of a socialist system, the situation at the ground level does not look promising. Lacking the core of the capitalist framework requited for the free market enterprises while having the desire to "jump ahead" and create the "best of both worlds," its bipolar mixture of communism and capitalism hard to compare to anything similar in another region. Regardless of their readiness and the Cuban government's assertion that socialism is going to remain unchanged on the island, Cuban businesses are moving forward in an environment that is ambiguous and somewhat chaotic. Still, there is hope for the emerging Cuban leadership in the private sector.

Nearly 400,00 Cubans have self-employment licenses, which is quite significant relative to its population size (Miroff, 2012, US-Cuba Relations, 2020). In addition, 3 million acres of state-owned land is now in the hands of private owners, and bars and restaurants are emerging all over Cuban cities (Miroff, 2012, US-Cuba Relations, 2020). While many small business owners perceivably embrace the changes, many companies struggle to create a sustainable business model in order to operate within a free market arena effectively. With rampant unemployment rates, a young generation without a clear vision for the future, and endemic poverty, many new Cuban "capitalists" were quick to jump on "bandwagon" of a free market without truly knowing what to do to create a sustainable business model (Bateman & Glennie, 2016, para. 4). Yet, in this convoluted environment with bipolar tendencies with both communism and capitalism elements, when it comes to its economic system, a new generation of Cuban leaders started thriving.

Research Challenges in Cuba

Doing research to explore the emergence of the new Cuban leadership was quite challenging. The paperwork we had to obtain prior to going to Cuba, in order to obtain our "educational license," was quite complex. As of right now, the U.S. does not allow any leisure and tourist travel to Cuba.

While getting a tourist visa, and doing research seem perfectly acceptable in other parts of the world, that was a much more complex undertaking in Cuba. All our research documents and related paperwork was submitted and approved prior to the true start of the research venture. This was the first of many hurdles to overcome, adding to the complexity of this research.

Additionally, there were a variety of logistical differences, in contrast to many other regions, such as, the inability to use credit cards and having to rely on cash-only transactions throughout the country. Failure to use research laptops, within 48 hours of landing in Havana upon receipt of a menacing desktop message that the laptop user is in a country with trade restrictions with the U.S., complicated matters quite a bit. Facing the reality of researching with no laptop was a bit hard to bear, but being prepared while doing research entails having hard copies of all the research material and not relying on any electronics, or access to print centers. Having a backup plan ensured the ability to overcome the unforeseen obstacle. One should go into an international research venture overprepared vs. unprepared.

Communications and access to our study participants was another obstacle. What in other circumstances could be considered routine matters, such as distributing our questionnaires and conducting interviews with entrepreneurial leaders, had to be carefully coordinated, taking spontaneity out of the entire process. Asking questions about the nature of their business, specifics of their business operations, and the obstacles their business encounters may be perceived as ordinary questions any business owner in the U.S. would not be reluctant to address. Getting on a "soapbox," criticizing the government, or analyzing the current state of the country's economy, is considered one's favorite pastime in many places of this world - not in Cuba. The seemingly mundane administrative questions were quite "adventurous," in the country with a still fully functioning old-style regime. For example, some of the research questions may be perceived as uncomfortable, or in some extreme cases, even dangerous for small business owners, still at the mercy of cumbersome business bureaucracy. Miguel Diaz- Canel administration increased penalties and performance standards for the country's 580,000 entrepreneurs in 2018, while increasing the power of government to inspect and punish the self-employment sector (Kuritzkes, 2018).

Being aware of the implications these questions and answers may have on the business owners, who were kind enough to participate in our study, required us to be ultra-sensitive and empathetic, not only to the content of our questions but to our very approach. We had to be ever cognizant of the implications of our interactions. For us, it was a research project. For our interview subjects, it could impact their livelihoods, and in some cases, their lives. The regular anonymity disclosure was reiterated throughout our interactions with each participant, not as a procedural matter, but as the main point. We kept emphasizing they can refuse to answer some or all our questions. The actual availability of research subjects was yet another challenge. However, the level of contact ensuring that they will be available once we arrive was much more intense than what one may perceive as normal, the reason being we had to go through several safeguard mechanisms ensuring nobody gets in "trouble" for their participation.

Due to similar reasons, the subjects may or may not show up for their scheduled interviews. And if they show up, at any point in time, they may ask us to delete their answers at any later time, up and until the actual publishing of our findings. In those circumstances, both the process and the outcomes of the undertaking existed in a very tenuous state.

Before conducting the Cuban research, contact with all subject establishments needed to take place several times beforehand, which is not always the standard practice. Later, we discovered that the owners of the enterprises had to get approval from what is best described as the Ministry of Commerce within Cuba. Upon arrival in Havana, we had to phone each company multiple times, to confirm the scheduled time, which made us nervous since we had minimal time in the country. Still, they insisted on a follow-up confirmation calls. To protect the anonymity of these establishments, the further sections will explain the nature of the business without the use of too many identifiable markers.

Our research ultimately included interviews with three different businesses in Cuba. One of the establishments was a small pub in the old city of Havana. The second was a youth sports society, specializing in boxing. However, the boxing center also incorporated two additional businesses in its operations, a coffee shop and a souvenir shop, thanks to the creativity of its owner. Three functional businesses were operating under one roof while employing 35–40 workers. The third small business venue we intended to study changed at the last minute.

Two hours prior to our scheduled interview, the owner of the third business cancelled. Upon discussion with our taxi-driver, we discovered that he owned a lucrative tourist business on the side, getting his leads with his "cover job" as a state taxi driver. His company operated a fleet of tour buses that were used for city tours, group tours of the larger island, private tours, and shuttle services. The business was registered under his wife's name, and the fact that he was actively pursuing leads through his taxi state job was both creative and risky.

Findings

Most Cubans are aware they cannot take the path from the central state planning to capitalism overnight. Moreover, the negative perception Western society has of communism is not shared by the emerging Cuban leaders. While they strive towards fewer restrictions and less controlled market, their general goals are not to immediately jump into free-market enterprises, or disparage the government system. Most Cubans don't even know what the free enterprise would look like within their existing system. They appear to be in favor of the pursuit of the best of both worlds-a Cuban version of a free market.

Cuban leaders were interviewed showed creativity, innovation, curiosity and bravery to carve out a new future. They have to work hard to overcome cumbersome bureaucracy in starting and maintaining their businesses, as opening a business and obtaining a business license may take a herculean effort in Cuba. The previously mentioned government taxi driver ended up with a lucrative business catering to a small segment of the tourist sector. Providing options for tourists, creates competition, inspiring many of his colleagues to engage in similar actions. The risk he willingly takes in pursuit of his business leads while utilizing his government taxi appears to be one of the "calculated risk" phenomena we encountered throughout Cuba. Everyone appears to be "pushing the envelope" just a bit further, and the overall atmosphere is not one of fear but one of hope and positive outlook. The flip side of the "risk coin" would be to lose his governmental job, which, if it happens, may not even be a major issue considering the rapid rate of his "side-job" development. The risk-taking encounters were so common that it makes one wonder if the government is turning a "blind eye" knowing it is incapable of taking care of its people otherwise while running the system on the premise of "caretaking" being its main purpose.

The concept of willingness to break the rules of accepted business practices and disobeying the governmental regulation are not necessarily praised within the United States or many other parts of the world. However, without understanding the Cuban business landscape and difficulties one encounters while opening and running any scale business operation, any criticism would be misplaced. Cuban leaders are continuously facing the dilemma of staying in business while rule-breaking while remaining deeply patriotic and supportive of their government. The leftover bureaucracy structure crafted by the hard-core communists is still suffocating the Cuban society as the wheels of change appear unstoppable. Raul Castro started implementing economic reforms that resemble the old-school Russian Gorbachev-style reforms (Mandell, 2014).

Cuban leaders must consistently reinvent themselves, pursue different strategies to get governmental support and adapt to whatever challenge presents itself. Several of the enterprise owners we talked to volunteered to renovate old historic district buildings in order to be able to open their businesses. Doing so expedites their business license, but it is still incredibly unique, considering they have no ownership interest in those buildings. The risk of that investment is that they can be ordered to vacate their establishments with little to no notice if that ends up being in government's interest. However, this approach gets them to the point of opening their business and making money quicker, which outweighs the risk of investing in a building they will not be able to occupy with their business in a long run. This type of creativity in order to thrive in one's business was not an exception, and was observed all over Havana.

The Cuban leaders we interviewed were proud of their country. They also were used to adjusting to the very unique obstacles of their transitioning society. The hesitance to talk or share their problems at times did not appear to be out of fear, but out of a sense of pride in the country's ability to survive and be sustainable, at a very high price to its people. Therefore, approaching Cuban leadership from any standpoint other than the willingness to learn without judgment would deprive one of the whole spectra of their unique experiences (Bateman & Glennie, 2016).

To summarize the results of our research of Cuban leaders, we had three emerging Cuban business leaders, who may not necessarily fall into a strict category of leadership, if compared to their U.S. counterparts. They were not running large companies, but they were signaling the quiet yet unstoppable shift in Cuban society and economy. They were true leaders navigating through quite cumbersome waters of doing private business in a socialist state, employing dozens of employees, and enhancing their country's chances of moving forward. The purpose of our study was to figure out how these leaders thrive in a country that is suppressing any independent businesses for decades, especially how they manage to combat all the obstacles that the Cuban state and external environment, in general, imposes on them.

What we have learned from doing our research into emerging Cuban business leaders, their creativity, perseverance, resilience, curiosity, bravery, and dedication, as they struggle to overcome the bureaucracy and multitude of other system obstacles are nothing short of amazing. They are also daring in their efforts to break the rules and restrictions imposed by their constraining society. Another quality of Cuban leaders is their superb education, which is one thing that Cuban government schools appear to be doing well, creating a generation of new business leaders who are critical thinkers, familiar with many theoretical and practical knowledge concepts needed for running a business. All leaders we encountered had quite impressive marketing, accounting, and market demand knowledge, which came in handy considering hiring many staffers is usually not an option, at least not at first. Cuban emerging leader is not only creative, resilient, and brave; he/she is also incredibly patient and hopeful, sensing the turn of the political tide within their country. Hope is one constant within the Cuban leadership reality. Due to the changes in US-Cuba relations and reversal of some of the educational licensing policies, we ended up having to complete our Cuban research in Mexico as introduced in the next section.

Mexican Leadership Research: Continuation of the Cuban Project

The UFP research grant's original 2019 itinerary involved two Cuban research projects. However, after our first trip, change in federal policies resulted in our educational license being revoked or deemed obsolete, preventing us from the completion of the second part of the Cuban project. If we were to complete our project, it would have to occur a location that was somewhat aligned with the demographic and geopolitical dynamics of Cuba. While there was no other country in the region with the similar complexities of the Cuban communist regime, Mexico shared enough of Cuban core geographic and developing country characteristics, such as unemployment, income, cumbersome bureaucracy, and volatile economy, allowing the completion of our project.

Therefore, through the ingenuity and quick thinking, Mexico became a hastily prepared contingency plan to enable us to preserve our research plan, initially developed for the second portion of the Cuba project. Though the sudden switch in the logistics was nightmarish, both for the researchers, entrepreneurial business owners, leaders, and employees, the rearranged planning and logistical preparation saved the day.

Study Overview

The basic premise of Cuban research was transferred to a context of Mexico. The first research question pertaining to the transfer from a communist to a free market economy was not applicable to Mexico, so we focused on the second question trying to identify 3–5 obstacle variables preventing the Mexican small business sector from moving into a more liberal enterprise model.

In January 2020, we successfully addressed the various obstacles that challenged our original plans and proceeded with our research in Mexico. As we began to embark on our project, despite the proximity and our familiarity with the country, we were quickly reminded that in the final analysis, Mexico's leadership realities are similar to its neighboring Caribbean nations. However, when it comes to the various struggles and challenges of small enterprises that permeate the region, each country has its unique complexities. Furthermore, we discovered numerous similarities in how small business entrepreneurs overcome those challenges.

Intersection of Leadership and Culture

Our research project in Mexico consisted of a study of three small enterprises and the leaders within those enterprises. As prior mentioned, Mexican research was not stand-alone research but a continuation of our Cuba research. The research questions and basic hypotheses were not changed in comparison to our Cuban research. While vastly different, there are some core similarities between the two regions. Mexico was definitely not selected at random. Citizens from each country have a strong family connection, love for music, dancing, and social interactions at the community level, with interestingly enough teaching styles quite similar (Brown, 2015). Moreover, each country has a very strong patriotic spirit and high literacy rate, but sadly scores high on the corruption index and unemployment rate (Government Stats- Compare Key Data on Cuba and Mexico, 2020).

We just made geographic and selection of enterprise adjustments. In the spirit of comparison, they were practitioners of the same challenges of their Cuban, Zambian, and Haitian counterparts, and the same levels of creativity and ingenuity in their responses to those challenges.

Research Challenges in Mexico

Our research project in Mexico, in one respect, could, in many ways, had all the characteristics that resembled a project that occurred in the heartland of the United States, taking place in Kansas, New York, or Arizona. Its proximity to the U.S., its familiarity with U.S. customs and practices, and its relative ease of access to the country's research subjects and its facilities. From another perspective, however, our team was reminded early and often that our research project in Mexico demonstrated all of the earmarks of other international projects, no different from those in Cuba, Haiti, Zambia, or any other global endeavor. Some logistical issues were due to miscommunication with the studied enterprises, causing us to extend our stay. Infrastructure was not a concern, but getting to some more remote locations was a bit of a challenge due to our unfamiliarity with the area. The timing and circumstances of the Mexican research project were also somewhat unorthodox.

The research plan in Mexico included three business operations in the Yucatan peninsula, including two private hotels in Riviera Maya and a small fishing enterprise in Tulum. The overall research plan was to study the enterprises similar in size, number of employees, and level of operational effectiveness, similar to those in Cuba. Mexico, which revealed a variety of fascinating practices and strategies that we had previously discovered in Cuba during our earlier projects.

In the case of the fishing enterprise, licensing and related government requirements were perceived as cumbersome. The owner of this particular fishing enterprise had a limited license, just for the fishing operation and selling its fish. But, as is typical of entrepreneurship, especially in developing world economies such as the Caribbean, the business continues to expand on the focus of its enterprise. In this case, the owner transformed his fishing operation into a restaurant, eventually selling food and alcohol on the premises that had begun to yield a comparable lucrative side business. Those side businesses, however, were not licensed, and subject to incurring fines. To summarize, the restaurant operation, including alcohol sale and night entertainment, thrived while not being properly registered. We encountered some remarkably similar circumstances in our study of Cuban establishments, in which the proprietor is running a bundle of three enterprises in one without a full-blown or license to cover all the various business operations. That pursuit of minimal or limited licenses for a multitude of businesses was a prevailing characteristic throughout the region.

Various forms of bribery, which, in turn, promulgate a blind eye to corruption, are also acceptable business practices in Mexico, as they are throughout the region. Even in the areas where there is a will to stop these practices, Mexican authorities have quite limited resources to make a true difference. The enforcement authorities are not only challenged by the bureaucracy of their enforcement duties, but they also impede the entry of foreign businesses into the country. Those businesses not familiar with the nuances of local business practices in the country, by definition, must seek the assistance of others to navigate the local traditions.

Additionally, tourists are continuously required to pay "fake fines" based on the demands of the local officials. If you can afford the expenses of foreign travel, the locals assume then you must have money to pay for fines. These questionable practices are not only considered to be acceptable, but rampant and expensive, and deter tourism or foreign travel. For example, business owners feel pressured to take care of local officials to avoid any trouble. Standing on their own moral ground is lonely and dangerous in some parts of the world. For example, entrepreneurs pay "tax" on local goods being transported from the beach to stores to avoid being fined each day by random police officers. What one may observe as an extraordinary practice in the United States is considered an acceptable cost of doing business in Mexico. Consequently, when conducting an international research, one must be prepared for unexpected or hidden expenses imposed upon foreign travelers, be it traveling in Mexico, Haiti, Cuba, Zambia, and those must be calculated in the overall budget for the research endeavor.

Findings

The leaders in Mexico were remarkably similar to those in Cuba, in Haiti, and in Zambia, demonstrating traits of perseverance, courage, innovation, and persistence. These qualities are not optional but are business sustainability and existence-driven. Each leader we studied encountered incredible challenges, ups and downs, and was multiple times on the verge of giving up, but persevered and succeeded. And remember, survival is a potent motivator.

From the perspective of an educated outsider, these unorthodox practices are typically interpreted to be arcane, primitive, and illegal. Upon closer analysis, however, they are deemed practical, acceptable, and even necessary for survival. The paradoxical bi-product of this vicious cycle of survival is a continuous creation of entrepreneurial leaders that are viewed to be the most creative, innovative, and ingenious in comparison to their counterparts who operate within functional economies. They are the personification of the expression, "necessity is the mother of invention." For most of us, our economic well-being is a matter of an improved lifestyle. For these entrepreneurs, however, it is a matter of survival.

Conclusion

Zambia, Cuba, Haiti, Mexico, with many other regions of the developing world, are undergoing transformation, with each having its own unique layers of difficulties impacted by different socio-cultural, economic and political realities. If we start off the basic premise, the Cuban economy may be perceived as semi-functional, albeit in a transitional turmoil from a pure communist to its own version of a free enterprise. Cuban failed state created the highest possible use of its natural resources for the longest possible time (ever since the embargo was imposed). Haitian reliance on foreign aid hinders its ability to develop its own resources to the best possible use, whereas Zambian over-reliance on its copper prevents the entire country from venturing into some other industrial sectors that would produce more of a return on investment. Out of the four countries presented in this chapter, only Mexico, while riddled with its own issues of corruption and criminal activity, is close to the concept of healthy consumer demand, sustainable business models (in specific sectors), and functional economy (again in certain areas).

Unlike Cuba, freedom of movement, communication, and engagement with the business owners was not an issue in Haiti, Zambia, and Mexico. However, some logistical issues with conducting research were still shared by each region. Transportation in Zambia and Haiti was quite a challenge due to damaged infrastructure and poor road conditions. In cases of Zambia, Cuba, and Haiti, the bulk of data collection had to take place manually, and literature review involved siting in libraries and pulling articles off the shelves versus an online search.

One of the most immediate commonalities of Mexico with Zambia, Cuba, and Haiti, was that most of their circumstances and practices are fundamentally survival -driven due to their sparse economies. In each of the countries we studied, their governments are heavily reliant on foreign aid and taxation imposed on its residents, and their enterprises. As a result, those enterprises are squeezed by the demands of their governments, and their survival is reliant upon their entrepreneurial leaders to engage in a variety of ingenuity and questionable business practices which include avoiding or minimizing those governmental demands while imposing inflated prices upon its customers to maximize its revenues. Those customers, in turn, will resort to any number of questionable, if not illegal practices to avoid the inflated prices. That cycle impacts the entire population, which escalates to a seemingly continuous reliance on foreign aid in some cases historical and some geopolitical ones.

Despite all of these obstacles, the new emerging leadership fully motivated to overcome any challenges is present in each of the studied countries. They focus on quality, innovation, technological achievements, curiosity, creativity, and persistence with little support within their communities and by the government. The studied motivational and personality characteristics influenced these emerging leaders to start up new businesses, persevere under the multitude of "obstacle" variables, and create a sustainable business model creating the multitude of highly functional leadership realities.

Reflecting on the overall experience across research studies in these diverse nations, I found that while the foundational principles of research remain similar, the preparatory work and conditions for research can vary greatly. The situation on the ground can heavily influence logistics, and the resulting challenges and opportunities will differ, as a result. This requires familiarity with culture, geography, history, economy, and politics within the target research area. In the context of business leadership, the researcher must understand acceptable business practices for the local environment. Beyond knowledge of the practices themselves, it is important to analyze how the environment has influenced those practices and ultimately why the practices operate as they do. This requires suspension of bias, to explore them in the context in which they exist. Lastly, the analysis of leadership effectiveness must also be made in terms of the cultural context.

Researchers venturing into international study ventures within the developing world, during periods of transformation, must be cognizant, diligent, and patient to employ practices that honor and value the cultural practices, while, at the same time, retain the highest standards and integrity of the research that circumstances allow. To conduct research in an international environment can be rewarding and exciting. While accommodating local customs, policies, and practices, one still should retain the integrity and rigor of the methodology of the discipline.

The landscape of global leadership is changing due to emerging markets, changing demographics, disruptive technology integration, innovation, and creativity of a new generation of entrepreneurs. Leadership realities in the developing world are nothing short of inspiring. We encountered resilience, persistence, stubbornness, bravery, motivation, and a fighting spirit. Overcoming all odds, these business leaders are passing the survival point, and their businesses are thriving. We hope this chapter enables the reader to take a much more expansive approach to assess leadership, developing a mindset that each country's leaders may have some similarities when it comes to traits that make them successful, but also some vast differences enabling them to operate in quite difficult settings.

The author of this chapter owes immeasurable gratitude to her fellow co-researcher Clifford D. Williams, whose business acumen, knowledge of languages, and familiarity of business practices made Haitian, Cuban, and Mexican research possible.

References

African Development Bank Group. (2017). *Annual report 2017*. https://www.afdb.org/fileadmin/uploads/afdb/Documents/Generic-Documents/AfDB_Annual_Report_2017_EN.pdf.

Augustin, E., & Robles, F. (2020). Cuba's economy was hurting. *The pandemic brought a food crisis. NY Times*. Retrieved from https://www.nytimes.com/2020/09/20/world/americas/cuba-economy.html.

Bateman, M., & Glennie, J. (2016). *Cuba must shun capitalism and seek development solutions from within*. https://www.theguardian.com/global-development/2016/nov/11/cuba-shun-capitalism-seek-development-solutions-within.

Beugelsdijk, S., & Welzel, C. (2018). Dimensions and dynamics of national culture: Synthesizing Hofstede with Inglehart. *Journal of Cross-Cultural Psychology*, *49*(10), 1469–1505.

Borenstein, S. (2019, January 12). *Why Haiti keeps getting hammered by disasters*. https://www.cleveland.com/world/2010/01/why_haiti_keeps_getting_hammer.html.

Brown, C. (2015). *Cuba and Mexico – a cultural comparison (CultureGrams World Edition)*. ProQuest.

Buss, T. F., & Gardner, A. (2005). Why foreign aid to Haiti failed and – how to do it better next time. *Foreign aid and foreign policy: Lessons for the next half-century*. 173.

Collins, David. (2008). Has Tom Peters lost the plot? A timely review of a celebrated management guru. *Journal of Organizational Change Management*, *21*. doi:10.1108/09534810810874804.

Daugherty, R., Zelihic, M., Deresa, C., Nga'mbi, H. C., & Ssekamatte, D. (2021). Empowering global leaders through workplace sustainability: A case of Zambian leaders. *The Journal for Transdisciplinary Research in Southern Africa*, *17*(1), 10.

Deming, W. E. (2000). *The new economics for industry, government, education* (2nd ed.). MIT Press. ISBN 0-262-54116-5. OCLC 44162616.

DesRoches, R., Comerio, M., Eberhard, M., Mooney, W., & Rix, G. J. (2011). Overview of the 2010 Haiti earthquake. *Earthquake Spectra*, *27*(1_suppl1), 1–21.

Feffer, J. (2016). *Cuba and capitalism*. https://www.huffingtonpost.com/entry/cuba-and-capitalism_us_56f52bf0e4b0ea8862ebf27f.

Gadzala, A. W. (2010). From formal-to informal-sector employment: Examining the Chinese presence in Zambia. *Review of African Political Economy*, *37*(123), 41–59.

Gavin, J., & Westwood, R. (2009). *International and cross-cultural management studies: A postcolonial reading*. Palgrave Macmillan.

Gordon, A., Plumblee, J., Higdon, G., Davis, I., & Vaughn, D. (2017). *Engineering aquaculture in rural Haiti: A case study*. Retrieved from EBSCOhost database.

Government Stats: Compare key data on Cuba & Mexico. (2020). Retrieved from https://www.nationmaster.com/country-info/compare/Cuba/Mexico/Government

Haiti Infrastructure, Power, and Communication. (2017). http://www.nationsencyclopedia.com/economies/Americas/Haiti-INFRASTRUCTURE-POWER-AND-COMMUNICATIONS.html#ixzz4xK9yt4vs.

Hillier, F. S., & Lieberman, G. J. (1995). *Introduction to operations research*. McGraw-Hill Publishing Company.

Hilger, S. (2008). 'Globalisation by Americanisation': American companies and the internationalisation of German industry after the Second World War, European Review of History: Revue européenne d'histoire, *15*, 4, 375–401, doi:10.1080/13507480802228531.

House, R., Javidan, M., Hanges, P., & Dorfman, P. (2002). Understanding cultures and implicit leadership theories across the globe: An introduction to project GLOBE. *Journal of world business, 37*(1), 3–10.

Jorge, A. (2003). *Privatization, reconstruction, and socio-economic development in post-Castro Cuba.* Institute for Cuban and Cuban-American Studies. University of Miami.

Kamwanga, J., & Koyi, G. (2009). *Impact of China-Africa investment relations: The case of Zambia.* African Economic Research Consortium.

Klitgaard, R. (2010). *Addressing corruption in Haiti.* American Enterprise Institute.

Koontz, H., & O'Donnell, C. (1972). *Principles of management: An analysis of managerial functions.* (2nd ed.). McGraw-Hill.

Kuritzkes, C. (2018). The End of Cuba's entrepreneurship boom. *Foreign Policy.* https://foreignpolicy.com/2019/07/15/the-end-of-cubas-entrepreneurship-boom/.

Mandell, L. (2014). *Capitalism in Cuba? It's closer than the U.S. may think.* https://www.pbs.org/newshour/nation/capitalism-in-cuba-its-closer-than-the-u-s-may-think.

Margolis, D. N. (2014). By choice and by necessity: Entrepreneurship and self-employment in the developing world. *The European Journal of Development Research, 26*(4), 419–436.

Mesidor, C. (2014). *The Haitian connection: How one entrepreneur is helping to redevelop the island nation.* (International Business) Earl G. Graves Publishing Co., Inc. Retrieved from EBSCOhost database.

Miroff, N. (2012). *Cuba is reforming, but wealth and success are still frowned upon.* https://www.businessinsider.com/cubas-economic-transition-2012-9.

Negi, R. (2008). Beyond the "Chinese scramble": The political economy of anti-China sentiment in Zambia. *African Geographical Review, 27*(1), 41–63.

Olalere, A. (2015). Complexity and leadership crisis in Africa. *International Journal of Public Leadership, 11*(3/4), 180–191.

Owens, B. (2018). The benefits and challenges of international research collaboration. *University Affairs.* https://www.universityaffairs.ca/features/feature-article/the-benefits-and-challenges-of-international-research-collaboration/.

Ozuomba, C. V. (2013). Impact of insurance on economic growth in Nigeria. *International Journal of Business and Management Invention, 2,* 19–31.

Park, M. (2016, October 11). Disaster divided: Two countries, one island, life and death differences. *CNN.com.* https://www.cnn.com/2016/10/11/americas/haiti-dominican-republic-visual-

Peart, J., & Knowles, L. (2018). Applying the stakeholder model to social entrepreneurship a practitioner approach. *Journal of multidisciplinary research, 10*(1-2). 85–95.

Porter, M. E. (1996, November-December). What is strategy? *Harvard Business Review, 74*(6), 65–67.

Scheinberg, S., & MacMillan, I. C. (1988). *An 11 country study of motivations to start a business.* Babson College.

Stahel, Walter. (2005). The functional economy: Cultural and organizational change. In *The industrial green game: Implications for environmental design and management.* The National Academies Press.

Thorpe, D. (2017). How this social entrepreneur is moving Haiti away from aid toward trade. *Forbes Magazine.* https://www.forbes.com/sites/devinthorpe/2017/01/18/how-this-social-entrepreneur-is-moving-haiti-away-from-aid-toward-trade/#405963c66526.

US-Cuba Relations. (2020). *Council on foreign relations.* https://www.cfr.org/backgrounder/us-cuba-relations.

Van Bracht, G. (2012). A survey of Zambian views on Chinese people and their involvement in Zambia. *African East-Asian Affairs, 1.* doi:10.7552/0-1-57.

Wanasika, I., Howell, J. P., Littrell, R., & Dorfman, P. (2011). Managerial leadership and culture in Sub-Saharan Africa. *Journal of World Business, 46*(2), 234–241.

Whitney, W. T. (2019). Protests in Haiti show signs of eventually producing change. *Guardian* (Sydney), 1893, 12.

Wie. (2009). *The fall of berlin wall in the eyes of china: From the "dramatic changes in east europe" to the "unification of the two germany".* https://www.kas.de/c/document_library/get_file?uuid=65a2687b-c011-babf-062c-9f3658742559&groupId=252038.

Winston, B. E., & Patterson, K. (2006). An integrative definition of leadership. *International Journal of Leadership Studies, 1*(2), 6–66.

World Bank Report. (2014). https://openknowledge.worldbank.org/bitstream/handle/10986/20697/WPS7134.pdf?sequence=1&isAllowed=y.

World Bank. (2020). *The World Bank in Africa.* https://www.worldbank.org/en/region/afr/overview.

World Bank. (2020). *The World Bank in Haiti.* https://www.worldbank.org/en/country/haiti/overview.

World Bank. (2018). *The World Bank in Zambia.* https://www.worldbank.org/en/country/zambia/overview.

Part III

Insights, Gaps and Future Directions

Jennie L. Walker

Part I set the foundation for exploring international leadership research, while Part II delved into the research process itself. Now in Part III, we turn to consideration of how we prepare future researchers, how we disseminate new knowledge gleaned from research, and, ultimately, how we maintain integrity of research practices in the field. Part III is structured into three parts: A. Teaching and Learning International Leadership Research; B. Publishing and Applications; and C. Concluding Thoughts: Zooming in on International Leadership Research Standards.

To conduct international research with integrity means to think through cross-cultural context, apply multiple perspectives and relevant research methodology to capture local context in a truthful and unbiased way. Most researchers plan and conduct research with integrity, however, as Martinson, Anderson, and de Vries (2005) reported, as many as one in every 100 U.S. researchers deliberately engage in some form of research misbehavior. Although researchers likely have good intentions, they may be unaware of the unique demands of international scholarship. "To cross cultural borders in research is a slippery and complicated endeavor, and good intentions, though essential, are not enough to help researchers make those crossings with respect for those they research and with their own integrity intact" (Miller Cleary, 2013, p. 1). This makes teaching and learning about international leadership research practices of fundamental importance to the field.

The first section begins with a deep dive into Teaching and Learning International Leadership Research through two chapters that build on one another. In Chapter 24, Tolstikov-Mast, Walker, Lemonte and Rosser-Mims begin with a discussion of internationalization of doctoral research education, including experiential learning and internships in other cultures.

They argue that curricula need to be more intentional in translating a commitment to internationalization into a comprehensive and practical strategy. The chapter advocates to review research education for curriculum internalization, and offers two examples of these efforts in practice. "Different cultures (culture itself, language, formal presentation, rules) can influence researchers' ways of understanding problems, methods, results and activities in the research process" (Welzer et al., 2017). This makes the integration of international and cross-cultural perspectives and distinctions in research approaches vital to scholars operating in diverse social contexts.

Walker and Tolstikov-Mast are then joined by Williams in Chapter 25 to look at ways to further enhance international research training. This chapter extends the discussion from the previous chapter by examining the perspectives and experiences of students themselves, the role of faculty in enhancing students' self-efficacy in this area, as well as additional ways that institutional support for international research can be put into place. While students may take research courses throughout their degree programs, they may not perform novel, hands-on research until the thesis or dissertation stages at the end of their programs. The authors discuss how integrating more and earlier research experience may better prepare students for their future career goals, but also may be critical in enhancing their self-efficacy with research practices while they are students. This is not only because of the practice of doing research, but also due to the faculty mentoring and support that take place during these activities. Faculty mentoring and support are critical to promoting socialization, scholarship, research, and career development, especially for students from underrepresented and historically marginalized groups (Felder, 2010).

Later in Chapter 27, Doctoral Leadership Programs: Preparing Stewards of the Leadership Discipline, Malakyan also critically examines how well doctoral programs are preparing future researchers. The chapter presents findings from a research study assessing 50 doctoral programs in leadership worldwide to understand the program purpose and goals, curriculum structure and program quality to determine whether they are designed to prepare stewards of the leadership discipline. Malakyan shares critical insights about the opportunities to better align program goals and curriculum in practice. His insights are echoed by other international researchers in the field. "Critically, while institutional barriers may be slow to dismantle, as individual scholars…we must recognize and take immediate opportunities to facilitate academic capacity-building and promote equitable collaboration" (Urassa et al., 2021).

Cross-cultural interactions are a hallmark of international leadership research, making cultural sensitivity of critical importance. However, the research context challenges those involved to consider not just how they personally interact with people from other cultures but how to navigate and interpret culture in the research itself. This requires reflexivity. "When we become cross-cultural researchers, we confront the importance of understanding ourselves, our cultural roots, how we live those routes or challenge them, where we are going, and what influences us along the way" (Miller Cleary, 2013, p. 7). This is an exercise in examining our motives and position of privilege in the research process. In Chapter 26, Race, Whiteness, Intersectionality, and Teaching International Leadership Research, Surbhi Malik, Dakin Kirby and Singletary Walker challenge us to do just that – examine our motives and privilege in research, especially with respect to race and intersectionality. This chapter is a compelling conversation between three scholars from different disciplines and racial backgrounds examining how the question of systemic racism in the United States is related to teaching international leadership research. The authors consider the role of their own positionality in teaching research methods and designs, and they offer resources for further exploration. Banfill builds on these personal reflections on culture in his experience in Africa as a doctoral student researcher. Chapter 28, Discovering the Behaviors of Effective Leaders in Africa: A Doctoral Student's Journey into International Leadership Research, explores lessons learned while working across cultures and in collaboration with a research team. He details how multiple pilot studies helped him shape and narrow his research focus.

Banfill and many other authors throughout this handbook point to the importance of research partners in other cultures, whether they be gatekeepers, stakeholders, translators or native experts on the topic or culture itself. Research collaborations are an underexplored and under-taught area of research preparation. "…opportunities for doctoral students and junior scholars to learn how to initiate and participate productively in an RPP [Research Practice Partnership] are limited, even though there is an increasing demand from junior scholars for such opportunities" (Henrick, Cobb, Penuel, Jackson, & Clark, 2017, p. 16). Henrick et al. (2017) go on to say that practitioners and experienced scholars alike have had few opportunities to "develop a sense of what a genuine partnership with researchers might look like" (p. 16). As several authors within this handbook discuss, research partners were instrumental for cross-cultural research. They also required investment of time and skill in building relationships and coordinating research activities. However, our conversations with authors revealed that few had any formal training or mentoring in how to develop research partnerships and maintain them, making this a consideration for research training. A focus on positive and productive cross-cultural teaming is needed to balance what has been deemed an over-emphasis on conflict within cross-cultural teams in leadership research.

> There is ample evidence to show that the international business and cross-cultural management literature has over-emphasized the difficulties, obstacles and conflicts caused by cultural differences rather than the positive dynamics and outcomes that stem from such differences. For example, researchers have expended less effort on developing new theoretical perspectives highlighting the positive characteristics of multicultural teams than explaining the liabilities associated with team diversity (Stahl, Miska, Lee & De Luque, 2017).

Cross-cultural and multicultural research teams are advantageous to add multiple perspectives to research design, analysis and interpretation (Youssef and Youssef, 2016).

The last chapter in section one deals with a less explored but very impactful area within international leadership research: International Research in Crisis Situations and Unprecedented Times of Uncertainty. In Chapter 29, Sadek examines the unique elements of conducting research in war zones and with displaced communities. Her insights underscore the importance of understanding the unique contexts of the research and the participants themselves. She argues that there is a significant lack of research conducted within these communities, particularly among refugee populations and with respect to leadership. There is a growing call for inclusion in international research for marginalized populations, such as immigrants, indigenous peoples, underrepresented ethnic groups, disabled peoples, and disadvantaged populations (Romm, 2018; Williams, 2015; Miller Cleary, 2013). Inclusion is defined not just through the sample for research but also in the broader study design and transformative research process that emphasizes caring and respect for the communities involved (Romm, 2018; Williams, 2015). Miller Cleary (2013) calls for international researchers to reframe research from a "do no harm" imperative to center on an "ethic of care and respect" (p. 11). Ultimately, these researchers and Sadek argue for a "transformative" approach (Romm, 2018), requiring a paradigm shift from simply taking knowledge from people to a humanitarian commitment focused on the well-being of those researched.

The second section in Part 3 looks at publishing of international leadership research and its various applications. In Chapter 30, International Publishing: Challenges and Considerations, Collins and Wipperman discuss the publishing process and challenges of international publishing in particular. The changing world of scholarly communication has brought about many controversial and hotly debated topics (Tennant et al., 2019), and publishing internationally can further add to the complexities. Collins and Whipperman present considerations for international copyright, as well as publishing contracts, publishing best practices, and considerations for finding and evaluating relevant publishing outlets. This chapter is unique, as graduate research programs often require students to become familiar with copyright and plagiarism guidelines, but do not necessarily delve into the finer details of the international publishing world.

Several of the authors in this section are concerned with the ever-changing global environment and how those changes necessarily impact scholarship and practice. As Uhl-Bien, Marion and McKelvey (2007) aptly pointed out, "Leadership models of the last century have been products of top-down, bureaucratic paradigms ... Complexity science suggests a different paradigm for leadership – one that frames leadership as a complex interactive dynamic..." (p. 298). Arkadiusz, Muriungi and Scardino focus on this complex interactive dynamic in leadership scholarship in Chapter 31, while Avdul looks more squarely at the dynamic practice of leadership needed in global organizations in Chapter 32. In Chapter 31, The Future Agenda for International Leadership Research and Practice, the authors say that leadership theories and models available thus far, while helpful in understanding leadership development, are frequently inadequate for a full understanding of the changing nature of leadership in the 21st century. They review existing literature and then propose a future agenda for research from the lens of servant leadership; virtual team leadership; and leadership in global crises. In Chapter 32, Benefits of Conducting International Leadership Research in an Ever-Changing Global Environment, Avdul begins with a discussion of the importance of international leadership research for global organizations. He then discusses the types of leaders that are needed to operate effectively in modern global environments. These typologies are meant to inform future international leadership research agendas.

Wickramasinghe rounds out the discussion of publishing and applications with the Personal and Professional Benefits of ILR in Chapter 33. She discusses how conducting international leadership research has impacted her life, translating into life lessons, lifelong relationships, scholarly growth and career advancements. By sharing her personal stories, she illustrates how international leadership research has ripple effects well beyond the scholarly and professional realms to enhance cross-cultural understanding and enrich one's worldview.

The final two chapters in the book discuss concluding thoughts on best practices, standards and frameworks that can contribute to the success of international leadership research. Chapter 34, Making Research a Success, is a conversation among eight experienced international researchers about the meaning of success in international leadership research. They discuss best practices, challenges, and rewards. The conversation is dynamic, as it illustrates diverse perspectives among these interdisciplinary researchers, while underscoring their mutual enthusiasm for the work. Throughout the handbook, various scholars have shared their lessons learned, many through trial and error. The final chapter in the book, Chapter 35, Lessons Learned: Doing Research with Integrity, offers a framework to guide the international leadership research process and a series of compelling questions for each stage of the research process, with the aim of helping scholars better prepare for and engage in responsible international leadership research. While it is unlikely that one model, or one book for that matter, could capture a very rich and complex field in totality, we do hope that this handbook will create an ongoing forum for communication, refinement of practices, and a community of support among international leadership researchers.

References

Felder, P. (2010). On doctoral student development: Exploring faculty mentoring in the shaping of African American doctoral student success. *Qualitative Report, 15*(2), 455–474.

Henrick, E. C., Cobb, P., Penuel, W. R., Jackson, K., & Clark, T. (2017). *Assessing research-practice partnerships: Five dimensions of effectiveness.* William T. Grant Foundation.

Martinson, B. C., Anderson, M. S., & De Vries, R. (2005). Scientists behaving badly. *Nature, 435*(7043), 737–738.

Miller Cleary, L. (2013). *Cross-cultural research with integrity: Collected wisdom from researchers in social settings.* Palgrave Macmillan.

Romm, N. R. A. (2018). *Responsible research practice.* Springer International Publishing.

Stahl, G. K., Miska, C., Lee, H. J., & De Luque, M. S. (2017). The upside of cultural differences. *Cross Cultural & Strategic Management.* doi:10.1108/CCSM-11-2016-0191

Urassa, M., Lawson, D. W., Wamoyi, J., Gurmu, E., Gibson, M. A., Madhivanan, P., & Placek, C. (2021). Cross-cultural research must prioritize equitable collaboration. *Nature Human Behaviour, 5*(6), 668–671.

Tennant, J. P., Crane, H., Crick, T., Davila, J., Enkhbayar, A., Havemann, J., Kramer, B., Martin, R., Masuzzo, P., Nobes, A., Rice, C., Rivera-Lopez, B., Ross-Hellauer, T., Sattler, S., Thacker, P. D., & Vanholsbeeck, M. (2019). Ten hot topics around scholarly publishing. *Publications, 7*(2), 34.

Uhl-Bien, M., Marion, R., & McKelvey, B. (2007). Complexity leadership theory: Shifting leadership from the industrial age to the knowledge era. *The Leadership Quarterly, 18*(4), 298–318.

Welzer, T., Družovec, M., Überwimmer, M., Gaisch, M., Füreder, R., & Costa, Y. (2017, May). Cultural awareness in research and teaching. In *Proceedings cross-cultural business conference 2017* (pp. 289–296). Shaker Verlag.

Williams, C. (2015). *Doing international research: Global and local methods.* SAGE.

Youssef, E. M., & Youssef, M. A. (2016). A critical investigation into cross-cultural research methodology: Some insights and literature review. *International Journal of Business Excellence, 9*(4), 441–462.

Part IIIA
Teaching and Learning International Leadership Research

24

Internationalization of Doctoral Research Education

Experiential Learning in Global Practicum and Research Internships

Yulia Tolstikov-Mast, Jennie L. Walker, Pamela A. Lemoine, and Dionne Rosser-Mims

Introduction

Internalization is the intentional process of integrating diverse global dimensions into the mission, administration and curriculum of an institution to allow teaching, research, and service to embrace a multidimensional and multi-value reality, and to make a meaningful contribution to a global society (de Wit, 2020; de Wit, et al., 2015; Knight, 2008). Ideas of higher education internalization are not new (e.g., Cavusgil, 1998). As a response to increased multiculturalism and globalization influences, higher education institutions have been designing internalization strategies and investing in global competencies of their students for several decades (de Wit, et al., 2015; de Wit, et al., 2017; Guri-Rosenblit, 2015; Mestenhauser & Ellingboe, 1998; Tight, 2019). At the same time, more work is needed to make curricula more intentionally international. de Wit (2020) states that additional efforts are needed to integrate global dimensions into the purpose, functions and delivery of higher education to "enhance the quality of education and research for all students and staff to make a meaningful contribution to society" (p. 9). Thus, the question for many institutions is "how to translate what seems to be a strong commitment to internationalization into a comprehensive and practical strategy" (Qiang, 2003, p. 260).

One of the least apparent internalization discussions is about research curriculum (Antelo, 2012; Kwiek, 2018; Woldegiyorgis et al., 2018). Research education is an integral part of every academic discipline; and research courses are offered in every department and with every degree. At the same time, not only that there is no commonly accepted definition of research internalization, most universities associate international research strategies with research production. For a measurable output (important for institutional or program accreditations), universities focus on faculty research, publications, and international partnerships; as well as a number of international doctoral students and a faculty international mobility (e.g., short-term periods of international collaborations, a visiting professor assignment) (Kyvik & Larsen, 1997; Rostan, Ceravolo, & Metcalfe, 2014; Woldegiyorgis et al., 2018).

Nevertheless, evidence demonstrates that international research has national variations in meanings and approaches, and requires specialized education (Kyvik & Larsen, 1997; Rostan, Ceravolo, Metcalfe, 2014; Woldegiyorgis et al., 2018). With increased global research interdependence, future

DOI: 10.4324/9781003003380-24

researchers need to learn simultaneously to engage in research of their home disciplines, multi-disciplinary and multinational research, and work in international research collaborations (Kwiek, 2018; Rostan et al., 2014; Trowler, 2012). For some disciplines, an international research curriculum could be a course or assignments throughout a program due to a lesser influence of an international environment on a study process and outcomes (e.g., hard sciences). Other disciplines (e.g., social sciences; health sciences, public policy) would benefit from a more robust and extensive international research curriculum (Rostan et al., 2014).

The focus of this chapter is on internalization of doctoral leadership research education. Authors' discussions and examples point out the importance of experiential learning approaches to prepare leadership scholars for research in diverse international leadership environments. Numerous international leadership studies (Nahavandi & Krishnan, 2018; Peterson & Hunt, 1997; Reiche et al., 2019) conclude that the meaning of leadership is tightly connected to a local context. Additionally, experience in diverse leadership practices is one of the main expectations for global leadership development and in succession planning (Lane, et al., 2017; Mendenhall et al., 2017). Therefore, doctoral programs that cultivate leadership scholars with international research interests should offer "on the ground" research training immersed in local leadership realities.

Need to Internationalize Doctoral Research Curriculum

Two arguments ground our support for a targeted international leadership research education: (1) research curriculum influences doctoral students' choices of perspectives and methodologies in their own research, and (2) rising numbers of international leadership dissertations call for special research education to ensure quality and rigor of these dissertation studies. While some doctoral programs claim internationalization, "the lack of clear definition as to what this means leaves this assertion without full substantiation" (Cavusgil, 1998, p. 82).

Influence of Curriculum on Research Agenda

Studies of doctoral research curriculum across subjects and countries revealed that doctoral students find research courses valuable for their scholarly development (e.g., Coronel Llamas & Boza, 2011; Pieridou, & Kambouri-Danos, 2020). The research curriculum helps doctoral students develop their identity as researchers and instill standards of planning and conducting research in specific settings (Pieridou & Kambouri-Danos, 2020). Moreover, exposure to diverse research methodology (methodological pluralism), multi-paradigmatic and multidisciplinary discussions lead students to adopting and applying the same approaches in their own research (Coronel Llamas & Boza, 2011; Kemp & Nurius, 2015; Vandermause, Barbosa-Leiker, & Fritz, 2014).

Kemp and Nurius (2015) explain that to cultivate researchers (learn, retain, reproduce research knowledge), it's essential to have a specific developmental effort to ensure mastery of research knowledge and skills. The plan is initiated in doctoral students' first year classes, moves to a navigation (application) stage during candidacy and dissertation, and continues in the maturation at the post-Ph.D. (early career) stage. The same long-term approach should be taken when teaching any type of research (Kemp & Nurius, 2015; Lyall & Meagher, 2012). Mastering multidisciplinary and multi-paradigm frameworks or unique methodologies requires curriculum rather than a brief training (one assignment, several readings, one course). Faculty need time and space to teach how to "both navigate and integrate diverse methodological and theoretical frameworks, and sophisticated communication and collaborative skills" (Kemp & Nurius, 2015, p. 135). Finally, doctoral students should have access to diverse intellectual ideas, alternative paradigms of knowledge production, and new experience (Jiang & Shen, 2019; Mu et al., 2018; Rizvi, 2010; Ryan, 2012) to help them move beyond "monocultural chauvinism" (Morris & Hudson, 1995, p. 73) to "a new international academic ethos" (p. 74).

Rise in International Leadership Dissertations

The second reason for the internalization of leadership research curriculum is an exponential increase in the number of dissertations on leadership topics across cultures and societal borders. According to ProQuest Dissertations and Thesis Global database (accessed on November 9, 2020), 63,831 dissertations have been produced on international, intercultural, cross-cultural and global leadership topics between 1980 and 2019 (Table 24.1). Data demonstrates a steep increase in the number of dissertations over the period of 39 years, with a 2, 3, or even 4 times increase in the past 20 years.

Table 24.1 Increase in International, Intercultural, Cross-cultural, and Global Leadership Studies: ProQuest Dissertations and Theses Global Database (accessed on Nov 9, 2020)

Subject	Number of Dissertations1980–2019				
	1980–1989	*1990–1999*	*2000–2009*	*2010–2019*	Total
International leadership research	3085	5430	11717	35211	58,146
Intercultural leadership research	10	23	62	270	388
Cross-cultural leadership research	20	53	152	262	502
Global leadership research	52	193	1487	2920	4,795
					63,831

A growing interest of emerging leadership researchers to engage in studies in culturally diverse contexts requires a diverse research curriculum to learn multiple ways to view and capture reality (Antelo, 2012; Rostan et al., 2014; Ryan, 2012; Trowler, 2012; Woldegiyorgis et al., 2018). If taught only traditional frameworks and methodologies in courses, doctoral candidates in dissertations might experience challenges in recognizing diverse paradigms and be faced with the obstacle of unlearning research behavior after it's formed (Miller Cleary, 2013; Miyazaki & Taylor, 2008; Pannucci & Wilkins, 2010). Development of a thinking process is complex and "takes into account the cognitive, affective, and behavioral domains of learning" (Cavusgil, 1998, p. 84). Thus, research internalization should not be limited to simply requiring an international study sample and conducting research in a different society, but reorienting research thinking on recognizing and incorporating local frameworks and research design as well as questioning foundational approaches for their universality (Cavusgil, 1998; Yao & Vital, 2016).

Overall, developing any kind of research readiness takes time and effort; and doctoral leadership programs with international research focus should consider a long developmental approach, including practice-driven curriculum strategies, rather than letting students experience international research only in their dissertations. The chapter offers two strategies for doctoral leadership research internalization, global leadership practicums and research internships abroad. These experiential learning programs are opportunities for immersion into societies to observe native leadership practices and for developing international research skills by engaging in research in a different country.

Experiential Strategies for Internalization of Doctoral Leadership Curriculum

Emerging studies in doctoral research curriculum demonstrate educational value of applied or experiential research learning (Stevahn, Anderson, & Hasart, 2016; Myers-Coffman et a., 2021). This learning helps understand meaningful insights of a study design, team collaboration, challenges and opportunities involved in conducting research, study timeframe, community engagement, and other aspects. According to data, these types of research courses increase confidence and preparation to do research independently (Myers-Coffman et al., 2021) and enhance meaningful application of research skills and students' appreciation of scientific inquiry (Stevahn, Anderson, & Hasart, 2016).

Learning International Leadership Research Through Cross-Cultural Immersion Experiences – Dr. Jennie Walker's Experience

Short-term cross-cultural immersion experiences can be effective vehicles to learn international leadership research methods and apply them in practice. Integrating these into the curriculum furthers the internationalization mission of an institution. This section will discuss research findings on the benefits of short-term cross-cultural immersion experiences in graduate student development generally, and specifically how research and scholarship can be built into them to teach international leadership research through experiential learning. The examples include both an in-country immersion prior to the COVID-19 pandemic and a shift to virtual immersion during the pandemic travel restrictions.

Benefits to Graduate Student Development

Short-term programs make international experiences accessible to graduate students who are often balancing full-time professional work, the demands of their personal lives and their studies (Canfield, Low & Hovestadt, 2009). Shorter-term educational experiences, defined as programs lasting eight weeks or less (Institute of International Education, 2018), have grown in popularity especially for graduate students. Many times, these experiences are just one to two weeks long. About half (51 percent) of graduate students participate in experiences that are two-weeks or less, a third (36 percent) participate in experiences that are 2 to 8 weeks long, and only 13 percent participate in study abroad programs that exceed 8 weeks (Sanger & Mason, 2019, p. 14).

There are several reasons cited for the popularity of these programs, such as lower cost, fewer scheduling limitations, less conflict with family and work obligations, and a more comfortable entrée into another cultural environment (Institute of International Education, 2018). They also may allow students multiple opportunities to gain experience in different cultural environments. For these reasons, graduate students are more likely to engage in limited- and short-term overseas experiences than the overall study abroad population (Institute of International Education, 2018; Sanger & Mason, 2019). Graduate students also participate in larger ratios, compared to the overall study abroad enrollment data. As many as 68 percent of Master's students and 30 percent of Doctoral students study abroad through short-term programs, even though 70 percent of them were not required to do so in their degree programs (Sanger & Mason, 2019). It is not clear how many of these programs integrate research experiences, as no published studies on the topic were identified.

The high participation rates in short-term study abroad experiences by graduate students, highlights a great opportunity for doctoral programs at institutions with a mission to internationalize curriculum. From a learning perspective, short-term immersion programs have shown positive changes in students' beliefs, attitudes, values and worldviews (McElhaney, 1998; Kiely, 2005), profound influence on students' intercultural competence (Black & Duhon, 2006; Williams, 2005), deepened empathy and care for others (King, 2004), and increased interest in international courses, travel and careers (Norris & Gillespie, 2009; Lewis & Niesenbaum, 2005). According to the Council of Graduate Schools (2013), graduate students in general need to develop global perspectives and skills due to the globalization of research, development networks, and new technologies for communication and collaboration. Having international experience may also benefit students when they pursue jobs, whether they plan to work in the academy as a professor, as a researcher for a think tank or in other organizations. The QS Global Employer Survey Report (2016) found that more than 80 percent of employers around the world said they actively sought graduates who had international study experience.

While shorter immersions can be stand-alone experiences, they are often integrated into a more comprehensive curriculum design, such as courses with build-in travel components, practicums, internships, conferences, service projects, labs, or consulting services. Faculty-led programs are considered to be optimal for learning in the context of coursework (Campbell, 2016; Mills, Deviney, & Ball, 2010; Slotkin et al., 2012). However, there are many vendors for short-term study abroad that partner with institutions to either fully lead these experiences or do so in conjunction with faculty. A more recent phenomenon is virtual study abroad in coursework, where faculty in different parts of the world arrange for virtual collaborations between their students, such as the X-Culture program (X-Culture, 2019). Given the way that COVID-19 has altered the modalities of higher education, virtual study abroad experiences will likely grow in popularity.

While some studies have shown limitations in learning, due to the compressed time frames, short-term experiences serve as "springboards" for learning and shifts in worldview (Jones et al., 2012), especially when program design is intentional and students are active participants in their experiences (Harris, Kumuran, Harris, Moen, & Visconti, 2018; Rowan-Kenyon & Niehaus, 2011). At the graduate level, learning objectives should consider more advanced levels of knowledge, higher levels of abstract thought, both breadth and depth in a discipline, and emphasis on higher level taxonomies of learning (analysis, evaluation, creation). At the doctoral level, learning objectives related to development as a researcher and scholar are particularly valuable.

Doctoral programs could create more and earlier opportunities for students to engage in research activities with faculty. For students aiming to research across cultures, short-term immersion programs with a dedicated research and/or scholarship component would be particularly valuable. While the foundational research (e.g., literature review, IRB requirements, participant communication and planning) could be completed prior to the immersion, faculty could mentor students in real time during the immersion in the application of research methods (e.g., interviews, working with international partners and participants, survey distribution and management). The short-form would also be helpful in streamlining scheduling and time commitments for students and faculty alike.

Example of a "Global Practicum" Experience for Doctoral Students

The Ph.D. program in Global Leadership at Indiana Institute of Technology includes a short-term cross-cultural immersion called the "Global Practicum." It is an optional 3-credit course designed to introduce students to indigenous or local leadership theories and practices by providing immersive experiential learning experience and travel to different cultural destinations. Global practicums are offered 2–3 times a year in different international locations with the central learning objective for students "to apply concepts studied in the classroom setting to real world international locations" (Indiana Institute of Technology, 2020). Students gain practical experience in other cultures, enhance their research skills, and engage in experiential learning. These experiences are also often coordinated with international research conference attendance, to engage students in further learning about research methods and applications. Course content and the length of time abroad vary based on the focus of the immersion. They are typically 8–10 days on average. Students have an option to design their own independent global practicum experience, as well.

In 2018, I was appointed to teach the Global Practicum course in Lima, Peru. Lima had been chosen specifically to coincide with the International Leadership Association (ILA) regional conference. The conference presented a specific opportunity to foster learning in leadership research and scholarship, and to provide students with networking opportunities with other leadership scholars in an international setting. ILA conferences are frequented by faculty and students in the Ph.D. program, as the focus of the organization compliments the program's focus on leadership and it appeals to a wide range of leadership professionals (e.g., researchers, faculty, consultants, practitioners) across cultures.

Faculty who are appointed to teach the Global Practicum course have freedom to design the experience, using the high-level objectives. In my case, I had limited time to design the experience as I wasn't appointed to lead the trip until about 6 weeks prior to the intended travel. In a normal situation, I would have had several months to plan. With more planning time, I would have incorporated an empirical research project into our agenda. An empirical study would have required advanced planning for research design, time to gain IRB approval and advanced communication with research partners and participants. It would have been beneficial for students to have faculty mentorship and peer support for a first empirical international research project. Faculty who have led other global practicums have incorporated specific research projects, collaborations with local not-for-profit groups in acts of service (i.e., service learning), and even joint research projects with local universities. Given the time limitation, I focused on leveraging further learning about research practices and application for students through participation in the International Leadership Association regional conference in Lima, Peru. This would allow students to attend scholarly sessions and network with other researchers.

Students taking the course for credit were enrolled in a standard 6-week summer session with an online classroom in Blackboard. Prior to the immersion, students participated in 3 weeks of online class sessions to prepare them. They had two live sessions, at the start of class and immediately prior to travel, to establish relationships with other students and the instructor. On a weekly basis, they then interacted in discussions in the online classroom. Sessions included an orientation to the immersion experience and local culture. Students had an opportunity to assess their global mindset and create a specific development plan they would work on during the course. Global mindset assessment and reflection was an important preparatory activity, as it allows students to directly pinpoint dispositions, knowledge and skills that they need to enhance to work well with others in a global context.

Since the degree program focused on global leadership specifically, students explored leadership research in the local culture and broader region and completed a research assignment analyzing leadership practices and culture in Peru. I also engaged students individually to ensure their logistical preparedness and support their individual development goals. The online classroom discussion forums provided an ongoing space for them to connect and coordinate plans along shared interests. For example, students were encouraged to share travel itineraries and extracurricular interests they intended to explore in the country. This led to students coordinating transportation, planning cultural visits together, and discussing specific research interests in more depth.

Since the immersion was designed to facilitate both cultural experience and international leadership scholarship experience, a major component of the preparation was to submit conference proposals to present at the regional ILA conference in Lima. Every student was encouraged to submit a proposal to present at the conference. Attendance at the conference was mandatory, but conference submissions were not. There were several reasons for this: the shorter than normal planning timeframe, readiness for a research presentation and the fact that some students did not take the course for credit. Half of the students had a presentation topic sufficiently developed to create a proposal, and most were accepted to present. I worked with each student to review and revise their proposals. I continued to work with them on a consultative basis to finalize their presentation slide decks for the conference prior to departure. This created a mentoring opportunity for each of them to move from student to scholar with support and guidance as needed.

On an administrative note, the complete immersion agenda was finalized prior to the start of the course. This meant that I arranged all in-country visits to cultural sites and outlined daily immersion activities more than a month prior to travel. This included working with a local tour operator, coordination with the regional ILA conference planner, managing schedules for local business visits and independent planning for daily transportation, meals and supplemental activities. Since two major objectives of the practicums include "practical experience in international cultures" and "experiential learning," the agenda for daily immersion activities balanced time as a group with time for individual exploration. "Practical experience" refers to the ability to attend to basic daily activities, such as shopping, transportation and ordering meals. Students were encouraged to step off the "beaten path" to immerse themselves in daily living within the culture and to interact with local people. More extensive visits to cultural sites were coordinated with a local tour operator who provided a multi-lingual guide who provided in-depth explanations for students. These visits were not just diversions; they were chosen to bring to life many aspects of the cultural research they performed in preparation for the trip. Understanding history, culture, politics and economics, for example, helps to inform leadership analysis in a cultural context. For example, students learned about the colonization of the indigenous peoples and ongoing marginalization in society that has influenced power dynamics and social advancement.

Nearly half of the trip was dedicated to the third objective of global practicums, "enhancing research skills." All students were registered to attend the full regional ILA conference activities, which included daily scholarly sessions and interactions with scholars. The social interactions provided students with the ability to discuss research agendas, strategies and methods in more depth than a typical conference session allowed. Research is often an intensely social activity, requiring skill in networking with stakeholders, gatekeepers, potential research partners and participants. In a typical higher education experience, students may work with one another in a class but do not always have facilitated opportunities to build networks with other researchers. In the context of international research, partners from the local culture can make the difference between success and failure in completing data collection. Many of the conference participants were from or working in South America. There were also many participants from other countries, such as the U.S.A. and Canada with deep experience researching in other cultures. Student presentations were well received, and the students themselves said that their confidence in presenting and discussing their research had grown.

I also arranged for a private dinner session with a local management consultant to provide first-hand perspectives on leadership in Peruvian society and organizations, as well as research practices. Students have experience with guest speakers in a class, but it is less common to have significant small group interaction and one-on-one conversation in a less formal context. The social nature of the dinner facilitated personal conversations about daily life in Peru, perspectives on family, culture and politics. These complimented discussions on leadership research, as students developed a more holistic perspective on the perspectives and concerns of local peoples. Upon return from the trip, students participated in another 2 weeks of online coursework, which consisted of reflections on various facets of the experience including cultural visits, daily living, scholarly conference sessions, and networking with researchers. They also completed a culminating research project that required them to analyze leadership theory and practices in the context of Peruvian culture. Those who presented at the conference were encouraged to publish their work, as well.

Student evaluations were overwhelmingly positive, citing their conference experiences and local cultural interactions to be equally valuable for them. The principle learning objective for the course was to apply concepts studied in the classroom setting to real world international locations. The central concepts were leadership, Peruvian culture, global mindset and international leadership research practices. By blending scholarly and cultural activities, the learning objective was fulfilled.

How the COVID-19 Pandemic Shifted Global Practicum Experience

While the Global Practicums at Indiana Institute of Technology have historically all required travel, it is important to note the impact of COVID-19 travel restrictions in 2020–2021 and how it shifted the program design. A Global Practicum to Costa Rica was planned for early 2020 in partnership with the University for Peace. As it became clear that there was a global health emergency developing, travel for the Global Practicum was postponed. However, given the planning that had already taken place, I worked with the University for Peace to reimagine a virtual immersion.

Since there were some existing examples of virtual immersions at other higher education institutions and through independent operators, I looked at the timeframes and designs that had been implemented. It was clear that these programs were largely either very short, full day programs (i.e., 1–2 days) or involved short sessions (i.e., 1–2 hours) spread over longer periods of time (i.e., 2–4 weeks). We gathered input from our students who had an interest in attending the virtual immersion. Many of them were concerned about having to take multiple full days off work. Conversely, some of them were concerned about too many part-days off of work throughout a longer term. We also needed to consider the integration of the immersion sessions into the existing curriculum and account for the fatigue that long virtual sessions can create. Since the Global Practicums included curriculum leading up to and following immersions, I ultimately decided to use our normal Global Practicum course timeline and create a 4-week format with pre-immersion curriculum the first two weeks, virtual immersion in week three, and post-immersion curriculum in week 4. The most significant change was that instead of one full week of immersion experiences, I curated immersions into one evening orientation and two half day sessions in the same week. This seemed to be the best solution to mitigate the scheduling concerns of the students, while retaining our learning objectives.

Over the course of 4 weeks, students would learn about Costa Rican culture and leadership across three contexts: non-profit, sustainable business and higher education. The first two weeks of pre-immersion curriculum included curated readings and multi-media on Costa Rican culture and leadership that culminated in a small group paper analyzing culture and leadership in the sector of their choice. Students also participated in a global mindset assessment and a weekly online class discussions to cross-pollinate and debate learnings they had through the materials. Additionally, there were supplemental readings on international and cross-cultural research. The research context was important, because one of the learning objectives was for students to prepare for and engage in an organizational analysis in one of three sectors represented in the immersion. Students chose their desired sector for analysis and were organized into small groups in week one to begin performing foundational research for their organizational analyses.

The immersion experience itself consisted of 10 hours of live, interactive sessions via Zoom that were organized into one 90-minute evening kick off session with the University for Peace and two half day sessions that were divided into two 90-minute sessions with breaks in between. There was also a debrief session at the end of each day for students to discuss their learning and feedback on the virtual format. The kick off session discussed Costa Rican culture from the perspectives of local residents and introduced University for Peace as the local partner for the immersion experiences. Day 1 of immersion focused on sustainability in both business and in higher education. It included a video tour of a sustainable coffee farm, a conversation with the owner of the operation, and a panel discussion with leaders at University for Peace on how they are leading international education during the pandemic and planning for the future. Day 2 of immersion began with a panel discussion by business leaders from multinational companies in Costa Rica to discuss their operations and leadership during this the crisis. It was followed by a visit to a non-profit organization dedicated to help and empower women and children affected by poverty and social vulnerability. Each session provided students with the opportunity to ask questions and discuss issues of interest to their personal and professional development.

Following the immersion week, students worked with their small groups to finalize their final project presentation. They were required to create a recorded presentation that identified a specific "problem" the sector and/or organization was facing; analyze the root of the problem and contributing factors in Costa Rican society and culture; evaluate leadership approaches that may mitigate or eliminate the problem in the context of Costa Rica, and then recommend actions the sector or organization could take to mitigate or eliminate the problem in the future. Students shared their final presentations with the class and also with their chosen organization at the end of the course.

The virtual format was novel for everyone involved – students, faculty, staff and partners. The feedback from the students was largely positive, saying that they got much more value out of the experience than they expected. Several commented on how they would like to see more of these virtual immersions built into existing courses, as a way to deepen their learning and engagement across cultures. The principle adjustment they recommended for the future was to take the 10 hours of virtual immersion and spread them out over the term. Instead of concentrated immersion sessions over 4 weeks, the students suggested spreading the Global Practicum course over the full eight weeks of a normal term with one- to two-hour immersion sessions throughout. This was surprising feedback, given the students' initial requests. However, the shift likely reflects the learning they themselves had during the experience. They found the sessions worthwhile enough to schedule weekly time to attend them. As faculty leading the course, I believe that the virtual immersion added great value to the course and opened the possibility of cross-cultural learning and interactions for those that may not have the flexibility or resources for travel. Involving an even greater portion of the student population in cross-cultural immersions through a virtual format is promising for furthering internationalization goals within higher education institutions.

Conclusion

Research has found that short-term immersion programs are beneficial across graduate programs to enhance student dispositions and preparedness to work across cultures. They have particular value for doctoral students preparing to become researchers and scholars in cross-cultural and global contexts. These experiences can be leveraged by faculty to create more and earlier experiences for students to participate in research and scholarly activities. This can more quickly help students adopt the new identities of researcher and scholar, because of the hands-on, real-time mentorship a faculty member provides in the process. Peer support during the shared experience also contributes to their formation, as they are able to experience and analyze cross-cultural experiences together, whether they are in-person or virtual. Ultimately, given their popularity among graduate students in particular, short-term immersion programs present an opportunity to foster greater internationalization in the curriculum in support of an institution's mission to do so. Virtual immersions are a promising vehicle to involve an even greater portion of the student population and further internationalization goals.

Internship Abroad at Troy University Global Leadership Ph.D. Program – Dr. Pamela Lemoine's and Dr. Dionne Rosser-Mims's Experiences

Troy University Global Leadership Ph.D. Program offers another unique example of leadership research internalization – research internships abroad. Designed with interdisciplinary focus, Troy doctoral program is grounded in empirical evidence from 312 leadership doctoral programs in the United States and 34 in other countries that leadership studies should focus on preparing leaders to tackle "environmental, social, and global challenges" (Malakyan, 2019, p. 329) and to produce international and cross-disciplinary solutions (International Leadership Association, 2018). Thus, doctoral leadership education requires a move from traditional to evolving modern interdisciplinary and cross-disciplinary doctoral program. Additionally, the importance of interdisciplinary focus for doctoral leadership programs is also supported by the International Leadership Association (2018). With modern leadership challenges rarely confining themselves to orderly categorization, doctoral programs are called to address education through multidimensional perspectives and different disciplines (Borrego & Newswander, 2010).

Global leadership was another emergent concept in the leadership field that became a foundation for Troy's doctoral program. The university defines global leadership as "the processes and actions through which an individual influences a range of internal and external constituents from multiple national cultures and jurisdictions in a context characterized by significant levels of task and relationship complexity" (Reiche et al., 2017, p. 553). While the academic field of leadership studies had been relatively slow to respond to globalization as evidenced by the small number of U.S. degree programs in global leadership and international courses in leadership programs, studies by the Global Leadership Forecast and the World Economic Forum suggested strong public and private sector demand for professionals trained in leadership, global politics, and cultures: all global leadership competencies (Global Leadership Forecast, 2018; World Economic Forum, 2015).

Planned during a time of a robust economy, the Troy University Global Leadership Ph.D. Program was intentionally created as a totally online program. The Chancellor's leadership team, deans from the College of Communication and Fine Arts, College of Education, Sorrell College of Business, College of Health and Human Services, Library Services, College of Arts and Sciences, and Library Services along with representative departments and faculty members collaboratively worked to design the program, the third doctoral program at Troy University, agreeing to broad outlines and embedding the program as a Global Leadership Program with three cognate areas and two specializations.

A Contemporary Doctoral Program: Application of Theory to Practice

Given the competitive marketplace for Ph.D. programs, the Troy committee was charged with developing guidelines which included requirements for the degree to be aligned with the needs of professionals working in a globalized society. Additionally, there was an expectation to attract students from both the domestic and international markets. To recruit scholar-practitioners, program components also needed to align to career development and preparation for non-academic careers. Thus, the program was designed to be fully online to meet the needs of working professionals; tied to career pathways with an emphasis both on creating "knowledge and practical guidance" (Jones, 2018, p. 819).

With no nationally agreed framework for doctoral programs (Loxley & Kearns, 2018), Troy University academic leaders and the doctoral program development committee had considerable discussions about Clark and Lunt's (2014) classification of "doctorateness." There were deep debates regarding which doctoral degree model should be used: Doctor of Education (Ed.D.); Professional Doctorate (P.D.); or Doctoral of Philosophy (Ph.D.) in the context of traditional versus non-traditional as well as evolving, contemporary doctorate programs (Armsby, Costley, & Cranfield, 2017; Jones, 2018). The Troy University Global Leadership Ph.D. program reflected elements of traditional and non-traditional modern doctorates: (1) centered on the scholar-practitioner –aligned with real work problems; (2) an interdisciplinary – constructivist approach tied to address practitioner needs; and (3) an international internship as a theory-to-practice and relevant real-world contextual application that situates the dissertation (Gault, Leach, & Duey, 2010; Jones & Warnock, 2015).

Ultimately, the program was termed by the Alabama Commission on Higher Education as an applied Ph.D. program that met regulatory and accreditation framework requirements in terms of descriptors, competencies, and outcomes to meet the needs of students who were not necessarily going to work as researchers, and who needed a relevant degree with employable competencies, and aligned with industry needs, and included experiential learning (Armsby, Costley & Cranfield, 2018; Townsend, Pisapia, & Rassaq, 2015).

Currently, the program is housed in the College of Education providing students access to interdisciplinary knowledge and skills and allowing them to study leadership within diverse cognate or specialization areas (interdisciplinary knowledge base). Also, students complete a core global leadership curriculum focused on leadership, leadership theory, and the global nature of today's workforce, in addition to completing an international internship and defending a dissertation.

Internships Abroad: Applied and Experiential Focus of Research Education

Two factors contributed to the idea of the internship abroad: importance to learn applied scholarly perspective and international research. Internships have evolved from apprentice work in medieval times for those learning trades and crafts to acquire skills so students might begin their own work. Early universities also practiced internships. Internships are still promoted as methods for employers to know job applicants have requisite employment skills. Internships provide theory to practice; transferable skills are important for students and for businesses and organizations looking for employable graduates.

In the United States, doctoral experience has traditionally included researching, reading, analyzing, synthesizing and producing new knowledge in Western context (Lam et al., 2019). It was not a prerogative of doctoral education to focus on transferable skills – pathways to activities outside of a traditional research production (Denicolo, 2016; Gibbs & Griffin, 2013; Hancock & Walsh, 2016; Kemp & Kemp, 1999a,1999b). Contemporary doctoral programs are promoting internships as methods to support graduates' readiness for employment (McGagh et al., 2016, Orrell, 2018). A major concern is to ensure that Ph.D. graduates are knowledgeable about career paths other than academia. With the recognition that full-time academic positions are not available as more work is directed to contingent faculty, Baryshnikov, DeVille, and Laugesen (2017) studied the need for Ph.D. graduates to explore other career fields. Duke and Denicolo (2017) posited the exploration of different career pathways for doctoral graduates should include the recognition "increased international mobility and preparation for a variety of career destinations outside of academia" (p. 1). Internships are included in some Ph.D. programs in Australia (Work-Integrated Learning) and the United Kingdom (Professional Internships for Ph.D. students, PIPS) to invest in the Ph.D. graduate's job readiness (O'Carroll, Purser, Wislocka, Lucey, & McGuinness, 2012). Offering an applied research program, Troy University decided to establish an internship as a curriculum opportunity to practice and enhance relevant knowledge and skills and bridge classroom and practice.

GLOL 8807 Internship in Global Leadership is an experiential learning course to prepare doctoral students for leadership roles across cultures and prepare scholars-practitioners with knowledge and skills in international research methodology (Hastings, Wall, & Mantonya, 2018). More specifically, the internship aims to offer practical application for global leadership theories in an international setting, including practicing international research skills. The internship is an innovative experience as it develops collaboratively through a working partnership between a doctoral student, faculty instructors, a faculty field advisor experienced in developing international education classes, and on-site/local mentoring partnerships. It also provides opportunities for students to professionally network, which can aid them in pursuit of employment once they complete the degree (Barger et al., 2016; Sykes & Sykes, 2017).

Experiencing International Leadership Research

Due to its international nature, the Global Leadership Ph.D. program is grounded methodologically both in research basics as well as in international research approaches (Yao & Vital, 2016). Yao and Vital (2016) reported doctoral programs lack preparation in the process of conducting international research important to understand interconnected diverse human realities. The authors suggest the need "for doctoral student researchers to be trained to work within international contexts" (p. 194) as it's uniquely "influenced by the intersections of difference, inequalities, and geopolitics" (p. 205).

One of the program's goals is to "expand international themes in the curriculum and research priorities" (Stromquist, 2007). During the development of the program curriculum, there was a specific focus to ensure both global leadership and specialization courses were designed and aligned to include international perspectives. Courses examine global leadership from various political, social, economic, legal, and cultural contexts and settings. They also include an exploration of changing environments in complex global and domestic organizations; and training in critical thinking and analytical skills to anticipate, analyze and find solutions for global leadership challenges.

GLOL 8807 Internship in Global Leadership goal is to help doctoral students and early career researchers to engage in opportunities to develop their cross-cultural and international understanding of research and prepare them for international engagements in dissertation work (Yao & Vital, 2018). Study results by Schmidt et al. on conducting international research (2012) emphasized the need for students to practice planning international research. This is when "the students participating in the project develop potential research themes involving their diverse disciplines, contact with their international partners about their research goals, design study purpose, and outlined interdisciplinary and context specific sub-questions (Schmidt et al., 2012).

Conducting research in an international setting brings differences to the Institutional Review Board permission process (Lebrón, 2017). GLOL 8807 Internship in Global Leadership offers students to practice how to approach research with international samples and in international context. The U.S. Department of Health and Human Services provides guidance in the *International Compilation of Human Research Standards* (2020). Doctoral students in internships review the guidance as well as requirements and boundaries of doing research with human participants in other countries (e.g., must comply with the U.S. and international ethical standards, concern for participants' rights and welfare within different ethical and international contexts, compliance with local regulatory legislation) (U.S. Department of Health and Human Services, 2020).

Opening a Doctoral Global Leadership Program and Planning Experiential Learning in the Time of COVID-19 Pandemic

The internship planning was underway as the program launched; and it required immediate modification with the Coronavirus pandemic. In August 2018, I was appointed to lead Troy University's program committee to develop the Troy University Global Leadership Ph.D. Program proposal for the Alabama Commission on Higher Education (ACHE). Dr. Dionne Rosser-Mims, Dean of the College of Education worked closely with the committee on the proposal, navigating the intricacies of ensuring that the proposal pieces met standards required by ACHE. The Alabama Commission on Higher Education approved the proposal in June of 2019 and subsequently, the Southern Association of Colleges and Schools (SACS) Substantive Change proposal was submitted and approved in September 2019.

In March 2020, the COVID-19 pandemic shut down the education of 220 million postsecondary students (World Bank, 2020). As COVID-19 infections spread throughout the world, higher education institution closures disrupted a $600 billion world-wide industry (Hechinger & Lorin, 2020). The disruption both displaced students and led to long-term impacts on higher education institutions in terms of pedagogical processes as well as economic losses. While education was seen as a necessity for success and critical to building human capital in terms of working in the global, knowledge economy, academic leaders around the world were forced to make decisions to curtail some programs, postpone expansion of others, and stop the launch of new programs. In a volatile, uncertain, and complex world economy challenged by a pandemic, Troy University launched the new Ph.D. program with a full cohort of 20 students on August 1, 2020. Never had application of global leadership skills been more in demand than with leaders world-wide who were dealing with complexity, ambiguity, chaos, and uncertainty due to COVID-19.

Virtual Research Internships Abroad

COVID-19 pandemic educational institution closures started in the United States in March 2020. There was immediate recognition that international travel could continue to be impaired and alternative methods of conducting international internships needed to be explored. For the purposes of the program in Global Leadership, international internships were defined as a course with a component of an educational experience (experiential learning) taking place in another country (Knight, 2015). With COVID-19, discussions moved to the use of virtual internships.

Virtual internships have been in use since the mid-2000s. Referred to as virtual, remote, telework (United Kingdom), tele-travail (Canada, France), and other terms specific to different countries, virtual internships are marketed in the 2020s as alternative methods for doing internships. A review of virtual internships posted online promotes virtual internships from colleges and universities, various formats and with differing amounts of time. Shorter internships (micro-internships) to full-year or multiple year internship experiences are tailored to the needs of students and connected to program requirements.

University internships are a thriving business. Examples at universities include the University of Rochester: Absolute Internship, Pontificia Universidad Catolica del Peru (PUCP)- Field School Program, and Institute for American Universities (IAU)- France, Spain, Morocco. UC (University of California-Davis) internships include UC Davis Programs Virtual Summer Internships; the UC Davis Widening Circles program, Omprakash, Team4Tech Virtual Ed Tech Internship, and the UC Davis Washington Program, an internship program and credit classes offered in Washington, DC. Columbia University offers a Virtual Internship Program (VIP) which provides internship experiences in marketing, public relations, consulting, public health, not-for-profit organizations, arts administration, and legal advocacy.

Troy University has both graduate and undergraduate internship opportunities: undergraduate internships include experiences with the Alabama state government, museums, social justice initiatives, the National Park Service, and other internships particular to programs at Troy. Global Leadership doctoral students have presented a plethora of potential internships as their interests have evolved in the first year of the program. Virtual internships voiced by doctoral students in the first terms of a new program offered ideas for internships including service, social justice, and public good, and were usually tied to one of the five specialization areas: organizational leadership, strategic communication, public administration, instructional leadership and administration, and higher education.

Examples from students include virtual internships with indigenous communities, marketing, mentoring, social justice projects, and working with public policy in countries outside the United States. Some students presented specific ideas; other students solicited input from faculty to help them consider how an internship to meet their particular needs might be structured and supported. There are also companies specializing in a virtual internship placement, willing to partner with universities and international businesses and ready to evolve as universities and programs work to meet virtual and face-to-face internship requirements. As Troy Global Leadership Ph.D. students move into their second year of the program in August 2021, planning for internships to take place within the third year of the program will continue.

COVID-19 closures were in place and there was recognition of the possibility international travel might continue to be impaired even into the future. Thus, exploration of virtual global internships became a focus until pandemic issues subsided.

Conclusion

The Troy University Global Leadership Ph.D. program reflected elements of traditional and non-traditional modern doctorates: (1) centered on the scholar-practitioner – aligned with real work problems; (2) an interdisciplinary – constructivist approach tied to address practitioner needs; and (3) an international internship as a theory-to-practice and relevant real-world contextual application that situates the dissertation.

Internationalization of Doctoral Research Education: Experiential Approaches

The chapter calls for the internationalization of doctoral leadership education, emphasizing the importance of international research curriculum. International research has national variations and is tight to context with leadership meanings and epistemologies. A systematic approach to international research knowledge and skills development would help prepare confident leadership researchers capable of understanding, designing, and conducting studies in different cultures using multi-disciplinary and multi-paradigm frameworks. Two curriculum examples demonstrate benefits of experiential learning with immersive activities: global practicum and internship abroad. Traditional doctoral leadership education lacks creative approaches to bridge education and practice. With emergence of new applied doctoral education models for researcher-practitioners and increase in global leadership learning, doctoral leadership programs should rethink curriculum activities. The main focus should be on acquiring knowledge through experience: applying scholarship to international leadership situations or designing collaborative systems to practice international research. Virtual offerings could help continue international training when travel is restricted.

References

Antelo, A. (2012). Internationalization of research. *Journal of International Education and Leadership, 2*, 1–6. doi:10.1177/1028315318762804.

Armsby, P., Costley, C., & Cranfield, S. (2018). The design of doctorate curricula for practicing professionals. *Studies in Higher Education, 43*(12), 2226–2237. doi:10.1080/03075079.2017.1318365.

Barger, D., Gordon, A., Plumblee, J., Ogle, J., Dancz, C., & Vaughn, D. (2016). Increasing student development through multi-level immersive learning: Clemson Engineers for Developing Countries case study. *International Journal for Service Learning in Engineering, 11*(2), 55–72.

Baryshnikov, Y., DeVille, L., & Laugesen, R. (2017). Math PhD careers: New opportunities emerging amidst crisis. *Notices of the AMS, 64*(3), 260–264. doi:10.1090/noti1483.

Bayerlein, L. (2015). Curriculum innovation in undergraduate accounting degree programmes through virtual internships. *Education & Training, 57*(6), 673–684. https://www.learntechlib.org/p/158710/.

Black, H. T., & Duhon, D. L. (2006, January/February). Assessing the impact of business study abroad programs on cultural awareness and personal development. *Journal of Education for Business, 81*(3), 140–144. doi:10.3200/JOEB.81.3.140-144.

Borrego, M., & Newswander, M. L. (2010). Definitions of Interdisciplinary Research: Toward graduate-level Interdisciplinary learning outcomes. *The Review of Higher Education, 34*, 61 - 84. doi:10.1353/rhe.2010.0006

Campbell, K. (2016). Short-term study abroad programmes: Objectives and accomplishments. *Journal of International Mobility, 1*(1), 189–204. doi:10.3917/jim.004.0189.

Canfield, B. S., Low, L., & Hovestadt, A. (2009). Cultural immersion as a learning method for expanding intercultural competencies. *Family Journal: Counseling and Therapy for Couples and Families, 17*(4), 318–322. doi:10.1177/1066480709347359.

Cavusgil, S. T. (1998). Internationalizing doctoral education in business: A call for action. *Thunderbird International Business Review, 40*(1), p. 77–85. doi:10.1002/tie.4270400108.

Clarke, G., & Lunt, I. (2014) The concept of 'originality' in the Ph.D. How is it interpreted by examiners? *Assessment & Evaluation in Higher Education, 39*(7), 803–820. doi:10.1080/02602938.2013.870970.

Coronel Llamas, J. M., & Boza, A. (2011) Teaching research methods for doctoral students in education: Learning to enquire in the university, *International Journal of Social Research Methodology, 14*, 1, 77–90, doi:10.1080/13645579.2010.492136.

Council of Graduate Schools. (2013). *Graduate education for global career pathways*. Council of Graduate Schools. https://cgsnet.org/graduateeducation-global-career-pathways-1.

Creighton University Graduate School. (2019). *Guidelines for differentiation among undergraduate, graduate, and professional courses*. https://gradschool.creighton.edu/sites/gradschool.creighton.edu/files/Guidelines-for-Differentiation-UG-Grad-Courses.pdf.

Denicolo, P. M., Duke, D. C., & Reeves, J. D. (2017). *Fulfilling the potential of your doctoral experience: Success in research*. Sage.

de Wit, H. (2020). Internationalization of higher education: The need for a more ethical and qualitative approach. 10th Anniversary Series. *Journal of International Students, 10*(1), i–v. 9–17. doi:10.32674/jis.v10i1.1893.

de Wit, H. (2017). Global internationalization of higher education: Nine misconceptions. In G. Mihut, P. G. Altbach, & H. de Wit (Eds.), *Understanding higher education internationalization. Global perspectives on higher education*. Sense Publishers. doi:10.1007/978-94-6351-161-2_2.

de Wit, H., & Hunter, F. (2015). The future of internationalization of higher education in Europe. *International Higher Education, 83*, 2–3. doi:10.6017/ihe.2015.83.9073.

de Wit, H., Hunter, F., Howard, L., & Egron-Polak, E. (Eds.). (2015). *Internationalisation of higher education*. European Parliament, Directorate-General for International Policies.

de Wit, H., Gacel-Avila, J., Jones, E., & Jooste, N. (2017). *The globalization of internationalization: Emerging voices and perspectives*. Routledge Taylor & Francis.

Denicolo, P. M. (2016). International developments in the purpose and process of the doctorate: Consequences for supervision, examining and the employment of graduates. In A. Fourie Malherbe & B. Aitchison (Eds.), *Postgraduate supervision: Future foci for the knowledge society* (pp. 1–14). Stellenbosch Sun Media.

Duke, D. C., & Denicolo, P. M. (2017). What supervisors and universities can do to enhance doctoral student experience (and how they can help themselves)? *FEMS Microbiology Letter, 364*(9), 1–7. https://doi.org/10.1093/femsle/fnx090.

Forest, J. F., & Albach, P. G. (Eds). (2007). *International handbook of higher education*. (1st ed.). Springer. https://www.springer.com/gp/book/9781402040115.

Gault, J., Leach, E., & Duey, M. (2010). Effects of business internships on job marketability: The employers' perspective. *Education+Training, 52*(1), 76–88. doi:10.1108/00400911011017690".

Global Leadership Forecast. (2018). DDI. https://www.ddiworld.com/research/global-leadership-forecast-2018.

Gibbs, K. D., & Griffin, K. A. (2013). What do I want to be with my PhD? The roles of personal values and structural dynamics in shaping the career interests of recent biomedical science PhD graduates. *CBE Life Sciences Education, 12*(4), 711–723. doi:10.1187/cbe.13-02-0021.

Guri-Rosenblit, S. (2015) Internationalization of higher education: Navigating between contrasting trends. In A. Curaj, L. Matei, R. Pricopie, J. Salmi, & P. Scott (Eds.), *The European higher education area* (pp. 13–26). Springer. doi:10.1007/978-3-319-20877-0_2.

Harris, V. W., Kumaran, M., Harris, H. J., Moen, D., & Visconti, B. (2018). Assessing multicultural competence (knowledge and awareness) in study abroad experiences. *Compare: A Journal of Comparative and International Education, 49*(3), 430–452. doi:10.1080/03057925.2017.1421901.

Hancock, S., & Walsh, E. (2016). Beyond knowledge and skills: Rethinking the development of professional identity during the STEM doctorate. *Studies in Higher Education, 41*(1), 37–50. doi:10.1080/03075079.2014.915301.

Hastings, L. J., Wall, M., & Mantonya, K. (2018). Developing leadership through "serviceship": Leveraging the intersection between service-learning and professional internship. *Journal of Leadership Education, 17*(1), 141–151. doi:10.12806/V17/I1/A2.

Hechinger, J., & Lorin, J. (2020, March 19). *Coronavirus forces $600 billion higher education industry online*. Bloomberg Businessweek. https://www.bloombergquint.com/businessweek/colleges-are-going-online-because-of-the-coronavirus.

Indiana Institute of Technology. (18, August, 2020). *Global travel* [Ph.D. in Global Leadership]. https://phd.indianatech.edu/travel/.

Institute of International Education. (2018). *Leading institutions by duration of study abroad and institutional type, 2015/16-2016/17. Open doors report on international educational exchange*. http://www.iie.org/opendoors

International Leadership Association (ILA). (2018). *Leadership program directory*. https://www.ilanet.org/Resources/LPD/index2.asp.

Jiang, J., & Shen, W. (2019). International mentorship and research collaboration: Evidence from European-trained Chinese PhD returnees. *Frontiers of Education in China 14*, 180–205. doi:10.1007/s11516-019-0010-z

Jones, M. (2018). Contemporary trends in professional doctorates. *Studies in Higher Education, 43*(5), 814–825. doi:10.1080/03075079.2018.1438095.

Jones, S. R., Rowan-Kenyon, H. T., Ireland, S. M., Niehaus, E., & Skendall, K. C. (2012). The meaning students make as participants in short-term immersion programs. *Journal of College Student Development 53*(2), 201–220. doi:10.1353/csd.2012.0026.

Jones, H. M., & Warnock, L. J. (2015). When a PhD is not enough: A case study of a UK internship programme to enhance the employability of doctoral researchers. *Higher Education, Skills and Work – Based Learning, 5*(3), 212–227. doi:10.1108/HESWBL-05-2014-0013.

Kemp, D. A. (1999a) *New knowledge, new opportunities: A discussion paper on higher education research and training*. Department of Education, Training and Youth Affairs.

Kemp, D. A., & Kemp, D. (1999b). *Knowledge and innovation: A policy statement on research and research training.* Department of Education, Training and Youth Affairs.

Kemp, S. P., & Nurius, P. S. (2015). Preparing emerging doctoral scholars for transdisciplinary research: A developmental approach. *Journal of Teaching in Social Work, 35*(1–2), 131–150. doi:10.1080/08841233.2014.980929.

Kiely, R. (2005). A transformative learning model for service learning: A longitudinal case study. *Michigan Journal of Community Service Learning, 12*, 5–22. http://hdl.handle.net/2027/spo.3239521.0012.101

King, J. T. (2004). Service learning as a site for critical pedagogy: A case of collaboration, caring, and defamiliarization across borders. *Journal of Experiential Education, 26*(3), 121–137. doi:10.5901/mjss.2015.v6n2p471.

Knight, J. (2008). *Higher education in turmoil: The changing world of internationalization.* Sense Publishers.

Knight, J. (2015). Updated definition of internationalization. *International Higher Education, 33*, 2–3. doi:10.6017/ihe.2003.33.7391.

Kyvik, S., & Larsen, I. M. (1997). The exchange of knowledge: A small country in the international research community. *Science Communication, 18*(3), 238–264. doi:10.1177/1075547097018003004.

Kwiek, M. (2018). International research collaboration and international research orientation: Comparative findings about European academics. *Journal of Studies in International Education, 22*(2), 136–160. doi:10.1177/1028315317747084.

Lam, C. K. C., Huu, C., Lau, R. W. K., de Caux, B., Chen, Y., Tan, Q. Q., & Pretorius, L. (2019). Experiential learning in doctoral training programmes: Fostering personal epistemology through collaboration. *Studies in Continuing Education, 41*(1) 111–128. doi:10.1080/0158037X.2018.1482863.

Lane, H. W., Maznevski, M. L., Mendenhall, M. E., & McNett. J. (2017). *The Blackwell handbook of global management.* Blackwell Publishing. doi:10.1002/9781405166355.

Lebrón, J. (2017). *Forming interdisciplinary scholars: An evaluation of the IES predoctoral interdisciplinary training program.* George Mason University. https://sites.nationalacademies.org/cs/groups/pgasite/documents/webpage/pga_186161.pdf.

Lewis, T. L., & Niesenbaum, R. A. (2005). Extending the stay: Using community-based research and service learning to enhance short-term study abroad. *Journal of Studies in International Education, 9*(3), 251–264. doi:10.1177/1028315305277682.

Loxley, A., & Kearns, M. (2018). Finding a purpose for the doctorate? A view from the supervisors. *Studies in Higher Education, 43*(5), 826–840. doi:10.1080/03075079.2018.1438096.

Lyall, C., & Meagher, L. R. (2012). A masterclass in interdisciplinarity: Research into practice in training the next generation of interdisciplinary researchers. *Futures, 44*, 608–617. doi:10.1016/j.futures.2012.03.011

Malakyan, P. G. (2019). International curriculum and conceptual approaches to doctoral programs in leadership studies. *International Journal of Doctoral Studies, 14*, 325–350. doi:10.28945/4254.

McElhaney, K. A. (1998). *Student outcomes of community service learning: A comparative analysis of curriculum-based and non-curriculum-based alternative spring break programs.* Hathi Trust Digital Library. https://catalog.hathitrust.org/Record/003987168/Cite.

McGagh, J., Marsh, H., Western, M. C., Thomas, P., Hastings, A., Mihailova, M., & Wenham, M. (2016). https://acola.org/wp-content/uploads/2018/08/saf13-review-research-training-system-report.pdf.

Mendenhall, M., Osland, J., Bird, A., Oddou, G. R., Stevens, M. J., Maznevski, M., Stahl, G. K. (Eds.) (2017). *Global leadership: Research, practice, and development (Global HRM)* (3rd ed.). Routledge.

Mestenhauser, J. A., & Ellingboe, B. J. (1998). *Reforming the higher education curriculum. Internationalizing the campus* [Abstract]. American Council on Education/Oryx Press Series on Higher Education. https://eric.ed.gov/?id=ED423813.

Mihut, G., Altbach, P. G., & de Wit, H. (2017) (Eds.). *Understanding higher education internationalization.* Sense Publishers.

Miller Cleary, L. (2013). *Cross-cultural research with integrity.* Palgrave Mcmillan.

Mills, L., Deviney, D., & Ball, B. (2010). Short-term study abroad programs: A diversity of options. *The Journal of Human Resource and Adult Learning, 6*(2), 1–13. doi:10.36366/frontiers.v29i2.396.

Miyazaki, A. D., & Taylor, K. A. (2008). Researcher interaction biases and business ethics research: Respondent reactions to researcher characteristics. *Journal of Business Ethics, 81*, 779–795. doi:10.1007/s10551-007-9547-5.

Morris, S., & Hudson, W. (1995). International education and innovative approaches to university teaching. *Australian Universities' Review, 38*, 70–74. https://www.learntechlib.org/p/80131/.

Mu, G. M., Zhang, H., Cheng, W., Fang, Y., Li, S., Wang, X., & Dooley, K. (2018). Negotiating scholarly identity through an international doctoral workshop: A cosmopolitan approach to doctoral education. *Journal of Studies in International Education, 23*(1), 139–153. doi:10.1177/1028315318810840.

Myers-Coffman, K., Ibrahim, M., Bryl, K., Junkin, J. S., & Bradt, J. (2021). Learning by doing: Student experiences in a mixed methods research course. *International Journal of Doctoral Studies, 16*, 031–046. doi:10.28945/4683.

Nahavandi, A., & Krishnan, H. (2018). Indo-European leadership (IEL): A non-Western leadership perspective. In J. L. Chin, J. E. Trimble, & J. E. Garcia (Eds.), *Global and culturally diverse leaders and leadership: New dimensions, opportunities, and challenges for business, industry, education and society* (pp. 105–123). Emerald Publishing.

Norris, E. M., & Gillespie, J. (2009). How study abroad shapes global careers: Evidence from the United States. *Journal of Studies in International Education, 13*(3), 382–397. doi:10.1177/102831530831974.

O'Carroll, C., Purser, L., Wislocka, M., Lucey, S., & McGuinness, N. (2012). The PhD in Europe: Developing a system of doctoral training that will increase the internationalisation of universities. In A. Curaj, P. Scott, L. Vlasceanu, & L. Wilson (Eds.), *European higher education at the crossroads* (pp. 461–484). Springer.

Orrell, J.(2018, April 30). Work integrated learning: Why is it increasing and who benefits? *The Conversation.* https://theconversation.com/work-integrated-learning-why-is-it-increasing-and-who-benefits-93642.

Parada, F., & Peacock, J. (2015). Quality of doctoral training and employability of doctorate holders: The views of doctoral candidates and junior researchers. In A. Curaj, L. Matei, R. Pricopie, J. Salmi, & P. Scott (Eds.), *The European higher education area: Between critical reflections and future policies* (pp. 593–612). Springer Open Access. doi:10.1007/978-3-319-20877-0".

Pannucci, C. J., & Wilkins, E. G. (2010). Identifying and avoiding bias in research. *Plastic and reconstructive surgery, 126*(2), 619–625. doi:10.1097/PRS.0b013e3181de24bc.

Peterson, M. F., & Hunt, J. G. (1997). International perspectives on international leadership. *The Leadership Quarterly, 8*(3), 203–231. doi:10.1016/S1048-9843(97)90002-3.

Pieridou, M., & Kambouri-Danos, M. (2020). Qualitative doctoral research in educational settings: Reflecting on meaningful encounters. *International Journal of Evaluation and Research in Education, 9*(1), 21–31. doi:10.11591/ijere.v9i1.20360.

Qiang, A. (2003). Internationalization of higher education: Towards a conceptual framework. *Policy Futures in Education, 1*(2), 248–270. doi:10.2304/pfie.2003.1.2.5.

QS Global Employer Survey Report. (2016). Retrieved from https://www.qs.com/qs-global-employer-survey-2016-reveals-desirable-graduates/.

Reiche, B. S., Bird, A., Mendenhall, M. E., & Osland, J. S. (2017). Contextualizing leadership: A typology of global leadership roles. *Journal of International Business Studies, 48*(5), 552–572. doi:10.1057/s41267-016-0030-3.

Reiche, B. S., Mendenhall, M. E., Szkudlarek, B., & Osland, J. S. (2019). Global leadership research: Where do we go from here? In *Advances in global leadership* (Vol. 12, pp 211–234). Emerald. doi:10.1108/S1535-12032 0190000012013.

Rizvi, F. (2010). International students and doctoral studies in transnational spaces. In M. Walker & P. Thomson (Eds.), *The Routledge doctoral supervisor's companion: Supporting effective research in education and the social sciences* (pp. 158–170). Routledge.

Rostan, M., Ceravolo, F. A., & Metcalfe, A. S. (2014). The internationalization of research. In F. Huang, M. Finkelstein, & M. Rostan (Eds.), *The internationalization of the academy. The changing academy – the changing academic profession in international comparative perspective* (Vol. 10). Springer. doi:10.1007/978-94-007-7278-6_7.

Rowan-Kenyon, H. T., & Niehaus, E. (2011). One year later: The influence of short-term study abroad experiences on students. *Journal of Student Affairs Research and Practice, 48*(2), 213–228. doi:10.2202/1949-6605.6213.

Ryan, J. (2012). Internationalisation of doctoral education. *Australian Universities' Review, 54*(1), 55- 63. https://files.eric.ed.gov/fulltext/EJ968523.pdf.

Sanger, J., & Mason, L. (2019). *Who's counting? Understanding the landscape of graduate learning overseas.* Institute of International Education.

Schmidt, A. H., Robbins, A. S. T., Combs, J. K., Freeburg, A., Jesperson, R. G., Rogers, H. S., Sheldon, K. S., & Wheat, E. (2012). A new model for training graduate students to conduct interdisciplinary, inter-organizational, and international research. *BioScience, 62*(3), 296–304. doi:10.1525/bio.2012.62.3.11.

Stevahn, L., Anderson, J. B., & Hasart, T. L. (2016). Community-based research (CBR) in the education doctorate: Lessons learned and promising practices. *International Journal of Doctoral Studies, 11*, 441–465. doi:10.28945/3620.

Slotkin, M. H., Durie, C. J., & Eisenberg, J. R. (2012). The benefits of short term study abroad as blended learning experience. *Journal of International Education in Business, 5*(2), 163–173. doi:10.1108/183632612112 81762.

Stromquist, N. P. (2007). Internationalization as a response to globalization: Radical shifts in university environments. *Higher Education, 53*(1), 81–105. doi:10.1007/s10734-005-1975-5.

Sykes, R., & Sykes, D. (2017). Learning the ins and outs of an industry virtually, using contemporary internship methods strengthens the student's expertise and better prepares them for future workplace environments. *International Journal of eLearning and Distance Education, 32*(10), 1–17. https://files.eric.ed.gov/fulltext/EJ1154 622.pdf.

Tight, M. (2019) Globalization and internationalization as frameworks for higher education research, *36*(1), 52–74. doi:10.1080/02671522.2019.1633560.

Townsend, T., Pisapia, J., & Razzaq, J. (2015). Fostering interdisciplinary research in universities: A case study of leadership, alignment and support. *Studies in Higher Education, 40*(4), 658–675. doi:10.1080/03075079.2 013.842218.

Trowler, P. (2012). Disciplines and interdisciplinarity: Conceptual groundwork. In P. Trowler, M. Saunders, & V. Bamber (Eds.), *Tribes and territories in the 21st century: Rethinking the significance of disciplines in higher education* (pp. 5–29). Routledge.

U.S. Department of Health and Human Services. (2020). *International compilation of human research standards 2020 Edition*. https://www.hhs.gov/ohrp/sites/default/files/2020-international-compilation-of-human-research-standards.

Vandermause, R., Barbosa-Leiker, C., & Fritz, R. (2014). Research education: Findings of a study of teaching-learning research using multiple analytical perspectives. *The Journal of Nursing Education, 53*(12), 673–677. doi:10.3928/01484834-20141120-02.

Williams, T. R. (2005). Exploring the impact of study abroad on students' intercultural communication skills: Adaptability and sensitivity. *Journal of Studies in International Education, 9*(4), 356–371. https://www.ie.org/Research-and-Insights/Graduate-Learning-Overseas.

Woldegiyorgis, A. A., Proctor, D., & de Wit, H. (2018). Internationalization of research: Key considerations and concerns. *Journal of Studies in International Education, 22*(2), 161–176. doi:10.1177/1028315318762804

World Bank Group. (2020, April 8). *The COVID-19 crisis response: Supporting tertiary education for continuity, adaptation, and innovation*. http://pubdocs.worldbank.org/en/621991586463915490/WB-Tertiary-Ed-and-Covid-19-Crisis-for-public-use-April-9.pdf.

World Economic Forum. (2015). *Global leadership index: Outlook on the global agenda*. Geneva, World Economic Forum, LLC. http://reports.weforum.org/outlook-global-agenda-2015/global-leadership-and-governance/\global-leadership-index/.

X-Culture. (2019). *For instructors*. https://x-culture.org/for-instructors/.

Yao, C. W., & Vital, L. M. (2016). "I don't think I'm prepared": Perceptions of U.S. doctoral students on international research preparation. *Journal for the Study of Postsecondary and Tertiary Education, 1*, 197–214. doi:10.28945/3489.

Yao, C. W., & Vital, L. M. (2018). Reflexivity in international contexts: Implications for U.S. doctoral students international research preparation. *International Journal of Doctoral Studies, 13*, 193–210. doi:10.28945/4005.

25

Enhancing International Research Training

Student Perspectives, the Role of Faculty and Institutional Support

Jennie L. Walker, Yulia Tolstikov-Mast, and Brenda Williams

Introduction

At the doctoral-level, research practices are traditionally learned through an apprentice model in which experienced researchers (i.e., faculty) provide instruction and then supervise apprentices (i.e., students) in conducting research. "By definition, the doctoral experience is a demanding new experience during which students move from being readers and 'consumers' of research to being producers of knowledge" (Gardner & Mendoza, 2010, p.xiv). Instruction takes place via a series of research courses. However, in many programs students may not have the opportunity to practice hands-on research until their culminating dissertation project. Considering the great importance of research at this level of education (Vaughan, Boerum, & Whitehead, 2019), integrating more experience into programs may better prepare students for future career goals and enhance their self-efficacy with research practices. This chapter extends the discussion on teaching international leadership research from the previous chapter by examining the perspectives and experiences of students themselves, the role of faculty in enhancing students' self-efficacy in this area, as well as additional ways that institutional support for international research can be put into place. The chapter concludes with one of the author's design thinking on crafting an international research course.

Perspectives and Experiences of Doctoral Students in International Research – Dr. Brenda Williams' Experience

To intimately understand the needs of students who engage in international research and how to best prepare them, it is helpful to begin with an exploration of some of their perspectives and experiences. The discussion in this section is based on a pilot study I conducted with a group of doctoral graduates to understand their real-life experiences in conducting international leadership research during their dissertations. The qualitative study was born from a concern that international research training is sometimes designed as an ancillary or "ad hoc" activity in doctoral programs with international focus. We cannot ask emerging researchers to produce international leadership scholarship without prior training. Rather, an intentional research skill set in conducting studies and reporting data should be developed before doctoral students engage in their dissertation research.

DOI: 10.4324/9781003003380-25

One such skill set is an understanding of multicultural factors and differences in data collection, data analyses and reporting of findings in qualitative research. The pilot study specifically explored students' experiences with multiculturality in their research. Multiculturality is necessary in qualitative research (Sands, Bourjolly, & Roer-Strier, 2007; Zhang & Guttormsen, 2016). Multiculturality is defined as, "The obstacles [and opportunities] created when interviewers exhibit…[multicultural backgrounds] during international field research projects" and where there is a consideration of, "…multicultural backgrounds create challenges and opportunities in data collection during in-depth interviewing…" (p. 233). We need to view, "multiculturality as a key methodological challenge during in-depth interviewing…" (Zhang & Guttormsen, 2016, p. 232) or we risk creating challenges, missed opportunities, and lost meaning in the interviewing process. Students as developing scholars need to have a keen awareness of the intersectionality of inequities, social justice and multicultural differences.

Data Collection

Graduates of a global leadership Ph.D. program were sent a qualitative survey on their experiences conducting international qualitative research during their dissertations. All students in the program had been required to complete one core course on international research methods. Questions on the survey included:

1. What experiences were the most challenging conducting a global research study?
2. How would you describe how you dealt with multicultural issues during the interview process (language, cultures, religion, etc.)?
3. What would you do differently in collecting and analyzing your data using a multicultural approach?

The graduates were also asked demographic questions, such as their year of graduation, dissertation topic, specialization and current employment.

Five alumni responded, offering insights on their experiences conducting qualitative research from 2018 to 2020. The respondents included four males and one female. Four of the five specialized in organizational management, while one specialized in academic administration. All five were currently employed in various occupations, including a director of clinical research and development, a data analyst, a lecturer/trainer, an engineer and a senior administrator in higher education.

Data Analysis

Four themes emerged in the qualitative survey: 1. Challenge to identify and communicate with sample itself; 2. Criticality of culture; and 3. Leverage multicultural resources and knowledge.

Theme 1   Challenge to Identify and Communicate with Sample Itself

The first survey question asked alumni about the most challenging experiences they had in conducting a global research study. Many responses centered on identifying and communicating with the sample itself. Respondents shared the challenges they had in contacting participants to interview. Once they were in communication, there were challenges with comprehension of the research questions and in follow-up. The challenges with the sample itself underscore the importance of preparing students for communicating with diverse participants who may be geographically distant, as well.

Theme 2 Criticality of Culture

The second survey question asked alumni about multicultural issues they encountered in the research process. There were many issues identified by the respondents, such as challenges due to differences in language, culture, nationality, ethnicity, religion, and tribal differences. There were additional barriers to research based on differences in free speech, ethics, politics; boundaries regarding respect; and difficulty conveying the importance of the study to the local culture. The responses to the questions on multiculturality show that the challenges permeated all aspects of the research process. Ultimately, one respondent said, "I would strongly advise researchers to be careful exploring the human phenomenon in a different culture."

Theme 3 Leverage Multicultural Resources and Knowledge

When asked what they would do differently in collecting and analyzing data using a multicultural approach, the respondents pointed to the importance of multicultural resources and leveraging multicultural knowledge. Alumni stressed the importance of finding a research partner within the culture itself and incorporating culture into the research inquiry. They highlighted the usefulness of mixed methods to more fully understand multicultural factors in the data gathering and analysis process. Better transcription software was highlighted as an important resource. Lastly, there were comments regarding thoughtful groupings and classifications of participants to better account for multiculturality.

Discussion

Alumni experience of international leadership research underscored the unique multicultural issues encountered in the research process. Their insights on what they would change in future research studies centered on better leveraging their knowledge of multiculturality and incorporating resources to help them do this. For this reason, it may be useful for those teaching international research methods to consider using The Model of Multiculturality (Zhang & Guttormsen, 2016, p. 234) as a methodological research tool to emphasize consideration of multicultural factors in research. This approach provides students the ability to apply a qualitative model to interviewing participants with a focus on how to appropriately and accurately interview and report findings within a multicultural foundation. It is critical that programs that train international researchers understand the unique context in which international research occurs and that it adds a layer of complexity to research that needs to be accounted for in research training. These students' experiences illustrate that even in a program that has one required international research course, further training, faculty guidance and hands-on experience may have helped them better navigate the international contexts in which they were researching. The next section explores the role of faculty in guiding students in international research training, specifically how they can enhance students' sense of self-efficacy.

Role of Faculty in Enhancing Students' Self-Efficacy in International Leadership Research

Doctoral education requires students to become comfortable with new identities as researchers and scholars. "In order to develop a research identity, doctoral students first need to see themselves as the creators of new knowledge in the field" (Dollarhide et al., 2013, p. 146). Research on graduate-level research training is relatively sparse (Shivy et al., 2003). However, two studies show that doctoral students have low self-efficacy with their identity as a researcher until they reach the dissertation stage. Dollarhide, Gibson, and Moss (2013) found in their study that students in the dissertation stage were the most likely to accept the responsibility for creating new knowledge. This is consistent with Lambie and Vaccaro's (2011) finding that self-efficacy increases with time over the doctoral program.

Faculty play a critical role in fostering both motivation to research and student identity development as a researcher. The process of professional identity development is a cycle of learning, practice, and feedback in which the new professional experiences dependence and autonomy in the search for individuation, professional viability, and internal locus of evaluation (Auxier et al., 2003). Faculty modeling, positive reinforcement and early involvement have been found to have a strong, positive influence on the research training environment (Shivy et al., 2003). When the interpersonal and instructional aspects of the research training environment were assessed for impact on student attitudes toward research, the interpersonal aspects were more important (Larson & Besett-Alesch, 2000). A study by Shivy et al. (2003) found that faculty advisors who were helpful, caring and involved with students drew them into research. Conversely, student ambivalence, anxiety and under confidence can diminish students' enthusiasm to perform research (Gelso & Lent, 2000). However, faculty workloads can make personal attention for each student challenging. This is a limitation of the traditional apprentice model for doctoral students.

An alternative or perhaps compliment to the traditional apprentice model is what Samuel and Vithal (2011) call a "community approach" to research development. This involves peer mentorships in addition to faculty mentorships. They use the example of scholarly writing groups where students support one another, which are sometimes integrated into programs. The extension of this idea to research would be in performing research as a cohort or in subgroups of the cohort. This model presents an opportunity to better support doctoral students by scaffolding their learning; that is, providing a more supportive structure between learning about research and then independently performing it. This may bolster persistence toward degree completion. It may also contribute to a higher degree of interdisciplinary learning via the perspectives of diverse students.

In the context of international leadership research, knowledge production tends to take place in other cultural environments. Globalization has allowed research on many subjects to go beyond geographical boundaries (e.g., Lezama-Solano et al., 2019). Therefore, creating opportunities for doctoral students to engage in research activities in other societies and cultural contexts becomes important for their learning. Without evidence, we cannot assume that graduate students coming from leadership degree programs have built a globalized perspective through the curriculum. At the same time, leadership scholarship and education have been challenged around the world for their limitations in this respect (Ashford & Sitkin, 2019; Chin, Trimble, & Garcia, 2018; Riggio, 2019). Criticisms include weak interdisciplinary collaborations, narrow views of leadership as a position, systematic biases in leadership conceptualization, and prevailing male-centric and Western-centric bias (Hino, 2019; Kellerman, 2012; Nahavandi & Krishnan, 2018; Riggio, 2019). Rost and Barker (2000) argue that leadership education does not address the complex relationships among people created by globalization.

It is incumbent upon leadership programs to infuse global and multicultural perspectives throughout the curriculum. In the case of doctoral students in globally focused programs, specific training in international research methods is critical. Institutional support for international research training currently takes a variety of forms and is not consistently available across universities or programs. The next section discusses some examples of how institutions are responding to the need for international research training.

Enhancing Institutional Support for International Research Training

There is currently no central resource in the field to guide institutions in training international research methods. An internet search of "international" and "cross-cultural" "research training" revealed that there is a myriad of approaches across institutions. There are resources offered through offices of international research, internal training courses for faculty and students, and external training sessions open to the wider field. Collected examples are not exhaustive but representative of current practices. It is important to acknowledge that publicly available information on international research training, scholarship, and curriculum is scarce and may not provide complete descriptions of available resources.

Offices of International Research

Several universities offer centralized resources for international research through dedicated offices of research. The Office of Global Research Engagement (OGRE) at the University of Florida assists international research endeavors by offering *resources* for funding, preparing proposals, connections to other researchers (Supporting Faculty to Build Knowledge Globally, n. a.). Similarly, the University of Michigan' Survey Research Center has an International Unit dedicated to supporting international survey design and implementation of survey infrastructure development and technical innovations (International Unit, n. a.)

One of the most comprehensive set of resources and standards for international research was found through The University of California (Berkeley) Human Subjects Research in an International Setting. It provides detailed checklists for researchers, along with clear ethical and regulatory standards related to the setting in which the research will be conducted. Researchers must demonstrate a clear understanding of local context (local laws, culture, tradition, and language, current political and social climate) in their research design and process. Investigators are encouraged to partner with local researchers. They are also required to reflect on and describe their expertise and specific qualifications (e.g., relevant coursework, background, experience, and training) (Human Subjects Research in an International Setting, n. a.). The guidance provided by this office reflects stringent training requirements for researchers so they may adequately demonstrate their preparation to collect valid and reliable data across cultures while minimizing bias.

Internal Training Courses in International Research

There are limited but promising examples of research curriculum within institutions that include international scholarly components, field experiences or methodologies. Some were offered as courses, while others were offered as training seminars, immersion experiences or facilitated access to research networks.

Course-Based Training

Most degree programs that offer an international research course have one or two courses available. Boston University's Global Study & Research initiatives supports international large and small scale studies to improve human condition, to enhance world primary health care among many other global areas through coursework. A search of 7000 courses revealed two courses, Psychology of Social Oppression and Children and Culture, that discuss cross-cultural research issues and alternative models of looking at diverse realities (Boston University Course Search, n. a.). Troy University's Ph.D. program offers a course called Internship in Global Leadership that has research components (Troy University, n.d.). The Center for Global Curriculum Studies at the Doctor of Education (Ed.D) degree program at Seattle Pacific University supports graduate students by facilitating international research connections in the field of education. Among many activities, the CGCS offers two on-campus doctoral seminars: "Research in Curriculum and Instruction" and "Trends and Research in Global Education," and supports doctoral students with resources in conducting international research on education-related topics (The Center for Global Curriculum Studies, n. a.). While the Ph.D. in Global Leadership Program at Indiana Institute of Technology offers two courses in its curriculum that incorporate international research: International Research Methods and Global Practicum (Indiana Institute of Technology, n.d.). Later in this chapter, Dr. Tolstikov-Mast discusses the design thinking behind the International Research Methods course she created.

Only one institution was found to offer a range of international research courses as a part of a concentration in Global Health: Renaissance School of Medicine at Stony Brooks University. The School offers courses such as Medical Spanish, International Research Elective, International Clinical Elective, and International Language Immersion that may be taken as elective credits (Curriculum, n.a.).

Seminar-Based Training

Two universities were found to offer seminars for international researchers. The office of the Vice President for Research at Brown University conducts an international research session on IRB policy on international research (International Research, November 17, 2020). While The Center for Global Curriculum Studies in the Doctor of Education (EdD) degree program at Seattle Pacific University offers two on-campus doctoral seminars: "Research in Curriculum and Instruction" and "Trends and Research in Global Education," and supports doctoral students in conducting international research on education-related topics (The Center for Global Curriculum Studies, n. a.).

Immersion Experiences

Several universities have established international research abroad programs for international scholarly training. New Jersey Institute of Technology is part of Global E3 (The Global Engineering Education Exchange Program), a group of leading universities around the world committed to educating internationally-experienced engineering graduates. One of the partners, the German Academic Exchange Service (DAAD) offers the RISE (Research Internships in Science and Engineering) professional research opportunities to spend a summer working with German doctoral students on serious research projects. This experiential program allows doctoral students to integrate the international undergraduates directly into the lab work and serve as personal and professional mentors (International Research Programs and Opportunities, n. a.).

Tufts University also embraced experiential learning and mentorship approach. Its Global Research Assistant Program (GRAP) allows Tufts students to work with Tufts faculty on at least an 8-weeks summer international research projects. The 2020 Global Research Assistant Program (GRAP) Projects are offered in physics, bioinformatics, biology, agriculture and animal leadership across 5 countries (Global Research Assistant Program, n.a.).

Long-term international research experience is part of Long Island University's Bachelor of Arts in Global Studies. The senior year research curriculum includes International Research and Internship Semester (IRIS). Students carry an independent international research project developing expertise on a global issue of their choice. Based on the proposal developed in their Junior year, students carry out their IRIS program at one of the LIU Global IRIS sites (Costa Rica, Australia, China, or Spain) or with one of LIU Global's partner organizations (e.g., Bali, Germany, Trinidad & Tobago, Thailand, and Morocco) (International Research and Internship Semester (IRIS), n. a.).

St. Mary's University (Texas) experimented with international research assignments where 27 undergraduate students (68% self-identified as Hispanic, and 52% as first generation/low income) engaged in field studies on the island of Roatán, Honduras. The field study is interdisciplinary with emphases on comparative psychology and environmental science. Students had the opportunity to design independent research projects, and the majority of the students had taken either statistics and/ or research methods courses or had been involved in smaller, independent research projects prior to attending the field study (Hill & Karlin, 2019).

Immersion experiences to conduct international research may be particularly impactful for student learning. Mu et al. (2018) and Jiang and Shen's (2019) research with Chinese students engaged in Ph.D. training outside of China revealed pressures to conform to Western academic authority, lack of acknowledgement of intellectual contribution of non-Western thinking (Mu et al., 2018). Thus, the exchange provided opportunities for doctoral students to interact across the globe to confront Western-centric research education, educating reflexive knowledge workers and make possible culturally inclusive and multiculturally appropriate research collaborations (Mu et al., 2018). According to Jiang and Shen (2019), a substantial number European-trained Chinese PhD returnees continued working in research partnership, exchanging Western-Eastern approaches to research and even publishing in co-authorship with their European supervisors.

Holliday (2017) also looked at the learning impact of immersion experiences in research by interviewing nine doctoral students at a British university: an American, living and working in Mexico, a Bangladeshi living and working in the UK and Kuwait, three British nationals, a German Iranian having lived and worked in the UAE, a Malaysian, a Mexican, and a South Korean. The purpose of the study was to look into a conflict between an approach to the British Ph.D. study and the cultural orientations of "international" students. Students revealed that the school and classroom environment helped them develop interculturality through reflexive engagements realizing that shared reflexivity among methodologically and culturally diverse colleagues is at the core of interculturality and understanding of cultural complexity. At the same time, students shared that functioning in English as a second language environment jeopardizes their intellectual credibility. Thus, urging us to think how we understand internationalization and the nature of academic knowledge and process, their intellectual credibility may be jeopardized due to language competence. The study concluded that in international research, when diverse colleagues interact with each other in new domains, it's no longer possible to talk simplistically about cultural differences and influence of cultural background on research.

External Training Sessions in International Research

There appears to be an opportunity for institutions to design and offer externally facing international research training, as few institutions were found to offer this. John Hopkins University Advanced Academic Programs offers a Certificate in International Research Administration Management. The program is designed to enhance competencies and skills in research contracts and agreements, regulatory affairs, research infrastructure, function, regulatory and ethical issues, and international research collaborations (Graduate Certificate, n. a).

Another example is the IIE-GIRE (Graduate International Research Experiences), a fellowship program for doctoral engineering students supported by the National Science Foundation (NSF). The program offers an opportunity to conduct innovative research abroad for 3 − 5 months and create research connections between doctoral' student's home and host institutions. IIE also offers enrichment webinars to introduce critical topics in the international STEM arena (About IIE-GIRE, n.a.). Another NSF initiative in international research is offered via the Integrative Graduate Education and Research Traineeship Program (IGERT). The program is designed to elevate the importance of offering interdisciplinary, international, and interorganizational (I3) research collaboration experiences for doctoral students (Schmidt et al., 2012).

In our exploration of how institutions are providing international research training, it appears that one of the most popular and expedient ways to provide this training is through coursework. While this may be the most straight-forward way to incorporate this into a degree program, our review shows that there are dynamic opportunities to also build in immersion experiences to practice skills and ongoing courses and seminars to further develop students and faculty alike. Since courses are a prime vehicle to introduce students to international research methods, the next section discusses one of the author's experience designing a course within a global leadership Ph.D. degree program.

Developing an International Research Course – Dr. Yulia Tolstikov-Mast's Experience

In 2011, as a Lead Faculty of a newly established online doctoral program in global leadership I had extensive discussions with doctoral students about their plans for dissertation research. Many students wanted to conduct studies outside the United States. If their choice was domestic research, students still planned to engage with diverse populations (e.g., immigrants, diverse gender, ethnicity or race groups, refugees, Native American groups). At that time, I was also working on a Russian followership study in Russia that reinforced for me unique expectations of international research even if a researcher is a member of the same cultural group. Conversations with my students and my own scholarly experience led me to embark on a long journey: development of a doctoral global leadership research course (that I taught for about six years) and later, proposing and editing this handbook with my colleagues.

The course design was an exciting and challenging process. Leadership studies had very limited conversations about an international leadership research process (e.g., Peterson, & Hunt, 1997), and the field had no textbooks to offer to emerging scholars. However, I was finding relevant publications in other fields and outside the United States (e.g., organizational psychology, bio-medics and bioethics, indigenous research in New Zealand) to address the learning objectives of the course (e.g., Anderson, & Steneck, 2011; Ryan, Leong, & Oswald, 2012; Smith, 2012).

The main purpose of the course was to introduce doctoral students to the international leadership research process, including influences of culture on leadership theory development, ethical research standards across cultures, cross-cultural approaches to rigor, international sampling, concept translations, publication standards and others. Diverse (Western and non-Western) course readings, discussions, and assignments introduced students to ideas that leadership research methods generally have a common bias towards Western or European ways of thinking. Thus, the class centered on how to capture evidence of authentic leadership and followership in diverse communities using an international leadership research paradigm.

The core course assignment was a four stages International Collaboration Project where students had to apply advanced research skills necessary to conduct original qualitative and quantitative research and advanced critical thinking skills as well as to demonstrate responsibility, accountability, ethical consciousness, and adherence to legal, professional and educational standards of global leadership. In addition, the course aimed to teach about integrity, rigor, and validity of international research, international sampling strategies, work with gatekeepers, culture-specific approaches to research design, and others. To develop as international leadership scholars, students were asked to journal throughout the course to reflect on challenges and rewards of conducting international research and working in international research collaborations, and their self-development as international leadership researchers.

Table 25.1 8-Week International Research Collaboration Project: Course Activities

Weeks	Phase	Tasks
1.	Project Planning	Introduction to the course. Class discussions and readings.
2.	Project Planning	Introduction to the project and an international partner.Assigning international teams and international team members introductions.Class discussions and readings.
3.	Project Planning	International teams start collaborating and discussing phases of the project.
4.	Phase 1	DUE
5.	Phase 2	DUE
6.	Phase 3	DUE
7.	Phase 4	DUE
8.	Debrief	Exchange written feedback between international partners (faculty collect and share combined feedback). Class discussions and readings. Individual Reflections

The main premise of the assignment was that as scholar-practitioners in the field of global leadership, doctoral graduates would be expected not only to understand global leadership content but also act as global leaders and participate in international research projects (including initiating, designing, and conducting them in collaborations with international research partners). The task of the assignment was to engage in a session-long international research collaboration to develop a draft of an international research proposal. Prior to the start of the session, I identified an international partner for a real-life simulation. The goal was to form several international teams (mixing my students with students/researchers in other countries) and task those teams to work on a simulation under the supervision of two professors, me and a professor at an international university.

Every stage of the project had a deliverable where teams had to produce a document addressing research-related questions thoroughly but scientifically concisely. Phase one, for example, encouraged research teammates to do some prior planning to determine feasibility of a study (e.g., consider each other's research training, including report on research skills and competencies of an international research partner to understand commonalities and differences in international research approaches, financial and legal considerations, rationale for a potential applied international research topic). The second phase asked to analyze unique contextual elements to consider in the study, explore ethical research traditions pertaining to their specific international research environment, discuss sampling strategies and identify potential challenges, and design informed consent form considering local expectations. Phase three required description of the research purpose and a brief theoretical framework (based on Western and non-Western scholarship), present philosophical assumptions to guide a study and identify any personal assumptions or biases that might impact research. The final phase four included a choice and explanation of a research method and design, a brief write-up of a method section, examples of potential interview questions or survey instruments (in English and a local language). Finally, to conclude the assignment, groups had to articulate study feasibility and importance (practical and scholarly) for global leadership. Rubrics helped guide students' work, and course professors served as consultants and mediators on the project. International quarrels were inevitable, and course professors helped both sides to stay focused on their joint project and on discussing and negotiating differences.

I was fortunate to partner with the universities and researchers in Peru (The Universidad San Ignacio de Loyola, Lima) and Russia (Saint Petersburg State University of Economics) to design and run the research project. As a coordinator, I learned to stay flexible and ready to adapt any day of the course. Relying on transparent communication with my international partners using WhatsApp, Viber, FaceTime to reach each other promptly across time zones and geographic distance was paramount. In Peru, I had to modify the project a week prior to the start of the course, as my students ended up working with only one researcher. In Russia, however, I was able to work with several groups (a class of upper level master's students and a group of scholars pursuing a Candidate of Science degree (Kandidat Nauk is the aspirantura) (Doctoral Programmes, n. a.).

Doctoral students learned that research expectations and approaches to research are not universal. For example, some business and social science Magistr degrees in Russia require a strong research preparation, thus, graduates have sufficient training to engage with the U.S. Ph.Ds. on research. A Candidate of Science degree does not require research courses but includes an independent research work under supervision and mentorship of a chair; countries have different start for semesters and academic years, informed consent is likely to be modified to meet local context and ethical research standards, some research topics are a no-go due to cultural or historical traditions, any translation of an interview protocol or survey instrument needs to be triangulated, etc. Like in any international professional interactions, doctoral students had to consider time zones, electronic communication protocols, intercultural communication challenges, pressure of deadlines or negotiation of tasks.

With Covid-19, many universities have been looking for opportunities to meet educational goals without travel. Virtual collaborations between international universities and programs could help add needed internalization to any curriculum including research curriculum. Class collaborations are challenging undertakings that require extra time and energy to put together. They also require additional administrative support and potential course releases.

I was excited to locate an article in the food science education area that described a similar experience with an international collaborative research course (Lezama-Solano et al., 2019). International Research Experience (IRE) graduate class at Kansas State University (KSU) offered an international sensory research project in collaboration with Tallinn University of Technology (TTU) (Estonia). Like in my course, the main part of IRE included remote learning where KUS students used Zoom and other social media to interact with students at TTU. However, IRE also included a travel component to the local site of their Estonian counterparts at the end of the course.

Schmidt et al. (2012) commented that collaborative research education experiences would benefit from having a participatory class culture and very engaged professors to motivate interactive teaching and learning. Collaborating teams should be presented with real-world problems that need research-driven solutions, and students gain research skills when they apply their knowledge to unfamiliar situations. Although I did not encounter any publications on international research collaboration in undergraduate, graduate, or doctoral leadership subject courses or research courses, scholarship suggests interdisciplinary learning that includes collaboration across national boundaries and cultural backgrounds are important to teach students to how to capture local realities and to face challenges in the field of international science (Borrego & Newswander, 2010; Morse at al., 2007; Omeri et al., 2003).

While this course provided a solid introduction to international leadership research, as Dr. Williams discusses in her survey of doctoral students additional, and ongoing skill building is important. Degree programs, institutional research boards and institutions themselves should consider the pre-requisite training their students should and will receive in international contexts and multicultural societies prior to conducting research in the field.

Conclusion

This chapter examined teaching international research methods through the perspectives and experiences of doctoral students themselves, the role of faculty in enhancing students' self-efficacy in this area, and additional ways that institutional support for international research can be put into place. Scholars argue that, typically, doctoral programs do not train students in how to conduct studies across societal, intellectual, paradigmatic layers to understand diverse stakeholder perspectives and participate in complex research teams to solve real life challenges (Borrego & Newswander, 2010; Lezama-Solano et al., 2019; Hollis, & Eren, 2016). Without a solid foundation of training, these novice researchers have challenges to function in varied and complex settings that characterize an increasingly globalized world. More importantly, the absence of comprehensive international research training limits the effectiveness of research itself to advance knowledge and practice. Institutions can rectify this situation with targeted research training and requirements and by infusing multicultural perspectives and considerations throughout curriculum and co-curricular experiences. There are larger scale opportunities, as well, for doctoral programs to proactively teach researchers to work across disciplines, cultures, and institutions.

References

About IIE-GIRE. (n.a.). *Graduate international research experiences.* https://www.iie.org/Programs/Graduate-International-Research-Experiences.

Anderson, M. S., & Steneck, N. H. (2011). *International research collaborations: Much to be gained, many ways to get in trouble.* Routledge.

Ashford, S. J., & Sitkin, S. B. (2019). From problems to progress: A dialogue on prevailing issues in leadership research. *The Leadership Quarterly, 30*(4), 454–460.

Auxier, C. R., Hughes, F. R., & Kline, W. B. (2003). Identity development in counselors-in training. *Counselor Education and Supervision, 43*, 25–38.

Borrego, M., & Newswander, M. L. (2010). Definitions of interdisciplinary research: Toward graduate-level interdisciplinary learning outcomes. *The Review of Higher Education, 34*, 61–84.

Boston University Course Search. ?A3B2 tlse=0.6pt?>https://www.bu.edu/phpbin/course-search/search.php?page=w0&pagesize=10&adv=1&nolog=&search_adv_all=%22cross-cultural+research%22+&yearsem_adv=*&credits=*&hub_match=all&pagesize=10.

Chin, J. L., Trimble., J. E., & Garcia, J. E. (2018). (Eds.). *Global and culturally diverse leaders and leadership: New dimensions and challenges for business, education and society.* Emerald Publishing.

Curriculum. (n.a.). Renaissance School of Medicine, Stony Brooks University. https://renaissance.stonybrookmedicine.edu/global_medical_education/curriculum.

Doctoral Programmes. (n. a.). *Education in Russia for foreigners.* http://en.russia.edu.ru/edu/description/sysobr/925/.

Dollarhide, C. T., Gibson, D. M., & Moss, J. M. (2013). Professional identity development of counselor education doctoral students. *Counselor Education and Supervision, 52*(2), 137–150.

Gardner, S. K., & Mendoza, P. (2010). *On becoming a scholar: Socialization and development in doctoral education.* Stylus.

Gelso, C. J., & Lent, R. W. (2000). Scientific training and scholarly productivity: The person, the training environment, and their interaction. In S. D. Brown & R. W. Lent (Eds.), *Handbook of counseling psychology* (3rd ed., pp. 109–139). Wiley.

Global Research Assistant Program. (n.a.). *Global tufts.* https://global.tufts.edu/GRAP-students#2020-global-research-assistant-program-(grap)-projects.

Graduate Certificate. (n. a). John Hopkins University advanced academic programs. https://advanced.jhu.edu/academics/certificates/.

Hill, H. M., & Karlin, M. (2019). Reflections on an international research immersion field study as a high impact practice to produce publishable papers by underrepresented undergraduates. *Frontiers in Psychology, 10*(601). doi:10.3389/fpsyg.2019.00601.

Hino, K. (2019). Are leadership theories Western-centric? Transcending cognitive differences between the East and the West. In R. Riggio, (Ed.), *What's wrong with leadership? Improving leadership, research, and practice.* Routledge.

Hollis, F. H., & Eren, F. (2016). Implementation of real-world experiential learning in a food science course using a food industry-Integrated approach. *Journal of Food Science Education, 15*(4), 109–119. doi:10.1111/1541-4329.12092.

Holliday, A. (2017). PhD students, interculturality, reflexivity, community and internationalisation. *Journal of Multilingual and Multicultural Development, 38*(3), 206–218.

Human Subjects Research in an International Setting. (n. a.). Berkeley Human Research Protection Program. https://cphs.berkeley.edu/international.html.

Indiana Institute of Technology. (n.d.). *Ph.D. in Global Leadership.* https://phd.indianatech.edu.

International Research. (November 17, 2020). Office of the President for Research. https://events.brown.edu/research/view/event/event_id/191837.

International Research and Internship Semester (IRIS). (n. a.). LIU Global. https://liu.edu/global/Academics/program-locations/International-Research-Internship-Semester.

International Research Programs and Opportunities. (n. a.). Undergraduate Research and Innovation. http://centers.njit.edu/uri/programs/international.php.

International Unit. (n. a.). Institute for Social Research, Survey Research Center. https://www.src.isr.umich.edu/services/international-unit/.

Jiang, J., & Shen, W. (2019). International mentorship and research collaboration: Evidence from European-trained Chinese PhD returnees. *Frontiers of in Education China, 14*, 180–205. doi:10.1007/s11516-019-0010-z

Kellerman, B. (2012). *The end of leadership.* HarperCollins.

Lambie, G. W., & Vaccaro, N. (2011). Doctoral counselor education students' levels of research self-efficacy, perceptions of the research training environment, and interest in research. *Counselor Education and Supervision, 50*, 243–258.

Larson, L. M., & Besett-Alesch, T. M. (2000). Bolstering the scientist component in the training of scientist-practitioners: One program's curriculum modifications. *The Counseling Psychologist, 28*, 873–896.

Lezama-Solano, A., Castro, M., Chambers, D., Timberg, L., Koppel, K., Chambers, E. IV., & Huizi, Y. (2019). Benefits, challenges, and opportunities of conducting a collaborative research course in an international university partnership: A study case between Kansas State University and Tallinn University of Technology. *Journal of Food Science Education, 18*(4), 78–86. doi:10.1111/1541-4329.12162 https://onlinelibrary.wiley.com/doi/epdf/10.1111/1541-4329.12162.

Morse, W., Nielsen-Pincus, M., Force, J. E., & Wulfhorst, J. D. (2007). Bridges and barriers to developing and conducting interdisciplinary graduate-student team research. *Ecology and Society, 12*(2), 429.

Mu, G. M., Zhang, H., Cheng, W., Fang, Y., Li, S., Wang, X., & Dooley, K. (2018). Negotiating scholarly identity through an international doctoral workshop: A cosmopolitan approach to doctoral education. *Journal of Studies in International Education, 23*(1), 139–153. doi:10.1177/1028315318810840. https://journals.sagepub.com/doi/pdf/10.1177/1028315318810840.

Nahavandi, A., & Krishnan, H. (2018). Indo-European leadership (IEL): A non-Western leadership perspective. In J. L. Chin, J. E. Trimble, & J. E. Garcia (Eds.), *Global and culturally diverse leaders and leadership: New dimensions, opportunities, and challenges for business, industry, education and society* (pp. 105–123). Emerald Publishing.

Omeri, A., Malcolm, P., Ahern, M., & Wellington, B. (2003). Meeting the challenges of cultural diversity in the academic setting. *Nurse Education in Practice, 3*(1), 5–22. doi:10.1016/S1471-5953(02)00026-4.

Peterson, M. F., & Hunt, J. G. (1997). International perspectives on international leadership. *The Leadership Quarterly, 8*(3), 203–231. doi:10.1016/S1048-9843(97)90002-3.

Riggio, R. (Ed.). (2019). *What's wrong with leadership? Improving leadership, research, and practice.* Routledge.

Rost, J. C., & Barker, R. A. (2000). Leadership education in colleges: Toward a 21st century paradigm. *Journal of Leadership Studies, 7*(1), 3–12. doi:10.1177/107179190000700102.

Ryan, A. M., Leong, F. T., & Oswald, F. L. (2012). *Conducting multinational research: Applying organizational psychology in the workplace.* American Psychological Association.

Samuel, M., & Vithal, R. (2011). Emergent frameworks of research teaching and learning in a cohort-based doctoral programme. *Perspectives in Education, 29*(1), 76–87.

Sands, R. G., Bourjolly, J., & Roer-Strier, D. (2007). Crossing cultural barriers in research interviewing. *Qualitative Social Work, 6*(3), 353–372.

Schmidt, A. H., Robbins, A. S. T., Combs, J. K., Freeburg, A., Jesperson, R. G., Rogers, H. S., Sheldon, K. S., & Wheat, E. (2012). A new model for training graduate students to conduct interdisciplinary, inter-organizational, and international research, *BioScience, 62*, (3), 296–304. doi:10.1525/bio.2012.62.3.11. https://academic.oup.com/bioscience/article/62/3/296/359554.

Shivy, V. A., Worthington Jr, E. L., Wallis Jr, A. B., & Hogan Jr, C. (2003). Doctoral research training environments (RTEs): Implications for the teaching of psychology. *Teaching of Psychology, 30*(4), 297–302.

Smith, L. T. (2012). *Decolonizing methodologies: Research and indigenous peoples* (2nd ed.). Zed Books.

Supporting Faculty to Build Knowledge Globally. (n. a.). International Research. https://internationalcenter.ufl.edu/faculty-engagement/international-research.

The Center for Global Curriculum Studies. (n. a.). Seattle Pacific University. https://spu.edu/academics/school-of-education/graduate-programs/doctoral-programs/center-for-global-curriculum-studies

Troy University. (n.d.) Ph.D. in Global Leadership. https://www.troy.edu/academics/academic-programs/graduate/global-leadership.html.

Valencia-Forrester, F. (2019). Internships and the PhD: Is this the future direction of work-integrated learning in Australia? *International Journal of Work-Integrated Learning, 20*(4), 389–400.

Vaughan, M., Boerum, C., & Whitehead, L. S. (2019). Action research in doctoral coursework: Perceptions of independent research experiences. *International Journal for the Scholarship of Teaching and Learning, 13*(1), 6.

Zhang, L. E., & Guttormsen, D. S. (2016). Multiculturality as a key methodological challenge during in-depth interviewing in international business research. *Cross Cultural & Strategic Management*. doi:10.1108/CCSM-07-2014-0084.

26

Race, Whiteness, Intersectionality, and Teaching International Leadership Research

Surbhi Malik, Erika L. Dakin Kirby, and Sarah Singletary Walker

Introduction

In August of 2020, we presented on a campus workshop entitled "Teaching Anti-Racism in the Undergraduate Curriculum." We work in different disciplines: Erika in Communication Studies, Surbhi in English, and Sarah in Management/Organizational Behavior. Our presentations were related but covered different aspects of the conversation. Later that evening, we received an email from Yulia – our colleague at Creighton and a co-editor of this *Handbook* – that laid out a compelling vision for an invited chapter by deftly weaving together our distinct approaches into a significant intervention for teaching international leadership research. Our presentations on anti-racism had reflected the urgency to address in our pedagogy the rapidly changing American racial landscape in the aftermath of the George Floyd and Breonna Taylor killings. However, Yulia's vision asked us to extend that vision outward, and to question what relationship, if any, existed between our discussion of systemic racism in the United States of America (USA) and teaching international leadership research.

This chapter addresses this question from the vantage point of three scholars with backgrounds in different academic disciplines who occupy different racial positions. The dialogue models the directions we need most in teaching international research: (a) cross-disciplinary conversations, (b) epistemic humility instead of "epistemic dominance" (Stein, 2017), and (c) a crosspollination of ideas that allows for challenging and changing our own assumptions, categories, and definitions of leadership. The U.S. national racial context is not easily visible within the contours of international leadership research; our dialogue makes it more manifest and traces the implications of that visibility for pedagogy. Indeed, making the structures of white supremacy and imperialism visible in international leadership research has vital implications for studying leadership everywhere.

This chapter is structured as a conversation with Surbhi serving as the facilitator and moderator. We have indicated the questions in italics and bold to set them off from the regular text. And since Surbhi also participates and offers her own insights, the different formatting of the questions allows us to demarcate the transition to the next question. We started out by individually writing out a few thoughts and identified some clear overlaps – such as intersectionality and pedagogical approaches – on which we based the initial questions. The conversation unfolded over email, which gave us more time to ponder what the others were saying. Since we came at this topic from different directions, we thought it might be more insightful if we could show our readers the underlying frame of the seemingly concrete ideas, not only in content but also through the Q&A format. We wanted to

DOI: 10.4324/9781003003380-26

model how an interdisciplinary conversation on international leadership research pedagogy can compel us to revise our standpoints and transform our future research trajectories. A conversation, we discovered anew, is an opportunity not simply to speak and share but to learn and change.

Conversation Among Authors

SURBHI: So, let me begin by asking you a little bit about your own positionality as a scholar doing research on and teaching about race. How does your own racial position, with all its contradictions and complexities, inform your teaching praxis? Or more broadly, how does your biography influence your pedagogy?

ERIKA: I identify as White, heterosexual, she/her/hers, Catholic, upper-middle-class, almost 50, a professor, and a mom. I grew up in a small city in North Central Iowa where the population was mostly White. I am a product of Catholic schooling from first grade through high school. I attended Buena Vista University for college, a Predominantly White Institution (PWI) in an even smaller town in Iowa with about 1,200 students. And since my family was lower income, our only travel was the occasional trip by car to the Twin Cities or Des Moines. So, my life into and through college never really took me out of my bubble of Whiteness.

Since college, I have lived in two major metropolitan areas: Omaha and Minneapolis/St. Paul. I attended the University of Minnesota-Twin Cities for my M.A. degree and the University of Nebraska-Lincoln for my Ph.D. Being exposed to new people and new perspectives in the Twin Cities started to shift my attention toward "isms"; I was calling myself a feminist when I started my Ph.D. program at age 24. I started seriously interrogating forms of oppression beyond sexism after living in (super segregated) Omaha and seeing the radicalized difference in living in White and BIPOC (Black, Indigenous, People of Color) bodies in my city, which at one point was the most dangerous city in the U.S. to be Black and male. I committed to teaching from a standpoint of anti-oppression in my 30s; later than I would like to admit, but early enough to raise children who continually question structures of privilege. Today, I teach courses on "isms" and privilege-oppression, especially as related to race and gender.

But the Black Lives Matter movement and becoming involved in antiracist efforts on campus and in my community really pushed me to think more deeply on how my Whiteness affects my views on the world. Frankenberg (1993) defines Whiteness as "[a] a location of structural advantage, of race privilege…[b] a 'standpoint', a place from which White people look at ourselves, at others, and at society…[and c] a set of cultural practices that are usually unmarked and unnamed" (p. 1). How does Whiteness impact my worldview?

As an example, I was at an Omaha Community Council on Racial Justice and Reconciliation meeting where 75-ish people of a wide mix of racial identities had gathered. One of my Black friends opened the discussion and asked: "So how do we achieve racial reconciliation in our city?" As might be expected, the Black and Brown people present spoke first…and then White people were asked why we were not speaking (and then a few did speak). After the meeting, I went to the Council and offered to do a "real" research project to see what people thought about achieving racial reconciliation. While my proposal was well received, looking back I can see how my Whiteness permeated all of this: (a) my feelings in the meeting itself reflected a right to (White) comfort, and (b) my thoughts that "this could have been done better" reflected White "only one right way to do things" thinking (see also Okun, n.d., on white supremacy culture). One element of Whiteness is the "authority" to determine what is/not knowledge, and I reproduced this by assuming that since the information was not gathered through structured research that it was not as legitimate (Le & Matias, 2019). But perhaps the leaders of that meeting accomplished exactly what they were trying to do! Who was/am I to question their approach? No matter how much I educate myself, I can still operate under the assumptions of Whiteness.

SARAH: I identify as a Black, heterosexual (she/her), married mother of one, and an ally to marginalized people. I am technically a "millennial" who prefers physical books to electronic texts. I do not really have a "home" base. My father served in the United States Air Force for 30 years. Thus, growing up, I lived throughout the United States and spent over six years living abroad. I moved to Germany at the age of two, and at one point in time, the only language I spoke was German. Later on, I attended Dillard University (DU), a small private, Historically Black College and University (HBCU) in New Orleans. My matriculation to DU was definitely about my race, but not in the way you might assume. Because my formative years were spent both living abroad, and in the Midwest, my mother wanted me to get the *Black* experience. In effect, she thought that my life as a Black female did not automatically mean that I understood what it meant to be Black. That is, attending an HBCU was meant to instill in me an awareness of Black culture. In some ways, her concerns were valid (i.e., I learned a lot about Black history at Dillard), and in other ways, I realized that lived experiences of individuals of the same racial background are not necessarily identical.

Immediately after graduating with my bachelor's degree from DU, I entered a doctoral program in Industrial-Organizational Psychology at Rice University in Houston, Texas. My mentor in graduate school inspired me to examine the everyday experiences of marginalized people (e.g., racio-ethnic minorities, pregnant women, LBGTQIA+, overweight). Overall, my research interests examine experiences of discrimination and bias in workplace settings. In addition, my research seeks to identify mechanisms for reducing displays of subtle forms of discrimination (e.g., microaggressions, incivilities). Most of my work examines status characteristics *other* than race (e.g., gender, pregnancy, weight, age, sexual orientation). As a graduate student, I *avoided* research examining race because I did not want to appear to be self-serving. That is, I did not want to seem as if I only studied groups to which I belong. Though I was not explicitly told so by anyone in my program, I felt that my legitimacy as a researcher *might* be diminished if I studied race. This was likely attributable to literature in social psychology which reveals that non-marginalized individuals who confront bias are perceived more favorably than their marginalized counterparts (see Ashburn-Nardo & Karim, 2019). Thankfully, I no longer feel this way, and in some ways feel quite the opposite. I relocated from Houston, Texas to Omaha, Nebraska about two years ago. In the last two years, race has become particularly salient to me. One might see the irony in this…I study bias and discrimination but had not previously felt significantly impacted by the constructs. Moving from one of the most diverse cities in the country (i.e., Houston) to Omaha has given me a new perspective on how our experiences vary based on where we live.

In considering how to answer the call to provide insight for pedagogy related to international leadership research, I spent some time reflecting on my beliefs about this discipline. My perception of cross-cultural (e.g., international) research has evolved. As a graduate student, I believed that international research was about collecting data *outside* of the United States. My schema was that international research might examine U.S. expatriates working abroad (Werner, 2002). In hindsight, using this framework most of the early international research literature can also be viewed from a Western (i.e., again, often in the United States) perspective, in that it sought to understand the experiences that individuals had when working in foreign countries.

In addition, my perception of international research also consisted of research which included samples from Asian, African, European, and Latin countries as being sufficient to meet the "threshold" for this distinction. Rather than understand the experiences of expatriates, this type of research sought to understand the perspectives of employees with non-U.S. origins. Today, I do not believe that international research is just about the *location* of study participants. Instead, I believe that to truly have informative international research studies, we need to do a better job at understanding the complexities (e.g., cultural differences) that transcend borders.

SURBHI: I immigrated from India to the United States, so the connection between the U.S. national racial domain and the international is baked into my immigration story. I encountered America in India before I landed on its shores. America was a part of the quotidian life in India: Barbie dolls, M★A★S★H, George Michael, and Tom Sawyer were part of our (middle-class, educated) cultural lexicon. These cultural artifacts were, of course, more than "products;" they narrated certain stories of American racial and gender ideologies and stirred our imagination of what America was or might be. This imagination was not always in sync with American realities of race and gender, I discovered later after immigrating. But the more important takeaway is that my experience exemplifies what Inderpal Grewal (2005) calls "transnational America," defined as the power of American nationalism to "produce American identities imbricated within a consumer citizenship that exceeded the bounds of the nation to become transnational" (p. 8). In India, I never questioned this American presence; I took it for granted. But a key moment In Lisa Lowe's (1996) book, *Immigrant Acts*, changed this. Drawing on Michelle Cliff's (1995) novel *Abeng*, Lowe (1996, p. 99) talks of a young girl who recites Wordsworth's poem "Daffodils" but has never seen a daffodil in her life. Seeing my own story reflected in Lowe's book made me question why I was reciting "Daffodils," or reading American literature and British literature, in India, even though this education was disconnected from the life around me. In fact, I gravitated toward studying the intersections between American Ethnic Studies and Postcolonial Studies during graduate school because it allowed me to draw a direct line from my education in a convent school in India, a remnant of British colonialism, to why I felt "at home" in the United States. My story integrates the connections between women's experiences across continents: it was, after all, an Asian American scholar's description of a girl in a novel by a Jamaican American writer which accurately described the experience of a recent Indian immigrant woman like me.

This tapestry of our life stories and disciplinary journeys underscores that we are situated at different distances from questions of race and international leadership research. Since our work is based in the U.S. context but we also see it as inextricable from the international domain, could you please elaborate on why the intersection between the national and the international is important to bring into the classroom in the first place?

SARAH: International leadership research provides us with a lot of context for understanding how varying geopolitical and historical factors impact leaders. Previous research reveals that some aspects of leadership are universally applicable across cultures (see Den Hartog et al., 1999). For instance, we know more about cultural differences that impact the ways in which leaders effectively communicate (Den Hartog & Verburg, 1997; Gelfand et al., 2007; House et al., 2002), lead change efforts (Valikangas & Okumura, 1997), and motivate followers as a function of the national context (Gelfand et al., 2017; Li et al., 2021). It is important to acknowledge that the extant literature provides us with a lot of context pertaining to the importance of understanding boundary conditions when leading globally. We believe that having research that focuses on nationalism is a useful *starting* point for conducting and teaching about research in this area. Gelfand et al. (2017) argue that future literature should move from being discipline specific to interdisciplinary in nature to better understand cross-cultural phenomena. Moving in this direction will remove some of the silos that exist in the literature. This is particularly true for leadership research as it is inherently interdisciplinary (i.e., leaders exist in every field) but the extant literature ends to be discipline specific. In addition to doing interdisciplinary research, we should do more work to understand the complexities associated with culture. That is, when considering the landscape of the literature, we should introduce concepts related to race, culture, and *intersectionality* in international leadership curriculum and research.

ERIKA: And as we think about pedagogy(s) of teaching international approaches to leadership, there are many (unexamined, ignored) ways that Whiteness and colonialism have shaped the paradigm – a Euro-supremacist politics of knowledge (see Stein, 2017; also, we follow the National Association of Black Journalists June 2020 style guide that whenever a color is used to appropriately describe race then it should be capitalized). Whites cannot achieve an "exteriority to the historical determinations of the place from which we speak, write, research, teach, organize, and learn" (Mitchell, 2015, p. 91). Therefore, to aspire to teaching leadership from a global perspective, we must seek to enact *epistemic justice* since "the racialized [White] framing principles of Western knowledge systems are deeply embedded" (Stein, 2017, p. 29). Speaking as a U.S. scholar, in this country we cannot talk about teaching leadership from a global perspective without teaching Whiteness, because it is seemingly invisible, the unspoken, the unmarked, upon which everything else is based. As McIntosh (1989) illustrates, many U.S. White students do not think that racism affects them because they are not BIPOC and they do not see "Whiteness" as a racial identity. And yet, race is only an issue because Whiteness exists (Le & Matias, 2019).

In other countries, a more general sense of Western- and Euro-supremacy, or the culture of the colonizer, might feel like more fruitful concept than "Whiteness." Regardless, we need to problematize the underlying notion in order "to understand the White imagination, especially in aspects of how and why (1) Whiteness centers Eurocentric curricula and discourse and (2) White educators may choose to ignore or deflect questions about their racialization in society" (Le & Matias, 2019, p. 21). Once educators recognize how they have "centered" Whiteness, a critical pedagogical perspective prompts us to consider what inequities need to be challenged in making pedagogical decisions (Pendakur & Fur, 2016). How can we balance Western/Eurocentric/White perspectives with alternative worldviews? For example, in international studies, Hagmann and Biersteker (2014) push for an "understanding that neither any single paradigmatic framework nor a native or foreign body of works should be supposed to be exclusively valid or claimed to be universally applicable" (p. 309).

In examining Whiteness in (leadership) education, Critical Race Theory (CRT) is an important epistemology organizing in legal studies that "challenges the ways in which race and racial power are constructed and represented" (Crenshaw, Gotanda, Peller, & Thomas, 1995, p. xiii). CRT scholars examine ways that racism and White privilege operate together to dominate institutions and systems. In general, CRT scholars posit that concepts of neutrality, objectivity, colorblindness (e.g., "I don't 'see' color"), and meritocracy must be challenged (see Gooden, 2012). From the opposite vantage, Critical Whiteness Studies (CWS) endeavors to reveal the invisible structures that (re)produce White supremacy and privilege (Applebaum, 2016). CWS advances the importance of vigilance among White people in examining the meaning of White privilege and how it is connected to complicity in racism. Foste (2020) uses CWS to examine student leaders and offers a discursive strategy of the *enlightenment narrative* where they are concerned with presenting themselves as racially conscious and progressive White student leaders and avoid any meaningful critique of racism and White supremacy. So, as we contemplate pedagogies to teach international leadership research, we need to center (and question) the culture of Whiteness.

SURBHI: Including international research in leadership curriculum offers a more capacious and inclusive approach. As recent scholarship attests, definitions of leadership are intimately bound to notions of whiteness and masculinity (Liu, 2020; Ospina & Foldy, 2009; Chin & Trimble, 2014). International leadership research, then, is a de-centralizing force, with the potential to dismantle power relations and hierarchies: it challenges the entrenched centers and models by bringing into view alternative forms of leadership, such as leadership styles of Australian women (Damousi, Rubenstein & Tomsic, 2014) or of educators in Asia (Hawkins, Herschock & Mason, 2007) or more community-based leadership models (Liu, 2020). As Helena Liu (2020, p. 135) puts it, anti-racist feminist theorizations of leadership greatly "expand the definitions of what is possible, where leadership no longer has to be located within heroic individuals." As such, the vocabularies of "cultural difference" and "cross-cultural contexts" are prominent in international leadership research. But I would argue that this language, so dominant in international research, is not always neatly aligned with the national vocabulary of "race." For example, Western dominance in the international context, or colonialism, is seen as something that happens in other countries, while we denote the domination of and violence against people of color within the United States as racism and not colonialism. The use of different vocabularies prevents us from seeing these two types of domination as connected.

Demonstrating for my classes that these two types of domination are indeed connected, and that the national and the international are co-constituted and intertwined, is important because it reorients our understanding of leadership research in two ways. First, it reminds us that the question of which leadership issues cross borders and are available for comparison is not neutral but "politically complicated" (Narayan, 1997, p. 86). For example, as John Hutnyk (2006, pp. 80–81) notes, British academia's avoidance of the history and anthropology of Asian labor organizational leadership reflects specific contradictory racial and colonial narratives of South Asian workers as both subservient and militant. On the one hand, this history was invisible because the South Asian workers were stereotyped as too meek to organize. On the other, this history evoked the "fear of restless natives" (Hutnyk, 2006, p. 81). The persistence of colonial ideologies, therefore, played a role in why academics eschewed this research. So, what we choose to research in international leadership needs to reckon with the question why this subject and not another, and what that choice says about our own theoretical frameworks. Second, the above example also shows that the connection between racism in the national and colonialism in the international domain helps us understand the extent to which the language of "cultural difference" obscures the brutal exclusions that racial and gender hierarchies enact. In other words, it is not enough to simply include examples of the "international" to study "cultural difference;" instead, it is important to establish how that very inclusion transforms our commonly accepted definitions of leadership and challenges the hierarchies between the West and the rest.

I want to transition now to thinking about what teaching of international research looks like in your classroom. What are the approaches you emphasize or guard against? Could you please share a few readings that you assign/would assign to teach students/ junior scholars about race, especially in the context of international research? What would you want students to take away from these readings or how do these readings significantly change their approach to international research or help them see the reverberations of race in the field?

SARAH: In developing scholars who are conducting international research, one of the areas for consideration in future research is an examination of intersectionality (Crenshaw, 1990). Recognizing that individuals living within the same country have different lived experiences is paramount for understanding boundary conditions of the constructs of interest. When conducting research, it is important to consider how both demographic (e.g., gender, race, ethnicity, age), contextual (e.g., location), and individual differences variables (e.g., personality) may have an impact on the experiences of leaders. For instance, Moorosi, Fuller, and Reilly (2018) recently published a case study that examined the experience of Black, female leaders employed as principals in three different countries (i.e., England, South Africa, United States). This work compared and contrasted their experiences serving in leadership roles while working in different parts of the world. An outside observer might assume that their racialized experiences would be very similar. However, the authors reported differences (and similarities) regarding their efficacy in leading others. Specifically, each of the principals had a similar lived experience with respect to their upbringing (i.e., came from working class backgrounds) and the types of student populations they served (i.e., majority Black). However, the pathway to their leadership positions varied significantly with one leader having explicit leadership training to move towards a principalship, whereas, another had no training in school administration and had to learn on the job. Future research may extend this work by identifying how their experiences differ from others (e.g., majority group counterparts, other marginalized groups) in similar positions, as well as to determine if their experiences are primarily a function of global context, racio-ethnicity, gender or perhaps a result of the interplay between some (or all of) these constructs (i.e., intersectionality). In addition to examining racial ethnicity, it is also important to examine intersectionality with respect to other status characteristics (e.g., sexual orientation, religion, family status).

Extending the conversation about intersectionality, it is important to acknowledge that a growing body of work examines ways to *teach* intersectionality in graduate programs. An interesting framework for library studies provides a model for redesigning curriculum to focus on intersectionality (Villa-Nicholas, 2018). This model consists of three parts: (1) making intersectionality salient in the classroom; (2) incorporating classroom assignments to facilitate learning about intersectionality (e.g., case studies, readings, classroom discussions); and (3) assessing cultural competency to examine student learning and/or behavioral change. When applied to international leadership, this framework would involve not only teaching established theory and models in international leadership curriculum, but also include content specifically related to race, culture, gender, and other status characteristics. In addition to including content specifically related to intersectionality, another approach might involve creating a course designed to examine a variety of ways in which intersectionalities have an impact on one's discipline. Naples (2009) provides an illustration of the ways in which one of her courses has evolved over time. Specifically, the article provides the reader with an understanding of how to introduce intersectionality in courses. Through written from the perspective of a faculty member teaching courses in Feminism, the author provides a series of questions (e.g., "What are the limits and possibilities of different approaches to intersectionality? How have social scientists taken up the call to intersectionality in their research?") that can be used by faculty teaching courses in a variety of disciplines. In each of these cases, whether it be weaving intersectionality throughout the entire curriculum (Villa-Nicholas, 2018) or developing a course (Naples, 2009) to delve deeper into understanding intersectionality, having these types of exposures likely results in increased cultural competency of individuals studying international leadership.

ERIKA: When teaching (leadership) research from a global perspective, White Supremacy Culture (WSC) should be emphasized. WSC is the ideology that White people and the ideas, thoughts, beliefs, and actions of White people *are superior* (see Showing Up for Racial Justice, 2019). WSC is centered in Western knowledge, which "is characterized as much by its particular content as it is by its organizing principles of progress, possession, universalism, certainty, and neutralization of difference: either through incorporation, erasure, or elimination" (Stein, 2017, p. 29). Okun (building on others) has compiled a list of behaviors/thoughts as to how WSC presents; I offer some in the context of teaching how to do international leadership research.

1. *Objectivity* is the belief that there *is* such a thing as being objective or "neutral," that people should think "logically," and that emotions are inherently irrational and should not play a role in professional work.

Lesson: Students must realize they have a unique (nonobjective) worldview that impacts how they view reality, ask research questions, and choose research methods. This translates to "assuming that everybody has a valid point and our job is to understand what that point is" (see Okun).

2. Valuing *quantity over quality* means that things that can be directly measured (e.g., number of people at a meeting) are more highly valued than things that cannot (e.g., the quality of relationality at the meeting).

Lesson: This value can certainly be tied to the ongoing debates about the inherent values of qualitative vs. quantitative scholarship (and mixtures of both, and alternative methods) and how we can "prove" each (especially with methods like autoethnography). We need to illustrate how multiple forms of research are valuable.

3. *Worship of the written word* is the WSC belief that "If it's not in a [insert form of writing here], it doesn't exist," which devalues the ways information is shared *outside* of writing in many cultures, such as oral traditions of storytelling and song as repositories of knowledge.

Lesson: We should teach students to share their scholarly findings in a multiplicity of forms, especially with groups that do not "worship" the written word. This involves challenging our own [White] beliefs about appropriate presentation(s) of results.

4. *Only one right way* is the belief there is one right way to do things, and once people are introduced to the "right" way, they will see the light and adopt it.

Lesson: Students need to interrogate this concept – emphasizing that when working with a community on a research endeavor, we need to learn about how the community "does things" and build our analysis from there. We do not inherently know the right way just because of our expertise.

5. *Paternalism* emerges when those *with* power think they are capable of making decisions for and in the interests of those *without* power.

Lesson: Most studies are constructed like this if we are being honest; we should teach students to include people who are impacted by the research in the research design when and if possible.

6. *Either/or thinking* assumes that things are good/bad, right/wrong, with us/against us; there is no sense that things can be both/and, which results in trying to simplify complex things.

Lesson: We need to teach students to be reflexive about when they have "either/or" thoughts and push to do a deeper analysis and come up with more than two alternatives in order not to simplify complex issues.

7. Ideas of *individualism* and "*I'm the only one*" emerge when people do not like to work in groups and "believe they are responsible for solving problems alone," partially because of a desire for individual recognition and credit.

Lesson: The structures of the academy and the indoctrination of first- or solo-authorship can make this tricky, but students should also realize the value in diverse perspectives on research teams and giving credit to all those who participate in an effort.

And of course, there are more facets of WSC that teacher-scholars could offer and frame in terms of research. Beyond WSC, additional lessons in Whiteness can also help in teaching and researching international leadership.

We should teach that *Whiteness does make a difference in the daily life of White people*. Professors can reinforce McIntosh's (1989) foundational work on the "invisible knapsack" where White privilege is likened to "an invisible weightless knapsack of special provisions, maps, passports, codebooks, visas, clothes, tools and blank checks." Some privileges are tied directly to knowledge and representation: "I can turn on the television or open to the front page of the paper and see people of my race widely represented" (#5)…"When I am told about our national heritage or about 'civilization,' I am shown that people of my color made it what it is" (#6)…and "I can be sure that my children will be given curricular materials that testify to the existence of their race" (#7). As one example of how a lesson could be formed from this, students could be assigned the first 20 articles that come up in a [database] search of [facet of leadership] and then be asked to log across the articles: (a) the racial identities and/or nationalities of who was studied, and (b) if the discussion of limitations involved some version of "we would have benefitted from a more diverse sample." This would illustrate how we continually make calls for more perspectives in research but do not always follow through because it is easier to represent/reproduce White/Western perspectives.

We should teach that *Whiteness can make White people racially arrogant, defensive, and/or "fragile"* – and give students tools to recognize this in themselves and others. DiAngelo (2011, 2020) offers that the insulated environment of racial privilege ("racial insulation") builds White expectations for racial comfort while at the same time lowering the ability to tolerate racial stress. She labels as universalism the idea that Whites are taught to see [our] perspectives as objective and representative of reality (also see McIntosh, 1989). Thus, "The belief in objectivity, coupled with positioning White people as outside of culture (and thus the norm for humanity), *allows Whites to view themselves as universal humans who can represent all of human experience*" (p. 59, emphasis added). Of import to achieving epistemic justice and valuing alternative ways of knowing is to ensure students understand that *racial arrogance* is a trigger of White Fragility:

> Because of White social, economic and political power within a White dominant culture… Whites are the least likely to see, understand, or be invested in validating assertions of racism and being honest about their consequences, which leads Whites to claim that they disagree with perspectives that challenge their worldview, when in fact, they don't understand the perspective (DiAngelo, 2011, p. 61).

This means we should teach students doing global leadership research to not (even unintentionally) assume their centrality in the research process.

We should teach *how Whiteness was [socially] constructed and is NOT biological* so these notions are not reproduced in research assumptions and designs. The 14-part podcast *Seeing White* discusses how Whiteness was socially constructed, from the days of bringing the first African people sold into chattel slavery in 1619 to modern constructions of Northern and Southern racism (Scene on Radio, 2017). Concentrating on the impact of Whiteness on research, Episode 8 on *Skulls and Skins* looks at the scholarly work of Samuel Morton and how he was trying to use skull shape to prove the superiority of White people, illustrating how nonobjective (even nonscientific?) research can be when immersed in WSC and when trying to "prove" racist thoughts. And to underscore the points of (re)considering power and colonialistic undertones in leadership research, the entire collection acquired by Morton was taken from public view in summer of 2020 so the skulls can be returned to the land for repatriation and burial (see Patel, 2020).

This lesson of Whiteness and research can then be furthered in terms of "scientific" knowledge on race as biological: (a) what has been amplified and (b) what has been minimized. Kendi (2019) suggests "racial science" should have ended once and for all in 2000 when the Human Genome project illustrated that in genetic terms, all human beings, regardless of race, are about 99.9% the same. This international research effort conducted from October 1990 to April 2003 to determine the DNA sequence of the entire human genome "gave us the ability…to read nature's complete genetic blueprint for building a human being" (National Human Genome Research Institute, n.d.). [And that when geneticists compare ethnic populations, they find there is more genetic diversity between populations within Africa than between Africa and the rest of the world (see Kendi, 2019).]

This "was arguably one of the most important scientific announcements ever made by a sitting head of state [President Bill Clinton] – perhaps as important to humans as landing on the moon – but the news of our fundamental equality was quickly overtaken by more-familiar arguments" of how to investigate the 0.1% of difference (see Kendi, 2019, p. 53). As echoed in *Seeing White* Episode 8: "Our science is about weapons, and capital…and not about how to heal and to create equality…I don't want to discard science at all, but I want to say that maybe we need to look at what forces are directing the kinds of questions our scientists are asking." This is the central question to help our students (re)consider the relationships between Whiteness and research: What forces are directing their questions? And do these forces allow a truly international perspective on leadership?

SURBHI: The central takeaway for my classes that teach international research is a critical reexamination of the terms of engagement with diversity and international perspectives. We especially reckon with how the efforts to include diversity, intersectionality, and cross-cultural perspectives are themselves susceptible to re-inscribing Western, colonialist paradigms. When we approach inclusion without changing the underlying, deeply entrenched "Western epistemological framework" (Stein, 2017, p. 33), we re-inscribe the same racial and gender dynamics that it purportedly aims to dismantle.

How do we include the diversity of international research in a way that dismantles the colonial epistemological framework and its attendant racial hierarchies? First, there is the question of "de-colonizing the syllabus." The term fundamentally urges us to not leave unchallenged or unques-tioned any part of knowledge production in our field, especially the cannon – the texts deemed indispensable and whose arguments often settle into an orthodoxy (Appleton 2019). For example, I include Chandra Mohanty's (2003) *Feminism Without Borders* in my "Transnational Feminism" course to illustrate how a text uses research on South Asian feminisms to challenge global feminist cannon's emphasis on an "ahistorical, universal unity" (p. 31) that does not dismantle ideas of First World dominance and Third World inferiority.

In fact, Mohanty's book offers a master class in pedagogical models on incorporating international research. For example, she critiques the "tourism" or "add-and-stir" model, which she defines as the attempt to include non-Western perspectives in the syllabus in the most superficial or perfunctory way and in which "the Euro-American narrative of the syllabus remains untouched" (Mohanty, 2003, p. 239). Such an additive approach depoliticizes the systemic effects of colonial paradigms into mere descriptions of "cultural difference." That is, "cultural difference" becomes a description rather than an analytical framework that deepens our insights into how power works in the realm of culture. For example, if we add South Asian feminism to a course on global feminist leadership to merely denote that women's leadership in the region deviates from the western norm rather than to function as an analytical framework that indicts colonial patriarchal dominance, that would signal a "tourism" approach. Instead, what we need to recuperate the political power of international re-search is the emphasis that the proliferation of new sites of research is not about addition or mul-tiplicity but an opportunity to theorize and offer fuller accounting of power structures at the global level. Keeping this in mind, Mohanty advocates that we follow a solidarity model of pedagogy that highlights points of connection and disconnection between the Western and non-Western feminist leadership but that also attends to the power/colonial relations between them.

Attending to colonial difference and its indissoluble residue of race means examining the asymmetries of power that situate Western leadership as the objective norm and reduce the different leadership approaches in "other" societies to "culture." I assign feminist philosopher Uma Narayan's (1997) book *Dislocating Cultures* because it delineates the asymmetries of power that automatically define differences in non-Western leadership styles (compared to the Western norms) as markers of "cultural difference" rather than as the complex products of historical, political, social, and economic factors. Narayan's book has important lessons for cross-cultural research, even though it is not specifically about international leadership.

The purpose of international leadership research, following Narayan's arguments, is not an endeavor of learning about "other" cultures. Instead, we must preface this research with the question of what is legible and recognizable to us as leadership in non-Western contexts in the first place and why. In other words, what do the modes of leadership recognizable to us say about our own epistemological frameworks? And how can we reorient and revise those frameworks to theorize new modes of leadership? In brief, this is not a question of bias that can be rectified with a less-biased stance, or ignorance corrected by knowledge, but of thinking about the global power structures that determine what kinds of leadership are recognizable and considered valid.

For example, in the course on "Transnational Feminism," of which anti-racist feminist leadership is a vital touchstone, I screen the Oscar winner Sharmeen Obaid-Chinoy's films that chronicle violence against women in Pakistan: *Saving Face* (2012), about acid attack victims, and *The Girl in the River* (2015) about honor killings. The frame I use to teach these films shares the aims of this *Handbook*: to not simply study the content of the research – in this case, not to learn the sociological truth of honor killings or acid attacks – but to study the problems of learning about "other" cultures. Watching these films and reading Narayan, my students and I discuss how these specific topics more easily cross over into America. We also discuss that while we might recognize the director Obaid-Chinoy as a leader-activist, she can also be interpreted as a "native-informant" figure giving us "insider information" about her/ their "culture." Other questions emerge: Do we recognize the Pakistani women who are the victims of acid attacks or attempted honor killings also as leaders? To what extent is our conception of leadership, especially feminist leadership, anchored in ideas of progress or forward movement demanded by Western epistemological frameworks? Is it possible for us to see stasis or a movement sideways as leadership? How can we read these everyday women's voices – which are not about status, power, or control, but about struggle against their circumstances – as leadership?

This is where the idea of "cross-pollination" between cultures, or what Vijay Prashad (2003) refers to as polyculturalism, becomes helpful. Following Prashad's theory, the power of cross-cultural work in the above example would be to not situate the Pakistani women, or their leadership, as fundamentally "foreign" or "other," but to harness it to reimagine what we mean by anti-racist feminist leadership in the first instance. "Cross-pollination" of cultures requires us to put these women's leadership in dialogue with our own notions of what leadership means. It means to recognize the specific points of dialogue and linkages – of history and knowledge – between the Pakistani women's resistance and American women's struggles that might not be associated with a movement or that might not necessarily result in a "triumph." This approach will help us imagine and nourish international leadership research as a site of cross-cultural work based on a recognition of common struggles that Western epistemological frameworks obscure.

SARAH: So how do I teach concepts related to diversity, inclusion, and intersectionality? I utilize a variety of approaches to examine these concepts. Below are some examples of my pedagogy and recommendations for how this may relate to teaching international leadership.

One of the most salient examples of teaching about diversity is actually in a course on diversity management. Early in the semester, I ask the students to read Minor's (1959) foundational work titled, "Body Ritual among the Nacirema" and ask students to discuss their impressions of the Nacirema. This short is written from the perspective of an individual who is encountering the Nacirema for the first time. The irony of the story is that the Nacirema (American spelled backwards) represent people living in America today. Prior to knowing what the story is about, students come up with a list of descriptions that consists of several negative stereotypes that suggest the culture is primitive, uncivilized, unorthodox, and perhaps misunderstood by outsiders. Prior to revealing information about the irony of the article, students have to grapple with how they may view cultures that they consider to be different from their own. After realizing that the article is written from the perspective of a more advanced civilization viewing American culture, the students are often surprised but also quickly understand how the terminology utilized in the reading relates to American culture. We conclude our discussion by identifying how our misperceptions can influence how we view others. I have found this to be a powerful example because the students in the course would not label American culture as being primitive or uncivilized. Yet, they do learn that one's perceptions can lead to erroneous conclusions about others. This type of activity may enable students to reflect in ways that align with the pedagogy used by Surbhi and Erika. In effect, students' perspectives take in a way that allows them to identify with marginalized individuals.

I would like to return to an example mentioned by Erika. It is worth noting that Erika and I teach in different disciplines, yet we incorporate some of the same readings in our courses. My students also read a piece by McIntosh (2007) that focuses on both White and Male privilege (i.e., unearned entitlement). The combination of both race and sex enables me to start having conversations about intersectionality and how the interplay of multiple status characteristics differentially impacts one's daily experience (i.e., and in the context of the course, work experience). I ask students in the class to make their own lists of ways in which they visualize (or experience) unearned entitlement. Reflecting on my experiences with this activity, I have found that POC, nontraditional college-age students, and LGBTQIA+ students generally are able to generate examples that differ from the lists that are provided by McIntosh (2007) and those examples generate riveting class discussions. Specifically, students provide explicit examples of ways they have experienced marginalization and we discuss these instances as a class. In these instances, students can learn from one another and better understand the importance of considering the implications of privilege on those who do (and do not) benefit from its existence. In learning more about Erika's framework, I am interested in how we might collaborate to make these discussions more impactful.

In having these classroom conversations, I find that it is important to create a space where students are able to acknowledge the different lived experiences of others. I have found that an effective way to do this is to include an article that frames bias as unethical management behavior (Banaji et al., 2003). Framing bias in this manner provides a nonthreatening context for students to have discussions about biases related to race, gender, and other status characteristics. In addition to reading about the examples in the article, students also take the Implicit Associations Test (IAT; Greenwald & Banaji, 1995) to examine the schemas they have about a variety of status characteristics. This approach enables students to acknowledge their own preferences and bias, and makes them less reluctant to engage in class discussions, and more open to figuring out ways to address bias.

This approach could be useful in the (re)design of courses in international leadership. Academicians in this area should consider modifying existing courses or even in creating a course that focuses on understanding how bias, culture, status characteristics, and intersectionality can help us better understand international leadership theory and typology. Case studies, articles, and other source material may be helpful in enabling individuals to better understand the biases that may impact individuals in leadership positions that have a global impact. Such an approach may also help inform future research studies. Coupled with Surbhi's suggestion of deconstructing the syllabus to change the manner of the conversations that we have about race, racism, and inclusion, this approach may enable students to develop a deeper understanding of ways to lead, manage, and interact with others.

This conversation on how we teach international research in three different disciplines has been enlightening. We all bring different approaches to it and reflect on how our own positionality inflects our teaching and research outcomes. How has this conversation made you think anew about teaching international research or yielded new understandings of leadership?

SURBHI: Coming from the fields of American Ethnic Studies, Postcolonial and Cultural Studies and Transnational Feminisms, I have been struck by the convergences these fields present with international leadership research. In order to understand how colonialism functions in our research methods and designs, we must reckon with why only certain kinds of knowledge about the non-Western world are deemed valid and legitimate. After all, in the neoliberal era, knowledge production by the "other" or about the "other" often becomes a source of profit and capital – including social capital, cultural capital, or psychological capital – exacerbating epistemic privilege or dominance (Mohanty, 2003; Stein, 2017). For example, important takeaways of anti-capitalist research in postcolonial/cultural studies, such as "inquisitiveness" and "nonjudgmentalness" about cultures (Vogelgesang *et al.*, 2014), are used to maximize corporate profits.

Two things are important here. First, our research designs need to incorporate a meaningful intersectionality, as Sarah discusses, which accounts for leadership through the intersecting hierarchies of race, class, sexuality, and nationality. Such critical intersectionality will include difference not to simply fill gaps in research but to de-center Western/White notions of leadership as domination, and it will allow alternative collective leadership structures to emerge as new points for theorization. Second, research that theorizes leadership as opposition to power, resistance to the status quo of hierarchies, and as an experience of shared vulnerability disrupts linear narratives of leadership formation and authority, especially the "assumptions of linear causation from race-ethnicity to leadership and from leaders to followers" (Ospina & Foldy, 2009, p. 892). In a research study, that would mean accounting for how leaders from marginalized groups change the narrative of race and are not just determined by it. Similarly, our research can benefit from thinking of followership as not simply derived from leadership but an important site for forming leadership.

In talking with Erika, I have been struck that even though colonialism has been studied as racialized and gendered, the language of Whiteness, more prominent in the national sphere, does not permeate the field of international research in a widespread way. For example, the vocabularies of "diversity" and "multiculturalism" serve to obfuscate the "ascendancy of whiteness" (Puar, 2007, p. 24) that lies at their core. There is, then, an urgent need to account for the role of Whiteness not only in colonial ideologies and practices but also in the more liberal inclusive projects of citizenship, education, and market participation (Lowe, 2015; Puar, 2007, p. 31). One way to capture the role of Whiteness in international leadership research studies would be to follow Liu's (2020; p. 130) suggestion that we "become adept at incorporating new language into our racial grammar, calling out the ways our organizations valorize *white* values, *white* perspectives, *white* needs and interests, *white* people and *white* leadership" (original emphasis). But at the same time, Whiteness is "not strictly delimited to white subjects" (Puar, 2007, p. 31), and racialized subjects too participate in the "project of whiteness" (Puar, 2007, p. 31) in research approaches. The ideas that we highlight in this dialogue, including interdisciplinary conversations, epistemic humility, and crosspollination of frameworks, can ensure more deliberate and intentional questioning of the possibilities and limits of the "international" in the way we design and teach research.

ERIKA: Getting this push from Yulia to think about how my commitment to teaching Whiteness might intersect with teaching an international leadership course/curriculum has been impactful. Writing and dialoguing with Surbhi and Sarah has deepened some of my thinking even while writing this chapter. Seeing how similarly Sarah and I teach about these issues across different disciplines was powerful. Moreover, I had not fully thought about how we regularly use "Western" to substitute for White. I am further struck by Surbhi's notion that separating international "creates a context in which racism 'over here' is seen as separate from culture 'over there'" and as such neutralizes racial hierarchies towards "cultural difference." This reiterates that using social identities as a space from which to interrogate our place as teachers-scholars – in addition to culture – is productive. We privilege and marginalize/oppress based on social identity categories. Students could consider multiple facets of where their (privileged/ oppressed) identities fall on a "diversity wheel" (e.g., https://www.jhsph.edu/offices-and-services/office-of-inclusion-diversity-anti-racism-and-equity/resources/) and reflect on how identity and culture are all connected to the way we view reality, ask research questions, and choose research methods. For example, while my racial identity of being White imbues a lot of assumptions…so does my national origin identity of being a U.S. citizen. I would not want to teach international research just about "culture" or just about race (etc.)…it is a both/and that this dialogue has crystallized for me.

SARAH: Hearing about the ways that others address the complexity of race in their classrooms was fascinating. Conceptually, I understand how my research and teaching has a natural fit with international leadership. I study and teach topics related to managing others with a particular focus on examining ways to make sure that marginalized individuals have opportunities and experiences that are similar to their non-marginalized counterparts. This experience, however, has made me realize how limited my perspectives are when considering the global (i.e., international) landscape. Moving beyond surface-level characteristics (e.g., gender, race, age), it is important to examine the ways that deep-level diversity characteristics (e.g., culture, experience) impact the ways in which we interact with and lead others. Working on this project has made me realize that there is a lot of work that is yet to be done and that it is particularly important to consider how the conversation needs to change. In considering intersectionality, how do leader and follower characteristics interact to have an effect on leadership effectiveness? Given the changing nature of work, to what extent does technology have an impact on the ways in which individuals lead others? Considering recent happenings (e.g., COVID-19 pandemic, increased salience of racial disparities from BLM, protest movements throughout the globe), what are the considerations for leaders who are managing international teams? Moreover, this work should be conducted across disciplines to gain a better understanding of best practices. Conducting interdisciplinary projects has the potential to change how we understand international leadership and potentially design frameworks to create a context for more inclusive teaching pedagogy.

Conclusion

Our hope is that the happenstance of Yulia "matching" us to write this chapter after our anti-racist teaching practice panel has elucidated some points about teaching international leadership that may have otherwise gone unspoken and therefore undone. In addition, we have tried to prepare instructors to acknowledge their own diverse identities when teaching. It is instructive to review the diversity wheel on a regular basis to remind ourselves where we have privilege that might give us advantages and oppression that might bring us disadvantages in teaching and doing international leadership research. As much as we like to think research is "objective," as teachers and researchers we are embodied beings. With every new mix of students, there are different power dynamics to negotiate within the class in addition to teaching about power in research/methods more broadly. Now more than ever, we need to interrogate power in our research in all disciplines, including international leadership.

References (teaching references have*)

Appleton, N. S. (2019, February 4). *Do not 'decolonize'…if you are not decolonizing: Progressive language and planning beyond a hollow academic rebranding.* http://www.criticalethnicstudiesjournal.org/blog/2019/1/21/do-not-decolonize-if-you-are-not-decolonizing-alternate-language-to-navigate-desires-for-progressive-academia-6y5sg.

Applebaum, B. (2016) Critical whiteness studies. In the *Oxford research encyclopedia on education.* doi:10.1093/acrefore/9780190264093.013.5.

Ashburn-Nardo, L., & Karim, M. F. A. (2019). The CPR model: Decisions involved in confronting prejudiced responses. In *Confronting prejudice and discrimination* (pp. 29–47). Academic Press.

Banaji, M. R., Bazerman, M. H., & Chugh, D. (2003). How (un)ethical are you? *Harvard Business Review, 81,* 56–64.

Burns, A., Martin, J., & Haberman, M. (2020, September 30). G.O.P. alarmed by Trump's comments on extremist group, fearing a drag on the party. *The New York Times.* Retrieved October 1, 2020 from https://www.nytimes.com/2020/09/30/us/politics/trump-debate-white-supremacy.html.

Chin, J. L., & Trimble, J. E. (2014). *Diversity and leadership.* SAGE.

Cliff, M. (1995). *Abeng.* Plume.

Crenshaw, K. W., Gotanda, N., Peller, G., & Thomas, K. (Eds.). (1995). *Critical race theory: The key writings that formed the movement.* The New Press.

Crenshaw, K. (1990). Mapping the margins: Intersectionality, identity politics, and violence against women of color. *Stanford Law Review, 43,* 1241–1299.

Damousi, J., Rubenstein, K., & Tomsic, M. (2014). *Diversity in leadership: Australian women, past and present.* ANU Press.

Den Hartog, D. N., House, R. J., Hanges, P. J., Ruiz-Quintanilla, S. A., Dorfman, P. W., Abdalla, I. A.,… Akande, B. E. (1999). Culture specific and cross-culturally generalizable implicit leadership theories: Are attributes of charismatic/transformational leadership universally endorsed? *The Leadership Quarterly, 10*(2), 219–256.

Den Hartog, D. N., & Verburg, R. M. (1997). Charisma and rhetoric: Communicative techniques of international business leaders. *The Leadership Quarterly, 8*(4), 355–391.

*DiAngelo. R. (2011). White fragility. *International Journal of Critical Pedagogy, 3*(3), 54–70.

*DiAngelo. R. (2020). *White fragility: Extended version* [Video]. Retrieved January 23, 2021 from https://www.pbs.org/wnet/amanpour-and-company/video/white-fragility-extended-version/.

Dickson, M. W., Den Hartog, D. N., & Mitchelson, J. K. (2003). Research on leadership in a cross-cultural context: Making progress and raising new questions. *The Leadership Quarterly, 14,* 729–768. doi:10.1016/j.leaqua.2003.09.002.

Foste, Z. (2020). The enlightenment narrative: White student leaders' preoccupation with racial innocence. *Journal of Diversity in Higher Education, 13*(1), 33–43. doi:10.1037/dhe0000113.

*Frankenberg, R. (1993). *The social construction of Whiteness: White women, race matters.* University of Minnesota Press. doi:10.4324/9780203973431.

Gelfand, M. J., Aycan, Z., Erez, M., & Leung, K. (2017). Cross-cultural industrial organizational psychology and organizational behavior: A hundred-year journey. *Journal of Applied Psychology, 102*(3), 514–529. doi:10.1037/apl0000186.

Gelfand, M. J., Erez, M., & Aycan, Z. (2007). Cross-cultural organizational behavior. *Annual Review of Psychology, 58,* 479–514.

Gooden, M.A. (2012). What does racism have to do with leadership? Countering the idea of color-blind leadership: A reflection on race and the growing pressures of the urban principalship. *Educational Foundations, 26*(1-2), 67–84.

Greenwald, A. G., & Banaji, M. R. (1995). Implicit social cognition: Attitudes, self-esteem, and stereotypes. *Psychological Review, 102*(1), 4–27. doi:10.1037/0033-295X.102.1.4

Grewal, I. (2005). *Transnational America: Feminisms, diasporas, neoliberalisms.* Duke University Press.

Hagmann, J., & Biersteker, T. (2014). Beyond the published discipline: Toward a critical pedagogy of international studies. *European Journal of International Relations, 20*(2) 291–315. doi:10.1177/1354066112449879

Hawkins, J. N., Hershock, P. D., & Mason, M. (2007). *Changing education: Leadership, innovation and development in a globalizing Asia Pacific.* Springer.

Hofstede, G. (1980). Motivation, leadership, and organization: Do American theories apply abroad? *Organizational Dynamics, 9*(1), 42–63. doi:10.1016/0090-2616(80)90013-3.

House, R. J., Javidan, M., Hanges, P., Dorfman, P. W. (2002). Understanding cultures and implicit leadership theories across the globe: An introduction to project GLOBE. *Journal of World Business, 37*(1), 3–10.

Hutnyk, J. (2006). The dialectic of "here and there": Anthropology at home. In N. Ali, V. S. Kalra, & S. Sayyid (Eds.), *A postcolonial people: South Asians in Britain* (pp. 74–90). Hurst & Co.

★Kendi, I. X. (2019). *How to be an anti-racist.* One World.

Le, P. T., & Matias, C. E. (2019). Towards a truer multicultural science education: How whiteness impacts science education. *Cultural Studies of Science Education, 14*, 15–31. doi:10.1007/s11422-017-9854-9.

Li, P., Sun, J. M., Taris, T. W., Xing, L., & Peeters, M. C. (2020). Country differences in the relationship between leadership and employee engagement: A meta-analysis. *The Leadership Quarterly.* doi:10.1016/j.leaqua.2020.101458.

Liu, H. (2020). *Redeeming leadership: An anti-racist feminist intervention.* Bristol University Press. doi:10.2307/j.ctvtv93zk.

Lowe, L. (1996). *Immigrant acts: On Asian American cultural politics.* Duke University Press.

Lowe, L. (2015). *The intimacies of four continents.* Duke University Press.

Matias, C. E., Viesca, K. M., Garrison-Wade, D. F., Tandon, M., & Galindo, R. (2014). "What is critical whiteness doing in OUR nice field like critical race theory?" Applying CRT and CWS to understand the white imaginations of white teacher candidates. *Equity & Excellence in Education, 47*(3), 289–304. doi:10.1080/10665684.2014.933692.

★McIntosh. P. (1989). White privilege: Unpacking the invisible knapsack. *Peace and Freedom Magazine,* July/August, 10–12.

McIntosh, P. (2007). *White Privilege and Male Privilege (1988). Womens Voices. Feminist Visions: Classic and Contemporary Readings.* Ed. Susan M. Shaw and Janet Lee. 3rd ed. New York: McGraw, 91–98.

Mitchell, N. (2015). Intellectual. *Critical Ethnic Studies, 1*(1), 86–94. doi:10.5749/jcritethnstud.1.1.0086.

Miner, H. (1956). Body ritual among the Nacirema. *American Anthropologist, 58*(3), 503–507. doi:10.1525/aa.1956.58.3.02a00080.

Mohanty, C. (2003). *Feminism without borders.* Duke University Press.

Moorosi, P., Fuller, K., & Reilly, E. (2018). Leadership and intersectionality: Constructions of successful leadership among Black women school principals in three different contexts. *Management in Education, 32*(4), 152–159. doi:10.1177/0892020618791006.

Naples, N. (2009). Teaching intersectionality intersectionally. *International Feminist Journal of Politics, 11*(4), 566–577. doi:10.1080/14616740903237558.

★Narayan, U. (1997). *Dislocating cultures: Identities, traditions, and third world feminism.* Routledge.

National Association of Black Journalists. (2020, June). NABJ statement on capitalizing black and other racial identifiers. Retrieved November 15, 2020 from https://www.nabj.org/page/styleguide.

National Human Genome Research Institute. (n.d.). *The human genome project.* Retrieved February 9, 2021 from https://www.genome.gov/human-genome-project.

★Obaid-Chinoy, S. (Producer and Director). (2015). *A girl in the river: The price of forgiveness* [Film]. HBO Documentary Films.

★Obaid-Chinoy, S. (Producer and Co-Director) (2012). *Saving face* [Film]. HBO Documentary Films.

★Okun, T. (n.d.). White supremacy culture. Retrieved January 23, 2021 from https://www.dismantlingracism.org/uploads/4/3/5/7/43579015/okun_-_white_sup_culture.pdf.

Ospina, S., & Foldy, E. (2009). A critical review of race and ethnicity in the leadership literature: Surfacing context, power and the collective dimensions of leadership. *The Leadership Quarterly, 20*(6), 876–896. doi:10.1016/j.leaqua.2009.09.005.

★Patel, K. (2020). Penn Museum to remove Morton Cranial Collection from public view after student opposition. *The Daily Pennsylvanian.* Retrieved September 24, 2020 from https://www.thedp.com/article/2020/07/penn-museum-morton-cranial-collection-black-lives-matter.

Pendakur, V., & Furr, S. C. (2016). Critical leadership pedagogy: Engaging power, identity, and culture in leadership education for college students of color. *New Directions for Higher Education, 174*, 45–55. doi:10.1002/he.20188.

Pillen, H., McNaughgton, D., & ward, P. R. (2020). Critical consciousness development: A systematic review of empirical studies. *Health Promotion International, 35*(6), 1519–1530. doi:10.1093/heapro/daz125.

*Prashad, V. (2003). Summer of Bruce. In M. Evelina Galang (Ed.), *Screaming monkeys: Critiques of Asian American images* (pp. 255–265). Coffee House Press.

Puar, J. (2007). *Terrorist assemblages: Homonationalism in queer times.* Duke University Press.

Scandura, T., & Dorfman, P. (2004). Leadership research in an international and cross-cultural context. *The Leadership Quarterly, 15,* 277–307. doi:10.1016/j.leaqua.2004.02.004.

*Scene on Radio. (2017). *Seeing white* [Podcast series]. Retrieved January 22, 2021 from http://www.sceneonradio.org/seeing-white/.

*Showing Up for Racial Justice. (n.d.). White supremacy culture. Retrieved January 22, 2021 from https://www.showingupforracialjustice.org/white-supremacy-culture.html.

Stein, S. (2017). The persistent challenges of addressing epistemic dominance in higher education: Considering the case of curriculum Internationalization. *Comparative Education Review, 61*(S1), 25–50. doi:0010-4086/2017/61S1-0003$.

Välikangas, L. & Okumura, A. (1977). Why do people follow leaders? A study of a US and a Japanese change program. *The Leadership Quarterly, 8*(3), 313–337.

Villa-Nicholas, M. (2018). Teaching intersectionality: Pedagogical approaches for lasting impact. *Education for Information, 34*(2), 121–133. doi:10.3233/EFI-180191.

Vogelgesang, G., Clapp-Smith, R., & Osland, J. (2014). The relationship between positive psychological capital and global mindset in the context of global leadership. *Journal of Leadership & Organizational Studies.* doi:10.1177/1548051813515515.

Werner, S. (2002). Recent developments in international management research: A review of 20 top management journals. *Journal of Management, 28*(3), 277–305.

27

Doctoral Leadership Programs

Preparing Stewards of the Leadership Discipline

Petros G. Malakyan

What is the purpose of doctoral education? This was the principal question asked by a group of researchers leading the Carnegie Initiative on the Doctorate (CID) in 2001. The Carnegie team proposed a general answer to this question by stating that "the purpose of doctoral education, taken broadly, is to educate and prepare those who can be trusted with the vigor, quality, and integrity of the field" (Walker et al., 2009, p. 161). Golde and Walker (2006) first introduced the term "steward of the discipline" as part of the CID initiative. They define stewards as "a scholar in the fullest sense of the term – someone who can imaginatively generate new knowledge, critically conserve valuable and useful ideas, and responsibly transform those understandings through writing, teaching, and application" (Golde & Walker, 2006, p. 5).

This chapter seeks to answer the above question by reviewing 50 doctoral programs in leadership worldwide in light of CID's purpose statement and the concept of "stewards of the discipline." The research question posed by CID in 2001 was as follows: "If you could start [your doctoral program] de novo, what would be the best way to structure doctoral education in your field to prepare stewards of the discipline?" This curricula question was chosen to address the following research questions below:

- What is the overarching purpose of doctoral programs in leadership?
- How are the doctoral curricula in leadership structured?
- How are the current trends of leadership employed in the doctoral programs in leadership?
- Is followership a part of the leadership curriculum?
- Given the way doctoral curricula are structured, how likely is it that doctoral programs in leadership will develop stewards of the discipline?

Challenges and Current Trends of Leadership Education

Study and research on leadership as we know it is primarily a Western phenomenon and endeavor. For instance, most leadership programs are in the United States (Guthrie, Teig, & Hu, 2018). According to the International Leadership Association's Leadership Program Directory (2019), leadership programs are disproportionately located in North America ($n = 1656$), Western Europe ($n = 224$), and Australia ($n = 51$). In other words, 97.5% of leadership education is offered in the Western world, while only 2.5% of leadership education is available in Asia, Eastern Europe, Middle East, and South-East Asia

DOI: 10.4324/9781003003380-27

(Malakyan, 2019). No doctoral programs in leadership are identified in Australia, South America, and countries with some of the world's largest populations, such as China and India.

Leadership studies seems both an attractive and challenging prospect. On the one hand, in the last 20–30 years, leadership studies have attracted sociologists, behavioral scientists, social psychologists, historians, philosophers, anthropologists, and political scientists, to name a few, thus making this interdisciplinary field of study an international phenomenon (House, Hanges, Javidan, Dorfman, & Gupta, 2004; International Leadership Association, 2019). On the other hand, the challenge of developing leaders through teaching, writing, and application remains an unfulfilled promise worldwide. Therefore, a question arises as to what the purpose of leadership education is, and more specifically, for this study, doctoral education in leadership.

The study of leadership has changed drastically since the second part of the 20th century. For instance, leadership studies moved from the "me" to the "we" paradigm. It is no longer about the leader but the relationship she is engaged in a given situation and context. Thus, leadership is not about the person anymore, but rather the process individuals are involved in by leading and following roles and functions (DeRue, 2011; Malakyan, 2014). Additionally, in the entrepreneurial and interdependent world of the post-industrial and digital eras, the scientific management statement, "I am my job," seems mostly irrelevant because individuals are expected to develop dynamic and multiple identities (i.e., leader, follower, manager, associate, partner, and team-member) in the global workforce (Burke & Stets, 2009; Collinson, 2006; DeRue & Ashford, 2010; Rost, 1993; Stets & Burke, 2014). The summary of current trends below in leadership research will serve as criteria to assess the quality of doctoral programs in leadership:

1. *Relationship-based leadership.* Leadership research has acknowledged that certain traits, such as inner drive, integrity, and authenticity, may make one an effective leader or a follower (Gardner et al., 2005; Kirkpatrick & Locke, 1991; Moorman, Darnold, & Priesemuth, 2013). Leading and following behaviors and functions are not static and can be traded in various situations (Malakyan, 2014). Thus, the international leadership research may consider studying leadership and followership as one continuum or the two sides of one coin, or the two interdependent variables of the leadership tango (Chaleff, 2012).
2. *Process-based leadership.* Leadership research is not about the person but the process of leading and following (Hollander, 1992). Thus, the international leadership research may depersonalize leadership studies by taking the person (noun) out of the process to study the process of leading and following (verb) or "leadship" and "followship" in context (Malakyan, 2015).
3. *Dynamic and multiple identity leadership.* The industrial paradigm of leadership that has stratified the workforce between leaders and followers (leaders do leadership, followers do followership) is an outdated paradigm for today's information and digital age. Thus, international leadership research may integrate personal identity theories, stemming from process philosophy and philosophical psychology, with leader-followership research to understand multiple and dynamic leader-follower identity formations in different cultural contexts.

Definitions

The key terms for this study are as follows:

- *Stewards of the discipline* – A person who generates new knowledge, conserves relevant ideas, and transforms knowledge and ideas into teaching, writing, and application (Golde & Walker, 2006, 9–14).
- *Purpose* – Doctoral programs in leadership aim to educate and prepare their students to become stewards of the discipline.

- *Structure* – Refers to the amount of content, research methods, and dissertation writing courses required for a doctorate degree in leadership.
- *Quality* – Refers to the adoption of contemporary leadership theories and methods courses that reflect the current trend of the research and scholarship on leadership. For this study, leadership theories that are process-based ("we vs. me") as opposed to leader-centered approaches to leadership ("me vs. we"), have been considered as "contemporary" leadership theories and "current trends" of leadership research.
- *Integration* – Refers to the integration of followership research with the curriculum structure of doctoral programs in leadership.

Method

In this study, the author reviewed and analyzed electronic documents (MS Word and PDF) of 50 doctoral programs in leadership worldwide through an internet-mediated research approach (Altheide, Coyle, DeVriese, & Scneider, 2013; Hewson & Buchanan, 2013; Hewson & Stewart, 2016). A computer-aided content analysis was employed to assess the purpose, curriculum structure, quality, and integrity of doctoral programs in leadership to understand the degree to which these programs prepare students of the discipline. The sample of doctoral programs represents a comprehensive list of Ph.D. programs in leadership studies and organizational leadership worldwide. The list of the 50 programs is provided in Appendix 27A.

The author analyzed the purpose statements of all 50 programs from the perspective of CID's proposed purpose statement on doctoral education in order to understand the degree to which the purpose of doctoral programs in leadership prepare "stewards of the discipline." The doctoral *curricula* were then analyzed, and the amount of content, research methods, and dissertation writing courses offerings were considered the criteria for program vigor. The type of leadership course offerings was analyzed to access the programs' quality based on the current trend of the research and scholarship on leadership. The integrity of the programs was assessed based on whether programs offered any stand-alone courses on followership. Finally, based on the study results on the programs' purposes, curricular structures, type of leadership courses, and the presence of followership courses in the program curriculum, the author attempted to understand the probability of doctoral programs preparing stewards of the leadership field of study.

Sample

The sample for this study was selected based on the following criteria: (a) doctoral programs that offer Ph.D. in leadership and organizational leadership (a total of 44 programs); (b) six doctoral programs that use the word "leadership" or "organizational leadership" on their doctoral degree titles, such as Ed.D. in Organizational Leadership, Postgraduate Diploma in Advanced Leadership Studies, Ed.D. in Leadership Studies, Doctor of Professional Studies in Organizational Leadership, Doctorate in Interdisciplinary Studies: Organizational Leadership, and Psy.D. in Leadership Psychology (See Appendix 27A); (c) programs that require more than 50 credit hours of coursework and dissertation writing or equivalent to 3–5 years of program duration; and (d) have an official website page. The rationale for choosing these specific criteria was to focus on doctoral programs that require original research and dissertation writing with the aim to prepare scholars for the field of leadership studies.

Forty-three out of 50 programs are housed in the United States. Of the remaining seven programs, one was in Belgium, one in Canada, one in France, one each in the Philippines and South Africa, and two in the United Kingdom, thus making a total of seven international programs in leadership. No doctoral programs in leadership were identified in Australia, Asia, and South America.

To the best of the researcher's knowledge and available online resources, this study's sample represents a comprehensive list of doctoral programs in leadership derived from the International Leadership Association (ILA) database and the Google and Yahoo search engines.

Procedure

A spreadsheet was created alphabetically according to each program's title and name; the education institution; URL address; the country where the program is housed; program purpose or goals; curriculum design; program descriptions; program learning outcomes; course titles and descriptions; research and dissertation courses; content courses; credit-hour requirements for the content, research, and dissertation courses; total credit hours requirements; and global or international focus. Additionally, the author copied the website information and the available program brochures and handbooks into an MS Word file or downloaded as a PDF document for review and analysis to identify explicit data on stewardship of the discipline, thus generating new knowledge, conserving ideas, and transforming knowledge and ideas into teaching, writing, and application.

For implicit data, systematic axial coding was employed to confirm whether any information on (1) generating new knowledge, (2) conserving ideas, and (3) transforming knowledge and ideas into teaching, writing, and application were identified in the body of the collected documents. Then, each program document was read and reviewed multiple times to code, tabulate, and record the concepts and categories of stewardship of discipline (i.e., generating, conserving, and transforming on a spreadsheet).

As noted in the study findings, programs that restricted access to curriculum or program information on their website were considered a study limitation. Thus, the validity and reliability of findings were contingent upon the website information available to the researcher.

Findings

Based on web searches using Google and Yahoo, the sample, which includes 50 available doctoral programs in leadership and organizational leadership, mostly Ph.D. degrees, indicates that 86% of doctoral programs in leadership are in the United States.

Program Purpose/Goals and Learning Objectives

To determine whether the doctoral programs in leadership prepare stewards of the discipline, the available program information, such as program purpose, goals, and objectives, have been analyzed by searching keywords from the definition of "Stewards of the discipline." See Table 27.1.

The above table indicates that the most commonly used terms among 50 doctoral programs in leadership worldwide are "knowledge," "scholar," "research," and "theory." More specifically, 35 programs explicitly use the word "knowledge" to describe their program purpose or goals. Two programs use the terms "generate new knowledge" and "create new knowledge." By explicitly using terms such as "scholar," "scholar-practitioner," "leader-scholar," and "scholarship," 35 programs claim that their program purpose is to prepare scholars and produce scholarship. Further, a total of 38 programs explicitly use the term "research" to exhibit their commitment to engage their students in research activities, and 34 programs used the term "theory" to show the theoretical nature of their program.

In addition, two programs use the term "steward" and "stewardship," and the word "discipline" was used by 15 programs. Information on whether the doctoral programs in leadership are intentional regarding "transform[ing] knowledge and ideas into teaching, writing, and application" (i.e., the adopted definition of stewards of the discipline), 22 programs implied transformation, transformative research, and ideas.

Table 27.1 Key Words for Stewards of the Discipline

Term	Description	Number of Programs
Stewards	"leaders as stewards of an organization"	1
Stewardship	One of the eight key domains for study: "stewardship"	1
Discipline	"Discipline"	4
	"Variety of disciplines"	2
	"Disciplines of leadership"	2
	"Leadership discipline"	2
	"Academic discipline"	5
Knowledge	"Knowledge"	35
	"Generate [and] create new knowledge"	2
Transform knowledge and ideas	"Transformation"	8
	"Organizational transformation"	10
	"Transformative research"	1
	"Bold ideas," "your ideas," "formulating ideas"	3
Scholar	"Scholar"	12
	"Scholar-practitioner"	4
	"Leader-scholar"	4
	"Scholarship"	15
Research	"Research"	27
	"Original research"	5
	"Scholarly research"	6
Theory	"Theory"	34

Curriculum Structure

Table 27.2 presents a summary of the program credit requirements and curriculum structure for 40 doctoral programs in leadership. The remaining ten programs (five national and five international) neither report on the curriculum structure nor provide a list of specific course offerings on their website.

Table 27.2 Program Credit Requirements and Curriculum Structure

Programs/ Curriculum Structure	Total Credit Hours	Content Course Credits	Research Methods Course Credits	Dissertation Course Credits	Field-Work/ Practicum/ Internship Credits
4 Programs	51–59	30–36 = 4 programs	9–15 = 4 prog	9–12 = 4 prog	
24 Programs	60–63	18–27 = 5 prog	6–9 = 5 prog	6–9 = 10 prog	6 = 1 practicum
		30–36 = 12 prog	11–15 = 13 prog	11–15 = 13 prog	
		39–43 = 6 prog	18–27 = 5 prog	18–27 = 1 prgr	
		45–48 = 1 prog	30–1 prog		
8 Programs	64–70	30–36 = 6 prog	6–9 = 2 prog	6–9 = 2 prog	6 = 1 internship
		45–48 = 2 prog	11–15 = 4 prog	11–16 = 4 prog	12 = 1 practicum
			21–23 = 2 prog	21–24 = 2 prog	
4 Programs	71–75	31–33 = 2 prog	12–13 = 2 prog	12–16 = 2 prog	
		43–45 = 2 prog	15–24 = 2 prog	17–18 = 2 prog	

The data in Table 27.2 indicates that the coursework for 40 doctoral programs in leadership varies from 51 to 77 credit hours. Thus, the analysis below has been divided into four categories: (1) programs that require 51–59 credits, (2) programs that require 60–63 credits, (3) programs that require 64–70 credits, and (4) programs that require 71–75 credits coursework.

1. The data summary of eight programs among 40 that constitute 20% of the doctoral programs require 64–70 credit hours of coursework is as follows:
    Content Courses:

    *   Six programs require 47–51% (30–36 credits) content courses with an average of 49%
    *   Programs require 69–70% (45–48 credits) content courses with an average of 69.5%
    *   The total average of content courses for all 8 programs is 59%

    Research Methods Courses:

    *   Programs require 9–13% (6–9 credits) research method courses with an average of 11%
    *   Programs require 17–21% (11–15 credits) research method courses with an average of 19%
    *   Two programs require 32–33% (21–23 credits) research method courses with an average of 32.5%
    *   The total average of research method courses for all 8 programs is 21%

    Dissertation Writing Courses:

    *   Programs require 9–13% (6–9 credits) dissertation writing courses with an average of 11%
    *   Programs require 17–23% (11–16 credits) dissertation writing courses with an average of 20%
    *   Two programs require 33–34% (21–24 credits) dissertation writing courses with an average of 33.5%
    *   The total average of research method courses for all eight programs is 21%

    Internship & Practicum Course:

    *   One program (10%) requires 6 credits of internship course with an average of 9%
    *   One program (10%) requires 12 credits of practicum course with an average of 14%
    *   The total average of internship and practicum courses for two programs is 12%

2. The data summary of four programs among 40 that constitute the 10% of the doctoral programs require 71–75 credit hours of coursework is as follows:

    Content Courses:

    *   Programs require 43–44% (31–33 credits) content courses with an average of 43.5%
    *   Two programs require 60% (43–45 credits) content courses with an average of 60%
    *   The total average of content courses for all 4 programs is 52%

    Research Methods Courses:

    *   16–17% (12–13 credits) are research methods courses with an average of 16.5%
    *   Programs require 21–32% (15–24 credits) research methods courses with an average of 26.5%

- The total average of content courses for all 4 programs is 22%

Dissertation Writing Courses:

- Programs require 17–21% (12–16 credits) dissertation writing courses with an average of 19%
- Two programs require 24% (17–18 credits) dissertation writing courses
- The total average of content courses for all 4 programs is 21.5%

3. The data summary of four programs, that constitute 10% of the 40 doctoral programs, require 51–59 credit hours of coursework. The content of these programs are as follows:

- 59–60% (30–36 credits) are content courses with an average of 59.5%
- 18–25% (9–15 credits) are research methods courses with an average of 21.5%
- 18–20% (9–12 credits) are dissertation writing courses with an average of 19%

4. The data summary of the 24 programs among 40 that constitute 60% of the doctoral programs require 60–63 credit hours of coursework and are described below:

Content Courses:

- Programs require 30–43% (18–27 credits) content courses with an average of 36.5%
- Twelve programs require 50–57% (30–36 credits) content courses with an average of 53.5%
- Programs require 65–68% (39–43 credits) content courses with an average of 66.5%
- One program requires 75–76% (45–48 credits) content courses with an average of 75.5%
- The total average percentage of content courses for all 24 programs is 58%

Research Methods Courses:

- Programs require 10–14% (6–9 credits) research method courses with an average of 12%
- Thirteen programs require 18–24% (11–15 credits) research method courses with an average of 21%
- Programs require 30–43% (18–27 credits) research method courses with an average of 36.5%
- One program requires 48–50% (30 credits) research method courses with an average of 49%
- The total average of research method courses for all 24 programs is 30%

Dissertation Writing Courses:

- Ten programs require 10–14% (6–9 credits) dissertation writing courses with an average of 12%
- Thirteen programs require 18–24% (11–15 credits) dissertation writing courses with an average of 21%
- One program requires 30–43% (18–27 credits) dissertation writing courses with an average of 22.5%
- The total average of dissertation writing courses for all 24 programs is 18.5%

Practicum Course:

- One program requires a 9.5–10% (6 credits) practicum course with an average of 9.75%

The remaining 10 doctoral programs in leadership, particularly international programs, put much emphasis on research initiatives throughout the duration of the program. For instance, some program curricula are divided into Ph.D. research and Ph.D. thesis or dissertation writing phases, while most U.S.-based doctoral programs in leadership seem to combine the research phase with the completion of content and methodology courses. In other words, doctoral programs that require less, or never require content courses, allow more time – between two and three years – for their students to engage in original research and dissertation writing, whereas programs with content course requirements tend to designate one or one-and-a-half years for original research and dissertation writing.

Quality – Current Trends in Leadership

This assessment criterion refers to the contemporary leadership theories and methods courses embedded in the leadership curricula that reflect the current trend of the research and scholarship on leadership. Table 27.3 is a summary of Appendix 27C: Content Courses on Leadership used in 50 Doctoral Programs.

The above list of content courses within 46 doctoral programs in leadership (four programs did not report courses or any curriculum structure on their websites) indicate that 6.3% of courses are advanced leadership and seminar courses, 6.9% are applied and practice, 19.7% are context-based, 1.9% are process- and relationship-based, 4.4% are complexity or systems-based, 26.6% are contemporary or current trends in leadership-based, 13.1% are foundational and theoretical, 11.9% are interdisciplinary, and 9.2% are other leadership courses.

Based on the guiding definition of the program quality, which presupposes teaching contemporary leadership theories, practices, and the current trends of the research and scholarship on leadership in context, 65.8% of courses taught in 46 doctoral programs seem to affirm the overall quality of the leadership discipline.

A total of 41 types of research methods courses have been identified among 46 doctoral programs in leadership (see Appendix 27B). Four out of the 50 programs did not report courses or curriculum structure on their websites. Thirty-eight programs offered qualitative and advanced qualitative research methods courses. The number of quantitative research methods courses among the 50 programs, including separate statistical research methods courses, was 31.25. A total of fourteen programs offered research design. The Research Methods course was 14, Research Seminar – 9, Program assessment and evaluation – 6, Survey Research – 5, Foundations of Research – 4, Mixed Methods – 4.

Table 27.4 indicates the types of methodology courses offered by 40 doctoral programs in leadership (10 out of 50 programs did not report courses or a curriculum structure on their respective websites):

The data on methodology courses indicates that 90% of doctoral programs in leadership offer qualitative and advanced qualitative research methods courses; 75% – quantitative and advanced quantitative; 62.6% – statistical courses; 35% – research design and advanced research design; 32.5% – advanced and applied research methods; 22.5% – research seminar. Courses such as Program Evaluation, Survey Research, Foundations of Research, Mixed Methods, Research Ethics, Empirical Research, Action Research, Research Critique, and Analysis of Research were used 15% or less. Only two doctoral programs (5%) required Global Leadership Research and Advanced Global leadership.

Integration – Followership in Leadership Curricula

Followership has not been taught consistently across doctoral leadership programs. In fact, only seven (14%) programs out of 50 offer a course on followership or on followers as a stand-alone course. However, the analysis of the doctoral leadership program website pages, brochures, catalogs, and course descriptions revealed that eight other doctoral programs (16%) use the "follower"-related terms in their

Table 27.3 Content Courses in Leadership Programs

Content Courses in Leadership Curricula	Number of Courses	Course Title
Advanced seminars or courses	20	Advanced leadership courses (13); Advanced leadership seminars (4); Leadership colloquium (3).
Applied and Practice	22	Applied Courses for Leaders; Applied Leadership Practices; Applied leadership research; Applied ethics (2); Art and Practice of Leading; Internship in Leadership; Change theory and practice; Ethics and Standards of Practice in Leadership; Instructional Leadership Theory/Practice (3); Leadership as Personal Practice; Leadership Styles and Reflective Practice; Leadership Theory, Research, and Practice; Leadership: From Theory to Reflective Practice; Leading Organizational Change: Theory and Practice; Leadership application; Leadership Practicum; Leadership Residency.
Context-based leadership	63	Cultural Leadership (10); Global Leadership (26); African American Leadership Studies; Business & Public Leadership; Community Based Leadership; Community College Leadership; Curriculum and Leadership; Dynamics of Race, Culture, and Gender in Higher Education; Ecclesial Leadership; Healthcare Leadership; Introduction to Doctoral Study in Global Leadership; Leadership and Accountability for Nonprofit Organizations; Leadership in School Improvement; Leadership Through the Ages: Biblical – Servant Leadership Model; Leadership, Public Relations and Stakeholder Engagement; Leading Non Profits and NGOs; Organizational leadership (13).
Complexity and systems-based	14	Complexity-based (6) – Analyzing Complex Problems; Complexity & Leadership Studies; Leadership in Complex Organizations; Leadership: Diversity and Social Justice in Complex and Global Organizations; The Complexity of Leadership Research; The Complexity of the Leadership Task.Systems-based (8) – Applied Leadership Practices: Integral Self and Systems Approach; Global Leadership, Systems & Policy; International Organizational Systems, Theory and Leadership; Leadership Pro-seminar: The Self and the System; Leadership: Advanced Systems Theory and Research; Leading Dynamic Systems with Multi-Dimensional Thinking; Leading the Organizational System
Contemporary and current trends in leadership	85	Adaptive leadership (2); Becoming a 21st Century Leader; Collaborative Leadership and Partnership; Contemporary Issues in Leadership; Contemporary Perspectives in Organizational Leadership Theory; Negotiations and Conflict Resolution for Contemporary Leaders; Current & Global Issues in

(Continued)

Table 27.3 (Continued)

Content Courses in Leadership Curricula	Number of Courses	Course Title
		Industrial & Organizational Psychology; Examines Current Theories Regarding Leadership; Dynamics of Race, Culture, and Gender; Emerging Theories of Leadership; Ethical Leadership (32); Creative leadership (7); Leadership and change (21); Group Dynamics and Team Leadership; The Neurobiology of Leadership; The Neuroscience of Leadership; Stewardship; Toxic Leadership; Leadership Analytics; Leadership and diversity (6); Leadership and sustainability (2); Leadership and environment (3); Teams (3); Trends in Organizational Leadership Research; Women, Leadership (2).
Foundations of leadership and leadership theory	42	Foundations of leadership (11); Leadership theory (23); Leadership studies (8).
Interdisciplinary	38	Interdisciplinary (4); Art and Practice of Leading; Art of Social Justice and Leadership; Creativity and Innovation (3); Creative Change and Transformational Leadership; Culture, Climate (2), and Change Leadership; Dimensions of Leading the Learning Organization; Empathy, Dialog, and the Ethic of Care; Entrepreneurial Leadership; Human Resources Leadership and Management; Leadership and Communications; Leadership and Consulting; Leadership and Corporate Social Responsibility; Leadership and Film; Leadership and History; Leadership and Law; Leadership and Learning Organizations; Leadership and Management Theory; Leadership and Motivation; Leadership and Peacebuilding; Leadership, Advocacy, and Policy Development; Leadership, Forgiveness, and Restorative Justice; Leadership, Justice, and Servanthood; Leadership, Public Relations and Stakeholder Engagement; Leading Learning; Managerial Economics for Decision Making and Leadership; Organizational Behavior and Leadership; Philosophical Concerns in Educ/Leadership; Psychology of Leadership (2); Strategic Leadership (6); Transformative Leadership for Civic and Community Engagement; Ways of Knowing: Teaching, Learning, Leadership.
Process- and relationship-based	6	Group process; Leader Decision Processes; Process Consultation and Facilitation Skills; Small group processes; Leadership and Peacebuilding: Conceptual Relationships and the Role of Outliers.
Other	30	

Table 27.4 Content Courses in Leadership Programs

Research Methods Courses	Programs
Qualitative and advanced qualitative	36
Quantitative and advanced quantitative	30
Statistical courses	25
Research design and advanced research design	14
Research methods, advanced, and applied	13
Research seminars	9
Program evaluation	6
Survey research	5
Foundations of research	4
Mixed methods	4
Research ethics	3
Empirical research	3
Action research	2
Research critique	2
Global leadership and advanced research	2
Analysis of research	2
Other research methods (see Appendix 27B)	24

program information: "followers," "followership," "leader-follower interactions," "role of the follower," "characteristics of followers," "leader and follower behavior," "global followers," "the relationship between leaders and followers," "dignity of the follower," "create followers," and "leader-follower relationship." In summary, 30% of doctoral programs in leadership mention the term followership or follower.

Discussion

In this study, the author assessed the purpose/goals, the curriculum structure, the quality, and the integration of followership in leadership studies of 50 doctoral programs in leadership worldwide to determine the extent to which these programs prepare stewards of the discipline defined by The Carnegie Initiatives of the Doctorate (CID). The study established some key results that are worth mentioning. First, since 86% of the doctoral programs in leadership have been primarily concentrated in North America, one may anticipate that Western leadership may well be the dominant perspective of the field of leadership study. Below is the context analysis of the purpose/goals, curriculum structure, quality, and integration of leadership-followership of 50 doctoral programs worldwide.

Program Purpose/Goals and Learning Objectives

What is the overall purpose of 50 doctoral programs in leadership based on what is reported on their website? To what extent does their program purpose meet the criteria of developing stewards of the discipline as defined by CID? The explicit and implicit finding of this study seems to confirm the working definition of the *stewards of the discipline* on multiple aspects of the inquiry. First, since 70% of the doctoral programs explicitly use the terms "knowledge" and "scholar" to describe their program purpose and goals, it can be concluded that 70% of the doctoral programs worldwide aim to enhance leadership knowledge, and by doing so, they intend to prepare scholars or stewards of the discipline. Second, the fact that 76% of the programs explicitly use the term "research" to characterize their program goal and 68% of programs are theory-based, it is reasonable to think that these programs seem committed to generating new knowledge and exploring new ideas through original research. Additionally, since 44% of programs imply transformation, transformative research, and ideas, and between 68 and 76 percent of doctoral programs in leadership show explicit and implicit evidence for knowledge creation, research, and the use of theory, it is more likely that these programs may develop the stewards of the discipline.

Curriculum Structure

This study shows that only 40 out of 50 doctoral programs in leadership worldwide report curriculum structures and the required courses on their program websites. Therefore, the analysis below represents 80% of the doctoral programs in leadership under four program categories: (1) four programs that require 51–59 credit hours of coursework (10%), (2) 24 programs that require 60–63 credit hours of coursework (60%), (3) eight programs that require 64–70 credit hours of coursework (20%), and (4) four programs that require 71–75 credit hours of coursework (10%).

1. Four programs with a 51–59 credit hours requirement are content-driven programs because the content courses occupy nearly 60% of the curriculum structure. Additionally, nearly 22% of courses are research methods courses that equip doctoral students with tools on how to conduct research. Only 19% of the programs are designed for original research through dissertation writing.
2. Twenty–four programs with the 60–63 credit hours requirement are too content-driven because the content courses occupy 58% of the curriculum structure with 30% research methods and nearly 19% dissertation writing. Additionally, one program offers a practicum course, 10% of the curriculum structure.
3. Eight programs with the 64–70 credit hours requirement are too content-driven programs because the content courses occupy 59% of the curriculum structure with 30% research methods and nearly 19% dissertation writing. Additionally, two programs, which comprise 12% of the curriculum structure, offer practicum and internship courses.
4. Eight programs with the 71–75% credit hours requirement are less content-driven programs because the content courses occupy 52% of the curriculum structure, with 22% comprising research methods and nearly 19% comprising dissertation writing. Additionally, two programs offer practicum and internship courses, comprising 12% of the curriculum structure.

A question is worth asking. How would curricula structures that require 52–60% coursework, 22–30% research methods, and 19% dissertation writing, along with a few internship and practicum courses (10–12%), across 40 doctoral programs in leadership prepare the stewards of the leadership discipline? The data of this study data is too insufficient to fully answer this question due to a lack of information about each of the content and methodology courses taught in each program that may be geared toward conducting original research.

Therefore, it is nearly impossible to determine the extent to which these programs generate new knowledge and conserve relevant ideas through content and methodology courses. However, the data seem to indicate the fact that the coursework-driven doctoral programs in leadership, predominately housed in the United States (see Table 27.2), allocate nearly 80% of the time and effort to complete content and methodology courses. Thus, with a nearly 20% curricular space for original research and dissertation writing, it seems that these programs designate insufficient time for doctoral students to generate new knowledge or theories through original research that might prepare them to become scholars and stewards of the leadership discipline. This finding is consistent with CID findings among doctoral students in humanities and social sciences. Much like in leadership doctoral programs, these students write their dissertation in their third or fourth year as their first substantial research project. Due to lack of preparation in how to conduct original research, one student reported "I did not get a chance to do a research project that involved primary sources in my field until I started the dissertation" (Walker, et al., 2009, p. 63).

Regarding the remaining 10 doctoral programs that do not report curricular structures or content courses, they tend to put more emphasis on conducting original research by allocating two to three years for original research and dissertation writing as opposed to content-driven programs. This finding is consistent with previous studies, which indicate that non-U.S. doctoral programs in leadership are predominately research-based and with few content course requirements (Malakyan, 2019). Can one argue that international leadership programs that are more research-focused seem to align well with the vision of the "Carnegie Initiative on the Doctorate" on how to develop stewards of the discipline? From the curriculum structure perspective, such an argument may have merit because the doctoral programs in leadership that require less or no content courses seem to have a greater potential to develop scholars and stewards of the leadership discipline than those who require more time and effort for mastering the existing knowledge (content courses) than creating new knowledge.

Quality – Current Trends in Leadership

The analysis of the data presented in Table 27.4 indicates the level at which the doctoral programs in leadership utilize and teach contemporary leadership theories and methods courses that reflect the current trend of the research and scholarship on leadership. The list of the 320 content courses have been categorized as:

- Advanced seminars or courses – nearly 6%
- Applied and Practice – nearly 7%
- Context-based leadership – 20%
- Complexity- and systems-based – 4%
- Contemporary and current trends in leadership – 27%
- Foundations of leadership and leadership theory – 13%
- Interdisciplinary – 12%
- Process- and relationship-based – 2%
- Other – 9%

Courses that represent the contemporary and current trends in leadership and are complexity- and systems-based, as well as context- and process-based, comprise 53% of the courses offered among 50 doctoral programs worldwide. Additionally, these courses, which seem to be leader-centered, make up 13% of the courses taught throughout the 50 programs. Other course categories, such as advanced, applied, foundational and theoretical courses, and interdisciplinary, among others, were difficult to assess as to whether they were leader-centered or process-based. This is another limitation of this study. Nevertheless, the data seems to have sufficient evidence to assume that more than 50% of courses show explicit evidence for a process-based approach to leadership study and research. Thus, the quality of the course contents offered in 50 doctoral programs in leadership meets the quality standards set by this study.

Moreover, the 41 different types of research methods courses offered by at least 40 doctoral programs in leadership (no data available for the remaining 10 programs) indicate that the most commonly used research methods courses are qualitative (90%), quantitative (75%), statistical (35%), research design (32.5%), and advanced/applied (22.5%) research methods courses. Few programs use contemporary research methods courses for leadership; for example, global leadership research (5%), field research, and research for leadership. Twenty-four research methods courses under the category "Other" (i.e., the complexity of leadership methods, ethnographic methods, narrative analysis, research synthesis for leadership, and research team, among others) appeared once. Thus, it can be concluded that, unlike the contemporary content courses in leadership, there is a scarcity of contemporary research methods courses tailored specifically to leadership research. Further, as reported in Table 27.4, there are 26 doctoral courses on global leadership, and only two programs offer research methods courses on global leadership research. Would graduates in leadership acquire skills to conduct global leadership research along with the master of global leadership knowledge? This question deserves attention from the curriculum designers in leadership.

Integration – Followership in Leadership Curricula

Only 14% of programs integrate followership courses in the leadership curricula and only 16% of doctoral programs use "follower," "followership," and related words, in their program and course descriptions. Whether the above percentages align with the attention paid to followership in the doctoral programs in leadership remains an unanswered question for this study due to limited information about courses and how they are taught. Nevertheless, it can be concluded that followership, as a stand-alone course or an integral part of leadership studies, seems not consistently taught or used across doctoral leadership programs. Additionally, teaching and research on followership remain scarce among the selected sample of doctoral programs, which indicates that leadership seems to still be taught from a leader-centered perspective. This study is limited to providing data on how many dissertation topics on followership have been produced by the doctoral programs in leadership.

The above finding is consistent with the 2019 study with a sample of 70 doctoral programs in leadership that indicated that "only 11 programs teach leadership from a process-based perspective, insofar as they either mention followership or leader-follower relationships in their study programs or include a course on followership" (Malakyan, 2019, p. 336). Hence, integrating the followership research education with leadership as one scholarly inquiry may provide not only a clearer focus but also a holistic approach to leadership and followership research as one academic continuum. Malakyan writes:

Given the widespread allegiance to the teaching of leadership from a leader-centered perspective, it is time to intentionally integrate theories of followership and leadership as one continuum or one academic endeavor to more fully understand the leader-follower relationship process in a given situation and context. Moreover, due to a number of paradigm shifts within leadership studies, such as changes from the industrial model of "me" to post-industrial "we" and from leader-centered theories to process-based and relational approach to leadership (Larsson & Lundholm, 2013; Shamir, 2007, 2012; Uhl-Bien & Ospina, 2012), it is the responsibility of academic institutions to promote less authoritarian and more democratic models of leadership for current and future organizational and community leaders and followers around the world (Malakyan, 2019, p. 339).

Developing Stewards of the Leadership Discipline

This study selected 50 doctoral programs in leadership that mostly comprised Ph.D. degrees and assessed program purpose/goals and learning objectives, curriculum structure, program quality, and integration of leadership and followership to determine the extent to which doctoral programs in leadership generate new knowledge, conserve relevant ideas, and enable doctoral students to transform knowledge into teaching, writing, and application, and by doing so prepare scholars, researchers, and practitioners as stewards of the leadership discipline. Although this study did not measure the teaching, writing, and application aspects of the selected 50 doctoral programs in leadership, attempts have been made to analyze data in light of four measures:

1. What do program purpose, goals, and objectives say about preparing stewards of the discipline?
2. How the program curricula are structured (the amount of content, research methods, and dissertation writing courses)?

3. What type of content and research method courses are offered as evidence for program quality?
4. How followership and leadership studies and theories have been integrated in content and research methods courses?

The study revealed that first, the purpose of 70% of doctoral programs is to enhance leadership knowledge, 76% of programs are research-focused, 68% of programs are theory-based, 44% of programs imply transformation, transformative research, and ideas to their program goals. Therefore, it is evident that these programs are committed to developing scholars that may well fit with the CID's definition of developing the stewards of the discipline. Second, the 40 doctoral programs that have a strong inclination toward a coursework-driven curriculum structure with an average of two-year coursework and one year conducting original research and writing may not be well structured to produce stewards of the leadership discipline out of their graduates.

However, programs within the remainder of 10, which require at least two years of research and dissertation writing and one-year coursework, maybe better structured to develop stewards of the leadership discipline. Third, the data shows that the overall quality of the 50 doctoral programs in leadership is high as they address both the contemporary and current trends of leadership theories. Additionally, since more than 50% of the content courses are context-, process-, complexity-, and systems-based courses, the quality of the content courses may well prepare doctoral students to become the stewards of the leadership discipline. However, the methods courses need to equip the doctoral students with leadership-related methodology tools. Fourth, the weakest area of the doctoral programs in leadership is the integration of followership and leadership research as one academic inquiry. Fifth, considering the fact that 86% of leadership programs worldwide are housed primarily in the United States, these programs may not be immune from teaching leadership that stems from a predominately Western individualistic and leader-centered perspective. Therefore, how leadership research is being taught in leadership programs in the world may determine what type of leaders will emerge for the 21st century digital and post-pandemic world.

In summary, the program purpose/goals and program quality may foster preparing stewards of the leadership discipline while the program curriculum structure and the discipline integration may hinder the development of stewards of the leadership discipline.

Future Directions for Doctoral Programs in Leadership

This study, which examined the existing doctoral programs in leadership worldwide, has revealed some gaps and opportunities for new directions in international leadership research. The study looked only at programs' available data on their websites and thus came with significant limitations. Nevertheless, some conclusions may be made for future research. Below are propositions for future directions for scholars and educators of leadership and global leadership research.

Proposition 1: Develop an international leadership doctoral curriculum that combines Western and non-Western leadership paradigms from Africa, America, Oceana, and other parts of the world that have not been fully integrated into leadership education which continues to be a Western educational endeavor as seen in the study sample. Therefore, doctoral students and leadership researchers may integrate intercultural leadership theories and approaches, and craft global leadership curricula that are multidisciplinary to address complexities of leadership across cultures in order to prepare stewards ("scholars-practitioners") of global leadership discipline (Tolstikov-Mast, Bieri, Walker, Wireman, & Vaiman, 2018).

Proposition 2: Studying leadership alongside followership as one continuum and for knowledge inquiry is the right thing to do. To omit or ignore one of the main variables from scientific inquiry, which has been the case with followership, makes the outcome of leadership research incomplete (Hurwitz & Hurwitz, 2015; Malakyan, 2015). Admitting that there is no leadership without followership, or without followers, there are no leaders is not enough (Cavell, 2007). We need to change our research agenda by studying leading and following behaviors and functions as one inquiry to address unresolved interpersonal, organizational, and global problems. For instance, collectivistic and relationship-oriented cultures may share their followership expertise with individualistic cultures on how to better combat the coronavirus pandemic. It should also be noted that collectivistic and relationship-oriented cultures prevented the spread of COVID-19 better than cultures with an individualistic and self-centered mindset.

Proposition 3: Developing stewards of the leadership discipline. The real leadership influence comes from the ethical quest for knowledge when doctoral faculty engage in apprenticeship relationships with the doctoral students or advisees to co-learn and co-create knowledge to address human, organizational, and environmental problems. CID considered this vision to be central and "foundational to the concept of intellectual community" (Walker, et al., 2009, p. 14). Thus, colleges and universities aiming for developing stewards of the leadership discipline worldwide is a noble cause.

There is a growing need for the education and development of national leaders worldwide with the aim to ensure intercultural dialogue, life betterment, and peace in the world (Andringa, 2001). The stewardship paradigm adopted by the Carnegie Initiative on the Doctorate presupposes an ability to share, enable, multiply, and sustain human, material, and environmental resources. It acknowledges the necessity for interdependence between the parties involved to develop collaborative and partnership programs to face global problems and challenges. It also enables parties to efficiently share and allocate resources and develop innovative ideas and methods to educate the next generation of the stewards of the leadership discipline toward global security and peace.

International leadership research and doctoral education that aims to develop stewards of leadership discipline may address several pressing global issues, such as global public health, poverty, economic inequality, environmental disasters, and abuse of human and natural resources. Thus, instead of engaging in arms races between nations, which leads to destruction, we may engage in developing stewards of global leadership.

References

Altheide, D., Coyle, M., DeVriese, K., & Scneider, C. (2013). Emergent qualitative document analysis. In S. Hes-se-Biber & P. Leavy (Eds.), *Handbook of Emergent Methods* (pp. 127–154). Guildford Press.

Andringa, R. C. (2001). *The Internationalization of Higher Education: Can the American Experience Advance Peace and Learning in the World?* Symposium at Peking University, China. Council for Christian Colleges & Universities.

Burke, P. J., & Stets, J. E. (2009). *Identity theory.* Oxford University Press.

Cavell, D. P. (2007). Leadership or followership: One or both? *Healthcare Financial Management, 61*(11), 142–144.

Chaleff, I. (2012). *Leading and following through tango.* Courageous follower blog: Archive for "video" category. *The courageous follower.* Retrieved from http://www.courageousfollower.net/blog/video/

Collinson, D. (2006). Rethinking followership: A post-structuralist analysis of follower identities. *The Leadership Quarterly, 17*(2), 179–189.

DeRue, D. S. (2011). Adaptive leadership theory: Leading and following as a complex adaptive process. *Research in Organizational Behavior, 31,* 125–150.

DeRue, D. S., & Ashford, S. J. (2010). Who will lead and who will follow? A social process of leadership identity construction in organizations. *Academy of Management Review, 35*(4), 627–647.

Gardner, W. L., Avolio, B. J., & Walumbwa, F. O. (2005). *Authentic leadership theory and practice: Origins, effects and development.* Emerald Group Publishing Limited.

Golde, C. M., & Walker, G. E. (Eds.) (2006). *Envisioning the future of doctoral education: Preparing stewards of discipline.* Jossey-Bass.

Guthrie, K. L., Teig, T. S., & Hu, P. (2018). *Academic leadership programs in the United States.* Leadership Learning Research Center, Florida State University.

Hewson, C., & Buchanan, T. (2013). *Ethics guidelines for internet-mediated research.* The British Psychological Society.

Hewson, C., & Stewart, D. W. (2016). *Internet research methods.* SAGE Publications.

Hollander, E. P. (1992). The essential interdependence of leadership and followership. *Current Directions in Psychological Science, 1,* 71–75.

House, R. J., Hanges, P. J., Javidan, M., Dorfman, P. W., & Gupta, V. Eds. (2004). *Culture, leadership, and organizations: The GLOBE study of 62 societies.* Sage Publications.

Hurwitz, M., & Hurwitz, S. (2015). *Leadership is half the story: A fresh look at followership, leadership, and collaboration.* University of Toronto Press.

International Leadership Association (2019). Leadership Program Directory. Retrieved from http://www.ila-net.org/Resources/LPD/index.htm.

Larsson, M. & Lundholm, S. E. (2013). Talking work in a bank: A study of organizing properties of leadership in work interactions. *Human Relations, 66*(8), 1101–1129.

Kirkpatrick, S. A., & Locke, E. A. (1991). Leadership: Do traits matter? *Academy of Management Perspectives, 5*(2), 48–60.

Malakyan, P. G. (2019). International curriculum and conceptual approaches to doctoral programs in leadership studies. *International Journal of Doctoral Studies, 14,* 325–350.

Malakyan, P. G. (2015). Depersonalizing leadership and followership: The process of leadership and followership. *World Journal of Social Science Research, 2*(2), 227–250.

Malakyan, P. G. (2014). Followership in leadership studies: A case of leader-follower trade approach. *Journal of Leadership Studies, 7*(4), pp. 6–22.

Moorman, R. H., Darnold, T. C., & Priesemuth, M. (2013). Perceived leader integrity: Supporting the construct validity and utility of a multi-dimensional measure in two samples. *The Leadership Quarterly, 24*(3), 427–444.

Rost, J. C. (1993). *Leadership for the twenty-first century.* Praeger.

Shamir, B. (2007). From passive recipients to active coproducers: Followers' roles in the leadership process. In R. P.-B. B. Shamir (Ed.), *Follower-centered perspectives on leadership: A tribute to the memory of James R. Meindl* (pp. ix–xxxix). Information Age Publishers.

Shamir, B. (2012). Leadership research or post-leadership research: Advancing leadership research versus throwing out the baby with the bath water. In M. Uhl-Bien & S. Ospina (Eds.), *Advancing relational leadership theory: A dialogue among perspectives* (pp. 477–500). Information Age Publishers.

Stets, J. E. & Burke, P. J. (2014). The development of identity theory. *Advances in Group Processes, 31,* 57–97.

Tolstikov-Mast, Y., Bieri, F., Walker, J., Wireman, A., &. Vaiman, V. (2018). Global leadership field and doctoral education: Advancing the discipline through a targeted curriculum. In J. S. Osland, M. E. Mendenhall, & L. Ming (Eds.), *Advances in global leadership* (Vol. 11, pp. 313 – 343). Emerald Publishing.

Uhl-Bien, M., & Ospina, S. M. (2012). *Advancing relational leadership research: A dialogue among perspectives.* Information Age Publishing.

Walker, G. E., Golde, C. M., Jones, L., Bueschel, A. C., & Hutchings, P. (2009). *The formation of scholars: Rethinking doctoral education for the twenty-first century* (Vol. 11). John Wiley & Sons.

Appendix 27A Sample of 50 Doctoral Programs in Leadership Worldwide

	Education Institution	Program name	URL
1	Alliant University	Ph.D. in Leadership	http://www.alliant.edu/asm/programs-degrees/Ph.D.-leadership.php
2	Alvernia University	Ph.D. in Leadership	http://www.alvernia.edu/academics/graduate/Ph.D./
3	Andrews University	Ph.D. in Leadership	https://bulletin.andrews.edu/preview_program.php?catoid=17&poid=14289&returnto=3661
4	Antioch University	Ph.D. Leadership and Change	https://www.antioch.edu/gslc/degrees-programs/business-management-leadership/Ph.D.lc-cross-sector/
5	Ashford University	Ph.D. in Organizational Development and Leadership	https://www.ashford.edu/online-degrees/business/phd-doctorate-organizational-development-leadership
6	Ateneo de Manila University	Ph.D. in Leadership Studies	http://www.ateneo.edu/sites/default/files/Ph.D.%20in%20Leadership%20Studies%20-%20major%20in%20Organization%20Development.pdf
7	Benedictine University	Ph.D./DBA Values-Driven Leadership	https://cvdl.ben.edu/Ph.D.-curriculum-leadership-organizational-change-sustainability/
8	Capella University	Ph.D. Business Management specialization Leadership	http://www.capella.edu/online-degrees/phd-leadership/
9	Cardinal Stritch University	Ph.D. in Leadership for the Advancement of Learning and Service	https://www.stritch.edu/Academics/Programs/EDHEP
10	Carolina University	Ph.D. in Leadership	https://catalog.carolinau.edu/program/doctor-philosophy/leadership#courses
11	Creighton University	Ed.D. in Interdisciplinary Leadership	https://gradschool.creighton.edu/programs/doctoral-degrees/leadership/interdisciplinary-leadership
12	Dallas Baptist University	Ph.D. in Leadership Studies	https://www4.dbu.edu/leadership/images/documents/PhD/GCSOL-PhD-brochure.pdf
13	Durham University	Ph.D. and Centre for Leadership and Followership	https://www.dur.ac.uk/business/research/management/leadership-and-followership/
14	Eastern University	Ph.D. Organizational Leadership	https://www.eastern.edu/academics/graduate-programs/phd-organizational-leadership
15	Gannon University	Ph.D. Organizational Learning and Leadership	http://www.gannon.edu/Academic-Offerings/Humanities-Education-and-Social-Sciences/Graduate/Organizational-Learning-and-Leadership/
16	Gonzaga University	Ph.D. in Leadership Studies	https://www.gonzaga.edu/school-of-leadership-studies/departments/ph-d-leadership-studies/curriculum/coursework
17	Grand Canyon University	Ed.D. in Organizational Leadership, with conc. in Org. Development	https://www.gcu.edu/degree-programs/edd-organizational-development

	Education Institution	Program name	URL
18	Indiana Institute of Technology	Ph.D. Global Leadership	http://Ph.D..indianatech.edu/
19	Indiana University of Pennsylvania	Ph.D. Administration & Leadership Studies	https://www.iup.edu/sociology/grad/als/
20	Indiana Wesleyan University	Ph.D. in Organizational Leadership	https://www.indwes.edu/adult-graduate/programs/Ph.D.-organizational-leadership/
21	INSIL International Higher Institute for Leadership in France	Postgraduate Diploma in Advanced Leadership Studies	http://www.insil.fr/programs/PALS_Ph.D._Leadership.htm
22	James Madison University	Ph.D. in Strategic Leadership	http://www.jmu.edu/grad/programs/snapshots/strategic-leadership.shtml
23	Johnson University	Ph.D. in Leadership Studies	https://johnsonu.edu/phd/ph-d-in-leadership-studies/online
24	Lancaster Bible College	Ph.D. in Leadership	http://catalog.lbc.edu/preview_entity.php?catoid=5&ent_oid=72&returnto=798
25	Louisiana State University--Baton Rouge	Ph.D. Human Resource & Leadership Development	http://lsu-hrld.blogspot.com/p/Ph.D.-prog.html
26	Louisiana State University Shreveport	Ed.D. in Leadership Studies	https://www.lsus.edu/academics/graduate-studies/graduate-programs/doctoral-program-in-leadership-studies
27	Marian University	Ph.D. in Leadership Studies	https://www.marianuniversity.edu/degree/leadership-studies-concentration/
28	North Carolina A&T State University	Ph.D. Leadership Studies	http://www.ncat.edu/ced/departments/lsad/leadership-studies/index.html
29	North Central University	Ph.D. in Organizational Leadership	https://www.ncu.edu/programs-degrees/doctoral/doctor-philosophy-organizational-leadership
30	Our Lady of the Lake University	Ph.D. Leadership Studies	http://www.ollusa.edu/s/1190/hybrid/default-hybrid-ollu.aspx?sid=1190&gid=1&pgid=7956
31	Pepperdine University	Ph.D. in Global Leadership and Change	https://gsep.pepperdine.edu/doctorate-global-leadership/courses/
32	Regent University	Doctor of Strategic Leadership	http://www.regent.edu/sbl/programs/program-summary/-tab-dsl
33	Regent University	Ph.D. Organizational Leadership	http://www.regent.edu/acad/global/degree_programs/doctoral/doctor_philosophy_organizational_leadership/home.cfm
34	Shenandoah University	Doctor of Professional Studies in Organizational Leadership	https://www.su.edu/education/leadership-studies/dprof-organizational-leadership/
35	Southern Baptist University	Ph.D. in Leadership	http://www.sbts.edu/doctoral/doctor-of-philosophy/concentrations/leadership/
36	The Chicago School for Professional Psychology	Ph.D. in Organizational Leadership	https://www.thechicagoschool.edu/washington-dc/programs/Ph.D.-organizational-leadership/
37	Thierry Graduate School of Leadership	Ph.D. in Leadership and Mastery of Change	http://www.thierryschool.be/postgraduate_programs_leadership/Ph.D._leadership_intro.htm

	Education Institution	Program name	URL
38	Troy University	Ph.D. in Global Leadership	https://www.troy.edu/academics/academic-programs/graduate/global-leadership.html
39	Union Institute and University	Ph.D. in Interdisciplinary Studies: Ethical & Creative Leadership	https://myunion.edu/academics/doctoral/ethical-and-creative-leadership/
40	University of Central Arkansas	Ph.D. in Leadership Studies	http://uca.edu/Ph.D.leadership/
41	University of Exeter	Ph.D. in Leadership Studies	http://www.exeter.ac.uk/postgraduate/research-degrees/business/leadership/
42	University of Guelph	Ph.D. in Management specialization in Organizational Leadership	https://www.uoguelph.ca/business/phd-management
43	University of Maryland - Eastern Shore	Ph.D. Organizational Leadership	http://www.umes.edu/ORLD/Default.aspx?id=12404
44	University of Minnesota	Ph.D. in Organizational Leadership, Policy, and Development	http://www.cehd.umn.edu/olpd/grad-programs/CIDE/Ph.D..html
45	University of Nebraska-Lincoln	Ph.D. Human Sciences specialization Leadership Studies	http://alec.unl.edu/leadership/Ph.D.-human-sciences-specialization-leadership-studies
46	University of Oklahoma	Doctorate in Organizational Leadership	https://pacs.ou.edu/graduate/doctorate-interdisciplinary-studies-organizational-leadership/
47	University of Pretoria and King's College London	Ph.D. in Leadership and Security Studies	http://www.up.ac.za/en/the-albert-luthuli-centre-for-responsible-leadership/article/2029977/-Ph.D.-in-leadershiphttps://www.kcl.ac.uk/alc/study-with-us/phd-research
48	University of San Diego	Ph.D. in Leadership Studies	http://www.sandiego.edu/soles/academics/Ph.D.-leadership-studies/
49	University of Victoria	Ph.D. in Leadership Studies	http://www.uvic.ca/education/psychology/future/Ph.D./leadership/index.php
50	William James College	Psy.D. in Leadership Psychology	http://www.williamjames.edu/academics/olp/leadership-psyd/index.cfm

Appendix 27B Types and Number of Research Methods Courses in Doctoral Leadership Programs

Types of Research Methods courses	Number of Programs	Types of Research Methods courses	Number of Programs
1. Action research	2	21. Principles of research	1
2. Analysis of research	2	22. Psychometric method	1
3. The complexity of leadership method	1	23. Qualitative a. Advanced qualitative	279

Types of Research Methods courses	Number of Programs	Types of Research Methods courses	Number of Programs
	1	24. Quantitative a. Advanced quantitative b. Applied quantitative	2541
4. Computer Analysis of Qualitative Data			
5. Content analysis	1	25. Research colloquium	1
6. Correlational method	1	26. Research critique	2
7. Discourse analysis	1	27. Research design a. Advanced research design	113
8. Empirical research	3	28. Research ethics	3
9. Ethnographic method	1	29. Research methods a. Advanced research methods b. Applied research methods c. Intermediate method	3721
10. Evidence-Based Practice	1	30. Research practica	1
11. Experimental design	1	31. Research prospectus	1
12. Field-based research	1	32. Research seminar	9
13. Foundations of research	4	33. Research synthesis for leadership	1
14. Global leadership research a. Advanced global leadership	11	34. Research team	1
15. Introduction to research methods	1	35. Scholarly argument	1
16. Marketing research a. Advanced Marketing research	1	36. Scholar-Practitioner	1
17. Mixed method	4	37. Survey research	41
		38. Survey of Applied Research Methods	
18. Narrative analysis	1	39. Statistics/Statistical Principle a. Advanced statistics b. Applied statistics c. Inferential statistics d. Intermediate statistics e. Multivariate statistics f. Regression analysis	8523151
19. Program assessment and evaluation	6	40. Tests and Measurements a. Advanced test and measurement	1
20. Structural equations	1	41. Verbal Data Analysis	1

Appendix 27C Types of Content Courses on Leadership used in 50 Doctoral Programs

1. Adaptive Leadership and Immunity to Change
2. Adaptive Leadership and Resistance to Change
3. Administrative and Policy Leadership Issues
4. Advanced Global Leadership
5. Advanced Global Leadership Studies and Research
6. Advanced Integration of Leadership: Self and System
7. Advanced Leadership Development Colloquium
8. Advanced Leadership Dynamics
9. Advanced Leadership Seminar
10. Advanced Leadership Theories
11. Advanced Leadership Theory and Research
12. Advanced Learning Theory and Design
13. Advanced Seminar: Leadership & Management
14. Advanced Seminar: Leading Organizational Change
15. Advanced Seminar: The Leader as Coach
16. Advanced Supervision and Leadership Theory
17. Advanced Topics in Organizational Development & Leadership
18. Advancing Leadership Theory
19. Advocacy for Change Leadership
20. African American Leadership Studies
21. Analyzing Complex Problems
22. Applied Courses for Leaders
23. Applied Leadership Practices: Integral Self and Systems Approach
24. Applied Leadership Research
25. Art and Practice of Leading
26. Art of Social Justice and Leadership
27. Assessment and Public Policy (for Postsecondary Analysis & Leadership)
28. Assessment Tools for Organizational Leadership
29. Becoming a 21st Century Leader
30. Biblical and Theological Foundations of Leadership
31. Business & Public Leadership
32. Change Agent
33. Change Theory & Practice
34. Change, Power and Conflict
35. Character and Ethics in Leadership
36. Collaborative Leadership and Partnership
37. Community-Based Leadership
38. Community College Leadership
39. Complexity & Leadership Studies
40. Conflict Management
41. Conflict Management for Leaders
42. Consulting Principles
43. Consulting to Groups
44. Contemporary Issues in Leadership
45. Contemporary Perspectives in Organizational Leadership Theory
46. Creating Change and Innovation

47. Creative Change and Transformational Leadership
48. Creativity and Innovation
49. Critical Leadership
50. Cross-Cultural Ministry Leadership
51. Cultural and Global Leadership
52. Cultural Competences in Organizational Leadership
53. Cultural Dimensions of Leadership
54. Culture, Climate, and Change Leadership
55. Cultures, Values, and Ethics in a Global Environment
56. Current & Global Issues in Industrial & Organizational Psychology
57. Curriculum and Leadership - 3 Credits
58. Curriculum, Culture and Instructional Leadership
59. Decision-Making Theories and Strategies
60. Developing Leader Capacity
61. Developing Leadership Capacities in Organizations & Communities
62. Developing Leadership Capacity
63. Dimensions of Leadership
64. Dimensions of Leading the Learning Organization
65. Dimensions of Leading to Serve
66. Dynamics of Race, Culture, and Gender in Higher Education
67. Ecclesial Leadership
68. Educational Policy and Leadership
69. Emergent Organizational Change
70. Emerging Theories of Leadership
71. Empathy, Dialog, and the Ethic of Care
72. Employee coaching
73. Entrepreneurial Leadership
74. Ethical and Creative Leadership in Group Dynamics, Organizations and Society
75. Ethical Dilemmas and Stewardship
76. Ethical Foundations and Influences
77. Ethics and Leadership
78. Ethics and Leadership in Global Environments
79. Ethics and Leadership in Organizations
80. Ethics and Leadership Studies
81. Ethics and Personal Leadership
82. Ethics and Social Responsibility in Leadership
83. Ethics and Spirituality in Leadership
84. Ethics and Standards of Practice in Leadership
85. Ethics in Leadership and Inquiry
86. Ethics, Governance & Social Responsibility
87. Examines Current Theories Regarding Leadership
88. Externship in Advanced Leadership
89. Field Studies in Global Leadership
90. Followership
91. Foresight and Strategy
92. Formal Organizations in Education
93. Foundational Theories of Leadership
94. Foundations of Ethical and Creative Leadership
95. Foundations of Leadership

96. Foundations of Leadership Theory
97. Global Consulting
98. Global Leadership
99. Global Leadership Development
100. Global Leadership Research
101. Global Leadership Seminar
102. Global Leadership, Systems & Policy
103. Global Perspectives on Leadership
104. Global Perspectives on Learning and Leadership
105. Group Dynamics and Team Leadership
106. Group process
107. Healthcare Leadership
108. Historical and Cultural Perspectives of Organizational Leadership
109. Human Resource Development
110. Human Resources Leadership and Management
111. Innovation in Global Leadership
112. Innovation, creativity, and change
113. Instructional Leadership: Theory/Practice
114. Integral Leadership Theory
115. International Organizational Systems, Theory and Leadership
116. Inter-organizational Leadership
117. Intercultural Leadership
118. Interdisciplinary Foundations of Leadership: Psychology, Management
119. Interdisciplinary Leadership Seminar
120. Interdisciplinary Leadership Studies
121. Intermediate Leadership Theories
122. Internship in Global Leadership
123. Internship in Leadership
124. Intra-organizational Leadership
125. Introduction to Doctoral Study in Global Leadership
126. Introduction to Leadership Studies and Ethics
127. Introduction to Servant Leadership
128. Leader Decision Processes
129. Leaders and Followers
130. Leadership Analytics
131. Leadership and Accountability for Nonprofit Organizations (for Nonprofit and Community Leadership)
132. Leadership and Applied Ethics
133. Leadership and Applied Ethics
134. Leadership and Change
135. Leadership and Classical Ethics
136. Leadership and Communications
137. Leadership and Consulting
138. Leadership and Corporate Social Responsibility
139. Leadership and Creativity
140. Leadership and Diversity
141. Leadership and Diversity
142. Leadership and Diversity
143. Leadership and Ecology Ethics

144. Leadership and Ethics
145. Leadership and Ethics
146. Leadership and Feminist Ethics
147. Leadership and Followership: Theoretical Bases of Leadership
148. Leadership and Film
149. Leadership and History
150. Leadership and Law
151. Leadership and Learning Organizations
152. Leadership and Management Theory
153. Leadership and Motivation
154. Leadership and Organizational Cultures
155. Leadership and Peacebuilding: Conceptual Relationships and the Role of Outliers
156. Leadership and Personal Development
157. Leadership and Personal Ethics
158. Leadership and Post-Modern Ethics
159. Leadership and Psychology
160. Leadership and Social Justice
161. Leadership and Spirituality
162. Leadership and Technology
163. Leadership Applications
164. Leadership as Personal Practice
165. Leadership Assessment
166. Leadership Capstone Experience
167. Leadership Coaching
168. Leadership Colloquium
169. Leadership Communication in Organizations
170. Leadership Development and the Use of the Self
171. Leadership Development Colloquium
172. Leadership Ethics and Morality
173. Leadership for Change
174. Leadership for Diversity and Educational Justice
175. Leadership for K-20 Diversity & Education
176. Leadership for Social Change
177. Leadership for the Future (Capstone Seminar)
178. Leadership Foundations
179. Leadership in a Global Society
180. Leadership in Complex Organizations
181. Leadership in Global Context
182. Leadership in Global Economy and Society
183. Leadership in Organizations
184. Leadership in School Improvement
185. Leadership Inquiry
186. Leadership Issues in Technology and Organizational Change
187. Leadership Lecture Series Seminar
188. Leadership of Cross-Cultural and International Management
189. Leadership Policy and Culture
190. Leadership Pro-seminar: The Self and the System
191. Leadership Practicum
192. Leadership Project: Living Case Study

242. Managerial Economics for Decision Making and Leadership
243. Marketing for Leaders
244. Mentored Leadership Internship
245. Models of Participatory Leadership
246. Moral and Ethical Foundations of Leadership
247. Nature of Leadership Essay
248. Negotiations and Conflict Resolution for Contemporary Leaders
249. Neuroleadership Research Lab
250. Nonprofit/Philanthropic Leadership and Management
251. Oral Communication for Leaders
252. Organizational Behavior and Leadership
253. Organizational Communication
254. Organizational Culture and Climate
255. Organization Development and Change
256. Organizational Governance
257. Organizational Leader
258. Organizational Leadership
259. Organizational Leadership stream
260. Organizational Leadership/Consulting
261. Organizational Science and Leadership
262. Organizational Strategy and Design
263. Organizational Theory and Design
264. Organizational Theory and Development
265. Personality and Developmental Theory
266. Perspectives in Organizational Leadership
267. Philosophical Concerns in Educ/Leadership
268. Planning for Change
269. Policy and Politics in Global Leadership
270. Policy Development at the Leadership Level
271. Politics, Organizations, and Leaders: Legal and Ethical Issues
272. Power & Influence in Leadership
273. Power, Politics, and Influence in Organizations
274. Process Consultation and Facilitation Skills
275. Professional & Business Ethics in Organizational Leadership
276. Promoting Resilience in Communities After Trauma
277. Psychology of Leadership
278. Psychosocial Dimensions of Leadership
279. Readings in Leadership
280. Research in Leadership Education
281. Research Synthesis for Leadership
282. Seminar in Servant Leadership
283. Servant Leadership
284. Service Theory: Evolution and Influences
285. Small-Group Processes
286. Social Construction of Leadership
287. Sociocultural Concerns in Ed/Leadership
288. Special Topics in Leadership
289. Stewardship
290. Strategic Decision Making

28

Discovering the Behaviors of Effective Leaders in Africa

A Doctoral Student's Journey into International Leadership Research

Frank Banfill

Introduction

It was quite a sight as I took my seat on the deck of the ferry that would take me from Tanzania's mainland to the Lake Victoria island of Ukerewe. The woman sitting across from me had a bucket with a live chicken in it. A young man in the row in front of her was holding two goats by a leash made of rope. My driver, interpreter, and their truck were parked in the middle of the open-deck ferry. I could easily see the shores of Ukerewe, as the island is just a short boat ride across the water. I was told that at one time Ukerewe was connected to the mainland, but severe storms had caused erosion. Although the sights were interesting, they were not particularly unusual. I had made many trips to the east African country and these sights were commonplace. Over the previous five years, I had helped U.S. organizations connect with Tanzanian churches for the purpose of community development, church starting, and leadership training. I was making two to three Tanzania trips a year all to the Mara Region which is in the north bordering Kenya, Lake Victoria, and the Serengeti National Park. I had spent significant time in Mara's villages talking to residents and community leaders. I had also spent considerable time with church pastors and leaders from a variety of Christian denominations.

This journey to Ukerewe, however, was first my visit to the island. This was the last stop on my dissertation research trip. I was scheduled to conduct a focus group with members from a church on the island. My research topic dealt with effective leaders in Tanzania, especially why these leaders were effective. To answer that question, my research methodology called for interviews of the leaders as well as a sampling of their followers. I felt that these followers could give insight and perspective on the question that I could not get from just interviewing the leaders. The Ukerewe church recently had a pastor that I had identified in pilot research as an effective leader. Through that pilot project I came to a definition of effective leaders within the context of the African Inland Church of Tanzania (AICT) denomination as pastors who could "grow the active numerical membership of a church over a five-year period and lead the church to conduct community development projects designed to improve the health, economics, or general well-being of the community" (Banfill, 2015, p. 31). This community work included establishing health clinics, programs for vulnerable children, water wells, community micro-banking for entrepreneurship and

DOI: 10.4324/9781003003380-28

more. These leaders were not only concerned about their own organizations but also their broader community. My task was to understand what behaviors made the Ukerewe pastor and the other pastors in my study effective. Was there any commonality?

I had already interviewed the Ukerewe pastor on the mainland, where he was recently transferred to work for the AICT. I had met with three other effective leaders and conducted focus groups with their followers. Now it was time for the final group. Will anyone show up to the meeting? Will they provide solid information that could be turned into usable data? Will I be able to communicate effectively with them through my interpreter? How will I tie together the information I have gathered so far on this trip to write my dissertation? There were many questions floating through my mind as we journeyed to Ukerewe.

I also paused to appreciate that fact that as a doctoral student studying global leadership, this was a great opportunity to be fully immersed in the research. Not only that, but the opportunity to study global leadership as a discipline was also a great opportunity for me. For several years, I looked for a doctoral program that would best fit my interests, which at the time involved international humanitarian concerns and leadership development. I had filled out the application for one program in general leadership, but circumstances at the time kept me from proceeding. Then a few years later when I came across the Ph.D. in Global Leadership program at Indiana Tech, I knew immediately it was the right fit. I was able to study leadership from a global perspective which added a certain richness to my studies that I have come to greatly appreciate. For example, a course on developing human capital included an exploration of working with global, cross-cultural teams. Indiana Tech's program offered a concentration in organizational management, and those classes were also taught through a global lens. As a practitioner of leadership and organizational development, I found this global perspective to be especially helpful in my work. The multicultural focus of the program heightened my awareness of the dynamics that culture plays in every organization. In particular, it helped me see how culture shapes people's perceptions and perspectives, which are critical factors that leaders must take into consideration if they are to lead effectively.

The time on the island of Ukerewe was the final leg of my journey into international leadership research as a student. From that journey, I discovered the benefits of doing pilot studies. I learned lessons related to questioning, culture, narrowing research, relationships, and flexibility in research. Now several years later, I continue to reap the personal rewards of that journey. It is my desire that those who are beginning their journey into international leadership research will be able to learn from my journey.

The Benefits of International Pilot Studies

I recall a faculty member in my doctoral program describing the dissertation as putting together a giant jigsaw puzzle. My dissertation puzzle was greatly aided by four pilot studies that I was able to conduct prior to my dissertation research. These four pilot studies became my four corner pieces and helped frame the research in a way that enabled the other pieces to fall into place. The studies told me what the puzzle would be about and showed me an obscured picture of a possible outcome of my dissertation research. One corner of the puzzle pictured how leadership was understood and the various ways it was implemented in Tanzania. The second corner showed multiple layers of culture and how those interacted with leadership. The third corner showed leadership in action, tangible results of leaders' decisions and activities over time. The final corner revealed that by understanding a specific leadership theory the rest of the puzzle could make sense.

It took four months from the time I was released by my committee chair to start working on my dissertation until the time I stood before the dissertation committee to defend my work. Now several years post-graduate, looking back at Ukerewe and that research trip to Tanzania, I realize that the success of that trip and the speed in which I was able to complete the dissertation process was tied to lessons learned during these pilot studies. van Teijlingen and Hundley (2001) explain that pilot studies in the social sciences "refers to mini versions of a full-scale study ... are a crucial element of a good study design" (p. 1) and they increase the likelihood of success in the main study. Doctoral students certainly do not need four pilot projects like I did for successful research. I was able to take advantage of the fact that I was already going back and forth to Africa. Students should, however, make sure that any pilot studies they do are well formulated ahead of time. My Ph.D. program director was instrumental in helping me think through these pilot projects so that I could maximize their potential for research and set a good foundation for my future dissertation research. Having an experienced researcher as a mentor was invaluable.

Experience conducting international research during a doctoral program is instrumental in preparing students for successful dissertation work in international leadership. Indiana Tech offers global practicums which are comprised of both university organized, and independent studies conducted abroad. The university not only offered but strongly encouraged its global leadership Ph.D. students to do at least one international research project. Doing global research was an integral part of the program, and it was a key component of my dissertation. Since I was already making trips to Tanzania as part of my profession, I incorporated these practicums into my travels under the guidance of the Ph.D. program director. During the four years I was in the doctoral program, I was able to conduct four pilot projects – three global practicums in Tanzania and one study in my home country of the United States. My first study involved validating the translation of a research in-strument. My second study sought to understand the meaning of leadership within the culture, and my third study was multi-faceted involving document analysis, a focus group, and a survey. The fourth study, conducted in the U.S., involved an interview with a Tanzanian national. When I started into the first study, I had no intention of doing three more. Those evolved as I progressed in my studies and as I had more opportunities to visit Tanzania.

These pilot studies were like direction signs on a roadway that not only guided where the dissertation should head but helped me connect with people along the way who ensured the outcome of the journey was successful. The pilot studies also helped me determine the variables to measure, how the variables could be related, and then in the case of my dissertation, why case studies would be an effective tool for generalization. These all contribute to strong research. Construct, internal, and external validity are important factors in research (Yin, 2014). Construct validity is defined as "the extent to which variables accurately measure the constructs of interest...Do the operations really get at the things we are trying to measure?" (Vogt & Johnson, 2011, p. 70). Internal validity is defined as "the degree to which one can draw valid conclusions about the causal effects of one variable on another" (Vogt & Johnson, 2011). While external validity is defined by Vogt and Johnson (2011) as "the extent to which the findings of a single research study apply beyond the study. It's another term for generalizability" (p. 134). The pilot studies contributed to each of these. Maxwell (2013) explained that pilot studies enable the researcher to understand "the concepts and theories held by the people you are studying" (p. 67). I found this to be true. I also found that the pilot projects were real-world lessons in international leadership research. They were lessons that I could not get in a textbook alone.

I recommend that doctoral students studying fields such as leadership, business, sociology, and related disciplines engage in international research as part of their doctoral work even if they are not in a global studies program. As globalization increases, the world becomes increasingly inter-connected (Adler & Gundersen, 2008). The rapid global spread of COVID-19 in 2020 taught us that. This inter-connectivity means that all leadership is becoming global leadership. Even small single location organizations find themselves connecting cross-culturally and internationally for supplies, personnel, and even markets (Froman, 2014). Understanding international research better positions a leader to lead effectively. While every student may not have the opportunity like I had to do four international pilot projects, each doctoral student can participate in global research at some level even if they cannot travel abroad. My fourth study took place over the phone with a Tanzanian who had immigrated to the U.S.

There are many opportunities for international leadership research that do not require getting on an airplane. When COVID-19 shut down large parts of many countries in 2020, video conferencing became a way of life for many (Thomason & Williams, 2020). It has also caused people to think of new ways to connect with people who are not face to face. The same concepts could be used in international research as well. In addition, as a result of globalization, a researcher typically does not have to look far to find people from other cultures and nationalities. Direct access to these groups are often available close to home. Most major cities around the world, certainly in the U.S., have large international populations. I once lived on a cul-de-sac in a Dallas, TX suburb that had five houses on it. Each house had a family of a different nationality. An Ethiopian couple owned the house to the right of ours. We are Americans, and on our left was an Indian family that we got to know quite well. Next to them was a Vietnamese family and then the last house was owned by a Chinese couple. I literally walked steps from my house into my neighbor's home and found myself immersed into another culture. Looking back now, many of the components of my research in Tanzania could be conducted today through Internet video conferencing and acquiring digital versions of artifacts and documents. Other components, such as the focus groups, would still be difficult to conduct today without the researcher's physical presence because a lack of technology and Internet access still exists in many parts of the world, including Tanzania. The point is the more the researcher can immerse himself or herself into the culture being studied the more dynamic the study will be, but there are ways to connect with a culture without physically being where it is most prevalent. As a result of my journey into international research through pilot projects and my dissertation, I discovered five helpful lessons for novice researchers.

Lesson One: Stop Assuming and Start Questioning

Early in my doctoral studies, I was introduced to the Multifactor Leadership Questionnaire (MLQ), an instrument originally developed by Avolio and Bass (1995). The MLQ is used to measure characteristics consistent with transformational leadership (Avolio & Bass, 2004). The more I studied transformation leadership theory in the early days of my doctoral program, the more convinced I became that transformational leadership characteristics were what was needed by the world's leaders to be truly effective. I decided that I wanted to research if local leaders in Tanzania demonstrated transformational leadership. Tanzanians predominately speak Kiswahili. I found a Kiswahili translation of the MLQ through a psychological assessments vendor. I had an upcoming trip to Tanzania where I was scheduled to speak to a gathering of leaders. I thought this would be the perfect opportunity to administer the MLQ and launch into international leadership research. I had everything figured out, but I needed my Ph.D. program director to sign off on the project so I would get credit for it.

My program director responded to my request with a simple but profound question, "Has the Kiswahili translation of the MLQ been validated?" I had never thought about that. I knew there had been years of research on the MLQ's use around the world. I assumed that if the instrument had proven validity in English then it would in Kiswahili as well. Following my director's advice, I contacted the MLQ's publisher to see if there was research on the validity of the Kiswahili translation. I was told that there was not any of which they were aware. There was a bilingual English-Kiswahili researcher who received permission to translate the MLQ, but there was nothing published on its validation. I began to understand that if people completing the instrument in Kiswahili do not have the same understanding of the questions as English speakers, then their results are not the same as in English. This would negate the instrument's validity and damage the credibility of my research. Chiumento et al. (2017) emphasized that in translating words and concepts between languages an approach must be taken to maintain "equivalence across the source and target languages…[moving] beyond the 'correct' word toward the meaning embedded within the language" (pp. 608–609). Their qualitative cross-language study of mental health research in South Asia showed the importance of equivalent concepts not just lexical equivalence.

The simple question from my program director was a foundational lesson to my understanding of international research: you can never assume the equivalent translation of constructs across cultures. The Kiswahili words in the MLQ translation may have been the equivalent to the words in the English version but did the words mean the same thing to a Kiswahili speaker as to an English speaker? I learned in that first pilot study that this is a fundamental question that must be answered before we can assign meaning to the data we gather in research. I learned as a novice international researcher that I had to stop assuming and start questioning.

I did administer the MLQ to 48 leaders during that trip to Tanzania, but as part of a validation process. This was used to assess how long it took the respondents to complete the MLQ, see what questions were left blank indicating a possible lack of understanding, and to generally observe how respondents approached the MLQ. In addition, three non-English speaking respondents were asked through an interpreter to read the Kiswahili MLQ and explain a sampling of the questions (Tsang et al., 2017). Besides administering the MLQ to these leaders, the validation included having the Kiswahili version translated back to English by two interpreters whose first language was Kiswahili (Sperber, 2004). One of those interpreters was also asked to verbally explain what each question meant to him so I could assess if the meaning he assigned was consistent with the meaning I assigned. A third interpreter reviewed the Kiswahili translation for spelling mistakes and typos. This process revealed that four of the 45 questions on the instrument needed translation corrections to be fully understood but the remaining questions were reliable. This validation process was consistent with the approach Chiumento et al. (2017) recommends in using multiple interpreters to quality check the work of translations.

I also discovered through this process the impact a person's level of education can have on their understanding. For example, with this group of 48 the average respondent had the equivalent of a U.S. sixth grade education, yet their average age was 42. This was because of the poor education system in Tanzania and the fact that in most cases students in upper grades must pay tuition to attend public school. Most Tanzanians live in extreme poverty, making tuition payments unfeasible. As a researcher, I learned that I had to ensure that communication took place on a level appropriate for the people being studied. I could not assume that a 42-year-old leader in a Tanzanian organization had an equivalent education and training as a 42-year-old leader in a comparable Western organization. This finding was consistent with a multi-national study of migrant worker healthcare providers conducted by Teunissen et al. (2017) which noted the importance of appropriate communication for a participant's education level. Language and how it relates to a person's education are important cultural considerations, but as I would learn in my next pilot study, culture is quite complex. There are multiple layers to any culture that are not readily apparent.

Lesson Two: Look for Layers of Culture

Building on the lessons learned in the first pilot study, I conducted a second pilot to understand how Tanzanian church leaders understood the term *leadership*. During my doctoral studies I learned that leadership as a construct varied by culture (April & Ephraim, 2006). Some societies did not have an equivalent word. Other societies did not understand leadership in the same sense as it is understood in the West. I felt it would be a helpful exercise if I could better understand Tanzanian concepts of the word. I had already done some leadership training in Tanzania, but never stopped to ask basic questions like the Tanzanian views on leadership. I had been guilty of doing what many Westerners do when they try to serve people in Africa – I came with Western answers when I did not even know the African questions. Americans are often characterized as being great doers but not so great listeners (Corbett et al., 2014). This second pilot study helped me learn to slow down and listen before I try to help.

Since the humanitarian work I was doing in Tanzania was in conjunction with local church and regional denominational church leadership, I already had access to church leaders. I noticed that church leaders, especially local pastors, were on the front lines of dealing with a variety of social challenges such as child mortality, caring for the sick who have limited healthcare access, hunger, poverty, and damaging cultural rituals such as female genital mutilation. Because of their proximity to people and their unique leadership role in communities, local church pastors are in positions where their leadership, or lack of it, can significantly impact a community (Davis, 1998; Patterson, 2014). Pastors and religious leaders, for example, often play a role in either connecting people to healthcare or bringing healthcare to the people. Some 40% of sub-Saharan Africa's health care services are provided by religious organizations (Patterson, 2014). In Tanzania specifically, the government relies on service agreements with faith-based healthcare providers to fill critical gaps in its national healthcare system (Maluka, 2018). Faith-based providers often offer broader care at lower costs to patients at a higher perceived quality than government entities (Olivier 2015; Maluka, 2018).

During these pilot studies and my other visits to east Africa, I began to see that if pastors were effective in their leadership then societal improvement was possible. I visited once impoverished communities that had been transformed economically and physically, as well as spiritually, because of church leaders. While my doctoral courses had given me a theoretical framework from which to approach my research (transformational leadership), it was being on the ground in east Africa that gave me the philosophical foundation for my research (social welfare). The question arose, however, whether my understanding of leadership was the same or similar to the Tanzanian's understanding. I define leadership as the movement of people toward a shared vision. Applying my definition to Tanzanian leadership, I would see these church leaders moving society to the vision of better communities by addressing these societal challenges. Is this how Tanzanian leaders see themselves? Do they see leadership as helping society improve?

In the second pilot study, I conducted seven in-depth one-on-one interviews in Tanzania. Five of the interviews were conducted in English with bilingual informants. Two of the interviews were conducted in Kiswahili and English with the assistance of interpreters. All of the interviews took place within the Mara region. Six of the informants were affiliated with the African Inland Church of Tanzania Mara & Ukerewe Diocese (AICT) and one with the Tanzania Fellowship of Evangelical Students (TAFES). Four of the AICT informants held denominational leadership positions, one was a local church pastor, and one managed an AICT-operated hotel. Ages ranged from 22 to 63, with all but one age 38 or younger. Six were males and one was female. They were chosen for the interviews because of their positions and my proximity to them while I was on a work-related trip.

In addition to general questions on definitions of leadership, examples of good leadership, how leadership is developed, and so forth, informants were asked questions about their tribal backgrounds and how leaders were established within their tribes. There are 128 different tribes in Tanzania (Oberlander & Elverdan, 2000), each with its own unique culture and many with its own language. So, it was imperative that the interviews included questions related to tribal experiences to grasp a full understanding of the topic. Since this was a work-related trip and not a dedicated research excursion, I knew going into it that the interview process would have to be flexible and meetings scheduled after I arrived in the country. The interviews themselves took place in a variety of places. Some while sitting in an automobile, some outdoors under trees, a couple occurred at a hotel, and one at a church. Basically, the interviews occurred wherever I could get access to the informants. Prior to the trip, I had a list of people I wanted to interview. There were others I decided to interview once I had the opportunity to engage with them during the trip.

One of the leaders in this pilot study described what it was like to be Maasai, which was his tribe. Male members of the tribe undergo a rite of passage at age 14 where they live on their own in the wilderness for a month. As a result, he said that Maasai men tend to be fearless, can stand for long periods of time, and can function on little sleep. He explained that many Maasai men are employed as security guards for these reasons. Leaders are chosen within the Maasai tribe based on three factors: contributing in tribal meetings, having many children and handling them well, and a history of leaders within their clan. Other tribes, however, had different approaches to leadership selection. One based it partially on whether a man had multiple wives. Polygamy was seen by many as a sign of economic success, and the belief was that the economically successful would make good leaders. There were also significant differences in how tribes viewed women. These cultural differences create dynamic situations that leaders must operate within, especially if a leader is not from the same tribe (culture) as those he or she is leading.

The results of that study not only informed my understanding of leadership concepts in Tanzania but provided valuable experiences that would later be used in the dissertation research. The study itself showed that Tanzanians' concept of leadership is very similar to Western concepts of leadership and that Tanzanians "desire authentic and transformational leaders who can solve problems and move people forward to a more desirable situation" (Banfill, 2015, p. 53). Although their concept was similar, the time frame in which they viewed the leadership process differed from how Westerners typically approach leadership. Westerners, especially Americans, think in terms of quick results. "What must be done to turn things around in the next 30 days" is a question that you would expect to hear from an American but not from a Tanzanian. These Tanzanian leaders saw leadership as a process that plays out over a longer period.

The opportunity to conduct this study gave me experience in formulating interview questions, conducting cross-cultural interviews using an interpreter, conducting cross-cultural interviews with bilingual Kiswahili-English speakers, and most importantly, learning to see life from the perspective of those I was studying. These were all skills that were drawn upon in the dissertation research. I discovered in this study that if I approached Tanzania as a single culture then I would miss significant understanding. For example, in Oberlander and Elverdan's (2000) study of malaria treatment in Tanzania, they found that local cultures influenced whether malaria treatments would be sought and if they were, how well treatment adherence would take place.

In my dissertation research, which included four case studies of effective Tanzanian leaders, subcultures became one of the focal points. You could not fully appreciate or understand what made the four leaders effective without understanding how they operated cross-culturally. This second pilot study helped me see the importance of understanding the culture within the culture. In Tivinarlik and Wanat's (2006) year-long ethnographical study of educators in Papua New Guinea, they noted that "to develop an appropriate educational system for an entire nation requires a sound understanding of the local cultural contexts in which the system will be implemented" (p. 1). Papua New Guinea, like Tanzania, is multicultural. Understanding local cultural contexts is foundational to understanding the whole. This is a good lesson for anyone conducting international leadership research.

Lesson Three: Pilot Studies Help Narrow Research Focus

International pilot studies not only can provide insights into the layers of culture, but they also can help the researcher better narrow his or her research focus. My third pilot study was the most extensive and significant of the four. It also was the most beneficial to the dissertation research from a practical perspective. It enabled me to identify the leaders that I would later study in-depth in my dissertation case studies. It also introduced me to existing data that would be helpful in the research. This study had three parts: administration of the validated MLQ and demographic survey of AICT church leaders, conducting a focus group of AICT denominational leaders, and evaluation of a five-year AICT church growth study for the Mara-Ukerewe Dioceses.

In the first part, 55 people completed the MLQ and survey during a previously scheduled denominational meeting. I utilized the help of an AICT leader who had received advanced education in the U.S. to administer the survey. Of the 55 respondents, 24 were identified as currently serving senior pastors. These 24 became the focus of the second part of the study, which involved a focus group of three denominational leaders. These leaders had extensive experience working with all 24 identified pastors and their churches. As a group, they discussed each of the 24 and came to a consensus on who they considered to be the most effective leaders and why. That discussion not only narrowed down the potential pool of pastors to be studied but it created a definition of effective leadership within their context. This would become the definition used in my dissertation and it drove the selection of study participants. In the third part of the study, I did an analysis of church data provided by the denomination to determine which churches had added the most members during a five-year period.

The outcome of the third pilot study was a list of the top four pastors who had led their churches to not only grow numerically but also to make significant contributions to their communities. This fit my developing philosophical foundation of African social welfare and the belief that leaders need to make a difference not only within the sphere of the organizations they lead but within their broader communities. These four pastors and their churches would become the focus of my dissertation research into the behaviors of effective leaders in Tanzania.

More than anything else, however, this third study gave clarity to what my research question would be. As I sat with the three leaders from the AICT at a coffee shop in the city of Mwanza and listened to them discuss the initial 24 leaders, the question of *why* kept coming to my mind. Why were some pastors successful in the eyes of these denominational leaders and not others? Why had some pastors turned around declining churches while others oversaw the decline of their churches? Why did some pastors make great efforts to improve the welfare of their communities while others did seemingly little? From a practical perspective, I felt that if I could understand the why then I would have valuable information that could help more Tanzanian pastors become effective leaders, which in turn would improve the welfare of many Tanzanians. My research was now taking shape. I knew what had happened leadership-wise across the dioceses, now I needed to find out why it happened.

My final pilot study did not involve getting on an airplane. It was an interview of a Tanzanian who had recently emigrated to the U.S. The interview focused on questions related to his pastor in Tanzania and if he demonstrated characteristics consistent with transformational leadership. This interview helped prepare me to conduct the focus group on Ukerewe island and the three others I did on the mainland during the dissertation research. It gave me the opportunity to test questions and practice interviewing a Tanzanian church member.

Thanks to these pilot studies, I now had the four corners of my dissertation jigsaw puzzle. As I looked at these corners, it occurred to me that a multiple-case study approach would be the best way to unlock the puzzle's meaning in a way that could best benefit a broad audience. Although I was a student, I also was a practitioner. My thinking was to use my academic pursuit to develop practical tools that could make a positive difference in people's lives. In that light, I felt case studies would be a good way to communicate my research findings because people, especially in Tanzania, relate well to stories (Tandi Lwoga et al., 2011). Each case study would be a unique story with real people in situations with which other leaders in Tanzania could relate. Collectively, these stories would provide deep insights into effective leadership that I felt could inspire others to lead in similar ways.

I decided to use multiple case studies following the advice of Creswell (2007) who said that if done properly, multiple cases allow for broader generalization of findings. Given that my purpose was to help leaders in Africa, I wanted the outcome of my work to be as applicable as possible to as many as possible. Also, at the time, much of the research related to global leadership was based solely on surveys, according to McCall and Mobley (2001). They questioned whether "surveys could ever encompass the complexity of global leadership" (p. 37). It was clear to me both through my coursework and these pilot studies that they were correct. My desire was to uncover some of those complexities, and I felt case studies would be a good way to do so. Creswell (2007) recommended that no more than four or five cases be used in a multiple case study. I settled on four cases for my study because I had identified in the third pilot project what I felt were four strong examples. The pilot studies were invaluable in framing the dissertation puzzle and narrowing my research focus to these four cases.

Lesson Four: The Importance of Relationships in International Leadership Research

The pilot studies did more than frame the puzzle, however. They were pivotal in developing relationships and rapport with nationals that would be critical to my larger study. The relationships developed over time leading up to my dissertation research trip enabled me to assemble a competent team to assist me while I was in country. That team included a cultural collaborator, two interpreters, and a driver. Without these relationships, it would not have been possible to arrange the focus groups, schedule interviews with the four pastors, or even manage the logistics of moving around the country to gather data. When I went to Tanzania to research for the dissertation, I had just seven days in country. I knew, however, that I could accomplish what I needed to do because I had relationships with competent people in the country. As a result of the time that I spent in Tanzania working on various leadership development and humanitarian projects, I had developed a collegial relationship with the team that would eventually assist me. We viewed each other as equals in terms of our abilities and social status, but I sought to elevate their importance and expertise. I tried to consistently express that I was there to serve them. I reiterated that they were the experts when it came to the culture, community needs, and understanding the people. I also made it clear that my research activities were born out of a genuine desire to provide them with information and tools to make them more effective as leaders. This approach was well received. I was viewed as their partner rather than as one seeking to establish power. As a result of this relational foundation, the support team was more than willing to give their time and energy to assist me.

These people worked with me in advance of the trip. One was my cultural collaborator who served as the point person in organizing the focus groups, pastor interviews, and interpreters. A cultural collaborator is what Webb (2012) calls a "specialized cultural informant" (p. 64) who can help a researcher better understand cultural meaning. My cultural collaborator was a respected leader within the denomination I was studying, and he had extensive experience working with Western NGOs. His role as my research point person involved many back-and-forth emails between us and a phone call to make sure he understood the research methodology prior to my trip. This was critical because the research design called for a specific approach to securing focus group members to ensure they had relevant information and that there was an element of random selection. I did not want, for example, the pastors handpicking the focus group members that would be discussing their leadership. From a practical standpoint, I needed to be sure that when I arrived at the appointed focus group meeting site people were there. This is a challenge in Tanzania where people often operate on a concept of time and calendaring much different than the West. The people who agreed to participate in the focus groups received multiple reminder calls. All four groups had four to five people show up for their meetings, which met the design requirements (Banfill, 2015). After my research trip, the cultural collaborator assisted me in understanding the cultural aspects of the data I analyzed, and he reviewed the accuracy of my findings.

In addition to his pre- and post-trip work, the cultural collaborator accompanied me on five of my eight interviews to translate. He also recommended the two other interpreters who assisted me as

I moved around the country. I had worked with both interpreters on past non-research related projects. Based on my experience with these two and the cultural collaborator's recommendation, I had great confidence in their translation abilities. I was able to rest assured that what informants were saying in the interviews was being accurately translated to me. This is critical to international research. Chiumento 2017 defines interpreters as "someone who translates from a source to a target language, transferring meaning based upon vocabulary, grammar, expression, context, and culture" (p. 606). They went on to explain that the "the interpreter is seen as an active co-constructor of data influenced by their intersubjectives…that involves seeking, contributing to, eliciting, or limiting the attainment of data" (p. 606). In other words, the quantity and quality of data is directly tied to the abilities of the interpreter. Therefore, when conducting international research using an interpreter, careful attention must be given to who is selected to fill this role.

I have traveled to 30 countries, mostly for my work in church and community development and to do leadership training. I have worked with many interpreters. Some were amazing in their ability to rapidly and accurately relay thoughts and concepts back and forth between presenter and audience. These interpreters are highly beneficial when teaching because they allow the presenter to get into a more natural speaking rhythm that keeps both the speaker and the audience from getting distracted. The result is better comprehension of the material by the audience and a better understanding of the audience and their concerns by the teacher. I have had other interpreters, however, who could only communicate concepts on a basic level and missed the richness of language.

I found across my travels that communication with non-English speaking audiences can be improved by doing three simple steps before engaging with them. These involved dialoguing with the interpreter prior to the translation time, previewing content with the interpreter, and being mindful of the language and illustrations used with the specific audience. I incorporated these in both my research focus groups and the pastors I interviewed during my dissertation study. The first step is to spend a few minutes dialoguing with the interpreter before needing them to translate. By carrying on a simple conversation, you get a feel for the interpreter's English abilities and how easy or difficult it is for him or her to understand you. You might learn, for example, if you tend to talk fast then you may need to slow down your speech so the interpreter can better follow you. Accents can also be difficult for interpreters, especially if they are not accustomed to translating diverse English speakers. I had an interpreter in the Ukraine who told me that he once translated a short talk of a man from Alabama who had a thick southern U.S. accent. He had no interaction with the man prior to being called to the stage of the assembly when the man was ready to speak. The interpreter understood the first few minutes of the man's talk and the last few minutes. He said that since he could not understand the middle portion due to the accent, he just made up the talk. The man with the heavy southern accent was never told what happened. In his mind, he had given a talk and everyone in the room had understood what he said. The reality was the audience understood something, but it was not what he intended to convey. Conversing with an interpreter before he or she translates can increase the comfort level and clarity of both the interpreter and the presenter.

The second step is to talk through with the interpreter in general terms what you are going to say to the group. With my research, I gave the interpreters a list of the questions that I was going to ask the interviewees. I talked the questions through with the interpreters ahead of time to make sure they fully understood what I was trying to get from each question. Now the actual interviews involved more than the pre-determined questions as I would interject new questions based on interviewee responses, but at least the interpreter was aware of where we were heading with the questions (Ladha et al., 2018).

The third step when communicating through an interpreter is to be aware of your language and illustrations, avoiding jargons, colloquialism and stories or illustrations with which the audience cannot relate. I learned this lesson the hard way years ago when speaking to a group in Haiti. I told a story about being in a cave. I started into the story but realized that the interpreter was using far more words to translate what I said then it seemed he should have. Finally, the interpreter turned to me and said "Sorry, but we don't have caves here. I had to explain to them what a cave is so that the rest of what you said would make sense." Talking through any stories or illustrations ahead of time with your interpreter will help eliminate experiences like this one.

As mentioned, I utilized the interpreters with the focus groups and pastor interviews. Some of the pastors I interviewed spoke English. Although I knew they spoke English, I did not know the level of their English, except for one who I had worked with previously as part of a community development project. Even with him, the interview was conducted through a Kiswahili interpreter in case there were words or concepts with which he was not familiar. The importance for all of this is clarity of understanding (Harvard Law School, 2020). Our goal as researchers is to understand as fully as possible what we are studying. Our research loses some of its meaning and potentially even its validity if we do not take care with how we utilize interpreters.

In addition to the translators and cultural collaborator, my research team included a driver named Barnabas. This man was especially fitting for this role because he was well respected in the AICT denomination having served as a pastor and at the time of my research, was a trainer of pastors in community development and outreach. Barnabas also had been a professional driver before going into the ministry. Although his English skills were minimal and my Swahili almost non-existent, we found ways to communicate. We also had a mutual respect developed over several years of working together on various community projects. Barnabas not only knew the roads, but he knew the people along the way to our various destinations. At one point after spending a couple hours traveling on a dirt road that seemed to me to be in the middle of nowhere, we stopped at roadside café for lunch. As soon as we walked into the building one of the patrons got up from his table and walked over to Barnabas to greet him. He was a pastor in the area who had worked with Barnabas in the past. It was reassuring to me that if we had car trouble anywhere along our journey there would be someone nearby that Barnabas could call to help us. His connections were encouraging, and they also gave me additional credibility with the people I met. If I was a friend of Barnabas, then in their minds I was someone they could trust. The relationship with my research team was invaluable to my project, and it also helped me appreciate the importance of flexibility.

Lesson Five: The Need for Flexibility in International Leadership Research

Flexibility is key with any kind of international assignment (Bersin, 2012), and that includes leadership research. I found that flexibility provided me an opportunity to gain insights into my research question that I would not have gotten otherwise. My dissertation design for data collection included touring communities by car with each leader. I wanted to observe them observing their communities. When leader #3 and I finished our interview, we began walking to the vehicle for our community observation drive. The leader noticed that a group was meeting in an adjacent building and invited me to accompany him there. The group was one of 32 savings and credit groups this leader had started throughout the region. These groups functioned as their own micro-banks. This impromptu visit gave me the opportunity to interview the group, which was comprised of 10 women. There were no pre-planned questions, only the opportunity to engage with these ladies and question them in the moment.

This unplanned focus group interview provided some of the richest cultural insights that I gained during my trip. It was discovered, for example, that these women not only benefited economically from micro-businesses they started with loans from the group but the gender-based violence they had faced was greatly reduced. The economic empowerment they received generated more respect from their husbands resulting in reduction in domestic violence (Banfill, 2015). This unscheduled visit provided a new window into the unintentional yet positive results of good leadership. It also opened a window into a greater understanding of the Tanzanian society within which these leaders operated. If we had stayed with the plan of doing a community drive after the interview rather than being flexible, I would have missed important information. While my natural inclination was to follow the research design without wavering, I had to remind myself that the research design was simply a way to get good data, but it was not the only way. It was a means to an end and not the purpose for what I was doing.

This lesson in flexibility was also a reminder of the need to observe everything when immersed in research like this. By sitting with the various focus groups and pastors I learned that data is all around the researcher. Documents and forms posted on office walls, the mannerisms of people in the groups, the way people in the communities responded when they saw these leaders, the leaders' mannerisms around their people, and so forth all provided insights into the research question. I took notes on everything I saw using data collection sheets I had developed as part of my research methodology (Banfill, 2015). The data collection sheets also included a checklist of items to photograph while I was at the various venues. These helped to ensure that I was consistent in the information I gathered. Leadership is a complex, multi-layered discipline (Adler & Gundersen, 2008). The researcher needs to be willing to follow the data trail if he or she wants to discover as much as possible about their subject. That requires flexibility.

As a result of the pilot studies and this systematic approach to data collection, even with the added flexibility, I found that writing the dissertation flowed much easier than I had anticipated pre-research trip. With the data well organized, the analysis was easier. The other piece that helped the writing was knowing that I was going to use case study methodology well before the dissertation research trip. The pilot studies significantly informed my study methods and gave me the confidence that a case study approach would reap my desired results. Since I was using a case study approach, I knew while I was doing the field work that I would be telling the stories of my four example leaders. This encouraged me to think like a storyteller while I was gathering data to ensure that I could paint a full and accurate picture of each leader.

The Ongoing Impact of My Journey

Looking back at my journey as a doctoral student, I see the importance of laying a good foundation for international leadership research. I was fortunate to be in a doctoral program that encouraged its students to do pilot studies like the ones I did, and the program provided regular opportunities for students to travel internationally to prepare them as researchers. I am glad that my first experience conducting international leadership research came before it was time for my dissertation research. I do not believe that the outcome of the dissertation would have been as robust and meaningful as it was without the earlier projects. From a practitioner's viewpoint, research is done to help improve the human condition or better organizations and institutions. My dissertation provided relevant information that has been used to develop leaders in Tanzania and improve the lives of those they lead. For example, I co-founded a college there and the leadership concepts I learned through my research become foundational to the school's approach to educating students. I discovered that the journey was about more than doing good research to earn a degree. It was about doing good research that not only fulfilled academic requirements but also made a lasting difference in people's lives.

Today, my day-to-day activities as a practitioner do not typically involve research and certainly not international research. My work now involves organizational strategy and the management of a non-profit organization that serves preteenager students across the U.S. What I have learned, however, through international research does significantly benefit my work. As noted, global leadership is a complex topic and global leadership research seeks to make sense of those complexities (McCall & Mobley, 2001). This has helped my work in evaluating the complexities of organizations and then bringing meaning to those complexities in ways that make sense to people both within and outside the organization. It is very meaningful in consulting work, organizational development initiatives, and even ongoing tasks such as writing grant proposals and major donor communications or preparing reports for a board of directors. Occasionally I do get to do research as part of my job and that is greatly aided by the perspectives gained from international research.

Besides bringing clarity to complexity, international research sees beyond the immediate. It tries to understand the dynamics of culture, the diversities of people, and the context in which people and organizations operate. These are issues that impact most organizations and having this international research background enables me to comprehend a fuller picture of our organization, its constituents, and even its potential. The organization I serve currently has more than 10,000 students in its program and expects to grow to 100,000 within the next few years. These students and their parents are incredibly diverse, and a background in global leadership and research is proving invaluable to me in helping guide the organization to best serve them. Simply put, my job is to build a world-class organization. My experience in global leadership research is helping me do just that.

References

Adler, N. J., & Gundersen, A. (2008). *International dimensions of organizational behavior* (5th ed). Thomson/South-Western.

April, K., & Ephraim, N. (March, 2006). *Implementing African leadership: An empirical basis to move beyond theory.* Presentation at the 1st International Conference on Values-Based Leadership, Stellenbosch University, South Africa.

Avolio, B. J. & Bass, B. M. (1995). Multifactor leadership questionnaire instrument and scoring guide. *Mind Garden.* https://www.mindgarden.com/16-multifactor-leadership-questionnaire

Avolio, B. J. & Bass, B. M. (2004). Multifactor leadership questionnaire: Manual and sample set. *Mind Garden.* https://www.mindgarden.com

Banfill, F. (2015). *Multiple case studies in effective Africa leadership: A study of the leadership behaviors of effective local church pastors in the Africa Inland Church Tanzania Mara and Ukerewe Diocese* (Publication No. 10263321) [Doctoral dissertation, Indiana Institute of Technology]. ProQuest Dissertations and Thesis Global.

Bersin, J. (2012, October 31). How does leadership vary across the globe? *Forbes.* http://www.forbes.com/sites/joshbersin/2012/10/31/are-expat-programs-dead/

Chiumento, A., Rahman, A., Machin, L., & Frith, L. (2017). Mediated research encounters: Methodological considerations in cross-language qualitative interviews. *Qualitative Research, 18*(6), 604–622. doi:10.1177/1468794117730121

Corbett, S., Fikkert, B., Perkins, J., & Platt, D. (2014). *When helping hurts: How to alleviate poverty without hurting the poor...and yourself.* Moody Publishers.

Creswell, J. W. (2007). *Qualitative inquiry & research design: Choosing among five approaches* (2nd ed.). Sage Publications.

Davis, R. H. (1998). *Contemporary Christian leadership in Africa Inland Church*, Kenya: *A model for east Pokot* (Publication No. 9904705) [Doctoral dissertation, Fuller Theological Seminary]. ProQuest Dissertations and Thesis Global.

Froman, M. (2014). *2014 National trade estimate report on foreign trade barriers.* United States Trade Representative. https://ustr.gov/sites/default/files/2014%20NTE%20Report%20on%20FTB.pdf

Harvard Law School. (2020, September 22). Cross cultural communication: Translation and negotiation. Program on Negotiation. https://www.pon.harvard.edu/daily/international-negotiation-daily/negotiating-in-translation/

Ladha, T., Zubairi, M., Hunter, A., Audcent, T., & Johnstone, J. (2018). Cross-cultural communication: Tools for working with families and children. *Paediatrics & Child Health, 23*(1), 66–69. doi:10.1093/pch/pxx126

Maluka, S. (2018). Contracting out non-state providers to provide primary healthcare services in Tanzania: Perceptions of stakeholders. *International Journal of Health Policy and Management, 7*(10), 910–918. doi:10.15171/ijhpm.2018.46

Maxwell, J. A. (2013). *Qualitative research design: An interactive approach* (3rd ed.). *Applied social research methods* (Vol. 41). Sage Publications.

McCall, M. W., & Mobley, W. (Eds.). (2001). *Advances in global leadership* (Vol. 2). Emerald Group Publishing Ltd.

Oberlander, L., & Elverdan, B. (2000). Malaria in the United Republic of Tanzania: Cultural considerations and health-seeking behaviour. *Bulletin of the World Health Organization, 78*(11), 1352–1357.

Olivier, J., Tsimpo, C., Gemignani, R., Shojo, M., Coulombe, H., Dimmock, F., & Wodon, Q. (2015). Understanding the roles of faith-based health-care providers in Africa: Review of the evidence with a focus on magnitude, reach, cost, and satisfaction. *The Lancet (British Edition), 386*(10005), 1765–1775. doi:10.1016/S0140-6736(15)60251-3

Patterson, A. S. (2014, Fall). Religion and the rise of Africa. *The Brown Journal of World Affairs, 21*(1), 181–196.

Sperber, A. D. (2004). Translation and validation of study instruments for cross-cultural research. *Gastroenterology, 126*(1 Suppl 1), S124–S128. doi:10.1053/j.gastro.2003.10.016

Tandi Lwoga, E., Stilwell, C., & Ngulube, P. (2011). Access and use of agricultural information and knowledge in Tanzania. *Library Review, 60*(5), 383–395. doi:10.1108/00242531111135263

Teunissen, E., Gravenhorst, K., Dowrick, C. E., Van, W. F., Van den, D. M., de Brun, T.,…Van den Muijsenbergh, M. (2017). Implementing guidelines and training initiatives to improve cross-cultural communication in primary care consultations: A qualitative participatory European study. *International Journal for Equity in Health, 16*(1), 145. doi:10.1186/s12939-017-0525-y

Thomason, B., & Williams, H. (2020, April 16). What will work-life balance look like after the pandemic? *Harvard Business Review.* https://hbr.org/2020/04/what-will-work-life-balance-look-like-after-the-pandemic

Tivinarlik, A., & Wanat, C. L. (2006). Leadership styles of New Ireland high school administrators: A Papua New Guinea study. *Anthropology and Education Quarterly, 37*(1), 1–20. http://www.jstor.org/stable/3651372

Tsang, S., Royse, C. F., & Terkawi, A. S. (2017). Guidelines for developing, translating, and validating a questionnaire in perioperative and pain medicine. *Saudi Journal of Anaesthesia, 11*(Suppl 1), S80–S89. doi:10.4103/sja.SJA_203_17

van Teijlingen, E. R., & Hundley, V. (2001). *The importance of pilot studies* (Social Research UPDATE No. 35). Department of Sociology, University of Surrey. https://aura.abdn.ac.uk/handle/2164/157

Vogt, W. P., & Johnson, B. (2011). *Dictionary of statistics & methodology: A nontechnical guide for the social sciences* (4th ed.) [Kindle version]. Sage Publications.

Webb, M. B. (2012). *Leadership emergence in the Church of God of Tanzania* (Publication No. 3566327) [Doctoral dissertation, Fuller Theological Seminary]. ProQuest Dissertations and Thesis Global.

Yin, R. K. (2014). *Case study research: Design and methods* (5th ed.). [Kindle version]. Sage Publications.

29

International Research in Crisis Situations and Unprecedented Times of Uncertainty

Lamia El-Sadek

Introduction

Understanding the ways in which leadership is lived and experienced within an Indigenous context is critical to both Indigenous research and leadership studies. Within the Indigenous traditions and history, there are many examples of leadership that are not rooted in power, but rather in the essence of the culture of the people. My experience as an international development and relief worker inspired my interest in Indigenous research, research conducted by Indigenous groups using their historic and cultural knowledge, and contributed to underlying generalizations, assumptions, and perspectives I hold about marginalized groups in general and refugees in particular. For instance, I worked with various Somali, Iraqi, Palestinian, Eritrean, and Syrian refugee groups for over ten years. While this experience provided me a deeper understanding of the situation and lived experiences of refugees, it was vital to recognize my own preconceived judgments about leadership within the refugee context and remain vigilant in my awareness of when these assumptions affect my perceptions.

The Unique Nature of International Research on Leadership

The world today is engulfed in chaos, wars, and unrest. During turbulent times, individuals naturally look for solace and wisdom from leaders who can ease difficult living conditions and provide stability in an increasingly tempestuous world. Leadership is an exceedingly popular idea, and because it is so widespread, leadership "may mean almost anything to anyone. It easily and often becomes an essentially contested concept" (Grint, 2005a, p. 1). Gemmill & Oakley (1992) posit the dilemma that leadership is often seen as "a catch-all solution for nearly any problem, irrespective of context. This astonishing spread suggests that leadership may have overtaken management as one of the dominant social myths of our time." (p.114).

In a world besieged by financial crises, terrorism and political scandals, the calls for post-heroic leadership have become commonplace (Badaracco, 2001, p. 120). Every day, we find calls for more global leadership in government, the private sector and in the nonprofit world. These calls for global leadership are more resounding and persistent during times of international crises and emergencies, which are becoming more recurrent unfortunately. But the true definition of global leadership and how it is achieved, is a very new and scarcely researched topic. Hence making response to these calls and their achievement even more difficult. Alvesson and Spicer (2012) outline the current breakdown

DOI: 10.4324/9781003003380-29

of leadership studies to be "underpinned by two dominant approaches: functionalist studies which have tried to identify correlations between variables associated with leadership, and interpretive studies which have tried to trace out the meaning making process associated with leadership" (p. 367). While Wood (2005) asserts that leadership is continuously emerging from the ongoing interactions of individuals and is inherently constructed through continuous processes of understanding and growth among subjects.

In non-Western societies, specifically, leadership can be complex to research. Many non-Western societies experienced tremendous and dramatic changes in recent decades as the result of international wars, political take-overs, colonialism, and accelerated integration into the global economy (Watson-Gregeo & Gregeo, 1992). These profound changes resulted in additional conflict and "multifarious array of cultural as well as linguistic practices and ideologies. Many communities, within one society, participate in multiple speech and educational traditions, resulting in hybrid practices" (Moore, 2004, p. 39). This perspective informs recent research on the relationship between identity and Lx learning (Siegel, 1996).

The unstable nature of international research in non-Western and Indigenous settings necessitate for researchers to consider consequences of their presence, questions, and research on their respondents and the community at large. During my research, I encountered backlash from community members who expressed their disapproval of the presence of an outsider. Backlash included resistance from the larger community, participants backing out mid-way, and lack of cooperation from local community members. Understanding the local context is key in such situations.

I first became interested in understanding leadership and the ways it is expressed by Indigenous communities through my work in international development and human rights, which has shown me first-hand the significance and urgent need for a global lens when doing research. As a practitioner, I experienced the rich and complex diversity and differences between cultural groups, and in some cases between groups within the same culture. The many nuances and intricate differences, and their implications for communication, complex social relationships and norms, meant that it is imperative to learn more about Indigenous and non-Western societies. This presented me with the serious challenge as I sought to find non-Western research. It was almost impossible to find non-Western research on leadership specifically, as if scholarship believes that leadership does not exist outside the realm of Western societies and how leadership is formed, viewed and practiced within that framework. Research on leadership within refugee communities was also scarce. This could be a result of the unstable and often traumatic circumstances in which these communities must live.

Elements of Research on Refugees

Around the world, large numbers of refugees, forced migrants and internally displaced people live in poverty under the threat of violence without basic human rights such as freedom of movement and opportunities for education and employment. Refugees are defined as people who were forced to flee from, and are unable to return to their own country, due to persecution and violence (Ghosh, 2000). According to the 1951 United Nations' convention:

> A refugee is any person, who, owing to a well-founded fear of being persecuted for reason of race, religion, nationality, membership of a particular social group or political opinion, is outside the country of his nationality and is unable or owing to such fear, is unwilling to avail himself of the protection of the country. (Kirui & Mwaruvie, 2012, p. 161)

The convention governing the specific aspects of refugee problems in Africa, a regional instrument adopted by the Organization of African Unity (OAU) in 1969, expanded the U.N. definition to include people who are forced to flee external aggression, internal civil strife, or events seriously disturbing public order. Refugees also include internally displaced persons (IDPs), who are defined as "people who were forced to flee their home but who did not cross a state border. IDPs benefit from the legal protection of international human rights law and, in armed conflict, international humanitarian law" (Kirui & Mwaruvie, 2012, p. 162).

The United Nations High Commissioner for Refugees (UNHCR) estimates that more than 11.3 million people are living in segregated settlements or refugee camps, 7.3 million have been there for 10 years or more, with 23.6 million internally displaced in their own countries (UNHCR, 2014a). Two-thirds of refugees have been stranded in exile for more than five years, with no hope of an end in sight. (UNHCR, 2014). Forty-one percent of the refugee population worldwide are children, while half of all refugees are women (UNHCR, 2014). Additionally, The World Health Organization (WHO) estimates that around 3 million of the displaced persons worldwide live with disabilities (WHO, 2010). Women and children contribute 75% of the over 1,491,706 IDPs in Nigeria alone (UNHCR, 2014).

According to the UNHCR (2014), more than 70% of refugees and IDPs are trapped in transitional situations whereby they had been displaced for five years or more. However, the number of refugees and internally displaced people (IDPs) continued to rise in 2014 and 2015, hence resulting in increased urgent and humanitarian aid to existing and new refugee populations. The severe circumstances in which the refugees live in are often dangerous and threatening (UNHCR, 2014). The International Organization for Migration (IOM) reported that 4,077 migrants died in 2014, and 40,000 migrants died since the year 2000 (IOM, 2014). Meanwhile, the true number of fatalities is likely to be much higher, since many deaths are not recorded in light of their unrecorded locations (Rubio-Goldsmith et al., 2007). With new global crises, the refugee predicament worsens. The humanitarian consequences of the crisis in Syria have reached an unprecedented scale.

Refugees suffer "the deepest form of poverty, the poverty of insecurity; not knowing where or when they will get the next bit to eat, or how they will cope with the families" (Doheny, 1997, p. 635). Refugees are facing a life where their past, their history, and their legacies are lost. In addition to being subjected to torture and extreme hardship in fleeing their homelands, refugees lose their wealth, their properties, their connections and sense of community, and have to start over in a new land. Additionally, their future is in jeopardy, for they are entirely dependent on others for survival. Refugees rely on the UNHCR, their host countries, and the help of local non-profit organizations for sustenance, accommodation, and survival. While the refugees struggle to survive, the resources of their host countries are also being stretched to their limits to address the growing number of new refugee groups (Said, 2001).

My doctoral dissertation investigated the informal leadership emerging within the refugee community and the impact of such leadership on women refugees, based on a critical theory framework. As a philosophy, critical theory emphasizes the importance of challenging the role and balance of power in social relations (Kincheloe, 2008). Critical theoretical approaches are concerned with the inextricable relationships between power, language, and ideology. In an Indigenous research philosophical context, critical theory helps challenge the 'norms' and 'status quo' by introducing a venue for alternative thoughts and outcome. Greater clarity about the role and impact of informal leaders within the forced migration context will inform the development of more effective humanitarian, social, political, and developmental responses (Allenby & Fink, 2005, p. 1035).

The research was conducted with a voluntary, convenience sample of Syrian refugee women over 18 years of age, who were known to the researcher as displaced persons assigned to a refugee settlement area in Cairo, Egypt. Participants were enlisted in-person by the researcher to complete a fifteen-question interview that should take approximately three hours to allow time for breaks in light of the traumatic nature of the lived experiences of the participants. Demographics such as education and professional background are critical to consider under an intersectional interpretive lens as they shed more light on whether participants received formal leadership training or opportunities. These demographics serve as part of their social identities; hence it was important to study whether they impact the women's emergence and experiences as leaders in that context.

The interviews started with a broad question inviting the women to talk about the experience of displacement and temporary settlement. Thereafter, the interview covered topics such as how the women perceived their situation, the struggles their community faces and their hopes for the future. The interviews were conducted in Arabic, with the support of a translator specializing in the Syrian dialect. The refugee women responded well to the long interview questions. The location for interviews was either at the participant's home or at the community center.

As a qualitative researcher, I observed and interpreted the various realities and themes that emerge (Creswell, 2007), particularly around the refugee women's understanding and lived experiences of leadership. I pursued this research from an ontological viewpoint; whereby reality is subjective and is defined by the participants themselves. A rigorous data collection process was followed by thorough data interpretation to highlight emergent themes. The participants had great difficulty recounting their past lives before their displacement and showed great sadness and grief, followed by sobering and hopeful discussions of their current situation and their future for their families.

The findings revealed a number of consistent themes that emerged from the portraits of the three leaders. A theme of women as survivors and champions within the refugee context has emerged, while the experience of leadership emergence was characterized by a theme of transformation through learning. A third theme that emerged was the perseverance and resilience through faith and spirituality, unique to the displacement, refugee experiences, and trauma. Hope emerged as a theme and characteristic of authentic leadership as demonstrated by the participants. Finally, the participants displayed lived experiences of servant leadership in serving their community and leading through service.

The themes emerging from my research study indicate that informal leadership among refugee women leaders emerges organically due to several factors. Trauma, extreme circumstances, danger, fear, faith, and hope are all among the founding factors for emergence of leaders within the refugee context. Rosser (2003) stated that women and men reflect differing patterns in roles as leaders, but women were rated as more effective leaders in every dimension of leadership. The refugee women leaders in the study embody effective and influential leadership, which has inspired and motivated their followers to pursue their aspirations and achieve self-realization, as well as obtain hope and enjoy a sense of community.

Indigenous Research

Indigenous research is a unique and exciting research area that spans across several disciplines. But Indigenous research is not new, Indigenous people have always done research by asking questions that were relevant to them. Indigenous communities used their historic and cultural knowledge and resources to answer those research questions. Recently, there is a growing movement of bringing "Indigenous communities into the academy, challenging the colonial institutional relations and practices that have constituted Indigenous peoples as objects of research rather than as authorities about their own ways of knowing, being and doing" (Coburn et al., 2013, p. 2).

Within the research domain of global leadership, studies have largely ignored research on leadership within an Indigenous context. Global leadership research has been primarily focused on organizational leadership, as well as traditional types of leadership. Non-traditional leadership, rooted in community service, has been linked to difficult and challenging situations whereby informal leaders emerge to counter the difficult circumstances the group is undergoing. Majority of scholarly research is conducted from a Western perspective, and in Western countries, hence it is rare to find research that studies the occupational status or conditions of immigrants in both (Spörlein et al., 2014). At its heart, the traditional view of leadership is based on "assumptions of people's powerlessness, their lack of personal vision and inability to master the forces of change, deficits which can be remedied only by a few great leaders" (Senge, 1990, p. 340). In this aspect, Indigenous leadership witnesses a major departure from the traditional view of leadership. Indigenous leadership is inherently different from traditional Western leadership models. An understanding of Ubuntu, an Indigenous way of leadership, offers a stark contrast to its Western counterpart.

Ubuntu is an African perspective of life and worldview, that is rooted in the culture, religion, and collective consciousness of Africans (Coetzee & Roux, 2001). Ubuntu is an alternative to self, individualistic and utilitarian philosophies more prominent in the West. A Zulu word, with parallels in many of the African languages, Ubuntu can be translated as 'humanness'. Under the Ubuntu ethics and tradition, fundamental human rights can only be conceptualized under a context of communal rights. Communities adhering to Ubuntu, live under the principles of harmony, hospitality, respect, care and community that embodies the fundamental interconnectedness of a community (Lutz, 2009).

Under Ubuntu philosophy, human rights can only exist with value and meaning, under a societal context that is founded on equitable rights of all beings. Chuwa remarks that Ubuntu ethics have strong implications with regard to "the subordinate position of individual rights in front of basic communal interests and well-being" (Chuwa, 2010, p. 11), meaning that the community takes precedence over the individual and that the communion of people takes priority over individual inalienable rights including self-autonomy. This community-focused leadership and way of being is only one example of the many diverse forms of Indigenous leadership, making clear how important it is to further leadership research within vulnerable populations.

Refugee Research

Researching and Understanding Ethical Considerations

When it comes to conducting international research of refugee leadership and any vulnerable population, there are many ethical and research considerations to adhere to. On top of the list, is displaced and persecuted populations, who face ethnic genocide, cleansing, and extermination. Gaining access to such population is nearly impossible, not only due to the dangerous and unstable nature of the situation, but also due to the risk which many community members could bring upon themselves by speaking with outsiders.

Brown et al. (2005) defined ethical leadership as "the demonstration of normatively appropriate conduct through personal actions and interpersonal relationships and the promotion of such conduct to followers through two-way communication, reinforcement, and decision making" (p. 120). While Ciulla (2004) asserts that "Ethics is at the heart of leadership" (p. 8), therefore leaders divorced from ethics may contribute to additional trauma, toxic stress, and harm.

This consideration is especially relevant with a vulnerable population as is the case with refugees. Not only is it vital to conduct research and design interviews with the ethical considerations of vulnerable and traumatized populations, such as refugees, but so is viewing the ethics of their leadership within their own unique context and lens, which may differ from our understanding of traditional leadership. For instance, during a field visit I met a community leader who is revered by their refugee community members, primarily because she was able to establish a communal law, that ensures no additional harm is manifested upon women and children. A communal law, devised by an individual, who may inflict some sort of harm or loss upon one person, to ensure the rights of another are unharmed, is certainly divorced from the traditional ethical leader. However, understanding and appreciating this unique experience, and recognizing their leadership as valid, is crucial to unveil the many layers often obscured when we conduct international research.

Makings of an Effective Leader

Through my interactions, I witnessed the refugee community's application of social identity theory (Tajfel & Turner, 1979), which posits that a group helps its members to define who they are, and to evaluate their status. Social identity theory includes the process of social categorization such as developing categories to define one's own group and construction of self-image and the process of linking linkage of self-worth and self- into group memberships (Tyler & Blader, 2002, 2003). In line with social identity theory, the group engagement model (Tyler & Blader, 2003) argues that "discretionary cooperative behaviors originating from the individual, are motivated by members' desires to maintain and enhance their social identities from the feedback they receive from their own group" (p. 350).

Upon further inquiry and conversations with community members, I began to understand that interpersonal treatment and a unique decision-making process are among the essential criteria of their views of social identities within their newly established micro-society. To them, a true and ethical leader, makes poised, fair, and sensible decisions. As with many informal leaders, the absence of an embedded structure to delineate expectations, roles and affiliation, makes it imperative that the leader effectively transfer messages to their followers, in this case their refugee camp community members, to show and reassure them of his efforts to work on their behalf.

The leader in this case consistently held 'town hall' type gatherings, whereby on the same day of each week, she would hold space for community members to come meet her, present complaints, requests, or seek her guidance. The consistent communication and messaging of this leader had a positive impact on the community members' sense of merging with the group. This is particularly critical within the context of a newly displaced community, whose members do not necessarily know one another, and have found solace and comfort in this sense of belonging, as well as having an informal leader who holds space for them.

Challenges for Researchers

Within the global context, researchers are very likely to come across a population that is going through a crisis, whether environmental, health-related such as a pandemic, political or humanitarian. Several of these crises present very difficult, almost impossible, challenges for researchers to overcome. With political and humanitarian crises specifically, study subjects often need to hide involvement, and thus present a major challenge to any researcher struggling to locate an appropriate sample (Gurdin & Patterson, 1987). In some situations, humanitarian conditions as well as persecution may present the researcher with having to work with a hidden and hard-to-access population. Access to participants, and retaining them, becomes increasingly difficult, the more turbulent circumstances become. Additionally, distrust of outsiders as well as security concerns, amid the lack of safety systems or infrastructure also increase in such cases. For example, as the war in Syria is considered a civil conflict, and an internal matter, many Syrian refugees felt that any conversations between an outsider and their fellow countrymen or women was a violation of the sanctity of their agency.

When working with vulnerable populations, the researchers may unintentionally cause additional harm to their participants. Populations in war zones or forcibly displaced groups such as refugees are considered vulnerable populations as they are a dis-advantaged sub-segment of the community requiring care and protections in research. A vulnerable group's freedom and capability to protect themselves from risks and danger is impacted (Shivayogi, 2013). In the case of refugee women, these circumstances are shared with many other women living marginalized existences. These populations have limited to no access to supportive resources, are living in insecure housing or tents, and consider their living situations as unfriendly and unsafe (Beller & Graham, 1993). Therefore, it is imperative for researchers to remain vigilant and show considerate awareness of any security threats to themselves or their participants.

Vulnerable populations must be awarded protection of their rights, well-being, safety with measurements of risk-benefit scales, privacy and confidentiality (Shivayogi, 2013).

With more than 11 million people displaced through-out the world, without access to their savings, wealth, assets, jobs or investments, a number of displaced community members might be involved in breaking the law by the possession of illegal drugs, shop-lifting, handling stolen goods, fraudulently obtaining income support payments from aid. In considering the tragic circumstances of displaced communities, it is critical to appreciate their desperation to finds any means for survival. Additionally, within the refugee context, displacement does not put an end to domestic and gender-based abuse or human trafficking, and therefore it is very possible to encounter women who in addition to being a refugee, are also 'on the run', from a violent ex-partner or a human-trafficker. As a result, these circumstances may make it critical for many refugees to avoid interaction with outsiders, thus potentially negatively affecting a researcher's ability to maintain a sample population.

Gap of International Research and Potential to Reduce Harm

The investment in international leadership research has the ability to reduce suffering in vulnerable populations. Even so, there remains a significant gap in research. While a range of authors have examined the origins, evolution, and politics of the global refugee context, this literature has not investigated the process by which leadership emerges and develops within the refugee context. According to Hutchinson and Dorsett (2012), there is a lack of qualitative studies on the significance of family, friends, and community in reinforcing refugee strength and leadership during the reset-tlement process. Previous research on immigrants and refugees has covered a variety of topics, from focusing on aspects of social exclusion ranging from literacy barriers for women and youth un-employment (Taylor & MacDonald, 1992) to lack of access to health care (Kemp & Rasbridge, 2004). However, little to no research has investigated the factors leading to leadership development and sustainability within the refugee context. In fact, there is a significant paucity of literature available on refugee resilience and leadership (Hutchinson & Dorsett, 2012).

One qualitative study conducted with the refugee community in Australia highlighted the impact of leadership's relationship to resilience (Schweitzer et al., 2007). Apart from receiving support from friends and family, refugee people also utilized leaders within their own ethnic community to help them survive and adapt to their new challenges and lives. Weine (2008) posited that refugee youth, especially, may face "added stressors from adjusting to new school environments, serving as cultural and linguistic liaisons for parents and transitioning from childhood to adulthood" (p. 516). The presence of additional international research on leadership in the refugee context has the potential to promote needed leaders within vulnerable groups.

Turton (2003) asserted that "there is no justification for studying, and attempting to understand, the causes of human suffering if the purpose of one's study is not, ultimately, to find ways of relieving and preventing that suffering" (p. 8). This study aims to bridge the gap between forced migration studies of social transformation and human mobility theories. The presence of an effective leader can positively influence the morale, living experiences, and the outlook of individuals un-dergoing significant traumatic challenges such as refugees (Sarcevic et al., 2011).

Another key element to working with displaced populations is understanding the true impact of this research on the global scale. As global researchers, it is imperative to intentionally develop strategies and frameworks ensuring the inclusion and centrality of culture in theory and practice. Realizing that by adding to the scholarly literature on refugees and forced migration, this type of international research can potentially make a significant impact on improving debates and informing the development of better policies as related to displaced populations' placement, livelihood, access to basic needs, development, and sustainability of refugee leadership. I hope that my research, rooted in critical feminist theory, can provide a critical standard against which to evaluate current policies related to refugee women.

Thus, within the international research context, and the research of refugees and displaced populations in particular, international researchers' outcomes may be synonymous with holding power over which conclusions and findings matter and control over whose perspective is uplifted. As Cram, et al. (2006) state, "researchers are knowledge brokers, people who have the power to construct legitimating arguments for or against ideas, theories or practices. They are collectors of information and producers of meaning which can be sued for, or against indigenous interests" (p. 177).

Data Collection

Through my research, I hoped to shed insight onto the lives and experiences of an often-forgotten minority group. Unlike other immigrants, the adaptation of refugees to their new environment and culture is more challenging, especially because a significant number of refugees are victims of torture or witnessed torture (Suarez-Orozco & Suarez-Orozco, 2001). Highlighting the distinction between immigrants and refugees is critical, in order to better understand the challenges that are unique to refugees and decipher the difficulty they find in adapting to their new homes.

Refugees in general, and women refugees in particular, are rarely studied by academic and research circles. Conducting literature reviews revealed the scarcity of research on refugee populations, a non-monolithic group, all of whom are unique as they come from different ethnic and religious backgrounds. This is crucial to keep in mind while conducting research with refugees, as Syrian refugees are not the same as Palestinian, Somali, Iraqi or Eritrean refugees for instance. By understanding the unique nature of the refugee group that a researcher is working with, we can further demystify Indigenous research in general, and refugee research in particular.

Understanding the range of different language dialects can have a significant effect on research. Language learning is viewed as "not simply a skill that is acquired through hard work and dedication, but a complex social practice that engages the identities of language learners" (Norton, 2000, p. 132). As an Arabic speaker, it was crucial for me to understand that just because my respondents and I may understand the same classical Arabic language, the unique Syrian dialect of which I was uneducated, as well as the nuances of regions, tribes, colonial influence and educational backgrounds played a significant role in the way I approached translation and communication with the respondents. Another critical element of international research with vulnerable population is the demonstration of authenticity and commitment to research that responds to people's cultural context. International policy and human rights reporting are often influenced by research findings and may result in continued overpowering of groups.

The Methods

As an international researcher and human rights and gender activist, I understood that immersing myself into the role of interviewer would provide me with "a unique opportunity to be the primary research instrument for this study" (Janesick, 2004, p. 19). My work as a relief and development worker has provided me with essential experience in interviewing and listening, two significant skills in qualitative research and portraiture. Additionally, I have worked for many years with Indigenous and other marginalized groups; therefore, these experiences shaped my approach to the research questions, data collection strategy, interview questions, and data analysis throughout this study. I was drawn to the study of leadership among refugee women because I have come to view them as key agents for empowerment and positive change in their communities. As an activist for over 10 years, I worked with many refugee groups in various stages of displacement and was struck by their determination and endurance. I also had the unique opportunity to work with informal women leaders within the refugee community, which is how I was introduced to the concept.

A qualitative interviewer is able to "delve into the souls of the participants and present their realities with great depth and credibility" (Rubin & Rubin, 2005, p. 21). The primary data sources for this study was semi-structured individual interviews with the selected female leaders and observation in the form of field notes. By collecting data from multiple sources, I will be able to "highlight specific events representative of the past, present and future that illustrate their journey and a view of their philosophical roots and direction, ideological and historical past, and practical plans for the future" (Lawrence-Lightfoot & Davis, 1997, p. 70).

Interviews

The interview questions revolved around the past experiences, or lives, of these actors; what life was like before displacement, their social and economic status beforehand, responsibilities held and their overall sense of accomplishment. Then the interviewer probed the actors about their feelings regarding their journey of displacement and seeking asylum, their sense of loss and grief, and how they are coping with this experience. The respondents were asked open-ended questions about how their gender has shaped their experience and view of leadership, reaction to their role within the community, and obstacles they may have faced due to their gender. The researcher asked the actors whether they can recall the circumstances or conditions which first prompted them to take a leadership role within their community, and how people became to view them as leaders.

Refugees undergo an intense, tedious and lengthy process of forced displacement consisting of two stages. The first stage is characterized by denial, whereby the possibility of removal is too traumatic to acknowledge (Scudder & Colson, 1982). After the move, the second stage is characterized by clinging to old norms, traditions, habits, realities and certainties. The second stage also features avoidance of all risks, including any new learning and economic opportunities (Scudder & Colson, 1982). Understanding how leaders emerge and develop within the refugee context is vital in uncovering the best survival and sustainability processes that refugees turn to in light of these stages.

It was critical to ensure that there were no interview questions that delved into specifics about the participant's personal lives that made the interviewees unwilling or uncomfortable about participation. The pool of potential participants was over 100, while actual participants were originally planned to range between 5 and 10 women refugees, only three were able to participate. This small participant number enabled me to gain a deeper understanding of participant experience and to develop a thick, rich description of that experience (Creswell, 2009). Lawrence-Lightfoot & Davis (1997) stress the significance of the balance that a qualitative researcher must keep between creating a good portrait and maintaining good scholarship. They assert, "the shaping hand of the investigator is counterbalanced by the skepticism and scrutiny that is the signature of good research" (Lawrence-Lightfoot & Davis, 1997, p. 13). A volatile and constantly changing schedule are stable elements of conducting international research during times of crises and war. It is critical to demonstrate flexibility and adaptability in the face of the recurrent waves of uncertainty, updates, and challenges. By allotting additional time to counter the expected delays and challenges, a global researcher plans for their downtime and ensures the research finishes on time and is completed.

Due to grave security considerations within the unpredictable refugee situation and the war in Syria, I had to cancel a number of interviews and communicate with my dissertation advisor on an alternate plan. Other incidents included several respondents who over time were unreachable or were facing persecution and had to flee. As an international development practitioner, I was accustomed to these unpredictable situations and planned for them ahead of time with contingency plans in the case that the original plan and timeline changes. Security concerns and threats often caused cancellation or changes of my schedule, hence having a contingency plan to work around these changes is vital for a robust research process.

As a researcher, I am interested in uncovering "the experience of becoming, accepting, rejecting, and presenting oneself (or not) as a refugee" (Rowe, 2006, p. 3). Refugees have an undeniable vulnerability in the formation of refugee identity due to a myriad of external elements such as society, humanitarian agencies, host governments, and the refugee's own culture and experiences (Rowe, 2006). Within the context of refugee women research, a critical dimension acknowledges the value of combining outsider-insider perspectives in understanding the experiences of minority women in the majority culture of male leaders (McCall, 2005). The women leaders are insiders in the community with a profound understanding of the challenges, lived experiences and views, hence they offer insider (emic) perspectives. Although these women leaders perfectly understand the culture and experiences of refugees, they can also offer outsider (etic) perspectives to the interpretation of leadership development within the refugee since they are outsiders from the predominant male leadership models within their communities. Intersectionality, therefore, offers this study a relevant critical interpretative framework to analyze and interrogate the lived experiences of refugee women leaders in a predominantly male leader communal context.

Toxic Stress and other Health Considerations

It is critical to make allowances and truly understand the health and psychological conditions of international research populations. Within the refugee context, there is a myriad of health, both physiological and psychological, issues and trauma with which an international researcher must acquaint themselves with in order to be able to communicate, work with and accommodate their research subjects. According to Müller et al. (2018), the major impact factors on refugees' health are "linked to experiences and exposure (1) in the country of origin, (2) in refugee camps and en-route to their transition or permanent new home, and (3) in the process of immigration into the host country and living in European asylum centers" (p. 153). Researchers cannot conduct research on a vulnerable population such as the refugee population without taking into consideration its physical and mental health.

Understanding the mental and psychological displacement takes on a population is crucial. Refugees and other displaced populations suffer from lack of health resources, and mental health resources in particular. While working with refugees, I was introduced to the impact of toxic stress and the layers of trauma which they underwent during displacement. Toxic stress is defined as the exposure to extreme, frequent, and persistent adverse events without the presence of a supportive caretaker. There is a paucity of literature related to toxic stress and child refugees (Murray, 2018). Researchers have found that displacement, loss of sense of community and ones' belonging, were associated with a significant increase in serious illnesses during adulthood. Illnesses include heart, lung, and liver disease, cancer, and bone fractures. The scientists reported that experiencing four or more ACEs during childhood significantly increases the risk for toxic stress (Murray, 2018). However, it has been clearly established that the prolonged brutal and traumatizing war in Syria is having a profound impact on the physical and mental health of child refugees at a distressing rate. (Murray, 2018, p. 271).

Mental health problems including "depression, anxiety and post-traumatic stress disorder are prevalent among asylum seekers and refugees, and the provision of mental health services for survivors of torture and organized violence is widely regarded as inadequate" (Kroll et al., 2011, p. 487). Additionally, children, women and older refugees are especially vulnerable groups lacking adequate healthcare and treatment (Carta et al., 2013). Kroll et al. (2011) raise serious concerns around "the lack of healthcare provision to refugees and asylum seekers in detention with communicable diseases and with HIV" (p. 488). Understanding the physical and mental health crises which my respondents were undergoing, impacted the way in which I approached the work in various ways such as allowing for adequate time, head notice for interviews, actively and empathically listening to the respondents' stories with their toxic stress and trauma in mind. This knowledge also uplifted the research findings and my evaluation of the characteristics of informal leaders within the community which I was studying. Informal leadership within the refugee context can be manifested in the form of qualities such as concern for people, empowerment, intuitive management, creative problem solving, and the ability to create a vision (Giannini, 2001).

As international researchers, this makes it imperative for us to appreciate the insurmountable stressors that many of our research subjects experience, most specifically in the case of refugees. As I learnt more about the conditions and extreme hardship of my research subjects, the daunting task of carefully planning how to approach this vulnerable, and traumatized, population became crucial. Meticulous and detailed preparation can help ease anxiety research subjects have, by breaking down the 'unknown' and 'distrust'. Providing detailed and anticipatory guidance to research subjects, encouraging questions and investing in clarity, are all good ways to lessen any additional stressors that might be created by the research interviews.

Eisner (1989) asserts that interviews are "…a powerful resource for learning how people perceive the situations in which they work…connoisseurship is aimed at understanding what is going on" (p. 82). The interviews with the actors initially took place in a local community guide's house, a place where they will feel comfortable and safe. This helped to create a setting that encourages "… expression of strength… vulnerability, weakness, prejudice, and anxiety" (Lawrence-Lightfoot & Davis, 1997, p.141) during interviews. This is where the role of a local guide, and the significance of having them as an ally, comes in. Investing in additional time for preparation and briefings with their support network, primarily the local guide, can help address several issues of contention beforehand.

Global Research Success Strategies

During my research, multiple interviews took place and contact was maintained for several years with several respondents. This period witnessed several respondents moving residence abruptly due to the nature of their displacement, with contact phone numbers changing as well. I addressed this challenge by scheduling recurring check-ins on my calendar to ensure contact information is current and updated, as well as obtaining contact information of family members in case my primary respondent was un-reachable. Additionally, with no access to Wi-Fi hotspots or internal routers, I lost contact with many potential research subjects and had to start over. Finding alternate ways to reach respondents through the collective community 'grapevine' communications and referrals were very helpful in this situation.

While conducting the interviews, I often brought with me cookies, snacks and little toys for their children. When the women started to prepare dinner for their families, I offered to help with the food preparation and cleanup. These gestures of support and gratitude for their participation were necessary to obtain their trust, but also to infuse a much needed air of pleasantness and joy for these vulnerable and displaced women. These initiatives were also culturally appropriate and considered gestures of good-will and friendliness. Many of the respondents mentioned feeling desperate, sad, lonely, and hopeless about the future. They were also vulnerable since they had no access to many support services, such as schooling for their children, no access to healthcare or medication to their ill loved ones or themselves. They felt socially isolated, vulnerable, impoverished, with their fate dependent on aid organizations and international treaties.

When conducting international research with Indigenous, or vulnerable populations, it is very dif-ficult not to feel the weight of what they are going through. While I visited my respondents' homes for interviews and collecting data, I often felt a sense of abandonment when departing. I also felt outraged and helpless that I was unable to offer them support. There were times when I felt that I was heavily imposing, burdening them and adding to their load and worries. Understanding, and preparing for, the impact of conducting research in these situations is key to successfully completing the research and telling their stories. These ethical considerations made me try my utmost to lessen any additional harm to them either through community resistance of my interview questions. I opted to work with respondents whose direct family members did not object to their participation in the study, to minimize any chances of their exposure to additional harm.

On the other hand, I was often in awe of how formidable these women were, I had tremendous respond for their resolve to survive and persevere. Seeing the crushing adversity which they went through, and in some cases were continued to be subjected to, yet witness their determination and ability to make a life for themselves and families, was truly inspirational. I knew that I was unable to bring on any outside support or alter the realities of the population which I am studying, and often had to resolve my feelings and position around this. The respondents understood my role and limitations as a researcher collecting data, and they neither expected advice or commitment to solve their problems. They often expressed that they simply appreciated being listened to with empathy.

Due to the lack of literature on conducting research during times of war and international crises, I was not prepared for being a bystander in such a volatile and desperate situation. I believe this is one of the main gaps in international research that needs to be immediately addressed. The scarcity of resources to support international researchers could be detrimental to a researcher who finds themselves in a whirlwind situation, not only facing the dangers and risk of working within a war climate, but also having to resolve such ethical issues of their involvement and mission while witnessing such tremendous desperation and adversity of the researched population.

Another important strategy is the indispensable employment of a trusted gatekeeper. In war and crises situations where circumstances are very fluid and constantly changing, having the support of a gatekeeper can be crucial. To gain access to respondents in the refugee context is very difficult, as many of them do not trust outsiders and are facing existential crises. A gatekeeper not only enables the researcher to gain access to respondents, but also translate the importance of the research from their own standpoint in a way that make sense to them in their current situation. The gatekeepers with whom I worked were informal leaders in their own right. In light of the acute vulnerability of this community, gatekeepers demonstrated a clear responsibility to protect them from exploitation by outsiders including researchers and journalists who came in temporarily to learn of their plight then often disappeared causing respondents to feel abandoned and isolated, in an already displaced reality (Berg, 2004).

With a displaced population, that is constantly on the move, and often assigned new homes without advance notice, it is significantly difficult to plan around regular meetings and to ensure participants' long-term commitment to the research. One strategy I adopted, was to work with the participants and their UN liaison officer, who was introduced to the research topics and made aware of the timeline as well as the major dates and deadlines. I met the liaison officer through community members who viewed them as a great and trustworthy advocate. In collaboration with the participants, we had requested that the liaison officer flag any upcoming relocations immediately and let us know. This is an informal process that I learnt from refugees in the area who informed me that families with young or sick children, a similar arrangement was made, where they were able to receive an advance notice. Fortunately, by anticipating potential hurdles, and demonstrating openness to strategies followed by the community itself, I was able to avoid this critical obstacle.

As a researcher, it is very difficult not to be impacted by the human experiences and raw emotions we come across during our research. When working with individuals who experiences multiple layers of trauma and loss, researchers are vulnerable to the emotional toll the research may have on them. I managed the difficult emotional and mental weight by adopting several strategies including meditation, reflection, therapy and journaling. I also scheduled self-care days, where I would intentionally take a day off every two weeks to ensure that I get a chance to disconnect and de-stress.

Drawing Conclusions

I have developed strong views about the various obstacles facing single and widowed refugee women, and the importance of developing leadership figures within their own unique cluster. While my experiences may have solidified my ability to understand and relate to the experiences of the study's participants, I abstained from reaching conclusions based on any preconceived notions. Finally, my theoretical framework introduced a necessary bias that framed both what I explored and how I interpreted the data collected. While this is appropriate and necessary, it is critical to highlight the specific lens from which I explored this study.

The benefits of being a practitioner and a researcher were immense and I am very grateful for them, however, not all global researchers have the benefit of working on global scales before conducting research. Therefore, it is imperative to have more investment in learning about conducting international research and understanding that non-Western societies are unique in their own right. By devising best practices for working on international research, this will further inform and enrich policy work, international relations, and human rights advisories, educational as well organizational (non-profit and corporate) growth and prosperity.

Empirical evidence suggests a pattern of centering research around Western societies. In a study on leisure patterns across the globe, Valentine et al. (1999) concluded that it was "abundantly clear that cross-national research is almost nonexistent in the leisure field" (p. 243), and they subsequently added that "we know very little about the leisure behavior, policies, and practices of *non-Western* countries" (p. 244). This pattern presented a major challenge for me when conducting international research, where I was unable to find empirical data and research to inform my study's design, methodology, and approach.

Without allocating the proper attention to international research, and the unique nuances and dimensions of working globally as researchers, the empirical data currently present will remain vastly lacking a critical global perspective. One of the key assumptions behind culturally responsive research is the founding principle that culture is an integral part of any research's context, as it relates to program, methodologies that researchers choose to conduct their work, and community context (SenGupta et al., 2004).

As Hopson (2003) asserts, it is important to recognize that "cultural differences are not merely surface variations in style, preference and behavior, but fundamental differences in how people experience social life, evaluate information, decide what is true, attribute causes to social phenomena and understand their place in the world" (p. 2). Within a global research framework, cultural and contextual factors include demographic depictions of communities and programs as well as a rich range of "values and the less vocalized issues of power, racism, class, and gender that continue to shape our societies" (Senese, 2005; SenGupta et al., 2004, p. 86).

When conducting and evaluating research, the awareness of, and commitment to, studies that respond to people's cultural context is central. Culture is therefore critical to the assessment of any research and methodologies' value and merit (Askew et al., 2012). Along with this is the "explicit recognition that culture is a methodologically and epistemologically relevant and vibrant construct that requires specific and focused attention within evaluation design, process, and implementation" (Chouinard & Hopson, 2016, p. 239).

As a global researcher, I believe that a cultural responsible research design process and methodology is one that recognizes that culturally defined practices, norms, and values lie at the heart of international research. When working with diverse, often rarely studied populations, it is imperative to recognize that this type of research requires resilience and diligence, as well as motivation to explore the rich ways in which the world's many cultures inform and impact all facets of life and human behavior.

International research is unusual in the complexity and wealth of cultural, ethnic, political, racial, ethical, and methodological dilemmas posed, due to the vulnerability of the respondents, but also considering the scarcity of similar research. Global researchers are embarking on a journey in unchartered waters, where they are unable to benefit and learn from previous explorations. In fact, contemporary global researchers are at the helm of making many prominent and extraordinary discoveries not only on their respective populations but also on the very nature of doing international research, which are set to tremendously benefit future researchers.

References

Allenby, B., & Fink, J.(2005).). Toward inherently secure and resilient societies. *Science, 309,* 1034–1036. s

Alvesson, M., & Spicer, A. (2012). Critical leadership studies: The case for critical performativity. *Human Relations, 65*(3), pp. 367–390. https://doi.org/wgb.

Askew, B., Monifa, G., & Jay, M. (2012). Aligning collaborative and culturally responsive evaluation approaches. *Evaluation and Program Planning, 35,* 552–557. 10.1016/j.evalprogplan.2011.12.011.

2001 Badaracco, J.(2001).). We don't need another hero. *Harvard Business Review, 79*(6, 120–162.

Bandura, A. (1986). *Social foundations of thought and action.* Prentice Hall.

Beller, A. & Graham, J. (1993). *Small Change: The Economics of Child Support.* Yale University Press.

Berg, B. (2004). *Qualitative research methods for the social sciences.* Allyn & Bacon.

Bischoff, A., Denhaerynck, K., Schneider, M., & Battegay, E. (2011). The cost of war and the cost of health care – an epidemiological study of asylum seekers. *Swiss Medical Weekly, 141,* w13252.

Blum, L. A. (1988). Gilligan & Kohlberg: Implications for moral theory. *Ethics, 98,* 472–491.

Brislin, R. W. (1970). Back-translation for cross-cultural research. *Journal of Cross-Cultural Psychology, 1,* 185–216.

Brown, M. E., Treviño, L. K., & Harrison, D. A. (2005). Ethical leadership: A social learning perspective for construct development and testing. *Organizational Behavior and Human Decision Processes, 97,* 117–134.

Campbell-Sills, L., Barlow, D. H., Brown, T. A., & Hofmann, S. G. (2006). Effects of suppression and acceptance on emotional responses of individuals with anxiety and mood disorders. *Behavior Research and Therapy, 44,* 1251–1263.

Carta, M. , Angermeyer, M., & Holzinger, A. (2020). Mental health care in Italy: Basaglia's ashes in the wind of the crisis of the last decade. *International Journal of Social Psychiatry, 66,* 321–330. 10.1177/0020764020908620.

Chattopadhyay, S., & De Vries, R. (2008). Bioethical concerns are global, bioethics is Western. *Eubios Journal of Asian & International Bioethics, 18*(4), 106–109. https://www.ncbi.nlm.nih.gov/pmc/articles/PMC2707840/

Chilisa, B. (2012) *Indigenous research methodologies.* Sage.

Chouinard, J., & Hopson, R. (2016). A Critical Exploration of Culture in International Development Evaluation. *Canadian Journal of Program Evaluation, 30,* 248–276. 10.3138/cjpe.30.3.02.

Chuwa, L. T. (2010). *African indigenous ethics in global bioethics: Interpreting Ubuntu.* Springer

Ciulla, J. B. (2004). *Ethics, the heart of leadership.* Praeger.

Coburn, E. (2013). Unspeakable things: Indigenous research and social science. Révolutions, contestations, indignations. *Socio, 2,* 121–134.

Coetzee, P. H., & Roux, A. P. J., (Eds.). (2001). *The African philosophy reader.* Routledge.

Cookson, S., Abaza, H., Clarke, K., et al. (2015). Impact of and response to increased tuberculosis prevalence among Syrian refugees compared with Jordanian tuberculosis prevalence: Case study of a tuberculosis public health strategy. *Confl Health, 9,* 18.

Cram, F. (2006). Talking ourselves UP. *AlterNative: An International Journal of Indigenous Peoples, 2,* 28–43. 10.1177/117718010600200102.

Creswell, J. (2008). Editorial: Mapping the field of mixed methods research. *Journal of Mixed Methods Research, 3,* 95–108. Journal of Mixed Methods Research.

Dapunt, J., Kluge, U., & Heinz, A. (2017). Risk of psychosis in refugees: A literature review. *Translational Psychiatry, 7*(6), e1149. doi:10.1038/tp.2017.119

De Hoogh, A. H., & Den Hartog, D. N. (2008). Ethical and despotic leadership, relationships with leader's social responsibility, top management team effectiveness and subordinates' optimism: A multi-method study. *The Leadership Quarterly, 19,* 297–311.

Den Hartog, D. N., & De Hoogh, A. H. (2009). Empowering behavior and leader fairness and integrity: Studying perceptions of ethical leader behavior from. a levels-of-analysis perspective. *European Journal of Work & Organizational Psychology, 18,* 199–230.

Duff, P., & Uchida, Y. (1997). The negotiation of sociocultural identify in post-secondary EFL classrooms. *TESOL Quarterly, 31,* 451–486.

Eisenbeiss, S. A. (2012). Re-thinking ethical leadership: An interdisciplinary integrative approach. *The Leadership Quarterly, 23,* 791–808.

Ekmekci, P., & Arda, B. (2017). Interculturalism and informed consent: Respecting cultural differences without breaching human rights. Cultura. *International Journal of Philosophy of Culture and Axiology, 14*(2), 159–172.

Evans, W. R., & Davis, W. (2014). Corporate citizenship and the employee: An organizational identification perspective. *Human Performance, 27,* 129–146.

Fox, M. W. (2001). *Bringing life to ethics: Global bioethics for a humane society.* State University of New York Press.

Gao, G., Ting-Toomey, S., & Gudykunst, W. B. (1996). Chinese communication processes. In M. H. Bond (Ed.), *The handbook of Chinese psychology* (pp. 280–293). Oxford University Press.

Gemmill, G. & Oakley, J. (1992) Leadership: An alienating social myth. *Human Relations, 45*(2), 113–129.

Geertz, C. (1973). *Interpretation of cultures*. Basic Books.

Ghosh, A. (2000). Antinomies of society. *Social Change, 30*, 195–197. 10.1177/004908570003000413.

Ghosh, B. (2007). Managing migration: Whither the missing regime? How relevant is trade law to such a regime? *Proceedings of the ASIL Annual Meeting, 101*, 303–306. 10.1017/s0272503700025945.

Giannini, S. (2001). Future Agendas for Women Community College Leaders and Change Agents. *Community College Journal of Research and Practice, 25*, 201–211. 10.1080/106689201750068416.

Grint, K. (2005a) *Leadership: Limits and possibilities*. Palgrave.

Henderson, K. A. (1994). Theory application and development in recreation, park, and leisure research. *Journal of Park and Recreation Administration, 12*, 51–64.

Henderson, K. A., Presley, J., & Bialeschki, M. D. (2004). Theory in recreation and leisure research: Reflections from the editors. *Leisure Sciences, 26*, 411–425.

Henderson, K. A., & Walker, G. J. (2014). Ethnic and racial research methods. In M. Stodolska, K. J. Shinew, M. F. Floyd, & G. J. Walker (Eds.), *Race, ethnicity, and leisure* (pp. 21–36). Human Kinetics.

Holzhauser, K. (2008). *Australasian Emergency Nursing Journal*, 11, 10010.1016/j.aenj.2008.02.005.

Hopson, J. (2003). General learning models, functional and neural mechanisms of interval timing, *Frontiers in Neuroscience*, 10.1201/9780203009574.ch2.

Hutchinson, M., & Dorsett, P. (2012). What does the literature say about resilience in refugee people? Implications for practice. *Journal of Social Inclusion, 3*(2)55–78.

Janesick, V. (2015). Oral history as a social justice project: Issues for the qualitative researcher. *The Qualitative Report*, 10.46743/2160-3715/2007.1648.

Kemp, C. & Rasbridge, L. (2004). *Refugee and immigrant health: A handbook for health professionals*. Cambridge University Press.

Kincheloe, J. (2008). *Knowledge and critical pedagogy*. Springer Press.

Kirui, P. & Mwaruvie, J. (2012). The dilemma of hosting refugees: A focus on the insecurity in Northeastern Kenya. *International Journal of Business and Social Science, 3*(8), 161–171.

Kohlberg, L., & Hersch, R. H. (1977). Moral development: A review of the theory. *Theory into Practice, 16*, 53–59.

Kroll, J., Yusuf, A., & Fujiwara, K. (2010). Psychoses, PTSD, and depression in Somali refugees in Minnesota. *Social Psychiatry and Psychiatric Epidemiology, 46*, 481–493. 10.1007/s00127-010-0216-0.

Lutz, D. (2009). African ubuntu philosophy and global management. *Journal of Business Ethics, 84*(3), 313–328.

McCall, L. (2005). The Complexity of Intersectionality. *Signs: Journal of Women in Culture and Society, 30*, 1771–1800. 10.1086/426800.

Moore, Leslie. (2004). Learning languages by heart: Second language socialization in a fulbe community (Maroua, Cameroon) [Unpublished Ph.D. Dissertation]. University of California Los Angeles. Chapter 5: Guided Repetition as Social Practice (pp. 269-313).

Müller, M., Khamis, D., Srivastava, D., Exadaktylos, A. K., & Pfortmueller, C. A. (2018). Understanding refugees' health. *Seminars in Neurology, 38*(2), 152–162. doi:10.1055/s-0038-1649337.

Murray, J. S. (2018). Toxic stress and child refugees. *Journal for Specialists in Pediatric Nursing: JSPN, 23*(1). doi:10.1111/jspn.12200.

Norton, B. (2000). *Identify and language learning*. Pearson.

Norton, B. & Toohey, K. (2001). Changing perspectives on good language learners, *TESOL Quarterly, 29*(1), 9–31.

Orlandi, M., Weston, R., & Epstein, L. (Eds.). (1992). *Cultural competence for evaluators: A guide for alcohol and other drug abuse prevention practitioners working with ethnic/racial communities*. U.S. Department of Health and Human Services; Public Health Service; Alcohol, Drug Abuse, and Mental Health Administration (ADAMHA); Office for Substance Abuse Prevention; Division of Community Prevention and Training.

Piccolo, R. F., Greenbaum, R., den Hartog, D. N., & Folger, R. (2010). The relationship between ethical leadership and core job characteristics. *Journal of Organizational Behavior, 31*, 259–278.

Racine, L., & Petrucka, P. (2011). Enhancing decolonization and knowledge transfer in nursing research with non-western populations: Examining the congruence between primary healthcare and postcolonial feminist approaches. *Nursing inquiry, 18*(1), 12–20. doi:10.1111/j.1440-1800.2010.00504.x.

Rowe, J. (2006). Non-defining leadership. *Kybernetes, 35*, 1528–1537. 10.1108/03684920610688568.

Rubio-Goldsmith, R., McCormick, M., Martinez, D., & Duarte, I. *A Humanitarian Crisis at the Border: New Estimates of Deaths Among Unauthorized Immigrants*. Immigration Policy Center.

Salanova, M., Lorente, L., Chambel, M. J., & Martínez, I. M. (2011). Linking transformational leadership to nurses' extra-role performance: The mediating role of self-efficacy and work engagement. *Journal of Advanced Nursing, 67*, 2256–2266.

Sarcevic, A., Marsic, I., Waterhouse, L., Stockwell, D., & Burd, R. (2011). Leadership structures in emergency care settings: A study of two trauma centers. *International Journal of Medical Informatics, 80*, 227–238. 10.1016/j.ijmedinf.2011.01.004.

Schein, E. H. (1992). *Organizational culture and leadership* (2nd ed.). Jossey-Bass.

Schweitzer, R., Greenslade, J., & Kagee, A. (2007). Coping and resilience in refugees from the Sudan: A narrative account. *Australian Journal of Psychiatry, 41*(3), 282–8

Scudder, T., & Colson, E. (2019). From welfare to: A conceptual framework for the analysis of dislocated people. *Involuntary Migration and Resettlement*, 267–287. 10.4324/9780429052293-15.

Senese, P. (2005). Territory, contiguity, and international conflict: Assessing a new joint explanation. *American Journal of Political Science, 49*, 769–779. 10.1111/ajps.2005.49.issue-4.

Senge, P. (1990). *The Fifth Discipline: The Art and Practice of the Learning Organization*. Doubleday/Currency.

SenGupta, S., Hopson, R., & Thompson-Robinson, M. (2004). Cultural competence in evaluation: An overview. *New Directions for Evaluation, 2004*, 5–19. 10.1002/ev.112.

Shivayogi, P. (2013). Vulnerable population and methods for their safeguard. *Perspectives in Clinical Research, 4*(1), 53—57.

Shweder, R. (1991). *Thinking through cultures: Expeditions in cultural psychology*. Harvard University Press.

Siegel, M. (1996). The role of learner subjectivity in second language sociolinguistic competency: Western women learning Japanese. *Applied Linguistics, 17*(3), 356–382.

Snow, K., Hays, D., Caliwagan, G., Ford, D., Mariotti, D., Mwendwa, J., & Scott, W. (2016). Guiding principles for indigenous research practices. *Action Research, 14*(4), 357–375.

Sousa, C. M. P., Coelho, F., & Guillamon-Saorin, E. (2012). Personal values, autonomy, and self-efficacy: Evidence from frontline service employees. *International Journal of Selection and Assessment, 20*, 159–170.

Spörlein, C., & Tubergen, F. (2014). The occupational status of immigrants in Western and non-Western societies. *International Journal of Comparative Sociology, 55*, 119–143.

Stone-Brown, K. (2013). Syria: A healthcare system on the brink of collapse. *BMJ, 347*, f7375. https://pubmed.ncbi.nlm.nih.gov/24327182/.

Suárez-Orozco, C., & Suárez-Orozco, M. (2001). *Children of immigration*. Harvard University Press.

The Nuremberg Code. (n.d.). https://history.nih.gov/display/history/Nuremberg+Code.

The United Nations Educational, Scientific and Cultural Organization. (2005). Universal Declaration on Bioethics and Human Rights, https://en.unesco.org/themes/ethics-science-and-technology/bioethics-and-human-rights.

Tajfel, H., & Turner, J. C. (1979). An integrative theory of intergroup conflict. In W. G. Austin & S. Worchel (Eds.), *The social psychology of intergroup relations* (pp. 33–47). Brooks/Cole.

Taylor, J., & MacDonald, H. (1992). *Children of immigrants: Issues of poverty and disadvantage. Bureau of Immigration Research*. AGPS Canberra.

Tepper, B. J., Lockhart, D., & Hoobler, J. (2001). Justice, citizenship, and role definition effects. *Journal of Applied Psychology, 86*, 789–796.

Tracey, J. B., & Tews, M. J. (2005). Construct validity of a general training climate scale. *Organizational Research Methods, 8*, 353–374.

Tyler, T. R. (1999). Why people cooperate with organizations: An identity-based perspective. In R. I. Sutton & B. M. Staw (Eds.), *Research in organizational behavior* (Vol. 21, pp. 201–246). JAI Press.

Tyler, T. R., & Blader, S. L. (2000). *Cooperation in groups: Procedural justice, social identity, and behavioral engagement*. Psychology Press.

Tyler, T. R., & Blader, S. L. (2002). Autonomous vs. comparative status: Must we be better than others to feel good about ourselves? *Organizational Behavior and Human Decision Processes, 89*, 813–838.

Tyler, T. R., & Blader, S. L. (2003). The group engagement model: Procedural justice, social identity, and cooperative behavior. *Personality and Social Psychology Review, 7*, 349–361.

van de Vijver, F. J. R. (2011). Capturing bias in structural equation modeling. In E. Davidov, P. Schmidt, & J. Billiet (Eds.), *Cross-cultural analysis: Methods and applications*(pp. 3–34). Routledge.

UNHCR (2014a). "Syrian Regional Refugee Response Inter-agency Information Sharing Portal: Regional Overview Datasheet, December 11, 2014." Geneva: UNHCR.

van Knippenberg, D., van Knippenberg, B., De Cremer, D., & Hogg, M. A. (2004). Leadership, self, and identity: A review and research agenda. *The Leadership Quarterly, 15*, 825–856.

Walumbwa, F. O., Mayer, D. M., Wang, P., Wang, H., Workman, K., & Christensen, A. L. (2011). Linking ethical leadership to employee performance: The roles of leader–member exchange, self-efficacy, and organizational identification. *Organizational Behavior and Human Decision Processes, 115*, 204–213.

Watson-Gregeo, K. A. & Gregeo, D. W. (1992). Schooling, knowledge, and power: Social transformation in the Solomon Islands. *Anthropology & Education Quarterly, 21*(1), 10–29.

Weine, S. (2008). Family roles in refugee youth resettlement from a prevention perspective. *Child and Adolescent Psychiatric Clinics of North America, 17*, 515–532. 10.1016/j.chc.2008.02.006.

Wood, M. (2005). The fallacy of misplaced leadership. *Journal of Management Studies, 42*(6), 1101–1121.

World Medical Association. (2013). Declaration of Helsinki – Ethical Principles for Medical Research Involving Human Subjects. Retrieved June 30, 2020, https://www.wma.net/publications/wma-doh-1964–2014/.

Part IIIB
Publishing and Applications

30

International Publishing

Challenges and Considerations

Sarah Wipperman and Nina Collins

This chapter discusses various challenges authors face in navigating the international academic publishing ecosystem from a scholarly communication perspective. Much of the information herein is based on the experiences of the authors as publishing specialists and scholarly communication librarians and on workshops taught by the authors for graduate students and faculty in the United States. Please note that the authors are not lawyers and none of the discussions in this chapter should be taken as legal advice. The chapter is intended to give readers a better understanding of common topics and issues in publishing so that, as authors, they can make more informed decisions about where and how to publish.

This chapter begins with a discussion of copyright concerns in publishing, which establishes a foundation for future sections. Many publishing-related topics, such as open access, disseminating research to increase visibility, and even ethical considerations, have roots in copyright issues; so, general, foundational knowledge in copyright concerns is often pivotal to these other discussions. In this section, the authors additionally discuss copyright protections in a global context, reusing third party content in a publication, and the intersection of copyright infringement and plagiarism in publishing.

The second section builds on the topic of author rights outlined in the first section and applies these concepts to contracts and publishing agreements. Here, the authors cover common parts of a publishing agreement and common options the author might have. The third section focuses on dissemination of works through publication, looking at vetting publication venues, publishing best practices, open access, and sharing work beyond publication. The chapter ends with a number of resources and recommendations for international publishing.

Copyright Concerns in Publishing

Copyright Internationally

Each country creates its own copyright laws, requirements, and exceptions, which means there is no such thing as international copyright law – one unified copyright law to rule them all. Different countries have different rules for what gets copyright protections, what is required in order to gain protection, and for how long those protections last. It is therefore important to become familiar with the copyright laws of the individual countries in which you live and work in order to understand how to best protect your own work and how to reuse works created by others (third party works).

DOI: 10.4324/9781003003380-30

How copyright is treated between countries can additionally be governed by trade agreements, treaties, or other means, which further complicates the issue (U.S. Copyright Office, 2021). One major treaty in this area is the Berne Convention for the Protection of Literary and Artistic Works, which sets out basic principles for protecting works and author rights. Of particular interest, the Berne Convention states that works from one country should be given the same protections in other countries as those countries give to their own people, protections should be automatic (i.e., no formal requirements in order to gain copyright protections), and that the duration of copyright last at minimum the life of the author plus 50 years (World Intellectual Property Organization, n.d.-a). According to the World Intellectual Property Organization (n.d.-b), to date, 179 countries are contracting parties to the Berne Convention, so many countries have laws that comply with at least the minimum protections set forth in the Berne Convention. The World Intellectual Property Organization also provides a free database, WIPO Lex (https://www.wipo.int/wipolex/en/index.html), that you can use to search for copyright laws by country as well as treaties and judgments (n.d.-c).

Copyright Protections

As a creator and user of copyrighted works, it is important to know what protections you may have over your own works as well as what rights may be associated with works that you may want to reuse. This knowledge will save you time during the publication process (e.g., when you may need to clear permissions) and also help you better understand to what you are agreeing in your publishing contracts.

Each country's copyright law lays out the types of works that receive copyright protection and what protections they receive, but we can again turn to the Berne Convention for some general guidance on what might be protected. Article 2(1) of the Berne Convention requires that protections include "every production in the literary, scientific and artistic domain, whatever the mode or form of its expression" (World Intellectual Property Organization, n.d.-a, (2)(a)), so countries that are signatories of this treaty protect works that at the very least fall within these categories. The Berne Convention also lays out minimum standards for protections, which include the following rights that should be exclusive to the author of the work:

- the right to translate,
- the right to make adaptations and arrangements of the work,
- the right to perform in public dramatic, dramatico-musical and musical works,
- the right to recite literary works in public,
- the right to communicate to the public the performance of such works,
- the right to broadcast,
- the right to make reproductions in any manner or form,
- the right to use the work as a basis for an audiovisual work, and the right to reproduce, distribute, perform in public or communicate to the public that audiovisual work (World Intellectual Property Organization, n.d.-a, (2)(b)).

As mentioned in the previous section, the Berne Convention additionally requires that these protections happen automatically and last for at least the life of the author plus 50 years.

Because the Berne Convention only provides minimum requirements, countries may provide additional protections and rights to creators. Note that some countries also provide limitations and exceptions to the exclusive rights outlined in their copyright laws. For example, the United Kingdom and the United States have broad reuse exceptions (fair dealings and fair use, respectively) outlined in their copyright statutes that allow copyrighted works to be used under certain circumstances without constituting infringement (see Copyright, Designs and Patents Act 1988 §§ 29–30, 2014, for fair dealings in the United Kingdom and 17 U.S. Code § 107, 2018, for fair use in the United States).

What Doesn't Have Copyright Protections?

In most countries, copyright protections last a relatively long period of time, often the life of the author plus 50 or more years (per the Berne Convention), but they do not last forever. Works that have fallen out of copyright are considered to be in the public domain and can be used without restriction (although you should always cite your sources, regardless of the copyright status). The length of copyright protection and what is considered to be in the public domain is dependent on individual countries' laws, so a work could be in the public domain in one country but not another. For example, Marcel DuChamps' work of art, L.H.O.O.Q (1919), is in the public domain in the United States (see U.S. Copyright Office, 2017) but is still protected by copyright in France. Under French copyright law, Code de la propriété intellectuelle Art. L. 123-1 (1997), none of Duchamps' works will be released into the public domain until 2038 (70 years after Duchamps' death). Creators may additionally choose to give up their rights to their work and release it to the public domain. Countries may have other considerations for what is in the public domain and what gets protections. The United States, for example, also lays out types of works that cannot receive copyright protections or have limited protections, including but not limited to ideas; short words, phrases, or slogans (e.g., you cannot copyright your name or a slogan like Nike's "Just Do It"; protections for slogans or words fall under trademark law); facts; public domain elements (e.g., things you would find in nature); and processes (which fall under patent law) (17 U.S.C. § 102(b), 2018; see also U.S. Copyright Office, 2017). It should be noted, though, that even though underlying facts or data may not have protections, the author's expression of those facts and data (e.g., through prose or data visualizations) may have copyright.

Reusing Content in Your Publication

Most publishers place the onus on authors to clear permissions for any works they reuse as part of their publication, and the authors are typically liable for any copyright infringement that might occur on the author's part. It is therefore important for authors to be able to understand and identify potential copyright concerns with the content they are reusing and to know when permission may be required.

As outlined in the previous section, there are a number of rights that are exclusive to an author, including the right to reproduce and redistribute a work (i.e., "publish" it) as well as the right to translate or otherwise create derivative works. As long as a work has copyright protections, you will therefore need to ensure that you have the rights to reuse the work, either through a license (e.g., Creative Commons), a copyright exception (e.g., fair use or fair dealings), or by getting permission from the copyright holder.

The following flow chart (Figure 30.1) represents one way to work through whether or not you need to seek permission for reuse. Keep in mind that different countries have different copyright laws and exceptions, and you will need to go through the workflow for each item you want to reuse. The workflow starts by determining if the work is under copyright and, if so, if it is under an open license (e.g., Creative Commons) you can use for your intended purpose. If the work is in the public domain or under a license you can use, you do not need to seek permission, but you should cite the original material and ensure that you are complying with any license requirements, if applicable. If not, you move on to the next step of the workflow, which asks if you need to use the *exact* work. If, for example, you need a picture of a horse but it can be any horse, it would be easier to try and find a public domain or openly licensed image of a horse instead. If you cannot use an alternative, move on to the final step of the workflow, which asks if you can use a copyright exception, such as fair use or fair dealings, which will vary by country. If you feel that you can use a copyright exception, you should document the exception you are using and your reasoning for why you are using it. If you cannot use an exception, you should then seek permission.

Sarah Wipperman and Nina Collins

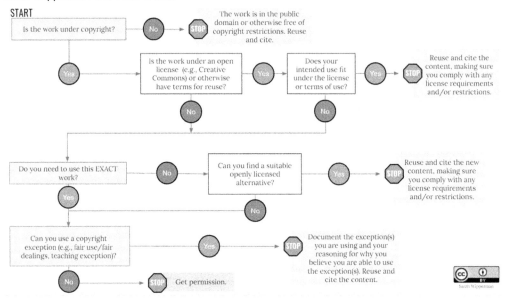

Figure 30.1 "Reusing Responsibly: Determining When to Seek Permission for Reuse". Flow chart outlining steps to determine if permission is required in order to reuse content. CC BY 4.0 Sarah Wipperman, 2020.

Creative Commons Licensed Content

Creative Commons licenses are a powerful tool for authors because they make it easier to find content that has been cleared for reuse by the creator. As previously discussed, many works are automatically protected by copyright in their country of origin with "all rights reserved," meaning that if you want to reuse a work in your publication, you will likely need to get permission from the copyright holder. Creative Commons licenses allow the author to keep copyright over their work with "some rights reserved," so as long as you are able to comply with the terms of the license, you can reuse the work (Creative Commons, 2020). For more information on Creative Commons licenses, go to https://creativecommons.org.

Seeking Permission

When all other avenues for reuse have been exhausted, it is time to seek permission. Getting permission can be a lengthy and potentially costly process, so if you are publishing, be sure to stay organized and leave plenty of time before your deadline.

The first step of getting permission is to find the rights holder, which can sometimes be difficult to determine. In many cases, the copyright owner is not the creator: Copyright holders can assign and transfer their rights to others (e.g., publishers) and often do so. If the creator has passed away, they may have transferred their rights to someone in their will, or their rights may have passed on to their heirs. Estates or societies may also handle the rights of a deceased creator. You may have to do some research in order to find the right copyright holder. For formal publications, contacting the publisher can be a good place to start this research. If the publisher does not own the rights themselves, they may know who does. For informal publications or other materials, contact the author directly. If you do not know the publisher or author of the work, try to find the original source of the content (e.g., where the material was first published or posted) and look for rights statements or other information on reuse.

Once you know who the copyright holder is, you should reach out to them for permission. Many rights holders will want to know the following:

- What are you reusing?

- How much are you reusing?
- In what way will you be reusing that work (e.g., publication, on a website, etc.)?
- For how long?
- Who will have access to the work (e.g., everyone, certain geographic distribution, etc.)?
- (If applicable) Publication details (e.g., publisher, title, format, cost, etc.).

The process for getting permission may vary: You may be asked to fill out a form in order to get permission, or you may simply need to email someone. While verbal consent could suffice, it is best to get permission in writing (and many publishers require it), and you should always cite work you reuse. Additionally, the copyright holder has no obligation to answer your query or give you permission to reuse their work, so "no reply" does not give you automatic permission to use the work. If you are unable to get permission to reuse a work, you will need to find an alternative option. Editing or otherwise making changes to the original work constitutes a derivative work, which would also require permission, so this is not a viable option in the absence of permission.

Copyright Infringement and Plagiarism in Publishing

As careful as an author may be in getting permission to reuse works, there could be instances where an author unintentionally commits copyright infringement or plagiarism. Copyright infringement and plagiarism often overlap but are two distinct concepts.

Copyright infringement involves violating the exclusive rights of the copyright holder (e.g., the right to copy, redistribute, publicly perform/display a work, create a derivative work, etc.), which typically extends to expressions of an idea (e.g., how an author phrases something) but not to the idea itself (for example, 17 U.S.C. §§ 102(b) & 501(a), 2018). Plagiarism generally involves passing off someone else's idea as your own or not properly citing the origin of the idea or materials.

Where copyright infringement has a legal basis in most countries and could have legal ramifications, plagiarism is an academic integrity or ethical violation that may not necessarily have any legal standing on its own unless another violation is taking place, such as copyright infringement or fraud. There are also a variety of ways in which plagiarism might be committed, from directly copying passages (which may also be copyright infringement) to minor similarities in phrasing or ideas to an author submitting multiple similar articles on the same topic or based on the same research (e.g., "salami-slicing") (Saunders, 2010, pp. 280–281). Beyond potential legal ramifications, plagiarism may carry other severe consequences such as expulsion or termination. Definitions and consequences of plagiarism are often found on individual university or employer websites.

In a publishing context, most author agreements ask the author to assert that the work is original and their own (see the Contracts and Publishing Agreements section for more information), but how a publisher determines whether or not a piece has been plagiarized and the actions they take can vary. Publishers typically post information on how they define and approach plagiarism on their websites as well as any information on tools they use, such as plagiarism detection software. These websites can also be useful sources for tips on how to avoid plagiarism. For example, see Taylor & Francis' Plagiarism Policies and Guidance for Authors (n.d.): https://authorservices.taylorandfrancis.com/editorial-policies/plagiarism/

Contracts and Publishing Agreements

Why Should You Read and Understand Your Contract?

When you sign a publishing agreement, it is a legal and binding contract between you and your publisher that will dictate how your work can be used and reused, potentially in perpetuity. This includes what *you* may or may not be able to do with your work in the future. It is therefore imperative to not only read the agreement but also understand the terms set forth. You should ensure that those terms align with your present and future goals for your work. The following sections are meant to help you understand commonalities among contracts and some of the basic legal concepts they contain. Nothing herein should be taken as legal advice.

Common Parts of a Publishing Contract

Publishing contracts can vary widely in their structure, length, and content. Because there is no standardized agreement, it can be difficult to anticipate what you may encounter in an individual contract. There are, however, some common parts or themes that many contracts have. Note that it is not guaranteed that these will appear in your contract or that they will appear as described.

Copyright Transfer or License

In order to publish your work, a publisher needs the right to at least reproduce and redistribute it. In order to gain this ability, publishers may opt for a copyright transfer or a license. In either case, you must ensure that you own copyright and are otherwise able to make the agreement with the publisher.

In a copyright transfer, you give up some or all of your rights to the publisher, who would then be a copyright owner (and in the case of a full transfer, you will no longer own rights to your work). Refer to the U.S. Copyright Office's *Copyright Basics* circular (2019) for more information on copyright transfers in the United States context. A license, on the other hand, can be an exclusive or non-exclusive agreement in which you retain your rights but give permission to the publisher to do certain things for a certain period of time (e.g., publish your work). An exclusive license means that you cannot give that same permission to another entity as long as your agreement with the publisher stands; a non-exclusive license gives you the ability to give multiple entities the right to reuse your work in the same way and at the same time (see also European Union, n.d.). Creative Commons licenses, for example, are non-exclusive licenses (Creative Commons, 2020).

In general, when publishing journal articles, authors publishing in a subscription journal can expect to sign a copyright transfer agreement or exclusive license agreement; authors publishing open access can expect to sign a non-exclusive license, typically retaining their rights and placing their work under a Creative Commons license.

Author Rights and Permitted Uses

Most copyright transfer agreements also include a section that describes how the author can reuse their work in the future. Remember, when you transfer your rights, you no longer own them and therefore must get permission from the (new) copyright holder (the publisher) to reuse your work unless your contract says otherwise. The following information tends to be more applicable to journal articles, but book agreements may have similar sections.

The author rights/permitted uses section can describe how the author can share their work. For journal articles, this can often be broken down as outlined in Figure 30.2, where the contract often describes what you can share, when and where you can share it, and other requirements for sharing. Journals may use different terminology for versions of your work or different definitions for sharing venues. If you do not understand the terms for how you can share your work, reach out to the publisher for clarification.

These sections may additionally outline other ways that the author might reuse their work, such as including a journal article in a book or building up on it for a future publication, reusing the article for teaching purposes, or how the abstract or figures might be reused.

Common Sharing Options in Academic Publishing Contracts

Common sharing provisions	What you can share	When you can share it	Where you can share it	Other requirements for sharing
Common sharing options	• Preprint¹ • Postprint² • Final version	• Immediately • After publication • After an embargo period • Never	• Repository (institutional, preprint/postprint, funding, etc.) • Personal website • Departmental website • Intranet of your employer's company • With colleagues	• Must include a specific statement or citation alongside the work • May limit sharing to a certain number of copies

¹ Version you initially submit for publication
² Version after peer review but before publisher-added formatting

Figure 30.2 "Common Sharing Options in Academic Publishing Contracts". Table showing common sharing provisions and options for sharing a work that may be found in publishing contracts. CC BY 4.0 Sarah Wipperman, 2020.

Representations and Warranties

Representations and warranties are general contract terms that essentially describe promises or assertions that a fact is true (*Glossary: Representations and warranties*, n.d.). What do you, as the author, promise and assert to be true, and what does the publisher promise and assert to be true? In many publishing contracts, the author must assert things such as that the work is their own and that they have not plagiarized the work, that they have the ability to enter into the publishing agreement, that the work is not libelous or slanderous, that they have not submitted the work for publication elsewhere, and that they have cleared any required permissions for third party materials. The publisher often promises to publish the work and give the author credit. These sections can be highly varied, so be sure to read each term and ensure that you are accurately representing your work.

Other Sections

There are a number of other sections that may be included in a publishing agreement. For example, there may be limitations of liability, mandatory arbitration, or indemnity clauses. Authors may be asked to disclose (or assert they disclosed) potential conflicts of interest and funding support for the work. They could be asked to consent to commercial electronic messaging from a publisher and their business affiliates. Book agreements may also outline royalties, deadlines, future publications or editions, the editorial process, and under what conditions the agreement might be terminated by either party.

Negotiating for More Rights

Once you have read your publishing agreement, you may find that you wish to retain more rights over your work. To do so, you may be able to use an author addendum or otherwise negotiate your contract. Publishers may have other agreements that might better meet your needs, or they may be willing to otherwise work with you to adjust the agreement terms or grant you additional permissions. While not ideal, if you cannot come to an agreement with the publisher that meets your needs, you can walk away and find a publisher that is a better fit. Once you sign the contract, though, you are bound by the terms within and lose your ability to negotiate the terms.

Publishing Your Work

Finding the Right Publishing Outlet

Choosing the right publishing outlet impacts how your work is disseminated, accessed, and read. Traditional journal publishing business models require authors to transfer copyright to the publisher; whereas open access publications may not require copyright transfer. Open access is the free, immediate, online availability of scholarly works, including re-use rights. Scholarly works made available by open access are free from paywall restrictions – requirements that readers or libraries pay to read the work (BOAI, 2002).

Open access publishing provides numerous benefits over paywalled scholarship, including increased usage and increased citations (Björk, 2017). Open scholarship is more freely accessible – and used – by practitioners and technicians in the field, as well as policy makers (JISC, 2019). Open access works are more easily accessed, therefore they are more likely to be used by researchers in the developing world. Educators cannot teach scholarship that they cannot afford to read. Open works are more likely to be used in teaching as well as research (SPARC Europe).

Open access can take many forms, including gold open access (born open) and green open access (self-archiving). Gold open access is the most widely known form of open access. While open access is free to read, it is not free to publish. The costs of publishing are often moved to authors in the form of article processing charges, or APCs.

While open access has numerous benefits, it is not without critique. For many researchers, particularly in the developing world, the fees associated with publishing act as a significant barrier to publication (Union, 2019). There are misconceptions that open access scholarship does not undergo the same degree of rigorous peer review as in journals that publish using the traditional business model. The widest misconception of open access publishing lies in deceptive publishing practices. Deceptive publishing, "is a practice whereby a company creates a journal on false pretenses for the purposes of defrauding authors, helping authors deceive their colleagues, or both" (OSI, 2019). Deceptive publishers are funded by authors, using APCs, and are commonly known as "predatory publishers."

The phrase "predatory publisher" was nearly always paired with "open access" when the term first came to prominence. Predatory publishers were described as publishers who exploit the open access publishing model by charging fees without providing scholarly rigor and quality publishing services (Butler, 2013). Predatory publishers are for-profit publishers, and operate without a commitment to publication ethics. They may cheat authors, deceive scholars into serving on editorial boards or even serving as peer reviewers (COPE, 2019).

While there are certainly bad actors in the world of publishing, not all publishers who fail to adhere to publishing industry standards do so deliberately. Eriksson and Helgesson (2018) correctly pointed out "the term 'predatory journal' unhelpfully bundles misconduct with poor quality." Furthermore, the term "predatory publisher" indicates sinister behavior on the part of publishers, and assumes authors to be innocent victims. In reality, some researchers deliberately choose "predatory" journals (Kurt, 2018). To best conceptualize this darker world of publishing, we use "deceptive publisher" and discuss expected publishing best practices to guide emerging scholars.

Publishing Best Practice

Deceptive publishers deliberately engage in deceptive publishing practices for the purpose of financial profit (OSI, 2018). They may mimic the look and feel of legitimate journals (false-flag journals), or imply affiliation with a legitimate or prestigious scholarly organization that may or may not exist (masqueraders). The largest category of deceptive publishers are the pseudo-scholarly journals. Pseudo-scholarly journals falsely claim to offer editorial and review services or claim credentials like indexing in reputable indexes or impact factor metrics. These claims are misleading or fraudulent. Often, the line between deliberate, fraud, and ineptitude is difficult to objectively discern. It is helpful to understand publishing best practices.

Scholarly publishers perform myriad tasks that add value to scholarly works (Anderson, 2018). While the editorial practices of scholarly journals happen behind closed doors, the publishing industry does have established standards of practice. The Committee on Publication Ethics (COPE) has developed *Principles of Transparency and Best Practice* for scholarly publishers (COPE, 2014). *Principles of Transparency* is a joint effort between the Open Access Scholarly Publishing Association, the Directory of Open Access Journals (DOAJ), COPE, and the World Association of Medical Editors.

Scholarly publishers are responsible for recruiting editors and editorial board members. They work with the editors to create policies and keep them updated. If necessary, they create and maintain contracts with sponsors that outline the roles of parties involved. This falls under Ownership and Management within the Principles (COPE, 2014). As it is not uncommon for deceptive publishers to mimic legitimate, well established, professional organizations or scholarly journals, the *Principles* make clear this is not acceptable practice.

Copyediting, typesetting, and registering an International Standard Serial Number of a new journal are professional publishing standards. ISSNs are issued by the ISSN National Centre in the publisher's home country. If the journal does not publish at least 5 articles per issue, the application for an ISSN will not be approved. It is not uncommon for deceptive publishers to launch many journals all at once; and, many of the journals will only have a few articles per issue. Deceptive publishers may also lie about physical location. For example, a journal titled the *American Scientific Journal of Advancement in STEM, Art and Humanities,* may have a business address in southeast Asia and used the ISSN registry service in that southeast Asian country.

Publishers market and brand the journal, detecting and cultivating relevant audiences (Anderson, 2018). One of the ways publishers reach relevant audiences is by indexing journal content with abstracting and indexing services. Publishers undergo lengthy application processes to have their content included in these discovery services. Once approved, they must maintain article-level metadata feeds to those abstracting and indexing services. Article-level metadata is data about each article, including: title, author, abstract, keywords, URL, and DOI.

Indexing and abstracting services are database collections of related content. These databases provide collected content with similar relevance, increasing findability of the works by scholars who are more likely to reuse it. Some notable examples of indexing services include Business Source Premier (by EBSCOhost), ERIC-Education Resources Information Center, Directory of Open Access Journals (DOAJ), and Journal Citation Reports (by Clarivate Analytics). Librarians are partners in the discovery and research process: They help maintain these databases and the classification schema that provide increased relevant discovery. The indexing and abstracting services most useful to scholarly audiences allow users to access relevant scholarship at multiple access points. For example, users of DOAJ can search for articles by title, abstract, keywords, author, ORCID, DOI, or language. Those databases that provide article-level access points allow users to discover the content *within* the journal, rather than simply providing information about the cover of the journal. Abstracting and Indexing services that do not provide article-level metadata – and access at these multiple access points – are not helpful in reaching relevant audiences.

Deceptive publishers will often lie about indexing in reputable indexes, or list abstracting and indexing services that are not real indexing and abstracting services (OSI, 2018). A journal should not claim to be indexed in Business Source Complete, or the Directory of Open Access Journals without having its content indexed there. Remember, a publisher must reach relevant audiences. Simply listing the journal in an online database that lists journal titles does not meet this goal. Users need to know if the articles *within* the journal are relevant to their research. Furthermore, listing a journal in a service that does not have user friendly search features does not meet this goal. It is important to be indexed with well-known services that scholars frequent to discover knowledge. Obscure services, unknown to scholars, are not likely to be used by scholars.

Deceptive publishers will commonly misrepresent the impact of scholarship published within their journals by falsely listing an impact factor. Journal Impact Factor (JIF) is a mathematical calculation of the number of times the articles published – in a given year – in that journal have been cited, divided by the number of citable research papers that were published in that given year. JIF is a trademarked term and is only assigned to journals indexed in Journal Citation Reports (JCR, by Clarivate Analytics). A journal that claims an impact factor, but is not indexed in JCR, is using some alternate metric. While there are many online services that offer alternative impact metrics, the criteria are subjective, not transparent, and cannot be reproduced (Xia & Smith, 2018).

The role of editors in the scholarly publishing process cannot be underestimated. Editors may have a contract with the publisher that has clear expectations and length of term appointment. Editors set the editorial policy, appoint the board, and recruit content and relevant peer reviewers. To effectively recruit relevant content and peer reviewers, editors should be engaged in the discipline. They should know the trends and key players in the disciplinary field of study. By continuing to talk with researchers in the field, editors stay abreast of trends and developments in the field and are better informed as to how a journal may need to change or grow in order to support the discipline. By contrast, deceptive publishers may list the same editor for many journals, across multiple disciplinary specialties. It is often a sign that a journal does not, or cannot, provide quality editorial rigor if it shares an editor with multiple other journals. In addition, deceptive publishers are known to list – as editors – individuals who have not agreed to serve.

Editors should have enough disciplinary experience that they can provide authority on content that falls within the scope of the journal. The editor is responsible for moderating peer review. This includes choosing and assigning peer reviewers to each manuscript. The editor should have enough experience in the discipline to vet peer reviewers as having relevant expertise. If the scope of the journal is too broad, the editor may be unable to effectively perform this expectation of the position. In the example listed above, the *American Scientific Journal of Advancement in STEM, Art and Humanities* has a very broad disciplinary scope. It is not reasonable to expect an editor to have disciplinary specialties in all these disciplines. As such, the editor cannot be expected to have vetted the disciplinary expertise of peer reviewers.

Editors work with Publishers to draft and enforce editorial policies. Examples of editorial policies include Peer review, Ethical Misconduct, Plagiarism, Conflict of Interest or Competing Interests, Corrections and Retraction, and Self-archiving policies. While it is the responsibility of the Editor to enforce these policies, the Publisher is expected to provide guidance for Editors in navigating concerns and potential violations of editorial policies.

It is the responsibility of peer reviewers to provide specific feedback to Editors. Peer reviewers evaluate the accuracy as well as the timeliness of the content. They may provide context or provenance for the content, relaying the importance of the content to the discipline. Peer reviewers will indicate whether or not an author provides strong evidence to support the conclusion and ensure data and conclusions match. Peer review takes time. Deceptive publishers will often accept manuscripts without suggesting changes, or employ an extremely fast peer review turnaround time.

Transparency in Publishing

One of the issues at stake with deceptive publishers lies in differentiating between those publishers that may not be well funded or who are inexperienced, and those publishers who engage in deliberate deception or fraud (OSI, 2018). It is important to avoid jumping to conclusions of fraud when the issue may be inexperience or limited resources. These gray areas make this issue difficult to directly confront. Transparency is key to helping authors assess the degree to which a publisher adheres to publishing best practice and scholarly rigor. A list of questions authors can use to help assess transparency and publishing best practice can be found in the Publisher Evaluation Tool (Appendix 30). In brief, publishers should adhere to the following:

- A journal's website should be clear about expectations, scope, and audience.
- The journal's name should not be overly similar to another journal.
- Journal contact should include the business address.
- Any publishing fees should be clearly listed.
- Editors and their contact information should be listed.
- Editorial policies should be clear and communicate expectations for both authors and peer reviewers.
- Policies should include research misconduct, publication ethics, and peer review.

Sharing Your Work after Publication

Publication is obviously an excellent way to disseminate your research, but there are a number of potential benefits for further sharing your work through other venues as well. While most of the content below pertains to journal articles or similar works, longer publication forms like books can also benefit from having a selection (e.g., a chapter) made available through other means.

First, unless you are publishing open access, many people will not be able to access and read your work without paying a fee or having a subscription (SPARC Europe, n.d.). This automatically limits the reach of your work and your potential audience. Many subscription journal publishers will not allow you to post the final version of your work on other sites, but even posting an earlier version (e.g., a preprint or postprint, as defined in the Contracts section), as long as your contract allows you to do so, can help increase your readership.

Second, you may want to reach an audience that extends beyond those who would normally encounter or read the journal or publication. This audience could include academics in other disciplines, practitioners in your field who do not have access to a subscription publication, or a general audience (Björk, 2017). Your publisher may also have a limited distribution range, which means that people in certain countries or locations may not have access to your work as well. Posting your work to other sites (again, subject to your contract terms) that may target a different, interested audience or allow for serendipitous discovery of your work could help to increase your visibility to those audiences.

Third, having your work in multiple places helps to ensure the longer-term preservation of your work. If, for example, your publisher goes defunct or otherwise ceases to exist, you and others may no longer be able to access your work. Maintaining copies of your work in other locations like the ones listed in the next section provides other access points in the future.

Where Can You Post Your Work?

As previously discussed, your publishing contract may limit where, when, and how you share your work. When you post your work in other locations or otherwise share your work, be certain that you are complying with your publishing agreement or otherwise have permission to do so. If you post your work or others' work illegally, you may be asked to take it down or even face legal consequences, which can be quite costly. For example, as a graduate student, biologist Diego Gomez posted another scientist's thesis online because he found it useful and wanted to share it with others; as a consequence, he faced up to eight years in prison for copyright violation under Columbian law (Catanzaro, 2017). The following will cover some common places academics post their work using the green open access model, and you can (and perhaps, should) employ multiple strategies for sharing your work, depending on your needs.

Institutional Repositories

Many universities maintain institutional repositories (IRs) to share the work created by their communities, so IR deposit tends to be limited to those who are affiliated with the university. These sites are typically built with longer-term preservation in mind and are often maintained by the university library system. IRs have varying levels of capabilities for storing and displaying content, so if you want to share a non-textual work, you may be limited in your ability to do so. IRs also tend to have permanent and/or stable URLs, which means that you can share the link as an open access alternative to your publication's URL without having to worry about dead links in the future. There may be certain people or teams dedicated to putting content in the IR or even clearing permissions, so check with your university library or other unit in charge of the IR to see what services might be available to you. OpenDOAR additionally maintains a list of repositories by country (n.d.): https://v2.sherpa.ac.uk/view/repository_by_country/

Other Repositories

There are a number of other repositories that exist beyond institutional repositories. There are preprint and postprint repositories (which are often subject-based) that are meant to house non-final versions of a work. As previously discussed, the preprint version of a work is typically the version you initially submit for publication; the postprint version of a work is typically after peer review but before publisher-added formatting. The benefit of these repositories is that they often have active communities, and you might be able to better target an audience interested in the subject area of your work. These repositories may be maintained by universities, societies, publishers, or a combination of entities, so they can also vary widely in scope and options available to depositors. Funders may also have designated repositories in which works that benefit from their grants funding must deposit. In some cases, publishers may deposit the work to those repositories on the author's behalf.

Personal Website

If you maintain a personal website or have a profile on your departmental website, this can also be a good place to post your work. While you may not have the same preservation capabilities as a repository available to you, personal or departmental websites may provide more flexibility in terms of display.

Academic Social Networking Sites

Academic Social Networking Sites (ASNS), like Humanities Commons, ResearchGate, and Academia.edu, allow academics to create profiles, network, and share their work with others. Note that commercial ASNS, like Academia.edu and ResearchGate, often operate on "freemium" models where you can create a free account but are encouraged to pay for a premium membership, and your information may additionally be used for advertising purposes on these sites. You should review the privacy policy prior to setting up an account.

Promoting Your Work

Once you have established which platform(s) you will use to further disseminate your work, they should become part of your promotional strategy. If you published in a subscription journal, you should post an open access version somewhere (if allowed by your publisher). If you published a book, you may even be able to post a chapter or portion of the book open access (again, if allowed by your publisher). Every time you promote your publication through social media, university communications, listservs, or other means, you should include a link to an open access version of your work (whether that be the link to the final version that you published open access or a link to an earlier version of the work posted to a platform). This will ensure that potential readers have access to some version of your work.

Recommendations and Considerations for the Publishing Process

The following section brings together many of the concepts previously outlined in this chapter and places them into context within the publishing lifecycle. At each stage of publication, the authors present various queries and recommendations to take into consideration as you go through the publication process and highlight resources that can help you accomplish your publishing goals. The resources and recommendations herein are not exhaustive but are meant to be a starting point that will help you make more informed publishing decisions.

Note: Parts of this section have been reproduced or adapted from Developing your Publishing Criteria, CC BY-NC-SA 4.0 *Sarah Wipperman (2020). Reproduced with permission.*

Pre-Publication

Establish Your Publishing Criteria

Answer the following questions to start establishing your publishing criteria for what is important to you in publishing your work. Once you start looking for a publication venue, you can use these criteria to determine how closely the publisher aligns with your goals and needs. Note that this guide is not intended to cover some of the more nuanced questions that individual disciplines face, and not all of these questions will be relevant for all fields. You may also have to prioritize some criteria over others based on your current needs.

- Where are you in the process?

  - Already have a manuscript, haven't started writing, etc.
  - Do you post to preprint servers, blogs, etc.?

- Where do you want to publish?

  - Do you have any journals/publishers in mind, or are you starting fresh?
  - Do you care if it is a commercial publisher? Society? University press? Open Access?

- Whom do you want to read this?

  - General audience, my field only, scholarly society, practitioners, international colleagues, policy makers, journalists, graduate students (e.g., a class), etc.

- What do you want to do with it once it is published?

  - Share it on an academic social networking site (ResearchGate, Academia.edu, Humanities Commons, etc.)? Institutional repository? Personal website? Departmental or lab website?
  - Are you comfortable sharing a non-final version?
  - Send it to colleagues? Others?
  - Use it in a conference presentation, online teaching, etc.?

- • Apply for a patent?
- • What is the nature of what you want to publish?

  - • Book, article, review, etc.
  - • Is it based on previously "published" work (e.g., dissertation, preprint)?
  - • Is this a more niche topic or more general audience in your field? Does it incorporate interdisciplinary research?
  - • Does it incorporate non-traditional elements? Multimedia? Data?

- • What is your timeline?

  - • Need this out ASAP, soon, no set date, etc.

- • Why are you publishing? Where are you in your career?

  - • Tenure and promotion, get a job, citations, share results, influence field/policy/teaching/practice, etc.

- • Do you have any funding requirements?

  - • E.g., a grant that requires you to publish open access
  - • Do you have a fund for publishing?

Create a List of Journals/Publishers

In creating your list, think about your publishing criteria: Does the journal/publisher meet your needs? Note that not all of this information may be found on a publisher website. Reach out to the journal/publisher with questions.

- • How much does it cost to publish?

  - • Do they charge per page? For color?
  - • Is there a fee to have your article be open access?

- • How much does it cost to read?

  - • For journals: If you are part of a university system, try to access the article from home when you are not logged on to any university websites or proxied in – do you hit a paywall?
  - • For books: What do similar books by this publisher cost?

- • What is the distribution?
- • Is it peer-reviewed? Is your intended section peer-reviewed? What type of peer-review do they use?
- • Is there an embargo?
- • Who owns the copyright to the work? (Note: "author retains copyright" can be misleading.)

  - • (Books) What happens if it goes out of print?
  - • Is it under a different license (e.g., Creative Commons)?

- • Check SHERPA/RoMEO (https://v2.sherpa.ac.uk/romeo) for sharing policies, double check publisher website to see how you will be allowed to share your work in the future and with whom.

  - • What can you share, when, and where?
  - • Are there restrictions on how many times you can share a link/reprint or with whom?

- Do you want this in an institutional repository? A preprint/postprint repository?
- (Journals) Do they have policies on preprint servers?
- Are you responsible for getting permissions for things you use in your work?
- What is their acceptance/rejection rate?

  - Talk to your subject librarian for more information.
  - Read other articles/publications from that journal/publisher.

- What are the major journals/publishers in your field? Where do your colleagues publish? Which publications do you like to read? This can be a good place to start.
- Reach out to your subject librarian for more information on journals/publishers in your field, databases, and other useful places to look
- Read journal policies/about page

  - What are the guidelines for submitting?
  - What audience do they try to reach? Does it match your intended audience?
  - Would your topic "fit" with what they are publishing?
  - (Journals and especially society journals) Who is the publisher? Who is the sponsor?
  - What is the turnaround time?
  - Do they have any author requirements, like having an ORCID?

Publisher Evaluation Tool

Evaluate your list of publishing outlets for publishing best practices and potential deceptive practices. Consider the audience you wish to reach and the efforts your journal undertakes to reach your audience. Review the scholarship published in these outlets and ask if you want your work published beside it. Consult your subject or liaison librarian and senior colleagues. Review the list of questions on the Publisher Evaluation Tool (Collins, 2021) in the appendix 30, or a similar review instrument to help you make informed decisions.

During Submission

- Rank your journal/publisher preferences based on your publishing criteria and submit accordingly.
- Be sure that your manuscript is formatted correctly and follows the journal guidelines.
- If you have co-authors, decide who will be in charge of copyright.
- Keep a folder with your preprint, postprint, publishing contract, and final version.

Reuse Considerations

- Reusing third party works

  - Keep track of any works you are reusing (e.g., images, tables, figures), who created it, where it was published, and where you accessed the content. This will make clearing permissions much easier once you get to the publication stage.

- Reusing your own materials

  - If you are planning on reusing your own materials, be sure that you have the right to do so. For example, if you previously published a paper that included a graphic you made, the publisher may have required you to transfer all of your rights to that graphic over to them. If that is the case (and unless your contract says otherwise), you may need to seek permission from the publisher in order to reuse your graphic, and you may additionally need to pay a fee. Be certain to read and understand the terms of your contracts.

- Whenever possible/appropriate, openly license your work (e.g., by putting it under a Creative Commons license) before publication so that you and others may reuse the work in the future.

- Reusing works from galleries, libraries archives, and museums

  - There may be additional copyright concerns when using works from galleries, libraries, archives, and museums. These institutions may require that you ask permission to reuse content from their sites even if the work itself is in the public domain. If, for example, you wish to reuse an image of a 1,000 year-old vase posted on a museum's website, there is clearly no copyright over the vase, but there may be some rights over the photograph of the vase. Photographs can have two forms of copyright: one over the contents of the image (e.g., the vase), and one over the image itself (e.g., how the creator arranged the vase, lit it, applied filters). In these cases where the object itself is in the public domain, you could choose to take a picture yourself, if you have the ability to do so, in order to avoid potential copyright issues with the high quality reproduction, or you could try to find an openly licensed photograph taken by someone else. These institutions may also request that you provide a certain attribution statement when reusing works from their collections. Check the institution's website to see if they have any such requirements or requests.

Publishing Contract Considerations

- Make sure it is clear about where/when/what you can share.
- You DO NOT have to just accept a click through agreement – write to your editor if you have questions or concerns.
- (For U.S. and Canadian authors) Use a SPARC Author Addendum to retain more rights (https://sparcopen.org/our-work/author-rights/#addendum).
- If they don't accept a SPARC addendum, try to negotiate for things that you want.
- If you can't get what you want, you can walk away (or publish knowing your restrictions).

Post Publication

- Sharing/further disseminating your work

  - Make sure that you are sharing in accordance with the publisher's policies. Different versions of your article will likely have different restrictions and requirements, so during the publishing process, you should be sure to keep a copy of each version for future use (e.g., version you submit, version after peer review, final version).
  - If you have an institutional repository, submit a copy.
  - Post to any Academic Social Networking sites you use and/or your personal/departmental website.
  - Share a link to the work on Twitter or other social media – be sure the audience can access an open access version of your work; include an additional open access link if the main work is behind a paywall.
  - Work with your university/departmental communications team to get the word out.

Translation Considerations

- Translations and copyright

  - Translations are a derivative work (see Copyright Protections) and are thus subject to copyright restrictions.

- Translating others' works

  - If the work is still under copyright, you will either need to use a copyright exception (e.g., fair use, fair dealings) or get permission from the copyright holder to make a translation of a work.
  - If you translate a work in the public domain, you may have some rights over your translation of that work (depending on the relevant country's copyright laws).

- Translating your own work (unpublished)

  - If you have not signed any agreements and are the copyright holder, you may translate your own work.

- Translating your own work (published)

  - If you have published in one language and want to translate the work to another, you may need to get permission from your publisher in order to do so. Check your contract or talk to your publisher.
  - Submitting a translated version of your work to another publisher is generally not permitted and is often unethical. Again, you may be subject to contractual limitations (e.g., you no longer own the copyright), and publishing the same work in a different language may additionally amount to self-plagiarism (Saunders, 2010).

Publishing is an important part of the research lifecycle and disseminating scholarly works, but it requires authors to make decisions about their work that will last for more than a lifetime. This chapter has provided some starting points and recommendations for making many of those decisions, including those regarding copyright and responsible reuse, understanding common aspects of publishing agreements, finding the right publishing outlet, and sharing and promoting a scholarly work after publication.

Scholars need to disseminate scholarship effectively and rigorously. By choosing transparent and ethical publication venues, authors can ensure that their work will benefit from publisher-added value, such as thorough peer-review, and distribution to a targeted audience. By making their work open access, authors can additionally ensure that their work will have the widest possible access and use through the removal of paywall barriers. Authors can benefit greatly from reusing copyrighted content responsibly, reading and understanding their publishing contracts, negotiating for more author rights as needed, and developing a strategy for promoting and sharing their work in other venues after formal publication. Through continued practice and implementation of the recommendations and strategies in this chapter, authors can lay a valuable foundation for responsible international scholarly publishing that can contribute to a successful scholarly career.

References

Anderson, K. (2018, February 6). Focusing on value – 102 things journal publishers do (2018 Update). *The Scholarly Kitchen.* https://scholarlykitchen.sspnet.org/2018/02/06/focusing-value-102-things-journal-publishers-2018-update/.

Björk, B.-C. (2017). Open access to scientific articles: A review of benefits and challenges. *Internal and Emergency Medicine, 12*(2), 247–253. doi:10.1007/s11739-017-1603-2.

Budapest Open Access Initiative | Read the Budapest Open Access Initiative. (2002). Retrieved December 1, 2020, from https://www.budapestopenaccessinitiative.org/read.

Butler, D. (2013). Investigating journals: The dark side of publishing. *Nature News, 495*(7442), 433. doi:10.1038/495433a.

Catanzaro, M. (2017, May 24). Colombian biologist cleared of criminal charges for posting another scientist's thesis online. *Nature.* https://www.nature.com/news/colombian-biologist-cleared-of-criminal-charges-for-posting-another-scientist-s-thesis-online-1.22057.

Code de la propriété intellectuelle, Articles L121-1 à L121-9 (2021).

Collins, N. (2021). Publisher evaluation tool. Purdue e-Pubs. Retrieved February 15, 2021, from http://docs.lib.purdue.edu/lib_fscm/33.

COPE. (2019). Discussion document: Predatory publishing. *Committee on Publication Ethics.* doi:10.24318/cope.2019.3.6

Copyright Act of 1976, 17 U.S.C. §§ 101-1332 (2018).

Copyright, Designs and Patents Act 1988, §§ 29-30 (2014).

Creative Commons. (2020, August 28). Frequently asked questions. *Creative Commons.* https://creativecommons.org/faq/#what-does-some-rights-reserved-mean.

Eriksson, S., & Helgesson, G. (2018). Time to stop talking about 'predatory journals.' *Learned Publishing, 31*(2), 181–183. doi:10.1002/leap.1135.

European Union. (n.d.). What is the difference between an exclusive and a non-exclusive license?. *European IP Helpdesk.* https://iprhelpdesk.eu/node/3189.

Glossary: Representations and warranties. (n.d.). Thomson Reuters Practical Law. Retrieved February 12, 2021, from https://content.next.westlaw.com/Document/I1559f7a3eef211e28578f7ccc38dcbee/View/FullText.html.

JISC. (2019). An introduction to open access | Jisc. (n.d.). Retrieved December 1, 2020, from https://www.jisc.ac.uk/guides/an-introduction-to-open-access.

Kurt, S. (2018). Why do authors publish in predatory journals? *Learned Publishing, 31*(2), 141–147. doi:10.1002/leap.1150.

OpenDOAR. (n.d.). Browse by country. Retrieved January 15, 2021, from https://v2.sherpa.ac.uk/view/repository_by_country/.

OSI Brief: Deceptive publishing | OSI global. (2019). Retrieved December 1, 2020, from http://osiglobal.org/2019/03/19/osi-brief-deceptive-publishing/.

Principles of Transparency and Best Practice in Scholarly Publishing. (2014). Committee on Publication Ethics. Retrieved on 3 December 2020 from https://doi.org/10.24318/cope.2019.1.12.

Saunders, J. (2010). Plagiarism and the law. *Learned Publishing, 23*, 279–292. doi:10.1087/20100402.

Sherpa Romeo. (n.d.). Retrieved January 15, 2021, from https://v2.sherpa.ac.uk/romeo/.

SPARC (n.d.). The SPARC author addendum. Retrieved January 15, 2021, from https://sparcopen.org/our-work/author-rights/#addendum.

SPARC Europe. (n.d.). Open access benefits. *SPARC Europe.* Retrieved December 3, 2020, from https://sparceurope.org/what-we-do/open-access/oa-benefits/.

Taylor & Francis (n.d.). What is plagiarism and why does it matter?. https://authorservices.taylorandfrancis.com/editorial-policies/plagiarism/.

Think. Check. Submit. (n.d.). Retrieved January 15, 2021, from https://thinkchecksubmit.org/.

Union, P.O. of the E. (2019, January 30). Future of scholarly publishing and scholarly communication: Report of the Expert Group to the European Commission. Publications Office of the European Union. http://op.europa.eu/en/publication-detail/-/publication/464477b3-2559-11e9-8d04-01aa75ed71a1.

U.S. Copyright Office. (2017). *Works not protected by copyright (Circ. 33).* Copyright Office, Library of Congress.

U.S. Copyright Office. (2019). *Copyright basics (Circ. 1).* Copyright Office, Library of Congress.

U.S. Copyright Office (2021). *International copyright relations of the United States (Circ. 38a).* Copyright Office, Library of Congress.

Wipperman, S. (2020, September 9). Developing your publishing criteria. Retrieved from https://osf.io/wfpuc/

World Intellectual Property Organization. (n.d.-a). Summary of the Berne Convention for the protection of literary and artistic works (1886). https://www.wipo.int/treaties/en/ip/berne/summary_berne.html.

World Intellectual Property Organization. (n.d.-b). WIPO-administered treaties: Contracting parties>Berne Convention. https://wipolex.wipo.int/en/treaties/ShowResults?start_year=ANY&end_year=ANY&search_what=C&code=ALL&treaty_id=15.

World Intellectual Property Organization. (n.d.-c). WIPO lex. https://www.wipo.int/wipolex/en/index.html

Xia, J., & Smith, M. P. (2018). Alternative journal impact factors in open access publishing. *Learned Publishing, 31*(4), 403–411. doi:10.1002/leap.1200.

Appendix 30 Check for Unethical Publishing Practices

Section 1	Y	N	IDK
Does the journal publish articles that have been plagiarized?	▋	▋	▉
Does the site include grammatical or spelling errors?			
Does the journal/publisher fail to disclose their geographic location; or, does the geographic location of the journal contrast with the title of the journal?	▋	▋	▉
Does the publisher list the same editor or editorial board for all of its journals?			
Is the turn-around time for peer review less than 10 days?	▋	▋	▉
Does the journal fail to provide detailed information about peer review?			
Is the first volume of the journal numbered something other than #1?	▋	▋	▉
Did the publisher open dozens of new Open Access titles all at once?			

Section 2	Y	N	IDK
Does the journal have very broad subject coverage?	▋	▋	▉
Does the journal ONLY list a P.O. Box or virtual office for the business address?			
Does the journal use Yahoo or Gmail email addresses for contact purposes?	▋	▋	▉
Is the only way to contact the journal through a "contact us" online form?			
Is the contact information for the editor the same as the website or journal?	▋	▋	▉
Did the journal contact you via email?			
Does the publisher fail to disclose the names of editorial board members or editors?	▋	▋	▉
Does the journal list the editorial board?			
Does the website have poor search functionality, or no search functionality at all?	▋	▋	▉
Does the website have dead links?			
Is the turn-around time for peer review less than 6 weeks?	▋	▋	▉
Does the journal make it difficult or impossible to find information about article processing charges, or use non-industry standard terms, such as "author side fee"?			
Does the journal lie about abstracting and indexing? (Such as saying it is indexed by Web of Science, when in fact it is not.)	▋	▋	▉

Check for Ethical Standards in Open Access Publishing

Section 3	Y	N	IDK
Is the journal or its publisher a member of the Open Access Scholarly Publisher's Association (OASPA)?	▋	▋	▉
Is the journal or its publisher affiliated with the Committee on Publication Ethics (COPE)?			
Does the journal list full contact information for the editorial board?	▋	▋	▉
Is the journal published by a reputable academic institution?			
Is the journal content indexed in reputable indexing/abstracting services?	▋	▋	▉
Does the journal post clear and transparent policies (such as information about author fees, licensing, corrections and retractions, peer review process, ethical standards and misconduct)?			
Have any of your colleagues published in this journal?	▋	▋	▉
Does the journal have policies for long-term digital preservation? (Perhaps they use LOCKSS)			
Review the scholarship published in the journal. Do you want your work published beside those works?	▋	▋	▉

Scoring the test

Section 1	Section 2	Section 3
If you answered "Yes" to any question in section 1, your suspicions should be raised. If you answer "Yes" to two or more questions in this section, you may wish consider another publication.	If you answered "Yes" to 2 or more, your suspicions should be raised. If you answered "Yes" to 4 or more questions in section 2, you may wish to consider another source. This publication may not adhere to expected publishing standards. Use your best judgment and speak with senior colleagues and librarians to learn more about this publication.	If you answered "Yes" to one or more of the questions in section 3, the publication demonstrates some expected publishing practices. Use your best judgment and be sure to speak with your academic community, including senior colleagues and librarians, to make your decision.

31

The Future Agenda for International Leadership Research and Practice

Arkadiusz Mironko, Rosemary Muriungi, and Anthony Scardino

Leadership Research in a Globalized World

Williams (2015) states that international leadership research considers three critical aspects: "thinking without borders; seeing the world through the eyes of others; and seeing what other people see, but thinking what they have not thought" (p. 2). Research undertaken from such a perspective considers multiple dimensions of leadership (Peterson & Hunt, 1997) that include indigenous ways of knowing versus modern ones; traditional and modern ways of leading; shared leadership vs individualistic leadership; technological leadership, and so on. Honoring multiple perspectives of leadership is a way of learning from one another. Not only is understanding leadership from other cultural dimensions important for our own learning, but it can also make us "think what others have not thought" (Williams, 2015, p. xxxiii).

Historically, with the rise of multinational corporations, leaders devised ways to lead and manage their teams spread across the globe (Mendenhall et al., 2012; Smith & Blanck, 2002) mainly by going to locations for short visits or longer expatriate stays (Collings, Scullion, & Morley, 2007). In later decades, with the internet, technology, and software solutions penetrating more of our work and life, corporate, academic, non-governmental and government leaders had to adapt to the faster pace of change. They responded by adopting new technologies that allowed for the transmission of data, information, and communication to be effective (Avolio et al., 2014; Caligiuri, 2006; Cascio, 2000; Maruping & Agarwal, 2004) in the virtual environment. The increasing complexity of interaction between the corporate headquarters, their subsidiaries, suppliers, distributors, and other stakeholders demands new ways to operate and lead.

In the following sections, the authors discuss the future of international leadership research within the context of servant leadership and followership; global virtual team leadership Research and practice; and leadership research and global crises. Recognition that service is a key aspect of leadership has gained traction in recent years. The digital age is here to stay and virtual teams are a reality of the modern age. Crises transcending national borders are on the rise and exploring leadership practices that can manage the unexpected is something international leadership research can contribute to.

DOI: 10.4324/9781003003380-31

International Leadership Research Utilizing Servant Leadership and Followership

Global Leadership

This section looks carefully at servant leadership and its connection to followership as it pertains to international leadership research. As more organizations experience growth in their scope of operations globally, the expectation of leadership to meet those needs has also grown. Research in global leadership focused on servant leadership can lead to bridging some of these leadership gaps. Literature revealed that traditional leadership methodologies have been challenged by increased complexities associated with dynamic change, and may not be relevant today (Suriyankietkaew, 2013).

Global leadership has been defined as "being capable of operating effectively in a global environment while being respectful of cultural diversity" (Harris, Moran & Moran, 2004, p. 25). While much of the literature on development of global leaders emphasizes that global leaders have some traits such as openness (Hall et al., 2001), cultural awareness (Adler, 1997), and cognitive capacity (Dalton, 1998), certainly filling the gap with deeper international leadership research to find great effectiveness would be advantageous.

The literature on global leadership provides many articles that state traits, characteristics, and attitudes of successful global leaders; but few attempts to lay a foundation on how to actually develop individuals into global leaders (Hall, Zhu, & Yan, 2001). Even though global leadership has lacked a universal definition, research on leadership competencies has often assumed competencies are universal (Tompson & Jody Tompson, 2013). Despite the plethora of advice and writing on global leadership, there is little effort to clearly define the concept. With few exceptions, much of the literature on global leadership tends to focus on lists of competencies and suggestions for improvement without offering a clear definition of global leadership (e.g., Brake, 1997; Rhinesmith, 1996). This is in part due to the fact that no theory of global leadership currently exists, despite the abundance of published leadership theories.

Servant Leadership and Followership

Servant leadership is a philosophy and set of practices that enriches the lives of individuals, builds better organizations, and ultimately creates a more just and caring organization. The global pandemic has underscored the need for transformational leadership styles, like servant leadership (COVID-19, 2020–2021). Servant leadership is a concept and style of leadership that can be the bridge noted in the previous paragraph as opposed to just any leadership as it embraces the whole person and globally this would lend itself to a more empathic result. According to Greenleaf (1977) the world is not only ready for but needs servant leaders; those individuals who inspire and empower others while wanting to serve first instead of lead first. Servant leadership is thus an expression of power, just like any other form of leadership, yet one that is applied for benefit others rather than the leader him or herself (Spears, 2004).

Laub (2004) referred to leadership as a process where leaders and followers, connected by one initiative, intentionally move to pursue a common objective. As such, leadership requires the initiative to create a change to meet an objective that is common not only to the leaders themselves but also to their followers. A follower is developed by the servant leader who presents himself as a role model so as to inspire followers, thereby enhancing his trust, information, and feedback (Lee-Kelley & Sankey, 2008).

One certainly cannot lead without followers, and leaders must inspire followers to want to follow. Servant leadership style transcends cultures in ways many other styles cannot for it embraces the uniqueness and the specialness of each person in the organization. According to Uhl-Bien et al. (2014) the oversight of followership is due in large part to the misunderstanding and confusion about the constructs of followership and how they relate to leadership. The idea is the leader is the servant, serving those who serve them, therefore creating trust and clearing a pathway of stronger connection and followership. An individual's ability to influence, motivate and enable others to contribute toward the effectiveness and success of the organization to which they belong (House, Hanges, Javidan, Dorfman, & Gupta, 2004). For Northouse (2004), leadership is also a process by which an individual can influence a group to achieve a common goal. Servant leadership or particular construct dimensions that seem to be applicable and relevant globally and cross-culturally. Irving (2005) explained that servant leadership is a valid and viable approach across cultures, but it requires more research for qualification. Irving stated that the servant leadership mode finds challenges in high power-distance relationships in which it is associated with a weak form of leadership.

Leaders who behave as servant leaders are truly present and have a propensity to be empathetic. A study on servant leaders suggests that servant leadership is a personal choice and brings accountability for the service to other people. Servant leadership in the workplace is said to grow from within the leader and can externally influence the organization. A follower is developed by the servant leader who presents himself as a role model so as to inspire followers, thereby enhancing his trust, information, and feedback (Lee-Kelley & Sankey, 2008). In order to inculcate feelings of ownership in the organizational decision-making process and employee's commitment, follower's autonomy is also encouraged. In addition, a creative and innovative atmosphere is also endeavored by servant leaders (Neubert et al., 2008).

Leader to follower compassion represents a dyadic process where the leader notices the suffering of the follower, feels empathic concern, and responds compassionately (Kahn, 1993; Lilius et al., 2008; Margolis & Molinsky, 2008; Miller, 2007). There is significant research evidence demonstrating a reliable association of empathic concern with actual helping behavior (Archer et al., 1981; Coke, Batson, & McDavis, 1978).

The importance of the leader follower relationship is certainly important, however equally important is to look at teams in this growing globalized, collaborative world. According to Irving's (2005) study, servant leadership and team effectiveness have a significant relationship. Irving also said that this relation encompasses multiple levels of team effectiveness, which include love, empowerment, vision, humility, and trust. Dannhauser and Boshoff (2006) found in their study that servant leadership, trust, and team commitment are all related. They cautioned that the relationship between trust and servant leadership has variance in terms of the structure, showing a larger gap in trust between the organization and the manager than in trust between colleagues. So, it seems there is much that can be learned from creating clear links between trust and followership.

Building Community Through Servant Leadership

The world has created an opportunity to connect with each other as never before. While many see the virtual nature of our interaction as a barrier, there are certainly great opportunities for research and development on both the leadership and follower side. Schaefer (2006) expounded on this idea: The person exerts his own energy of will, or power of choice, in order to realize the end. The end, as a motive, is not, however, the efficient, but the final cause or purpose of the choice. The motive is the reason why the person chooses, not the cause compelling him to choose. While it would be ideal to cite and provide COVID-19 leadership materials and citations, at the time of writing this we are in the midst of the pandemic.

A complex adaptive challenge of building community, such as that posed by the coronavirus pandemic cannot be successfully navigated by the leader acting alone (Heifetz & Laurie, 2001); a top-down hierarchical approach is unlikely to be successful in a context when facing a crisis that is so unpredictable and complex in nature. There is no leadership without people willingly following; in other words, followership is the choice we have in a democracy, not leadership.

The attributes of an effective leader when facing adaptive challenges have been previously described (Fernandez & Shaw, 2020); they include but are not limited to accountability, trustworthiness, and integrity. However, in a crisis, perhaps the most important of all is emotional intelligence and emotional stability that will allow a leader to place the interests of others above their own in servant leadership (Doraiswamy, 2012). Servant leadership that emphasizes empowerment, involvement, and collaboration is a particularly effective form of leadership in faith-based schools, colleges, and universities (Wheeler, 2012) and it is a leadership style that becomes more critical in a crisis (Doraiswamy, 2012).

Working remotely and being physically disconnected is a fairly new phenomenon. The idea here is to deeply research how to stay connected with other followers globally and otherwise as to not just to sustain and grow, and to feel connected to all things that matter, like mission, vision, and community. When the path ahead is complex and highly uncertain, a core ingredient of people's willingness to follow leaders is their faith in those leaders and their actions. Accordingly, evidence indicates that trust in leaders and authorities is critical for leaders' capacity to secure compliance with their policies (Jimenez & Iyer, 2016) and for encouraging followership more generally (Dirks & Skarlicki, 2004). But where does this trust come from? There is much opportunity for research globally and otherwise, to look at levels and types of leadership that can build this trust. It is clear that these ideas are more relevant for democracies around the world, we need to remember that not all concepts follow all political, governmental, and economic systems.

There are several characteristics of servant leader. However, we will focus here on three, beginning with awareness. Awareness is a quality within servant leaders that makes them acutely attuned and receptive to their physical, social, and political environments (Northouse, 2016). The global platforms many of us work from today present a great opportunity for more research, especially on trust in terms of followership. The next servant leader characteristic to focus on is Stewardship; it is all about taking responsibility for the leadership role entrusted to the leader (Northouse, 2004). Stewardship requires deeply listen to what is needed, and not necessarily applying our own interpretation or assessment of need. It means operating in service of and not in control of. By looking closer at this need, we can create a greater connection and, therefore, possibly have a deeper connection even with the physical distance. The final servant leadership characteristic to mention is building community. Servant leadership fosters the development of a community to provide a place where people can feel safe and connected to others. The central goal of servant leadership is to create healthy organizations that nurture individual growth, strengthen organizational performance and in the end produce a positive impact on society (Northouse, 2016).

While all characteristics link to each other, these three lead to greater empathy. Empathy is the ability to put yourself in the position of the person to whom you are speaking and to understand them better. To Spears (2004), empathy implies that you accept the person but can, if you need to, "refuse to accept certain behaviors or performance." This is an important differentiation that many otherwise good leaders occasionally forget. Empathy may be a soft skill, but it does not imply a softness in the performance that the team accepts. It is possible to empathize entirely with a team member whilst engaged in a disciplinary process because it is the behavior or performance that is at issue. This area can be evolved by linking the empathy and its impact on servant and global leadership.

Therefore, future study in international leadership research and creating a place to connect people is essential, especially with all the shifts in the political economy, social justice and even more broad-based lack of leadership in many areas of our lives (personal and professional). With our virtual world expanding, even before this pandemic (COVID-19, 2020-21) we appear to be connected through technology, but are we really? While many may feel they can make the virtual platform as personal and connected as possible, it still lends itself to distancing the physical and the deep connections that happen there. However, a great area of study could be the delicate balance between the virtual and physical platform and how to truly inspire people to follow you no matter what format you use.

Research on servant leadership and followership will need to be updated to today's pandemic and post-pandemic world. There are no guidebooks or handouts on how to be a leader during the unprecedented time of this pandemic (Covid-19, 2020-21) or shift on social change however if you fail to reinvent and adapt, you and your organizations will stall and fail. This is the time to bridge this gap through international leadership research.

Exploring the Future Direction of Global Virtual Team Leadership Research and Practice

The theories on servant leadership and leadership styles across the globe for a couple of decades now find a new application in the virtual world. Global virtual team leadership (GVTL) research is a budding and growing field. The focus of GVTL research is largely on cross-cultural communication, interpersonal and organizational trust and finds that trust may be built relatively quickly, but it can also be fragile and temporal (Jarvenpaa & Leidner, 1999). While the study by Reiche et al. (2017) focusing on relationship complexity and task complexity suggests that leaders must focus on a broader context of global team participants to be effective in leading their teams. Although some of the earliest research in the field date decades back now, with the COVID-19 pandemic, many companies' employees have increasingly retreated into the comforts of their home from where they need to work, motivate, manage, and lead their teams. To be effective in this new virtual environment one needs to often diametrically shift the approach towards their team as remote communication and collaboration require different sensitivity and skills (Kayworth & Leidner, 2002; Lee-Kelley & Sankey, 2008), both as a follower and as a leader.

Early research in this area focused on how teams can communicate via Information and Communication Technology (ICT). Maruping and Agarwal (2004), for example, offer three key interpersonal processes: (a) conflict management, (b) motivation and confidence building, and (c) affect management. Traditional global leadership research generally focuses on trust, knowledge of participants' cultures (Alon & Higgins, 2005; Mendenhall et al., 2017; Morrison, 2000), along with dos and don'ts of leading in the new setting. Research on GVTL attempts to determine the scope of global leadership tasks (Caligiuri, 2006) and defines a set of global leadership competencies and skills (Beechler & Javidan, 2007; Bird, Mendenhall, Stevens & Oddou, 2010; Mendenhall et al., 2012; Osland, 2008). Other research focuses on the development of assessment instruments (Spreitzer, McCall, & Mahoney, 1997) and training programs for global leaders (Pless, Maak, & Stahl, 2011). The latest research on global virtual teams seeks to understand specific global leadership competencies that are necessary in the virtual environment (Osland et al., 2020).

Some of the GVTL research focuses on four characteristics of virtual team leadership as identified by Zhang and Fjermestad (2006): physical distance, communicational distance, organizational distance, and cultural distance. They also identify three important leadership traits in the virtual team context that are discussed: communication competency, environmental alertness, and influence power (Avolio et al., 2004). Virtual team dynamics have been found to be critical to fully engage employees and promote collaboration (Jarvenpaa & Leidner, 1999; Maznevski & Chudoba, 2000; Schulze & Krumm, 2017).

Pitfalls easily avoided in face-to-face interactions, such as context and body language, can pose detrimental challenges on virtual teams and may be harder to spot and avoid (Jarvenpaa & Leidner, 1999). The goal for the International Leadership Research (ILR) going forward is to bridge the gap between traditional leadership and international leadership by examining emerging trends in the post-COVID-19 world and their impact on the future of the workforce.

The overarching question of this section is, What International Leadership Research can do for leaders of virtual teams going forward? With the changing work environments, due to improving technologies, the impact of the pandemic, or other events, new challenges emerge. Future research may need to explore how to keep virtual teams motivated, engaged, productive, and in good mental and physical health long term.

To be effective in the long-term, global virtual teams need to maintain a high level of inspiration towards common goals. Inspiration creates the highest levels of engagement, it is what separates the best leaders from everyone else, and it is what employees want most in their leaders. Bain & Company's research identified 33 distinct and tangible attributes that are statistically significant in creating inspiration in others, according to Horwitch and Whipple (2016). Empowerment, vision, and direction are a few of those elements that drive the performance of teams. Future research can test which of these elements is also indispensable for the success of GVT leadership.

While leadership researchers using traditional approaches have to build relationships to gain access and, most frequently, interview those in leadership roles, with global virtual teams operating online they generate a lot of data (Presbiterio, 20202). Although there are operational, security, and privacy challenges to consider, agreements can be made about the use of data and methods deployed to offer anonymity. Currently, due to the rapid changes because of the pandemic and the existing availability of technology able to accommodate most office-related tasks, and the rising demand for remote work, we are experiencing a shift in leadership skills (Degbey & Einola, 2020). The current scenario presents itself as a fruitful ground for research to both examine the past and attempt to guide into the future our work environment. Organizations and their teams need to adapt and become more flexible in order to respond to the increasing uncertainty in light of ongoing technological change and unforeseen events, such as a pandemic (Ansell, Sørensen, & Torfing, 2020).

GVTL in times of Volatility, Uncertainty, Complexity, Ambiguity - VUCA and Virtual Teams

Under these changing circumstances, VUCA is becoming a popular framework representing the challenging times; it stands for: Volatility, Uncertainty, Complexity, Ambiguity (Bennett & Lemoine, 2014). The framework allows leaders to develop responses to situations where they do not have sufficient information to offer responses, such as in a developing crisis or unexpected scenario. In business as in everyday life, we rarely have complete information when making decisions. Global leaders of virtual teams have to be responsive in the scenarios where some VUCA elements are present and offer direction, assurance and motivate their teams (Johansen, 2012). Turning challenges into opportunities requires inherent skills and the ability to recognize exogenous circumstances to frame and communicate future direction. These elements provide many opportunities for further research as well. The study of Seow, Pan and Koh (2019) identifies the need of implementing a study of VUCA elements in university curriculum to prepare students for success in a volatile, uncertain, complex, and ambiguous work environment. Situations in which many leaders find themselves often fit the elements of VUCA, and they are not easily generalizable. Going forward, researchers can frame these terms into specific scenarios to provide generalizable theoretical frameworks, or also use the VUCA elements in applied scenarios, hence, providing examples and answers from which further theory development can take place.

With subsequent studies, VUCA has developed into BEVUCA - Business excellence in a volatile, uncertain, complex, and ambiguous environment (Saleh & Watson, 2017). According to the studies of Kanji (1998), business excellence is measured by the satisfaction of customers, employees, and stakeholders and not by profits alone. While Porter and Tanner (2012) link business practices and performance to assess business excellence. The BEVUCA framework allows business leaders to maintain business excellence offered by their companies in uncertain times.

Improvisation in times of change is important to the success of a team in times of uncertainty. In their research, Vera and Crossan (2005) test the impact of improvisation on innovative performance in teams and find that teams which receive training have a positive impact of improvisation on innovative performance. Leaders often tend to fall back on past experiences, however, in the VUCA environment there may be no precedent. Under these conditions, leaders may be required to seek advice, data, guidance, and then improvise in making decisions and leading their teams (McChrystal et al., 2015). Future research in this area can explore the effectiveness of improvisation by leaders whether they are open to the risk or avoid the risk involved with ad-hoc improvised decisions. Also, what tools do leaders use to make decisions without complete information should be explored further? Whether they use logic, systematic approach or they are using feeling skills in approaching the problems. The decision-making process in the virtual environment by leaders and followers alike needs to be examined from both practical and theoretical perspectives.

New Directions for GVT Leadership Research

To answer many arising questions regarding leadership across the globe, servant leadership, and leadership in the virtual environment, new approaches to formulating the questions will be necessary. With the faster pace of change and increasing uncertainty in many areas of professional and personal lives, the research will also need to anticipate and study rising trends, however imperfectly. For example, what will be the geographic impact on corporate staffing strategies? Will companies leverage the technology effectively to source talent from where it resides (Mironko, 2018) without the requirement of people working from their offices?

The goal for ILR going forward is to bridge the gap between traditional leadership research and international leadership in the virtual world. New research opportunities on GVTL remain largely unexplored in the area of race, age, gender, ethnicity, and bias. An effective leader is one who can lead their teams by leveraging the team's diversity, talents of its participants, set direction, and diffuse conflict (Zander, Mockaitis, & Butler, 2012). Some research was done for example in the study of Maloney et al. (2016) where they propose guidelines to improve contextualization and avenues to explore context theorizing in both traditional and virtual teams. For example, the challenge of how leaders in the virtual work environment will be able to determine equitable performance evaluation and promotion processes will need to be examined from both practical and research perspectives. In the future researchers in the area will need to re-contextualize their studies to accommodate new changing conditions. Until the pandemic, working virtually was largely reserved for large multinationals, while post-pandemic, most businesses that can move to virtual mode have done so.

Flexjobs, a company that offers a listing of remote employment opportunities, maintains the list of industries and companies employing most of the remote workforce. According to their ranking: healthcare and computer/IT are taking the lead, education, sales, and customer service industries follow the lead. While lately, fields of business, accounting, and finance see the increasing numbers of remote workers (Jay, 2020, January 12). Attention will need to be paid to the context of the studied questions and subjects affecting the impact of workforce diversity on the performance of virtual teams. Traditionally the leaders and team members in global virtual teams may have not met each other before. In the post-pandemic world the team members, whether globally dispersed or local, may have worked in the same office space for years. Therefore, we may want to explore how the existing relationships, tacit knowledge of teams may influence future GVTL performance.

Conflict and its impact on global virtual teams' effectiveness may be another direction of research to be pursued further. Some studies indicate that conflict when resolved may lead to better team performance (Derven, 2016; Kankanhalli, Tan, & Wei, 2006). While Martínez-Moreno et al. (2015) examined the effects of team self-guided training on conflict management in virtual teams. They tested the ability to mediate conflict by separate sets of teams that had training and another set without training in ability to communicate synchronously. The study found that self-guided training along with feedback improves the ability to manage conflict in virtual team settings. Further, Mendenhall et al. (2017) address ambiguity as an aspect of global complexity in traditional global teams. The ambiguity between leaders and GVTs may need further exploration as well. Setting and communicating clear expectations in virtual teams can be challenging even when one is familiar with cultural differences (Derven, 2016).

Recently, Nordbäck and Espinosa (2019) examined characteristics of effective coordination of shared leadership in global virtual teams. Using interview data from a number of teams in two companies in the software industry, they found that shared leadership had a more positive effect on team effectiveness when shared leadership was coordinated both implicitly and behaviorally. They found that in teams that are more diverse members are less likely to share the same leadership expectations. While, behavioral leadership coordination delivered by explicit actions coordinating activities of the team increases in importance with a higher degree of shared leadership (Nordbäck & Espinosa, 2019). They conclude that shared leadership may have both advantages or be detrimental to the team's success. Future studies may explore the effectiveness of teams in other industries and across different leadership styles.

Further, research in the area of GVT leadership can determine a need for training for both leaders and teams to make them more effective. As virtual teams are here to stay, cross-cultural awareness of leaders and team members is of increasing importance (Lippert & Dulewicz, 2018). Studies of the subject indicate that very few leaders, only about 10%, had formal training in cross-cultural awareness (Black & Mendenhall, 1990). This is also an area for further exploration as much of the research on the cross-cultural awareness points towards cross-cultural misunderstandings in teams (Lokkesmoe, Kuchinke, & Ardichvili, 2016), this must be further exacerbated by the international dimension of teams. Shedding more light on these issues through robust research from both leadership and managerial perspectives would be beneficial for leaders as well as teams.

Leadership Research and Global Crises

The Merriam-Webster online dictionary defines a crisis as "an unstable or crucial time or state of affairs in which a decisive change is impending" (n.d., para 6). From a scholarly perspective, Seeger et al. (1998) describe a crisis as "a specific, unexpected, and non-routine event or series of events that create high levels of uncertainty and threat or perceived threat" (p. 233). In the context of organizational leadership, Prewitt and Weil (2014) offer an insightful take on what crisis leadership looks like:

> Crisis has its genesis in the values, beliefs, culture, or behavior of an organization which become incongruent with the milieu in which the organization operates. A leader, who is able to read the signals of looming crisis and understands how to harness the exigency brought on by the situation, can diminish the potential dangers and take full advantage of the resulting opportunities. (p. 72)

Crisis leadership, therefore, goes beyond responding to a crisis to being proactive in anticipating unexpected events and putting together a mechanism to mitigate crises before they happen (Firestone, 2020). As Sutcliffe and Christianson (2013) suggest, unanticipated events do not occur in a vacuum; "their seeds are sown long before turmoil arrives in small problems, mistakes, of failures that go unnoticed, ignored, misunderstood, or discounted, and subsequently escalate into crises or catastrophes" (p. 2). In this section, I discuss how international leadership research can create awareness of leadership practices around the world that could help in dealing with crises of a transnational scope such as the refugee crisis and climate change.

Servant leadership and leadership in virtual space are two approaches of leading in crisis moments in an interconnected world. The concept of leaders being servants (Greenleaf, 1977) has the potential to heal a hurting world. In many indigenous cultures around the world, serving humanity was a way of honoring planet earth and all its creations (Harris, 2017; Schaefer, 2006; Wildcat, 2009). People were considered custodians of the planet (Harwood-Jones, 2010; Suzuki & Knudstson, 1992) and were expected to safeguard mother earth.

Virtual leadership (Schmidt, 2014) is a reality of the modern age. Adjusting to the digital landscape, as a strategic tool at our disposal, is one way of leading into the future. COVID-19 has demonstrated how leading technological innovations have allowed the world to hunker down behind closed doors while work and social interactions occur in virtual space (Bryson, Andres, & Davies, 2020; Cooley, 2020; Rosen, Joffe, & Kelz, 2020). International leadership research plays an important role in revealing how servant leadership is practised in when global crises occur and how virtual leadership fits into the picture.

Leadership Around the World

Much of the existing literature on leadership is from a predominantly Western lens (Dickson, Hartog, & Mitchelson, 2003). Undertaking leadership research that honors and incorporates multiple worldviews from around the world is one way of navigating the fluid and often ambiguous nature of the modern era (Valk, Belding, Crumpton, Harter, & Reams, 2011). Living in a more globally connected world has collapsed physical boundaries and brought people from diverse backgrounds and cultures together. The global village has also become more complex and fast-paced. Social media and easy access to information technology have changed the way people interact and influence one another. Advances in technology have broadened the extent to which humankind can influence society. Thriving in this interconnected landscape necessitates an appreciation of how other people view and live in the world around them. As human development evolves, leadership needs to keep pace (Stogdill & Bass, 1981).

Depending on which part of the world one hails from, leadership can be attributed to many factors. In societies where leadership is vested in individuals or a single entity, leadership is often autocratic or authoritarian. Examples of autocratic and authoritarian leadership abound among the countries that have dictators at the helm (Van de Vliert, 2006). In communities where leadership is more distributed, leadership tends to be a shared responsibility with the common good being at the forefront as opposed to individual gain. An example of shared leadership is the *Njuri Ncheke* Council of elders in the Ameru community of Kenya. According to Kamwaria et al. (2015) the "Njuri-Ncheke made and executed community laws, listened to and settled disputes, and passed on indigenous knowledge and rites across the generations. It also handled matters related to religious values, economic system, and political unity of the Ameru" (p. 43).

In addition to leadership practices, terms conferred to leaders vary depending on the stature or characteristics they exhibit. Williams (2015) gives examples of two Arabic terms attributed to leaders. "The general term for elites is *aaliyatul-qaum*, meaning 'high profile people', but *al-kheirou fi al-qaoum* is also used, meaning 'the best of men'" (p. 76). Another aspect of terms ascribed to leaders is differences in meaning across cultures. Dickson, Hartog and Mitchelson (2003) described how the act of being "cunning" is perceived in two countries. In Columbia, "cunning" is understood to be a factor contributing to "outstanding leadership," while in Switzerland cunning" is seen as "inhibiting

[to] outstanding leadership" because it is perceived as "being sly and deceitful" (p. 735). The examples cited here shed light on how leadership attributes can look very different depending on the country and culture, and highlight the importance of international leadership in bringing such differences to light.

A researcher's own biases have the potential to influence the outcome of research with little room to incorporate differing viewpoints encountered during their research. An open mind that immerses itself in the reality of the research participants would augur well for all the parties involved. Researchers may be tempted to report what they perceive to be important to the person or organization the research is meant for and forget that representing the views of the research participants is as equally important. Williams (2015) highlights how:

> Researching another country can create a feeling of intellectual impunity, because repercussions are minimal for researchers once they finish. Yet the consequences of bad practice can harm local research participants, hosts and assistants, local and other visiting researchers, and the reputations of universities and organizations. (p. 80)

The reason for undertaking international leadership research (Dickson, Hartog, & Mitchelson, 2003) shapes research questions, choice of research participants, and the outcome of the research. If the purpose of conducting international leadership research is to prove a predetermined outcome, for example "that leadership practices are common across cultures," then this negates the aim of using research to learn about leadership practices of other cultures, which may differ from those of a researcher.

An overarching question for any international leadership research would be in whose interest the research is conducted (Williams, 2015). In cases where the research participants or populations studied do not speak the language of the research instrument used; do not fully appreciate the purpose of the research; how research findings will be used; and how their perspectives on the research topic will be represented (Barrett & Cason, 2010; Halai & William, 2012), whose knowledge is disseminated? And how is this knowledge created, categorized, and stored? In other words, who owns the knowledge acquired from international research and how do others obtain the right to use such knowledge? These are important questions to ponder when conducting leadership research on the international scene.

From an ethical standpoint, colonial legacies continue to affect interactions between ethnic groups, distribution of leadership responsibility, property rights, and land demarcation, among other issues (Alemazung, 2010). Conducting international leadership research ethically is one way of honoring the worldview of other cultures and "decolonizing" international research which does not often consider indigenous ways of knowledge (Smith, 2002). An article from Warwick Education Studies (n.d.) describes "decolonization" as:

> the undoing of colonial rule over subordinate countries but has taken on a wider meaning as the 'freeing of minds from colonial ideology' in particular by addressing the ingrained idea that to be colonised was to be inferior. Decolonisation then offers a powerful metaphor for those wanting to critique positions of power and dominant culture. (para 1)

In what the article refers to as "academic research decolonisation," potential areas that researchers using the "decolonizing methodology" can explore in their research include questioning "assumptions" on how power dynamics play into the selection of research problems; the "relationship between the researcher and research participants; inclusion of the voices of indigenous communities in "academic research" and being conscious of distorting the knowledge acquired from research findings that contributes the perception of "subordinate groups" (paras 2–8). Ignoring this would put in question the credibility, validity, and integrity of the research process and impact the population studied adversely.

There is a tendency to overlook the legacy of colonialism (Washington, 2007) when undertaking international leadership research and "the othering of people within world research" is "often done with meticulous methodology" (Williams, 2015, p. 84). It is important to understand cultural nuances ascribed to terminologies within local contexts (Schlebusch, 2010) that may label "others" in derogatory terms (Corry, 2013) that are only known to people within the locality, and which are oblivious to external players. Such labeling could create unnecessary problems for researchers not adequately prepared to undertake overseas research (Ferreira, 2008) and with limited knowledge of the location or population being studied.

Research participants in countries that were colonized could perceive the researcher as an extension of colonialism and can influence the conduct and outcome of the research done. It would be prudent for researchers embarking on the research of international scope to familiarize themselves with the history of countries that were colonized and how colonial legacy affects the worldviews of both the researcher and the research participants. Conducting international leadership research with this consideration in mind helps the researcher to assess how a history of colonialism influences research of national, regional, and global issues.

Viewed from another practical angle, is how organizations managed by expatriates from Western countries inform the leadership style best suited to the local context in which international organizations operate. Nkomo (2011) highlights "tensions and contradictions between stereotypical colonial images of 'African' leadership and management and proposed counter-images that often reflect the excesses of cultural relativism." Researchers studying how leadership manifests itself in organizations that straddle national borders could help global leaders and managers to adopt leadership practices that serve their organizations in a manner that embraces the diversity represented in them.

In world affairs, developed countries (Washington, 2007; Williams, 2012) influence the global agenda and discourse that is often driven by multinational corporations and international organizations (Dickson, Hartog, & Mitchelson, 2003), in what (Tomlinson, 2008) refers to as "cultural imperialism." Karan (2019) illustrates how the colonial mindset affects global health due to "unequal power" dynamics. The standoff between the World Health Organization (WHO) and the United States of America in 2020 speaks to how power plays out on the global arena. As the biggest donor to WHO, the United States (US) stretched its muscles to demand that certain conditions be met by the global health organization if the organization expected to continue receiving funds from the U.S. When this did not happen, the U.S. withdrew its membership to the organization (Bloom, Farmer, & Rubin, 2020; Higgins-Dunn, 2020; Ortagus, 2020) and ceded its role as a leader in global health (Wetter & Friedman, 2020).

Leadership Research in the Digital Landscape

Leadership today transcends geographical space to incorporate the virtual landscape created by information technology. Understanding how leadership takes place in the digital space is worthy of international research (Kane, Phillips, Copulsky, & Andrus, 2019; Larson & DeChurch, 2020). The popularity of opinion leaders and influencers is usually measured in terms of social media following (Weeks, Ardèvol-Abreu, & Gil de Zúñiga, 2017) and not by the expertise or personal interactions that make it possible to gauge the influencer's character (Neubauer et al., 2017). Leadership research can navigate this uncharted space to ensure that social media platform owners foster responsible use of their platforms and hold users accountable for their online activity. The alarming rise of misinformation and alternative facts on social media channels (Anspach & Carlson, 2020) calls for innovative and responsible leadership in the digital space (Douglas, Ready, Kiron, & Pring, 2020; Dubey, 2019).

Recent fact-checking incidences by social media powerhouses such as Twitter (Qiu, 2020) and Facebook (Horwitz, 2020) of content posted on their sites by their users are but two examples of how leadership in the digital space is sorely needed. Leaders are expected to make decisions for the organizations or communities they serve based on credible and reliable information. Followers rely on their leaders to communicate information that is truthful to them. Politics present a good example of how misinformation affects governance (Anspach & Carlson, 2020). The recently concluded U.S. elections demonstrate how alternative facts can be used to rally electorates to vote by swaying them towards certain political candidates, or dissuading them against political opponents (Chang, Chen, Muric & Patel, 2020).

Cybersecurity and privacy concerns are other considerations to make when exploring leadership in cyberspace. Hacking of individual, organizational, and government systems (Fidler, 2017; Hanson, O'Connor, Walker, & Courtois, 2019) have an adverse effect on those affected. When a foreign country succeeds in interfering with the way another country's governing infrastructure and a people's choice to elect their preferred leader, the potential for foreign influence in that country's internal affairs is increased (Norden & vanderwalker, 2017). Interference in a country's political systems by foreign countries relates to power and influence. International research could help in identifying triggers of cybersecurity attacks and offer ways for individuals, organizations, and countries to protect themselves against such attacks.

Leadership Research and Crisis Leadership

The ongoing Coronavirus pandemic has upended our world since December 2019 (Grint, 2020; Tourish, 2020) and has called attention to the ability of leaders to manage the unexpected (Grigorescu & Costovici, 2020). Crises of global reach frequently bring out the crisis of leadership to light. Tourish (2020) offers the following insights on how Coronavirus has also been a crisis of leadership, largely due to the complex and unknown dynamics of the virus:

> Decision making is particularly hazardous when we have poor evidence to guide us and face unpredictable outcomes. Mainstream leadership theories are of little help, since an environment of radical uncertainty means that leaders have less information, expertise and resources to guide them than is often assumed. Undaunted, populist leaders exploit uncertainty to suggest that simple solutions will work. I suggest that the responses of such leaders have been characterised by incompetent leadership, denialist leadership, panic leadership, othering leadership and authoritarian leadership. (para 1)

Success in mitigating the health pandemic and managing its effects has depended on the response provided by leaders at all fronts (Pisano, Sadun, & Zanini, 2020). In countries such as South Korea, Japan, Singapore (Forman, Atun, McKee, & Mosialos, 2020) and New Zealand (Jamieson, 2020), the pandemic was taken seriously from the outset and was managed effectively (Forman, Atun, McKee, & Mossialos, 2020). In countries such as the United States, where the response was not coordinated and conflicting signals were communicated about the virus and its management (Forman, Atun, McKee, & Mosialos, 2020; Yong, 2020) and Brazil (Malta, Murray, da Silva, & Strathdee, 2020), the pandemic continues unabetted with harrowing effects (Klein, Book, & Bjørnskov, 2020; Milani, 2021; Mirvis, 2020). In all cases, political and public health leadership have made the difference between containing the pandemic or not.

Countries that had visionary leadership informed their nationals on how to avoid infection and what to do if they were infected (Forman, Atun, McKee, & Mosialos, 2020; Jamieson, 2020). From a public health leadership lens, leading experts in managing pandemics and communicable diseases such as Dr. Anthony Fauci and the Center for Disease Control (CDC) in the United States, were downplayed by their own government for political reasons (Desikan, MacKineey, & Goldman, 2020; Hennekens et al., 2020). The leadership of the world's leading health organization – WHO – in managing the pandemic and giving timely guidance to countries on how to manage COVID-19 was also heavily criticized (Middleton, Adongo, Low, & Magaña, 2020). Research in both aspects of political and public health leadership would be instrumental in developing a blueprint that would inform preparedness (Gostin, 2020) for future pandemics of the magnitude of the Coronavirus in order to minimize the damage to so many critical areas of life (Nicola, 2020).

In an age where social phenomena of global nature afflict all humanity, research on how leadership across cultures manifests itself would be instrumental in finding novel ways of leading that honor mother earth and its inhabitants. As Williams (2015) reiterates, "reporting research effectively using international style, for academic, professional and public audiences" is vital "to achieve change across the world" (p. xxxiii). The centuries old wisdom of indigenous communities coupled with modern Science can deter further degrading of planet earth to maintain the harmony that many indigenous cultures have protected over the millennia.

Concluding Thoughts – The Road Forward

An appreciation of the specific context and legislation (Dawson & Peart, 2003), ethical considerations (Hammersley & Traianou, 2011), and the importance of preparedness are all key underpinnings for undertaking leadership research in international settings. Research that embraces multiple facets of leadership as understood and practiced around the world would create a platform for learning why people lead the way they do. Embracing multiple leadership practices would also create a deeper appreciation of leadership principles that work within specific contexts and how these are applied.

With the impact of Coronavirus being experienced globally, international leadership research might well be the vehicle to usher in a new era where cross-cutting leadership perspectives lead to a better world where all humanity thrives as opposed to a way of leading that caters to a select few. Exploring the wisdom of elders in indigenous communities – a valued component of indigenous leadership – could well be the missing link that is needed to leverage modern leadership theories and concepts. When leaders' responses to crises are based on ethical and values-based principles such as those espoused in servant leadership, they provide a shared sense of purpose with their followers (Ahern, 2020).

Advancing international leadership research through critical exploration of servant leadership and other leadership styles, will create new findings for theory and practice with respect to deepening connections between leader and follower. Equally important is to look at virtual teams in an increasingly globalized and collaborative world. Global research needs to expand to look not just at gaps in leadership but new contexts for it. Better understanding the interconnectedness of leadership globally is paramount.

References

Abdul, H. B., Sajjad, N. K., Siti, M. A., & Yasir, H. M. (2019). Transformational leadership style, followership, and factors of employees' reactions towards organizational change. *Journal of Asia Business Studies, 13*(2), 181–209.

Adler, N. J. (1997). *International dimensions of organizational behavior* (5th ed.). Thomson South-Western

Adler, N. (1997). Global leadership: Women leaders. *MIR: Management International Review, 37*, 171–196. http://www.jstor.org/stable/40228426.

Ahern, S., & Loh, E. (2020). Leadership during the COVID-19 pandemic: Building and sustaining trust in times of uncertainty. *BMJ Leader*. 10.1136/leader-2020-000271

Alden, C. (2011). *Foreign policy analysis: New approaches: Understanding the diplomacy of war, profit and justice*. Routledge.

Alemazung, J. A. (2010). Post-colonial colonialism: An analysis of international factors and actors marring african socio-economic and political development. *The Journal of Pan African Studies, 3*(10), 62–84.

Alio, M. et al. (2020). By refugees, for refugees: Refugee leadership during COVID-19, and beyond. *International Journal of Refugee Law, 32*(2), 370–373. https://www.ncbi.nlm.nih.gov/pmc/articles/PMC7543544/

Alon, I., & Higgins, J. M. (2005). Global leadership success through emotional and cultural intelligences. *Business Horizons, 48*(6), 501–512.

Ansell, C., Sørensen, E., & Torfing, J. (2020). The COVID-19 pandemic as a game changer for public administration and leadership? The need for robust governance responses to turbulent problems. *Public Management Review, 23*, 1–12.

Anspach, N. M., & Carlson, T. N. (2020). What to believe? Social media commentary and belief in misinformation. *Political Behavior, 42*, 697–718. doi:10.1007/s11109-018-9515-z#citeas.

Arar, K., Örücü, D., & Waite, D. (2019). Understanding leadership for refugee education: introduction to the special issue. *International Journal of Leadership in Education, 23*(1), 1–6. https://www.tandfonline.com/action/showCitFormats?DOI=10.1080%2F13603124.2019.1690958.

Archer, R. L., Diaz-Loving, R., Gollwitzer, P. M., Davis, M. H., & Foushee, H. C. (1981). The role of dispositional empathy and social evaluation in the empathic mediation of helping.

Avolio, B. J., Sosik, J. J., Kahai, S. S., & Baker, B. (2014). E-leadership: Re-examining transformations in leadership source and transmission. *The Leadership Quarterly, 25*(1), 105–131.

Avolio, B. J., Zhu, W., Koh, W., & Bhatia, P. (2004). Transformational leadership and organizational commitment: Mediating role of psychological empowerment and moderating role of structural distance. *Journal of Organizational Behavior: The International Journal of Industrial, Occupational and Organizational Psychology and Behavior, 25*(8), 951–968.

Bailey, C. (2013, September 2). Why every great leader is also a great follower. http://danblackonleadership.info/archives/3997.

Barrett, B., & Cason, J. W. (2010). *Overseas research practices: A practical guide*. Routledge.

Beechler, S., & Javidan, M. (2007). Leading with a global mindset. In M. Javidan, R. Steers & M. Hitt (Eds.), *Advances in international management* (Vol. 19, pp. 131–169). Elsevier.

Bennett, M. (2004). Becoming interculturally competent. In J. Wurzel (Ed.), *Toward multiculturalism: A reader in multicultural education* (2nd ed., pp. 62–77). Intercultural Resource.

Bennett, N., & Lemoine, G. J. (2014). What a difference a word makes: Understanding threats to performance in a VUCA world. *Business Horizons, 57*(3), 311–317.

Betts, A. (2017). *Refuge: Rethinking refugee policy in a changing world*. Oxford University Press.

Bird, A., Mendenhall, M., Stevens, M. J., & Oddou, G. (2010). Defining the content domain of intercultural competence for global leaders. *Journal of Managerial Psychology, 25*(8), 810–828.

Black, J. S., & Mendenhall, M. (1990). Cross-cultural training effectiveness: A review and a theoretical framework for future research. *Academy of management review, 15*(1), 113–136.

Bloom, B. R.; Farmer, P. E., & Rubin, E. J. (2020). WHO's next – The United States and the World Health Organization. *The New England Journal of Medicine, 383*, 676–677. doi:10.1056/NEJMe2024894.

Brake, T. (1997). *The Global Leader. Critical Factors for Creating The World Class Organization*. Chicago, IL: Irwin Professional Publishing.

Bryson, J. R., Andres, L., & Davies, A. (2020). COVID-19, virtual church services and a new temporary geography of home. *Tijdschrift voor Economische en Sociale Geografie, 111*(3), 360–372.

Caligiuri, P. M. (2006). Developing global leaders. *Human Resource Management Review, 16*, 219–228.

Campbell, K. M., & Doshi, R. (2020). The coronavirus could reshape global order. *Council on Foreign Relations*. https://www.foreignaffairs.com/print/node/1125706.

Cascio, W. F. (2000). Managing a virtual workplace. *Academy of Management Perspectives, 14*(3), 81–90.

Chang, H., Chen, E., Muric, G., & Patel, J. (2020). Characterizing social media manipulation in the 2020 U.S. presidential election. *First Monday, 25*(11). https://www.jstor.org/stable/pdf/resrep25214.pdfhttps://journals.uic.edu/ojs/index.php/fm/article/view/11431.

Coicaud, J.-M., & Warner, D. (2013). *Ethics and international affairs: Extent and limits*. United Nations University Press.

Coke, J. S., Batson, C. D., & McDavis, K. (1978). Empathic mediation of helping: A two-stage model. *Journal of Personality and Social Psychology, 36*(7), 752.

Colbry, S., Hurwitz, M., & Adair, R. (2014). Collaboration theory. *Journal of Leadership Education, 13*(4), 63–75.

Collings, D. G., Scullion, H., & Morley, M. J. (2007). Changing patterns of global staffing in the multinational enterprise: Challenges to the conventional expatriate assignment and emerging alternatives. *Journal of World Business*, *42*(2), 198–213.

Cooley, L. (2020). Fostering human connection in the COVID-19 virtual health care realm. *NEJM Catalyst Innovations in Care Delivery*.. https://www.ncbi.nlm.nih.gov/pmc/articles/PMC7371327/.

Corry, S. (2013). Savaging primitives: Why Jared Diamond's "The World Until Yesterday" is completely wrong. *The Daily Beast*, 30 January 2013. https://www.thedailybeast.com/savaging-primitives-why-jared-diamonds-the-world-until-yesterday-is-completely-wrong.

Dalton, M. A. (1998). Developing leaders for global roles. In C. F. McCauley, R. S. Moxley, & E. Van Velsor (Eds.), *The center for creative leadership handbook of leadership development* (pp. 379–402). Jossey-Bass.

Dannhauser, Z., & Boshoff, A. B. (2006, August). The relationships between servant leadership, trust, team commitment and demographic variables. In *Servant Leadership Research Roundtable Proceedings*.

Dawson, J., & Peart, N. S. (2003). *The law of research: A guide*. University of Otago Press.

Degbey, W. Y., & Einola, K. (2020). Resilience in virtual teams: Developing the capacity to bounce back. *Applied Psychology*, *69*(4), 1301–1337.

Derven, M. (2016). *Four drivers to enhance global virtual teams*. Industrial and Commercial Training.

Desikan, A., MacKineey, T., & Goldman, G. (2020). Let the scientists speak: How CDC experts have been sidelined during the COVID-19 Pandemic. *JSTOR*.

Diamond, J. (2005). *Collapse: How societies choose to fail or survive*. Allen Lane.

Diamond, J. (2012). *The world until yesterday: What can we learn from traditional societies*. Penguin Books.

Dickson, M. W., Hartog, D. N. D., & Mitchelson, J. K. (2003). Research on leadership in a cross-cultural context: Making progress and raising new questions. *The Leadership Quarterly*, *14*, 729–768.

Dirks, K. T., & Skarlicki, D. P. (2004). Trust in leaders: Existing research and emerging issues. *Trust and Distrust in Organizations: Dilemmas and Approaches*, *7*, 21–40.

Doraiswamy, I. R. (2012). An analysis of servant leadership in family owned businesses. *International Journal of Social Science & Interdisciplinary Research*, *1*, 169–174.

Douglas, A., Ready, C. C., Kiron, D., & Pring, B. (2020). The new leadership playbook for the digital age: Reimagining what it takes to lead. *MIT Sloan Management Review*. https://sloanreview.mit.edu/projects/the-new-leadership-playbook-for-the-digital-age/.

Drury, S. (2004a). *Servant leadership and organizational commitment: Empirical findings and workplace implications*. http://www.regent.edu/acad/sls/publications/conference_proceedings/servant_leadership_roundtable/2004/pdf/drury_servant_leadership.pdf.

Drury, S. (2004b). *Employee perceptions of servant leadership: Comparisons by level and with job satisfaction and organizational commitment* [Doctoral dissertation]. Available from Dissertations & Theses: A&I. (Publication No. AAT 3146724).

Dryden-Peterson, S., & Hovil, L. (2004). A remaining hope for durable solutions: local integration of refugees and their hosts in the case of Uganda. *Refuge*, *22*(1), 26–38.

Dubey, A. (2019). This is what great leadership looks like in the digital age. World Economic.

Forman, R., Atun, R., McKee, M., & Mosialos, E. (2020). 12 Lessons learned from the management of the coronavirus pandemic. *Health Policy*, *124*(6), 577–580. https://www.weforum.org/agenda/2019/04/leadership-digital-age-leader/.

Fernandez, A. A., & Shaw, G. P. (2020). Academic leadership in a time of crisis: The coronavirus and COVID-19. *Journal of Leadership Studies*. https://www.ncbi.nlm.nih.gov/pmc/articles/PMC7228314/

Ferreira, W. F. (2008). Conducting research and sponsored programs overseas. *Medical Research Law and Policy Report*, *7*(14), 441–449.

Fidler, D. P. (2017). *Transforming election cybersecurity*. Cyber Brief. Articles by Maurer Faculty, 2547. Maurer School of Law, Indiana University.

Firestone, S. (2020). What is crisis leadership? *Biblical Principles of Crisis Leadership*, 7–21.

Goldsmith, M., Greenberg, C. L., Robertson, A., & Hu-Chan, M. (2003). *Global leadership: The next generation*. Financial Times Prentice Hall.

Gostin, L. O. (2020). The great Coronavirus pandemic of 2020—7 critical lessons. *The JAMA Forum*, *324*(18), 1816–1817.

Greenleaf, R. K. (1977). *Servant-leadership: A journey into the nature of legitimate power and greatness*. New York: Paulist Press.

Grigorescu, A., & Costovici, D.-A. (2020). Managing the unexpected: The first effects of COVID-19 outbreak on the global economy. Stategica: Preparing for tomorrow, today. International Academic Conference (8th ed.), Bucharest, October 15–16, 2020. Tritonic Publishing House.

Grint, K. (2020). Leadership, management and command in the time of the Coronavirus. *Leadership*, *16*(3), 314–319.

Halai, A., & William, D. (2012). *Research methodologies in the 'South'*. Oxford University Press Pakistan.

Hall, D. T., Zhu, G., & Yan, A. (2001). Developing global leaders: To hold on to them, let them go! In W. H. Mobley & M. W. J. McCall (Eds.), *Advances in global leadership* (Vol. 2, pp. 327–349). JAI.

Hammersley, M., & Traianou, A. (2011). *Ethics in qualitative research*. SAGE.

Hanson, F., O'Connor, S., Walker, M., & Courtois, L. (2019). *Hacking democracies: Cataloguing cyber-enabled attacks on elections. Policy Brief Report No. 16/2019*. International Cyber Policy Center.

Harris, M. L. (2017). *Ecowomanism: African American women and earth-honoring faiths*. Orbis Books.

Harris, P. R., Moran, R. T., & Moran, S. V. (2004). *Managing cultural differences – global leadership strategies for the 21st century* (6th ed.). Butterworth- Heinemann/Elsevier.

Harwood-Jones, J. (2010). Custodians of the planet? *The Journal of New Paradigm Research*, *21*(3-4), 231–243.

Heifetz, R. A. (1994). *Leadership without easy answers*. Belknap.

Heifetz, R. A., & Laurie, D. L. (2001). The work of leadership. *Harvard Business Review*, *79*(11).

Hennekens et al. (2020). The emerging pandemic of Coronavirus and the urgent need for public health leadership. *American Journal of Medicine*, *133*(6), 658-650. https://www.ncbi.nlm.nih.gov/pmc/articles/PMC7270735/.

Higgins-Dunn, N. (2020). World Health Organization asks the U.S. to reconsider withdrawing from international group. CNBC. *Health and Science*. https://www.cnbc.com/2020/08/06/world-health-organization-asks-the-us-to-reconsider-withdrawing-from-international-group.html.

Hill, L. A. (2008). Where will we find tomorrow's leaders?. *Harvard Business Review*, *86*(1), 123.

Hollenbeck, J. P. (2001). A serendipitous sojourn through the global leadership literature. In W. H. Mobley & M. W. J. McCall (Eds.), *Advances in global leadership* (Vol. 2, pp. 15–47). JAI.

Horwitch, M. & Callahan, M. W. (2016). *How leaders inspire: Cracking the code. An analytical approach to inspirational leadership*. Bain & Company.

Horwitch, M., & Whipple, M. (2014). Leaders who inspire: A 21st-century approach to developing your talent. Bain & Company, Inc. [Web:] http://www. bain. com/Images/BAIN_BRIEF_Leaders_who_inspire. pdf. Accessed 2 March 2021.

Horwitz, J. (2020). Facebook's fact checkers fight surge in fake coronavirus claims. *The Wall Street Journal*. https://www.wsj.com/articles/facebooks-fact-checkers-fight-surge-in-fake-coronavirus-claims-11585580400.

House, R. J., Hanges, P. J., Javidan, M., Dorfman, P. W., & Gupta, V. Eds. (2004). *Culture, leadership, and organizations: The GLOBE study of 62 societies*. Sage publications.

Irving, J. A. (2005). *Exploring the relationship between servant leadership and team effectiveness: Findings from the non-profit sector*. http://www.regent.edu/acad/sls/publications/conference_proceedings?servant_leadership_roundtable/2005/pdf/irving_exploring.pdf.

Jamieson, T. (2020). "Go Hard, go early": Preliminary lessons from New Zealand's response to COVID-19. *SAGE Journals*, *50*(6-7), 598–605.

Jarvenpaa, S. L., & Leidner, D. E. (1999). Communication and trust in global virtual teams. *Organization Science*, *10*(6), 791–815.

Jimenez, P., & Iyer, G. S. (2016). Tax compliance in a social setting: The influence of social norms, trust in government, and perceived fairness on taxpayer compliance. *Advances in Accounting*, *34*, 17–26.

Johansen, R. (2012). *Leaders make the future: Ten new leadership skills for an uncertain world*. Berrett-Koehler Publishers.

Kamwaria et al. (2015). Recognizing and strengthening the role of the Njuri Ncheke in devolved governance in Meru County, Kenya. *Journal of Educational Policy and Entrepreneurial Research (JEPER)*, *2*(10), 42–47.

Kane, G. C., Phillips, A. N., Copulsky, J., & Andrus, G. (2019). How digital leadership is(n't) different. *MIT Sloan Management Review*, *60*(3), 34–39.

Kanji, G. K. (1998). Measurement of business excellence. *Total Quality Management*, *9*(7), 633–643.

Kankanhalli, A., Tan, B. C., & Wei, K. K. (2006). Conflict and performance in global virtual teams. *Journal of Management Information Systems*, *23*(3), 237–274.

Karan, A. (2019). *Opinion: It's time to end the colonial mindset in global health*. https://www.npr.org/sections/goatsandsoda/2019/12/30/784392315/opinion-its-time-to-end-the-colonial-mindset-in-global-health.

Kayworth, T. R., & Leidner, D. E. (2002). Leadership effectiveness in global virtual teams. *Journal of Management Information Systems*, *18*(3), 7–40.

Kahn, W. A. (1993). Caring for the caregivers: Patterns of organizational care-giving. *Administrative Science Quarterly*, *38*, 539–563.

Kim, Y. J. & van Dyne, L. (2011). Cultural intelligence and international leadership potential: the importance of contact for members. *Applied Psychology: An International Review*, *61*(2), 272–294.

Larson, L., & DeChurch, L. A. (2020). Leading teams in the digital age: Four perspectives on technology and what they mean for leading teams. *The Leadership Quarterly, 31*, 1–18.

Laub, J. A. (1999). *Assessing the servant organization: Development of the servant organizational leadership assessment (SOLA) instrument* [Unpublished doctoral dissertation]. Florida Atlantic University, Boca Raton.

Laub, J. (2004). Defining servant leadership. A recommended typology for servant leadership studies. *Proceedings of the Servant Leadership Research Roundtable*. Retrieved October 5, 2004.

Lee-Kelley, L., & Sankey, T. (2008). Global virtual teams for value creation and project success: A case study. *International Journal of Project Management, 26*(1), 51–62.

Leslie, Jean (2015). *The leadership gap: How to fix what your organization lacks*. Center for Creative Leadership.

Lilius, J. M., Worline, M. C., Maitlis, S., Kanov, J., Dutton, J. E., & Frost, P. (2008). The contours and consequences of compassion at work. *Journal of Organizational Behavior: The International Journal of Industrial, Occupational and Organizational Psychology and Behavior, 29*(2), 193–218.

Lippert, H., & Dulewicz, V. (2018). A profile of high-performing global virtual teams. *Team Performance Management: An International Journal.* doi:10.1108/tpm-09-2016-0040.

Lokkesmoe, K. J., Kuchinke, K. P., & Ardichvili, A. (2016). Developing cross-cultural awareness through foreign immersion programs. *European Journal of Training and Development, 40*(3), 155–170.

Maloney, M. M., Bresman, H., Zellmer-Bruhn, M. E., & Beaver, G. R. (2016). Contextualization and context theorizing in teams research: A look back and a path forward. *Academy of Management Annals, 10*(1), 891–942.

Malta, M.; Murray, L., da Silva, C. M. F. P., & Strathdee, S. A. (2020). Coronavirus in Brazil: The heavy weight of inequality and unsound leadership. *Eclinical Medicine.* https://www.ncbi.nlm.nih.gov/pmc/articles/PMC7380224/.

Margolis, J. D., & Molinsky, A. (2008). Navigating the bind of necessary evils: Psychological engagement and the production of interpersonally sensitive behavior. *Academy of Management Journal, 51*(5), 847–872.

Martínez-Moreno, E., Zornoza, A., Orengo, V., & Thompson, L. F. (2015). The effects of team self-guided training on conflict management in virtual teams. *Group Decision and Negotiation, 24*(5), 905–923.

Maruping, L. M., & Agarwal, R. (2004). Managing team interpersonal processes through technology: A task-technology fit perspective. *Journal of Applied Psychology, 89*(6), 975.

Maznevski, M. L., & Chudoba, K. M. (2000). Bridging space over time: Global virtual team dynamics and effectiveness. *Organization Science, 11*(5), 473–492.

McChrystal, G. S., Collins, T., Silverman, D., & Fussell, C. (2015). *Team of teams: New rules of engagement for a complex world*. Penguin.

Mendenhall, M. E., Osland, J., Bird, A., Oddou, G. R., Stevens, M. J., Maznevski, M., & Stahl, G. K. (Eds.). (2017). *Global leadership: Research, practice, and development*. Routledge.

Mendenhall, M. E., Reiche, B. S., Bird, A., & Osland, J. S. (2012). Defining the "global" in global leadership. *Journal of World Business, 47*(4), 493–503.

Merriam-Webster online dictionary (n.d.). Definition of crisis. https://www.merriam-webster.com/dictionary/crisis.

Middleton, J., Adongo, P. B., Low, W. & Magaña, L. (2020). Global network for academic public health statement on the World Health Organization's response to the COVID-19 pandemic. *International Journal of Public Health, 65*, 1523–1524.

Milani, F. (2021). COVID-19 outbreak, social response, and early economic effects: A global VAR analysis of cross-country interdependencies. *Journal of Population Economics, 34*, 223–252.

Miller, C. (1995). *The empowered leader: 10 keys to servant leadership*. Broadman and Holman Publishers.

Miller, K. I. (2007). Compassionate communication in the workplace: Exploring processes of noticing, connecting, and responding. *Journal of Applied Communication Research, 35*(3), 223–245.

Milliband, D. (2017). *Rescue: Refugees and the political crisis of our time*. Simon & Schuster/TED.

Mintzberg, H. (1973). The nature of managerial work. *International Journal of Leadership Studies, 8*(1), 67–75.

Mironko, A. (2018). The impact of human capital and skill availability on attraction of foreign direct investment (FDI) into regions within developing economies. *International Journal of Management, 9*(3), 139–163.

Moldoveanu, M. & Narayandas, D. (2019). The future of leadership development. *Harvard Business Review*, March–April 2019. https://hbr.org/2019/03/educating-the-next-generation-of-leaders.

Morrison, A. J. (2000). Developing a global leadership model. *Human resource management, 39*(2-3), 117–131.

Neubauer, R., Tarling, A., & Wade, M. (2017). *Redefining leadership for a digital age*. Global Center for Digital Business Transformation and metaBeratung GmbH. Retrieved from https://www. imd. org/globalassets/dbt/docs/redefining-leadership.

Neubert, M. J., Kacmar, K. M., Carlson, D. S., Chonko, L. B. & Roberts, J. A. (2008). Regulatory focus as a mediator of the influence of initiating structure and servant leadership on employee behavior. *Journal of Applied Psychology, 93*(6), 1220.

Nicola, M. et al. (2020). The Socio-economic implications of the Coronavirus pandemic (COVID-19): A review. *Elsevier Public Health Emergency Collection.* https://www.ncbi.nlm.nih.gov/pmc/articles/PMC7162753/.

Nkomo, S. M. (2011). A postcolonial and anti-colonial reading of 'African' leadership and management in organization studies: Tensions, contradictions and possibilities. *SAGE Journals, 18*(3), 365–386.

Nordbäck, E. S., & Espinosa, J. A. (2019). Effective coordination of shared leadership in global virtual teams. *Journal of Management Information Systems, 36*(1), 321–350.

Norden, L., & Vanderwalker, L. (2017). *Securing elections from foreign interference.* Brennan Center for Justice at New York University School of Law. https://www.brennancenter.org/sites/default/files/publications/Foreign%20Interference_0629_1030_AM.pdf.

Northouse, P. G. (2004). *Leadership theory and practice* (3rd ed.). Thousand Oaks, CA: Sage.

Northouse, Peter G. (2016). *Leadership: Theory and practice* (7th ed.). SAGE Publications, Inc.

Ortagus, M. (2020). *Update on U.S. withdrawal from the World Health Organization.* Press Statement. U.S. Department of State. https://www.state.gov/update-on-u-s-withdrawal-from-the-world-health-organization/.

Osland, J. S., Mendenhall, M. E., Reiche, B. S., Szkudlarek, B., Bolden, R., Courtice, P., ... Terrell, S. (2020). *Perspectives on Global Leadership and the COVID-19 Crisis. Advances in Global Leadership* (Vol. 13, pp. 3–56). Emerald Publishing Limited.

Osland, J. S. (2008). Overview of the global leadership literature. In M. E. Mendenhall, J. S. Osland, A. Bird, G. R. Oddou, & M. L. Maznevski (Eds.), *Global leadership: Research, practice, and development* (pp. 34–63). Routledge.

Peterson, M. F. & Hunt, J. G. (1997). International perspectives on international leadership. *The Leadership Quarterly, 8*(3), 203–231.

Pisano, G. P., Sadun, R., & Zanini, M. (2020). Lessons from Italy's response to Coronavirus. *Harvard Business Review.* https://hbr.org/2020/03/lessons-from-italys-response-to-coronavirus.

Pless, N. M., Maak, T., & Stahl, G. (2011). Developing responsible global leaders through international service-learning programs: The Ulysses experience. *Academy of Management Learning & Education, 10*(2), 237–260.

Porter, L., & Tanner, S. Eds. (2012). *Assessing business excellence.* Routledge.

Presbitero, A. (2020). Foreign language skill, anxiety, cultural intelligence and individual task performance in global virtual teams: A cognitive perspective. *Journal of International Management, 26*(2), 100729.

Prewitt, J. E. & Weil, R. (2014). Organizational opportunities endemic in crisis leadership. *Journal of Management Policy and Practice, 15*(2):72–87.

Qiu, L. (2020). Hey @jack, Here Are More Questionable Tweets from @realdonaldtrump. *The New York Times.* https://www.nytimes.com/2020/06/03/us/politics/trump-twitter-fact-check.html.

Ramalingam, B. Wild, L. & Ferrari, M. (2020). Adaptive leadership in the Coronavirus response: Bridging Science, policy and practice. Coronavirus Briefing Note. ODI. https://www.odi.org/sites/odi.org.uk/files/resource-documents/032020_pogo_coronavirus_adaptation.pdf.

Ray, J. (2020, January 12). *100-top-companies-with-remote-jobs-2020.* https://www.flexjobs.com/blog/post/100-top-companies-with-remote-jobs-2020/.

Reiche, B. S., Bird, A., Mendenhall, M. E., & Osland, J. S. (2017). Contextualizing leadership: A typology of global leadership roles. *Journal of International Business Studies, 48*(5), 552–572.

Rhinesmith, S. H. (1996). *A manager's guide to globalization: Six skills for success in a changing world.* Irwin Professional Pub.

Rosen, C. B.; Joffe, S., & Kelz, R. R. (2020). COVID-19 moves medicine into a virtual space a paradigm shift from touch to talk to establish trust. *Annals of Surgery, 272*(2), e159–e160.

Saleh, A., & Watson, R. (2017). Business excellence in a volatile, uncertain, complex and ambiguous environment (BEVUCA). *The TQM Journal.*

Scardino, Anthony J. (2013). Servant leadership in higher education: the influence of servant-led faculty on student engagement [Dissertations & Theses]. 25.

Schaefer, C. (2006). *Grandmothers counsel the world: Women elders offer their vision for our planet.* Shambhala Publications, Inc.

Schiller, B. (2012). *Can citizen scientists be our first line of defense in environmental disasters? Fast Company.* www.fastcoexist.com/1681099/can-citizen-scientists-be-our-first-line-of-defense-in-environmental-disasters?.

Schlebusch, C. (2010). Issues raised by use of ethnic-group names in genome study. *Nature, 464*(7288), 487.

Schmidt, G. B. (2014). Virtual leadership: An important leadership context. *Industrial and Organizational Psychology: Perspectives on Science and Practice.* doi:10.1111/iops.12129.

Schulze, J., & Krumm, S. (2017). The "virtual team player" A review and initial model of knowledge, skills, abilities, and other characteristics for virtual collaboration. *Organizational Psychology Review, 7*(1), 66–95.

Schuyler, A. (2006). *Systems of ethics.* University of Wisconsin, Madison.

Seeger, M. W., Sellnow, T. L., & Ulmer, R. R. (1998). Communication, organization, and crisis. *Annals of the International Communication Association*, 21(1), 231–276.

Seow, P. S., Pan, G., & Koh, G. (2019). Examining an experiential learning approach to prepare students for the volatile, uncertain, complex and ambiguous (VUCA) work environment. *The International Journal of Management Education*, 17(1), 62–76.

Smith, L. T. (2002). *Decolonizing methodologies: Research and Indigenous peoples*. New York, NY: University of Otago Press.

Smith, P. G., & Blanck, E. L. (2002). From experience: Leading dispersed teams. *Journal of Product Innovation Management: An International Publication of the Product Development & Management Association*, 19(4), 294–304.

Spears & M. Lawrence (Eds.). *Practicing servant leadership* (pp. 9–24). Jossey Bass.

Spears, L. C. (2004). The understanding and practice of servant-leadership. L. C. Spears & M. Lawrence (Eds.), *Practicing servant leadership: Succeeding through trust, bravery, and forgiveness* (pp. 9–24). Wiley.

Spreitzer, G. M., McCall, M. W. Jr., & Mahoney, J. (1997). The early identification of international executive potential. *Journal of Applied Psychology*, 82(1), 6–29.

Stahl (Eds.). *Developing global business leaders: Policies, processes, and innovations*. Quorum Books.

Starr, H. (2006). *Approaches, levels, and methods of analysis in international politics: Crossing boundaries*. Palgrave.

Stogdill, R. M., & Bass, B. M. (1981). *Stogdill's handbook of leadership* (2nd ed.). Free Press.

Suriyankietkaew, S. (2013). Emergent leadership paradigms for corporate sustainability: A proposed model. *Journal of Applied Business Research (JABR)*, 29(1), 173–182.

Sutcliffe, K. M., & Christianson, M. K. (2013). *Managing the unexpected. Center or positive organizational scholarship*. Executive White Paper series. Michigan Ross School of Business.

Suzuki, D., & Knudstson, P. (1992). *Wisdom of the elders: Sacred native stories of nature*. Bantam Books.

Tomlinson, J. (2008). *Cultural imperialism: A critical introduction*. ACLS Humanities.

Tompson, H. B., & Jody Tompson, G. H. (2013). The focus of leadership development in MNCs. *Fast Company Magazine*.

Tourish, D. (2014). Leadership, more or less? A processual, communication perspective on the role of agency in leadership theory. *Leadership*, 10(1), 79–98.

Tourish, D. (2020). Introduction to the special issue: Why the coronavirus crisis is also a crisis of leadership. *SAGE Journals*, 16(3), 261–272.

Treverton, G. F., & Bikson, T. K. (2003). *New challenges for international leadership: Positioning the United States for the 21st Century*. Issue Paper, RAND Corporation. https://www.rand.org/pubs/issue_papers/IP233.html.

Uhl-Bien, M., Riggio, R. E., Lowe, K. B., & Carsten, M. K. (2014), Followership theory: A review and research agenda. *The Leadership Quarterly*, 25(1), 83–104.

Valk, J., Belding, S., Crumpton, A., Harter, N., & Reams, J. (2011). Worldviews and leadership: Thinking and acting the bigger pictures. *Journal of Leadership Studies*, 5(2), 54–63.

Van de Vliert, E. (2006). Autocratic leadership around the globe: Do climate and wealth drive leadership culture? *Journal of Cross-Cultural Psychology*, 37, 42.

Vera, D., & Crossan, M. (2005). Improvisation and innovative performance in teams. *Organization Science*, 16(3), 203–224.

Vogelgesang, G., Clapp-Smith, R., & Osland, J. (2014). The relationship between positive psychological capital and global mindset in the context of global leadership. *Journal of Leadership & Organizational Studies*, 21(2), 165–178. 10.1177/1548051813515515.

Warwick Education Studies. (n.d.). *What is decolonising methodology?* https://warwick.ac.uk/fac/soc/ces/research/current/socialtheory/maps/decolonising/#:~:text=what%20is%20decolonising%20methodology%3F%20Decolonisation%20itself%20refers%20to,to%20critique%20positions%20of%20power%20and%20dominant%20culture.

Washington, H. A. (2007). *Medical apartheid: The dark history of medical experimentation on Black Americans from colonial times to the present*. Doubleday.

Weeks, B. E., Ardèvol-Abreu, A., & Gil de Zúñiga, H. (2017). Online influence? Social media use, opinion leadership, and political persuasion. *International Journal of Public Opinion Research*, 29(2), 214–239.

Wetter, S. & Friedman, E. A. (2020). U.S. Withdrawal from the World Health Organization: Unconstitutional and Unhealthy. In S. Burris, S. de Guia, L. Gable, D. E. Levin, W. E. Parmet, & N. P. Terry (Eds.). *Assessing legal responses to COVID-19*. Public Health Law Watch.

Wheeler, D. W. (2012). *Servant leadership for higher education: Principles and practices*. John Wiley & Sons.

Wildcat, D. R. (2009). *Red Alert! Saving the planet with indigenous knowledge*. Fulcrum Publishing.

Williams, C. (2012). *Researching power, elites, and leadership*. SAGE.

Williams, C. (2015). *Doing international research*. SAGE Publications. Kindle Edition.

Wilson, S. (2020). Pandemic leadership: Lessons from New Zealand's approach to COVID-19. *SAGE Journals*, *16*(3), 279–293. doi:10.1177/1742715020929151.

Yong, E. (2020). *How the pandemic defeated America*. https://www.mfprac.com/web2020/07literature/literature/Infectious_Dis/Covid19-DefeatedNation_Yong.pdf.

Zander, L., Mockaitis, A. I., & Butler, C. L. (2012). Leading global teams. *Journal of World Business*, *47*(4), 592–603.

Zhang, S., & Fjermestad, J. (2006). Bridging the gap between traditional leadership theories and virtual team leadership. *International Journal of Technology, Policy and Management*, *6*(3), 274–291.

32
Benefits of Conducting International Leadership Research in an Ever-Changing Global Environment

David N. Avdul

Introduction

Businesses and other types of organizations have always sought new and innovative ways to lower costs, increase efficiencies, grow revenues, and meet organizational objectives. This tendency has led to various globalization efforts and movements which have spanned the last 100 years or so (DeNisi & Griffin, 2019). Earlier globalization movements included pre- and post-World War II phases, where mechanical power, technological advances, and eventual governmental support made it economical to pursue goods made in other countries. According to Baldwin (2018), we are now exiting globalization 3.0, which consisted of factories crossing borders to make physical goods, low wages, and advanced technology, with workers and local communities struggling to adapt. And We are now entering globalization 4.0, which is estimated to disrupt service-sector and professional-level employees in advanced economies. These employees and their jobs may be exposed for the first time to artificial intelligence and global competition, due to advanced digital technologies. In other words, telemigration of services, instead of goods, is taking hold (Baldwin, 2019).

Globalization is ever-changing and is impacted by a variety of factors. Political uncertainty exists in many regions of the world, which impacts partnership policies and international agreements (Kleine & Minaudier, 2019). Anti-immigration sentiment and policies, which have been on the rise since the 2008 global financial crises, impact globalization, as organizations may be less inclined to move operations abroad or hire foreign workers (Vogt, 2019). Recently, countries have shown a willingness to withdraw from regional economic alliances meant to promote free trade, such as the United States' withdrawal of the Trans-Pacific Partnership under President Donald Trump and the United Kingdom's impending withdrawal from the European Union. But other countries like China are promoting globalization. As of April 30, 2019, 131 countries and 30 international organizations had signed agreements with China on joint construction efforts across the globe on their Belt and Road Initiative (Hui, 2019).

It is clear that globalization is ever-changing, but is here to stay in one form or another. Thus, organizations must be prepared to adapt to shifting global environments in which they operate. Being prepared means employing flexible processes, modern and digital technologies, nimble strategies and global partnerships (Ungson & Wong, 2008). At the same time, even more important is having leaders in place who operate effectively and motivate and engage employees in fast-paced and changing global environments. The purpose of this chapter is to focus on international leadership research and its

DOI: 10.4324/9781003003380-32

importance for global organizations. I discuss the types of leaders that are needed to operate effectively in modern global environments and provide insight on the following eight reasons for vitality of international leadership research. Those are to:

- identify and refine global leadership competencies;
- help organizations succeed with expatriate assignments;
- conduct better change management;
- help spur innovation;
- further understand leadership styles across societies;
- help leaders navigate ethical challenges;
- enhance communication;
- facilitate high performing global teams.

Identify and Refine Global Leadership Competencies

One benefit of conducting international leadership research is that the findings can help pinpoint and refine global leadership competencies, which can be used to identify and groom future leaders in organizations. While doing so is not a guarantee of success with global initiatives, it can serve as a starting point for organizations that wish to promote and train global leadership talent. Leadership competencies are important to study and refine because employee performance is greatly affected by leaders' qualities and behaviors; great leaders bring out the best in people (Kouzes & Posner, 2017). Leaders make differences in organizations, and if employees are satisfied with their leaders, they are motivated to perform well (Shehzad et al., 2019).

Overall, there is not a shortage of research to assess global leadership competencies. Mendenhall et al. (2013) posited that social scientists have delineated over 160 competencies that influence global leadership effectiveness. But additional research in this area can lend a hand in a variety of ways. First, it can help narrow down extensive lists of global leadership competencies already put forth by some researchers and consulting firms. Second, it can help to distinguish further between competency types, which can provide focus and clarity on competencies that are realistic and attainable.

To help understand the vast amount of global leadership competencies that exist today, it is useful to list some of the models that have already been developed. These frameworks were selected based on prevalence in leadership research and linkage to the eight benefits of additional research discussed in this chapter. The first model is the Global Competencies Inventory (GCI), developed in 2000 by Bird, Stevens, Mendenhall and Oddou. It was designed to assess personal qualities linked to effectiveness where cultural norms and behaviors differ from one's home country or region (Mendenhall et al., 2013). The GCI measures leadership competencies deemed critical when interacting and working with people from other cultures. The GCI measures the following dimensions of global competencies, grouped into three main factors:

- perception management. Nonjudgmentalness, inquisitiveness, tolerance of ambiguity, cosmopolitanism, and interest flexibility;
- relationship management. Relationship interest, interpersonal engagement, emotional sensitivity, self-awareness, and behavioral flexibility;
- self-management. Optimism, self-confidence, self-identity, emotional resilience, non-stress tendency, and stress management (Falconer, 2014).

The Global Executive Leadership Inventory (GELI), developed by Kets de Vries, is a global leadership model that utilizes self-assessment and a 360-degree feedback approach to gather feedback from others. It is primarily used to assess global leadership competency in executives (Kets de Vries,

2016). The GELI analyzes competency levels within the following 12 global leadership dimensions: (a) visioning, (b) empowering, (c) energizing, (d) designing and aligning, (e) rewarding and feedback, (f) team building, (g) outside orientation, (h) global mindset, (i) tenacity, (j) emotional intelligence, (k) life balance, and (l) resilience to stress (Kets de Vries, 2005).

The Thunderbird Global Mindset Inventory (GMI) was developed to measure and predict performance in global leadership, as it was surmised that most people in the world live and work with people like themselves (Thunderbird, n.d.). The GMI helps determine who may be able to employ a global mindset, which consists of communicating, conducting business, and influencing people who are different from them (Javidan & Walker, 2012). The GMI measures a manager's profile of global mindset in three dimensions: (a) intellectual capital, (b) psychological capital, and (c) social capital. Intellectual capital is a leader's ability to demonstrate global business savvy, cognitive complexity, and a cosmopolitan outlook (Javidan, Bullough, & Dibble, 2016). Psychological capital is represented by a passion for diversity and a quest for adventure and self-assurance. Leaders demonstrate social capital when they show intercultural empathy, interpersonal impact and diplomacy in their interactions towards others. Intercultural empathy is needed to prevent false assumptions towards people, increase knowledge to prevent incomplete comprehension, and to increase the skill needed to promote the right actions (Javidan & Walker, 2012).

Conger and O'Neil's (2012) framework for global leadership capacity is a third notable model. It includes three main clusters of skills deemed necessary for effective global leadership, referred to as: (a) baseline competencies, (b) skills and knowledge capabilities, and (c) a global leadership mindset. Baseline competencies are shown when people enjoy learning new things and are energized by meeting with people from other cultures. Leaders who exhibit baseline competencies demonstrate a catalytic learning capability, sense of adventure, entrepreneurial spirit, and sensitivity and responsiveness to cultural differences. Global skills and knowledge capabilities, the second cluster, are demonstrated when leaders show sophisticated networking competence, cultural literacy, context-specific learning, and overall leadership of multi-cultural teams. Individuals who exhibit these capabilities are not only energized by learning about new cultures, but also have the ability to navigate through them, network, and persuade partners to achieve common goals. A global mindset, the third cluster, involves strategic decision-making. Leaders who demonstrate a global mindset are comfortable with cultural complexities, view uncertainty of international markets as an opportunity instead of a burden, and think in global contexts and with an extended timeframe.

Ding's (2013) model for successful global leadership includes five components, which all revolve around trust. The central theme of the model is that without trust, relationship-building and overall leadership will fail. The first peripheral component in the model is innovation. Global leaders must be innovative thinkers and promote innovation throughout the organization in order to be effective. Second, global leaders must view the world as a whole and demonstrate a global mindset in their thinking and actions. Excellent communication is the third attribute. Global leaders must be able to successfully communicate the mission and goals of the organization to their co-workers and subordinates. The fourth element is leading by example, as leaders must practice what they preach. The last component is a focus on performance. In order for global leaders to be effective they must be able to evaluate diverse employees fairly and consistently based on their performance (Ding, 2018) (Table 32.1).

Organizational leaders today should take reasonable and realistic approaches to global leadership development, as research and competency lists like these continue to evolve and be refined. They should select a global leadership assessment instrument or framework that best suits their overall business strategies, with the understanding that identifying it is just the first step towards finding and developing high potential global talent. Once selected, leaders should ensure selected competencies are specific and visible in their organizations and ingrain them throughout, especially in their human resources practices (Conger & O'Neill, 2012; Rosenbusch & Terrell, 2013).

Table 32.1 Global Leadership Competencies

Instrument or Framework	Competencies
Global Competencies Inventory (2000)	Perception management. Nonjudgmentalness, inquisitiveness, tolerance of ambiguity, cosmopolitanism, and interest flexibility Relationship management. Relationship interest, interpersonal engagement, emotional sensitivity, self-awareness, and behavioral flexibility Self-management. Optimism, self-confidence, self-identity, emotional resilience, non-stress tendency, and stress management.
Global Executive Leadership Inventory (2004)	Designing and aligning, emotional intelligence, empowering, energizing, global mindset, life balance, outside orientation, resilience to stress, rewarding and feedback, team building, tenacity, visioning
Thunderbird Global Mindset Inventory (2010)	Intellectual capital through cognitive complexity, cosmopolitan outlook, and global business savvy Psychological capital through a passion for diversity, a quest for adventure and self-assurance Social capital through diplomacy, intercultural empathy, and interpersonal impact
Global Leadership Capability Framework (2012)	Baseline competencies. Catalytic learning capability, entrepreneurial spirit, responsiveness and sensitivity to cultural differences, sense of adventure Skills and knowledge. Context-specific learning, cultural literacy, leadership of multi-cultural teams, sophisticated networking competence Global mindset. Comfortable with cultural complexities, systems thinking in global contexts with an extended time perspective, view uncertainty as an opportunity
Ding's Global Leadership Model (2013)	Trust, innovative thinker, global mindset, effective communication, lead by example, focus on performance

Talent acquisition professionals can start by taking a strategic and long-term approach to identifying potential candidates, not only assessing the fit of a candidate to a certain job but also a fit for future requirements, which helps with succession planning (Deters, 2017). Once employees are hired, needs assessments can be administered to high potential leaders to identify gaps in global leadership development, and training and development can be conducted accordingly, using formal testing and evaluation methods. The performance appraisal and management process should include elements of global leadership development, and rewards systems can be designed to reward and encourage the development and enhancement of the desired traits and skills (Conger & O'Neill, 2012). In an ideal setup, employees would need to demonstrate fluency in the selected global leadership capabilities prior to being groomed, trained or sent on international leadership assignments (Lawrence, 2015).

Help Organizations Succeed with Expatriate Assignments

Another way that international leadership research can assist organizations today is with the selection and training of expatriates for international assignments. Expatriates are employees, either parent-country nationals or third-country nationals, who have been sent by a firm to work in another country on a long-term assignment (DeNisi & Griffin, 2019). Expatriate assignments are important to analyze because they are commonly viewed as an excellent way to develop global leaders (Collings, Scullion, & Caliguiri, 2019). Successful expatriate assignments can yield immense benefits when managed properly, such as the transfer of important technical and managerial knowledge, better control of foreign subsidies, enhanced communication, and more secure business transactions (Feitosa, Kramer, Kramperth, Kreutzer, & Salas, 2014). Once repatriated, expatriates are expected to use their international experience to increase performance and knowledge-sharing at their home facility (Mehore & Gankar, 2016). But expatriate assignments are time-consuming, costly, and complex. The Society for Human Resources Management (SHRM) stated that the cost of a three-year international assignment could exceed $3 million, with organizations still reporting a failure rate of 42 percent (Society for Human Resources Management, 2017). With high costs and much at stake, it is worth the investment to develop a refined and rigorous selection and training process for expatriates.

Additional international leadership research can help with the selection process of expatriates for overseas assignments. Similar to the identification of global leadership talent, more insight on global leadership competencies can help organizations identify individuals most suited and motivated for the challenges of working and living abroad. Some firms focus on leaders' technical skills when selecting expatriates, but while technical skills are important they do not ensure success on expatriate assignments (Varma et al., 2001). Also, past performance in one country is not a good predictor of success in another because cultural differences such as work ethics, performance expectations, and balancing of work and personal life differ from country to country (Bader et al., 2018). A better approach towards expatriate selection is to take a deeper dive into the leadership capabilities and competencies of individuals, identify their strengths and weaknesses, and then find ways to enhance and develop these persons. For instance, seeking out employees who score high in certain competencies, such as cultural intelligence, learning goal orientation and language ability is a good way to find excellent candidates for expatriate assignments (Feitosa, Kramer, Kramperth, Kreutzer, & Salas, 2014). Cultural intelligence reflects a learner's capacity to acquire, retain and interpret various types of information and experiences, and is a key determinant in promoting creativity, shared leadership, and trust (Huang, He, & Zhai, 2020). Learning goal orientation is the motivation to learn for the sake of gaining knowledge or learning a new skill. Employees who score high on this dimension are more open and receptive to training and development, a key attribute needed when working in unfamiliar environments or cultures (Feitosa et al., 2014).

Additional global leadership research can help select and refine training tools and methods which help to prepare and train expatriates for international assignments. A reasonable first step in training and development is to conduct a self-awareness assessment on participants. A self-awareness assessment is an exercise that engages participants to reflect on their own values, attitudes, and behaviors, and can be combined with 360-degree feedback to help make leaders aware any cultural barriers which may exist (Cumberland, Herd, Alagaraja, & Kerrick, 2016).

Cross-cultural training is another method that is often used by organizations to help leaders prepare for expatriate assignments. But while cross-cultural training is usually helpful to leaders (Bader et al., 2018), it is also likely inadequate to fully prepare them for the adjustment of living, working, and leading abroad (DeNisi & Griffin, 2019). A more comprehensive approach for preparation of expatriates is to use didactic training techniques, which includes classroom learning, formal education programs, and self-learning. Also, providing expatriates with experiential opportunities is good preparation for international assignments. For instance, short, global assignments can help individuals start to develop responsible global behaviors. Business trips, the opportunity to work on global teams, and even volunteering in another country can help to build global capability prior to immersing someone on a longer-term expatriate assignment (Rosenbusch & Terrell; 2013; Cumberland et al., 2016).

Another way that global leadership research can help with expatriation is to demonstrate how expatriate assignments can be translated into positive leadership growth exercises for employees, keeping in mind that the goals of the assignment still need to be realized. Strong organization, concise planning, and frequent communication by human resources professionals are critical towards making the expatriate experience into a leadership and growth opportunity and making the experience enjoyable overall (DeNisi & Griffin, 2019). Human resources professionals need to take active roles in managing the expatriate process, including viewing expatriation as a continuous career development exercise instead of a one-time task and opportunity to send someone abroad (Mehore & Gankar, 2016). While time-consuming, human resources professionals should take ownership of expatriate assignments and have a stake in expatriates' success. They must identify gaps in expatriates' careers and apprise them on potential future global assignments, aligning them with opportunities that will be challenging and provide career growth. Frequent communication and checking in is vital for expatriate success. Cole and Nesbeth (2014) found inadequate company communication, insufficient preparation, and inadequate and inflexible policies to be key reasons why expatriate assignments fail.

Conduct Better Change Management

More research on global leadership can help organizations conduct better change management. Change management, as defined by PROSCI, a leading management consulting firm, is the discipline that guides how individuals are equipped and supported to successfully adopt change in order to drive organizational outcomes and success (Prosci, n.d.). Change management is based on behavioral science technology, and provides a structured and intentional approach to move organizations from a current state to a desired end-state. Change management efforts can be domestic or global in scope (Mendenhall et al., 2013). Global change management includes international mergers and acquisitions, global expansion, and the implementation or integration of global policies and technologies. More research on global leadership can help organizations succeed with global change in a number of ways. For instance, it can help to clarify how leaders' behavior influences and impacts global change efforts. Leaders' behaviors should not be underestimated as to the impact it can have on global change initiatives. Active and visible sponsorship by senior leaders has been cited consistently by PROSCI as the top contributor to success with change management initiatives (Prosci, n.d.). Leaders' behavior sends signals to employees as to what is important and where to place focus, including in dealing with change initiatives (Yukl, 2010).

Based on early studies on behavioral leadership, leaders can primarily influence change by initiating more structure and by influencing people (Bass, 1985). One idea for additional global leadership research is to analyze which of these approaches, and to what extent, is most impactful for change management. For instance, if it was found that additional structure had more positive influence on the adoption of new global, operating procedures in one country, then more time could be spent on managing the processes for change, which includes developing and maintaining performance standards, meeting deadlines and establishing communication protocols. Conversely, if influencing people and relationship-building was found to be more effective in a different country, then leaders could place more emphasis on workers' job satisfaction, expressing appreciation for performance, motivating individuals and listening.

Going hand-in-hand with understanding leaders' behavioral impact on change management is better understanding of senior leaders' overall impact on the success or failure of global change efforts. While gaining senior management buy-in is certainly not new for change management, having visible and engaged leaders still seems to be a problem because leaders themselves often times experience stress and anxiety with change and are not eager to embrace it (Clemmer, 2021). Some leaders make mistakes in assuming that transformational change will occur through excellent management of processes and people or with the implementation of a new technology instead of getting involved themselves. Others may choose to defer leadership altogether, causing employees to disengage (Kim & Mauborgne, 2014). Additional research can provide insight on the impact that engaged senior leaders have on change management, or the downside of disengaged leaders. It could also provide a better understanding of what it means to be actively engaged, and help to bring forward novel approaches to leading global change management efforts.

John Kotter, in his 1996 noteworthy book *Leading Change*, provided insight on the importance of creating a successful leadership coalition for change, and noted that failing to create a powerful guiding coalition is a major error that is often committed. A powerful leading coalition consists of individuals who possess power - in terms of formal titles, reputations, information and expertise, and the capacity for leadership. Influential leaders are critical for change to take place because they help to establish overall direction for key projects, align people correctly, and successfully motivate and inspire them. Kotter's model has been used successfully in a variety of industries, even in policing, where it has been applied recently to help address challenges in homeland security information sharing (Lambert, 2019).

Third, the power dynamic of leaders and authority needs to be examined in more detail in the context of global change management. Specifically, new research could glean insight on the power and influence needed to successfully drive change, including the type of power, how the power is exercised, and the influence the leader has on subordinates, peers, and superiors (Yukl, 2006). From a global perspective, cultural dimensions of other nations would need to be considered in tandem with the power dynamic. It is likely that global leaders who demonstrate a lower power distance dynamic would be most successful with global change management initiatives. According to Morrison (2001), global leaders who demonstrate affective traits and behaviors are more likely to have success. Such traits include embracing other cultures, connecting with people from other cultures and taking an interest in them, trusting them, and demonstrating integrity.

One final recommendation relating to change management and international leadership research is to expand understanding of existing change management models to determine their applicability and fit on a global level. For instance, it would be insightful to analyze Kotter's (1996) eight-stage process for leading change and its applicability in different regions of the world. Based on the skills and dimensions identified in leadership research to be an effective global leader, many of the stages would seem to align well in many regions and cultures. Empowering employees, creating a guiding coalition, and generating short-term wins are some examples. However, creating a sense of urgency, and how is this accomplished, might prove to be more difficult in some regions where timing and the meaning of deadlines are often misunderstood (Varner & Beamer, 2011). ADKAR, the change management model developed by PROSCI, is another popular change management model that could be analyzed on a global scale. ADKAR is an acronym for awareness, desire, knowledge, ability, and reinforcement, and represent five key building blocks for implementing change (Prosci, n.d.).

Help Spur Innovation

Another benefit that can be realized with additional international leadership research is to help organizations spur innovation. While spurring innovation is a longer-term proposition, the potential is great because international leaders are in unique positions to help solicit creativity and innovation from their global teams. Also, parallels exist between the competencies needed for effective global leadership and leaders who serve as champions and promoters of innovation.

The inherent diversity of international teams is positive for innovation (Hewlett, Marshall & Sherbin, 2013). Individuals from different cultures have unique viewpoints and influences that have shaped their personalities and thinking throughout their lives, and this is a vast resource that needs to be tapped. Innovative leaders must learn to draw from their team members' distinctive backgrounds and experiences to solve problems, develop new ideas, and uncover innovative solutions, many of which may not be thought of in domestic or homogeneous settings (Amabile & Khaire, 2008;

Hewlett, Marshall & Sherbin, 2013). Leaders need to be developed to embrace diversity as an advantage and adopt a leadership style that encourages open communication and celebrates sharing of diverse ideas, even if they end up failing. They should take strategic steps to promote innovation by hiring dissimilar talent, developing innovative partnerships, and making innovation a visible strategic goal. Overall, they need to spend less time managing processes and more time finding ways to create a dynamic team and environment where individuals are free to share their thoughts (Amabile & Khaire, 2008). But promoting innovation through diversity is not just a concept, it yields real business results. A McKinsey report which examined 366 public companies in a variety of countries and industries found that more gender and ethnically diverse groups performed significantly better than homogenous groups. Also, study found that more diverse companies developed significantly more innovative ideas and had less inherent biases that contributed to similar thinking than more homogenous organizations (Boozer, 2020).

L'Oreal is an example of a company that adopted unique approaches to harness innovation. L'Oreal has over 3,000 research and innovation positions on staff across its global workforce and maintains a visible commitment to launching highly innovative and personalized products. The company launched the L'Oreal Technology Incubator in 2012, where employees collaborate with foremost leaders in academia, technology, and design across multiple countries, helping to bring forward new ideas (L'Oreal, 2019). L'Oreal visibly endorses an open innovation strategy that connects itself to a global ecosystem of startups and partnerships. It has successfully tapped into its global and multi-cultural talent to gain a competitive advantage. Since the late 1990s, the L'Oreal Paris brand specifically targeted and nurtured a pool of managers with mixed cultural backgrounds to help them serve regional and national markets. They then built product development teams around the multi-cultural managers. This approach has been extremely successful, and has helped L'Oreal in numerous ways. For instance, it has helped to identify new product opportunities, assist with cross-cultural communication, and adapt products, services and business models to local conditions (Doz & Hong, 2013).

Effective global leaders have massive potential to spur innovation due to the similarities that are evident between the competencies of effective global leaders and those who promote innovation. Thus, as leaders develop and gain global leadership competency they will also be building themselves up to serve as promoters of innovation. For instance, Conger and O'Neil's (2012) aforementioned competencies in their global leadership capability framework are all positive for building an innovative culture: (a) demonstrating a catalytic, or collaborative learning style, (b) an entrepreneurial spirit, (c) a sense of adventure, and (d) a responsiveness to cultural differences. Further, the building blocks of Thunderbird's Global Mindset Inventory align well with increasing innovative capacity, as they include comfort with risk-taking, the ability to collaborate and engage with others, a quest for adventure, and a willingness to test one's ability (Thunderbird, n.d.). Ding's model lists innovative thinking as one of its five main components for successful global leadership (Ding, 2018).

Another parallel identified between global leadership research and innovation is networking capability. The ability to build and utilize networks has been found to be critical for both innovation (Barsh, Capozzi, & Davidson, 2008; Chesbrough, 2003; Hemphala & Magnusson, 2012) and effective global leadership (Conger & O'Neill, 2012; Javidan & Walker, 2012). Regarding networking for innovation, Barsh, Capozzi, and Davidson (2008) found that well-developed connects and networks actually had a greater impact on innovation than individuals' intelligence and creativity. Chesbrough (2012) noted a shift to a more open way of innovating due to more comfort with knowledge-sharing and a realization that not all innovative efforts will come from within organizations. From a global leadership perspective, effective networking is key as well. Effective global leaders recognize the need to network and build successful relationships and with key stakeholders, both inside and outside of the organization. They do so by establishing trust, demonstrating cultural literacy and validating their expertise (Conger & O'Neill, 2012).

Further Understanding of Leadership Styles Across Societies

More international research is essential for better understanding of leadership styles and their effectiveness in countries across the globe. The findings will help organizational leaders understand which leader attributes, qualities and behaviors will be most useful in engaging employees and facilitating high performance in various regions. Culture will influence what types of leaders' styles will be most effective (DeNisi & Griffin, 2019), and more research on leadership and culture is vital to understanding this dynamic in more detail.

The Global Leadership and Organizational Behavior Effectiveness (GLOBE) study, is a large and important research project that examined the interrelationships between societal culture, societal effectiveness and leadership. The study was conducted across 62 different countries and sampled managers from a variety of industries (House, Hanges, Javidan, Dorfman & Gupta, 2004). The findings are extremely valuable in helping to define and clarify cultural differences across countries and understand how leaders' styles might be effective or ineffective. The researchers built upon Geert Hofstede's study of national culture by examining nine key dimensions of culture: (a) uncertainty avoidance, (b) assertiveness, (c) gender differences, (d) performance orientation, (e) humane orientation, (f) in-group collectivism, (g) institutional collectivism, (h) power distance, and (i) future orientation. They utilized leadership dimensions from their culturally implicit leadership theory (CLT) to understand the relationship between the dimensions of societal culture and certain leadership dimensions. The six leadership styles that were examined within the CLT were: (a) performance-oriented, or innovative and visionary leadership, (b) team-oriented leadership, (c) participative leadership, (d) humane leadership, which involves being empathetic, (e) autonomous leadership, which involves being concerned more with one's own actions and ideas without input from others, and (f) self-protective leadership, which places status on the "face" of the team. A key benefit from the massive research effort was the ability to determine the strength of association between the CLT leadership dimensions and the cultural dimensions. As an example, leaders who are charismatic, team oriented and participative are likely to thrive in a high-performance orientation society. Another important finding of the study was that culturally contingent leader characteristics tended to outnumber universal ones. All cultures universally agreed that some traits both make effective leaders and inhibit them. For instance, being honest and planning ahead were traits of effective leaders while being irritable, egocentric and ruthless inhibited effective leadership (Globe Project, n.d.).

Research like the GLOBE study has helped immensely with understanding cultural differences and their relationship to leaders' traits and behaviors. Other leadership styles, such as a transformational leadership style, should continue to be examined to determine its applicability in regions of the world in the context of the CLT. For example, it can be ascertained that transformational leaders would most likely thrive in societies that take a performance-oriented, team-oriented, and participative approach to leadership because they seek to establish strong connections with followers to motivate them. Also, transformational leaders want to empower followers instead of keeping them weak or dependent (Sendjaya, Sarros, & Santora, 2008). Transformational leaders seek to build organizational vision and shared focus based on trust and partnership. Followers often times feel admiration for transformational leaders, which motivates them to go above and beyond their normal work duties (Bass, 1985).

Transactional leadership is a more rigid and traditional leadership style where leaders keep formal distance from followers. Transactional leaders operate within strict command-and-control environments, like in the military, and rely on rewards for excellent performance and punishment for poor performance. Transactional leaders place emphasis on their own needs and feel they are in the best positions to make the key decisions for the organization (Yukl, 2010). Transactional leadership is still widely used and respected in various regions of the world. In the context of the CTL, countries of the world which place less focus on team-orientation and participative leadership and more focus on autonomy would endorse a more transactional leadership style. Hierarchical structures are likely to be effective in these countries, as transactional leaders are not likely to seek out followers for decision-making or input, but instead rely on them to maximize output and elevated performance (Bass, 1985).

Help Leaders Navigate Ethical Challenges

Additional international leadership research can help leaders navigate ethical challenges that come with working across many different societies. This is important, because although all leaders face ethical challenges, global leaders deal with them more frequently and in different ways than their domestic counterparts (DeNisi & Griffin, 2019). For example, global leaders face ambiguity with ethics as what is deemed moral in one country may be unscrupulous in another. Also, ethical standards, local laws, and headquarter organizational values may not be well aligned. Examples of business practices that vary drastically across the globe are health and safety concerns, equal opportunity and promotion, compensation, child labor, environmental issues, and even asking personal favors in business settings (Morrison, 2001). More research can help uncover ethical challenges that global leaders face in various countries and regions of the world, and suggest best practices for dealing with them.

Ethics is important to understand in detail on an international level because global organizations now more than ever are tasked to go beyond normal business operations to solve social issues such as human rights abuses and environmental issues, and thus practice responsible leadership (Mantikei, Christa, Sintani, Negara, & Meitiana, 2020). To combat some of the aforementioned pressures organizations have embraced certain themes and modified their strategic goals. Conscious capitalism, where financial goals and social goals are deemed complementary, is one example. A second example is promoting the "triple bottom line," where firms focus on profitability, the way people are treated, and protecting the environment (DeNisi & Griffin, 2019). Tackling these issues requires leaders who truly believe in them and are committed to them, both in their decision-making and their actions. It also requires new ways of thinking as it relates to conducting business and treating employees.

More international leadership research can assist with developing and enhancing formalized instruments for dealing with global ethical challenges. Instruments like these can help assess leaders' characters, feelings, and motivations, and provide valuable insight to them which they may not be aware. One such instrument is the Global Competence Aptitude Assessment (GCAA), which helps to measure levels of self-awareness, honesty with oneself, and the ability to be open-minded and respectful of diversity (Kaushik, Raisinghani, Gibson, & Assis, 2017). Other instruments help to place focus on a leader's ability to practice environmental stewardship and the ability to balance local and global perspectives (Mendenhall et al., 2013).

Some researchers have proposed that a link already exists between leadership capability and ethical behavior, and this needs to be explored further through research. For instance, Morrison (2001) suggested a link between ethics and three main leader competencies come forward in leaders of global companies: (a) the ability to be a good observer; (b) the ability to ask tough questions; and (c) the ability to understand what is core to the organization. Good observers were found to effectively observe and interpret behaviors, open up to people, and show empathy. They allow themselves to get close to people and build relationships, which helps people build trust in them and view them affectionately, diminishing the risk they will patronize any form of abuse. Second, ethical global leaders ask tough questions and put pressure on their organizations to operate ethically. They do so because they realize their global world is more complex, and is thus more susceptible to ethical traps and violations. Third, ethical leaders understand what are considered to be the core standards in the organization, and abide by them. This can be challenging at times because issues such as environmental concerns and even paying for gifts and dinners may hurt the company's competitiveness in certain regions of the world.

More international leadership research is to help uncover what it will take for global companies and their leaders to operate and behave ethically. Multi-national organizations need to build on advances that have already been made in behaving ethically and fostering social responsibility (Brenkert, 2019). They need to include a strong ethical component in their training and development programs for executives and hold their leaders accountable for their behavior. Leaders' behavior is vital because it sends a message to employees about what is considered right and wrong (Shieh, 2011). Leaders set the example, and if leaders make ethics a core value others are likely to follow (Kouzes & Posner, 2017).

Enhance Communication

Another way that global leadership research can assist organizations is to provide insight that enables leaders to communicate more effectively. Thoughtful communication is imperative for leaders to function and thrive in complex and difficult environments (Eldridge, 2020). Leaders need to communicate effectively to all levels of employees to send clear and concise messages that influence behavior and show employees where to place focus. Without effective communication it will be difficult for leaders to establish and cultivate meaningful relationships (Varner & Beamer, 2011).

Organizations need their global leaders to place emphasis on understanding culture in order to successfully communicate. At a basic level, culture is the shared values and beliefs of people, which permeate throughout the region and create a common value system (Shieh, 2011). Culture represents ways of behaving, feeling, thinking, and determining how things get done (Jaruzelski & Katzenbach, 2012). Culture is a complex phenomenon, and it takes time to understand the nuanced differences in foreign countries, all of which are taken for granted by locals. Language differences and managerial styles are communication elements that vary by culture. Organizations need to assess levels of cultural competency in their leaders and foster multi-cultural understanding and cultural sensitivity in order to successfully communicate and operate (Rosenbusch & Terrell, 2013). Organizations should develop leaders to be mindful of their communication in other cultures and countries to reduce misunderstandings, miscommunication and conflict at different levels (inter-/intra-organizational, interpersonal, within a group, etc.).

More research on global leadership and communication can help to highlight the importance communication has on conducting global business. Virtually everything is impacted one way or another by communication, and as the world has become increasingly interconnected, communication differences have become magnified, making effective communication even more vital (Lawrence, 2015). For instance, business negotiations are impacted by communication methods, and it is vital that leaders choose the most appropriate words when presenting conditions or terms (Ungson & Wong, 2008). Legal differences make communication difficult in other countries, and may alter the way leaders need to communicate and what may or may not be appropriate to communicate. Decision-making is impacted by communication methods and style, as is overall business messaging in various regions of the world. Nonverbal language in intercultural communication is important to understand as well. Items like eye contact, facial expressions, gestures, touching, and silence differ from country to country, and are complicated by the fact that different groups within a culture may use different nonverbal ques (Varner & Beamer, 2011).

More research on global leadership and communication can assist organizations to build a common global communications strategy. Such a strategy can help global leaders navigate the complex environment in which they operate. An effective global communications strategy starts with developing a concise and well-thought out mission statement that can convey the company's purpose and inspire followers (Lawrence, 2015). A second element of the strategy is to find ways to develop cohesive work teams, which helps to build relationships and help employees perform better together. Communicating outwardly to stakeholders and government officials is a third part of the strategy, which is typically longer-term and may take years to fully develop. Finally, promoting inter-cultural communication as core competency for leaders is imperative. In this way, companies can place emphasis and focus on the importance of tailored and specific messaging for their international leaders.

Ultimately, better communication can help organizations avoid conflict and misunderstandings and thus operate more effectively on a global level. Grooming leaders who are sensitive to cultural differences and who seek to build cohesion among a diverse group of employees and business partners is vital. Training leaders to pay attention to communication and informing them how communication is ubiquitous and impactful in global business settings will help them and their organization achieve their objectives. In addition, a specific global communication strategy can provide organizations with a strategic and targeted long-term approach towards reaching its intended audiences in a culturally sensitive way.

Facilitate High-Performing Global Teams

Another benefit of international leadership research is to utilize the findings to help global leaders build cohesive and effective work teams. This is essential in today's work environment where organizations evolve and grow and technology connects people across the globe. Developing high-performing global teams is no easy task. Global teams have inherent challenges due to the fact that members come from different backgrounds and cultures, work in different physical locations, and communicate differently. But effective global teamwork, if achieved, can be a huge competitive advantage. When people work together effectively on a team, their diverse perspectives open up opportunities not possible with one viewpoint (Rao & Weintraub, 2013). Also, effective teamwork combined with a continual learning has consistently shown to help organizations develop capabilities beyond their normal reach (Senge, 1990).

Additional research on international leadership can offer insightful feedback on global team composition and size, and how to set up a team for the best chance of success. Keller and Meaney (2017) posited that teams should be kept fairly small, constituting six to ten members. They found teams smaller than six members generated slower and poorer decisions due to a lack of diversity and bandwidth, but teams larger than ten members tended to be ineffective because sub-teams started to form, which encouraged divisive behavior. Larger teams also may find it challenging to include everyone's opinions in the group's decisions, which makes it difficult to foster broad participation and bring out diverse viewpoints (Govindarajan & Gupta, 2001). Selection of team members is important for team composition, and people should be selected based on managing and technical skills but also social skills, which can help with facilitating participation and resolving conflicts (Champion, 2015).

More international leadership research can help bring forward ways to enhance leaders' cultural awareness and competency to build effective teams. Studies have demonstrated a positive relationship between the degree of cross-cultural competence of their leaders and multinational team performance (Matveev & Nelson, 2004). Leaders who can demonstrate high levels of cultural competency are more likely to build successful global teams because they seek out opportunities to collaborate with their international team members, network, and go out of their way to try and find ways to bring people together. They view the diversity of the international team as an advantage instead of a liability, and foster strong teamwork by showing empathy towards team members' viewpoints while making concerted efforts to include them in decision-making (Rosenbusch & Terrell, 2013).

The effect of technology on global team effectiveness is another area that should be researched further, especially as virtual teams are commonplace in global business today. Many employees now work completely remotely or from their homes, a work-practice that has been accelerated by the Covid-19 crisis. But while this dynamic may seem to be damaging for teamwork, web-conferencing systems like Zoom may have actually shown to help bring people together (Hacker, Vom Brocke, Handali, Otto & Schneider, 2020). This may be positive for global teamwork because organizations were forced to adapt and implement technology to help people stay connected. It is worth researching further because newer technology like web-conferencing may help alleviate some of the typical problems associated with global team membership, such as global team members feeling isolated and alone (Champion, 2015).

Conclusion

Effectively managing through the complexities in a fast-paced and ever-changing globalized world is difficult, but without effective leaders it is virtually impossible. There is no doubt that more international leadership research is needed, not only to advance knowledge and understanding in the field, but also to continue to uncover and refine real-world benefits for multi-national organizations. The possibilities are vast.

I imagine a utopian organization where all eight benefits listed in this chapter can be fully realized in multi-national organizations with additional research and findings. In this scenario, an organization has used best-practice research to define a visible list of global competencies which align with the corporate strategy and are embedded throughout the organization, helping to identify, train and develop future global leaders. Its human resources staff manages the expatriate process efficiently and assists leaders with career development and repatriation. The organization conducts excellent change management with engaged and fearless leaders and has high-performing global teams who regularly stay in contact with one another and offer diverse viewpoints in an open and risk-free environment. Innovation is a core competency and is embedded within the corporate culture, and global leaders are adept at understanding and adapting their leadership style according to region. Leaders demonstrate strong ethics, and communication is done in a thoughtful and strategic way, taking cultural differences into consideration.

Is the scenario listed above possible? Maybe, but even it if is more research will be needed, because globalization is constantly changing and global leaders in the 21st century are asked to do more. Modern leaders must not only effectively lead their global organizations but also take a cosmopolitan outlook in their mission. Ethical treatment of people, social injustices, mass migration, climate change, and dealing with a worldwide pandemic are some of the challenges global leaders face today. For all of the aforementioned reasons, and others, there may never be a better time to tout the need for more international leadership research to develop effective and engaged global leaders. It is an absolute must.

References

Amabile, T. M., & Khaire, M. (2008). Creativity and the role of the leader. *Harvard Business Review*, 10, 100–110.

Bader, K., Froese, K., & Kraeh, A. (2018). Clash of cultures? German expatriates'' work-life boundary adjustment in South Korea. *European Management Review*, 15(3), 357–374.

Baldwin, R. (2018, May). *Why will future globalization be so different* [Video]. Ted Conferences. https://www.ted.com/talks/richard_baldwin_why_will_future_globalisation_be_so_different.

Baldwin, R. (2019). Globalisation 4.0 and the future of work. *Economistas*, 63–75.

Barsh, J., Capozzi, M., & Davidson, J. (2008). Leadership and innovation. *The McKinsey Quarterly*, 1, 37–47.

Bass, B. M. (1985). *Leadership and performance beyond expectations*. Free Press.

Boozer, J. (2020, Feb.). The military finds strength in its diversity. *National Defense*, 106(795), 4.

Brenkert, G. (2019). Mind the gap! The challenges and limits of (global) business ethics. *Journal of Business Ethics, 155*, 917–930.

Champion, D. (2015, June 22). The leadership behaviors that make or break a global team. *Harvard Business Review, 4*.

Chesbrough, H. W. (2003). *Open business models: How to thrive in the new innovation landscape.* Harvard Business School Press.

Chesbrough, H. W. (2012). Open innovation: Where we've been and where we're going. *Research Technology Management, 55*(4), 20–27.

Clemmer, J. (2021). Thrive in turbulent times with agile leadership: Change management is an oxymoron. *Leadership Excellence, 38*(1), 16–19.

Cole, N., & Nesbeth, K. (2014). Why do international assignments fail? *International Studies of Management and Organization, 44*(3), 66–79.

Collings, D., Scullion, H., & Caliguiri, P. (2019). *Global talent management* (2nd ed.). Routledge.

Conger, J., & O'Neill, K. (2012). Building the bench for global leadership. *People & Strategy, 35*(2), 52–57.

Cumberland, D., Herd, A., Alagaraja, M., & Kerrick, S. (2016). Assessment and development of global leadership competencies in the workplace: A review of literature. *Advances in Developing Human Resources, 18*(2), 301–317.

DeNisi, A., & Griffin, R. (2019). *HR5.* Cengage.

Deters, J. (2017). *Talent management: Successful selection of global leadership talents as an integrated process.* Emerald.

Ding, H. (2018). New era: Collaborative global leadership model. *International Journal of Innovation and Research in Educational Sciences, 5*(1), 82–87.

Doz, Y., & Hong, H. J. (2013, June). L'Oreal masters multiculturalism. *Harvard Business Review.* https://hbr.org/2013/06/loreal-masters-multiculturalism.

Eldridge, C. (2020). Communication during crisis: The importance of leadership, messaging, and overcoming barriers. *Nursing Management, 51*(8), 50–53.

Falconer, T. (2014, Feb/Mar). Discovering and developing global mind-sets: Global competencies inventory (GCI) & intercultural effectiveness scale (IES). *Human Resources Magazine, 18*(6), 5.

Feitosa, J., Kramer, W., Kramperth, A., Kreutzer, C., & Salas, E. (2014). Expatriate adjustment: Considerations for selection and training. *Journal of Global Mobility, 2*(2), 134–159.

Globe Project. (n.d.). Retrieved January 10, 2020, from https://globeproject.com/.

Govindarajan, V., & Gupta, A. (2001). Building an effective global business team. *MIT Sloan Management Review, 42*(4), 63–71.

Hacker, J., Vom Brocke, Handali, Otto, & Schnedier. (2020). Virtually in this together – how web-conferencing systems enabled a new virtual togetherness during the COVID-19 crisis. *European Journal of Information Systems, 29*(5), 563–584.

Hemphala, J., & Magnusson, M. (2012). Networks for innovation – but what networks and what innovation? *Creativity and Innovation Management, 21*(1), 3–16.

Hewlett, S. A., Marshall, M., & Sherbin, L. (2013). How diversity can drive innovation. *Harvard Business Review, 12*, 30.

House, R., Hanges, P., Javidan, M., Dorfman, P., & Gupta, V. (2004). *Culture, leadership and organizations. The GLOBE study of 62 societies.* Sage.

Huang, C., He, C., & Zhai, X. (2020). The approach of hierarchical linear model to exploring individual and team creativity: A perspective of cultural intelligence and team trust. *Mathematical Problems in Engineering,* 1–10. doi:10.1155/2020/2025140

Hui, Z. (2019). BRI ushering in a new type of globalization and global governance. *China Today, 68*(7), 28–31.

Jaruzelski, B., & Katzenbach, J. (2012). Building a culture that energizes innovation. *Financial Executive, 28*(2), 32–35.

Javidan, M., Bullough, A., & Dibble, R. (2016). Mind the gap: Gender differences in global leadership self-efficacies. *The Academy of Management Perspectives, 30*(1), 59–73.

Javidan, M., & Walker, J. (2012). A while new mindset for leadership. *People & Strategy, 35*(2), 36–42.

Kaushik, R., Raisinghani, M., Gibson, S., & Assis, N. (2017). The global aptitude assessment model: A critical perspective. *American Journal of Management, 17*(5), 81–86.

Keller, S., & Meaney, M. (2017, June). High-performing teams: A timeliness leadership topic. *The McKinsey Quarterly,* 1–7.

Kets de Vries, M. (2005). *Global executive leadership inventory.* Pfeiffer.

Kets de Vries, M. (2016). *Telling fairy tales in the boardroom: How to make sure your organization lives happily ever after.* Palgrave Macmillan.

Kim, W., & Mauborgne, R. (2014, May). Blue ocean leadership. *Harvard Business Review,* 1–14.

Kleine, M., & Minaudier, C. (2019). Negotiating under political uncertainty: National elections and the dynamics of international cooperation. *British Journal of Political Science*, *49*(1), 315–337.

Kotter, J. P. (1996). *Leading change*. Harvard Business Review Press.

Kouzes, J., & Posner, B. (2017). *The leadership challenge. How to make extraordinary things happen in organizations* (6th ed.). John Wiley & Sons, Inc.

Lambert, D. (2019). Addressing challenges to homeland security information sharing in American policing: Using Kotter's leading change model. *Criminal Justice Policy Review*, *30*(8), 1250–1278.

Lawrence, T. (2015, May). Global leadership communication: A strategic proposal. *Creighton Journal of Interdisciplinary Leadership*, *1*(1), 51–59.

L'Oreal. (2019, August 5). *L'Oréal named to fast company's inaugural list of the 50 best workplaces for innovators* [Press release]. https://www.prnewswire.com/news-releases/loreal-named-to-fast-companys-inaugural-list-of-the-50-best-workplaces-for-innovators-300896395.html.

Mantikei, B., Christa, U. R., Sintani, L., Negara, D. J., & Meitiana. (2020). The role of responsible leadership in determining the triple-bottom-line performance of the Indonesian Tourist Industry. *Contemporary Economics*, *14*(4), 463–473.

Matveev, A. V., & Nelson, P. E. (2004). Cross cultural communication competence and multicultural team performance perceptions of Americans and Russian managers. *International Journal of Cross Cultural Management*, *4*(2), 253–270.

Mehore, B., & Gankar, S. (2016). Better process leads to peak performance: A role of human resources management function towards expatriation and repatriation process – An overview through existing literature. *Journal of Indian Management Research and Practices*, *1*, 1–12.

Mendenhall, M. E., Osland, J. S., Bird, A., Oddou, G. R., Maznevski, M. L., Stevens, M. J., & Stahl, G. K. (2013). *Global leadership* (2nd ed.). Routledge.

Morrison, A. (2001). Integrity and global leadership. *Journal of Business Ethics*, *31*, 65–76.

Osland, J. (2008). Global leadership. *AIB Insights*, 10–11.

Pedersen, P., & Pope, M. (2010, November). Inclusive cultural empathy for successful global leadership. *American Psychologist*, *65*, 841–854.

Prosci. (n.d.). Retrieved January 10, 2020 from https://www.prosci.com/adkar/adkar-model.

Rao, J., & Weintraub, J. (2013). How innovative is your company's culture? *MIT Sloan Management Review*, *54*(3), 29–37.

Rosenbusch, K., & Terrell, S. (2013). Global leadership development. What global organizations can do to reduce leadership risk, increase speed to competence, and build global leadership muscle. *People & Strategy*, *36*(1), 40–46.

Sendjaya, S., Sarros, J. C., & Santora, J. C. (2008). Defining and measuring servant leadership behavior in organizations. *Journal of Management Studies*, *45*(2), 402–424. doi:10.1111/j.1467-6486.2007.00761.x

Senge, P. M. (1990). *The fifth discipline*. Currency.

Shehzad, M., Anjum, S., & Furquan, M. (2019). Leadership traits and their effects on employees. *Advances in Social Sciences Research Journal*, *6*(7), 324–329.

Shieh, C. (2011). Management innovation, corporation core competence and corporate culture: The impact of relatedness. *Applied Economics Letters*, *18*(12), 1121–1124. doi:10.1080/13504851.2010.526567

Society for Human Resources Management. (May 1, 2017). Retrieved January 24, 2021 from https://www.shrm.org/resourcesandtools/tools-andsamples/toolkits/pages/cms_010358.aspx.

Thunderbird. (n.d.). Retrieved January 10, 2020 from https://thunderbird.asu.edu/faculty-and-research/najafi-global-mindset-institute/global-mindset-inventory/three-capitals.

Ungson, G. R., & Wong, Y. Y. (2008). *Global strategic management*. M. E. Sharpe, Inc.

Varma, A., Stroh, L. K., & Schmit, L. B. (2001). Women and international assignments: The impact of supervisor-subordinate relationships. *Journal of World Business*, *36*(4), 380–388.

Varner, I., & Beamer, L. (2011). *Intercultural communication in the global workforce* (5th ed.). McGraw-Hill.

Venter, E. (2016). Bridging the communication gap between generation y and the baby boomer generation. *International Journal of Adolescence and Youth*, *22*(4), 497–507.

Vogt, I. J. (2019). The impact of the financial crisis on European attitudes toward immigration. *CMS*, *7*(24). doi:10.1186/s40878-019-0127-5

Yukl, G. A. (2006). *Leadership in organizations* (6th ed.). Prentice Hall.

Yukl, G. A. (2010). *Leadership in organizations* (7th ed.). Prentice Hall.

33

Chronicles of an International Leadership Researcher

Personal and Professional Benefits of ILR

Amanda S. Wickramasinghe

Introduction

International leadership research encompasses a variety of areas, including international policy, global narratives, and thought processes that help us understand the different dimensions of the world (Parker & Karlsson, 2014). Princess Diana, Mother Theresa, and Nelson Mandela – such profound international leaders – have made powerful impacts in our societies, and as a world, we are thankful for their contributions. Through their influence, the needle on leadership has moved by bringing awareness to international issues such as hunger, poverty, disease, segregation, injustices, and the importance of kindness and caring. International leadership research helps to shine a much-needed light on the complex issues we are encountering as a global community.

The international community is interconnected. Local economies are impacted by the global economy. For instance, the cell phones we purchase at a local store are usually researched, designed, manufactured, and distributed from different countries and involve collaboration across multiple countries. Conducting international leadership research is becoming more prevalent as economies and corporations are becoming more globally oriented. Since most companies have similar approaches to product development, leadership has had to evolve and transcend these borders and boundaries (Freshwater et al., 2006). As the world is shrinking there is more of a demand for international leadership research. Conducting such research gives rise to many personal and professional benefits.

The best types of personal and professional benefits consist of helping researchers see beyond their own horizons and make connections to understand how new knowledge applies to real-world situations (Bush & Jackson, 2002). For example, all types of research focus on discovering new methods and approaches that can enhance our daily lives. With the expansion of the global economy, international leadership research is increasingly relevant as it provides a foundation for nations to work together from a macro and micro level to solve challenges such as import/export of goods, services across borders, and pressing issues such as solving climate change and reducing gender inequality. According to the United Nations' environmental program, or-ganizations such as the World Health Organization (WHO), United Nations (UN) and other global corporations are working together to remedy issues by using international leadership research (un.org, 2021). We need global leadership to address these demands and complexities.

DOI: 10.4324/9781003003380-33

In the year 2020, there were calls for change and action with protests based on social and racial inequalities and a global pandemic causing an economic downfall (Detert & Roberts, 2020). Thus, we need international leaders to be resilient when leading through such challenging times (social injustice and global pandemics) and to knowledgeably collaborate across cultures and societies. Leaders also need to adopt to and understand new environments, while proposing long term solutions to systemic challenges.

Key elements of international leadership include fostering thinking patterns around global development topics such as world poverty, global hunger, global warming, global epidemics/pandemics, and racial inequality. International leaders must bring substantial creative thinking regarding global development (Parker & Karlsson, 2014). With this approach, international leadership research could provide an in-depth analysis and knowledge of how leaders in different countries mesh their cultural, political, business, and country-specific practices with their own individual leadership styles. This type of research can be utilized to support current leadership and to develop future leadership models for scholars and practitioners.

As an international leadership researcher, I have conducted multiple studies (on women and global leadership, work life balance, global competencies, cultural upbringing, virtual leadership globally, and cultural intelligence) with leaders worldwide. For this chapter, I focus on my experiences and journey as well as the professional and personal benefits of international leadership research (Ikenberry, 1996). It is important to note, that both my personal and professional benefits have overlapped; my personal benefits have transferred and shaped my professional growth, similarly, the professional benefits have impacted my personal development. The professional benefits include expanding knowledge about leadership within different countries, connecting with international leaders while increasing professional networks, and presenting research at international conferences (Parker & Karlsson, 2014). The personal benefits include recognizing and understanding cultural practices, maintaining an open mind, and developing a global mindset while traveling (Benabou & Tirole, 2000).

The narrative in this chapter addresses the benefits gained while conducting a qualitative phenomenological study of the work-life balance issues of women leaders. My research explored the lived experiences of Sri Lankan female leaders through semi-structured interviews. The underpinnings of the research were based on Giele's framework (Giele, 2008) and an instrument was developed through a series of interview questions to understand the challenges facing women who were practicing work life balance. I was curious to understand the institutional barriers and other issues facing Sri Lankan women leaders, such as the need to balance their work and family responsibilities. I chose Sri Lanka because I was born there, and most of my life has been in and still is in the United States, conducting the study gave me a newfound perspective on Sri Lankan women leaders. I found that Sri Lankan women leaders have ample opportunities to follow their dreams because education (The Education Act of 1940) is entirely free (Wickramasinghe, 2020). Moreover, as I engaged in research to inquire how they managed work and family responsibilities, I found that they valued family more than work (Wickramasinghe, 2020).

Another example was a qualitative phenomenological study of global leaders exploring the lived experiences of international leaders in multiple countries including Singapore, Germany, South Africa, Sudan, Greece, India, and the United States. The candidates were selected based on the following criterion sampling: 10 years of international experiences and having worked and lived in multiple countries (Creswell, 2014). The study utilized an interview process comprised of open-ended questions to gather rich data sets. Participants represented Fortune 500 companies, non-governmental organizations, and the United Nations, as well as leadership consulting firms and global universities. The study aimed to understand how global competencies shaped participants' leadership styles; additionally, the study analyzed participants' cultural upbringing and whether this factor contributed to their leadership skills (Bush & Jackson, 2002).

Often, to truly understand the professional and personal benefits of international research, there must be a time for reflection (Engelbrecht et al., 2016). I kept a journal throughout my travels and documented adventures, lessons, and life-changing moments. Journaling was an integral process to self-reflect and identify with special moments that impacted my life, such as riding an elephant in Sri Lanka, eating local delicacies in Jamaica, and participating in high tea events in London, England. It also helped with examining other positive and negative insights that I experienced while I was conducting foreign research. For example, some of the positive insights were meeting various leaders; conversely, the negative experiences were the ways that travel is sometimes unpleasant, tiring (and costly). There were also life lessons such as realizing that not all leaders are open to sharing personal information during the interview process which limits data gathering. Further, I realized that some leaders had lesser knowledge about leadership, it seemed that they were naturally born leaders. Furthermore, journaling gave me new insights for future research such as gender equality, reducing patriarchal systems, and improving the quality of education in developing nations. Additionally, there were several lessons from mistakes I had made, and from the journal I was able identify mistakes and pitfalls of my research methodology, approaches, and cultural nuances and this enabled me to reflect on how I can improve.

Professional Benefits of International Leadership Research

International leadership research not only benefits scholars and leaders, but there are professional benefits for the leadership researchers themselves. By traveling and engaging with communities in different countries to pursue such research studies, and by conducting interviews, administering questionnaires and surveys, and engaging in observations of leaders, you come to understand different and potentially even new patterns of leadership. As a researcher, you gain specific leadership knowledge and even expertise, all of which can help you advance your career (Loitch, 2019). For instance, while engaging in conversations with leaders in Brussels, I learned the importance of keeping the message simple, especially when delivering speeches to a global audience. Keeping it simple helps a broader audience to understand your intended message; this has propelled my career to enable me to connect with a global audience.

My experience as a researcher has opened several doors professionally through researching multiple countries. These experiences have enhanced who I am as a person and who I will be in the future. They also have contributed to my development as a researcher and enhanced my career credentials. More specifically, international research has given me a chance to engage in a state of mind where the possibilities are enriching and where there is a constant cycle of discovery and growth. Additionally, conducting research has contributed to developing competencies such as cultural intelligence (CQ), cultural empathy, cultural fluency, learning about inclusivity and developing diversity consciousness. These skills are interconnected with professional growth and with the practice of leadership. Below, I discuss each of these elements in further detail.

Expanded Knowledge from Researched Countries

For me, the best part of conducting international leadership research is traveling to countries abroad (Ghemawat, 2005) and learning about a country in more depth, compared to just being a tourist and seeing things only on the surface. For example, from conducting research, I have learned so much about Sri Lanka. To enhance my research, I wanted to understand their rich history, customs, traditions, and national holidays. To gain an in-depth understanding, I read multiple history books, articles, journals, and even travel books such as Sri Lanka- Cultural Smart, National Geographic Traveler (country specific books) and Lonely Planet (country specific). Reading books about the rich history of the country allowed me to understand that there was an extensive history dating back to thousands of years prior to the colonization of Sri Lanka (the kingdom era) (De Silva, 2005; Schrikker, 2007; Wickremeratne, 1985). It is important to note that the country was colonized by the Dutch, Portuguese, and British, and this knowledge has served me well in my efforts to converse with Sri Lankan women leaders. These conversations benefited my research efforts because it allowed me to understand how to create instruments to conduct further research. While engaging in such conversations, I realized their perspectives, history, and struggles (in male-dominated work industries, women were responsible for the home and family responsibilities, dealing with sexual harassment, and inequity), which was advantageous as I analyzed data transcripts. They were impressed that I was well-versed in their cultural practices. For example, I learned about colonization, and how the history of the country impacted the upbringing of Sri Lanka's leaders. Because they were colonized by the British, their second language is English, which is taught in school from an early age. This fact benefited the country's economic development and connection to the world community and economy (De Silva, 2005; Wickramasinghe, 2020; Wickremeratne, 1985). However, the negative colonization consequences were severe as the colonizers absorbed the country's natural resources (gems and precious stones), ports, and prohibited Sri Lankans from governing their own country.

Additionally, ancient history about the kingdom and its leaders contributed to my overall view and understanding of Sri Lanka. Notably, all this new knowledge has helped me develop my own leadership frameworks and understanding of the ways that countries have different types of leadership styles in different eras (Bucher, 2015). Depending on the era and governance, not all leaders governed in the same direction, and there were multiple styles utilized. Additionally, I learned about the languages that are utilized in certain parts of the country, since different regions use different dialects (De Silva, 2005). The Sinhalese dialect is the primary language (the mother tongue) of Sri Lanka, and Tamil is found mostly in the Northern region of the country (De Silva, 2005). Certain parts of the country practice different religions (Boyle, 2009; De Silva, 2005). The primary religion is Buddhism, but you will also find devoted Christians, Hindus, and Muslims in Sri Lanka. Faith has significantly impacted Sri Lankan leaders and their principles. For example, when they open a new branch or a new location of a company, they have a Buddhist ceremony with multiple monks to bless new beginnings, and all the employees from all religions participate as a sign of respect (Boyle, 2009). Notably, all these experiences have enhanced my cultural intelligence and my ability to work across countries and borders. By having a thorough understanding of the languages, history, cultural nuances, and leadership styles of different places, this has enabled me to create new leadership frameworks that work specifically for Sri Lanka.

Furthermore, the education system in Sri Lanka is fascinating. I learned about the Free Education and Health Care Act, which was implemented after 1948 – once the country gained its independence from the British (Schrikker, 2007). Based on the research that I have conducted, I have learned about Sri Lanka in more depth than I could have just by reading a travel magazine or article. I have learned about how the country's government operates, its local and community contributions, and the guiding principles of the country, such as respect for adults. The mother figure is often seen as a goddess in the country (Wickramasinghe, 2020), which has implications for respecting women.

Overall, knowing the history of the country benefits a researcher professionally by learning to work there when given the opportunity. Understanding a country in a thorough manner will allow the researcher to collaborate with global companies within the country and understand study participants at a more nuanced level (Bush & Jackson, 2002). As a researcher, I appreciate a chance to travel and advance society through research, as well as to help those who are unable to travel to learn from a researcher's experiences, stories, and adventures (Ghemawat, 2005). All of this brings me to my trip to Canada.

I was in Ottawa, Canada, to present my research at an international leadership conference. One of the fondest memories of this specific conference is that I was sharing a panel discussion with two other scholars and another practitioner. One night, we made arrangements to meet for dinner to discuss our panel discussion. We met at a local Thai restaurant in Ottawa and had a splendid dinner where we shared a great meal, discussed the logistics and organization of our panel, and shared our stories. Our stories encompassed our leadership journeys, our mistakes, successes, and a few "aha" moments. What I found most profound about each of these leaders during our dinner conversation was their ability to be resilient. Each leader had worked in foreign countries, adjusted their leadership styles, adapted to new situations, and substantially rearranged their lives to pursue their dreams and travel the world. Listening to their stories gave me respect for each of their journeys and showed me the importance of resiliency and why it is essential to adapt. Recently, I extended an invitation to my colleagues from Ottawa to speak at a leadership seminar that I was hosting. She spoke of her experiences with international development (the struggles, the adjustments, and pivoting to new climates) and this certainly illustrated the nature of international development research work. By listening to her experiences, this has inspired my future research endeavors such as working in rural countries and adjusting my outlook. I would not have come across this experience had I not traveled to Ottawa and made it a point to get to know my colleagues and share our stories.

Research has given me opportunities to visit different countries with a purpose: to recognize how people live, understand their collective goals, cultural nuances, and histories, plus notice the differences in countries' infrastructures. I often return from my travels eager to share my memories (with students, mentors, families, friends, and other travel enthusiasts) to impart a spark in them for traveling and learning from other nations. Knowledge from these countries has given me new ideas for research proposals such as access to education for women and girls, and new methods to improve the quality of drinking water for new studies. It inspires me to work on grant writing with my research teams, which adds to my overall professional growth as an international researcher.

Connecting With International Leaders

Learning from international leaders is incredibly valuable personally and professionally. As an international leadership researcher, the greatest reward for me has been the adventures found while learning from leaders who are from diverse cultures and backgrounds. Researching international leaders through interviews and surveys gave me an insider's knowledge and access to understanding. For example, I learned what steps they take to manage a crisis and subsequent resolutions. Through conversations about their professional journeys and personal success stories along with their struggles, each of these leaders' ability to connect inspired me to continuously write about leadership theories within journals, through articles, and even books from the knowledge that I have acquired. Even better, the stories that were shared included the importance of leadership knowledge. From a young age, I was fascinated with how leaders worked, operated, and guided others. I was astonished by the amount of multitasking it requires to be a leader; I have now realized that one of the best professional benefits is learning leadership skills from other great leaders. Skills such as patience, empathy, resilience, agility, and creativity have served me well in my career. I also learned the negative aspects of poor leadership such as abuse of power, status, control, and dictatorship – which has served as lessons of what not to do in leadership; I was able to share this knowledge in my research.

Currently, with the popularity of social media, world news cycles, and various international platforms, different leaders are in the spotlight for both positive and negative reasons, and information is more readily available (Bailey & Schantz, 2017). Partly because of this, there is also more interest generated about leadership in other countries. Understanding global leadership styles requires in-depth analysis; therefore, a significant number of research studies should be conducted and developed about different types of leaders from various countries. Studies such as focusing on the leadership styles of different world leaders would be of professional benefit to a researcher trying to identify leadership characteristics. Passing down knowledge from a leader to a researcher is a critical part of leadership growth since "There may be benefits from sharing knowledge and experiences with colleagues from different backgrounds" (Skene, 2007, p. 1).

As a researcher who has conducted international leadership qualitative studies over the years, finding study participants was always difficult since not all leaders fall under the robust research criteria. For example, I met great leaders, but they have never engaged in international work. For one of my studies, the criteria for the participants consisted of 10 or more years of international work experience, and that itself reduced the number of qualified participants that I could interview, which of course, makes finding participants challenging (Creswell, 2014). The journey to recruit a study sample required a lot of patience, but often the enthusiasm for my research led to additional referrals for participants.

For example, through my conversation with colleagues, I learned a great deal about a particular female leader in the Sri Lankan automotive industry. They told me that she would be a perfect candidate for my study. I did some research, reviewed her profile on LinkedIn, and realized she indeed was an ideal study participant. Her LinkedIn profile revealed that we had several mutual connections, and I asked our mutual connection to make an initial introduction. I have noticed that it is always better to connect via mutual acquaintances to establish credibility, and to foster a sense of comfort and trust at the forefront of the research process (Barnard, 2018). At the end, she agreed to participate, and I was able to interview her successfully.

In another example, I was trying to reach a CEO of a prominent Fortune 500 global corporation. Although I emailed multiple times, I received no response. Very likely, this email went to junk mail or was ignored because the communication lacked that personal touch (even with my extensive credibility). I learned long ago that being persistent and patient pays off eventually. Therefore, I will continue to reach out and be proactive with my communication.

Some of the leaders I have interviewed for my global competencies study have given me multiple recommendations and personal connections and have made formal introductions to help reach other leaders. For example, a leader (whom I admire and have formed a relationship with) who works in South Africa learned that an individual he knows from Afghanistan would be an ideal candidate for my study. That individual works for an international nonprofit involved in solving global hunger. Thus, my contact from South Africa emailed his acquaintance from Afghanistan (and copied me on the email) and gave me a great introduction. With that, I was able to have another study participant, but now from Afghanistan.

Overall, networking is crucial in research work. It consists of meeting new people, developing friendships and continuous learning, and even collaborating on professional tasks (Barnard, 2018). Conducting international leadership research has given me a once-in-a-lifetime chance to meet people who are making great changes in the world. Some of these global leaders include past presidents of different countries, ambassadors, United Nations representatives, educators, best-selling authors, NGO leaders, and other company heads. Associating with these leaders and being in the same professional circles has opened many doors for me. The numerous conversations that I have had helped me learn from their successes and sometimes their failures. They have also connected me with others to develop new collaboration possibilities (Freshwater et al., 2006).

Expanding Leadership Knowledge

Studying leadership has given me the opportunity to learn by observing other leaders. From my latest study on the competencies of international leaders, I learned how they were raised, their cultures, and how their upbringing had led them to be who they are as leaders (Groysberg, Lee, Price, & Cheng, 2018). By listening to their leadership journeys, I noticed how they intuitively applied elements of servant leadership, transformational, or transactional leadership, depending on the situation. One of the study participants spoke to me about being culturally grounded and that it had served him well during his tenure as a global leader. He specifically emphasized that regardless of where he was in the world, he still remembered the values his parents taught him; he was therefore able to carry out his vision by being authentic and grounded in his traditional values and beliefs. Another leader shared the importance of remembering humble beginnings and the steps that she took to become a leader. The lesson behind this story is to remember your past and what you have learned so that you treat others with respect and decency (Weber, 2020). I have also learned how to overcome challenges like communication barriers, increase motivational levels and effectively work across boundaries from my research. One of my aspirations is to join the United Nations. Expending leadership knowledge through my own research has propelled me one step closer to the direction.

While working with faculty in Sri Lanka, I learned that their research styles are different from what I was taught from my Western research training. With that, I adapted to the Sri Lankan research methodologies. For example, Sri Lanka is a conservative country with strict cultural practices, and to carry out most research topics, many levels of approval must be acquired before commencing a study. Sometimes, specific topics might be considered controversial, and having an open mind to understand what is allowed in that specific country is necessary so that one does not disrespect local traditions. Although it is a natural tendency to pass judgment, international researchers should not let personal biases alter research efforts, especially for controversial topics (Ghemawat, 2005). Going through such an experience taught me to expand my leadership knowledge by being receptive to learning from others.

Chances to Collaborate & Build Relationships

Collaboration allows people to grow together (Freshwater et al., 2006), and to utilize and enhance their own skill set (Gino, 2019). This is how leaders can learn from each other and develop a unique perspective about accomplishing a task collectively. For example, I was recently asked to contribute a book chapter to one of my mentor's latest publications. She was also one of my professors that I sought guidance from. Our research aligned, and we started working on a paper where we get to collaborate and bridge our ideas together as well as interview global women leaders. Recently I met scholars at an international conference only to realize we had similar research interests and should work on a study together. Thus, I have partnered with them to conduct a study about women uplifting other women. Being proactive in building new connections in the past prepared me to look for and take advantage of new opportunities. As an international leadership researcher, I recommend that you keep your eyes open for research partners, and small or large projects, begin conversations with peers, merge or develop ideas, and put research thoughts together.

In any career, one of the most important aspects is the ability to build good relationships (Ibarra, 2015; Zalis, 2018). A great professional relationship could be an opportunity for mentorship, advocacy, sponsorship, and recommendations (Ibarra, 2015; Murphy et al., 2017; Zalis, 2018). In order to build strong successful relationships, you have to build trust and respect. When I was conducting my research with Sri Lankan leaders, I learned that trust and respect are essential in any part of the world (Frei & Morriss, 2020). Each culture has a different set of rules, traditions, cultural nuances, and celebrations that are adhered to and followed (Prentice, 2004). Respect must be given and received when working in an international context to demonstrate that you are genuinely interested in understanding your partner's culture and background (Loitch, 2019). However, the way cultural groups show respect differs. In India and Sri Lanka, respecting adults (parents, family, extended family, aunts, uncle, teachers, and the elderly) is taught from a young age and is part of the collective cultural values. When a teacher walks into the classroom, for example, all students stand up to show respect and greet teachers by saying good morning ma'am [or sir]. In Western parts of the world, when a teacher walks in, the standards are different, and you will not likely see the same behavior patterns as in the Eastern part of the world (Dial-Benton, 2012). By keeping such cultural differences and knowledge in mind, this will assist you as a researcher when working with international colleagues.

When researchers are respectful of cultural protocols and systems, potential international research partners are more likely to converse and share their thoughts. Once the foundation of mutual respect is established, it is more likely that collaborations and communication will develop along positive lines (Frei & Morriss, 2020).

Being respectful of each other is a great way to begin any relationship regardless of the relationship's objective. A few years back, as a doctoral student in a public policy course, I had a chance to listen to a guest speaker who was a former U.S. Ambassador. The speaker was a delightful gentleman and extremely experienced in international affairs. He had traveled to over 100 countries, worked in multiple international settings, and was heavily involved in humanitarian efforts. Six months later, our paths crossed in Brussels, Belgium. We were both attending the same international conference in Brussels and served on the same panel. While I was in Brussels, I received an opportunity to learn more about the ambassador and develop a friendship. In between conference sessions, I met with him and we discussed our common interests, professional work history, and personal upbringing. The conversation allowed us to build a relationship, no doubt partly because I was respectful of his time and listened intently when he was sharing his story. I appreciated that he took the time to listen to my story and learn about me as well. Before the conference was over, we had already created a friendship based on trust and respect. The lesson behind the story is always keep an open mind when building relationships (especially as an international leadership researcher) as you will never how these connections (and collaborations) will advance your professional life.

From International Conferences to Local Projects and Leadership Development Consulting

Conducting international research offers a chance to present your studies and findings at global conferences to a community of international peers. Belgium, Sri Lanka, Belize, and Canada are just a few countries where I was fortunate to attend and present at international conferences. In Belize, in addition to sharing my study about higher education and technology, I had an opportunity to work in Placentia, Belize to provide children in local towns with iPad technology to further their education. Learning about Belize and the country's roots and struggles, led me to help advance education in Placentia through the charity efforts conducted by the conference's board. I have been to Belize a number of times, and with each visit I learn something new about its culture, perspectives, and carefree (live free) attitude. Through my international leadership research and engagement with the local community in Belize, I realized that local children were so eager to learn but did not have the means (e.g., books, laptops, internet, and electricity). Through the conference board and outreach efforts, I was able to help some of these school children by donating laptops to advance their education - the best money I have ever spent.

International leadership research has inspired me to engage in leadership consulting where I could apply theories, models, and frameworks to benefit leadership across societies. As a scholar, I am able develop leadership plans such as change diagnosis implementation and interventions based on leadership research knowledge and experiences. This is all based on the experiences I have gained by traveling to other countries and conducting research with diverse leaders. These approaches have been tried and tested, and I can see why certain types of leadership work for certain situations. I can then utilize these approaches in my leadership development programs and create custom leadership training (Cummings & Worley, 2019). Leadership training programs such as country-specific foreign training – identifying cultural norms, how to greet others, food etiquette, how to develop diversity consciousness, inclusive leadership, advancing women's leadership policies, and effective communication channels for employees who are planning for international assignments.

As discussed above, the vast array of experiences with conducting international leadership research has afforded me multiple opportunities and numerous pathways. This allows me to engage in work that I find rewarding such as working with global teams, assisting with NGOs, creating classes for learning management systems, teaching graduate students about global leaders, and sharing the importance of incorporating cultural training and consulting in the human resources management and the importance of inclusivity.

Personal Benefits

All my international leadership research experiences have impacted my life both personally and professionally. The lessons I have learned have guided me as a professional, I have utilized those lessons in my daily decision making (career choices, life choices, and how to devote my time). Therefore, the lines are definitely blurred between personal and professional benefits – they are interconnected. Some of the personal benefits include understanding cultural practices, customs, and traditions; and, therefore, developing an open mind and a global mindset.

My professional life has changed who I am as a person, as I devoted most of my younger life to advancing my career. Thus, my personal life has become my professional life. Recently, I was interviewed for my work in international leadership research, and the interviewer asked me what I would be doing if I was not a leadership scholar. My response to the question was that I would be traveling around the world, hiking, experiencing different foods, meeting different people, and contributing more towards charity. Then, the interviewer responded by saying it seemed that my personal and professional life had integrated so much that it had become one. During the interview process, I realized that my career has never been a burden, rather it has always been quite rewarding. There are always some barriers such as stress, or long nights transcribing data from the interviews – I must say, transcribing and analyzing data are the most time-consuming parts of research.

Understanding Cultural Practices, Customs, and Traditions

Understanding cultural practices, customs, and traditions stems from the notion of successfully working across cultures (Triandis, 2006). Researchers need to realize the distinctions between cultural practices, customs, and traditions. Furthermore, researchers need to have cultural mindfulness, cultural awareness, and high levels of cultural quotient, which allows them to navigate across cultural settings and backgrounds successfully (Triandis, 2006).

For example, some foreign names have fascinating origins and may be difficult to pronounce for a non-native speaker. However, taking a few minutes to ask how to pronounce a name correctly not only shows respect and it also shows that you care to learn. By demonstrating these skills, one puts communication lines at ease. Furthermore, being competent and well-versed about different environments are critical.

One of my favorite parts of a new culture experience is trying new foods. In Belize, I recognized that some of their curries were made from coconut milk (that is similar to Sri Lankan curries). Through my personal curiosity, l learned that local cuisine in Belize was influenced by the Indian workers who were brought there by the British Empire during colonization (Sen, 2017). I have found that many cultures have more similarities than differences, especially with food and family celebrations. Much of my personal curiosity was influenced by international leadership research, as the research has opened my eyes to new perspectives, backgrounds, and foreign assignments. Finding similarities and also understanding the clear distinctions have greatly benefited me as an international leadership researcher.

Open Mindedness/Global Mindset

Being placed in situations where there is a great deal of uncertainty is common for international researchers. One of the greatest assets of international leadership research is for the researcher to understand the importance of keeping an open mind (Lord, 2015). Some of the most successful researchers of the 21st Century have accredited their successes to having an open mind (Lord, 2015). Having the ability to try something different, appreciate it, and adapt to it is important within the host country (Ghemawat, 2005).

Successful leaders who have developed a global mindset and are continuously expanding that understanding will enhance their ability to lead global entities. Global mindset is the ability to adapt to new regions regardless of personal biases and having a willingness to learn and discover new possibilities globally (Javidan, 2010). As Javidan (2010) stated, "Leaders who have a high level of global mindset are more likely to succeed in working with people from other cultures" (p. 2). I definitely find this to be true in my personal experience. I have learned to appreciate other cultures, norms, and principles of leading, and each of these factors have contributed to my global mindset development. Examples of this include working with teachers in remote villages and learning from them how to utilize limited resources. Additionally, this assists with working with the local/grassroot communities to advocate for education policies and implementing new education systems. During my research experiences, I have learned that some teachers and students in rural villages around world with the fewest resources such as internet, electricity, running water, and a lack of computers tend to complain less and try to do more with their limited resources. These lessons have opened my mind and shown me to be successful you do not necessarily need the latest resources, but people can do so much with so little. Rather than complaining, doing what I can with what I have is an important lesson.

A large part of having a global mindset is the ability to be comfortable in rather uncomfortable settings (Javidan, 2010). The more experience I gain by conducting research, the more comfortable I become in different, new, and unknown intercultural situations, whether I am approaching a leader or having a simple conversation with locals. At Glasgow University in Scotland, I visited a local café that served haggis. Haggis is a Scottish delicacy composed of sheep heart, liver, and lung; and I was a bit apprehensive to try it (Miller, 2019). However, remembering to be open minded – I ate the meal that ended up being quite delicious.

An international leadership researcher needs to have the skill set to collaborate with an international organization and cultivate global connections. Some of the steps I have taken to develop a global mindset are the following: learning multicultural personality traits, examining and understanding possible biases, being curious, and learning the importance of general adaptability as well as flexible leadership styles. A few years ago, in Beijing, China, I had to use an interpreter since I do not speak Mandarin. My interpreter was a delightful young woman, and I had the opportunity to get to know her quite well. She shared with me her life story, struggles, adventures, successes, and future aspirations. She was from a small village far away from Beijing but had come to Beijing for college and job opportunities, leaving her family and home behind. I was able to connect with her through empathy, by relating to her journey, and sharing my story with her as well.

In Sri Lanka, I learned to change my thinking process. Even though I was born a Sri Lankan, I was raised in Southern California. I did not have knowledge about Sri Lankan culture and did not comprehend how businesses are conducted and how the responsibilities of women leaders are demonstrated. Even after having recognized these differences, I had to learn to think like a Sri Lankan woman leader to truly embrace their daily struggles (experiencing male dominant societies, sexual harassment, and professional misconduct) and successes. This ability was not intuitive or natural but a result of my attempting to see life through local women's experiences, focusing on keeping my biases at check, and keeping an open mind.

Some of these women traveled miles to get to work and had to wake up at 4:00 in the morning, cook lunch for the entire family, prepare the children to go to school, and take care of the chores. I learned that a lunch is composed of rice and multiple decadent and delicious curries that are uniquely packed for each family member versus in the Western part of the world where perhaps a ham and cheese sandwich or a peanut butter and jelly sandwich is considered sufficient.

Adaptability is critical to an open mind. Adaptability allows a researcher to adjust their actions and adjust to the current situation. Without adaptability, researchers remain stagnant and unable to move forward. Often, with adaptability, there is competitive advantage. Researchers who are open to change and adapting to changing environments have an advantage compared to others who are resistant to change. Researchers who are receptive to adapting often have an opportunity to explore alternatives, examine risk and uncertainties, change traditional structures, and leverage existing resources (Reeves & Deimler, 2011). One of my original research proposals was exploring the lived experiences of female global leaders, and after much deliberation with my mentor, she informed me that by just researching women, I was alienating an entire population. Thus, she suggested that I adapt and rethink my research to include men and reform the leadership framework. By doing so, I adapted to a new research setting to make my findings applicable to a larger global community. This is a perfect example of adapting and be open to new ideas and perspectives.

Over the years, I have realized that things do not necessarily go according to plan when conducting international leadership research. Ultimately, as a researcher you must adjust accordingly (Prentice, 2004). For example, my research team is currently in the process of working with a university in Nigeria for which we are developing training modules and research methodologies for leadership. Although we had a robust outline in terms of research and development, we realized after our initial consultation with the university liaison that we have to restructure the entire program to align with the Nigerian values and policies as we had originally structured it to be more Western-centric. As a team, we learned a valuable lesson about being open-minded and listening to their requests and perspective before we imposed what we deem to be correct. This experience contributed to my personal development as a researcher because it illustrated that I need to build rapport and relationships before any business is conducted. Again, this emphasizes the importance of being open to new experiences.

Conclusion

My learning has literally spanned the globe. Through my experiences and education, I would encourage others to follow this pathway, and I would offer a call to action for international leadership research. From conducting research – I have grown; when I started conducting international leadership research, I was not only physically young but mentally young as well. Opportunities that arose from research have made me a stronger person and have also changed who I am completely. As a leader, I have realized it is a good to sometimes take a pause and to reflect. Sometimes, I take time to self-reflect and to understand how I can improve myself, and I can see how I have grown over the years. I have realized that by doing research, some of the personal benefits I have gained are cultural sensitivity, having an open mind, having more flexibility for travel, and having a better understanding of cultural practices – all while learning even more about customs and traditions, building confidence, and developing a global mindset.

In the past, it is hard to believe that I was a shy person, so much so that I was apprehensive to talk to new people. But over the years, through conducting international leadership research and speaking to people, and through various assignments, I slowly emerged from that shyness and fear of being rejected. By interviewing prominent leaders, I have gained immense confidence and have strengthened my belief in myself. I have realized that I am capable of interviewing anyone; even though I have made my fair share of mistakes. I have realized that as a global leader it is all about confidence, and if you lack the confidence, it is quite obvious to others. Gaining confidence in myself has helped me grow as a person and has helped me in many more ways than I can describe. In addition, this growing confidence will help me with my future endeavors as well. My research has been personally and professionally transformative.

As leadership styles evolve with technology, global relations, and cross-cultural collaborations, even more research opportunities will arise. As researchers, we must seek out all opportunities to advance our knowledge about international affairs as well as expand our research agendas due to the many challenges we face in our world. Research agendas could include topics such as learning to work cross-culturally, becoming well versed in international affairs, learning how to lead global virtual teams, and ways to encourage multiple countries to work together to solve the world warming crisis.

My advice to future researchers, doctoral students, and aspiring scholars – do not be afraid of pursuing international leadership research. Initially it will be difficult – just like a riding a bicycle for the first time, you need someone to hold you; eventually however, you are fully capable of riding the bike by yourself. Initially, find a mentor or research partner and collaborate with someone who is more experienced; someone who can guide you through the process slowly but surely. Take on this challenge and it will be well worth it in the end. The learning, growth, and insight on global leadership is an ever-expanding field, rich with possibilities.

I hope the chapter has a served as source of inspiration to help you as a researcher, student, or practitioner to get a better understand of the immense possibilities with ILR and that this has provided insight into some of the downfalls as well. Perhaps, some of the experiences will apply – however, some may not. Regardless, you can create your own path. My suggestion to future international leadership researchers is to be open to international work as it will empower you and showcase the real struggles that some parts of the world are encountering. It will certainly provide a wide perspective of leadership experiences and engage your mind as well as your heart while doing so. This is one way we can change the world for the better, through international leadership research.

References

Anderson, D. L. (2015). *Organization development: The process of leading organizational change* (3rd ed.). Sage Publications.

Bailey, K., & Schantz, A. (2017). Here's what research can teach you about being a better leader. *World Economic Forum.* https://www.weforum.org/agenda/2017/08/heres-what-research-can-teach-you-about-being-a-better-leader/

Barnard, J. (2018). *How professional networking can improve your career progression.* https://virtualspeech.com/blog/how-professional-networking-can-help-your-career

Benabou, R., & Tirole, J. (2000). Self-confidence: Intrapersonal strategies. *Woodrow Wilson School Working Paper No. 209.* doi:10.2139/ssrn.220788

Bush, T., & Jackson, D. (2002). A preparation for school leadership: International perspectives. *Educational Management & Administration, 30*(4), 417–429. doi:10.1177/0263211X020304004

Covey, S. (2002). *Steven Covey on time management matrix from the 7 habits of highly effective people.* Simon & Schuster.

Creswell, J. (2014). *Research design: Qualitative, quantitative and mixed methods approaches* (4th ed.). Sage.

Cumming, T. G., & Worley, C. G. (2019). *Organizational development and change* (11th ed.). South-Western, Cengage Learning.

De Silva, K. M. (2005). *A history of Sri Lanka.* Penguin Books.

Detert, J. R., & Roberts, L. M. (2020, July 16). How to call out racial injustice at work. https://hbr.org/2020/07/how-to-call-out-racial-in-justice-at-work

Dial-Benton, C. J. (2012). *Experiences with discrimination: From deep within.* Xlibris.

Edinger, S. (2012, February 15). East meets west: Who has better leaders? *Harvard Business Review.* https://hbr.org/2012/02/east-meets-west-who-has-better

Engelbrecht, L., Spolander, G., Martin, L., Strydom, M., Adaikalam, F., Marjanen, P., Pervova, I., Sicora, A., & Tani, P. (2016). Reflections on a process model for international research collaboration in social work. *International Social Work, 59*(4), 438–451. doi:10.1177/0020872814531305

Frei, F. X., & Morriss, A. (2020, May). Begin with trust. *Harvard Business Review.* https://hbr.org/2020/05/begin-with-trust

Freshwater, D., Sherwood, G., & Drury, V. (2006). International research collaboration: Issues, benefits, and challenges of the global network. *Journal of Research in Nursing, 11,* 295–303. doi:10.1177/1744987106066304

Giele, J. Z. (2008). Homemaker or career woman: Life course factors and racial influences among middle class families. *Journal of Comparative Family Studies, 39*(3), 393–411. http://www.brandeis.edu/departments/sociology/pdfs/Giele2008.pdf

Ghemawat, P. (2005, December). Regional strategies for global leadership. *Harvard Business Review.* https://hbr.org/2005/12/regional-strategies-for-global-leadership

Gino, F. (2019). Cracking the code of sustained collaboration. *Harvard Business Review.* https://hbr.org/2019/11/cracking-the-code-of-sustained-collaboration

Groysberg, B., Lee, J., Price, J., & Cheng, Y. (2018). The leader's guide to corporate culture. *Harvard Business Review.* https://store.hbr.org/product/the-leader-s-guide-to-corporate-culture/R1801B

Hannay, M. (2009). The cross-cultural leader: The application of servant leadership theory in the international context. *Journal of International Business and Cultural Studies, 1,* 1. http://www.aabri.com/manuscripts/08108.pdf

Ibarra, H. (2015). *Act like a leader, think like a leader.* Harvard Business School Publishing.

Ibarra, H., & Scoular, A. (2019, November). The leader as coach. *Harvard Business Review.* https://store.hbr.org/product/the-leader-as-coach/R1906G

Ikenberry, G. (1996). The future of international leadership. *Political Science Quarterly, 111*(3), 385–402. doi:10.2307/2151968

Javidan, M. (2010, May 19). Bringing the global mindset to leadership. *Harvard Business Review.* https://hbr.org/2010/05/bringing-the-global-mindset-to.html

Loitch, P. (2019). *5 advantages of professional networking.* https://thethrivingsmallbusiness.com/what-are-5-advantages-of-professional-networking/

Lord, M. (2015). Group learning capacity: The roles of open-mindedness and shared vision. *Frontiers in Psychology, 6,* 150. doi:10.3389/fpsyg.2015.00150

Maxwell, J. (2008). *The leadership handbook.* Yates & Yates.

Miller, N. (2019, January 24). *Why Scotland loves haggis.* http://www.bbc.com/travel/story/20190123-why-scotland-loves-haggis

Murphy, W. M., Roberts Gibson, K., & Kram, K. E. (2017). Advancing women through development relationships. In S. R. Madsen (Ed.), *Handbook of research on gender and leadership* (pp. 361–377). Edward Elgar Publishing.

Parker, C. F., & Karlsson, C. (2014). Leadership and international cooperation. In R. A. W. Rhodes & P. Hart (Eds.), *The Oxford handbook of political leadership* (pp. 580–594). Oxford University Press. doi:10.1093/oxfordhb/9780199653881.013.026

Prentice, W. C. H. (2004). Understanding leadership. *Harvard Business Review.* https://hbr.org/2004/01/understanding-leadership

Schrikker, A. (2007). *Dutch and British colonial intervention in Sri Lanka, 1780-1815.* BRILL.

Sen, T. C. (2017). *Curry: A global history.* Speaking Tiger.

Skene, L. (2007). Undertaking research in other countries: National ethico-legal barometers and international ethical consensus statements. U.S. National Library of Medicine. *PLOS Medicine, 4*(2), e10. doi:10.137/journal.pmed.004010

Triandis, H. C. (2006). Cultural intelligence in organizations. *Group & Organization Management, 31*(1), 20–26. doi:10.1177/1059601105275253

U.N. org. (2021, January 26). *Global climate litigation reports 2020 status review.* https://www.unep.org/resources/report/global-climate-litigation-report-2020-status-review

Weber, M. J. (2020) Women of Sri Lanka: Family first. In M. J. Weber & K. Cissna (Eds.), *A global perspective on women in leadership and work-family integration: Breaking balance*(pp. 01–19). Cambridge Scholars Publishing.

Wickramasinghe, A. (2020). Women of Sri Lanka: Family first. In M. J. Weber & K. Cissna (Eds.), *A global perspective on women in leadership and work-family integration: Breaking balance* (pp. 107–122). Cambridge Scholars Publishing.

Wickremeratne, L. (1985). Colonialism in Sri Lanka: The political economy of the Kandyan highlands, 1833–1866. *The Journal of Asian Studies, 44*(2), 417–417. doi:10.2307/2055965

Zalis, S. (2018, February 23). *Forget networking: Relationship building is the best career shortcut.* https://www.forbes.com/sites/shelleyzalis/2018/02/23/forget-networking-relationship-building-is-the-best-career-shortcut/?sh=328d1600bf7d

Part IIIC

Concluding Thoughts: Zooming in on the International Leadership Research Standards

34

Success in International Leadership Research

Franziska Bieri, Yulia Tolstikov-Mast, Kem Gambrell, Patricia Goerman[1], Kathy-Ann C. Hernandez, Wanda Krause, Zeina N. Mneimneh, and Jennie L. Walker

Introductions – What Brings us to International Research?

YULIA TOLSTIKOV-MAST: We have very exciting contributors with diverse and extensive expertise in international research. Those scholars represent experiences within the area of Leadership Studies, as well as outside of the leadership field.

Some disciplines like cross-cultural psychology, organizational psychology, international education and some others have been engaging in discussions on rigor and unique research approaches in international studies. They have actually been doing it for decades. The leadership field didn't have that discussion for a long time. However, we currently see a sharp increase in intercultural scholarship with very limited conversations about an international research methodology and research process. With that, all our experts outside of the field of leadership can really help us apply their practices and help establish international leadership research standards and an agenda.

We have many exciting questions to discuss with our contributors about their views on international leadership research, growth as international scholars, the interdisciplinary approaches and future directions in international leadership studies. But before we start, it would be great if the contributors could introduce themselves.

JENNIE WALKER: I am a lead faculty member for leadership degrees at University of Arizona Global Campus and also an adjunct for Global Leadership in the PhD program at Indiana Tech. Before that, I worked at the Thunderbird School of Global Management in the Najafi Global Mindset Institute. I'm currently a GLOBE researcher and I do projects independently in international leadership research as well.

KEM GAMBRELL: I am a faculty member and chairperson in the doctoral program of Leadership Studies at Gonzaga University in Spokane, Washington. I have been doing research for the last twenty-plus years with the Lakota which is a sovereign nation and an indigenous group of peoples in the United States.

WANDA KRAUSE: I am program head of the Global Leadership Program and Associate Professor in the School of Leadership at Royal Roads University, in Canada. My work has taken me to

DOI: 10.4324/9781003003380-34

many different universities abroad, such as the London School of Economics, UK, SOAS, University of London, UK, University of Qatar, Qatar Foundation, and American University of Sharjah, UAE. I've lived most of my adult life abroad and mostly in the Middle East, for some time in Europe and mostly in Germany, the UK, Qatar, the UAE and Egypt. My research and work has been focused on Middle East socio-political issues. My PhD is in Politics of the Middle East. I've been mostly interested in understanding and researching the impact of women's organizations and networks on civil society to understand transformation and change.

ZEINA MNEIMNEH: I am an assistant research scientist in the Survey Methodology Program and the Director of the International Unit at the Survey Research Center, University of Michigan. One of the main objectives of our unit is to build survey research capacity in international settings. I have been involved in international survey research for more than 20 years with a focus on cross-cultural comparability and I currently chair the Comparative Survey Design and Implementation (CSDI) annual workshop. CSDI provides a venue for researchers and practitioners across the world to share their research and experience in conducting international and cross-national surveys.

PATRICIA GOERMAN: I'm Patti Goerman and I am the leader of the Language and Cross-Cultural Research Group in the Center for Behavioral Science Methods at the US Census Bureau. I've been working there for over 15 years now. We are a team that focuses on the development and pretesting of multilingual survey instruments through methods like cognitive interviews and focus groups. I did my PhD in sociology at the University of Virginia. My dissertation research was qualitative and focused on Latino immigrants to the United States, branching out to new receiving areas within the country. As a result of that work I also got the opportunity to visit El Salvador to volunteer with a group called Nursing Students Without Borders. Those experiences really paved the way for my later career. For my dissertation, I interviewed over 70 Spanish-speaking immigrants and heard their stories firsthand and for the volunteer work in El Salvador I interpreted and taught health related classes but I also got to see what people's lives were like in a small village and to speak with people who had family members in the United States. Incidentally, I was there when a 7.7 magnitude earthquake struck in 2001 and our group was stranded for a while due to earthquake damage to the airport. Both of those experiences were really eye opening. One of the things I have carried with me to this day is the importance of including different voices and perspectives in my research.

I'm also on the Executive Steering Committee of the Comparative Survey Design and Implementation group, along with Zeina Mneimneh. Being at the Census Bureau, we focus more on within-US surveys but I've really benefited from collaborating with researchers who do surveys across nations and finding out about the methods they use to achieve more parallel data. Many of the same survey methods can be used within a country when the aim is to include people who speak different languages.

KATHY-ANN HERNANDEZ: My name is Kathy-Ann Hernandez, and I am faculty in the College of Business and Leadership at Eastern University, specifically in the PhD program in organizational leadership, and I am also co-chair of that program. I have lived in three countries and even though I've been here for 20 years, I still consider myself an outsider-within; these international experiences color my perspective. My research focuses on the Black diaspora and understanding the immigrant perspective within the Black American or African American story as well as focusing the lens on the experience of people like me – African and/or African-Caribbean people who have come to the US from their respective contexts.

YULIA TOLSTIKOV-MAST: Kathy, you and Faith Ngunjiri are pioneers in describing and using a unique research design, auto ethnography.

Yes, thank you for bringing that up, Yulia. My experience with collaborative autoethnography is that it holds great potential for addressing some of the cross-cultural communication challenges and understanding that attend to both researchers and participants in international research.

FRANZISKA BIERI: I am originally from Switzerland, trained in the United States. Now, I'm in Bulgaria. I'm a sociologist by training. My dissertation was a qualitative study about the campaign against conflict diamonds and how NGOs, the diamond industry, and governments work together to develop the Kimberley Process. Lately I've been working more quantitatively. In one project, I was working with Bulgarian and Swiss colleagues together to implement a school leavers survey in Bulgaria to study what happens to youth once they leave education and what are the different work experiences depending on their education and other factors.

YULIA TOLSTIKOV-MAST: I'm originally from Russia, moved to the United States in 1996, received my Master's degree in Communication at Purdue University and went on to Memphis, Tennessee, where I graduated with a Ph.D. in Communication from The University of Memphis. Prior to relocating to the United States, I had B.A. in Russian, Literature, and English, taught Russian as a second language to diverse international student groups, worked with international students and in international business. Pretty much my entire professional career is about something international: traveling, working with internationals, or doing international research and training. My research highlight is a multistage qualitative study on Russian followership (2014–2019). It's a very exciting project, and I've learned tons about myself as an international researcher and about being engaged in international scholarship.

I also developed a doctoral course on global leadership research about seven years ago now. This course was the starting point for me to think conceptually about international leadership research, its quality, rigor and so forth. Thus, the ideas merged into the course. The course inspired me to think about the book. And the book's mission gathered us all together today.

Defining International Leadership Research

YULIA TOLSTIKOV-MAST: Prior to this meeting, we asked you to send us your thoughts on two questions: how do you understand international leadership and how can your experience with international research add and enrich international leadership studies knowledge and practice? Based on your responses, I see two camps – which is very interesting. The first camp includes leadership scholars who said international leadership is influencing people across cultures and in different contexts where leadership is not equal to a leader. The second camp had a more applied focus and most of the respondents in this camp were non-leadership scholars. They viewed leadership as a tool to articulate policies, to engage in leadership development, create changes within their organizations and so forth.

At the same time, both camps have commonalities. Leadership and non-leadership scholars said context and multidisciplinary lens are very important. Also, it's critical to have research standards to represent diverse voices. So, it seems everyone contributing to this conversation is on the same page about reasons to talk about international research as a process and standards of that process to know how to capture diverse reality, experiences and voices as close to their true representation as possible.

Let's just see if anyone has any comments about those differences and commonalities?

KEM GAMBRELL: As you were talking and reading our responses some of the things that were resonating for me and I think this has been part of my process in engaging in intercultural and cross cultural international research is that I grew up in the United States. Growing up in this very Western, individualistic, and I would say ethnocentric paradigm in that when we talk about leader, leading, and leadership in a way that leadership still bounces from that leader or our individual perspective. But as I continue to do my own research and as I was listening to the question the group had responded to, the thing that was interesting for me and I think continues to be deconstructed in my own process is that when I now think of leadership, I think of relationships. I think of people, I think of mutual influence and power sharing, if that's even such a possible thing, but rather this joyful mix of individuals coming together with a shared purpose to accomplish something. And of course, that's pretty generic. But I now believe that leadership is not about an individual. And I think one of the things that it sounds like this group is toying with and perhaps because of our research is that it's showing us that when we think of leadership, and when we talk about leadership, especially in an international context, we have to move it away from this individualistic paradigm. And we are moving it away from a culturally centric paradigm towards being more cross cultural and even trans-disciplinary. But the move is into this broader understanding and how individuals come together to make things happen. So perhaps the point is that we can stop talking about leadership through that individual paradigm and be open to more of the phenomena of how we engage with each other in relationship to get things done, and to accomplish our goals or our intents.

ZEINA MNEIMNEH: I have a follow up on that. This is very interesting. The way I initially viewed international leadership research is one that is linked to a decision-making process or an output. So, the data that are being collected as part of an international leadership research are used by entities who can develop a policy, a law, an intervention, or similar activities to improve life circumstances and wellbeing of their communities. This is somehow different than how the earlier conversations and how Kem described international leadership research which seems to be more process focused. So my question is: is it the process or the output that defines the leadership angle. It seems to me it is both.

YULIA TOLSTIKOV-MAST: Thank you, Zeina. I think it's an exceptional discussion and I'm waiting for the rest of our panel to jump in. Our positions show diverse approaches to international leadership in terms of paradigms, and Kem with her research with the indigenous nations, focus on how we can represent those diverse voices through conversations and give back to the community of our study participants. And Zeina is talking about how to use data. In this case, international research is viewed as an input to produce something useful that people can implement to make lives better. That's why the applied nature of international research is something that jumped at me right away. I think it really shows the diverse approaches to international research.

JENNIE WALKER: I'll have more to say about this when we get to the question about the interdisciplinary nature of leadership. But I would add to this particular conversation that I think that there are personal motivations and decisions that are made by each international leadership researcher about fundamentally, what their aims, and really legacy for their research is intended to be. While we'll see some differences across disciplines around what the scientific tradition of leadership means or should mean for a researcher and how we conduct ourselves, I would say that the decisions here are sometimes quite personal - especially in international leadership research when we're looking at distinctions in working with other cultures who also view the research in different ways. For me, I'll just speak personally, the reason that I do international leadership research is fundamentally motivated by a desire to have a better understanding of human experience in the world, whether it be in organizations or societies. And I also really would like to create positive change in individuals and also in groups, specifically in the workplace. I pursued my doctorate for that very reason. I was working in global leadership development in corporations for several years and thought we could do better. We could do better by the people that worked there. We could do better by the way that we interacted with and formed relationships with people in other cultures, especially in field operations. And so it's this idea of positive change that really motivates me. There's a lot of depth of discussion around what that means and what the applied nature of that is, but the intent here is that it affects people's lives in positive ways to make them more satisfied and fulfilled in their working lives. That's my perspective.

KATHY-ANN HERNANDEZ: Okay, I just wanted to add a quick perspective here. I know we have moved along in our discussion about the definition of international research to focus a bit more closely on the outcomes of research, but I would like go back to the definition of international leadership. From my perspective as an immigrant coming here, I have embraced the concept that I don't have to go abroad to do international research, especially as it relates to my own work focused on the Black diaspora. Eugene Robinson has written a book called *Disintegration: The Splintering of Black America* (2011). In it, he explores the question about what we mean when we talk about Black America. Well, what is Black America? We have people who have come to the US from Africa. We have people who have come here from the Caribbean. We have people who have been born here. Among these various groups, there are still these cultural divides and cultural misunderstandings; there are different ways of understanding leadership and inspiring followership that need to be addressed for us to move together effectively. It is important to recognize that and bring it to the discussion. It is especially critical as we think about the global village that we are involved in and working with, including virtual teams and people from different cultures. How do we lead in those spaces which are very permeable now and what are some of the issues that attend those kinds of spaces and conversations? In particular, how do we go about naming and being attentive to the various cultures that exist within even one given context?

YULIA TOLSTIKOV-MAST: Thank you, Kathy. That's a very important point. It's time to move on to other critical questions. But first, let's conclude the conversation about a definition and meaning of international leadership research. It seems our responses ultimately focused on what we call reliability, validity, or trustworthiness. We put emphasis into quality and what quality is and how we make sure the research is quality. I gathered it's important for all of us to represent the people we research to the best of our abilities with rigorous research skills that are international research skills, something that is unique and not traditionally Western, and we need to understand that uniqueness more and of course evaluate and discuss these standards further. Earlier in our discussion we briefly mentioned when we first got engaged in international research. Any other comments to add to that in terms of your initial experiences?

KATHY-ANN HERNANDEZ: I first began doing international research for my dissertation. I was looking at the issues affecting academic achievement and engagement of African American high school students and African Caribbean high school students. I collected data in the US, and I also traveled to the British Virgin Islands to collect data there. But what was interesting to me was that when I met with my methodologist, his immediate recommendation was that we needed to compare the different samples on the outcome measures. I said, "No, I don't want to do that!" At the time, I wasn't fully aware of the methodological issues around such comparisons, but I was developing my own philosophy and a paradigm that I wanted to bring to this work. From a deeply instinctive place, I knew this was not the approach I wanted to bring to my work. I vehemently opposed the proposition because I felt it just was not going to be a fair comparison. And so, I think that was the genesis of my framing of an intentional way of speaking into how different spaces require different questions and different mindsets. It became even clearer to me as I collected the data and interacted with students in the US and then in the British Virgin Islands. I saw first-hand how the same questions that I was asking, and the same survey I was administering were becoming very different tools when used in each context. I realized that it would require further sophistication and different ways of thinking about how to go about this well. I've continued to think about that over the years and, I would say, adopted a political position about what is required to do this well.

KEM GAMBRELL: I really appreciated what Kathy-Ann just said, because one of the insights that I've gained in my research. I really want to give a shout out to indigenous researcher and methodologies that have come out in the last 10 years or so, especially since Linda Tuhiwai Smith put her first research book out. But, our indigenous research methodology colleagues talk a great deal about what Kathy-Ann just mentioned, and that is: First, to ground our work in the place in space that we're in, but to also really work to understand that space, especially as international researchers who are often not from those other cultures. We have to really sit solidly in our own positionality but also allow and challenge, if you will, that paradigm that we hold. And so when I think of what Kathy-Ann was saying and how Western researchers insist upon this very almost sterile scientific method, kind of thing that removes the humanity and the understanding of nuanced differences in how we engage with the world as individuals. And I believe, if we're truly doing ethical research, we understand that one way of being or model doesn't fit all. One research method doesn't fit all and that it helps to really spend the time and understand where we're at and how the people that we have the honor and privilege of engaging with, how they view the world. It is our work to challenge our imbedded understanding, not necessarily higher or better than our own, but rather to honor both those places and spaces.

YULIA TOLSTIKOV-MAST: Thank you, Kem. It's a good segway to move to the next question.

Changing Perspectives on and Practices in International Leadership Research

YULIA TOLSTIKOV-MAST: Maybe we start with sharing if and how our perspectives on international research changed over time?

JENNIE WALKER: Sure. Well, I'll be building on what Kem just added, because I agree with that perspective. When I thought about this question, how did my perspective change over time for me as a researcher, I was trained to approach the process scientifically and to avoid forming personal relationships with participants. The idea was you would create bias by having a relationship with the participants. However, through the years, I found that in international leadership research relationship is a critical entree into the research itself. Because without trust, sharing information is difficult and it can even be prohibitive among different people and across different cultures. So, I believe that the Western scientific method is framed in a way that doesn't capture human dynamics or doesn't always capture them. This idea that trust and relationship are important for us to be able to share information, especially when leadership research, like much research, will often ask questions that are quite personal about beliefs and values and rationale for making certain decisions or behaving in certain ways. So, in short, I would say that my perspective has really changed around the importance of relationships to be able to conduct the research, especially in a genuine and authentic way.

YULIA TOLSTIKOV-MAST: Thank you. Zeina, would you like to jump in? I know we are talking about the importance of non-scientific, non-Western approaches. But at the same time both scientific and non-scientific are complementary and add collective value to understanding reality. Has anything changed in your view on international research compared to your initial experiences?

ZEINA MNEIMNEH: Yes. Thank you. I think maybe before I comment on how my perspective changed, I'd like to comment on the engagement of participants and local cultures and the partnership idea. While most of the examples have been focused on in-depth studies, engagement of local stakeholders is an essential component of any quantitative cross-cultural research. The success of any research be it qualitative or quantitative, we deal more with the latter, depends on who is on the ground collecting the data. If the researcher does not have a solid and transparent relationship with the entity that is collecting the data, the chance that things will go wrong is much higher, we have seen this in several of the international projects we were involved in. So trust, transparency and a common objective of serving the communities that are being studied should be shared by all international and local stakeholders involved in the project. Now when you are implementing a cross-national study in many countries, as an international researcher, it is impossible to establish this directly with the thousands of respondents that are being interviewed. Thus, the focus is on understanding the culture and building a relationship with local collaborators and partners and training the people who are in the field to understand the process and the value of valid data. One challenging area is how to train the individuals who are interviewing respondents and collecting thousands and thousands of interviews to implement this process in a standardized manner and collect unbiased data. It could come down to some tension between variance and bias. Because when you have interviewers use their own approach and when you compile all the data across all the interviewers you could see clustering effects or interviewer effects which could affect the quality of your data since you are adding another layer of variation that is not driven by the respondents.

The tension between standardization and adaptation (of the approach) exists not only at the level of an interview within a culture but also across cultures when they are being part of a single cross-cultural study. You want to localize your approach to the specific culture but you also want to have some level of standardization for comparability purposes. There is a lot of literature written about this and we have written some but we still don't know what is the right balance between localizing procedures, meaning adapting it as much as possible to the current context, and standardizing some aspects of the procedures to remove variations that are due to design and implementation and that do not reflect true variations. So, this balance between how much I need to standardize and how much I need to localize is very, very difficult to solve when the core objective of these cross-cultural studies is comparability. And the more countries or cultures you bring in, the harder it gets. Researchers sometimes push for adding as many countries and cultures as possible to their initiatives, but, in reality, sometimes adding very diverse cultures and trying to standardize procedures across extremely diverse countries might not work.

Now, one important practice that we encourage every researcher to implement especially in "standardized" cross-cultural studies and that helps with the adaptation of the survey questions to the local cultures is cognitive interviewing. The objective here is while you have a "standard" set of questions that you would like to ask across all the cultures or countries, these questions are heavily tested and adapted to the local culture. So while the question phrasing might look different across cultures, the construct that you are measuring is the same. And the way we do this is to conduct rounds and rounds of what we call in-depth cognitive interviewing to capture the cultural nuances. I'm sure Patti can talk a lot more about this topic.

YULIA TOLSTIKOV-MAST: Zeina. Before we move to Patti could you talk to your transformation?

ZEINA MNEIMNEH: Yes. Honestly it is not my own personal transformation only as much as it is a transformation that I've seen in cross-cultural quantitative research over the past two decades. Many coordinated cross-cultural studies started with the notion that there is a standard questionnaire that needs to be implemented as such across all cultures and countries if comparability of the data is to be achieved. While there was some flexibility to allow countries to do some changes to the questionnaire, the changes were very limited. First, there was a worry that this will impact the comparability of the data. Second, when you are conducting large cross-national surveys, anytime you want to implement any change, you need to spend resources to change the questionnaire, program it, test it, etc... And when you are doing this in many countries and many languages, especially if there is no central funding, this becomes a limiting step. Now things have changed since then. There are many models now that are more tolerant and flexible to local changes as long as the constructs being measured are the same, this is especially the case when there is central funding to coordinate the different studies across the different sites. Thus, it is very important for funders to realize that if the objective is to get reliable, valid, and comparable data cross cultures then funding for central infrastructure and coordination is essential.

PATRICIA GOERMAN: One point that Zeina brought up was the issue of cognitive interviewing to pretest survey questions. I don't know if everybody here is familiar with that method so I'll say a few words about it. Pretesting survey questions through cognitive interviews is an important way to include the voices of people with various backgrounds and from different social locations in the development of survey questions. We've been talking about the interdisciplinary nature of international leadership research and survey methodology itself is very interdisciplinary. The cognitive interviewing method comes from the field of cognitive psychology originally, and it has been adapted over the years for use in survey development. When survey methodologists are developing a survey instrument it is important to have as diverse a team involved in the development of the questions as possible. And, as Zeina mentioned, if the survey instrument will be used across different cultures, languages or even countries, the more contexts that will be included in data collection, the more difficult it is to have people from all those different backgrounds as part of the team developing questions. Often when multilingual questionnaires are developed, the team develops one language version first and then they move onto the translation phase. That often means that you don't have the perspective of people from all of the relevant languages or cultures involved in the original question formulation. So, one way to bring those voices in at some point during the development process is through cognitive interviewing, where researchers pretest the draft questions with respondents of different backgrounds. In my office, we have a lot of experience with pretesting Spanish language questions in the United States. Of course, "Spanish speakers" in the United States is not a uniform group. When we do pretesting of Spanish translations we include people from a variety of different countries. And when we test in any language we try to include both men and women, people with different educational levels and people with different family or living situations. Depending on the topics of the questions involved, we try to make sure we're including people that would go down every different path in the survey and answer in different ways. The goal is to sit down with people and ask them to go through the survey questions to find out how they interpret them and how they come up with their responses. We try to make sure that they interpret each question and response option the way the survey designers intended and if not we make edits and retest. Usually many surprises come up in testing. We often assume that people will interpret things in a certain way but it's impossible to account for all of the different life situations and experiences people will have or their interpretation of various terms, especially when you're dealing with translation. So cognitive interviewing is a really nice way to include the voices of the people that will ultimately be represented by your data in the development process. A group of experts, even if from different cultures and language groups, would have a hard time accounting for all of the life situations and perspectives of the respondents who will ultimately answer the survey.

YULIA TOLSTIKOV-MAST: Very good. Thank you so much for commenting and clarifying it, Patti. I don't know if any of you had previously engaged in discussions with scholars from multiple disciplines and paradigms. Typically, they are pretty ego driven (smile), not very inclusive, and can get confrontational. Not as peaceful and attentive like we're having right now. Usually when you put together qualitative and quantitative researchers, there is a push and pull and I'm just excited that we are sharing our perspectives with so many different angles and with mutual understanding that every perspective counts and, quantitative as well as qualitative paradigms have value.

Meaning of Success in International Research

YULIA TOLSTIKOV-MAST: The central question for our discussion is the meaning of success in international research. How do we understand success, especially when it comes to international leadership research? What do we see as barriers or challenges to that success? I'd like to start with Wanda and Kathy and if it's okay, and maybe Kem after that.

WANDA KRAUSE: Thank you, Yulia. I'm going to build on some of the things that have been said already, especially by Kathy, Jennie and Zeina. But I think it's important for us to ask what success is and perhaps to understand what success in research is not. That's kind of where I like to begin. So, we often think of success and research by looking at citation numbers or things like quantitatively how many languages a piece of research has been translated into. So these are the kinds of metrics that are usually used to determine research success. And from all the conversation we've had so far I'm really delighted, really happy to hear, some keywords that feature in my objectives for successful research emerging from all of your conversations and that is number one culture. So being very, very focused on culture. The second thing that I've heard quite often so far in our call today is around the personal. So, being aware of who we are in the research. These elements are key to understanding and defining what success. I also heard the words international and global. I want to highlight global in a way of defining what success is too because, as we're defining what is good for everyone, and Zeina had pointed out, I think that we need to look up what the local impact is and to really consider the context. And, as she pointed out rightly 20 years ago, that's when I first began my research, it wasn't just for everybody, it wasn't really a global sense; it was really a Eurocentric perspective of what needs to happen. And so now our research has developed to be more attuned to and very aware of what is required for solutions and change and specific problems in their local context. So yes, these challenges and problems can be global. But they're also contextualized and very local politics on economic situations and cultural conditions. So a couple of things to that I'd like to highlight. First of all, we just talked about how our perspectives have changed. And one thing I'll point out for myself personally is the change that I have observed in myself relates to that Eurocentric perspective and for me that's really critical to understand what success is. And so if our research reflects a development, not just in terms of understanding the context and being attuned to the context but development within ourselves. I think that is success to be measured. Because I think success isn't just about serving the community. I think that's first and foremost. And I think, in terms of servant leadership that comes first, obviously. If we are a changed person, I think that is part of what we can consider for success. So I know in my example, I thought when I began research in the Middle East, I had this understanding of democratizing the Middle East that was very Eurocentric. It was not only Eurocentric but very American, rooted in American democracy, even though I'm Canadian. And so, spending most of my adult life in the Middle East, I got to know the different models and historically the different models of what could be aligned with democracy. I got to really appreciate and change my perspective around consensus building and what collaboration could mean. It could be very different from our western models of democracy, not just in the West, but more particularly in North America. To really appreciate the context and what the context requires of us in terms of our adaptability is important. The goal is to come up with solutions together collaboratively, thereby serving the community in a way that's rooted in culture, rooted in the dynamics that relate to, for example, poverty, or different perspectives − in fact, perspectives that have been marginalized within those communities themselves. It is important to understand that marginalization of ways of knowing, being and doing isn't just about the larger context in a country. It is also being attuned to and aware of the power dynamics within those communities. One major way to measure success is to relate to, for example, the SDGs, the Sustainable Development Goals. I won't say that that's the only one because there are many goals, but it's the one that I work with the most. Ticking boxes will not mean success. It's how we go about it.

I'm not sure if it's been mentioned so far, but I did want to jump in earlier and address something. One of the questions that Zeina put out in terms of outputs as a measurement of success, I think relates to this question, too. I think with leadership, it's outputs but those outputs are also, for me, the process. So, if we are engaging in a way where we're holding space and we're allowing for transformation, for me that's success. In this case, I'm just simply holding space and not necessarily jumping in and leading as an individual or leading even collaboratively. It's just holding space for the conversations to emerge and happen so that people within their own communities can strategize and think of ways to address, for example, a problem. And so just holding space and looking at how things transform throughout that whole process is for me success because success is about change. It's about making a positive change. And it doesn't have to come from me, it can come from individuals, if I hold that space or enable that space to happen even if I have nothing really to do with it in real time. Success is positive change where needed. And so, that process or the piece to make that happen comes back to inquiry. Inquiry is about deep listening, it's about dropping our biases and assumptions and beliefs about the way the world should be and just being present. It doesn't mean that I'm necessarily facilitating that process, but just holding that space, creating opportunities for people who have been marginalized or who don't have a chance to speak, either because of their political positions or because of poverty or situationally where they're located along whatever spectrum.

My goal has been to bring in women's voices who have been marginalized in the literature and so that includes poor women, or people in places where researchers don't normally go into. For example, in Egypt, we would normally go into Cairo. And so, with my work I brought my research to places and areas where people don't want to stay for a number of reasons. First of which is poverty and sometimes an assumption that it's too risky. Now, Egypt right now is too risky to do much research, but often we hold a bias around risk that doesn't really exist. To build on what's been said before, success is also the degree to which our research is informed by and shaped by the cultures in which it takes place, in particular, the different cultures, not just the dominant culture. So, to be really attuned to what those different cultures are, especially those which are marginalized. Success, then, is further related to the degree we are aware of ourselves, that is, the self in those systems and the degree to which we can acknowledge who we are in those systems and how we influence those systems. We're full of biases. I don't think that we're ever able to peel back all our biases. But just to be aware of how we're impacting the data and, as has been mentioned, the degree to which culture is understood.

I think Zeina said if you don't understand the culture, then it is important to at least, at minimum, link in and making relationships with stakeholders on the ground who are there and, allowing space for them to determine the research as well. But I think it's really important to spend time in those cultures and we're not talking about a few weeks. It's months, it's years to really understand before putting solutions forward. However, I don't think solutions should be put forward on one's own; I think it's always got to be a collaborative effort. I think barriers would be around our own biases, so not knowing, not really being able to be self-aware enough to at least know some of our biases. We need to think very carefully about how those biases might be impacting the kinds of questions we're posing; how we are shaping our questions and the constructs in which those questions are embedded as in our own cultural constructs. So, to be very, very aware of them.

Another barrier is obviously not knowing who all the pertinent actors are for any project or research we're working on. A barrier is also not recognizing our own actions in relation to our research. And, further, not recognizing the systems that are in place: the overarching political systems, the systems of the structural elements of oppression, whether that's economic or political or otherwise. These are some of the barriers that come to mind.

KATHY-ANN HERNANDEZ: I'm going to limit my comments to qualitative research, and I will talk specifically about collaborative autoethnography. Success is gauged by if I've really listened and heard the perspectives, and if in our conversations, in our collaborative meaning-making, we have moved closer to bridging some of the power differential–some of the cultural divides, to really hear each other–and to understand the meaning that is coming out. If it's phenomenology, then am I really understanding the experience as the participants have presented it? What is their lived experience of whatever the phenomenon is? I think the other thing is what we call in our work multivocality. I just submitted an article to a journal and we went through so many rounds of revisions and the recommendation by the editor was that we only share themes that represented the majority of the participants; had we had 17 of them. I challenged that. For me, that's not success. Multivocality speaks to how I can honor and represent the multiple voices that are present in a space. Not only do we have to look carefully at the methodologies we are using, but we also have to push back and challenge ill-informed assaults to the methods. To take the recommended approach of this editor would have been to silence certain voices. Even though we talk about representing marginalized views in our work, the very approach to data analysis that we practice often silences those voices and leaves them out of the picture in the very sanitized article that makes its way to the public. So, this is what I wrote to her:

As a qualitative method, CAE not only adheres to traditional approaches of data analysis and interpretation, but it also challenges it. The method is built on extracting perspectives of the collective but not privileging that collective perspective at the expense of the individual. As one of the co-authors of the book that describes the nuances of this method, I continue to value adherence to this approach. Indeed, I, along with the co-authors of the book have been mindful to represent multiple voices of participants that did not conform neatly to a common theme/idea to give voice to the range of individual perspectives--multivocality. We view that as a strength of CAE and a salient aspect of what is considered to be a finding.

And so, I think for me, that is success: To what extent have I really represented and honored the voices, even though they were different from mine and from what we consider to be the finding? I think that's also a finding.

KEM GAMBRELL: I absolutely agree with what Wanda and Kathy-Ann were saying. I think Wanda landed very beautifully looking at multiple aspects of how we could define success. From a Western scientific method and specifically, how faculty are conditioned, the institution of Higher Education defines success and research by how many publications we get out the door. And so again, a paradoxical metric. But one of the other things that I think I would add to the success conversation is that if I am, as Wanda and many others have talked about, if I am truly in relationship with my participants, if I have done my due diligence of being in local communities and understanding their needs, success also is in recognizing whether or not the data or the knowledge or the information that I'm collecting is really mine to do something with. For those of us that do qualitative methodology what we understand is, there are times that we are extremely blessed with people's stories. And as Shawn Wilson writes, research is ceremony. We find ourselves often having the opportunity of being blessed and honored with narratives, experiences, and stories from people's lives that really actually might not be ours to publish. So, part of my own discernment and my growth as a researcher is to get cleaner and cleaner about understanding when I have just sat in relationship with somebody, and perhaps 95% of what they said I can use and I can use in terms of greater community findings and benefits and those kinds of things, but perhaps 5% of what I heard is not mine to share. It was just, if you will, a sacred moment that I was privileged enough to bear witness to. So, for me, part of that success, again, is that relationship and being close enough in relationship with those individuals or those organizations where I got to see their vulnerable moment. And it's not mine to share, but rather to hold sacred.

YULIA TOLSTIKOV-MAST: What a valuable discussion! To finish up and move to our next question, I think what all of us are saying is international research success is when I am representing my study participants' realities correctly and capturing context correctly. Collaboration is something that everyone pointed to as another element of success. Collaboration with gatekeepers, partners, study participants, local community, and local researchers. Also, success is in understanding our limitations and boundaries as researchers. As Kem just said, international research success is to make sure we do not only represent our study participants with integrity, but also do not overstep and mention something that we cannot based on ethical considerations or even local traditions and local culture.

I might be a little radical when it comes to success in international leadership research. I was looking at cross-cultural management scholarship and all their traditional discussions about the importance of capturing cultural differences and local societal nuances. At the same time how to do it or how to keep researchers accountable for conducting true international research are not popular discussions. So, in terms of that radical approach and to foster commitment to rigorous international research, I was thinking about an analogy of the Hippocratic Oath. Before doctoral students graduate from programs where they have an international leadership research curriculum and an international leadership research dissertation, these doctoral students pledge an International Research Oath. This is where, in front of their peers, they acknowledge (even pledge) their commitment to uphold specific international research and ethical standards. The goal is not only to celebrate their graduation but to show commitment to be an international researcher of integrity: a responsibility of connecting to study participants and representing them and their realities as correctly as possible.

Advancing the International Leadership Field – Inward and Outward

YULIA TOLSTIKOV-MAST: How can we make people from different disciplines more aware of the international leadership field? What about interdisciplinarity and how can we advance our understanding of the international leadership research process?

JENNIE WALKER: One thing that I wish is that the interdisciplinary nature of international leadership studies was better understood and discussed among scholars. I think that that's a responsibility of those of us who work in the field that clearly see these connections, to make that clear, and to emphasize that in our work. I had worked in global leadership development for several years before I pursued my doctorate, and at that time I wasn't aware of any global leadership doctoral degrees or international leadership research. So, when I looked at doctoral programs, I was confused about which program to apply to. Now, today there are a handful of programs that are constructed to be interdisciplinary but at the time this didn't really exist, and it wasn't that long ago. I mean, we're talking about 15 years ago. I looked at programs in business management, organizational industrial psychology, and cross-cultural communications, but none of them seemed to truly fit my interests. Since I specifically wanted to know how global leaders were best developed, ultimately, I decided to pursue a doctorate in higher education because the program allowed me to look at leadership development from an educational, and psychological perspective. I was fortunate that I had several mentors in international management programs that were able to influence my research as well. This allowed me to bring in those interdisciplinary connections that I saw and then felt when doing research, but other scholars didn't seem to acknowledge this. I'd say, in the first three to four years of my academic career, first as a postdoctoral fellow and then as a professor, it was really an exercise in trying to convince traditional business school professors that I even belonged in the field of Leadership Studies. I was fortunate that my supervisor at the time, who was an esteemed scholar in global leadership, he understood this interdisciplinary nature of the field and had recruited me for it.

However, many of the business professors I worked with both at the university where I worked and also at academic conferences, they openly questioned my qualifications because my degree was in higher education. For me, my saving grace with the critics was my actual experience working with executives in the field of business. They gave me a pass, if you will. After 10 years in the academy, I now have confidence that my intuition served me really well in choosing my path and in knowing that this was an interdisciplinary field, but it was really a hard road. I think that, as a result, there were many times where my contributions were not valued. These disciplinary silos that remain, I view as problematic in the field. I would suggest to those of us who work in this field that it is up to us to continually reinforce the message of where these interdisciplinary connections are in our work to make it visible to those who were trained in siloed disciplinary traditions.

PATRICIA GOERMAN: This discussion has been very interesting to me because I entered the field of survey methodology with a background in sociology. I think the interdisciplinary nature of survey methodology is parallel in a lot of ways to the interdisciplinary nature of leadership studies. Survey methodologists come from many different disciplines. There aren't very many graduate survey methodology programs in the United States. In my research center at the U.S. Census Bureau, almost every one of us has a background in a different discipline. As I mentioned earlier, my degree was in sociology. My research center also includes psychologists, linguists and anthropologists, a political scientist and of course some folks with survey methodology degrees. I think this situation is really beneficial because we all contribute different methods, literatures and perspectives to our collaborations.

In my view, an important way to make people aware of interdisciplinary research opportunities and to foster connections is to organize sessions at conferences across different fields. If I'm attending a sociology or survey methodology conference I can reach out to people interested in similar topics from other fields. Perhaps I can organize a session and solicit abstracts from people in different fields. The American Association for Public Opinion Research (AAPOR) is a survey methodology conference that Zeina and I both attend and that includes people from many different disciplines. I co-lead a Cross Cultural and Multilingual Affinity Group that meets at the AAPOR conference. That type of thing is another way to increase networking among people interested in the same topics. I have presented at sociology, anthropology and Latin American studies conferences over the years. It has been really eye opening to meet scholars from different backgrounds at those different meetings. Aside from organizing panels or sessions at conferences it can be great to volunteer to edit a special issue for an academic journal or a book such as this one. I have really enjoyed learning more about International Leadership studies through this collaboration.

ZEINA MNEIMNEH: I totally agree with Patti. I also would like to say two things about success. One thing that I believe is an indicator of success, and I think we need it for the future direction of international leadership, is capacity building. Local capacity building. It's challenging because a lot of the time you are limited with what you can do in terms of building capacity in the local culture, given the funding that you have. I'm sorry that I am always bringing the issue of funding, but, in reality, it is a big issue for us in terms of good quality or successful international research. When a researcher is interested in collecting data in an international site to understand a social phenomenon, there are at least two ways of doing this. One way, and this is where most of the funding or funded projects do is a researcher in the US, Canada, or Europe leads the study, collaborate with a local researcher to collect the data and then jointly analyze it. This is one model. Another model that we really push hard for is to build survey research capacity in the local country. Now, this would require more funding because efforts are not only spent on collecting the data but also on building local and sustainable infrastructure for collecting better data. Like helping local entities move to a more solid method of data collection by using let's say tablets instead of paper and pencil, training local staff on how to do cognitive interviewing, and building quality control systems. Local capacity building is essential because that's the only way that you could sustain scientific research in the local culture. That is not to say that there is not already some level of infrastructure and capacity there, but I think there is definitely more work to be done on in terms of bringing it one step further.

In terms of the multi-disciplinary and the future direction, I agree with Patti that in the field of survey methods, we are extremely interdisciplinary, the field itself is interdisciplinary. Most people who are trained as survey methodologists come from different disciplines. But what I think is still missing and that is really essential for cross-cultural leadership research, is making cross cultural survey research more of a sub-discipline. There is a lot of debate about whether the methods that are implemented in single studies are also applicable to multicultural projects. Sometimes it is, sometimes it is not. As a methodologist, there are theories that we are lacking. There are psychological theories we are lacking. There's theories from the sociology field. There's ethical operation that we are lacking. I mentioned the Comparative Survey Design Initiative (CSDI) that brings many of those people together but we need to be more proactive in attracting researchers from other disciplines to these multi-disciplinary workshops and sustaining the active discussion to push the field forward. Many of us go and present and then leave and do our own research. Some of us later might collaborate on a specific project, but there hasn't been a vehicle that maintains this consistent interaction to produce educational material for future social science researchers who are interested in cross cultural comparability.

YULIA TOLSTIKOV-MAST: Thank you, Zeina. Great contribution.

Future Directions of International Leadership Research

YULIA TOLSTIKOV-MAST: To close our discussion, let's think about future directions in international leadership research. We already mentioned local capacity building, multidisciplinary conferences, course development, workshops, special journal issues and sustaining interactions after all those engagements. Anything else you would like to add to the list of suggestions?

WANDA KRAUSE: I wanted to speak to capacity building and Kathy-Ann's comments to focus on the local as part of the global. We have so many issues in our own backyard and these issues are related to race, injustice, community development, or challenges of marginalization. I think we need to tap into what's happening in our localities, Europe or in the West in general, and tease those issues out as they emerge. Right now, I'm sensing, with little posts that I'm putting out regarding anything related to injustice or racism – and that has been in context with what's happening in the US with Black Lives Matter – that there is greater reception. I'm pleased to see that people are paying attention now to some of the posts I put out. And they wouldn't have paid as much attention six months ago, perhaps it's just because we finally have things appearing in the news. So, I think it's about tapping into our time, it's tapping into the events that highlight gaps, racism issues and linking them to the international because these issues are shared. It's important to be very attuned to bringing more people into the conversation, who are lit up by what's happening in their communities, and bridge that with what's happening in other communities because the contexts are different, but in essence, the challenges are pretty much the same. And so we can come up with solutions that can attend to the different contexts by inviting people from those different contexts to the conversation, to the same table. Thank you.

KEM GAMBRELL: I think for me, when I think of the future of international leadership and international leadership research and I think it's been said, but I think our job is to continue to unpack in our own worldviews. In those methodologies and methods that we're trained in, it is important to expand our own understanding so that we can share deeper and broader understanding with, let's say, those that we do research with. I also think this applies literally to the field of research, including how we understand our own lenses, our own positionality and what we're bringing to the table working to not over-project, but to be curious with other ways of understanding. I've mentioned it already, but a number of indigenous researchers have helped me into thinking differently about my own worldview and how I come into relationship with others, whether it's through my research or through my teaching or just through my everyday life. I think our job is to continue to be curious about not just those that we are doing research on and with but also be curious about and challenge how do we continue to understand and unpack how we make sense of the world as researchers and community. And again, given the point about our current discontent in the United States around issues of racism, marginalization and white supremacy, I think the first thing that we can do is to unpack our own privilege and really work to consider how do we think about our own worldview and how do we step back from again kind of this sterile Western scientific methodology.

JENNIE WALKER: The only thing I would add, thinking about our audience for the book and understanding that many people who are interested in this topic are likely to be doctoral students or newly developing researchers, is that I think that there's a tendency for people to focus on their education and their credentials over experience in the field. Wanting to take research classes and be involved in conferences and research projects right out of the gate is important. But I would say that it's equally, if not more important, that people are focused on getting experience in the field living and working across cultures. Because while we can develop an appreciation of cultural differences through education, it's my personal experience, and bias really, that our experience in other cultures and intimately with people from other cultures is critical to mature a more simplistic appreciation of cultural difference and similarities into a real disposition for being able to conduct both well intentioned and culturally responsive international leadership research in a way that provides deeper wisdom and a stronger skill set to adequately navigate complexities and then interpret findings appropriately.

YULIA TOLSTIKOV-MAST: Thank you, Jennie. Thank you everyone. I think it was a very exciting and unique conversation among the professionals with diverse methodological and cultural backgrounds as well as experiences with different types of research. I appreciate everyone's contributions and please, let's stay in touch! All those great suggestions – let's sustain interactions and do something good for the field of international leadership studies.

Note

1   This chapter is released to inform interested parties of research and to encourage discussion. Any views expressed are those of the authors and not those of the U.S. Census Bureau.

35

Lessons Learned

Doing Cross-Cultural and International Research with Integrity

Jennie L. Walker, Franziska Bieri, and Yulia Tolstikov-Mast

Introduction

This handbook was created to illuminate the complexities of international leadership research across cultural contexts and stages of the research process. While the scope of the volume cannot possibly address all contexts, it is our hope that it aids in the development of researchers – current and future – in the field. As editors, we originally framed the handbook with the stages of the research process in mind along with underexplored and emerging topics we found compelling in the field. What we found, however, was that the authors who responded to our call for chapters brought forth many additional considerations. This is the beauty of multidisciplinary collaboration. By opening our query to a diverse network of researchers worldwide, we identified additional questions, considerations and emerging research practices that may be known within a discipline or network of researchers but not necessarily to the wider field.

This final chapter in the volume reflects the combined perspectives of the editors and authors that rethink, build on and provide alternative approaches to conducting research in cross-cultural and international contexts. The differences are not just process oriented; they challenge the very assumptions built into commonly accepted research practices. Therefore, this chapter will look at how the assumptions and research process must look different for cross-cultural and international research in the field of leadership and beyond. We present a model that captures these considerations, and suggest that all researchers may want to consider this model to remain responsive to diversity in any research context. We also propose a series of questions for researchers to consider as they embark on their research journeys.

Research Process Revisited

A search for "research process" often results in a diagram of a singular research process that typically includes planning, research design, data collection, data analysis, and conclusions.

Discussion of the process is usually quite linear with steps to be completed in sequence and places a first focus on development of the research question. For example, Gelling (2015) reviews multiple models for research from the perspective of the nursing field (e.g., Moule, Aveyard & Goodman, 2016; Gerrish & Lacey, 2010; Taylor, 2010), saying that there are 10 different stages of the research process that are "common to all research" (p.44) including developing the research question, searching and evaluating the literature, selecting the research approach, selecting research methods, gaining access to the research

DOI: 10.4324/9781003003380-35

site and data, pilot study, sampling and recruitment, data collection, data analysis, and dissemination of results and implementations of findings. As another example, Offermann, Levina, Schönherr, and Bub (2009, May 7) present a comparison of research processes in the field of design science that includes several authors and both quantitative and qualitative methodologies (e.g., March & Smith 1995; Nunamaker et al. 1990; Peffers et al. 2008; Takeda et al., 1990; Vaishnavi & Kuechler, 2004/2005)) that illustrates the commonalities in approach. There is acknowledgement that some steps in the process are iterative and refer back to other steps, but the processes are framed similarly to what Gelling (2015) describes. They argue that a more expansive view and use of research methods would benefit their field. Maxwell (2019) also writes a compelling critique of qualitative research methods across fields, saying, "Despite the importance of research design for both qualitative and quantitative research, there has been little systematic investigation, in the literature on research design, of the concept of "design" itself" (p. 1). He notes that research design has important implications for how a study is conceptualized, planned, implemented, and for how validity and ethical issues are addressed. We agree.

Figure 35.1   Common Steps in a Linear Research Process Model.

The simplicity of a singular, linear model has utility in focusing students across disciplines on key activities of research process. Some methods, especially in qualitative methodology, do discuss a non-linear approach to data collection and analysis, but the dynamic approach is generally isolated to these steps. For research within a shared or known cultural context, research may indeed have a more linear process, as there is often a foundation of shared knowledge and perspectives. However, the oft presented linear process model does not represent the complexities of international research or research in diverse cultural contexts, because there are contextual considerations that are not linear; they need to be considered and reconsidered throughout the process. We suggest a shift away from a linear model with steps to one with fluid and multi-directional stages.

Perhaps most importantly, our critique of traditional research process is that it does not sufficiently account for or place emphasis on the disposition of the researcher and context of the study to carefully consider the ethical and culturally relevant foundations for the study. The insights within this handbook reveal dynamic interplay between researcher and the research environment throughout the research process. They also point to additional considerations and steps that may be required for international research studies.

In Part I of the handbook: Philosophical and Conceptual Traditions, authors raise critical questions about the degree to which international leadership research captures diverse perspectives globally, the inclusivity of definitions of "leadership" we use, whose leadership knowledge we use and whose leadership questions we should ask in research studies. Professors in research courses dutifully encourage students to look for "gaps" in the literature as a way of identifying research needs in the field. However, these authors are pointing out that valuable pursuits of knowledge may not just be in the gaps; they may be in questioning the very assumptions that created the literature to begin with or in the incomplete representation of worldviews. In doing so, they may find that their questions open formative self-reflection, as well. "When we become cross-cultural researchers, we confront the importance of understanding ourselves, our cultural roots, how we live those routes or challenge them, where we are going, and what influences us along the way" (Miller Cleary, 2013, p. 7). This is precisely why we asked authors to include reflections in their chapters, to illuminate how the research process has expanded their perspectives and worldviews.

Many of the authors' accounts acknowledge the importance of having an ethic of care and a humanitarian commitment to participants and communities involved in research. However, their experiences often share this as the result of experience, not as a part of their research training or process. Ethic of care includes being conscientious about "othering" people in international research. "Othering" is the act, whether it is intentional or not, to classify people, groups and societies as "alien" and thereby negate their shared humanity. This can happen through classifications ("tribal people") and verbiage ("illegal people"), stereotypical portrayals, and oversteps with intellectual property rights, such as ownership of ideas and recordings (Williams, 2015). To be inclusive in research means attending to this ethic of care and humanitarian commitment from the inception of the research idea through the implementation of research process to the integrity of the conclusions. Part II of the handbook looks at these considerations throughout stages of research.

In Part II of the handbook, International Leadership Research Processes: Core Issues in Study Design, Data Collection and Analysis, major topics throughout include research ethics and disposition for research. We are optimistic that most trained researchers operate within known ethical frameworks, planning and conducting research with integrity. However, analyses of ethical behavior among researchers does reveal reports of intentional actions that violate responsible conduct of research (Anderson & Steneck, 2011; Martinson, Anderson, & de Vries, 2005). Furthermore, even researchers with good training and positive intentions might be unaware of different notions and practices with respect to ethics that impact cross-cultural and international scholarship and collaborations, unintentionally finding themselves in ethical dilemmas. "To cross cultural borders in research is a slippery and complicated endeavor, and good intentions, though essential, are not enough to help researchers make those crossings with respect for those they research and with their own integrity intact" (Miller Cleary, 2013, p. 1). A chapter in this handbook titled Ethical and Legal Considerations in International Leadership Research by Gabrielle Blackman focuses on these issues in international context in detail. Authors throughout the volume surface numerous ethical concerns about the preparation of researchers to work in different contexts, whether they be a different sector (e.g., government), a different society (e.g., indigenous societies), a foreign political environment or a different diversity group (e.g., LGBTQ in another culture). While contextual considerations may typically fall in the research planning step of a traditional linear research process diagram, authors throughout the volume illustrate a plethora of unique considerations that extend well beyond planning.

The Ethical Global Research Project at The University of Edinburgh synthesizes many of these contextual considerations well, dividing them into four categories: place, people, principles and precedent (Reid et al., 2021). This research group is comprised of more than 200 researchers across 60 distinct disciplines and 30 countries. The researchers state that these four considerations are "Interconnected Threads" that are relevant at every stage of research. They also underscore that global research is neither linear or predictable. This is in line with our analysis of this volume of research perspectives. Instead of definitions or standard guidelines for the four Interconnected Threads, The Ethical Global Research Project offers questions for researchers to consider (Reid et al., 2021):

- Place: What will work in this context?
- People: Who will help us bring our best effort and draw in the support that we need?
- Principles: What worldview and values will best guide us?
- Precedent: What do we need to follow or challenge in established ways of working?

These considerations are novel when looking at widely socialized research models.

Part II of the Handbook surfaced the great importance of research collaborations in international research. This is rarely noted in process models for research. We believe this to be an underexplored area of research and one that is critically important across cultures. As the authors discuss throughout different chapters, research partners were instrumental for cross-cultural research. They also required investment of time and skill in building relationships and coordinating research activities. However, our conversations with authors revealed that few had any formal training or mentoring in how to develop research partnerships and maintain them, making this a consideration for research training.

Finally, in Part III: Insights, Gaps and Future Directions, the authors examine teaching and learning in international leadership research, the dissemination of knowledge through publication and application to practice and to the field of research, and end with an examination of research standards. As the editors and several authors in this volume discuss in Part III, much of the learning we had in international research contexts was through discovery rather than formal learning. By building these considerations into a model for research, we believe they would become part of formalized research training and that this would better prepare researchers and better serve the people and societies that they research. The title of this chapter, Doing Cross-Cultural and International Research with Integrity, reflects the intricate relationship between researcher disposition, the research context, research process and research ethics. We believe that research integrity is not just a checkpoint in the research process, such as in the review by an institutional review board. It is necessarily part of the disposition development of a researcher to work across diverse contexts and to acknowledge and create space in the research and research education alternative world views (Chilisa, 2012; Kovach, 2009).

Research Framework for International & Diverse Contexts

The framework we see emerging from this volume takes the focus away from the steps of the research process and places it on the ethical foundations for research and the contextual

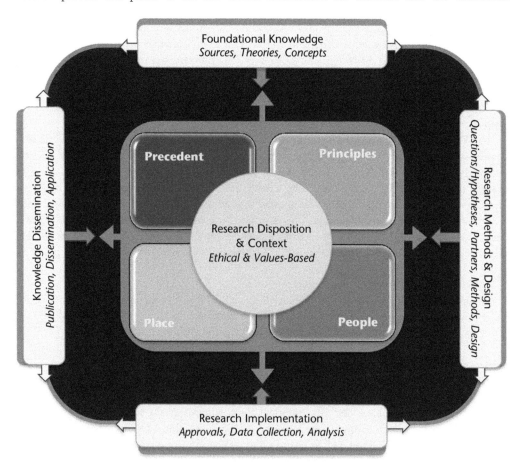

Figure 35.2   Research Framework for Cross-Cultural and International Research.

considerations of people, place, principles and precedent (Reid et al., 2021). These serve as the heart of the dynamic model and provide lenses through which the researcher navigates the research process. Rather than linear steps, we present stages in the model that reflect setting a foundation for knowledge, research design, research implementation and knowledge dissemination. While some components of the research process may begin in sequence, such as review of foundational knowledge to begin to identify a research question or hypothesis, the arrows in the model reflect the need for researchers to revisit stages to reflect, refine and even reconsider before moving to another stage. There is also an ongoing connection with the disposition for and contexts of research, as there are likely to be discoveries throughout the process that influence research stages.

Critical Questions at Each Stage of Research

As this volume has reinforced the complexity of research across cultural contexts, we suggest reflective questions for each stage rather than a checklist. These questions will help researchers think through each stage of research and the specific nuances of their research environment and sample. After all, ethics and integrity are relevant throughout the research journey. We thank all of our authors in this handbook and also those listed in our references for inspiring many of these questions.

Disposition and Context for Ethical and Values-Based Research: Principles, People, Place, Precedent

Disposition
- How does and will my personal background (e.g., culture, class, gender, sexual orientation, political affiliation, age, academic discipline, nationality) shape my interests, the research questions, and the study? What steps can I take to address, acknowledge, avoid or use those unique perspectives?
- What are my philosophical assumptions or "conscious positionality", and how will this shape the study?
- How can I create multi-level perspectives for the study?
- Whose leadership or followership questions do I ask? Who will benefit? Whose knowledge do we capture?
- What relationships and connections will I need to conduct the study (e.g., gatekeepers, research partners, local communities)?
- What additional training might I need to conduct the study?
- What role do I aim to have in this study as a researcher (e.g., scientist, advocate, collaborator, activist)?

Principles
- What worldview and values will influence decision making in the research process?
- How might I need to navigate these in culturally relevant ways?
- What worldview and values guide the research question?
- What harm could this research bring and to whom? How will I mitigate this?

People
- What is the relationship between myself and those involved in the research, in terms of power and socio-cultural differences?
- How will I respectfully navigate the relationship?
- Who are the stakeholders for this project?

- What are the intentions, needs, impacts, wisdom and fears of stakeholders?
- Who are the gatekeepers for this project? How will I gain access/trust?
- Who is a necessary or beneficial partner or collaborator for this project?
- What expectations, agreements and protocols will we use for working together?
- Who will be the beneficiaries of the knowledge and findings?
- What is the emotional and psychological context for research?
- Are there humanitarian concerns (e.g., instability, crisis, abuse, neglect) involved that we need to be aware of?
- What do I need to do to build my own capacity (e.g., training) or the capacity of the research team for this study?
- During this project, do I need to build in specific support to attend to the well-being of myself and/or the research team?

Place
- What is the context in which the research in occurring? Are there multiple sites, cultures and/ or disciplines to consider?
- What are unique research considerations based on the setting where this study will occur?
- What are the local values and existing local knowledge on the topic? How will the study capture and integrate those insights and build upon them?
- Are there particular political, legal, social or cultural considerations for where this research will take place?
- In terms of research ethics, are there unique challenges to foresee and plan ahead for?
- How will I embrace diversity in a local leadership context (e.g., gender, race, disability, sub-cultures, etc.)?
- What macro-level considerations do I need to account for in this context (e.g., crisis or risky environment, indigenous context, political, legal, economic, government, religious, ethical influences)?
- When suggestions for "problems" and future directions for research are formulated, do they account for place-based and strengths-based solutions?

Precedent
- How has history shaped current and future challenges with the topic?
- How is research conducted in this area?
- What is the current political, social or legal environment with respect to this topic and/or my affiliations as a researcher?
- How will I navigate potential challenges with the topic or me personally as a researcher?
- What research methods have previously been used with this topic and in this context? What were the strengths and limitations of previously used research methods?

Foundational Knowledge Stage: Sources, Theories, Concepts

Sources
- What or who are the sources of knowledge on this topic?
- What types of literature or media are available to understand the topic?
- Are there sources or worldviews that are not represented in published literature that need to be sought out to understand diverse and/or culturally relevant perspectives on this topic?
- What academic fields are represented in the literature? Do I need to pull from other disciplines or non-academic sources (e.g., cultural expressions, popular culture)?
- Are the sources I have found credible? How is credibility being defined in this study?

- Have I balanced rigor with culturally relevant information that may not be in premier journals?
- Are there sources beyond my primary language that need to be sought out? How will I access and interpret these?
- Are field interviews needed for novel topics that do not have sufficient published or accessible research?

Theories/Concepts

- What theories/concepts are pertinent to understanding the topic?
- What is the origin of the theories/concepts?
- Do the theories/concepts apply to the context of study?
- Are there other disciplines or traditions that need to be explored?
- Have I considered culture-specific leadership theories, concepts and models?
- Does the theoretical/conceptual framework chosen capture local cultural contexts?

Research Methods & Design Stage: Questions/Hypotheses, Partners, Methods & Design

Questions/Hypotheses

- What is the topic, issue or problem to be addressed? Why is it important/significant? Who is it important/significant for?
- What principles and values are implicit or explicit and need to be considered in this research?
- When looking at the topic, issue or problem, what are the needs, benefits and impacts involved and to whom?
- How should questions or hypotheses be framed for the context of the study?
- Does this study appropriately account for local/global dynamics, if relevant?
- Does this study appropriately account for macro/micro-level views, if relevant?
- What will the lens for this research be and why (e.g., emic or etic)? Are both needed?
- Do the research questions or hypotheses allow for diverse or multidisciplinary perspectives for this area of study?

Partners

- To what extent can international research collaborations contribute to my study?
- Who will serve as my partner(s)? How will we work together?
- How will the research collaboration influence the study plan? What do we need to follow, or challenge, in established ways of working as a research team?
- How will I incorporate a communication and feedback loop throughout the partnership to allow for candid observations, sharing of challenges (especially ethical in nature), suggestions and requests?
- Which authorities and community leaders need to be involved in the project (e.g., governments, traditional authorities, policy makers, service providers, practitioners)?
- Is there a need or benefit to engage support in global academic networks?
- Will funding agencies be involved? If so, how will this impact the research or acceptance of findings by the research community and those involved in the study?
- If I decide not to have a partner in the research, do I need some preliminary or ongoing guidance on the local context? Who will aid me with this?

Methods

- Which methodology best answers the research questions/hypotheses? Does it fit the study intent and context?

- Do I have the expertise myself or within a research team to effectively execute this research design? Who else do I need to involve?
- Have I considered non-traditional, unique, indigenous or mixed methods designs and methods (e.g., oral communications, artistic expressions as vehicles for knowledge)?
- Are there other methods or a blend of methods that would better capture local perspectives with respect to the research study intent and question?
- How can the study be designed to make the research impact more significant to those studied, to marginalized groups, or to marginalized academic voices?
- Have I researched what is known about interpersonal communication in local culture and information sharing to anticipate and prepare for issues arising with data collection (e.g., interviews, focus groups, observations, survey translation, appropriate questions, response biases, agreeability norms)?
- Have I engaged in sufficient pilot testing, where possible, and optimized the instruments, including any necessary translations of multilingual research?

Design
- What is my detailed plan for performing research? Does it account for local contexts, partners and identified or potential challenges?
- How will I recruit a local sample in a culturally relevant way?
- Does my sample represent ample and appropriate diversity for my study? If not, how will I reach a diverse sample?
- What is a culturally relevant approach to gathering informed consent where I am performing research?
- Is anonymity culturally relevant, or does it reduce the validity of the study in the eyes of the community involved (e.g., indigenous methods)?
- Will participants speak other languages, multiple languages, or have barriers to certain modes of communication (e.g., literacy, computer access, privacy concerns, cultural norms)? How will I address translation and transcription in my research design?
- What form of pilot study will help me answer some of these questions?
- Considering the population involved, what are traditional ways of communication and sharing knowledge?
- What culturally relevant ways have I identified for gathering data? Is a multi-modal approach needed?

Research Implementation Stage: Approvals, Data Collection, Analysis

Approvals and Organizational Support
- Which international, national and local research standards and organizations govern my project? What approvals will I need? When rules and policies differ, whose rules apply?
- Do current organizational or institutional policies support the research design and/or processes? Will I need to advocate for policy change to pursue this project?
- What regulatory conflicts may I encounter with this research? How will I ethically navigate these?
- What protocols are in place to ensure research ethics, adhering to both standards of the host country of the researchers and the country, context where the study occurs?
- What ethical dilemmas might I encounter in this research? How will I ethically navigate these?
- How can integrity be ensured when national standards and oversight differ?
- How can collaborators verify that research processes and products meet appropriate standards for integrity?

- Do I need to gain any specific expertise to ensure quality research process in this area of the world?

Data Collection
- What is my role as a researcher in the data collection process? Will I personally be able to collect data within this cultural context, or will I need a partner?
- How does my background shape the interview process or accessing potential respondents for quantitative surveys?
- What process will I use for note taking or other data collection? What may be cultural concerns regarding these choices?
- What tools or instruments will be used in the data collection? Have they been validated for this sample or context? If not, do they need to be before proceeding?
- How can I ensure unbiased data collect? Is that possible? If not, what biases need to be acknowledged and managed?
- Do our data collection processes present any potential risk or discomfort for the participants or end users, or for researchers or partners?
- How do I gather data in a way that demonstrates an ethic of care, respect and inclusion of diverse perspectives with respect to the research topic and context?
- What tools or processes do I need to create to ensure understanding and participation in the spirit of the research design?
- Are multiple modes needed to reach the desired sample or accommodate diverse needs?
- What challenges or obstacles may derail the data collection plan? What alternative plans do I have for data collection?
- Have I ensured rigor and integrity in my data collection?

Analysis
- How does my personal background (e.g., culture, class, gender, sexual orientation, political affiliation, age, academic discipline, nationality) shape my interpretation of the results? What steps can I take to address, acknowledge or avoid, if appropriate, the influence of my personal background on the analysis?
- What conscious or unconscious biases need to be controlled for in the analysis, and how will I ensure this?
- What contextual issues in this study could complicate analysis? How will I manage this?
- What am I not seeing in my analysis that someone else would take note of (e.g., participants, local partners, stakeholders)?
- Who can I consult with to gain additional perspective?
- Have I properly cleaned and screened data (for quantitative research) before moving forward with analysis? What do outliers mean in the context of this study?

Knowledge Dissemination Stage: Writing, Publication, Application

Writing
- Who is the audience that I am writing to and for?
- How did my personal background shape this study? Are those unique perspectives acknowledged and credited appropriately?
- Before publication, which conferences or other forums might be appropriate to submit to, share this information and gather additional input from the research community?
- Thinking back at the initial outlook in the planning stage on the study impact, has this research met the goals outlined?

- Have I assessed my conclusions through the lens of people, place, precedence and principles to ensure culturally relevant interpretations?
- Is generalization or transference possible or antithetical to the research method/findings (e.g., indigenous methods)?
- Are there readers among my sample, research partners, collaborators or stakeholders who can check for comprehensiveness, quality of analysis and cultural representation?
- How can this paper be interpreted and used?

Publication/Other Dissemination
- What is the academic contribution to my field?
- Considering reciprocity with my research participants and the community where research was performed, how and where else may I need to distribute knowledge from this study?
- In addition to academic publications, where else could I make findings available for stakeholders or policy makers?
- Is open access desirable for this publication to reach the right audiences?
- Which publication outlets or other ways of disseminating findings may also be relevant for co-authors or research partners who may be abroad?
- How can we share research findings in ways that honor those involved and have a positive impact?

Application
- What contribution to practitioners in the field does this research make?
- What specific relevance do the study findings have for specific groups or organizations (i.e., locally, nationally, globally)?
- What would I have done differently or better in the future? How might I share these learnings with other researchers?
- How will this research inform my teaching and service to my organization, institution and the field? What implications does this research have for these parties?
- How will this research influence policy or procedural changes to research at my organization/ institution and in the field? How can I serve as an advocate for this (e.g., requesting diverse library holdings, revising course objectives and curriculum)?
- What opportunities might there be for consulting or coaching to disseminate learnings and influence practice based on the findings?
- How might I advocate for or contribute to the evolution of research practice? What does this mean for current projects?
- What will I do to ensure positive impacts of our project are sustained, and any potential negative impacts are mitigated? What can I do to stay alert to these impacts?
- What and who will help me translate research to effectively shape policy and practice in different global contexts?

Conclusion

While cross-cultural and international research is not a new phenomenon, this book has illustrated the need for more robust preparation for researchers, especially during their formative education. It has also demonstrated the value of creating an outlet for experienced researchers to share their insights and learnings, not just their research findings, when working across cultures and societies. We recognize that the framework presented here is an initial attempt to capture a very rich and complex field, and that this volume is necessarily limited in its scope. However, are hopeful that this handbook will help to create an ongoing forum for communication among cross-cultural and international leadership researchers that will continue to invite and explore these issues further to make the framework stronger over time. Most importantly, we hope that the insights presented in the handbook will pave the way for strong and culturally relevant collaborations across cultures and societies.

References

Anderson, M. S., & Steneck, N. H. (Eds.). (2011). *International research collaborations: Much to be gained, many ways to get in trouble*. Routledge.

Anderson, M. S. (2011). What can be gained and what can go wrong in the context of different national research environments. In M. S. Anderson & N. H. Steneck (Eds.), *International research collaborations: Much to be gained, many ways to get in trouble*. (pp. 3–7). Routledge.

Chilisa, B. (2012). *Indigenous research methodologies*. Sage.

Du Plessis, H., & Raza, G. (2004, March 11–20). *Linking indigenous knowledge with attitudes towards science among artisans in India and South Africa: A collaborative cross-cultural project*. Paper presented at the conference on Bridging Scale and Epistemologies, Alexandria, Egypt.

Gelling, L. (2015). Stages in the research process. *Nursing Standard (2014+), 29*(27), 44.

Gerrish, K., & Lacey, A. (2010). *The research process in nursing*. John Wiley & Sons.

Kovach, M. (2009). *Indigenous methodologies: Characteristics, conversations and contexts*. University of Toronto Press.

March, S. T., & Smith, G. F. (1995). Design and natural science research on information technology. *Decision Support Systems, 15*(4), 251–266.

Martinson, B. C., Anderson, M. S., & de Vries, R. (2005). Scientists behaving badly. *Nature, 435*(7043), 737–738.

Maxwell, J. A. (2012). *Qualitative research design: An interactive approach* (Vol. 41). Sage Publications.

Maxwell, J. A. (2019). *Qualitative research design*. Sage Research Methods.

Miller Cleary, L. (2013). *Cross-cultural research with integrity: Collected wisdom from researchers in social settings*. Palgrave Macmillan. doi: 10.1057/9781137263605.

Moquin, H. (2007). *Postcolonial reflections on research in a Inuit community: Learning in community*. Proceedings of the joint international Adult Education Research Conference and the Canadian Association for the Study of Adult Education, University of Glasgow, Scotland.

Moule, P., Aveyard, H., & Goodman, M. (2016). *Nursing research: An introduction*. Sage.

Nunamaker Jr, J. F., Chen, M., & Purdin, T. D. (1990). Systems development in information systems research. *Journal of Management Information Systems, 7*(3), 89–106.

Offermann, P., Levina, O., Schönherr, M., & Bub, U. (2009, May 7). Outline of a design science research process. In Proceedings of the *4th International Conference on Design Science Research in Information Systems and Technology* (pp. 1–11).

Peffers, K., Tuunanen, T., Rothenberger, M. A., & Chatterjee, S. (2008). A Design Science Research Methodology for Information Systems Research. *Journal of Management Information Systems, 24*(3), 45–77.

Peffers, K., Tuunanen, T., & Niehaves, B. (2018). Design science research genres: Introduction to the special issue on exemplars and criteria for applicable design science research. *European Journal of Information Systems, 27*(2), 129–139.

Reid, C., Calia, C., Guerra, C., Grant, L., Anderson, M., Chibwana, K., Kawale, P., & Amos, A. (2021). Ethics in global research: Creating a toolkit to support integrity and ethical action throughout the research journey. *Research Ethics*. doi: 10.1177/1747016121997522.

Takeda, H., Veerkamp, P., & Yoshikawa, H. (1990). Modeling design process. *AI Magazine, 11*(4), 37- 37.

Taylor J. (2010) Preparing a research proposal. In K. Gerrish & A. Lacey (Eds.), The research process in nursing (6th ed., pp. 93–103). Wiley-Blackwell.

Vaishnavi, V., & Kuechler, W. (2004). *Design research in information systems*. LNCS.

Williams, C. (2015). *Doing international research*. SAGE Publications. doi: 10.4135/9781473920361.

Index

Note: *Italic* page numbers refer to figures; **Bold** page numbers refer to tables and page numbers followed by "n" denote endnotes.

For Product Safety Concerns and Information please contact our EU
representative GPSR@taylorandfrancis.com
Taylor & Francis Verlag GmbH, Kaufingerstraße 24, 80331 München, Germany

www.ingramcontent.com/pod-product-compliance
Ingram Content Group UK Ltd.
Pitfield, Milton Keynes, MK11 3LW, UK
UKHW011457240425
457818UK00022B/875